9448

LIBRARY
St. Michael's College Prep H.S.
19292 El Toro Rd., Silverado, CA 92676

P9-EDF-010

Short Story
Criticism

Guide to Gale Literary Criticism Series

For criticism on	Consult these Gale series
Authors now living or who died after December 31, 1959	*CONTEMPORARY LITERARY CRITICISM (CLC)*
Authors who died between 1900 and 1959	*TWENTIETH-CENTURY LITERARY CRITICISM (TCLC)*
Authors who died between 1800 and 1899	*NINETEENTH-CENTURY LITERATURE CRITICISM (NCLC)*
Authors who died between 1400 and 1799	*LITERATURE CRITICISM FROM 1400 TO 1800 (LC)* *SHAKESPEAREAN CRITICISM (SC)*
Authors who died before 1400	*CLASSICAL AND MEDIEVAL LITERATURE CRITICISM (CMLC)*
Black writers of the past two hundred years	*BLACK LITERATURE CRITICISM (BLC)*
Authors of books for children and young adults	*CHILDREN'S LITERATURE REVIEW (CLR)*
Dramatists	*DRAMA CRITICISM (DC)*
Hispanic writers of the late nineteenth and twentieth centuries	*HISPANIC LITERATURE CRITICISM (HLC)*
Poets	*POETRY CRITICISM (PC)*
Short story writers	*SHORT STORY CRITICISM (SSC)*
Major authors from the Renaissance to the present	*WORLD LITERATURE CRITICISM, 1500 TO THE PRESENT (WLC)*

ISSN 0895-9439

Volume 15

Short Story Criticism

Excerpts from Criticism of the
Works of Short Fiction Writers

David Segal
Editor

Jeffery Chapman
Laurie DiMauro
Christopher Giroux
Margaret Haerens
Drew Kalasky
Thomas Ligotti
Associate Editors

Gale Research Inc. • *DETROIT* • *WASHINGTON, D.C.* • *LONDON*

STAFF

David Segal, *Editor*

Jeffery Chapman, Laurie Di Mauro, Christopher Giroux, Margaret A. Haerens, Kelly Hill, Drew Kalasky, Thomas Ligotti, *Associate Editors*

Pamela Willwerth Aue, Christine Bichler, Martha Bommarito, Matthew McDonough, *Assistant Editors*

Jeanne A. Gough, *Permissions & Production Manager*
Linda M. Pugliese, *Production Supervisor*
Donna Craft, Paul Lewon, Maureen A. Puhl, Camille P. Robinson, Sheila Walencewicz, *Editorial Associates*

Sandra C. Davis, *Permissions Supervisor (Text)*
Maria L. Franklin, Josephine M. Keene, Michele Lonoconus, Shalice Shah, Kimberly F. Smilay, *Permissions Associates*
Jennifer A. Arnold, Brandy C. Merritt, *Permissions Assistants*

Margaret A. Chamberlain, *Permissions Supervisor (Pictures)*
Pamela A. Hayes, Arlene Johnson, Keith Reed, Barbara A. Wallace, *Permissions Associates*
Susan Brohman, *Permissions Assistant*

Victoria B. Cariappa, *Research Manager*
Maureen Richards, *Research Supervisor*
Maria Bryson, Mary Beth McElmeel, Donna Melnychenko, Tamara C. Nott, Jaema Paradowski, *Editorial Associates*
Maria E. Bryson, Stefanie Scarlett, *Editorial Assistants*

Mary Beth Trimper, *Production Director*
Catherine Kemp, *Production Assistant*

Cynthia Baldwin, *Product Design Manager*
Barbara J. Yarrow, *Graphic Services Supervisor*
Sherrell Hobbs, *Macintosh Artist*
Willie F. Mathis, *Camera Operator*

Library of Congress Catalog Card Number 76-46132
ISBN 0-8103-8930-4
ISSN 0276-8178

Printed in the United States of America
Published simultaneously in the United Kingdom
by Gale Research International Limited
(An affiliated company of Gale Research Inc.)
10 9 8 7 6 5 4 3 2 1

The trademark **ITP** is used under license.

Contents

Preface   vii

Acknowledgments   xi

Preface

A Comprehensive Information Source
on World Short Fiction

*S*hort Story Criticism (SSC) presents significant passages from criticism of the world's greatest short story writers and provides supplementary biographical and bibliographical materials to guide the interested reader to a greater understanding of the authors of short fiction. This series was developed in response to suggestions from librarians serving high school, college, and public library patrons, who had noted a considerable number of requests for critical material on short story writers. Although major short story writers are covered in such Gale series as *Contemporary Literary Criticism (CLC)*, *Twentieth-Century Literary Criticism (TCLC)*, *Nineteenth-Century Literature Criticism (NCLC)*, and *Literature Criticism from 1400 to 1800 (LC)*, librarians perceived the need for a series devoted solely to writers of the short story genre.

Coverage

SSC is designed to serve as an introduction to major short story writers of all eras and nationalities. Since these authors have inspired a great deal of relevant critical material, *SSC* is necessarily selective, and the editors have chosen the most important published criticism to aid readers and students in their research.

Approximately eight to ten authors are included in each volume, and each entry presents a historical survey of the critical response to that author's work. The length of an entry is intended to reflect the amount of critical attention the author has received from critics writing in English and from foreign critics in translation. Every attempt has been made to identify and include excerpts from the most significant essays on each author's work. In order to provide these important critical pieces, the editors will sometimes reprint essays that have appeared in previous volumes of Gale's Literary Criticism Series. Such duplication, however, never exceeds twenty percent of an *SSC* volume.

Organization

An *SSC* author entry consists of the following elements:

- The **Author Heading** cites the name under which the author most commonly wrote, followed by birth and death dates. If the author wrote consistently under a pseudonym, the pseudonym will be listed in the author heading and the author's actual name given in parentheses on the first line of the biographical and critical introduction.

- The **Biographical and Critical Introduction** contains background information designed to introduce a reader to the author and the critical debates surrounding his or her work. Parenthetical material following the introduction provides references to other biographical and critical series published by Gale, including *CLC, TCLC, NCLC, Contemporary Authors,* and *Dictionary of Literary Biography*.

- A **Portrait of the Author** is included when available. Many entries also contain illustrations of materials pertinent to an author's career, including holographs of manuscript pages, title pages, dust jackets, letters, or representations of important people, places and events in the author's life.

- The list of **Principal Works** is chronological by date of first publication and lists the most important works by the author. The first section comprises short story collections, novellas, and novella collections. The second section gives information on other major works by the author. For foreign authors, the editors have provided original foreign-language publication information and have selected what are considered the best and most complete English-language editions of their works.

- **Criticism** is arranged chronologically in each author entry to provide a useful perspective on changes in critical evaluation over the years. All short story, novella, and collection titles by the author featured in the entry are printed in boldface type to enable a reader to ascertain without difficulty the works discussed. Also for purposes of easier identification, the critic's name and the publication date of the essay are given at the beginning of each piece of criticism. Unsigned criticism is preceded by the title of the journal in which it appeared.

- Critical essays are prefaced with **Explanatory Notes** as an additional aid to students and readers using *SSC*. The explanatory notes provide several types of useful information, including: the reputation of a critic, the importance of a work of criticism, and the specific type of criticism (biographical, psychoanalytic, structuralist, etc.).

- A complete **Bibliographical Citation,** designed to help the interested reader locate the original essay or book, follows each piece of criticism.

- The **Further Reading List** appearing at the end of each author entry suggests additional materials on the author. In some cases it includes essays for which the editors could not obtain reprint rights.

Beginning with volume six, *SSC* contains two additional features designed to enhance the reader's understanding of short fiction writers and their works:

- Each *SSC* entry now includes, when available, **Comments by the Author** that illuminate his or her own works of the short story genre in general. These statements are set within boxes or bold rules to distinguish them from the criticism.

- A **Select Bibliography of General Sources on Short Fiction** is included as an appendix. Updated and amended with each new *SSC* volume, this listing of materials for further research provides readers with a selection of the best available general studies of the short story genre.

Other Features

A **Cumulative Author Index** lists all the authors who have appeared in *SSC, CLC, TCLC, NCLC, LC,* and *Classical and Medieval Literature Criticism (CMLC),* as well as cross-references to other Gale series. Users will welcome this cumulated index as a useful tool for locating an author within the Literary Criticism Series.

A **Cumulative Nationality Index** lists all authors featured in *SSC* by nationality, followed by the number of the *SSC* volume in which their entry appears.

A **Cumulative Title Index** lists in alphabetical order all short story, novella, and collection titles contained in the *SSC* series. Titles of short story collections, separately published novellas, and novella collections are printed in italics, while titles of individual short stories are printed in roman type with quotation marks. Each title is followed by the author's name and corresponding volume and page numbers where commentary on the work may be located. English-language translations of original foreign-language titles are cross-referenced to the foreign titles so that all references to discussion of a work are combined in one listing.

Citing *Short Story Criticism*

When writing papers, students who quote directly from any volume in the Literary Criticism Series may use the following general forms to footnote reprinted criticism. The first example pertains to material drawn from periodicals, the second to material reprinted from books:

[1]Henry James, Jr., "Honoré de Balzac," *The Galaxy 20* (December 1875), 814-36; excerpted and reprinted in *Short Story Criticism,* Vol. 5, ed. Thomas Votteler (Detroit: Gale Research, 1990), pp. 8-11.

[2]F. R. Leavis, *D. H. Lawrence: Novelist* (Alfred A. Knopf, 1956); excerpted and reprinted in *Short Story Criticism,* Vol. 4, ed. Thomas Votteler (Detroit: Gale Research, 1990), pp. 202-06.

Comments

Readers who wish to suggest authors to appear in future volumes, or who have other suggestions, are invited to contact the editors by writing to Gale Research Inc., Literary Criticism Division, 835 Penobscot Building, Detroit, MI 48226-4094.

Acknowledgments

The editors wish to thank the copyright holders of the excerpted criticism included in this volume, the permissions managers of many book and magazine publishing companies for assisting us in securing reprint rights, and Anthony Bogucki for assistance with copyright research. We are also grateful to the staffs of the Detroit Public Library, the Library of Congress, the University of Detroit Mercy Library, Wayne State University Purdy/Kresge Library Complex, and the University of Michigan Libraries for making their resources available to us. Following is a list of the copyright holders who have granted us permission to reprint material in this volume of *SSC*. Every effort has been made to trace copyright, but if omissions have been made, please let us know.

COPYRIGHTED EXCERPTS IN *SSC*, VOLUME 15, WERE REPRINTED FROM THE FOLLOWING PERIODICALS:

America, v. 155, November 15, 1986 for "Poised for Fame: Andre Dubus at Fifty" by Joseph J. Feeney. © 1986. All rights reserved. Reprinted by permission of America Press, Inc., 106 West 56th Street, New York, NY 10019 and the author./ v. 155, November 15, 1986. © 1986. All rights reserved. Reprinted by permission of America Press, Inc., 106 West 56th Street, New York, NY 10019.—*American Imago*, v. 34, Fall, 1977. Copyright 1977 by The Association for Applied Psychoanalysis, Inc. Reprinted by permission of the publisher.—*Arizona Quarterly*, v. 45, Summer, 1989 for "Robert Coover's 'Writing Degree Zero:' 'The Magic Poker' " by Wayne B. Stengel. Copyright © 1989 by Arizona Board of Regents. Reprinted by permission of the publisher and the author.—*Book Week-New York Herald Tribune*, October 20, 1963. © 1963, New York Herald Tribune Inc. All rights reserved. Reprinted by permission.—*Book World—The Washington Post*, January 12, 1986. © 1986, *The Washington Post*. Reprinted with permission of the publisher.—*Books*, August 25, 1963. © 1963, renewed 1991, *The Washington Post*. Reprinted by permission of the publisher.—*The Centennial Review*, v. XXXV, Fall, 1991 for "Of Suitcases and Other Burdens: The Ambiguities of Cynthia Ozick's Image of Germany" by Hans Borchers. © 1991 by *The Centennial Review*. Reprinted by permission of the publisher and the author.—*Commentary*, v. 61, June, 1976 for "American Jewish Writing, Act II" by Ruth R. Wisse. Copyright © 1976 the American Jewish Committee. All rights reserved. Reprinted by permission of the publisher and the author.—*Commonweal*, v. CXV, December 2, 1988. Copyright © 1988 Commonweal Foundation. Reprinted by permission of Commonweal Foundation.—*Critique: Studies in Contemporary Fiction*, v. XXXIV, Summer, 1993. Copyright © 1993 Helen Dwight Reid Educational Foundation. Reprinted with permission of the Helen Dwight Reid Educational Foundation, published by Heldref Publications, 1319 18th Street, N.W. Washington, DC 20036-1802.—*Critique: Studies in Modern Fiction*, v. VII, Winter, 1964-65; v. XXV, Winter, 1984; v. XXVIII, Fall, 1986. Copyright © 1964, 1984, 1986 Helen Dwight Reid Educational Foundation. All reprinted with permission of the Helen Dwight Reid Educational Foundation, published by Heldref Publications, 1319 18th Street, N.W. Washington, DC 20036-1802.—*Encounter*, v. XXII, January, 1964 for "Satire and Melancholy" by Michael Frayn. © 1964, renewed 1992 by the author. Reprinted by permission of the author.—*Essays in Literature*, v. 15, Spring, 1988. Copyright 1988 by Western Illinois University. Reprinted by permission of the publisher.—*Genre*, v. 13, Summer, 1980 for "Parody as Exorcism: 'The Raven' and 'The Jewbird' " by J. Gerald Kennedy. © copyright 1980 by the University of Oklahoma. Reprinted by permission of the University of Oklahoma and the author.—*Hadassah Magazine*, v. 55, June, 1974 for an interview with Bernard Malamud by Curt Leviant. Reprinted by permission of the publisher and Curt Leviant.—*The Hollins Critic*, v. XXIV, February, 1987. Copyright 1987 by Hollins College. Reprinted by permission of the publisher.—*The Hudson Review*, v. XXXIII, Winter, 1980-81; v. XXXVI, Winter, 1983-84. Copyright © 1980, 1983 by The Hudson Review, Inc. Both reprinted by permission of the publisher.—*John O'Hara Journal*, v. 5, Winter, 1982-83 for "The Unity of John O'Hara's 'Waiting for Winter' " by Edgar McD. Shawen; v. 5, Winter, 1982-83 for "John O'Hara's 'Alone': Preview of Coming Attractions" by Charles W. Bassett. Both reprinted by permission of the respective authors.—*Judaism*, v. 28, Winter, 1979 for "Malamud's Short Stories: A Reshaping of Hasidic Tradition" by Marcia B. Gealy; v. 36, Fall, 1987 for "The Theme of Responsibility in Bernard Malamud's 'The Mourners' " by Irving Halperin. Copyright © 1979, 1987 by the American Jewish Congress. Both reprinted by

Reprinted by permission of the publisher, Catherine Rainwater and William J. Scheick./ v. 25, Summer, 1983 for "The Art of Cynthia Ozick" by Victor Strandberg. Copyright © 1983 by the University of Texas Press. Reprinted by permission of the publisher and the author.—*The Times Literary Supplement,* n. 4540, April 6-12, 1990. © The Times Supplements Limited 1990. Reproduced from *The Times Literary Supplement* by permission.—*TSE: Tulane Studies in English,* v. XVIII, 1970. Copyright © 1970 by Tulane University. Reprinted by permission of the publisher.—*Twentieth Century Literature,* v. 19, April, 1973. Copyright 1973, Hofstra University Press. Reprinted by permission of the publisher.—*The Village Voice,* v. 25, November 26, 1980 for "Little Wishes" by Judith Gies. Copyright © The Village Voice, Inc. 1980. Reprinted by permission of *The Village Voice* and the Literary Estate of Judith Gies./ v. XXXII, January 20, 1987 for "Going the Distance" by Ellen Lesser. Copyright © News Group Publications, Inc., 1987. Reprinted by permission of *The Village Voice* and the author.—*VLS,* n. 22, December, 1983 for a review of "In Bed One Night and Other Brief Encounters" by Caryn James. Copyright © 1983 News Group Publications, Inc. Reprinted by permission of *The Village Voice* and the author.

COPYRIGHTED EXCERPTS IN *SSC,* VOLUME 15, WERE REPRINTED FROM THE FOLLOWING BOOKS:

Alter, Iska. From *The Good Man's Dilemma: Social Criticism in the Fiction of Bernard Malamud.* AMS Press, 1981. Copyright © 1981 by AMS Press, Inc. All rights reserved. Reprinted by permission of the publisher.—Bilik, Dorothy Seidman. From *Immigrant-Survivors: Post-Holocaust Consciousness in Recent Jewish American Fiction.* Wesleyan University Press, 1981. Copyright © 1981 by Dorothy Seidman Bilik, Wesleyan University Press. Reprinted by permission of University Press of New England.—Brophy, Brigid. From *Don't Never Forget: Collected Views and Reviews.* Jonathan Cape, 1966. Copyright © 1966 by Brigid Brophy. Reprinted by permission of the author.—Brown, Jane Gibson. From "Woman in Nature: A Study of Caroline Gordon's 'The Captive',", in *The Short Fiction of Caroline Gordon: A Critical Symposium.* Edited by Thomas H. Landess. University of Dallas Press, 1972. Copyright 1972 The University of Dallas Press. Reprinted by permission of the author.—Cowan, Louise. From "Aleck Maury, Epic Hero and Pilgrim," in *The Short Fiction of Caroline Gordon: A Critical Symposium.* Edited by Thomas H. Landess. University of Dallas Press, 1972. Copyright 1972 The University of Dallas Press. Reprinted by permission of the author.—Dvorak, Paul F. From an introduction to *Illusion and Reality: Plays and Stories of Arthur Schnitzler.* Translated by Paul F. Dvorak. Peter Lang, 1986. © Peter Lang Publishing, Inc., New York 1986. All rights reserved. Reprinted by permission of the publisher.—Elkin, Stanley. From *Pieces of Soap.* Simon & Schuster, 1992. Copyright © 1992 by Stanley Elkin. All rights reserved. Reprinted by permission of Georges Borchardt, Inc. on behalf of the author. In North America and the Philippines by Simon & Schuster, Inc.—Field, Leslie. From "Portrait of the Artist as 'Schlemiel (Pictures of Fidelman)'," in *Bernard Malamud: A Collection of Critical Essays.* Edited by Leslie Field and Joyce Field. Prentice-Hall, 1975. © 1975 by Prentice-Hall, Inc., Englewood Cliffs, New Jersey. All rights reserved. Reprinted by permission of the editors.—Gass, William H. From *Fiction and the Figures of Life.* Alfred A. Knopf, 1970. Copyright © 1971 by William H. Gass. All rights reserved. Reprinted by permission of the author.—Gordon, Caroline. From *The Collected Short Stories of Caroline Gordon.* Farrar, Straus, Giroux, 1981. Copyright © 1981 by Caroline Gordon.—Gordon, Lois. From *Robert Coover: The Universal Fictionmaking Process.* Southern Illinois University Press, 1983. Copyright © 1983 by the Board of Trustees, Southern Illinois University. All rights reserved. Reprinted by permission of the publisher.—Grebstein, Sheldon Norman. From *John O'Hara.* Twayne Publishers, Inc., 1966. Copyright © 1966 by Twayne Publishers, Inc. All rights reserved. Reprinted with permission of Twayne Publishers, an imprint of Macmillan Publishing Company.—Harap, Louis. From *In the Mainstream: The Jewish Presence in Twentieth-Century American Literature, 1950s-1980s.* Greenwood Press, 1987. Copyright © 1987 by Louis Harap. All rights reserved. Reprinted by permission of Greenwood Publishing Group, Inc., Westport, CT.—Helterman, Jeffrey. From *Understanding Bernard Malamud.* University of South Carolina Press, 1985. Copyright © University of South Carolina 1985. Reprinted by permission of the publisher.—Hershinow, Sheldon J. From *Bernard Malamud.* Ungar, 1980. Copyright © 1980 by The Ungar Publishing Company. Reprinted by permission of The Continuum Publishing Company.—Howe, Irving. From *Celebrations and Attacks: Thirty Years of Literary and Cultural Commentary.* Horizon Press, 1979. Copyright © 1979 by Irving Howe. Reprinted by permission of the Literary Estate of Irving Howe.—Kennedy, Thomas E. From *Andre Dubus: A Study of the Short Fiction.* Twayne

Hortense Calisher

1911-

American novelist, short story writer, and autobiographer.

INTRODUCTION

In her short stories, novels, and novellas Calisher portrays the psychological tribulations of urban characters with a precise and intricately stylized language that often verges on the poetic. An intelligent and artful chronicler of Jewish intellectual life in New York City, Calisher extended her early reputation as a short story writer with ambitious and diverse novels, interspersing elliptical science fiction narratives with Jamesian realism and iconoclastic studies of socially marginalized characters. Yet, despite her achievements in the novel, Calisher has been particularly esteemed for her short fiction, where her verbal virtuosity and psychological insight flourish in a more constrained format. Commenting on her mastery of the short story, Doris Grumbach stated, "Calisher's accomplishment is that she lifts the tale out of the commonplace, carrying it away from the harness of hard fact by her fine verbal textures. . . . Sudden awarenesses, epiphanies of character are her métier, which is perhaps why, to my mind, her stories seem more impressive than her novels."

Biographical Information

Calisher was born into a middle-class Jewish family in New York City, where she has lived for most of her life. Much of her early fiction is a portrait of her childhood; in the "Hester Elkins" stories, her father is indelibly rendered as a cultured Southern gentleman whose humorous, ambling conversations are contrasted with her mother's nagging fixation with industry and practicality. A German-Jewish immigrant, Hedwig Calisher evidently stifled her daughter's affection with constant anxiety about the family's financial security and their social status as Jews in America. Calisher's intellect and imagination were stimulated from an early age by her relationship with her father, who read German and Hebrew, and by the cultural ambience of New York, whose museums, theaters, and concert halls enthralled her. However, despite this early inclination toward the arts, Calisher did not begin to write fiction until she was in her late thirties. She graduated from Barnard College in 1932 as an English and Philosophy major, and was hired as a social worker in New York's Department of Public Welfare. After marrying an engineer and raising two children, Calisher began to write poems and stories, and by 1951 she had published thirteen stories, seven of which appeared in *The New Yorker.*

Major Works

With the publication in 1993 of her novella *Age,* Calisher had produced eleven novels and six collections of short stories and novellas. Her first story collection, *In the Absence of Angels,* established her as an already mature and important short story writer. Typical of Calisher's vision is the opening story, "In Greenwich There Are Many Gravelled Walks," about the struggles of a young man and woman to cope with the chaotic excesses of their dysfunctional parents. "Time, Gentlemen!" sketches the quintessential portrait of Calisher's childhood home: the indolent, garrulous father lingering over a breakfast of black butter and fried calves' brains, and Hester giddy with amusement over her punctilious mother's ineffectual struggles to send him to work. Calisher's other collections include a number of novellas, such as *Extreme Magic,* which details a man's emotional survival tactics following the death of his entire family in a fire, and *The Railway Police,* the bizarre story of a congenitally bald woman who decides to publicly embrace her marginalized identity. With the publication of *The Collected Stories of Hortense*

Calisher in 1975, Calisher was widely recognized as a pre-eminent master of the short story.

Critical Reception

While Calisher's books have been effusively praised by many reviewers in newspapers and journals, others have complained that her style is overly affected and idiosyncratic, and academic critics have virtually ignored her works. Possibly this is due to Calisher's determination to write for her own audience and her stated conviction that critics rarely interpret a work correctly. Her predilection for producing a willfully diverse body of work has also presented difficulties for commentators eager to assess her overall stature as a writer. In spite of this lack of consensus, individual critics have extolled her narrative prowess. The respected author and critic Anne Tyler has concluded that Calisher's stories "are all a form of amber, sealing unforgettable moments in time. And Hortense Calisher is better at this sort of sealing than any other writer I know of."

PRINCIPAL WORKS

SHORT FICTION

In the Absence of Angels 1951
Tale for the Mirror: A Novella and Other Stories 1962
Extreme Magic: A Novella and Other Stories 1964
The Railway Police and The Last Trolley Ride 1966
The Collected Stories of Hortense Calisher 1975
Saratoga, Hot 1985
Age 1987

OTHER MAJOR WORKS

False Entry (novel) 1961
Textures of Life (novel) 1963
Journal from Ellipsia (novel) 1965
The New Yorkers (novel) 1970
Queenie (novel) 1971
Herself (autobiography) 1972
Standard Dreaming (novel) 1972
Eagle Eye (novel) 1973
On Keeping Women (novel) 1977
Mysteries of Motion (novel) 1983
The Bobby-Soxer (novel) 1986
In the Palace of the Movie King (novel) 1994

CRITICISM

Gertrude Buckman (essay date 1951)

[*In the following review of* In the Absence of Angels, *Buckman extols Calisher for the absence of sentimentality in her work and the poignance of her melancholic characterizations.*]

It is always gratifying to make the acquaintance of a writer of intelligence and feeling; it is these qualities which most clearly mark the work of Hortense Calisher, whose stories in the last few years have made their quiet, cogent bids for our attention. Miss Calisher is an eminently sober writer; without affectations or flashiness, without recourse (with the one exception, perhaps, of **"In Greenwich There Are Many Gravelled Walks"**) to immediate dramatic circumstances, she regards the human situation, the relation of one to one, of one to the destroying "everybody," with exactitude, compassion and restraint.

All these stories [in *In the Absence of Angels*] are essentially sad, or rather, sorrowful, for most of her characters suffer from their difference, their isolation, their concern with those terrible needs of the human being which for most of us seem destined never to be fulfilled. This might seem maudlin if Miss Calisher had in her any extravagance, either of matter or method; it might prove thoroughly depressing, if her clarity of vision at close hand did not have its more important extensions, permitting her to hold, with calmness and maturity, to the "long view" which adumbrates the possibility, at least (even if only by inescapable, ironically necessary contrast), of a more satisfactory existence.

It is a pity that this long view does not take in lighter-hearted areas. Miss Calisher seems quite undisposed toward humor, except of a rather grim sort, as in **"Heartburn,"** a kind of allegorical fantasy of a tormenting inhabitant of a person's body which can only be expelled by being passed on to another who has expressed disbelief in its existence. This is not, of course, an amusing story—Miss Calisher's intention is never to entertain—it simply expresses her recurrent theme in slightly different terms. The difference, however, is not unwelcome; it lends an air of sprightliness to a collection which suffers somewhat from almost doggedly explicit seriousness. The total effect of these stories is a little overwhelming, a little like the day of her heroine in **"The Woman Who Was Everybody,"** "a labyrinth" through which we follow "an infallible, an educative thread—to a monster's door."

Miss Calisher's explicitness is the result of a virtue; she is a thoughtful and conscientious writer, and her choice of words pleases and rouses admiration for its precision, honesty and taste. Her use of language lies somewhere between science and inspiration. But she disdains short cuts, she will not make those concessions to the imagination, those delightful leaps of language or idea which might provide the relief of laughter to modify our plight even in a world which is giving us all such a hard time, the world in which, "in the absence of angels and arbiters from a world of light, men and women must take their place."

Gertrude Buckman, "Unfulfilled Yearnings," in The New York Times Book Review, November 18, 1951, p. 46.

Robert Gorham Davis   (essay date 1962)

[Davis is an American educator and critic. In the following review of Tale for the Mirror, *he lauds Calisher's linguistic flair and her ability to identify with her characters.]*

Hortense Calisher is a superb raconteur. Her delight in telling a story is infectious; there is shared relish in the pauses and interruptions, the expected sidelights, the suddenly broadened prospectives or nostalgic glimpses of the past. Almost always she causes the reader to look forward with regret to the ending. With it will vanish the small, distinct, illumined world, apparently quite solid, where even in this brief stay one has come to feel at home. The comparative brevity of the thirteen stories in this collection [*Tale for the Mirror: A Novella and Other Stories*] keeps their author from becoming involved in the too great complications of character and perception which some critics thought to be the fault of her otherwise brilliant recent novel, *False Entry*.

The narrative pleasure which Miss Calisher so readily and gracefully communicates is partly explained by her skill in the practice of her art, especially in finding the exact phrase to define a mood or explain a gesture. But even more, it comes from a deeply affectionate identification—rare nowadays in so conscious an artist—with the material that goes into her stories.

First in giving these fictional worlds solidity is the sense of place. **"What a Thing, to Keep a Wolf in a Cage!"** begins with a woman walking up the Via Aurelia Antica "in the sauterne Roman sunlight." The title story [**"Tale for the Mirror"**] and another, **"Mrs. Fay Dines on Zebra,"** use to very different advantages the atmosphere of old houses along the river roads some twenty-five miles up the Hudson, "a landscape from which individuality still rose like smoke, in signal columns blue and separate and clear." Others, like **"The Scream on Fifty-seventh Street,"** could have been written only by someone who had lived in New York from childhood and had seen the neighborhoods changing—the New York of "parks muted with dust and pavements oscillating with power."

More important than place are the people, who of course are always affected by place. The central characters are as often men as women, and each has a particular history; yet emerging from the stories is a kind of composite biography which gives the collection the fascination of an indirect novel. The background is both Southern and Jewish, with the double sense of family this entails—a large, happy, active, inventive family with multitudinous relatives and retailers. Inevitably, the earliest memories, going back to World War I, are the most nostalgic. Later come marriage, children, a period abroad, divorce, years of intense loneliness and deep uncertainty.

A few of the endings are merely anecdotal, but mostly the stories turn inward, as their characters themselves are forced to do, asking what tale they can tell the mirror when they have to face it in the morning. Sometimes they do their telling to psychoanalysts: a wife, "on the outside," waits bitterly for her husband to get over his love affair with himself. Sometimes—with no psychiatrist but the self to listen—they lie awake at the "hour past love, the courtroom of the night, when the soul, defending, shrank to the size of a pea." Sometimes it is children who force the self-evaluation in a relationship which permits no evasion, "the knife we are impaled upon." There are also, in the stories, characters who have happy memories of their childhood and who sleep well after making love.

The title story at first seems merely an amusing, gossipy novella about an Indian charlatan who moves into a neighboring house with his female entourage. Gradually, without losing any of its humor or relish for picturesque details, it gathers to itself most of the serious themes of the other stories. In a delicately maintained balance that is characteristic of Miss Calisher's work at its best, the moral complexities of *Tale for the Mirror* are steadily intensified without diminishing the need to see its fantastic entanglements, and life itself, lucidly and wisely for what they are.

Robert Gorham Davis, "Questions at Dawn," in The New York Times Book Review, *October 28, 1962, p. 5.*

Brigid Brophy   (essay date 1963)

[Brophy is an Anglo-Irish novelist, dramatist, and critic. Many of her novels and plays are farcical satires of middle-class morality and hypocrisy, and her criticism is known for its provocative and acerbic iconoclasm. In the following excerpt from a review originally published in 1963, she admires Calisher's artistry and characterizes her style as European in its sympathies.]

Hortense Calisher is an American of European sympathies, taut artistry and stupendous talent. European culture in the very act of being déraciné—and letting out a mandrake shriek—is the motif Miss Calisher builds into a grand fugue in *False Entry*, published here last year, a huge novel you can nibble round for twenty or thirty pages before you are suddenly in, hurtling through its exciting plot, dazzled by its delicacy and stunned by its sheer Dickensian creativeness. Her effects are necessarily smaller but at their best just as cogent in *Tale for the Mirror,* which consists of thirteen stories, all bearing the marks of having had to earn their living. Literally, they are magazine stories: it is sad that the only one which could be called so derogatorily is the one from the *New Yorker*. The atmospheres range from suburban to Southern to Yiddish; there is even a superb period piece set at a 1918 victory parade, as condensed in its evocations as a bit of dusty bunting. The themes are mostly metaphors of loneliness. In the title story—the longest—the hero is led, through a Jamesian series of social scenes, to recognise that himself is no less isolated in American society than his Indian and possibly charlatan neighbour. Loneliness is tied into a neat, rather Dorothy Parker parcel in a story about two solitary American women in Rome, and carried to a chill intensity in **'The Scream on 57th Street'**, a story about—

or, I rather think, a story which achieves the classic expression of—widowhood.

Occasionally Miss Calisher's intricate prose flattens into doodling, her narrative swoops towards sentimentality or melodrama and she herself seems engulfed in a second's loneliness, where she cannot believe her own imagination. But she is only plummeting in an air pocket. One even comes to accept her scoopings, like those of a supreme soprano. Most of the time her decorative manner is as firm and economic as rococo wrought iron. Her talent is a naturally brilliant exotic, cutting a figure of stylish idiosyncrasy. Muscular and slender, it picks its fastidious way over the mudflats, leaving a print beautiful, elaborate and rare.

Brigid Brophy, in a review of "Tale of the Mirror," in her Don't Never Forget: Collected Views and Reviews, 1966. *Reprint by Holt, Rinehart and Winston, 1967, pp. 159-60.*

Adrian Mitchell   (essay date 1964)

[*An English poet, dramatist, novelist, and critic, Mitchell was an exponent of the pop poetry movement of the late 1960s and early 1970s. His work is notable for its mass appeal and its fervent political commitment. In the following review, Mitchell commends Calisher's* Extreme Magic *for its compassion and psychological insight.*]

Compassion is not easy. It is much simpler for a contemporary author to take a quick look at the tense, jagged world of 1964 and decide to submerge its real surface in easy bitterness or pity, gall or maple syrup.

Hortense Calisher, as readers of *In the Absence of Angels, False Entry,* **Tale for the Mirror** and *Textures of Life* already know, takes the hard way. The sophisticated are often so occupied with their own reflections that every other face takes on their features. Not Miss Calisher, for all her worldliness. *Extreme Magic,* a collection of eight short stories and one short novel, is alive with a compassion which works—because it is built from the exactly observed details of human lives.

Read her brief, apparently spare, story **"The Rabbi's Daughter."** A middle-class girl, trained to be a concert pianist, takes her baby to join her husband in the ugly, industrial city where he has had to accept a factory job. A less complex writer might have told this with a straight snarl at social conditions or a snicker at the girl's ingrained snobbery. Miss Calisher, while she shows the conditions and the snobbery, gives us something else as well. She *becomes* the girl and forces the reader to assume the same identity. Through her eyes we see the significant physical symbols of her life. Here the girl finds her piano in the hovel that is her new home:

> She opened the door. There it was, filling the box room, one corner jutting into the entry to the kitchenette. Tinny light, whitening down from a meager casement, was recorded feebly on its lustrous flanks. Morning and evening she would edge past it, with the gummy dishes and the

clean. Immobile, in its cage, it faced her, a great dark harp lying on its side.

That paragraph, with its juxtaposition of plain and colored sentences, its rhythm and its exactness, gives some idea of the music of her prose. Sometimes she plays more lightly as she describes a young girl's first visit to France or a dinner party dilemma never faced by Emily Post— what do you do when the other ladies, including your hostess, start taking off their blouses at table? (Miss Calisher's answer: take off your own, if you happen to be wearing a fresh black corset decorated with a Star Ruby.)

Occasionally, usually when circling in on a character, she drops into her only bad habit, a nudging knowingness most extremely expressed like this: "In her size forty-two Liberty lawn and wide ballibuntl hat she might just have stepped off a veranda in Tuxedo or Newport, from one of those corners where dowagers affixed themselves." Even so, her nudges can be effective jolts, carrying more knowledge than knowingness: " . . . the sickening qualm, the frightful inner blush of the inappropriately dressed."

In **"Two Colonials"** she traces, with wicked accuracy, an odd European alliance between a German refugee professor and a new and vacuous English recruit to the faculty of a Midwestern college.

"Extreme Magic," the 83-page story with which the collection concludes, is concerned with the crippling isolation of a human being. Miss Calisher is a skilled heart and brain surgeon. She can never be content to mourn this condition; she must always search for a possible cure.

Guy Callendar, her protagonist, has drifted into the antique business after the death of his wife and three children. Miss Calisher builds him detail by detail—his unpretentiousness, his preference for dogs over cats, his fair ability as a straight cook, his fear of the young and the manner of his becoming "a man who could only like." Guy, for all his numbness, has to encounter other people, and these encounters drag him step by step to a position from which he can see the return of life. His counterpart, the restaurant-bar owner Sligo, who wants to die, can only react to his personal revelation with drinking bouts which culminate in the destruction of his own bar and his own mind. Guy's revelation is opposite, it leads him to move toward the world again, to tidy the barn in which he lives as if in preparation for life's revisitation. It is as strongly stated, as truly startling, as the best works in the Calisher canon.

Adrian Mitchell, "Finding What Is Human," in The New York Times Book Review, *May 17, 1964, p. 4.*

William Peden   (essay date 1964)

[*Peden is an American critic and educator who has written extensively on short fiction. In the following excerpt from his* The American Short Story: Continuity and Change, *Peden observes that most of Calisher's fiction is set in New York and depicts failure in relationships and values.*]

Most of the stories of Hortense Calisher, collected in *In*

the Absence of Angels (1963), *Tale for the Mirror* (1962), and *Extreme Magic* (1963), concern New Yorkers; an occasional later story takes place in Europe, but she is at her best with her American pieces. Several of these are about incidents in the life of Hester Elkin, who appears as child, adolescent, and young adult; among the best are **"A Box of Ginger"** and **"The Watchers"** from *In the Absence of Angels,* **"Time, Gentlemen"** and **"The Coreopsis Kid"** from *Tale for the Mirror,* and **"The Gulf Between"** from *Extreme Magic.* Hester's milieu is the comfortable one of Manhattan apartment dwellers in the first quarter of the twentieth century, a bustling, active world of a large Jewish family with many cousins, uncles, and aunts "so close-knit that all its branches lived within round-the-corner call of each other." Hester's Virginia-born father, who had immigrated to New York in the early 1880s, is the center of this small universe, which Calisher recalls with affection and re-creates in detail, its sights and sounds, its smells, the clothes its inhabitants wore and the food they ate and the experiences they encountered, from the death of a grandmother to the ritualistic breakfast routine of Hester's father or a child's observation of Armistice Day in New York. All this is effectively rendered, simple without lapsing into the trivial, warm-hearted without being sentimentalized.

Many of Calisher's stories are set at a far remove from this sheltered world. They take place in a society in which the concept of order, harmony, and happiness has been blurred almost beyond recognition. In them, the loss of love, the failure of marriage, the inability of human beings to communicate with each other are central themes. The narrator of the title story of her first collection ["In the Absence of Angels"], for example, concludes that "in the absence of angels and arbiters from a world of light, men and women must take their place": these stories indicate that men and women are poor substitutes.

The failures of Calisher's people are not just the defeats of specific human relationships, but the failures of traditional social and personal values in a world so fragmented and beset by stress and tension that the values have become either unrecognizable or unattainable. The young intellectual of **"The Woman Who Was Everybody"** is aware that she is one of the "rejected"; she tries to escape the "gray encroaching smutch of averageness" by a meaningless affair with a young technician, but knows that after the "desperate wrenches, the muffled clingings of love-making," she will still be alone and unwanted. The senator's wife of **"The Night Club in the Woods"** tries to buy a romantic past that never actually existed. The young man who has "moved up" from Fourteenth Street to Sutton Place yearns for the past, when love illuminated a relationship that has lost its meaning. The husband and wife of **"Saturday Night"** have become "strangers . . . too far apart even for conflict . . . sharing the terrible binding familiarities of the joint board, the joint child . . . and the graceless despair of the common bed." The widower of the novella **"Extreme Magic"** is isolated after the death of his wife and children. The protagonist of another novella—a form in which Calisher excels—is similarly separated from the world of accustomed relationships and responses by hereditary baldness (**"The Railway Police"**).

Calisher narrates these stories of human failure and fallibility with grace and insight; the grayness of her people's lives is lightened by her pervading compassion. The main character of **"If You Don't Want to Live I Can't Help You,"** from [*Extreme Magic*], is typical. After a trying day, which includes a visit to her death-and-failure-obsessed nephew and her participation in commencement exercises during which she is honored for her academic achievement, Professor Mary Ponthus reflects: "I'm of the breed that hopes. May this one [a student] want to live. *Maybe this one wants to live.* And when you see that, that's the crux of it. We are all in the dark together, but those are the ones that humanize the dark."

William Peden, "Metropolis, Village, and Suburbia: The Short Fiction of Manners," in his The American Short Story: Continuity and Change, 1940-1975, *revised edition, Houghton Mifflin Company, 1975, pp. 30-68.*

Joan Joffe Hall   (essay date 1966)

[*In the following review of* The Railway Police *and* The Last Trolley Ride, *Hall censures Calisher for what she views as needless narrative complications and stylistic convolutions, particularly in the second novella.*]

Somewhere between one of her earlier novels, *Textures of Life,* and *Journal from Ellipsia,* published [in 1965], Hortense Calisher moved from a stylized view of the actual world to fantasy, from the very terrestrial, even mundane, love of a young couple into outer space. In these two new short novels, *The Railway Police* and *The Last Trolley Ride,* this planet is turned into a backdrop for very strange, occasionally otherworldly, events. Both are highly idiosyncratic narratives, the one of a bald lady who decides to proclaim her baldness, the other of an elderly man named Jim who has a friend named Jim and who tells the story of youthful love and a mythical trolley line.

It's hard to avoid comparisons: *The Railway Police* is the better of the two. There's something too archly coy about *The Last Trolley Ride.* The convolutions of the sentences, the fake suspense about who is telling the story and about what finally did happen, falsify, it seems to me, the essential simplicity of the story itself. Jim and his friend return to a small town after World War I and court the Pardee girls, who live neglected on the outskirts of town, selling fritters. On the remarkable day when the trolley line, a folly from its inception, is retired, everyone goes on a picnicky last ride. When the return ride is temporarily stalled, Jim and Emily sneak off into the bushes, but the friend and Lottie stay on the trolley. It later turns out that plump and sexy Lottie is frigid, that the mate has to starve her to get his sex, that she leaves him after conceiving the child whom Jim and Emily bring up with their own. The trolley itself is a symbol of fate, of the past, of a simpler life; and also of an unruly universe, the universe of folly (its inventor has a miniature replica of the system, which functions perfectly—in his basement). All this is clear enough, except that Hortense Calisher for some reason feels obliged to jazz things up, to obscure the narrative line, to turn the characters and events into enigmas, to make the inventor fabulously rich and cultivated; in short, to create mystery where there is none.

Miss Calisher's style is, at its best, witty and ripe with insights; words melt in her mouth like the Pardee girls' fritters. But she has such an appetite for language, for seasoning in every sentence, that at its worst her style can become opaque, no medium for discovery and elucidation, a risky idiom for narrating events, dangerous for long fiction. Perhaps the brevity of **The Railway Police** is crucial to its success.

There's plenty of suspect mystery and initial obscurity in **The Railway Police,** but the story is finally compelling. A social worker of thirty-nine who wears wigs because she is absolutely bald decides, after seeing a vagrant thrown off a train by the railway police, to announce her baldness, to give up her pretense of hair, to obliterate all evidence of her place in the world, her home and job, to become a vagrant. She begins by leaving her girdle and stockings in the train lavatory and ends by monkishly carrying a bowl and watching from under a viaduct as the sun comes up. In one wonderful scene she throws all eighteen of her wigs off their wig blocks in what she believes is a gesture of farewell, but comes to acknowledge as a salute—hello wig blocks, the essence of the human head.

The intricacies, the subtleties, the cerebrations of Miss Calisher's style work better here, partly because the woman, who narrates the story, is herself involuted and complicated (as Grandfather Jim is not), and partly because the story is no idyl, but tense and metaphysical. A kind of metaphysics of baldness: the heroine's baldness, her deformity, is her humanity, and the story asks us to consider what it means to be human.

> Joan Joffe Hall, "Two Tickets to Tomorrow,"
> in Saturday Review, New York, Vol. XLIX,
> No. 25, June 18, 1966, pp. 39-40.

David K. Kirby   (essay date 1973)

[*Kirby is an American critic and educator. In the following excerpt, he interprets Calisher's short story, "Heartburn," as a variation on the fairy-tale theme of the princess and the frog.*]

It is difficult to live in an age of unbelief. Our faith in the old institutions may be dead, but the institutions themselves die hard. Like rejected suitors who won't take no for an answer, they continue to haunt us, and occasionally, whether out of desperation or because we suddenly realize that we were wrong, we take them back again. As a result, all the old relationships—with church, state, family, friends—are under continual scrutiny, a fact that we will have to live with for some time to come. We have all read *Who's Afraid of Virginia Woolf?* or at least we have seen the movie. We know that the answer is "We are all afraid," but we don't really know why, and so the search for new answers about old relationships continues.

What may surprise us is that this search is sometimes cast in a literary form that seems highly unsuitable for the purpose: the fairy tale. Yet examples abound. In a widely-read anthology which is representative of the best recent short

fiction, John Hollander's *American Short Stories Since 1945,* there are no less than three stories which are patterned after the familiar fairy tale of the princess and the frog. They are "Angel Levine" by Bernard Malamud, **"Heartburn"** by Hortense Calisher, and "Miriam" by Truman Capote. In each of the three stories, a character (the princess) is disturbed by a mysterious and unwanted guest (the frog); in each, the princess-character can be released from his or her unhappiness only if he or she believes in the frog-character . . .

In Hortense Calisher's **"Heartburn,"** the basic elements of the fairy tale are retained, but there is a violent and frightening twist which has its parallels in several of the darker tales of the Brothers Grimm. Again, there are two characters who share an unhappy relationship; again, the key to their mutual happiness is that one character must believe in the hidden truth of the other. The princess-character in **"Heartburn"** is a neurologist with an unusual patient, one who seems to have some kind of small animal lodged in his chest. The animal-in-the-chest is contagious and may be passed on to another, but only under one condition; that the second party publicly avow his disbelief in the reality of the animal. The patient acquired the animal while investigating an inexplicable epidemic at a boys' school; it is believed that a chap named Hallowell had the ability to inflict the animal on the other boys. The patient has searched the world for Hallowell; despairing of that, he has sought medical care from the finest specialists. Interestingly enough, none of the doctors actually state their disbelief in the animal; rather, they tolerate the patient as one who may be mentally disturbed and, in order to rid themselves of him, refer the patient to yet another specialist.

The parasite, despite the discomfort it causes, has one salutary effect; it forces the host to be completely candid, for his *true* story must be disbelieved if the animal is to be passed on to another. In all fairness to the patient, however, it should be noted that he has not come to victimize the neurologist; rather, he is genuinely interested in a cure. Thus both men need for the neurologist to believe: the patient, for the sake of his own sanity, needs someone who will do more than humor him; and the doctor needs to believe in order to protect himself.

But the credulity of the neurologist only goes so far, and he declares his disbelief. Instantly, the patient falls forward onto the doctor's desk. There is a shadowy movement, and something "small, seal-covered, and ambiguous" leaps for the doctor and disappears into his mouth, which has been inconveniently left open out of shock and surprise. (The animal is described earlier as "a form of newt or toad," so that the idea of the princess kissing the frog is treated here with a curious yet appropriate literality.) Thus we see the fairy tale reversed: the princess chooses not to believe, and the promised catastrophe is brought to pass. Ironically, in Calisher's story the frog-character becomes a prince again anyway, or at least he reverts to being a normal and happy mortal. Fairy-tale justice is always poetic justice.

> David K. Kirby, "The Princess and the Frog:
> The Modern American Short Story as Fairy

Tale," in The Minnesota Review, *Vol. 4, Spring, 1973, pp. 145-49.*

Ellen Cronan Rose (essay date 1975)

[*In the following review of* The Collected Stories of Hortense Calisher, *Rose considers the collection to be a self-contained portrait of its author and offers a mixed assessment of Calisher's narrative skills.*]

An *oeuvre,* as every critic knows, is the body of an author's work and in the autobiographical *Herself,* Hortense Calisher says that "if a writer's work has a shape to it—and most have a repetition like a heartbeat—the *oeuvre* will begin to construct him." [*The Collected Stories of Hortense Calisher*] constitute an *oeuvre* and construct a portrait of the artist that her seven novels and four novellas neither modify nor significantly augment. In collecting them, Arbor House has given us an opportunity to see and assess that portrait.

Writers have great rises and slumps in ego. You spend your life doing something, and if it's misinterpreted it seems wasteful, but I don't suppose there's really any critic except posterity.

—Hortense Calisher, Conversations, *1967.*

It appears, in cameo form, in the most engaging of the stories, **"Mrs. Fay Dines on Zebra,"** originally published in *Ladies Home Journal* and first collected in *Tale for the Mirror* (1962). Ostensibly a fantasy, the story is a revealing self-portrait of the storyteller Hortense Calisher, here disguised as the *diseuse* Arietta Minot Fay. Mrs. Fay is the last of the Hudson River Minots, a family distinguished by its unique and now outmoded talent for entertaining. "No Minot had ever had a salary." Instead they had attached themselves to various wealthy patrons as "jesters, *fonctionnaires* attending the private person only," prized for their wit, intelligence, charm, that *je ne sais quoi* called style. The widowed Mrs. Fay, her bank account standing at a somber $126.35, needs to find a rich husband; the Minot in her requires him to be a patron as well, who will appreciate her talents.

Watching Arietta Fay identify and capture her patrons, we are watching Hortense Calisher at work. Like the Minots, Calisher is "not a knave, beyond a certain French clarity as to the main chance." She has entertained her patrons superbly for 25 years, perhaps because—like the Minots—she has "attached herself to honorable patrons" who read *The New Yorker* and *Harper's Bazaar* and the best of the women's magazines. Arietta Fay procures a patron and a subsistence by her uncanny tact as a storyteller. Calisher's **Collected Stories** are a dazzling display of that tact at work.

The successful jester knows his patron, supplies his de-

mand even before it is articulated. As Calisher says in *Herself,* "when you write under the likelihood that a magazine will take your work, you will not be able to prevent taking your tone from it." Reading the **Collected Stories,** you can identify the wry sophistication and sardonic detachment of the *New Yorker* stories, the well-bred and tasteful sentimentality of those that flattered the readers of *Mademoiselle* and *Charm.* Always you are conscious of the general public, represented for me by the anonymous librarian who pasted on the flyleaf of *Queenie* her handwritten judgment that "Hortense Calisher always *writes* well."

If Hortense-Arietta has an Achilles heel, it is just that. "Words!" she exclaims in **"Little Did I Know,"** another story with a *diseuse* heroine. "I was drunk on language. I collected words in all shapes and sizes, and hung them like bangles in my mind." In *Herself* she admits that this may lead "to a rhetoric which, loving its own rhythms, may stray too far from sense," as it does when, in **"The Rabbi's Daughter,"** a baby gazes at us "with the intent, agate eyes of satisfaction." What is agate about satisfaction? What is satisfying about agate?

This rhetoric endangers the bulk of Calisher's fiction, the stories and novels representing "those flights from the subscribed-to-ordinary" that Calisher says are for her "the heights of literature." There remains a small and precious residue. Even Arietta Fay must have had some private moments, when she wasn't spinning tales for her patron.

"Imagination, which speaks in dithyramb, can never equal the rough, fell syllable of memory," says the narrator of *False Entry.* Calisher's tongue is restrained by the stringencies of memory in her autobiographical fictions, the Hester-Kinny Elkin stories that replicate her family, and the two novels, *False Entry* and *The New Yorkers,* that imaginatively build on that foundation. In the Elkin stories, that Calisher wisely put at the center of this collection "where they may radiate" (and do), verbal felicities are at the service of memory. Adjectives do not pirouette, but evoke the smells and tastes and atmospheres of childhood. In the best of these stories—**"The Gulf Between," "The Sound of Waiting," "The Middle Drawer"**—personal memory is transformed into universal truth as the child becomes "us" and the parents "them" in an eternal drama of growth and mutability.

Comparing the Elkin stories to the tales told by Arietta, one wonders why Calisher deserted the syllables of memory for the dithyrambs of the entertainer. Like Mrs. Fay, she performs superbly, knowing "every periphrasis" of her stories, "every calculated inflection and aside," every knack of pleasing. But even Arietta Fay knows that "in this taxable world," patrons are hard to come by and that the decline of the private patron signals the decline of "his factotum." Can a world which rations its fuel and chastens its cuisine afford a retainer who dines on her charm? Calisher's *oeuvre,* represented by the **Collected Stories,** constructs a portrait as exquisite as the full-length portrait in ivory of Arietta's forebear, Yves Minot—and just as out of date.

Ellen Cronan Rose, in a review of "The Collected Stories of Hortense Calisher," in The

New Republic, *Vol. 173, No. 17, October 25, 1975, pp. 29-30.*

Anne Tyler (essay date 1975)

[*Tyler is an American novelist and short story writer who is known for her fictional portraits of family life in works such as* Searching for Caleb *(1976), and* Dinner at the Homesick Restaurant *(1982). Often considered a Southern regionalist, Tyler has been most influenced by and is frequently compared to Eudora Welty. In the following review of* The Collected Stories of Hortense Calisher, *Tyler extols Calisher's virtuosity with the short story form.*]

Years ago, Hortense Calisher wrote a story called **"Time, Gentlemen!"** in which she described the conflict between two different perceptions of time—that of her father, a Southern Victorian gentleman born in 1862, and that of her mother, 22 years younger and infinitely crisper, brisker, and less relaxed.

In that story (which I can practically quote verbatim, so thoroughly did I enjoy it back in college), the mother does the housework with her hat on, in a vain effort to remind her husband that the rest of the world is already out shopping or running businesses. The father, meanwhile, seems to have forgotten he *has* a business, and the morning slips past him while he buys his sweepstakes tickets from the newsboy, consumes a breakfast of black butter and calves' brains (which have to be poached, and then breaded, and then fried), and welcomes such odd visits as that of the furniture-feeder—the man who comes monthly to oil the various gargoyles and griffins of the household.

The paradox, as Hortense Calisher points out, is that for all his lack of haste, her father never once missed a train, or lost his customers, or suffered any of the other defeats that time administers to most people. No, it is the mother who ends up kicking the dining-room clock, for "time is her enemy, and, she knows, the natural enemy of us all; it is not fair that my father's naive trust in it works for him as pragmatically as some people's trust in God."

Now Hortense Calisher's stories have been collected in one volume—including **"Time, Gentlemen!"** and the other semiautobiographical "Hester stories." As anyone who has ever grown a little dotty over a particular writer knows, there is a certain greedy satisfaction in having such a collection at your fingertips, even if you've read nearly all the pieces in separate volumes before. Also, for me, it's nice to see what good judgment I showed as a college student.

The first realization you'll come to in this collection is that, at least in her perception of time, Hortense Calisher is her father's daughter. *The Collected Stories* is a fat, solid book; the pages are dense with print; the plots are built up slowly. We have all the time in the world, she seems to be saying; let me tell you these stories properly. And she does.

A bucktoothed spinster smiles "as if she were holding a mashed daisy in her mouth." A woman's long, pointed shoes look like "dachshunds' muzzles." A mother's grief for her dead child is conveyed by describing a kindergarten bathroom, with its "miniature basins and pygmy toilets and hooks about three and a half feet from the floor." Events are told not necessarily in chronological order, but as they occur to the speaker—as, perhaps, a Victorian gentleman might relate them, unwrapping them layer by layer like the leaves of one of his fine old panatelas.

"A story is an apocalypse," Hortense Calisher says, "served in a very small cup." But her style is so leisurely and expansive that one of *her* stories seems more like an apocalypse served in a gravy tureen. Like her father, however, she loses no customers with lack of haste. She has a gift for persuading people to adopt her own view of time—to suspend impatience, forget that urgent desire to find out how things end, and submerge themselves in details that open rooms off other rooms. I suspect that this is why I have always preferred her short stories to her novels—not that the novels are of lower quality, but that to sustain this degree of intensity for any length of time is too exhausting for the reader.

Nearly all of her stories convey a deep sense of *breakage*—the only word I can think of that is strong enough to describe the splits that exist between one character and the rest of the world, or between one way of life and another. In several pieces the outsiders are Jews, but the theme is not really anti-Semitism; the characters' Judaism is simply a kind of shorthand to show their condition of outsidedness.

Even the comedy is provided by outsidedness of some sort. A gawky Southern spinster, incongruously transplanted to New York, stumbles into membership in the Communist Party. In **"Songs My Mother Taught Me,"** the heroine's traditions of tact, graciousness, and scrupulously mended underwear lead her into stripping to her Merrie Widowe Waist-Pincher at a formal banquet.

There is a whole group of stories where the division is between the "watcher" and the "watched." They are truly painful; I recommend reading them in the bosom of whatever family you can gather round you. Every inch of the landscape of loneliness is described in them so thoroughly—the unmarried aunt at the edge of the family funeral, the shopgirl slogging through her despairing routine, the widow waking at night to listen for a scream that, like those high-pitched whistles for dogs, can be heard only by those who are abysmally lonesome.

And when an attempt is made to bridge the divisions—which rarely happens in these stories—the result is more divisions. A divorced father, joyously celebrating his new marriage, finds himself split from his son. A woman tries to form some deeper connection with her lover, only to alienate him forever. Loneliness is our permanent condition, Hortense Calisher seems to be saying—or, at any rate, it is some people's.

But the warmest and most delicately wrought of these stories are the ones in which the division is between past and present—our present selves yearning over our past selves, like the middle-aged woman of **"The Nightclub in the Woods"** watching the newlywed couple dance. In fact, her lonely night club is not really so different from the long-lost Victorian apartment of **"Time, Gentlemen!"**: that "old place, lit up as bravely as a fishbowl against the dark shadows of eternity . . . falling through the clear ether silently, with all its house lights on."

Nightclub or fishbowl, P.S. 146 or a dead woman's dresser drawer—they are all a form of amber, sealing unforgettable moments in time. And Hortense Calisher is better at this sort of sealing than any other writer I know of.

> Anne Tyler, "Tales of Apocalypse Served Up in a Tureen," in The National Observer, November 22, 1975, p. 21.

Elaine Kendall   (essay date 1985)

[*Kendall is an American journalist and critic. In the following review of* Saratoga, Hot, *she assesses Calisher's use of the novella form.*]

"Some stories cling to the pen as novels do," Hortense Calisher has said, trying for more than the high or low moments of life; reaching for the essence of the life itself. The eight fictions in this collection [*Saratoga, Hot*] belong to that arbitrary category, qualifying by ambitiousness of purpose rather than complexity of plot, number of characters or length alone. Although these particular tales are layered and complex, calling them novels embroils the reader in an unnecessary academic riddle. When is a story not a story?

"Saratoga, Hot" shifts back and forth from the time that Tot, the well-meaning but undirected scion of a prominent horse-owning family, is the driver of a sports car involved in a serious accident. Nola, his date for the evening, suffers injuries that leave her lame. Traumatized by an overwhelming sense of responsibility, Tot is unable to settle upon a permanent career, supporting himself by managing a series of racing stables—work with little security but enough perks to make life comfortable. Horse owners, especially the lucky ones, are generous with their spare houses and cars, only too happy to include a personable young man in their festivities. When Nola has recovered sufficiently, Tot marries her, and they share this peripatetic and uncertain life.

Calisher is completely at ease with the run-down elegance of the Saratoga season; as familiar with the foibles of the horse owners as with the assorted gamblers, gangsters and sycophants who go with the territory. Simultaneously a love story, an acutely observed satire and a nostalgic commentary on the era when racing was the sport of kings, off-limits for the rabble, [**"Saratoga, Hot"**] seems closest to the author's stated purpose of creating "an apocalypse in a very small cup."

"Gargantua" is set in the hospital where the young writer's mother is desperately ill. For the first time in her life, the narrator is completely on her own. At the time the story takes place, the treatment for her mother's anemia is cooked liver, and with all the food in the world to choose from and only her own taste to consider, the daughter finds herself preparing liver for herself, as if the inexorable progress of her mother's disease could be halted by her participation in the cure. There's a circus in town, and the

unearthly shrieks of the gorilla, Gargantua, float up through the hospital window, lending a surreal dimension to the scene, turning the adolescent back into a child while the mother briefly becomes a parent instead of a patient. "Gahd," the daughter says, "Gah-hd" . . . an outgrown high school expression. "Must you?" the mother asks— "looking at me in the only way she ever seemed to, at two spots just above my temples, where all this future of mine could apparently be seen, already horning on the head— 'the word is *God.*' " Although the respite is short, a point has been made. Years later, as the writer herself is recovering from surgery, her memories of that interlude sustain her. Her mother's illness has educated her; provided her with the support and resilience she needs to regain her strength. "My mother and I have been here together all this time. . . . We are Gargantua."

"The Passenger" takes place on the Chicago-to-New York train, a long enough ride for character development, drama and resolution, as well as the social commentary essential to these stories. The writer is returning home after a television interview, although from the courteous service and well-maintained amenities on the train, we seem to be in an earlier period in the history of transportation. The club car is lively and crowded, offering far more scope for fiction than an airplane. For the sort of "small novel" Calisher has in mind, air travel is useless. She has embarked on this trip not only because trains are relatively dependable even in bad weather but because "of what happened to me on one, 15 years ago. Do I desire merely a replay of that wildly extraterritorial moment? Or do I also hope against hope, to lay down, while still alive, the burden it left me with?" Although the replay doesn't happen and is never described, the reader's curiosity is not only aroused but satisfied by the events and encounters that do.

"Sound Track" and **"Real Impudence"** are attempts to explore new territory—the shallow and often sleazy netherworlds of rock music and pop success. These stories show signs of strain, as if the writer were struggling to overcome her distaste for her themes. The tone seems uncharacteristically judgmental; the dialogue invented rather than overheard; the targets disintegrating under Calisher's close scrutiny.

In the end, the terminology doesn't matter. The treatments seem the right length for the subject; neither stretched short stories nor abbreviated novels but forms particularly and meticulously tailored to suit each occasion.

> Elaine Kendall, in a review of "Saratoga Hot," in Los Angeles Times Book Review, June 21, 1985, p. 5.

Hortense Calisher with Gregory Fitz Gerald and Peter Marchant   (interview date 1986)

[*Fitz Gerald is an American poet, short story writer, critic and educator, and Marchant is an American writer and educator. In the following interview, they question Calisher about her development as a writer.*]

[Fitz Gerald and Marchant]: *To what extent does autobiographical material enter into your fiction?*

[Calisher]: My first stories, which appeared in the *New Yorker* and later became known as the Hester stories, are very much what writers traditionally begin with: they were stories about my family. Even under my hand, however, the material began to change. Since I was a young writer, I didn't realize what was happening. Still, strange things were happening in the stories that I found I couldn't abide by. Even though I tried very hard to get down on paper exactly what the experience meant to me, it became evident that that actual experience was fading out, to be replaced by my rendition of it. I wrote about eight of those stories and then a story called **"In Greenwich There Are Many Graveled Walks,"** which I showed to a friend, Julian Muller, who had helped me get published. He had seen all my early stories before they found their way into print. When I showed him this one, he asked whether these were people I literally knew. I answered that I knew people *like* them, or that these characters had attributes of people I knew. He said, "Congratulations, you've written your second novel."

Characterization is a composite of attributes of people you know?

Yes, as I think it is for many writers. There are romans à clef like *Point Counter Point.* I assume Aldous Huxley tried very hard to represent very accurately the personalities of many famous English people he knew—D. H. Lawrence, Katherine Mansfield, Middleton Murry, Augustus John. Even if writers are not working so self-consciously, they unconsciously draw upon all of their experiences and people they knew in the mysterious way in which writing is born. The actress Irene Worth was telling me the other day how she collects the gestures of people she observes in a kind of storehouse of gesture for her art. Novelists probably don't operate quite that self-consciously; however, you will notice in Henry James's notebooks that he records incidents or stories that he might use in his fiction. I've tried that, but it never works. Such notebooks are interesting to look back to, but they are not a treasure house.

When I first met you, I was your graduate student at Iowa. You had that marvelous course in the novel, early on in your own career. Later, you went from writing short stories to writing novels. Would you discuss that development in your career?

Actually, at that time I was working on my first novel, *False Entry,* which took me about seven years to write. It was published about ten years after my first book of short stories. When that book of short stories appeared, I gave a long interview to Harvey Breit of the *New York Times.* He asked the question posed to all writers of short stories: "When are you going to write your novel?" I had thought it a publisher's question, since publishers have always felt that novels make more money, that they make a career as short stories do not. I told Harvey that if a writer can say everything that needs to be said in seven thousand words, why use seventeen thousand or seventy thousand?

A work ends formally for me as a writer when I can feel inside a sense of resolution; I cannot prolong it. At that time I had no idea I was going to write a novel, and I was sure that I wasn't going to write one just because someone thought I should. In time the novel came: this thing began to gather in me, just as stories had. For years I carried with me a sheet of yellow paper on which I had written notes for it, but I had done the same thing for short stories. I would have a whole page of key phrases that would be embodied in the short stories, key phrases that meant something only to me. Actually, the notes for some of the short stories were longer than for that first novel.

Often the best stories, or even novels, come with their endings in mind before I begin to write them—not the end scene so much as the end sentence or the end language. I had that end import for *False Entry* for years before I actually wrote it. That novel took me a long time in part because I had young children and I had to learn how to be a full-time writer. Also I was approaching, with some trepidation, this lengthy work, and I discovered that it takes time, it takes reverie. I had never taken as long with a book. My later novel, *Mysteries of Motion,* also took a long time.

Once you mastered the novel form, did you find it difficult to return to the short story?

Yes, I remember being told that by the editor of the *New Yorker,* William Maxwell, who had seen it to be true among many writers with whom he had worked. I *have* done it, but I do find that my short stories are longer after having written novels. I recall my former agent Bernice Baumgarten telling me, just before taking me to lunch with the eminent editor of the *New Yorker,* Katherine White, who was to be my editor but was ill at the time, "Katherine always feels so awful when a short-story writer turns into a novelist." I will not tell you what I replied!

I wish you would!

It was obs . . . not for everyone's ears, because I thought it rather a nerve of her to say.

I have always been impressed with your short stories, for a certain magic they have. I am impressed in particular by characterization and style. For example, I recall the character in **"The Hollow Boy."** *Is there any background for that story that you are willing to share with us? Who was that boy?*

It is an entirely imaginary character.

It is a very fully realized imaginary character then.

He is an immigrant boy, and his parents are working very hard to open a restaurant. They are very stingy German types of a certain class that I *did* know. The setting is New York, and he is beginning to open out to his world. Everything that his parents buy for his birthday is really for the restaurant, however. He has a friend whose family is somewhat like the family of a high school friend of mine—excitable, Socialist–Labor Party types. Her father was an amateur violinist who worked in the garment industry; the women in the family were all excitable Russians who talked about art all the time. They were very warm—not that mine weren't—and I loved them all. The friend may have been partly me.

It's interesting that you should mention that, since I thought your making the narrator an adolescent boy was an accomplishment.

And yet male writers create female characters all the time. As I have said in the preface to my collected short stories, I see no reason why we women should not make Bovarys of boys and men.

I get the strong impression from what you say and write that you are not entirely sure at the beginning of the story what its form or direction will be, that there has to be an element of organic development which comes from within. Is that correct?

I may not be entirely sure of the direction, but I have a strong sense of the story's organic import—it's a theme, something like a round, beautiful globe that I hope to bring into being. At the same time, I may not be sure of the line-by-line narrative development—that comes at the point of the pen.

Speaking of the point of the pen, I might add that I am impressed by the subtlety and flexibility of your style. Do you work very hard at style?

No!! Indeed, some reviewers have seen my style as a limitation, especially those who feel that style ought to be absolutely colorless, like the agar in which micro-organisms are suspended. Somerset Maugham was supposed to be the embodiment of that personless style. If critics value that personless style, they will criticize writers for having a "lapidary" style, to use a term once applied to my writing. I, too, believe that style ought not to be decorative.

But one could see another meaning of the term lapidary: *a person who examines a gem through a magnifying glass in such a way that the gem's strong points and beauties are emphasized.*

This is an old literary argument that is never going to be resolved. Fashions come and go.

I read the passages on critics in Herself *with great sympathy. I wanted to say, "Right on!" I agree that there is much bad criticism. What do you see as the value of* good *criticism?*

Good critics bring us to literature. Bad criticism results from the critic's ego getting between the work and the reader. There is always the critic who wants to make a name by using a book or author to create his own work of art. When a critic feels that he is an artist—and very few are—he is less concerned with interpreting the writer than with self-aggrandizement. On the other hand, if the critic comes to literature as Edmund Wilson did, he is passionate to bring people to the things he loves.

Has any criticism affected your creative work?

Very little, I should say—except to make me angry. I want to answer critics, and sometimes I do. However, generally I avoid criticism myself, in the intervals between books. Writers learn quickly, if they are steady writers, that this engine they have inside themselves wants to keep going.

The satisfaction of having successfully finished a book lasts about two weeks, and then I want to be writing again. I enjoy criticism at that point because I want to discover what I think about a work, and I do that best at point of pen.

You mentioned a critic who had misunderstood your book The New Yorkers *and had damaged it seriously in his review.*

He was on the staff of the *New Yorker* and had himself just published a book. Often newly published writers are asked to review books. He was an odd choice, however, since he had just published a collection of business portraits, one of which was of the Piggly-Wiggly grocery stores. In any case, he was asked to review a novel of mine, *The New Yorkers,* (a companionpiece to *False Entry,* the two of them being a long chronicle of American life). He literally wrote that he didn't understand my book, so everybody thought it must be my fault. Nobody thought it might be his! Afterward he wrote me the most curious letter of apology. I wished he had published it, but no one else saw it. I don't know that the review killed the novel, but it was the main review in the *New York Times.* Reviews can make or break a book. What else can I say?

Do such reviews adversely affect your writing?

For a while, but the only cure is to go on writing, to have something else to move on to. In fairness, I should add that I do not remember the good reviews, either. I changed publishers once, and I had to exhume from my archives what the new publisher wanted as a backlog of cuttings. Although I never systematically keep them—I am forever tossing cuttings into drawers here and there—I did have quite a few. I was quite surprised by the nice things people had said about my work, but such things do not penetrate a writer's consciousness. If they did, perhaps many of us would stop writing.

Have you ever been interested in writing science fiction?

I have written fiction about space, but I am determined that it not be considered science fiction. We must be aware that an enormous amount of our future lives will be involved in space—space shuttles, space labs, and so forth are going to be part of our everyday world. There are space museums all over the country, and yet most adults walk around in them as though they were in fantasyland.

We are dealing with the next stage in the development of transportation. I'm interested in transportation as part of America's myth. I don't write with that interest in mind, but I have written two novellas—**"The Railway Police"** and **"The Last Trolley Ride"**—and in the latter there is a kind of folklore passage about transportation and what it means to America, and to all of us on this planet. Scientists, I'm sure, would agree that space now offers new challenges in transportation.

I'm interested too in the moral implications, as there always are whenever we begin to do something of this magnitude; that is, moving out into space: what are the far-reaching effects on humans of this movement into space? For, of course, I am a humanist; I believe that the impulse of literature is humanistic. My husband says that I'm going to have a hard time convincing people that some of my later writing isn't science fiction, but I'm going to try. I wrote a book called *Journal from Ellipsia,* which was classified as science fiction. People thought I knew a great deal about science, but I didn't. I was fascinated by the vocabulary of astrophysics.

Your husband, Curtis Harnack, is also a novelist. What is it like for two novelists to be married to each other and to work together? Many would consider that an impossible situation.

It depends on *which* two novelists! We are very closely married. Both of us had been married to nonartists, and we find an extra closeness because we share the same kind of work. We are very different as novelists. We come from different parts of the country: I would be considered an urban novelist, while he comes from the great heartland—Iowa—and has written very affectingly about that part of the nation. When he began to write, those books were considered so-called farm novels and were very unfashionable. That's all changed now, and the city is beginning to get it in the neck. It helps that we have different styles; but we like each other's work. What really makes it possible for our lives is that we both go off into our own separate places where we are thinking about our work rather than each other. Some who are not writers might resent in their spouses that kind of immersion.

So the usual fears of competition don't apply at all?

No, we root for each other, and not artificially. Most people anticipate there would be plate-throwing; I can conceive of myself throwing a plate, but not over literature.

What are your writing habits?

I'm a morning writer. I get up very early, and I don't want to talk to God or man, or husband, and he feels the same. I work until I have to stop—no definite time. You learn your own habits. Having written as long as I have, I know that toward the end of a book I can write longer into the day. Everything begins to fuse and come to its natural resolution; once you have laid down the paths, what was tentative at the beginning has direction. As I finish, I can write eight hours a day, I can work long days revising first drafts of my fiction, but those are exhausting days. I hate them!

Do you consider yourself a feminist?

In *Herself* I tried to examine the situation of a writer who is a woman. I was speaking more to other writers than to women generally. I wrote about several oddities like the affect of a woman as opposed to a man's: George Eliot's curls were ridiculous, but Walt Whitman's beard was sincere.

I've been a feminist since the beginning, in my way. There is a story I wrote called **"The Rabbi's Daughter,"** which is reprinted occasionally in feminist collections. I'm not a doctrinaire feminist: I would never join any movement, I suppose, because I have to *speak* for myself. As one involved with the word, I have to make the words; I cannot allow any group to speak for me politically.

Generally, however, I believe that America is particularly backward in its treatment of its writers who are women. I feel much more comfortable in England and Europe because no one approaches me as a *female* writer or a *woman* writer abroad, but here I have to explain, as I am now explaining, that a writer who is a woman is just that, not necessarily a *woman* writer.

I was one of the first to use domestic life in my fiction because it was part of my experience. Men write out of their own experience, but the burden is still on the writer who is a woman to explain, even to justify, her material. Giving birth, which is rather important to life, was not considered so important to literature. It was just considered something women do. I never felt that the whole area of human expression was not open to me as a person, and I still don't.

Hortense Calisher, Gregory Fitz Gerald, and Peter Marchant, in an interview in Southwest Review, *Vol. 71, No. 2, Spring, 1986, pp. 186-93.*

Thomas Mallon   (essay date 1987)

[*Mallon is an American novelist, biographer, critic, and educator who garnered acclaim for his masterful and voluminous study of diaries,* A Book of One's Own: People and Their Diaries *(1984). In the following review of* Age, *he questions the efficacy of Calisher's ornate style and the verisimilitude of her portrait of an elderly couple.*]

Rupert and Gemma, the aging main characters of Hortense Calisher's new novella [*Age*], have the kind of fading, genteel glamour that their names convey. He is a poet "who no longer writes much" and she is an architect "who no longer builds." Thirty-five years into what is a second marriage for both, they mostly devote themselves to each other. Their union is both sensible and deep, and it is still, on occasion, confirmed in the physical: "Our naked bodies are more of a match now, brought to resemblance by the Palladian lines of aging."

What distresses them most, as Gemma puts it, "is that one of us will inevitably be left behind." To obviate this fate they decide each to compose what they variously call an almanac, an archive and a dialogue (a diary, really) to serve as "company—to the one of us who survives. To be read by him or me—only afterward." This joint program of journal-keeping gives the book its central premise and the characters their chief problem: having to decide, finally, if what is planned as consolation may not eventually present just as much opportunity for torment. (Jane Welsh Carlyle's diary, one may remember, gave her husband, Thomas, a nasty posthumous shock.)

Age has some other subjects and activity, too. The reader learns of the violent death of a daughter from Gemma's first marriage ("I have no place to accommodate my feelings about Francesca, so I do without them") and becomes acquainted with Rupert and Gemma's old friends, Kit and Sherm, the latter a nicely drawn specimen of the overpraised man of American letters, his head an "oversized benignity" that "looks so well on rostrums." Residing in

Rupert and Gemma's Manhattan house is their tenant, Mr. Quinn, a sporty nonagenarian who once played tennis with Bill Tilden and who still wears a "Prince of Wales V-neck sweater." Gemma envies "this gofer from the past" who "is having an amateur old age." The best scene in *Age,* ludicrous and moving, involves the passing of Rupert's first wife, Gertrude, at the Plaza Hotel, attended by not only Rupert and Gemma but also two nuns from a hospice for the dying (an institution supported by another, more recent, husband of Gertrude's). "May one ignore the shrewd narcissism of the dying?" asks Gemma. "Or must one skip to it?" Gertrude's theatrical exit succeeds in impressing not only the characters who witness it but the reader as well.

Age is technically complicated as short novels go, sometimes unfortunately so. The narrative is carried by the alternating diaries-in-progress, but the entries tend to advance themselves on wisps of dialogue and prose poetry, and the antiphonal voices of Rupert and Gemma are not particularly distinct—though there's a point to be made by this, of course. In her 17th volume of fiction, Ms. Calisher remains splendidly capable of aphorism ("Guilt coarsens the tongue"), but just as often she will have one of her diarists strain toward the unauthentic generalization: "Women museum curators tend to stay younger than their age." Likewise, her elegant imagery ("Age must sing its own voluntary, in a chorus of one") has a tendency to overdress itself: "that night-blooming plant of our era, carbon monoxide." Her observations of the behavioral symptoms of aging—"sudden cabs, untoward purse-fumblings, a sense that one has talked too much, or else been silent without knowing it"—are generally sharp, if not particularly unexpected.

Rupert and Gemma may be admirable, even heroic, in their "gestures against death." Watching her sew on a button, he remarks approvingly: "To be under imminent sentence. . . . And threading a needle." And yet one wonders whether their decision to face death head-on, their preoccupation with it, isn't a kind of premature defeat, less inspiring than evasion would be, and perhaps morbidly atypical.

Last June I had the pleasure of dining with some women of the class of 1927 who had returned for their reunion at Vassar College, where I teach. Charles Lindbergh's landing, made the month they graduated, came up only because I (age 35) made a point of asking about it. The women themselves, several years older than Rupert and Gemma, seemed much to prefer conversing about Oliver North, Gary Hart, the compact disk players their children had given them for their birthdays. There is something, finally, annoying about the still reasonably robust Rupert and Gemma being so insistently focused on the supposedly essential. The unexamined life may not be worth living, but one ironic result of *Age* is that it makes one wonder if it isn't better to live as if there's *every* tomorrow, right up until death brings its unwanted relief.

Thomas Mallon, "To the One Left Behind," in The New York Times Book Review, *October 18, 1987, p. 14.*

Sylvie Drake   (essay date 1987)

[*Drake is an Egyptian-born American drama critic. In the following negative review of* Age, *she takes issue with Calisher's liberal use of mundane details in her portrait of the protagonists and faults the writing as overwrought and self-conscious.*]

What to make of this slender novel/novella [*Age*] by Hortense Calisher? It is as fragile and paradoxical as the state of its protagonists, a spunky pair—he a poet, she an architect—who are confronting the last frontier: the uncharted territory of age.

These two, Rupert and Gemma, have made a pact in their 70s to keep separate journals of their life together. The journals are to be read only when one of them dies, which means only the survivor gets to read both. It's a curious, not entirely logical idea, troubling even to the characters as characters.

It allows Calisher the conceit of giving us introspective views of the same life seen through different angles of a shared prism. In this case, it's two views of a marriage in which events by now are few and mostly unremarkable. The device, an opportunity for close examination of the *emotional* process of aging, is oddly used.

Calisher focuses on the minutiae of living—the descending spiral of energy and autonomy, the extended concerns that creep up on people as age treacherously advances.

Not a bad approach, theoretically. This zeroing in on the particular can, and often does, have echoes in the universal. But Calisher is hit and miss. Too much of the time she focuses on minutiae that remain minute. Nor does she achieve enough distinction between the voices of Gemma and Rupert.

Though she claims to alternating chapters being written by these alternating members of the couple, they sound exactly alike, which is frequently confusing.

Much more problematic, however, is Calisher's idiosyncratic style. She writes in strangely unfinished sentences. Without verbs. Like this. Usually. Too often.

While striving for simplicity, this overaffection for truncated phrases becomes merely eccentric. Just as perplexing is the fact that she'll career from something as exquisite as "those sunbelt clothes that look like food coloring" or "the sun splashes all with afternoon paint" to something as improbably awkward as " 'Now you tell me. What you've been up to. *I've* told you. What I.' "

On balance, the cleverness of "cheese smacking of the best cholesterol," the perception of "What youth does is make me uncertain I am still in the world" or the happy economy of "It's where you say what you should never think" do not make up for too much of the rest of the self-conscious writing. There is an unshakable awareness here of a writer at work.

Elizabeth Forsythe Hailey's *Joanna's Husband and David's Wife* utilized the similar idea of a husband and wife contributing to a single memoir (in this case a husband comes across his wife's record of their life together and injects his own vastly different perceptions of it). While it is not the same story and has nothing to do with age, there was a color and individuality in those characters that we miss in Calisher's manicured volume. Too much gentility is part of it, but *Age* natters where it should speak. It is embroidery rather than a work of the heart—or to borrow Rupert's words: "A progression of replicas almost without matter, without devotion to any original."

Sylvie Drake, *"Charting the Frontier Called Age," in* Los Angeles Times Book Review, *December 13, 1987, p. 11.*

Calisher on gender and writing:

There does seem to be a tendency, here [in the United States], to distinguish between men and women writers. I think it's based on the rather strange distinctions that are made in this country in dividing things into the feminine and the masculine; there are things that are right for females to do, and things that are right for males to do.

Actually, the male writer in America suffers from this more than women do. We suffer critically in the sense that we are usually reviewed by women writers, by other women generally, and it's a great accolade to be finally reviewed by a man, but this is incidental in this country. The fact that so many of our male writers must flex their virility muscles in peculiar ways must be hard on them. They have to fight through the generation of writers that grew up with me, and in a way repeat the thing that Hemingway did to show that although he was an artist, he could shoot bears or fish. Many young writers still have this difficulty, and I think it comes from the fact that it's not quite all right in America for a man to be an artist. I think it's much, much easier, now; in fact, many of the young male writers I know aren't out shooting bear and seem quite secure.

Hortense Calisher, Conversations, *Rand McNally & Co., 1967.*

Louis Harap   (essay date 1987)

[*Harap is an American editor and critic whose work has focused on Jewish contributions to American culture. In the following excerpt from his* In the Mainstream: The Jewish Presence in Twentieth-Century American Literature, 1950s-1980s, *Harap discusses the theme of Jewish acculturation in America as it is manifested in Calisher's fiction.*]

Whatever inhibiting influences existed in the 1940s and 1950s . . . novels with Jewish characters and some with acculturation themes continued to appear. A recognized short story writer like Hortense Calisher was not at all reluctant to draw occasionally on her experience as a Jew. She wanted to be herself, "what I was," and "it simply never occurred to me" not to treat her own mode of experience as a Jew in America with her ethnic "mixture." This is borne out in her stories. Unlike most Jewish writers of recent generations who were East European, she came of a second-generation German-Jewish father and a first-

generation German-Jewish mother. Her family lived in the South in comfortable circumstances. Calisher asserts that "with some Jews later," she was "compromised" because she "had no recent *shtetl* tradition"; indeed, she had never heard of the *shtetl* until she later read about it and "met its traces in friends." She was even suspected of trying to conceal an awareness of the *shtetl* and a knowledge of Yiddish, so much were such signs of origin taken for granted by many. These stories dealing with Jewish characters are largely limited to the German Jews, whom she knows best. Her stories, written during the 1940s and 1950s, show a particularly lively awareness of anti-Semitism. She had little patience with self-deception concerning Jewishness. Her sequence of stories about Hester Elkins from age ten to marriage contain few allusions, but one of the stories, **"The Old Stock,"** published in the *New Yorker* in 1950, concerned a self-hating Jewish mother. The story evoked a storm of disapproving mail and even newspaper comment. In her autobiography, *Herself* (1974), Calisher writes that the story "touched on the same self-hatred and secret fears; I have dared to imply that Jews are not impeccable."

In the story Hester and her mother go to the South Farm in the Catskills. The mother in the story is obviously based on her own mother as described in her autobiography, a self-hating German Jew who despised East European Jews as endangering her social position and who, in the vivid words of the story, which might also describe her own mother, gave a "prim display of extra constraint . . . in the presence of other Jews whose grosser features, voices, manners, offended her sense of gentility all the more out of her resentful fears that she might be identified with them." Mother and daughter visit an old local aristocrat, Miss Onderdonk, with whom they were acquainted from other years at the farm. Miss Onderdonk complains, "I told Miss Smith she'd rue the day she ever started taking in Jews." Mrs. Elkins replies, "I thought you knew that we were—Hebrews." " 'Say it,' Hester prayed, . . . say 'Jew.' " With the self-assurance of the bigot the old lady observes, " . . . ain't no Jew. Good blood shows any day. . . . Can't say it didn't cross my mind. Thought that the girl does have the look." Back at the farm, Mrs. Elkins' hostile attitude toward her fellow Jewish guests also aroused the epistolary ire of some Jewish readers. Calisher observes in her autobiography that in this story she had excited such vehement defensive responses because she had "expressed some of these tormenting self-doubts of even the most outwardly impregnable Jew—rich, assimilated, cosmopolitan, living an easy life scarcely subject to slurs, much less oppression. . . . Are 'we' anything like 'they' say we are? . . . I had explored what must never be admitted to enemy forces—that there are divisions in our ranks,— . . . hierarchies. I had turned up the under side of our snobberies."

Anti-Semitism is explored in other stories, in **"Two Colonials"** and **"The Hollow Boy."** Social anti-Semitism at college is treated in **"One of the Chosen."** At a twenty-year reunion of his college victory crew, for which he was coxswain, David Spanner is reminiscing with Number One oar, Anderson, "effortlessly debonair and assured." After catching up on the past, Anderson tells Spanner,

"Remember the house I used to belong to? . . . The one that got into the news in the thirties because they hung a swastika over the door. Or maybe somebody hung it on *them*. . . . Could have been either way." Then, more confidentially, "You know, Davy. . . . I wanted to take you in. . . . A few of us together could have pushed it through—but all the others made such a God-damned stink over it, we gave in. I suppose you heard. . . . If we hadn't been so damned unseeing, so sure of ourselves in those days. . . . Ah, well, . . . That's water over the dam."

He gave Spanner a "brotherly slap on the back, and turned away embarrassed. Standing there, it was as if Spanner felt the flat of it, not between his shoulder blades, but stinging on his suddenly hot cheek—that sharp slap of revelation."

Calisher remarks in her autobiography that, after these short stories, "I could not write of Jews again until [the novel] *The New Yorkers* [1964]." In that novel her Jewish characters accept their Jewishness in a relaxed manner. The central character, Judge Mannix, tells his rabbi, "every martyr's already half self-made, don't you think? . . . We all half chose to be victims—to be the chosen." Because, I suppose, they reject either extreme, defensiveness or intimidation, about their identity. The earlier stories had been written from this conviction. They resisted both hypersensitivity and outright anti-Semitism in others.

Louis Harap, "The Jewish Decade: The 1950s," in his In the Mainstream: The Jewish Presence in Twentieth-Century American Literature, 1950s-1980s, *Greenwood Press, 1987, pp. 21-51.*

Kathleen Snodgrass   (essay date 1993)

[*In the following excerpts from her* The Fiction of Hortense Calisher, *Snodgrass discusses the central themes of Calisher's work—including the journey of personal self-discovery, the gulfs of miscommunication which sunder relationships, and the persistence of family experiences in present conflicts—as evidenced in her short stories and novellas.*]

Between 1948 and 1953 Calisher published eleven autobiographical stories; a twelfth appeared in 1965. In all but three of the stories, the protagonist is Hester Elkins and the narrator, her adult self looking back at crucial episodes in her youth. The stories are replete with details of a time long past (the earliest takes place during an Armistice parade in New York City), yet these are anything but exercises in nostalgia.

In his Introduction to the 1984 edition of ***Collected Stories,*** John Hollander argues that the autobiographical stories—grouped together here for the first time—interconnect but not in a "novelistic" way: "The continuity that does exist is provided more by an authorial sensibility and critical consciousness than by the family and the German-Jewish middle-class Manhattan of their milieu." However, beyond the unity created by the adult narrator's consciousness, there is, in fact, a novelistic unity. The theme of initiation clearly dominates each of the twelve

stories: each culminates in a moment of epiphanic self-awareness. If the stories were to be rearranged in a biographically chronological order, that theme becomes at once more encompassing and more defined: a single (albeit, episodic) narrative takes shape, dramatizing Hester Elkins's rites of passage from childhood through adolescence to early adulthood.

The often uneasy triangle of parents and child looms large in these stories. By temperament and acculturation, Mr. Elkins is a turn-of-the-century Southern gentleman; the Austrian-born Mrs. Elkins, a twentieth-century dynamo. One is an easygoing and adoring father; the other is a demanding and hypercritical mother. The young Hester firmly allies herself with her father and his strategy for living; as the narrative progresses, however, what seemed once a neatly defined either-or reality becomes—given Hester's increasingly charged love-hate relationship with her mother—clouded and complex.

Hester's coming of age falls into distinctive stages corresponding to definite clusterings of stories. In the earliest stage, as seen in **"Time, Gentlemen!" "May-ry,"** and **"The Coreopsis Kid,"** the central relationship is between Hester and her father. But even as Hester basks in his uncritical love and warm, expansive nature, chinks in his armor appear. Although Mr. Elkins is only a peripheral figure at best in the second group of stories—**"A Box of Ginger," "The Pool of Narcissus,"** and **"The Watchers"**—the essentially romantic approach to life he embodies is found to be woefully inadequate. Mrs. Elkins's brand of realism dominates the next group of stories, **"The Gulf Between"** and **"Old Stock."** Then, in two stories of emotional impasse—**"The Sound of Waiting"** and **"The Rabbi's Daughter"**—neither realism nor idealism seems to provide a strategy for living. Only in **"Gargantua"** and **"The Middle Drawer"** does Hester finally achieve a moment's delicate balance of two seemingly opposed sets of values.

The first group of stories introduces not only Hester's parents, mismatched in years and in temperament, but also Hester as the child between them—though not yet torn between them. The mood of **"Time, Gentlemen!"** is sweetly elegiac, as the narrator remembers, thirty years later, the daily ritual of getting Mr. Elkins off to work. Mrs. Elkins is only a peripherally disapproving, nagging presence, at war with her husband's "Victorian sense of time." Like an English bartender calling "Time, gentlemen" at closing, she would clear her house of late-morning revelers. Mr. Elkins is described in loving detail:

> My father, born in 1862, and old enough to be my grandfather when I entered the world a year after his marriage to a woman twenty-two years younger than he, was by birth therefore a late Victorian. . . . [A] precocious, Alger-like energy—in his case combined with some of the bright, fairy-tale luck that comes to the third sons in Grimm—was to keep him all his life younger in appearance and temperament than others of his span. . . .

Each workday morning sees a struggle between Hester's parents: "a parable in which Conscientious Practicality, my mother, strove to get Imaginative Indolence, my father, out of the house somewhere nearer to nine than noon." That Mr. Elkins's business runs smoothly enough without him counts for little in Mrs. Elkins's mind; she craves "the appearance of frenzied toil."

On this particular day (a quintessential one, really) young Hester is her father's ally and co-conspirator. His leisurely breakfast—calves' brains, first blanched, then sautéed—followed by meandering conversations with a succession of tradesmen, is matched by Hester's feigning illness so as to stay home from school. Both triumph: Mr. Elkins is still home at noon; Hester is home for the day. At the story's—and the day's—end, Mr. Elkins delights in the company of his family gathered around the dining room table: "We are all together with him in the now. . . . The lamps are lit for the night, against that death which is change."

By situating that evening "in the now," a timeless present, the adult narrator still allies herself with her father. And yet, she also remembers, "with an Eurasian aching," her parents' "dividing voices." They may be as different from each other as two continents, but the adult Hester now acknowledges what her childhood self could not: that she is native to both.

In **"May-ry,"** Hester is once again the enthralled witness to a family drama which her father dominates. This time, however, she is not her father's ally: "He was the kindest man in the world, yet when the time came, it was my father who was purely unkind to our colored maid."

Mrs. Elkins is again the censorious outsider, her disapproval this time directed at Mr. Elkins's easy, jocular relationship with their maid, Mary (pronounced "May-ry" by the Richmond-born Mr. Elkins). For ten years, the two have had an understanding: Mary's periodic drinking binges have been explained away as attacks of rheumatism. Although Mary is thirty-years old, Mr. Elkins considers her a child "and he loved all children. Just so long as she kept herself seemly in front of him . . . she was only doing what was expected of her." So long as Mary drank outside the house and kept up her side of the long-standing fiction, Mr. Elkins was content. His home remained sacrosanct, protected from realities he would rather not face; hence, his adamant refusal to listen to Mary when, having decided to resign, she wants the truth finally out in the open:

> [He] positively refused to consider, to treat, to discuss, to *tolerate* a hint of what she wanted to tell him and he knew as well as she did. That she'd been lying all these years and wanted the dear privilege of saying so.

Mary finally screams out the truth and leaves, never to return. Decidedly the Southern patriarch, Mr. Elkins is fiercely protective not only of his home but also of his long-held belief that blacks are essentially childlike.

"Time, Gentlemen!" and **"May-ry,"** companion stories, dramatize what is at once one of Mr. Elkins's most and least admirable attributes: his determination to make his home a refuge. Her father's staunchest ally in **"Time, Gentlemen!"**, Hester becomes his reluctant judge in **"May-ry,"** and in so doing, takes a step back, however unconsciously, from her father's approach to life.

Mr. Elkins is again a dominant figure in **"The Coreopsis Kid,"** a story which celebrates his unconditional love; for the first time, however, Mrs. Elkins is a presence to be reckoned with. Hester is a tall, ungainly nine-year-old, an only child who feels increasingly expendable and unlovable as her mother's second pregnancy comes to term. At a family garden party in the fall of 1918, Hester identifies herself with many of the party-goers, Mr. Elkins's elderly retainers, who "swam knowingly toward him out of the sea of incompetents." Convinced, as only a nine-year-old can be, that the birth of a sibling will leave her, very literally, out in the cold, a banished waif, Hester especially identifies with Mr. Katz, the oldest and feeblest of her father's retainers: they two "were the worthless people, whom the practical people could not forever afford." Her father was the magnanimous one, "[b]ut with Mrs. Elkins, some businesslike reason for being was expected." The war's end and the baby's arrival signify the end of an era:

> the probable end of a halcyon time, after which expenses like herself and Katz, unless they could justify themselves in the meantime, might not be rescuable, even by her father, from her mother's measurement of worth.

Hester becomes even more convinced of her own unlovableness when she compares herself to her female cousins: "a rosy wreath. . . . as closed to her as if they had locked hands against her, meanwhile interchanging the soft passwords of their pet names." Seeing her face's reflection—"sallow, shuttered, and long"—she concludes that "It must lack some endearing lineament, against which people and language might cuddle. For it, a nickname was a status to be earned."

The story ends with two celebrations, the Armistice Day parade and Hester's private rejoicing in the knowledge that neither love nor a nickname "was a status to be earned." The discovery is a serendipitous one. Sent to collect Mr. Katz, whom Mr. Elkins has invited to the parade, Hester spots a photograph of her three-year-old self "in white corduroy bonnet with lining frilling her solemn face," inscribed by her father: *Regards. From the Coreopsis Kid."* Mr. Elkins, a manufacturer of fine soaps, talcums, and toilet water, including "Coreopsis of Japan," had heralded the birth of "The Coreopsis Kid" with eight hundred telegrams. Here is the reassurance Hester has craved: she has always been lovable and worthy of a nickname in her father's eyes.

Still, the closing paragraph reveals how fragile and provisional Hester's personal armistice is. Like countless other well-wishers of the parading soldier, Hester holds an orange to throw. She is loathe to let go of this concrete symbol of her happiness:

> It was round, perfect, like the world at this moment. If there was a flaw in it, it could not yet be seen. She held onto it for as long as she could. Then, closing her eyes tight, she threw it.

A world war may have ended, but Hester still sees the world as divided into warring camps; her familial dilemma persists: "there was no pleasing them—the practical ones. Yet they had to be pleased."

As the narrative progresses, however, a more complex configuration evolves from the young child's unambiguously black-and-white view. In the next group of stories—**"A Box of Ginger," "The Pool of Narcissus,"** and **"The Watchers"**—"the practical ones" prove to possess more interesting dimensions than the young Hester had imagined. And, just as the realists gain a certain ascendency, the romantics lose ground.

In **"A Box of Ginger,"** Mr. Elkins is again the patriarch warding off painful truths. On the funeral day of his brother he cannot bring himself to tell his ninety-three-year-old mother of her son's death (having let her believe, through letters Mr. Elkins wrote in his brother's name, that her son was out West recuperating). Mrs. Elkins urges her husband to read the most recent "letter" to his almost totally blind mother, but it is Hester's nine-year-old brother, Kinny, feeling very adult and important, who volunteers for the task. His grandmother, quickly seeing through the sham, realizes that her son is dead. The story ends with grandmother and grandson embracing: "they rocked back and forth together, in a moment of complicity and love."

Mr. Elkins's tender-hearted, essentially romantic approach to life is not denigrated (even his wife joins him in countenancing a comforting lie over a painful truth) but neither does it triumph, as in **"Time, Gentlemen!"** and **"The Coreopsis Kid."** And, in two other stories—**"The Pool of Narcissus"** and **"The Watchers"**—the adolescent Hester becomes more acutely aware. In both stories Hester is still essentially an observer absorbing crucial lessons.

A tall, gawky twelve-year-old in **"The Pool of Narcissus,"** ill at ease in her party dress of "lavender voile, its color harsh against her olive-brown hands," Hester longs for the looks and bearing of Mrs. Braggiotti, the widowed mother of her friend, Clara, who "with her tilted nose, masses of true blond hair, and bud mouth, was just what every shag-haired girl staring into the Narcissus pools of adolescence hoped to see." A moment's clear-sightedness threatens that romantic vision when Hester observes Mrs. Braggiotti

> wearing a pince-nez that mercilessly puckered the flesh between her brows, giving her the appearance of a doll that had been asked to cope with human problems.

For a time, Hester manages to dispel any such unflattering and disquieting images of her idol.

Following Clara's birthday party, she and Hester accompany Mrs. Braggiotti and her unByronic suitor, George, to his soda fountain. There, Hester witnesses a brief but disturbing scene:

> Mrs. Braggiotti pushed George away sharply. "My shoe! Oh, you've got dirt all over my shoe!" She bent down to brush it, real distress on her face.
>
> "What is it you *do* want, Etta?"
>
> . . . "Why, I don't want anything, George," she said, in the same tone with which she had refused the sundae.

Hester has heard enough to want out of "the dim island of the store . . . with its promise of suspension, of retreat" from the outside world. Her romantic idol unmasked as a paper doll with an emotional depth to match, Hester runs out into the cold, eager for "people she could jostle, buffet, and embrace." In **"The Coreopsis Kid,"** a younger Hester despaired of her long, sallow face, so painfully different from those of her conventionally pretty cousins. Here, she sees herself in a new, more flattering light: "Looking down at her hands, she thought suddenly that they were a good color; it was the lavender voile that was wrong."

In **"The Watchers,"** however, she learns to be wary of too much difference, of an unconventionality that leaves one too far out in the cold. Now fourteen years old, Hester has found another role model: her spinster aunt, Selena, who, like Mrs. Braggiotti, seems at first enviably detached from mundane concerns. Selena proves to be an even more chillingly cautionary figure, not because of anything she does, but, rather, because of Hester's closer identification with her.

Initially, Selena's aloof, Bohemian airs fascinate the silently rebellious teenager:

> Spare and dark-haired, the color of a dried fig, she wore odd off colors, like puce and mustard and reseda green. Although they did not become her, she carried them like an invidious commentary on the drab patterns around her, and her concave chest was heavily looped with the coral residue of some years' stay in Capri as an art student, in her youth.

Hester envisions her aunt "living in the narrow, high rooms of one of the single houses she associated with the very rich . . . from which the humdrum truth of people would be inscrutably barred"—a house all the more alluring since inimical to Hester's noisily busy "family of Philistines."

She is subsequently bewildered to discover that her idol is pathetically eager for those Philistines' acceptance. Following Hester's grandmother's death, the Elkins household bustles with activity, and Selena, her "cheeks . . . hennaed with an unaccustomed tinge of participation," performs the humble tasks assigned her. When, before long, someone else takes over, Selena joins Hester on the sidelines. What Hester admired and sought to emulate in Selena is losing its romantic aura:

> For a long time the two of them sat there watching, while between them grew a tenuous thread of communion, as between two who sit at the edge of a party or a dance, sipping the moderate liqueur of observation, while around them swirl the tipsier ones, involved in a drunkenness the watchers do not share.

Heard but not spoken in Hester's simile is the word, "wallflower."

At the story's close, Hester and Selena, her name unaccountably missing from the list of family mourners, are left behind. Hester,

> In her mind, like a frieze . . . saw the added-up

picture of Selena, always watching tentatively, thirstily, on the fringe of other people's happiness, and fear grew in her as she became suddenly aware of her own figure. . . . It was watching, too.

More often than not, throughout the autobiographical stories, Hester's avidity for close, critical observation is cast in a far more positive light.

The teenage Hester of the next two stories, **"The Gulf Between"** and **"Old Stock,"** is both observer and participant in familial and social dramas that further complicate her view of adulthood. **"The Gulf Between"** opens six months after the death of Mr. Elkins's mother; his economic losses necessitate their moving from a spacious apartment—Hester's home since birth—to another half its size. Mrs. Elkins's "village-sense of disaster," for so long frustrated by affluence, rises or, depending on one's perspective, sinks to the occasion.

On this dismal moving day, "as always in time of crisis, her face had the triumphant look of disaster confirmed." She makes the transition as unpleasant as possible, setting out dinner in cartons on the kitchen—rather than the dining room—table, as if to "forcibly show her family the ugly pattern of tomorrow"—a pattern as much her design as one imposed upon them. When Mr. Elkins mildly protests the unnecessarily Spartan trappings, Mrs. Elkins responds with a cruel *non sequitur,* reminding her husband, twenty-two years her senior, that it is time the children realized their father isn't growing any younger. "[A]nxious as always to deny the ugly breach, to cover it over with the kindness that bled from him steadily," Mr. Elkins turns his attention to Hester and her brother. An outraged Hester comes to her father's defense by taking the offensive. Hurtful *non sequiturs* are not solely her mother's domain: " 'I wonder what I would have looked like,' she said in a hard voice, 'if you had not married her.' "

Later that night, Hester wakens to her parents' bitter quarreling. In much the same way that she fixed herself and Selena "like a frieze" at the conclusion of **"The Watchers,"** so now she envisions her parents, frozen in place, poles apart:

> On the one side stood her mother, the denying one, the unraveler of other people's facades, but resolute and forceful by her very lack of some dimension; on the other side stood her father, made weak by his awareness of others, carrying like a phylactery the burden of his kindliness.

Hester's view of her parents' essential strengths and weaknesses suggests an impossible dilemma. What use to bridge the gulf between two so fundamentally flawed? Just as Hester's domestic world has shrunk to the confines of the small apartment, where, significantly, the young Mrs. Elkins is now sole matriarch, so, too, has her perspective on the triangular relationship of parents and child. In the closing lines of the story, Hester, seeing herself "flawed with their difference . . . falling endlessly, soundlessly, in the gulf between. . . . began to weep the sparse, grudging tears of the grown."

In **"Old Stock,"** a story that occupies the same time frame

as **"The Gulf Between,"** Hester discovers other treacherous gulfs, but, disquietingly, ones all too easily bridged in the adult world.

The story opens with Hester and her mother on a train bound for the Catskills. The family's fortunes are still in decline, "but it would have been a confession of defeat for Mr. Elkins had he not been able to say during the week to casual business acquaintances, 'Family's up in the country. I go for weekends.' " Mrs. Elkins—blonde and beautiful, "whose blurred handsomeness bore no denomination other than the patent . . . one of 'lady' "—is also intent on keeping up appearances. Today, however,

> there was that added look Hester also knew well, that prim display of extra restraint her mother always wore in the presence of other Jews whose grosser features, voices, manners offended her sense of gentility all the more out of her resentful fear that she might be identified with them.

In contrast to her mother, all containment and silent censure, Hester, "feeling the rocking stir of the journey between her thighs," is exhilarated by "a verve of waiting" for whatever life holds:

> nowadays it seemed to her that she was like someone forming a piece of crude statuary which had to be reshaped each day . . . that she was putting together from whatever clues people would let her have, the shifty, elusive character of the world.

Soon after their arrival at the farm, Hester discovers that the world is shifty in ways she had not imagined. Mother and daughter escape the company of their fellow Jews to visit, as they have the two years before, the very Gentile Miss Onderdonk, an aging, laconic spinster and proud member of the "old stock," her dearest possession a "Leather-Bound Onderdonk History."

The laconic spinster has dismissive words enough for the vacationing Jews and for Mrs. Elkins's informing her that she, too, is "Hebrew":

> "Never seen the Mister. The girl here has the look, maybe. But not you."
>
> * * *
>
> "Does you credit," said Miss Onderdonk. "Don't say it don't. Make your bed, lie on it. Don't have to pretend with me, though."
>
> * * *
>
> "Had your reasons, maybe." Miss Onderdonk tittered, high and henlike. "Ain't no Jew, though. Good blood shows, any day."

Hester speaks out—" 'We're in a book at home, too. . . . "The History of the Jews of Richmond, 1729-1917" ' "—but hers is a Pyrrhic victory. She has fought back, but on Miss Onderdonk's narrowly snobbish terms: "She had not said what she meant at all." Later, upon returning to the farm, Hester is further confused by a radical realignment: the sight of her mother striking up a friendship with one of the formerly-scorned Jewish women from Manhattan, "one of the ones who said 'gorgeous.' "

At the story's end, it is dusk and "A thin, emery edge of autumn was in the air"—fitting atmospheric conditions for the bleak, abrasive reality Hester now contemplates. About to enter the dining room, she steels herself for the "equivocal adult eyes":

> Something would rise from them all [the diners] like a warning odor, confusing and corrupt, and she knew now what it was. Miss Onderdonk sat at their table, too. Wherever any of them sat publicly at table, Miss Onderdonk sat at his side. Only, some of them set a place for her and some of them did not.

The *New Yorker* publication of **"Old Stock"** precipitated a slew of censorious letters to the magazine and an angry newspaper article penned by a Cleveland rabbi. In *Herself* Calisher writes that her "sin was double":

> I had expressed some of these tormenting self-doubts which even the most outwardly impregnable Jew . . . may still be born with: Are "we" anything like "they" say we are? Are we defensively proud of being whatever we are because we have to be? . . . Would we really rather not be what we are? Worse, I had explored what must never be admitted to enemy forces—that there are divisions in our ranks. Not only divisions, but hierarchies. I had turned up the underside of our own snobberies.

Like Hester, the young adult protagonists of **"The Sound of Waiting"** and **"The Rabbi's Daughter"** see only a series of numbing, inescapable compromises. Floundering in a world of closed doors, yearning for a "bright, fairy-tale luck," Kinny (Hester's brother) and Eleanor (like Hester in all but name) despair of effecting a viable compromise between the romantic approach to life and an emphatically fact-bound one. At this stage, they are overwhelmed by the web of circumstance.

In the Introduction to her *Collected Stories,* Calisher describes Kinny and Eleanor as "youth revolving before the prospect of the world and not yet aware who they are." They are certain only of what they don't want out of life: Kinny despises his drudgery-ridden job as a welfare worker; Eleanor panics at the thought of joining the ranks of the many "shriveled, talented women."

The twenty-one-year-old Kinny, recently graduated from college and living with his widowed father, is all too painfully attuned to "The Sound of Waiting." Working for the welfare department, now swamped with victims of the Depression, Kinny is tortured by "the driving sense of alienation, of constriction, that sent him out more and more on his free Saturday afternoons and Sundays." Kinny is waiting for his life to happen, and the waiting is all the more difficult when he contrasts his with his father's youth.

In **"Time, Gentlemen!"** Mr. Elkins's "fairy-tale luck" was merely alluded to; here, the saga of "the self-made American with the imprint of . . . the *bon vivant,* the *fin de siécle* beau-to-be," is fleshed out. Kinny envies not his father's business successes but his amorous conquests: there was always, in Mr. Elkins's anecdotes, "an undercurrent that spread beneath his talk, moving provocatively under the lace of words like a musky perfume—the sense of beautiful women."

"[L]istening to the echoes" of himself one Sunday afternoon, Kinny imagines waking his napping father—now in his seventies, his world shrunk to the confines of the apartment—to ask:

> "For what is it I wait?" Instantly the fantasy shrank, and he winced at the picture of the clumsy byplay that would really occur, knowing that between them lay the benumbing sleep of the years, a drowse from which it was not possible to wake.

Instead, Kinny rushes out into the street, finding an illusory purposiveness in its activity. With no destination in mind, he nonetheless finds himself knocking at the door of one of his clients, a prostitute: "After the first compromise, he thought, all others follow." The prostitute is a poor substitute, indeed, for those beautiful women of his father's youth.

A similar sense of constriction permeates **"The Rabbi's Daughter."** Eleanor is "a thin fair girl whom motherhood had hollowed, rather than enhanced." A Juilliard-trained pianist with hopes of a professional career, she has become a weary housewife with neither time nor energy for practicing. Until her hawk-eyed aunt points out her work-coarsened hands—" 'So . . . the "rabbi's daughter" is washing dishes!' "—Eleanor has been blind to "the compromises that could arrive upon one unaware, not in the heroic renunciations, but erosive, gradual, in the slow chip-chipping of circumstance."

Eleanor's dread of those compromises deepens when she arrives at a house that her engineer-husband has just rented in the Midwest. The "door-cluttered box" is scarcely large enough for Eleanor's piano, which, in a moment of optimism, she had imagined practicing daily. Still in her travelling suit, as though loathe to admit she is "home," Eleanor plays a Beethoven andante and adagio—not, however, the scherzo movement. Her mood darkens considerably when she wonders: "will the denied half of me persist, venomously arranging for the ruin of the other?" At the story's end, Eleanor breastfeeds her hungry infant: " 'This one is still "the rabbi's daughter." ' " . . . At once it began to suck greedily, gazing back at her with the intent, agate eyes of satisfaction."

Both **"The Sound of Waiting"** and **"The Rabbi's Daughter"** end on a somber note of capitulation; the two protagonists have arrived at the kind of impasse that the adolescent Hester had long feared would come about.

Two stories, **"Gargantua"** and **"The Middle Drawer,"** stand apart from the rest, focusing as they do on Hester and her mother. The adult narrator recalls, with an admixture of love, anger, and gratitude, enduring lessons her mother taught her. Published in 1948, **"The Middle Drawer"** is Calisher's first autobiographical story, **"Gargantua"** (1967), the last; nonetheless, they are companion pieces.

The college-bound Hester of **"Gargantua,"** still a gawky adolescent impatiently awaiting a miraculous sea change that will transform her into a beautiful, self-assured adult, craves confirmation of her potential from her mother:

> I wanted her to look at me squarely, not to tell me who I was . . . but to see me both for what I was and what I wasn't yet: a ragged creature but ready to be magnificent. . . . But that was the simpler part of it. . . . I thought I hated her, yet I wanted her to tell me how to be just like her.

But her mother, in the hospital recuperating from an operation, sees (or at least, comments on) only Hester's clumsiness, laziness, and general ineptitude.

Hester, temporarily the woman of the household, enacts a nightly ritual. She finds herself inexplicably mimicking her mother, dining nightly on liver, the same dish—"plain, primal, a meat to be eaten without sauce"—her mother, suffering from postoperation anemia, must eat. When Mrs. Elkins learns of this, she suddenly sees her daughter in a startlingly new light:

> She was a woman of reserve . . . but this was one of the few times in our life together that I could be dizzyingly sure I had pleased. "You did it so that when I come home . . . so that you . . . " she said.
>
> Wasn't this why I had done it, in part? Head bent, I nodded.
>
> But in the matter of secrets, I was still in-between, no match for her. Her nose breathed in sharply. . . . "You're *rehearsing*!" she said.
>
> . . . I saw that I had confused her, not as the chick can sometimes confuse an adult, but as the grown confuse the grown. She had lost her pure version of me. I was opaque.

It is clear to the reader that Hester's act is a rehearsal on several levels. In a practical sense, Hester is preparing herself for the liver dinners she will soon cook for her mother. On another level, she is, perhaps, anticipating a time in the unforeseen future when she will be an invalid regaining strength; it is a rehearsal for some unhoped for contingency down the line. On yet another, deeper level, Hester is rehearsing for adulthood. Physically and temperamentally unlike her mother, she is imitating her in a small but concrete way. Mrs. Elkins, on the other hand, is eager that her daughter be like her in another way altogether: she wants Hester to become one of the sharp-eyed, sharp-eared realists.

Rarely light-hearted, Mrs. Elkins finds daily amusement in the bellowings of the gorilla, Gargantua, one of the attractions of the Madison Square Garden circus. She is especially amused to have to call Hester's attention to the low roars that Hester had taken for the city's anonymous sounds. She is more irritated than amused, however, when Hester mishears another, human bellowing, coming from the Irish woman in the next room. Hester hears " 'Oh Lord. . . . Let not *my* will . . . but THINE . . . be done.' " Her mother's harsh " '*Listen*! . . . When are you ever going to start listening and looking at the world around you!' " focuses Hester's attention, and she hears: " 'Oh Lord. . . . Let not *thy* will . . . but MINE . . . be

done.' " At that moment, the adult narrator knows, "the satiric spirit . . . entered [her] life."

A wonderful concatenation of events follows:

> Three things then happened simultaneously. My mother and I burst out laughing—together. From the Garden, Gargantua began his morning calling. . . . And my father entered the room.
>
> He didn't belong here, we felt that at once, not in the cozy nest we had all made for ourselves—the two of us, the unknown Irish girl, and Gargantua.

That mother and daughter should "burst out laughing—together" marks a decisive and welcome truce in their strained relationship. As surprising, in light of all the other autobiographical stories, is their silently shared reaction to Mr. Elkins's presence.

There is yet another, sweeter surprise in store for Hester. Mrs. Elkins has caught a brief glimpse of Gargantua in her daughter's absence:

> "I guess I've been here too long. . . . But I swear to you, darling. It looked like nothing so much as an enormous old slice of liver."
>
> So we'll never know, I said to her back then, what Gargantua really is. . . . And I didn't much care, for she had said "darling."

The adult narrator remembers all of this when she is in the hospital recovering from a serious operation. At the story's close, Hester does not remember but instead imagines her mother's comforting words:

> "The beast that haunts us, the nameless," she says, "why it's nothing but an old slice of liver. Or while I say it is, in this merry-dark way whose lilt you hear yet—it *is* only that. There are things I can't decree away from you—such things, my darling. But while I say it is only that, I hold back the beast."

Throughout the story, Mrs. Elkins tries to help her daughter in real and lasting ways by insisting she closely attend to the world about her. All her married life, Mrs. Elkins has felt that she has had to constantly watch over her husband, the family dreamer. She does not want her daughter to be, like him, in need of such vigilance. The adult Hester tries to pass the lesson on to her own children in "a certain old, dull meal" of liver she sometimes serves them: " 'I'm the scourge, but *listen. Look about you in the world*!' "

In an imaginative sense, Mrs. Elkins is her grown daughter's protector, just as Mr. Elkins had been the young child's, but there is a crucial difference: Mr. Elkins, the denier of ugly realities, did all he could to banish the beast from his home; Mrs. Elkins does not deny but transforms the " 'beast that haunts us, the nameless' " into something harmlessly mundane, even ludicrous.

In **"The Middle Drawer,"** the adult Hester momentarily "hold[s] back the beast" for her mother, a gesture that illustrates the great extent to which she has absorbed her parents' best qualities. The story opens a week after Mrs.

Elkins's death. Having returned home to nurse her mother through her final months, Hester, key in hand, is on the verge of unlocking her mother's private drawer:

> There were no revelations to be expected . . . ,
> only the painful reiteration of her mother's per-
> sonality and the power it had held over her own,
> which would rise—an emanation, a mist, that
> she herself had long since shredded away, part-
> ed, and escaped.

What follows—Hester's bitter memories of past hurts—is ample proof that she has not escaped and probably never will. As the story unfolds, the reader discovers that the "reiteration of her mother's personality" remains both a burden and a legacy.

"[M]otherless since birth and almost immediately step-mothered by a woman who had been unloving, if not un-kind," Mrs. Elkins had grown to be a guarded woman, rarely capable of the "animal warmth" the young Hester craved. Instead, between them

> the barrier of her mother's dissatisfaction with
> her had risen imperceptibly, like a coral cliff
> built inexorably from the slow accretion of care-
> lessly ejaculated criticisms that had grown into
> solid being in the heavy fullness of time.

One of the main sources of contention was Hester's passion for reading:

> To her mother, marrying into a family whose
> bookish traditions she had never ceased trying
> to undermine with the sneer of the practical, it
> was as if the stigmata of that tradition, appearing
> upon the girl, had forever made them alien to
> one another.

"One remote, terrible afternoon," Mrs. Elkins grabbed a book from Hester and tore it in two. Filled with "the cold sense of triumph . . . at the enormity of what her mother had done," Hester accused her mother of thinking only of money; later, however, she realizes "that her mother, too, was whipped and driven by some ungovernable dream she could not express, which had left her, like the book, torn in two."

Hester's love-hate relationship with her mother continues into adulthood: she wants both "to earn her mother's ap-proval at the expense of her own," and to "find the final barb . . . that would maim her mother once and for all, as she felt herself to have been maimed." Hester has the chance when she returns home to nurse her mother who is dying of breast cancer. She finds her mother

> moving unbowed toward the unspoken idea of
> her death, but with the signs on her face of a piti-
> ful tension that went beyond the disease. . . . It
> was clear she was suffering from a horror of
> what had been done to her and from a fear of the
> revulsion of others. It was clear to Hester, also,
> that her father and brother had such a revulsion
> and had not been wholly successful in conceal-
> ing it.

When Mrs. Elkins asks Hester if she would like to see the mastectomy scar—an unmistakable plea for reassur-ance—Hester is engulfed by childhood memories of "the

thousands of incidents when she had been the one to stand before her mother, vulnerable and bare, helplessly await-ing the exactitude of her displeasure."

In the next moment—the climactic moment of this story and, indeed, of the cycle of autobiographical stories—Hester delivers not the long-anticipated "final barb" but the loving lie:

> "Why . . . it's a beautiful job, Mother," she
> said, distilling the carefully natural tone of her
> voice. "Neat as can be. I had no idea . . . I
> thought it would be ugly." With a step toward
> her mother, she looked, as if casually, at the
> dreadful neatness of the cicatrix. . . .

Later, after her mother's death, Hester contemplates her mother's unwitting bequest: "fortitude. . . . But pity—that I found for myself."

The stories written after this first autobiographical story declare otherwise, however; Hester has learned something about pity from her father. What she did achieve on her own was the successful distillation of her parents' best qualities: steeliness and a keen, critical perspective from her mother; kind-heartedness and a sympathetic eye from her father. She has come to "read" the world the way Ran-dall Jarrell advises one should read good poetry: "with an attitude that is a mixture of sharp intelligence and of will-ing emotional empathy, at once penetrating and gener-ous."

"The Middle Drawer" ends with Hester's recognition and acceptance not only of her mother's legacy but also of "the innumerable small cicatrices imposed on us by our begin-nings; we carry them with us always, and from these, from this agony, we are not absolved." These words also mark the end of the autobiographical stories, as they appear in Calisher's *Collected Stories.* But the fitting close both to Hester's oftentimes stormy relationship with her mother and to the autobiographical stories as a whole appears in the concluding paragraph of **"Gargantua"** (published twenty years after **"The Middle Drawer"**): "The people one lives with and loves can be like cornucopias in the mind; even after they are dead, we can abstract their rich-es, one by one." Just as Hester has "abstracted the riches" of her parents, incorporating within herself their finest qualities, so Calisher, with a perspective at once piercing and embracing, has extracted the rich marrow of her early life, transforming it into stories at once powerfully evoca-tive of a now distant past and startlingly contemporary in their sure, sensitive delineation of a young girl's rites of passage. . . .

. . . . .

In the works previously examined, Calisher's protagonists enter what they had once feared: "the great enclosure of the norm." There are, however, very different kinds of ex-traditions and initiations in some of Calisher's fictions. In the novellas *The Railway Police* (1966), *Survival Tech-niques* (1985), and the novel, *On Keeping Women* (1977), the protagonists cut themselves loose from the ties that once bound them to the textures of everyday life, shedding their conventional lives like dead skins. The unnamed pro-tagonists of the novellas speak out through their actions, sloughing off possessions and identities to become literal vagrants, while the aptly named Lexie in *On Keeping Women* finds her liberation in language.

The heroine of **The Railway Police**—an attractive, financially independent social work supervisor—has, in her own mind, lived a life of pretense: since adolescence she has literally concealed "the felony of [her] private difference"—congenital baldness. The novella opens on her spur-of-the-moment decision not only to divest herself of wigs but also to "be out of the organized world"—to become a street person. The train has just pulled into, appropriately enough, Providence, when the railway police apprehend a ticketless passenger, a young vagrant, "just a hairsbreadth too unshaven." The protagonist, impeccably groomed and polished, from her hat and coiffed wig to her gloves, pinpoints and embraces what sets him apart:

> It takes keeping up, any posture of what you are not, takes a sense of fitness to the point of fashion, and the vagrant won't bother with that sort of thing, not for that purpose, he's too honest for it, or else he wants to be spotted; maybe it's his very function in life to wander about thus exposed so that others may find their signals in him.

With "a kind of suffragette swelling, part yearning and part vengeful," she rejects "orthodox womanhood" and sets out to become not only a vagrant but also, and more significantly, just such a signal to others.

Even as she takes immediate, practical steps to divest herself of possessions and identity—her first decisive move is to discard her wig box—she, like so many of Calisher's characters, breaks free of the past only after immersing herself in it. Through memory, she charts the hitherto submerged current that has led to this decision. Not surprisingly, the matter of her baldness dominates three particular episodes from the past.

In her youth, she broke off an engagement with a man for whom her baldness—and possibly that of the child she was carrying—posed no problem: it was a simple physical fact. Upon his refusal to marry her if she aborted their child—" 'Children can learn to be bald' "—she rejects both his condition of marriage and its accompanying assertion. To her mind, "To be acceptable, such decisions must come to the bald—from the bald." In the years that follow, she, like Pierre Goodman in *False Entry,* remains solitary. Feeling herself to be a private outcast, she dedicates herself to society's outcasts.

In the second decisive encounter, the protagonist is, for a brief time, exhilarated by the possibility of real intimacy. She falls in love not at first sight but at first hearing a man in an art gallery, anxious to purchase a Picasso, rhapsodize about baldness:

> "Kept thinking of it all the time I was away. Most of all in Bangkok. Monks with shaved heads, widows too. . . . Modern Giacometti, sculpture without curls. . . . [Y]ou've never seen the glory of the unadorned human head before."

Here, at last, is a man who might treasure what the pro-

tagonist has—or, more accurately, lacks. Still, she keeps her baldness a secret until, one night in bed, she joins him completely naked from head to toe. Believing she has shaved her head for him, he proceeds, though clearly appalled, with love making—until, that is, she nuzzles her head against his lips, literally rubbing his face in the bare facts.

The protagonist then makes a quasi-religious pilgrimage to Bangkok, to those shaved-headed monks and widows. However, she quickly rejects "group solutions to both philosophical problems and practical ones." It is only when she is no longer consciously searching for signs that she finds one in a pariah dog that, she remembers, "rolled his eyes up at me, unmistakably me, and slowly thumped his tail. . . . He lifted his coattails to me . . . in signal." She returns to New York, to her old routines, forgetting the moment until, that day on the train, "One of [the vagrant's] coattails flipped up" in a signal she now understands.

When she makes her debut as a vagrant, she does so on her own, idiosyncratic terms. Neither an unimaginative pragmatist, like her first lover, nor too much the aesthete, like her second, she is, rather, a pragmatic aesthete:

> I took a plaid car-blanket of consoling warmth and color, and a change of inner and outer clothing. . . . At the last moment I add a short veil of gauze.

> The veil was connected with a slight ambition of mine . . . For it's entirely possible to be both honest and frivolous. . . . So, for Paris in the spring, I carried gauze.

And in her Abercrombie shoulder bag, the Picasso painting of two bald-headed lovers, a farewell gift from her former lover.

She chooses the setting for her debut—the neighborhood she knew as a social worker—as carefully as she did her apparel:

> The viaduct is a particularly coveted one, having at its opposite arch a public convenience, far enough away so that there is no smell. . . . Fires are not allowed by the city, of course, nor sleeping, but several niches . . . are excellent for either. The neighborhood, too, still a family one though on the fringe . . . attracts a remarkably high class of loiterer. . . .

Until now, she has carefully stage-managed the particulars of her radical transition. But in flight from a policeman determined to help her, she suddenly loses all self-confidence: "it was a long way between signals. . . . I needed to be told that taking something off could be as positive and worthy as putting something on." In a Chinese restaurant where she has taken refuge, she finds the reassuring sign when the waiters return her payment for tea in a salad bowl—symbolically now a begging bowl—and bow her out into the street. Returning their bow, she feels herself to be a secular monk: just as others have been her signals, so now she becomes one herself—if only, as yet, to those sympathetic waiters. In the novella's Whitmanesque conclusion she celebrates a universal reciprocity:

> In the inexhaustible doubleness of the world, are there signals everywhere, wild as grass, that unite us? Or must we unite them?

* * *

> Come, you narks, cops, feds, dicks, railway police, members of the force everywhere! Run with us! If the world is round, who's running after who?

On this, the symbolically fitting dawn of the first day of spring, she curls up to sleep, back-to-back with a fellow vagrant: "And so—I was born"—not only as a street person, however. In shedding wigs, in giving up the "struggle against the facts like a fly trying to get out of the cosmos," she finally has made peace with her own difference. Now she can assert what once she rejected: "Children can learn to be bald"; they (including she) can learn not to disguise difference but to proclaim it, literally out-of-doors.

Almost twenty years after writing **The Railway Police,** Calisher would again explore a solid middle-class citizen's rebirth as a street person in **Survival Techniques,** one of the "little novels" collected in **Saratoga, Hot** (1985). The similarities are striking: both unnamed protagonists find in society's marginal figures the signal they have been waiting for; both view their solo flights not as escapes but as true entries into a more authentic life. The differences are equally striking. The woman in **The Railway Police** has always felt different by reason of her baldness; not so the retired shopkeeper of **Survival Techniques.** He is breaking away not only from a way of life but also from his wife of thirty-five years. His passage, then, from apartment down to street corner is all the more wrenching.

The novella charts his careful transition from one world to another. For most of his adult life, his Viennese burgher's wife and his shopkeeper's routine have kept him on the straight and narrowly middle-class path. With retirement, fretting about making ends meet, his perspective on his little world begins to change. He notices first that "There is no other street so brilliantly prime for certain conveniences, for certain people." Four steam heat vents provide warmth in winter; four subway entrances provide toilets and, in inclement weather, shelter "for certain people."

Just as the heroine of **The Railway Police** found her "signal" in a vagrant, so also does the protagonist of **Survival Techniques.** The street's three regulars first attract him by their peculiar dress and demeanor: they do not worry about keeping up appearances or making ends meet. Even more arresting is their dignity and self-containment: they beg neither for handouts nor for pity.

The protagonist's transition from apartment to street corner is not only gradual; it is also furtive, so as to keep his wife in the dark as long as possible. While she is away working part-time, he spends longer and longer stretches of time on the street, an apprentice watched over by his "three mentors." As his attraction to the street grows, his distaste for apartment life intensifies: "My stay up here

was only a hibernation, in which the vision of the street was always with me." That long hibernation ends after a year's deliberation and rehearsal and coincides not, as in **The Railway Police,** with the first day of spring but with the year's first real snowfall: a morning "damp with promise."

While the woman in **The Railway Police** hopes to become a "statement," not a "mystery," the protagonist of **Survival Techniques** aspires to be both: a disquieting and willfully enigmatic presence. He takes refuge, even from his wife, in an impassive silence, refusing either to proclaim or to explain his new vocation. Not surprisingly, the novella concludes not with a celebration of universal kinship but with an admonition from one who is now "outside" to those "who could still pass a body by":

> You yourself were faithful feet. Each day, stopping longer. As if we were the authority to complain to. Dot, dot, your rhythm goes. . . . Dot, dot. And carry your burden on. For we do not beg. If we would beg, you could get past us. I could tell you how.
>
> The best way is to know nothing about us.
>
> That is why I keep my eyes lowered. Never look into them.

. . . . .

The protagonists of three other Calisher works—the novellas, **Extreme Magic** (1964) and **Saratoga, Hot** (1984), and the novel, *Standard Dreaming* (1972)—also cast off "fears like skins," but not in preparation for solo flights. After periods of stasis and emotional withdrawal, they reenter that "great enclosure of the norm" from which they had once thought themselves permanently estranged.

In its almost schematic progression, **Extreme Magic,** Calisher's second novella, establishes in a capsulized form the pattern of reentry. For almost ten years Guy Callendar has viewed himself as other people's "extreme," a "triple amputee at the sight of whom even the single-legged may take heart." A house fire killed his wife and children, leaving him survivor and beneficiary. "When the indemnity money came in, thousands upon thousands of it," a mental hospital gently steered him towards its "own necessary fantasy of the goodness and wholeness entirely residual in the world." Now, for seven years, he has known a measure of calm and satisfaction as an antique dealer in upstate New York:

> Sheer luck had . . . nudged him into a modus vivendi whose limits so exactly modulated to his own—one exactly useful to a man able to move on, unable to forgive himself for it.

He has also found solace in the "safe visual goodness" of a tree-enclosed space.

In a week's time, the span of the novella, Callendar comes to see himself and the world in very different terms. "Perspective," a key word throughout, first appears when Callendar contemplates his estrangement from ordinary relationships:

> Perspective was what any man carried on his

back, not a cross, but an easel to which pictures were supplied slowly, always with an unknown hand. He merely knew better than most what had happened to him. . . . Some men trage-dy. . . . pushes altogether out of their sphere.

The first disruption of his well-ordered life occurs when he pays an unexpected visit to an innkeeping couple down the road on their day off. Callendar stumbles into a terrify-ingly bizarre scene: Sligo is aiming darts as close as possi-ble to Marion, who stands in front of the bull's-eye. Al-most as alarming is Marion's command: " 'On't move,' " said the rigid hole of her mouth. . . . " 'He only has two more.' " Their Monday ritual ends when, last dart thrown, Sligo slumps into drunken unconsciousness.

Marion is her husband's acquiescent victim—" 'We suffer the same' "—who claims she wants to be left alone: " 'One gets on better without talking. Pity is fatal.' " Even as she asks Callendar not to return because she " 'can't afford the perspective,' " she sends out a muted cry for help: " 'Is it sick of me? That I stay.' " Marion, Callendar's contempo-rary, reminds him of his earlier self: an extreme case in need not of distant pity but of immediate intervention. He resolves to be there the following Monday.

When he returns to his safe, hemmed-in acreage, Callen-dar's once fixed perspective is again disturbed, though not unpleasantly, by a sixteen-year-old girl in a bikini. Alden's youth and naïveté are a relief after his nightmarish experi-ence; still, it disconcerts him to learn he has been her "view": "it never struck him that anyone could look in on his solitude." But upon hearing that he has been Alden's "view," he gains a larger, faintly disquieting angle of vi-sion: "He stared . . . at [her] image of this clearing, mi-nuscule in [her] distance, across which [walked] a toy man . . . toy solitary."

When, the next Monday, Callendar and Alden kiss, "He had his perspective. He was the one who was unnatural here"—"here" encompassing the girl and his safe enclo-sure. Even as they embrace, Callendar has made his choice: "in the silence a quarter-mile from the highway, he could hear within himself the sound of lives, regular as rockets, riding to their Monday smash." What he hears and responds is not only the cruel ritual down the road:

> Around him, real cars whizzed loud as imagi-nary ones . . . people . . . were on the move. He wanted to . . . call out to them—I'm with you again. I'm part of the violence.

The night before that second Monday, Callendar performs a seemingly mundane domestic chore that both foreshad-ows and rehearses some great change: "there was really no need for this house-cleaning. But he had an urge to *see* the barn[/house] as empty as it had been when he came." Set-tling into a sleeping bag on the lawn, Callendar gazes af-fectionately and nostalgically—his perspective that of an outsider: "The barn was what he loved; he had rescued it"—as it had rescued him.

At the second Monday's "smash" at the inn Callendar finds that Sligo, too, has cleaned house. Standing in the midst of his bar's wreckage, waiting for the sedative Mari-on has just administered to take effect, Sligo smashes his fist through a glass showcase which holds a purportedly historic but in fact bogus diamond ring. The association between it, himself and his marriage are clear enough: with this final act of destruction, he has passed judgment on three deceptions.

The scene that follows recalls the climactic scenes of *False Entry* and *The New Yorkers:* Pierre and Ruth, finally able to unburden themselves of painful memories, free them-selves to move on. To Callendar, her necessary audience, Marion unfolds the twenty-year-old lie that set in motion the " 'double dream.' " Sligo, a count's Irish groom, passed himself off as his employer to Marion, then a seven-teen-year-old student at a posh boarding school. Her guilt stems from having used her background—" 'Speech, tastes, needs, a million discriminations people like me . . . didn't even know we were born with' "—as a weapon against Sligo. Callendar responds with a demand he has only recently made of himself: " 'Pity *yourself*. . . . So you can leave here. . . . So we can go.' "

Waiting for the ambulance that will take Sligo away, the two stand on the riverbank, contemplating a view, literal and symbolic, he had turned his back on:

> they stared into the blind current of the river, and beyond it, into a current wider than it or any harbor, into that vast multiplicity where there might be no sure order of good or evil, but surely a movement. . . . He knew it was there, this force that had flung him out, and drawn or flung him in again, this movement which, like some god of unbelievers . . . both took away, took away—and gave. This was nothing to make ei-ther a religion or an unfaith of; it was merely the doctrine . . . which lived somewhere in the tough, central dark of those to whom it hap-pened. For extreme cases there was sometimes—an extreme magic.

If this were a forties' Hollywood movie, violins would swell in the background, rising to a crescendo as the sun sets on the river. Instead, the two turn their backs on the sunset's glow and walk towards the ambulance's "treach-erous glare."

At the novella's close Callendar not only fully faces "that vast multiplicity"; he also remembers "How it felt to be only half alone—in all its separate lights and darks"; he is on the verge of reentering, with Marion, "the double dream, [where] one no longer tallied these, or dared."

Callendar's closest fictional counterpart is Pierre Good-man, whose passage from false to true entry repeats itself in so many of Calisher's subsequent works. Both men, in their early forties, survive familial tragedies and shrink from real intimacy. Callendar becomes Marion's confi-dant much the same way Goodman becomes Ruth's.

Both works end on a note of somber optimism: *False Entry* with Goodman's realization that "Nothing concluded but the power to go on"; *Extreme Magic,* with Callendar's re-membering "how it felt to be only half-alone.". . .

There are unmistakable parallels [in *Saratoga, Hot*] with *Extreme Magic,* published twenty years earlier: calendars, emblematic of the characters' controlled lives, figure in the opening paragraphs of both works. *Extreme Magic* opens with Guy Callendar gazing at "*the Resourceful Calendar*—for 1846. . . . a tightly integrated little universe"; *Saratoga, Hot* opens with a reference to the protagonists' predictable (albeit, nomadic) life. Nola and Tot, a married couple in their early thirties, survive by following the horses: "it makes a calendar, both for the day and the year."

Like Marion and Sligo in *Extreme Magic*, Nola and Tot have a symbiotic relationship in which both are victims, but Tot bears the additional guilt of the physically unscathed. Three years before the narrative begins, Tot was the driver in an accident that permanently crippled Nola, then a college girl he had just met. Tot is burdened not only by guilt but also by the barely-submerged fear that Nola does not want "to live out any calendar. . . . Or rather, since he was driving that day, she will live"—for his sake. Their calendar, then, is a bridge over an emotional abyss neither wants to peer into: better to focus on the sequence of events. On this particular day, however, a series of unexpected events and encounters will disrupt both the day's calendar and the carefully planned scenario of their particular "double dream."

The action takes place in Saratoga, New York, where they have come for the August racing season. This is Tot's world, where only money and horses confer status. At the same time, even the lowly hot walkers, whose job it is to cool down the horses after racing, feel important. Tot belongs to both strata: without money or a horse, he nonetheless has a privileged status by reason of his lineage. Significantly, we never learn his patronymic, only his given name, Tottenham, his mother's illustrious surname and the only one that counts in the horse-racing world. His marginally privileged status is summed up in the name's diminution to "Tot."

Dependent as he and Nola are "on the secondhand largess" of Tot's rich, horsey relatives for both jobs and possessions, they treasure their one month in Saratoga where they can live in their own house, however small, even doll-like. Their world is one of constricted movement and cramped, separate spaces: "the crazy little porch, only doormat wide" is Tot's domain, where, each predawn day, he lists the day's activities "bestride the railing, one foot dangling, and scans left-right, sky and ground, as if the view will open for him"; nights, he often perches precariously on the roof, an easy climb from the house's porch. Given the limitations of space and movement, Tot understandably needs "his own porch" and roof. At the same time, they are sentry posts from which he can watch over his prized possessions: his house and Nola. Although Tot regrets Nola's reluctant but all-too-often necessary dependency on him, he nevertheless wants to maintain a delicate balance of mutual dependency.

The tiny living room is Nola's painting studio where, following the few hours at the track spent sketching—all the time she can physically bear—she spends her days painting the pictures that, despite potential buyers, she will store in the attic. Their bedroom is "really her dressing room and just big enough for a double bed, [where] they sleep instead, by her insistence, on separate, less than

twin-width beds, since she may wake at any time for a pain pill." Awake or asleep, their lives are defined, joined and partitioned by Nola's physical condition.

As this particular day dawns, Nola and Tot enact what is for him one of the day's most pleasurable rituals: "this once per day," Nola leans on him while descending their rickety front steps. Today, however, a cat, made tame by Nola's attentions, entangles itself in her skirt—as always, a long one to hide her crippled leg. Nola stumbles, Tot catches her: "Is that why the heavy orthopedic shoe shoves out in reflex?", hurling the cat under the wheels of a passing car. Insisting on her right to put it out of its misery, she, unaided, negotiates a descent that Tot anxiously details:

> Brushing him aside, she grasps the railing with both hands. This means swinging the inert leg with the big shoe as a separate weight, which he has never seen her do upright. . . .
>
> So she negotiates the first step. The second step creaks as she lowers herself on it, between cane and railing. That movement, with him ready, she has something done. For the last step, using the cane and a balancing talked of but never dared, she brings herself to the ground.

With one blow of a log, Nola smashes the cat's head, then instantly reverts to her dependent state: "She takes two steps toward him, a third tottering one. He receives her on his chest." "Tottering" back to Tot, to the status quo of mutual dependency, she seemingly negates a demonstrable capacity, physical and emotional, for greater autonomy.

The traumatic episode results in a deliberate break with the day's calendar: Nola announces that this is the one day of the season she will spend the day with Tot at the track. There, Tot once again offers to help her on the uneven ground, but

> she does not cave toward him. She stands, and stands on her own feet, eye to eye. . . . She takes his arm, but almost like any woman. "A house is so—static. Any house. Here—everything moves."

More than a physical achievement, this standing on her own feet—along with the pointed remark about houses—marks a subtle change in their relationship.

At the track, Tot has two unsettling encounters that parallel Nola's more dramatic and physical disruptions of the norm. The first is with a newcomer to the Saratoga scene, Gargiola, whose car had struck the cat. A wealthy man with mob connections, eager to breach Saratoga's closed society, he initially strikes Tot as a Damon Runyon caricature, a lovable gangster with faulty grammar—until Tot notices that "The eyes are not just a character's." Gargiola sees all too well that Nola " 'takes things hard' "—too hard: " 'Women had ought to scream. My girls scream at any little thing.' " Like Lexie, in *On Keeping Women*, Nola keeps things in.

Tot's second encounter is with a very different sort, a Lord Momsey who urges Tot to ride his polo pony in a match.

Despite his riding ability and a loverlike admiration for the thoroughbred, Tot refuses: " 'I can't risk it. Family matter.' " Years earlier, when a riding injury temporarily invalided him, leaving Nola to the care of her alcoholic mother, Tot vowed never again to ride.

These two very different encounters highlight Tot's over-protectiveness and his unconscious, contradictory desire both to deny and to preserve what sets her apart from other women. He does not want to hear her scream as other women do: Nola is a thoroughbred; Tot, her hot walker determined to help her maintain her characteristic calm. At the same time, Tot does not want to acknowledge her infirmity; he cannot bring himself to tell Lord Momsey why he will not ride: "He has never known how to say it."

Tot's desire to blot out Nola's physical problems is clearly evidenced later that day. Before their setting out for a party he presents her with two gifts. The first is an heirloom wedding dress:

> The dress, austere with lace at the top, wild with it below, nestles the long neck, pointed chin and piled hair just as he expected; the skirt hides as he had hoped. . . . But the dress is after all a wedding one, with that double effect—when used for other occasions which such dresses bring. As a sometimes exacting painter of herself, she will have seen that she is aged by wearing it. Yet can she see how behind that double-edged veil the thirties cast, he can still see the girl, in flawed outline?

The second gift completes the disguise: "A slender, cream-colored Parisian walking stick." The maternity shop's salesgirl called it a " 'fun accessory,' " but Tot intends it to be a veiled necessity, a substitute for Nola's Salvation Army cane. They both know, however, that long after dress and walking stick are retired to her closet, the cane will remain a "fulcrum ever between them."

In the novella's climactic scene, both Tot and Nola are mobilized, thanks to Gargiola who, like Sligo in *Extreme Magic,* smashes glasses and illusions. Arriving home from the party, Tot and Nola find a flower-flooded porch—Gargiola's tribute to Nola's early-morning bravery—and Gargiola himself, suitorlike. He has come to woo Tot's inside knowledge of the track; when he makes the mistake of offering money in exchange for information, Nola intervenes. With so little to give or call her own, she provides the crucial advice free of charge: " 'here you build the barn before you build the house.' "

In that cramped living room a grateful Gargiola jumps up, breaking one of Nola's treasured champagne glasses. From this point on, however, he is neither a suppliant nor a bull in a china shop. He insists on his right to pay for the glass; furthermore, he wants to buy not one but a whole slew of Nola's paintings, despite her insistence that she make a gift of one. His response—" 'So you keep your foot on your husband's neck, huh? Better you scream' "—mobilizes her:

> Dropping the stick to the floor, she has lifted the stoutly framed still life from the mantel and clasped it in front of her. . . . Leaning on the picture as if it is not in midair and not held by

herself, she is walking toward that man—not to Tot. . . .

Gargiola . . . doesn't move. . . .

He takes it.

Now she will fall forward on him.

She stands.

Earlier in the narrative we learned that as a child Nola had played a game with her father; he would stand and she would fall into his arms. Ever since her accident she has been Tot's child-wife, tottering toward him. But Gargiola, though a kindly father figure, will not treat her like a child.

Just as Guy Callendar urges Marion to pity herself if she would move forward, so Gargiola jolts Nola out of a self-pitying paralysis. Before falling asleep, she murmurs, " 'And the attic—.' " She, along with her work, is prepared to leave the confines of a safe space and her paintings will leave the attic for the market place. She contemplates, emotionally and artistically, a wider world: " 'And then I'll paint you—' she says in her sleep. 'Over and over. Oh, what a relief it will be. To paint life-size.' "

At the moment Nola stood unaided, Tot felt "a peculiar thrill . . . this feeling of separateness" and of liberation. At the novella's close he also contemplates a more normal life: "It occurs to him that with time, passing through the small leeways others allow themselves, he and she may end up like everybody else." And, just as Nola looks forward to painting life-size, Tot envisions a more active and, at the same time, more grounded life. He wants an end to their nomadic existence: "Waiting for the horses he wouldn't want to be without, but not following them": "Maybe he can get a horse now."

The novella opens with Tot straddling his porch's railing; at its close he climbs up only to slide off the roof—"He always wanted to." Like Nola's taking those few, unassisted steps, Tot's descent from the heights marks a crucial moment of transition from stasis to motion. Soon, he will be straddling—and, no doubt, occasionally falling from—horses.

Throughout the novella there are echoes of another drama of growth and change, Ibsen's *A Doll's House.* Long before Gargiola says to Nola, " 'You're—a doll,' " the connection has been made, beginning with Tot's and Nola's doll-like house and the similarity of their names to Ibsen's Nora and Torvald, who, like Nola and Tot, have been married eight years. Both women are strong-willed yet girlish, especially in their husbands' eyes. The climactic scenes in both works occur after parties for which the women have been costumed by their husbands—Nora, in a Capri peasant girl's dress; Nola, in a wedding gown. Coached by Torvald, Nora performs the tarantella; silently urged on by Tot, Nola performs merely by walking with the aid of a graceful walking stick, as though not a cripple. Both have two decisive encounters with men who seek access, via the women, into their husbands' closed worlds. Both Krogstad and Gargiola, by shattering illusions, are instrumental in forcing the two women to stand on their own.

Calisher's novella does not pale in this comparison; in fact, the opposite may be true. Ibsen's Nora undergoes a jarringly abrupt aboutface—one moment the wheedling child, the next, a doctrinaire suffragette. (Ibsen also had his misgivings, as evidenced in the several versions of the ending.) Calisher's Nola experiences a more complex, more believable transformation, all the more so because no doors slam.

Unlike Ibsen's heroine, the protagonists of **Extreme Magic**, **Standard Dreaming**, and **Saratoga, Hot** are not escaping but "returning animals." They have come out of long hibernations, out of dead-end enclosures, to face—quietly, without histrionics—the "treacherous glare" of a vital, chance-ridden world.

> *Kathleen Snodgrass, in her* The Fiction of
> Hortense Calisher, *University of Delaware
> Press, 1993, 136 p.*

FURTHER READING

Bibliography

Snodgrass, Kathleen. "Hortense Calisher: A Bibliography, 1948-1986." *Bulletin of Bibliography* 45, No. 1 (March 1988): 40-50.

   Comprehensive primary and secondary bibliography which includes separate listings for individual stories and essays by Calisher, interviews, and reviews of her works.

Criticism

Allen, Bruce. Review of *Saratoga, Hot. Saturday Review* 11, No. 4 (July-August 1985): 76-7.

   Praises Calisher's technique and style.

Auchincloss, Eve. "Good Housekeeping." *The New York Review of Books* 11, No. 10 (25 June 1964): 17-18.

   Offers a mixed review of *Extreme Magic*, considering some of the stories to be derivative and superficial.

Bader, Eleanor J. "The Triumph of Age." *Belles Lettres* 4, No. 2 (Winter 1989): 7.

   Reviews Calisher's *Age* and Alice Adams's *Second Chances*, praising both authors for their ebullient, insightful portraits of aging characters.

Bolger, Eugenie. "Endangered Species." *The New Leader* LIX, No. 2 (19 January 1976): 18-19.

   Lauding her control of narrative pace and atmosphere, Bolger hails Calisher as a master of the short story form.

Brown, Rosellen. "Trying for the Life." *The New York Times Book Review* (26 May 1985): 10.

   Faults Calisher for the extravagances of her style, but generally commends her narrative skill.

Cassill, R. V. "Feminine and Masculine." *The New York Times Book Review* (22 May 1966): 4-5.

   Extols Calisher's artful synthesis of narrative, symbol, and theme in *The Railway Police and The Last Trolley Ride*.

Davenport, Guy. "Caution: Falling Prose." *National Review* XVI, No. 28 (14 July 1964): 610.

   Contains a positive review of *Extreme Magic: A Novella and Other Stories*.

Emanuel, James A. Review of *Tale for the Mirror: A Novella and Other Stories*, by Hortense Calisher. *Books Abroad: An International Quarterly* 37, No. 2 (Spring 1963): 205.

   Praises Calisher's technique and sensibility.

Grumbach, Doris. Review of *The Collected Stories of Hortense Calisher*, by Hortense Calisher. *The New York Times Book Review* (19 October 1975): 17-18.

   Hails Calisher's achievements as a short story writer.

Lee, Charles. "People and Love." *The Saturday Review of Literature* XXXIV, No. 48 (1 December 1951): 37, 43.

   Praises Calisher's psychological acuity and her use of concrete description.

Newquist, Roy. "Hortense Calisher." In his *Conversations*, pp. 62-70. New York: Rand McNally & Company, 1967.

   An interview with Calisher in which she discusses such topics as her work and her attitude towards her critics.

Peterson, Virgilia. "Mystery Stories." *The Reporter* 35, No. 8 (17 November 1966): 66-7.

   Concedes that Calisher is a consummate stylist and an astute observer of character, but complains that the extravagance of her language hinders reader comprehension.

Phillips, Robert. Review of *The Collected Stories of Hortense Calisher*, by Hortense Calisher. *Commonweal* CII, No. 10 (7 May 1976): 317-19.

   Appreciates the psychological acuity and stylistic beauty of Calisher's short stories, which Phillips considers to be far more successful than her novels.

Rabinowitz, Dorothy. "New Books." *Saturday Review* 3, No. 2 (18 October 1975): 17-18.

   Praises Calisher's style and traditional narrative skills as they are displayed in *The Collected Stories of Hortense Calisher*.

Shinn, Thelma J. "Growing, Growing, Grown: Fiction of the 60's." In her *Radiant Daughters: Fictional American Women*, pp. 125-82. New York: Greenwood Press, 1986.

   In a few pages devoted to Calisher, asserts that her fiction unravels female stereotypes and sensitively renders mother-daughter relationships.

"Stingless and Catlike." *The Times Literary Supplement*, No. 3268 (15 October 1964): 933.

   Includes a positive review of *Extreme Magic*.

Additional coverage of Calisher's life and career is contained in the following sources published by Gale Research: *Contemporary Authors*, Vols. 1-4, rev. ed.; *Contemporary Authors New Revision Series*, Vols. 1, 22; *Contemporary Literary Criticism*, Vols. 2, 4, 8, and 38; *Dictionary of Literary Biography*, Vol. 2; and *Major 20th-Century Writers.*

Robert Coover

1932-

(Full name Robert Lowell Coover) American novelist, short story writer, playwright, poet, and critic.

INTRODUCTION

A respected contemporary experimental writer, Coover intends in his fiction to startle and fascinate the reader, believing, with fellow American author John Barth, that literature has reached a state of exhaustion. In his search for new approaches to literature, Coover produces works in which the distinction between fantasy and reality becomes blurred. By placing standard elements from fairy tales, popular culture, biblical stories, or historical events in a distorted context, he attempts to deconstruct the myths and traditions which people create to give meaning to life.

Biographical Information

Coover was born in Charles City, Iowa, and, at the age of nine, moved with his family to Indiana, where his father worked as a newspaper editor. He displayed an early interest in writing, creating short stories and poems while a young boy and later writing for school newspapers. Coover attended Southern Illinois University at Carbondale, then received his B.A. from Indiana University at Bloomington in 1953. After graduation, he served in the U.S. Navy from 1953 to 1957. Coover published his first work, *One Summer in Spain: Five Poems,* in 1960, then earned his M.A. in 1965 from the University of Chicago. He has since taught in universities throughout the United States.

Major Works

Coover uses familiar mythic or popular cultural materials as well as various literary forms and techniques to illustrate his belief that history and truth are human inventions. By making readers aware that they are reading fiction and by subverting myths, Coover attempts to alert his audience to significant new literary patterns. He based much of *Pricksongs and Descants,* his first short story collection, on such sources as the Bible, fairy tales, and familiar everyday events, arranging them into original, unexpected forms. For example, "The Brother," told from the perspective of Noah's sibling, relates the tale of those who helped build the ark but were left to drown, and "J's Marriage" tells about the events surrounding the birth of Jesus Christ from Joseph's point of view. "The Babysitter," a

kaleidoscopic story often cited as the best of the collection, exemplifies Coover's tendency to portray a single event from multiple perspectives. In a style suggestive of cinematic montage, he combines over 100 discrete paragraphs to create a shifting plotline and to develop various possibilities as to which of the versions, if any, is true. Coover also focuses on the act of writing to explore the relationship between art and reality. In "The Magic Poker," the narrator reminds the reader that he invented the scenes and characters and can manipulate them as he wishes, and "Beginnings," the concluding story from *In Bed One Night and Other Brief Encounters,* reflects the difficulty of writing when reality, history, and truth are invalidated. As Jackson I. Cope has explained, "Beginnings" is a "metafictional representation of a writer's block, a writer's futile retreat to an island to get started on a new work only to find himself knee-deep in unworkable ideas and crumbs of first sentences." Coover again uses the illusory qualities of film in *A Night at the Movies; or, You Must Remember This* to unify the components of the stories in this collection, to identify the function of cinema in modern American society, and to question the reliability of events captured on film, in memory, or on paper.

Critical Reception

Critics generally agree that Coover is notable for his experimental approach to fictional forms and for his originality and versatility as a prose stylist, frequently comparing him to John Barth, Donald Barthelme, and Thomas Pynchon. Paul Gray commented that "Coover has earned his reputation as an avant-gardist who can do with reality what a magician does with a pack of cards: Shuffle the familiar into unexpected patterns."

PRINCIPAL WORKS

SHORT FICTION

Pricksongs and Descants 1969
The Water Pourer 1972
The Hair o' the Chine 1979
After Lazarus: A Filmscript 1980
Charlie in the House of Rue 1980
A Political Fable 1980
The Convention 1981
Spanking the Maid 1981
In Bed One Night and Other Brief Encounters 1983
A Night at the Movies; or, You Must Remember This
    1987

OTHER MAJOR WORKS

One Summer in Spain: Five Poems (poetry) 1960
The Origin of the Brunists (novel) 1966
The Universal Baseball Association, Inc., J. Henry Waugh,
    Prop. (novel) 1968
A Theological Position (collection of plays, including *A*
    Theological Position, Rip Awake, The Kid, and *Love*
    Scene) 1972
The Public Burning (novel) 1977
Gerald's Party (novel) 1986
Pinocchio in Venice (novel) 1991

CRITICISM

William H. Gass (essay date 1970)

[*Gass is an American fiction writer and critic. Widely praised for the virtuosity of his prose style, he is among the most conspicuous modern proponents of the view that literature's sole meaning lies in the aesthetic forms an author creates with language. In the following essay, he favorably assesses Coover's use of experimental methods in* Pricksongs and Descants.]

Before us we have several stacks of unread cards, maybe as many as a week's worth, and when in the course of the game we discover them, turning their faces toward us, they are placed in overlapping layers on the table. There these thin and definite narrative slices play us, though of course we say that we are playing them. Most of the fictions in Robert Coover's remarkable new volume [*Pricksongs and Descants*] are solitaires—sparkling, many-faceted. Sharply drawn and brightly painted paragraphs are arranged like pasteboards in ascending or descending scales of alternating colors to compose the story, and the impression that we might scoop them all up and reshuffle, altering not the elements but the order or the rules of play, is deliberate. We are led to feel that a single fable may have various versions: narrative time may be disrupted (the ten played before the nine), or the same space occupied by different eyes (jack of hearts or jack of diamonds), fantasy may fall on fact, lust overnumber love, cliché cover consternation. The characters are highly stylized like the face cards. We've had them in our hands before: Swede, the taciturn guide; Quenby, his island-lonely wife; Ola, their nubile daughter; Carl, the fisherman out from the city . . . and in other stories there are others equally standardized, equally traditional.

Just like the figures in old fairy tales and fables, we are constantly coming to forks in the road (always fateful), except here we take all of them, and our simultaneous journeys are simultaneous stories, yet in different genres, sometimes different styles, as if fantasy, romance and reality, nightmare and daydream, were fingers on the same hand. In **"The Elevator,"** several types of self-serviced trips are imagined for its fourteen floors plus B, and the fact that the story is in fifteen numbered paragraphs seems as inevitable as the fourteen lines of the sonnet.

One of the most impressive pieces in the book in this regard is called **"The Babysitter."** She arrives at seven-forty, but how will her evening be? ordinary? the Tucker children bathed and put away like dishes, a bit of TV, then a snooze? Or will she take a tub herself, as she seems to have done the last time? Will she, rattled, throttle the baby to silence its screaming, allow it to smother in sudsy water? Perhaps her boyfriend will drop over for a spot of love? and bring a sadistic friend? Or maybe a mysterious stranger will forcibly enter and enter her? No—she will seduce the children; no—they will seduce her; no—Mr. Tucker, with the ease and suddenness of daydream, will return from the party and (a) surprise her in carnal conjunction with her boyfriend, (b) embrace her slippery body in the bath, (c) be discovered himself by (i) his wife, (ii) his friends, (iii) the police . . . or . . . All the while the TV has its own tale to tell, and eventually, perhaps, on the news, an account will be given of . . . While the baby chokes on its diaper pin? While the sitter, still warm out of water, is taken by Mr. Tucker? While both she and the children are murdered by Boyfriend & Friend? No . . . But our author says yes to everything; we've been reading a remarkable fugue—the stock fears and wishes, desires and dangers of our time done into Bach.

Within the paragraphs, the language, which is artfully arranged and colored for both eye and ear, reads often like a scene set for the stage:

Night on the lake. A low cloud cover. The boat
bobs silently, its motor for some reason dead.

Or it has the quality of an image on the oblong screen
which is being described for us because we've been carried
away into the kitchen and yet wish to miss nothing: what's
happening now, dear?

Mark is kissing her. Jack is under the blanket,
easing her panties down over her squirming
hips.

The present tense is often salted with a sense of something
altogether over.

I wander the island, inventing it. I make a sun
for it, and trees—pines and birch and dogwood
and firs—and cause the water to lap the pebbles
of its abandoned shores.

While the collection is dominated by the paragraph as
playing card, there are short pseudo-dramas and sections
of monologue, too, as well as patches of more traditional
narrative, for this is a book of virtuoso exercises: alert, self-
conscious, instructional, and show-off. Look at me, look
at me, look at me now, says the Cat in the Hat. Indeed,
Coover is the one to watch—a marvelous magician—as
the last piece, **"The Hat Act,"** suggests; a maker of miracles, a comic, a sexual tease, befooler of the hicks and ultimately a vain rebuilder of Humpty Dumpty, murderer of
his own muse, a victim of his own art . . . mastered by
it, diddled, tricked, rendered powerless by the very power
he possesses as an artist:

At times, I forget that this arrangement is my
own invention. I begin to think of the island as
somehow real, its objects solid and intractable,
its condition of ruin not so much an aesthetic design as an historical denouement. I find myself
peering into blue teakettles, batting at spider-
webs, and contemplating a greenish-gray growth
on the side of a stone parapet. I wonder if others
might wander here without my knowing it; I
wonder if I might die and the teakettle remain. . . . Where does this illusion come from,
this sensation of "hardness" in a blue
teakettle . . . ?

A number of our finest writers—Barth, Coover, and Barthelme, for example—have begun to experiment with
shorter forms, as Beckett and Borges before them, and in
many ways each wishes to instruct us in the art of narration, the myth-making imagination. The regions they have
begun to develop are emphatically not like the decaying
South, the Great Plains, or the Lower East Side; they are
rather regions of the mind, aspects of a more or less mass
college culture; and therefore the traditions—the experience—they expect to share with their readers is already
largely "literary": Greek, often, with Barth's *Lost in the
Funhouse,* though a broader spectrum of language received via TV, magazine, movie, and newspaper occupies
Barthelme in *Unspeakable Practices, Unnatural Acts,*
while biblical stories, fairy tales, and the myths and fables
of popular culture most concern Coover in the short pieces
he's collected here, as well as in some others which he has
yet to reprint.

Barthelme rewrote Snow White. Coover rewrites Little

Red Riding Hood (and who is the woodman but Beanstalk
Jack?); gives us a beautiful new Hansel and Gretel; adds
to our knowledge of Joseph and Mary (how did he take
it?); injects as much bitterness as flood into the story of
Noah; leans toward goatboy allegory in a tale titled **"Morris in Chains,"** etc., and at all times contrives to counter,
even to destroy, the meaning and power of the original.

Coover himself remarks, in a dedicatory preface addressed
to Cervantes and placed with predictable perverseness
well within the body of the book, that

The novelist uses familiar mythic or historical
forms to combat the content of those forms and
to conduct the reader . . . to the real, away from
mystification to clarification, away from magic
to maturity, away from mystery to revelation.

No wonder, then, that in the tale about the Ark, it's not
the high and dry Coover writes about, but the abandoned,
the drowned.

It is finally significant, I think, that the experimental
methods which interest Coover, and which he chooses to
exploit so skillfully, are those which have to do with the
orderly, objective depiction of scenes and events, those
which imply a world with a single public point of view,
solid and enduring things, long strings of unambiguous action joined by tight causal knots, even when the material
itself is improbable and fantastic; and the consequence of
his play with these techniques is the scrambling of everything, the dissolution of that simple legendary world we'd
like to live in, in order that new values may be voiced; and,
as Coover intends them, these stories become "exemplary
adventures of the Poetic Imagination."

It is also characteristic of this kind of writing to give covert expression to its nature, provide its own evaluation;
so that the imagined reader, dressed in red riding, bringing
a basket to her wolf-enclosed granny and hesitating momentarily before the cover of the cottage, finally opens the
door with the thought

that though this was a comedy from which, once
entered, you never returned, it nevertheless pos-

Coover on *Pricksongs and Descants*:

"The Elevator" was in fact a generative story for [*Pricksongs and Descants*]. It gave me an idea for constructing a
new kind of book of short fictions and I used it for awhile
like a structural analogy for the book as a whole, in terms
of what the stories would be like and how to organize them,
pattern them out, and so on. Eventually I moved away from
such a rigid plan, but it was what got me going. If there's
an "anchor" story in the set, it's **"The Magic Poker."** Having got the basic idea, concept, of the book from **"The Elevator,"** and some of the story ideas as well, I kept moving
toward the completion of the book, watching for the story
that would say, now it's done, this completes it. And that
story was **"The Magic Poker."**

Robert Coover, in The Radical Imagination and the
Liberal Tradition, *1982.*

---

sessed its own astonishments and conjurings, its tower and closets, and even more pathways, more gardens, and more doors.

This reader, too, will subscribe to that.

William H. Gass, "Pricksongs & Descants," in his Fiction and the Figures of Life, *Alfred A. Knopf, 1970, pp. 104-09.*

Susan Kissel   (essay date 1979)

[*In the following essay, Kissel analyzes the relationship between audience and artist in Coover's short fiction.*]

In today's smaller, more sophisticated literary audience the contemporary fiction writer seems to have found a new freedom "from the compromising demands of a mass audience . . . [freedom] to explore the peculiar elements of his craft and reinvigorate the art" [Frank Gado in the introduction to *First Person: Conversations on Writers and Writing*]. Robert Coover has been one of many writers who has voiced his relief in being able to forgo the "broad audience" with its " 'Head Start' cultural vocabulary" to reach out to "people who will read such ventures, recognize value, and try to see that it is transmitted in one way or other." The resulting relationship between sophisticated reader and sophisticated writer in Coover's own works, however, is not always an harmonious one.

As Robert Coover has explained in his prologue to "Seven Exemplary Fictions" in *Pricksongs and Descants,* the artist's present task is one of dogged perserverance in the face of fears about the failure of his literary art. Now more free than ever before to pursue the subtleties of his fictional craft, he must be very careful not to push too far into unknown territories of uncertain contour and uncertain value. His task requires both boldness and delicacy; when he sets forth to create "exemplary adventures of the Poetic Imagination, high-minded journeys toward the New World and never mind that the nag's a pile of bones," he cannot ignore the aged and fragile form which sustains him. As the contemporary writer attempts to develop increasingly complex literary metaphors and literary techniques, there are uncertain results ahead as everyone—especially the uncertain adventurer, "barber's basin on [his] head," himself—recognizes.

In setting out for the "New World" of fiction, the contemporary writer is, of course, as Robert Coover recognizes, attempting in large part to satisfy his own desires and his own curiosity. Yet he is also responding to the demands of a sophisticated literary audience which shares his interest in adventurous creations and in new sources of artistic energy. The risks of the modern writer's undertakings and the difficulties of his labors may lead him at times to conclude that the knowledgeable and sophisticated reader, for whom he is twisting the metaphoric vehicle into new and entertaining forms, expects too much for the little he must give. As the narrator of Barth's "Title" in *Lost in the Funhouse* complains: "It didn't used to be so bad. It used to be less difficult. Even enjoyable. For whom? Both of us. . . . Once upon a time you were satisfied with incidental felicities and niceties of technique: the unexpected

image, the refreshingly accurate word-choice, the memorable simile that yields deeper and subtler significances upon reflection. . . . The narrator gathers that his audience no longer cherishes him. And conversely." The contemporary writer reveals his resentment of his reader's demands in his fictional portrayals of modern audiences, both literary and otherwise. In them he finds a "hostile impatience" for new and cruel delights—as when Pynchon's playgoers in *The Crying of Lot 49* take pleasure in a drama in which: "For about ten minutes the vengeful crew proceed to maim, strangle, poison, burn, stomp, blind and otherwise have at Pasquale, while he describes intimately his varied sensations for our enjoyment. He dies finally in extreme agony. . . ." As the director Driblette later tells Oedipa, the play "was written to entertain people. Like horror movies."

Several stories in Robert Coover's *Pricksongs and Descants* serve also to portray this cruelty and insatiability of the modern audience in its quest for engaging entertainment. In **"A Pedestrian Accident,"** for instance, the street crowd which gathers around the crushed pedestrian, Paul, is largely hostile to him: "On some faces Paul saw compassion, or at least a neutral curiosity, an idle amusement, but on most he saw reproach. There were those who winced on witnessing his state and seemed to understand, but there were others—a majority—who jeered." It is only that bawdy entertainer, Mrs. Grundy, who can finally please the crowd with her indecent remarks and her mocking belittlement of Paul's personal significance. She gives the crowd what it wants—an engaging story and the release of laughter needed to turn Paul's plight into diverting, escapist, raucous entertainment. In Coover's **"Panel Game"** Mrs. Grundy's younger, more attractive counterpart, the Lovely Lady, similarly titillates the Audience while helping to put the Bad Sport panelist into a noose. As she pokes fun at the Bad Sport, he is hanged to the sound of laughter, once more that of an audience being entertained.

Such audience demands for what William Wordsworth referred to at the outset of the nineteenth century as "extraordinary incident" and "outrageous stimulation" generally hurt the performer-artists of Coover's works as well as innocent victims such as Paul and the Bad Sport. Mrs. Grundy is the notable exception—a successful performer. She fares very well at the hands of a "great" audience which "never failed her" and profits, as well, by turning Paul's catastrophe into amusing, sideshow entertainment. Other performers in this collection of stories, however, find themselves unable to satisfy the crowds of spectators which gather to watch them without, in some way, hurting themselves. The two circus performers in **"Romance of the Thin Man and the Fat Lady,"** for instance, find that they must give up their new-found physical attraction and excitement for one another to allow those of us in the audience to "[hold] fast to our precious metaphor" of what they should be and the comedy they should suggest of "the ultimate image of all our common everyday romances." They must sacrifice their personal happiness in order that they might "win back their public, found to be an integrant of their attachment, after all." As entertainers, they discover that they are bound to their audience and to each other through that audience, as well.

Robert Coover further explores the performer's dependence upon the responsiveness of his audience in **"The Hat Act"**—a story in which he depicts most vividly the difficult relationship of the contemporary artist and his audience. In this story Coover's magician reveals a pitiful inability to continue to meet skillfully the increasing expectations of his audience—expectations which he arouses himself only in part through the growing difficulty and cleverness of his tricks. The audience, while pleased at first with the sudden appearance of a rabbit from the magician's hat, quickly becomes bored with the initial trick, and even with the sudden appearance of a *number* of rabbits and a *number* of doves as well; the crowd desires something different, something unexpected, to remain happily entertained. In his effort to gain audience applause, the magician "bows, stuffs, pitches, smiles, perspires"; his performance becomes a "desperate struggle" in which he is described as "perspiring from overexertion," "gasping for breath," and "trembling with anxiety" in order to continue to astonish and please those who sit in judgment upon his skills. Clearly, the magician is uncertain of the consequences of several of his tricks; they require such superhuman skill and are so complex in nature that he can no longer remain in control. Nevertheless, he seems driven to continue the act, compelled to find another extraordinary trick, and eager to regain the admiration of his audience.

The magician not only fails completely in each of these objectives, but his mistakes prove disastrous, finally, for both himself and his audience as well. He becomes frantic not to fail when he is unable to withdraw his assistant from the hat into which he has made her vanish. Driven into a frenzy by audience displeasure, he stamps upon the hat in anger and, too late, "kneels, utterly appalled and grief-stricken, in front of it." As the magician's hands are bound and he is led off the stage, a sign is erected which reads:

THIS ACT IS CONCLUDED
THE MANAGEMENT REGRETS THERE
WILL BE NO REFUND.

The metaphor of the failing magician is a powerful one through which Coover suggests both the comedy of the artist's perspiring efforts to please and the horror of his possible failure to control his art; if he cannot master the techniques of his evolving craft, both the artist and his audience, it is clear, will experience fearful losses.

Coover suggests that the contemporary artist—bound as he is to his audience as performer, magician, and funhouse designer, and sensitive as he must be to the expectations and desires of those he entertains—nevertheless must not let his readers exert ultimate control over his efforts. Instead, Coover indicates that the contemporary artist must often find himself disappointing his audience—disappointing himself in fact—as in **"Romance of the Thin Man and the Fat Lady"** where, in responding to the "precious metaphor" of the circus couple's relationship, the narrator reveals "we are irritated to discover their limits, to find that the Ludicrous is not also Beautiful. . . . Well, let us admit it, perhaps it is ourselves who are corrupted.

Perhaps we have seen or been too many Ringmasters, watched too many parades, safely witnessed too many thrills, counted through too many books. Maybe it's just that we've lost a taste for the simple in a world perplexingly simple."

To help his audience regain a taste for the perplexing possibilities inherent in the simple story, Coover repeatedly explores the basic myths of our cultural heritage and restores to these familiar stories the horror, irony, and comedy of their age-old human dramas: of Little Red Riding Hood in **"The Door"**; of Hanzel and Gretel in **"The Gingerbread House"**; of Noah's Ark in **"The Brother"**; and of the Virgin Birth in **"J's Marriage"** (as well as in *A Theological Position* from the collection of plays which bears its title). These simple stories of human betrayal, human misery, and human desire reveal Coover's premise that the fiction writer can only repeat the past and repeat himself, however cleverly.

Robert Coover knows all too well that the simple story, however viewed, will not satisfy the experienced tastes of the modern audience. In **"Klee Dead,"** for instance, the narrator admits that his "show" has been "Pretty dull stuff. Hardly the kind of show to keep crowds about, especially when there's a circus in town, and it goes without saying that they're all moving on. So may we. . . . I'm sorry. What can I say? Even I had expected more. You are right to be angry. Here, take these tickets, the city clerk, obsequious fool that he is, refused them, you might as well go. I owe you something and this is all I have." This final, apologetic narrative gesture reminds the reader that the writer is limited to the basic human experience in his fantasies and myths and that the stories to be found there will not astound or shock or uplift with their familiarity. Fiction can provide only a lesser stimulation in our amusement-oriented culture. The narrator's ironic offer of circus tickets in **"Klee Dead,"** then, comments upon the modern reader's insatiable appetite for novelty and sensation in arm-chair entertainment—an appetite which the reader shares with the much less sophisticated circus and street crowds he disdains.

The picture Robert Coover creates of the modern audience, then, is not always a flattering one; he suggests that the contemporary literary audience, with its intelligent, sophisticated readership, is guilty of the mass audience's exploitive, hostile demands for entertainment. The reader has seen too many thin men and fat ladies and "safely witnessed too many thrills," Coover suggests, to continue to be amused by the familiar circus of fiction with its dilapidated funhouse attractions. And yet Coover implies that the artist cannot afford to please his disappointed audience with new, bizarre tricks, without finally destroying the whole show and becoming, himself, the monster-magician dragged off the stage at the end of **"The Hat Act."** The audience's disappointment is one which the author, at times, shares; as the narrator of **"Klee Dead"** laments, "Even I had expected more." So, too, the author-creator-spectator-protagonists of Coover's novel *The Universal Baseball Association, J. Henry Waugh, Prop.* and his short play *Love Scene* expect more of the dramas they both direct and despair to see played out before them.

But the final voice is not that of the disappointed and failed creator-artist; it is that of the author as Ringmaster exhorting his audience to rediscover with the narrator of **"Romance of the Thin Man and the Fat Lady"** the "ring around the rings" in the seemingly simple world of circus entertainment:

> We can hang on to nothing. Least of all the simple. . . . So, damn it, let us hoot and holler and thrill and eat peanuts and cheer and swill the pop and laugh and bawl! Come on! All us Thin Men! All you Fat Ladies!.

> *Susan Kissel, "The Contemporary Artist and His Audience in the Short Stories of Robert Coover," in* Studies in Short Fiction, *Vol. 16, No. 1, Winter, 1979, pp. 49-54.*

Larry McCaffery   (essay date 1982)

[*McCaffery is an American educator and critic. In the following excerpt from* The Metafictional Muse: The Works of Robert Coover, Donald Barthelme, and William H. Gass, *he examines various experimental techniques employed by Coover in* Pricksongs and Descants *in order to "magically transform reality . . . into fresher, more useful fictions."*]

In **"The Hat Act,"** the last of the twenty-one fictions collected by Coover in **Pricksongs and Descants,** a magician appears on stage and performs a variety of feats of wizardry. As he performs, we are given the reactions of an impatient, highly critical audience. Although they applaud vigorously and laugh at especially spectacular successes, they are also easily bored; if they are not constantly provided with new feats, their cheers and whistles soon turn to silence and then to loud boos.

"The Hat Act" tells us much about Coover's short fiction because, like the magician, Coover continually presents the fabulous and improbable to surprise us and jar us out of our expectations. Like the magician's audience, we are forced to view the ordinary perpetually transformed into new shapes and patterns. Indeed, the magician in **"The Hat Act"** is representative of all the fiction-makers in Coover's work from the religious fanatics in *The Origin of the Brunists* to J. Henry Waugh to Richard Nixon in *The Public Burning.* All these characters are actively engaged in the magical transformation of daily reality into their own systems. The magician is an especially appropriate symbol of Coover's fiction-maker, for anthropologists suggest that creative art may well have sprung initially from magic and magical representations.

Whereas Coover's longer works tend to examine the broad base of fictional systems through which we perceive the universe, his short fictions usually deal much more directly with *literary* fictions, the sources of their appeal, the problems which face those who want to create them, and the way in which they affect our relationship to reality. In addition, Coover wholly abandons the quasi-realistic framework employed in his novels and relies instead on either prenovelistic formal strategies (such as are found in fairy tales, romances, and fables) or on wholly nontraditional, experimental techniques. The effect of both these

approaches is to emphasize through form the invented, purely fictive nature of the story before us; rather than trying to give the illusion of having reflected empirical reality (the goal of the realistic novelist), Coover hopes to magically transform reality—which, in his terms, has already been fictionalized by the time it reaches human consciousness—into fresher, more useful fictions. Or, to use Coover's own words, "The world itself being a construct of fictions, I believe the fiction maker's function is to furnish better fictions with which we can reform our notions of things." Meanwhile by flaunting his artifice and fictional design, Coover establishes a distance between reader and text; as with the works of Rabelais, Sterne, and many modern metafictionists, his stories offer the reader a dialogue instead of identification—a dialogue which is directed at the story we are reading. Coover's stories always present their characters, events, symbols, and other literary devices as literary elements drawn from a much larger set of possible relationships. Thus the reader is continually made aware that the pattern set before him is arbitrary and can be broken, that other perspectives are possible, and that the reader and Coover are engaged in a game of choices. A character in the introductory piece to **Pricksongs** makes this clear when he says that what will follow is "an elaborate game, embellished with masks and poetry, a marshalling of legendary doves and herbs." Like Lévi-Strauss's handling of mythic material, Coover's approach emphasizes the transformational possibilities of elements and directs our attention to pattern and structure rather than to content. By accepting the transformational possibilities within language and fabulation, Coover suggests, we observe the exemplary process of the artist countering the effects of both death (stasis) and randomness (chaos)—a process which also helps demonstrate his central point about the dangers of allowing our fictions to rigidify.

In order to insure that his readers respond to his stories as fictional arrangements, Coover often uses plots, characters, imagery, and other aspects of design which are drawn from a variety of well-established sources: from fairy tales, biblical stories, tall tales, folk legends, cultural stereotypes, and other familiar literary motifs. Like other contemporary manipulators of myth (John Barth, John Fowles, Iris Murdoch, Ishmael Reed, Barthelme), Coover relies on this sort of material precisely because our responses to it are pre-set; since the material is familiar and our responses predictable, Coover can manipulate these expectations by rearranging the familiar patterns into unfamiliar—but frequently wondrous or liberating—shapes. Coover hopes that his strategies will create in their formal manipulations a sort of freedom from mythic imperatives which [Alain] Robbe-Grillet has recently described: "As his imagination manipulates the mythological material, the novelist establishes his freedom which exists only in language."

Coover's use of prenovelistic forms suggests one of the reasons why his stories, paradoxically, may seem modern or experimental. Because these forms are ancient and have been largely ignored since the rise of the novel (at least until recently), they may today seem fresh and innovative. Coover's intentions can also be compared to musical structures, an analogy hinted at by the title of his collected stories, *Pricksongs and Descants.* The puns in the title—the "death-cunt-and-prick songs" mentioned by Granny in **"The Door"**—suggest the primary motifs of many of the stories: sex, death, violence, and the grotesque. But "descant" and "pricksong" are also basically synonymous musical terms. Coover has defined "descant" as follows: " 'Descant' refers to the form of music in which there is a *cantus firmus,* a basic line, and variations that the other voices play against it. The early descant, being improvisations, were unwritten; when they began writing them, the idea of counterpoint, of a full, beautiful harmony emerged." One useful way to view many of Coover's short fictions is as variations of or "counterpoints" to the basic line of the familiar mythic or literary "melody." His comment about the "full, beautiful harmony" which emerged from the descant emphasizes the positive aspect of his intention. Not merely wanting to debunk myth and pattern, Coover hopes to use them to design new, harmonious forms.

One of the ways Coover attempts to create new perspectives on familiar material is simply by telling the familiar story from an unfamiliar point of view. Coover's biblical tales, for example, rely on this method (these stories include **"The Brother," "J's Marriage,"** and **"The Reunion"**). In **"J's Marriage"** we are told of Joseph's surprised response to Mary's mysterious impregnation and of their subsequent marriage. Joseph's bewildered and annoyed reaction to the pattern of his life gives us a new outlook on this story. Coover invents many details which weren't important to the myth, but which are crucial to his manipulation of it: what, for example, was their sex life like after they were married? (nonexistent, except for one instance which may have been only a dream). What sort of relationship did Jesus have with Joseph? (they ignored each other). How did Joseph die? (of consumption at a tavern, his face resting in a glass of wine). Joseph, who is referred to only by a Kafkaesque "J," is a slightly parodic forerunner of the modern existential man; like the townsfolk of West Condon, he strains to find meaning and significance in the seemingly irrational events of his life. Joseph differs from Coover's other major characters, however, because he is unable to create a workable system whereby to put the pieces of his life together. Mary's explanation of her pregnancy is difficult for Joseph to accept because he is unable to reconcile it with any rational conception of God:

> She explained to him simply that her pregnancy was an act of God, and he had to admit against all mandates of his reason that it must be so, but couldn't imagine whatever had brought a God to do such a useless and, well, yes, in a way, almost vulgar thing. . . . No power of mental effort provided a meaningful answer for him; it was simply unimaginable to him that any God would so involve himself in the tedious personal affairs of this or any other human animal, so inutterably unimportant were they to each other.

Unable to find a framework in which to organize such events, Joseph at last "simply gave in to it, dumped it in with the rest of life's inscrutable absurdities." Without the inclination to accept even the "tragic fiction" (in this he resembles Paul Trench), Joseph dies ignobly, thinking of his life that "in spite of everything, there was nothing tragic about it, no, nothing there to get wrought up about, on the contrary." Thus Joseph provides a gloomy example of a man unable to accept the aid of fictional systems.

In **"The Brother"** Coover again retells a familiar biblical story—Noah, the ark, the flood—from a new and revealing perspective. The story centers not on Noah and the other survivors of God's wrath, but on Noah's unnamed brother—one of the victims. From this angle Coover capitalizes on many dramatic ironies by presenting the frightened "other side's" point of view. Told in an unpunctuated Joycean monologue which uses an incongruously modern-sounding idiom, the story quickly wins our affection for Noah's brother. This brother even helps Noah build the ark, mostly to humor "him who couldn't never do nothin in a normal way just a huge oversize fuzzyface boy." As the brother reports it, Noah before the flood is a pretty ludicrous figure; we see, for example, the bemused attitude of the brother and Noah's neighbors as they watch the building of the huge ark on the top of a hill ("How the hell you gonna get it down to the water?" someone asks), the reactions of Noah's not-so-amused wife ("She's over there hollerin at him how he's getting senile and where does he think he's sailin to and how if he ain't afraid of runnin into a octypuss on the way he oughta get back home"), and so on. Because we know what will follow, our reaction to even the humorously reported scenes is strained; certainly the fact that there is no biblical logic provided to help justify what is happening emphasizes the human aspects of the scene and makes Noah's refusal of aid to his brother seem cruel and cold.

The three stories grouped under the heading of "The Sentient Lens" are complicated metafictional examinations of the hold which fictional patterns and designs have over us. On one level, they may even be viewed as replies to a specific literary approach: the "new realism" of Robbe-Grillet with its "camera-like" objectivity. A truly realistic narrative, according to Robbe-Grillet, requires such an objective method, for only in eliminating all tendencies in the direction of anthropomorphism, including the elimination of all metaphors and analogies, can a writer allow objects their own identity and free man from a constricting humanism. Rather than appropriating the humanistic lie that "man is everywhere," the writer must acknowledge the inevitable, final gulf between himself and all things which are "other." The eyes of man must "rest on things without indulgence, insistently: he sees them but he refuses to appropriate them, he refuses to maintain any suspect understanding with them, any complicity; he asks nothing of them; toward them he feels neither agreement nor dissent of any kind." A writer who wishes to capture this true state of man's relationship to the world must attempt to furnish some sense of this total "otherness" of things outside himself. According to Robbe-Grillet, this can best be achieved in fiction by relying on neutral descriptions of objects and events, descriptions which are "cleansed" and "uninfected" by analogy and metaphor and which are therefore "camera-like" in their objectivity. As he explains:

To describe things, as a matter of fact, is deliberately to place oneself outside them, to confront them. It is no longer a matter of appropriating them to oneself, of projecting anything onto them. Posited, from the start, as *not being man,* they remain constantly out of reach and are, ultimately, neither comprehended in a natural alliance nor recovered by suffering. To limit oneself to description is obviously to reject all the other modes of approaching the object: sympathy as unrealistic, tragedy as alienating, comprehension as answerable to the realm of science exclusively.

It would be difficult to imagine a literary or philosophical viewpoint which would more directly oppose that of Coover than the views just summarized. Given Coover's definition of man as metaphor maker, any such claim to objectivity or realism would naturally be viewed with distrust; Robbe-Grillet's strategies would, therefore, be seen as futile efforts to ignore the fact that man is forever trapped within his own fiction-making machinery. For Coover the very notion that a writer can duplicate the supposedly neutral, objective vision of a camera would be ridiculous. As we have already seen, Coover fully accepts the Kantian suggestion that man's relation to the "objective world" is always mediated by categories of the mind; these categories insure that when man deals with the world, his perceptions from the outset are symbolic; they are, in effect, "contaminated" by man *by definition.* In the "Sentient Lens" stories, Coover parodies some of Robbe-Grillet's ideas by making the *camera itself* an involved, humanistic narrator.

The scenes of each of the "Sentient Lens" stories are reported to us as if seen through the lens of a camera. But in keeping with Coover's intentions, the lens which narrates the action is a "sentient" lens, not neutral at all but very responsive to the scene it is observing. In the following passage from **"Scene for Winter,"** for example, Coover allows the lens to relate the scene in images which are obviously anthropomorphic in nature:

> The snow has folded itself into drifts, or perhaps the earth itself is ribbed beneath, cast into furrows by fallen trees and humps of dying leaves— we cannot know, we can only be sure of the surface we see now, a gently bending surface that warps and cracks the black shadows of the trees into a fretwork of complex patterns, complex yet tranquil, placid, reflective; the interlaced shadows and polygons of brightly daylit snow suggest the quavering stability of light, the imperceptible violence and motion of shadow.

Not only are the images presented here in "humanized" language, but also the lens is responding actively to what is happening. Thus, when an unexpected noise occurs, the lens is obviously excited with anticipation:

> Brief sharp crackling sound! . . . Again! Next to us, up close: the columnar trunk of a great pine. Crack! In the wood. Yes, again! The subtle biting voice of wood freezing. We hesitate, expectant, straining to hear it again—but our attention is suddenly shaken, captured by a new sound, an

irregular crumpling smashing noise that repeats itself four or five times, stops, then sounds again.

The second of the "Sentient Lens" stories, **"The Milkmaid of Samaniego,"** is one of Coover's most interesting examinations of the way fictional patterns dominate our perceptions of reality. The scene, again reported through the restrictive eye of a lens, is anticipated for us long before it actually begins; we are told that a milkmaid is approaching, though "we've nothing present to let us suppose it." Instead of focusing on the milkmaid, however, at first we see only a man with yellow teeth chewing vacantly on a hunk of bread. Although our field of vision centers on this man, something seems to suggest that a milkmaid is approaching. Thus we become "aware" of her, despite the fact that we cannot yet actually see her:

> We are, then, aware of her undeniable approach, aware somehow of the slim, graceful pitcher, the red kerchief knotted about her neck, her starched white blouse and brightly flowered skirt, her firm yet jubilant stride down the dusty road, this dusty road leading to the arched bridge, past the oaks and cypresses, twisted wooden fences, the haphazard system of sheep and cattle alongside the occasional cottage and frequent fields, fields of clover, cabbage, and timothy, past chickens scratching in the gravel by the road, and under the untempered ardor of the summer sun.

This unseen but somehow perceived landscape with the milkmaid approaching owes more to painting than to literature for its specific, almost inevitable details. We can "see" the milkmaid in much the same way that we can anticipate the events in Coover's biblical stories or fairy tales; the basic pattern or design has yielded these details to us so often that we can "create" the scene even before it physically appears in front of us. The lens/narrator explains this sense as being "almost as though there has been some sort of unspoken but well understood prologue, no mere epigraph of random design, but a precise structure of predetermined images, both basic and prior in us, that describes her to us before our senses have located her in the present combination of shapes and colors."

This scene, then, is created out of the same sort of "mythic residues" that were the materials of many of Coover's other stories; and because of the power of these residues to rigidify our responses, it is difficult for us to respond to this scene in any way other than conventionally. Like the cowpokes in Coover's play, *The Kid,* the lens is suspicious of elements which threaten to disrupt these familiar conventions and patterns. Of the man who has mysteriously intruded into the scene, for example, the lens comments unapprovingly that "even had the ambiguity of our expectations allowed a space for him . . . we probably would not have had him just at the bridge, just where our attention might at the wrong moment, be distracted from the maid." Noticing other unexpected elements about the man—his "tattered black hat," his "torn yellow shirt," his "fixed and swollen right eye"—the lens adds that "these are all surprises, too, and of a sort that might encourage us to look for another bridge and another milkmaid, were such a happy option available."

Fortunately the "real" milkmaid appears, exactly matching our expectations except in some trivial details (her kerchief is daffodil yellow instead of red, for instance). The process of her approach is described in careful detail until the lens is again distracted by some actions of the man: "As she walks her skirt flutters and twists as though caught by some breeze, though there is none. Here—but the man, this one with the tattered hat and bulging eye, he stands and—no, no! the maid, *the maid!*". Fully content to rest in the groves of convention, the lens wants only to present the familiar scene without interruption. But when the scene dissolves into a conventional, idyllic farmyard, another gratuitous element—a young boy—appears. The lens begins to describe the boy, emphasizing his sexual qualities, and then attempts to return to the pre-set material: "Not more than a dozen paces away, a tall lad, dark and fine boned with flashing brown eyes and bold mouth, curries a thickchested coal-black bull, his sturdy tanned— but no more of that! for, in short, he looks up, they exchange charged glances." As is typical of Coover, *the established pattern* here is shattered, the narrator having lost control of his material. Despite the pleas of the lens ("No! not—!"), the young boy, whom we have probably expected to be *defending* the maid from the attack of the old man, is soon attacking the milkmaid himself, tearing at her dress, knocking the pitcher of milk from her head.

When the dissolve is concluded and we see the original scene again, the familiar elements can no longer create the proper picture; with the aid of the unkempt, yellow-toothed man, the milkmaid tearfully sets her stoneware jug aright. Initially frightened by his appearance, the maid soon accepts the intruder and his friendly intentions. Silently they contemplate the pattern which has led them to this moment: the sun, the road, the now empty pitcher. The man indicates that other sources can compensate her for her loss; withdrawing some coins from his pockets, he shows them to the maid: "They are few, but of gold and silver. They look, to tell the truth, like nothing less than a whole private universe of midsummer suns in the man's strong dark hand. . . ." The story concludes with the empty pitcher—now discarded and unneeded in the presence of the new alternatives, although originally a central element in the design—shattering into fragments:

> The pitcher, thought at first to be stable in the grass at the foot of the bridge, is actually, as we can now see, on a small spiny ridge: it weaves, leans, then finally rolls over in a gently curving arc, bursting down its rust-colored veins into a thousand tiny fragments not unlike the broken shells of white eggs. Many of these fragments remain in the grass at the foot of the bridge, while others tumble silently down the hill into the eddying stream below.

The Spanish epigraph to this story [*mira que ni el presente esta seguro* (look, not even the present is secure)] has already suggested that the elements of the present secure scene will not always remain certain.

The "Sentient Lens" stories are typical of the way Coover constantly places shifting alternatives before us—a process that will reach new proportions with Richard Nixon's fumbling efforts to make sense of the Rosenberg case in *The Public Burning*. In all of Coover's work the suggestion seems to be that fixed perspectives are false perspectives and that attributing "meaning" to events may be useful but should always be done with the awareness of alternative possibilities. Like Donald Barthelme, Coover often mockingly thrusts significance in the reader's face, even in situations where interpretation seems unlikely. This "game" of interpreting symbols is openly played in **"Panel Game,"** the earliest and most significant of the "Exemplary Fictions" which were collected in *Pricksongs*. Set up as a kind of closet drama (a favorite form for Coover), **"Panel Game"** presents an "Unwilling Participant" who is chosen to sit on a television game show panel in the midst of several mysterious, possibly allegorical figures (an "Aged Clown," a "Lovely Lady," and "Mr. America"). Soon the "Merry Moderator" is introduced and the Unwilling Participant is plunged into a complex, incomprehensible game whose rules he does not understand. Urged on by the moderator ("But what does it mean? *What does it mean?*"), he senses that the game has something to do with deciphering language but no useful rules or connections seem to emerge; like all of Coover's major characters, the poor participant finds meaning everywhere and cannot separate his own fancy from the intentions of the game. He also resembles many of Coover's later characters, such as the West Condonites in [*The Origin of the Brunists*] and Nixon in *The Public Burning*, in demonstrating a fundamental distrust of transformation and process as he frantically tries to assign fixed meanings, to shape patterns, and to create order from the mass of ambiguous, confusing signs that lie all around him.

In **"Klee Dead,"** another metafictional tale which deals with the perils of interpretation, a self-conscious narrator finds it impossible to play his role as an all-knowing storyteller who is supposed to explain why one Wilbur Klee has committed suicide. This narrator knows very well that the reasons behind a suicide are usually much too complicated to be presented neatly in a story of this sort. He does manage to point out several potentially revealing signs (Klee's dentures, a scrap of paper which may be a suicide note), but he also confesses that these may well be only "lifelike forgeries." He demonstrates at several points that he *can* present realistic stories with all the expected details and soothing illusions about cause and effect, but these stories have nothing to do with Klee (except in some vague, anagrammatic way) and are, in fact, simply parodies of the realistic method. In the end we are left with "virtually nothing. . . . And a good fifteen, twenty minutes shot to hell."

Perhaps Coover's most surreal story, **"The Marker,"** presents another allegorical quest for vital artistic forms in today's world. In it we find a young man named Jason preparing to go to bed with his wife. After putting a marker in his book, he turns out the light and begins to search the room unsuccessfully for his wife. Totally disoriented and confused, Jason—the artist/quester—wanders around the room, trying to use the familiar reference points to guide him, until, at one point, he arrives back where he had started; eventually, with the aid of his wife's laughter, he finds his bed and begins to make love to his wife. While thus engaged, Jason momentarily wonders with alarm "if this is really his wife," but he rejects these thoughts "since there is no alternative possibility." Most of Coover's characters who deny the possibility of other views meet unhappy ends, and the case is no different with Jason: soon his lovemaking is interrupted by a police officer and four assistants who burst into the bedroom unannounced. Horrified, Jason discovers that although it is his wife who lies beneath him she is now a rotting corpse, which "follows him punishingly in movement for a moment, as a sheet of paper will follow a comb." Throwing off the past, then, even a hideously disfigured corpse, is evidently not an easy task; and, as Jason discovers, the consequences of paying so much loving attention to something which is dead are serious indeed. The police officer makes sure that Jason will no longer create anything when he "pulls out Jason's genitals flat on the tabletop and pounds them to a pulp with the butt of his gun." Just before leaving, the officer delivers a speech which unmasks the metafictional intent of the story:

> "You understand, of course," he says, "that I am not, in the strictest sense, a traditionalist. I mean to say that I do not recognize tradition *qua* tradition as sanctified in its own sake. On the other hand, I do not join hands with those who find inherent in tradition some malignant evil, and who therefore deem it of terrible necessity that all customs be rooted out at all costs. I am personally convinced, if you will permit me, that there is a middle road, whereon we recognize that innovations find their best soil in traditions, which are justified in their own turn by the innovations which created them. I believe, then, that law and custom are essential, but that it is one's task to review and revise them. In spite of that, however, *some things still make me puke! . . . Now get rid of that fucking corpse!"*

This speech neatly summarizes Coover's own fictional approach which denies that tradition is "some malignant evil" to be "rooted out at all cost"; Coover instead suggests that a "middle ground" should be established that recognizes that "innovations find their best soil in traditions." The officer's pretentious, scholarly-sounding explanation is, of course, totally incongruous to the grotesqueness of the situation and resembles similar insertions that are found in Barthelme's works. The speech is also typical of the way in which metafictional self-reflections arise in Coover's stories in places we least expect them. The implications of the officer's speech really cut two ways: it is about time, it is suggested, that the "lights be turned on" for many writers who have been making love to something long dead—like, say, the realistic novel; on the other hand, the officer's "middle road" also hints that if writing nowadays must involve anything disgusting or ugly then, liberal though he is, it too should be rejected—or, as the narrator of **"The Magic Poker"** says, "There's nothing to be gained by burdening our fabrications with impieties. Enough that the skin of the world is littered with our contentious artifice . . . without suffering our songs to be flattened by savagery."

Pricksongs and Descants also contains a series of structurally related stories that are Coover's most radical departures from realistic norms to date. In these stories, as with

the best fictions of Borges and Nabokov, the structure itself is used to serve his central thesis about the dangers involved in dogmatic perspectives on our fictional systems. These stories—which I have elsewhere labeled Coover's "cubist stories"—can be usefully approached by comparing Coover's intentions with those which generated the cubist revolution in painting earlier in this century. Making analogies between different art forms should always begin by respecting their differences, but in this case the cubist analogy seems to me to be especially helpful in identifying a context in which we can respond to these experimental stories.

Even a cursory glance at Coover's cubist stories (**"The Magic Poker," "The Gingerbread House," "The Elevator," "Quenby and Ola, Swede and Carl,"** and **"The Babysitter"**) reveals that they share with the cubists' works a general reaction against mimetic methods of presentation and emphasize instead the formal manipulation of the artist's elements. More significant for my analogy with cubist painting, however, is the fact that, like the cubists, Coover forces his audience to deal with the elements of his works as mere artifacts or conventions and creates a deliberate ambiguity of event which directly parallels the cubists' spatial ambiguity and which confounds his audience's desire for outer referents. Picasso's rejection of realism and his developing spatial ambiguity was partially a response to his own interest in primitive art (which ignored mimetic principles in terms of perspective and proportion in favor of a subjective interpretation) and in the somewhat earlier experiments of Paul Cézanne. These interests influenced Picasso to move far beyond Matisse and the Fauvists, who were using color with an unprecedented freedom and arbitrariness in the period just before Picasso produced what is generally regarded as the first cubist masterpiece, *Les Demoiselles d'Avignon.* In creating *Les Demoiselles* Picasso broke away from perhaps the two most important characteristics of European painting since the Renaissance: the classical norm for the human figure and the spatial illusionism of one-point perspective. By running together planes otherwise separated in space and by combining multiple viewpoints into a single form, Picasso boldly created a precedent of great significance for the later cubist paintings. As we will see, Coover's cubist stories are developed via structuring devices that are closely related to these two key methods of departure from representational norms.

As should be evident from our discussion of his other works, Coover shares with the cubists the relativistic view that the role of the artist is not to render reality unambiguously but to create realities whose ambiguities suggest something of our own relationship to the world. Robert Rosenblum's discussion of the larger implications underlying the cubist method also helps define Coover's intentions:

> For a century that questioned the very concept of absolute truth or value, cubism created an artistic language of intentional ambiguity. In front of the cubist work of art, the spectator was to realize that no single interpretation . . . could be complete in itself. And in expressing this awareness of the paradoxical nature of reality and the

need for describing it in multiple and even contradictory ways, Cubism offered a visual equivalent of a fundamental aspect of twentieth century experience.

Coover's cubist stories create exactly this vision of "multiple and even contradictory" views of reality; like cubist paintings, they are consistently structured to force the viewer to consider competing realities as equally "real" or true. Their method of presentation is fairly easy to describe; in many ways the process is similar to watching film rushes of the same scene shot several times from different angles, the action moving slowly forward in spurts and sputters because of so many retakes. Basically, Coover assembles all the elements of a familiar, often even banal situation—characters, setting, symbols, imagery—and then starts the story on its way. But as soon as any sort of clear pattern begins to establish itself, he stops the action, retraces his steps, and allows other plot lines to develop. The later plots sometimes complement the earlier ones and at other times directly contradict them; but all variations are allowed to exist as possibilities and none is insisted upon as the "real" one. After all, the stories seem to suggest, because *any* of the possible actions is purely an invention, why should our view of the situation be limited to any one perspective of it? Coover's method, it should be emphasized, is a more radical departure from realistic norms than the multiple presentations of other works which might be labeled cubistic (Durrell's *Quartet,* Faulkner's *The Sound and the Fury, As I Lay Dying,* or *Absalom, Absalom!* Gide's *The Counterfeiters*). In reading these earlier works, the reader cannot accept any *one* perspective as leading to the truth; but there is still the sense in these works that a locus of truth is present, not within the text itself but within the *reader,* who assembles the different elements simultaneously and then decides on the proper interpretation. But with Coover's stories it is a fruitless task to attempt to separate fantasy from reality, the "real" perspective from imaginary or distorted ones, just as similar inquiries into cubist paintings or a "cubist movie" like *Last Year at Marienbad* lead only to dead ends.

In presenting all the forks of the road, Coover abandons one of realistic fiction's strongest conventions—that the author should choose one specific narrative "path" and then follow it to a conclusion. Writers have relied on this convention for an obvious reason: they believe this is the way the objective world operates. Coover abandons this principle, just as the cubists abandoned one-point perspective, because the assurance of the existence of the objective nature of reality has faded. [Many] modern artists have rejected realistic conventions because, to quote John Weightman, "Any realism of social context is out of the question, because reality is infinite and multifarious and can only be rendered by partial and mutually exclusive grids. There are no plots in nature, so that to tell a story in terms of cause and effect is to accept a naive linear fiction."

Probably the simplest of the cubist pieces is **"The Elevator,"** a story which Coover has said generated most of the others. The story clearly shows Coover's approach and opens as follows:

Every morning without exception and without so much as reflecting upon it, Martin takes the self-service elevator to the fourteenth floor, where he works. He will do so today. When he arrives, however, he finds the lobby empty, the old building still possessed of its feinting shadows and silences, desolate though mutely expectant, and he wonders if today it might not turn out differently.

What follows this opening section are fourteen different short sequences, each numbered and each describing different elevator trips for Martin. The total number of sequences, fifteen, corresponds to the fourteen floors of the building plus the basement, but the sections do not follow each other in any apparent temporal or causal order. We learn, for example, that Martin has an uneventful ride, fights or doesn't fight an office bully, takes the elevator to a nonexistent fifteenth floor, makes love to or is repulsed by the elevator operator as they plunge to their death, and so on. Coover has commented that this story "is based purely on number and musical analogues," a cryptic remark which does, however, suggest some useful ways of considering these cubist stories. The musical analogy has already been suggested: one way to view the different sections in **"The Elevator"** is as variations or counterpoints (the "pricksong" or "descant" idea) to the familiar plot line (an ordinary ride in an elevator). The concept of number is also important. For example, the magical number seven figures prominently in the story's development, as it does in many of Coover's works: it has been seven years since Martin began working in this building; there are usually seven people in the elevator; what is probably the most important scene takes place in the seventh section. More importantly, mathematics provides a key analogy with what Coover is doing here, an analogy suggested by the epigraph Coover chose for **Pricksongs** taken from Valéry's "Variations on the Eclogues": "Therefore they set me this problem of the equality of appearance and number." Like a mathematician toying with the different possible permutations of a set of given elements, Coover constructs **"The Elevator"** (and his other cubist pieces) so that each section can be seen as a permutation or transformation of the set of original elements (the main characters, the plot possibilities, the symbols employed, and so on).

Although at the end of **"The Elevator"** Martin decides not to take the elevator trip at all, we should not assume that the other sequences were all fantasies, daydreamed by Martin as he actually stands before the elevator. Readers who try to recreate the "real events" of any of the cubist stories will be frustrated and will have misunderstood their nature. As with Duchamp's *Nude Descending a Staircase,* what we are given here is not a static picture of reality but the presentation of a process, a way of looking at things. The fact that different sequences contradict one another should not disturb us any more than the fact that the same curved and rectilinear shapes are used to confound the anatomy of the human form and guitar in Braque's *Man with a Guitar* or Picasso's *Ma Jolie* [*Woman with Guitar*]. In **"The Elevator"** all the events, including the contradictory ones, are allowed to freely intermingle. Each of the events within the story's "set" is equally real—or fictional—for every sequence creates its own reality as it is presented.

As is true of all the cubist stories, **"The Elevator"** is clearly linked to Coover's more conventional fiction. Death and sexual violation dominate the action here, just as they do in nearly all the stories in *Pricksongs.* Also typical is the way Coover creates his characters and situations in a flat, nonrealistic manner. But as presented by Coover, seemingly infinite possibilities are held within this small set of elements. Martin himself senses this as he considers the nature of the Kantian categories: "This small room, so commonplace and so compressed, he observes with a certain melancholic satisfaction, this elevator contains them all: space, time, cause, motion, magnitude, class. Left to our own devices, we would probably discover them." Yes, the possibilities of an elevator used as a literary or metaphysical symbol are indeed almost limitless; and perhaps if left to ourselves, we would figure them all out eventually. But meanwhile Coover starts us on our way. If we look at the elevator as a literary symbol, for instance, we find that many of the obvious possibilities have been anticipated: the elevator as a social microcosm; the elevator as a phallic symbol; the elevator as a coffin; the elevator as a jail—"He steps inside: this tight cell! he thinks with a kind of unsettling shock"; "Martin imagines suddenly he is descending into hell. *Tra la perduta gente,* yes!" Critics of practically any persuasion should be able to find something of interest here.

The elevator also allows Coover to exhibit his delight in verbal forms, his ability to control a dizzying variety of styles—a quality which he demonstrates in all his work. Thus the style in the individual sections switches rapidly from the apocalyptic ("I, Martin, proclaim my omnipotence! In the end, doom touch all! MY doom! I impose it! TREMBLE!"), to pornographic parody ("His gaze coolly courses her belly, her pinched and belted waist, past her taut breasts, meets her excited stare"), to a bawdy, colloquial joke ("But hey! theres this guy see he gets on the goddamn elevator and its famous how hes got him a doodang about five feet long"). The story thus implies that you aren't taking advantage of the possibilities which are open to you.

Perhaps Coover's most successful cubist story is **"The Babysitter."** In his prologue to *Pricksongs,* Coover speaks admiringly of the "synthesis between . . . reality and illusion, sanity and madness, the erotic and the ludicrous, the visionary and the scatalogical," and in this story he makes this synthesis vital. The tale is composed of over one hundred short sections which weave a variety of alternative possibilities. The elements of this story are drawn from familiar territory: a teenage babysitter arrives, middle-class parents depart for a party, the babysitter settles down for an evening of television, diaper changing, and perhaps some making out with her boyfriend Jack if he should stop by. These elements, despite their fragmentation, make up a plot line we are all familiar with, but other combinations are possible; relying on material drawn mainly from cultural stereotypes and myths, television shows, and pornographic clichés, Coover conjures up a variety of our society's stock fears and wishes, fantasies and dangers.

"The Babysitter" is therefore composed of the same sort of shifting, contradictory possibilities as **"The Elevator."** Here, too, the many switches in voice and style provide Coover with the chance to parody a variety of literary conventions and styles and to keep the borderline between fantasy and reality fluid at all times. Most readers—especially upon their first reading of the story—are probably tempted to figure out which of the sections are "real" and which are merely the converging, overlapping "fantasies" experienced by the principal characters of the story. Coover allows us to do this kind of sorting throughout the first part of the story, but gradually he begins to allow the various "fantasies" to intermingle *with each other*—an obvious impossibility in terms of realistic norms. Thus one of the scenes begins with Jack, the babysitter's boyfriend, fantasizing about seducing the babysitter with the assistance of his friend Mark: "Mark is kissing her. Jack is under the blanket easing her panties down over her squirming hips." But this scene is suddenly interrupted by the entrance of Mr. Tucker—an appearance seemingly imagined by Mr. Tucker earlier in the narration. At this point the reader must ask himself how Mr. Tucker's fantasy was able to intrude upon the fantasy being experienced by Jack. The answer, of course, is that Coover is not interested in the fantasy/reality distinction we are trying to impose; that these two plot elements are here fused should not bother readers any more than the fact that the cubists often run together planes otherwise separated in space or use a single line to suggest two different subjects or features.

Although it soon becomes obvious that it is impossible to untangle the different levels of reality in **"The Babysitter,"** beneath the shifting plot lines there are certain social implications. Coover uses the television programs which the babysitter watches (spy stories, westerns, convoluted love stories) to mirror the sexual aggressiveness and more covert hints of violence in the Tucker household and at the party; appropriately enough, during several of the rape scenes, images from the television set are reflected over the bodies of the participants. Coover is careful, however, to leave the idea that the television is *causally related* to the social context of violence completely up to our own discretion. Other parallels are less subtle: before the two boys decide to visit the babysitter at the Tuckers', we see them playing a pinball game which is described in parodically sexual and sadistic terms: "He pushes a plunger with his thumbs and one ball pops in place, hard and glittering with promise. . . . He heaves his weight gently against the machine as the ball bounds off a rubber bumper. He can feel her warming up under his hands." Later in one of the rape scenes, this metaphor is repeated: "The television lights flicker and flash over her glossy flesh. 1000 WHEN LIT. Whack! Slap! Bumper to bumper. He leans into her, feeling her come alive." That people are confused enough to direct their sexual feelings toward machines in this story is not really surprising, for every character (including the children) seems driven by sexual obsessions of one sort or another. This sexual obsessiveness is as evident at the drunken cocktail party attended by the Tuckers as it is back at their house; gossip and lewd jokes make up the main topic of conversation, and the central event of the evening is the game of "Get Dolly Tucker Back in Her

Girdle Again," played to the delight of all on the living room floor. Coover's story thus demonstrates the way in which sex and violence are peculiarly intermixed in our society's public and private fantasies, its various forms of entertainment, even in its most mundane activities. Obviously, however, the social message of this story is slight and presented heavy-handedly. Actually Coover seems to use the cliché implications he draws much like Donald Barthelme in many of his stories—simply as further literary elements which can be manipulated for ironic or parodic purposes.

The two other interesting cubist stories in *Pricksongs,* **"The Magic Poker"** and **"The Gingerbread House,"** are both based on fairy tales. In **"The Gingerbread House"** Coover presents forty-two short sections to create a variety of possible outcomes to the familiar Hansel and Gretel fairy tale. The tale is notable in part for its development of the overtones of sex and violence contained in the original story, a development created by the innuendoes of language rather than by overt action. **"The Gingerbread House"** is also a good example of the way in which Coover deliberately undercuts, reverses, or obscures the familiar associations we may have brought to the story. Rather than simply altering the pattern, he allows parts of the original story to engage other possibilities openly. For example, he draws in materials or characters extraneous or contradictory to the original story (such as the dove or the man with white hair). At other times he suddenly switches the symbolic or allegoric implications we are familiar with. For instance, rather than having the black witch (evil, experience) kill the dove (purity, grace), Coover has the young boy (innocence, goodness) brutally do the job. Indeed, the basic opposition between the two innocent children and the evil witch is undermined by a variety of hints pointing to a willing sexual connection between them. In addition to such basic reversals, Coover plants an overabundance of familiar images and symbols (doves, butterflies, flowers, colors, etc.), but he does not allow them to grow and establish their familiar pattern (or *any* pattern, for that matter). Thus we probably notice that some sort of color imagery is being employed in this story, because specific colors recur in section after section. But when we try to establish a consistent "meaning" in this color imagery, we find that our analysis is mocked; the final meaning of colors, like whiteness in *Moby Dick* or *The Narrative of Arthur Gordon Pym,* remains ambiguous. As the reader/critic, we are placed in exactly the same position as many of Coover's characters: in trying to sort out the ambiguities before us, we are inundated with meaning, surrounded by what Neil Schmitz has termed "iconic words, ostensible keys to ostensible meanings."

"The Magic Poker," the most complicated of Coover's cubist stories, is composed of various fragments of fairy tales, legends, myths, and speculative histories. It opens with a godlike narrator busily setting the stage for some expected visitors:

> I wander the island, inventing it. I make a sun
> for it and trees—pine and birch and dogwood
> and firs—and cause the water to lap the pebbles
> of its abandoned shores. . . . I impose a hot

midday silence, a profound and heavy stillness.
But anything can happen.

As was the case in **"Klee Dead,"** the narrator occupies the center of the stage; as other scenes and characters are introduced, he never allows us to forget that they are *his* scenes and creatures, the products solely of his imagination. When the central symbol of the story—the magic poker—is introduced, he proudly reminds us that he alone is responsible for its being there: "It is long and slender with an intricate worked handle, and it is orange with rust. It lies shadowed, not by trees, but by the grass that has grown around it. I put it there." From the beginning we see the narrator's obsessive control over the fiction he is building, his fumbling efforts to keep us entertained, his ambivalence about what he is doing. He resembles many of Coover's victims of artifice, struggling to understand the nature of what he is creating and often confusing his inventions with reality. He is another of Coover's magicians, a self-conscious Prospero who represents Coover himself; as he manipulates the different elements of his story, he is hopeful of entertaining us but also constantly reminds us that it is he who pulls the doves from the hat. The story therefore has the dual focus which we find so often in Coover's work: on the one level, we watch the highly artificial characters struggling to work out their fictional destinies on a magical island; at the same time, we observe the narrator trying to assemble the story, self-consciously considering *his* destiny as a creator of stories.

As the narrator begins to sketch in the details and characters of his story, he also becomes increasingly aware of his constructions as *objects.* Indeed, in much the same fashion as Waugh's Universal Baseball Association or Nixon's fantasies about the Rosenbergs in *The Public Burning,* the story itself gradually becomes a fiction which slowly assumes a reality of its own and begins to envelop its creator. At one point, the narrator admits that his metaphors seem to be developing a stubborn sense of "reality" and "hardness" of their own:

> At times, I forget that this arrangement is my
> own invention. I begin to think of the island as
> somehow real, its objects solid and intractable,
> its condition of ruin not so much an aesthetic de-
> sign as an historical denouement. I find myself
> peering into blue teakettles, batting at spider-
> webs, and contemplating a greenish gray growth
> on the side of a stone parapet. I wonder if others
> might wander here without my knowing it; I
> wonder if I might die and the teakettle remain.

Clearly, the problems facing this narrator lie at the heart of all of Coover's work. The process we observe in **"The Magic Poker"** is that of a fiction gradually assuming its place in the world, with its creator often mistaking his "aesthetic design" for the design of the universe. Eventually, "by some no doubt calculable formula of event and pagination," the narrator disappears entirely into his creation, with only the island remaining behind: "The lake is calm. Here a few shadows lengthen, a frog dies, a strange creature lies slain, a tanager sings."

The narrator not only succumbs to his own invention but also faces the same sorts of problems that all modern writers do. As Neil Schmitz summarizes, "Throughout 'The Magic Poker' the narrator is . . . bemused, at once the systematizing writer and a witness to the fecundating power of words. Traditional fiction, like the mansion in which nineteenth century novel-lives might well have been lived, is wreckage; Coover himself a vandal writing on its deserted walls" ["Robert Coover and the Hazards of Metafiction," *Novel* 7 (1974)]. As the narrator examines the wreckage of language and symbols that lie strewn around him, he occasionally strains too hard and gives in to excesses. In the cottage where he has been imagined, the caretaker's son squats over a teakettle and produces a "love letter." But the narrator intervenes, aware that his absolute power of invention has allowed him to go too far; in the process of analyzing what he is doing, he provides a good example of how Coover undercuts his use of symbolism by alluding to its presence:

> A love letter! Wait a minute, this is getting out of hand! What happened to that poker, I was doing much better with that poker, I had something going there, archetypal and even maybe beautiful, a blend of eros and wisdom, sex and sensibility, music and myth. But what am I going to do with shit in a rusty teakettle?

The magic poker which the narrator manipulates with such evident delight resembles the literary elements in all of Coover's stories in that it can be transformed into whatever is needed. Thus the poker appears at one point as the familiar archetype of fairy tales which, when kissed by a beautiful girl, changes magically into a handsome enchanted prince. It also can usefully serve the narrator as a phallic symbol or, more generally, as a symbol of creativity (much like the writer's equally phallic pen). It is later employed, however, as a *parody* of these symbols, as when one of the girls "kisses the rusted iron poker, kisses its ornate handle, its long rusted shaft, kisses the tip. Nothing happens. Only a rotten taste in her mouth." In another variation, the poker repulses any magical suggestions at all: when the girl discovers it, she finds it "not so rusty on the underside—but bugs! *millions* of them!". Less conspicuously, but more practically, the poker is also put to use as a substitute for the missing leg of a piano, as a magic can, as a weapon, as a kettle stirrer, and even as a convenient simile for the narrator himself: "Yes, and perhaps tomorrow I will invent Chicago and Jesus Christ and the history of the moon. Just as I have invented you, dear reader, while lying here in the afternoon sun, bedded deeply in the bluegrass like an old iron poker." Here the narrator literally becomes the cumulative symbol of the story, and he withdraws permanently into his language. As Neil Schmitz explains this withdrawal:

> **"The Magic Poker"** thus turns sinuously in upon itself. Figurative language, Coover's enchanted poker, remains that instrument that . . . releases the writer from his metafictional anality, his obsessive control over the fiction he is creating. . . . Coover envisions an escape into language, the writer's essence. . . . Language grows on this "invented island" and finally reclaims the artifice of Coover's narrator.

"The Magic Poker" effectively draws together many of the concerns we have seen operating in much of Coover's short fiction. Using a familiar form, he restructures the elements of this form into new shapes which deny the adequacy of our previous perspectives. At the same time, the central problem of all of Coover's work emerges: how does man maintain his precarious balance between using and appreciating his inventions, and becoming lost within them? Like many of his stories, **"The Magic Poker"** deals with fictions in a literary sense and metafictionally examines the relationship between a writer and his inventions.

> *Larry McCaffery, "Robert Coover and the Magic of Fiction Making," in his* The Metafictional Muse: The Works of Robert Coover, Donald Barthelme, and William H. Gass, *University of Pittsburgh Press, 1982, pp. 25-98.*

Coover on writing:

Borges said we go on writing the same story all our lives. The trouble is, it's usually a story that can never be told—there's always this distance between the sign and the signified, it's the oldest truth in philosophy—and that's why we tend to get so obsessive about it. The important thing is to accept this unbridgeable distance, and carry on with the crazy bridge-building just the same.

Robert Coover, in Genre, *1981.*

Richard Andersen   (essay date 1983)

[*Andersen is an American critic and educator. In the following essay, he discusses "the role of the fiction maker" in a selection of Coover's short stories.*]

The role of the fiction maker is the central concern of Robert Coover's work. Yet it has been inadequately discussed by the critics, who, more often than not, have commented on Coover's stories as individual pieces rather than as an *oeuvre* in which a single theme is developed. My essay attempts to correct both this oversight as well as another, namely, the shockingly small amount of attention that has been given to Coover's uncollected works.

Much has been said about the fact that Coover's fictions invite their readers to participate with their author in games of wit and satire. But there is more to these stories than fun and games. Coover makes a conscious attempt to return to his readers their desire for the thrill of discovery—if they ever had one. He wants to free them and not a few writers from the blind alley of exhausted forms and ideas that characterize so much of contemporary literature.

To free themselves and their readers from the deadening effects of convention, today's writers must challenge the assumptions they've inherited from the past, determine what has become obsolete, and sally forth into new worlds of fiction, says Coover. Never mind that the only vehicle available is a pile of bones. Use the familiar and worn out to combat the content of hackneyed forms and to conduct audiences to the real. Take them away from magic to maturity, away from illusion to revelation.

I will show you how to do this, says Coover, barber's basin on his head. I will lead you beyond structural games to the less frequently seen side of props and mirrors. I will show you how to make clear rather than deceive. I will give you new and indispensable funds of information about writing and human nature.

To make his readers constantly aware that his fictions are an art form as well as a comment on the human condition, Coover creates elaborate artifices into which he places his characters and their events. Because these personae and their actions tend to be types drawn from the popular culture, however, they enrich rather than balance the artifices Coover has erected. Furthermore, these familiar characters create in the readers' minds stereotypical responses that the author can manipulate by sending them in unexplored directions.

Coover's attempts to wean his readers from their conventional approaches to fiction fall into two categories. The first category involves the reinterpretation of stories that have been accepted uncritically for long periods of time. By providing these stories with alternative perspectives, Coover hopes to free his readers from some of the cultural clichés they have unconsciously assimilated. "Our old faith," says Coover, "—one might better say our old sense of constructs derived from myths, legends, philosophies, fairy stories, and other fictions which help to explain what happens to us from day to day, why our governments are the way they are, why our institutions have the character they have, why the world turns as it does—has lost its efficacy. Not necessarily is it false; it is just not as efficacious as it was."

The second category into which the remainder of Coover's works may be placed concerns stories that present fiction as a variety of narrative possibilities. These stories are designed to subvert their readers' accepted literary conventions and traditional ideas about human nature and help them recognize and attain higher levels of artistic consciousness.

> Most of society's effort goes into forging the construct, the creative form in which everybody can live—a social contract of sorts. . . . Whatever form they set up is necessarily entropic; eventually it runs down and is unable to propel itself past a certain point. When it does that it becomes necessary to do everything that has been taboo: wear women's clothes, kill the sacred animal and eat it, screw your mother, etc. A big blast reduces everything to rubble; then something new is built. . . . Artists recreate; they make us think about doing all the things we shouldn't do, all the impossible apocalyptic things, and weaken and tear down structures so that they can be rebuilt, releasing new energies. [Coover in Frank Gado's *First Person: Conversations on Writers and Writing,* 1973]

Coover's principal method for liberating his readers from sensibilities that have been deadened by the familiar is irony. Speaking of himself and other contemporary writ-

ers whose tendency was once to reject traditional narrative forms, Coover says, "We are turning back to design and there is an attraction towards modes of inquiry and creation that we rejected as we moved into this Era of Enlightenment. These forms . . . have a certain beauty, and now a potential for irony exists in them. . . . They *are* useful after all." Irony enables Coover and his readers to distance themselves from traditional narrative forms without isolating themselves from the human content of those forms. Consequently, Coover's readers are able to enjoy his poking fun at literature's inherited conventions without losing their concern for the human condition. The result is a healthy sense of humor and the awareness of a changing consciousness.

Of the many works not included in Coover's collection of twenty-one short stories [*Pricksongs and Descants*], "The Reunion," "The Dead Queen," and "The Mex Would Arrive at Gentry's Junction at 12:10" serve as models for the reinterpretation of stories that have lost their efficacy. Coover explains the creative genesis of **"The Reunion,"** a retelling of Christ's Resurrection, this way: "The problem of Christian belief bothered me: it wouldn't leave me alone and yet I couldn't solve it. Then I found a vibrant way to understand the matter: I imagined a character like Jesus, created him in my own mind, and carried this thing on with him. Rather than try to discuss the historical arguments for his existence or non-existence, or to investigate what had happened to the Gospel texts and how much we could depend on the various parts, I merely took the story itself and, involving myself in it, considered various variations." The story, which does not remain faithful to the original, begins with Doubting Thomas telling the apostles about how important it is to "confront reality honestly and bravely, one's own wishes be damned." Just as Thomas convinces Christ's followers that they have relied too heavily on the myth of the Messiah, however, Christ, who has been hanged rather than crucified, appears and accepts a chair offered to him by the doubting apostle. Unfortunately, Christ's head can no longer be supported by his broken neck and the physical effects of his hanging dominate the scene: "Again the head rolls off the man's shoulder, and now dangles over the back of the chair, staring upside down, at the circle of straight faces that stare. Thomas sees that the man cannot, by himself, return the head to the shoulder, but neither he nor anyone else in the room can bring himself to help the man. Instead he stares down at the stark and brittle body whose head has disappeared behind its back. The man in the chair does not move. Nor does he ever move again. It is a long and cheerless night."

"The Reunion" is a pivotal work for Coover. It sacrifices the humor and bitter but human sensitiveness of his other Bible retellings for a more explicit delineation of the author's belief that his readers should consider Christian myths "not as literal truth but simply as a story that tells us something metaphorically about ourselves and the world." By shifting the metaphor from Christ's redemption to mankind's overconfidence in myths, however, Coover opens up the possibility for different versions as well as different interpretations of traditional stories. A symbol for this idea may lie in the fact that none of the retellings ends with a period, thereby suggesting that they can continue in a variety of ways. Furthermore, by rewriting, as opposed to retelling, the story of Christ's Resurrection, Coover exposes the undershaft of religious myths and provides his readers with an ironic commentary on how fictions, which have no more meaning than people assign to them, can be formulated into truths.

"The Dead Queen," a reinterpretation of the familiar fairy tale "Snow White and the Seven Dwarfs," begins at the funeral of the wicked Queen, who was jealous of Snow White's beauty. Prince Charming and his new bride are supposed to live happily ever after, but the Prince, who is also the story's narrator, has his doubts. Snow White, in his eyes, seems to be "utterly heartless," though not malicious, "like a happy child at the circus, unaware of any skills or risks. . . . She's suffered no losses, in fact that's just the trouble, that hymen can never be broken, not even by me. . . . This is her gift and her essence, and because of it, she can see neither fore nor aft, doesn't even know there is a mirror on the wall." Reflecting upon the crimes the Queen committed against Snow White, Prince Charming wonders if the allegedly evil stepmother had been motivated to poison Snow White for reasons other than jealousy: "She'd sent that child of seven into the woods with a restless lech, and he'd brought her back a boar's heart, as though to say he repented of his irrational life and wished to die. But then, perhaps that had been what she wanted, perhaps she had ordered the boar's heart, or known anyway that would be the Hunter's instinct, or perhaps there had been no Hunter at all, perhaps it had been that master of disguises, the old Queen herself, it was possible, it was possible."

Pondering alternative versions to the traditional story sobers Prince Charming, who finds himself troubled by things about which he had not given much thought: "the true meaning of my bride's name, her taste for luxury and collapse, the compulsions that led me to the mountain. . . . " Suddenly, it dawns on the Prince that the Queen might have been trying to save him from Snow White, to break the pattern of the fairy tale, and to free its characters from its traditional bonds. Believing that he retains the power that his fiction maker bestowed upon him for his own purposes, Prince Charming wrenches open the coffin, throws himself upon the Queen, and kisses her in the hope of restoring her to life. The Queen, however, does not return Prince Charming's kiss: "She stank and her blue mouth was cold and rubbery as a dead squid." No doubt this is the taste left in Coover's mouth by writers who try to repeat traditional formulas.

Speaking about other fairy tales that Coover has reinterpreted, Neil Schmitz claims that they are "little more than adulterated versions of the TV cartoon, *Fractured Fairytales.*" He says that Coover's professed aim to introduce his readers to new narrative possibilities is laboriously achieved. "In brief, it is only a different kind of effect that Coover strives to produce in his fiction by deconstructing the 'familiar form'. The result is not a transcendence of that form, but rather a transposition of its elements" ["Robert Coover and the Hazards of Metafiction," *Novel* 7 (1974)].

Certainly there is some truth to Schmitz's observations. Coover's retelling of "Snow White and the Seven Dwarfs," like the *Fractured Fairytales,* depends upon an audience whose perception of the original story enables them to understand the comment the satiric version is making. However, Coover's representation of innocence lost and the broadening of a person's consciousness go beyond the gently ironic parodies of the television cartoon. More than a display of technical wizardry, Coover's fairy tales provide their author with universally accepted metaphors through which he can effectively relate his ideas about fiction and the human condition.

In **"The Mex Would Arrive at Gentry's Junction at 12:10,"** Coover demythifies Hollywood's version of the Wild West. The story opens with Sheriff Henry Harmon, a parody of the role Gary Cooper played in the film *High Noon,* fretting about the arrival in town of don Pedo, a Mexican antithesis of everything "Hank" stands for. To further emphasize the disparity that exists between his two protagonists, Coover gives each one his own narrative voice. Hank, as might be expected, is described in terms of the language and conventions the Mexican undercuts: "The sheriff of Gentry's Junction, erect, tall, lean, proud, his cold blue eyes squinting into the glare of the noon sun, walked silently, steadily alone, down the dusty Main Street, the jingle of his spurs muffled only slightly by the puffs of dust kicked up by his high heels." In contrast with Hank, don Pedo, whose name means "fart," is described by a voice that has been influenced by the Spanish language: "The wanted unwanted Mexican he stands at the bar. He laughs and laughs and he drinks. He is short to the extreme, nor is he lean. Squat. Squat is the word, and dark with brown watery eyes. Not severe. Not honest. . . . It is assumed that all the womans die beneath the Mexican, later or sooner. It is the, how you say? the legend."

While don Pedo throws into disarray the order and completeness of which the sheriff is so fond, Hank tries to round up a posse from among the townspeople, who seem to be more afraid of him than of the fun-loving bandit. While the sheriff bullies the town's most prominent maintainers of the status quo, the banker, the storekeeper, and the minister, into covering him during his face-off with the bandit, don Pedo seems to be breaking up all of the town's conventional attitudes. He is seen burning the sheriff's legal papers, winning at cards with a hand of five aces, making love with Hank's virgin fiancée, and "demonstrating for the little school children the enormity and joyous function of his genital member" while their teacher is "bound and gagged to her desk. . . . They applaud in childish glee as the Mexican he with the prodigious protuberance destroys a something-or-other that the schoolmarm has been guarding for years: POP! there she goes."

In a showdown that in many ways resembles the final scene of Eugene Ionesco's *The Killer,* in which a detective captures a mass murderer only to be convinced by him that life is not worth living, the sheriff makes his stand against don Pedo. With every Western cliché having been accounted for, however, Coover reverses the conventional procedures that brought him to this point in the story.

When Hank steps forth to challenge the bandit to draw on him, he notices that the villain is not standing spread-legged in the middle of the street, but sitting on a bucket, picking at his teeth, and playing with a watch. When Hank notices that the watch is his, the Mexican returns it to him without protest. Reaching down to disarm don Pedo, Hank senses that everything seems wrong. The gunfight is not going according to the script. Villains are not supposed to fart while being arrested and their guns should have notches in their handles. The bandit's are old and rusty; one of them has no hammer. Tossing the guns away, Hank concludes that the Mexican is a fraud. When he signals his back-up crew to come forward and bring a rope to hang don Pedo, however, he hears a click. He reaches for his guns, but his holsters are empty. The Mexican has stolen the sheriff's pistols while being disarmed. Spinning toward the bandit, Hank's astonished face greets a silver bullet from his own gun. As the bandit rides off into the sunset, he can hear behind him the sounds of celebration. The storekeeper, the banker, and the preacher, those keepers of convention and resisters of originality, "swing with soft felicity from scaffolds and the golden whiskey he runs like blood."

Although **"The Cat in the Hat for President"** and **"Beginnings"** do not retell or reinterpret familiar stories, they follow a line of attack that is similar to the one Coover employed in **"The Reunion," "The Dead Queen,"** and **"The Mex Would Arrive at Gentry's Junction at 12:10."** Basically, Coover's attack in these allegories is four-pronged: he begins by identifying the metaphor that has outlived its usefulness; he then demonstrates through parody the subjective nature of the metaphor and points out the danger of substituting fiction for truth; finally, he releases the imaginative forces that created the metaphor into new constructs. As Coover dismantles the popular culture's substitutions for truth, however, he paradoxically revitalizes them by providing new perspectives from which they may be approached. "Working with cultural givens and trying to improve them," he says, "is a rewarding endeavor. Sometimes a work will coincide with the 'Head Start' cultural vocabulary of the broad audience; sometimes it won't. There's not much to be done about it, really. So I just have to continue the enterprise for itself. There will always be some people who will read such ventures, recognize value, and try to see that it is transmitted in one way or other."

"The Cat in the Hat for President" is a spoof on the hoopla that attends the way Americans choose their national leaders. Nevertheless, the author's role in these works is similar to the one he has played in all of his preceding fictions:

> The role of the author, the fiction maker, the mythologizer, is to be the creative spark in the process of renewal; he is the one who tears apart the old story, speaks the unspeakable, makes the ground shake, then shuffles the bits back together into a new story. Partly anarchical, in other words, partly creative—or re-creative. The organizers of society—the politicians, chiefs, bureaucrats—will go ahead and rebuild the thing from time to time, but that's not what the storytellers

are doing. . . . I enjoy the fun of stirring things up, breaking the rules, punching holes in the structures so as to see through to the mysteries—even if only to rediscover what it was you liked about society when it was still all of a piece. The artist's role, then, is priestly in a way; he's there, at his best, as a voice of disturbance.

Representing the organizers of society in **"The Cat in the Hat for President"** is the story's narrator, Mr. Brown, whose life in business has been long, successful, and dull. Ironically, however, many of Mr. Brown's attitudes are similar to those of Coover and the anarchical protagonists of his other fictions. Like Doubting Thomas of **"The Reunion"** and don Pedo of **"The Mex Would Arrive at Gentry's Junction at 12:10,"** Brown believes in the fictional nature of the reality man has created: " 'Liberal', 'conservative', 'left', 'right', these are mere fictions of the press, metaphoric conventions to which politicians sooner or later adapt." Nevertheless, Brown needs the familiar as much as anyone else and so finds comfort in the traditional.

Attempting to free Brown and those who share his point of view from the illusions of order that their fear of reality has produced is the Cat in the Hat, a character from Dr. Seuss's children's stories, whose antics are about as unpredictable as any story by Coover. Brown sees the Cat as better suited for a circus than a political convention and inherently destructive, "but what," he rationalizes, "is destroyed except nay-saying itself, authority, social habit?" Eventually, Brown, who is chairman of the political party, capitulates to the enthusiastic response the Cat's unorthodox approach to politics has created and agrees to support his candidacy for the Presidency.

On the day of his nomination, however, the Cat appears on the convention floor wearing a pair of roller skates and holding up a cake on a rake. On top of the cake is a goat balancing an umbrella on his nose, and on top of the umbrella wobbles a fishbowl with a protesting fish inside. Soon the whole assemblage falls and the entire hall is engulfed in water from the fishbowl. The fish, which is now of Leviathan size, swallows up all the delegates and then spews them forth into a glass-encased arena that happens to be the fishbowl on top of the umbrella that is being balanced by the goat who is standing on top of the cake that the Cat in the Hat is balancing on his rake. "Now you can see / What I can do!" announces the party's nominee, "I can give you / Something new! / Something true / And impromptu! / I can give you / A new view!"

Although Brown can appreciate the liberating perspectives offered to him and to the party's delegates by the Cat in the Hat, he suspects the Cat might be a greater threat to the status quo than a new metaphor for appreciating the old ways. His friend, Clark, however, comforts him with the thought that any great liberation is necessarily accompanied by a sense of loss. "What we must do, Mr. Brown," says Clark, echoing Coover in his prologue to the collected stories in *Pricksongs and Descants,* "is help all men once more to experience reality concretely, fully, wholly, without mystification, free from mirages, unencumbered by pseudo-systems."

As valuable as the Cat's alternatives to conventions may be, however, they are resisted by educators, labor leaders, businessmen, minority groups, priests, poets, bureaucrats, warriors, journalists, and others who have located for themselves a verity in the traditional. What follows is the Cat's assassination and an apocalyptic orgy that echoes those of Coover's three novels: *The Origin of the Brunists* (1966), *The Universal Baseball Association, Inc., J. Henry Waugh, Prop.* (1968), and *The Public Burning* (1977). Seen in this light, **"The Cat in the Hat"** can be read not only as another appeal for Coover's readers to accept numerous and imaginative possibilities in literature, but also as a metaphor for the tolerance of extremities that can separate people from the "human constant," and "carry us out to something new where these old ways of identifying ourselves will seem sad and empty."

What Coover often seems to preach in **"The Cat in the Hat for President"** he actually practices in **"Beginnings,"** a short fiction that challenges its readers to suspend their disbelief and accept a story about a writer who, "in order to get started" on a work he has in mind, "went to live alone on an island and shot himself. His blood, unable to resist a final joke, splattered the cabin wall in a pattern that read: It is important to begin when everything is over." In other words, says Coover, once people kill the rigidifying conventions with which they approach literature, they will be able to enjoy fictions that have been enriched by infinite numbers of imaginative possibilities.

Beginning a story, says Coover's narrator, is always difficult because, traditionally, a beginning implies an end. By beginning his story with an end, however, and later ending it with a beginning, the narrator achieves a sort of constant middle in which virtually anything can happen: a man is born at the age of thirty-two with a self-destruct mechanism in his gonads; the writer begins a story in which the first-person narrator is the story itself; a friend of the writer borrows his typing ribbon for a clothesline and mistakes his story for a grocery list, nearly poisoning them both; Jesus cannot raise Lazarus from the dead and is embarrassed in front of a crowd of expectant onlookers; God turns Noah into salt; a soldier who has been in a foxhole for fifty years forgets who the enemy is, crawls out of his hole one day, and is shot; to keep Adam from starving, Eve turns herself into an apple. There are more stories, but Coover's point is made: whether the stories are plausible, concern what the protagonist does or what the characters do, they all contain narrative possibilities that, because they take place within the context of a fiction, are also valid. Moreover, Coover does not conclude any of the possibilities he presents. Each remains, as Coover believes fiction should be, an open-ended challenge to his readers' imaginations.

"The Reunion," "The Dead Queen," "The Mex Would Arrive at Gentry's Junction at 12:10," "The Cat in the Hat for President," and **"Beginnings"** effectively measure Coover's dedication to defending the creative process against the dogmatic imperatives of convention. Accepting this role, he says, "gave me an excuse to be the anarchist I've always wanted to be. I discovered I could be an anarchist and be constructive at the same time." By chal-

lenging his readers' conventional visions of the world through parodies of stories with which they are familiar, Coover also dramatizes how necessary fictions are to the human imagination. More than aesthetically admirable, they are a kind of utility that people rely on to enrich their lives. When man loses sight of the fictional nature of his creations, however, he tends to dogmatize them. Consequently, the forms in which these fictions appear become rigid and resist the appearance of new constructs and the fresh ideas that usually accompany them. The point at which fictional forms become dogmatic, Coover is saying, also marks the time for them to be broken up and to have their energies released into new perspectives. These new perspectives, however, represent more than a variety of views regarding narrative constructs; they are also metaphors through which life can be further comprehended and appreciated.

> *Richard Andersen, "The Artist in Coover's Uncollected Stories," in* The Southern Humanities Review, *Vol. XVII, No. 4, Fall, 1983, pp. 315-24.*

Caryn James   (essay date 1983)

[*In the following essay, James offers a favorable review of* In Bed One Night and Other Brief Encounters.]

Robert Coover's stories are mind games with a heart. *In Bed One Night and Other Brief Encounters* humanizes language games and literary theorizing, and, remarkably, does so by using cartoonish characters and a nearly anonymous narrative voice. While these nine very short pieces don't amount to much in themselves, they are miniature demonstrations of the control Coover displays in his more substantial work. Like a literary juggler, he keeps all the parts of his fiction in motion, balancing rhythm, word play, and the central image of the author creating his story. Or does the story create the author?

"Beginnings," written in 1972, masterfully explores this question. "In order to get started, he went to live alone on an island and shot himself," reads the first line. What he starts is the story we're reading: "He began a story in which the first person narrator was the story itself, he merely one of the characters, dead before the first paragraph was over." This circular undercutting of cause and effect is the most facile part of **"Beginnings."** Reaching for substance, Coover brings the author-character to life, making him implausible, mundane, unique, and universal. The island becomes a postlapsarian Eden, complete with Eve (this time she's the one who gives up a rib), children, and the distractions and rewards of family life. He awakens one morning, "tangled in first lines like wrinkled sheets," but he also runs out of peanut butter and lets the coffee boil over. Peanut butter and first lines are equally tangible in this world where imagination and reality merge.

Though the more recent works are slighter, they share some characteristic Coover effects. "here's what happened it was pretty good" is the first line of **"An Encounter."** **"The Old Man"** starts, "this one has to do with an old man." Such stories belong to the second generation of metafiction: Coover not only writes about self-conscious storytelling, he assumes that we are aware of his self-referential posture. There's no need to introduce us to the pervasive but protean "he," the author-character at the center of most of his fiction.

In **"The Tinkerer"** and **"The Fallguy's Faith,"** this unnamed "he" is the vehicle for speculations about authorship. Full of playfulness, **"The Tinkerer"** presents an inventor who "took a chance and invented mind / set it walking around jumping up and down," only to see it run amok "through plate glass windows over precipices," and to discover he'd created not mind, but love. He goes on, "frantically inventing serenity." While **"The Tinkerer"** comes to life, **"The Fallguy's Faith"** illustrates what happens when Coover's humanizing power fails to take hold. Here, the character falls "like a discredited predicate," questioning whether he has fallen *merely to have it said he had fallen.*" Even as an intentionally sketchy, abstract figure, the fallguy cannot carry the story. He lacks both the human quality of the inventor and the vitality of "mind" or "love"—which careers around the city, proving along the way that, for Coover, character is no less fluid than reality.

Coover's literary theorizing is more subtle in **"Debris,"** an atypical piece. The main character finds a woman, or perhaps the image of a woman, lying on a beach. As he tries to recall a song, the misplaced melody or words become a metaphor for the woman. But the characters are not just linguistic symbols brought to life—the shadow of a relationship hovers, keeping them grounded in reality. "what went wrong between us he asks because he needs a little cheering up / why did you wash up in this bad light?" The metaphor does not represent the reality of the woman or the relationship; the metaphor *is* reality, Coover suggests, and vice versa.

A few comic stories leave metaphor behind. The best, **"In Bed One Night,"** is a literary slapstick in which several strangers are assigned to share the same bed—social security cutbacks seem to be the problem. An old lady searches for her dentures, her one-legged brother lies at the foot of the bed, a drunken worker fucks a fat woman, and a skinny Oriental cowers, as the owner of the bed registers his shock: "*wha—?!* he cries out in alarm." Coover skillfully orchestrates this pandemonium in a breathless, unpunctuated style. Even when his comic technique is so emphatically in the foreground, he keeps an eye on the complexity of authorship. In his most farcical moments or his most deft and restrained moods, Coover is relentlessly energetic about one question. His fiction insists on asking where its own creativity comes from, and just as insistently answers that it exists only in the active process of writing and reading.

Caryn James, in a review of "In Bed One Night and Other Brief Encounters," in VLS, *No. 22, December, 1983, p. 3.*

> **Lois Gordon on Coover's writing:**
>
> Coover has developed a style unique among his contemporaries, mixing so-called fact and fiction with realism and surrealism, merging narrative line with adjacent and "descanting" poetic or fragmentary evocations of moral, mythic, historical, philosophical, and psychological dimensions. He writes in virtually every form, including short story, poetry, fairy tale, filmscript, drama, and novel. Within each, he demonstrates a remarkable diversity of styles and manipulates the trappings of every conventional literary form from old comedy to theater of the absurd; he also translates or transposes techniques associated with other art forms—e.g., film montage and operatic interludes. Any of these might then be transformed into the most extreme forms of parody. Coover has the uncanny ability to reproduce or mimic verbally the written, spoken, or even kinesthetic styles of literally hundreds of historical or popular figures. He can also arouse the emotions traditionally associated with tragedy. Regardless of length—and he has published noticeably long and short fiction—his work is always rich and difficult. Throughout, one would have a hard time finding an ill-chosen word or awkward phrase.
>
> *Lois Gordon, in her* Robert Coover: The Universal Fictionmaking Process, *1983.*

Lois Gordon   (essay date 1983)

[*Gordon is an American educator and critic. In the following excerpt from* Robert Coover: The Universal Fictionmaking Process, *she provides an overview of Coover's short fiction.*]

Coover's novels focus on the human need for rituals in a world of time and flux. These "games," as one character calls them—of religion, art, history, and science—appear to organize and give meaning to life's intrinsic disorder. Coover sets up elaborate situations and vast canvasses on which to chart the survival or decline of those who construct and observe these rituals.

The short fictions, perhaps because they are short, differ in several ways. They take for granted the need for sustaining mythologies, but they focus on neither the deepest longings which motivate them nor the grammar of the creative mind that designs them. Most distinctively, they do not spell out the individual's creative/destructive involvement in his imaginative constructs. Instead, most of these short pieces, which include stories, plays, and filmscripts like the **Pricksongs, Hair O' The Chine,** *After Lazarus,* **Charlie in the House of Rue, A Theological Position,** and **Spanking the Maid,** are self-reflexive, metafictional exercises. They often concentrate on archetypal roles or situations, or on generally familiar myths or Bible and folktales—those moral lessons generations have accepted as "exemplary." Coover takes the old designs and familiar stories and attenuates the ambiguities or metamorphic nature of their every detail. Whether dealing with a Bible story or Red Riding Hood, or a modern archetype like "the babysitter," he exposes the arbitrariness of every given. Serious, ethical implications that have until now been overlooked are suddenly illuminated, as are unsuspected dimensions of human character. At times, Coover focuses on a legend's "unimportant" characters; sometimes he rewrites a fable entirely; other times, he only partially restructures it. Implied throughout is an indictment of our unthinking embrace of these mythic exampla and the foolish if not self-destructive lives we have modeled after them.

Although there is an enormous variety in the short pieces, Coover's "play" with familiar tales (especially fairy and Bible tale) is particularly interesting. To be sure, the reader's subsequent associations with, say, "Little Red Riding Hood," "Hansel and Gretel," or "The Three Little Pigs"—or even Shakespeare's *Tempest* or the New Testament's Lazarus or Hollywood's Charlie Chaplin—are never the same. Coover rejects Eliot's dictum that we live in the living moment of the past in the present (and vice versa), which suggests an ever-evolving historical/moral continuity. Although like Lévi-Strauss, he would seem to believe in persistent, omnipresent myths (e.g., all men in all societies create legends that define good versus evil), and although he would appear to believe that such structures may be useful at times, he is, in these pieces, artistically most concerned with the distorted representations of human nature in the classic Western myths and the ill effects of holding on to unworkable archetypes.

Closely examined, Coover's tales expose a variety of complex problems regarding so-called human virtue and moral truth. Implied is the notion that, like any other written documents (e.g., the chronicles of history), fairy tales or Bible stories distort the rich and often unfathomable, ambiguous nature of human experience. The Noah story, for example, carefully considered, contains less than salutary truths about human and divine justice—i.e., an inherent selfishness about the Noah who would abandon his brotherhood and a cruelty about the God who could author such a scheme. Coover's **"The Brother"** tells the story of Noah's gentle, generous, and appropriately nameless brother who, for many months, assists in building the ark. When the floods begin, however, he and his already pregnant wife are left to drown in the rains. The likely abandonment of such a couple compels the reader to question his preconceived mythology of God's so-called bounty and Noah's "elect" status as progenitor of a new race.

This type of realistic scrutiny of such familiar myths runs through Coover's work. In another sort of fable, he transforms the safe materials regarding ritual initiation into more disturbing revelations about human nature. He refurbishes the proverbial gingerbread house and restyles the crossings of any number of bridges; youth becomes involved in the complications of moral uncertainty and the intimate connections between life and death, beauty and the corrupt.

Again exposing the underside, variability, or ambiguity of human behavior implicit in popular myths, Coover focuses on minor characters—or at least those frequently ignored. **"J's Marriage"** [Joseph's] relegates Jesus to the background and is instead concerned with Mary's immaculate husband and his growing despair over her condition. Coover rearranges details and amplifies what suddenly appear to be crucial personal considerations—e.g., Mary's attitude toward marital sexuality and Joseph's loneliness.

Sometimes he retains only the most general or vaguely recalled details of a familiar story. His brilliant **"The Magic Poker,"** an island tale with Prospero and Caliban figures, concentrates on the richly diverse yet similar textures of imagined and real experience. It also concretizes the existential confrontation with contingency.

Coover merges details from several sources. In **"The Gingerbread House"** and the later *Hair O' The Chine,* which incorporates much of this, are Jack and the Beanstalk, Little Red Riding Hood, the woodsman, Hansel and Gretel, Beauty and the Beast, Adam and Eve, and Mary and Joseph, among others. Some of the stories (**"The Elevator,"** **"The Babysitter,"** **"The Train Station"**), while not literary archetypes, reconstruct archetypal situations and portray the variety of fears and fantasies implicit in them.

Finally, among the most interesting works (although most could fit into this category) are the metafictions like **"The Magic Poker,"** **"The Elevator,"** **"The Babysitter,"** **"The Hat Act,"** **"Quenby and Ola,"** *Hair O' The Chine, After Lazarus,* and the plays of *A Theological Position.* Many of these are written in a highly structured form, yet while they deny specific plot or characterization, like a cubist painting, film montage, or in many ways like symbolist poetry, they give rise to continuously metamorphic designs that reflect the nonfixed nature of both reality and human possibility. Their subject is process, and in each Coover captures an instant in time, or a specific landscape in space, or a single aspect of human nature. Then he suggests the infinitely rich possibilities that may grow out of, or cancel, one another in that specific time, space, or character. Once again, the transformational quality of the fictions mirrors the existential universe. Events lack final definition, and characters lack fixed motivation; meaning remains unshaped and unspecific. The author-narrator lacks final control over his medium. Coover's subject is process or structure rather than meaning.

These pieces evoke the reader's keen sense of the infinite possibilities of both the word and the world, and like the novels, they have an open-endedness in content, form, and meaning, also akin to much contemporary sculpture and collage. They propel an endless number of shifting surfaces into space—the infinite possibilities between felt, read, and then translated meaning, which the reader experiences. The act of imposing imagination upon the plenitude of experience is shared by Coover's persona and reader; the game of living is again reflected in the game of reading.

In many of these metafictions (**"The Magic Poker,"** **"Quenby and Ola,"** *Love Scene*), the author's voice is announced as subject ("I wander the island, inventing it"), and it expresses all the pleasures and complexities of writing a story. Here is a writer-magician, often pulling words, rabbits, or islands out of hats, self-consciously creating myth, wrestling with words and created landscapes—both God-creator of a verbal universe and victim of its emergent arrangements. Literature, rather than philosophy, religion, or politics, now structures the universe—tentatively.

The short fictions, then, share the vision of the novels regarding the flux of reality and the power and danger of frozen mythologies. Stylistically, their fusion of realism and surrealism within multiple levels of shifting imagery and a variety of prose styles bears the Coover signature. Again, he often utilizes a strong narrative line in order to counterpoint in fragmented juxtapositions of imagery the fluid and unfixed nature of human psychology, morality, and external phenomena. Finally, he creates an open-ended and infinitely evocative, almost metaphysical style in order to accommodate what seems to be his vision of the human striving for physical and spiritual harmony, to illustrate that the violations (or harmony) of the flesh are the violations (or harmony) of the spirit—to tie this world to the next and demonstrate the means by which one may connect his finitude with something more lasting. Once more, imagination is endowed with deity.

The title **Pricksongs and Descants** well expresses Coover's vision, as does the other apparatus appended to the stories—i.e., a prologue and dedication to Cervantes, two epigraphs, and, in the cloth edition, a dedication to the Virgin of the Post and a particularly interesting cover design. The two epigraphs are

> *He thrusts, she heaves.*
> —JOHN CLELAND, FANNY HILL

> *They therefore set me this problem of the equality of appearance and numbers.*
> —PAUL VALERY, "VARIATIONS ON THE ECLOGUES"

Cleland's "he" and "she," connected to Válery's "they," suggest the difficult though possible unity ("the problem") that exists between flesh, mind, and spirit. The cloth edition's tribute to the Virgin of the Post (on the dust jacket) similarly unites mystery and sexuality. Since it does not appear in the paper edition, it is quoted here in full:

> Once, some time ago and in a distant land, I met a young maiden, known to her tribe as the Virgin of the Post, and she gave to me, amid prurient and mysterious ceremonies, a golden ring. Perhaps it was a local custom, a greeting of sorts. Perhaps a message, an invitation, a mission even. Some peculiar Moorish device of transport and return. Wand-scabbord. Open-sesame. Who can say? It bears on one edge an indecipherable legend, a single cleft rune, not unlike the maiden's own vanished birthmark, and I am inclined to believe that portentous inscrutability may in fact be the point of it all. Now, to that Virgin, I offer these apprentice calculations of my own, invented under the influence of her gifts, begging her to remember the Wisdom of the Beast: "If I carry the poison in my head, in my tail which I bite with rage lies the remedy."

A "golden ring" and "mission," "transport and return," the "prurient and mysterious," distant lands, tribes, and wand-scabbords: "portentous inscrutability" is perhaps the object and lesson, as Coover says, "the point of it all." He has already set up the polarities and materials for des-

cant—the maiden and beast, as well as the dualities of mind and matter. In addition, he announces his method, his use of narrative line from fairy tale or myth in order to explore the counterpointing mystery of experience. The wisdom of the beast would seem to be that there does indeed exist a bond between life and death, pain and recovery, gratitude and humility, mind and body, the organic and inorganic, sexuality and spirit.

The cover design of the cloth edition is interesting too, a detail from a Bosch painting of *The Seven Deadly Sins* united with an image of Christ and love—ironically two traditional and diametrically opposed mythic or moral views of human experience—which Coover perhaps utilizes as emblems of complimentarity. Finally, that he should reach back to older sources (Bosch and Válery) and that Válery should be writing "Variations" on an even older literary comment adds an additional and ironic breadth to his statement. . . .

That Coover is dealing with traditionally irreconcilable materials and that he seeks to create new alliances, is clear in his dedication to Cervantes, apostrophized for his transformation of the exhausted romance into the novel form. Coover makes clear that, like Cervantes, he too is responding to a new world vision, one in which mimetic, teleological fiction has become unworkable.

Lois Gordon, in her Robert Coover: The Uni-

A sketch of Robert Coover by Lewis Thompson.

versal Fictionmaking Process, *Southern Illinois University Press*, 1983, 182 p.

L. L. Lee   (essay date 1986)

[*Lee is an American critic and educator. In the following essay, he studies the moral vision Coover presents in* Pricksongs and Descants.]

Robert Coover's *Pricksongs & Descants* would appear to be exemplary illustrations of the "post-modernist" story, stories, that is, which call into hard question received attitudes towards art, towards communication, towards traditional moral ideas, and, finally, towards the existence and/or being of the human person. Such stories tend to come to rest in language and language structures; for language is all we "know." "Men live by fictions," Coover [said in an interview with Larry McCaffery in *Genre*, (Spring 1981)]. And his aim? "The world itself being a construct of fictions, I believe the fiction maker's function is to furnish better fictions with which we can re-form our notions of things." Or, as Larry McCaffery appropriately suggests, Coover, as artist, "counters . . . the effects of both death (stasis) and randomness (chaos)," in order to "demonstrate his central point about the dangers of allowing our fictions to rigidify." But "fictions" are structures made by language.

However, to argue that Coover is writing only a kind of "metafiction," a fiction about fictions, is to misread these works. For they are more than questions or denials of humanistic value systems as embodied in language; they are also assertions, and often affirmations, about human existence outside of language, assertions that such existence is problematical and difficult, but. . . .

For Coover's act, his writing, must also be seen as, perversely, traditional—and, perversely, moral and didactic. He calls into question and responds, and usually in the same story: as Morris the shepherd in **"Morris in Chains,"** sings, in his "old," i.e., traditional, song, "Now if my tune obscure should seem / The meaning overlong / Consider less than life a dream / And more than death a song / And more than death a song." Life, it would appear, is song, i.e., art itself—but, of course, life itself is what is finally important, life as the complete human experience. Therefore Coover will look at it not from a single vantage point, either of language or traditional morality, but from two sides at once.

Nevertheless, one must grant that to understand how Coover presents his double vision, one must examine his way of presenting (not telling) his "fictions" (fictions, since they are very rarely "stories" in the usual sense, despite our having to admit that they are "stories"—"the central thing for me is story," Coover claims, perhaps a little self-defensively). And so his "way" is through certain thematic matters, both formal and of content.

The first major formal (and contentual) theme is the disappearance of the artist. This may seem a purely "modernist" idea: Joyce (or was it Stephen Dedalus?), after all, had his artist stand aside, paring his fingernails. For Flaubert, too, the artist was nowhere to be seen, although he was ev-

erywhere in the work—but, above all, the work was the *artist's work*. However, the reflexive self-consciousness expressed in the post-modernist work, the awareness that the work of art *may* be only about itself, makes for a qualitative difference. And the result of this self-consciousness is a doubt as to whether the artist creates his own work or whether the work is somehow the product of language itself, separate and suprahuman.

There are "I's" in the fictions who may sometimes pretend to be an author, the author, perhaps even Robert Coover, but most of the time they do not even pretend that. Even when he does pretend, the "I" tends nevertheless to become a character who is obviously "made." In **"The Magic Poker,"** the "I" says, "I wander the island, inventing it." He is both in and outside his work. Later, speaking of the caretaker's son, he asks, "Didn't I invent him myself . . . ?" but then wonders "if it was not he who invented me. . . . " And in the same short section, he becomes the caretaker's son, animal-like, with a shag of hair between his buttocks, and then the "tall man" who is also a kind of prince—and a transformed magic poker. With the disappearance of the artist as authority, all seems relative.

Too, more often than not, the "I" is being controlled by someone else—who is not the author, with the political, economic, social views of the author, not another narrator within the work, but, rather, what David Hayman has called the "arranger," a someone who is both in and out of the work, who orders it—and yet has no responsibility and no existence beyond the work. He is, at bottom, the "relations" that make up the work.

A purely formal, corollary, thematic is the direct manner of telling the stories. Stories are given from different points of view—**"Morris in Chains"** begins with a "narrator," one of the "civilized," telling of the capture of the shepherd Morris; shifts to Morris' stream-of-consciousness ramblings; and then returns to the narrator, alternating throughout the story; differences are clearly signalled in this story by having Morris' thoughts be enclosed in parentheses and lack capitals whereas the narrator's voice is orderly, i.e., his-her "grammar" is perfect. But in this use of language we begin to see Coover's moral teaching: Morris, on the one level is free, and yet he is surrounded by civilization and so controlled; the narrator is constrained by his-her own language.

Or stories are told as several stories (as examples, **"The Elevator"** and **"The Baby Sitter"**); or the point of view is within the story but is not that of an author's or a character's—in "The Sentient Lens" the point of view is that of a non-substantial "we" (or maybe "I-eye") which observes with human senses but almost without a human sense, for the sentient subject both exists and doesn't, i.e., this is the dream(er)'s point of view and "we are, ergo we doubt ourselves."

Or events are non-sequential—that is, time and order are arbitrary, irrational, "unrealistic." Morris' sections seem simple flashbacks to his life before his capture, although one cannot be sure—certainly, however, they are given in the present tense, the tense of living, but the sections turned over to the narrator are all in the orderly, and dead, past. In **"Quenby and Ola, Swede and Carl,"** this shift of events is given not just through flashbacks or flashforwards, those ordinary devices of the modernist experimental novel, but rather because events are *happening* out of the accepted sequence. The story is the result, then, not of the "intent" of the artist, but of the perspectives of the work of art itself. And thus we are back to the "arranger." Such a work appears, then, objective, non-judging. But this appearance is deceiving; the multiple possibilities of events are a better device for the moralist than pounding assertion on a simple theme.

The second major theme is one of "formal" content, but this is not meant as a bad play on words. It is, rather, a thematic that differs from the arbitrariness of sequence, for the artist, the author, does enter clearly into the work—in order to make a positive statement: that is, the past, especially the art of the past, continues to affect us, to shape *our* art. For example, Coover uses, again and again, the fairy story; he uses the work of Cervantes; he uses Irving; he uses the Bible. He cannot escape using them—they are the necessary culture (one must add that he uses more than the past—he uses, if oddly, the expectations and clichés of modern television; once more the example is **"The Baby Sitter."** But this too is the necessary culture).

But that art is not there simply for allusion. It gives echoes indeed, it gives the ordinary surface structure. Nevertheless, these other stories are not used in a one-to-one, allegorical relationship. Rather, they are likely to be conflated, i.e., several of them are used in one fiction; or a character knows what acts he must perform because he already knows the story he is in. The woodcutter of **"The Door,"** the first story, remembers "the old formula: fill the belly full of stones"—he is, then, also the huntsman of the Grimm brothers' version of Little Red Riding Hood who, having cut the wolf open to release the girl and her grandmother, fills that wolf with stones and sews him up. But in Coover, he hasn't yet done so. Such art, in upsetting the formula, makes for a deeper structure yet, one that suggests innumerable meanings. In short, such a structure insists that shapes can, indeed must, have a multiplicity of meanings.

The third major theme, though, is a counter-theme that does not appear at first to be so. It is the "playing" of the author—and here I mean Coover—especially his playing with language. To play with language is no doubt to doubt its absoluteness, but such play is also an assertion of value: language is what we humans are—it is not simply an extension of the human; moreover, to play is to enjoy; we enjoy, or should enjoy, ourselves. Too, Coover himself has remarked that "formal games reflect on the hidden games, more so in an age without a Final Arbiter." The games of language and art do somehow say something about the moral ideas of a culture.

And the last, and second counter, theme is the sanctioning of the ancient and honored belief in the value of the natural as opposed to the urban, to that which is made—by humans. For example, **"Morris in Chains"** is a miniature *Brave New World,* almost too insistent on its denial that

the rulers of the new world, the representatives of the city, lack emotion, almost clichéd in its insistence that the shepherd knows and feels far more than these people of the *civis* (who go so far as to have absolute control over the weather and whose only crickets are artificial, but "authentic" enough to fool the pastoral Morris). The natural is also the sexual; sex is a good, an affirmation of life. Morris has castrated his lead ram in order to keep his sheep population down; civilization presses upon the flock and too many lambs make their flight difficult. But Rameses, the ram, attempts to kill Morris in revenge—and Morris understands, indeed forgives.

And, as I noted earlier in citing Morris' song, life is art; there is no song in the City except as Morris, fleeing through its parks, creates it; song is life is art is natural. Moreover, when the voice of the narrator claims that the pursuit of Morris was "a merciless hacking through the damp growths of our historic hebephrenia," one must suspect a moral statement behind this. That is, for the "civilized," Morris' pastoral life represents a childish stage in human development; Coover is almost Wordsworthian here—we do and perhaps must give up immediacy to be "adult," but that is a great loss, since this kind of adulthood is a regression from life, not a growth into it. In other stories, e.g., **"The Door: A Prologue of Sorts,"** Coover shows that there is a positive kind of maturation, one that does take us into real adulthood.

Still, immediate experience, unmediated experience, the story asserts, *is* possible. The language of civilization (civitas) kills that immediacy. Morris' language is uneducated but that in itself affirms that his words are the things themselves; signifier is actuality. His nemesis, Doris Pelorus (the plays in her name, the possible etymologies, are enormous and insulting to her), is learned, pedantic, most correct in her language—and spiritually dead since she "lives" only in abstraction(s). At the end of the **"Romance of the Thin Man and the Fat Lady,"** the voices of the barkers announcing the circus attractions are also those of the uneducated—but here both context and the kind of language, the running together of words, the comic mispronunciations, the sheer laziness of tongue, work for the opposite effect from the language of Morris. The barkers are speaking *commercialeze* on a low level; they are, then, speaking abstractions, not truth. (The joke and the paradox is that all this insistence upon immediacy, upon real presence, is contained in a work that deliberately doubts real presence.)

One may take that introductory story, **"The Door: A Prologue of Sorts,"** as the type story of the collection, developing this congeries of thematics. For the title itself calls attention to the *concrete made*—a door can be seen, a prologue is an "idea." But, too, a door can be, is, here, a symbol, the result of "idea." All is multiple; nothing is simple.

The story is told more or less chronologically, but it is not told straightforwardly. Its basis is Little Red Riding Hood, yet, although one must keep the fairy story in mind, one cannot read Coover's fiction as a mere version. Coover's story begins with what one might call an authorial voice talking about a him, the "father"; shifts to an unpunctuated, uncapitalized, not quite "stream-of-consciousness," the "grandmother"; returns to the "authorial" voice talking about a her, the "daughter." The father awaits, foresees, the arrival and passage of his daughter on her way to the grandmother's house; the grandmother, in her bed, recounts her own autobiography as a pattern for life and also awaits the girl; and then the daughter stands outside the cottage door, relieved and anxious at the same moment, awaiting her future, the crossing of the threshold. Nothing occurs; all is expectation. But at the same moment everything has already been enacted.

And each of these "voices" brings in one or more other fairy stories as a structural device. The "door," then, is the actual door of the grandmother's house, but, in a sense, it is also these fairy stories of Little Red Riding Hood and of Jack and the Beanstalk and of Beauty and the Beast.

Now, of course, the relationships between these stories and Coover's are multiplex. First, one must remember that, although they give structure to Coover's own work, they are not his work. One needs also to consider the innumerable interpretations of these particular fairy stories; they can mean almost what one wills. And yet, at the same moment, Coover has *a* meaning, one that may be found in Bruno Bettelheim's reading of the fairy story [in *The Uses of Enchantment,* 1976]: Bettelheim sees fairy stories as illustrating the maturing process for children, a maturation that is sexual as well as social. Maturation in all senses is a basic good in Coover's story. Here is the obverse to the attitude of the "civilized" in **"Morris in Chains."** And even though one cannot limit either the fairy story or Coover's fiction to this, "maturation" is the didactic element in both.

Coover's work has a father who is first the Jack of Jack and the Beanstalk, now a grown man, but who is also, as I have noted, a woodcutter as well as being the hunter of "Little Red Riding Hood" who saves the girl from the wolf—yet this father's attitude towards his daughter obviously has "Freudian" overtones, for he is both father and "Ogre," Jack become the Giant—and also the wolf. ("And he'd thought the old Giant had lived in heaven, the poor bastard"; but, of course, the Giant hadn't; there was no Eden; the Giant was only another Jack. There is no salvation in these cautionary tales. The woodcutter mentions an "Old Man," who is, no doubt, God—but His purposes, as always, are incomprehensible). At one moment the father thinks that he wishes "her the joy, . . . both of them for that matter": and obviously the "them" is his daughter *and* the wolf (who is the girl's husband). But one wonders if the father doesn't also *know* that he is both father and wolf ?

The grandmother is double too; as she lies in the bed waiting for her granddaughter, she momentarily takes over the story, becomes the narrator (her "stream-of-consciousness" is almost more direct talk than "stream," but, like Morris' language, it functions to suggest immediacy and therefore truth). She reports that she had, long before, been called Beauty and had married the Beast; she knows that life is ambiguity, a mixture of good and evil, of violence and love. Still, by implication, her life has been elemental, and, like her language, somehow true, although

Coover suggests that she also represents class structure; she was no woodcutter's daughter. That is, he brings the whole world into his story, a deliberate attempt at universality.

But who, then, really, waits for Little Red Riding Hood? Not the traditional grandmother. Not even, perhaps, the traditional wolf. And yet both the father and the grandmother are traditionalists; they are aware that there is evil in the world; indeed, to repeat, the father is aware that evil is in himself. But what they want to do is to warn, to educate, Little Red Riding Hood.

The story has one more pattern that reinforces this "maturation" thematic, a pattern that speaks directly to the reader's own life. For it is also an initiation story, metaphorically a birth story; by passing through the door, the girl is born into the world—a world, we may assume, of evil, force, violence, power. And yet one must notice that, at the end, she is relieved to be so born, escaping *into* the house where the wolf-lover is and out of the forest where the father-wolf is. She has matured; she is a woman, achieving sexual knowledge and leaving childhood behind. For, propelled by the sun (which is time), she crosses the threshold into adulthood, even though she is aware that "this life was a comedy from which, once entered, you never returned. . . ." But the maturation of the individual is not the whole of Coover's point. For evil and threat are on both sides of the door; she cannot escape the wolf. The wolf is also the world and she, like the reader, cannot avoid it.

L. L. Lee, "Robert Coover's Moral Vision: 'Pricksongs & Descants'," in Studies in Short Fiction, *Vol. 23, No. 1, Winter, 1986, pp. 63-9.*

Heide Ziegler   (essay date 1986)

[In the following excerpt, Ziegler discusses the structure and content of Spanking the Maid.]

In 1982 Robert Coover published **Spanking the Maid,** a text subtitled *A Novel.* Judged by its length, however, **Spanking the Maid** is a novelette, not a novel. Thus the subtitle calls attention to itself. **Spanking the Maid** presents us with something unexpected or novel, which pretends, moreover, to be chosen at random: *a* novel. Yet at first sight nothing in Coover's novel justifies the reader in expecting something unexpected or random. The structure of the text contradicts this expectation, just as its lacking bulk contradicts the pretentiousness of the subtitle. **Spanking the Maid** consists of a series of short chapters, involving two characters, the master and the maid, who daily repeat the same ritual: the master spanks the maid. This ritual is invoked whenever the maid inadvertently makes a mistake. Gradually, these mistakes take on a life of their own: a blanket, perfectly spread, appears to crumple itself. The apparently random develops an unexpected logic by which it perpetuates itself and thereby acquires the status of necessity. As a result, the master needs to spend more and more time studying manuals to teach him the perfect technique of spanking, for his ideal is the perfection of his power, mirrored in and justified by the perfection of the maid's daily chores. Yet, as he unsuccessfully tries to raise her to the level of this ideal, he in turn becomes dependent on her mistakes, and by implication on her existence, as the precondition of his own power: "Sometimes, especially late in the day like this, watching the weals emerge from the blank page of her soul's ingress like secret writing, he finds himself searching it for something, he doesn't know what exactly, a message of sorts, the revelation of a mystery in the spreading flush, in the pout and quiver of her cheeks, the repressed stutter of the little explosions of wind, the . . . dew-bejeweled hieroglyphs of crosshatched stripes."

Master and maid are like God and man, or like author and reader, and for all of them the day of creation is drawing to a close. For while the text repeats the same scene—spanking the maid—with few, if any variations, the time of day for the action changes from morning to late in the day. As night approaches, the master, not having been able to achieve his ideal, begins to look for the "mystery" that will explain to him why he ever had to spank the maid in the first place. In like manner, God might be looking at the imprints He has left in the human soul, treating them as "hieroglyphs" that may bear a message for Him. And the author looks at the weals he has left on the "blank page" of the reader's naked behind, since these traces are like "secret writing," revealing to him something he did not put there.

Spanking the Maid becomes an extended metaphor for the relationship between author and reader, and it thematizes their mutual dependence to the point of excluding all other concerns—just as the necessity of domination and submission will eventually infiltrate every experience of master and maid and change it into a pretext for the repeated ritual of attempting to perfect their relationship. As a consequence, Coover's text becomes increasingly hermetic and its values radically ambivalent. For example, the bedroom of the master, the locale of the novel's action, is separated from the garden by nothing but a glass door, and the garden is always in sight. But neither master nor maid ever enter the garden, which could, or perhaps should, be read as a metaphor for life, so that it becomes either the garden of paradise lost or the imaginary garden of forbidden lust. The bedroom on this side of the glass door thus becomes the realm of reality where a daily ritual of pain is performed that represents the *conditio humana*. As a result of existing in a circumscribed place, lust has become perverted into pain, but then both lust and pain cannot ever exist except when under the pressure of limitation. The exclusiveness of the bedroom represents the rationale as well as the dilemma of the text; it is the locus of the author-reader relationship. Since there is no alternative to this relationship, executed in the form of perverse ritual, the form of perverse ritual is rendered the only genuine value the text contains. Paradoxically, for Coover the novel as genre has to become hermetic in order to survive.

Heide Ziegler, "A Room of One's Own: The Author and the Reader in the Text," in Critical Angels: European Views of Contemporary American Literature, *edited by Marc Chénetier, Southern Illinois University Press, 1986, pp. 45-59.*

Wayne B. Stengel   (essay date 1989)

[*In the following essay, Stengel cites "The Magic Poker" as an example of Coover's attempt "to destroy the myths of contemporary literature and to examine the very nature of the writing process."*]

Robert Coover's **Pricksongs and Descants** is not only a superb short story collection but a work that attempts to destroy the myths of contemporary literature and to examine the very nature of the writing process. Despite lavish talents, Coover has been a neglected figure on the American literary scene because his prose consistently investigates the conflicts that beset modernist writing as well as the act of composing that produces them. Frequently regarded as a precocious metafictionist, a lesser Barth or Pynchon, whose prose puzzles recall experimental American writing of the late sixties at its most synthetic, Coover is actually a highly poetic, extremely sophisticated prose philosopher whose fictions have always questioned the self-reflexivity of the American metafictionist movement. He has much in common with the anti-mythological writer that Roland Barthes sought in his 1957 essay "Myth Today," the one who would produce what Barthes calls writing degree zero, language that assiduously attempts to extract all its false, mythic content.

In paralleling Barthes' program, Coover's stories attain a sparsity, purity, and elegance that signifies far more than Coover's declaration of his own presence in the text. Rather, these stories reflect the presence of a tough-minded yet supple intelligence in their analyses of many myths, including what Barthes considers one of the most dubious myths of literature: the literary mythos itself, the belief that literature must exclusively concern itself with the dissemination of ideas or feeling, that it should contain an explicitly defined subject-object relationship, or take the goal of instructing an audience how to think, act, or respond.

Perhaps the easiest way to analyze Coover's accomplishment in **Pricksongs and Descants** is to examine one of the best and most difficult stories in the collection, **"The Magic Poker."** "The Magic Poker" resembles several other of Coover's stories in the collection: it is told in a long series of brief, montage-like film clips or images that might be found on a loop of film several minutes long. Coover's storytelling has definitely been influenced by film, and especially by film theorists such as Eisenstein, who uses editing and montage devices to elicit Pavlovian behavioral responses from his audience. Where Coover diverges from a film-maker like Eisenstein, and from modernist collage writers like Dos Passos or Doctorow is in his assertion of the contradictory, indeterminate nature of historical reality. Coover is not a collage-maker who attempts to assert wholeness or unity by shoring his fragments against the ruin of twentieth-century art and life. Rather he is a practitioner of indeterminate field theory who, like Heisenberg or Wittgenstein, questions how much even the investigator may know or understand about the phenomena which he discovers and in part creates. Accordingly, the force and clarity of **"The Magic Poker"** emerges once a reader understands three of Coover's dominant concerns in the story: first, he believes the myths of literary modernism must be challenged before an audience can appreciate the questions and inquiry inherent in much contemporary writing; second, he feels the reader should become the controlling consciousness of a work of fiction rather than being controlled by the author's voices or vision; and third, Coover contends that only by violating male conceptions of art, storytelling, writing, and sexuality—the phallic magic poker of the title—can the reader perceive the violence and manipulation of the masculine imagination.

The premise of **"The Magic Poker"** is that a male authorial presence creates an exotic, potentially magical island and then populates it with a debonair, pipe-smoking figure dressed in a white turtleneck, and a hirsute, degenerate creature identified as the son of a former caretaker of the island. As the story progresses, this latter figure seems to deteriorate further while performing a series of increasingly barbaric acts. In addition to one male figure of sophistication and urbanity and another of primitivism, the male narrator posits the arrival of two women on the island, Karen and her voluptuous, unnamed sister whose sensuous body and tight-fitting gold pants signify for many readers, and perhaps especially for the male reader, the male-generated myths of sexual wantonness and sexual accessibility.

Within a few pages, Coover's story resonates with an abundance of signs which would seem to evoke a logical or causal signification. For example, the urbane lord of the manor who awaits the sisters in a sumptuous but crumbling mansion appears to be a God-like Prospero figure for whom this entire island may well be, as it is for any reader, an elaborate imaginative construct. Similarly, the hairy beast running wildly across the landscape and watching the sisters from the shadows of a summer cottage that either he, the narrator, or both of them have vandalized, becomes a likely Caliban. He seems an animalistic being, perhaps on a lower plane of evolution than the other characters, but a man to whom Coover, like Shakespeare, gives far more capacity for human sympathy and understanding than he does to his manipulative Prospero.

With a further turn of the symbolist or semiological screw, Coover's Prospero and Caliban equivalents become Freud's ego and id, respectively, while the brave new world that the magician figure and the male narrator have created seems sometimes to resemble Eliot's wasteland and sometimes a lush, tropical paradise which rejects the arrogance and destructiveness of society's attempts to civilize it. Furthermore, the most obvious sign or symbol in the story, the magic poker of the title, which the male narrator tells the reader he places where the two sisters will find it, becomes, after the sisters fondle it, the elegant lord of the manor himself. Therefore the magic poker seems a sign that signifies, in sexist fashion, the phallus; masculinity; the power of magic, art, or the imagination; and the pen or pencil that creates this story.

As one can gather from this cursory discussion of the hypotheses and technique of the story, the ultimate fascination of **"The Magic Poker"** is its complete refusal to resolve or even choose among any of its interpretive possibilities. In "Myth Today," Barthes tells us that myth is that form of depoliticized speech in which the signified is made

to appear as the natural, logical, or causal result of the signifier, where the form of the signifier largely usurps its meaning, and in which historical process is denied and transformed into a process of nature. The cumulative force of Coover's story achieves just the opposite effect. Here is a work whose mutually contradictory narrative options and film-clip technique of overlapping, repetitive, yet highly conflicting images create a vision of unlimited possibilities which completely cancel themselves out and defy conventional literary interpretation. The final effect of **"The Magic Poker"** is to produce, as Barthes advocates in "Myth Today," a writing degree zero which scrupulously demythologizes not only varieties of consciously wrought literary writing but previous conceptions of literature itself.

Yet for all its self-abnegation, for all its short-circuiting of sign system, **"The Magic Poker"** is anything but nihilistic. Throughout this story, Coover consistently adheres to three values: his respect for the resilience and inviolability of the imagination; his unwavering belief in storytelling as an imaginatively privileged trope for and analogue to history; and his insistence that the feminine imagination is equal to the male's. The reader finds these three uncompromised positions everywhere in a story that seems otherwise to be rigorously and intentionally decentered.

The pervasively ironic underpinnings of **"The Magic Poker"** emerge in Coover's characterization of the tall, suave Prospero-type, who desires to seduce, or in some way possess, the female arrivals on his island, as the reader soon sees. Or is it the masculine narrator of the story who attempts to control these women through this magician? Regardless, as befits this voraciously open-ended story, these male attempts at seduction fail. Instead, the tale reveals how intellects that confuse power with imagination inevitably become lost in their own abstractions.

> The tall man stands, one foot up on the stone parapet, gazing out on the blue sunlit lake, drawing meditatively on his pipe. He has been deeply moved by the desolation of this island. And yet, it is only the desolation of artifact, is it not, the ruin of man's civilized arrogance, nature reclaiming her own. . . . Leaning against his raised knee, staring out upon the vast wilderness, hoping indeed he has heard a boat come here, he puffs vigorously on his pipe and affirms reason, man, order. Are we merely blind brutes loosed in a system of mindless energy, impotent, misdirected, and insolent? "No," he says aloud, "we are not."

This passage displays a high concentration of the forces that drive **"The Magic Poker."** A character in the story, although one created by the God-like authorial presence of the narrator, rationalizes that reason, man, and order, that invincible triad of classical, humanist thought, are the bonds that tie his chaotic, increasingly primitive island universe together. Meanwhile, this world rapidly reverts to a wilderness in a story that juxtaposes warring images of seduction, destruction, and betrayal. Furthermore, this magician argues that the desolation he sees around him is only that of artifact, of a man-made world, or perhaps of a writer's vision of reality, and not nature vengefully attacking civilization's arrogance. His rhetoric immediately causes the reader to question a Prospero's assertions while it delineates the major themes of this story.

Actually, the character is desperately seeking control in a fiction in which he is not even a principal player. Earlier in the story, the male narrator acknowledges he has invented his Prospero figure as well as the two sisters who come to his island. Moreover, this narrator wonders at the same time if this Caliban, the caretaker's son, hasn't invented him and his own imagination. Furthermore, the narrator justifies Barthes' warning about all myth and mythmakers by denying history of all kinds. As he makes the following observation, the narrator confuses history with aesthetic design:

> At times, I forget that this arrangement is my own invention. I begin to think of the island as somehow real, its objects solid and intractable, its condition of ruin not so much an aesthetic design as an historical denouement. . . .

Here the narrator has made the mistake of denying the importance of aesthetic imagination. Even if this island exists only in his art, it can enter the minds of his readers and thus become a part of their imaginative experience, surviving there as a form of history and reality. Doubtlessly this island is real for anyone who actively encounters this story and chooses to imaginatively enter its terrain.

As the narrator proceeds, the reader can easily hear the barely constrained male rage that motivates his voice. This man feels deeply threatened because the myth of the male writer's control has been so thoroughly undermined by the very women he has invented to kiss his magic poker. Here he crudely contemplates his dilemma:

> "I have brought two sisters to this invented island," I say. This is no extravagance. It is indeed I who burden them with curiosity and history, appetite and rhetoric. If they have names and griefs, I have provided them. In fact, I add, "without me they'd have no cunts."

Until at least mid-twentieth century, literary, social, psychological, and even sexual myths held that the magic poker, the magician's wand, his means of instrumentation, mechanization, and production of the art of writing, is largely a male domain. Consequently, much of the aesthetic tension of the last half of **"The Magic Poker"** derives from the violence the story generates in deciding who shall wrest control of the previously masculine magic poker: the narrator, or the women he thinks he has invented and invited to his island. Once his seduction plans falter, Karen's sister momentarily gains possession of the poker and transforms it first into a cigarette, then into a walking stick, and finally into a rifle before the narrator's astonished eyes. Next she offers the narrator the poker as a means of wantonly breaking a perfect pane of glass herself.

With this series of elliptical, contradictory images, the story simply reinforces what it has suggested throughout. This scene implies that the act of writing by men or women should be at once creative and destructive, focusing only to digress, a centrifugal as well as centripetal force. Therefore, a kind of aesthetic violence can be a highly creative energy. Impartially, the story makes its female characters as naive about art as its narrator and Prospero figure are. Appalled at what they discover of the Caliban-like creature's scatological destruction of a summer house on the island, the sisters lecture the reader about the emptiness of lust and desire, completely unaware that this work and their existence in it germinate in seemingly empty feelings of lust and desire. Meanwhile, the jarring, contentious frames of the story demonstrate that the writing process itself can be a literal battle for power, for control and possession of ideas, images, and technique.

Finally, the magic poker would seem to represent the penis, or male pride and control of women and literature. Correspondingly, the women in the narrative become, like the clear, transparent pane of glass in the otherwise ravaged mansion, objects to be broken and penetrated once men come to fear the transforming force of the female imagination able to appropriate the magic poker. Therefore, **"The Magic Poker"** may be read as an elaborate allegory about writing as a sexual act, an activity motivated and perpetrated by the fear of castration. Yet before the critic moves from Roland Barthes to Jacques Lacan to explain the force of this story, the wary reader can see that Coover has purposefully and carefully designed his magic poker to mean both less and more than any individual theorist or anti-theoretical critic might be able to discover in it. The male narrator, finally a surrogate for Coover and all the masculine voices in the tale, announces as he approaches the conclusion of this storytelling that his revels, like those of the story's Prospero, now are ended:

> I am disappearing. You have no doubt noticed. Yes and by some no doubt calculable formula of event and pagination. But before we drift apart to a distance beyond the reach of confessions . . . listen; it's just as I feared, my invented island is really taking its place in world geography. . . . Yes; and perhaps tomorrow I will invent Chicago and Jesus Christ and the history of the moon. Just as I have invented you, dear reader, while lying here in the afternoon sun, bedded deeply in the bluegreen grass like an old iron poker.

Just as the narrator's male dominance and ego begin to wane, he discovers an element of his lasting potency in spite of himself. He recognizes an act of invention is a kind of reality and history as surely as the actual existence of Chicago, Jesus Christ, and the moon. Moreover, where has the overwhelming majority of humanity discovered its conceptions of Chicago, Jesus Christ, the moon, and the magic poker itself if not first on the printed page? Thus **"The Magic Poker,"** which seems in its final pages an allegory of sexual politics, eventually becomes a metafictional investigation of the difference between fiction and reality, art and life, yet a metafictional inquiry pursued from a perspective the metafictionists even in the heady sixties never formulated.

This story ultimately asks, Who is the magic poker? The narrator, the tale's Prospero, its Caliban, Coover himself, or perhaps even the hypothesized dear reader? Or does the author merely imagine a reader, ideal or otherwise? Or is the magic poker a kind of conduit between this writer and his ideal reader? To undermine the myth of reader-response, the narrative even questions the existence of the writer-reader relationship. Ultimately one senses that Coover wonders, and with immense justification, if once he invents a reader and gives him or her so many interpretive possibilities, whether Coover, the author, has any role in the text, or even whether he should. In fact, after the story is composed, should Coover reign as final proprietor and arbiter of the text? Furthermore, in what locus does a story so ingeniously unconstructed as this germinate and center? In the mind of the writer, or of the reader, or in some uncharted way station between the two? What the dying male writer ultimately learns in the last pages of this story is a valuable, even affirming insight from a text which some critics shortsightedly find empty and meaningless: any kind of narrative, even one as superficially jumbled and discordant as this overedited filmic story, becomes a kind of history and reality for the resilient, humane imagination aware that time must mean change and invention. That is, all good storytelling has the power to be a version of history, however elliptical and problematic its technique, particularly when it forms a poetic analogy with a changing world by dramatizing that world's resistance to change.

In a violent, extremely decentered text, **"The Magic Poker"** unleashes several frightened male voices ignoring history, demanding aesthetic design, and seeking control by asserting man, order, and reason. Meanwhile, their masculine enclave veers towards chaos and extinction. The violence of Coover's writing has frequently been noted by critics but seldom understood. His narrators are often men who deny possibility, change, options, and history, even while Coover's montage technique suggests the endless, overlapping permutations and combinations of the historical and imaginative processes. Consequently, this male rage attacks the women who invade its island universes, particularly when these women gain control of the magic poker of art, imagination, and sexual potency. Correspondingly, just as this story threatens to degenerate into the violence of its masculine consciousness, the tale returns to a more primitive state in the myth of its origins and the origins of all storytelling. Nearing his story's conclusion, Coover enfolds the folk tale version of the legend of the magic poker within it. Using this embedded frame tale or fabliau device, Coover localizes the myth of the narrative impulse. Here we have the classic fairy tale of the king who will reward anyone who can remove his daughter's gold pants (as provocatively filled as Karen's gold pants) with both her hand in marriage and the all powerful scepter of his kingdom, the magic poker. It is no young King Arthur but a dwarfish, hairy gnome—easily analogous to our Caliban—who steals the magic poker and with it removes the woman's pants. She kisses the magic poker, transforming it into an elegant gentleman in a white turtleneck—our Prospero. In turn, this surrogate Prospero slays the ugly gnome with the magic poker. Inevitably, his chivalric heroism transforms the princess not into the knight's happy bride but into a bereaved widow. This innermost source of narrativity affirms what all of **"The Magic Poker"** implies: storytelling is sometimes a

patriarchal structure, and women, if often its sources of enchantment, can also be its victims and its dupes.

Conclusively, **"The Magic Poker"** admits of many of the mythologies of modern and postmodern literature: Freudian psychology, symbolism, feminism, and semiology, as well as principles of collage fragmentation and montage editing. Additionally and most importantly, **"The Magic Poker"** epitomizes the Barthian search for a zero degree of writing that expunges all these myths or any one theory that wants to impose any narrow, self-contained signification on an elaborate, inexhaustible system of signs. **"The Magic Poker"** thus becomes an extended, unending dialogue, an echo chamber for all the theories it teasingly entertains and, finally, interpretively disavows.

"The Magic Poker," like all of the tales in **Pricksongs and Descants** and much of Coover's writing, insists that art must be a constructively violent act that creates by first refuting and then destroying previous patterns of aesthetically imposed reality. Among these impositions is that bankrupt variety of male domination of the magic poker, that pen or penis which wants to superimpose a false, rational order on an emotionally and sexually uncharted world, and maintain it. In advocating aesthetic violence and sexual equality, Coover's fictions write a new kind of indeterminate history. As **"The Magic Poker"** ends, Karen and her sister escape the sexual snares of this Prospero and leave his island—with him as a virtual prisoner in their boat. Putting Prospero between her legs, Karen's sister draws from inside her pants not Prospero the man, the magician, or the storytelling, but the only symbol worth possessing: the magic poker itself. With this triumphant reversal of sexual roles and narrative situations, Coover is certainly implying that should woman gain definitive control of imaginative power and authority in society, a feminine literary age might be as sexually manipulative as art sometimes has been under the reign of men.

Coover is a legitimately revolutionary writer in his contention that the human need for sexual control produces a kind of aesthetic violence which has begun to change men and women's conceptions of what fiction should be. Indeed all of Coover's works, from his determinedly unconventional conventional religious novel, *The Origin of the Brunists,* to his metaphysical speculation on the nature of God and baseball, *The Universal Baseball Association,* to his audacious rewriting of history in *The Public Burning,* and finally to his most recent novel, the critically condemned, violently convoluted murder mystery, *Gerald's Party,* are pricksongs and descants, chants both sacred and profane: pricksongs, male voices in complaint against the tyrannies of society and sexuality; and descants, voices extolling the greater glory of God while wondering where God is, who he is, what his machine might be, and how it controls the machine of Coover's fiction. Like the metafictionists, Coover rejoices in the artificiality of literature and the indeterminate nature of authorial control. Triumphantly unique, he has always asked what literature is, who invented the author anyway, and what might constitute a more moral kind of aesthetic control.

Wayne B. Stengel, "Robert Coover's 'Writing Degree Zero': 'The Magic Poker'," in Arizona

Quarterly, *Vol. 45, No. 2, Summer, 1989, pp. 101-10.*

Coover on storytelling:

The central thing for me is story. I like poems, paintings, music, even buildings, that tell stories. I believe, to be good, you have to master the materials of the form you're working in, whether it's language, form and color, meter, stone, cameras, lights, or inks, but all that's secondary to me. Necessary but secondary. I know there's a way of looking at fiction as being made up of words and that therefore what you do with words becomes the central concern, but I'm much more interested in the way that fiction, for all its weaknesses, reflects something else—gesture, connections, paradox, story. I work with language because paper is cheaper than film stock. And because it's easier to work with a committee of one. But storytelling doesn't have to be done with words on a printed page, or even with spoken words: we all learned that as kids at our Saturday morning religious experience in the local ten-cent cinemas. Probably, if I had absolute freedom to do what I want, I'd prefer film.

Robert Coover, in Robert Coover on His Own and Other Fiction, *1981.*

Thomas E. Kennedy   (essay date 1992)

[*In the following excerpt from* Robert Coover: A Study of the Short Fiction, *Kennedy analyzes the thematic and metaphorical aspects of* A Night at the Movies; or, You Must Remember This.]

The thematic and metaphorical coherence of *A Night at the Movies* gives it a unity not often seen in a short story collection. [Jackson I.] Cope goes so far as to call the book "a novel plotted on the experience of attending that range of continuity enveloping discontinuity which used to constitute an actual night spent at the movies." If it is a novel, however, it is not one in any strict sense, and since a number of its components have previously appeared on their own—several years before the publication of the collection in 1987—and stand well on their own, it does seem more appropriate to view the work as a collection of fictions on the related "cinematic" themes of nostalgia, memory, the pursuit of identity in metaphor, and the function of film for contemporary American society.

Film is experience safely captured as surely as the experience which we survive to encapsulate as memory. Apart from the discovery of new facts, nothing new can happen to disrupt the known contours of what is safely in the past, what is "complete," so to speak, just as nothing can change the sequence of a film in the can. Or can it?

[**"The Phantom of the Movie Palace",** the] opening to the collection, seems to play on the static nature of "completed" film, merging cinematic scene and known films into a composite experience in a fiction whose universe consists of a projectionist, a theater, a screen, and seemingly all the films ever made up to about 1950.

"The Phantom" opens with a series of parodies of film genres and stereotypes—science fiction, gangster film, "the handsome young priest with boyish smile" (though here crooning to a man in the next toilet stall), horror, "a man with an axe in his forehead" panicking a movie audience which begins to blend and change places with the film in the way that B-movies and television thrillers occasionally make heavy-handed use of metafilm strategy.

The point of view shifts to the projectionist "changing reels in his empty palace," yearning for the past. He "keeps" the theater, cleaning and sweeping it daily, although there is no one to clean up after and no one comes to his palace anymore. No sooner does the projectionist appear than the fiction slides off into yet another film composite: a legionnaire lost in the desert climbs aboard a sinking luxury liner. Mischievous children plan to stick a hornet's nest in the truant officer's pants. An orphan girl is crawling up a ladder to the hayloft where "some cruel fate awaits her," suggested by a close-up of the holes in her underwear—or are they water spots on the old film? The projectionist stops the movie for a closer look, but the aged film is "forever blurred, forever enigmatic." "There's always this unbridgeable distance between the eye and its object."

Meaning itself seems to pursue both the images on the screen and the projectionist. He wanders the opulent old movie palace, turning on lights, floodlights, and the popcorn machine, and explores its secret rooms and subterranean tunnels where, it is said, there is access to "even deeper levels . . . linkages to all the underground burrowings of the city." But "dark anxiety . . . drives him back up into the well-lit rooms above . . . to the homely comforts of his little projection booth."

He switches lights off "as he goes, dragging darkness behind him like a fluttering cape," while the cat woman seduces the hayseed superhero and the ingenue sings her only line again and again—"Love!" in a film packed with matings and battle. The high priestess comes on to the ape man, who can think of little else but to call for his elephants.

The projectionist experiments, superimposing films upon one another, crossing them; he assaults "a favorite ingenue . . . with a thick impasto of pirates, sailors, bandits, gypsies, mummies, Nazis, vampires, Martians, and college boys, until the terrified expressions on their respective faces pale to a kind of blurred, mystical affirmation of the universe."

Or he turns off the projector lights and fills the theater with the sound of "blobs and ghouls, robots, galloping hooves and screeching tires, creaking doors, screams, gasps of pleasure and fear."

Some of the stratagems he invents himself; others come to him by accident. Films stick together, and images transpose. He drives stampedes through upper-story hotel rooms, beards a breast, clothes a hurricane in a tutu. "He knows there is something corrupt, maybe even dangerous, about this collapsing of boundaries, but it is so liberating . . . and it is also necessary."

The projectionist understands that the crisis the film characters are made to suffer in this way "is merely the elemental crisis in his own heart." Image follows image for pages of collage and juxtaposition. "He recognizes in all these dislocations . . . his lonely quest for the impossible mating, the crazy embrace of polarities, as though the distance between the terror and the comedy of the void were somehow erotic—it's a kind of pornography." He continues, image upon image upon image, "just to prove to himself over and over again that nothing and everything is true."

His experiments proceed, become more daring, ingenious, dangerous. He turns two projectors on their sides, causing the image and gravity of two separate worlds to intermingle, but something happens. He seems to have lost the ingenue. Has she fallen from the film? Escaped perhaps? He feels the pain of his loneliness—perhaps she is out there in the movie house itself? He leaves his projection room to look for her and finds these words cut into the movie screen: "Beware the Midnight Man!"

Light and images flare through the theater. He flees back to the projection room but is blocked by "thickets of tangled film spooling out at him like some monstrous birth." He cuts through but finds his projectors are gone. "It's as though his mind has got outside itself somehow, leaving his skull full of empty room presence." But "she" has been there and written a message in lipstick: "FIRST THE HUNT, THEN THE REVELS!"

Tentacles of film seem to be trying to strangle him. He flees again and throws the light switches, but nothing happens. "The ingenue's insane giggle rattles hollowly through the darkened palace." He continues through the menagerie of film images, though his objective is unclear. The prose becomes Chandlerian (as he falls 30 feet down the grand foyer wall: "It's a long way back down, but he gets there right away," and then, as he wanders into a *Casablanca*-like scene, mock-Chandlerian, à la, say, Bob Hope in a haunted house ("There's a cold metallic hand in his pants. He screams. Then he realizes it's his own").

But in fact, he is still lying curled up on the floor after his fall, though now in the middle of an 18th century ballroom, people minuetting around him while musketfire sounds from the streets. He looks up and sees the ingenue on the mirrored ceiling. The ballroom tips, and all the film images slide out into the public square, "where the terror nets them like flopping fish." "He is pulled to his feet and prodded into line between a drunken countess and an animated pig," then marched along the thickly carpeted aisle to the guillotine which is "rising and dropping like a link-and-claw mechanism."

The projectionist looks for the exit and protests that he does not belong there; the drunken countess tells him it is "the vages [wages] of cinema." "It's all in your mind," says an usherette, pointing the way to the guillotine with her flashlight, "so we're cutting it off." As he is positioned and the blade drops, he finds himself "recalling a film he once saw (*The Revenge of Something-or-Other*, or *The Return of, The Curse of* . . .), in which—".

Cope points to the importance of the link-and-claw imagery that runs through the story—the mechanics of the pro-

jector, the machine that sends forth the images. Machine and man, projector and projectionist, make up a solipsistic universe in which all activity consists of finding metaphors for "the elemental crisis in his [the projectionist's] own heart . . . a lonely quest for the impossible mating, this crazy embrace of polarities . . . the terror and comedy of the void." (The link-and-claw "theory" will appear again in the pages to follow.)

And in the end, as with the hero of Barth's *Lost in the Funhouse,* the projectionist's existence mixes with the films, is lost in the films, and *becomes* the metaphor for himself, losing his head. Finally it is all in his mind, and the only way out is to cut it off, the irony presumably being that loss of mind is a continuance of mindless activity, the projectionist's empty and solipsistic pursuit of nostalgia and metaphor even as meaning pursues—and eludes—him.

In **After Lazarus** language pretends to be film in much the manner of [**Pricksongs and Descants**'s] "The Sentient Lens"—"Scene for 'Winter.' "

Starting with titles and credits and a hollow voice repeatedly crying "I have risen!" the narrative fills in background by describing camera angles, light, shadow. The camera follows the main street of clay houses. "No trees, grass, flowers; no animals; everything is empty and silent. The doors are all closed, the windows shuttered. Long steady contemplative takes." In the background, unfocused, is a cathedral. The camera moves into the side streets and becomes increasingly unsteady. The searching camera begins to follow an old woman down the rutted street to the cathedral.

There is funeral music, a priest, a procession of gaunt men—their faces identical with that of the priest—and 12 pallbearers also "duplicates of the priest." Behind the coffin come the mourners, all women; dust rises but does not dull the glitter of their hard-polished shoes. The camera rises to the face of the dead man in the casket, also identical to the others. The road is lined with mourners dressed in black, hundreds of them, all with the same face as the priest. The procession proceeds to the cemetery, where pictures of all the dead also reflect the same face and where "weeds, flowers, grass grow wildly." The camera stops at an open grave, and the pallbearers lower the casket in. "Suddenly the hands of the corpse lift tremblingly from his chest."

The resurrected corpse crawls out of the grave. A pallbearer flings him back in. There is a community wail, then silence, and the pallbearer is all alone in the cemetery. The road to the village too is desolate. He runs back to the village, followed by the camera. It, too, is empty.

Again the hollow voice is heard: "I have risen!" The pallbearer returns to the house from within which is heard the sound of a heartbeat. He rushes inside. There is a black dress and shawl on a chair; the pallbearer hurriedly pulls on these clothes and looks up to see himself—"the pallbearer standing before her". He goes into the next house and repeats these actions while the heartbeat continues. There is a succession of pallbearers, a succession of dresses and shawls, a succession of heartbeats. The pallbearer produces from "her" skirts further dresses and shawls, undoes his fly and produces yet another shawl and dress. A similar succession of tricks occur with a white flower.

The pallbearer runs out into the street, follows the sound of the funeral music, bounds into the cathedral, finds the robes of the priest, pulls them on, orders another pallbearer to don the robes of the assistant, who in turn orders another pallbearer to don the robes of a lesser assistant, and so on. The procession begins again while the pallbearer watches from the cathedral doors. Then he stumbles down the steps, joins the procession, and climbs into the casket. The pallbearers proceed to the cemetery and lower the casket "toward the camera" into the grave. Darkness is followed by silence, a scraping sound like that of mice in a wall, then silence again, with which the piece concludes.

It is interesting to note that **After Lazarus** is devoid of prophets or religious analogies and has none but the very faintest of similarities to the story of Lazarus told in John (11:1-44), which has provided so many proverbs in our literature—including, inter alia, Kierkegaard's famous "sickness unto death" (11:4) and the often quoted, sometimes ironically, "Jesus wept" (11:35). There is no Jesus here, no Martha, no Mary, no Thomas, no Lazarus even, nor any sign of the necromantic act that finally inspires Caiaphas to begin plotting Jesus' death (11:53). There is only a village of like-faced people, a funeral procession, a corpse that crawls out of the grave only to be flung back by a pallbearer—a rejected resurrection, so to speak—who will ultimately change roles with the priest and the corpse in a reenactment of the apparently continuing ritual of funeral, "resurrection," and rejection of resurrection, a series of role changes and reenactments.

Why?

There are many layers of meaning to John's brief account of the raising of Lazarus—the humanity of Christ; indications of the dual purpose of his role as savior of the nation and of the individual; a dramatic element foreshadowing his threat to the existing order; and that order's crafty response. But the meaning of Coover's resurrection story seems more elusive.

I note that both Cope and [Richard] Andersen say little or nothing about this piece, while [Lois] Gordon goes on at some length. But ultimately she sheds little light on this cryptic mock filmscript of a fiction other than to conclude, "[T]he variety of one's associations with this filmscript will depend, as ever, upon his literary and psychological history. . . . [T]he appeal of the work is clearly more emotional than rational . . . a poetic transcription of archetypal dream landscapes."

It would be difficult to deny the grain of truth in such sweeping statements, but I find myself hard-pressed to provide a cogent interpretation of this fiction. Certainly, there are intriguing elements in it as well as repeated details that tantalize with apparent significance (the polished shoes of the women, the scraping sound like mice in the wall—scratchings from the grave? or the sound of the movie projector?). But what is the ultimate *experience* of the piece?

Are we witnessing the triumph of ritual over substance?

Of costume and role over identity? Why indeed does the pallbearer fling the resurrected corpse back into the grave and run for his life? Why do all others disappear at that moment? Why does everyone have the same face? Why are we made witness to the long train of cross-dressings until the pallbearer finally finds a costume that unites his identity in the priest (the unity of male and female perhaps)? And why does he only then proceed to take on the role of the corpse? And is he "dead"? Was the original corpse dead before it climbed out of the coffin? Is it suggestive that this *formally* filmic tale of rejected resurrection follows a tale of execution (**"The Phantom of the Movie Palace"**) that is filmic in *content*? Does its superior title (which appears above the title) on the book's contents page, **"Weekly Serial,"** "mean" something, or is it there purely for effect? Are we to make assumptions about the streets being without vegetation while the graveyard abounds with wild growth (perhaps calling to mind Wallace Stevens's "The vegetation abounds with forms")?

Or are these literal inspections of detail irrelevant here? Are we indeed merely witnessing an emotional, irrational exercise, a series of "archetypal dream images," a psycholiterary mirror designed only to evoke a response from our own literary and psychological histories?

Unlike Coover's other biblical stories, **"J's Marriage"** and **"The Brother,"** After Lazarus is almost completely devoid of human psychology, but I do not see here the sharp metafictional elements one finds in his other "nonhuman" stories, such as **"The Hat Act"** or **"The Leper's Helix."** The images we are shown *are* dreamlike, perhaps archetypal, and like a dream they do certainly intrigue. . . .

[*Charlie in the House of Rue*] is billed as comedy, though existential horror peers through the cracks. [The piece] moves on a stream of transforming images in a world where nothing is fixed; and a dreamlike mobility prevails. The Charlie Chaplin we know from silent films, though never directly named, finds himself in an opulent house. He wanders from room to room, helping himself to available goodies, cigars, drinks, but the people he encounters are all rueful, dour, closed off, indifferent to his polite approaches.

There is a fat, mustachioed cook glowering over a bowl of soup in the kitchen; an old, top-hatted, goateed man at the drink trolley in the library; a silent-flicks policeman wearing a helmet; an elegant lady (perhaps the ingenue of the book's opening piece); and a maid. Charlie's attempts at communication with these gloomy, unresponsive people begin to go awry; as he tries to repair the damage caused by his errors, things only get worse, in classic slapstick manner.

But matters escalate, and the situation becomes increasingly uncertain and bizarre. He reaches for one thing only to find it has been transformed, in a moment's lights-out darkness, to something else. He throws a pie in the face of the cook and discovers it is really the face of the elegant woman. Classic slapstick comedy situations abound, but with a twist of *huis-clos* surreality: bypassing Chaplin's sentimental underpinnings, the piece evokes true existential terror in a world of timeless repetitions and unpredictable transmutations.

Charlie has set the house in motion, a series of motions that he struggles vainly to keep up with. He discovers the elegant woman with a noose around her neck about to plunge off the balustrade. Desperately, he entertains her with a comic juggling act to distract her from her intentions. Her face softens, she watches, but he slips and accidentally knocks her over the balustrade, from which she twitches and writhes at the end of the rope.

He races about trying to cut her down, to save her, but is foiled in slapstick fashion again and again. Events in the other rooms where he seeks help or tools to cut the rope become increasingly grotesque. The maid, naked now, attacks him with a pair of scissors and, trying to cut off his moustache, stabs his nostril. The policeman clubs him and himself with his billy club. The cook goes berserk, beating Charlie brutally with the corpse of a decapitated hare.

The lights go on and off from time to time, leaving an altered situation. Bloody and bruised, Charlie finds himself in the library, which is now in good order again despite his most recent unleashing of chaos there. But a coffin is in the center of the room. The lid slowly rises, and blackness shines from within. The corpse in it, the old goateed man from the drink trolley, begins to sit up, but the lid slips and decapitates him. The lid rises again, and the headless corpse climbs out (yet another of the book's resurrections).

Charlie flees and finds the elegant lady again, still hanging from the rope, dead now. He piles a chair on a table on a stand and shinnies up to cut her free, but the furniture topples out from beneath him. He grabs for the corpse and clings to it to keep from falling. He dangles there, bruised and bleeding, his pants down around his ankles, as the light fades and everything else with it. His weeping face seems to ask, "What kind of place is this? Who took the lights away? And why is everybody laughing?" If comedy is a mask for suffering, the two merge here and are both illuminated. Charlie's wanting to know why everybody is laughing, while he clings to a hanged corpse, brings to mind Eliot's "laceration / Of laughter at what ceases to amuse."

Charlie in the House of Rue is a remarkable accomplishment. Perhaps more than any other piece in the book, it reproduces the experience of film at the same time that it clearly transcends the natural and imposed limitations of that medium. The story reaches deep into the heart of the material for an experience far more profoundly moving than Chaplin was able or willing to try and, in doing so, turns popular culture into an astonishing piece of innovative art.

The reader is advised of a moment's pause while the operator changes reels. While the reader-viewer waits, Coover presents **"Intermission."**

The piece begins, appropriately enough, with a young woman at the movies going to the lobby during intermission for refreshments. There she meets a man who invites her outside, where she is kidnapped by gangsters. Nearly 20 pages follow of preposterous events experienced by this character reminiscent of Terry Southern's *Candy* (1955), let loose in Spielberg's *Raiders of the Lost Ark* (1981): naive scenes of jungle dramas, escapes, Valentino abductions, more escapes, romances, near drownings, a further escape in a hot-air balloon from which she falls out over the movie house, half naked, nearly starved, just in time for the end of the intermission.

But something strange has happened. A cartoon is showing, but no one is laughing (the opposite of the situation that concludes *Charlie in the House of Rue*). The theater is full of dead people with flattened faces. She is about to scream when she feels a clawlike grip on her shoulder (Cope's link-and-claw theory again, though wearing thin).

At first she is frightened, but finally she realizes that "the claw only wants her to watch the movie, and hey, she's been watching movies all her life, so why stop now, right? Besides, isn't there always a happy ending? Has to be. It comes with the price of the ticket."

The amusement here seems as light as what it parodies, and it moves us breezily to the following piece.

"Cartoon,"—the same film perhaps that the heroine of **"Intermission"** sits watching in the icy clutches of the claw, waiting for her happy ending—begins: "The cartoon man drives his cartoon car into the cartoon town and runs over a real man." Coover once again brings to mind another recent Spielberg epic, *Who Killed Roger Rabbit?* (1988), in which a real actor drives into an eerily convincing "Toon Town." Spielberg dazzles with technical wizardry, but Coover is doing deeper work with the concepts of reality, realism, and fiction.

The cartoon man in a cartoon car in a cartoon town runs over a real man. Wronged, but not badly hurt (he compares it to a paper cut), the real man fetches a cartoon policeman while the cartoon man gets a real cop. A huge cartoon dog chases off the cartoon policeman while the real policeman proceeds to arrest the real man. A real cat chases the cartoon dog, but is in turn chased by a cartoon woman who seduces the real policeman by removing and giving him her cartoon breasts, which he has ogled with cartoon eyes after shooting the real cat.

The cartoon woman goes off with the cartoon dog as the cartoon man sets a cartoon dinner table for the real man, getting him to place the dead cat on it; when he does so, the cutlery runs off screaming. The real man leaves in the cartoon car, which has shrunk to handsize by the time he gets home. He finds his wife in bed with a cartoon man, which experience, she indicates, hurts as little as being hit by a cartoon car (like a paper cut).

"Ah," says the real man, and he "feels a stinging somewhere, though perhaps only in his reflections." He hears a policeman's whistle, "but he knows this is no solution, real or otherwise. It would be like scratching an itch with legislation or an analogy." In the mirror, he sees he has grown a pair of cartoon ears "like butterfly wings," which he wags "animatedly . . . or perhaps being wiggled by them," thinking there is hope for him yet.

The illusion here is achieved by the juxtaposition of the

words *real* and *cartoon*. The reader responds to the cue words automatically, envisioning a "real" man in interchange with an "unreal" one (a cartoon figure), but in fact our real man is nothing but the noun, *man*. This "man" performs the acts of verbs; for example, he walks alongside the cartoon policeman, concerned about the cartoon policeman being suspended above the pavement. The reader "sees" a real man walking sensibly beside an impossible comic figure, but in fact the two figures, a cartoon and a noun, are equally comic. The straightman is even skimpier than the comic. One thinks of Gass's remark that discovering that characters in fiction are only words is something like suddenly discovering that one's wife is made of rubber.

The question seems to be how are we "real" persons affected by our interchanges with "cartoon" (or fictional) characters? Perhaps we begin to grow cartoon ears (with which to listen to reality) or find that our "reflections" (mimesis) "sting." If half the world around us has grown flat as a cartoon in our eyes, and if what we see in the "mirror" finally is turning into a fiction, where do we turn to find what is "real," to find something that can affect us more profoundly than a paper cut?

It is interesting to reflect that this might well have been the cartoon that "the claw" forced the heroine of **"Intermission"** to watch. That young woman, whose experience is as unreal as a movie romance or a weekly serial, sits in a movie palace full of corpses, confident that if she only continues to watch the film the happy ending she has paid for with her ticket will come along.

From the cartoon we turn to what the movies used to give us as "realism"—the travelogue. **"Milford Junction, 1939: A Brief Encounter,"** however, is a travelogue superimposed upon the dim background of Noel Coward's *Brief Encounter* (1944). The result is a parody so dry it is barely humorous, combined with a drama so vague it is barely discernible.

As often as not, either the subjects of the old trailer travelogues, like Milford Junction (or Churley or Ketchworth, the other towns mentioned in the narration) were hardly worthy of such attention, or the filmic rendering was so inept as to render the place a drab and unlikely tourist site.

Coover plays with the inanity of the narrator's monologue in such films, cleverly achieving glimpses beneath the dim surface. The parody, however, seems to suffer from a degree of the oppressive, pointless, forced dramatic detail of its object. Readers interested in an appreciation of the piece are referred to Cope, who seems to find some greater virtue in it.

In **"Top Hat"** dance becomes fiction and movement metaphor, though again, as always, the dance here is in language, in words. This is one of the dazzlements of this book: Coover's skill at transforming film genre into fiction. There is a sharp irony in his bringing this off in a culture where film is the ultimate medium, where the highest praise of a fiction is its selection for adaptation to film, the more expensive the better, dismal as such adaptations generally are.

But Coover successfully adapts in the opposite direction, bringing Fred Astaire from silver screen to book page and pitting him, as a maverick in white tails, against the establishment, achieving what the loner in contemporary American myth is no longer allowed: victory over the crowd.

Our *Night at the Movies* concludes with **"You Must Remember This,"** a fictional reworking of what is probably the most prominent film myth of the post-World War II era, *Casablanca*.

A number of insinuated elements in the film become explicit in the fiction, and the result is general destruction of the story and disorientation of the characters. Ilsa Lund appears to Rick as in the film, requests the letters of transit as in the film, pleads, demands, and threatens as in the film, and, as in the film, Rick defies the pistol in her hand and overpowers her with the sheer moral force of his stance. But then things begin to go awry when Rick breaks the code of romance: he takes hold of Ilsa's breasts and thrusts his pelvis into her buttocks.

"Is this right?" she gasps. "I—I don't know!" he groans. "I can't think!"

The story turns from romantic implication to sexual explicitness. There follow some 20 pages of sexual abandon; scenes of Ilsa and Rick partaking of one another in most conceivable manners are intellectualized as a Norman Mailer might have done in homage to a Henry Miller. . . .

The romantic theory is hilariously undone, and the legend deromanticized with brilliant comic meditations (despite the tin Norwegian accent given Ilsa—nearly as dismal as Meryl Streep's Karen Blixen). Rick and Ilsa are left in a kind of contemporary manual of good bedroom manners in the age of erotic enlightenment before the era of HIV.

Slowly, however, the force of their passion, as passion's force will, begins to dwindle. The background music ("As Time Goes By") begins to have the annoying effect of "mice in the wall," last heard from in *After Lazarus*. Ilsa begins to wonder how she got mixed up with Rick in the first place; perhaps it was simply because "he seemed so happy when she took hold of his penis" in Paris. She speculates on why he takes things so seriously and expects to understand things, as Americans do. "He is an innocent man, after all. This is probably his first affair." Rick, too, begins to have his doubts. "Maybe she was stupider than he thought."

Finally, they discover that the story has gone wrong. All of the other characters, those from Casablanca as well as those from Paris, are waiting expectantly downstairs in the bar for Rick and Ilsa to play their part. Ilsa's identity begins to dissolve as she becomes conscious of the fiction she is participating in. "Maybe," Rick muses, "making up stories is a way to keep . . . from going insane." "Maybe memory itself is a kind of trick, something that turns illusion into reality and makes the real world vanish before everyone's eyes like magic."

In the end, they realize that the story, the memories, have gone awry, and they try to resume the lines of the script that has given them their legendary identity. But their cover is blown; their identities and their world have vanished "like magic."

"You Must Remember This" is a strong comic close to the collection. It is a fictional examination of a Hollywood legend that perhaps more than any other has taken hold of the imagination of the postwar Western world, convincing us that we believe the individual memory of pleasure and happiness is less important than our responsibility to serve and preserve the democratic society in which we live.

But, Coover seems to say, the roles assigned us by that legend do not quite fit. Self-denigration is not a mask we easily don in reality. In recent years society has been ruled by pleasure and memory has become a trick, supported by Hollywood, to turn illusion into reality so convincingly that we no longer quite know what the nature of the real world is: It has disappeared as if by magic.

"And then?"

This sums up well the task Coover has taken upon himself in his volumes of short fiction. By disrupting the traditional flow of the legends that define us, he challenges the reader to define him- or herself. He takes our "mythic residue" away from us and leaves us with a question—the question on the lips of every listener squatting around the fire listening to every storyteller: "And then?"

That is Coover's answer for us. The very question.

Coover's major collections of short fiction span nearly 20 years from the first volume to the third, and their concerns throughout are metafictional. They deal, via illusion, with the techniques and illusions of popular fiction and film that we use to create our identities. Coover plays with these popular illusions to attract the reader into a fiction where those established, conventional ploys will be stripped away, bringing the reader into confrontation with deeper functioning levels of fiction. In the end perhaps little more remains after the old illusions have been stripped away than new illusions.

Nonetheless, the process frees us of that Coleridgian film of familiarity that dulls the force of conventional fiction. We are delivered to the strange new existential magic that awaits us in Coover's elevators, behind his pulsing doors, in his reworked fables, fairy tales, and biblical humanizations, in his verbal renderings of TV game shows, cartoons, silent movies, and Hollywood films, and amidst the ruins of his fictional islands, where destruction becomes an act of creation, the only possible beginning an end.

It is difficult to imagine American short fiction over the past three decades without Robert Coover. He emerged with the wave of innovation of the 1960s, but his work is not like that of the other innovators of that time. In fact, his work is not quite like anything seen before, though his influence continues to prevail. In his tales, which frighten us and make us laugh and never quite satisfy, we find an antidote for the mental poison of our times.

> *Thomas E. Kennedy, in his* Robert Coover: A Study of the Short Fiction, *Twayne Publishers, 1992, 153 p.*

Coover on why he writes:

Because art blows life into the lifeless, death into the deathless.

Because art's lie is preferable, in truth, to life's beautiful terror.

Because, as time does not pass (nothing, as Beckett tells us, passes), *it* passes the time.

Because death, our mirthless master, is somehow amused by epitaphs.

Because epitaphs, well-struck, give death, our voracious master, heartburn.

Because fiction imitates life's beauty, thereby inventing the beauty life lacks.

Because fiction is the best position, at once exotic and familiar, for fucking the world.

Because fiction, mediating paradox, celebrates it.

Because fiction, mothered by love, loves love as a mother might her unloving child.

Because fiction speaks, hopelessly, beautifully, as the world speaks.

Because God, created in the storyteller's image, can be destroyed only by His maker.

Because, in its perversity, art harmonizes the disharmonious.

Because, in its profanity, fiction sanctifies life.

Because, in its terrible isolation, writing is a path to brotherhood.

Because in the beginning was the gesture, and in the end to come as well: in between what we have are words.

Because, of all the arts, only fiction can unmake the myths that unman men.

Because of its endearing futility, its outrageous pretensions.

Because the pen, though short, casts a long shadow (upon, it must be said, no surface).

Because the world is re-invented every day and this is how it is done.

Because there is nothing new under the sun except its expression.

Because truth, that elusive joker, hides himself in fictions and must therefore be sought there.

Because writing, in all space's unimaginable vastness, is still the greatest adventure of all.

And because, alas, what else?

> *Robert Coover, in* Contemporary Novelists, *1986.*

Pierre Joris   (essay date 1993)

[*In the following excerpt, Joris looks at Coover's use of cinematic conventions in* A Night at the Movies; or, You Must Remember This.]

Robert Coover's work is extremely refreshing. Though highly conscious of the necessary self-reflexive nature of fictional forms, Coover has managed to avoid the trap of gratuitous parody, of repetition for the sake of repetition. Even when working with "musty and mouse-nibbled leaves of old periodicals" (as he did, for example, in *The Public Burning,* a novel whose language—especially the dialogue—is based on the historical 1950s speeches and writings of Eisenhower, Nixon, and consorts), he manages to "in-form" his creations with new energy and meanings. One reason for this may be that Coover, while fully aware of the re-presentational nature of all writing, has not limited himself to a self-conscious recycling of those forms belonging to the history of the novel. His vision of where we are, though highly comic as it emerges in his works, especially the short fictions, is relatively pessimistic:

> We seem to have moved from an open-ended, anthropocentric, humanistic, naturalistic, even—to the extent that man may be thought of as making his own universe—optimistic starting point, to one that is closed, cosmic, eternal, supernatural (in its soberest sense), and pessimistic. (*Pricksongs and Descants*)

It is in reaction to this state of affairs that Coover conceives the writer's mission [articulated in *Pricksongs and Descants*], which is to "use familiar mythic or historical forms to combat the content of those forms and to conduct the reader . . . to the real, away from mystification to clarification."

Thus *A Night at the Movies* is the conscious utilization of the familiar mythic and historical forms of another cultural genre: film. As we have seen, every writer is also and may be foremost a reader. Today we would need to amend that statement and say that she or he is also a viewer of films. The movies, which have to a great extent usurped the social function (and also very often the Aristotelian strictures) of the traditional eighteenth- and nineteenth-century novel, are in this sense essential documents of our present and thus, I submit, probably not only more accessible, but may be also more appropriate than say, *Clarissa* or even *Don Quixote,* to tell the story of our contemporary dilemmas or to criticize our culture. This is not to suggest that the re-flexive movement, which makes conscious and ironic or parodic use of older, "exhausted" forms, is not present. To the contrary, Coover's subtitle "You must remember this" ironically points out that film, although a contemporary cultural form, is also and at the same time already a form of the past, or better, a form "with a past"—and thus no innocent ingenue, no matter how much it would like to present itself as such.

Indeed, although the formal reference of the writing is to the medium of film, and although each one of the individual fictions that make up the book is directly related to film, the book as a whole tries to suggest the complex *social occasion* of "going to the movies," of spending "a night at the movies." That situates the event in the past and in opposition to either today's (low-brow) television culture or its (high-brow) art-cinema culture. Coover delights in constructing a nostalgic framework meant to remind us of 1940s and 1950s outings: rather than the one feature film we are likely to take in today when we are able to get off the television-couch, this is a full evening's worth of "entertainment," including previews, serials, adventure flicks, shorts, comedy, kiddie-films, a travel documentary, a musical interlude and a "main feature." Such a program cannot but reproduce a certain haphazard quality, a randomness alien to any Aristotelian notion of the well-wrought book, of the "novel" as a coherency mirroring a supposed cosmic coherency. But it is exactly that haphazard quality that serves the postmodern sensibility of complexity, discontinuity, randomness all the better. "Fictions," the term Coover uses to define the genre of his book, is a concept that more accurately describes our imaginings concerning our contemporary world than the idea of "the novel."

Coover's imitation of the genre(s) is unabashed from the very beginning: the traditional "table of contents" has been replaced by a "program," followed by this rejoinder often found in old movie theaters or programs, and reproduced down to the erratic capitalization of the words, here usurping the place of the literary exergue: "Ladies and Gentlemen May safely visit this Theatre as no Offensive Films are ever Shown Here." The reader smiles, detecting a clear note of sarcasm, and, of course expecting the opposite. . . .

This essay is not the place to propose or attempt a full analysis of the many fictions making up *A Night at the Movies.* We will have to make do with a close look or, better, with several medium-range shots (what French movie parlance calls "des plans américains") montaged with a few zooms and panning or travelling shots of the first story. But this is no loss. That story, a dazzling tour de force of writing, can serve as paradigm for the whole book: it is, simultaneously, a comic parody of just about every imaginable movie genre, a stern fable on the porous boundaries between "fiction" and "reality," an astute analysis and critique of the author's role, a philosophical meditation on the illusionary nature of time and the effectuation of the apocalypse announced in the text's first sentence.

The title itself, **"The Phantom of the Movie Palace,"** puns on the title of a well-known film, hiding and thereby highlighting another cultural genre, namely opera. Opera is a genre that, like film, partakes both of the theater and of literature. It is, moreover, also a genre that, like the novel and like silent movies, has often been declared dead. Something dead, then, although still somehow present, intruding, looming, or letting its shadow fall upon the present: that is, of course, the very definition of a phantom.

At the most superficial level of "realistic" analysis, **"The Phantom"** can be read as a funny and highly moral tale: in an old, slightly decrepit, and totally deserted movie theater, a lonely projectionist, refusing to acknowledge that the good old days—or "the age of gold" as Coover puts it—are over, locks himself so deeply into the fictitious world of old movies and movie characters that he finally goes insane, believing himself to be a character in an old historical movie, about to be guillotined. A rational medical diagnosis would describe the illness as paranoid schizophrenia, or if we wanted to invent a new, more literary term, "iconic schizoparanoia." At this level of analysis a basic moral tail wags the story: The wages of the refusal to live in the present, i.e., real world, are madness, insanity. This is, however, an unsatisfactory "explication de texte," not only because it rides roughshod over the very complexity and involutedness of the text itself, but also because it is unable to read the re-flexive nature of the moral it draws from its own flawed reading of the text. The un- or ir-reality it blames the character for wanting to live in is, of course, also that of writing, of fiction itself, and therefore such a moral would ultimately have to condemn all fiction as "only" re-presenting reality and thus never being the thing present to itself.

The most obvious mistake of such an analysis lies in the fact that it abstracts a linear plot—or tries to force the text into Aristotelian strictures—and thus falsifies the text. It is, indeed, more than a simple misreading; it presupposes a willed simplification of the textual matter itself bordering, consciously or unconsciously, on willful deception. To get to a more nuanced reading of Coover's story, in order to uncover the multilayeredness and interweaving of text and meaning, we need, first of all, to go to that text itself, to its texture. Coover's writing is anything but linear, expository prose. One way to describe its complex gestalt would be to compare it to Möbius strip—that paradoxical topographical figure where inside and outside turn into each other, creating a space literally indescribable by Euclidian means.

One could consider this Möbius strip topography of the text as its strategy, whereas its tactics are those of montage, i.e., a technique the early modernist writers brought into literature from film and that has been central for most innovative poetry and prose ever since. Coover's formal procedures or tactics thus actually imitate, parody, represent those of the genre he is "writing about." Writing is always a re-writing of an earlier text, although in the present case this applies not only to matters of "content," but also to the formal procedures used in creating the text; in Derridaian terms it is not just a repetition of the trace, but a repetition of the angle at which the stylus hits the clay of the tablet—thus also a matter of stylistics.

A simple example of the text's Möbius strip strategy can be found early in the text, in pages 14-15. Coover has started his fiction by presenting, in four paragraphs, by means of rapid montage, scenes from various film genres: science-fiction, gangster, family drama, and pornography. (Further along, the story will show scenes from a Foreign Legion movie, a kiddie comedy, a Western, a Tarzan flick, and many more). This is done without any contextualization; i.e., the reader cannot know or decide where he or she stands, if she or he is purely an outside spectator watching the films with detachment, or some kind of eavesdropping participant inside the scene or frame. The

fifth paragraph at first continues this pattern. The opening sentence—"The man with the axe in his forehead steps into the flickering light."—indicates simply another shift of genres: we are now in some kind of horror movie. The second sentence—"His eyes, pooled in blood, cross as though trying to see what it is that is cleaving his brain in two."—confirms the setting while already cross-breeding genres by shifting from pure horror to some (intentional? non-intentional?—we cannot say as yet) form of comedy, or at the very least, to a parody of the horror film.

The third sentence—"His chest is pierced with a spear, his groin with a sword."—broadens both the horror and comic possibilities, thereby intensifying the parodic dimension. The fourth sentence opens with the logical continuation of the actions depicted by the first three sentences (or shots): "He stumbles, falls into . . . " Up to this point the language has been purely descriptive of an external action. Now, in the middle of the fourth sentence, it changes and presents us with what we take, or have to take, at first glance, for a metaphor: "He stumbles, falls into a *soft splash of laughter and applause.*" Our initial understanding of the completed sentence suggests that what we have here is a rhetorical trope where the spatial "into" replaces a temporal "as"—i.e., as the man falls, or at the same time as the man falls, the audience (who or where that as yet unnamed audience is, we do not know) begins to laugh at the horror-comic antics. The fifth sentence seems to confirm this reading, opening as it does with "His audience, still applauding . . . "; its end reassuringly indicates that what we have witnessed is indeed "only" a movie that has come to its end as the audience "rises now and turns towards the exits."

However, the middle segment of that sentence—"as the light in the film flows from viewed to viewer"—is both enigmatic and disturbing. What is happening here? It cannot simply mean that the light of the movie-projector, and thus of the movie, goes out while the house-lights come on, for the sentence unambiguously states that it is the light "*in* the film" that now changes direction and flows from viewed to viewer. The sentence can semantically only suggest that what has been seen now becomes what sees, that the relationship of viewer and viewed is inverted. The horror movie now views the audience that in the next sentences (in fact three short sentence fragments setting the scene *staccato*) does indeed become the actor of another classic horror scene of that genre: "Which are locked. Panic ensues. Perhaps it is a fire."

The next sentence buttresses the previously intuited insight: indeed the projector, i.e., the (light of the) horror movie did not go out / end, for we are now told that "Up on the rippling velours, the man with the split skull is still staggering and falling, staggering and falling." In the next sentence the viewers of the original horror film are now viewed as caught in their own horror film:

> "*Oh my god! Get that axe!*" someone screams, clawing at the door, and another replies: "*It's no use! It's only a rhetorical figure!*" "*What—?!*" This is worse than anyone thought. "*I only came for the selected short subjects!*" someone cries irrationally.

In the middle of this new film-scene further twists and layers appear in the strange dialogue ("It's only a rhetorical figure" and "I only came for the selected short subjects"), which we will come back to later. But this is not all yet: the last sentence of the paragraph introduces yet another twist:

> They press their tear-streaked faces against the intractable doors, listening in horror to their own laughter and applause, rising now to fill the majestic old movie palace until their chests ache with it, their hands burn.

Now the audience, the viewers of the first film, has not only become the viewed of a second horror scene; but also, in the final twist of the paragraph, as actors in that scene, the viewers—the auditors, to be more precise—of themselves in their role as audience of the very first horror scene. The effect of these switches between observer and observed, viewer and viewed, inside and outside, in which the one seems at will to turn into the other in a whirling dervish dance of change of perspectives is exactly what I have called the Möbius strip strategy. The other set of terms that could, of course, be substituted for the one used above is "reality" and "fiction." Clearly the boundaries between fiction and reality, between object and subject, between viewed and viewer are porous indeed.

This basic stratagem operates throughout Coover's story, both on the micro-level of the sentence and on the macro-level of the story-line. Briefly, in the latter, the main character, the projectionist, moves from the reality of his movie theater into the fiction of his films, in a *chassé-croisé* chase with the eternal ingenue character of his films who crosses over from the fictions of the films into the projectionist's reality-theater. The gateway for that crossing over consists also in a transformational process. The projectionist, erotically fascinated by what he perceives to be holes in the underwear of a young ingenue climbing a ladder leading to a hayloft, is however aware that they are "just water spots—it's an old film," thus producing another one of the strange places where "fiction and reality meet." But his desire, "his lonely quest for the impossible mating, the crazy embrace of polarities," pushes him to conjoin the two.

To bridge the "unbridgeable distance between the eye and its object" he manipulates his old films (by means of filmic, literary, and painterly techniques: collage, montage, frottage, overlay, décollage) only to find that the ingenue has vanished—escaped through the water-marks that have shape-shifted or are they the stiletto heel marks of the incarnation of another ingenue? "a mad scatter of vicious little holes" in the middle of the screen. Thus, these holes in the screen are the gateway from one reality into another, but it is not as if the scatter of holes were random black holes: they spell out a semantically laden sentence in block letters: "Beware the Midnight Man!"

His comic gift allaying any queasiness we may have at the inevitably arising suspicion that "nothing and everything is true" (or, to use Hassan I Sabbah's harsher version of the same realization, that "nothing is true, [and so] everything is permitted"), Coover guides or rather rides us through these masterfully effected transformations and

dislocations in a universe—or universes—where polysemy is not so much a metaphoric quality of individual words, but rather a metonymic function of syntax, and especially of that larger syntax structure we call narrative.

> The hero, trying simply to save the world, enters the fun house, only to be subjected to everything from death rays and falling masonry to iron maidens, time traps, and diabolic life-restoring machines, as though to problematize his very identity through what the chortling fun-house operators call in their other-worldly tongue "the stylistics of absence." [**"The Phantom of the Movie Palace"**]

As behooves a good metafictioner, Coover's text is fully conscious of its own turns and twists, and on one level can be read precisely as an investigation and critique of the role of the fiction writer. The "Mad Projectionist" thus becomes another figure of the contemporary author: not the god-like creator of exquisite "true" fictions he is supposed to control completely, he is the technical manipulator of already existent data—images or words or stories—that he controls only to a limited degree. In that sense, and to go back to the suggestions made in the first part of this essay, in the traditional novel something "long forgotten" is dragged out, something that was hidden is revealed: the author as magus or demi-urge makes present what was not and would have remained thus without his mediation.

By contrast, in Coover's version of the author as projectionist, writing splices together everything we already know. We have seen and re-seen these films hundreds of times: there is no hidden origin, no long-buried truth that is finally revealed by the author. The Mad Projectionist shows us *and himself* what we have known all along although we did not know that we knew it. ("I think I have been in this movie before," a contemporary idiom has it, while we could speculate, had we but the time, on how close this comes to Nietzsche's "Eternal Return.")

The Mad Projectionist *qua* author realizes how little control he has over the iconic cultural representations he handles, in this case, "his" characters and story-lines, and how "meaning" is independent of both his own will and of that of his characters:

> They seem then, no matter how randomly he's thrown the clips together, to be caught up in some terrible enchantment of continuity, as though meaning itself were pursuing them (and him! and him!), lunging and snorting at the edge of the frame, fangs bared and dripping of gore.

But he also senses the dangers lurking, for "he knows there's something corrupt, maybe even dangerous, about this collapsing of boundaries," although it is simultaneously liberating, and thus he cannot stop even if at times he feels "like he's caught out in no-man's-land on a high trapeze with pie on his face." When things go wrong, he has the authorial faith that "an expert touch of his finger on a sprocket soon restores time's main illusion." But even that faith in minimal technical control seems a delusion, for in this story, at least, the author as Mad Projectionist does get caught in the web of his "creations" and remains unable to extricate himself. When he is led to the guillotine, the mob screams "The public is never wrong!" while a voice on the public address system (a voice that among other things is also the anonymous voice of the literary critic) recounts the crimes of the condemned. These "crimes" read like an encapsulated indictment of the innovative prose writer from Cervantes' time to today, proffered at the moment when the abstracted voice of the "critic" has taken it upon himself to produce justice and occupy the center of the stage:

> . . . creatures of the night, a collection of the world's most astounding horrors, these abominable parvenus of *iconic transactions,* [my italics] the shame of a nation, three centuries in the making, brought to you in the mightiest dramatic spectacle of all the ages!

And so we are in a way, led back to the opening paragraph of this essay, in a circular or, I would hope, spiral motion, which, as this is not fiction, can only try and fail to imitate the spiral of Coover's story. The end of which is no end, for although the Mad Projectionist caught in a movie of a movie seems to and, yes, gets guillotined, the dropping blade makes him "surrender himself finally . . . to that great stream of image-activity that characterizes the mortal condition," enabling him to re-turn, to re-run ("it's a last-minute sort of rescue") a film he once saw "(*The Revenge of Something-or-Other,* or *The Returns of . . .*)" as the Möbius strip twists one more time.

The apocalypse acknowledged in the opening sentence has indeed happened, but it is now only one old story-line among many others, and, as on a Möbius strip there is no beginning or end. The essential aspect of the apocalypse, namely that it signals the end, is denied, especially as he who tells it is there after the end. In an open universe, the apocalypse can only be local, limited, and therefore bereft of final, eschatological meaning. If Coover's story and writing techniques have so far been seen mainly under their spatial strictures—the Möbius strip is essentially a topographical gestalt, it is time now to look at the lessons they teach in matters of time, not some absolute time, but under the guise of "timing."

The End of the World or apocalypse is also the end of time and the beginning of eternity. This concept of the apocalypse presupposes a linear, one-directional concept of time that in turn is the basis for the inevitability of events and thus for our sense of the essentially "tragic" nature of those events in the human sphere. *Que sera, sera.* The song, in its nostalgic whining, in fact gives the essence of the notion of the tragic: fate. The apocalypse is thus the ultimate tragic event. But Coover's apocalypse is apoplectically funny. What has happened? The answer, to abbreviate and oversimplify to the extreme, is: film. Or, better, the lessons concerning time that the art of the moving picture has given us.

Tragedy / Comedy: it is as if these literary "genres" were finally a matter of relative speed. A cinematic lesson we have all experienced: at the end of a run-of-the-mill entertaining, exciting, sometimes funny, gangster period-piece, the director wants to introduce a sense of the tragic. He does it with the slow-motion technique. Bonnie and Clyde die under a hail of fast bullets, but these bullets are slowed

down so that we, the spectators, should conceive of these bullets as moving slowly, inexorably, inevitably towards their targets. In that slowness, in that infinite moment of suspension just before the bullet breaks the skin and draws blood, originates the tension between our desire to avoid, deflect, arrest the event and our realization of the unavoidable, inexorable nature of the event, i.e., of "fatedness." The bullet was sent on its path long before we became conscious of its progress and target; it is an absolute event in a linear time frame that we cannot change or even inflect. We can only be impotent spectators. That tension is exactly what we call the tragic.

Comedy, on the other hand, resides essentially in the destruction of that moment of suspension, and of the tension thus created, by speeding up movement to the point where cause (the fate prescribed from before time) and effect happen simultaneously: the man collapses as / or even before the trigger is pulled. As Coover puts it: "Cause (that indefinable something) is a happy ending. Or maybe not." And the reverse holds true too: take a basic slapstick pie-throwing scene, slow it down until the pie moves only by infinitesimal increments towards the face of the unaware victim, and you have tragedy. Every comedian knows that "timing is all." Coover's statement that he considers "tragedy as a kind of adolescent response to the universe—the higher truth (being) a comic response" seems, to me, to express exactly that new knowledge of time. Once we are aware that time is not that absolute, sternly linear pattern that makes tragedy possible, but a malleable thing that can be speeded up or slowed down, abolished or created, twisted or re-run, then tragedy and comedy can become interchangeable, depending on how we read or see the world. Then, of course, an end of time, an apocalypse, becomes just one of many cosmic jokes, eternally recurring, like a bad joke that has us in stitches even as our heads rest on the block. And maybe it is our laughter that is also the signal for the guillotine to drop, the guillotine that is, as Coover puts it, that "gigantic ticket chopper" granting admittance to the movie theater of our Möbius strip world.

Pierre Joris, "Coover's Apoplectic Apocalypse or 'Purviews of Cunning Abstractions'," in Critique: Studies in Contemporary Fiction, *Vol. XXXIV, No. 4, Summer, 1993, pp. 220-31.*

FURTHER READING

Criticism

Andersen, Richard. *Robert Coover.* Boston: Twayne Publishers, 1981, 156 p.

> Discusses the role of the "fiction maker" in Coover's fiction. Andersen includes an annotated bibliography.

Chénetier, Marc. "Ideas of Order at Delphi." In *Facing*

Texts: Encounters between Contemporary Writers and Critics, edited by Heide Ziegler, pp. 84-108. Durham, N.C.: Duke University Press, 1988.

> Comments on myth and fable in "Aesop's Forest."

Cope, Jackson I. *Robert Coover's Fictions.* Baltimore: The Johns Hopkins University Press, 1986, 151 p.

> A detailed study of Coover's fiction.

Durand, Régis. "The Exemplary Fictions of Robert Coover." In *Les Américanistes,* edited by Ira D. Johnson and Christiane Johnson, pp. 130-37. Port Washington, N.Y.: Kennikat Press, 1978.

> A French critic's perspective on Coover's fiction.

Gado, Frank. "Robert Coover." In his *First Person: Conversations on Writers & Writing,* pp. 142-59. Schenectady, N.Y.: Union College Press, 1973.

> Interview with Coover in which he discusses his literary influences, the writing process, and formal and thematic aspects of *Pricksongs and Descants.*

McCaffery, Larry. "Robert Coover on His Own and Other Fictions: An Interview." *Genre* XIV, No. 1 (Spring 1981): 45-63.

> Interview in which Coover discusses the role of the contemporary writer in America as well as his work in short fiction, the novel, poetry, and the theater.

Siegle, Robert B. "Coover's 'The Magic Poker' and the Techniques of Fiction." *Essays in Literature* VIII, No. 2 (Fall 1981): 203-17.

> Examines Coover's narrative technique in "The Magic Poker."

Additional coverage of Coover's life and career is contained in the following sources published by Gale Research: *Contemporary Authors,* Vols. 45-48; *Contemporary Authors New Revision Series,* Vol. 3; *Contemporary Literary Criticism,* Vols. 3, 7, 15, 32, 46, 82; *Dictionary of Literary Biography,* Vol. 2; *Dictionary of Literary Biography Yearbook: 1981;* and *Major 20th-Century Writers.*

Andre Dubus

1936-

American short story writer, novelist, and essayist.

INTRODUCTION

Characterized as a Southerner who seldom writes about the South, Dubus is known for his realistic fiction which explores the desires, disillusionment, and moral dilemmas of contemporary American society. He is noted for his deft creation of believable characters in everyday circumstances, and his fiction often contains detailed descriptions of meals, drinking sessions, and physical activity. Critics particularly acknowledge Dubus's realistic portrayal of the thoughts and emotions of his female protagonists.

Biographical Information

Dubus, who grew up in a middle-class Southern family, has credited his lifelong Catholicism with sharpening his sense of curiosity about people and their actions, calling it the foundation of his compassion toward others. He served as an officer in the U.S. Marine Corps before entering the University of Iowa in 1964 to pursue graduate studies in writing. By 1966, Dubus was living in Massachusetts, the setting for many of his works, and teaching modern fiction and creative writing at Bradford College. His first novel, *The Lieutenant,* was published the following year. Throughout the 1970s and 1980s, Dubus continued lecturing and writing short stories and novellas which were published to generally favorable reviews. In 1986 he lost one leg and nearly died in a highway accident that occurred when he stopped to help two stranded motorists. During his rehabilitation, Dubus wrote and published a collection of essays, *Broken Vessels,* several of which specifically reflect the physical and emotional pain of this experience.

Major Works

Dubus is best known for his well-plotted, realistic stories which typically center on the turbulence, and sometimes the violence, of male-female relationships. Although his characters often attempt to escape the pain of unstable marriages through infidelity, as in the stories of Dubus's first collection, *Separate Flights,* and in the title story of *Adultery, and Other Choices,* their promiscuous affairs usually intensify, rather than relieve, their dissatisfaction. Catholicism is a strong and generally positive presence in Dubus's fiction. The lifelong struggle to reconcile the rem-

nants of one's religious training with the desires and demands of contemporary American life is a central theme in each of the four novellas and two short stories which comprise *The Last Worthless Evening.* In "A Father's Story" from *The Times Are Never So Bad,* a man whose daughter has killed someone in an automobile accident seeks comfort through religious ritual and a compassionate priest. Two stories from this collection revolve around abused women: "The Pretty Girl" describes a man who terrorizes his ex-wife and her lover, and "Leslie" concerns a disillusioned woman beaten by her drunken husband.

Critical Reception

Dubus has received generally favorable critical attention throughout his career, particularly for his ability to explore the ethical contradictions of society through the perspective of ordinary people whose everyday lives are laced with ambivalence and moral conflict. Dubus's sensitive portrayal of the inner lives of both men and women in his fiction and his craftsmanship of style and technique have merited critical praise. Nonetheless, and perhaps because they are so accurately portrayed, Joyce Carol Oates has called Dubus's characters "resolutely ungiving and uncharming," and Charles Deemer asserts that Dubus's work, though powerful and socially relevant, can be "depressing to read" in spite of its essential humanity.

PRINCIPAL WORKS

SHORT FICTION

Separate Flights   1975
Adultery, and Other Choices   1977
Finding a Girl in America   1980
The Times Are Never So Bad   1983
Voices from the Moon   1984
We Don't Live Here Anymore   1984
The Last Worthless Evening   1986
Selected Stories   1988

OTHER MAJOR WORKS

The Lieutenant   (novel)   1967
Broken Vessels   (essays)   1991

CRITICISM

Walter Sullivan   (essay date 1975)

[*In the following excerpt, Sullivan praises Dubus's ability to create convincing settings and believable characters, while he contends that the stories in* Separate Flights *are all "variations on a single theme."*]

Andre Dubus . . . is a southerner who almost never writes about the South. Most of the stories in *Separate Flights* take place in New England or the Middle West, and on a superficial level they have a great deal in common with the work of Sillitoe, for they are filled with images and acts of sex. Dubus is good with quick strokes, slight details that bring whole sequences into focus. In **"We Don't Live Here Anymore"** four young women at a party come out of the kitchen wearing sheepish grins, all having discovered that the others were pregnant when they married. So of course the marriages are going sour, and the husbands and wives begin to trade off with each other. Minor characters, people seen briefly in bars or at filling stations, give Dubus's work an enhanced sense of reality and an enriched texture.

What I do not like about Dubus's stories is the cumulative effect of the collection as a whole, the sameness of characterization from one piece to the next, the obsession with sexual congress and crumbling affections. For example, almost without exception the men, whatever their ages or

morals or professions, are given to physical exercise. They run before breakfast; they work out at the gym. Men and women drink and smoke too much, so that one gets the feeling that Dubus cannot discover what business to put them to: when they are out of bed, they do not know what to do with their hands. This is a small matter, and one which a writer of Dubus's talent could easily rectify, but the obsession with sex gives me more serious concern. [Fiction writer Alan] Sillitoe's people drink and fornicate because they are poor and bored and ignorant and desperate: such is the state of things in Nottingham. But has the whole world become an extension of this English hopelessness? Are the possibilities of literature reduced in our time to variations on a single theme? This is not the place to attempt to answer such large and serious questions, but I wish . . . Dubus would address . . . these matters. . . .

"We Don't Live Here Anymore" is a novella about two couples in academia, their children, their infidelities, their sad endurance of the death of love. Here as elsewhere Dubus refuses to oversimplify. The narrator is enamored of his best friend's wife. His own wife has a fling with his best friend. But Dubus is too good a writer to make the ending either happy or clean. Edith will stay with her husband. And Jack, whose story it is, may or may not leave Terry, for whom he no longer cares. But the children will not go away, and fate will not deliver solutions in neat packages. So after a good deal of adultery and much argument and pain, the tale concludes on a snowy Sunday morning with nothing solved and nothing to do except take the children riding on their sleds.

"If They Knew Yvonne" is the only work in this collection which probes Dubus's southern and Roman Catholic upbringing. The South furnishes the weather, the glitter of sunlight on the Gulf, and the church is the enemy to be dispensed with as a sign that one has grown up. This is an old theme and one that invites cheap shots: from the beginning the vulnerability of the human Christ has never been in question. But Dubus uses a light touch: he is fine at depicting the young lovers who try to resist temptation; the priests are humane; the general tone is comic; the ending is tender rather than harsh.

Finally there is **"Miranda Over the Valley"** which in my judgment shows Dubus at his best. The point of view is that of a freshman in college, pregnant and three thousand miles from her boyfriend and her home. She and Michaelis, the undoubted father of her child (for she has had intercourse only once), agree to marry. She will drop out of school, care for the baby while he goes on to become the lawyer he has always planned to be. But her parents say no. I can conceive that a good many readers of my generation might feel that the parents are overdrawn, and that the story in general is stacked against them. But for me the scene in which the three people whom Miranda loves most and on whom she has depended for support talk her into having an abortion is fully realized. Mother and father press the case; Michaelis is a silent collaborator.

Logic is all on the side of death. Of course Miranda's plans to keep her baby are naive: she can have no notion of how much trouble babies can be and of what discord they can bring when they come unplanned into the world to force a marriage. But she knows that she loves Michaelis, and she loves and wants the baby, and her life is not the same once she has agreed to the abortion. Things go on, it is true. Days pass as before. The sun rises; the same people, at least the ones that matter to Miranda, walk the earth. And she never even sees the child. But all of her relationships are changed; her capacity for love is gone, replaced by a hateful and destructive passion. To get inside the mind of a woman and to portray her joy and her agony as Dubus has done here is accomplishment indeed. We have no right to ask him to do better.

Walter Sullivan, "Erewhon and Eros the Short Story Again," in The Sewanee Review, *Vol. LXXXIII, No. 3, Summer, 1975, pp. 537-46.*

Gene Lyons   (essay date 1977)

[*Lyons is an American author and critic. In the following review, he describes the stories in* Separate Flights *as snapshots of late twentieth-century American life and asserts that Dubus's fiction is characterized by finely crafted characters and believable circumstances.*]

Madison Avenue and the organized churches aside, marriage has few defenders these days, and if a social unit can be invented that will move more lawn mowers, console TV sets, station wagons and automatic corn poppers than the nuclear family, the only place you will be able to see a married couple will be on educational television. At first glance Andre Dubus's *Separate Flights,* published in 1975 seems to be one more brief for the prosecution. After ten years of marriage here is how the narrator and protagonist of the novella **"We Don't Live Here Anymore"** talks about the institution:

> For some years now I have been spiritually allergic to the words husband and wife. When I read or hear husband I see a grimly serene man in a station wagon; he is driving his loud family on a Sunday afternoon. They will end with ice cream, sticky car seats, weariness, and ill tempers. In his youth he had the virtues of madness: rage and passion and generosity. Now he gets a damp sponge from the kitchen and wipes dried ice cream from his seat covers. He longs for the company of loud and ribald men, he would like to drink bourbon and fight in a bar, steal a pretty young girl and love her through the night. When someone says wife I see the confident, possessive, and amused face of a woman in her kitchen; among bright curtains and walls she offers her husband a kiss as he returns from the day sober, paunchy, on his way to some nebulous goal that began as love, changed through marriage to affluence, is now changing to respectable survival. She is wearing a new dress. From her scheming heart his balls hang like a trophy taken in battle with a young hero long dead.

His own marriage is not even remotely like that; nor is the marriage of his best friend Hank, whom he is cuckolding, and who before the end of the story will have returned the favor. But this is the stance they like to assume when the need for excusing themselves from the sins of egomania seizes them. Now drinking with the boys is one thing, but anybody who longs for fist fights is a sentimentalist: either he had very few in his youth or he watches far too many cowboy movies. And as for the one-night stand, it is likely to be the leading cause of marriage. No amount of masculine or feminist posturing has been able to conceal or change that. In our culture anyway, casual copulation seems to make almost everybody sad.

The vision behind Dubus's fiction is sober, unsparing and exact, but never pitiless. With one or two exceptions, stories like **"The Doctor,"** or **"In My Life,"** which are so short and comparatively slight as to seem almost unfinished, any of the novella and seven short stories contained in *Separate Flights* might serve as textbook examples of what one means by calling a fiction writer a "craftsman." Dubus puts his stories together like a man with one eye on the future and declines to argue, as I have done in the first paragraph, with contemporary cant and delusion. Each of the stories has its own voice and point of view, as if Dubus were telling his readers rather flatly that: "Here is the way they lived inside American houses in the latter third of the 20th century. This is what they said and did and what they cared about and cried over. You may draw your own conclusions." In many ways he is like Joan Didion without the name brands and the grotesquery, perhaps because his characters live in New England, Iowa and Louisiana rather than in California. In the absence of God they construct their small melodramas out of an inability to live without some kind of myth, and in one way or another those melodramas involve the departure of love and the incipient discovery of mortality. It is time and faithlessness—religious and sexual—that destroys spontaneity. The way back always seems shorter than the way out, particularly if one has no good reason to return. It bears mentioning that Dubus is, or was at least—it is impossible to tell from the stories themselves—a Catholic.

I find I must correct myself. Some of the characters in one of his stories, **"Miranda Over the Valley,"** do live in Southern California. The Miranda of the title is a Boston University freshman who discovers on Halloween that she was impregnated by her high school boyfriend just before leaving Los Angeles. Her parents fly her home to poolside to talk her out of marriage and into an abortion, offering her more or less as a bribe a Christmas trip to Acapulco with her lover, a conscience-stricken young man who plans to become a poverty lawyer. Her mother is abortion's most strenuous advocate:

> ". . . What are you going to be, pussycat—a dumb little housewife? Your husband will be out in the world, he'll be growing, and all you'll know is diapers and Gerbers. You've got to finish college—" . . . She looked at Michaelis; he was watching her mother, listening. "You can't make marriage the be-all and end-all. Because if you do it won't work. Listen: from the looks of things we've got one of the few solid marriages around. But it took work, pussycat. Work." Her eyes gleamed with the victory of that work, the necessity for it. "And we were older. I was twenty-six, I'd been to school, I'd worked; you see the difference it makes? After all these years with this guy—and believe me some of them have been like standing in the rain—now that I'm get-

ting old and going blind from charcoal smoke at least I know I didn't give anything up to get married. Except my independence. But I was fed up with that. And all right: I'll tell you something else too. I'd had other relationships. With men. That helped too. There—" she lightly smacked the table "—that's my confession for the night."

But her face was not the face of someone confessing.

Her father puts it even more simply: "Listen sweetheart, I know you can work. That's not the point. The point is, why suffer?" Miranda, however, cannot help but suffer; she is the suffering kind, and flying to New York with her mother for the abortion is not to her like having a hangnail treated. Unlike her roommate in Boston she is no good at casual lovemaking; both the trip to Acapulco and her relationship with Michaelis are off at the end of the story and "her mother's eyes (and, yes, her father's too) were hesitant, vulpine. How can we get our daughter back? the eyes said. We have saved her. But now how do we get her back?"

I hope that the reader will not jump to conclusions from a summary that necessarily simplifies a story that is, after all, about a young woman making an important decision, a story, if you will, about the impossibility of one's youthful expectations. It is not possible to determine, on the evidence at hand, what Dubus thinks about abortion as an abstract legal, moral or even theological question; I suspect he would say it doesn't matter to the story. The things to notice are the author's fictive gifts and his discipline, the carefully restrained wit and compactness of his characterizations.

The protagonists of **"We Don't Live Here Anymore"** have all four made the opposite, or at least one of the other choices on the unmarried pregnancy question. We have heard one of the husbands. Here is the other:

> . . . A love affair is abandon. Put the joy back in fucking. . . . It doesn't even matter if you love Terry. You're married. What matters is not to hate each other, and to keep peace. The old Munich of marriage. You live with a wife, around a wife, not through her. She doesn't run with you and come drink beer with you, for Christ sake. Love, shit. Love the kids. Love the horny wives and the girls in short skirts. Love everyone, my son, and keep peace with your wife. Who, by the way, is not invulnerable to love either.

The complications that ensue between and among two couples who know one another with sufficient intimacy to feel sympathy and even a kind of love all around are so sad, so harrowing when they all decide to confess to each other and tell the "truth," and so perfectly calibrated for time and place and character (academics in a small Massachusetts town in the late 1960s) that anyone who has ever lived in such surroundings may wonder from time to time whether Dubus has been eavesdropping upon the souls of people he has known, and perhaps even upon his own.

Having said all of this, it must also be reported that in its very exactitude and spurning of rhetorical melodrama,

Dubus's style occasionally disappoints the very expectations that it raises. Observing his wife, who after all is only 30—she sounds at times and is spoken of as if she were twenty years older—the narrator of **"We Don't Live Here Anymore,"** who describes her as "the prettiest girl I had ever seen; or rather, the prettiest girl I had ever touched," sees in her "that sad, pensive look that married women get after a few years," and castigates himself for having abandoned her emotionally. But after a while one wonders whether or not he, and by extension the author, has not come by his "tragic" detachment a little too easily. None of Dubus's characters tries very hard to be good; if any of them have serious work to do besides measuring the velocity of their fall into helplessness it is rarely reported. Much as I admire the skillful presentation of the novella I am prone to wonder, after a while, as George Orwell wondered over Graham Greene's Scobie from *The Heart of the Matter,* whether or not "if he really felt that adultery was mortal sin, he would stop committing it; if he persisted in it, his sense of sin would weaken."

Similar reservations qualify my admiration for **"If They Knew Yvonne,"** a piece that seems more memoir than fiction about a young man's reconciliation of sexuality and Catholic puritanism in Louisiana—Dubus was raised and educated there—during the 1950s. Again, anybody *that* guilty over masturbation probably would either have quit or become considerably less pious about it. In any case Dubus's nice evocation of his protagonist's betrayal of his first lover, the Yvonne of the title, in a moment of callow adolescent braying is in itself worth the price of the book, as is the evocation of the boyish innocence of his sister's 5-year-old son that ends it. It is in moments like Yvonne's shaming that it all begins, this war between men and women, and reading the story might well help to effect a minor truce or two. Not all women were so blamelessly exploited then as they sometimes like to remember, and not all men were or are so proud of exploiting.

"Separate Flights," the title story of the collection, displays the same strengths as the others, and there the steadiness and integrity of Dubus's style lends force to an otherwise familiar figure: the middle-aged, middle-class person whose life has come to nothing. Very little that is out of the ordinary or even detectable to anyone but her husband—when he is paying attention—happens to Beth Harrison. She drinks too much, fantasizes lovers she is too timid to take, dries out for a while, and when her youngest daughter Peggy goes away to college yields to boozing again. When her husband wonders if her discontent has been caused by the onset of menopause she admits to a form of slow-motion suicide: "I'll die of lung cancer, wearing a tampax."

There is one passage in **"Separate Flights"** that epitomizes both my admiration for and reservations about Dubus's work, and perhaps the best way to deal with my own ambivalence is to try it out on you and let you decide for yourselves. It occurs during a passage discussing Beth Harrison's insomnia:

> She knew this much, though: she was not equipped to solve a problem of this sort. Until now she had always dealt with problems that

had alternatives and you weighed them and made a choice, like buying one dishwasher instead of another. But now the buyer's instinct was useless: what was needed was a probing insight into herself, and this was a bitter and unprofitable task. For when she did try to explore herself she found—oh God: she found nothing.

That part of my critical sense that responds to the tight economy of Dubus's writing is pleased; another part of me is made uneasy at the invocation of the familiar suburban Nada and wishes that in this story as in others Dubus would be a bit less craftsmanlike and more adventurous in both plot and theme. But I may be asking for an essay instead of a story by asking that. Dubus might very well respond that he doesn't exactly know why his characters feel so sad, or that what he knows is no more than what we can all read about in any issue of *Newsweek* or *Ms.* So I leave it up to you.

In any case Andre Dubus is exactly the kind of writer who has been well served by publishing with Godine, for while that house is hardly unknown, it treats a book of short stories like these in a way that a large publishing house would not. ***Separate Flights*** is not only very handsomely designed and printed but it is still in print and very much available now, almost two years since its publication date. Had it come out with a large commercial press it would very likely have died unmentioned in about three months, and would long since have been remaindered. In the long run Godine will probably do well with the book; Dubus is too good to languish unread. One has only to read a few pages to know that one is reading the genuine thing.

> Gene Lyons, "Eavesdropping on the Quotidian," in The Nation, *New York, Vol. 224, No. 8, February 26, 1977, pp. 248-50.*

Anatole Broyard   (essay date 1977)

[*Broyard was an American author and critic. In the following review, he suggests that the title story of* Adultery, and Other Choices *is most reflective of Dubus's talent for storytelling.*]

Freshening up the subject of adultery in fiction is no mean feat and Andre Dubus does a good job of it in the long title story of ***Adultery and Other Choices.*** Edith and Hank Allison have what Hank describes as "a loving, intimate marriage," and to a degree, this is true. Hank is both tender and passionate with Edith, he respects her, and he wants and needs the stable structure of their life together.

Yet Edith feels that Hank, who is a novelist and teacher, "is keeping himself in reserve," that "with his work he created his own harmony, and then he used the people he loved to relax with." While such a relationship lacks the romantic extravagance that so many of us hope for in the unreasonable depths of our hearts, it succeeds for perhaps the same reason. Its demands can comfortably be met. Relaxing with someone can be dressed up as love, especially when a man brings to his wife the intense afterglow of his work.

But the arrangement cannot afford any further qualifications. When Hank admits that he is having an affair, that is bad enough: when he adds that he does not believe in the "unnatural boundaries of life-long monogamy," there is for Edith no longer any *raison d'être* in their marriage. She has given herself to Hank, and he has given her back. She does not know what to do with the stranger she has suddenly become. Is she liberated or abandoned? She can't tell.

When Edith tries to defend and rediscover herself by having an affair with Jack Linhart, she exchanges her emotional security for the peculiar chess game, for the acrostics of adultery. But adultery turns out to be only a kind of pressure cooker compared to the leisurely feast of marriage. Edith feels that she and Jack "made love too much, pushing their bodies to consume the yearning they had borne and to delay the yearning that was waiting." She finds it difficult to live, or love, in spasms.

How does one enjoy adultery? Edith wonders, looking at Debbie, one of Hank's students and his latest mistress. In her affair with Hank, Debbie "had come without history into not history"—how can that be enough? Who can live on it?

Edith articulates her own needs when she falls in love with Joe, a former Catholic priest. Before her, Joe was a virgin, and she feels that "she holds his entire history in her body." While this is too much to expect of love, it does throw some perspective on what love ideally strives for. When Joe dies of cancer, Edith understands that one of the things love does is to console us for the fact of death. Love is a flirtation with immortality: nothing less will do. Her marriage with Hank is not profound enough to fortify her against death, and perhaps that function is its only ultimate justification.

Not all of the stories in ***Adultery and Other Choices*** are as satisfying as this one. Several stories about childhood seem to be, like virtually all stories about childhood, lugubrious. The looking back in this kind of fiction is usually the least dimensional form of nostalgia. It is difficult enough to make an adult interesting, and a child's vulnerability may have been turned into a tired cliché by post-Freudian fiction. In the end, it seems that such stories are most moving to the author himself and that what the reader feels may be only a detached pity that does not even pass through art.

Army stories are not much better, and Mr. Dubus has written some of these too. Like adultery, Army life offers a temporary intensity with severely limited references. More successful is a story called **"The Fat Girl,"** in which an unattractively stout girl diets herself into beauty, marriage, and what is generally regarded as a reasonably happy life, only to discover that she has also dieted away her appetite for that life, that, in some way, her fatness was part of her essence and now she is only a mannequin of other people's expectations.

In the title story of ***Adultery and Other Choices,*** Mr. Dubus appears to have found his best voice. Even without the help of some good moments in the lesser stories, this one alone will make it worth your while to go out and get the book.

Anatole Broyard, "Some Good Moments," in
The New York Times Book Review, *November 20, 1977, p. 14.*

Edith Milton   (essay date 1978)

[*In the following review of* Adultery, and Other
Choices, *Milton commends Dubus's exploration of gender roles, conflicts, and relationships in contemporary
American society.*]

During his first meal in America, Martin Chuzzlewit observes a curious native custom: there are about 20 diners
around the table, of whom, Dickens tells us, five or six are
"ladies, who sat wedged together in a little phalanx by
themselves," and who, at the end of the meal's only
course, file out. "And there," says Dickens, "was an end
of *them.*" He goes on to observe that Martin, snob, egoist
and Victorian though he is, finds such separation uncomfortable, but that the American gentlemen "now lounged
about the stove as if a great weight had been taken off their
minds by the withdrawal of the other sex."

If the distance between the sexes here appeared extreme
even by the norms of an Englishman of the 1840s, it is
hardly surprising that the chasm has lasted over the years,
refusing even now to be entirely bridged. Or that the ordinary progress of sexual relationships, courtship, marriage,
adultery, has been treated consistently more shyly in
American fiction than it has in European: shrouded in allegory by Hawthorne and Faulkner, wrapped in wishful
thinking by Hemingway and Mailer, and speared by Philip Roth and others on the sort of satire reserved in cozier
cultures for political opponents. There are of course exceptions to this; most notably Henry James, who explored
relationships between men and women, father and daughter, friend and friend, lover and lover, with more insight
than Dostoevski and more precision than Flaubert. But
then, he spent his life abroad.

And an extraordinary number of American writers who
stayed at home have chosen to remain on their own side
of the sexual divide as well. Being men, they have either
written only about men, or permitted into their fiction no
woman but the one inevitable in a man's life, his mother.
America has given fond succor to the image of man entangled in the maternal web, popular in all fiction since fiction
first began. But America has also been a nursery for,
among others, the sea novel and the war novel, the furthest fictional reaches I would think possible from the
womb.

In his recent collection of short stories, ***Adultery and
Other Choices,*** Andre Dubus considers this puzzle of separation and discomfort in American life. He examines a
variety of relationships; family relationships, friendships
between women, camaraderie between men, marriage,
adultery. He writes of men and women in isolation from
each other, and of men and women together. But, most
particularly, he focuses on that monstrous division between the two, possibly conceived in nature, probably exaggerated by our culture and our values, and described by
Dubus in poignant detail as an integral part of his characters' daily lives. I can think of no one who has drawn a

more precise map of that no-man's land between the sexes
than he has in this collection and in his earlier *Separate
Flights.* And even in fiction written by women or journalistic accounts of how women live, it would be difficult to
find as painful or as accurate a description of the futilities
of keeping house as there is here in **"Andromache"** or in
his earlier **"We Don't Live Here Anymore."**

The force of women absent is as palpable as their presence
is. And the influences of marriage and passion are far less
powerful in these stories than a more negative pressure, a
vacuum in communication which begins as silence between husband and wife, and ends by inhaling husband,
wife, children and society into a conspiracy of isolation.
Where love, or even the desire for love, exists, life is sane;
in **"Graduation,"** for instance, where a much-used girl decides to become a virgin again. Or in **"Cadence,"** in which
a young officer candidate for the Marine Corps counsels
his friend, Paul, " 'to get a girl again. There's nothing like
it. . . . *Noth*ing. It's another world, man.' " Secure in his
affections, he can afford to weigh his needs against the dehumanizing demands of the Corps, and leave. But Paul
has long since been sucked into the void which existed between his parents. He has signed the Marine contract because he thinks it will please his father, and because the
recruiting captain had appeared "like salvation . . . wearing the blue uniform and manly beauty that would fulfill
Paul's dreams." In the confusion in which he lives, he
needs the clear certainty of masculine order and approval,
and the story ends as, his friend gone, he dissolves "into
unity with the rest of the platoon."

Dubus himself spent five years in the Marine Corps, which
exists in several of these stories as the antithesis of all
things instinctual, sexual and growing. It is not, in itself,
really evil, or even inhuman. But its humanity springs
from the need for silence, for peace from women and from
life, and for the certain ritual which will replace the uncertainty of understanding.

> 'Nothing growing, nothing moving,'

says one Marine to another in **"Corporal of Artillery."**

> 'Nothing but Marines,' Fitzgerald said.

> 'Like I said: nothing,'

answers the first. And in **"The Shooting,"** Sergeant Everett, admiring a photograph of himself taken to commemorate his killing of a sad, paranoid sailor, sees himself in it
"forever poised in peaceful silence," the prototype of the
successful, well-adjusted military man.

The best of the stories about Marine Corps life, and perhaps the best story in the collection, is **"Andromache,"**
which makes explicit the conflict between the male compulsion for protocol, bravado and death, and the paradoxical female need to nurture and sustain what will only end
by destroying itself. To nurture and sustain, moreover,
without disturbing the great male rituals. The story, which
is written from the point of view of Ellen, a Marine Officer's wife, widowed by his latest quest for adventure, recalls their last Christmas together and her attempt to give
a Christmas party for her husband's men. The party is a
failure; the complex arrangement of Marine manners

keeps the enlisted men from showing up. Ellen is hurt, but represses her anger at the waste of her food, her effort, in the all-encompassing need to be a good sport, to pull in her stomach, to mourn, finally, in silence. *"Be a strong Marine,"* she says to her small son as he starts to cry at his father's funeral. While her daughter has already learned the lesson of self-repression, and, at the age of nine, knows as much as her mother does about control and selflessness in the face of the male needs and abandonments which have been the lot of military wives since Andromache.

But, by extension, all wives are military wives, and the Marines only the most potent of those institutions in which a man can feel his manhood safe from interruption. There is some security even in the lesser sports. In poker, for instance, and in golf. Men jog together to express their friendship and to get away from their wives, and though families speak often to each other with affection, they speak around secrets and gaps of the unspeakable.

The center of the book's first three stories is the child, Paul, who grows up to be the young Marine of **"Cadence."** In **"An Afternoon with the Old Man"** he is urged by his mother on an expedition into male territory with his father. Silent at home, his father becomes drunk and expansive on the golf course, courting his son's affection with praise and grape soda, while Paul feels he has become his mother's spy in this land forbidden her. In **"Contrition"** a French horn is the symbol of all that is not articulated between his parents, and Paul's own inadequacies in the face of that. And in **"The Bully"** his misery at the hands of the class bully is balanced against his helpless imitation of the bully's sadism, and his identification with his lonely death.

Ambivalence is the pivot of Dubus's world, which is a world in splinters, where men and women face in opposite directions, and Catholic mother and Protestant father do not meet sufficiently even to disagree. A man, to feel himself a man, must sacrifice himself on the altar of masculine ritual, and even adultery stems from routine and a sense of what one owes oneself more than it does from real feeling.

It is impossible to escape the suspicion that most of these stories have an autobiographical source, especially those in which Dubus patently disparages the masculine ideals of the protagonist. Most of the women emerge triumphantly human; Ellen of **"Andromache,"** Bobbie, the restored virgin of **"Graduation,"** and Louise, **"The Fat Girl,"** who goes on a diet just long enough to discover that fat is what she is, and that any love worth the name can find her under the blubber. These women, and Paul's unposturing, gently failing friends, are the valiant of the earth; the others are oppressed by their maleness as by a burden. It is his ability at once to understand the strong and to exonerate the silly which makes Dubus's writing enormously engaging.

The title story, **"Adultery,"** is the last and longest in the book, and in it Dubus tries to arrive at some sort of accommodation for all the fragments of his universe. The accommodation is uncomfortable and difficult, for the reader, I think, as well as for the characters, since it invokes a sexual answer for a spiritual need, and a spiritual answer for a sexual one; a combination which presents notable problems of perspective also in D. H. Lawrence, of whom Dubus often reminds one.

In **"Adultery,"** Joe Ritchie leaves the priesthood not because he has lost faith, but because he feels the need to complete himself by being loved by a woman. " 'I must have a woman,' " he says to himself when he is drunk. But the need is much more than physical, and he sees women as beings beyond the grasp of religion, beings whose nature combines passion and instinct, and whose visits to his confessional are merely "a distant and dutiful salute to the rules and patterns of men."

He is a marvelously Romantic figure; but to fulfill himself he chooses a rather colorless partner, Episcopalian Edith from Winnetka; the wife of a philandering, callow writer, she has already had several affairs, but keeps a clean house. Soon after they fall in love, they discover that Joe is dying, and their adultery transforms itself into a sort of earthbound sacrament, a statement of the flesh made to a distant God in the face of imminent death.

It is a story large in scope and complex in ambition, and finally Edith's journey from vacuity to pathos does become moving. But there is no question that Dubus is at his best when he examines the shards of his particular universe, when he charts the islands of domestic and military routine which define the seas of incomprehension on which his characters live. Putting the pieces together, he is less convincing; one feels the scale of Eternity jarring against the smallness of his people.

But Dubus is an exact and a compelling writer. The power of all these stories is very great, and the direction of the last is interesting. One wonders of what Dubus may be capable when he knows the path better; when he can describe the way to salvation with the same easy authority with which he describes the mined wasteland which stretches between lives.

> *Edith Milton, in a review of "Adultery, and Other Choices," in* The New Republic, *Vol. 178, No. 5, February 4, 1978, pp. 33-5.*

Judith Gies   (essay date 1980)

[*In the following review of* Finding a Girl in America, *Gies suggests that Dubus is at his best as a fiction writer when he explores and depicts the details of ordinary people's lives.*]

Andre Dubus is a writer of unusual gifts. At his best, he captures the almost imperceptible erosions of daily life— the slow disintegration of marriages, the loosening of bonds between parents and children, the leaking away of self-respect. And he records the small gains— reconciliations, fresh starts, efforts to keep the machinery of our lives in working order. He writes with sensitivity and exactitude about ordinary people whose common lot is a narrowing of options.

And nowhere are the options more limited than in this

new collection [*Finding a Girl in America*], which includes 10 stories, all previously published, and a new title novella. In earlier collections, notably *Separate Flights,* Dubus wrote with equal clarity about men and women and he recorded the treacherous shifts in their relationships with intelligence and subtlety. But here he has narrowed his focus—the book might as well be called "Being a Man in America"—and the author's perception of this condition is disheartening. In one way or another, the men in these stories are all casualties, victims not only of sexual warfare but of fallout from the male myth. For Dubus's characters, manhood is a series of endurance tests—in the marines, at the bar and the typewriter, and in the home, where they struggle with what one exhusband remembers as "the old male-burden of having to be strong for both of them."

Dubus himself was a marine, and he often writes about peacetime soldiers, some of whom are more at home on the base than they are in the outside world. In **"The Misogamist,"** a marine corporal puts off his impending marriage for as long as possible, then abandons the idea altogether: "he glimpsed the concrete details of his life as male and military, uniforms and gear and troops, and his needs for a woman had no surrounding details at all, they all ended in something abstract." Although most of these characters carry their battles into the domestic arena, they nearly all seem to have been bested; they are divorced fathers, jilted husbands and lovers, men adrift. It is sexual suicide with a vengeance.

Nevertheless, their stories sometimes work very well. **"Killings"** is a grim account of an ordinary man driven to an extraordinary act—the revenge of a father on his son's murderer, which of all "male-burdens" must surely be one of the weightiest. The story is strangely ambivalent, and its implications are chilling. Like some of Dubus's best work, it is about ferocity, an aspect of love that the author reserves primarily for the relationship between parent and child. In **"The Winter Father,"** a divorced father of two struggles to maintain a fragile connection with his children through a succession of "entertaining" weekends. After one of these visits he returns them to their mother with apparent equanimity, yet the next morning, scraping the inside of his windshield, "he realized the grey ice curling and falling from the glass was the frozen breath of his children."

Even more effective is **"Delivering,"** the story of two young boys coming to grips with their parents' separation. Because it is recounted without sentimentality, the struggle of the children to marshal their puny defenses is all the more touching.

Most disappointing is the title novella, a continuation of a saga begun in *Separate Flights* and continued in *Adultery and Other Choices.* Hank Allison, now 35, is working on his third novel and teaching at a New England women's college. His wife has divorced him after a futile attempt to combat his infidelities with some of her own. Formerly an advocate of open marriage, and veteran of countless shallow affairs, Hank now contents himself with seeing his 13-year-old daughter, running and drinking

with his friend Jack, and finding a girl in America—namely, Lori, the latest in a series of willing students.

But Hank is tired now of "all this trifling around," and he is outraged by the revelation that a previous lover (more spirited than the current one) has aborted his child after telling him to go to hell. Now he is looking for monogamy, with a child-woman who compares homework techniques with his daughter and seems unlikely to interfere with his writing (or his running or his drinking). It's nearly impossible to sympathize with the self-indulgent maunderings of this born-again puritan. For one thing, his priorities are all too clear: "Knowing he is foolish, he still wishes she [Lori] were shorter. . . . Hank never wishes he were taller." That pretty much says it all, although I like Hank's ex-wife, Edith, who was an infinitely more substantial character in *Adultery* than her cameo appearance here would suggest.

The stories are uneven, and the vision somewhat bleak, but when Dubus is good, he is very good indeed, and this collection is worth reading.

Judith Gies, "Little Wishes," in The Village Voice, *Vol. 25, No. 48, November 26, 1980, p. 42.*

Gilberto Perez   (essay date 1980-81)

[*In the following excerpt, Perez offers a critical overview of* Finding a Girl in America, *suggesting that Dubus's stories provide a believable context for the dramatization of significant moral issues.*]

The stories in Andre Dubus's new collection, *Finding a Girl in America,* . . . often deal with losing, and with looking again for a girl in America. In one story, set before and during the Second World War, a man from Texas has a girl in his home town who seems ideal for him, but after he joins the Marines he gets to cherish his life with the troops, keeps her waiting for years, and finally cannot bring himself to marry her; he breaks her heart but the real loss, we are left in no doubt, is his. The greater loss seems to be the woman's in another story of conflict between marriage and career, which deals with a young pitcher of major-league potential who unknowingly neglects his wife in his devotion to the game. Even when not on the road, he has been virtually absent on the nights before pitching, needing "to enter the rhythm and concentration that would work for him when he actually had the ball in his hand"; and on the day when he is to pitch the decisive game of the season his wife tells him she's leaving him for another man. "Can't a man try to be the best at what he's got to do and still love his wife?" he pleads with her, but he can see it's no use, she's in love with the other man, an unglamorous small-town dentist with a wife and two kids of his own. Although the pitcher's impulse is to give his wife's lover a beating, he realizes he must do something that, like many of the demands of his profession, is "unnatural": he sets to regain that rhythm and concentration he needs for the game. Having lost his wife, he loses the game too, but not because he didn't pitch very well. His future looks bright, the pain caused him by his wife will pass, and what future can she have with that married dentist? Dubus tends to uphold in this book the values of that eroded institution, marriage: against the Marine who forsook his girl, against the wife who wouldn't stick by the pitcher and his dreams of being the best.

Skill as a refuge from pain, the pitcher's skill at his decisive game or that displayed, in another story, by a boy adeptly delivering newspapers from his bicycle with his younger brother in tow while knowing that, earlier that morning, their mother left home for good: this, among other things in the book, reminds one of that other eroded institution, Hemingway. Hemingway explicitly comes up at one point in the title novella, when the protagonist, a thirty-five-year-old writer named Hank Allison who teaches at a college in Massachusetts, mentions *A Farewell to Arms* to a woman he's in bed with. She hasn't read it, has little interest in literature, which is the chief reason Hank stops seeing her, the only woman his own age he has had an affair with since his divorce. Not that Hank shares the pitcher's aspirations to reach the top in his career—he sees himself "just as an unknown, average, .260-hitting writer"—but he thinks his work "the best of himself," and places it first in his life even if his relationships with women turn out to suffer in consequence.

That was apparently his main problem with Monica, who told him so when she left him. She was the third young girl in a row, all students, to leave Hank after a year or more with him:

> None but Monica had told him why, in words he could understand. The other two had cried and talked about needing space. When the first left him he was sad, but he was all right. The loss of the second frightened him. That was when he saw his trap.

Now over a year has passed since Hank last saw Monica, and another student, Lori, a year younger, has taken her place. From this present time, narrated in the present tense, the novella makes its frequent excursions into Hank's past, the first occurring right at the beginning. High on the Tequila they are drinking in bed together, Lori tells him something about his previous girlfriend that hurts and enrages him beyond what he had thought possible: Monica had been pregnant by him and had had an abortion. That child unknown to him till now, done away with on Monica's wishes, Hank feels strongly was equally his—he's given to using the first person plural when talking about his women's pregnancies—and he very much would have wanted it. His rage at his former girlfriend is wholly understandable, the moral issues raised by abortion much more complicated than allowed for by the familiar argument one can imagine Monica using to justify herself, about the baby being part of the woman's body and thus for her to do with as she sees fit. Still, what did Hank expect? Readily performed abortions are part of the code of sexual behavior that gives students freedom to sleep with their professors without much thought of an enduring attachment—the freedom Hank has benefited from. And his marriage, from which he has a daughter by now pretty close in age to his girlfriends, ended as a result of his making it an "open" marriage in order to satisfy his itch for sexual experimentation.

I respect Dubus's earnestness, and his ability to dramatize these moral issues in the story of Hank Allison; but I think he relies on too simple a scheme in casting Monica as the frivolous girl who makes Hank see the error of his ways, and Lori as the serious girl who, as it turns out, truly loves him. Taken individually, they are both believable characters: the brief sketch we get of Monica is sufficient, and the fuller portrayal of Lori—her doubts about herself, her one unsatisfactory sexual experience prior to Hank, her quietness in contrast with the aggressive flirtatiousness (and probable infidelities) of her mother—makes it convincing that she should have fallen in love with Hank. But the place Dubus assigns the two of them in Hank's life is too pat. Not only has Hank lost all desire for sexual experimentation, he can't even make love to Lori after he hears from her about the abortion, and in a touching scene near the end he tells her he can't again: "Ever. With anyone. Unless both of us are ready for whatever happens . . . I'm going to court you. And if someday you say you'll marry me, then it'll be all right . . . " Yes, she says right then and there, since that's what she's wanted herself but in her shyness hasn't expressed in all the time she's been sleeping with him: lucky for Hank to have found an old-fashioned girl to coincide with his belated conversion to old-fashioned courtship and marriage.

Gilberto Perez, "These Days in the Holocene," in The Hudson Review, *Vol. XXXIII, No. 4, Winter, 1980-81, pp. 575-88.*

William H. Pritchard   (essay date 1983-84)

[*Pritchard is an American author and critic whose criticism is known for its personable tone. In the following excerpt, he calls Dubus's portrayal of the everyday lives and secret agonies of ordinary people perceptive and realistic.*]

As for Andre Dubus, whose fourth collection of short fiction [*The Times Are Never So Bad*] earns him the title of seasoned veteran, one would not wish him to be at all other than he is. Which is also to say that he has not "developed" from the best work of his first collection, *Separate Flights,* of eight years ago. That book, like Dubus's subsequent collections, opened and/or closed with the stories that constitute his best work: **"We Don't Live Here Anymore"** and **"Separate Flights,"** from the first book; **"Adultery,"** from *Adultery and Other Choices;* **"Finding a Girl in America,"** the title story of his third collection; and in the new one, **"The Pretty Girl"** and **"A Father's Story."** To say that he hasn't developed is not meant as a complaint, since the first in line of these works, the novella **"We Don't Live Here Anymore,"** contains in essence all he has to "say" about life: there is man, there is woman, there is marriage and children, there is adultery and separation (or reconciliation); there is running, there is coffee and bacon and smoking in the morning; there is beer, often paced by shots of tequila and whiskey, at night. There is also, more explicitly than before—in the final story to the new collection—a Catholic, wounded, guilty sensibility:

> I have said I talk with God in the mornings, as I start my day, and sometimes as I sit with coffee, looking at the birds, and the woods. Of

course He has never spoken to me, but that is not something I require.

This from the man who has kept silent about a hit-and-run accident in which his daughter was involved. Divorced, having learned to live alone, he discovers an aloneness beyond the one he thought he had learned to inhabit. Of course, the "point" of **"A Father's Story,"** as in Dubus's other work, does not consist in some truth about life, or morality, or the individual talent. More than most contemporary writers of fiction, his work is its own reward: it feels something like an offering to whatever gods have allowed him to set down the burden of what he has to say.

Dubus writes as if Hemingway and Faulkner still mattered to an American writer, and this is refreshing and intelligent. To be sure, he is very much a Man's Writer, writing out of his sense of difference from the other sex in such an expressive way that the word "macho" is shown up for the cheap cliché it is:

> . . . I've known a lot of women who didn't need booze or drugs or a workout, while I've never known a man who didn't need one or the other, if not both. It would be interesting to meet one someday. So I flex into the spray, make the muscles feel closer to the hot water, but I've lost it, that feeling you get after a workout, that yesterday is gone and last night too, that today is right here in the shower, inside your body; there is nothing out there past the curtain that can bring you down, and you can take all the time you want to turn the water hotter and circle and flex and stretch under it, because the time is yours like the water is . . . it's what you lifted all that iron for, and it'll take you like a stream does a trout, cool and easy the rest of the day.

With such sensitivity is this iron-pumper, assaulter of his wife and her lover, Hemingwayish dumb-ox, endowed. But the lead story which he begins as the teller of, has room for more than the inside of his poetic head, and it moves later to a third person treatment of his wife, Polly, the "pretty girl" of its title. Dubus is the sort of inclusive consciousness that cares about pumping iron but also cares about point of view. I can't praise enough his realistic sense of place and of things Northwest of Boston, along the Merrimack, all that Catholicism and beer and sex and guilt. It is Jack Kerouac crossed by Henry James, and the result is a unique American talent which I hope continues to prosper.

> *William H. Pritchard, "Some August Fiction," in* The Hudson Review, *Vol. XXXVI, No. 4, Winter, 1983-84, pp. 742-54.*

Steve Yarbrough   (essay date 1986)

[*In the following critical assessment of Dubus's short stories published between 1977 and 1985, Yarbrough praises Dubus's narrative technique and suggests that his skill as a fiction writer is best showcased in his longer short stories.*]

Andre Dubus has published two novels and four novellas, but his growing reputation rests most securely on his short stories. Those stories may, with some qualifications, be divided into three groups, based upon the way in which the stories are structured: closely related to structure, characterization is handled differently in each of the three types of stories.

In the first of these groups, the stories limit themselves to what Henry James called "the detached incident." Narration is straightforward. We begin at one point in time and move ahead until the incident that gives the story its life has finished taking place. Characterization depends solely upon the characters' responses to the incident in question. In Dubus's work, **"The Doctor"** and **"The Dark Men"** best exemplify this type of story.

The stories in the second group have no clearly defined beginning or end. The thread of the narrative may spin itself first one way, then another. In the most characteristic of these stories, Dubus relinquishes purely narrative interest, giving away the outcome of events in the first few lines. The focus is not on what is going to happen to the characters; it is instead on what *has* happened to them, on what has made them the people they are. The narrative assumes the shape of a circle. Examples of stories in this group are **"Townies"** and **"In My Life."**

The majority of Dubus's short fiction falls into the third category. Most of the stories in this group are compressed novels. Several years, or even several decades, of a character's life may be packed into one tight paragraph. However, the same might be said of stories in the previous group. But the stories in the third class differ from those in the second in two important respects. First, they tend to be much longer, and the extra room allows a heavier reliance on scene—as opposed to summary—than a shorter story does. Second, whereas the stories in the second group have no recognizable beginning or end, the stories in the third group do. They are narratives in a more conventional sense. We are led to believe that something important *is* going to happen to the characters; and while we do examine their pasts, we also see them responding to events in the fictional present. Notable stories in this group are **"Separate Flights"** and **"The Fat Girl."**

"The Doctor," in the collection *Separate Flights,* illustrates Dubus's ability to draw characterization from the isolated occurrence. The story is brief, about 2500 words; it has a simple plot. Art Castagnetto, an obstetrician who lives in a rural community near Boston, goes jogging one quiet Sunday morning and encounters disaster along the way. A slab of concrete has tumbled off the edge of a bridge and trapped a child beneath the shallow waters of a brook. While Art struggles vainly to lift the slab, the child drowns. The following morning, troubled by a vague but nagging memory, Art returns to the scene of the accident and makes a discovery: in the yard of the house that stands near the bridge lies a coiled garden hose; had he cut off a piece of the hose and placed one end of it in the child's mouth, the child would have been able to breathe until the slab could be lifted. He walks home, takes his pocketknife out, cuts a section out of his own garden hose, and places it in the trunk of his car.

Through careful use of detail, Dubus sets the scene for the

tragedy that will, in one small way, change Art forever. The morning on which the accident occurs has signaled the beginning of spring. He has put away his sweat suit, preferring to jog in shorts and tee-shirt. Running down the road, he enjoys the freshness of the morning, breathing "the scent of pines and, he believed, the sunlight in the air." The brook, frozen all winter, has now begun to run clearly. The sights of the first warm Sunday of the year are all welcome: a mile or so past the bridge, he sees a family sitting at their picnic table reading the paper; a bit farther he sees a young couple washing a Volkswagen, and they look at him and wave. "All up the road it was like that: people cleaning their lawns, washing cars, some just sitting under the bright sky; one large bald man lifted a beer can and grinned."

When Art turns and starts home, the peaceful morning is suddenly cracked open: "Then something was wrong—he felt it before he knew it. When the boys ran up from the brook into his vision, he started sprinting and had a grateful instant when he felt the strength left in his legs, though still he didn't know if there was any reason for strength and speed." At the bridge, he finds the child and fights to free him. As his efforts fail, a sense of incredulity overcomes him. That such a morning could be torn by tragedy seems unthinkable: "He refused to believe it was this simple and this impossible." Yet his strength is not enough. The morning turns ugly:

> The sky changed, was shattered by a smoke-gray sound of winter nights—the fire horn—and in the quiet that followed he heard a woman's voice. . . . He turned and looked at her standing beside him in the water, and he suddenly wanted to be held, his breast against hers, but her eyes shrieked at him to do something, and he bent over and tried again to lift the slab. Then she was beside him, and they kept trying until ten minutes later, when four volunteer firemen descended out of the dying groan of the siren and splashed into the brook.

Art returns home and drinks all afternoon. Sitting in his backyard with his wife, he suddenly begins to cry. The next morning "an answer—or at least a possibility—was waiting for him, as though it had actually chosen to enter his mind now, with the buzzing of the alarm clock." He rises, walks down the road, sees the garden hose lying near the scene of the accident, then goes back home, cuts a section out of his own garden hose and places it in the trunk of his Buick. The story's concluding sentence nicely sums up what seems to be Art's dominant character trait; it also indicates the child's death will have a long-lasting effect on the doctor. "His fingers were trembling as he lowered the piece of hose and placed it beside his first-aid kit, in front of a bucket of sand and a small snow shovel he had carried all through the winter." Objects for use in routine emergencies fill the trunk of Art's car. But, whereas a scraped knee or an automobile halted by snow might be considered routine, death by drowning, in a shallow brook on a perfect morning, is anything but routine. The addition of the hose is an attempt to insure preparation for the once-in-a-lifetime crisis. Yet the experience has been so shattering for Art—who prides himself on being pre-

pared—that it is unlikely he can ever again consider himself truly ready for all eventualities.

"The Dark Men," a story from *Finding a Girl in America,* is about an Office of Naval Intelligence investigation of Commander Joe Saldi, a Naval pilot currently stationed aboard a carrier. Saldi's friend and superior officer, Captain Deveraux, is visited by two ONI investigators, who acquaint him with Saldi's guilt (though Deveraux refuses to let them tell him exactly what Saldi is guilty of) and ask to see the pilot. Deveraux stalls long enough for Saldi, who as yet knows nothing of the investigation and is planning to go ashore, to leave the ship; then he tells the ONI men they will have to come back that night. Later the captain goes ashore himself, has Saldi located and brought to a bar. There the captain tells his friend of the investigation. That afternoon, when the ONI men return to the ship and ask for Saldi, Deveraux informs them that Saldi, in an apparent suicide, has taken his plane and flown out to sea. There has been no radio contact for more than an hour.

Deveraux feels animosity, if not outright hatred, for the ONI men. He is conscious of the contrast in appearance between himself and Saldi, on the one hand, and the ONI men on the other. Both Saldi and Deveraux spend time outside, in the sun, and their faces are healthy; they both wear Navy whites and openly display insignia of rank, as well as campaign ribbons, on their uniforms. Everything about the ONI men, in contrast, suggests blankness, anonymity: "Their faces were drained of color, they were men who worked away from the sun. They wear dark civilian clothes, and the captain feels that their dress defies him: "They were from the Office of Naval Intelligence . . . and although they called him Captain and Sir, they denied or outmaneuvered his shoulder boards by refusing to wear their own." The ONI men look "for the dark sides of other men."

Just as the last scene of **"The Doctor"** draws all the elements of that story together to form a single, clear impression of character, so does the concluding scene of **"The Dark Men."** Having already learned of his friend's final action, Captain Deveraux walks the flight deck, waiting for the return of the ONI men, Foster and Todd:

> When they emerged from the island and moved toward him, walking abreast and leaning into the wind, he was standing at the end of the flight deck. He saw them coming and looked away. The sun was going down. Out there, toward the open sea, a swath of gold lay on the water. When they stopped behind him he did not turn around. He was thinking that, from a distance, a plane flying into the sunset looks like a moving star. Then shutting his eyes he saw the diving silver plane in the sunset, and then he was in it, his heart pounding with the dive, and the engine roaring in his blood, and he saw the low red sun out of the cockpit and, waiting, the hard and yielding sea.
>
> "Commander Saldi is not here," he said.
>
> "Not here?" It was Foster. "Where is he?"
>
> "Out there."

Saldi's suicide is a slap in the blank faces of the ONI men. Deveraux's complicity in the affair allows him to share responsibility for the act of defiance. When he envisions the plane diving, streaking toward the sea, he manages to share further in the act of defiance by imagining himself in the cockpit.

Both **"The Dark Men"** and **"The Doctor"** render the detached incident vividly and invest it with significance. The narration in both stories is straightforward; there are no flashbacks. The scenic method is relied on almost exclusively in both stories. What we know about the characters, we know because of their responses to a single situation.

While narration is straightforward in those stories, it is anything but that in the stories that fall into the second group. **"In My Life"** is the story of a white woman, the first-person narrator, who has been raped by a black man named Sonny Broussard. The story both begins and ends with Broussard's execution. Sandwiched in between the beginning and the ending are the rape itself, an account of the narrator's failed marriage, and affairs with three different men. The story is only about 2500 words long. It can cover so much ground only because Dubus makes very effective use of summary.

In the following passage, the first four sentences summarize the narrator's marriage. The transitional phrase "one morning" signals the beginning of the scene in which the marriage actually ends:

> It seems after you get to be twenty-five there's nothing but married men. I was married when I was eighteen, we had to, but I miscarried, and inside of two years I couldn't stand the sight of him. His name was Brumby, and I came to hate that name, and I would pronounce it hating. I'd say, "Okay, *Brum*by." One morning I woke up and he was gone. I went in the kitchen and there was a note on the table, with the salt shaker resting on it. I was grinning when I picked it up. It said: I'm sorry, I'll send money. Brumby. I laughed, I was so glad he finally took it on himself to leave.

The night of Broussard's execution is a temporal base that keeps Jill from seeming a disembodied voice wandering through events. Thoughts of the execution continually intrude, forcing themselves into Jill's consciousness and the narrative. All other events, even though they precede the execution, are viewed in light of it. The circular form allows the central event to remain dominant throughout. Dubus's skillful use of summary enables us to form a surprisingly complete impression of Jill's life—thus, the title of the story.

A story similar in design is **"Townies."** The first section of the story begins when an elderly security guard at a small college finds the body of a murdered coed lying on a snowy bridge one night. Instead of phoning the police or the ambulance, he kneels and strokes her cheek, his mind drifting back to the many times in his life when he looked at other coeds, young and attractive, and wondered what it would feel like to touch one of them. The series of flashbacks is framed by the old man's kneeling and

touching the murdered girl. The section ends right where it began.

Section two begins with a man named Mike following a girl across campus. He overtakes her on the footbridge and, in a brutal scene, beats her to death. As he walks away after the murder, he too recalls incidents involving various coeds from the college. Like the security guard, Mike is a townie, but an unemployed one: he lives off the coeds that he manages to lure into sexual relationships. The dead girl was the most recent of his lovers.

Perhaps more than any other story Dubus has written, **"Townies"** renounces all purely narrative interest. The coed's death is divulged early, in the opening paragraph of section one; section two, which actually precedes section one chronologically, does not lead up to the girl's death but begins with it. What maintains interest is Dubus's deft examination of character. Each section probes a townie's response to the constant presence of the coeds.

The security guard's life in the town has been one of muted desire. He recalls, for example, a time when as a young man he saw a group of the girls standing on a street corner waiting for the bus to Boston:

> It was a winter day. When he saw them waiting for the bus he crossed the street so he could walk near them. There were perhaps six of them. As he approached, he looked at their faces, their hair. They did not look at him. He walked by them. He could smell them and he could feel their eyes seeing him and not seeing him. Their smells were of perfume, cold fur, leather gloves, leather suitcases. Their voices had no accents he could recognize. They seemed the voices of mansions, resorts, travel. He was too conscious of himself to hear what they were saying. He knew it was idle talk; but its tone seemed peremptory; he would not have been surprised if one of them had given him a command. Then he was away from them. He smelled only the cold air now; he longed for their smells again: erotic, unattainable, a world that would never be open to him. But he did not think about its availability, any more than he would wish for an African safari.

Recognizing that they come from a different world, the security guard has always remained passive around the coeds. His first active response to their presence only occurs when he reaches out and strokes the cheek of the girl Mike has murdered.

It is ironic that Mike, who cares nothing for the girls, is able to have them at will. They are his meal tickets. He accepts money when they offer it; when they don't offer it, he steals it. Whereas the security guard has always been so keenly aware of the sight and smell of the girls, Mike is aware of what they own—their expensive clothes, their stereos, their Volvos. He hasn't limited himself to the girls: for twenty-five dollars he once agreed to go to bed with "the one college fag, a smooth-shaven, razor-cut boy who dressed better than the girls." The next morning he woke, looked at the young man's face, and wanted to kill him.

Mike's responses are all angry, and they all result from

greed. The murder he finally commits results not from his anguish at losing a lover but from the bitterness he feels at losing the right to sleep in Robin's comfortable room, to spend her money and drink her liquor.

"Townies" is about closed worlds. Though Mike manages to work his way into the girls' beds, he no more fits into their world than the security guard would. It seems natural for the narrative to form a complete circle: just as the story ends where it begins, so does the life of a townie.

The stories in the third group are not so quick to relinquish the power of suspense. None of the stories has a complicated plot, yet Dubus does work to elicit concern for what is going to happen to the characters. While he examines the characters' pasts, just as he does in a story like "Townies," he also presents an ongoing action. The result is a group of compressed novels.

One of Dubus's finest stories is "Separate Flights," the title story in his first collection. Beth Harrison is a forty-nine-year-old grandmother who smokes too much, drinks too much, can't sleep, and has stopped believing in love. Her youngest daughter, Peggy, will soon be leaving their home in Iowa to attend a New England college. Facing the fact that in September she will be left alone with her husband Lee—whom she despises—Beth increases her drinking, and her frustration grows more intense.

The symbol of Beth's isolation is the separate flight. Whenever she accompanies Lee to a convention, he insists on their taking separate flights, so that if one plane crashes, Peggy will still have one parent left. But to Beth, this only means that she might die alone, among strangers. On one such flight, she meets a silversmith and toys with the idea of going to bed with him during their layover in Chicago, but nothing comes of it. For weeks after the flight, she lies in bed beside her husband and masturbates, tantalized at the thought of his catching her. As her life slides further out of control, Beth concludes that her best friend, for the rest of her life, will probably be booze.

In "Separate Flights," the narrative is tightly bound by Beth's perceptions. We see only what she sees. When Beth observes her daughter at a cookout, the description is filtered through her consciousness: "Then she looked to her right, at Peggy, her blue eyes made brighter by contact lenses, her cheek concave as she drew on a cigarette, faint downy hair on her face catching the sunlight." When Beth walks into the living room late one night and, flipping on the light, discovers Peggy making love to her boyfriend Bucky, she sees "Peggy's face hidden inside the dress she was shrugging into, and Bucky with his naked back turned, snapping trousers at the waist." The author of a work of fiction is never really absent from his story, but Dubus makes himself seem so throughout "Separate Flights." The strict third-person limited point-of-view forces us to share Beth's perspective, to feel the impact events have on her.

Flashbacks are an important tool in this story. They work well here chiefly because they are so skillfully woven into the narrative. An especially subtle transition occurs after a flashback that begins while Beth is talking with Robert Carini, the silversmith, on the plane. As she talks, she gazes out the window into "clouds so thick she couldn't see the wing behind her." The flashback begins in the middle of their conversation, takes us back to the airport lounge, where, waiting to board the flight, Beth has two drinks. When she gets on the plane, she meets Carini. They begin talking, and Beth soon finds herself revealing the facts of her stale life to the stranger, telling him things she has told no one else. The conversation she and Carini have at the end of the flashback overlaps the conversation that was taking place when the flashback began. We only realize the flashback has ended when we read "she was watching Robert's face; he suddenly squinted and she turned to the window: they had broken through the clouds into a glaring sky that was blue and clear as far ahead as she could see." The transition is effortless. The flashbacks in "Separate Flights" are all handled with the same ease. They provide brief but illuminating glimpses of Beth's past without disrupting the narrative flow.

Flashbacks are not such an important tool in "The Fat Girl," from *Adultery & Other Choices.* This story covers a period of seventeen years in the life of a fat girl named Louise, focusing on her battle against chocolate bars and peanut butter.

As a child, Louise eats little at meals, and no one can figure out why she keeps growing. But Louise knows: she grows because of the four, five, or six chocolate bars she eats each night, she grows because of the peanut butter sandwiches she tucks under her shirt and slips up to her room. She continues to grow until her senior year at college, when her roommate Carrie talks her into dieting. That year she loses seventy pounds. She meets and marries a handsome lawyer, for whom she cooks lavish meals each night while starving herself to stay thin. But when she becomes pregnant, she rediscovers the joy of overeating and decides that her identity is bound to obesity, that being Louise means letting her appetite reign. Gluttony is her favorite thing.

Dubus uses summary passages extensively in "The Fat Girl." One advantage of summary is that when it is employed properly, it facilitates the passing of time. Dubus's summaries work well because they are full of concrete details:

> It started when Louise was nine. You must start watching what you eat, her mother would say. . . . The two of them would eat bare lunches, while her older brother ate sandwiches and potato chips, and then her mother would sit smoking while Louise eyed the bread box, the pantry, the refrigerator. Wasn't that good, her mother would say. In five years you'll be in high school and if you're fat the boys won't like you; they won't ask you out. Boys were as far away as five years, and she would go to her room and wait for nearly an hour until she knew her mother was no longer thinking of her, then she would creep into the kitchen and, listening to her mother talking on the telephone, or her footsteps upstairs, she would open the breadbox, the pantry, the jar of peanut butter. She would put the sandwich under her shirt and go outside or to the bathroom and eat it.

Louise eats, time passes—and we see how far back the roots of her secret passion reach. Such passages help Dubus develop his character quickly.

He does not, however, rely exclusively on summary. There are several scenes which draw us closer for greater intensity. When Carrie asks Louise to diet, for instance, we move out of a summary passage into a brief but effective scene. When, near the end of the story, Louise and her husband Richard argue about the weight she has put on, there is again a scene. Dubus's sense of selection here is infallible.

The compressed novel seems to be the ideal form for Dubus. It allows him to probe more deeply into the characters than a story limiting itself to the detached incident can, and it allows him to forge a dramatic narrative, something the shorter, "formless" stories do not do.

A few of Dubus's stories do not fit neatly into any of the three groups. For instance, **"Delivering,"** from *Finding a Girl in America,* focuses on a single incident—a woman's leaving her husband and sons—but Dubus uses flashbacks to fill in information about the characters' pasts. **"Andromache,"** from *Adultery & Other Choices,* is a circular narrative—we learn in the opening paragraph that the protagonist's husband has been killed in a plane wreck, then 7500 words later we return to virtually the same point—but it differs from **"In My Life"** and **"Townies"** in that, after delving into the past, the narrative moves back toward the fictional present in a basically straightforward fashion.

Dubus's reputation is deservedly growing: his most recent collection, **The Times Are Never So Bad,** received enthusiastic reviews in such publications as *Newsweek, Vanity Fair,* and *The New York Times Book Review.* Even those reviewers who have praised Dubus's work, though, while duly noting his ability to draw fully realized, complex characters, have tended to ignore the more technical aspects of his fiction. But it is precisely his mastery of narrative technique that enables him to convey his insight into character.

Steve Yarbrough, "Andre Dubus: From Detached Incident to Compressed Novel," in

---

Dubus on short story writers:

"Short story writers," insists Dubus, "simply do what human beings have always done." Like "good counselors who won't let you get by with the lack of honesty and commitment we bring to abstractions . . . short story writers simply do what human beings have always done. They write stories because they have to; because they cannot rest . . . because they are human, and all of us need to speak into the silence of mortality, to interrupt and ever so briefly stop the quiet flow, and with stories try to understand at least some of it."

Andre Dubus, as quoted by David Toolan, in "Harshness to Poetry, Poetry to Revelation," Commonweal, 22 November, 1991.

Critique: Studies in Modern Fiction, Vol. XXVIII, No. 1, Fall, 1986, pp. 19-27.

Joseph J. Feeney   (essay date 1986)

[*In the following excerpt, Feeney comments on the breadth of biographical, psychological, and social circumstances which have influenced Dubus's fiction.*]

Blurbs and pictures on the dustjackets of his books seem to tell it all. He looks like a teamster or a bearhunter: solid build, bushy beard, blue cap marked "Captain," jeans with a wide leather belt. He is a baseball addict, was a Marine for over five years, carries an axehandle in his car trunk and has a strong social conscience. He calls himself a "cradle-Catholic," often attends daily Mass, has been married three times and likes vodka with pepper grains. He gives salty interviews, writes careful prose, creates superb stories and shows unusual insight into women and boys in his fiction. He has been awarded Guggenheim and National Endowment for the Arts fellowships, dislikes James Joyce and has published stories in such places as *The New Yorker, The Paris Review, Harper's* and *The Sewanee Review.* He is admired by Joyce Carol Oates and John Updike, has almost a cult following and yet is not well known.

Yet a biographical sketch of Andre Dubus would not be complete without one more detail. On July 23, 1986, while being a Good Samaritan to a man and a woman who had been involved in an accident on Route 53 north of Boston, Mr. Dubus was himself seriously injured and spent his fiftieth birthday in Massachusetts General Hospital comforted by his wife Peggy and their daughter Cadence. Supported by his family, his friends and his faith, he is determined to continue his creative writing and not allow himself to be daunted by any physical disability.

Born in Louisiana on Aug. 11, 1936, and living now in blue-collar Haverhill, Mass., Andre Dubus (pronounced Duh-*beusse*) has sprinkled bits of his past in his novels, short stories and novellas. He writes about boyhood in small Louisiana cities, life in the Marine Corps (on an aircraft carrier, a Pacific island and West Coast bases), graduate school in Iowa, and college teaching, marriage, children and "Ronnie D's" bar in the Merrimack Valley near Haverhill. Out of this material he has already gotten nine books: first a novel, *The Lieutenant* (1967), then four books of stories, **Separate Flights** (1975), **Adultery & Other Choices** (1977), **Finding a Girl in America** (1980), and **The Times Are Never So Bad** (1983). Each of these collections included a novella—Dubus's best form. And these four novellas, interrelated by recurring characters, were published together in his sixth book, **We Don't Live Here Anymore** (1984). The same year brought Dubus's superb **Voices From the Moon,** a well-reviewed novel that views the same events from six different perspectives. In 1984, he also published, in limited edition, **Land Where My Fathers Died,** a thirty-seven-page detective story of multiple perspective that also appeared in the magazine *Antaeus.* Dubus's ninth book, **The Last Worthless Evening** (1986), is a collection of six short stories and novellas.

What does he write about? The best answer, I suppose, is

marriages—their relationships, tensions and adulteries—and families, especially the children. Dubus is a careful observer, and his perceptions of human feelings, attitudes and reactions are unusually acute. Furthermore, as an artist, he can communicate these perceptions through carefully invented characters, situations, events, dialogues and phrases. Take as an example this description of a thirty-six-year-old man visiting his young lover in **"Going Under"**: "In her purple sweater and pants she is lovely, and he presses his face into her shoulder, her hair, he is squeezing her and her heels lift from the floor, then he kisses her and breathes from deep in her throat the scorched smell of dope. He looks at her green eyes: they are glazed and she is smiling, but it is a smile someone hung there: Miranda is someplace else."

Dubus's fiction tells about the hope of love and the lack of love and the death of love. His characters wish terribly for lifelong love but, to their sadness, rarely find it; rather, in Dubus's fiction as in American society, all too many marriages and families fail. "All adultery is a symptom," he writes, and in his best work he examines the illnesses of American marriages and families and the underlying "failures of the human heart." In *Voices From the Moon,* he even describes a shattered family trying to formulate their own stumbling explanations for their pain and loss: "The trouble was love," or "It's divorce that did it," or "She had outlived love." In other stories and novellas certain characters are even able to foresee the collapse of love. In **"Separate Flights,"** Beth Harrison, who has long stopped loving her insurance-man husband, muses about her young daughter: "Now her seventeen-year-old, Peggy, was in love and she liked to talk about her plans, with this grownup tone in her voice, and there was nothing to do but listen to her, not as you listen to a child who wants to be a movie star, but to a child whose hope for friends or happiness is so strong yet futile that you know it will break her heart."

The divorced fathers, too, grieve for their lost marriages and wounded children. In **"The Winter Father,"** Peter Jackman remembers: "He and Norma had hurt each other deeply, and their bodies had absorbed the pain. . . . Now fleshless they could talk by phone, even with warmth, perhaps alive from the time when their bodies were at ease together. He thought of having a huge house where he could live with his family, seeing Norma only at meals, shared for the children, he and Norma talking to David and Kathi; their own talk would be on extension phones in their separate wings: they would discuss the children, and details of running the house. This was of course the way they had finally lived, without the separate wings, the phones. And one of their justifications as they talked of divorce was that the children would be harmed, growing up in a house with parents who did not love each other, who rarely touched, and then by accident. There had been moments near the end when, brushing against each other in the kitchen, one of them would say: Sorry." And, in a passage I find hard to forget, the same Peter Jackman, with rueful humor, epitomizes the awkwardness of the divorced father who has visitation-rights every Saturday: "He thought of owning a huge building to save divorced fathers. Free admission. A place of swimming pool, bad-minton and tennis courts, movie theaters, restaurants, soda fountains, batting cages, a zoo, an art gallery, a circus, aquarium, science museum, hundreds of restrooms, two always in sight, everything in the tender charge of women trained in first aid and Montessori, no uniforms, their only style warmth and cheer."

Dubus can also be harsh in his honesty. In the novella **"We Don't Live Here Anymore,"** the narrator, Jack Linhart, is having an affair with his best friend's wife, Edith Allison. As they are lying together, Jack recalls an evening when he and his wife Terry were with the Allisons and two other couples: "Once at a party Terry was in the kitchen with Edith and two other wives. They came out grinning at the husbands: their own, the others. They had all admitted to shotgun weddings. That was four years ago and now one couple is divorced, another has made a separate peace, fishing and hunting for him and pottery and college for her; and there are the Allisons and the Linharts. A deck-stacking example, but the only one I know." Then Edith tells him a truth about her husband, her daughter, and herself: "He needs us, Sharon and me, but he can't really love anyone, only his work, and the rest is surface."

"I don't believe that."

"I don't mean his friendship with you. Of course it's deep, he doesn't live with you, and best of all you're a man, you don't have those needs he can't be bothered with. He'd give you a kidney if you needed one."

"He'd give it to you too."

"Of course he would. But he wouldn't go to a marriage counselor."

It is with such harsh honesty, as well as with strong, sexually explicit language and a spare prose style, that Dubus avoids sentimentality. As a writer he has developed a distinctive voice: long clear sentences (usually compound), vivid detail for physical objects, accurate description of human emotions and reactions, and understated, smoothly flowing sentences at moments of intensity. His language is generally simple and direct, but for accuracy he is willing to use the unusual or formal word: "impuissant," "misogamist," "Faustian." Though he occasionally uses humor and irony, his voice is usually serious, emotionally powerful and simultaneously sympathetic to, but distant from, his characters. His narration is calm, his dialogue good, his words carefully chosen and edited. At his best, writes Joyce Carol Oates, Dubus creates novellas that are "triumphs of voice"—a voice of style that has the quality of "unhurried precision."

Even Dubus's metaphors, though original and effective, have a certain dispassion to them: "Like a cat with corpses, [my wife] brings me gifts I don't want"; "His marriage was falling slowly, like a feather"; "He feels they are not at a hearth but are huddled at a campfire in a dangerous forest." In one short story, **"The Pitcher,"** an unfaithful wife effectively uses the metaphor of her baseball-player husband as she tells him, "All summer I've been feeling like I was running alongside the players' bus waving at you. Then he came along."

Dubus often adds breadth and perspective by putting his

individuals or families in some larger social, literary or religious framework. Some characters come out of themselves by meeting friends at Timmy's Bar; others look to books or plants or records (classical by day, jazz at night). Dubus's Marines find models of bravery in Corps legends, especially the heroes of the Chosin Reservoir. Some characters worry about friends or brothers serving in Vietnam; others feel concern for the blacks in the South or the poor on the streets of New York City. Another man in *Voices From the Moon,* the owner of two ice-cream stores, has an effective social conscience: he "was good to his workers" and "did not keep them working so few hours a week that he could pay them under the minimum wage"; he was even "planning a way for all workers, above their salaries, to share in the profits, and was working on a four-day week for his daily and nightly managers, because he believed they should be with their young families." (This was a man who had fallen in love with his son's ex-wife. Dubus's moral universe is never a simple one.)

Dubus also broadens his fiction's scope by literary allusions. He quotes a passage from Conrad's *Heart of Darkness,* takes a title from St. Thomas More (*The Times Are Never So Bad*), and at various moments refers to, or echoes, such writers as Conrad (*Lord Jim*), Hopkins, Hemingway, Balzac, Tolstoy, Shakespeare, Kipling, Faulkner, Zola, Kate Chopin, Rhys, Colette, de Maupassant, even Joyce, as well as his great literary hero and teacher, Chekhov. For a writer who is at heart a realist, he makes surprisingly frequent use of Greek myth: one man, lying with his love in his arms, "kisses her until she warmly wakes and encircles him with her squeezing arms; he ascends; he is Prometheus; and he pauses in his passion to gently kiss her brightened eyes." Andromache, Oedipus and Icarus make their appearances, and in a celebration of fidelity Dubus uses Aphrodite, the Greek goddess of love and fertility, to comment on contemporary America. Musing about his friend Jack Linhart, who has stayed married despite mutual infidelities, Hank Allison thinks, "Jack is right. He's glad now they stuck it out. He and Terry. He said I've got a good friend who's also my wife and I've got two good children, and the three of them make the house a good nest, and I sit and look out the window at the parade going by: some of my students are marching and some of my buddies, men and women, and the drum majorette is Aphrodite . . . and she's leading that parade to some bad place. I don't think it's the Styx either. It's . . . some big open field with brown grass and not one tree, and nobody's going to say anything funny there. Nobody'll laugh. All you'll hear is pants and grunts. Maybe Aphrodite will laugh, I don't know. But I don't think she's that mean. . . . "

Far more than to society, literature, or mythology, though, Dubus looks to Catholic belief and practice to broaden the perspectives and expand the framework of his fiction. Sometimes it is an occasional "O Jesus" or "Dear Jesus"; sometimes his characters pray or go to Mass or talk about "Holy Saturday"; sometimes there is a religious allusion in a Dubus title—**"Contrition," "Bless Me, Father," "Sorrowful Mysteries."** Other characters wonder about God's absence, like the wife who had lost her own faith during college and, thinking about her husband, "did

not know whether Lee believed or not. She could not remember ever talking about God to him." There are priests and brothers in his stories, too, most of them good men and wise counselors. Many of Dubus's fictional boys go to Catholic schools (he, himself, attended a Christian Brothers' high school, where he wrote his first stories), and one young boy finds God through guilt: Having almost drowned a young cat, he "looked up into the rain at God." This does not stop the boy, though, from killing the cat the next morning.

As a moralist, Dubus values fidelity, truth, justice and innocence even as he vividly records the failures of marriage and family. His characters sometimes interpret their actions in terms of morality, and one or two of his people go through a process of moral reasoning in the pages of his stories (a dangerous practice for a storyteller, but Dubus keeps it under control). He will even try to redefine a moral term, to make clear that fidelity in marriage involves far more than sexual fidelity. This he does in **"The Pitcher,"** as a wife talks to her baseball-player husband: "It wasn't the road trips. It was when you were home: you weren't here. You weren't here, with me."

"I was here all day. . . . And all those times on the road I never went near a whorehouse."

"It's not the same."

Dubus also has a strong sense of the sacraments. His characters go to confession or to Mass—folk Masses, parish Masses, quiet weekday Masses. For one character, the Eucharist is a way to avoid loneliness, for another, a way to praise God, for a third, "The Eucharist is the sacrament of love and I needed it very badly those five years" during a bad marriage. And young Richie Stowe himself, in *Voices From the Moon,* wants to become a priest, even as, at book's end, he first experiences the appeal of the hair and arms and hand-touch of young Melissa Donnelly.

More originally, some characters manifest what might be called a "religious imagination," as they use some religious framework or story or phrase to interpret their own experiences or someone else's situation. One young white man from southern Louisiana reads of a black man, Sonny Broussard, who is to be executed for rape and sees his condemnation and death as parallel with Christ's. In another story a suburban housewife, though she has lost her faith, still "tried to pray. She wanted to fall in love with God. . . . Cleaning the house would be an act of forgiveness and patience under His warm eyes." One fifty-four-year-old father comes to love his daughter more in her weakness than in her strength, and realizes that here he resembles God, who loves us humans in our very weakness. And young Richie Stowe from *Voices,* almost thirteen and a daily Mass-goer, "felt always in God's eye," "knew God saw and loved those who suffered, yet still saw and loved him," and was certain that Christ had been in him when he finally forgave his parents for their divorce: "Everyone had to bear a Cross as Christ did. . . . Two years ago his mother moved out and then they were divorced and he [Richie] carried that one, got himself nailed to it, hung there in pain and the final despair and then released himself, commended his will and spirit to God, and something in him died—he did not know what—but afterward, like Christ on Easter, he rose again, could love his days again, and the people in them, and he forgave his parents, and himself too for having despaired of them."

These perspectives expand the world of Dubus's fiction and, together with his spare style, help to control the intensity of emotion and sentiment in his work. But, I should make clear, Dubus is not primarily a novelist of society or literary allusion or religion. His focus is always on his wounded people, with their complex lives and motives, their infidelities and violence and adulteries and "demons," and their unspoken hopes for forgiveness and goodness. Like Virgil, Dubus knows the *lachrymae rerum*—the tears evoked by human experience—and he unfailingly treats his characters with immense and deep compassion.

One more thing should be said: Andre Dubus is a careful artist and craftsman. He loves to write prose; he writes every day on a regular schedule, and lets his story "gestate for a long, long time." He never does an outline, and "usually begins with a 'what if.' An idea just comes to me." At that point he needs to know many details about his characters: "I make note of things that may never get into the story. I want to know if they believe in God; if so, do they belong to an organized religion? Ever since the Surgeon General's report on smoking I've thought it was important to know whether or not a character smoked, because it said something about a character . . . I make notes on the age, the family. The hardest part is to get the characters' employment. I have to find them a job, and then I have to find out something about the job." And when he is ready to write, he writes with great care. Once happy to produce one thousand words a day, he is now content with one hundred. Interestingly, he tapes all of his prose before completing it, testing his word-choice and sentence-rhythms by hearing as well as by seeing. Only then is he prepared to publish.

> Joseph J. Feeney, "Poised for Fame: Andre Dubus at Fifty," in America, Vol. 155, No. 14, November 15, 1986, pp. 296-99.

Andre Dubus with Patrick H. Samway   (interview date 1986)

[*In the following interview, which took place prior to his debilitating automobile accident, Dubus discusses literary and religious influences on his work.*]

[Samway]: *What authors or works of literature have influenced you?*

[Dubus]: Chekhov the most. I cut my teeth on Hemingway, not stylistically or thematically, but because I did a research paper on him as an undergraduate. I learned a lot about the craft, not so much from reading his work, but about his approaches to writing. He gave me advice: Do physical exercise after writing and forget what you have written; don't think about it; let your subconscious think about it; always stop when you're doing well; save the rest for the next day and stop in midsentence (I still do that). I've violated that rule twice in my career; I went

ahead and got too excited and I finished the scene of a story. And you know, you live another twelve lives before you get back to your desk the next day—with interruptions by your family, your friends, your enemies and your bills. By the time I get back to my desk the next day, I don't even remember the story. Those two mornings after I violated that rule, I just walked up and down in the den all morning trying to remember what was supposed to happen next and attempting to get it in the story. It's wonderful advice. So I learned about writing from Hemingway.

Chekhov is the one that taught me to look more deeply, with more compassion and compression. Marvelous writer. I was writing my second novel when I read his story "Peasants." I was writing a novel that wasn't any good—just a bunch of scenes that anybody can put together. Something like some bad John O'Hara. I read "Peasants" one afternoon after writing and I thought that was strange; Chekhov said he couldn't write a novel because he couldn't write narrative, but in this story he's covered in thirty pages an entire year and dealt with both one family and one peasant village—a microcosm of most of Russian society after the freedom of the serfs. Now how did he do that? Then I reread it and it's all scenes, almost. And I saw how he wrote thematic scenes and compressed them into thirty pages and dealt with peasants, religion, booze, the innocence of children and their future as peasants. I threw away those two or three chapters and said, "It's time to learn how to write!" I began trying to learn how to write. That was in 1968 and I have been trying that ever since. And every time I read something great by Chekhov, I think, "Well, I've got a long way to go," which is the reason I keep doing it, I guess.

What about some of the Southern authors?

Faulkner—big influence. When I was younger, my inner thoughts were in Faulknerian rhythms. I never read Faulkner while I wrote. I still don't read his works while I'm writing. Only a couple of people I know have noticed some Faulknerian rhythms in my fiction. Richard Yates is one of them. Faulkner wrote action so well. He could create movement that is also suspended at the same time—and it's not slow motion. It's as though you can see each moment of the motion, but the motion is still moving, as in "Barn Burning" when Ab Snopes throws the rug on Major de Spain's porch, and Sarty Snopes is on the mule, kicking the mule, and Ab reaches out and pulls his hand back. Faulkner's rhythms show all the speed of throwing the rug and the rug thumping and the lights going on in the house and people coming down and the boy's fearful heart and the mule starting to move out. Faulkner has not really stopped the action because there is still motion going on. Perhaps the best example is in "Pantaloon in Black" when Rider kills the cheating Birdsong, who goes for his revolver as Rider takes out the razor to kill him; you get each detail of the movement—the razor blade in his fist and then its unfolding as it slashes Birdsong's throat before the blood even spurts. It's beautiful! I never tried to imitate that. I know that's where my long sentences come from and the focus on detail when I'm writing some action. I have also been influenced by Gina Berriault and Nadine Gordimer.

What about Flannery O'Connor?

No, she frightens me. I don't read her much. I wish I had never read that quote of hers where she said that she writes about sacraments that nobody believes in. Every time I read her stories I look for the sacraments and get lost in the story. A friend of mind gave me good advice, but I can't take it; he said, "Forget what Flannery O'Connor said, just read her stories." But I can't. I'm always looking around for baptisms and Communions. I wish she had never said what she did. I don't know. I have a story, **"Miranda Over the Valley,"** which is full of Catholic symbols and allusions, and yet few have mentioned them in critiques of this story. On the other hand, I hoped nobody would because they were for me.

What about your own Catholicism? How important is that to you?

I think it pervades my writing, because for a long time I wrote about people who had no relationships with the deity since I was curious about living like that. But I have always been a Catholic. I think my Catholicism has increased my sense of fascination and my compassion. When I write about Catholics, I get very excited because there are a lot of ethical problems Catholics can get into.

For example?

Well, if a person is a real Catholic, almost anything is an ethical problem, and that person can either resort to the rules the person has been taught, such as the Ten Commandments, the Six Commandments of the church, or the person can move on to the New Testament and think about the ass being in the ditch. A Jesuit once said to me in high school: "You will never meet anybody who has committed a mortal sin. You have as much chance of doing that as you have of meeting someone who has committed a capital crime, because it is almost impossible to commit a mortal sin." Right? There has to be so much premeditation; you have to be as cold about it as a businessman or a hit man, and most people don't do that. That's why I think seven years is not a bad sentence for most murderers, because most murderers are one-time murderers who kill a friend or someone in the family and would never do it again. I think most of them say, "Oh, my God," when they realize what they have done. Aren't ninety percent of our murders committed among family and friends?

Would you identify yourself as a Catholic writer?

Yes, always have.

What does that mean in terms of your writing?

Well, I see the whole world as a Catholic, so I can't help but see my characters through the eyes of a Catholic. The story I just finished, **"Blessings"** [printed in Delta], has, I think, a lot of religion in it, including secular sacraments. But, like many American families, these characters are not churchgoing people. The family in **"Blessings"** went through a good deal; there are a lot of blessings in the story.

John Updike said about Joe Ritchie in **Voices From the Moon** *that the church still functions as a standard of measure. Do you agree with Updike's assessment?*

Yes, I do. I still think the main problem with the United States is that we lost God and we lost religion and we didn't replace God or religion with anything of value. It doesn't bother me if people (including my own children) don't have religion, as long as they replace it with a philosophy. We are raising my daughter Cadence as a Catholic. I like very much what the young priest said when he had all the parents of the children to be baptized over to the rectory the week before the baptism: "You are raising your child Catholic in the same way you are going to feed your child certain foods. It is good for the child, and at a certain age the child may say, 'I don't want this,' but you have to start it with a certain nutrition." Now if Cadence finds another philosophy later on, then I don't consider her religious training a failure. I don't consider her lost—a spiritual loss. This country hasn't found any philosophy except money—and selfishness. I find the United States a very nonspiritual country, and I think that is largely the problem. In fact, we might need an enforced agape for survival, and in this way maybe people will be good again. I've seen the whole of my fictive world through the eyes of someone who believes the main problem in the United States is that we have lost all spiritual values and not replaced them with anything that is comparable. We just pretend all this. We never have been a Christian country. As a matter of fact, there never has been a Christian country. Has there ever been a country that didn't kill its enemies, oppress the poor and bring the strong and the rich to power? Well, it saddens me and angers me. Maybe that's why I'm fascinated by the mystics, those who transcend all that drowns me. The mystics remain in harmony with the earth and their fellow human beings and, yet, are above it all as they enjoy union with God. It's like an opera! It's beautiful!

> *Andre Dubus and Patrick H. Samway, in an interview in* America, *Vol. 155, No. 14, November 15, 1986, pp. 300-01.*

Art Seidenbaum   (essay date 1986)

[*In the following review of* The Last Worthless Evening, *Seidenbaum asserts that Dubus's stories and novellas are detailed reflections of everyday life rather than purely fictional creations.*]

Andre Dubus seems to have absorbed life rather than created it. His people, whether aboard an aircraft carrier or bending elbows at Timmy's tavern, have individual voices and separate hopes and particular tragic memories, but they also have a generic quality in common. Humanity is the easy word, probably the right one.

Dubus' people are neither celebrities nor scoundrels. Sometimes victims of circumstance and occasionally heroes of circumstance, they are wrapped in a reality each of us can recognize because the conversations and the contexts are so right. This collection of six stories [*The Last Worthless Evening*], four of them long enough to be called novellas, has moments of violent death, almost all of them surprising exclamation marks in lives otherwise hardly punctuated.

"Molly" is about the discovery of sex but more about mother-daughter relationships and the odd costs of being an accepting parent. **"After the Game"** is about a baseball pitcher who became paralyzed on the mound but is more about a man being lonely—in another land and language. **"Land Where My Fathers Died"** is about an accident that looked like murder but more about family loyalty and even love. Family is a major theme moving the people in these stories—the delight from it, the dangers in it.

"Rose" is probably the most ambitious story because the title character is an unattractive, uncommunicative woman who hangs out in Timmy's as a "silent partner"—a regular who rarely speaks, part of the bar surface but not the surrounding conversations. Her story, when she finally tells it, is of being abused and exploited, of being humiliated until the lives of her children were at stake—and then how she lost her children even while trying to protect them.

While Dubus' fiction copies the life around him, it may have infused his own life. I was reading the galleys for this book in Boston, on vacation in a hotel room. I was also reading the Boston Globe for my daily dose of world and local calamity. **"Rose"** has a paragraph about human relations, each to each:

"If there is damnation, and a place for the damned, it must be a quiet place, where spirits turn away from each other and stand in solitude and gaze haplessly at eternity. For it must be crowded with the passive: those people whose presence in life was a paradox; for, while occupying space and moving through it and making sounds in it they were obviously present, while in truth they were not: they witnessed evil and lifted neither an arm nor a voice to stop it, as they witnessed joy and neither sang nor clapped their hands. But so often we understand them too easily, tolerate them too much: they have universality, so we forgive the man who watches injustice, a drowning, a murder, because he reminds us of ourselves, and we share with him the loyal bond of cowardice. . . . "

There was a story in the Globe one day about Dubus, how he had stopped at a violent roadside accident to help the victims, how his having stopped to be a good Samaritan—having refused to "stand in solitude"—caused another hideous accident. Dubus' leg was amputated. But he was pleased to be alive, to be able to continue his work.

He described himself in that story as a "minor writer." His own stories confute such public modesty. His fiction and his person are full of the goodness that men do.

Art Seidenbaum, in a review of "The Last Worthless Evening," in The Los Angeles Times Book Review, *November 23, 1986, p. 6.*

Ellen Lesser   (essay date 1987)

[*In the following review, Lesser observes that in* The Last Worthless Evening, *Dubus goes beyond the geographic and thematic boundaries that evolved in his previous fic-* tion *to explore wider social issues and that the length and pacing of a novella is uniquely suited to Dubus's style.*]

With an author's first or second book, reviewers talk about promise; with a third or fourth, they speak of delivering on it. With his eighth book of fiction, Andre Dubus joins that small group of writers beyond the vocabulary of promise or even delivery—the ones who have settled in and are going the distance. In his previous story and novella collections, and his one short novel, **Voices from the Moon,** Dubus has carved out a territory recognizably his own: geographically, the towns north of Boston along the Merrimack river; thematically, a moral landscape of adultery, divorce, sexual searching, colored by an inescapably Catholic perspective on guilt and sin. Some of the stories in **The Last Worthless Evening** are set in that familiar Massachusetts town, with its ubiquitous neighborhood bars, its leather factory and small local college. Yet this new volume represents a departure for Dubus. His reach is broader here, taking in subjects from race relations to child abuse, baseball to Vietnam veterans.

As a storyteller, Dubus is protean in his sympathies. In **"Land Where My Fathers Died,"** ostensibly a kind of detective novella, he uses shifting personae, moving with equal ease through the minds of the young Greek dishwasher who's walking home drunk on a freezing night and goes into an open office to find a dead doctor; the lawyer who runs marathons and sleeps with his college intern to silence the dissatisfied "little bastard" inside him; and the second generation Armenian high school girl who goes to the doctor for diet pills, and "wanted to be dead," she thinks she's "so fat and ugly." **"Molly,"** the longest of the book's four novellas, explores the friendship between a single mother and her daughter—getting at the story, again, through more than one point of view. Dubus traces Molly's initiation into sex and womanhood with such sensitivity and confidence that it's hard to imagine a woman writer doing it any better.

The collection's powerful final novella, **"Rose,"** unravels the story—told to the narrator at Timmy's, the bar where both he and Rose are regulars—of a family turned into a small hell by the father's violence. "I hate Jim Cormier," the narrator declares, "and cannot understand him; cannot with my imagination cross the distance between myself and him, enter his soul and know how it felt to live even five minutes of his life." And yet Dubus does go on to cross that distance, to bring the reader, for a few moments at least, inside the soul of the child beater, drinking beer and gazing "at the drying diapers, as if they were not cotton at all, but the whitest of white shades of the dead, come to haunt him, to assault him an inch at a time, a foot, until they won, surrounded him where he stood in some corner of the bedroom, the bathroom, in the last place in his home that was his. His *quercencia:* his cool or blood-smelling sand, the only spot in the bullring where he wanted to stand and defend, to lower his head and wait." You sense, on finishing **"Rose,"** that even the darkest corners of the spirit are open to Dubus.

Developing the complex history required for the impact of a story like **"Rose"** demands more leisure and breadth than much of today's highly compressed short fiction affords; it seems natural that Dubus has turned more and more to novellas. The form is ideally suited to his method—the unhurried, meticulous accretion of gesture, observation, reflection. By the time you reach the end of his 40 or 60 pages, the last line hits you with the accumulated heft most often associated with the close of a novel. But Dubus can still jump right in and knock you out with a much shorter story. In **"Dressed Like Summer Leaves,"** 11-year-old Mickey Dolan, on his way home from school in camouflage pants and T-shirt, passes by Timmy's bar just as a Vietnam vet Marine comes out for air and mistakes him for "Charlie." Mickey gets drawn into the bar and the haunted, volatile world of the veterans drinking there. By the time he escapes, shirt torn, to walk home "like a tattered soldier," he's seen and heard a good deal—in as tense and well wrought a 12 pages as I can remember.

In an age of quick-fix epiphanies, Dubus's style is unfashionably discursive. A treatise on Southern bigotry, or a digression on the nature of evil, might tempt the reader to say, "Shut up and get on with the story." But Dubus makes you want to listen. The man who retells Rose's story remarks, "We like to believe that in this last quarter of the century, we know and are untouched by everything." Andre Dubus knows a lot, and it has touched him deeply.

> *Ellen Lesser, "Going the Distance," in* The Village Voice, *Vol. XXXII, No. 3, January 20, 1987, pp. 50, 52.*

Andre Dubus with Thomas E. Kennedy (interview date 1987)

[*Kennedy is an American author, educator, and critic. The following excerpt is taken from an interview that was originally published in the February 1987 issue of* Delta *and is based on conversations and correspondence between Kennedy and Dubus during an eighteen-month period of time in the mid-1980s. Below, Dubus discusses his characters, his works, and the writing process.*]

[Kennedy]: *Contemporary American fiction seems to me to harbor two basic kinds of writer and critic: those who hold that fiction is about people and events, and those who hold that it is about language and perception and imagination. Writer-philosopher William H. Gass has said, "That novels should be made out of words and merely words, is shocking really. It is as though you had discovered that your wife were made of rubber." You, on the other hand, seem to care very much, even tenderly for your characters. Frederick Busch has said that your characters "are bent beneath a weight that Andre Dubus, one feels, would bear for them if he could—their utterly plausible and undefended humanness. . . . " Do you think of your characters, in a literal sense, as people?*

[Dubus]: Yes, I think of my characters in the literal sense as people. They make me cry when they do things I wish they hadn't done. I remember having Peter Jackman, in **"Going Under,"** in the shower for three days. I was worried about him. I wrote **"Adultery"** because Edith started getting my attention and saying, "Man you left me in a

slutty mess [at the end of **"We Don't Live Here Anymore"**]; how about coming back and seeing how I'm doing?" Yeah, I think of the characters as people.

Do your characters dictate their own actions (as E. M. Forster said his did on the famous Passage to India*), or are they galley slaves, as Nabokov claimed his were when asked this very question in* The Paris Review *some years ago?*

They dictate their own actions and, boy, sometimes I am really happy with what they do and, other times, as with Polly shooting Ray [**"The Pretty Girl"**], I am disappointed. If Nabokov's characters are galley slaves, I might understand why; while having flu in Iowa years ago, I was reading *Lolita*, getting a hard-on, then I got well, and never remembered to pick it up again. I do not think any good writer has characters who are galley slaves. I don't like Camus's fiction, although I admire the man deeply, and his essays, but to me, his characters are always acting out his philosophy. I can't read Sartre's fiction or plays for the same reason. I prefer the essays. I think most of the act of writing is intuitive. I think the act of good writing is intuitive, but it comes from a very conscious intellect. That might be a trick answer. I always find fiction taking turns that I have not forseen, and do not understand, but I feel to be inevitable and right. When that doesn't happen, the story dies. . . .

Sometimes I get the feeling your characters are victims of Frank Sinatra and Tony Bennett: In the thrall of cocktails and bluesy bar rooms and the guy or gal that got away.

Yes. A lot of the characters—that's a very good reading—are victims of the songs of the 40s and 50s. I think that music had a deleterious effect on a lot of us because it made many of us believe that marriage was not a beginning of a very difficult vocation, the most difficult one that we would undertake, but that it was in fact the happy ending, and that we would all dance happily through life and that those of us who lost a woman would indeed have drinks in the bluesy bar room and sing, "Set em up, Joe, I've got a little story you ought to know." . . .

Are the emotional problems of your characters caused by being in a confusing stage of social evolution where traditional marriage is breaking up faster than traditional bonding needs can evolve to the new social situation?

I think you're asking me to tell you that marriage is over, jealousy over, that all those feelings I have had since childhood have changed in the latter quarter of the twentieth century. I do not believe any of this. I see sexual love between two people who marry more as a deep and abiding friendship, a tolerant and forgiving friendship which also involves sharing each other's bodies. I believe the commitment to write and the commitment to love are so much alike. A friend of mine wrote to me after he read the manuscript of **"Finding a Girl in America,"** and he said, "Hank has finally learned that loving is as hard and takes as much discipline and working commitment as writing does." . . .

In my opinion, you write startlingly well from the point of view of a woman. I'm thinking of Edith in **"Adultery,"** *of Beth in* **"Separate Flights,"** *and of Miranda in* **"Miranda**

Over the Valley," to name three. To what do you attribute this ability? Is the jump from one heart to another of equal distance whether from man to man or man to woman?

Nadine Gordimer, in her introduction to her selected stories, deals with this entire problem by saying that all writers are androgynous, and I believe it. I am stunned—and I am not putting you down, my friend—at how often I am asked in interviews how I can write about women, when I meet women all the time who write well about men, and I think the real answer to your question is, as you say, the jump from one heart to another is of equal distance whether from man to man or man to woman. I think that is the answer. There is something universal in all of us. Some female characteristics I would not be able to write about without asking a woman, but I've spent a lot of time asking women, and I have always been interested in women. I have always enjoyed talking to women, I love women. If you are interested in a certain type of person, and you love the type of person, it is not that difficult to become them and write about them. I think I would have a lot easier time writing about a woman than I would, for instance, about a fictional Ronald Reagan. . . .

Do you think of yourself as an American, at home in the American culture, in the daily life surrounding you, or are you alienated from it, or from aspects of it? Do you have faith in the political and social patterns of America?

Yes, I am American at home in the American culture and in the daily life surrounding me. I am alienated from aspects of it, especially in the direction that American politics is going—that is, nationalizing and sanctifying greed, but calling it something else. I do not have faith in the political and social patterns of America. I see the country getting more and more greedy and I deeply believe that if the country is going to continue to be based on greed and selfishness, that it doesn't really deserve to survive, but of course the victims of this greed and selfishness deserve to survive so what do you do about that? You can't have a revolution. The government has all the guns, and besides, my scant knowledge of history tells me every time there is a revolution, the mother-fuckers who take over do the same thing. I am absolutely in favor of socialized medicine or some sort of national medical care. I don't think anyone should be afraid to get sick. I don't think the poor should have rotten teeth in their mouths. I don't think our friend's baby should have died in Maine because she couldn't afford medical care. I am in favor of people who work at a place jointly owning that place. I guess that's socialism. I like two views—Tolstoy's, if you have a culture based on Christian values where each person is trained to help the other, then you will still have murderers and rapists, but you will not *create* any. We certainly create them. And I like what Einstein said in an essay that our education is all wrong, we should not be taught to compete; we should be taught to work for the common good.

You write a lot of stories about murder and violence—"The Pretty Girl," "Killings," "The Shooting," "Townies," and in **The Times Are Never So Bad,** *you use a Flannery O'Connor epigraph about how violence strips the personality to what is eternal. Is this violence a reflection of American*

consciousness, of your own, of both, or more of an attempt to reach that eternal vision of the human personality?

I think it is mostly a reflection of American consciousness. I think if I lived in Canada or Denmark, I probably wouldn't write much violence. One of my son's girlfriends was mugged. My twenty-one-year-old daughter risked her life because a person was pointing a gun at the window of a teacher my daughter was going to visit. Someone else very close to me was raped. And I can't read the paper, even the local one, without coming across violence. I see this country as becoming a very violent country and I react to it. I do not think my own consciousness is violent. The eternal vision of the human personality: Well, Peggy read me that quote from Flannery O'Connor, and I stole it because it was wonderful for an epigraph and is probably true in some cases. I think my attitude about violence is expressed in **"Killings."** As in **"Man's Fate,"** the assassin comes back from stabbing this guy, and they are all talking about the wonderful new world they will have under communism, and he says, "What about me?" And you realize the act of killing has removed him from nature and the same thing with Matt Fowler in **"Killings."** Once he kills a human being, he has violated nature and is forever removed from it. . . .

For five and a half years, you were a captain in the Marine Corps—a warrior artist. How did that feel?

If you mean by warrior some berserk blood-stained guy enjoying killing people, I never had that feeling. If you mean a professional soldier, that is what I felt like. I didn't want a war. As a young man, I wanted to live an active life and keep that apart from my artistic life. But I resigned from the corps because my father died. Only later did I realize it was my father's death that gave me the freedom to resign. My respect for him and my need for respect from him were not greatly diminished by distance and by age. I do not think I would have had the courage while he was alive to explain to him that I was leaving a good and secure and honorable, in those days, profession, and was going to take a family of one wife and four children to Iowa City for an assistantship of $2,400 a year. . . .

Which of your contemporaries and which of the younger generation of writers do you read and find exceptionally good?

This is dangerous. I am bound to leave somebody out. there are so many. John Yount and Paula Fox, I think, are America's greatest living novelists. I think Gina Berriault is our greatest living short-story writer. I think Nadine Gordimer is internationally a great short-story writer and an equal of Gina Berriault. I like Tobias Wolff, I like Raymond Carver. I like the galleys of the first book of stories I just read by a woman named Sharon Sheehe Stark (*The Dealers Yard,* 1985; *The Wrestling Season,* 1986). I like Susan Dodd (*Old Wives' Tales,* 1984; *No Earthly Notion,* 1986). I do reread Chekhov. I like a book of stories by Nancy Huddleston Packer called *Small Moments,* published by the University of Illinois Press which published my old friend Mark Costello's *The Murphy Stories.* Contemporaries. Contemporaries. I like Thomas Williams, Mark Smith, I like Kate Chopin, though she is not a contemporary. I like Philip Caputo. Not only for nonfiction (*Rumor of War*) but his two novels. I once tried to convince Dick Yates to read Caputo's novels, and he said, "Well, I don't read novels by journalists." Well, I don't either, I have a prejudice, but I told him Caputo's not a journalist. I found an old quarterly that no longer exists, I was going through it one night to see who was in there with me and what became of them, and there was Philip Caputo. He had some poems there, and the biographical thing said he was going off to Spain to write a book of poems and stories called *A Rumor of War*. My hunch is he made the right move in making it autobiographical. I like very much his second two novels. I am also a fan of Joseph Wambaugh. A lot of people raise their eyebrows at that, but I think he's the only man who can tell us what it is really like to be a policeman in a large city, and in his first novel—he has the Watts riot from the point of view of the police, and it is wonderful. He does contrive, he is clumsy, but too many novels I read contrive and I think it is one of the built-in flaws of the novel. But he is honest and good. R. G. Vliet, a book called *Solitudes,* is one of the best American novels I have ever read. Nobody knows anything about it. Matter of fact, nobody knows anything about Paula Fox or Gina Berriault either.

Are you a voracious reader?

I guess. I don't read as much as I want. I find that during the baseball season I tend to either watch or listen to the Red Sox. That's 162 games. I don't think I miss more than ten a year. I also find that sometimes when I am writing intensely, I don't have the kind of energy it takes to do good reading at night, and I will then turn to detective fiction which I do not think is a minor form. It just takes less *literary* intensity to read.

Which of your own fictions do you feel most satisfied with? Do you regret any?

I guess I'm most satisfied with **"Adultery."** I don't know if it's the best, but it took four hundred typed pages, seven drafts, seventeen months of work spread over maybe two or three years. And I tried to put into there everything I knew about God, death, and women, and marriage. You ought to by now open a beer and say, "So why didn't you use the cover of a matchbook, asshole? Postage stamp?" But I am most satisfied with it, I guess, because it threw me off the saddle so many times and hurt me, and I kept giving up.

"Going Under" did the same thing to me. I kept quitting it. I feel very good about **"The Pretty Girl"** which wasn't even as hard to write, but it was very draining. I feel good about a story called **"Waiting,"** which came from a hundred-page novella which was no good, and the total time on that seven-page story was fourteen months. And I feel a certain satisfaction for a story called **"Delivering"** because on a Sunday afternoon, I was taking my daughter Nicole to her riding lessons, and I decided to do something I rarely do and that is make up a story. And I decided to write about a little boy and no more sensitive little boys like my autobiographical things, but a tough little boy—decided on the situation and the story was done, the first draft was done in five days, and it was just about complete.

Since *Voices from the Moon* is fairly recent, I feel good about that, but I even feel maybe better about something I was working on last January [1985] in Montpelier, a short novella of fifty-three pages called **"Rose,"** which I think took more chances than a lot of other things I've done. I do not think I regret any of them. Some of them I don't like anymore, but that's because I was younger when I wrote them and could have done them better, so I don't put them in collections. I don't even regret *The Lieutenant* having been published. If I wrote that now, it would be a *good* hundred-page novella, but as it is, it is a weak two-hundred page novel, but there are real people in it so I don't regret it. If I regret, I don't send it off. By the time I send it off, I know I have taken it as far as I can, and there is really nothing more I can do with it. My only regret would be if I had been lazy or copped out. . . .

How often do you write? And how much do you get done on a good day?

I write seven days a week when I am writing something. Not always. Things happen. Flu, colds. But that's my intention. Sometimes I intentionally take time off. Right now I'm working on a novella that I haven't worked on in over a week because I went to the University of Arkansas, but I was going to take a break from it anyway because I was starting to hate it, and the vacation has done me good. I'm ready to get back to it. A good day to me doesn't depend on the number of words, but on how well they got written. Many days if I get a hundred words I'll say that's fine. Other days I suddenly get two thousand. I probably average three to five hundred.

Each morning I start by reading the last page I've written which has been interrupted in half sentence, half scene, and I look at the words in the margin. They tell me where the scene is going, at least where it was going the day before; then I read from the beginning making small changes, but mostly I read from the beginning to get into the story. It is damn near impossible for me to just pick up where I left off because so much has happened from the time that I left off until the time that I have picked up again: dealing with the builder, the house, the phone, the child, hunting, having fun, drinking, who knows? When I write a novella, I only read the section that I am working on or else it would take two hours to finally get back to work. Then, when I finish that first draft in long hand, I tape it, and I listen back, and I think the taping is very valuable because as you can see, by then I have read much of the story or novella, some passages, hundreds of times. Reading them aloud makes me concentrate more, and then listening back points out very quickly to me repetitions, lines of dialogue that I don't need, rhythms that I should work on, and then with luck, I type the final draft. . . .

I've heard various descriptions of the process of writing. Some say it is like feeling your way through a dark room, others like viewing a landscape in lightning. Hemingway, I believe, said that sometimes it is like drilling for oil, other times like mining coal. Strunk and White say it is "a question of learning to make occasional wing shots, bringing down the bird of thought as it flashes by." What is it for you? Meditation, inspiration, mining, drilling, trial and error?

First, I would like to add a quote by Updike that I like very much. He said it was like driving at night. You can only see as far as your headlights are showing you, but if you keep driving you'll get there. For me, it is less inspiration or meditation than trying to see what you are trying to write, working very hard, trying to find the words and the rhythm to go with it. . . .

What is the objective of fiction? What is fiction's highest aim and greatest accomplishment?

I think the first objective of fiction is to give pleasure. That can be the kind of pleasure that makes the reader continue to turn the page, to want to find out what is going to happen. There are other forms of pleasure. There is the pleasure of insight, there is the pleasure of good company. I think that is the first objective. And without achieving that you can't get the rest. I think the next objective is through the pleasure to draw the reader out of himself or herself and take that reader into a search where both of you go in without knowing the answer. Look for some questions, watch some people dramatize the questions, live with those people and see if you and the reader can come up with an insight into the truth. That insight might be that there is no answer [chuckles], that insight might be terrible. So it is pleasurable, musical, enjoyable on a high level, and also sometimes on a level more prone to titillation, and in the process of this dance, we confront the difficulties of life and we try to understand, we confront mortality, we try to live other lives, to leap into the heart of another and understand.

> *Andre Dubus with Thomas E. Kennedy, in Kennedy's* Andre Dubus: A Study of the Short Fiction, *Twayne Publishers, 1988, 176 p.*

Thomas E. Kennedy   (essay date 1987)

[*Kennedy is an American author and critic whose* Andre Dubus: A Study of the Short Fiction *was published in 1988. In the following essay, he traces theme and style in Dubus's works.*]

The fiction of Andre Dubus began to appear in the 1960s, a decade whose leading new writers were anything but realists. To the sixties, the very concept of an objective, comprehensible reality was suspect, a house of lies hammered together of truisms, party promises, and straight-faced socio-political lunacies, a place as contrived as the linear fiction so many of the decade's writers sought to escape.

Overloaded perhaps with the quotidian gore of foreign war and domestic strife being spewed forth daily by the media, many American fiction writers began to retreat to more purely imaginative realms, testing, pushing at the accepted technical limits of their craft. The decade was invaded by the variety of Latin American magical realism and *ficciones,* the Barthelme jump-cut, the Cooverian replay series with variations, the Hawkes time shuffle, the Burroughs page shuffle, the Barthian anti-illusionist illusion. It was a decade whose best-selling novels depicted American society as a madhouse run by a madwoman or kinked by a catch clause, whose heroes were a wild nihilistic Gingerman, an epic Onanist, a computer-assisted goatboy; a decade when William H. Gass pronounced absurd the views of fiction "as actually creative of living creatures"; a decade whose novels took the form of psychoanalytic rants climaxing in lengthy primal screams, of cold-blooded facts fleshed into bloody fiction that followed real-life killers to the gallows, of subjectivized journalism parading as instant historical novel; when even an established realist like Malamud was fictioning birds that talked and artists that debated with the devil over the form and content of a hole in the ground. In the years to follow, a "new fiction" and a "superfiction" would be proclaimed which, in retrospect, seem less "new" than reactionary, in a non-pejorative sense of the word—a rejection of the form which had evolved in the immediate past century to hearken back to techniques closer to those of subjective-romantics such as Hawthorne or Poe or to the absurdist strategies of Gogol or the earlier experiments of Sterne. The story of manners—developed to fine subtleties and nuances by Flaubert, Chekhov, and James, who used the intricacies of human behavior as metaphor for the drift of movement of the spirit, making their abstractions from the mystery in which human beings daily live—was largely rejected as insufficient to deal with the immediate political pressures seen to be stifling the spirit of humanism.

And people just plain wanted something *new.* They wanted out of the realm of logic, linearity, cause and effect, and into the world of the imaginative literalist, where meanings deeper than logic dwelt.

Into this environment came Andre Dubus, ex-Marine Corps Captain, pursuing a master of fine arts degree in the mecca of American university writing programs, his hair unruffled by the burgeoning wave of post-modernism. While writers like Barth, Barthelme, and Coover set about the quest for a new, perhaps more complex grasp of reality, an overview, Dubus set quietly, indefatigably forth in his fictional exploration of what human beings do to one another in the pursuit of love—not overview, but close-up. From the start of his literary career, Dubus has written about the world, the real world in its own terms through a strategy of literal verisimilitude. His stories fulfill Goethe's two-century-old definition of the story as concerning itself with an event which might really have happened though it went unreported.

John Updike has said that Dubus beat the neo-realists to it by twenty years, but Dubus's fiction is neither "K-mart realism" nor "hick chic;" there is a kind of lush spiritual core to his work which seems not present in the work of so-called minimalists like Carver.

Perhaps the most lucid keynote of Dubus's work is found in his **"If They Knew Yvonne,"** published in 1969 and selected by Martha Foley as one of the year's *Best American Short Stories.* The story follows the struggle of a young Catholic to find his way out of the *via negativa* into which he has been thrust by the Brothers and back into the word with his Faith intact; the journey finds its completion in a line from St. John, in which Christ prays to the Father,

"I do not ask that You keep them out of the world, but that You keep them from evil."

This is a problem central to the fiction of Dubus. How to live out one's part in a material world with spirit intact, if not unscathed by evil? How to negotiate the *via affirmativa* of human society without being spiritually poisoned by it. How to live well, to *grow* well.

Unlike, say, Barth, Dubus leaves the process of solving his technical writing problems on his desk; the only problems addressed by his stories are directly human, moral ones. The world of Dubus's fiction is one in which the word *sin* again becomes valid, for it is a world in which men and women are responsible for their actions—and their *inaction* (**"The Pretty Girl"**), capable of wrong and perhaps also, therefore, of *right,* capable at least of seeking to avoid evil, at the very least of regretting the evil for which they are responsible and, in their commitment to this, of approaching love, communion with the God who gave to men the new command: to love one another.

In an age obsessed by sexuality, the complex reality which we lump under the word love seems largely to have been relegated by contemporary culture to soap opera, song lyrics, and growth psychology. Much of the fiction of human relationships—Roth, Fowles, even Updike—seems to focus more on the physical and passionate hungers concerned with the individual's relation to himself and his own personal survival and freedom than with the further reaches of communion embodied in the concept of love. Perhaps this is due to despair of finding a grasp of the concept at once functional and profound; perhaps to fear of venturing from the outposts of cynicism to which contemporary western man has been delivered; perhaps to the absence of an objective spiritual frame of reference capable of housing it. Dubus doffs the armor of cynicism for an examination of the vulnerable spirit.

In the fiction of Andre Dubus, love is treated in a direct, unashamed way, devoid of cynicism or dark laughter. It is as natural and sustaining an element as air or water. Without it, the spirit shrivels, demons of madness are unleashed (**"Going Under"**), priests lose contact with their Faith (**"Adultery"**), mothers and fathers lose contact with one another (**"Separate Flights," "Molly"**), and with their children (*Rose*). With it, Dubus's characters know pain, but also come to understand both the distance from and closeness to the beloved and to experience sacramental moments of communion, "the sad and joyful longing of love the saints feel for God" (**"Deaths at Sea"**). Yet even love, even a love of pure motive, has consequences and effects which are ambiguous, which exact a price of the purity at the core of the individual human heart. Thus, the father who covers up his daughter's hit-and-run crime in **"A Father's Story"** must admit to himself, "I love her more than I love truth," and it is a hard moment for him—one whose consequences touch the remainder of his life.

As the body of Dubus's work grows to reveal its greater patterns, his treatment of human love becomes even more clearly a spiritual direction away from the hunger concerned with the individual's relation to himself toward those further reaches of communion.

The hunger of Dubus's characters to transcend the solitude bounded by their flesh is where their progress toward the communion of love begins. Examples of this theme can be found in every one of Dubus's nine books of fiction.

Perhaps nowhere in his work is that progress more completely rendered than in the three novellas on which this essay focuses: the first about a marriage which devolves from passion to pity; the second about an act of adultery purer than the marriage it degrades; the third about abortion and responsibility.

The major focus of all three is on two couples: Hank and Edith, Jack and Terry. Hank is a writer, Jack a teacher. They are friends, colleagues. They run together, drink together, and wind up sleeping with each other's wife. Both marriages were a result of unplanned, youthful pregnancies prior to the liberalization of abortion.

While each of the novellas stands alone, the three together are a distinct entity whose central character proves to be Hank; it is finally in Hank's consciousness, in the third novella, that the deepest vision of what happens to the two couples comes to bloom, though this final vision would not achieve its fullest impact without the preliminary visions presented in the first and second novella via Jack/Terry and Edith/Joe Ritchie, respectively. Hank's presence is central to all three, even where he is off stage, but in the third, all of the characters' experience culminates in his liberation from cynicism.

The first of the three novellas, **"We Don't Live Here Anymore,"** (collected in *Separate Flights,* 1975, and in *We Don't Live Here Anymore,* 1984), is told in the first-person voice of Jack Linhart, who is "surrounded by painful marriages that no one understands. But Hank understands his, and I think for him it has never been painful, the pain was Edith's." (Hank's pain is to await another death, in the third.)

Jack is Edith's lover. She sought him out because she was hurt that Hank had cheated on her with a French exchange student. Jack feels cheated by marriage itself; his wife is a sloppy housekeeper and has a violent temper, and he no longer desires her. He regrets the passing of his youth, yearns to fall in love, get drunk, have a fight in a bar. The first optimism of his love affair with Edith has him think, "I will love them both," wife and mistress, but clearly his conscience (or as Terry puts it, "his cold, guilty face") will not permit this duplicity for long.

Interestingly, Jack is less honest with his wife, on the surface, than Hank is with his. He keeps secret his affair until he can maneuver Terry into an affair of her own, denying her suspicions until they are both in the same boat of guilt—and even then he waits a while. Hank, when confronted with Edith's direct question of whether he is having an affair with "that phony French bitch," answers simply: *Yes.* When she begins to question him about it and about what it means, he warns her that she had better be as tough as her questions because he intends to start answering them. Jack, on the other hand, sculpts his conversations with his wife, selecting details to avoid problems and realizes that he has "lost all dedication to honesty." Likewise, making love to Terry, he thinks of Edith, then immediately projects the dishonesty into her mind and suffers the resultant isolation in the midst of intimacy. Edith, too, looks at Hank and thinks of Jack and concludes to herself that "it is all lies now." Jack yearns for romantic love, but disdains marriage, feels trapped. Coming home at the end of the day seems like a journey to "some nebulous goal that began as love, changed through marriage to . . . respectable survival . . . " A happy marriage seems to him as unlikely as "a happy tiger in a zoo." If Jack is trapped in his marriage, Hank uses his as a place to relax from his adventures: " . . . he moved out from it on azimuths of madness and when he was tired he came back. While Edith held to the center she had been hurt . . . Now she had a separate life too and she came home and they sat in the kitchen with their secrets that were keeping them alive . . . "

At one point, Jack worries whether Hank knows about him and Edith, but experiences an insight into Hank's thoughts—that he knows and doesn't care: "Edith can't touch me and you can't either, what matters here is what matters to me." Hank displays his cynicism as a virtue: "It doesn't even matter if you love (your wife)," he tells Jack. "You're married. What matters is not to hate each other, and to keep peace . . . You live with a wife, around a wife, not through her . . . "

Jack's discontented yearning and Hank's contented cynicism seem equally expressions of hungers to satisfy the self.

Of the four adults in the first novella, Terry alone identifies the essence of the longer progress they have set out upon. Towards the end, she comes home depressed from an evening of "sordid, drunken adultery" with Hank and accuses Jack of hating her. He denies it; she demands:

> "How would you know if you hate me? You don't even know me. You say, 'You are what you do.' But do you really believe that? Does that mean I'm a cook, an errand runner, a fucker, a bed maker . . . a Goddamn *cleaning* woman . . . You just love someone who looks like me . . . you love the tricks . . . the fucking and spaghetti sauce . . . "

Only at that point does Jack come out with the truth. His response to this incisive clarification of what is wrong? He says, "I love Edith." Terry is angry, hurt, confused, but determines to be loyal to her love for Jack, to serve it with herself—ideas that we see verbalized in the second novella, where Joe Ritchie defines love as "a series of gestures of escalating and enduring commitment." Alone of all four characters in the first novella, Terry takes on this commitment to another person.

Finally, Jack does not leave her. He stays, out of pity. By now everything is out in the open. Jack feels awkward knowing that Hank knows, but Hank—who has completed a new book during the time Jack and his wife were having their affair, says, "I ought to dedicate my novel to you . . . You helped get it done. It's so much easier to live with a woman who feels loved." Again, Hank's cool distance, Jack's guilty conscience: selfish motivations from opposite poles of the ego.

The novella closes with a scene of Jack and Terry's now passionless life together—she loves, he does not—while Hank takes up with a nineteen-year-old girl, and Edith has an affair with another man. The ending seems one of rather grim acceptance; there *is* something pitiful in Terry's determination to win back Jack's love and something depressing in Jack's fatalistic acceptance of his life with her. Yet what is the alternative picture? Hank and Edith's impending dissolution; Hank's cynicism; Edith's desperation. The story is finished, but not yet complete.

In the second novella, **"Adultery"** (collected in ***Adultery and Other Choices,*** 1977, and in ***We Don't Live Here Anymore***), Hank and Edith begin not only to experience the consequences of the passions for which they have taken down the walls of inhibition, but also to learn of a wiser love, the mystery which occurs—as Edith's lover, Father Joe Ritchie, puts it—with "the leap the heart of man takes toward the heart of God"—or towards the heart of another human being, "the series of gestures with escalating and enduring commitment" which is Ritchie's definition of love.

The adultery in this book is not that of Edith's affair with the fallen-away priest, but the general adulteration of her marriage, of the love between her and Hank who have ceased to be Miltonian "fit, conversing mates." Father Ritchie does not experience his love for Edith as a sin; he only fears it might be a sin as long as she is still involved in her poisoned marriage; were she to leave Hank and marry him, the priest would feel at peace with God again.

In this novella, Dubus follows the direction of Edith's spirit—her disconnection from the daily tasks of her life which she began to experience when she learned of Hank's infidelity—his *philosophy* of infidelity—and "she could no longer find his heart . . . Watching him talk she saw his life: with his work he created his own harmony, and then he used the people he loved to relax with. Probably it was not exploitative. Probably it was the best he could do . . . Death stalked her now—as though let in by the breach opened by Hank's adulterous heart."

Death. Both love of God and love of man or woman in Dubus's fiction are necessitated finally by the awareness of death. Without love, that awareness is unbearable, life a dimension stalked by demons. With love—with the act of love and the commitment of love—"our bodies aren't just meat . . . they become statement, too, they become spirit," as Father Ritchie expresses it. In "the leap of the heart to God," heart to heart, a transubstantiation takes place which lets us transcend our isolation and brings us to terms with time and mortality—the quotidian agonies with which conscious man must live.

This, finally, is what Edith learns in the second novella. Finally she is able to release herself from Hank, from their marital charade. After she leaves Joe Ritchie at the hospital, dying of cancer, she comes home to bed; Hank reaches for her, but she resists him. He tries to insist, to override her grief with his passion, and she tells him that they are all dying—not only Joe, but Hank and herself, too, and that that is what they had lost sight of. She gets out of bed, then, and returns to the hospital to sit by Joe's bed, waiting for him to wake once more so she can tell him that she will leave Hank, for she wants him to know that their love has given her that strength.

In **"Finding a Girl in America"** (published in the collection of the same title in 1980 and in *We Don't Live Here Anymore*), the irony at last is that an unwanted pregnancy in the first novella trapped Hank prematurely into a marriage from which he sheltered his ego with cynicism, while here an unwanted abortion, more than a decade later, visits him with pain that flays the last hide of cynicism from his spirit, leaving him in torment. This time he is alone. Edith, having re-experienced love with Joe Ritchie, has become strong enough to leave Hank, to dissolve the adulterated marriage—the point at which **"Adultery"** ended. Now, alone, Hank is taking up with one young girl after another, each of whom leaves him after a year or so. Deprived of the grounding of his marriage and homelife, he is hurt and vulnerable. From his latest girl, Lori, he learns that the one before her, Monica, had been pregnant by him and had an abortion without ever having let him know. Hank rages, weeps, falls asleep to dream about the dead fetus being boiled to death on the beach while he lays alongside his daughter in the sunshine.

Throughout the remainder of this third novella, Hank is haunted by the dream, and his potency deserts him before that image of the dead, boiled fetus on the beach. The image recurs in his brain and is suggested in the landscape: a stranded lump of kelp—viewed out of the window of a restaurant where he sits enjoying the sight of his daughter nourishing herself on beefsteak—becomes a dark suggestion. Finally, Hank realizes that he is no longer capable of, no longer desires an act of copulation which is not fully motivated by the will to take full responsibility for its consequences. Here we follow Hank's progress to the ultimate comprehension which he has been equipped to reach only by Edith's having cut him loose from his cynical mooring to his home. There is an interesting parallel between Joe Ritchie in **"Adultery"** and Hank in **"Finding a Girl in America"**: both hunger to expose their souls, the priest in his sermons, Hank in his writing. The priest finally recognizes his hunger for what it is: the loneliness at his core focusing outward: "He realized now that beneath his sermons, even possibly at the source of them, was an abiding desire to expose his soul with all his strengths and virtues and weaknesses to another human being . . . a woman."

Similarly, in the third novella, Hank at one point cannot understand why a woman he is involved with does not express an interest in reading his fiction; he feels her lack of interest as a lack of interest in that which is best in him, his reality. Both these yearnings are expressions of the hungering ego seeking to transcend itself: Joe Ritchie's hunger leads him from celibacy to the love of another human being; Hank's, in the last of the novellas, also finally turns his thoughts away from himself. His hurt at the woman's indifference to that deepest part of himself inspires him to grieve for Edith, for what she had suffered when she was with him: "the loneliness of not being fully known." Grieving here for another's pain of loneliness, Hank has come a long way from the man of the first novella who could chuckle that he was freed to complete his

novel because his best friend had abated Edith's loneliness for him, made her feel loved.

Finally, this is a Hank who has learned to suffer—and more importantly to empathize with the suffering of others—not that there is virtue in suffering, but that, as the novella's Saint Exupery epigraph suggests, "Sorrow is one of the vibrations that prove the fact of living," and to be indifferent to the sorrow of others is to choose the solitude from which our unimpeachable passions hunger to be free.

Joyce Carol Oates on Dubus's characters:

Andre Dubus's fiction is perhaps an acquired taste, for his characters are resolutely ungiving and uncharming. Most of them drink beer in vast quantities and contend with periodic hangovers; all of them are addicted to one thing or another, which Mr. Dubus examines with an extraordinary sympathy—drinking, smoking, black coffee, Quaaludes. When their various addictions fail they tend to think, like Ray [in **"The Pretty Girl"**], "it's time to do some more terrorizing." In the main, however, their addictions comfort them and give them reasons to keep on living. Where another writer might dramatize his characters' plights in order to reveal and exorcise their strategies of delusion, Mr. Dubus has other intentions. Like the hard-drinking protagonist of **"The Captain,"** who has survived an unspeakably grueling experience in the war, he has learned "of how often memory lies, and how often the lies are good ones."

Joyce Carol Oates, in her "People to Whom Things Happen," in The New York Times Book Review, *June 26, 1983.*

This Hank is tormented by an abortion and in love with a nineteen-year-old girl who is trying to learn how to live well and to avoid the promiscuity and cynicism about love she feels her sisters are developing. Hank now sees his own daughter growing up. He sees the promiscuity of the young as a drain on their possibilities, as trapping them into temporary episodes of loveless monogamy which limit their experiences of friendship with others in a way far worse than his generation had been trapped by the unwanted or perhaps merely untimed pregnancies. He sees that Jack and Terry's marriage has outlasted Jack's restless desires and begun to thrive again, has grown to a family, that Jack now cherishes Terry as a friend.

Here, then, finally, at the end of **"Finding a Girl in America,"** Hank sees the end place of the egoistic desire which has characterized him through the first two novellas, and that place is "death and solitude." Love without responsibility is love without communion. It ends in death and solitude. He has transversed the maze of hunger and come to its belly, a place where the freedom reached is "the wrong freedom"—a freedom from human company, entry to solipsism.

The freedom that these four characters began to grope toward in the first novella—primarily Jack and Hank, whose egos needed it most, but also Edith and Terry, for whom perhaps the progress is more clarification of what they already know than development—was a freedom from the self, a freedom sought in desire and passion and achieved finally, as best it can be, by recognizing the consequences of the solipsistic yearning upon one another, and themselves, a point at which the envelope of human solitude opens to the possibility of human communion.

Thomas E. Kennedy, "The Progress From Hunger to Love: Three Novellas by Andre Dubus," in The Hollins Critic, *Vol. XXIV, No. 1, February, 1987, pp. 2-9.*

Eva Hoffman   (essay date 1988)

[*In the following review of* Selected Stories, *Hoffman suggests that in Dubus's fictional explorations of love and its corruption, everyday objects, circumstances, and relationships transcend the ordinary.*]

Emotional veracity is surely one of the most elusive elements in fiction. Just how do we decide that we trust a writer's voice? The sound of authentic feeling is different for each writer, and it cannot be easily parsed; and yet it is what determines whether we decide to put ourselves in an author's hands, or to balk at even the most brilliant insights or the most touching incidents or the most unexceptionable views. Andre Dubus is a writer whose work depends almost entirely on the persuasiveness of that sound. He consistently forgoes cleverness, formal rigor and any number of special effects. His note is a fragile one, and is sometimes too closely adjacent to the sentimental. And yet, when he hits it right, the cadences of that unverifiable but convincing truthfulness give his writing a simple and surprising power.

Mr. Dubus, who lives in Haverhill, Mass., is the author of a novel and six previous books of short fiction. He has been a quietly appreciated literary presence for over 20 years; his *Selected Stories* (most published elsewhere between 1975 and 1988) reminds us how much of a specific, unmistakable place he has come to carve out and occupy. Geographically, the fictional Dubus country is situated north of Boston, in the rural hamlets and unpresumptuous small towns of the Merrimack Valley. Spiritually, it is a place distinguished by its unvarnished and illuminated ordinariness.

We are accustomed, in today's fiction, to characters who are wretched, or disconnected, or down and out. But Mr. Dubus's people don't even have the glamour of poverty, or neurotic despair, or ennobling restlessness. Their occupations are of the near-invisible sort: they own ice-cream parlors or work as bartenders or waitresses, or are college students of the middling kind or college teachers of undefined tenure status. There tends to be something pre-postmodern in their indifference to worldly success, in their resistance to clocks and office regimen and schedules. ("She regarded [the clock] as . . . a conscience run on electricity," it is said of the protagonist in **"The Pretty Girl,"** "and she was delighted, knowing that people had once lived in accord with the sun and weather, and that punctuality and times for work and food and not-work and sleep were later imposed upon them, as she felt now they were imposed upon her.") What matters to them most are not the temp-

tations of upward mobility, but their dilemmas as wives and husbands and fathers and lovers.

It is in these usually hidden lives that Mr. Dubus finds his material—and his drama. For despite the unprepossessing privacy of his characters, a typical Dubus tale usually turns on, or builds toward, a highly dramatic, often violent situation: a father who vows revenge for his son's death and who achieves it, in its ambiguous sweetness, through murder (**"Killings"**); a young woman who has been raped by her husband and who is driven, eventually, to pull the trigger on him (**"The Pretty Girl"**); a woman who is having an affair with a former priest and who decides, as she prepares for his death from cancer, to end her open and false marriage (**"Adultery"**).

But the immediate interest of these short stories and novellas resides not so much in the explosive premises and the detonating endings as in the concrete, sensuous detail, in the patient stitching of modest observation. Nothing is too humble for Mr. Dubus to notice, and his even, unjudging tone pays no heed to pretension, or to knowing snideness. People in these stories flip pancakes and dress in parkas in the morning, pour bourbon and worry about what young people are doing to themselves with drugs, and proffer and accept signs of affection without the benefit of irony or self-irony, or even self-consciousness.

Lacking stylishness or skepticism, or sharp wit, Mr. Dubus's people are endowed with a forbearing acceptance that comes close to both passivity and a kind of knowledge. They are allowed to live out their natures, and their fates. The protagonist of **"The Fat Girl"** lets herself, after a long interval of heroic thinness, go to fat again with a triumphant luxuriance, as if fat were her destiny. Others move along the trajectory of their longings toward grief or love or moments of vision with a hypnotic and unconflicted certainty.

Especially toward love. Now that one has an overview of two decades of his work, it is evident that love is at the center of Mr. Dubus's fictional morality, its presence the greatest virtue, its corruption the only sin.

The word "sin" is pertinent, for many of the characters in these stories are active Roman Catholics, and their belief in the redemptive powers of human love derives directly from their religious faith. In **"Voices From the Moon,"** a priest has this to say to a 12-year-old boy who is trying to reconcile himself to the frightening discovery that his father is about to marry his older brother's former wife: "Think of love. They are two people who love each other, and as painful as it is for others, and even if it *is* wrong, it's still love, and that is always near the grace of God."

To speak about matters of sentiment with such unadorned forthrightness is to take considerable risks, and in its reaches of sympathy, as well as in its resolute plainness, Mr. Dubus's fiction has a certain daring. His range of characters is wide: young marines in basic training facing the first test of their endurance, and middle-aged family men who want to test themselves no more; young women trying to decipher their own hearts, and mothers who know the futility of trying to convey what they know to their sons. His protagonists are divided nearly equally between men and women, and despite the almost defiantly traditional views voiced in these stories on the matter of gender ("it was womanhood they were entering, the deep forest of it, and no matter how many women and men too are saying these days that there is little difference between us, the truth is that men find their way into that forest only on clearly marked trails, while women move about in it like birds"), Mr. Dubus has the courage to imagine women from within their subjectivity, and to do so with considerable understanding. He is not afraid to be utterly serious in his accounts of jealousy, or the pain of divorce, or filial attachment. He makes us feel the full force of family passions.

He is particularly fascinated by the love between fathers and daughters, and there are several such bonds in these stories which are almost disturbing in their intensity. In **"A Father's Story,"** one of the most forceful and disconcerting tales in this collection, a father chooses to save his daughter by covering up her crime, and possibly colluding in the death of a young man she accidentally ran over. A believing Roman Catholic, toward the end of the story he confronts his God. "I could bear the pain of watching and knowing my sons' pain, could bear it with pride as they took the whip and nails. But You never had a daughter and, if You had, You could not have borne her passion."

"A Father's Story" has enough momentum and sheer fervor to stay this side of pathos; but Mr. Dubus does not always avoid the melodrama that is the natural defect of his virtues. The thin line he walks becomes particularly tricky when he is negotiating questions of sexuality. The sensibility of these stories is warmly physical and erotic, but he relies too much on scenes of people engaged in tender congress. He is too preoccupied with virginity. Sometimes he substitutes a conventional response for the more strenuous work of the imagination. In **"Rose,"** a story about child abuse, the episodes are horrendous, but the language of suffering is almost entirely and conventionally pathetic. Indeed, too often in these stories there is a disjunction between the extremity of the situations and the persistently compassionate tone; it is as if instead of confronting the sometimes troubling conundrums he sets up (is it really all right to murder your son's murderer?), Mr. Dubus prefers to let them dissolve in the amniotic fluid of his empathy.

But in his more effective stories—and those, here, predominate by far—the light of Mr. Dubus's acceptance is a source of clarity and of strength. His voice neither aggrandizes nor belittles, but it accords even the most mundane gestures and objects their exact, just dignity. Really, what he gives us is an unastonished account of his characters' puzzlements and desires, and those small moments in which momentous movements of the heart happen. In the process, he recovers their largeness and significance. Mr. Dubus is a writer who works within a well-defined sphere of concerns. But if you're willing to listen to the nuances of his music, you'll find that, in his own register, he has near perfect pitch that can transfigure the commonplace.

> *Eva Hoffman, "Taking a Chance on Pathos,"* in The New York Times Book Review, *November 6, 1988, p. 7.*

Richard Eder   (essay date 1988)

[*An American critic and journalist, Eder received the Pulitzer Prize for criticism in 1987. In the following review of* Selected Stories, *he suggests that Dubus's fiction is sometimes marred by excessive writing.*]

Like Raymond Carver, Andre Dubus sets his stories largely among the blue-collars and other Americans who confront impossible demands with narrow means.

Unlike the austere and finely voiced Carver, Dubus endows his constricted lives with large-scale emotions. Rage, lust, longing, violence and despair are painted with deep-hued, tumultuous colors in [**Selected Stories**] this selection of the author's work over the last 15 years.

In one story, a father whose son has been shot dead by the estranged husband of his girlfriend, kidnaps the killer, shoots him and buries him. In another, a wife stabs her husband to death after he has raped her, beaten up her lover, and set a circle of fire around the house where she is staying.

And in a third, a domestic brawl escalates after a man throws his young son across the room for interfering with his view of the television set. The boy's arm is broken. His mother smashes the television set. The husband sets their house on fire, nearly burning their two daughters to death. After rescuing them, the wife runs her husband over with their car.

Dubus is no minimalist.

What he is, is harder to decide. If he made spaghetti sauce—and from the many scenes in which someone cooks a meal as a kind of redeeming truce, one suspects he does—it would be intensely flavored, dark red, bursting with extra meat, and redolent of six different herbs. It would be savory and strangely wearying.

The passions and desperations are rendered so vividly that the reader is shaken, first, and then numbed. Sex is explosive, rage a choking sensation, sorrow is worse than dying, religious scruples are a burning agony. Not that Dubus would use such phrases. There is not a cliché in the entire book; and everything is made from scratch and at triple strength.

Dubus writes of the lives of those who are not quite at the bottom of the social and economic scale. They haven't given up yet; they are still struggling painfully. They have enough of the American Dream to dream it, but not enough to get a piece of it. They are choked and desperate.

"Who's going to buy one?" screams the husband in **"Rose"** after his wife breaks the television screen with his beer bottle and runs to tend their son's broken arm. "It's the only . . . peace I've got."

Behind the horror of that grotesque cry, there is the pity. Class is a theme that recurs in these stories, many of them set in the depressed Merrimack Valley of northeastern Massachusetts. Dubus uses passion and violence, as Gorky and Dreiser did, to declare that the world is arranged to drive the poor mad.

How do you portray the life of quiet desperation, so that

the desperation is not lost in the quiet? With great subtlety, as Carver does; but even then, the quiet can take over. Or else, by making the quiet scream. That is Dubus' method. Often it pierces us; often, it deafens us.

He is so extraordinarily, uniquely right about so many things. Nobody writes about fatherhood, for example, with such raging compassion. In **"Killings,"** he makes us feel how sheerly unbearable it is for a father to have his son killed.

Like so many parents, the father had mourned his child dozens of times in his imagination—when he crossed the street alone for the first time, went skating, drove the family car.

And now, "all the fears he had known while they were growing up, and all the grief he had been afraid of, had backed up like a huge wave and struck him in the head and swept him out to sea."

It is searing perception, that sentence, yet it cools even as it burns. The rhetorical wave image disperses itself. And the story's crowded step-by-step narrative about how the father and a friend abduct and kill the killer, is excessive. So it is in **"Rose"**; and in **"The Pretty Girl,"** where the wife stabs the husband who has raped her and who comes back in the simple belief that she had enjoyed it.

It is not the outsize incidents that furnish the excess, though. Dubus makes an astonishing fictional case for them. What mars many of the stories—some of them potentially brilliant—is the excessive writing.

Like one of the fathers he understands so well, Dubus can't let his offspring go, trust it, and be silent. He tends to tell us so much about each of their lives, each of their emotions, each of their shifts and compulsions, that the gesture, tone and spirit are swamped by the author's voice. Evocation becomes an ornate accretion of detail.

Dubus' style can be a kind of cloud cover over an extraordinary landscape. Sometimes it altogether blots out his wit and passionate sense of the shapes of men's and women's lives in hard times. Sometimes, these show through dimly and intermittently. And sometimes, the view is unimpeded; and what a view it can be!

"Winter" is a discerning picture of the awkwardness of a divorced father with his two children. **"Anna"** and **"Townies"** are taut and ironic accounts of the divisions of class and wealth in a small town. **"Delivering"** is a splendid story of a boy who fights pain and takes responsibility when his mother leaves home.

By far the finest of the stories, almost a novella in scope, is **"Voices From the Moon."** It tells of the effect of two disruptions on the fabric of a family's life. One is the departure of the mother, Joan, after 27 years, to live alone in the same town and work as a waitress. The other is the decision of Greg, the father, to marry his oldest son's divorced wife.

It is an eventful story; there is love, anger and painful acts of growing in it. And yet it is oddly peaceful. Dubus has created a pond so still and crystalline that the lines of disturbance and reconciliation display their complex and graceful geometry.

The focus is the tender sensibility of the youngest boy, who works his way blindly into understanding. But the portraits of the other family members are vivid and memorable. The finest is of Joan. Her love "had died of premature old age," Dubus writes. She leaves "simply because she had outgrown, not so much Greg, as her marriage to him." The author evokes the spare and independent life she makes for herself; it is a stirring image of growing up while growing old.

"Voices" is told in a style that is partly purged. Dubus retains the warmth, involvement and elaborateness, but he lets air and light in, as well. It is one of his later stories; it would be nice to think that it promises a clearer, less impeded view of his formidable gifts in the work to come.

> *Richard Eder, "Stories from Scratch at Triple Strength," in* Los Angeles Times Book Review, *November 20, 1988, p. 3.*

John B. Breslin   (essay date 1988)

[*Breslin is an American author, educator, and Roman Catholic clergyman. In the following essay, he examines the influence of Catholicism on Dubus's fictional exploration of human relationships.*]

"I am fifty-one years old, yet I cannot feel I am growing older because I keep repeating the awakening experience of a child: I watch and I listen, I write in my journal, and each year I discover, with the awe of my boyhood, a part of the human spirit I had perhaps imagined, but had never seen or heard."

Thus the narrator of **"Rose,"** the concluding story in Andre Dubus's collection (1986), *The Last Worthless Evening.* At some risk to my critical credentials, I find that narrative voice remarkably close to its author's and revelatory of the imagination that stands behind a considerable body of work published over the past two decades. Dubus began by publishing a full-length novel in 1967 that grew out of his studies at the Iowa writers' school and, more to the point, out of his experience in the Marines. *The Lieutenant* has only recently come back into print, thanks to a small publisher in Cambridge, Massachusetts. Since 1967 Dubus has concentrated on shorter forms, stories and novellas of varying lengths, five collections worth, and a separately published short novel, *Voices from the Moon.* Whatever the form or the setting, however, the watching eye and the attentive ear are always in evidence, and with them the shock of discovery. Dubus picks his venues carefully, each reflecting his own lived experience: Catholic schools in Louisiana; the male-dominated world of the military; and, more recently, the Merrimack Valley northwest of Boston, an uneasy meeting point of town and gown amid the rubble of obsolete mills and factories. What they have in common for the reader is an assurance of authenticity, not just for the places, with their *bayous* or ward rooms or desolate winter roads, but more importantly for the troubled human beings—Dubus's stock in trade—who with their distinctive accents, prejudices, and graces, attempt to puzzle out the meanings of the lives they've been dealt and have frequently messed up.

A consciousness of sin permeates the atmosphere of these stories, which is not surprising in a writer who answers, "Catholic," when asked for a proper adjective to describe his work. Dubus accepts our flawed condition as a given, but he manages to view his characters' failings with a compassion that bespeaks an equal conviction that grace is powerfully at work in the world. In a number of stories this pattern of sin and grace is played out within a specifically Catholic setting, but just as often, the characters have no religious convictions or, at most, exhibit a vestigial sensibility of the divine in lives otherwise determined by an overtly secularized culture. But moral questions remain, questions shaped and colored by family values, ethnic heritage, military ethos, and intellectual training. And it is to these moral issues that Dubus relentlessly returns, exploring their demands and their paradoxes in the lives of middle Americans of the mid-twentieth century.

Take Dan Tierney, the hero of Dubus's first novel, *The Lieutenant*. Thrust into the command of the Marine detachment on an aircraft carrier, Lieutenant Tierney gets caught up in an attempt to save a weak young recruit from his perverted tormentors, only to find his efforts are futile against the engine of military justice and a naval captain's determination to clear his ship, and his command record, of any sexual taint. Tierney's insistence on following his conscience sabotages his own career.

Like many first novels, it is a story of innocence lost, and it suffers from the genre's neat moral divisions of heroes and villains. But it sounds themes that Dubus will pick up and develop in his later and more sophisticated treatments of military life. One of these is the deep resentment felt by regular officers against the faceless and powerful intelligence arm of the military, the "dark men" of a later story. In both cases they violate the unspoken covenant that binds servicemen together, embodying in its place the impersonal force of authority that values order above all else. Dubus's sympathies clearly lie with someone like Captain Devereaux who warns his pilot friend of the investigation into his personal life. The competing values are neatly summarized as the investigators stand with the captain on the flight deck of his carrier and he informs them that their prey is not on board:

> "He's out there . . . "
>
> "Out there?" Foster said. "You let him fly? In a million dollar . . . "

Captain Devereaux looked at him, and he stopped.

This subversive, anarchic strain runs through many of these stories, and not just the military ones. Dubus's characters are apt to take the law into their own hands to avenge or protect family or friend. He makes no abstract moral judgment on these tribal loyalties, and it is clear that the psychic price of such action comes high. As the man who has just murdered his son's murderer in **"Killings"** tells the story to his wife, "the words had no images for him, he did not see himself doing what the words said he had done; he only saw himself on the road." And later,

as his wife sleeps beside him, "he shuddered with a sob that he kept silent in his heart." Whether or not the murder is even discovered, Matt has been marked, like Cain.

Perhaps the most powerful of these stories of private judgment—and Dubus's best in my estimation—is also one of his most explicitly Catholic. **"A Father's Story,"** in *The Times Are Never So Bad*, gives us the first-person account of Luke Ripley, the divorced owner of a stable, who spends an hour early each morning in prayer and random reflection on his life before he rides off on one of his horses to the local church where, with his good friend Father Paul and a handful of others, he celebrates Mass. This daily pattern, Luke feels, brings him as close to his center as he has even been, but he has no illusions about mysticism or holiness. In his awareness of the gap between intention and accomplishment he captures the genius of sacrament and ritual, the essence of the Catholic imagination:

> But I cannot achieve contemplation, as some can; and so, having to face and forgive my own failures, I have learned from them both the necessity and the wonder of ritual. For ritual allows those who cannot will themselves out of the secular to perform the spiritual, as dancing allows the tongue-tied man a ceremony of love.

Into this calm comes the shock of family disaster. During her annual summer visit Luke's twenty-year-old daughter, Jennifer, accidentally hits someone with her car on a dark road and returns to wake Luke in the middle of the night. What he does, he does instinctively to protect his daughter. But the story is told retrospectively, and so at each stage—as he drives to the scene, finds the body, returns to tell her the boy is dead, and finally smashes the damaged fender into a tree at church—we hear as well his reflections, his awareness that efforts to spare Jennifer count also as sins against the boy and his family: "my first sin against him, not stopping for Father Paul, who could have given him the last rites, and immediately then my second one, or, I saw then, my first, not calling an ambulance to meet me there." Later still, he rehearses the confession he will never make to his priest-friend, because he knows he would not act on his advice to go to the police: "He will not hear anything of failure to do all that one can to save an anonymous life, of injustice to a family in their grief, of deepening their pain at the chance and mystery of death by giving them nothing—no one—to hate."

But what is most extraordinary about this story is its ending, and the risk Dubus takes in having Luke recount a dialogue with God from his morning reflections. Distinguishing between his sons and his daughter, he tells God he would have called the police if one of his boys had come to him, but would do again what he did for his daughter. "But you never had a daughter and, if you had, you could not have borne her passion." To God's further accusation that he therefore loves weakness, Luke responds. "As you love me," and heads out to saddle his horse for Mass.

At a reading Dubus gave of the story several years ago, a friend of mine heard him say that a young woman had told him, "Daughters have stories, too." That reaction echoed several I heard from women of various ages when I taught the story in class. They felt that Luke had done his daughter more harm than good in trying to protect her, but fathers of daughters also told me that even if they did not approve of Luke's decision, they understood it. Dubus has clearly touched a live nerve in our sexually egalitarian society; it is a tribute to the power of his writing, however, that the story is never mistaken for a tract. It remains Luke Ripley's narrative—credible, even sympathetic, because Dubus has made Luke that way.

In the later novel, *Voices from the Moon,* Luke Ripley turns up again, this time in a bit part as the stable owner on whose horses young Richie Stowe experiences a merging of body and spirit remarkably similar to Ripley's own: "He had learned to make his spiritual solitude physical and, through his flesh, to do this in communion with the snow and evergreens, and the naked trees that showed him the bright sky of winter."

Indeed, Richie is in many ways a twelve-year-old version of Luke; he, too, finds in daily Mass the same centering; and he, too, is caught up in a family drama, but one largely out of his control. What is tearing the Stowe family apart is the divorced father's decision to marry the ex-wife of Richie's older brother Larry—a plot line that skirts dangerously close to soap opera, and is only saved by Dubus's ability to give each of the characters involved an individual voice and a history that in conjunction make for a dialogue of generations. Family bonds, however, shredded by divorce, remain strong enough to lend credence to the mother's prediction that Larry and his father will eventually be reconciled.

Meanwhile, Richie is undergoing his own personal testing which provides the narrative frame for the novel. Coming home from Mass, in the first chapter, he meets Melissa Donnelly who smokes and seems otherwise worldly and alluring to the young priest-to-be. In the final chapter, after we have seen each member of the Stowe family at his or her most vulnerable, Richie goes out to meet Melissa for an innocent tryst that he imagines as a major temptation against his religious calling. But Dubus leaves the matter much more ambiguous in the novel's final words: "(Richie) saw in the stars the eyes of God too, and was grateful for them, as he was for the night and the girl he loved. He lay on the grass and the soft summer earth, holding Melissa's hand, and talking to the stars."

Certainly Richie's confessor, who early in the novel counsels the boy to have compassion and forgiveness for his father ("even if it *is* wrong, it's still love, and that is always near the grace of God"), would not see Melissa as a competitor to Christ. Dubus treats the demands of Catholicism seriously and refuses to reduce religious experience to good feelings, but just as firmly he rejects Jansenism and its world-denying instincts. Human love may be fractured, sometimes even a distorted mirror for God's grace, but it remains for us here and now the only glass to see through darkly.

Which brings me to a final group of three interlocked stories that appear in different collections. Dubus explores the permutations of human love in the lives of two couples joined and divided by friendship and sexual appetite. Here, too, Dubus risks the low comedy possibilities of *Bob*

and Carol and Ted and Alice by focusing his stories on the sexual tribulations of four middle-class inhabitants of a Massachusetts college town. Hank Allison and Jack Linhart teach together, run together, and genuinely think of themselves as each other's best friend. ("There are several men I love and who love me, all of us married, passive misogynists, and if we did not have each other to talk to we would probably in our various ways go mad.") But as the first story, **"We Don't Live Here Anymore,"** opens, Jack is having an affair with Hank's wife, Edith, for which he feels the guilt of betrayal though he knows that Hank rejects monogamy in principle and has had numerous affairs with his female students. And by the story's end Jack's wife, Terry, has reciprocated by sleeping with Hank. These transpositions are important elements of plot, but the story is Jack's as he struggles to comprehend his own deepest drives and frustrations. What does it mean to be married to a woman who continues to love him when his own passion has died? Is being a father enough to hold such a marriage together? Jack shares Hank's doubts about the value of monogamy and is willing to experiment with an alternative, but he lacks his friend's deep cynicism: *There are two kinds of people,* Hank said. *The unhappy ones who look it and the unhappy ones who don't.* In the end Jack decides to stay with Terry for reasons he intuits but can't express.

For the other two stories (**"Adultery"** and **"Finding a Girl in America"**) the focus shifts to Edith and Hank, but without the first-person narration that made Jack Linhart both more puzzling and more immediate. Dubus uses **"Adultery"** as the title of the collection in which it originally appeared but wryly appends "& Other Choices." These three words suggest a subtle commentary on the moral issue behind the erotic entanglement, yet also turn aside heavy-handed moralizing. We become what we choose, Dubus insists, and nowhere more so than in our loving. For a while Edith believes she can accept Hank's philandering and match it; and he wants to believe that by condoning her affairs he will achieve a guiltless freedom. But Edith, like Jack Linhart, cannot finally separate sexual love from commitment, and when she falls in love with a forty-year-old ex-priest named Joe Richie, who is dying of cancer, she begins to realize the hollowness of her marriage.

Dubus divides **"Adultery"** into four parts, using the love story to frame Edith's reflections on her life with Hank in the long second section. The effect is to make of her deepening love for Joe a prism through which both Edith and the reader can perceive her need to act even though her choice to divorce Hank offers no consolation since Joe will soon be dead.

Joe himself is another of Dubus's overtly religious creations, a near relation of both Luke Ripley and Richie Stowe, who finds in the Eucharist a symbol and center for all his loves. Because he experiences something sinful in his relationship with Edith (though not the simple *fact* of adultery), he stops receiving Communion. Were she to divorce Hank and marry him, Joe would return to the sacrament. There is a casuistry here, but one of symbol rather than of law, that parallels Luke Ripley's bold concluding dialogue in **"A Father's Story"** with his daughter-less

God. Joe, too, "loves in weakness," but the love proves strong enough to free Edith from Hank's loveless marriage arrangement with her. She recognizes that her ability to leave Hank is Joe's final gift to her, just as her announcement of it as he lies dying is her gift to him.

The conclusion of the trilogy is, fittingly, Hank's. **"Finding a Girl in America"** opens with him apparently in the midst of still another affair with one of his students: "On an October night, lying in bed with a nineteen-year-old and tequila and grapefruit juice, thirty-five-year-old Hank Allison gets the story." And it is not a pretty one. He has been, without his knowledge, the father of an aborted child from a previous affair. The image of that fetus haunts his waking and sleeping hours, forcing him to face the consequences of his own choices. "I don't want to have to say no to anything, not ever": the life philosophy he had enunciated for Edith when she first discovered his infidelities has borne this terrible fruit.

Coming to terms with that reality is the burden of the story, and Dubus nicely rounds off the trilogy by having us see Hank deal with it by turning to the central people in his life—Edith, Jack, his thirteen-year-old daughter Sharon, and Lori, the girl at the beginning of the story. Joined together by their daughter, Edith and Hank have achieved reconciliation in their divided lives, and she is able to offer him comfort in his grief as well as forgiveness. Jack tells him to marry Lori, and his encouragement has the added weight of someone who has refused to give up on his own marriage. Watching Sharon with Lori, Hank realizes that "he does not want her girlhood and young womanhood to become a series of lovers, he does not want her to become cynical and casual about making love. He does not, in short, want her to be like his girlfriends."

But he also knows that Lori is not like his other girlfriends, either. She may be the latest of his student mistresses, but by story's end he has determined that she will also be the last, and he asks her to marry him with all the trepidation of a young man courting his love. The circle has been completed, not so innocently, perhaps, as at the end of a Shakespearean comedy with all the young couples neatly paired off, but with enough resolution and reconciliation to give us hope, and some comfort for the pain suffered on the journey to self-knowledge.

The comic vision implied in this trilogy, and in Andre Dubus's work in general, is profoundly Christian, and, more specifically, profoundly Catholic in inspiration. Dubus looks at the world around him and sees sin and brokenness, but he refuses to despair. For behind the physical detail his eye so sharply sees and behind the psychological nuance his ear so deftly notes, he perceives a presence that understands and forgives us more generously than we do others and better than we can ourselves. For those characters with a sensitivity to sign and sacrament (Luke, Richie, Joe) that presence finds a local habitation and a name in the Eucharist where the mystery of God-in-flesh continues daily to play itself out. For the rest there are hints and guesses, mostly in moments of vulnerability when their deepest loves and loyalties are threatened: Edith at Joe's deathbed, Hank worrying about his teenage daughter, Captain Devereaux protecting his old friend.

The grace that Bernanos's cure found to be everywhere and in everything often works strangely, even paradoxically, in a world hell-bent on denying its presence, but work it does, quietly and inexorably, not to save us from pain and suffering but to give them meaning by rescuing faith, hope, and love from our icy despair or lukewarm diffidence.

By watching and listening and, most of all, by writing, Andre Dubus continues to celebrate the human spirit in which it is possible, he insists, to see the power of God and God's grace at work. He is a writer who needs and deserves a wider audience. The recent bestowal on him of a MacArthur Fellowship acknowledges his achievement so far and will, I hope, gain him more attention as an important contemporary writer working within a rich Catholic tradition.

> *John B. Breslin, "Playing Out the Patterns of Sin & Grace," in* Commonweal, *Vol. CXV, No. 21, December 2, 1988, pp. 652-56.*

Anne Tyler   (essay date 1989)

[*Tyler is an American novelist, short story writer, and critic. In the following review of* Selected Stories, *she characterizes the collection as "deeply rewarding," and Dubus as a writer who assumes moral responsibility for his characters.*]

A woman and her grown son are sitting after hours in the restaurant where she works, discussing the son's unhappiness. The woman says, "You know why I like my waitress friends so much? And what I've learned from them? They don't have delusions. So when I'm alone at night . . . I look out my window, and it comes to me: we don't have to live great lives, we just have to understand and survive the ones we've got."

A man struggling along on his own after his wife has left him reflects, "It is not hard to live through a day, if you can live through a moment. What creates despair is the imagination, which pretends there is a future, and insists on predicting millions of moments, thousands of days, and so drains you that you cannot live the moment at hand."

And a newly divorced father of two young children tries to adjust to solitude:

> He separated his days into parts, thought about each one, and learned that all of them were not bad. When the alarm woke him in the winter dark, the new day and waiting night were the gray of the room, and they pressed down on him, fetid repetitions bent on smothering his spirit before he rose from the bed. But he got up quickly, made the bed while the sheets still held his warmth, and once in the kitchen with coffee and newspaper he moved into the first part of the day . . . as near-peaceful as he dared hope for . . .

These three—citizens, all, of Andre Dubus's sad, brave, gritty fictional world—have in common a heartening willingness to confront head on the conditions of their lives. There is nothing unique about the conditions themselves.

Heaven knows, modern literature is full of lonely, muddled people in reduced circumstances, drifting (as many of these characters do) toward self-destruction on a tide of booze and violence. But most other writers are content simply to plop their characters in these straits and leave them there. Most other stories end, or rather, trail away, in a flat refusal to look beyond the fistful of pills, the black eye, the morning hangover. Andre Dubus is not so easily satisfied. He forces his people to question their situations, sometimes coming up with answers and sometimes not, but nearly always demonstrating conscience and intelligence. In short, he feels morally responsible for his characters, and it's this sense of responsibility that gives his work its backbone.

Selected Stories contains twenty-three pieces, two of which have never before appeared in book form. Longtime admirers of Dubus's work will be pleased to see that each of his many concerns is fully represented. **"The Pitcher"** and **"After the Game"** reflect his passion for baseball; **"Cadence"** draws upon his experience in the Marines; and **"If They Knew Yvonne"** and **"Adultery,"** among others, reveal his deep Catholic roots. What's most important, though, is the overall effect. The storekeepers, bartenders, construction workers, short-order cooks, and housewives in these stories are so lovingly detailed, their inner worlds so thoroughly explored, that we close the book with the feeling that we've finished a group of novels—rich, teeming, bountiful novels at that.

In **"The Pretty Girl,"** which is perhaps the most stunning piece in the collection, a ruffian named Ray rapes his estranged wife, beats an ex-lover of hers to a pulp, and surrounds her house with a circle of flames. It would be hard to imagine a character more despicable. Yet when he shows up in her bedroom one night, there is something bewildered and wounded and, yes, even likable about him. "I just want to talk," he says, and, "What did I ever do anyways?" and, "No, come on: what did I do?" The story calls up the most complicated emotions. It's an unblinking story; it refuses, absolutely, to screen out the messy other side of things, the stray doubts and the "yes, buts" and the mitigating circumstances.

In **"Killings,"** a father grieving for his murdered son is appalled to find the murderer at large, released on bail and casually appearing about town. Finally the father can stand it no longer; he kidnaps the man and shoots him through the head. To us readers, revenge is sweet; we feel a clear sense of satisfaction as he pulls the trigger. But here again, we're not allowed to get off so lightly. We're shown the careful tidiness of the murderer's apartment; we see how meekly and reasonably he behaves when he still has some hope of being spared. (Forced to drive at gunpoint, he asks, "You wouldn't have the gun cocked, would you? For when I put on the brakes.") And yet none of this lessens our feeling of wicked satisfaction; that's what makes the story so affecting.

"A Father's Story" examines the reaction of a middle-aged man—a devout Catholic—when his daughter confides that she has hit somebody with her car. The father might conceivably save the victim's life by reporting the accident at once, but he thinks instead of his daughter's life, and he chooses to keep it a secret. If it had been one of his sons, he says, he would not have done so. Why? he imagines God asking. Does he love his sons less? No, the father says. "But You never had a daughter and if You had, You could not have borne her passion."

> So, He says, you love her more than you love Me.
>
> I love her more than I love truth.
>
> Then you love in weakness, He says.
>
> As you love me, I say . . .

Another writer might have told the same story but stopped a bit sooner, omitting the question of daughter versus sons, omitting the dialogue with God. That's not Andre Dubus's style. He has a way of stepping forth, however thin the ice.

In **"Voices from the Moon,"** a man is shattered by the news that his ex-wife and his father have fallen in love. He goes to his mother for comfort, which, amazingly, she manages to give him. She predicts the gradual way his hurts will heal, the step-by-step manner in which he and his father will regain their old closeness until one day they can actually sit down to dinner together without dwelling on the past. It's this long, astonishing speech of hers, ending with her remark about not having to live great lives, that elevates the story from soap opera to literature. Another writer might have been content merely to define the situation and then turn away, conveniently ignoring the knotty question of how these people will proceed from here on out. But Dubus forges ahead—again, unblinking.

Not all of the stories work equally well. A few come to an end before the act of forging ahead can be accomplished; several are marred by a dreamlike, rhythmic writing style that suggests the author may have put himself into a trance with his own words.

> For a long time she had not been afraid of people or the chances of a day, for she believed she could bear the normal pain of being alive: her heart had been broken by girls and boys, and she had borne that too, and embarrassment and shame and humiliation and failure, and she was not one of those who, once or more wounded, waited fearfully for the next mistake or cruelty or portion of bad luck.

Also, an introduction would have been welcome—a word from Dubus about why certain stories were included and others left out, and perhaps a brief glance backward over the twenty-some years of his career. But it may be greedy to wish for that, when what we've been given is so much: a fine, hefty, deeply rewarding collection from one of this country's ablest writers.

> *Anne Tyler, "Master of Moments," in* The New Republic, *Vol. 200, No. 6, February 6, 1989, pp. 41-2.*

Freddie Baveystock (essay date 1990)

[*In the following review of* Selected Stories, *Baveystock characterizes Dubus's fictional treatment of human conflict and crisis as psychological in origin and execution and suggests that the longer works are most reflective of the author's considerable insight and perception.*]

Only eight of Andre Dubus's fifty-odd short stories or novellas have already been published in this country, in two paperback editions which are now out of print. So the appearance of these twenty-three *Selected Stories* is to be welcomed by anyone interested in short American fiction. Dubus has only ever written one novel, *The Lieutenant*, which, were he to write it now, he reveals in an interview with Thomas E. Kennedy in *Andre Dubus: A study of the short fiction*, "would be a good hundred-page novella . . . [not] a weak two-hundred page novel". Indeed, this latest volume proves that the long short story is Dubus's great strength: four of the stories account for nearly one half of the book, including the seventy-page **"Voices From The Moon"**, which, with its six different narrative viewpoints, has all the impact of a novella.

Dubus's repeated use of these forms sets him apart from the writers of the American neorealist school with whom he is often lazily lumped together by British critics. Certainly he shares with Raymond Carver, Richard Ford and countless others a preference for the small-town setting, but it is not Dubus's aim to capture the hardships of these ostensibly "small" lives in haunting, spare prose. At his best he does something else altogether, which is to probe the mental, moral and emotional turmoil of these people as they attempt to lead honest and good lives but find themselves failing, often disastrously.

In order to achieve this, Dubus goes unswervingly for the crisis point (the book contains a large number of murders, rapes and violent beatings). His approach, however, is predominantly a psychological one, and he eschews the apparatus of the crime novel (of which he is an avid reader), suspense and mystery. This is not to say that Dubus's writing is undramatic: in **"Killings"**, we follow a man as he sets out to murder his own son's murderer, out on bail, and in **"The Pretty Girl"**, a husband's repeated harrassment of his estranged wife escalates into rape. The next time he returns, she has a gun and kills him.

The focus on violent death does become repetitive, and, when it is used to lend the stories a conclusiveness that they otherwise lack, leaves an unpleasant taste. Dubus claims (again in Kennedy's book) that the violence of his stories "is mostly a reflection of American consciousness. . . . I can't read the paper, even the local one, without coming across violence." Although he obviously doesn't condone this violence—we are not meant to feel much sympathy for Polly in **"The Pretty Girl"** as she allows her husband to bleed to death—Dubus is clearly drawn to people *in extremis*.

One of the book's long *tours de force*, **"Rose"**, perhaps best exemplifies this. It is unique among Dubus's stories in that it makes use of an uninvolved framing narrator. Having got to know the narrator through drinking together in the local bar, the solitary Rose finally tells him her story, one which recurs many times in various forms in this volume: she married young, hopeful and Catholic, and before long found that she and her husband were unable to cope with

being poor and having three tiny children. While Rose descends into a torpor, her husband becomes increasingly violent towards their son, until the evening he bodily throws the boy across the room. This awakens Rose's maternal instincts, and in the ensuing mêlée, he also tries to set fire to their apartment with the two girls inside. In desperation, Rose rescues her daughters, but in doing so, murders her husband.

This harrowing tale is related by the narrator with a Faulknerian sense of inevitability (Dubus's long, looping sentences, as well, often echo Faulkner's prose rhythms). Although the story's unconventional conclusion—that Rose is a worthy mother of her children—is made ambiguous by the presence of the garrulous and opininated narrator, it bespeaks Dubus's fiercely moral vision. The story shows up Dubus's strengths and weaknesses: while his concentration on Rose's torment gives the tale a relentless narrative and emotional power, it precludes any wider exploration of the issues raised. Rose's action is decisely swift, and there is no turning back.

The majority of Dubus's work is centred on a single consciousness, often to undeniable effect; Joyce Carol Oates has called these stories "triumphs of voice". Yet the multiplicity of characters and viewpoints in **"Voices From The Moon"** comes as something of a relief. This tale of family discord provoked by the father's decision to marry his son's ex-wife is undoubtedly the book's highlight. Each of the six characters is fully fleshed out, and, moreover, a resolution is reached without recourse to the gun. The son finds himself being comforted by his mother's words: "we don't have to live great lives, we just have to understand and survive the ones we've got".

In the longer stories, Dubus brings to bear what Thomas Kennedy calls his "unabashed humanism" with masterly insight and precision, but these qualities are absent from a good many of the shorter works: this volume's compendiousness does not always serve Dubus well. No such distinction is made by Kennedy's book: in his introduction he writes of "the relief of doffing the armor of criticism and opening one's heart to . . . characters as near to living creatures as fictional creations can be", and indeed he proceeds to trace Dubus's themes through all of his short stories with a total absence of discernment. Dubus deserves better.

Freddie Baveystock, "Crisis Points," in The Times Literary Supplement, *No. 4540, April 6-12, 1990, p. 376.*

FURTHER READING

Criticism

Holmes, Jon. "With Andre Dubus." *Boston Review* IX, No. 4 (August 1984): 7-8.

    Essay based on an interview with Dubus in which he

comments on his childhood and real-life influences on
his fiction.

Kennedy, Thomas E. *Andre Dubus: A Study of the Short Fiction.* Boston: Twayne Publishers, 1988, 176 p.
> In-depth thematic and stylistic analysis of Dubus's short
> fiction.

**Additional coverage of Dubus's life and career is contained in the following sources
published by Gale Research:** *Contemporary Authors,* **Vols. 21-24, rev. ed.;** *Contemporary
Authors New Revision Series,* **Vol. 17;** *Contemporary Literary Criticism,* **Vols. 13, 36; and**
Dictionary of Literary Biography, **Vol. 130.**

Caroline Gordon

1895-1981

American novelist, short story writer, and critic.

INTRODUCTION

Often associated with the Southern Literary Renaissance and the Southern Agrarian movement, Gordon is best known for fiction which synthesizes elements of mythology, Southern history, and Roman Catholicism. Although she was primarily devoted to the cultivation of the novel, Gordon first established her reputation as a writer of short stories. Preoccupied with the hero's journey of classical mythology, Gordon sought to reveal the universality of human nature throughout history in her fiction. She stated: "The proper work of fiction will be both timeless and temporal, temporal in its definition of a particular society at a given moment in history, timeless in its repetition of the archetypal pattern of behavior."

Biographical Information

Gordon was born on her grandmother's farm, Meriwether, located in Todd County, Kentucky. She was educated by her father, who taught classics at an academy for boys in southern Tennessee, where she became the only female student. In 1924 she married poet Allen Tate, to whom she was introduced by writer and friend Robert Penn Warren. In the 1920s the couple made two extended trips to Europe, and while in Paris they associated with such expatriate writers as F. Scott and Zelda Fitzgerald, Ernest Hemingway, Gertrude Stein, and Ralph Cheever Dunning. Gordon published her first short story, "Summer Dust," in the fall 1929 issue of *Gyroscope*, a literary magazine in which her husband had published his poetry. With "Summer Dust," Gordon realized her ability to write provocatively about nature and to sensitively capture the mood, local dialects, and cultural characteristics of the American South. During the 1930s Tate and Gordon frequently hosted such literary figures as Ford Madox Ford, Katherine Anne Porter, and Robert Lowell at their home, Benfolly, in southern Tennessee. During this period Gordon struggled with her roles as wife, mother, and writer, often referring to herself as a freak: "The work I do is not suitable for women. It is unsexing. I speak with real conviction here. I don't write 'the womanly' novel." Gordon and her husband moved frequently as she served as teacher, lecturer, or writer-in-residence at various American universities. In 1947 she converted to Roman Catholicism, which profoundly affected her fiction. She believed that the artist had a moral obligation to serve, praise, and worship God through art. In her 1964 essay, "Letters to

a Monk," published in *Ramparts,* she wrote: "I was nearly fifty years old before I discovered that art is the handmaiden to the Church." Gordon died in 1981 at San Cristóbal de las Casas, Chiapas, Mexico.

Major Works

Gordon's short stories are noted for their diverse subject matter, their keen evocation of mood, and their thematic progression from the secularism of Southern Agrarianism to Christian concepts of salvation and redemption. Three of Gordon's stories set during the Civil War—"The Ice House," "Hear the Nightingale Sing," and "The Forest of the South"—exemplify her focus on the past and portrayal of the decline of the antebellum South. Another popular historical work, based upon a true incident involving a young white woman who was captured and adopted by a Cherokee tribe, is "The Captive." The protagonist of her novel *Aleck Maury, Sportsman* is prominently featured in several of Gordon's stories—including "Old Red," "One More Time," "To Thy Chamber Window, Sweet," and "The Last Day in the Field"—and reflects her interest in the epic hero's journey "as he endeavor[s] against misfortune." Maury, like Gordon's father, is a teacher of classics for whom hunting and fishing represent a means of liberation from the constraints imposed by family and society, the physical limitations of his advancing age, and the decline of the Old South. Among Gordon's stories occurring in more contemporary settings are "The Waterfall," an autobiographical account of events at Benfolly, and "The Olive Garden," a story concerning a man suffering psychic trauma caused by his experiences in World War II. The popular story "The Brilliant Leaves" concerns death, betrayal, the role of men and women in contemporary society, and the conflict between innocence and experience. Gordon's famous story "One against Thebes," first published as "The Dragon's Teeth" in 1961, is a rewriting of "Summer Dust." Although the two stories are similar in their focus on the social milieu of the South and their use of identical mythical allusions, the theme of "One against Thebes" links the journey of the hero of Greek myth with that of the individual in the Christian quest for salvation, a theme representative of Gordon's later novels.

Critical Reception

Critical reception of Gordon's short stories has been very favorable. She was awarded a Guggenheim Fellowship in creative writing after the publication of "Summer Dust" and "The Long Day," and she also won second prize for "Old Red" in the 1934 O. Henry competition. At times her stories have been compared to those of Daniel Defoe, William Faulkner, and James Joyce for, respectively, her employment of foreshadowing, recurring characters and Southern settings, and shifting points of view. According to Frederick P. W. McDowell, Gordon's "stories preeminently reveal her use of the vivid detail for establishing mood, for conveying subtleties of psychological shading, and for achieving the expansiveness of meaning that in literature we associate with symbolism."

PRINCIPAL WORKS

SHORT FICTION

The Forest of the South   1945
"A Narrow Heart: The Portrait of a Woman"   1960; published in journal *The Transatlantic Review*
Old Red, and Other Stories   1963
"Cock Crow"   1965; published in journal *The Southern Review*
The Collected Stories of Caroline Gordon   1981

OTHER MAJOR WORKS

Penhally   (novel)   1931
Aleck Maury, Sportsman   (novel)   1934; also published

as *The Pastimes of Aleck Maury: The Life of a True Sportsman,* 1935]
The Garden of Adonis   (novel)   1937
None Shall Look Back   (novel)   1937; also published as *None Shall Look Back: A Story of the American Civil War,* 1937
Green Centuries   (novel)   1941
The Women on the Porch   (novel)   1944
The House of Fiction: An Anthology of the Short Story, with Commentary   [with Allen Tate]   (anthology) 1950; revised edition, 1960
The Strange Children   (novel)   1951
The Malefactors   (novel)   1956
How to Read a Novel   (criticism)   1957
A Good Soldier: A Key to the Novels of Ford Madox Ford (criticism)   1963
The Glory of Hera   (novel)   1972

CRITICISM

William Maxwell   (essay date 1945)

[*An American novelist, short story writer, nonfiction writer, and author of children's books, Maxwell was a frequent contributor of reviews to the* New Yorker. *In the following review, he offers a mixed assessment of the* The Forest of the South.]

Four of the stories in [*The Forest of the South*]—"**The Ice House**," "**The Long Day**," "**The Brilliant Leaves**" and "**All Lovers Love the Spring**"—are good. "**Her Quaint Honour**" is excellent. The others are slight or, more often, exasperating.

Surprise and suspense are not necessary ingredients of the modern short story, but if they are missing then they must be replaced by smaller tensions, so that the reader, abandoning his interest in the outcome of the story, is completely held by every detail of its architecture. There are no such tensions in these stories, no courting of interest by any of the traditional story teller's devices. Miss Gordon is never sentimental, though her subject matter—the Civil War, Southern plantation life, young love, the frustration of the middle-aged—invites sentimentality. There is a fundamental honesty both in the writing of these stories and in the writer's conception, but both are frequently canceled out by an equally fundamental dullness, which comes mostly from the fact that, although the characters speak like living people few of them ever seem to be alive.

One can't help wondering if this is deliberate, an act of taste, since Miss Gordon can create character, just as she can, and now and then does, write with feeling, imagination and humor. Most of the time one crabbed unwieldly sentence follows another, as if there were always, standing at her shoulder, an admonisher, telling her to keep her writing low in key, unexciting, unemotional, factual and flat. Certain admirable effects are gained by this method, especially if a writer is dealing with death by violence, one of Miss Gordon's favorite themes. But if carried on ad infinitum the crabbed style is exhausting and the dogged reader ends up demanding more, as a result of his pains, than Miss Gordon, gifted though she is, has to offer.

There is also in these stories a regrettable lack of clarity. "We were up long before day and were loading the horses at first dawn streak. Even then Tom didn't want to go," a story will begin; or, "At 3 o'clock he came out on the gallery," and it sometimes takes pages before the reader is able to make out that "I" is a pioneer woman and Tom is her husband, that "he" is a boy approaching manhood. Nothing is gained by this initial obscurity. Sometimes in the body of a story one is obliged to go back and figure out what has actually happened, and the endings are often the most ambiguous of all, not because of the complexity and subtlety of the writer's ideas, as Henry James's endings are ambiguous, but by virtue of Miss Gordon's inexplicitness. The action of all these stories is carefully motivated, however, and the ideas, once they are recognized, are simple and direct.

The novelist nearly always reveals himself as well as his characters, the short story writer seldom. Of the seventeen stories in this collection, one is wholly objective, eleven are told from the point of view of a man or a young boy and only five from the point of view of a woman or a little girl. There are other women writers—notably Nancy Hale—who have written about men, from a man's point of view and with a man's knowledge. But Miss Gordon's ability is really astonishing in that she handles with more than competence such special and exclusively masculine interests as 'possum hunting, poker and the curing of tobacco, handles them with absolute first-hand knowledge and as a man would handle them. In one of the stories a woman remembering her girlhood says:

> Unless they [the boys] needed me real bad they didn't want me along and when they started out for the stable would pretend they were going to see a man about a dog or even that some animal was being bred out in the stable lot, to keep me in the house. Every Friday night before I went to sleep I used to make up my mind that I wouldn't have anything to do with them, but when Saturday morning came I'd get out and follow them, far enough behind so that they wouldn't notice, pretending I was playing something by myself. Do you remember that when you were a child there were some people you couldn't stay away from because it seemed like there wasn't any use in being anywhere else?

This heartbreaking little aside is possibly the key not only to Miss Gordon's knowledge of 'possum hunting and the curing of tobacco leaves, but also to the mystery of why some of these stories are well written and moving, the work clearly of an artist in full possession of her powers, and others so unsatisfactory. The little girl who tags along after boys, unwelcome, persistent, an outcast learning, nevertheless, the secrets of a world she is never going to be accepted into, must ultimately pay for knowledge thus acquired by not knowing, at times, what use to make of it.

William Maxwell, "Of Southerners and the South," in New York Herald Tribune Weekly Book Review, *September 23, 1945, p. 4.*

Vivienne Koch   (essay date 1946)

[*Koch is an American critic. In the following review of* The Forest of the South, *she discusses Gordon's thematic focus on the past and Southern history and culture.*]

For almost two decades Caroline Gordon has been writing about the forest of the South. I know of no other prose writer except William Faulkner who has remained so purely identified with that locale. And it is precisely because both Faulkner and Miss Gordon have seized upon the South with their imaginations and not merely with their eyes and ears that they are able to draw a South that for all its jumble of rich vegetation one can recognize as a *forest;* they have not, like antiquarians or historians, become distracted by the trees.

To consider **The Forest of the South,** a collection of short stories, ranging in composition from 1928 to 1944, is to see in cross-section, as it were, Caroline Gordon's development as a prose artist. For, while we must arbitrarily rule out a consideration of her novels here, it happens to be a fact that some of these stories represent aspects of themes which she develops more fully in her novels and, often, as in the Aleck Maury stories, and in **"All Lovers Love the Spring"** (in which the central character is the nuclear prototype for the cousin in *The Women on the Porch*) they are literally shavings from the novels, or preliminary drafts which have their special validity.

As in her novels, it is possible to detect in almost every one of these stories, ranging in setting from Civil War days to modern times, the almost invisible canvas of the past. It is not necessarily a canvas *on* which the action is painted (although this is true in **"The Captive," "The Forest of the South,"** and others) but a canvas rather more like a backdrop effecting a dimension *against* which the theme is played. What this yields for the texture of the stories is a curious psychological depth in which, while each character rotates on his own particular axis, as one goes farther into the past the spatial lines of the receding perspective do not converge, as commonly occurs in historical fiction, but instead continue miraculously parallel. In *Penhally,* a Civil War novel, the pastness of that past is sensitively worked in through old Nicholas, his memories of his boyhood, of his parents' tales and of their memories. Thus the perspective is extended back 60 years further so that the structure of life at Penhally by its myriad connecting lines with another century gains additional reality and sanction.

But it is more than merely nostalgia for a lost grandeur, raised by loss to mythic proportions, which goes into Miss Gordon's powerful penetration of the past. Nostalgia, to be sure, may be the initial impulse directing the artist that way. But Miss Gordon is too intelligent, informed and objective toward herself to over-rely on the carrying power of an impulse. For while one can deal with the surface of the past as an antiquarian, or record its structure of event as a historian, or apprehend its sensibility as a poet, Miss Gordon's method is none of these. Her way is, rather, the fusion of all of them, a combination making it possible for the past itself to come into action, at times, as protagonist or agent. In her work, the past is always accruing upon itself.

"Summer Dust" (1928), her second attempt at fiction, while yet episodic and uncertain of the short story limits, foreshadows clearly the way in which this fusion was later to operate. The overt pattern of the story is the insistent impingement of the world's evil upon the imaginative resources of a child's innocence. Yet, enveloping the particular problem of childhood is the fine tissue of circumstance which flows from the special psychological structure of the South. Thus, the past (and innocence) is not merely Sally's preoccupation with the delicious fairy tale of the little princess, with whom, both by social credit and imagination, the child has identified herself. (On her peach-picking expedition with her playmates Sally thinks: "I'm not a nigger, . . . I'm the only one who's not a nigger.") The past is in the forest in which Sally gets lost with her horse, in the sick old Negro woman endowed by local legend with a mysterious witch-like strength whom she is made to visit, in the white tenants whose malicious but slyly just denunciation of her family suggests an opaque background of deprivation and degradation. The totality of these events combine into that evil summer dust which conspires to invade the cool green herbage of Sally's innocence.

In **"The Long Day"** written later that year, but more successfully integrated and pointed, Miss Gordon deals with another aspect of the South, its past and its present. It concerns a crime of passion viewed through the eyes of a little white boy. We never know whether Joe has "cut" his wife or whether, as he tells the boy, it is she who has "done cut herself." The ambiguity is sustained through the very end when Joe, sensing the situation is closing in on him, runs, "crouching like a dog . . . into the tall weeds. . . . Henry watched the yellow ripple spread slowly across the field." The fulcrum of the story is Joe's own sense of guilt, a sense which is a social inheritance, and which is left deliberately unrelated to the reality of his offense. Joe is guilty in his own eyes regardless of who has done the "cutting" or what the provocation was.

"The Captive," well-known to Miss Gordon's admirers, and commonly classified as a *tour de force* of the "adventure" story genre serves to illustrate the growth of her resourcefulness in dealing with the past. Written in 1931, the story, on the surface, is a fast-moving, first-person narrative in which the escape of a pioneer woman from the Indian captors who have slain her children achieves a kind of Robinson Crusoe-ish freshness and ingenuousness. The credibly archaic, yet not fussed-up, diction of the narrator, Jinny, the intimate and detailed knowledge of Indian life and custom, the fine, naturalist's eye for fauna, flora and terrain, all re-enforce the level of realism at which the tale can be meaningfully enjoyed.

Nevertheless, the particular brilliance of **"The Captive"** lies in its subtle blending of the natural and the supernatural. The element of the supernatural, moreover, flows not merely from Jinny's ignorance and superstition, but, significantly, is generated by her inner need. Thus for exam-

ple, it is not accidental that it is by following her dream that Jinny escapes her captors. The dream (a magnificent piece of prose which, even detached from the context, would stand up on its own terms) is composed of fragments of Jinny's past (her beaux, her community life) and fragments of a dimly perceived future (the vision of the stockade, "The white people . . . all over the land") held together by the curious white light of the dream, by the cabin made of bleached bone (the bones of the burnt children she cannot bear to remember even subconsciously) "White, with patches of green on them." The whole dream and its ultimate fruition in reality becomes welded into a strangely symbolic view of both Jinny's individual destiny, and the supra-individual future of America and her expanding West.

By 1934 Miss Gordon is functioning in the matrix of the Aleck Maury stories in which the past, although overtly neutralized, lurks richly in the psychic life of the central figure. **"To Thy Chamber Window, Sweet," "One More Time,"** and **"Old Red,"** comprises an affectionate, humourously nostalgic group of which **"Old Red"** is by far the most ambitious story. It is a very representative one for examining the more mature habits of Miss Gordon's art. The plot is Time; and it is a plot with which Aleck Maury will have no truck:

> *Time,* he thought, *time!* They were always mouthing the word, and what did they know about it? Nothing in God's world! He saw time suddenly, a dull leaden-colored fabric depending from the old lady's hands, from the hands of all of them, a blanket pulled about between them, now here, now there, trying to cover up their nakedness. . . . But time was a banner that whipped before him always in the wind! He stood on tiptoe to catch at the bright folds, to strain them to his bosom. They were bright and glittering. But they whipped by so fast and were slipping always ever faster. Where, for instance, had this year gone? He could swear he had not wasted a minute of it, for no man living, he thought, knew better how to make each day a pleasure to him. . . .

The unstated equation between Aleck Maury and Old Red, the elusive fox of his hunting days, raises the memories of the old sportsman to a symbolic pitch in which his own evasion of the humans who would hunt him down as ruthlessly as any animal quarry takes on a heroic gallantry, a gallantry with a tinge of pathos to it because *we* know it is time who is the real antagonist. In this story, then, the past sensed through the rich texture of Maury's sensibility (he is the kind of individualist only the old South could afford to produce) has a double function—as if cause and effect were inseparable, as if protagonist and antagonist were locked in a beautiful but piteous embrace.

In **"Tom Rivers"** (1935) the view of the past is less integrated and the pastness of the old Southwest seems to be merely a peg upon which to hang some fine tales of riding, fishing, drinking, poker, and the varied violence of frontier life. This story can be thought of as a notebook for scholars for, because of its loose, episodic structure, it is easier to discern the minute facets of craftsmanship and knowledge which go into Miss Gordon's carefully wrought re-presentations of the past. Her accurate and masculine handling of sports, games and fighting shows up the strain of objective observation which the more complex themes in other stories cunningly assimilate to the central direction. **"Tom Rivers"** dramatizes Miss Gordon's excellence as a writer of prose which is not "feminine," something one cannot claim for many women artists of our time who, like Katherine Mansfield and Virginia Woolf, almost always write in a feminine hand.

In the late thirties there appears a shift in the tone of Miss Gordon's writing, which, since her subject seems to remain constant, has escaped her critics. **"The Forest of the South,"** the hauntingly prophetic title piece of this collection, **"Hear the Nightingale Sing,"** (1944) and her recent novel, *The Women on the Porch,* all represent this shift. While the approach is still "objective," while the narrative point of view shifts as fluidly as before from omniscient spectator to individual characters, there is a heightened connection between interior and exterior event, between environment and character which can only be vaguely suggested by the term symbolism.

"The Forest of the South," depicting the gradual enslavement of a Yankee lieutenant before the insidious claims of the enemy, is a beautiful illustration of this symbolism. Early in the story, Lt. Munford, oppressed by the too bright and shimmering atmosphere enveloping the southern manor in which he is quartered, and vaguely disturbed by the presence there of its crazed mistress and her over-grateful daughter, sees a puppy, the soldiers' pet, who scampers toward him and "then fell on her back with her habitual gesture of outstretched paws. He thrust out his toe to poke her gently in the belly, and then withdrew his foot, frowning. 'Get up!' he said harshly." Thus the ambivalence of his growing feeling for Miss Mazereau is subtly established by means of a natural detail of manor life. Later, when he observes the girl more closely, he notices her eyes: "The lids were heavy, so heavy that they dimmed the brilliance of her glance. And the lids themselves had a peculiar pallor. Wax-white, like the petals of the magnolia blossom. When he had first come into this country he had gathered one of those creamy blossoms only to see it turn brown in his grasp. . . . " This is a precise metaphoric foreshadowing of the shocking dénouement, where not only does his betrothed turn brown in his grasp, but the stain spreads to his own hands as well.

So drenched is the story in this objective symbolism, the progress so complicated by the richly evocative detail, that the movement takes on a mountingly cumulative power which finally transforms a "love-story" into a curious nexus of ambiguity: a Poe-like decadence of climate and situation gradually invades the victors, who are left inheriting the evil they have supposed they came to put down. The allegory is left hovering in a state of perilous and daring tension between the natural and the supernatural, a tension which is relieved at the very end only by Lt. Munford's stunned recognition that he has been conquered by the cost of conquest. Those who like immediate political parables can shift the terms of the relationship to whatever conquered country they prefer.

In **"Hear the Nightingale Sing"** the same paradox is handled from another point of view and here again the conqueror is destroyed by the conquered. Again the "enemy" is represented by a woman, and although the delicately handled theme of the suppressed sexuality of the girl who is "overfond of animals" is not as complex as that of **"The Forest of the South,"** it is valuable for much the same kind of judgment. Here again the alternating impulses of protectiveness and violence are brought into focus as the terms of conduct in love and in war.

There is one further aspect of Miss Gordon's relationship to her imaginative centre, the South, which, as I have previously intimated, is rare in writing about that region. It is her extraordinarily keen insight into the caste structure of the South, in which the psychological complexities of what it means not "to be a nigger" or poor white trash, and, by indirection, what it means to be one are given the kind of exposition from which the sociologist might learn. **"Her Quaint Honour"** (1938) is a powerful example of this valuable type of social evidence: caste relationship, as a matter of fact, is the real theme of the story. But the oppositions are not over-simplified as in so much "liberal" interpreting of the south. Instead, caste loyalty comes into conflict with other equally strong values and the struggle thus set up can be resolved only in paradox in feeling or event.

> *Vivienne Koch, in a review of "The Forest of the South," in* The Sewanee Review, *Vol. LIV, No. 3, July-September, 1946, pp. 543-48.*

Louise Cowan   (essay date 1956)

[*Cowan is an American educator, critic, nonfiction writer, and editor whose writings have concentrated on the Fugitive movement. In the following excerpt, Cowan offers a stylistic and thematic analysis of "The Brilliant Leaves."*]

[In her] short story, **"Emmanuele! Emmanuele!"** Caroline Gordon has seized upon the Claudel-Gide contrast as a vehicle for an exploration of two opposite attitudes toward the artist's function. A young admirer of the celebrated Guillaume Fäy is discussing Fäy's journals with the poet Raoul Pleyol:

> "In his journals he dares face himself. It is more than most of us can do . . . "
>
> Pleyol said heavily: "It is more than any of us can do . . . Do you think that a man sees himself when he looks into a mirror? He sees only the pose he has assumed. If you want to see yourself look into the eyes of your friends—or your enemies—who are made in the image of God."
>
> Heyward said stubbornly: "An artist's first duty is to confront himself."
>
> Pleyol brought his big hand down on the desk. "An artist's first duty is the same as any other man's—to serve, praise, and worship God."

Pleyol's is the orthodox Christian position, one which Miss Gordon has displayed with increasing boldness in the last few years—in her anthology *The House of Fiction* (edited jointly with her husband, Allen Tate), in her critical essays on various writers, in her novel *The Strange Children,* and now in the story **"Emmanuele! Emmanuele!"** But it is a position implicit in the Southern background in which she was irrevocably steeped.

In that it is concerned with a young man's struggle to assimilate his heritage, Faulkner's *Absalom, Absalom!* may be taken as representative of the Southern conception of the artist. On the basis of this interpretation, it is instructive to contrast it with Joyce's *Portrait of the Artist as a Young Man,* in which, as the maturing Stephen Dedalus becomes more dedicated to his art, he finds he must progressively sever the ties that bind him to humanity. Finally, at the end of the work, it is "to forge the uncreated conscience" of his race that he sets out. His purpose is to bring into being a kind of truth that has not existed in life itself, and he is fully cognizant of the dangers inherent in such a task. In Faulkner's novel, on the contrary, Quentin Compson finds himself increasingly bound to a way of life, a group of people, and even a certain set of events— unwilling though he may be—as he is placed ever more surely in the position of viewer. His task has been to uncover what is already in existence, to uncover it and place it in the proper position to be recognized and known. His painful identification with the truth he sees and his suffering acceptance of his role are revealed in his cry, "I don't hate the South! I don't hate it!"—the antithesis of Stephen's cold rejection of his native land.

The difference in the two attitudes may be traced to the artist's conception of himself: as subject to the creator and the laws of his creation or as artificer of an independent order. Modern Southern writers in general have regarded their task as the discovery of an already existent pattern in actual experience rather than as the imposition of an ideal pattern upon experience. Their unanimity of attitude is not traceable to a conscious aesthetic (for there has been no traditional Southern theory of art), but to an instinctively coherent way of dealing with the world, a way inherited from their culture and underlying their own personal vision of life. This world view can best be described, I think, by the word *sacramental,* since it is a way of looking at the physical universe as existing both in its own right and as a sign. But, to the Southerner, matter is not in any simple fashion an embodiment of spirit. Objects and creatures are real in themselves, and yet they are also mysteries, reflecting God and each other in a network of resemblances which at times illumine and at times veil the relationship between the creator and his creation. The mode of thought resulting from this attitude is analogical, and, though it is of course far older than the American South, it is not encountered consistently elsewhere in literature written in English since the seventeenth century.

What I have termed the sacramental attitude Caroline Gordon has described in a recent article ("Some Readings and Misreadings," *Sewanee Review,* Summer, 1953) as a "patient, passionate portrayal of natural objects" which, in being based on "a recognition of the natural order," she can only consider Christian, at least "in hope." She finds this kind of writing in Yeats and in the nineteenth-century

masters of the art of fiction, from whom she learned her techniques. But many of the great nineteenth-century novels she finds to have a more direct indebtedness to Christianity, one grounded in revelation rather than in immanence, for they embody unconsciously "the strange and original plot" of the Christian scheme of redemption. From the study of her masters—Flaubert, Turgenev, Chekhov, James, and the early Joyce—she gained not only her distinguished technical competence but an architecture basically Christian, one consistent "in hope" with her heritage. Moreover, her own creative imagination has given a remarkable integrity to the two traditions within which she has worked; and, though the surface of her novels (before *The Strange Children,* in 1951) moves toward destruction and despair, the "current in their depths" moves in a strongly different direction.

"My stories, I think, are all one story, and as yet I hardly know what the plot is," Caroline Gordon has written. "Like most fiction writers, I seem to spend my life contemplating the same set of events. Each novel is what I make of those events." It is perhaps her short stories that provide the key to what is "the same set of events," since they are of necessity more tightly constructed than the novels and less involved in an expansive enveloping action. Of the stories published in *The Forest of the South* (1945), more than half deal with the special betrayal involved in the man-woman relationship. In his admirable article "Caroline Gordon and the Historic Image" (*Sewanee Review,* Fall, 1949), Andrew Lytle has remarked in Miss Gordon's writings the theme of man's inadequacy to woman and has given as demonstration a detailed analysis of the short story **"The Brilliant Leaves."** This inadequacy of man is truly one of Miss Gordon's persistent themes and the consequent turning away of the woman one of the principal events in her stories. But there is another betrayal in **"The Brilliant Leaves,"** another event, so that I may perhaps be forgiven if I consider the story further, taking advantage of Mr. Lytle's perceptive criticism. In this brief narrative, a boy watches helpless while the girl he loves falls to her death from a rocky ledge that she has wilfully insisted upon their climbing. The account would be one of unmitigated and senseless horror without the modifying and enlarging effect of the recurrent imagery which informs the story and, in reality, carries its meaning. At the beginning, when the boy goes to keep an innocent assignation with the girl in the woods, he must pass his mother and his aunt, who are sitting on the gallery, gossiping about the people who live in the white houses—the little white houses which, in the boy's eyes, cluster on the hill in all the solidarity of the featureless but encompassing world which cups his life. It is the boy who listens to the women on the porch recount the tale which is at once the prelude to and the recapitulation of the main story, and it is the boy who carries to the girl the tale of betrayal by inadequacy—the story of an old maid, Miss Sally Mainwaring, who, when a girl, descended a ladder to find her father, shotgun in hand, and her lover disappearing into the bushes. The woman's fate begins to be seen as an ironic parallel to the young couple's when the boy proposes marriage to the girl and is answered, "They wouldn't let us; we're too young." By the time the pair comes to the falls, the reader has been prepared for the powerful extensions of meaning in Miss Gordon's careful description:

> They came out of the hollow and were on the brow of the mountain again. In front of them was a series of limestone ledges that came down one after another like steps. Gushing out from one of them, filling the whole air with the sound of its rushing, was the white waterfall they called the Bridal Veil.

This is the "ladder" the girl is to descend when her foot slips and she falls backward; and like Miss Sally Mainwaring, she is to find no human lover waiting for her below. But, before the accident, standing over the precipice, her face moist from the spray, she urges the boy to attempt the climb behind the falls. "I like doing things with you," she confides, and, his cheeks burning, he consents against his better judgment. Later, we know from her failure to see the boy when he finally reaches her—though her eyes are open—and from her screams when he tries to lift her up that she feels herself bitterly betrayed.

My stories, I think, are all one story, and as yet I hardly know what the plot is. Like most fiction writers, I seem to spend my life contemplating the same set of events.

—Caroline Gordon

But though the girl is betrayed, so too is the boy, albeit in a less simple manner—by his trust in the benevolence of the surrounding world. When he first leaves the chatting women on the porch to follow a path into the woods, he halts once and looks back, seeing the women and unconsciously knowing them for what they are: the women for whom life—that inner life of joy and adventure—has stopped. They are "on the shelf," viewing experience from the outside, and their concern is with the civilized and conventional white houses. As the boy enters the woods, he sees under his feet the "brilliant, fallen leaves" and remembers his aunt's comment about them the day before, when she had returned from a walk; the entrance to the woods was "positively spectacular," she had said; but she had gone no further into the woods. The dazzling colors of the autumnal leaves were, like everything else for her, a matter for conversation. But in the boy's mind they are connected with the passion and excitement of the ripened moment, now when the two young people stand on the threshold of maturity, when their adolescent love has changed in its character. "It's different, isn't it?" the girl comments and, when she is questioned, replies, "Last time we were here the woods were just turning green." But after she has fallen from the ledge, the full comprehension of the plight of the leaves is left to the boy, who, running for help, understands them now, though only on the periphery of his own extremity:

> He ran slower now, lurching sometimes from side to side, but he ran on. He ran and the brilliant, the wine-colored leaves crackled and broke under his feet. His mouth, a taut square, drew in, released whining breaths. His starting eyes fixed the ground, but he did not see the leaves that he ran over. He saw only the white houses that no matter how fast he ran kept always just ahead of him. If he did not hurry they would slide off the hill, slide off and leave him running forever through these woods, over these dead leaves.

Time has frozen for the boy, and, with a nightmare-like clarity, he sees into the depths of his relationship with nature. He is engaged in an efforted and painful flight that takes him nowhere, with help from society beyond his reach. He is ineffectual and alone, and he sees that eternity could be like this one suspended moment. The fallen, brilliant leaves now are known for what they are: dead and dry bits of vegetation, cut off from their source; and likewise the boy must recognize the life of innocent joy and delight (the green leaves) irrecoverably gone and the dazzling and exciting life of adventure and passion (the brilliant leaves) heartbreakingly deceptive.

It has been written of Turgenev, whom out of the whole world of novelists Miss Gordon most resembles, that his women are strong, his men weak, and chance all-powerful. One might be tempted to substitute death (or time) for the word *chance* and to let the statement stand for Caroline Gordon's chief theme, particularly after a reading of **"The Brilliant Leaves."** But, though, as Mr. Lytle has suggested, the boy is inadequate to the girl in the grim drama, his inadequacy derives from his strength. Both are defeated by the conditions of human life—by being committed to nature, which carries within itself the principle of its own dissolution. The defeat is more painful in being of necessity solitary.

"The Brilliant Leaves" is almost parabolic, so clear, hard, and precise are its analogical formulations. And when we look back over Miss Gordon's novels, we realize that indeed it is a kind of parable, or—perhaps more properly—a dumb-show in which the events of the novels are acted out in shortened and pantomimic version. The constant set of events in all the novels revolves around man and woman, caught in mortality and seeking self-realization. Woman attempts to find fulfillment in love, whereas man looks outward to some aspect of "the world." Both become aware of their defeat at about the same time: a crisis may precipitate its sudden discovery, or it may lie hidden under the surface of an increasingly meaningless life. Two paths are open to the woman: to fall over the precipice into utter destruction, as does the girl in **"The Brilliant Leaves,"** or to become one of the women on the porch, as does Miss Sally Mainwaring in the same story. But the men must engage themselves in perpetual flight. And for both sexes, the common enemy Death is constantly at hand, and, as time wears on, increasingly more bold in revealing himself.

Louise Cowan, "Nature and Grace in Caroline Gordon," in Critique: Studies in Modern Fiction, *Vol. 1, No. 1, Winter, 1956, pp. 11-27.*

An excerpt from "The Captive"

The Cherokee, Mad Dog, had been sitting there broiling the deer nose on a rock that he had got red-hot in the flames. When it was brown he brought it over and gave it to me. Then he went back and sat down, sullen like, not saying anything. The fire shone on his black eyes and on his long beak of a nose. When he moved, you could see the muscles moving, too, in his big chest and up and down his naked legs. An Indian woman would have thought him a fine-looking man, tall and well formed in every way, but it frightened me to look at him. I was glad it was the old chief and not him that had taken me prisoner. I was glad, too, that the chief was old. I'd heard tell how particular the Indians are about things like that. I thought the old chief would likely do what he said and keep me for his daughter, but if it was Mad Dog he would have me for his wife.

I thought the meat never would get done, but it finally did. The Indians give me a good-size piece off the haunch and I ate it all, except a little piece I put in Dinny's mouth. He spit it out, but I kept putting it back till he got some good of it. Then I took him down to the creek and scooped up water in my hands for him. He'd been fretting because my milk was giving out, but the water and the juice from the meat quieted him a little. After we'd both had all the water we could drink I went back up the hill and sat down on a log with Dinny laying across my knees. It felt good to have his weight off my arms, but I was afraid to take my hands off him. I was feared one of them might come up and snatch him away from me any minute.

He laid there a while a-fretting and then he put his little hand up and felt my face.

"Sadie . . . " he said. "Sadie . . . "

Sadie was the oldest girl. She played with him a lot and fondled him. He'd go to her any time out of my arms.

I hugged him up close and sang him the song Sadie used to get him to sleep by. "Lord Lovell, he stood at the castle gate," I sang, and the tears a-running down my face.

"Hush, my pretty," I said, "hush. Sadie's gone, but Mammy's here. Mammy's here with Baby."

He cried, though, for Sadie and wouldn't nothing I could do comfort him. He cried himself hoarse and then he'd keep opening his little mouth but wouldn't no sound come. I felt him and he was hot to the touch. I was feared he'd fret himself into a fever, but there wasn't nothing I could do. I held his arms and legs to the blaze and got him as warm as I could, and then I went off from the fire a little way and laid down with him in my arms.

Caroline Gordon, in her The Collected Stories of Caroline Gordon, *1981.*

Caroline Gordon with Catherine B. Baum and Floyd C. Watkins   (interview date 1966)

[*Watkins is an American educator, critic, nonfiction writer, and editor. In the following interview conducted in 1966, Gordon discusses the source, structure, themes,*

and various critical interpretations of her short story "The Captive."]

[Watkins writes in a prefatory note: "In the winter of 1966, Caroline Gordon taught creative writing at Emory University. She consented to spend an evening with Catherine B. Baum, my wife, and me. Mrs. Baum and I asked her many questions, most of them about that remarkable short story of the life of Jinny Wiley among the Indians, **"The Captive."** A valuable aspect of the interview is the fact that Miss Gordon did not reread the story. She pulls her comments out of the pure material of memory—out of the past. Here, she seems almost to be Caroline Gordon at the time of the writing of the story.

Questions and answers are taken from the tape recording of the conversation. We have made editorial deletions, but no additions."]

[*Watkins and Baum*]: *Did you follow your source closely?*

[Gordon]: Yes. I did. I'm trying to think if I changed it in any way. Now the source, the old book that the story is based on, is called the *Wiley Captivity and the Founding of Harman's Station.* [The critics add in a footnote: "The full title is *The Founding of Harman's Station with an Account of the Indian Captivity of Mrs. Jennie Wiley and the Exploration and Settlement of the Big Sandy Valley in the Virginias and Kentucky,* by William Esley Connelley (New York, 1910)."] I thought it was such a wonderful story, and it seemed to me that the story was almost written, and I got the notion that I could finish it. This old man had done such a wonderful job, the man who wrote the book—Connelley, a local historian.

I would agree, but I think yours is still much more wonderful and I'm sure of some of the differences, but not all of them.

Well, since I wrote it so long ago, I think I might say, without flattering myself too much, I think my story is art. He wasn't trying to create a work of art. He's an historian. I'm not an historian. I'm a fiction writer. I saw it in fictional terms. But now I think he has the soul of an artist, or he could never have done those pictures. I think the pictures are perfectly wonderful. I'm very much impressed by them, and when you gave me the book the other day, and I looked at them, I felt exactly as enthusiastic as I did when I wrote that story.

Do you know any other modern writers who have written captivity stories?

Janet Lewis wrote a book called *The Invasion* about the Chippewa that I thought was wonderful. That was maybe twenty or twenty-five years ago—a wonderful book. It wasn't exactly an Indian captivity.

You've read a good many captivities?

A few, not many. This one just sort of leaped at me and led me by the heels. Donald Davidson's great grandmother was captured by the Indians and taken to Canada, and her husband, I think his name was Andrew, went all over the country looking for her, and finally he was in a boarding house in Canada and she was a servant waiting on the table, and he recognized her and took her back to Tennessee.

It's a wonder Davidson hasn't written something about that.

Isn't it. I've often wondered about that. I don't think he has. Do you?

Not that I know of. Have you ever been in the country where Jinny lived?

Well, now, that's a strange thing. Year before last, summer before last, I went down to eastern Kentucky to a writers' conference. I'd never been in eastern Kentucky before in my life, and I was very much interested in the country. I saw little low hills, and they would plant corn clear to the top of the hill, or tobacco—something I never saw before. One of my colleagues offered to drive me over to Hindman, Kentucky, to see James Still, a novelist whose work you may know. And as we drove over I kept looking at the landscape and finally I said to him, "You know, I have the strangest feeling as if I had been along here before, and I just never have." And then we go along about twenty-five miles, and I saw a sign which said "Jinny Wiley State Park." Now I've never been up in that country where she was, you know. By that Paint Creek—and there's one called Mud Creek. I've never been up there.

When you read this book that you used as a source, were you looking for a source for a story? Or when did you realize that you wanted to write a story about her?

I was in the stacks in the Vanderbilt library, and I took this book down idly. I suppose this is the first thing I wrote about the pioneer period. I think I wrote it before *Green Centuries*. And I took it down and looked at it, and I got very excited about it. I thought it was wonderful, and I read it at first just because I found it so interesting. And then the idea of finishing the story came to me. It seemed to me that the story was there. I don't think I thought about it much at the time. I just knew I had to write that story.

How much longer was it before you wrote it?

I can't remember. I do remember this—that I suffered more writing it than any story I ever wrote—than any short story. Well, it's a long story really. I think I was on it for about six weeks, and I remember, when I got through with it, I got some white satin and embroidered pink roses on it for my daughter's doll dresses because I felt as if I had been living in the wilderness for weeks from jerky—you know those venison meats. And I really was exhausted, and I felt I needed to coddle myself. Well, actually, I don't think I read the story over more than two or three times since I wrote it.

Do you like to reread your own work?

I can't bear to touch any of my short stories.

Can't bear to reread them or can't bear to revise them? Or either one?

Well, revising is an entirely different thing, but I can't bear to read them after they're written.

Why?

Well, I'm primarily, I guess, a novelist, and I used to feel about writing short stories sort of like I was making a journey through a dark wood and finally got out on the outside and was set upon by wolves. (Laughs.) I used to wish I wouldn't get an idea for a short story. (Laughs.) I don't like to write them. I mean I don't like to write novels either, but, well, I've been interested in this phenomenon in publishing. When the publishers get hold of good short story writers, Katherine Anne Porter, Flannery O'Connor, J. F. Powers, they try to turn them into novelists, and nearly always they suffer dreadfully over long periods of years trying to write this novel that they ought not to have to write. And whenever they write they do their own work—like short stories. And it's a little the same way with me. I wasn't cut out to write short stories.

I would have to argue that you're very much cut out to write both. Do you object to rereading a novel less?

Yes. Uh-huh. I have picked up my novels and reread them interested to find out what was going to happen. (Laughs.) Because they go out of your mind. When you've finished a book, it's gone. I can't remember the names of some of the characters.

Back to Jinny, why did you omit her pregnancy and the birth of the child as described in the source? She had a child by her husband after she was captured.

Just too much.

And would the dog be [omitted for] the same reason?

Yes. Now, I remember one thing. I started the story when the Indians came, and there's a passage where she sees one of her daughters tomahawked, and then she sees her fourteen-year-old son, sees an Indian tomahawk him, and she thinks, "Well, I can't get any more help from him." And then it goes on. Well, my editor, Maxwell Perkins, in the course of our long and happy association, made me three suggestions, and he made me one about this story which I pass on to my pupils. He said—"Caroline, where are you going to go from there?" He said, "If a woman looks at her fourteen-year-old son while he is being tomahawked and her chief emotion is that she can't get any more help from him, she is wound up to such a pitch that she is beyond the borders of reality and you can't handle her in fiction."

That's not a selfish thought on her part?

Well, I don't think so, no. I think it's—well—a parallel in *The Red Badge of Courage*. The soldier looks up and sees that the sun, the red sun was pasted in the sky like a wafer. Well, that's an impressionistic rendering of the way we react when we've had all we can take. The apparatus that registers horror-emotion isn't working for a while.

That's the best answer I've heard to this frequent query about Jinny's emotions.

Well, I believe Maxwell is right about that. I saw at once he was right about that. I've always remembered it and tried to practice it. And I went back and built the story up a little more. As I recall it starts with her husband,

Tom Wiley—it starts something like, "We were up before daybreak and loading the horses, and even then Tom wasn't a mind to go," as I remember. And, then she persuades him to go and that gets him off the scene, you see. And then, the Indians begin to hoot and holler and she is afraid of them; that is, she hears owls and she suspects that they're Indians. And then as I recall a neighbor comes in, and then she gets the children to play a game. They all dance. It came from Maxwell's suggestion that you couldn't start with her keyed-up so high.

The children sing a song at this point—"Hog-drovers, hog-drovers, hog-drovers we air." Does that foreshadow in any respect the fate of the daughters? Foreshadow the coming of the Indians in that story?

I don't remember.

"Hog-drovers, hog-drovers, hog-drovers we air, A-courtin' your daughter so sweet and so fair."

"Kin we git lodgin' here, O here . . . ?"

"No pig-stealing drover kin git her from Pap." And I thought possibly that the hostility of the hog-drovers in that song might foreshadow the coming of the Indians to Jinny's family. Is that too farfetched?

I think in a well-constructed story every single stroke helps, you know, the structure. It's all one fabric. But I don't believe that that really is symbolic of Indians. The Indians are on the scene already with their imitations of the hoots of owls. No, I think that's a little farfetched.

Well, I've been misteaching my class for years.

Well, you must remember that I may be wrong. And I haven't read the story. Perhaps I should have read the story before coming here tonight.

No, I think you remember it well. Did you know that song, "Hog-Drovers," as a child?

I got it from Andrew Lytle. He used to sing it often.

You know he used it in a story.

Which story is it?

"Jericho, Jericho, Jericho."

Did he? Well, I had written this one before he did. (Laughs.)

Where did you hear the story about "Pa'tridge in the Pea Patch," or the song rather? Do you remember that one?

Yes, I do. "Kickin' up her heels. Call the little gal to milk her in the pail." I don't remember, but for *Green Centuries* I have a bale of notes, of pioneer customs and ways. Yes, it's about this thick, the way people live. And you know you collect things. I'm trying to recall now, but I think that I wrote **"The Captive"** before I started collecting material for *Green Centuries*.

Was there an actual song about Vard Wiley, or did you—?

I made that up. (Laughs.) My only essay into verse.

You mention eating smoked herring in Virginia. And a man who had never read your story was telling me about remembering eating smoked herring when he was a child in Virginia. Did you know this from your own experience?

Oh, yes. My family used to get, in Kentucky, used to buy kegs of salted roe herring. They sent them from, oh, Richmond or Baltimore every year, and it was our favorite breakfast—with hot biscuits.

What's a dog alley?

Dog alley?

In a house.

Do I say "dog alley"? Do I? Usually it's dog run.

Well, I have always called it dog trot.

Yes. Clarence Nixon, you know him? Well, he said that too.

Dog trot?

But dog run was the—. I'm surprised at myself for saying dog alley. Dog run was the phrase I heard. Well, you know what it is, the hall. But the dogs lay there.

Now you added, if I'm not mistaken, all the story of Lance Rayburn's courtship of Jinny Wiley.

Yes.

Well, did this have its own source or was this invented, so to say?

Invented.

What about the story of the old man who dressed in women's clothes and teased old man Daugherty while he was in swimming. Do you remember that one?

Oh yes.

Did you invent that one, or had you heard it?

I heard it. It happened in our neighborhood. (Laughter.)

It may interest you to know it happened during my father's childhood also.

Well, those things—it's the archetype appearing, you know. They're archetypal, and people do these same things. It's right interesting to a fiction writer. For that reason I think Jung, the psychiatrist, is much more interesting than Freud because he calls your attention constantly to the—well, he believes that the archetype is operating right now. I had a student once in New York, a boy from Indiana, who was writing a story called "Lament for a Southern Guitar." That's a nice title, isn't it? It was about a hillbilly boy who had come to the city to look for his friend, a crooner who'd made good on the big time. And he looks for him everywhere and finally finds him in some low dive, a wreck, taken to marijuana or something. Anyway, this young man was also—I had a course in mythology which I'd worked up—and he was taking that course too, and one day he said to me, "Miss Gordon, I just found out what I'm doing." So I said, "Well, what are you doing, Frank?" He said, "I'm writing an Orpheus." And I'd never mentioned Orpheus to him in connection with his story, though I had thought often that this is really a re-enactment of the myth, a version. So I think you find those things happening all the time.

Where did you ever hear dialect like Jinny's? Did you know country speech?

Sure.

As a child?

Why of course I can talk several dialects if I want to. I don't speak them socially. (Laughs.) The new grammarians speak of the dialect of the President of the United States or the dialect of the Queen of England. But now neither of those worthies would keep their jobs if they spoke in dialect.

In true dialect?

Yes, I can speak in dialect anytime I want to, and often do. But I must resent being told that I customarily speak dialect as some of the new grammarians maintain. I remember Flannery O'Connor sending me a story a few years ago, asking me for comment, and I wrote back, "Yes, I'll give you my comments on the story, but I'll tell you now I'm not going to give any advice to any young writer who is under the impression that *slurp* is a verb." So she sent me a good many stories over the years for comment, but she never again, in my presence at least, used *slurp* as a verb.

Where did you get the names for Mad Dog and Crowmocker? Those seem like very legitimate names and they're not in the source.

I got them out of some books about the Cherokee Indians, I forget just which ones.

You didn't make up the fact that Indians cooked the noses of deer on hot rocks? Is it Jinny or one of the Indians who cooks the nose of the deer?

I had forgotten that, but I'm sure I didn't make it up.

I think the Indian cooked it and brought it to her.

Well, I'm sure I didn't make it up. I just couldn't.

It sounds like a special delicacy, like pigs' feet or something of that sort.

You know, in the Cherokee nation the deer clan was, I believe, the most esteemed clan. Who was it that said that the braves of the nation were concentrated in the deer clan? It produced the men who had the greatest influence among the white people. Well, of course, my hero in *Green Centuries* is Dragging Canoe, and his father, Atta Kulla Kulla, was one of those Indians—I think there were six—who were sent to London. They were painted by Sir Joshua Reynolds, and in that book was the great warrior Oconostota. And when he came back he told his people—he reviewed his career as their leader in war—and he said he'd done everything exactly right when they went out on the warpath. He had stopped on the right side of the tree. You know, of course, that every move they made was prescribed as ritual. He does everything exactly the way he should have done it. But across the water there was a medicine or religion more powerful than theirs, and it was no more use. And then Atta Kulla Kulla took this up and the

white men called him "the little carpenter" because he could make a treaty so neatly with the white man, which of course the white man never kept and never intended to keep. (Laughs.) The letters that were exchanged between our hero John Sevier and people like that and the Indian chief were very moving. The Indian chiefs meant what they said. But John Sevier didn't mean a word he said, nor did the other white men. Well, anyway, Dragging Canoe told the Indians not to have anything to do with the white man—not to take his guns, not to take those bolts of stroud cloth they loved so much, not to take the beads, and not even to take the cow. He treated with Spain, with France and England, and really had set himself up, you see, to overthrow the white man. But of course, he couldn't. One thing that's interested me is that almost every Indian tribe had its Pocahontas, and the Cherokee Pocahontas was a woman named Nancy Ward. She was a member of the deer clan. She was what they called a ghigau. I don't know how to pronounce it: g-h-i-g-a-u. It was a matriarchal organization, you know. And she sat with the men in the long house and waved the swan's wing; that is, she had the power of veto. That's the only power she had. But she could veto anything when she waved the swan's wing.

If I can switch to the subject of technique, why did you let Jinny tell her own story instead of having someone tell it about her? Is that a fair question?

No. No. You know I never thought of it at the time. But instinctively I imagine—well, I just think it's better told that way. After all, one of the technical inventions of modern times is the interior monologue—getting into the character's consciousness—something that Tolstoy never did, or Thackeray or Dickens. But that's one of the things we've learned, and I don't think I could have gotten the story across as well. I don't think so. I think the first question that anybody who writes a story or a novel has to face is the point of view. Now I think most writers solve the problem unconsciously; they don't stop to think about it. And I didn't at the time; I just did it that way. But since then I've had to think about these things, deduce theories, you know.

As Jinny remembers her former life, what's the purpose of that passage? There are several pages where she recalls her grandmother and her courtship—does she do that before or after the young captive comes?

I think she did it before; I'm not sure. Well I think, looking back on it—the forest was a great menace to the pioneer, you know. That's one reason they cut the trees down, looted the country. In a way they were afraid of it. Certain men that were very bold like Daniel Boone fell in love with it and didn't want to be out of the forest. But the pioneer just had a hatred of the forest. And in the forest, you lost your individuality.

Does that happen to Jinny?

Well yes, yes. I think there's one passage—something about people that lived and nobody ever knew what became of them or something like that. After all she had lost her husband and her children, and she was away from everything she'd ever seen before and with strange people.

And I think it's only natural that one way of asserting your individuality is through your memories. Of course old people, when they get pinned down, we say, it's a commonplace, that they begin to dwell in the past.

Is the theme of the loss of the wilderness a part of this story, a theme maybe not unlike that in Faulkner's The Bear?

Well, of course an awful lot of nonsense has been written about Faulkner's stuff, but I don't know. I don't ever think of my stories as having a theme.

Do you use a different term?

No. Theme is old-fashioned to me. The Victorians used to talk about the theme or the moral. I think people talk about themes nowadays as being Victorian. Instead of saying the moral, they say the theme. We're getting into deep water, aren't we?

I have some of that feeling about the word. But I think that a story may have a meaning even though it's not necessarily a moral—and a meaning you may talk about.

The writer might not see it that way.

Does he object to the idea or to the word?

Who?

The writer. The idea of meaning or theme or moral to a story—these are very bad terms, but if you could get rid of the terms would he object to the idea?

Well, I expect my kind of writer would. But I'm a little bit peculiar. I think that that in a way is the way Dante describes the process in this letter that he wrote to his patron Can Grande della Scala. You remember that there was a man, another poet, who was supported by this nobleman, and he said to Dante one day, "Why is it that everybody likes to read my poems and so few people like to read yours?" Dante said, "Because there are so many of you and there's only one of me." Then a few days later, Can Grande della Scala said to Dante, "Why is it that everybody likes to read so-and-so's poems and so few people like to read yours?" And Dante evidently had his full share of vanity; so he sat down and wrote him this letter which I think is a very valuable thing. And he said, "In order to read my poetry, you've got to read in four different ways." And then he set forth four levels. He said you've got to read first on the literal level, then on the allegorical level. That is to say, you can say something and at the same time say something else. I can say, "He got up and left the house." Well, if he's a character in my story, he got up and left the house, but his getting up and leaving the house, allegorically, may mean all sorts of things. And then I accept Dante's four-fold level completely. He said there is a moral or tropological level: "Ought he to have got up and left the house?" (Laughs.) And on the fourth level, anagogical, well, I don't think fiction writers often hit it and only the greatest poets, like Milton and Dante, who treat of heavenly matters. Now, I think this story fits in that category. And it's certainly mostly on the literal level and, I don't know, maybe Dante's allegorical level is the same as the theme. I dislike the word *theme* though.

I dislike allegory more than I do theme. You don't?

Well, allegory has been around ever since Aesop, and I don't think you can get rid of allegory. *Theme,* well, we haven't had it long.

Well, I'll try to avoid it from now on, then.

No. No.

Why is "Lord God, I sure was lucky to get away from them Indians" such a good ending? My daughter laughed about that ending for five minutes after she had finished the story.

Well, now you see you and I were in disagreement a few minutes ago. Putnam, a poet that I used to know—he's dead now—liked this story very much. And he disliked that ending. He thought I should have cut it off when she gets there into the blockhouse.

You don't agree with him?

No, I don't. I think it's necessary to round it off. And I'm glad to see you like it.

I think it's such an understatement, for one thing. It's a very mild and simple way to sum up something.

Well, and I think it's characteristic. That's why I was a little astonished when my student wrote this paper that she wasn't of heroic stature. I think it helps to put her up on a pedestal by putting her in the proper perspective. She lived to be ninety-seven, and her husband died soon after she got back. She married again and had a whole 'nother breed of children. There was a Negro man named Ananias who had a very large family and our family's doctor, Cousin Robin, told Ananias that he really didn't think his wife could have another child; it would endanger her health. Then after a while Ananias came and reported that Susie was that way again. And Cousin Robin said, "But, Ananias, I told you. Susie could not have another child." He said, "It's the Lord's will, Doctor." And Cousin Robin, who was an agnostic like most men, said, "Don't talk that way to me. The Lord never had but one child himself."

I like that too. Do you think country people have better memories than most city people? Take Jinny. She remembers specific birds when she was escaping and the way the light shines and exact fears. Would that be true to the country character of Jinny?

Of course.

Why can't city people remember that well?

They don't have time. They don't have time—they're always rushing to go somewhere.

I heard a person at Georgia Tech the other night say that country people could remember so well because they had so little to remember.

Oh, well, that's urban nonsense. They're trying to remember, and to look at things. City people don't have time to see they're so rushed.

Will you accept—if you won't take the word theme—*will you accept the word* symbol?

Oh, yes.

Would you say that the lights on Jinny's trip back from the wilderness could be regarded as symbolic?

The lights?

Yes. She sees lights as she wades in the water that shine peculiarly to her through the forest. Would this be because of her psychological state?

I don't remember that, but I should think so. She was in a very wrought up condition because, well, you know the dream she had when the captive comes to her with the buffalo skull lamp, and in her dream she sees the fort built by the man who comes to rescue her.

That dream shows her the exact way to escape, doesn't it?

Absolutely.

Is that supernatural?

Of course it is. Now that dream, you see, that's one reason that story's so good. That old man, Mr. Connelley, had that dream in there. I don't know whether I, a raw fiction writer at the time, would have ever had nerve to invent it. It was already there, you know. You remember his wonderful picture of the captive. It's very moving. So I just buttressed it a little on each side. I think you see Lance Rayburn there and all sorts of things like that. But it's very bold. Well, it's a little of what nowadays they call extrasensory perception, a term unheard of when I wrote that story and certainly in her day. Well, symbol, symbol and theme, I think one reason I'm so impatient with the word *theme* is that it so often gets in the way of symbol. And I'm old enough now to have people write critically about my work. Well, there are three young men writing about it now, and each one of them finds out symbols that never entered my head.

Can they be valid if they didn't enter your head?

I don't believe they're ever valid if they enter your head. (Laughs.) I really don't. I mean it's like if you say, now I'm going to have a young woman in my story who symbolizes greed, she'll never do it. You create a character and years later you might look back on it and say, well, you know now, that Anna Maria symbolizes greed.

If that's the case though, why can't the reader put into a story any symbolism he wants to put into it?

He often does, but he ought to be ashamed of himself.

How does he know when he ought to be ashamed of himself?

Well, I think if he were brought up on Dante's four-fold level of interpretation, he'd know. That's one of the things I try to teach them—what a symbol is. A symbol is a sign.

Is Jinny's failure to try to escape more before the dream any kind of moral or cultural weakness on her part? Has she given up to her life with the Indians too much?

Well, I think that question is sociological—almost. I will not charge you with that crime, but almost. The woman is human. She has seen all her children killed. She saw a man tortured to death. She herself was in danger of being tortured. I think that's brought out very plainly. She's

frightened to death. She has a kind of minor nervous breakdown. I would have been dead or nuts by this time, and I think most modern women. She is of heroic stature, but still she is a human being. And how can you say, how can anybody say, that she's lacking in moral fiber? I think she's got about forty times as much moral fiber as almost any woman I know.

Does the fact that all the men are gone from the fort who might help Jinny except this one old man—might we call that symbolic?

Now, I don't think so. No. What are those men doing? They're looking for Jinny. This man hasn't gone. His name is Henry Skaggs and he was a famous Indian fighter, but he is very old and feeble. Very likely they brought him along for all his skill in trailing and all that. And that's why he's left there. I think, when people don't recognize a symbol when they see it, they make symbols where there aren't symbols.

I have a hard time making my point in language you will accept, but one of the things that's striking in this story to me is the hardship of frontier life on the women. And even in the story when you see two deer together, a buck will bump the female.

Bucks have been bumping females for thousands of years.

But maybe they bumped them harder on the frontier than at any other time.

I doubt that the pioneer woman had a harder time than the woman who lives today. Margaret Mead, the anthropologist, in one of her books, she says that the young married woman who is a mother too today does I think it's eight times as much work as her grandmother did. In the first place, there always used to be a grandmother or an old maid aunt who loved to keep the baby. Nowadays the association with the older generation is considered to be poisonous. No grandmother is allowed to come into the house with her grandson except on special occasions. And this young woman, if she lives in the city, if she lives an urban life, is a chauffeur, a laundress, a therapist, well—as a doctor I know from Princeton said to me, "Most of my patients are young married women, and they all work as hard as *five* women; they do the work of five women."

Do you think they might bear up under a captivity like Jinny had?

No, because their nerves are at a different tempo. No, I don't think they could. She was an outdoor woman, and as I recall she was a dead shot, loved to shoot, and she was a sportswoman, so to speak. And no, I don't think they would know how to protect themselves at all in her circumstances. They couldn't possibly have done it. But a woman who lived that way didn't think she underwent such hardships.

Do you think that the frontiersmen in this story have a culture inferior to ours?

Well, I don't know. I think our culture is in an awfully bad way, but I can't say theirs is superior. Each age you know has its hazards. That's one of those categorical questions I couldn't answer. Could you? You answer it.

Caroline Gordon, Catherine B. Baum, and Floyd C. Watkins, in an interview in The Southern Review, *Louisiana State University, n.s. Vol. VII, No. 2, April, 1971, pp. 447-62.*

James E. Rocks   (essay date 1970)

[*In the following essay, Rocks offers a stylistic and technical analysis of Gordon's short fiction.*]

From the beginning of her extensive career as novelist and critic, Caroline Gordon has written short fiction. Her earliest story, **"Summer Dust,"** appeared in late 1929—two years before her first novel, *Penhally*—and her recent belletristic writing has been in the short fiction genre. The majority of her stories date, however, from 1929 to 1945, when most of them were collected in **The Forest of the South.** A second volume, **Old Red and Other Stories** (1963), reprinted eight from the earlier collection and added five of her recent ones; both of these volumes are now out of print.

The appearance of this second collection recognized Miss Gordon's popularity as a short story writer. Because her best work has been in this form, a study of the shorter fiction can provide the reader with a good perspective on the body of her writing. Her achievements in the technique and craft of fiction are widely recognized and praised; the stories, as well as the novels, exemplify her inheritance of the Jamesian tradition of fiction. But Miss Gordon is not very successful in controlling the larger form: the novels produce the effect of a series of parts that do not cohere into something larger. The stories are particularly important for an understanding of her work not only because they are distinguished examples of her craft but because they crystallize many of the themes that dominate all her writing. Often, in fact, they are condensed statements of the problems she confronts at length in the novels.

In this study I have read Miss Gordon's short fiction with two questions in mind: how do her stories reveal a preoccupation with certain themes and techniques and how, interpreted together, do the stories show the development of her career from the secularism of the agrarian ethic to an acceptance of the Christian myth of salvation? Some of her stories are key examples of the progress of her quest toward Catholicism; others need to be seen in relation to these important stories. And because her short pieces are scattered in magazines and collections and because only a few of them are widely known, my purpose is to provide a general view of her short fiction. Many of her stories deserve fuller readings than they have received before or than I have given them here. I hope the detail I have sacrificed has made way for a clearer presentation of the dominant pattern of her thought and art.

A reading of her stories in chronological order reveals something of the broad outlines of her development as an interpreter of the South and of the growth of her ideas about man's material and spiritual existence; and such a reading also shows that her theories of fiction did not really change, for her earlier stories are as carefully crafted in the impressionistic manner as are her later ones. But the chronological approach to her short fiction is limited, because it does not allow the reader to see how an appreciation of her fiction is enhanced by the juxtaposition of stories written at different times in her long career.

A more meaningful approach to an overview of Miss Gordon's short fiction is to arrange her stories by subject into three groups. To be sure, all of the stories are interrelated, for they treat the same principal theme—natural and supernatural grace. A concern for man's condition in relation to a historical tradition informs every work of fiction that Miss Gordon wrote. But one group is centrally concerned with the burden of history, particularly Southern history, and parallels the themes of *Green Centuries* (1941), *None Shall Look Back* (1937), and *Penhally* (1931), respectively the exposition, crisis, and catastrophe of her portrayal of the Southern tragedy. Several stories that define the Negro personality fall conveniently into this group because they treat the question of racial identity in the South. A second group features Aleck Maury, the subject of her most popular novel, *Aleck Maury, Sportsman* (1934). The half-dozen stories about him are far less diffuse than the novel and present the themes of this saga with greater drama and meaning; moreover, these stories provide some insight into Caroline Gordon herself, who appears in several of them in the guise of the character Sarah.

"The Presence" (1948), the last of the Maury stories published, shows an important transition in Miss Gordon's thinking—from an ethic rooted in the values of agrarianism to one reaching toward the divine grace of the Christian myth. As a Roman Catholic convert in the early fifties, Miss Gordon saw that a sole reliance upon material values will destroy the necessary spiritual life that man must ultimately accept. *The Garden of Adonis* (1937) and *The Women on the Porch* (1944) show her working toward the scheme of redemption portrayed in her two most recent novels, *The Strange Children* (1951) and *The Malefactors* (1956). Her latest short stories, the third group, are concerned with precisely these problems of the Christian life and anticipate a novel reportedly in progress; this autobiographical fiction returns to very much the same situation treated in her first story, **"Summer Dust."**

These three groups—stories about history, Aleck Maury, and the Christian myth—include almost every work of short fiction she has written. There is one exception, however. **"The Brilliant Leaves,"** probably her finest work in the short form, resists convenient labels. Nowhere in Miss Gordon's fiction are so many natural facts rendered symbolic; none of the stories is more indicative of her themes and techniques. A perfect union of form and content, this story dramatizes a theme central to her works, that of the betrayal of woman by man. Because **"The Brilliant Leaves"** provides an approach to the interpretation of her fiction as a whole, it deserves separate—and, indeed, initial—consideration. Despite its apparent simplicity this narrative is rich and subtle.

"The Brilliant Leaves" plays a variation on the theme of innocence and experience: a young couple pays the supreme price of physical or emotional death for a newly acquired knowledge about each other and themselves. Evelyn and Jim, the intelligence of the story, represent life, youth, and the immediate present, and stand in marked opposition to his mother and aunt, who sit during the story on the veranda of a staid summer resort and thus remind the reader of the inhabitants of Swan Quarter in *The Women on the Porch*. To young Jim they represent the tedious milieu of adult convention which inhibits his youthful vigor. They are discussing the once high-spirited Miss Sally Mainwaring, who a long time before had climbed down a ladder, a symbolic descent from innocence, to meet her lover; when he ran off frightened she reentered the enclosure of the house to remain unmarried for the rest of her life. The apparently casual topic of conversation between the mother and the aunt foreshadows the action that follows.

Jim leaves the resort and goes into the woods, which are resplendent with the brilliant red leaves of autumn. When he meets Evelyn she says that a telegram from Miss Mainwaring to her mother almost kept her from meeting him; in the context of the events that follow, Miss Mainwaring could have prevented Evelyn from placing a mistaken trust in her lover. Like the spinster, and by extension many of Miss Gordon's heroines, Evelyn makes excessive demands of her lover. Her vision of love is romantic; impetuous and reckless, she disregards consequences, whereas Jim is cautious and heedful. Because Evelyn wishes to return to the beauty and innocence of an earlier encounter, she asks Jim to find a meeting place that is still mostly green like summer. While descending the mountain ledge into a valley below, suggestive of Miss Mainwaring climbing down the ladder, Evelyn slips into the chasm of Bridal Veil Falls. Like her, Evelyn is betrayed by a weakling lover, who does not or cannot save her from disaster; each woman had placed too much faith in her man, who in turn had not prevented her from taking the course of action that precipitated her emotional or physical death.

> "The Brilliant Leaves," probably her finest work in the short form, resists convenient labels. Nowhere in Miss Gordon's fiction are so many natural facts rendered symbolic; none of the stories is more indicative of her themes and techniques. A perfect union of form and content, this story dramatizes a theme central to her works, that of the betrayal of woman by man.
>
> —*James E. Rocks*

After determining that Evelyn is near death, he climbs the ledge: "He ran and the brilliant, the wine-colored leaves crackled and broke under his feet. His mouth, a taut square, drew in, released whining breaths. His starting eyes fixed the ground, but he did not see the leaves that he ran over. He saw only the white houses that no matter how fast he ran kept always just ahead of him. If he did not hurry they would slide off the hill, slide off and leave

him running forever through these woods, over these dead leaves." Jim knows in this moment that he cannot reach the porch, that indeed he is cut off from the aid of society. The brilliant leaves, symbolic of his passion, now crack and break under his feet; they are dead because with Evelyn's fall he discovered that his life of passion had deceived him. Gone too is the life of innocent delight, represented by the green leaves of the ledge that they had descended together. The shared experience of youthful passion maturing into love is ended in paralysis or death near a rushing cataract, suggestive both of vital life and, more important, of destruction. His lover lies with her brown hair tangled in the ferns, a seedless and flowerless plant, which like the leaves and the seasons is symbolic of some aspect of their tragic love. Evelyn's propensity for catastrophe is indicated earlier in leaf symbolism: twice her eyes are compared to the look of leaves that lie at the bottom of a running brook; residing deep in the vitality of her being is the hint of death. Loss, alienation, and betrayal are the principal themes of this story and, indeed, of much of Miss Gordon's fiction. Alternatives are suggested in her later fiction, and in most situations an awareness of one's place in a historical tradition is required before any scheme of salvation is possible.

Until her conversion to Roman Catholicism, Miss Gordon defined her tradition in terms of the history of the South, which provides the ethical imperatives of her fiction, particularly the novels. Several of her stories portray pioneer America, the period of the Civil War and Reconstruction in the South, and post-World War II Europe; they attempt to examine the conflict of cultures and the probabilities for restoration of order after chaos.

"The Captive," her longest short story, delineates pioneer America. A dramatized study in cultural anthropology like *Green Centuries*, **"The Captive"** presents the point of view of a white person in contact with the alien Indian culture, which, like the later Negro culture in America, elicits a curious mixture of revulsion and fascination from the white observer. These are the attitudes of one—for example, Jinny, the narrator of this story—whose knowledge and understanding are limited solely to the superstition that infrequent contact perpetuates.

In appropriately simple and ungrammatical language, similar to dialect stories in Southern local color fiction, Jinny recounts the massacre of her children and the movement with her Shawnee captors into the impenetrable woods, which signify estrangement and confusion, as they do in *Green Centuries*. When she moves away from the security of her home and the white civilization, the Indian way of life becomes more natural and Indian sexuality more attractive, but she resists change by keeping her mind alive to the past in elaborate plans of flight and vivid dreams, which demonstrate her profound feelings of guilt, fear, and aversion during her stay in this unfamiliar social order. Her escape to the fort is a return to a more comprehensible world from a withdrawal into alienation, a kind of descent into hell, which leaves her presumably wiser. But she takes no advantage of subsequent evaluation and interpretation, for she tells her story from the perspective of the immediate action—a technique that contributes to the popularity of this favorite anthology piece.

Three of Miss Gordon's short stories are set during the Civil War and Reconstruction. **"The Forest of the South,"** the title work of her first collection of short fiction, takes place in romantic Natchez. After the death of her father and the destruction of their home, Eugénie becomes seriously deranged; although her actions and words seem rational, her faint, mysterious smile, expressionless eyes, and strange manner betray a deep emotional shock, not unlike that of the South itself. When Lieutenant Munford, a Yankee soldier responsible for the care of these two women, and one of Miss Gordon's few respectable Northern characters, asks Eugénie to marry him, she takes him to a deserted plantation where a Confederate soldier asks him whether he is prepared to assume the responsibilities of marriage to such a woman.

The lush vegetation of the plantation gardens accentuates the difference between the beautiful Southern climate and the cold and snow of his Connecticut home, where Munford will have to send Eugénie after they are married. He is convinced of the evil of slavery, but his observation of plantation culture causes him to think that the South is not what he had originally imagined. He is oppressed more than once by the bright stillness of the sun and the moonlight shining on the plantation grounds, illuminating generally his new realization of Southern culture and particularly his love for the voluptuous, romantic yet distracted Southern belle.

Despite the innumerable problems suggested by such a marriage, for Munford there seems to be some promise of reconciliation between the victorious and paternalistic North and the defeated South. Before he answers the Confederate's query, Munford looks out the window of the run-down mansion: "The window frame was dark and gauzy but beyond stretched a green meadow. Light played everywhere upon it, the same luminous, quivering light that yesterday at this hour had struck through the leaves at Villa Rose." As Munford sees it, the meadow prophesies a successful future; the potential conflicts are minor in the light of his new, redemptive love. But dramatic irony operates effectively in the story to undercut such a hopeful vision: the light that shines about Munford tends to distort reality, and his union with Eugénie suggests as much disorder as possible order. Eugénie signifies a ravished South, fallen into a knowledge of loss and despair; Munford represents an ever-optimistic North, still confusedly innocent.

Contrasted with the fading elegance of Natchez is the setting of poverty in **"Hear the Nightingale Sing,"** a story similar to *None Shall Look Back* in its statement on the irrevocable end of the ante-bellum South. Through this simple narrative of Southern hatred for the callous invaders from the North run nostalgic reflections on the past mingled with a harsh sense of the future doom of a defeated homeland. Barbara, the principal reflector of the events in the story, is another of Miss Gordon's indomitable women, seeking desperately to recreate sweet memories of the past. Unlike the ecstatically happy nightingale in Keats's ode, the nightingale in the ballad that comes to

Barbara's mind is drawn from the legend of Philomela and thus sings sorrowfully of misfortune. The strong-willed Barbaras of the South met their severest test during the Reconstruction, the political chaos of which so thoroughly demoralizes the second and third generations of Llewellyns in *Penhally*. **"The Ice House,"** set during this period, is a scathing comment on the general attitude of Northern commercialism. The spring season, with new green "creeping up through the clumps of brown sedge grass," contrasts ironically with the charnal-house odor rising from the decaying, moss-covered bodies. Death often suggests the cyclical renewal of life, but in **"The Ice House"** all life is suspended, because the ideals and values that motivated both antagonists in the Civil War are no longer even memories to the survivors. **"The Ice House"** dramatizes the indifference of profit to life or the memory of life. Because of the subtlety of language, which relates the gruesome situation while not overtly evaluating its morality, this story, like much of Miss Gordon's fiction, contains a potentially explosive emotion within a framework of understatement.

A more recent historical period, that of post-World War II Europe, provides the setting for a story which articulates an idea that runs throughout Miss Gordon's fiction—man's need for a myth and a tradition to give continuity and a sense of meaning to life. In **"The Olive Garden"** the central intelligence, Edward Dabney, returns after the war to a former habitation on the French Riviera and reminisces about the people who once seemed indestructible but who are now all dead or departed. This story juxtaposes youth with age, past with present; overall is the implicit suggestion of the invincible human will to recreate and perpetuate. Withstanding all chaos, both social and natural worlds maintain a continuity despite change; even wars—the confrontation between myths—cannot alter the course of human endeavor, even if it takes the form only of memories retained from a happier time. Not only do the themes of conflict in this story stand comparison with Miss Gordon's Civil War fiction, but also the character of the intellectual Dabney, with his expatriate background, looks ahead to the alienated individuals in her last two novels, *The Strange Children* and *The Malefactors*. Unlike Dabney, these people, who represent the modern dissociated sensibility, do not retain from their sense of the past any optimism for the future.

These short stories about history are concerned with the problems of the union or disunion of apparent opposites. So, in part, are the stories about the Negro, who, Chester Eisinger writes, plays a "curiously limited role" in Miss Gordon's fiction: "an introduction to all evil"—"the violence of life and the lust of man"—is presented through the Negro, he argues [in *Fiction of the Forties*, 1963]. The Negro is a minor character in Miss Gordon's dramatization of the Southern ethic, particularly in the larger panoramas of the novels. The ante-bellum families in her fiction are indulgent masters or employers, and except for the knowledgeable Negro hunters and fishermen in *Aleck Maury, Sportsman* or the faithful, somewhat Uncle Tomlike Winston of *None Shall Look Back* or the misunderstood Maria of *The Women on the Porch*, the Negro is rarely an actor in her works; rather, he provides back-

ground and is pictured as indigenous to the Southern locale, but has little more function than menial servitude.

The Negro is the subject of much talk, little of which is
very flattering, and is the repository of curious habits and
superstitions, many of which take on significance in the
white world of the novels. The whites have little or no
sympathy for the Negro in general, because they wonder
whether he is deserving of normal human emotions. They
are continually interested in him, however—as a subject
for study rather than as the recipient of understanding and
acceptance. In *None Shall Look Back* and *Penhally* the
Negroes flee the plantation, as Lucy and Charles comment, like rats deserting a sinking ship. For Lucy [of *None
Shall Look Back*] finally, the Negro is a "furtive and forever alien race," a description that in general sums up Miss
Gordon's portrayal of the Negro in her fiction. There are,
of course, a few notable individuals who transcend their
position, but the majority fit her essentially traditional
view of the Negro.

"The Long Day" shows the Negro's happy mask, behind
which lurk the compulsive and destructive emotions that
negate rationality. The adult white world permits the boy
Henry, the observer of the action, to learn the disillusion-
ing truth about the Negro capacity for violence. Whereas
"The Long Day" describes a white youth's contact with
the Negro, **"The Enemies"** relates a young Negro's observation of his own race. The experiences form for Eugene,
the somewhat puzzled intelligence, a kind of initiation into
the intensely passionate and religious nature of his people.
Confusion also defines the basic attitude of Jim, the white
tobacco farmer who is the narrator of **"Her Quaint Honour,"** which derives its title from "To His Coy Mistress."
[Andrew] Marvell's poem ridicules female chastity, traditionally a matter of some concern to the Southern male.
But the problem for Jim takes on an added dimension because the woman whose honor he finds himself defending
is Negro. The story directs its irony at both Jim and the
Negro couple: the black code of honor is almost a parody
of white morality in its intensity, and a white man is forced
to protect a black woman he thinks is responsible for the
altercation. Honor is indeed a strange and peculiar matter
in the world of these characters.

Miss Gordon's first story, **"Summer Dust,"** belongs generally with the Negro stories and provides a significant transition between them and the Aleck Maury group. Sally,
the reflector of the action, senses her estrangement from
the people around her. Much like the alienated young girls
of Carson McCullers' fiction, she finds that she cannot
penetrate the others' private worlds; youth and social convention force her into a fairy-tale fantasy of godmothers,
crystal palaces, and gypsies. The story is divided into four
sections: the first dramatizes Sally's sense of difference
from both Negro and poor white and the sad realization
that conflict does exist between the races and among the
classes of white society. The second is a tranquil pastoral
interlude, which provides an escape from this very social
world into the seclusion of nature. The third, which bal-
ances with the first, shows her growing fear of an old
Negro woman who Sally believes is a witch. In the fourth
part, the apparent sophistication of her elder brothers'

"adult" world excludes Sally from its masculine conversation. She kicks the dust up around her in a cloud, drifting
off into the imaginative retreat of her fairy godmother's
palace in the wood.

The importance of **"Summer Dust"** to the group of Negro
stories lies in its description of white attitudes toward the
Negro, who functions as only one manifestation of the social reality in which Sally must learn to live, yet it is certainly a significant one. As Miss Gordon's fictional guise,
Sally (or Sarah) appears in a number of her works, including a recent one, **"One Against Thebes,"** which returns to
the material of **"Summer Dust"** and which will be discussed subsequently with her latest fiction. As a first published effort **"Summer Dust"** is a remarkable achievement:
the point of view recalls the Jamesian mastery, the style
is richly descriptive, and the structure is carefully balanced. Furthermore, the story illustrates Miss Gordon's
early and continued interest in the question of man's place
within a particular social milieu.

The problem of identity is central to these stories; both
white and Negro experience some sort of new awareness,
however incommunicable, in contact with one another.
This quest for identity is the burden of each of Miss Gordon's characters: Aleck Maury, for example, the subject
of the second group of stories under discussion here,
spends a lifetime in search of his rightful position in the
agrarian society of the modern South. A quaint eccentric,
Maury was patterned on Miss Gordon's own father, and
so it is not surprising that she appears in several of the
Maury narratives as a kind of observer character. As in
"Summer Dust," her participation behind the fictional
mask of Sarah or Sally in **"Old Red,"** *Aleck Maury,
Sportsman,* and *The Strange Children* can be interpreted
as her own search for meaning and understanding within
the Southern milieu. In one story, **"The Petrified
Woman,"** Miss Gordon is a spectator of the world which
envelopes all her fiction.

Aleck is a character of small importance in **"The Petrified
Woman,"** which belongs generally, however, in this group
of stories. Here, as elsewhere, Miss Gordon shows that
Sally remains forever an enigma to him, partly because she
represents changes that come with progress, a phenomenon of modern life that he finds at best of dubious value.
Through her persona, Miss Gordon reveals that she understands and respects her father; in fact, there is a decided attitude of hero worship present in the novel and stories
dealing with Aleck.

As young Sally in **"The Petrified Woman,"** Miss Gordon
indulgently observes the eccentric members of a family at
a reunion. As witness to the violent marital crisis between
her country cousin and his city wife, Sally learns that Tom
has become demoralized through Eleanor's dominating
influence, that she, like the lamia, or the petrified woman
that Sally saw in a carnival sideshow exhibit, was capable
of destroying him slowly and subtly, despite her outward
appearance of charm and pleasantness. Tom is a weakling,
however, susceptible to her insidious treatment; he somehow fails to satisfy her and thus becomes an antagonist.
In fact, Eleanor and Tom are remarkably similar to the
many estranged married couples in Miss Gordon's fiction,

particularly the novels. One could say that, as Sally in this story, the young Caroline Gordon is observing a phenomenon central to her fiction—the man-woman conflict through the failure of love. **"The Petrified Woman"** can be read, therefore, for its significant insight into her other works.

A vulnerable man is the ready victim of a strong-willed woman in Miss Gordon's fiction. The battle of the sexes was not unknown to Aleck Maury, who often met defeat and frustration at the hands of a wife who wished to convert him from the sportsman's ethic to social responsibility, from independence to dependence. Near the age of seventy, Aleck rejects a second subjugation. In **"To Thy Chamber Window, Sweet,"** Aleck, the born raconteur, entertains a household with stories from his past and quotes passages from Milton, Swinburne, and Shelley's modified ballad about romantic love in a pastoral setting, "The Indian Serenade," one line of which provides the story with its title: "And a spirit in my feet / Hath led me—who knows how? / To thy chamber window, sweet!" One of the women boarders thinks that Aleck is addressing this amorous outpouring to her, but she fails to realize that he most likely does not even realize the meaning, so caught up is he with the sound of his own voice. Later, as if aware that he might be snared by another "protectress," he decides to escape to a new fishing retreat.

Through the technique of the concealed narrator, Miss Gordon is here able to portray Aleck as a ribald if not slightly ludicrous Falstaff figure. In the other Maury stories, however, the serious implications far outweigh the humorous ones. In **"The Last Day in the Field,"** narrated by Aleck, the season of Indian summer corresponds to a time in Aleck's advancing years, the last burst of vigor before the winter of a man's life. His leg cramp has already given him a year's discomfort, and around him, in nature, he sees the approaching moment of death—the autumn leaves blaze with color but falling to the ground, the elderberry bushes hanging closer to the earth as frost creeps higher each night. The natural world offers him a terrifying example of the process of death and decay.

While hunting on the last day of the season with another man, whose youth Aleck envies, his leg begins to pain him, but when they find another bird cover he knows he has to hunt it. "In the fading light I could hardly make [the bird] out and I shot too quick. It swerved over the thicket and I let go with the second barrel. It staggered, then zoomed up. Up, up, up, over the rim of the hill and above the tallest hickories. I saw it there for a second, its wings black against the gold light, before, wings still spread, it came whirling down, like an autumn leaf, like the leaves that were everywhere about us, all over the ground." For a moment Aleck could identify with the hunted bird, soaring high in its last moments of life but falling to the ground, dead on the shriveled leaves. The natural world reflects Aleck's own awareness of diminishing activity and approaching death. His narrative explicitly reveals at several points that he recognizes nature's example, yet in certain instances—as in his description of the felled bird—the reader is allowed to draw the comparison. The subtlety, finally the achievement, of this deceptively simple story

rests in the dichotomy between physical sight and mental insight, which exists in much of Miss Gordon's fiction because it is an intrinsic possibility of her narrative techniques while, at the same time, one result of her artful use of symbolic naturalism. Her characters see what is about them but often fail to realize the significance it possesses for them.

Aleck's often unconscious concern with the passage of time is again apparent in his narrative, **"One More Time."** Once more in his life a specific event discloses that he is growing old. His former friend, Bob Reynolds, accompanied by his wife, whom Bob, in their womanless world of sport, had never mentioned to Aleck before, and who is, like Aleck's wife, solicitous and over-protective, comes to the inn "one more time" in order to drown himself on the river he used to love as a vigorous sportsman. Bob's suicide, rather than the act of a coward, was a refusal to accept years of inactivity; to die on a site of former triumph would be a noble repudiation of subsequent physical decline. Because it is part of the stern and often cruel ethic of the sportsman to reject defeat, the story clearly supports the suggestion made by some critics that the Maury code is reminiscent of Hemingway's.

Time is also central to the most famous of Miss Gordon's stories, **"Old Red,"** which telescopes the whole novel into one revelation, intensifying meaning through a structure based on the juxtaposition of various moments in time, which, as Aleck's constant obsession, appears in various guises in the story. His awareness of advancing age and a sense of pending death is a fatalistic view of existence, one which he has always challenged with the ethic of carpe diem: "But time was a banner that whipped before him always in the wind." About him, at his wife's ancestral home, Merry Point, time hangs in heavy folds, smothering his staid mother-in-law, who in turn deadens her spinster daughter. Together, like the women on the porch, they try to hide in time, namely the past, which Merry Point represents because it is changeless through the generations; the home as permanence provides a fitting setting for Aleck's thoughts of past, present, and future.

The story itself is carefully structured on the passage of time, which has symbolic meaning in the context of Aleck's experience. The first section takes place in the evening at dinner, the moment of social intercourse; here Aleck perceives the older generation, the Allards, and the future one, represented by his daughter and son-in-law, all of whom are alien to him. In Aleck's mind, past, present, and future freely associate in this part of the story, inspired by a return to the family group. Section II corresponds roughly to his immediate present (and hopes for a foreseeable future), during which he must seize every opportunity for his sporting activities. He compares these pastimes with the previous experiences of hunting Old Red with Uncle James—memories which in Aleck's view of life retain an immediacy of the present. Another attitude towards the past is represented in Aleck's son-in-law Stephen—Allen Tate, perhaps—who is writing an essay on John Skelton.

Stephen's attitude toward the past, like that which motivates the Allard women at Merry Point, is stultifying to

Aleck because it negates the vitality of the present by turning the mind to the performances of a past better left forgotten. (Aleck's is precisely the attitude adopted by Stephen's daughter Lucy, the central intelligence of *The Strange Children*.) For Aleck, Stephen incarnates this futile reliance on the dead past: the scholar's "serious, abstracted face . . . was like that of a person submerged." Aleck's attitude toward Stephen's work is indicated in a subtle juxtaposition of the vital spring season—significantly, the time of the story—and the subject of the young man's researches into dusty volumes: "Mister Maury looked out at the new green leaves framed in the doorway. 'John Skelton,' he said, 'God Almighty!' "

The third section takes place late the same evening, while Aleck is in bed. Symbolically it is the night time of his life, one of those moments which, in all the Maury narratives, inspire thoughts of his own past and prospects for an uncertain future. Everything in this room, where he slept the night his wife died, takes on menacing shapes and creates weird shadows, as if the past were about to close in on him. And, indeed, it does, in his mind, which conjures up memories of his wife, who, having changed into a different person after their marriage, tried to make him over into the man she thought he should be. But she had lost the struggle, as the others will when they try to confine him, he thinks. Like the hunters giving chase to Old Red, society will never cease trying to mold him in its own image. But Aleck decides that he will escape from them, just as Old Red always could; he makes plans to leave Merry Point the next morning, looking to a future of unending sports, until finally the "real, the invincible adversary" captures him, as it took his wife many years before. Aleck knows that he cannot avoid the final confrontation with death but that he can run from the death-in-life state that society would try to impose on him.

This structure, with its chronological progression suggestive of the large outline of man's past, present, and future, informs a story of great complexity—the first of the Maury narratives published, one should note. The technique of interweaving various moments in time within the broad pattern indicated gives this story a degree of perfection that none of the other Aleck Maury works possesses. In **"Old Red"** the themes of the Maury stories grow out of a masterful pattern, in which every detail contributes to the total achievement. The technique of the central intelligence, employed likewise in **"The Presence,"** allows for a richer, more fluent style not possible when Aleck narrates, as he does in *Aleck Maury, Sportsman*. This style, like that used in the passage in which Aleck remembers Old Red, does seem appropriate, it might be said, to Aleck's more profound thoughts.

In **"Old Red"** the fox becomes a symbol of Aleck, who visualizes it as a projection of his own conflict between freedom and confinement, heightened by an awareness of the passage of time, the central theme of this story and, ultimately, of the total narrative. Aleck has sought freedom in the natural world but has had to pay a high price for that freedom, because the social world has required his conformity. He understands that he is different from others but he knows too that his ethic provides a deeper insight into man's condition and a more responsible participation in earthly existence.

There is a tragedy implicit in Aleck Maury's code, however. His pursuit of nature requires a flight from the social world, an escape which tends to isolate the modern man from the immediate problems around him. For Aleck, who in large part epitomizes the traditional values of the ante-bellum South, the concerns should be those of the modern South, to which he is openly indifferent. Aleck is not unlike Rion in *Green Centuries,* who insulates himself from society and eventually meets defeat at the hands of nature, against which he constantly fights to keep alive. Ironically Aleck too will end as Rion does: although his survival does not depend upon his outright struggle with nature, it will eventually be determined by the process of natural aging and decay. Aleck centers his life in the very world which will ultimately take his life, and even though he is aware of the "invincible adversary" he plunges deeper into nature, of which death is its agent.

Maury's salvation in the natural world can be only a tentative one, however, in the larger scheme of Miss Gordon's philosophy. Like most of the characters in her early novels, Aleck worships nature, not the God of nature, who becomes the source of grace and finally salvation in the last two novels. Although Aleck is not a particularly religious man, in **"The Presence"** he finally senses a need for a higher reality to save him from his present life and from the fear of death.

In **"The Presence"** Aleck discovers that all womanhood, save his blessed Aunt Victoria, is the scourge of man. At a boarding house—an impermanent world, lacking associations—Maury learns that the owner has been violating the sportsman's code of fair play by seeing another boarder clandestinely. When his wife discovers the adultery she is prostrate with grief; lying insensate on her bed in a "kind of death" she reminds Aleck of a shot bird. But the wife is not guiltless because she denies her husband any forgiveness; she is incapable of the selfless gift of Christian charity.

To Aleck, man is a victim of every woman's wiles and domination. Only Aunt Victoria in his long life of servitude to women remains as the incarnation of queenly womanhood, like Juno, he says, and finally, like the Blessed Virgin Mary, to whom Aleck and Victoria prayed the night she died. The memory of Victoria, whose sanctity, nobility, and grace placed her in the presence of the divine Mother, recalls his former devotions and prayers. Aleck's speaking the Angelic Salutation at the end of the story does not indicate conversion but a sudden awareness that the hour of his own death may be near. He is suddenly humbled, paying homage to his sainted aunt in his prayers to Mary. This story, written about the time of Miss Gordon's own conversion, suggests the new religious dimension that *The Strange Children* and *The Malefactors* would take. Aleck reaches for a salvation higher than the natural world, as Miss Gordon does herself in her latest work.

Miss Gordon has published very little fiction in the past fifteen years. These recent writings do clearly illustrate, however, the nature of her development from agrarianism to Catholicism and recapitulate earlier ideas that fit into the mold of her Christian faith. **"Emmanuele! Emmanuele!"** relates the history of the unfortunate marital relationship between a French author, Guillaume Fäy and his wife, Thérèse, whom he calls Emmanuele ("God with us") because he considers her his only existence, his source of oneness with the divine. Robert Heyward, the central intelligence, enters into the old writer's personal life and emerges from his acquaintanceship with a sad awareness of the man's compelling genius, of his tragic married life, and of the ambiguity of love. It is others, not the artist, who are strange, he concludes after knowing Fäy.

The character of Fäy is based on André Gide, whose own wife burned his lengthy correspondence to her, an event that threw Gide into prolonged despair. The facts of this fictionalized portrait are similar in many respects to Gide's own life: the journal, the homosexuality, the narcissism, the courtship of his wife, and the kind of fiction (such as Fäy's *Le Frère Prodigue*) are all incorporated into this story. Heyward learns to respect the master's awareness of self and his search for the deep personal meanings which he has candidly recreated in his writings. Heyward's confrontation with Pleyol, the poet-diplomat and Christian, who represents Paul Claudel, with whom Gide carried on a long correspondence, provides the crux of the story, at least as far as Miss Gordon's ideas are concerned. The dialogue on the responsibility of the artist, with Gide-Fäy and Claudel-Pleyol taking opposite positions, is central to her latest fictional phase.

Pleyol contends that Fäy's works are not art because Fäy is unsure of what he wants to say. Heyward agrees but argues that Fäy has never stopped seeking, that he dares to face himself in his journals: "An artist's first duty is to confront himself." In response, Pleyol asserts, "An artist's first duty is the same as any other man's—to serve, praise and worship God." Heyward accuses Pleyol of turning his back on Fäy when he discovered that Fäy was "unfortunate." Pleyol replies that he repudiated Fäy when he learned that Fäy loved the abyss better than life.

Heyward prefers Fäy's aim, and so does Miss Gordon, as it would appear from the tone of the story; yet her later fiction and criticism have extolled Christian values as a foundation for literature, an attitude derived in part from Jacques Maritain. And in *How to Read a Novel* she criticizes Gide for formlessness, for double-mindedness, and for a sole reliance on self-expression. But, on the other hand, her own writings have been primarily a confrontation with the self in a given social world, and her present work is a return to her past in an effort to examine her artistic development. In the novel reportedly being written now she figuratively sits down before a mirror, just as Fäy does when he is composing.

Is there then a conflict of aims within Miss Gordon, a rejection of the artist's Christian duty for one which necessitates personal revelation despite the consequences? Not at all, to be sure, for she has continually emphasized both the artist's need to portray a particular social reality with frankness and his responsibility to reveal the divine ordering of the world through artistic form and structure. These two aims can be compatible, and she has made them so. By examining the self and offering it as an example of the human condition, one will fulfill the ultimate responsibility of the Christian writer. In her latest two novels particularly, the characters are presented to serve as illustrations of the scheme of redemption, the archetypal quest for salvation. For example, she suggests that Hart Crane, portrayed as Horne Watts in *The Malefactors,* was seeking God, even if his actions might have indicated a far different goal. In dramatizing the conduct of life, the concern of the novel as she defines it, all passions of the human soul are valid if they serve to reveal the Christian way of life.

Although Heyward defends Fäy he realizes that the French writer feels guilty and strange around his wife, as if she possessed a pernicious secret with which she could destroy him. His existence seems enclosed in the secretary where his letters to her are kept, and when he learns that she burned them he does die emotionally. Thérèse Fäy is another of Miss Gordon's dominating women who challenge a man's love with acts of cruelty or neglect. Thérèse demanded what Fäy could not give her; so she made him suffer. To what extent she was guilty herself; what she did finally mean to him—both were problems left unresolved after the correspondence was destroyed. Thus the relationship remains vague and uncertain, as it did in the case of Gide and his wife, and as it does so often between Miss Gordon's fictional characters. But because Heyward is fascinated with Thérèse, and because of Fäy's apparent regard for his wife, Miss Gordon seems to be saying here that man must look to woman for knowledge of himself—an idea that she presents most fully in *The Malefactors.*

The novel that Miss Gordon says she is writing now is an autobiographical portrait of the artist as a young woman, the aim of which is to recreate the past that formed her artistic vocation. Several sections of it have appeared as short stories. **"A Narrow Heart: The Portrait of a Woman,"** the first part to be published, carries the title that the finished work will presumably bear; fictions by Flaubert and James, among her artistic mentors, have inspired the two-part title. In this chapter, set in a room at Merry Mont at nightfall, which betokens an approaching death, Miss Gordon recollects how at the age of four she began to comprehend the calling which would obsess her thereafter. The artist, she says, is a haunted seer, compelled to perform his task but always aware that there is an indefinable presence that menaces him, keeping him on the appointed path. "On this road which we are condemned in early youth to travel we may expect, I gather, to be challenged at every turn. The challenge takes the form of a test that is repeated over and over. What is demanded of us is that we recognize the true, the beautiful, the timeless under its accidental appearance" [*Transatlantic Review,* Spring, 1960]. As long as the artist can follow the chosen path, illuminated by the golden light of his vocation, he can hold back the presence of those hovering shadows, she continues. The mood of **"A Narrow Heart"** is paradoxically that of a death-wish—the setting and imagery substantiate this view—as if the compulsion to create has at last defeated her. Miss Gordon is not very explicit in her romantic definition of the artist; she states that the novelist has special ways of knowing but does not choose to elaborate further in this curious and beguiling story.

Miss Gordon envisions the artist, then, as a kind of knight-errant, who in his quest (for salvation?) undergoes the trials of initiation into a knowledge of the human condition. The artist is a potential hero, and it is with heroes that she is fundamentally concerned in this novel, as the latest chapter, [which originally appeared as the short story] **"Cock-Crow,"** has revealed. In **"A Narrow Heart"** she mentions her family, particularly the Meriwether clan, whose pride, discipline, and grim temper she could admire so completely. In **"Cock-Crow"** she continues this praise, indulging in rapture over the very name "Merry Mont." This self-contained world, rooted in time and space, bred heroes, she maintains, like her younger brother, who became the intelligence of **"Her Quaint Honour."** Her family had to be heroic, she argues, because their lives were a constant struggle to survive and endure the losses brought about by the Civil War. There is a revival of chauvinism and a reaffirmation of agrarianism, along with self-pity and nostalgia for the lost glories of a former world, when she writes that losing the Civil War not only was bad for the South but was "a calamity for the whole world." Or, "The consciousness that one belongs to an 'oppressed minority' stiffens the moral fibers against the strains to which they will be subjected later on."

Miss Gordon explains in [**"Cock Crow"**] one of her most revealing works, that she has made a lifelong study of the hero, who must combat the only enemy, Death. In her fiction, Nathan Bedford Forrest (in *None Shall Look Back*) and Aleck Maury exemplify the hero that she describes here. She also explains what the Civil War meant for her as a Southerner when she writes further about the hero: "When a man is faced with death, energies which he was not aware he possessed are rallied in the effort to preserve

Gordon with her husband, Allen Tate.

the life which, until that instant, may not have seemed to him as precious as it truly is. War which, now under one guise, now another, pits man against his arch enemy, Death, has always provided a favorable climate for the growth of the hero, as well as for the study of his ways and deeds." The hero is in decline today, then, because he must be recognized in the only way a man can prove himself a hero—in combat; such confrontations are lacking now, she adds with singular casualness.

Finally, two other remarks in [**"Cock Crow"**] are relevant to a clearer reading of her fiction. With surprising understatement she writes at one point: "Women, of course, are always on the look-out for heroes"; they compel them to action (life is doing, she contends) and bestow the laurels of victory. Also, the great novelist who has himself descended some way into the abyss will better know the existence of the characters in his novels—a tacit acceptance, then, of Gide-Fäy and of Hart Crane. She concludes this essay-story with a skillful narrative of the life of Heracles, the greatest of heroes, one whose extraordinary future was heralded by a cock crow the night after he strangled the serpents in his cradle. Heracles ("glory of Hera") toiled against all ravaging monsters, and because he chose the life of Virtue rather than of Pleasure he stands in her opinion as the archetypal hero in quest of the good. But Heracles was likewise a fallible man—victim of his own error and victim of the whims of the gods. In her opinion he knew the abyss but redeemed himself nonetheless.

Heracles is the subject of a poem that Fäy is writing and figures as the archetypal hero of salvation in **"One Against Thebes,"** the second chapter to be published of this proposed novel. [The critic adds in a footnote that **"One Against Thebes"** was first published as **"The Dragon's Teeth"** in the Autumn 1961 issue of *Shenandoah*.] It is a retelling of her earlier initiation story of youthful alienation, **"Summer Dust,"** but in **"One Against Thebes"** the style is more fluent, allowing the moments in time to flow one into another more meaningfully. To compare the two stories is to recognize Miss Gordon's stylistic development. Moreover, there is a change of emphasis in this later work: whereas the young girl in **"Summer Dust"** is a participant in the action, this one is an observer of the kind of world—like that of **"The Petrified Woman"**—which has provided the material and vision for all of Miss Gordon's fiction. The situations of this later story follow **"Summer Dust"** exactly except for an additional section, in which the young child hears the various classical myths that entice her imagination—those of Heracles, Prometheus, Cadmus, and Oedipus, the one who was against Thebes, a hero who descended into the abyss. Does Miss Gordon think of herself as an Oedipus, as the title would suggest? Does she sense an alienation from this world (the young girl of **"Summer Dust"** certainly does)? Was she, like Joyce, an exile who was compelled to interpret the society she left? Furthermore, does she see a capacity for the heroic in every man, like the young Negro boy Son, who as a baby strangled a snake? A partial affirmative can be offered to each question, but the total picture must remain incomplete until the novel is published.

These last three stories tantalize the reader of Miss Gordon's fiction. Although there are no really new ideas in them, they are curiously open-ended and fragmentary. The complete work might well provide answers to questions raised by these latest stories; it seems now as if the novel will be a fitting confirmation of the attitudes which her whole career has fostered. Even if this projected novel is never completed, however, Miss Gordon's fiction will still reflect a development that has reached a more or less inevitable conclusion. Her short fiction is a trenchant illustration of her spiritual growth; it delineates the themes that constitute her mind and the techniques that form her art. These stories reveal the conflicts arising between dominant women and weak men, who fail to meet the test of woman as guide. They portray the theme of initiation into a particular tradition or society and the resultant quest for identity; special attention is often directed to the problems of the artist, as observer of and participant in his world. Miss Gordon's own search for order, stability, and permanence—salvation, in fact—finds as meaningful an expression in these stories as in the novels; her evolution from secular agrarianism to the Christan myth is represented perfectly, for example, in the Aleck Maury narrative. Indeed, Caroline Gordon's career can be seen in terms of her short fiction, a flourishing genre in the twentieth century, particularly among Southern writers, to whose distinguished company she has added the prestige of her impressive talent.

> James E. Rocks, "The Short Fiction of Caroline Gordon," in TSE: Tulane Studies in English, *Vol. XVIII*, 1970, pp. 115-35.

Louise Cowan (essay date 1972)

[*In the following essay, Cowan discusses Gordon's portrayal of the modern epic hero in several of her "Aleck Maury" short stories.*]

Caroline Gordon's angle of vision—the vantage point from which she regards the moving configurations of human existence—is primarily epic. As an intrinsic structure, that is, as one of the fundamental generic patterns, the epic is concerned with the ongoing of history. Within its broad expanse everything is sacrificed to an essentially eschatological thrust; for nothing less than the outcome of the human enterprise hangs upon the success of its heroic quest. Domestic life must be set aside for epic endeavors, even though the feminine spirit encloses the action as guide and goal. "Women, of course, are always on the look-out for heroes," Miss Gordon has written in **"Cock-Crow"** (*The Southern Review,* Summer, 1965), a portion of *A Narrow Heart,* her novel in progress. The hero, she tells us, is one who pits himself "against odds so desperate that only the continual exercise of heroic virtue" can save him. And his ultimate adversary is always hidden. "A hero—any hero—spends his life in combat with the common, the only enemy, Death." Each of the characters about whom Miss Gordon is writing in *A Narrow Heart* (whom, as she explains, she has known—or heard of—in her own life) she sees as standing "on the edge of an abyss":

An abyss so deep and dark that no human eye

has ever penetrated it . . . I know, too, that some of them—it may be "the bravest and the best"—came to their dooms because they would not capitulate. Through a kind of mistaken bravery. It was the one rash step forward, the setting of the foot on what should have been solid ground but which, instead, was thin air, that sent them hurtling headlong into the abyss.

If Miss Gordon's characters hurtle into the abyss, they do so as epic and not tragic figures. Epic heroes do not struggle as tragic heroes do against the gods. Theirs is not a lonely battle within themselves, a striving to find interior dimensions of being; rather, epic heroes endeavor to maintain manliness and courage in a communal and cosmic realm, obeying whatever divine imperatives are given them, following a code of honor in a society that is in perpetual disorder.

But though the world about which an epic poet writes is frequently disunified and confused, and though the hero himself may be blinded into taking a fatal false step, it is nonetheless a requisite that the imaginative light by which the writer views his scene be clear. No moral ambiguities must cloud the poet's—the novelist's—mind if he is to depict the heroic. Indeed, the chronicler of the hero needs a far greater certainty about the purpose of life, as well as an infinitely broader perspective, than his model, his paradigm, could possibly possess. Consequently an epic poet is always in search of an underlying myth that can account for the extraordinary behavior of the true hero, who is moved by forces that he can neither comprehend nor control.

Miss Gordon's chief effort as an artist—like that of most other significant twentieth-century writers—has been to find a usable sacral system—a myth—in a society increasingly secular and consequently detached from the major symbols within its own cultural heritage. The Christian structure, which, for Western society, appropriated the mythic house of the gods and provided for centuries our major cultural figures, has gradually lost its imagistic concreteness and become associated in the modern mind with a set of moral principles by which one ought to live or with fossilized phrases and gestures. The effect has been thus to deprive Christian dogma of its connection with "the world's body"—to leave it abstract and bloodless, operative only in deliberately spiritual and moral realms. Perhaps in response to the decline of the Christian extra-rational expression, a structure of more ancient symbolic patterns was brought to modern attention early in the twentieth century by the publication of Sir James Frazer's *The Golden Bough* and further emphasized by the findings of various historians of religion, the work of the Cambridge anthropologists, and the writings of C. G. Jung. This archaic and essentially Eastern outlook is based on primordial myth, the archetypal mode of thought that, manifest and clear in Greek mythology, has come to be recognized by anthropologists and psychologists as at once the dominant mode of thought in primitive cultures and the very ground of the individual psyche. Interestingly enough, what this discovery has done is to reanimate early Christian images, making possible an incorporation of the two tropologies.

When T. S. Eliot wrote of the "mythical method" in Joyce's *Ulysses* [in "*Ulysses,* Order and Myth," *Criticism: The Foundations of Literary Judgment,* 1958, edited by Mark Shorer], he was referring to the age-old body of pagan myths as it was given form in Homer's *Odyssey,* omitting any mention of the other symbolic structure present in the novel and discoverable through more or less overt references: the Christian religious and cultural tradition. In the same way, his notes to *The Waste Land* send his readers to the vegetation cults and to the *Bhagavad-Gita* or even the Old Testament, but only peripherally to any portion of the Christian mysteries. And yet, in both these twentieth-century works Christian symbols operate as fully and organically as do pagan myths; in fact, it is by means of parallels between the two sets of analogies that a reader can discern the full significance of the depicted present. Eliot maintains that "manipulating a continuous parallel between contemporaneity and antiquity is a simple way of controlling, of ordering, of giving a shape and a significance to the immense panorama of futility and anarchy which is contemporary history." But, as I have indicated, it is not simply "antiquity" with which contemporaneity must be aligned. There is that other, more recent, body of tag-ends and surprisingly persistent relics with which the present-day writer is tantalized and troubled—the Christian master images derived from what Christopher Dawson [in his *The Historic Reality of Christian Culture,* 1960] has called "the historic reality of Christian culture." Still embedded vestigially in the very life of the people and their folk arts, these medieval modes of thought and feeling are to be encountered in their complete paradigmatic form in *The Divine Comedy;* and to this work writers in our time have turned, either knowingly, as have Miss Gordon and most other serious artists, or unknowingly, as have many lesser "makers" who are, willy-nilly, entangled in the literary tradition that Dante shaped.

[In his 1961 study, *Dante, Poet of the Secular World*] Erich Auerbach has maintained that it is only by Dante's time that the "mimetic content" of the Christian story sank into the imagination of Western man. "The story of Christ fundamentally changed [the European] idea of man's fate and how to describe it." But this transformation took place "far more slowly than the spread of Christian dogma." Auerbach attributes to Dante the creation of a vision which permeated history: "a testimony to the reality that is poetry, to the modern European form of artistic mimesis which stresses the actuality of events." The "concrete reality" of Beatrice, for instance, is depicted with a fidelity unknown before the thirteenth century. For Dante, Auerbach maintains, personal experience "expands into the universal" and becomes a part of reality in general, with "earthly particularity held fast in the mirror of a timeless eye." Accordingly, in Dante's poem earthly life is seen to be enclosed in the spiritual world; yet the reality of events, historical order and form, are not lost. Auerbach refers to St. Thomas's dictum: "When a more perfect form supervenes, the previous form is corrupted: yet so that the supervening form contains the perfection of the previous form, and something in addition." The Christian faith, then, if we agree with such critics as Auerbach, was given its cultural and poetic form by Dante, as the religion

of the Olympic gods was ordered by Homer. Before Homer a matriarchial order prevailed, governing a tribal, matrilineal society that shaped all life by custom (as before the Christian Middle Ages there was Hebraic law out of which Christianity came). These even older forms are contained within the forms that perfected—or fulfilled—them. Thus it is Homer and Dante who have chiefly affected the Western imagination: so much so that, despite the progressive secularization of culture, the symbols they produced still lie deep in the minds of modern men. The writer needs to discern these powerful forces, not simply in order to give form to chaos, as Eliot has suggested, but so that he may express life more nearly as it is actually experienced and thus avoid its oversimplification and, further, the banalization of his art.

Eliot and Joyce—as well as Pound, Yeats, Faulkner, and most other major twentieth-century writers have been busy at this task of reconciling the polarities of ancient myth and Christian mystery and thus reanimating sacred presences in a world largely "neutralized" by its rationalism. Death in particular has been the subject of exploration by present-day writers, with its alternative images of entrance into the darkness of the underworld and ascension to the fields of light. Sacrificial death, the shedding of blood, vegetation, water, the polarities of earth and sky and of darkness and light—these motifs have all been fruitfully used by many writers to reawaken a sense of the paradoxical nature and hence the mystery of existence. In particular, the masculine-feminine polarity has been consistently explored as a vehicle for restoring the fulness of the supernatural to modern life, since both pagan myth and Christian faith make use of the union of opposites to portray the radical paradox of being.

No writer in our time has been more concerned with this reconciliation than Caroline Gordon. Her early novels deal overtly with neither pagan myth nor Christian mystery; but, concerned with the polarities of thinking and feeling, they dramatize the feminine and masculine principles in a devastated society that cannot surrender itself to love and integration, where death is the over-arching enemy. It is not until her fourth novel (*The Garden of Adonis,* 1937) that archaic myth and Christian symbolism manifest themselves more or less specifically in her work. *Green Centuries* (1941) makes explicit use of ritual and myth. And by the time of *The Women on the Porch* (1944), these modes are expressly reconciled and the sacramental union between lovers is made possible, signalling a union of myth and mystery, nature and grace. *The Strange Children* (1951) and *The Malefactors* (1956) command a wide range of Christian paradigms, with archetypal materials providing the substrate of both novels. For the last fifteen years Miss Gordon has been working on a double novel, the upper pattern of which is to be entitled "A Narrow Heart: The Portrait of a Woman" and the lower pattern, to be published first, to be called "The Glory of Hera." She has written of this double structure:

> The upper pattern purports to be my own auto-
> biography but is actually the history of the lives
> of certain members of my family who have been
> associated, to some extent, with public
> figures . . . The lower pattern winds serpent-

wise through the upper pattern of action and deals with the archetypal world which the present day Jungians and the archaic Greeks inform us lies at the very bottom of every human consciousness.

Miss Gordon's **"One against Thebes,"** a revision of an earlier story **("Summer Dust")** looks provocatively like the germ of the plan for these two novels. In this story a child (the writer herself) pursues her path down a dusty road, with her shadow, a Negro girl, and a kind of Demeter figure, a Negro woman carrying a basket in which she is to gather peaches. A black boy runs beside the two children, making a trail in the dust which "might have been made by a great snake, a serpent as large as any one of them, hurling itself now to one side of the road, now to the other . . . ." The child thinks "how she and the other girl and the boy and even the old woman seem to move in its coils." Mythological materials are linked in this story with the child's present experiences, which take on the aspect of a journey and a quest. There is the story of "Son" killing a snake when he was a year old, as Hercules strangled the serpents in his cradle; there are the Greek myths of Heracles, Erectheus, and the dragon's teeth recounted by the child's father (Aleck Maury) to a skeptical brother, Tom. There is also a visit to see the ancient Aunt Emily, who is said to drink blood, like Tiresias and the other greedy shades inhabiting the underworld. The child sees her own progress down the dusty road as a quest for the "crystal palace" of a fairytale, where there will be a gold crown, silver slippers *and a veil of silver tissue, embroidered with the sun and the moon and the stars. . . ."* If she can make her way through the obstacles in her path, she will end by attaining a union with the entire cosmos.

Miss Gordon prefaces her story with a passage from *Oedipus at Colonus:* "That way you shall forever hold this city, / Safe from the men of Thebes, the dragon's sons" (translation by Robert Fitzgerald). Oedipus is the speaker of these lines, to Theseus, the noble king of Athens who has provided protection for the old wanderer at the end of his days. Thebes, the city from which Oedipus has been exiled, was founded by men who sprang up from dragon's teeth sown by Cadmus and has been ever since a center of internecine conflict, incredible suffering, and misfortune. In the drama, a few lines after the passage quoted, Oedipus speaks of being driven "by an insistent voice that comes from God." He has followed his vocation, then, in coming to this sacred grove of the Furies and says farewell to life with dignity and selflessness, absorbed, one feels, into the bosom of the gods.

One can only speculate on Miss Gordon's choice of title; but since it speaks quite clearly of the life dedicated to following "an insistent voice," it seems possible to consider her story a parable of the artist, following a vocation in the path of the serpent, seeking the crystal palace, encountering undeserved suffering, and redeemed finally from the doomed city of Thebes to bless the fortunate and just city of Athens. It is the child herself who will become the "one against Thebes," but at the same time her father, Aleck Maury, like the aging Oedipus, is also in a sense pitted against the forces of death and destruction. The child—in the earlier story Sally Maury, the daughter of Aleck—is

here referred to simply as "the child." She is the young artist, called by an inner voice to a life of observation, of absorption, of re-mythologizing. Like the little girl in **"A Narrow Heart: The Portrait of a Woman"** (*The Transatlantic Review,* Spring, 1960), she is preoccupied with the qualities of things, with trying to know them as they are and as they establish themselves in consciousness. As an Antigone figure, she will have to guide and direct the humbled Oedipus and later take the part of the gods in struggle against the rationalistic edicts of Thebes. She will stand, like her father, as one against Thebes and will help to keep the city safe from the dragon's sons. But the artist is not, in Miss Gordon's view, the hero. The artist—the poet—is a seer, whose consciousness gives form to the total history of man. True, he observes the hero and appreciates him, understanding his courage and his mission because both have an inner voice to guide them, both are aware of dragons, both stand solitary over the abyss. Nevertheless, the artist has a different kind of toil: to construct an image of that essentially epic struggle. And though in this story Miss Gordon's referential imagination allies the child's father with the tragic figure of the old Oedipus, her view of him throughout the Aleck Maury stories has been cast in an epic, not a tragic, mold.

Another recent piece of short fiction to be incorporated into *A Narrow Heart,* **"Cock-Crow,"** mentioned earlier, centers on the story of Hercules, or Herakles, and is important in illuminating Miss Gordon's chief subject, which she calls "Two branches of a lifelong study: the life and times of the hero." In it we are reminded that, after the incident of the infant's slaying of the serpents, Tiresias recommended that the child's name be changed from Alcides to Herakles "because he would eventually become the glory of Hera." Miss Gordon goes on to mark many implicit parallels in the life of this powerful, violent god to events connected with the story of Christ—Alcmena hears the cock crow three times after the infant has strangled the serpents; the child is of course the son of a god and a mortal woman; during a time of withdrawal to Mt. Cithaeron, he chooses in a vision a maiden named Virtue over one named Pleasure; he shows "premonitory respect" for virginity; he seems to follow "some inner voice." Heracles suffered terribly throughout his life, sometimes, Miss Gordon points out, "when he was crazed by the gods for their own inscrutable purposes." But as long as he was in his right mind, he never deserted his calling—"a life of toil." His toil was conflict, and his chief work was a "lifelong combat with the monstrous, in whatever guise it showed itself." Today, in contrast, we are occupied most of the time, she tells us, with "watching the dragon coil and uncoil in the 'earth of our own hearts'." The mythic hero who kills dragons foreshadows the coming of the one who conquered sin and death. But the primordial darkness remains within us, despite the victory of the light that the darkness could not comprehend.

One can speculate a bit further and conjecture that Miss Gordon's current novels, long under construction, depict these two basic realities to which contemporary man is related—the two supernatural dimensions in which he is enmeshed, with or without his awareness. The "lower pattern" of which she speaks is the primordial world of archetypes that, as she says, "lies at the bottom of every human consciousness." The "upper pattern" is no doubt a story of Christian conversion and of the workings of grace in a particular life, located in a specific place and time—a Dantesque story which will preserve the "actuality of events." As Ezra Pound has written of Dante [in *The Spirit of Romance*], "he gives us not the action itself but its reflection in his own heart." There should be no misunderstanding of Miss Gordon's method in this work that she calls her last novel. She is not tempted to narcissism or introspection; she is at last writing the novel that, as she says, Ford Madox Ford predicted she would write. She is giving form and shape to her own experience, objectifying it and yet portraying it from within, keeping its historicity and at the same time perceiving in it the movement toward eternity. Her comments give strong evidence that she has come to see the "figure in the carpet" within her own work—that underlying pattern which has given form and structure to her artistic vision over the years.

With its "upper" and "lower" stories, Miss Gordon's writing is epic in accord with the two symbolic structures of which I have been speaking. On the mythopoeic level, the epic journey symbolizes a quest for the integration of the component parts of man; it is a search for wholeness, for the union of earth and sky gods. It requires a descent into darkness; its obstacles are women and death. Its virtues are magnanimity and valor. In contrast, the Christian epic speaks allegorically of the progress of the soul; a glimpse of love and joy—what Jacques Maritain calls a "flash of reality"—impels it on its quest. The obstacle to be overcome is sin; the journey is toward grace, toward light out of darkness; but there is nevertheless a confrontation of the abyss. Woman is the mediatrix of grace in this journey, the Beatrice figure who impels and guides.

That Caroline Gordon's novels—her long fiction—possess an epic cast should not be difficult to demonstrate, since even a cursory reading of them uncovers a largeness of canvas that customarily goes with the heroic mold. But I should like to maintain that even her short stories are shaped by an epic vision, though one may be obliged to consider many of them fragments of that wide and majestic outlook. In all of her stories the man does what he "must"; he follows a code of honor that is fundamentally destructive to the feminine ancestral principle. Miss Gordon's early novels demonstrate his unvarying defeat; but as her works reflect more of the Christian eschatology, her epic vision changes its tone from tragic to comic.

In one group of short stories written early in her career, Aleck Maury is the central epic hero—a man who has found in his youth the "secret life" of joy and danger in the ritual of the hunt. He must ponder what it is in nature that wild creatures, dogs, and hunters sense—something which renders life incalculably precious. It is this search for the life abundant that pulls Maury away from home and family in a lifelong pursuit of hunting and fishing—in a lifelong flight, too, as it turns out, from his mortal enemy, death. Miss Gordon's later work demonstrates more openly her reconciliation of the pagan and Christian tropologies, but these short pieces contain in their depths the same twofold view of reality.

Miss Gordon has said that she cannot bear to reread her short fiction, whereas she can confront her novels with some equanimity. One might suggest that this reluctance to look again at particular pieces she has written stems from the very nature of the two media; a short story is nearly always an embodiment of an insight that focuses everything on an immediate *now,* whereas a novel tends to move along at a less intense pace. Miss Gordon's long fiction is a masterly achievement; but then so is her shorter work. And the Aleck Maury pieces, supplementing the novel *Aleck Maury, Sportsman,* are of particular importance in her canon. Because they illumine several aspects of her entire body of work—the double mode of her imagination, the epic structure of her vision, and the central object of her concern, the hero—the Aleck Maury stories are worth a good deal of study.

Aleck Maury is both classics professor and hunter—a man with a vocation and an avocation; that is to say, a man divided. He represents the outcome of a choice Western civilization made some generations before his birth—to pursue a natural and not a supernatural good. For those who believe that Miss Gordon is uncritical in her devotion to the Southern Agrarian way of life, an analysis of Aleck Maury's "epic journey" should dispel the misapprehension if, indeed, a close reading of all her early work does not. Just as Rives Allard in *None Shall Look Back* represents a kind of "Hercules Furens"—or an Achilles: a man crazed by the impossibility of an ideal and so looking into the eyes of death with erotic longing—so Aleck Maury represents the next stage in the steady decline of the hero. But if Rives is the modern Achilles, a tragic epic hero, then Aleck Maury is the modern Odysseus—the comic epic hero who must live by his wits and come to terms with women. But Maury is the product of a land in which there is no longer any active faith, even in a desperate "lost cause"; for, though the South which he represents and loves has kept to a precious heritage of courtesy and hospitality, its essential deism contains within itself no principle of regeneration. The noblest ideals of the old South have been cut away from their roots: its splendid and living classicism has become the scholarly speciality of a sensitive and cultivated man who no longer views the Greek and Roman ethic as an imperative. The vital Southern love of the land and its conviction of the need for guardianship has declined in him to a self-indulgent passion for hunting and fishing; its communality has become a solitary quest for what must be a *secret* life of joy; its public figures have dwindled to private "characters." No, Aleck Maury is no grand epic figure; he has grown up after a devastating war which has virtually destroyed his people (he faces a land in desperate disorder), yet his concern is not to restore the patria so much as to find a separate peace. He has his inner voice, his calling; he is "one against Thebes"; he shows a persistent gallantry in the face of what he calls "a sad life." But he avoids confronting the abyss. He steers away from open conflict. His constant struggle is to avoid entrapment in any kind of responsibility; he tries desperately always to preserve his own identity, but for no political or communal service. Miss Gordon's portrayal of Maury is respectful and tender; yet she unsparingly makes clear his fault—and the failure of the society that produced him. What was once a shared way of life has declined—as I have indicated earlier—because of its lack of connection with the transcendental elements of its faith. The catastrophe of the Civil War has destroyed the South's vital political genius. Remaining in the Southern culture—as almost nowhere else in the modern world—is a strong sense of immanence—of the sacredness of nature. But, as Allen Tate has remarked, once a society has had the higher revelation, it cannot go back to a lower one; thus Aleck Maury could not, if he would, recapture the vitality of the pagan myths. His life moves ever more constantly toward privacy and self-centeredness; he must frenziedly grasp for an experience of the inner life of nature, knowing finally that he is alone in his pursuit, that all his family and friends have lost the sense of nature as a great repository of widsom, as a sacred book that must be read and pondered.

The portrait of Aleck Maury that emerges from Miss Gordon's writing is, as I have indicated, a loving one. But to suppose that it is simply an affectionate tribute is to misunderstand her artistic integrity. She is not a romantic nostalgist. Neither is she a "constructionist" in the sense of shaping material to fit her ends, something that would be strongly tempting to a writer of her wit and sense of parody. Rather, she is employing the actual materials of her life—her family, her region—to depict, as Dante did, the universal in the historic particular. Again and again she makes use of Christian and Greek presences in the domestic context of her stories; at times these representations seem little more than private puns, placed there for the amusement of the author; but to consider even the smallest details in this manner is to miss the completeness and solidity of her artistic vision. In an interview on her story **"The Captive"** (*The Southern Review,* Summer, 1971) she has referred to "the archetype operating right now" and goes on to say of her use of symbols that it is largely unconscious: "I don't believe they're ever valid if they enter your head," she comments; yet she is clear in her defense of the four-fold medieval allegory, a fairly conscious method of depicting the analogical dimensions of meaning. In the face of this apparent contradiction we must be content, I think, to surmise that Miss Gordon's creative imagination works in the two modes that we have been discussing, the primordial set of symbols remaining dark to her, but the Christian allegory knowable, because referring to familiar people in her life and to conscious beliefs.

In the first story about Aleck Maury, **"The Burning Eyes,"** (incorporated verbatim into the novel *Aleck Maury, Sportsman*), the boy encounters the beginning of his vocation. He has grown up in a womanless home, Oakleigh, where the ground is barren under the huge oak trees. "There are no flowers on the lawn, not a shrub breaks the stark outline of the house where it rises among black trunks," Aleck Maury recalls. "I know now that this was because no woman's hand had tended Oakleigh since my mother's death and I used as a child to wonder if it was because grass and flowers would not grow in that soil." The house itself is lifeless and austere. "I thought of the house as having an expression not sinister yet curiously blank, a sort of withdrawnness from which you could not escape. . . . " The boy surveys the landscape before him "standing on a stump," and for him the world is "a curv-

ing dark stretch of woodland" and an "old, red, winding road." When he is eight years old, "life, the secret life, that is compacted equally of peril and deep excitement" begins one night as he is taken on a possum hunt by a Negro servant, Ralph, whom Aleck thinks of as a kind of Cyclops because he is seven feet tall and has only one eye. The boy believes Ralph's wife's story that he "poked [the other one] out on them old brambles" while he was hunting. When he and Ralph and the dog Ming go out together into the dark woods, it is a bright moonlit night; the dog bounds ahead of the hunters and gives out a "loud, ecstatic note"; Ralph carries the boy along to the foot of a tree wherein a possum has taken refuge. The boy looks up into the dark foliage of the tree; he sees the round, golden eyes of the possum. "They regarded me steadily, or rather they regarded nothing. They glowed, and it was as if there was nothing in the world but whirling blackness and, set in it, those immense, those golden orbs." The boy loses track of time, is caught in the blend of blackness and gold. Finally, the gun shatters the experience. "A coarsely furred grey ball dropped onto the dead leaves at our feet."

This is the boy's first encounter with death; he is led to see it as an enemy in the life of nature which he seeks to share. That it must come to the quarry is part of the shared ritual; yet, though he accepts the death of the victim, Aleck Maury is never able to surmount his dread and horror of what is to be his lifelong adversary.

"The Burning Eyes," then, depicts a joyless world, the "waste land situation" of the epics—a gloomy house, a barren soil, a dark forest, tree stumps, a one-eyed guide, a domineering woman (his sister), a trip into the darkness. Into this gloom comes an encounter with the ecstasy of the hunt; the boy looks into the heart of life in the possum's eyes, and the grey ball that falls at his feet onto the dead leaves is what is left after the transport of communion. From here on, Aleck Maury will live a life of singleminded dedication in his desperation to keep communion with the primordial life of things. That one must spill blood to do so is the familiar paradox of the hunt, though he never loses his compassion for the life he spills or his love for the dogs and men who participate in the chase.

The dominant imagery in the second of the Aleck Maury stories, **"The Last Day in the Field,"** speaks of life remaining past its due season in something that otherwise should be dead: "That was the fall when the leaves stayed green so long," the story begins. Elderberry bushes hit by light frost still stand up straight against the stable fence. "The lower, spreading branches had turned yellow and were already sinking to the ground but the leaves in the top clusters still stood up stiff and straight." Aleck Maury views the bushes and thinks, " Ah-ha, it'll get you yet!' . . . thinking how frost creeps higher and higher out of the ground each night of fall." These and other details reinforce the importance of Aleck Maury's leg, crippled by rheumatism, which, even though Aleck's interior delight at hunting has not abated from his childhood, makes this indeed the last day in the field. His piety toward the hunt, his skill, his craft—all have grown, over the years, into a body of wisdom revealed to the reader by means of contrast. Joe Thomas, a young man who owns two fine dogs that have been trained in Kentucky and are ready for the field, asks Aleck to go hunting with him when the weather is right. On the morning after a sufficiently heavy frost, Aleck is up, tapping at the boy's window, making breakfast, and taking the lead, eager to pursue the only life that holds transcendent joy for him. The boy is sluggish, hard to awaken, slow to react, and yet in the field impatient, too hasty, careless. Aleck savors each detail and, despite the growing pain of the leg, takes his time. In his memory, the whole enveloping action of a shared lifetime of hunting is re-evoked: people, places, dogs, events. "I looked at him [the big dog] and thought how different he was from his mate and like some dogs I had known—and men, too— who lived only for hunting and could never get enough no matter how long the day was." But this is a long day, this last one. The leg is a crippling hindrance; evidence of Maury's pain abound. "Man, you're sweating," Joe says. Aleck explains it as the result of hot work, but he knows that he cannot continue much longer:

> The sun was halfway down through the trees, the whole west woods ablaze with light. I sat there and thought that in another hour it would be good dark and I wished that the day could go on and not end so soon and yet I didn't see how I could make it much farther with my leg the way it was.

They come to "as birdy a place" as Maury has ever seen; and he knows he will have to hunt it despite the pain. The dogs have covered a bevy of birds; but Joe, careless and over-eager as he has been all day, takes "one step too many" and the birds explode into flight. Both hunters fire, and both get their birds. But the covey is gone, and no singles seem to remain. Suddenly Joe sees the big dog pointing: he has uncovered a single. "Your shot," Aleck tells the boy. But in a gesture of maturity and magnanimity— such as Wiglaf makes to the old Beowulf—Joe steps aside for Aleck Maury to have the last shot:

> I went back and flushed the bird. It went skimming along the buckberry bushes that covered that side of the swale. In the fading light I could hardly make it out and I shot too quick. It swerved over the thicket and I let go with the second barrel. It staggered, then zoomed up. Up, up, up, over the rim of the hill and above the tallest hickories. I saw it there for a second, its wings black against the gold light, before, wings still spread, it came whirling down, like an autumn leaf, like the leaves that were everywhere about us, all over the ground.

Again the experience of communion is bound up in the experience of death. Aleck Maury is intensely aware of his own mortality—of being "in the fading light." For the first time during the day he shoots too quick and must try again. The bird, struck and mortally wounded, takes on the appearance of more intense life for a few moments as it suddenly soars "above the rim of the hill and above the tallest hickories." It appears to hang there, "its wings black against the gold light," before its rapid descent as a part of universal mortality. It is "like an autumn leaf," in its fall, "like the leaves that were everywhere about us, all over the ground." Maury, the viewer, is aware of his own participation in the death of what he hunts. Death the

great enemy is closer to him now than it was in **"The Burning Eyes."** And it is from death, approaching him by the inexorable march of time that he flees, though in this story he is simply caught up and merged in that death without rejecting it. And the experience of discovering a noble dog and of helping to educate a young hunter make the story more affirmative than negative.

When we next encounter Mr. Maury in the short stories— in **"To Thy Chamber Window, Sweet"**—he has been in flight for some time. He is a vagabond after the loss of his wife, as he had been essentially while she was living. Like Odysseus, Aeneas, and the Arthurian Knights, he is a wayfarer, seeking a grail. Like Odysseus and the mad Lancelor, he is dependent upon the hospitality of various groups of people, particularly women; but he must be careful not to be captured by any of them. In **"To Thy Chamber Window, Sweet,"** he barely escapes in time from the feminine lures of a Mrs. Carter. In the manner of Aeneas sneaking away from Dido, Mr. Maury leaves without confronting the blue-eyed widow who has been charmed by his reading of poetry and hopes to ensnare him in the soft wiles of womanly concern. She has attempted to manage his diet, has compared him to her dead husband, has taken him on a romantic ride with her out to Rainbow Springs. Ahead of him the road, "banked on either side with roses, seemed to disappear in a tunnel of live oak branches." Mr. Maury shows at this point that he has already chosen the masculine companionship of Jim Yost, the fisherman, over the sweet dominion of Mrs. Carter. During the night, when Yost has decided to leave for the Suwanee [sic] River, Aleck Maury is suddenly seized with the inspiration—as from a god—to go with him. He sends word to Mrs. Carter by her Negro boy, takes off with Jim Yost, and murmurs to himself a line from *The Odyssey*: *"And snatch'd his rudder and shook out more sail . . . "* Like Odysseus leaving Calypso, like Aeneas deserting Dido, Mr. Maury has escaped from feminine charms to pursue his epic quest.

In **"Old Red,"** Mr. Maury comes to visit his wife's girlhood home, Merry Point, and is virtually captured by her mother and his daughter Sally. In this story he comes to realize that he is no longer hunter but hunted: in order to preserve his freedom in the face of encroaching old age, he sees that he will have to resort to the wily tactics of a fox. He has taken up fishing now, after having to relinquish the hunt; and it serves him well as a solitary occupation in which he is deeply in communion with nature, pitting his wits and his skill against living creatures in their own environ. That Maury is seeking some sort of answer to the mystery of being becomes even more apparent in these stories of his later life, wherein he desperately moves from place to place, looking for sufficient creature comforts (which ironically have to be provided by women) while he can pursue the only activity for which he has any zest.

The first paragraph of **"Old Red"** indicates his changed position. Maury is deprived of some of his autonomy; and by use of a familiar symbol in her writing—the window— Miss Gordon indicates his feeling of entrapment: "When the door had closed behind his daughter, Mister Maury went to the window and stood a few moments looking out." He is a guest in someone else's—not master in his own—house; he is expected to behave in a "sensible" manner; he feels that his daughter has assumed some sort of command. There are overtones of *King Lear,* wherein Lear is treated as a naughty child by his "pelican daughters," though certainly Sara is more likely—one would think—to prove a Cordelia to him than a Goneril or Regan. But all his life, it seems, as he says in a later story, he has been in servitude to women. And in **"Old Red"** he still threshes against that imprisonment.

> He stood looking down at his traps all gathered neatly in a heap at the foot of the bed. He would leave them like that. Even if they came in here sweeping and cleaning up—it was only in hotels that a man was master of his own room—even if they came in here cleaning up he would tell them to leave all his things exactly as they were.

He tells himself that he will stay only a week, "no matter what they say."

If **"Old Red"** is the first story in which Mr. Maury's active misogyny appears, it is also the first time we are aware of his gluttony; it is as though his insatiable hunger for the texture and concreteness of life is expressed in his voracious appetite as well as in his constant search for a new body of water and plentiful fish.

At the dinner table, relishing the hot batter bread and Merry Point ham, Mr. Maury hears his daughter and her new husband and his wife's mother and sister ask him what he does with his time. He thinks to himself:

> *Time!* They were always mouthing the word, and what did they know about it? Nothing in God's world! He saw time suddenly, a dull, leaden-colored fabric depending from the old lady's hands, from the hands of all of them, a blanket that they pulled about between them, now here, now there, trying to cover up their nakedness . . . . But time was a banner that whipped before him always in the wind! He stood on tiptoe to catch at the bright folds, to strain them to his bosom. They were bright and glittering. But they whipped by so fast and were whipping always ever faster. The tears came into his eyes. Where, for instance, had this year gone? He could swear he had not wasted a minute of it, for no man living, he thought, knew better how to make each day a pleasure to him. Not a minute wasted and yet here it was already May. If he lived to the Biblical three-score-and-ten, which was all he ever allowed himself in his calculations, he had before him only nine more Mays. Only nine more Mays out of all eternity and they wanted him to waste one of them sitting on the front porch at Merry Point!

This is the traditional *carpe diem* theme, turned to the modern world, where indeed linear time is man's enemy. And Aleck Maury, for all his moments of mythic awareness of what Mircea Eliade [in *Cosmos and History,* 1950] calls the Great Time, of time opening out into eternity (which is what he experiences in hunting and fishing), cannot live in that sacred time. He lives in *profane duration,*

time which is measured by a standard outside human life and which carries on inexorably toward an end of things.

Mr. Maury manages to get away from the house to fish by making his way to the Willow Sink—not much of a pond, but better than nothing. On the way an image rises in his mind, one that comes to him less frequently in his old age: "the wide field in front of his uncle's house in Albermarle, on one side the dark line of undergrowth that marked the Rivanna River, on the other the blue of Peters' Mountain. They would be waiting there in that broad plain when they had the first sight of the fox." He recalls one fox to whom the hunters have given a name—Old Red, who always showed himself on the ridge. The hunters always hoped to cut him off before he made it to the mountain. But he always lost them. "A smart fox, Old Red."

That evening, lying awake in the room where he had slept the night after his wife died, the moon shining brightly on the wallpaper, the shadows all advancing toward him, Aleck thinks of Molly. It was as though she has been retreating from him throughout their marriage. The death of their first child and her turn to religion had made them opponents. "For many years they had been two enemies contending in the open . . . Towards the last she had taken mightily to prayer." She had prayed over him, constantly seeking to make him what she thought he ought to be. But toward the last, during her illness, she must have realized that she had "wasted herself in conflict," and had neglected to be ready for "the real, the invincible adversary [who] waited . . . ." Struggling to go to sleep, Aleck suddenly finds himself in his reverie in the midst of the fox hunt. "He was always of those going around to try to cut the fox off on the other side. No, he was down off his horse. He was coursing with the fox through the trees." Aleck has identified himself now with the quarry. "The trees kept flashing by, one black trunk after another":

> And now it was a ragged mountain field and the sage grass running before them in waves to where a narrow stream curved in between the ridges . . . . But the fox's feet were already hard on the mountain path. He ran slowly, past the big boulder, past the blasted pine to where the shadow of the Pinnacle Rock was black across the path. He ran on and the shadow swayed and rose to meet him. Its cool touch was on his hot tongue, his heaving flanks. He had slipped in under it. He was sinking down, panting, in black dark, on moist earth while the hounds' baying filled the valley and reverberated from the mountainside.

He gets up and smokes a cigarette. Afterwards he plans his stratagem for the next morning. He will tell his daughter that his old kidney ailment has recurred and that he'd better return to Estill Springs for the waters, which had helped him last time. He knows that if he hurries, he can have a fly in the water half an hour after he gets off the train.

If **"Old Red"** records a narrow escape for Aleck Maury, **"One More Time"** teaches him, by analogy, that there is no final escape. He has come to Mrs. Rogers' inn, where he was headed after leaving Merry Point. Here he encounters an old fishing crony who has come back to the familiar place for "one more time"—to die. Wasting away with a terminal illness, Reynolds drowns himself in the Blue Pool, where Aleck remembers him "sitting in a boat in the middle . . . and looking up to the top of the gorge . . . and saying that from this one spot you can see nearly a whole mile of the Elk." Maury had wondered the night before Reynolds' death "how it would be to know that there was something inside you that would give soon and that you could only live as long as it lasted . . . . Would you want to stay very quiet so you might live longer or would you tell yourself there was nothing the matter and try to have as good a time as you could?"

This is the fundamental question about death for the modern. How does one face the unconfrontable? A notable failure to accept death with equanimity has followed upon the scientific revolution that produced the modern world. The seventeenth-century loss of the culture attendant upon Western Christendom left the modern with an "angelic" religion, such as Aleck Maury's wife seems to possess. The mythic patterns of life, the "old verities" continue among people who seem entirely secular in attitude and who do not consider themselves Christian—such as Aleck Maury. Maury knows what it is to commune with himself—and through himself with the spiritual reality within the universe. This activity, in which he engages when he is hunting or fishing, is the only relief he can find for the intolerable burden of approaching the end of things which death seems to have in store for all men. He cannot raise these separate and discrete moments to the level of faith, and hence cannot view death as an *end* in an entirely different sense: as Telos, fulfillment of purpose.

When we next encounter Aleck Maury in the short stories (in **"The Presence"**), he has been living for twelve years at the Mowbray house as a boarder. Jim Mowbray's wife, Miss Jenny, whom he admires and loves, has made Maury renounce fishing after he almost drowned getting out of his boat. His overweight now is a decided disadvantage to him; yet he cannot give up his relish for fine food. Miss Jenny is a talented cook, herself a Junoesque woman, and she loves humoring the Doctor, as she calls Mr. Maury. Consequently, as he puts it to himself, he has not been engaged for some time in any high enterprise that calls for the favor of the gods; he has had no epic adventure. The domestic has apparently conquered the heroic quest.

Mr. Maury is now seventy-five, frankly obese, cantankerous, and solitary. His capacity for interpreting life is keener however than it was in his youth. He is more aware than ever before of the symbolic patterns embedded in ordinary experience: Nothing in the other boarders' life and manners evades his keen scrutiny. Miss Gilbert, a fellow boarder, is abstractly pure and angelic, and Mr. Maury loathes her. She dresses constantly in white, tilts her aquiline nose into her drinking cup, and tries continually to interest him in spiritualist readings. In direct opposition to her is another boarder, Riva Gaines, a divorcee with a child, who represents the abstraction of flesh from spirit as Miss Gilbert exhibits the contrary. Mrs. Gaines is a predatory woman, using her sex as a means to personal happiness, seeking to snare and seduce men. In contrast

to both of these is Miss Jenny (Mrs. Mowbray), who manages the boarding house and gives it her tender concern. She is warmly feminine and maternal, proffering Mr. Maury neither moral advice nor the mere shallow formula of coquetry, but biscuits swimming in melted butter, chicken and dumplings, and quince preserves. He has connected her with Juno, the goddess of the hearth, the Queen of Heaven. As she is his ideal of womanhood, her husband is the kind of man he most admires: a huntsman and an accomplished dog-trainer, who can continue the quest in field and stream that Aleck has had to renounce. Though Aleck is no more reconciled to death now than he was when he was younger, he can endure to go on indefinitely in this manner, with the two Mowbrays satisfying vicariously his intense desire for life.

At the beginning of the story, Miss Jenny is away visiting her sick father. The household is awry; Mr. Maury is uncomfortable without her presiding presence. Nothing is as it should be; Mrs. Gaines neglects her child, the food is not up to par, Miss Gilbert preys upon Mr. Maury as a potential convert to her spiritualism. When Jenny Mowbray returns, Mr. Maury relaxes into the warm aura of love that her presence provides. At dinner, "She wore a camellia in her brown hair; her face, flushed from the ardors of the kitchen, was almost as pink as the petals of the flower." (*Old Red and Other Stories*) When she speaks of her ill and aging father, however, Mr. Maury thinks of his pursuing enemy death:

> Before him a vista seemed to open, a tunnel, whose low, arched side oozed dark mist. At the far end a stooping, shawled figure slowly raised a clumsy, bandaged hand. From the dank walls the moisture poured faster; the figure was dissolving in gray mist; he could no longer see even the feebly raised right hand . . .

Mr. Maury turns to Jenny. "My kidneys trouble me a great deal," he says. She listens to him sympathetically.

The warmth of this domestic haven is shattered when the discovery is made that Miss Jenny's husband is courting the young widow and that the Mowbrays will seek a divorce. Aleck is left with no one to turn toward for shelter; more, he is left with a knowledge of the impossibility of earthly happiness, the insufficiency, once more, of the natural world to sustain the human spirit.

Oddly enough, however, when Mr. Maury is left alone on the dark veranda of the house, with his world destroyed, it is in bitter thoughts of women that he occupies himself rather than in grief over the betrayal of his cherished Miss Jenny. "Women!" he has exclaimed to Miss Gilbert a bit earlier. "I've been watching them. They'll rock the world if they don't look out!" Reflecting on his situation, he thinks to himself, "There were no women in his life now, and yet he seemed to have been in servitude to them all his life."

In this state of darkness and despair, he recalls the death of his Aunt Victoria, who like Miss Jenny had also been described as "Junoesque." He had often thought of her as Hera, Queen of Heaven, and had confused her with that lady to whom she made him pray when he said his rosary:

"Hail, holy Queen, Mother of Mercy, hail our life, our sweetness, and our hope." He recalls that, when she died, she had seemed to see something beyond him, something to which she responded with expectancy and recognition. The story ends with this recollection. Aleck Maury has reached his goal, found his grail, has confronted directly the "meaning" of life in his memory of his aunt's faith. What he will do with this epiphany is not indicated, though he ends his reverie with a prayer: "pray for us sinners, now and at the *hour . . .* of our death."

Thus ends the epic journey of Aleck Maury, a man who, for all his gentleness and apparent traditionalism, is a romantic and a modern—a "superfluous man," as Turgenev characterized the figure. He turns away from society to the hunt, not for any shared ritual—for his is a solitary pursuit—but for a romantic quest to seek in nature what Wordsworth called the "visionary gleam." Like Rousseau's "solitary walker," he finds in society the chains that would bind him to routine, the forces that would corrupt his delight. He savors the Rousseauistic "sweet sentiment of his own existence" in field or stream; and his relationship to nature itself is not sacramental and submissive, but calculating and eventually cunning. It is his own mind that nature gives him: "My mind to me a kingdom is"—he once cites this line from Sir Thomas Dyer. Maury's delight is, like that of the Renaissance poet, in knowing. But as Thomas Aquinas has pointed out, loving is superior to knowing; for whereas in knowing, everything enters into one's self, in loving one is drawn out of oneself to something higher—to the beloved.

Unlike the narrator in *A Sportsman's Sketches* who does his solitary walking to gain the wisdom of the serfs, to observe the human community, Maury prefers to be alone or to have a single companion, with whom he has no relation, except on a limited basis. When he deals with the folk, it is to trick wisdom out of them. He alters nature, as in such instances as his placing pieces of iron in a pond to make trout breed. He constantly thinks that he can "figure out" the laws of nature and is continually in search of devices to make fish seek the hook more readily.

Further, in his attitude toward his own learning, the classics exist for him as a kind of enhancement of life; he does not make of his study an entrance into wisdom and love. He is a modern Cartesian man: split between mind and body and desperately seeking wholeness. He is a modern pantheist, repelled by the womanishness of religion, having to seek the sacred far apart from society and, as long as he has a pond or a stream, not needing a God.

Like another modern epic hero, Melville's Ishmael, Aleck Maury is a thinker, a scholar, a classics teacher. Like him, he feels cut off and alone; his mother died in his youth; he is impelled forward by an insatiable desire to know. Unlike Ishmael, he is of good family, well off, brought up with care and devotion by Negro servants. He is more whole than his New England counterpart; he has escaped Puritanism and rationalism; he understands that he must *do* as well as know, must *be* in order to know. Ishmael's initial epiphany occurs apparently when he gazes into the depths of the water, whereas Aleck Maury as a boy has caught a glimpse of the reality in nature when he looks

into the glowing eyes of a possum about to be killed. And, after he can no longer hunt because of his encroaching infirmities, he spends his time avoiding anything that will interfere with his fishing. Hunting and fishing have been for him existentially a ladder reaching to the high levels of spiritual reality; but Aleck Maury is not able to ascend its rungs without looking back. He must connive, conceal, lie, deceive in order to eke out the pleasure that crowns his life. He lacks faith in the permanence and universality of what he discovers, seeing himself as peculiar, the only man alive who cares about the intricate and delightful order of natural life in all its details. He looks upon death as ending one's participation in nature and hence fears it as the great enemy, since it will by definition sever the life of joy. "I'd rather be a slave in the land of the living," the shade of Achilles says in *The Odyssey,* "than King in the realm of the dead."

In Maury's old age, he is like another nineteenth-century epic hero, Stepan Verkhovensky, in Dostoevsky's *The Possessed.* Stepan too is a classical scholar, a teacher without faith, who longs for the beauty of another era. Both seek in the natural order the fulfillment of the soul, and both are doomed to failure in this quest—though Stepan finally finds his goal in the holy Russian soil and in the New Testament brought to him on his deathbed by a gospel woman. We do not know how Aleck Maury ends; but the marks of his imprisonment in a realm of natural good are unmistakable.

In his last story, as we see, he has become an utter wanderer, a displaced person who must seek room and board—who has, in effect, no place to lay his head. He has possessed the "kingdom of his mind," his classics; he has revelled in hunting and fishing, the close, poetic communion with nature. He has significantly been denied a Beatrice as guide. For, despite his love for his wife, she has somehow failed him. He has never known his mother. His daughter, though friendly and concerned, is not his kind of person, he thinks; she's more like his sister-in-law than like her mother. But one feminine relationship has provided an unconscious paradigm that his memory has never relinquished: Aunt Victoria did not, like Molly, pray over him; on the contrary, she made *him* pray. At her death, he remembers, she "uttered a cry and raised her head from the pillow," looking past him at something that he cannot see, over his shoulder. "He turned and saw nothing. Another softer sound broke from her and her head fell back on the pillow and she was still." He remembers that he had wondered, on his knees, what it was that she had seen.

Two visual images have thus made up the poles of Aleck Maury's life—the one of a possum blazing down at him, illuminating all of creation with an inner fire; and the other of an old woman looking up and beyond him toward something transcendent that is nevertheless a real "presence." Both visions are on the boundary of death, both are ultimate testimony to something in reality that lies behind the face of nature. The boy spends his entire life searching unconsciously for what his Aunt must have seen. But he seeks it on the lower level, by looking into the burning eyes of the natural world, rather than by construing it metaphysically, looking beyond nature into the heart of being.

It is only when he himself stands on the borderline of death, in his old age, that he is ready to choose: he is at the *hour* (and Miss Gordon underlines this word) that is for the Christian the moment of choice.

What I am maintaining, then, is that Miss Gordon's dominant angle of vision is epic, that within this epic vision she sees life as manifesting a "lower" and an "upper" pattern—the first mythological and archetypal, the second historical and analogical. The central movement within her world is a movement toward death: a death that can be either the loss of everything held dear or the fulfillment of desire. The Aleck Maury stories, written for the most part in her early years (and admittedly here read in the light of her later work!) hold a paradigmatic position in her canon—partly because they openly demonstrate her chief theme: that the modern epic quest manifests itself as a futile search to find in nature the ground of being; but principally because they present to us so clearly the character of the modern comic epic hero: Aleck Maury—at one and the same time heroic, admirable, pitiable, and finally lost in his commitment to a private inner voice that, in the end, calls him to no communal quest, gives him no chance of regaining Ithaca or founding the new Troy, and leaves him in retreat, ever more defenseless against the wrath of Juno.

The Dantesque method is present in the Aleck Maury stories as a use of "characters in her family" whom she sees as symbolic personages representing conditions of souls in quest of salvation. The memory of Aunt Victoria to which I have already referred is like an image of Beatrice that could still, even at this late moment, save him. But Beatrice required of Dante that he examine his conscience, change his heart, renounce the earthly paradise, weep bitter tears of repentance, and move toward the spheres of light. One cannot say how Maury responds to this new turn his "inner voice" has taken, whether in effect the wanderer becomes, like Dante, a pilgrim. It is enough for us—and for the artistic integrity of the stories—that he is brought face to face with a revelation that, still, across the years, has the power to confound and redeem. For the reader, at any rate, profane time has been cast in the light of the sacred.

Louise Cowan, "Aleck Maury, Epic Hero and Pilgrim," in The Short Fiction of Caroline Gordon: A Critical Symposium, *edited by Thomas H. Landess, The University of Dallas Press, 1972, pp. 7-31.*

Jane Gibson Brown (essay date 1972)

[*In the following essay on "The Captive," Brown disputes earlier interpretations of the story, examining it as "a narrative of endurance and initiation," heroism, and salvation.*]

Caroline Gordon's **"The Captive"** has been either ignored or else misunderstood since its publication in *Hound and Horn* in 1932; and, on a cursory examination, the story with its apparent structural simplicity and its abundance of highly dramatic detail seems deceptively open to dismissal or misinterpretation. Certainly readers unfamiliar

with Miss Gordon's work as a whole might tend to lump her with such writers as Kenneth Roberts, who have written engagingly, if somewhat superficially, of the American frontier; in fact, as Vivienne Koch observes [in "The Conservatism of Caroline Gordon," in *Southern Renascence,* edited by Louis D. Rubin, Jr. and Robert D. Jacobs, 1953], the earliest critics maintain that the story should be "commonly classified as a *tour de force* of the 'adventure' story genre." Since Miss Gordon's conversion to Catholicism, however, Miss Koch and others have attempted to see the piece, written prior to that conversion, essentially as a Christian allegory almost sectarian in its emphasis.

An extreme example of these later critics is Larry Rubin who interprets the work [in his "Christian Allegory in Caroline Gordon's 'The Captive,' " *Studies in Short Fiction* V (Spring 1968)] as a "Christian vision of sin, predestination, justification by good works, and redemption through Christ's agony on the Cross." For Mr. Rubin, the Indians in the story are "forces of evil (Mad Dog represents the devil incarnate)," whereas Jinny Wiley is equated with the old Adam. Furthermore, he suggests that the white youth burned and tortured by the Indians functions as a Christ symbol. Hence, according to Mr. Rubin, the story's ending, in which Jinny utters the simple, "Lord God, I was lucky to git away from them Indians," is to be understood as an expression of thanksgiving for salvation with "Lord God" a "formal ministerial usage."

Both extremes—the earlier condescensions and the later theological analyses—do an injustice to the artistry of Caroline Gordon. The classification of **"The Captive"** as a historical romance is, as Miss Koch suggests, a simplistic misreading. Indeed, it would seem that such an interpretation merely confuses the enveloping action of the narrative with the central action.

Mr. Rubin, however, forces the various elements of the story into abstract theological categories, and in doing so, fails to reconcile the literal level with the archetypal pattern which is the central action of the narrative. His reading, then, is an oversimplification of quite another kind; for his exegesis, since he fails to notice the thematic significance of the wilderness or the use of ritual within the Indian tribal culture, is a dismissal of the enveloping action as part of the story's organic structure. More importantly, the characterization of Jinny Wiley as a tough frontier woman is insignificant to his allegorical reading. But neither enveloping action nor depth of characterization can be ignored if, after long years of neglect and misunderstanding, the story is to be read correctly.

That Miss Gordon's historical sense is at work in her art is readily apparent. In an interview with Catherine B. Baum and Floyd C. Watkins, she herself acknowledges her dependence upon a genuine interest in the American conquest of the wilderness. In answer to the question, "Did you follow your source closely?" Miss Gordon replies:

Yes. I did. I'm trying to think if I changed it in any way. Now the source, the old book that the story is based on, is called the *Wiley Captivity and the Founding of Harman's Station.* I thought it was such a wonderful story, and it seemed to me that the story was almost written, and I got the notion that I could finish it . . . ["Caroline Gordon and 'The Captive': An Interview," *Southern Review* VII (Spring 1971)]

Moreover, as Miss Gordon further states, what she did was to take the historical story and fictionalize it. Thus she has made of the tale a work of art embodying myth, symbol, and archetypal action working up out of history and not down out of abstraction.

Basically, **"The Captive"** is a narrative of endurance and initiation in which the main character, a spirited and over-assertive woman named Jinny Wiley, learns the code of the wilderness while she is held captive by a group of Indian warriors who are the true inheritors of the land. It is through this ultimate understanding of the mysteries of "a sacramental nature" that she achieves a heroic stature and her own salvation. Living in ignorance of her proper role as a frontier woman, Jinny, through trial and suffering, is introduced by the Indians to the ultimate presences of a nature animated by the divine, a nature to which she must finally be submissive; and, indeed, she does receive the wisdom of the wholeness of nature, and her feminine function in the masculine world of the frontier is at last apparent to her.

The action of the narrative can be easily summarized. Jinny Wiley tells her own story of captivity and escape in the early American frontier. Living in a region near the Ohio River, she insists that her husband go into the settlement to sell ginseng and buy salt. During his absence, the unmanned home is mistakenly attacked by Cherokees who seek blood revenge against Tice Harman for his murder of an Indian brave. The Wiley house is burned, and all but the youngest child are killed and scalped. Jinny and the baby, who is later killed, are then forced to journey with their captors for days to reach a sacred and secret tribal stronghold, where the white woman is held for months, protected against the lust of the young warriors only by an old chief who claims her as a daughter and teaches her Indian skills and customs. Although Jinny occupies herself with thoughts of escape or deliverance by the settlers, she is ignorant of the region in which she finds herself and cannot discover the correct way out of the camp. She makes one abortive attempt to escape but is frightened by the wilderness and returns, preferring the security of living among her captors to the dangers of the unknown. Finally a warrior's growing lust for her becomes apparent at a time when a white youth is brought into the camp to be tortured and killed. The old chief, as a result of the warrior Mad Dog's prowess in battle and his successful capture of the boy, sells Jinny to the lustful victor as his wife. But the brave has no time in which to claim her, for he is sent out on a hunting party for provisions. Obsessed with fear and revulsion, Jinny has a dream in which a vision of the dead white youth appears to her and leads her to the safety of the white settlement. On the morning after, when Jinny is left alone by the hunters, she runs from the camp, carefully tracing the path of the youth in the dream. Days later, after a severe journey in which the Indians nearly recapture her, Jinny makes a desperate river crossing and reaches the protection of a settlement fort.

Certainly, on the literal level, the narrative is a tale of dramatic adventure akin to the ever-popular sagas of the American colonial experience. However, a larger significance of the action underlies the surface movement. Indeed, the myth of the frontier is only a particular historical extension of the archetypal experience of an emerging culture, as old as time and life itself.

The narrative actually begins with an expression of Jinny Wiley's fearlessness and impetuosity when she persuades her husband against his better judgment to leave her unprotected. This assertion of her will over Tom Wiley's is a kind of daring born out of her unwillingness to play the role of a submissive wife. Yet it goes against the dictates of the frontier, a community of hunters and woodsmen where women, as a rule, are never left alone.

> We were up long before day and were loading the horses at first dawn streak. Even then Tom didn't want to go.
>
> . . . I was bound he should make the trip, Indians or no Indians. I slapped the lead horse on the rump. "Go along," I said. "I'd as soon be scalped now and have done with it as keep on thinking about it all the time."

This daring of Jinny's begins to emerge as foolhardiness when it becomes apparent that no other woman in the community would permit herself to be left so helpless against the constant threat of an Indian attack, especially in a time when the relations between Indians and whites are severely strained. But Jinny allows herself to be left because she is a proud frontier woman whose flirtations with danger reach the level of hubris. Even when she senses with the first owl hoot of the Indians the threatening danger closing in on her, she recalcitrantly refuses to change her course of action. Relying on self alone in ignorance of the accidental in nature, she proceeds.

> But I couldn't get my mind off something a man said to me once when were out hunting on the Hurricane, and I made him go right in on a bear without waiting for the other men folks to come up.
>
> "You're brash, Jinny," he said, "and you always been lucky, but one of these times you going to be too brash."
>
> Sitting there listening to them owls calling and wondering how much longer it would be before Tom got home, I got to thinking that maybe this was the time I was too brash. For I knew well there wasn't another woman in the settlements would have undertaken to stay on that place all day with nothing but a parcel of children. Still I said to myself it's done now and there's no undoing it and the first thing I know Tom will be back, and tomorrow morning it'll fair up, and I'll be thinking what a goose I was to get scared over nothing.

Jinny is a woman of unfeminine pursuits and interests. She hunts with men and exposes herself unnecessarily to dangers with which no woman can properly cope. And she clearly cannot comprehend the masculine code of behavior in a threatening wilderness. Indeed, she understands even less the feminine need for protection in an environment antagonistic and hostile to human weakness. The Hog-Drovers Song, which her children sing and which she does not truly hear, is a corrupted presentation of the masculine protectiveness of woman. The Hog-Drovers are refused lodging in the song because the farmer's daughter they wish to court must be protected until her proper suitor arrives. The Drovers are several who seek an entrance into the household and the implied connotation is they are plainly up to no good. In reply to the question of lodging, the father, with the appellation "No pig stealin' drover," suggests that the crude courtiers wish to steal the virtue of the daughter; and, indeed, the young girl herself from the safety of her father's house. Thus, the guardianship of woman is a masculine role which Jinny refuses to recognize and to which she will not submit. This lack of submission to her own femininity has already exposed her to danger at the hands of Lance Rayburn, a rapacious suitor of her youth. Both the Hog-Drovers Song and her recollection of Rayburn foreshadow the later withdrawal of chief Crowmocker's protection at a time when she most needs it, an event which finally reveals to Jinny the essential helplessness of women without men. Therefore, it is significant that even when, with the increasing danger of the Indian attack, a neighbor comes to offer the protection of his household, Jinny accepts this shelter only on her own terms, out of an ignorance of Indian ways.

> . . . I thought I'd best go over to the Borderses'.
> It was my judgment, though, that there wasn't
> any hurry. Indians hardly ever come around before nightfall.

This final stubborn hesitation, an additional act of hubris, renders Jinny and her children vulnerable to the attack and brings about the destruction of the Wiley household. Joe, the eldest son, who is supposed to be the man on the place, is ironically too young to accomplish any of the earlier boasts he has made about his conduct in the event of an attack. As his mother sees him fall under the warrior's tomahawk, she knows that the last male effort to prevent her capture has been thwarted. Her seemingly cruel comment, "I seen him go down and I knowed I couldn't git any more help from him," is a tough, harsh but human response in a confrontation with one's enemies in the thick of the fight where there is no time for mourning. It is a perfectly logical and consistent statement for a woman in Jinny's circumstances to utter. However, ultimately Jinny's loss of her son and her resulting helplessness point to the larger significance of her captivity. Indeed, she can no longer rely on herself alone but must seek both the companionship of the chief and the guidance of the white youth. But only after she has been utterly isolated and down on her luck can Jinny be initiated into the oneness of nature. Thus, she herself must suffer for her ignorance and hubris. Mad Dog's murder of her baby, Dinny, during the flight from the white pursuers to the Indian encampment, removes the last trace of her past; and her inability to prevent this murder reveals to her the nature of her own weakness when confronted with forces beyond her control. Even the old Crowmocker, who claims her as a replacement for his lost daughter, eventually casts her into the worst possible bondage as the wife of Mad Dog. Thus,

through a series of terrible misfortunes Jinny is educated into a knowledge of the code of the masculine frontier, the world of the whites. Yet it is ironic that those who hold her captive and threaten her most severely teach her the most important lesson of her life.

This lesson, an acceptance of her proper place in the pattern of creation, is first revealed to Jinny in rudimentary fashion during the flight through the woods, when old Crowmocker boils tea for her and the baby to get them to sleep and later when he applies a poultice to Jinny's swollen feet so that she can continue the journey. Implicit in this medicinal use of vegetation is the idea that nature can be employed as the ultimate restorer. In contrast to Crowmocker's use of nature as a providential aid to man, Tom Wiley has taken ginseng, itself a sweetish herb valued medicinally, into the settlement to sell for salt. The Indians, Miss Gordon is careful to show, use natural salt licks. Thus, this action of Wiley's points to the fact that the white man exploits nature but the Indians, as true inheritors of the wilderness, accept gratefully that which is given to them. To be sure, when Mad Dog buys Jinny, the young brave gives the old chief silver brooches, but this exchange is only part of the formal rite of betrothal. And thus the silver is symbolic in its usage. Indeed, Crowmocker is really more impressed with Mad Dog's prowess in battle than with his gift, for the Cherokee chief is perhaps the last warrior who truly understands the rituals defining man's dependence upon nature, or he expects to have no heirs in his craft.

As the last of the true inheritors, Crowmocker's reverence for nature as restorer and the medicine man as its priest exemplifies the old chief's worship of the highest art of nature, an art beyond the capabilities of the mere warrior or hunter. Indeed, he understands the primary function of nature as the giver and sustainer of life itself. And it is through the healing power of medicine that Crowmocker understands the Great Spirit that informs the natural world.

> He said he was a chief but he might have been
> something better. He might have been a medicine man. He had the gift of it from his grandmother. His own mother died when he was born,
> he said, and his old granny raised him. He told
> me about how she would take him into the
> woods with her looking for yarbs and roots, and
> how she knew where everything grew and which
> roots would be good to take and which had no
> strength in them. He said that after I was adopted into the tribe he would tell some of her secrets
> to me, but the Spirit would be angry if a white
> woman knew them.

In contrast to Crowmocker's deeper understanding, Jinny herself possesses a kind of knowledge of the wilderness shown in her ability to identify the various trees, to mark the change of seasons, and to distinguish the unknown parts of the woods from the familiar. But this knowledge is superficial, a mere notation of external phenomena. She cannot know, as an intruder, either the essential spirit of the wilderness or the transcendent meaning of the trees, herbs, and animals she can correctly name.

However, the religious life of the tribe and the Indians'

worship of the spirit of nature is manifested to her when Crowmocker explains the ancestral significance of the painted beasts on the cliffs walling in the encampment and also points out the burial mounds. As true inheritors and knowers of the wilderness, the Indians' piety toward their bestial and human predecessors is consistent with the larger view of nature as one family presided over by the Great Spirit. And although Jinny does not at first believe that the painted bear will crush any white who enters the sacred stronghold, she senses that the supernatural aspect of nature is something real and living among the tribe. Indeed, it is on the grassy knoll where all tribal celebrations and rituals are held that Jinny sits and gives her memory and imagination the freedom to keep alive the presences of her lost family and her past. In seeing the house and children whole and alive, she begins to participate in the spirit of nature with the knowledge that the dead are with her still. The Lance Rayburn episode (he has since died mysteriously) and the recollection of her late grandmother point to Jinny's gradual ability to hold communion with the dead. Moreover, the Rayburn memory reminds her of her loyalty and devotion to Tom Wiley, which foreshadows the desperate refusal to become Mad Dog's wife.

Apart from her leisure on "the barren," Jinny is made to do squaw's work, so that her captivity forces her to perform a purely feminine role, though at home she has not even finished weaving cloth for her children's clothes.

> I did a lot of work while I was with the Indians. It was hard on me at first but I got used to it.
>
> . . . . .
>
> I got so after a while that the Indian way of doing things seemed natural to me.

The "naturalness" of the Indian customs and her own particular role in the tribe serve to curb her impetuosity when she attempts an unprepared escape, making her realize in time that she is ill-equipped for such an extravagant gesture. Her return to camp is the first step in her acquisition of respect for danger and her acceptance of restrictions which later, at the proper moment, enable her to exhibit in her escape not foolhardiness but genuine courage.

Similarly, her experiences at the Indian salt lick further enlighten Jinny, and she becomes heir to a knowledge of beasts denied to ordinary men. As she moves deeper and deeper into the unveiling of mysteries, she recalls tales which show the artificial, debased character of the white world. The episode of Vard Wiley dressing up as a woman and chasing the old schoolmaster Daughtery naked from the swimming hole reveals to her evils inherent in her own culture: violations of the basic order of nature. When she laughs at the tale, she feels strange sitting in the woods. Moreover, a dream vision of the Indian bone house, where her own spiritually dead people frolic, again reinforces her sense of the taint of original sin which man brings with him into the wilderness.

Even the Indians finally are not exempt from this original sin. The Cherokee community itself is on the decline. As Crowmocker tells her, bees swarm out of season and the war whoop which used to mean joy now only hides the braves' fear. The game vanishes from the salt lick and the hunters must range farther and farther from the camp in order to obtain food. This shrinking of the wilderness, as Crowmocker knows and tells Jinny, is bound to result in strife between the Indians and the whites. The conservation of the wilderness is, then, for the Indian an ultimate concern. Thus, they do not take pelts which are too thin, whereas Lance Rayburn gloried in their indescriminate acquisition. Therefore, it is really this threat of a ruined creation which the whites present to the Indians. And old Crowmocker's prophecy of the vanishing wilderness points to the essentially feminine nature of the Cherokee nation.

> The white people . . . The white people are all over the land. The beaver makes no more dams and the buffalo does not come to the lick. And bees swarm here in the ancient village. Bees swarm on the graves of our fathers. . . .

It is evident that the Indians are violated by the whites; and yet they reply in kind, mistaking Tice Harman's house for the Wiley's, becoming perverse themselves and misusing a power which they derive from their closeness to nature. And in trying to adapt to the white man's world of bullets and firewater, they further debase the spiritual function of the hunt and other essential rituals. In trying to possess the wilderness, then, they begin to lose it.

Jinny herself is caught between the evils of the two cultures. Although while living among the Indians she greases herself to remove the taint of her white skin, she is never formally brought into the Cherokee nation. Thus, she preserves and strengthens her own cultural heritage by putting to use only the best of Indian wisdom. When the white youth is brought to the camp to be tortured and burned, Jinny recognizes her own identity as white and her own helplessness to prevent the murder. One of her truest utterances comes when she confronts the boy face to face and says:

> "I can't do nothing," I said. "I'm a white woman, but I can't do nothing. Christ!" I said, "there ain't nothing I can do."

And, indeed, there is nothing she can do for the boy. However, her understanding that she is utterly helpless prepares her for the salvation which comes to her in the dream. Moreover, she accepts herself for what she really is, a white woman in a dangerous, masculine world. Therefore, when Mad Dog buys her from the old Cherokee, she relies on the only help left to her in the nocturnal vision of the dead youth, who leads her out of the dark hostile world into the light. The light is symbolic of Jinny's knowledge that she must remain true to the providential scheme of things. Thus, she sticks to the water in escaping, although she often doubts the certainty of its path to safety. Similarly, she wastes little time in hunting rabbits with the old knife. Following a more feminine instinct, she boils wild greens and nourishes herself in order to keep up her strength. She does not, then, run wildly without rest, shelter, or food. She now knows the importance and the order of endurance.

In the last scene of the story at a river crossing, Jinny passes her final trial through her heroism and proper assertion of will. Like the white youth who in a vision shows her the path, an old man of the fort provides her with a way across the river on the raft. However, provided with this simple protection, Jinny must alone save herself. Thus, as the old man prays and the raft becomes unhinged, Jinny poles her way to safety. Miss Gordon seems to suggest two important concepts here. In both episodes, one with the youth and the other with the old man, there is the strong suggestion that both the masculine and the feminine working in a proper balance are necessary for a right order of being. Moreover, there is also the significant implication that one must work with the spirit of nature, that simple prayer is not enough.

Jinny acknowledges her newfound humility and the wisdom of nature in her last statement when she is safely inside the fort. Contained in the "Lord God, I was lucky to git away from them Indians!" is her declaration that she has not relied on herself alone, as she formerly did. The word "lucky" used in this context implies that Jinny knows something of endurance itself, that it is ultimately a matter of luck, even if one is submissive and properly diligent. In the end she has been lucky, just as Dinny, the children, and the white youth were unlucky. For all that she has accomplished in the tempering of her pride and the acquisition of wisdom, her luck, then, is only a gift bestowed upon her as a kind of grace. That she has no thoughts of her family is logical enough, so soon after the desperate danger which she has faced. Jinny's period of mourning has been given its due on the barren. It is her lot to endure. And she has earned that prerogative.

Jane Gibson Brown, "Woman in Nature: A Study of Caroline Gordon's 'The Captive'," in The Short Fiction of Caroline Gordon: A Critical Symposium, *edited by Thomas H. Landess, The University of Dallas Press, 1972, pp. 75-84.*

Robert H. Brinkmeyer, Jr.　(essay date 1982)

[*In the following excerpt, Brinkmeyer offers a mixed assessment of Gordon's* The Collected Stories, *faulting the volume's organization and arguing that Gordon's short fiction is most successful and aesthetically pleasing when viewed from a chronological perspective.*]

The Collected Stories is, with a few exceptions, a collection of superb, often flawless short fiction. Any doubt that Gordon was a master craftsman is laid to rest with . . . *The Collected Stories,* where, in one finely wrought story after another, she captures the exquisite complexity of life and the imagination.

As the collection of her stories shows, Gordon's most noteworthy achievement as a writer is that throughout her very long career, spanning over five decades, she kept her work almost uniformly fine—this despite the fact that she passed through several stages of development which drastically altered her thought and art. After she joined the Catholic Church in 1947, for example, she wrote [in "The Art and Mystery of Faith," *The Newman Annual* (1953)] of the upheaval in her life, saying that she felt "a little as if I had all my life engaged in the writing of a novel and

only recently had discovered that the plot is entirely different from what I thought it was." "I was nearly fifty years old," she wrote [in "Letters to a Monk," *Ramparts* 3 (December 1964)], "before I discovered that art is the handmaid to the Church." In navigating during her lifetime several similar shifts in outlook, Gordon maintained her artistic balance and her work weathered remarkably well; only late in her career, when she struggled to forge a unity of classical and Christian vision, did her fiction begin to show signs of a serious falling off.

As rich and profound as *The Collected Stories* is, the volume has its flaws, the most serious of which is its organization. Throughout her career Gordon maintained an ongoing search for the best way to view and write about the world; and as her outlook on life developed and changed, so did the shape and texture of her art. For this reason, Gordon is most intriguing when read chronologically, beginning with her first story **"Summer Dust"** (inexcusably absent from *The Collected Stories;* it should have been included with the rewritten version, **"One Against Thebes,"** published over 30 years after the original, which is in the volume) and working through her entire canon.

Unfortunately, *The Collected Stories* is arranged neither chronologically nor in the manner the stories were originally collected in her two previous volumes, *The Forest of the South* (1945) and *Old Red and Other Stories* (1963). Instead (and one presumes this was Gordon's wish rather than Robert Penn Warren's, who wrote the volume's introduction), the stories are arranged into four groups, loosely tied together by theme and content. What is lost in this arrangement is the opportunity to follow Gordon's developing vision and technical innovation. This loss far outweighs what is gained by the juxtaposition of different stories on a similar theme. Moreover, Gordon's writing changed so radically during her career that it can be downright confusing—and distracting—to find several stories from different periods set together, linked only by arbitrary similarities of subject. A thematic arrangement just doesn't work with a writer who changed as persistently as Gordon did.

Gordon's early work, beginning with **"Summer Dust"** (1929) up through her fifth novel, *Green Centuries* (1941), depicts heroic characters struggling to assert order and meaning in a shadowed world. At the heart of these heroes' solitary stands against death and disintegration lie a stoic acceptance of man's depravity and a desire to forge a code of courageous dignity. As heroic and noble as these characters are, the dark forces of life inevitably destroy them and—we understand now—their fragile edifices of order. Gordon's strong bond of sympathy with her heroes (derived primarily from her extensive early education in the classics), allowed her to maintain a healthy tension between her dark vision of existence and her need to assert some vestige of meaning amidst life's pain; this tension helped prevent her works from becoming merely shrill cries against the world's unfairness.

Sometime in the early 1940s Gordon's thought and art began to shift. With *The Women on the Porch* (1944) and several stories which followed until her conversion to Roman Catholicism in 1947, she began searching for a larger system of order which would transcend personal heroics. Where these works, like her earlier fiction, center on the difficult quests for order in a threatening world, now disorder is finally brought into check; emerging from crises of despair, Gordon's heroes arrive at the understanding that an overarching tradition exists, rooted in eternity, which can bring them the unifying order they seek. Gordon at this point seemed to be unsure of the nature of this tradition, at times suggesting it rested with Christianity (*The Women on the Porch*), at others with classicism (**"The Olive Garden,"** reprinted, fortunately, for the first time in *The Collected Stories*). Probably because she was herself wavering between accepting one of these two traditions, she was able to keep her fiction free from easy reconciliations and heavy-handed dogma—elements which flawed Gordon's fiction during the next few years.

In 1947 Gordon joined the Roman Catholic Church, a step which gave her a tradition and authority by which to structure her life and art. With her newly embraced faith, Gordon believed, her art took on a greater depth and profundity, since it now took on what Flannery O'Connor called "the added dimension"—that is, the Church's vision of world and eternity. Whether or not Gordon's artistic vision deepened is an arguable point, but clearly her work from this period—notably her two novels *The Strange Children* (1951) and *The Malefactors* (1956) and her long story **"Emmanuele! Emmanuele!"** (1954)—took a new shape. While these works are more openly concerned with the transcendent, they lack the deeply-felt love for heroic struggle which gave her earlier work such strength. Rather than celebrating man's valiant efforts to achieve private dignity, the post-conversion works show such struggles as rooted in vanity and destructive pride. Only by abandoning these personal struggles and by giving oneself to the Church, these works suggest, can a person achieve fulfillment and unity.

To communicate her religious vision to an audience she saw as secular and unsympathetic, Gordon adopted strategies of shock and distortion; these she hoped would compel her readers to abandon literal interpretation and look beyond to the religious message embodied in the work. Unfortunately Gordon's strategy, usually centering on a dramatic and unprepared for conversion experience near the end of the work, often appears forced and unconvincing, the result of her didacticism rather than her fidelity to human experience. The reader feels cheated rather than enlightened.

After *The Malefactors* (1956) and up until her death in 1981, Gordon struck out with her fiction in a new radical direction: she tried to merge her Christian and classical visions. Following the lead of Jacques Maritain, she developed a definition of Christian art based on archetypal patterns rather than on literal subject matter. Great literature, she . . . [wrote in "On Learning to Write," *Four Quarters* 12 (January 1963)], "comes into being when one of those timeless patterns reveals itself in time and conflict in which human beings are involved"; and true artists are those who intuit these archetypal patterns and structure their work by them on some deep level. Works so constructed, Gordon said, were ultimately Christian because since archetypes embody the full range of human endeavor, they finally lead to the Christian mysteries. With her new theory of fiction came a renewed interest in heroes, whom she now likened to the ancient battlers; from wrestling with evil, Gordon's heroes gained knowledge which could lead them to the discovery of God. Perhaps because she was trying to accomplish too much, most of the work from this period (**"One Against Thebes"** is an exception), is sketchy and uneven, written as if from a tentative hand. *The Glory of Hera* (1972), her only novel from this period, suffers from these faults.

To grasp the complexity and multiplicity of a long and varied career like Gordon's is next to impossible with *The Collected Stories*—unless the reader breaks with the book's arrangement and reads the stories chronologically. Few, however, will read the book this way, and so, as worthwhile and important as this collection is, its organization ultimately steers readers away from much of the meaning and significance of Gordon's short fiction. . . .

Robert H. Brinkmeyer, Jr., "New Caroline Gordon Books," in The Southern Literary Journal, *Vol. XIV, No. 2, Spring, 1982, pp. 62-8.*

Howard Baker   (essay date 1982)

[*An American writer and critic, Baker was cofounder of the literary magazine* Gyroscope *in which Gordon published her first short story "Summer Dust." He was also a personal friend of Gordon and among the expatriate writers who congregated in Paris during the 1920s and 1930s. In the first part of the essay below, Baker praises Gordon's keen evocation of her origins and experiences in southern Kentucky in* The Collected Stories of Caroline Gordon, *calling her a master of the genre. In the postscript, he provides a stylistic analysis of her methods.*]

For a long time I believed that Caroline Gordon's superior skill in telling a story stemmed from her being, more often than not, an expatriate, as it were, from the scenes about which she was writing. She had the advantage, I thought, of unusually long perspectives when she called up scenes which she once had known intimately. Her chosen settings did lie almost exclusively among the low, wooded hills and red-earthed tobacco fields of Todd County in southern Kentucky, where she had spent her childhood and early maturity. Here the families of intermarried, no longer affluent landlords lived in stately faded dwellings among the poor houses of their tenant farmers.

Twenty out of the twenty-three stories in the handsome new *Collected Stories* do in fact give us unforgettable pictures of the spirited, highly variable, often troubled lives of men native to this part of Kentucky, along with views, just as remarkable, of womenfolk who could gather themselves much more comfortably together at dinner tables and on long gallery-like porches. There is a tightness of a "family connection" here, and also a discord of the frictions that can brew in it. The result is a vision with a roundness and a peculiar realism of the ways of life in Todd County, which could be recreated vividly, with great feeling, when recalled from distant places. In fact, all of Caroline Gordon's work, these short stories and the roster of the novels as well, shows a clarity of perspective, a vividness of feeling, which have hardly been matched by the other writers of her generation.

I think now that there is a great deal of merit in the expatriate theory, but it does not explain as much as it ought to. It has had, in any event, the finest of precedents in the education of a story-teller whose triumphs in the art will probably never be equaled: Ulysses, reciting his tale in the court of great-hearted Alcinous; . . . and as it happens, Homer has taken scrupulous care at the start of his poem to reveal the most important fact about the origins of Ulysses' mastery. Ulysses, Homer says in the translation of Robert Fitzgerald, had had an opportunity "to see the townlands and learn the minds of distant men," while he was carrying in his heart an overwhelming nostalgia for his home in Ithaca.

The same may be said for Caroline Gordon. After working in Paris during the latter part of 1928 with her husband Allen Tate, who had been awarded one of the first of the Guggenheim Fellowships, and exploring with him the examples of ancient arts and of the most modern of arts which were at hand in that enormously complex capital, she found herself in July 1929 living at a remote spot in Finistère. She had already begun a novel in Paris and had this to say to her friend Sally Wood in a letter written on board ship on the way back to America at the end of the year: "I have four short stories to show you, all written in the last six months. I never could write short stories until I went to Brittany and then I broke out with 'em like a rash."

Of these four stories, the three which are readily identifiable were delivered in Brittany with all the traits of Todd County impressed on their countenances. One, **"The Long Day,"** tells the afterlude of a deadly contest between a young black man and his woman. Through the long day a white boy is waiting around at the gate of the cabin, hoping his older black friend will shake off his troubles and keep his promise to go fishing with him. The black man is waiting around too, hoping that the woman in the cabin will start recovering from the damage she has suffered at his hand. When she does not, when he sees her dead eyes looking at him, he starts running from the house, "crouching like a dog, diving through the tall goldenrod," toward the woods. In Todd County a man, smitten by a curse of the gods, flees blindly, with no place to go.

So it is too at the end of the novel *The Garden of Adonis*, which was written soon after **"The Long Day."** In this rural tragedy an unlucky, poor white tenant farmer crushes the head of a landowner who has seemed to preside over his string of disasters. After gazing stupidly at the bloodied piece of oak in his hand, the man drops it and starts running "faster and faster through the clover toward the distant woods." *With no place farther to go!* Given these circumstances I suppose there is never any secure place to go, in Todd County or anywhere. In this fiction, however, the force of this truth comes out with unique power.

Violence, stupefying violence, bursts like an underground river from hidden caves in these rocky forests. In **"The Ice House"** the skeletons of many soldiers must be disgorged from the pit where they had been put out of sight, in order to be given proper burial. Here the afterlude of wartime violence is shaped around the necessarily hardened feelings of the hired help, digging up the bodies, and around the unnecessary but probably inevitable chicanery of the contractor who had come down from the North to carry out these pointless services. Although the letters to Sally Wood show that violence was acceptable as a literary commodity, even convenient to a mind "running as mine does," still our author handled violence from the beginning as a manifestation of what can and does go on under the surface of life. Sometimes it is not gruesome; sometimes it is full of pathos, as in **"The Brilliant Leaves"**; sometimes it is comic, highly comic, as in **"The Petrified Woman."**

One might argue that the countryside around Concarneau in Brittany had just the peculiarities that it took to trigger the imagination of Caroline Gordon. The wooded hills with their pastures and patches, vegetable gardens and small fields of grain, straggling plots of fruit trees, with lanes winding among them, all this in the heat of July could have seemed to be transparently, or perhaps mysteriously familiar. Nor, given the sensitivities in her make-up, would she have passed lightly over the strong traditions which still persisted among the people of that *département*. The Breton is a man of small but hardy enterprises, respectful of family and of the Catholic faith, and is unbending in his dislike of centralization. It was a good place for a writer to gather her own faculties and memories together so that they would become something that resembled a well-shaped, well-turned, well-painted vessel.

I have moved slowly over the first stories because I think we can see in them the clear imprint of the hand of a master. One story, however, the first of them all, cannot be treated in even a very slow summary manner: it has an ever-renewing sap in it, such as that which our Chinese gold-miners attributed to the rhizomes of the Heavenly Ailanthus which they brought with them to California. **"One Against Thebes"** in most ways is an enlarged telling of Caroline's first short story, **"Summer Dust,"** which appeared in the *Gyroscope*, November 1929. The first version is set out in the purest of country talk, the symbolism is allowed to remain only implicit: I wish that *The Collected Stories* had included both versions. Although I think that **"Summer Dust"** is much the better told, I am happy to settle for **"One Against Thebes"**: . . . A black woman and her children, and our author herself as a child, are walking along a dusty lane in Kentucky. They are going with a pail or two and a basket to the large, decayed Old House to bring home some peaches from the ruined gardens. The children plow their feet through the dust. One of them, Son, runs ahead, lurching from one side of the road to the other, leaving behind a trail which causes the child to think that "it might have been made by a great snake, a serpent as large as any of them, hurling itself now to one side, now to the other, and thinks, too, how she and the other girl and the boy and even the old woman seem to move in its coils."

On the way home she walked along the side of the road to avoid the serpentine trail that Son's feet had left in the dust. Son himself had broken off a big cattail and when he came up to the crooked track, "he would whack the dust—as if he were trying to beat a snake to death." The long coiling imprint in the context of the story is transparently symbolic.

Quite clearly it stands for death . . . and probably for other gloomy underworld marvels, as Professor Maury tries to explain to the girl and some of the boys that same night. Such a track might have been made by the deadly Lernaean Hydra, the first of the monsters that Heracles killed. One snake was definitely among the largest in the tribe of reptiles—the snake which Heracles strangled in his cradle while he was still an infant. Nevertheless, there was still a hoard of venom floating around in his world, some part of which would overcome him on the day of his death, striking him as he stood before the altar of Zeus attired in the ceremonial robe, the poisoned ceremonial robe, which Deineira, Heracles' too fallible, too loving wife had prepared for him.

From Brittany and the *Gyroscope* of 1929 there stretches a trail which is not snake-like but encouragingly straightforward, leading to the last of the completed novels, *The Glory of Hera.* This was a crowning work. It seems already to be sadly forgotten. Fiction, like so many of our endeavors, has become pretty thoroughly addicted to the showy and the frivolous. *The Glory of Hera,* with Heracles as its hero, carries the clearly enunciated serpent theme in the first Todd County short story to the farthest reaches of the imagination.

The perspectives which can be cast backwards from distant vantage points have the merit of illuminating the past, as I have said, but they fail, I think, to reach into certain dark pockets in the events which they are revealing in the round. These dark pockets may be the most important of all. Brittany, despite the security it gave the backwards view, could not possibly have interpreted the workings of the minds of the black man and the white boy in **"The Long Day."** That, like other irrationalities in the stories, had to come from somewhere else. Those unwanted violences, or badly misdirected quirks of temperament, are the linchpins that collapse and bring each story to its end.

Curious instances abound. The older boys are smugly discourteous toward Professor Maury that evening when he tries to tell them a few facts about Heracles. He is angered and points out their preference for living their lives as ignoramuses. "He couldn't talk to children for a long time without getting tired, but he couldn't talk to grown people either. . . . " He was doomed to become, quite understandably, an unusually lonely man. And in the middle of the Theban story the little girl attends, wondering, to allusions to other unwanted but apparently somewhat humorous violences: she overhears her brother say to another boy, "Sure, she was there. With the baby! Right there in the courtroom!" And then she hears this: "What'd the judge say?" And the reply: "Said he reckoned Virgil'd know what the age of consent was next time. Told him next time he reckoned he'd be able to figure *that* out." I have to ask myself, what point of vantage accounts for

such insight into the ruffling of lives in Todd County, or in any county?

For Caroline Gordon's own sketch of that vantage point we might try joining her, still as a child, in the top of an enormous tree growing beside her home, and surveying with her the vista of Todd County spread out to its utmost beneath a bright summer sky.

She composed, by way of introduction to a novel which was to be called *The Narrow Heart,* what appears to be an autobiographical overture. These allusive pages, rehearsing themes and counterthemes, came out in the Fall 1972 issue of the *Sewanee Review,* edited by her old friend Andrew Lytle, under the title "A Visit to the Grove." Some fragments of it are so frank a confession of her understanding of herself as a writer that I want to quote them exactly as they are, without interposing any commentary:

> . . . I have wandered afield. I must return to the tree in which I perch while I survey the countryside.
>
> The only earth I knew then was the red earth of my native valley, and it seemed to me—on that day, at least, that the road which I could glimpse through the trees crawled through the valley like a great, wounded serpent, dragging its length between places where water bubbled up out of the earth between darkly leaning rocks. . . .
>
> Early in life I began forming those habits which today constitute so large a part of my professional equipment: the habit of a certain kind of observation. . . . From my early childhood any natural object, animate or inanimate, could arrest my attention. But I observed them, I now begin to suspect, because I wanted to show somebody else how that tree stretched its branches or how that river flowed or how that bird or beast moved or. . . .

Or how a landmark that had become visible from the top of the tree revealed itself, outside, and inside:

> The house, low, rambling, and greyish in color, stood in a grove of lofty oaks. John Barker had left his land dotted with these groves to provide building sites for his descendants. . . . At Summertrees the grown people sat in the living room to talk. In a far corner of the room stood what was called a "missy bed," *full of cats!*—a bed on which any number of cats were free to repose and on which nobody else ever reposed. A child could stand beside that bed and sink her hands deep into a blanket of warm, palpitating fur.

Or again it was a path that led

> . . . into a country stranger even than the region which lay back of the house, which was called "the Tink Woods" because the skeleton of a woman—a "Thing," the Negroes called her—had been found cradling the skeleton of a child in its arms in the crotch of a huge sycamore shortly after "the War."

A "certain kind of observation" was obviously an item in her professional equipment which could zoom back and forth through untold reaches of space and time . . . while always staying exactly on target.

The possession of such a faculty has occurred more than once before, or so we are told by authors in whom I take a good deal of stock, and all writers of passable fiction doubtless possess at least a sizable modicum of it. But he who was most richly endowed, in my opinion, was Icarus-Menippus, speaking through the mouth of Lucian of Samosata. Here was a mortal who had fastened an eagle's wing to one arm, and to the other the wing of a great vulture, a vulture by choice in order not to disguise his true nature too thoroughly from the eyes of the gods and thus to invite *hybris*. But reaching the moon on his flight, he took full advantage of the eaglewing. By flicking it rapidly in front of his face, he made use of the powers of vision of Zeus's spy-eyed bird. He studied our earth, with each of its flawed little crooks and crannies. According to Erasmus, this is how the picture shaped itself out:

> . . . In short, if a man like Menippus of old could look down from the moon and behold those innumerable rufflings of mankind, he would think he saw a swarm of flies and gnats quarreling among themselves, fighting, laying traps for one another, snatching, playing, wantoning, growing up, falling, and dying. Nor is it to be believed what stir, what broils, this little creature raises, and yet in how short a time it comes to nothing itself; while sometimes war, other times pestilence, sweeps off many thousand of them together. [*Praise of Folly*, John Wilson, trans., 1668]

Of course the violent or the pathetic irrationalities in Caroline Gordon's stories do not take on so dark a cast as this. But they are there, those harsh irrationalities are there, and at the same time they are presented with a sympathy to which I want to do as much honor as I possibly can.

One must consider what a good story *was:* how the concept of a prose fiction narrative could best be defined in the days of Caroline's training. One sees that whatever else these stories may be, they are well balanced. If the endings are not "happy endings" the final effect is the enlargement and enhancement of the spirit. Ford Madox Ford, Caroline's mentor in defining their craft, made the ending the crux of the fiction writer's problem. English prose fiction, he went on to say, had its ancestry in the classical Spanish masters of the picaresque, not in the native Euphuistic or Arcadian romances (though many authorities, "swayed perhaps by patriotism," deny this . . .), and the first triumphant writer was Daniel Defoe in *Moll Flanders,* with his plain style and his ability to foreshadow the inevitable end at the beginning of each paragraph and each episode, and of the picaresque work as a whole.

This mastery—of having the first sentence foreshadow the last—which I maintain is a mastery in which Caroline Gordon shared, begs for some small illustration, and I ask the reader's indulgence now that I am about to insert a double-layered excerpt from the pages of Defoe. The event I have in mind could be reprinted as a short story under the title "The Heist of the Baronet." Moll Flanders, "the engaging, good-natured, humane cutpurse"—Ford's words—living as nature and necessity dictated, allowed a

self-infatuated baronet to lead her to tea and a couch, a banquet and a great bed . . . and seeing him drunk, she makes off with his gold watch, his silk purse of gold, his fine periwig and silver fringed gloves, his sword and fine snuff-box. Moll pities so noble but so wayward a man. She finds a means to have each of his proud fineries restored to him, and of course, along with them, some measure of his self-esteem . . . for which, naturally, she received generous honorariums.

The second level of the story, fear of the pox, "that dart which strikes fatally through the liver," began early to bring disquiet into the narrative. With this fear as his conscious motive, the baronet contrives to see Moll again. His fears quieted, put in fact wholly out of mind, he reenacts the earlier drama with her with such fervor that he sleeps the night out in her darkened alcove, and she comes to him naked again in the morning. Her great hope is that she would become his honorable kept-woman. For Moll such hopes, as usual, were destined to be dashed, and she resorts to new shifts to keep herself alive.

The interplay of an "upper pattern" of consciousness with "the lower pattern" figured powerfully in Caroline Gordon's "habit of a certain kind of observation." The upper pattern in the workings of the baronet's mind is to try to safeguard his wife from the possibility of contracting a dread disease, the lower pattern causes him to hurry underground, to contend with serpents and beautiful lost rivers, to flirt again with death. For Defoe the patterns can go side by side, interwoven, because the one that could end in death can be cleansed at the last moment by repentance and divine mercy. Moll Flanders lives to enjoy the last years of her life in perfect happiness. And so, for Defoe, the cutting edges of the view of the earth from the moon are not quite so damaging to our egotistical sense of things. Something like this, however, something much less coarse than Moll Flanders' sense of trust in divine mercy, but rather something Greek and finally traditionally Roman Catholic, is what Caroline Gordon shares with us when the irrational fatal blow is delivered before our eyes.

Having laid out this chart of the view from the top of the tree, with its resemblances to the eagle-eyed view from the moon, I turn abruptly to the orientation it gives in respect to certain crises in the life of the passionate sportsman, the now elderly Professor Maury. Stories suggested to Caroline by incidents in the life of her father, the Aleck Maury of the superb novel, are among the best, certainly the best known, in *The Collected Stories.*

In **"Old Red"** the man, long a widower, has grown so attached to modest, distant fishing resorts, that he finds his style stifled when he returns to the bosom of his "family connection." Nothing moves him so much as the memory of an old black woman in Florida *who could smell the fish* swimming around in the right cove on one side or another of the lake. But here in Kentucky a funeral is about to take place, the thought of which stifles him unendurably. The ruffling of all of the family collected together! In the night he succumbs to a dream-vision, in which he himself is that famous old red fox, who always eluded the hot, shuffling pack of dogs and hunters by taking to watery trails under dark cliffs, by going underground. . . . The next morning he has his bags packed and is on his way to the train, leaving for still another haunt by still another lake.

Then later, in **"The Presence,"** his rapture at the escape he made by following the lower pattern of his consciousness, is reversed. After years at another haunt, when his physical condition denies him the field and even the native fishing canoes, he keeps close to his hospitable small boardinghouse. A younger surrogate does the hunting, his wife does the cooking, the comforting, the nursing. His fellow boarders have their quirks and sprightlinesses. One of them, a trim divorcée, has a cast-off girdle of Aphrodite plastered to her belly, of which Mr. Maury has only a pleasantly confused awareness. He is happy; he has sublimated his chagrins. Sometimes, petting his host's young setter and carrying the harvest of quail to the cookhouse, he feels that he himself is "making his way home, at day's end, by the slanting rays of sun, his heavy game bag on his shoulder." Then abruptly the blow falls. His trim fellow-boarder has carried the hunter, his only friend, off and is sending the wife, the one woman on whom he could lean, into exile in some other county, totally out of reach. . . . He will have to go somewhere else now. But there is no place to go. Perhaps only, it seems, toward a presence which his foster mother had seemed to see somewhere above her just before she died.

In other stories it is a shattering, only slowly to be realized, fact that Tom Rivers, as real a creature as any on earth, could disappear utterly, as if swallowed into the black hole in which some of the rivers made their departure from Todd County.

And shattering, too, the topsy-turvy motions of the "upper pattern" and the "lower pattern" playing one against the other in the young woman, the brave, ungentled filly, in **"The Brilliant Leaves."** This girl is not yet bold enough to deal with a lover, but daring enough to challenge him to go to the river with her and to try to make a passage through the open space against the cliff behind the torrent known as Bridal Veil Falls. She slips, is dashed down, mortally hurt, a brown heap, on the rocks below. He gets to her, finds her so badly injured that he scrambles down the mountain and runs for help, going faster and faster. "He saw only the white houses that no matter how fast he ran kept just ahead of him." The brilliance of the autumn leaves on the ground that day had been spectacular.

There are two or three additional stories to which I would like simply to call attention. In honor of Defoe and the picaresque technique we ought to remind ourselves that **"The Burning Eyes,"** with its marvelous interchange of directions, with darkness and illumination at the end, was first printed as a short story in *The Magazine* in 1934. In reality it is an episode taken from the beginning of the novel *Aleck Maury, Sportsman*. . . . That **"The Waterfall"** is a remarkably faithful account of life at Benfolly, the Allen Tate–Caroline Gordon historic southern house in Tennessee, which the little girl, who is not Caroline now but probably her daughter Nancy and "the connection" is not family but literary relatives—this little girl avoids explaining to a visitor, a man marked for *hybris*, that the river with its magnificent falls which she has been showing

him to his great delight, came out of the mountain just above them and sank underground not far below. . . . That there is an uncanny, powerful story called **"The Olive Garden"** toward the end of the book, in which a man's whole personality seems to desert him among the ruins of war-spent Cap Brun. And from the cliff overlooking the sea, the city behind him only a grisly ghost, peopled with ghosts, he thinks of the caves on the edge of the water far below, where Ulysses once had been, which if need be could harbor a new race of men, such as that which Deucalion had brought forth, and thinks that even now he can hear "the heroes murmuring to each other."

"Emmanuele! Emmanuele!" remains one of the grandest of the stories. On the surface so unlike Todd County, so full of the overripe fruit of the north African Mediterranean shores, and yet in the end, when the scene shifts to the somber fields and lanes of the Channel coast of France, how complete is the return to that other, familiar world! In the north the sensual, narcissistic aesthete, who resembles André Gide, is out of his element. He finally finds himself entrapped in a sinkhole. His wife, Emmanuele, who is a country gentlewoman still rooted to the honest soil of her estate, has burned his letters. His finest work! His full revelation of himself! She has turned his precious genius into ashes! "Emmanuele!" he cries . . . *the eyes that had gleamed so merry, so mottled! They would be black now—twin prisons in which a creature that had once sported in the sun would sit forever in darkness.* As Menippus put it: What stirs this little creature raises and yet in how short a time it comes to nothing itself.

Never have I known an art of storytelling so lean and elegant as that which we have been considering. One final example, narrowed down to no more than three or four sentences, will say everything that most needs saying. The very title of the story, as good titles invariably do, gives a very palpable essence of the whole. **"The Last Day in the Field"** will say to anyone who knows something about Aleck Maury that the sportsman is in the act of retiring from quail hunting, resigned to the art of the rod and lure on stream or lake. To bring down the last bird of the day, Aleck has to use his second barrel. The bird staggered, "then zoomed up. Up, up, up, over the rim of the hill and above the tallest hickories. I saw it there for a second, its wings black against the gold light, before, wings still spread, it came whirling down, like an autumn leaf, like the leaves that were everywhere about us, all over the ground." For man and bird, for both, the end of the season had come upon them, as if they had been one and the same creature.

. . . . .

In an effort to present a closely knit view of these stories in a complicated literary landscape, as I see them from the top of my own tree, I have omitted references to other indispensable commentary on the art underlying this fiction, including that of Caroline Gordon herself. Assuming that the reader may not be familiar with earlier discussion, I feel I should add a few notes that may clarify certain particulars.

In general the critical vocabulary to which our author became more and more attached derives from Henry James. In my opinion it is a difficult, needlessly abstract array of key terms. For that overall view of experience "from the top of the tree," in which the near and the far may be seen, with the present and the past interwoven in it, the Jamesian term is "the central intelligence." In letters and in the University of Dallas syllabus on writing, Caroline Gordon said she wished that James had called it "the central consciousness," not intelligence. This speaks for her unhappiness with the more abstract term.

In the syllabus, she frames, or encloses, the central consciousness with a peripheral fringe of discoveries—i.e., the concrete details included in the story. This periphery is visualized as beginning with an opening at the top and coming to a close at the bottom. For this peripheral structure she uses a metaphor at another place in the syllabus which describes a rock at the top of the pool splitting the inflow of the stream so that the currents travel unevenly together until they are finally united at the foot of the pool. Such a rock as this fulfils the standard set by Defoe: in the first sentence the last sentence is implicit.

At the beginning of **"Old Red"** for example there appears a sentence—"it was only in hotels that a man was master of his own room"—which is the notch at the top of the periphery, the rock at the head of the pool. Along with this is the remark that a minnow bucket is "glinting in the last rays of the sun," in the room in which the man would like to be his own master, even though the room is in his daughter's house. He would like to be permitted to keep his fishing gear close at hand, at the foot of his bed, in case of a need for sudden departure.

Knowing as we do that in **"Old Red"** Mr. Maury, even as he is settling into his daughter's house, is turning his mind seriously ahead toward an early departure, and in very fact the departure does come more quickly than he himself had anticipated, because a blasted unavoidable family gathering at a funeral is going to take place: in these circumstances we find ourselves compelled to attend with a peculiar delight to the events, the concrete details that figure in the abbreviated visit. These are the peripheral "discoveries." And as it happens, no term could seem to be better suited to the juxtaposition of the passionate sportsman with the gifted, entranced intellectual, who is his son-in-law, when they are fishing together in a leaky rowboat in a pond near the house. The heavy older man had taken his place in the bow. Seated up there he could make perfect casts, while watching with admiration the expert play of the muscles in the wrist of his casting arm. The younger man did very well, considering the disadvantages of his position, and his fits of abstraction and his overly conscientious concern about handling the boat. Mr. Maury, noticing all this out of the corner of his eye, suffered a pang of pity: people were like that, too full of their work to enjoy anything. And instantly the bleak thought struck him that it was he, not the younger man, who was the lonely one, it was he who was trying to live in a world with nobody but himself in it.

Although peripheral discoveries as applied to the central consciousness—once both are understood—works wonders in the imagination, I find other terms hard to accept.

I resist it when I discover that Henry James, with what I regard as a strangely perverse taste for abstractions in his criticism, criticism only, pronounces such a detail as the glinting minnow bucket in the opening passage an example of "solidity of specification."

The "upper and lower" patterns of consciousness took on an importance of great significance by the time *The Glory of Hera* was being written and would have been essential to the strange, ambitious work which was in progress at the time of the author's death. For the final distinction between these patterns, I quote Donald E. Stanford, the editor of [*The Southern Review*] in the memorial tribute prefixed to the Summer 1981 issue, who in turn is quoting Caroline Gordon:

> The upper pattern purports to be my own autobiography but is actually the history of certain members of my family. . . . The lower pattern winds serpent-wise through the upper pattern of action and deals with the archetypal world which the present day Jungians and the archaic Greeks inform us lies at the bottom of every human consciousness.

When speaking of levels or layers of consciousness in the stories, I thought it more appropriate to use the terms in an ordinary way, without specific Greek or Jungian implications, recognizing simply that human beings justify their conduct most often by tempering their compulsions with whatever rationalizations seem to be most suited to the purpose. And it is also true that in our author's work the mythological and Jungian explanations came later than the last of the stories.

As for the technical principle I have tried to describe—the long perspectives underlying the narratives—one exception occurs in **"Mr. Powers,"** which was obviously written at Benfolly about the Tates' early life at Benfolly. It is a solid little realistic story, but perhaps by that very fact one of the least interesting.

On the other hand **"The Olive Garden,"** which I have called both uncanny and powerful, casts a hypnotic spell which I shall venture to describe in greater detail. In the late summer of 1932, after Caroline had received a Guggenheim grant, the Tates moved to a villa, the Villa Les Hortensias, at Cap Brun, near Toulon, the French naval base on the Mediterranean coast. Ford Madox Ford and Biala lived at the Villa Paul not far away. John Peale Bishop and other literary people were in the area. Though each pursued his work with intensity, there were many gatherings of friends, often with impromptu picnics on the lovely sea-facing bluffs. One picnic, however, for its sheer extravagance, will probably retain a place in literary annals for a long time. Some dozen friends had gone by small boat into one of the hidden coves under the red cliffs at Cassis. There on a shingle beach a feast of *coq-au-vin* and shellfish was boiled up, while an old native carried bottles of wine on foot down the steep trail on the cliff. Radcliffe Squires in *Allen Tate* (1971) records a count of sixty-one bottles of wine.

It was here that one of Allen Tate's most memorable poems, "The Mediterranean," had its inception: the banqueting of the picnickers suggesting the spare but prophetic first meal eaten by Aeneas and his followers on Italian soil:

> And we made feast and in our secret need
> Devoured the very plates Aeneas bore.

Here, as is too typical of the author and his times, Tate's poem ends, not with the sense of triumph, at long last, which the founders of the Roman people enjoyed, but with the commonplace sense of the crush of our own modern empire upon us.

Caroline's story seems still to have the shadows of "feast and carousal" hanging over it. The abandoned villa Les Hortensias makes a touching appearance at the beginning of the story. But meanwhile World War II has overrun Cap Brun from all directions—the imagined year is *circa* 1947—leaving craters in the earth and only tangles of living trees in the fig and olive gardens: desertion, emptiness, unpeopled darkness. It seems that the time has come now when it is necessary to start all over again. To start before Aeneas' arrival, before Ulysses': to start from scratch, with a fresher race implanted on the globe. The olive garden is Gethsemane, I think. And the whole effort is directed, as I said earlier, toward a far from commonplace realization of perceptions which are deeply Greek and traditionally Roman Catholic.

> Howard Baker, "From the Top of the Tree," in The Southern Review, *Louisiana State University, Vol. XVIII, No. 2, Spring, 1982, pp. 427-41.*

FURTHER READING

Bibliography

Griscom, Joan. "Bibliography of Caroline Gordon." *Critique* I, No. 1 (Winter 1956): 74-8.
Bibliography of works by and about Gordon.

Sullivan, Mary C. "Caroline Gordon: A Reference Guide." In *Flannery O'Connor and Caroline Gordon: A Reference Guide,* edited by Robert E. Golden and Mary C. Sullivan, pp. 193-308. Boston: G. K. Hall and Co., 1977.
Annotated bibliography of Gordon's works and critical and biographical studies about her, including a chronological listing of Ph.D. dissertations.

Biography

Horsford, Howard C. "Letters of Caroline Gordon Tate to Sally Wood Kohn, 1925-1937." *The Princeton University Library Chronicle* XLIV, No. 1 (Autumn 1982): 1-24.
Relates Gordon's life between 1925 and 1937 based upon her correspondence with friend and writer Sally Wood.

Makowsky, Veronica A. "Caroline Gordon: Amateur to Professional Writer." *The Southern Review* 23, No. 4 (Autumn 1987): 778-93.
Provides excerpts from Makowsky's biography on Gor-

don, cited below. This essay follows the early years of Gordon's career and marriage to Allen Tate, the rigors of their life as struggling writers in the United States and Europe, and the literary personalities with whom they associated: Ford Madox Ford, Ernest Hemingway, F. Scott and Zelda Fitzgerald, Robert Lowell, and Leonie Adams.

———. *Caroline Gordon: A Biography.* New York: Oxford University Press, 1989, 260 p.
Analysis of Gordon's life and work. Discussing Gordon's Southern heritage and her life experiences, Makowsky asks: "What formed Caroline Gordon's imagination and the themes of her work? Who set her standards for serious art? Did male mentorship hurt or benefit her work and her reputation?"

Ross, Danforth. "Caroline Gordon, Uncle Rob and My Mother." *The Southern Quarterly* XXVII, No. 3 (Spring 1990): 9-22.
Anecdote concerning Gordon's early life on her family's farm, Meriwether, where she was born and spent her early years, and her adult years at Benfolly in Clarksville, Tennessee, where she and her husband Allen Tate lived in the 1930s. A distant relative of Gordon, Ross also chronicles Gordon's relationship with various family members.

Waldron, Ann. *Close Connections: Caroline Gordon and the Southern Renaissance.* New York: G. P. Putnam's Sons, 1987, 416 p.
A detailed account of Gordon's life and career.

Criticism

Alvis, John E. "The Idea of Nature and the Sexual Role in Caroline Gordon's Early Stories of Love." In *The Short Fiction of Caroline Gordon: A Critical Symposium,* edited by Thomas H. Landess, pp. 85-111. Irving: The University of Dallas Press, 1972.
Analyzes Gordon's treatment of love and sexuality in five of the stories collected in *The Forest of the South.*

Baro, Gene. "A Leisurely Hunter, a Man at Bay." *The New York Times Book Review* (20 October 1963): 4.
Review of *Old Red, and Other Stories,* in which Baro praises Gordon's success at evoking direct experience and transforming the reader into a participant in the "Aleck Maury" stories.

Blum, Morgan. "The Shifting Point of View: Joyce's 'The Dead' and Gordon's 'Old Red.' " *Critique* I (1956-1958): 45-66.
Discusses Joyce's use of shifting points of view in his short story "The Dead" and analyzes Gordon's employment of the same technique in "Old Red."

Hendry, Irene. "Southern Stories." *The Kenyon Review* VIII, No. 1 (Winter 1946): 168-69.
Review of *The Forest of the South,* claiming that the selection and arrangement of stories is suggestive of Gordon's novels.

Rubin, Larry. "Christian Allegory in Caroline Gordon's 'The Captive.' " *Studies in Short Fiction* V (October 1967-July 1968): 283-89.
Argues that "The Captive" reflects the Christian vision of original sin, predestination, and redemption.

The Southern Quarterly XXVIII, No. 3 (Spring 1990): 9-88.
   Special issue devoted to Gordon. Essays by Veronica
Makowsky, Ashley Brown, and Larry Allums are in-
cluded.

Additional coverage of Gordon's life and career is contained in the following sources published by Gale Research: *Contemporary Authors,* Vols. 9-12, 103 [obituary]; *Contemporary Authors New Revision Series,* Vol. 36; *Contemporary Authors Permanent Series,* Vol. 1; *Contemporary Literary Criticism,* Vols. 6, 13, 29; *Dictionary of Literary Biography,* Vols. 4, 9, 102; *Dictionary of Literary Biography Yearbook: 1981;* and *Major 20th-Century Writers.*

Shirley Ann Grau

1929-

American novelist and short story writer.

INTRODUCTION

Best known for her novels and stories set in the region surrounding the Mississippi River delta, Grau is the author of the Pulitzer Prize-winning novel *The Keepers of the House,* which traces three generations of an interracial family in Alabama. Her three collections of short stories have been praised for meticulous craftsmanship, precise characterization, and deft evocations of the connections between characters and their natural surroundings in the Deep South.

Biographical Information

Grau was born into a wealthy family in New Orleans. She attended private schools in New Orleans and in Montgomery, Alabama, receiving her college education at Newcomb College, Tulane University. Grau considered becoming a classics scholar or an English professor before embarking on a literary career after one year of graduate study. Her first work, the short story collection *The Black Prince, and Other Stories* was published in 1955 and won critical approval from reviewers who hailed Grau as a promising new voice in Southern fiction. That same year, Grau married a university professor. In the ensuing decades she has written several novels and short stories while dividing her time between homes in New Orleans and Martha's Vineyard.

Major Works

Grau's short fiction has been collected in three volumes published at long intervals in her career. The first compilation, *The Black Prince, and Other Stories,* contains the meticulous prose and masterful descriptions of nature that critics consider characteristic of her works. Set in the bayous along the Mississippi River, the title story concerns a black satanic figure who exhibits supernatural powers, and Grau's portrayal of natural landscapes and primitive characters was highly praised by reviewers. Her second volume, *The Wind Shifting West,* was published in 1973. Each of the stories focuses on a moment of self-awareness in the life of the protagonist, from a middle-aged wife who engages in adultery for the first time, to a schoolgirl who faces a lonely year as the only black child in an all-white school. Grau's third collection, *Nine Women* (1985), again

depicts a wide range of characters, but all are female. In the highly praised "Letting Go" a young wife separates from her husband, frees herself from her domineering parents, and sets out to make a life of her own. Other protagonists reflect a less optimistic outlook, most notably the lone survivor of an air disaster who boards flight after flight hoping to meet death in a second accident.

Critical Reception

Initial reviewers of *The Black Prince, and Other Stories* enthusiastically acknowledged Grau as a brilliant new writer of Southern regionalist fiction, and her most successful works have drawn on her knowledge of the natural surroundings and social life of the Deep South. Her modest output of subsequent works, however, failed to live up to the extravagant claims of her early proponents. Nevertheless, according to critic Mary Rohrberger, Grau's talent as a short story writer "is immense though not revealed by a simple surface reading; for what is beneath the surfaces and interacting with them is what is characteristic of the short story genre, and Grau has mastered the genre."

PRINCIPAL WORKS

SHORT FICTION

The Black Prince, and Other Stories　1955
The Wind Shifting West　1973
Nine Women　1985

OTHER MAJOR WORKS

The Hard Blue Sky　(novel)　1958
The House on Coliseum Street　(novel)　1961
The Keepers of the House　(novel)　1964
The Condor Passes　(novel)　1971
Evidence of Love　(novel)　1977

CRITICISM

John Nerber　(essay date 1955)

[*In the following review of* The Black Prince, and Other Stories, *Nerber hails Grau as "one of the chief literary discoveries of recent years."*]

Judging from this extraordinary collection of nine short stories [*The Black Prince, and Other Stories*], Shirley Ann Grau is quite likely to be one of the chief literary discoveries of recent years. One has to go back to Eudora Welty's first book, *A Curtain of Green,* for a comparable performance. Without being in the least like Miss Welty—though both are Southern writers concerned with the Southern scene and people—Miss Grau has the same unmistakable authority, the instinctive feeling for form and language (obviously strengthened by a lot of hard work) and that pervasive relish for the wonderful particularities of human nature that are part of the equipment of the born writer.

That Miss Grau is dedicated cannot be doubted, nor that she is an accomplished storyteller in the old magical sense of the word. The title story, for example, **"The Black Prince,"** a folk tale of a mysterious, godlike (or satanic) young Negro's sudden appearance in a backwoods hamlet and the discord he sows by his very presence, is easy-flowing, idyllic and inevitable as Isak Dinesen's *Winter's Tales,* and for the same reasons. Both writers have an essential sense of mystery, a special awareness and belief in invisible things.

Yet, and at the same time, Miss Grau can write as vigorously and powerfully of a Negro convict just released from prison and running amok with lust, or the gentle and qui-

etly sustained story of a woman and her daughter, in **"The Girl With the Flaxen Hair,"** and how they clothed poverty with pride and the fury of things dreamed—a story as inevitable and classic in its way as Faulkner's "A Rose for Emily."

Miss Grau's Southern world is violent and gentle; it contains both Negroes and whites. But it is, curiously, a new world. It differs subtly from that of any other Southern writer, just as her characters have been caught in certain new undertones—they have become Americans rather than remaining regional Southerners. Their speech rhythms have changed significantly. Miss Grau may well be the first to record it.

These stories reveal a fresh and extremely gifted young writer. There can be little question of her ability to write. She has the additional endowments of warmth, compassion, perception and humor. And, unless this reviewer misses his guess, she can be considered as already safely enshrined in the best anthologies of short stories. The discerning reader can only await the real promise of her next book.

> *John Nerber, "Violent and Gentle," in* The New York Times Book Review, *January 16, 1955, pp. 4-5.*

Anatole Broyard　(essay date 1973)

[*Broyard was an American essayist, short story writer, and a former editor of the* New York Times Book Review. *In the essay below, he offers a mixed assessment of* The Wind Shifting West.]

In [*The Wind Shifting West*], Shirley Ann Grau shows an impressive range: her stories stretch from fairly good to pretty bad. She is very much a Southern writer, with many of the virtues and flaws this description implies. Southern fiction, for example, seems to have a soft spot for the freaky, the sort of thing Tennessee Williams is famous for: ladies who are spiritually on their last legs, who "imagine" things, who look as if they've been tenderly brought down from the attic, and are given to talking to themselves in a rather "dicty" way. Hot nights, moss hanging from the trees, the heavy scent of magnolias, snakes in the hollows, a nostalgia for feudal living, an elocution that encourages bombast—all this may have influenced the Southern style of writing. And a history of intimate domestic contact with black people may have encouraged the development of a sort of white voodoo, which is the Southern writer's equivalent of the Absurd.

Faulkner and Flannery O'Connor were good enough to salvage something out of this tattered anachronism—at least in their best work. Less talented authors tend to fall into the bayou or swamp, into inscrutable wisdom of the South. All too often in fiction, the South seems to be looking back. "Immemorial" was Faulkner's favorite word, and characters in Southern books are always gazing off into the pathos of distance and remembering. People grow older by hungering for what they have left behind. The cornfields are always ripe for picking. Every night you can hear the dying cry of the field mouse as the owl swoops down. The stars are invariably crossed.

In their favor, Southern writers have an environment that might still be called heterogeneous. They have a sense of tradition that is useful as a contrapuntal line. If their language is sometimes debased, the corruption is of their own making—not "the media's." They believe in mystery, in refreshing contrast to the quiz-kid omniscience of too many Northern writers.

Of the 18 stories in *The Wind Shifting West,* the best and the worst are those which are most typically Southern. **"Stanley,"** the last and longest story, shows us a 46-year-old black butler watching a rich white man almost twice his age reminisce in his wheel chair. The old man sits in a greenhouse especially built for him—to keep from drying up?—and the huge cage of tropical birds beside his chair is constantly replenished, as if to deny such a thing as death. The old man has had a colorful life—one of his last remarks is about the condors of San Ysedro—but the butler already feels that his own is over. His experience has not rejuvenated him. All he looks forward to is going *back* to the town where he was born to sit on the porch and recall his childhood, the only part of his life worth looking back on.

"Homecoming" is a bitter blow at Southern sentimentality and love of ritual. A girl is notified that a boy who gave her his ring before going to Vietnam—a boy she hardly knew—has been killed in action. Her mother, who has all too coincidentally lost her husband in another war, treats the occasion as a widowing of her daughter and invites her friends to a "wake." The girl is galled by her loveless bereavement, and her last words to the memory of the boy are almost an emancipation proclamation for Southern writing: " 'Good-by,' she said in a very light whisper. 'You poor bastard.' "

In **"The Thieves,"** an aging girl waits for her lover to propose to her. One night, his indecisiveness so annoys her that she helps a thief, who was trapped by the police in her backyard, to escape. This is her rebellion against the convention and the "safety" of marriage. When her lover does propose, it is too late. She has already seen beyond him, into an unfillable void, and answers with "Go away, little boy."

"Beach Party" is a very deft story about a good-looking woman of 40 who is seduced on her brother-in-law's boat as they go to pick up her husband, who has foolishly—symbolically?—splintered his mast in showing off. Though it begins promisingly enough, the story settles for more deftness and an imposed pessimism. After making love, the woman says ". . . that's all there's left . . . some weed on the anchor and some salt dried on our skin." The brother-in-law replies with, "There isn't ever much left, when it's done," and the reader wonders why not? Why isn't there much left? And, in fact, after a moment's reflection, anyone can see that the truth of the story has been sold short for the price of neatness, so the author can quit while she thinks she's ahead.

"Last Gas Station" is pure backwoods Beckett. A family that runs a gas station progressively diminishes by deser-

tion, traffic mysteriously increases, abandoned cars clutter the roadside, and so on. **"Pillow of Stone"** is a broken-English slander against Creoles, a folk opera in which a pregnant daughter braves heavy seas to reach her dead father's bedside so "he can rest" once he knows that she has "come with one to take his place."

There are a few more O.K. stories and a few inconsequential vignettes, snapshots that didn't develop well: like one of a young teen-ager absorbing the death of a skindiver at a beach party with about the same degree of discomfort and understanding that she might feel if she swallowed her chewing gum.

Miss Grau has sharpened her tools, but they cut too easily through her characters. Her formal preoccupations sometimes have the effect of cramping their style, of keeping them from being fully themselves. *The Wind Shifting West* would be a more interesting book if they all broke through the plotted trajectories of her stories to the incalculable reaches we sense in them.

> *Anatole Broyard, "Quitting While She's Ahead," in* The New York Times, *November 1, 1973, p. 41.*

William Peden   (essay date 1974)

[*Peden is an American critic and educator who has written extensively on the American short story and on such American historical figures as John Quincy Adams and Thomas Jefferson. In the following review, he assesses the strengths and weaknesses of* The Wind Shifting West.]

Twenty years ago Shirley Ann Grau, then in her early twenties, published her first book, a collection of stories about whites and blacks in her native Louisiana. I was doing a lot of reviewing then, and I thought *The Black Prince* one of the most impressive "firsts" I'd seen in a long time. Now, several novels (including her Pulitzer Prize-winning *The Keepers of the House*) later, we have her second collection, *The Wind Shifting West,* eighteen stories ranging in setting from an unspecified South to the east coast. The stories are thoroughly professional throughout, completely competent from beginning to end, but slightly disappointing: I sometimes felt that I'd read several of them before under many different professional names and in many magazines.

On the other hand, Miss Grau certainly knows what she's about, she knows how to build a scene, she knows how to move her characters around and how to dispose of them at the proper time. She is at her best, it seems to me, when her angle of vision is that of a girl or a woman, as it is in the very good title story ["The Wind Shifting West"] of a wife's casual introduction to adultery with her brother-in-law; or in **"The Beach Party,"** in which a teen-aged girl is introduced to dates and to death; or in what seems to me her best story, **"The Way Back,"** a relatively brief, unpretentious and completely convincing depiction of the end of an affair.

The collection is also highlighted by two effective, low-keyed stories centering around white-black relationships and problems. **"Eight O'Clock"** depicts a racial disturbance as viewed through the eyes and consciousness of a young black child; **"The Other Way"** concerns the only black child in a recently-integrated class.

When she tries too hard or strays too far from the usual, I find Miss Grau less convincing. **"The Patriarch,"** reminiscences of an eighty-five-year-old egoist, is entertaining but seems preposterous. **"Three,"** about a college student, her husband, and the ghostly apparition of her first husband who was killed in Vietnam, is a valiant effort that doesn't come off; **"The Last Gas Station,"** surreal and apocalyptic, I found silly and unconvincing; and **"The Lovely April,"** the author's fling at old-fashioned "sothren gothic," generates some early tension and suspense but ends up a bore.

> William Peden, *"The Recent American Short Story," in* The Sewanee Review, *Vol. LXXXII, No. 4, October-December, 1974, pp. 712-29.*

Grau on storytelling in *The Black Prince*:

In *The Black Prince* I was trying to create a kind of legendary, mythological time, a non-real approach, a storytelling in the legendary sense of storytelling. That's something I still want to do because I think the realistic story has rather sharp limits. Perhaps myth-making is the way to go. Certainly, in *The Black Prince,* there is no realistic attempt, that's pure myth-making.

> *Quoted by John Canfield in his "A Conversation with Shirley Ann Grau,"* The Southern Quarterly, *Winter 1987.*

Paul Schlueter   (essay date 1981)

[*Schlueter is an American educator and critic whose books include* The Novels of Doris Lessing *(1973) and* Shirley Ann Grau. *In his criticism he is "particularly interested in the relationship between the arts (especially literature) and religious faith (especially Christianity)." In the following excerpt from his study of Grau, Schlueter discusses the most accomplished stories in* The Black Prince, and Other Stories *(1955) and* The Wind Shifting West *(1973).*]

Grau's critically acclaimed first book [*The Black Prince and Other Stories*] seems in retrospect the kind of talented though contrived collection of lyrical tales so often identified with a youthful writer. Her sharp awareness of sensory stimuli, particularly the visual, is evident in most of the stories in the book, as is her fairly obvious use of symbolism, particularly symbolism based on biblical or other traditional sources. The frequent lack of any substantial plot in these stories, or of plots lacking any legitimately developed conclusions, may attest to their author's relative inexperience as a writer of fiction, but even so the tales are finely etched, intuitive glimpses of life in the rural South, often with impoverished blacks as characters, and with Grau's consistently fine sense of atmospheric detail always

present. Certain touches seem contrived; for example, almost every story features some object or other that is a glittering silver color.

In general, the stories in this collection that are concerned with blacks are more effective than those concerned with whites; the former seem imbued with a sense of mystery, with echoes of folklore and myth often emphasized. She handles dialect well, and she never sentimentalizes or patronizes her characters. She creates believable, well-rounded human beings, people who, regardless of color or social level, remain firmly memorable. In short, with her first book Grau made a solid though not flashy or spectacular debut as a writer. Although only three of the stories had appeared separately in periodical form before the appearance of the collection in book form, most of the nine stories have been subsequently reprinted in other anthologies.

"White Girl, Fine Girl," Grau's first professionally published story, is set in Clayton County in an otherwise unidentified Southern state. Stanhope is the state capital, and Kilby, seven miles away, is the site of the "colored prison." Jayson Paul Evans, just released from the prison after serving most of a twenty year prison term for manslaughter, moves through the countryside to Stanhope to see Aggie, the widow of Mannie, whom he had killed in a fight resulting from Mannie's finding him and Aggie together. Entering the Pair-a-Dice Bar, Jayson meets Joe, who has also been a lover of Aggie's but who prefers a peaceful conversation to conflict. Jayson finds out that Aggie now has been "born again" and has nothing to do with men, especially since her oldest girl was sired by Jayson at the time Mannie caught the two. As he heads toward Aggie's house, the children (each with a different father) throw stones and pieces of brick at Jayson—as they had earlier at Joe—simply because he is walking down their street. As the children and Aggie flee the house, Jayson, bloody from the onslaught of stones, rampages through it and encounters his daughter. As Jayson leaves, satisfied, for the bar, the daughter follows him, evidently curious to know her father, till he halfheartedly throws a stone after her and she leaves. The story ends when Jayson enters a house to have sex with a white woman, evidently a surrogate for the light-skinned Aggie.

The story is not a complicated one, except insofar as Aggie's various lovers and their respective children need to be kept separate. Jayson's time in prison, from his point of view, is to some extent Aggie's fault, since her provocative nature led both him and Joe to have sexual relations with her. And Joe, although out of prison while Jayson has been in, has fared no better with the independent Aggie, who wants nothing to do with any man. Similarly, the stone-throwing incident with the girls is paralleled with Jayson's almost leisurely tossing a stone at his daughter; just as Aggie and her children, having "gotten religion," want nothing to do with him, so Jayson, in turn, wants nothing to do with his daughter. And, finally, his going to a white woman is also parallel to his attempting to go to Aggie, with the added irony of his choosing a white woman rather than merely a light-skinned one; earlier, in the tavern, Joe had pointed to the white girl pictured on the Jax beer poster and had advised Jayson to find one like her.

Further parallels are referred to earlier in the story: as Jayson leaves the prison, he skips a stone across the river, almost to the other bank, as if to suggest that although the other bank is close, it is still too far to be reached easily, just as in prison the outside world was close enough to touch, but was not available to Jayson. When he encounters two small black boys in the woods, their immediate response is to pull a knife, just as he had an ice-pick with Mannie, leading to his imprisonment.

But the primary emphasis in the story is on "casting the first stone," on Jayson's sensing the need of avoiding retribution, even though Aggie cannot do so. For Jayson, having spent many years in prison for killing a man, now has no desire to seek revenge against Aggie, only an urge to see her and the daughter he had sired by her but never seen, and thereafter to return to life as he had known it prior to prison.

Grau is especially effective with atmosphere in this story, but the plot is somewhat contrived, with parallels between separate incidents in the story and with biblical and mythic parallels being both ironic and too obvious: Jayson (Jason?) is cast out of the comfortable home he has known for many years (prison) and immediately heads for Pair-a-Dice (both Paradise and chance) to renew relations with Aggie, but ends up with forbidden fruit of another sort with a white woman.

"The Black Prince," originally published as "The Sound of Silver," is a successful blending of naturalistic detail with fablelike mystery, and with more than a few of the biblical echoes found in the other stories in this collection. The story opens with an epigraph, lines from Isaiah 14:12 that effectively indicate Grau's intention in the story: "How art thou fallen from heaven, O Lucifer, son of the morning!" For "The Black Prince" in this story is clearly identified with one with supernatural abilities and appeal, as well as the ability to seem to appear and disappear without warning.

Alberta Lucy, light-skinned beauty in the impoverished community in which the story takes place, is introduced throwing a stone, as in the previous story, but at birds, not people. And as she hears the sound of the birds, an added whistle is also heard, that of a man suddenly appearing from around a tree. When asked, he says he "just come straight out the morning," and tells Alberta her full name, even though she has never seen him previously. As he leaves without sound, she joins her friend Maggie Mary Evans to work in the fields. At lunch he appears to both girls, tells his name—Stanley Albert Thompson—and leaves, without even a depression in the pine needles and grass to indicate where he had been seated.

In time he joins the crowd at Willie's Bar and wins several fights in which he is involved. Willie, who makes corn liquor to sell in addition to running the bar, is also interested in Alberta, but can only watch as the two spend the silver that Albert seems never to run out of. In addition, Albert has a watch and ring—the only ones in the hamlet—worth as much as all the money seen in a year thereabouts.

Indeed, when Alberta visits his shack (lit with candles instead of the more common lamps), he takes some wax from candle-drippings, rolls it around, and makes new silver coins until Alberta's dress pockets are full.

Thereafter they are inseparable at Willie's, even though the community is irreparably split because of a long-dormant feud that has arisen again, to some extent because of Stanley Albert's presence. Once a man named Pete Stokes shot at Stanley Albert but missed; a chase ensued in which the thick bushes "seemed to pull back and make way" for him as he chased Pete, who was never seen again, dead or alive. The story ends with Willie's casting four silver bullets (from melting down the coins paid him by Stanley Albert) and shooting Stanley Albert dead-center in the chest. As he attempts to stand after being shot, Stanley Albert's eyes become two polished pieces of silver, and a black pool of blood forms on the floor. But he is not killed; he and Alberta disappear, and in the ten or so years following, many calamities occur, including Willie's dying when his barn burns. And thereafter the couple become part of a legend:

> And kids sometimes think they hear the jingle of silver in Stanley Albert's pocket, or the sound of his watch. And when women talk—when there's been a miscarriage or a stillbirth—they remember and whisper together.
>
> And they all wonder if that's not the sort of work they do, the two of them. Maybe so; maybe not. The people themselves are not too sure. They don't see them around any more.

So the story ends—mysteriously, abruptly.

The mythical parallels in this story are obvious and require little comment. Stanley Albert evidently is a "fallen Angel," an angel of light, of the morning, one who, like Lucifer, comes to lead others to evil and/or death. Without pushing biblical echoes too far, one can see numerous ways in which this story relates to some of the same motifs found in the other stories in this collection, particularly the emphasis on a "prince of darkness" visiting earth with destruction and fire. Interestingly enough, one character with which the story begins, Maggie Mary, does not seem part of this motif (she is dropped by the middle of the story), even though her name is clearly a variation on Mary Magdalen.

Grau's powers of imagination and ability to evoke an atmosphere of mysterious uncertainty are at their best in this, the title story in this collection, even if the substance of the story is no more tangible than Stanley Albert's own presence. As evocative presence, the story excels; but whatever conflict there is in the story seems contrived and unequal. Indeed, one cannot help but identify more with Willie than with any other character in the tale, simply because he undergoes a more meaningful alteration because of the "prince" than does anyone else. After all, Alberta merely seems to have found her prince in Stanley Albert, the highest bidder for her favors, while Willie's business and eventually his life are snuffed out by the actions resulting from the "black prince's" coming to his bar. . . .

Of all the stories in this collection, **"The Girl with the**

Flaxen Hair" is the one with most of the quality of a fairy tale or myth. Lily, young daughter of the town dentist, notices new neighbors moving into the vacant house sharing the block with her own family's house, and soon discovers a beautiful yellow-haired girl her own age named Rose, and her parents, living there. Rose's father is found to be a mere barber, but her mother, daughter of a famous though dishonest politician elsewhere in the state, prefers to embellish the reality of the family with tales of grandeur and glory. Lily's father, a commonsensical dentist, is not taken in by Rose's mother, but Lily's mother finds her to be charming. Rose's father leaves, ostensibly to study music in his native France, and the remaining members of the family carry on as if nothing is amiss.

Yet much is amiss, as Lily's father discovers early one winter morning when he sees Rose sneaking out in the dark to steal coal from the piles in the railroad yard. The truth, then, is that though fiercely proud, the two remaining members of the family are impoverished. When spring comes, Rose continues her early-morning forays, and on one particular day, when the train schedule has been changed, she is struck and killed by a speeding passenger train. Her mother then leaves the town forever, and life in the town resumes its routine as it had been two years earlier.

Lily in time grows up, we are told in the last paragraph of the story, and as she matures she cannot always recall what her own father looked like, but she will always remember Rose and the almost legendary politician Rose and her mother had so often described, complete with shiny boots and a blue coat with silver buttons. Though she presumably learns, as her father had told her, that the politician was a fake, the image she has of him and the "girl with the flaxen hair" will remain with her as long as she lives.

Much of the fairy-tale quality of the story, at least insofar as Lily is concerned, results from the fairly obvious comparison between the two girls. Lily, despite her name, is far from bland or pale, and her tomboy antics, even when she injures herself, do not noticeably alter her realistic awareness of the life around her. Rose, though, is a far paler girl, and although she once endures a dental extraction without any sort of grimace or complaint, she does in reality reflect a less substantial, more ethereal personality. It is almost as if Rose and her mother, by so completely living a lie and by so assiduously maintaining the facade of respectable gentility, are less able to adapt to the realistic demands of life than are Lily and her family, who matter-of-factly accept the comings and goings of life. Hence when Rose is killed, the entire myth that Lily had built up around Rose is embellished to the point of being perpetual truth, with Rose's image a far more substantial one than the relatively unclear one her own living father reflects. Even the story's title resembles that found in a collection of fairy tales, such as those by Hans Christian Andersen, and so we are not surprised when this golden daughter of the morning dies, leaving the sorrowful neighbor girl to embellish the reality with permanence. . . .

Differing from the other stories in this collection in that it concerns fairly sophisticated city dwellers, **"Fever Flow-**er" is a sensitive account of the tensions between Hugh and Katherine Fleming, divorced parents of three-year-old Maureen, and their respective lives apart from each other. Katherine, aged twenty-five, prepares to leave the house for her ex-husband's one-day-a-week visit with Maureen; the one detail about Katherine we are likely to remember, other than her loveliness, is the fact that "she was not quite human. She did not need anyone." Hugh, though, has remarried and will be a father again shortly. Maureen, her room decorated by her mother as would be the room of a much older girl, becomes the focal point between the two parents, at least in part because neither really wants her very enthusiastically, Katherine because she is basically narcissistic, and Hugh because as a businessman he does not get as much return from supporting Maureen as the support costs him.

On this day together, Hugh and Maureen first play happily in the house with Hugh giving her her bath, something he rarely does, and then with the two of them going to the park for the day. While there, she takes him into the heavily humid conservatory where exotic plants that flourish in the heavy atmosphere—orchids in particular—saturate the air with their fragrance. Maureen, wearing an orchid pinafore, is clearly intended to appear one with the plants and the humid atmosphere. The flowers, we are told, "were forced to grow to gigantic size in half the time, they were beautiful and exotic and they did not last." To some extent this fits both Maureen and her mother, for both are beautiful and exotic, and the joy Hugh has experienced with both women in his life is doomed to diminish and eventually become extinguished. Taking Maureen home, Hugh finds that she does not want to take off her orchid dress, despite the overwhelmingly oppressive humidity.

It remains for Annie, the housekeeper, to best present a point of reference by which the others in the story can be evaluated. Deeply religious, Annie reads (in Paul's letter to the Galatians) that one should "Walk in the spirit and you shall not fulfill the lusts of the flesh. . . . The fruit of the spirit is joy." As Annie reflects on the passage, she sees both Hugh and Katherine burning in hell while she, Annie, takes Maureen by the hand to heaven.

Grau parenthetically tells of the future for each of the persons in the story, with none of them achieving anything close to happiness, and with Maureen herself going through three divorces before she settles down on the west coast; this is almost as if it were a prophetic utterance on Grau's part, based at least in part in Annie's self-righteous fanaticism. One tends to sympathize with Hugh, who is better out of the marriage with Katherine than he would have been had the marriage continued, and with Maureen, who is only a child. Yet Hugh is fully as self-centered as his ex-wife (significantly, she demanded the divorce) in his seeing personal relationships in commercial terms, and Maureen is obviously growing up to be as spoiled and self-conscious of her beauty as her mother had been.

Maureen is the "fever flower" of the story's title, the orchid growing too fast in the heavy atmosphere of the hot-house environment; unable to survive in the "normal" outside atmosphere, she, like the flower, thrives in the un-natural aura of high humidity, lush attention, and careful nurturing. Though Maureen has a fever at the story's end, this, it seems to me, is merely a physiological means of drawing the comparison even more tightly between the child and the greenhouse plants she had seen that afternoon. Were it not for Grau's parenthetical comment about Maureen's subsequent life, we would surely think, from the story's last lines—"She did not turn again: she had stopped crying. And lay there, beautiful and burning"— that she, like the orchids, would soon die, burned out before normal maturity has even occurred. Such, however, is not the case; Maureen like her mother is destined to be a person who could completely cut herself off from the past. Just as Katherine had never seen Hugh once they were divorced, so one can deduce that Maureen, as she grows up, will also cut herself off from her parents, as they—Katherine because of her narcissism, Hugh because of his new family—occupy less and less of Maureen's life.

Although not a complicated story, **"Fever Flower"** does work rather well on the levels of both the realistic story and the symbolic underpinnings, even though a more experienced writer would have been able to intertwine the two more subtly than Grau did at the time the story was published. Still, it remains one of the more effectively realized of the tales in this collection. . . .

Given the highly favorable critical reception of *The Black Prince and Other Stories* and the frequent appearance in magazines of subsequent stories by Grau, it was naturally only a matter of time till an additional collection was published. Yet when *The Wind Shifting West* appeared nineteen years after the earlier collection, the critical reaction was decidedly antagonistic. While the book is not the "unmitigated disaster" that it was called by a reviewer in the *Washington Post* [27 November 1973], it was also surely not so consistently rewarding as the earlier collection. And while some of the stories are sharply evocative and memorable, most are merely competent, lacking much emotional drive and substance, and a few are simply disappointing. Two of the stories are early draft versions of works subsequently expanded and published as novels: **"The Patriarch"** is a previously unpublished synopsis of *Evidence of Love*, . . . and **"Stanley"** is an early version of portions of *The Condor Passes*. . . . The remaining sixteen stories, all but two of which originally appeared in periodical form, deal to a great extent with isolation and displacement, especially concerning women, and one of the stories, a very successful one, is Grau's only published effort at creating an end-of-the-world atmosphere.

[**"The Wind Shifting West"**] is about Caroline Edwards, a reluctant sailor with her husband Robert on his new boat. A "great sailor," he is smoothly competent, even further alienating and isolating her from the life he and their small daughter enjoy. So, while her family goes out sailing, she joins the others at the family reunion. When word comes that Robert has broken his mast through carelessness, she goes with her sister's husband Giles to the rescue. Giles, though, goes the long way, to a deserted cove, where he seduces Caroline before going after Robert. Caroline, dissatisfied after the experience, acknowledges that there is not much left after the act, just some weed on the anchor and some salt dried on their skin, and she is bothered by the absence of feeling. Just as her husband was too occupied with his boat to notice her as a person, so her brother-in-law is too intent on his goal to detect the degree of unhappiness she feels.

A slick, deft story, **"The Wind Shifting West"** is an adequate though undistinguished account of the despair beyond words a person may feel when he feels completely alone, even while in the presence of many other people. Caroline finds that she has nothing to say at the family reunion other than small talk about how this person has grown since last year, or how that person has changed. In a vigorous family like Robert's, Caroline's pale, untanned appearance is distinctly out of place. Hence even seduction offers the potential of being noticed, though here too she is disappointed because of Giles' self-assured manner and his too-confident air of superiority, even in knowing that she will give in to his seductive approach. But after the sexual act, Caroline feels neither more fulfilled nor more emotionally moved, neither guilty nor intrigued, by the encounter; she remains as alone as before. . . .

"Homecoming" is, as a *New York Times* critic termed it [1 November 1973], a "bitter blow at Southern sentimentality and love of ritual." A nineteen-year-old boy whom the protagonist, Susan, barely knew has been killed in Vietnam, and the occasion of his death leads her relatives to treat the occasion as a major death in the family. Since her father had also been killed in war, her mother especially considers the death an occasion for wholesale mourning. Susan is not at all upset, but the manner in which her mother and their friends exaggerate the closeness of the two teenagers—her mother constantly reminds her that the two would have gotten married, with her fervent denials proving useless—is such as to cause Susan to retreat into her own room, even further reinforcing the others' conviction that she is bereaved. Susan then realizes that she too "is obeying a set of rules" and that the boy's being dead really will not change anything for her, despite all that her mother is saying. In other words, she can see her mother's desperate attempts to force sympathy on her as a way to have a "good time," as a major incident in the humdrum life her mother experiences. The story ends with Susan whispering to the dead boy, "Good-by, you poor bastard," as she rejoins the others gathered to commiserate.

Grau's tone is especially good in this story, for it would not have taken much for a touch of complete cynicism to enter in, with the mother made comical instead of pathetic or Susan hard-boiled instead of aloof. As it is, Susan remains as alone as she had been previously, but she has reached a level of understanding she had not had, not even when she first heard of the boy's death. For now she realizes *why* her mother reacts as she does, why death is an occasion for people to come together to share the experience. And even if in this case the emotional depth of the "loss" is radically overestimated, the occasion still serves as a form of ceremony by which sharing can occur.

Hence in joining the people in her house at the story's end, Susan reflects a degree of maturity her earlier rebelling against her mother's excited planning did not reflect. It is a convincing story, one that makes a serious point without resorting to the extremes of either comic ridicule or grotesque caricature. And just as Susan can now understand her mother, so we too can understand a bit better the emotion of personal and communal reaction to death. . . .

Of all of Grau's fiction, long as well as short, ["The Last Gas Station"] is evidently her one foray into the realm of the apocalyptic, into the kind of "end-of-the-world" fiction so often identified with such forms of fiction as speculative or science fiction. And even though the setting is the same one used so often in Grau's earlier work, a small bayou town below New Orleans in the Mississippi delta region, the very combination of the setting with the events in the story combine to make this an extremely effective tale, surely one of her stories that deserves far wider circulation.

The story, in brief, is of a family of a father and four boys who operate a run-down gas station on a four-lane highway heading straight to the South. Indeed, the highway becomes a kind of deity to the narrator, the youngest boy in the family, not only because the family cat had been killed on the road, but even more because, as a continually living entity, the highway seems to breathe. The family gradually diminishes in number as first Bruce leaves, then the father dies, Mark leaves, and then there are just Joe, the eldest, and the narrator, the youngest, left.

As Mark leaves, after a fight with Joe, he says, "Cain killed Abel. The end of the world is coming," and this is indeed what seems to occur. At first there was too much traffic on the highway, all heading South (i.e., toward the gulf), with everyone wanting gasoline. When the station's tanks are depleted, the two surviving boys notice the great number of cars abandoned alongside the highway, then the highway itself closed as a result of a massive pile-up, and then no traffic at all. As Joe, still not knowing what has caused the changes in traffic past the station, decides that they too will leave, the narrator runs away and hides out of fear of Joe's anger and instability, until Joe too leaves, at which time the narrator returns to the empty station. But there is no more electricity, just total silence, not a single thing moving in any direction. And as the story ends, the narrator knows what he will do when the next car passes—if there is ever again another car or anything else moving in the world.

Many stories, of course, have been written about the "last days," the apocalyptic day when life will cease because of one catastrophe or another. Whether man-made or natural, the "end of the world" concept carries with it an inherent fear for many civilized people because of its promise of total disruption of the smooth, normal way civilized life is expected to function. An account of the end of life in a futuristic society has one effect upon us, and a realistic account of such cessation of life in a major urban setting quite a different one. Yet it remains true that the most fearful accounts of the final great cataclysm are those seen from the perspective of a rural setting. As with Walter Van Tilburg Clark's classic tale, "The Portable Phonograph," we realize that if the effects of the conflagration are so intense here in the hinterland, what must it have been like in urban centers?

In **"The Last Gas Station,"** moreover, we experience these final days not through the eyes of relatively sophisticated observers, but through the eyes of a young, presumably uneducated boy who has had no contact with the outside world through any of the various forms of communication, not even any contact with others outside his family of similarly unlettered males. On one level, the story may seem to deal with a mere extreme form of sibling rivalry, as first one brother and then another flee. But Mark's comment about Cain and Abel may be nearer the point, for the story does have an aura of biblical doom, as if the world is coming to an end, with no place left to escape to, and with no survivors. And the setting, similar to one used by Grau many times in more conventional stories to establish a sense of place or mood, here serves all the more to heighten the horrors of what must be "out there," out where the protagonist cannot see but where he would like to be, just so he could know what has happened. One has not the slightest expectation of the events in this story when he begins to read it, for it seems like merely one more variation upon a familiar, even trite, theme. But Grau's accomplishment in the story is a fine one, to a great extent because of the very understated, calm manner in which apocalyptic horror is suggested, not shown directly. . . .

One of Grau's better characterizations of an eccentric is "Mr. Robin," a little man coming in on the train as **"The Lovely April"** opens. Evidently rather simpleminded and prone to unconventional behavior (such as coming to church wearing a hat, under which his head sports a pancake topped with a fried egg), but basically innocent, harmless, and a victim rather than a victor, Mr. Robin lives comfortably as a result of being from a well-to-do family. And this day, he comes to live in a small town where he would be more protected than he could be in the city. In time he parasitically attaches himself to the family of the narrator, and he sits throughout the day talking to the black cook, Oriole, in the narrator's home. Oriole, a powerful woman who had rid herself of several husbands previously, comes to love Mr. Robin, she misses him when he is not in her kitchen, and she wishes to protect him at all times. When Mr. Robin's father writes to have him returned to the city, Oriole sells her farm, packs up her belongings in a wagon, and leaves to take Mr. Robin to the train. The train is barely out of town before it has to stop because of a granite monument sitting on the tracks. During the melee which follows, Mr. Robin walks out of the train unnoticed, presumably taken by Oriole up to the high ridges of the hills where they can live together.

This is an unusual story in at least one major respect: it is one of the few examples in Grau's work where humor is deliberately introduced and where it fits the subject matter. Akin to the frontier tall-tale, **"The Lovely April"** is an ironic commentary on various forms of social intercourse, including the powerful woman saving the weak man, the "love conquers all" concept in which even color differences are overlooked by those involved, the "God's fool" idea of the simple man being in some indefinable way closer to truth and virtue than those more cynical souls around him, and so on. The monument was presumably placed on the tracks by Oriole, since she is more powerful than most of the men mentioned in the story, and it would be only through this means that she could "save" Mr. Robin. And the story takes on some of the mythic quality so prominent in Grau's earlier collection of stories and which is almost wholly absent from this one. It is an amusing story and a serious story at the same time, and it is among the best pieces in this book. . . .

Just as Grau's career as a novelist has experienced its ups-and-downs, with some of her work decidedly inferior to others, so her short story output has varied widely. Her skills as a novelist, however, have shown genuine growth with her last two novels, but her more recent short stories are far from her best efforts. *The Black Prince and Other Stories* was a most distinguished debut for a writer of short stories, to a great extent, no doubt, because Grau knew her milieu and subject matter and was able to dig out the riches potential in such material.

As she has changed focus, however, her work has lost much of the deep interest in her own world and the people inhabiting that world. On the one hand, it seems valuable for her to move away from the provincialism of the Gulf Coast region so emphasized in her first books, and in the recent novels she has found the expanse in which she can develop character and theme. In her more recent short fiction, however, she seems unable to develop characters as much as seems necessary, nor to probe more vigorously into the subjects about which the characters are concerned. In some recent stories she seems to have taken the easy way out—not just those dealing with topical issues, but even more with those handling familiar subjects or variations on the one central issue of this collection, the isolation and solitude experienced by women, in particular, who find death or some other force out of their control altering their expected directions in life.

The Wind Shifting West would no doubt be a stronger collection if it had been limited more selectively to, say, another nine stories. Some of the tales in this collection are solid and well worth comparing with most of those in the earlier collection. Some are successful forays into new (for Grau) territory, such as the apocalyptic **"The Last Gas Station."** Yet such a large number of these stories are so embarrassingly weak that one wishes he could avoid discussing them at all, were it not necessary for the sake of completeness in treating her output of short fiction.

To say that her shorter work is a "mixed bag" would be to say the obvious, but it would not offer any answers to the questions of why her career as a writer of short fiction developed as it did, nor would it be possible here to offer such suggestions. One must note, however—and bemoan—the fact that, as rich a book as *The Black Prince and Other Stories* was, *The Wind Shifting West* was, to the same degree, a disappointing book.

Still, Grau remains an important figure in the history of the American short story, and indeed her lasting status as a writer may be more as a writer of the shorter form than of the novel. A number of her stories remain uncollected, and although the total output of such stories is not as great as that of, say, Flannery O'Connor, she fully warrants the claim that at her best, in terms simply of the quality of her

best work if not in terms of quantity of production or consistent productivity, she ranks with O'Connor, Eudora Welty, and Carson McCullers. Hence the failings found in her second collection of stories should not be construed to suggest that her overall career as a storywriter is in dispute, only that she remains as inconsistent in quality in the writing and publishing of the story as of the novel.

> *Paul Schlueter, in his* Shirley Ann Grau, *Twayne Publishers, 1981, 158 p.*

Mary Rohrberger   (essay date 1983)

[*Rohrberger is an American educator and critic whose works include* Hawthorne and the Modern Short Story *(1966) and* The Art of Katherine Mansfield *(1977). In the following essay, she surveys Grau's short fiction.*]

Grau on becoming a writer:

I've been writing stories for a very long time. When I was a tiny child, I remember printing my stories so they looked more like print than handwriting. There is never a place in anybody's life when you say, O.K. this is it, I'll do it. You drift, openings come to you, and you take them. You end up in places you never dreamed you'd end. Chance plays a great part. For example, I started out very much wanting to be a classics scholar. . . . [But] when I popped out into the real world, I could see that the university system could absorb about one classics scholar a year in their teaching ranks, so that had to go—purely practical. Because I like universities and I like teaching, I thought, I'll get a Ph.D. in English and teach and write. It seemed like a good idea. I think it would not have been. But, anyway the head of the department said no women would be teaching assistants in his department. And then I said, well I can't go into a thing until I've tried it. I can't try it here, and I don't see a reason in the world to beat my head on that. I didn't like the rules of the game, so I quit. Just about then my free-lance pieces began to show. So I said, O.K., follow where the doors open.

Quoted by John Canfield in his "A Conversation with Shirley Ann Grau," The Southern Quarterly, *Winter 1987.*

The problem with Shirley Ann Grau is that she has consistently refused to stand still and conform to the stereotypes critics and reviewers have created for her. The problem of course, is not hers but ours, for we have consistently failed to understand the complexity of her statements and the excellence of her forms. Rather than try here to treat the corpus of her fiction, I have decided to examine the short stories, starting with the earliest and coming to ones she is currently working on for collection in a new anthology. My hope is to demonstrate not only her extraordinary skill in the short story genre, but also the development of that skill, and by so doing to stimulate a continuation of the recent flurry of scholarly activity devoted to examination of her work.

Had critics and reviewers been familiar with Grau's first published stories, their initial judgments concerning her proper métier might have been different, for the stories published during her college years exhibit a range more in line with catholic than regionalist tendencies.

"For a Place in the Sun" appeared in April 1948 in *Surf,* an intercollegiate magazine published at Tulane University. Grau was then a nineteen-year-old sophomore at Newcomb College. The protagonist of the story, a young man named Dan, has been injured by a falling crate and is unable to take a job driving a large van. The job signifies for him escape from his cramped and penurious circumstances, but it also signifies the advent of manhood and the assumption of a power role.

Dan is his mother's favorite son and subconsciously he seeks comfort in and from her. At the same time, he wants her approval and her admiration. Though injured, he is trapped not by his body but by his state of mind. The fuzzy whiteness in the form of tiny puffs of clouds that he hallucinates, the blades of grass he tears from the ground and scatters, his throbbing pain replicated in the landscape, the fog and marshes and odor of decay are all correlatives of his inner being.

His mother is also of two minds. Torn between her desire to care for her first born and her knowledge that she must at least try to motivate Dan to activity despite his injury, she speaks to him cautiously and fearfully. Struck by what she says but unable to deal with it, he escapes to the barn, to a milking stool where he sits breathing heavily and gazing vacantly at a row of milk cans. His vacant gaze is similar to the painful void and the dank hollows he wants to escape. Enshrouded by fog and blinded by his own egoism, seeing only shadowy forms, Dan opens the gate to the pasture lot, knowing the animals' escape will prevent his brother Will from taking the job Dan believes is his.

Although the plan to thwart his brother succeeds, Dan does not prevail. Will realizes what has happened; moreover, the knowledge does not bother him. Secure in himself, he is neither annoyed nor angry, and he has no need to tell his mother or to lash out at Dan. In the end, Dan stretches his leg in the sun to ease his pain, but "not even the clear yellow rays that seeped through the cloth could ease it or warm the cold loneliness within him."

This remarkable story is told in fewer than two thousand words. Nothing is stated overtly; everything is related indirectly through image patterns. The notable skill of the storyteller is evident from the first image of expected pain to the cyclic return to pain at the end of the story. The details of setting and action function to reveal the psychologic makeup of the characters as well as their inner conflicts. Modern in form with an *in medias res* beginning and lack of complicated plot, the story ends with an epiphany that embodies the entire experience.

The first issue of a new literary magazine, *Carnival,* published at Tulane in May 1949, contains a second story, **"So Many Worlds,"** a short-short story, less than one thousand words. This time Grau handles a different kind of people, a different social class, and uses a somewhat different form. In **"So Many Worlds,"** two people enter a restaurant and are seated by a waiter. The young wife, clothed in fur and diamonds, clearly dominates and man-

ages her confused and gesticulating husband. A short paragraph moves the couple to the outside. It is after a rain, and he points to a puddle: "Look, a world at your feet." "That," she says, is the "other side of the looking glass," the "upside-down world." As she hurries him away, his glance falls back to the puddle of blackness where "their two reflections lay bent and grotesque, and made a single pattern." In **"So Many Worlds,"** rising action moves to what in a traditional story would be climax. But instead of climax a transitional paragraph begins the pattern of images that builds to the epiphany.

The December 1949 issue of *Carnival* provides another story, **"The Shadowy Land,"** not long by any means, but better than twice as long as anything Grau had done before. The story's more complex plot is arranged in a traditional order—exposition, conflict, complication rising to climax and falling then to denouement. With more characters and a mingling of social classes, this story is Grau's first "Southern" story. Set in New Orleans during the Mardi Gras, the story contains white "masters" of French extraction and black "servants." Her skill at handling dialect at this early stage in her career is evident here, as well as in the speech of the poor whites in **"For a Place in the Sun"** and the speech of the moneyed class in **"So Many Worlds."** The protagonist is a white girl child named Barbie, who is dressed for the Mardi Gras as a "little southern lady" (in the words of a passing drunken Yankee) and is carried about for most of the day on the shoulder of her "faithful servant" John. John, whose own little boy is left behind, is called into service because Dilsey, Barbie's black nurse, refuses to take her. Dilsey, with wide white apron and knife strapped to an inner thigh, is going out to look for her husband who has left her, and she means to kill him. Barbie, in her role of naive protagonist, is carted about all day, while the drama of the chase takes place just outside of her immediate consciousness. But Barbie is not entirely innocent. Indeed, it is in this ambiguity that the power of the story resides, for no costume or role can hide the thrill the child experiences when she feels the knife on Dilsey's thigh and understands its purpose or the fear she experiences over that which she is too young to analyze. Barbie wakes into a shadow land in which the shadows are never dispelled, and her day is peopled by antic figures acting out grotesque patterns replicating nightmares. Nor is there hope of spring awakening consequent to the penitential fasting. At the end of the story, still being carried on John's shoulder, Barbie drowses while the cold wind blows the tears on her cheeks.

As a college senior, Grau published two more stories in 1950 in *Carnival,* in the October and December issues. Another four-thousand word story, **"The Lonely One"** focuses on a black family, particularly on Cissy, who believes her lover Brett is not coming back to her. Brett, the very model of a machismo figure of legend who drinks more, fights better and loves stronger, does however come back, and of course kills Cissy's new friend Sam. Based more in simple irony of circumstance than in the power of image, **"The Lonely One"** is the least successful of Grau's early stories, though her evocative skill is still evident in such descriptive passages as the first paragraph, where she speaks of the "hemlock shoulder of the ridge," or in the descriptions of the dancing couples or the trumpet player "wailing great mistakes."

"The Things You Keep" is also based in irony of circumstance. May's lover comes home to their small apartment to tell her he is leaving her. At the end of this very short piece, May stands before a mirror watching herself cry. Not as simple as this summary indicates, the story is carried forward on two levels—the overt level of linear plot resulting in the man's leaving and a covert level composed of patterns indicating that trouble spots should have notified her long before he did. Both levels come together in the final paragraph.

The last story published by Grau in *Carnival* appeared in the October 1951 issue at a time when she had entered graduate school and was working on a master's thesis. She never finished the master's thesis but during this period she began to write the stories that would appear in *The Black Prince*.

"The Fragile Age" is like nothing she had done before. It is a comic piece, a carefully controlled satire on literary study and the vagaries of the university. Mrs. Perse has disappeared into the library for four days before her husband realizes her absence and takes his problem to the dean. The ineffectiveness of the dean, the creeping and laborious working of Perse's aged mind, and the tottering Mrs. Perse, whose excitement at locating a source which can result in the birthing of a lifetime dream, generate sufficient energy to delineate and define the objects of satire and lead to the story's humorous climax. In the vaults of the library, at the far end of one of the corridors, Stravos and Michaels, two graduate assistants, find Dr. Perse illuminated by a lamp and glowing with inner light. His wife is absent, but her manuscript is there on a desk. She has, Perse exclaims, located the source of *Beowulf*! Her pursuit has not been in vain. Concurrent with Perse's announcement, Stravos and Michaels find in the center of the polished seat of the library chair a "little pile of grey dust." Evidently, like the one-horse shay, Mrs. Perse goes off all of a piece—"all at once and nothing first," her excitement acting like an orgasm sufficient to shatter her into particles of dust but not great enough to scatter the particles and disperse them into the air. In locating the source of *Beowulf* she finds her own source, too, in the little pile of grey dust. The title, "The Fragile Age," seems perhaps too restricted in its application if it is taken to apply only to the actually aged, but if as metaphor it is attached to the whole academic community whose pursuits are dry as dust, the story takes on considerably more meaning. The metaphor, of course, can be carried further, but Grau makes little attempt to do so, seeming content in this story lightly to skim surfaces.

The Black Prince, published by Knopf in 1955, contains nine stories, three of which were published earlier: "Joshua" in *The New Yorker;* "White Girl, Fine Girl," in *New World Writing* and "The Black Prince," in *The New Mexico Quarterly*. Several differences are apparent among the stories published in *Carnival* and the stories published in *The Black Prince:* the later stories are considerably longer; more fully developed plots follow either the traditional or the epiphanic line; more characters are involved and they are developed in more complex ways. Despite the additional complexities made possible by the additional length, however, basic devices remain the same. The writing style remains poetic and evocative; images still cluster into patterns, subsurfaces function in analogical modes.

In the move to longer stories, Grau's effort was toward a more careful and precise rendering of the experiential, while at the same time holding to that rich suggestiveness made possible by symbolic structures. The distinction to be made is not exactly between the romantic and the realistic or the intuitive and the empirical. That would be too easy. Rather, it is more between the direct and the subtle. What Grau was aiming for was a realistic rendering of a total experience, but only if "total experience" is taken to mean a meshing of the affective and the cognitive. Grau makes the point herself in her comment on "The Black Prince" prepared for an anthology of literature:

> Fiction, as I see it, is basically and always realistic. What else can it be? I know nothing beyond my experience and the experiences of people like me. If my expression becomes too personal, my symbols too intimate, my readers no longer understand. The demands of communication force me—partially at least—into the common mold of thought. I find myself dancing around the edges of meaning, trying to cut off a bit of the truth here, a bit there, trying to express, to shake the limitations of experience, above all to communicate my vision of the world. And, like most writers, I sometimes lose patience and abandon the reasonable realistic paths for the simple direct truths of mythmaking.

In this comment made thirteen years after the publication of *The Black Prince,* Grau was not suggesting that "The Black Prince" is easier to understand than stories which do not partake of the quality of legend. She uses both the words "direct" and "oblique" to describe her method and she is talking about means of communicating.

I should like to extend her points by suggesting that the "college" stories in their brevity and concentration on essence, are marked by a common analogical mode. Indeed, most of the stories in *The Black Prince* collection are closer to the dream mode than to the realistic. Five of the stories portray black characters in situations common to folk ballads. The other pieces of the collection, with the exception of "Fever Flower," are initiation stories, told in the first person by a white adolescent (two female and one male). But even these in one way or another partake of the stuff of legend. There is a pattern whereby Grau moves increasingly toward the more realistic, but we need to remember that the stories in *The Black Prince* are also early stories. And though movement can be seen away from the college stories, similarities persist.

In "White Girl, Fine Girl," the opening story in *The Black Prince,* the voice of a storyteller is clearly evident; the tone is conversational, the overt purpose descriptive, the style imagistic, subtly rendering areas of thematic concern. Just released from prison, Jayson Paul Evans tests his manhood and his will. When he leaves the road to enter a field, he moves at a jogging trot, taking long steps and swinging his arms, testing his "flight." It is difficult

THE WIND SHIFTING WEST

The wind blew out of the south, cold and wet as southern winds always were.   It had been blowing for a week, not hard but very steady. And the fog got thicker every day.   Makoniky Head and the old grey house perched on its back got dimmer and dimmer, day after day, until by Thursday morning they had disappeared completely.

"Well," said Caroline Edwards cheerfully, "there they go."

"What, honey?" Robert Edwards squatted at the far corner of the porch, his black hair glistening with damp.

He was doing something with a length of rope.   Caroline asked: "Is that the new anchor line for the Chere Amie?"

"This line?"   He didn't look up, but his tone was startled.

"Wrong?"

"Jib sheet."

"Oh.   Yes, I suppose it would have to be."

"Honey, you'll never make a sailor."

"Well, the Head has disappeared, that's all I was saying."

From the typescript of "The Wind Shifting West."

to avoid identifying Jayson with jay birds. The first clue appears when Jayson talks to a "dusty black crow" that is scratching on the "bare red earth." Aggressive and boastful, Jayson wants to drive away other "birds," throws stones and has stones thrown at him, sings a song without either rhyme or meter, steals food, "borrows" a skiff from two boys by the force of his size and determination.

Jayson is determined to seek out Aggie, the woman for whom he went to prison, and to assume the authoritative role not only in her and her daughters' lives but also in the reestablishment of his former business. But Jayson has reckoned without Aggie, who will have nothing to do with him, and he has not counted on his daughter acting out a stereotypical female role. His acceptance of the "Jax Poster" girl who is "white or nearly white" as a substitute for Aggie satisfies for the moment his need to prove himself and to assert the dominance of his position. Trusty lieutenants await his wishes; the girl of his dreams is his. His triumphant entry into town is completed, his masculinity restored. How long it will last is a question providing ironic overtones for the end of the story. Similarly, the title of the story sets the irony at the beginning, and image patterns throughout the story reinforce the irony, identifying town and prison, Jayson freed and Jayson trapped, Jayson as potent force and Jayson as impotent, the rebellion of the women and their submissiveness, white girl, fine girl and the Jax beer poster.

Many similarities exist between Jayson Paul Evans and Stanley Albert Thompson, the black prince of the title story ["The Black Prince"] who "comes walking out of the morning fog." Both men are associated with jays (as is Jay Mastern, who impregnated Maggie Mary Evans); both exude virility; both use songs in their association with women, though Jayson's songs are harsh and sometimes scolding and Stanley Albert Thompson's song is soft and melodious; both have superior muscle prowess and "win" their fights. There are, however, essential differences. Stanley Albert Thompson is a real figure of myth, a supernatural power, a force so seductive he can attract all women and enrage all men, a dispenser of death and of everlasting life, a successful wooer of the woman he chooses—Alberta. The seduction scene where Stanley Albert Thompson woos Alberta is one of the most memorable in all of Grau's writing—chiaroscuro joins with rhythms of sound and meter arranged in circular patterns to lead to the night flight of the betrothed couple. Alberta is a fitting mate for Stanley Albert Thompson, a woman made to his specifications to fit the role of princess of the night. Filled with devil lore (the flight through the air, the silver bullet, the alchemy, the play on the name—S.A.T.A.N.), the story has the dimensions of legend, being at once powerful and lyrical in its effect.

"Miss Yellow Eyes" presents a variation on the theme of the perfect couple. Where Stanley Albert Thompson and Alberta are purely black, Chris and Lena have had their color so mixed with white that their skin is light enough for them to pass over the color line, and this is their ambition. They will go to Oregon where it is easy to pass, and they will be white. They are a handsome couple—Lena,

all gold colored with light brown hair and ivory skin and eyes flecked with yellow, and Chris, with pale blue eyes and a suntanned face and brown gently waving hair. The narrator of the story is Lena's younger sister Celia, who calls Chris the handsomest man she has ever seen, and says she is more than half in love with him herself. For Celia, Chris becomes a model of conduct and stature whose actions are honest and straightforward and noble. Called into the Army during war time, Chris believes he has an obligation to go. Pete, brother to Celia and Lena, has a different opinion. He is angry and frustrated over the segregated life he is forced to lead, over the fact that the country drafts black men as well as white men but allows black men few other equalities.

Three other characters, two actually present in the story and one not, complete the cast of persons: the old gris-gris woman whom Lena goes to in time of despair (after she goes to a priest); Lena's mother, a cook in "one of the big houses on St. Charles Avenue"; and the absent father, whose presence is marked by a photograph. The missing husband and father becomes a symbol for all the men unable to function in a society that takes away their manhood. The war kills Chris. Pete, whose effort to cut off his finger to save himself from the draft results in his cutting off his hand instead, is left maimed and too angry and bitter to function. Only the women are left—the mother, still working as a "fancy" cook; Lena, broken and empty in spite of her prayers to supernatural forces; and Celia, her good sense and moderate responses replaced by the hysterical outbursts of the closing scene.

With Chris dead, Pete believes himself justified, and he taunts mother and sister:

> "But me, I'm breathing. And he ain't. . . . Chris was fine and he ain't breathing. . . ."
>
> "Chris boy . . . you want to cross over . . . and you sure enough cross over . . . why, man, you sure cross over . . . but good, you cross over."

Unable to take anymore of Pete's taunting, Lena attacks him, and accidentally hits him on the stub of his arm. Missing his footing, he falls, screaming softly to himself: "Jesus, Jesus, Jesus, Jesus."

Pete's call on Jesus, together with a motif of "crossing over," strongly suggests the image of Moses leading his people across the waters and, as in the spiritual, a cry to the Pharaoh: "Let my people go." Moses, a prototype of Christ, is successful; but Chris (a modern Christ?) is unsuccessful in leading his people to freedom.

"The Way of a Man" and **"Joshua"** complete the roster of stories about black people. The former, a heavily ironic story of the initiation of a young man into a world of crime and debt, contrasts with the latter, another initiation story, but one whose protagonist finds through his initiation some positive values.

In **"The Girl with the Flaxen Hair,"** Grau uses a first person narrator, the young girl Lily, who tells the story from an adult perspective. The point of view is particularly useful both in the presentation of the voice of the protagonist and in the perspective provided, for time, memory, and voice are major themes. Lily, a "tomboy" type, has a mother enamored of a misty Southern past and a down-to-earth dentist father who tries to keep "reality" in the forefront of his life and that of his wife and daughter. The Ramond family that moves nearby is a reverse image of the first family. There is a father who apparently cannot cope with reality, a mother attempting to live a lie, and a daughter Rose, a "sheltered" type, who accepts the lie. It is in the interaction of the two families and the conflict that arises that the tension of the story lies. Images also participate in the counterpoint—the wounded limbs, for example, Lily's cut hand ripped open by a splinter that she virtually ignores and her mother does not even notice, and Rose's wasp stings that create chaos and confusion and that are still wrapped long after the ache is gone; Lily's father's slow moving hand wounded by the bite of a child who was having his teeth examined and Mr. Ramond's hands moving so fast over a piano keyboard that they become a blur; Lily's black hair and sun-tanned skin and active life and Rose's yellow hair and fair skin and languid movements; the mother's real possessions which she values less than Mrs. Ramond's imagined ones; Rose's dream vision of a fairy tale marriage to a phantom groom and the coffin in the baggage car she lies in for her ride back to Jefferson City; and most important of all, the real father whom Lily forgets and so makes disappear and Mr. Ramond who actually disappears.

"The Bright Day," also told in the first person, is the slightest story in the collection. Charlotte, a young woman recently married, finds herself caught in a moral dilemma that threatens to break up her marriage. Unable to stand firm against the family, she gives in, and although she halfway realizes that timber and brick and cement do not create a home, she will not let herself come to complete realization. When she feels faint because of her subconscious recognition of the truth, she blocks that recognition and attributes her condition to the heat of the day.

If **"The Bright Day"** is the slightest story in the collection, **"Fever Flower"** is the best. On first perusal the opening paragraph seems innocent of symbolic overtones, but, as the story continues, patterns emerge, and one can be shocked to discover (so easy is the reading) that the images presented in this paragraph will later coalesce to form the major metaphor of the story, extending it beyond local significance to microcosmic proportions. A single word "Cadillacs" in the first paragraph carries over to the second, where locale magically becomes particularized as the modern South and limited even further to the affluent members of that land together with their servants. Before long, however, locale is identified with artificial growth, forced feeding, tropical gardens and attitudes that create tropical gardens, hot houses where children can only writhe and burn. The fever flower of the title refers both to the hot house orchids, blooms forced to grow outsized and defying normal time patterns, beautiful, exotic, and soon used up, and to Maureen, small daughter of Katherine and Hugh Fleming, who will be formed beyond her years and so distorted, her normal growth perverted by the environment in which she lives.

Identification of Katherine and Maureen is skillfully made

by means of the orange juice both mother and daughter drink and spill and by Katherine's vision of the proper kind of room appropriate for a child of three—not a nursery, but a young girl's room with vanity table and mirror and perfume atomizers and ruffled organdy. Another device Grau uses to establish identification is the montage, a kind of voice-over projection into the future, typically presented as inset or parenthetical passages. In these we learn what will happen when mother and daughter, both used up, both not quite human, settle into lives of narcissistic display.

The sexual base of the forced growth is suggested throughout the story but comes to climax at the story's end, which identifies Annie's vision of torment and destruction prior to the apocalypse with the child's burning up with fever. Annie is the child's Irish nurse who desires the child for her own and hates both mother and father for their interference and for their lusts. A Bible reading woman, she prefers the New Testament to the Old. But her preference for the Epistles marks her fixation on lusts of the flesh, and though she thinks she cannot understand the Apocalypse, she creates her own vision of torment: "Joy. The lusts of the flesh. The chaff which shall be cast in the fire. Hell Fire. Which was like summer sun, but stronger seven times."

Annie's vision for Maureen resides in a Gaelic song: "A love to have . . . And strong arms to carry you away." Perhaps Annie does not realize that the man she summons for Maureen is called too soon, though the little lady appears in her feverish sleep already to have received him. Her hair is damp and sticks to her skin; her cheeks are flushed; her color is high. Shadows give her face the illusion of age. At the end her crying has stopped and she lies there "beautiful and burning."

"One Summer" is an initiation story told in the first person by an adolescent boy who finds that the death of his grandfather miraculously propels him into the role of a man. With his new status come realizations frightening in their implications as the boy experiences his first presentiment of death. Like the other stories, the surface of this one is gloss, so smooth and effortless to read that the rendering of the texture of the experience seems its only purpose. But beneath the surface, underpinnings of image patterns made clear by means of repetition and juxtaposition point to meaning worth reaching for.

At its publication *The Black Prince* received rave reviews from all of the right critics and places. But though the critics wrote in superlatives, the superlatives were based in initial impressions, and no one went further in an effort to analyze the stories to see just where their merits lay. Indeed, the major impression that the critics seem to have taken away with them was that the stories were written by a young Southern woman and that she would carry on the tradition of Southern writers, especially women, and take her place among other Southern regionalist writers of the time. Novels followed the publication of *The Black Prince,* all published by Knopf: *The Hard Blue Sky* (1958), *The House on Coliseum Street* (1961), the Pulitzer Prize winning *The Keepers of the House* (1964), *The Condor Passes* (1971)—each succeeding one better than the last, though it was becoming more and more difficult for reviewers to make their assumptions about Grau's work jibe with the work she was producing. And all the while she continued to write short stories, publishing them regularly both in the popular magazines and in the literary journals. A number of these were collected in the volume, *The Wind Shifting West* (1973).

Stories in *The Wind Shifting West* demonstrate many of Grau's mature interests, as well as her continuing and remarkable narrative skill in the genre of the short story and her ability to handle forms and points of view extraordinary in their range and gradation. A fiction that can loosely be classified as a "ghost story" (**"Three"**) or one in the "science fiction" mode (**"The Last Gas Station"**) take their place in the same collection with pieces of topical interest (**"The Other Way," "Eight O'Clock One Morning"**), with stories that circle back to Grau's earlier interests typified in *The Black Prince* (**"Pillow of Stone"**), to those that adumbrate novels to come (**"The Patriarch,"** anticipating *Evidence of Love,* 1977, and **"Stanley,"** *The Condor Passes*), and with stories, including several of the above, that demonstrate a continuing effort to hide the technical and formal underpinnings in a dazzling and seemingly effortless surface display. The volume also exhibits virtuosity in perspectives employed. Whereas point of view in *The Black Prince* was basically limited to children or primitives, viewpoint in *The Wind Shifting West* extends to include people of all ages, both sexes, and different social classes in a variety of settings.

"The Wind Shifting West," the title story, is set not on a Southern coast but on one in the Northeast; point of view is third person focused through the protagonist, Caroline, a woman approaching middle-age; and nothing more spectacular happens than a first infidelity. Caroline and Robert Edwards, with their nine-year-old son Guppy, have for ten years been joining the rest of the Edwards family in their summer houses on the coast. Routines are so well established that people and actions fit into their places as easily and neatly as Mrs. Edwards, the matriarch of the family, fits words into her Double Crostics. Though it is very early in the season, Robert is enthusiastically preparing to sail across the sound in a visit he makes annually. Caroline stays home to tend the geraniums and then visits the home of her mother-in-law where other members of the family have gathered, including Giles van Fliet. Half English and half Dutch, with his continental ways and speech patterns, Giles seems even more out of place in the Edwards family than does Caroline. Both are physically different; both ostensibly accept the Edwards pattern of living but, consciously in Giles' case and subconsciously in Caroline's, secretly despise it; both are inlaws, unrelated to each other.

Caroline's dissatisfactions seem trivial—displayed as they are in an array of small incidents which begin as soon as the story does. In ten years of marriage she has not learned the right terms for the accouterments of a boat; in ten years she has not succeeded in diminishing the use of her son's nickname or in influencing her son to her own point of view; in ten years she has never really fitted into the family or its interests; and in a year and a half she has not

kissed her husband goodbye because Robert does not want to embarrass their son. Caroline's preoccupation with her age is another indication of her frame of mind. The "little twinge" in her back is also a "twinge in her soul"; she responds with annoyance to her nephew's pleasure in her physical appearance, to her mother-in-law's blunt comments, to Giles' cool presence.

A ship to shore call begins the intensification of the conflict. A mast has been ripped from Robert's new boat, and he and Guppy are stranded at their friend's place. The ship to shore conversation between Caroline and Robert acts as an objective correlative for their growing estrangement. Robert is annoyed because she does not know the procedures necessary for communication. He and Caroline talk at the same time and at cross purposes with neither hearing the other. When Giles takes the phone, he begins a pattern of action to which Caroline acquiesces as the story continues. Giles' obvious admiration for his mother, whose fidelity to her husband he comments on, is in stark contrast to his own behavior. When Caroline realizes that he keeps bathing suits in a variety of sizes on his boat for the women they will accommodate, she questions him about his marriage. His response makes it clear that his own infidelities are kept separate from his marriage and in his own mind have no bearing on it.

Giles, who handles his power launch with the same skill he apparently handles women, is set in counterpoint to Robert, the "sailor who has just lost his mast." Ironically, Caroline uses Robert's symbolic "unmanning" as part of her rationalization for her behavior and eventually her acquiescence. In the end, however, it is she who is diminished, as she half realizes. The anchor with some weed attached and still wet from the staying of the boat is the only mark (besides the salt dried on their skin) of their action. Already a cynic, Giles comments: "There isn't ever much left when it's done." Perhaps Caroline will come to know finally that she has made nothing better; she has simply exchanged partners in a power struggle. The wind having blown from the south, now blows from the west, but the south wind will come again as it always does and, with it, more fog.

Grau writes with such compassion for characters and understanding of their situations that it often comes as a surprise that the world she creates is usually negative in its aspects—the characters being enshrouded in fog a whole lot more than they bathe in sunlight. **"The Beach Party,"** another story set on the Northeast coast, makes the point effectively. Frieda, the youngest member of the beach party, feels out of place, not only because of her age but because she does not "know the symbols." She finds herself frustrated and annoyed, feeling "just the way she had when as a child, she found a floating bottle and a message too blurred to read." At the ocean, she is afraid. She knows that her fear has to do with the dark color and with the sound and the motion of the surf. The "unknown opaque distances of the ocean" frighten her. By the end of the story, Frieda has learned to read the symbols. A boy has drowned, but it seems no more horrible than everything else—than live lobsters steamed to death, than the evidence of dead creatures in the sea wrack all around, than the press of a male body, than the releasing of sperm and the process of ovulation that is simply a part of the movement of life toward death. But knowing the truth does not make it easier to accept. She makes her way back home grateful for the radio, "safe inside its tinny shell." In the end, the beach party in all of its aspects is a symbolic representation—a prelude for death. **"The Land and the Water,"** another story in the collection, makes essentially the same point. Water, symbol for life, is also symbol for death. In the story, as the sky darkens overhead, the water becomes a lead-colored gray.

The two stories from which novels emerged—**"The Patriarch"** and **"Stanley"**—are among the most fascinating in the collection. *The Condor Passes,* into which **"Stanley"** grew, was published in 1971 and so actually preceded the publication of **The Wind Shifting West.** In the short story Grau goes back to a favorite image—the green house, an artificial environment, created to house and nourish plants not ordinarily grown in the real environment and birds not ordinarily kept in captivity. The green house provides an environment helpful to the old man in that it aids in his breathing and provides a springboard for his memory of South America where he made his fortune. There is now nothing left of the South America he knew except the old man's memory of it, for he has outlived all of his contemporaries.

The old man is clearly presented in bird images. Stanley's responsibility to rid the bird cage of dead birds every morning is tied to the old man's need to be sheltered from a recognition of his coming extinction. When the old man identifies the hawk that flies low over the green house as a condor, he foreshadows his own death, for with his death, the condor passes. There is nothing left of him but memory and that only in the minds of the people who actually knew him. When they are gone he will be extinct—as we all will be.

"The Patriarch" seems a mature reflection on and restatement of **"The Black Prince"** of the earlier collection. Edward Milton Henley, aged eighty-eight, is another and much more fascinating "black" prince, who could indeed be a real son of the morning, for if "truth lies beyond fulfillment of desire, in satiated appetite, then the conventional wisdom of western morality" is, indeed, the "sobbing end of shabby gentility," and paradise lost was actually gained.

Evidence for the identification of Edward Milton Henley as the patriarch is abundant. He is the "father," a mirror image of his own father, whom he sometimes thinks looked at him as through the "wrong end of a telescope." Named after John Milton, he grows up at a time when life is a preparation for paradise and death entry thereto. His father's house is gothic and its talisman is a rainbow lantern. Virtually ignored by his parents, the high point of his young life is the time he nearly dies; but he enjoys the experience—the sensation of floating in the air or swimming in water. Even in health, one of his recurring dreams is of being dead. During his illness he talks constantly—"in tongues," his mother thinks. In his desire for darkness, the covenant for him becomes not everlasting light and life but

its underside—the dark side, in other terms, the irrational and hedonistic as opposed to the rational and ascetic.

As an adult Henley eschews dualities, the base of western philosophy, preferring to think of life as a stage parade where one role is exchanged for another by a simple change in costume; and what he ironically describes as perhaps "a senile astigmatism" is more a statement of his metaphysics. Along with dualities, Henley rejects "twos" in his later life, saying he is haunted "by that absurd number." Indeed, he rejects "twos" even in denying the life-sustaining role of women, creating as he does a situation as near as he can get to fathering a son without a woman. The various women in his life, including his four wives, are simply conveniences, there for his physical pleasure or objects of his mental titillation, the subjects of taunts. Nor is he bound by a need for women, a fact he proves in the four years he spends with Guido.

At the end of the story, shifting abruptly from first person to third (a feat hardly ever tried in a short story), Grau focuses on Anthony, already an old man, who is watching his father talking to his grandchildren in the grape arbor. The scene seems dramatic, unreal, reminding Anthony of an illustration of a patriarch or prophet in a book of Bible stories. And when his father raises his hand in a greeting to him: "It was, the Reverend Henley thought with a shudder, altogether like a blessing."

Given the tantalizing and complex nature of the subject matter of **"The Patriarch,"** it is easy to see why Grau extended it to *Evidence of Love.* Indeed, in extending it, she put "the flesh on the bones and the skin on the skull."

Grau is now putting together a collection of short stories [*Nine Women*] consisting of newly written pieces. At my request, she sent me **"Summer Shore"** and **"Letting Go."** It seems hardly fair to readers to comment on pieces not yet published, but the temptation is great, especially since the collection will be ready for publication, the author says, sometime this year.

"Summer Shore" seems, at first reading, a simple narrative about a couple comfortable with themselves and each other, married thirty-two years, and content in and with their family rituals. The story takes place, however, not at the beginning of a season but at its end. Image patterns of wintery blasts, approaching age, sudden death, imminent changes, and threatening transitions overpower signals of calm and sun, false in their implications. The people, regardless of how compassionately treated and understood, prove at close look to be insular, opinionated, parochial in their views, cliquish, provincial, bored—a backside presentation, what Katy sees when she looks at the aging summer crowd all facing toward the sea. Katy sees but will not allow herself to understand. She hides inside her house, her wooden shell, protected by her role as wife of the "ranking male member of a tribe" and by her family surrounding her. "How can it end," the poet Donald Davie asks, "This siege of a shore that no misgivings have steeled, / No doubts defend?" Grau uses these lines for epigraph. In Christian terms, one thinks of the apocalypse and of destruction before the raising of the new Jerusalem.

Is this why Katy thinks suddenly: "Next year in Jerusalem"?

Lines from Emily Dickinson begin **"Letting Go"** as well as provide its title: "As freezing persons recollect the snow—/first chill, then stupor, then the letting go." In the story Mary Margaret needs to run to keep from letting go into the "comfortable silences" provided by her parents and their home. Although she believes she hates the pattern of the parents' lives; still, in growing up and in marrying, she patterned her own life in basically similar ways. She has accepted the idea that regular habits and moral behavior ward off troubling thoughts. She has conformed to expectations. At twenty-three she was secretary to a senior vice-president and on her way to being executive assistant. At twenty-four she married, and though her parents disapproved of the match, still she did not basically change the pattern of her life. She worked and carefully tended the apartment and regularly, every Wednesday, visited her parents to attend with them the Perpetual Novena, even after her husband Edward refused to go with her. When she and Edward decide to divorce, she wonders whether she already has had all her parents have—apparently comfortable lives. They are so used to each other that they never quarrel; indeed they have never showed emotion to her, not even when she was growing up. But they do care for her; they are simply inarticulate people who behave as they have to. Mary Margaret's acceptance of a job in Oklahoma City is an effort to escape, to put the old patterns behind, to seek for something else, but the temptation to stay behind is so great that she needs to invent a fearful beast to guard the doors of her parents' house to keep her from reentry. She does not know that crowded highways, exhaust-filled air, and the bustle of city life form their own patterns that in time can also, like the Perpetual Novena, provide protection—at least up to a point.

As a short story writer, Grau's talent is immense though not revealed by a simple surface reading; for what is beneath the surfaces and interacting with them is what is characteristic of the short story genre, and Grau has mastered the genre. Southern female writer she is, by accident of birth and genes. Southern regionalist writer, she is not. Nor are her skills confined to revealing and commenting on "the genuinely native particulars of a scene" in time, as Frederick J. Hoffman would have it. Rather, like that of other important writers, her work transcends particulars, excellent as she is at rendering them.

> *Mary Rohrberger, "Shirley Ann Grau and the Short Story," in* The Southern Quarterly, *Vol. XXI, No. 4, Summer, 1983, pp. 83-101.*

Jonathan Yardley   (essay date 1986)

[*Yardley is an American journalist and critic. In the following essay, he favorably appraises* Nine Women.]

In these nine short stories [in **Nine Women**]—her first story collection in more than a dozen years—Shirley Ann Grau is writing about women in moments of decision and crisis. They are women of different circumstances and ages, but they have in common a Southern upbringing that stresses manners, decorum and reticence, as well as an awareness that their lives have reached moments they cannot avoid and from which they cannot turn back. Their crises vary in magnitude, from questions of identity to matters of life and death, but each of them has to make a choice, whether conscious or not, that will permanently alter her life.

Grau is now and always has been deeply concerned with the lives of women, but it would be a mistake to characterize her as a "feminist" writer. In the first place there has never been a hint of rhetoric or dogma in her work; she is among other things kindly disposed toward men, and disinclined to dismiss them as brutes or oppressors. Beyond that, she is in the best and broadest sense of the term a domestic writer, one whose principal subject is family life in all its complexities and who prefers to examine her characters in human rather than political terms.

A characteristic story—and in my judgment the finest in the book—is **"Letting Go."** Its protagonist, Mary Margaret McIntyre, is a young married woman who each week comes to her parents' house: "I come every Wednesday for supper and the novena. Perpetual novena. That was how I learned what eternity was—like the novena, it goes on and on without end." Her husband does not come with her, because for no good reason he is despised and ridiculed by her hard, narrow, self-satisfied mother and father. Wednesday nights are a form of torture for her, yet she comes because "I have honored [my parents] for all my twenty-nine years, and I am not about to stop now." Finally, though, she comes to understand that what she gives is not returned, that her parents only demand attention and obeisance; at last she breaks away from the perpetual novena, hard though it is for her to do so, and begins to shape a life that can truly be her own.

These moments of revelation and decision are not always so clear or dramatic. In **"The Beginning,"** a black woman looks back on her childhood, living with a mother who adored her, who told her that her father was a prince, "a Hindu from Calcutta, a salesman of Worthington pumps," and that she herself was "the Indian princess in her palanquin, the treasure of the mahal above Leconte's Drugstore." Eventually she learns that none of this is true, but also that this knowledge is beside the point: "And so I passed my childhood disguised to myself as a princess. I thrived, grew strong and resilient. When the kingdom at last fell and the castle was conquered, and I lost my crown and my birthright, when I stood naked and revealed as a young black female of illegitimate birth, it hardly mattered. By then the castle and the kingdom were within me and I carried them away."

Several of the women are widows, missing their husbands in different ways and seeking new satisfactions in their new lives. One, rejecting the pleas of her embarrassed children, takes employment as housekeeper for an eccentric old man; when he dies, she develops an enriched understanding of the fate that awaits her as well. Another, also recently widowed, reluctantly but determinedly makes the rounds at her country club on the first day of its summer season; in her grief and loneliness she drinks too much gin, but she is also "truly glad to have had this day, one of my dwindling supply, to have had the sun and the bitter sea taste in my mouth." Still another, a young woman who survived an airplane crash in which her husband and children were killed, is obsessed with a belief that her survival was an error and that she must rejoin her family; she flies constantly now, waiting for the plane that will crash and bring about this reunion.

In all of these stories there is an awareness that fate is capricious. "Funny thing," Mary Margaret McIntyre thinks, "luck and the difference between living and dying." Even as these women seek to master their lives, they know that they cannot: "These things, they were all of them beyond her reach. Forces changing her life, and beyond her control. Impersonal, like wind and rain. Unquestioned." There is in their lives a "thing that crouched waiting in the shadows," a fate they have no choice but to accept, however shocking and painful it may prove to be.

Thus it is that Angela, a successful businesswoman, accedes, even if with apprehension and grief, to her lesbian lover's desire to have a child; Barbara, a prosperous middle-aged woman, permits the dissolution of her own marriage on the same day as her daughter's wedding; Katy, also prosperous and middle-aged, accepts her role as "wife of the ranking male member of a tribe" which observes annual rituals that are at once tired and life-giving. None of these women is conspiring in her own oppression or abuse; each is simply coming to terms with what fate has dealt her, and trying to make the best of it.

To describe these stories as I have may make them seem morose, even morbid, but quite the contrary is the case. Irony and self-deprecating wit are much in evidence, and so too is Grau's keen eye for the manners of middle-class life along the Louisiana coast. There are no flash and dazzle in these stories, and their tone is like Grau's prose: measured, reflective, uninsistent. But their quiet can be misleading; Grau is a serious writer, and her subject is always the essential business of life. It is fine to have her back after so long an absence.

> *Jonathan Yardley, "Shirley Ann Grau's Stories from the New South," in* Book World— The Washington Post, *January 12, 1986, p. 3.*

John Canfield   (essay date 1986)

[*In the following review, Canfield discusses themes and technique in* Nine Women.]

Nine Women is Shirley Ann Grau's first book since her novel *Evidence of Love* (1977) appeared nearly a decade ago. While the years between 1977 and 1985 have not been prolific ones for this Pulitzer Prize-winning author of two previous collections of short stories and five novels, they have given Grau time for fertile reflection. Written at the rate of slightly more than one a year, each story in *Nine Women* deals with a woman who is looking back as she attempts to cope with change and somehow organize a late-middle-age pattern of living. In nearly every case the woman has reached a crisis point. The crisis may have been perpetrated by a deliberate action on her part: a

planned divorce after a daughter's marriage; or it may have been unforeseen: a husband's sudden death. But in nearly all the stories, the protagonist is forced into an isolated life of introspection. She becomes a solitary woman ordering the world around her through a hard-won bravery. When Myra in **"Widow's Walk"** returns to the beach resort the summer after her husband, Hugh, has died, she discovers that although her friends remind her of Hugh, "Hugh did not live in them. Hugh was dead. She was here alone."

Through Myra and her other characters Grau addresses an increasingly common situation for American women. Whether they isolate themselves of their own volition or find themselves left alone by a divorce or a husband's death, they face the problem: how does a single woman survive economically, psychologically, and physically? Ironically, one of the few really "sustaining couples" in *Nine Women* is Angela Taylor and Vicky Prescott, upper-middle-class lesbian lovers in **"Home."** These two professional women—Angela is a real estate agent while Vicky owns an "exclusive" boutique—face a crisis when the younger Vicky reveals to the middle-aged Angela that she wants to have a baby.

The wide range of women Grau writes about evidences a careful examination of contemporary American society. In several stories she examines women from upper-middle-class backgrounds, an area with which she has a great deal of familiarity. Yet in another story, **"Housekeeper,"** Grau looks at a maid telling a story about herself and the man she worked for, Dr. Hollisher. In **"Ending,"** Barbara Eagleton, an upper-middle-class southern black, realizes on the night of her daughter's wedding that her long contemplated divorce from her husband is about to become a reality. She tells her husband, "It could have been our twenty-fifth anniversary. That would have been so neat and precise. I could say I was married for twenty-five years. Now I'll have to say I was married for twenty-four and eleven-twelfths years." And in **"Letting Go,"** Grau writes about the secretary, Mary Margaret MacIntyre, who tries to break away from her working-class Catholic parents, with their ritualistic lifestyle and stubborn ways that have already caused the demise of her marriage.

With this variety of characters comes a range of narrative techniques and interesting minor thematic developments. In some ways, Grau's new collection of stories provides a retrospective embodiment of her earlier works. In **"Hunter,"** a story about a woman's psychological recovery from an airplane crash in which her entire family was killed, the reader observes the same events from several different points of view, paralleling Grau's narrative technique in *The Keepers of the House* (1964). The overpowering sense of place and time as ordering principles in her first novel, *The Hard Blue Sky* (1958), recurs in **"Summer Shore,"** a story about a woman facing another one of her family's ritualistic, end-of-summer parties at the family beach property.

The unity of *Nine Women* inheres strongly in the sense of retrospection. Nearly every story deals with a woman recalling past events. Sometimes, as in **"Flight,"** a dying woman relives an entire short story in flashback; whereas in other stories, notably in **"Summer Shore,"** the "real-time" action triggers questions about the past, the right answer to which might help to bring order to the present. In **"Housekeeper,"** Grau layers the flashback process. Mrs. Emmons remembers her job as Dr. Hollisher's housekeeper and then in the process of that reflection re-members bracelets she wore on the job to let the doctor know where she was in the house, which in turn triggers a memory about wearing bracelets during her childhood days. Again, this kind of layering of the past and discus-sion of the past's influence on the present harkens back to Grau's work with this theme in *The Keepers of the House.*

Grau's devotion to what she calls "a certain facility with words," that is to say, her dedication to superb craftsman-ship, intensifies the thematic and dramatic unity of *Nine Women.* She maintains a control over her language—a power which has become a point of pride for this skilled writer. Her prose is polished and elegant, while the obser-vations are keen and selective. On the first page of the first story, the reader gets to know a mother's voice:

> She whispered words like that, singsonging them in her soft high voice that had a little tiny crackle in it like a scratched record, to comfort me when I was a baby. Her light high whisper threaded through all my days, linking them tightly to-gether, from the day of my birth, from the first moment when I slid from her body to lie in the softness of her bed. . . .

Then, in **"Summer Shore,"** Grau paints a quick landscape:

> For three days the wind had blown from the northeast, dragging black, fast-moving streaks of clouds across a gray smeared sky. In the sum-mer houses along the coast and meadows of Chenier Cove shutters rattled day and night, doors crashed open and closed, chimneys back-winded soot across ceilings, windows leaked in the heavy rainsqualls.

While it is obvious that *Nine Women* results from Grau's slow, deliberate look at her world, it is also obvious that such keen insight will become still greater. With *Nine Women* Shirley Ann Grau continues to grow as a writer, showing that she transcends the pejorative "regionalist" label attached to her by many critics. If in another eight or ten years she brings out another collection of stories with the range and acuity of this one, the wait will be well worth it.

> John Canfield, "Women Alone," in The Southern Review, *Louisiana State University, Vol. XXII, No. 4, Autumn, 1986, pp. 904-06.*

Thelma J. Shinn (essay date 1986)

[*In the following excerpt, Shinn discusses the depiction of women in Grau's short fiction.*]

Shirley Ann Grau presents women with the strength and self-confidence to challenge the unchallengeable—to throw bricks even at the "hard blue sky." As [Ann] Petry's narrator in *Country Place* described his female cat as "much closer to the primitive than a male cat," so too have Grau's strong women been called primitives by Lou-ise Gossett [in her *Violence in Recent Southern Fiction,* 1965]. "In Miss Grau's first fiction the Negro is largely an-other primitive whose violence expresses uninhibited pas-sions and temper," Gossett says of *The Black Prince and Other Stories* (1955). Other primitives are the bayou Cre-oles of Louisiana who people her pages.

In contrast to the primitives are the city-bred Southern women. We meet . . . the surviving version of the South-ern lady here, and Grau shows the conflicts produced by the survival of this anachronism in modern society. . . .

The first three stories of *The Black Prince* deal with Grau's black primitives, who accept violence as part of life. Violence is often, in fact, honest and constructive, an attempt to deal immediately with the problems which con-front them. **"White Girl, Fine Girl"** shows how one woman protects herself from becoming a victim. Aggie's husband Mannie has been murdered by her lover Jayson, who is now returning from prison. Aggie's son by her mar-riage died from drinking lye, and since then she has had three daughters, one by Jayson and one by his friend Joe. Joe warns the returning Jayson that "Aggie got plain mad" after that. "So she ain't having nothing to do with no men. She don't let anybody come in her house no more. And she got the kids so they don't let their daddies walk down the street. They got to go round the next block or the kids throw rocks at them. And they big enough to hurt." Jayson, however, risks the rocks to reach the house and wreck all he can. He is less rough with his daughter, Alice Mary, whom he had never seen before, and purpose-ly doesn't hit her with the rock he throws at her to stop her from following him. If a woman needs to protect her-self, perhaps a daughter needs to know her father at least. The story is violent but affirmative and humorous as well; all the cast are survivors.

The legendary Alberta in [**"The Black Prince"**] attracts and then follows the virile but satanic Stanley Albert Thompson into the realm of fantasy. But Alberta is no lost dreamer, nor is she left behind as are Welty's worshipping women. She is "a handsome girl, taller than most people in her part of the country, and light brown. . . . She was not graceful—not as a woman is—but light on her feet and supple as a man." This independent young woman will commit to love only on her own terms: she "shook her head, no, she would walk; no man needed to lead her." She even bargains with Stanley: "I don't see as how I could stay though . . . I don't see as how. You ain't give me none of the things you said." She is willing to fight for what she wants; when Willie attacks Thompson, "quietly, smoothly, in a single action, without interrupting her step, Alberta picked up a bottle . . . and swung it against Wil-lie's head." A fitting model for a strong woman, she leaves to wander with her man, loving but equal. . . .

The blacks in **"Miss Yellow Eyes"** seem somewhat less isolated and more contemporary than those in the other two stories, but Lena, to whom the title refers, retains the primitive strengths. She is very fair, and she and her hus-band Chris hope to move to Oregon and pass for white. However, Chris is wounded in the war and dies in a field hospital. When her brother Pete, who lost a hand to avoid the draft, taunts her—and himself—with the wisdom of his choice and the hopelessness of her plans, she breaks out of her depression by hitting him. Lena's violence serves no constructive purpose, perhaps, but we have difficulty not approving. As Gossett says, Grau's primitives are "un-complicated, outgoing people whose actions are made violent more by circumstance than by flawed human nature." Lena is a precursor of women who become so frustrated by social restrictions on constructive outlets that their energies are channeled into destruction.

Grau's bayou primitives appear first in **"Joshua."** In her first novel, *The Hard Blue Sky* (1958), Grau will trace the maturation of a young woman; in **"Joshua," "The Way of a Man,"** and **"One Summer"** she concentrates on the maturation of boys. **"Joshua"** gives us only a brief glimpse of a bayou mother as she tries to protect her son from too early an initiation into manhood. The father has decided to send Joshua to "run my [fishing] lines," but the mother refuses to let him go: "You ain't sending that little old boy out where you scared to go." She loses; mothers in this primitive world cannot stop the inevitable maturation of their children any more than they can stop any other act of nature, such as a hurricane. Their nobility lies in their willingness to try. These women share their husbands' labors and have acquired an equality born of knowing that they are not dependent. They speak their minds and never hesitate to fight for what they want.

Grau's more civilized types do not have the same core of self-respect, although they reveal great strength and determination at times—almost always misdirected. The Southern lady is best seen in Mrs. Ramond and her daughter, **"The Girl with the Flaxen Hair."** Mrs. Ramond is introduced as a daughter as well; she lives on the legends of her father, Senator Winslow, and her carefully selected memories. Rose is a fragile girl who "had a face like a Botticelli angel" and whose hopes for the future were centered around her mother's plans for a dazzling wedding. Even after they are deserted by Mr. Ramond—apparently because he was made to feel too much beneath his "aristocratic" wife—the two continue to live genteelly with no means of support. Rose sneaks out at night to gather coals at the railroad yard for heat, until one night she is killed by a train which had changed its schedule. The two Ramonds are trapped in the mystique of the Southern lady, and the excessive fragility and ultimate destruction of the daughter echo the death throes of the tradition itself.

A more modern mother and daughter are shown in **"Fever Flower,"** but modernity alone is no improvement over the stereotyping of the past. The divorced Katherine Fleming cannot even convince herself that she is concerned about her daughter Maureen. Katherine is not selfishly pursuing a wild life; her idea of happiness is solitude, preferably lying in a hot tub: "She had a perfect body; she was a superb animal. But she was not quite human. She did not need anyone." She has furnished Maureen's room as if the small girl were a teenager, trying to skip the "awkward growing years, the child years" that demand parental responsibility and to push Maureen into the "four or five years of the girl's first beauty." For Katherine these would

be the best years they could share, even though she would probably see very little of Maureen and both would "realize that they did not really like each other very much." Like Lil in Petry's *Country Place,* Katherine is eager to be free to live her own life.

Despite rare moments of affection, for her father (remarried and expecting another child) Maureen is a risky investment: "He was spending quite a bit of money on his daughter and he could not quite convince himself that it was worth it." Maureen will pass through three husbands before she too chooses the advantages of solitude in "a beautiful, very expensive apartment for one." Rose Ramond, the Southern belle, may have been a dying blossom; but Maureen, the "fever flower" of her parents' sicknesses, scarcely improves the garden.

> *Thelma J. Shinn, "A Strategic Retreat: Fiction of the 50's," in her* Radiant Daughters: Fictional American Women, *Greenwood Press, 1986, pp. 75-124.*

FURTHER READING

Criticism

Cantwell, Mary. "Lives in Short." *The New York Times Book Review* (9 February 1986): 17.
    Negative assessment of *Nine Women.*

Clapp, Susannah. "Displaced Persons." *The Times Literary Supplement* (15 November 1974): 1278.
    Reviews *The Wind Shifting West,* noting that "people buffeted and slightly out of phase with their surroundings provide Mrs Grau's best stories."

Cole, Diane. Review of *Nine Women,* by Shirley Ann Grau. *Ms.* XIV, No. 7 (January 1986): 91.
    Positive assessment, concluding that *"Nine Women* should send new readers to discover Shirley Ann Grau's world of strong women of the South."

Hall, Joan Joffe. "Lives Alone." *The New Republic* 169, No. 21 (24 November 1973): 30-1.
    Discusses subjects and themes in *The Wind Shifting West.*

Pearson. Ann. "Shirley Ann Grau: Nature Is the Vision." *Critique* XVII, No. 2 (1975): 47-58.
    Examines the function of natural setting in Grau's fiction.

Peden, William. "Vibrant World." *The Saturday Review,* New York, XXXVIII, No. 5 (29 January 1955): 16.
    Reviews *The Black Prince, and Other Stories,* noting that Grau "is a very promising young author."

Poster, William S. "Fiction Chronicle." *Partisan Review* XXII, No. 2 (Spring 1955): 275-82.
    Includes a favorable review of *The Black Prince, and Other Stories.*

Rich, Barbara. "Short and to the Point." *The Women's Review of Books* III, No. 11 (August 1986): 12-13.

> Includes a favorable assessment of *Nine Women*. According to Rich: "*Nine Women* is Grau at the top of her considerable form: the prose spare, the characterizations deep."

Thompson, Sharon. "Long Time Passing." *The Village Voice* 31, No. 15 (15 April 1986): 52, 54.

> Praises theme and technique in *Nine Women*.

Yardley, Jonathan. Review of *The Wind Shifting West,* by Shirley Ann Grau. *The New York Times Book Review* (23 December 1973): 11-12.

> Praises Grau's depiction of contemporary life.

Additional coverage of Grau's life and career is contained in the following sources published by Gale Research: *Contemporary Authors,* **Vols. 89-92;** *Contemporary Authors New Revision Series,* **Vol. 22;** *Contemporary Literary Criticism,* **Vols. 4, 9;** *Dictionary of Literary Biography,* **Vol. 2; and** *Major 20th-Century Writers.*

Bernard Malamud

1914-1986

American novelist and short story writer.

INTRODUCTION

Malamud ranks as one of the most significant contributors to contemporary American literature. The fictional world developed in his short stories, most often urban and Jewish, combines elements of realism and fantasy and centers on the struggle for survival by characters who face the particular hardships of modern existence. Their survival depends on their ability to combat life's inevitable suffering by breaking through the barriers of personal isolation and finding human contact, compassion, and faith in the goodness of themselves and others. The typical Malamudian protagonist stumbles through this process in a tragic yet comic way, evoking both pity and humor.

Biographical Information

Malamud was born in Brooklyn, New York, to Russian Jewish immigrants. Much of his youth was spent working in his parents' grocery store, and critics contend that the Jewish-immigrant milieu of many of his short stories and novels was derived from these experiences. He attended high school in Brooklyn and received his Bachelor's degree from the City College of New York in 1936. After graduation he worked in a factory and as a clerk at the Census Bureau in Washington, D. C. Although he wrote in his spare time, Malamud did not begin writing seriously until the advent of World War II. Becoming increasingly aware of the horrors of the Holocaust, Malamud began questioning his religious identity and started reading about Jewish traditions and history. He explained: "I was concerned with what Jews stood for, with their getting down to the bare bones of things. I was concerned with their ethnicity—how Jews felt they had to live in order to go on living." In 1949 he began teaching at Oregon State University. While there he published two novels and his first short story collection, *The Magic Barrel,* for which he received a National Book Award in 1959. Malamud left Oregon State in 1961 to teach creative writing at Bennington College in Vermont, where he remained until shortly before his death in 1986.

Major Works

Themes of suffering and charity are typical of Malamud's most studied short stories. "The Loan," for instance, cen-

ters on the unsuccessful attempt of a widower to persuade an erstwhile friend and his wife to grant him a loan so he can obtain a headstone for his wife's grave, while "The Mourners" portrays the conflict between an elderly tenant—who suffers from the guilt of having long ago deserted his wife and children—and his landlord, who wants to evict him. The need for interaction with others is a major theme in such stories as "The Magic Barrel," in which a young rabbinical student who previously had devoted his time to study realizes that he has been hiding from life and that redemption can be found in love for another person. The commonality of human experience figures prominently in many stories, particularly "Angel Levine," in which the protagonist, a white Jew who initially refuses but then accepts aid from a black, Jewish angel, announces to his wife at the story's conclusion that "there are Jews everywhere." "The Jewbird" and "Man in a Drawer" deal respectively with the rejection of one's heritage and unwanted responsibility. In "The Jewbird," Cohen, an assimilated Jew, murders Schwartz, a Yiddish-speaking crow who symbolizes the Jewish traditions Cohen has rejected. "Man in a Drawer" centers on the reluctance of a tourist to smuggle the stories of a Russian writer out of the Soviet Union. Although Malamud does not directly address the Holocaust in his fiction, its legacy often informs the suffering of his characters. The protagonist from "The German Refugee," for instance, commits suicide upon learning that the Nazis have executed his wife who converted to Judaism after he abandoned her and fled to the United States. In the stories from *Pictures of Fidelman: An Exhibition,* Malamud addresses the relationship between art and life through an episodic portrayal of Arthur Fidelman's attempts to become a successful artist in Italy. As in "The Jewbird," Malamud's stories often mix elements of fantasy and reality. "Talking Horse," for example, features a centaur, while "Idiots First" concerns a confrontation between a Jewish man and the Angel of Death.

Critical Reception

In assessing Malamud's short stories, many commentators have examined his works in relation to American literature. Critics, for instance, have compared "The Jewbird" to Edgar Allan Poe's poem "The Raven" and the stories in *Pictures of Fidelman* to Henry James's stories about Americans in Europe. Others assert that many of Malamud's motifs and symbols have antecedents in Jewish folklore and Hasidic traditions. "The Jewbird," for example, features a talking animal—a common element in Jewish folklore—while "Idiots First" incorporates the common folk literature motif of a mortal in conflict with an Angel of Death. However, despite the preponderance of Jewish characters and subject matter in Malamud's oeuvre, critics argue that Malamud's stories extend beyond Jewish literature. As Leslie Field has explained: "[Just] as Hawthorne was never interested in merely portraying his characters in a Puritan society in order to dissect Puritanism, so Malamud has never been overly concerned with depicting American Jews in order to discuss Judaism." Scholars have also written extensively on Malamud's use of the *schlemiel,* or unlucky bungler, as a character-type, his combination of Yiddish and English to achieve a language rich in tension and ambiguity, and the allegorical nature of his stories. In summing up Malamud's short fiction, Jay L. Halio has remarked that "if [Malamud's] most characteristic theme is that of human suffering brought on by failed communication and failed charity, his typical response to such situations is an unsentimental insistence that the realities of human existence must be faced."

PRINCIPAL WORKS

SHORT FICTION

The Magic Barrel   1958
Idiots First   1963
Pictures of Fidelman: An Exhibition   1969
Rembrandt's Hat   1973
The Stories of Bernard Malamud   1983
The People, and Uncollected Short Stories   (unfinished novel and short stories)   1989

OTHER MAJOR WORKS

The Natural   (novel)   1952
The Assistant   (novel)   1957
A New Life   (novel)   1961
The Fixer   (novel)   1966
The Tenants   (novel)   1971
Dubin's Lives   (novel)   1979
God's Grace   (novel)   1982

CRITICISM

Granville Hicks   (review date 1958)

[*Hicks was an American literary critic whose famous study* The Great Tradition: An Interpretation of American Literature since the Civil War *(1933) established him as the foremost advocate of Marxist critical thought in Depression-era America. Throughout the 1930s he argued for a more socially engaged brand of literature. After 1939 Hicks sharply denounced communist ideology, which he called a "hopelessly narrow way of judging literature," and in his later years adopted a less ideological posture in critical matters. In the following excerpt, he favorably reviews* The Magic Barrel, *noting Malamud's concern with human responsibility.*]

Malamud's first novel, *The Natural,* published in 1952, was a wildly original extravaganza of baseball. In his second, *The Assistant,* which appeared last year, he wrote, with calm, deep assurance about a Jewish storekeeper. It is in the world of Jewish storekeepers and their like that most of the stories in *The Magic Barrel* are laid. In *The Assistant,* which seems to me one of the important novels of the postwar period, Jewish experience is used as a way of approaching the deepest, broadest problems of love and fear, of communion and isolation in human life. So, too, in *The Magic Barrel*: the more faithfully Malamud renders Jewish life, the wider his meanings are.

Malamud's stories often have a legendary quality, whether his method is realistic, as **"The First Seven Years,"** or fantastic, as in **"Angel Levine."** In these particular stories there are echoes of the Bible: the allusion to Jacob and Rachel in the title of the first, the paraphrase of Job in the opening of the second. He does not merely allude to legends, however; he creates them. [**"The Magic Barrel"**], for instance, seems to be the kind of tale that is handed down from generation to generation in a culture that depends on oral tradition. This and certain of the other stories appear to have been brought to the exactly right shape by a process of attrition.

His stories are varied, more varied than I had realized as I encountered them in magazines. **"A Summer's Reading"** has a deceptive simplicity that reminds me of Sherwood Anderson. **"The Lady of the Lake"** ends with a twist that would have amused O. Henry, though Malamud, needless to say, has not written it for the sake of the twist. Some stories are put together with textbook precision, but others pass themselves off as mere anecdotes. Although compassion is obviously Malamud's great quality, he has many resources, among them the comic inventiveness of such a story as **"Behold the Key."**

The question Malamud asks more often than any other is: what are the limits of human responsibility? In **"The Last Mohican"** he develops the theme with a rare combination of humor and pathos, whereas in **"Take Pity"** he approaches it by way of fantasy. More often he is quietly matter-of-fact, as in **"The Bill"** and **"The Loan." "The Loan"** will serve as an example of what Malamud can do. Here are Lieb the baker and his wife, aging and ill, and here is Kobotsky, also aging and ill, who asks Lieb for money so that he can place a stone on his wife's grave. That, in the midst of so much physical suffering, the three can undergo profound agonies of soul, Kobotsky in asking a favor, the others in deciding whether or not to grant it, becomes, in Malamud's hands, a triumph of the human spirit.

> Granville Hicks, "The Uprooted," in The Saturday Review, *New York, Vol. 41, No. 20, May 17, 1958, pp. 16, 39.*

Irving Howe   (review date 1958)

[*A longtime editor of the leftist magazine* Dissent *and a regular contributor to the* New Republic, *Howe was one of America's most highly respected literary critics and social historians. He edited several volumes of Yiddish poetry and fiction, and his historical work on Eastern European Jewish immigrants,* World of Our Fathers: The Journey of the Eastern European Jews to America and the Life They Found and Made *(1976), received a National Book Award. In the review below, originally published in 1958, he defines the stories in* The Magic Barrel *as realistic fables.*]

It is very hard to describe the stories in *The Magic Barrel* with any sort of exactness—and not because they are so weird or exotic but because they are genuinely original. Part of the shock of pleasure in reading them comes from the discovery that one's initial response is mistaken. One reacts, first of all, to Malamud's painfully familiar setting: the Jewish immigrant neighborhood of the depression years. Here, predictably, are the Jewish grocery-man dragging in cases of milk each morning, the Jewish baker slowly expiring over his ovens. Somewhat later in time comes the Jewish graduate student fumbling his way through Rome, eager to grasp knowledge of the Gentile world yet perversely oppressed by a strange Jew, an archetypal *nudnik,* who in his unqualified shamelessness represents the claim that each Jew has on all others: the claim of trouble.

Malamud's stories bring back, for a page or two, memories of half-forgotten novels: the cramped, grey, weepy aura of "American Jewish" fiction. But then one learns that Malamud is not so easily "placed," and that if it is legitimate to admire the care with which he summons the Jewish immigrant world, an important reason is that he treats it as no writer before him—except perhaps Daniel Fuchs—has ever done.

For in each of Malamud's best stories something surpris-

ing happens: it is as if the speed of the movie reel were crazily increased, as if the characters leapt clear of the earth, as if a Chagall painting snapped into motion and its figures, long frozen in mid-air, began to dip and soar. The place is familiar; but the tone, the tempo, the treatment are all new.

In what way? Malamud, as it seems to me, moves not to surrealism or fantasy but to a realistic fable in which the life cycle is exhausted at double-time: a wink, a shrug, a collapse. Everything—action, dialogue, comment—is sped up, driven to a climax in which a gesture compresses and releases an essential meaning, and the characters, hurtling themselves across a dozen pages, rise to a fabulous sort of "Yiddish" articulateness of gesture and speech.

Now, in any obvious sense this is not realism at all: the stories seldom plot along accumulating incidents, and they frequently diverge from strict standards of probability in order to leap-frog to dramatic moments of revelation. Nonetheless, their essential economy, the psychological pattern to which they remain loyal, can be called "realistic": for they aim at verisimilitude in depth, they are closely responsive to a serious public morality, they wish ultimately to indicate that this is the way things *really* are. Malamud spurs the realistic story to a pace so feverish as to leave behind the usual stylizations of realism, but the moral and psychological intentions that are typical of realistic stories continue to operate in his work.

This is a procedure with obvious dangers. Partly they are inherent ones, since his stories usually involve gambling everything on one or two paragraphs; partly they seem the result of a manner that Malamud shares with a good many other recent American Jewish writers: a jazzed-up, slapdash, knock-em-down-and-hit-em-again approach to language and action. In his inferior stories Malamud depends too much on hard and flashy climaxes, so that the most beautiful aspect of his novel *The Assistant*—its hum of contemplativeness, its quiet humane undertone—is not to be found here. And too often Malamud's stories seem excessively brilliant on the surface, a ruthless dash for effect, and then one has the feeling that one is being bullied and blinded by a virtuoso.

In each of Malamud's best stories something surprising happens.

—Irving Howe

But these are incidental faults, and at his best Malamud has worked out for himself a kind of story that is spectacularly successful. In **"The Loan,"** Kobotsky, an impoverished Jew, comes to his old friend Lieb, an aging and harassed baker, to ask for some money. Years ago they had quarreled, but still a spark of feeling survives. Among his other troubles Lieb now has a second wife, Bessie, who shares with him the tears of poverty and adds some salt of her own. Kobotsky begs for his loan on the ground that his wife is sick, but Bessie, who must make the final decision, remains unmoved; then Kobotsky tells the truth, his wife has been dead for five years and he wants the money to buy a long overdue stone for her grave. Bessie, who can identify with a wife in a grave more easily than with a wife in a hospital, begins to weaken. Gathering force and lyricism, the story now speeds along to its climax: through a device I shall not disclose, Malamud achieves another reversal, this time to show that Bessie's heart has again hardened and Lieb will not be able to help his friend. The last paragraph:

> Kobotsky and the baker embraced and sighed over their lost youth. They pressed mouths together and parted forever.

Now by any usual standard this ending is melodramatic and most improbable: Jews like Kobotsky and Lieb do not press mouths together. But in the story the ending works, since it embodies what Malamud could neither have represented through ordinary realism nor risked stating in his own right: the beauty of defeat as a kind of love. And the reason it works is that Malamud has prepared for surprise by leading us so surely from one moment of suppressed intensity to another that the burst of pressure which creates the final excitement also dissolves any lingering expectations of ordinary realism. It is for similar reasons that one does not find it disturbing that in the superb title story ["The Magic Barrel"] a matchmaker who has arranged for a meeting between a rabbinical student and his (apparently) sluttish daughter, should watch them on the sly, chanting "prayers for the dead." Such incidents, in Malamud's stories, are not symbolic; they are synoptic.

At his best, then, Malamud has managed to bring together that sense of the power of external circumstance which so overwhelmed writers a few decades ago and the concern of more recent writers for the gratuitous sign that declares a man's humanity even as it is being crushed. The settings contribute an atmosphere of limitation, oppression, coercion: man is not free. The action and language preserve, through the renewing powers of imagination, the possibility of freedom.

Malamud is one of the very few American writers about whom it makes sense to say that his work has a distinctly "Jewish" tone. He writes as if the ethos of Yiddish literature, the quiver of *menschlichkeit,* had, through a miraculous salvage, become his possession. And he preserves this heritage with an easiness, a lack of self-consciousness, that makes most American Jewish writers seem local colorists exploiting accidental associations. Malamud can grind a character to the earth, but there is always a hard ironic pity, a wry affection better than wet gestures of love, which makes him seem a grandson of the Yiddish writers. How this has happened I cannot say, for my guess would be that Malamud does not have a close knowledge of Yiddish literature; but perhaps the moral is that for those who know why to wait, the magic barrel will reappear.

> *Irving Howe, "The Stories of Bernard Malamud," in his* Celebrations and Attacks: Thirty Years of Literary and Cultural Commentary, *Horizon Press, 1979, pp. 32-4.*

Samuel Irving Bellman   (essay date 1964-65)

[*Bellman is an American educator, biographer, and critic. In the excerpt below, he critiques earlier criticism of Malamud's fiction and posits that Malamud's stories depict a reconstructed, baneful society which is partially mitigated by his deceptively oblique but recurring themes of new life and redemption.*]

" 'A wonderful thing, Fanny,' " Bernard Malamud's poor little tailor Manischevitz tells his wife, who has just been resurrected by a Negro angel (at the end of the story **"Angel Levine"**). " 'Believe me, there are Jews everywhere.' " "Cronin," Malamud tells us at the beginning of **"A Choice of Profession"** (a recent story which is included in *Idiots First*), "after discovering that his wife, Marge, had been two-timing him with a friend, suffered months of crisis." These two tachistoscopic flashes provide important clues to the Great Malamud Mystery that has been beguiling readers for over a decade. Stated simply, the mystery is this: what is Malamud really getting at, in his weird hopespun stories of suffering storekeepers and a host of other insulted and injured types? His last books have been enormously successful with the critics and the upper middle-brow readers: *The Assistant* (1957) is one of the most talked-about novels of the postwar period, the story collection *The Magic Barrel* (1958) won the National Book Award, and his academic novel *A New Life* (1961) has also come in for a great deal of respectful praise. If it is too much to ask why Malamud should be singled out above such consistent prize-winners as Flannery O'Connor, George P. Elliott, and J. F. Powers (to name only three), since his books do not seem markedly superior to theirs, what then is the secret of Malamud's charisma or literary power?

Style, surely, it cannot be, for Malamud's diction is not seldom gratingly inappropriate. Contents then? At first reading, Malamud's stories generally leave the reader little to wonder about. The central figure is a drab, down-and-out little nobody who invites our instant pity (and sometimes contempt) because of his hard luck—Sobel the shoemaker's helper, Fidelman the expatriate art student, Morris Bober the unsuccessful grocer, Seymour Levin the novice college instructor, Marcus the weak-hearted tailor, Etta the Roman widow who is twice betrayed. Always, it seems, the central character is poverty-stricken—no money in hand and the wolf at the door. If money is not the problem, it will be a matter of another kind of poverty: judgment, perhaps, or resiliency, or even just plain luck. Harmonizing with the drabness of the agonist and many of the other characters is the dull and cheerless setting: skies are gray, buildings are ancient and decrepit, the entire prospect is at best depressing.

Malamud seems, on the surface at least, to be giving us the "natural history of man": man is born, man suffers, and then man dies. If Malamud sometimes stops short of this last step, he will substitute the perversion of hope: wanhope (despair), misguided hope, or miserable resignation. Even when the supernatural is invoked, as happens occasionally when Malamud resorts to allegory to dramatize the plight of his marginal folk, life is a pretty sorry affair. Once in a long while there is an almost unbelievable happy ending (as in **"Angel Levine"**), but the effect is that of a momentary respite on the part of Malamud's forces of doom: before long, we fear, things will be back to normal.

We used the term "at first reading." Malamud has a tendency to seed his tales and novels with all sorts of suggestive passages that prey on the mind and cause the reader to reread and rethink Malamud's experiments in misery. . . .

In **"The Last Mohican"** (included in *The Magic Barrel*) there is the shameless parasite and *Jewish Refugee from Israel,* Shimon Susskind, with his strange way of standing motionless, "like a cigar store Indian about to burst into flight." . . . At the end of **"Naked Nude"** (included in *Idiots First*) the reckless art student Fidelman outwits his sadistic captors and steals his own painting. "In the pitch black, on the lake's choppy waters, he saw she was indeed his, and by the light of numerous matches adored his handiwork."

In other words, there is something special about the coordinates Malamud chooses to graph man's progress along the road of life, and this particular quality—or series of graphic locations—contrasts sharply with the all-too-familiar story line of Malamud's fictions. Yes, the curve runs predictably from birth to suffering to death, or to false hope (or wanhope), but there are strange divagations in the curve, and it is a mistake to describe it only in terms of its origin, midpoint, and endpoint, as many have been tempted to do. Malamud, for all the apparent simplicity of his plots, for all the obviousness of his subject matter, is actually a very complicated writer, complicated enough it seems to have snared his reviewers into falling for easy answers to profound questions or meeting the Malamudian ambiguity of meaning by merely describing it, in oblique or fragmentary terms.

Malamud has been read as an allegorist, a fabulist, a romancer asserting the need of the modern American artist to transcend the stultifying realism or naturalism which has so restricted fictional art. He has been excessively patronized for his quaint Jewish themes, and stereotyped with baffled admiration. Thus Ihab Hassan in *Radical Innocence: The Contemporary American Novel* (1961):

> Malamud's vision is preeminently moral, yet his form is sly. It owes something to the wile of Yiddish folklore, the ambiguous irony of the Jewish joke. Pain twisted into humor twists humor back into pain. The starkness of suffering, the leaden weight of ignorance or poverty, the alienation of the Jew in a land of jostling Gentiles—all these become transmuted, in luminous metaphors and strange rhythms, into forms a little quaint or ludicrous, a bittersweet irony of life, into something, finally, elusive.

Understandably, it has become good form to take particular notice of the search-for-love aspect of Malamud's fictions, a feature that mid-twentieth-century writers (Graham Greene, J. D. Salinger, William Styron, George P. Elliott, etc.), following Erich Fromm and other public-relations-minded psychoanalysts, have made *de rigueur* in their studies of fragmented modern man in a pluralistic society. Thus Ben Siegel, in "Victims in Motion: Bernard

Malamud's Sad and Bitter Clowns" (*Northwest Review,* Spring, 1962), speaks of "Malamud's reluctance to give up on anyone. Each being is unique, responsible, imperfect, and redeemable. No one is beyond redemption, and in most instances love is the surest means of attaining it." And Jonathan Baumbach, in "The Economy of Love: The Novels of Bernard Malamud" (*The Kenyon Review,* Summer, 1963), points out that "Bernard Malamud, in his fables of defeated love and failed ambition, has extended the tradition of the American romance-novel, has made the form into something uniquely and significantly his own. . . . Malamud's fiction delineates the broken dreams and private griefs of the spirit, the needs of the heart, the pain of loss, the economy of love. . . . The amount of love a man is able and willing to commit to life is, in Malamud's universe, the measure of his grace."

With the appearance of Malamud's new collection of short stories, *Idiots First* (which contains material published between 1950 and 1963), it is possible to come to a clearer understanding of just what Malamud is getting at in his fictions, and of just what significance some of his less obvious or subliminal ideas have, set against the background of his gray, forbidding, Thomas Hardyan world. To begin with, Malamud appears to confront the reader with a reconstructionist view of society and man's position in it. Life victimizes poor Jews, does it? We'll make the best of it—*and* the worst of it—and let their tribe increase. But up to now Jews have been a vanishing breed? The same solution for both problems: safety in numbers, and spread the misery around. "Believe me, there are Jews everywhere." So in *The Assistant* Frank Alpine, the Italian delinquent, atones for all his wrongs to Morris Bober's family and then converts to Judaism, suffering the pain of circumcision ("The pain enraged and inspired him."). In **"Angel Levine"** we are reminded that there are black Jews too, and they are also capable of being hurt. And in the stories in *Idiots First* we are introduced to entire new categories of Jews—if they don't suffer themselves, they help others suffer: the butler and the Angel of Death in **"Idiots First"**; the father confessor, complete with cassock and biretta, in **"Still Life"**; the bird family in **"The Jewbird."** There is even another gratuitous conversion to Judaism, the German wife of a refugee critic in **"The German Refugee"** (after her conversion she is martyred by the Nazis).

Malamud's partial Judaization of society is a daring literary expedient at best. One of its most interesting features, the spontaneous conversion, is apt to cause resentment in otherwise sympathetic readers. Thus Ihab Hassan in *Radical Innocence,* comments ironically on Frank Alpine's conversion: "The act is one of self-purification, of initiation too, in Frank's case, but it is also an act of self-repudiation, if not, as some may be tempted to say, of symbolic castration." But there is a certain poetic justice in reversing the basic idea of Karl Marx's destructive *World Without Jews* or the "friendly" story by Philip Wylie some years ago in which all Jews suddenly vanish at the stroke of midnight, to the eventual shame and discomfort of their enemies. And there is the psychological element too (as indicated above), what Kenneth Burke calls the "socialization of losses"—a rhetorical device which minimizes an adverse circumstance by projecting it onto others. Still, the "conversion" theme by its very nature demands an embarrassing sentimental credulity from the reader. Thus Philip Roth's tale, "The Conversion of the Jews" (which appeared in *The Paris Review* after Malamud's *The Assistant* was published), in reversing Malamud's Judaization tendency reads like a hallucinatory tour de force.

Two special matters relating to Malamud's partial Judaization of society must be examined here. One is touched on in Milton R. Stern's review of *Idiots First,* "All Men Are Jews," in *The Nation,* October 19, 1963. Quoting Malamud to the effect that " 'All men are Jews . . . although few men know it'," Stern develops a reductivist view which encompasses *all* of society, not merely special categories such as converts, birds, and a number of other particular types. Malamud, Stern implies, brings all men down to a specified—i.e., Jewish—condition. "Malamud's compelling force as one of our major talents comes from his ability to evoke the sense of helplessness, anonymity and dislocation that besets the modern psyche. It is precisely in this sense that he identifies his Jews as modern everyman."

There is a charming academicism in equating Malamud's submerged Jewish *misérables* with the majority of humanity, which is more fortunate because it is less vulnerable to the besetting horrors of oppression, poverty, and privation. Jews and non-Jews both, it appears, can observe their common humanity in Malamud's fictions; since there is such a heavy Jewish cast in the various novels and stories, we move outward from the "Jewish problem" to the universal human problem, which is not very different after all. But such a reading of Malamud is precisely what was meant earlier by the suggestion that Malamud has snared his reviewers into falling for easy answers to profound questions or into evading the Malamudian ambiguity of meaning by partially paraphrasing it.

For example, one of Malamud's finest and most representative stories, **"The Magic Barrel"** (in the story collection of that name), deals with a rabbinical student, Leo Finkle, who seeks a wife but is unable to love. He tries a marriage broker, Salzman, and rejects all the proffered candidates. Finally, he discovers a picture of Salzman's daughter and insists on making a match with her—even though she has become a prostitute and her father will not hear of a meeting. So a match is made. "He . . . concluded to convert her to goodness, himself to God," Malamud says of Finkle before he nags Salzman into arranging a rendezvous. And when Finkle sees her, "her eyes—clearly her father's—were filled with desperate innocence. He pictures, in her, his own redemption." Familiar enough, in the experience of Western Man, from the allegory of Jerusalem the faithless wife and God's forgiveness (Ezekiel 16), the story of Mary Magdalene, and the traditional saintly-prostitute motif in Russian literature (Dostoevsky, etc.), to say nothing of modern American writers like Steinbeck? A surface familiarity, no more. Even recalling cases we have known in which men married prostitutes and there was mutual regeneration, this tale does *not* make kinsmen of us all, and is not translatable into universal terms.

Consider. Finkle, before he discovers the prostitute's picture, is acutely miserable because of the emptiness of his life—"unloved and loveless." "Out of this, however, he drew the consolation that he was a Jew and that a Jew suffered." Salzman is a weird, almost supernatural figure, half devil, half cupid or pan, who constantly shadows Finkle (like the unshakable Angel of Death in **"Idiots First"**) and in fact seems to have planned the match . . . even though he says his daughter has died to him, and, when Finkle meets her (under a lamp post), Salzman waits around the corner, chanting prayers for the dead. Such characters in so deliberately ambiguous a story are certainly not emblematic of the modern psyche. Nor are very many characters in *Idiots First*: a poor Jewish father contending against the Jewish Angel of Death (who goes by the name of Ginzburg); a Jewish storekeeper in Harlem seeking marriage with a Negro woman; a Jewish art student in Italy beset by adversities; a Jewish blackbird (who has other Jewbird relatives) victimized by "anti-Semeets" and later killed by another Jew, whose son he has helped greatly; another Jewish storekeeper who goes broke; a Jewish clothier who dies of a heart attack caused by a fight between his two employees, a Pole and a Sicilian.

In other words, Malamud's partial Judaization of society is so limited a process, involving as it does only special categories of individuals, that it should not be confused with a generalized process covering the entire population. But related to Stern's view in "All Men Are Jews" is the idea developed by Leslie Fiedler that American culture itself is becoming quite Jewish and that Americans *as* Americans are the Jews of the present age. Ever the class-conscious ex-Marxist ferreting out conflicts and social upheavals, pinning labels, and descrying portents of the coming societal revolution, Fiedler rises to extravagant new heights as he thunders home this view in article after article and even in his recent novel, *The Second Stone.*

Where Stern's reductivist view refers to the human condition, Fiedler's view relates to culture and politics. But Fiedler has simply come to see everything, including American literature, in Jewish terms. All of his cultural experience is recast so that it comes out Jewish, and even when he is dealing with a specifically Jewish work (i.e., Malamud's *The Assistant*) he must re-Judaize his material: "This is a book which ends with a conversion and circumcision of its central character to Judaism. What *The Assistant* really suggests is that, after all, Jews are the best Christians and that a good Christian might as well get circumcised and face up to this fact." Here Fiedler's point in re-Judaizing Malamud is that Malamud, like other contemporary Jewish-American writers, is de-Judaizing his material.

True, Stern's and Fiedler's extremist positions show what might be made of the plausible argument that Malamud extends his Jewish materials somewhat beyond their natural bounds. But Stern is quite unwarranted in attributing a *reductively Jewish* literary effect to Malamud just as Fiedler is unwarranted in crediting him with a de-Judaizing strategy: the cause of Christianity, after all, is hardly advanced when Alpine converts to Judaism. Yet there is a modest measure of usefulness in the generalizing views advanced by Stern and Fiedler, the usefulness of a discountable (i.e., partially salvageable) claim. To a degree, as Stern argues, Malamud's tales of Jewish suffering illustrate the miseries of all humanity (although Malamud's suffering Italians should not be left out of account), and to a degree, as Fiedler insists, Jewish writers, comedians, and toy and wine producers remind Americans of the Jewish cultural tradition, and the hostility Americans encounter abroad is reminiscent of the geo-political hostility long familiar to Jews. The usefulness of such arguments is reflected in the limited suggestive quality of the generalizations, not in their literal applicability.

But [in "The Jew as Mythic American," *Ramparts* (1963)] Fiedler is even more usefully suggestive in regard to Malamud when he pursues his class-dislocation scheme to a shocking conclusion: "At the moment that young Europeans everywhere (even, at last, in England) become Imaginary Americans, the American is becoming an Imaginary Jew. But this is only one half of the total irony we confront; for at the same moment, the Jew whom his Gentile fellow-citizen emulates may himself be in the process of becoming an Imaginary Negro."

This tendency, if that is the right word, seems to go back to a European work of fiction, Kafka's novel *Amerika* (published after his death in 1924), in which the crypto-Jewish protagonist Karl Rossmann, an incurable victim of persecution, bureaucracy, and mischance, applies for a job and after being ignominiously downgraded is asked his name. "So as no other name occurred to him at the moment, he gave the nickname he had had in his last post: 'Negro.'" One thinks of the Jewish jazz musician who undertook to live as a Negro in Harlem some decades ago, and of Norman Mailer's essay "The White Negro" (in *Dissent,* 1957). But even more significant here are two of Malamud's stories in *Idiots First*: **"Black Is My Favorite Color"** and **"Naked Nude."** In the first, a Jewish liquor store operator in Harlem repeatedly tries to assimilate with Negroes, only to be spurned and beaten for his pains. In the second, Fidelman the *schlimihl* art student in Milan, steals a Texan's wallet, is pursued by the carabinieri, and seeks refuge in a brothel where the debased brothel operators enslave him. In his spare time Fidelman draws. "Scarpio pointed to a street scene. In front of American Express here's this starving white Negro pursued by a hooting mob of cowboys on horses. Embarrassed by the recent past Fidelman blushed."

Is there a special point to Malamud's reconstructionist view of society, whereby non-Jews turn into Jews and some Jews begin turning into Negroes (**"Angel Levine,"** **"Black Is My Favorite Color,"** etc.), much to their discomfort? Yes, Malamud suggests. The world is losing its oxygen and becoming unfit to live in; people grow desperate in their plight (like fish out of water), turn black perhaps, sicken unto death, and make a pitiful spectacle as they fight a losing battle. Not all are affected . . . at least at the beginning. We see rich, pompous Jews (**"Idiots First," "The Cost of Living"**) and even some very ordinary types (Professor Krantz in **"The Maid's Shoes,"** Feuer in the dramatic sketch **"Suppose A Wedding"**) who appear relatively untouched by the lethal conditions in the atmosphere. This situation of decay and death, of selective, encroaching evil and its fey victims is not at all what

we have called the "natural history of man," suggested to the reader by a first reading of Malamud. There is an actual poison in the air, and some unfortunates succumb to it early in the game.

"The Jewbird" is a striking illustration of the baneful world that Malamud projects. "The window was open so the skinny bird flew in. Flappity-flap with its frazzled black wings. That's how it goes. It's open, you're in. Closed, you're out and that's your fate." Like a refugee from some nameless destruction Schwartz the Jewish blackbird seeks shelter in the apartment of salesman Harry Cohen, near the lower East River. Triply reduced as an earnest of what is to befall him, the winged Negro Jew (an inverted Angel Levine, doomed to ignominious destruction) cannot explain to the puzzled Cohens how he came to be what he is. Is he an old Jew changed into a bird by somebody? "'Who knows?' answered Schwartz. 'Does God tell us everything?'" From the outset Cohen hates him and tries to drive him away. Ironically, Schwartz came in the window because he was escaping from "anti-Semeets." Although he takes a liking to Cohen's dull-witted son and helps him out with his schoolwork, Schwartz is treated no more kindly by Cohen. Finally, after a campaign of terror Cohen severely torments the bird and then murders him. Afraid to leave Cohen's dwelling because the "anti-Semeets" would get him, Schwartz dies at the hands of a Jewish "anti-Semeet." Note: once doomed to blackbirdhood, the unfortunate but unsavory Schwartz has no basis for survival; one of his innumerable "natural enemies" will be sure to get him. It is his utter inability to change his appearance or his habits (he insists on remaining a smelly, unkempt moocher) that infuriates Cohen and drives him to murder . . . a murder without remorse, because to Cohen Schwartz is only an imposter and a *schnorrer*.

In Malamud's poisoned world the precipitating factor bringing on painful destruction is very often an utterly human event: the death or defection of a spouse. Once the family is no longer cemented together, the oxygen in the atmosphere thins out progressively and the surviving spouse finds it harder and harder to exist. If he (or she) does not actually die, life becomes a source of misery and emptiness and the individual is literally left gasping for breath. In **"Black Is My Favorite Color"** Nathan the Harlem liquor store operator courts Ornita, who rejects him not only because she is Negro but because of her husband: dead, he is still alive in her memory. "'Nat,' she answered me, 'I like you but I'd be afraid. My husband woulda killed me.'" And Nat's fruitless courtship brings her only suffering. The two Italian widows, in **"Life Is Better Than Death"** and **"The Maid's Shoes,"** are *twice* displaced and rendered wretched—after their husbands' deaths they take lovers who use them and leave them in a state of limbo. In **"A Choice of Profession"** a man with a well-paying job, "Cronin, after discovering that his wife, Marge, had been two-timing him with a friend, suffered months of crisis." He deteriorates and in the process harms a girl who comes to him for help.

In **"The German Refugee"** Oskar Gassner, fleeing the Nazis, leaves his Gentile wife behind and considers himself well parted from her. Then, discovering that she has converted to Judaism and been killed by the Nazis, he commits suicide. In **"Idiots First"** Mendel, with the hand of death upon him, begs tearfully for an instant's time to get his idiot son on the train, and sums up for the implacable Angel of Death his doomed life: " 'All my life . . . what did I have? I was poor. I suffered from my health. When I worked I worked too hard. When I didn't work was worse. My wife died a young woman. . . . ' " The same pattern is seen in Malamud's poor-little-storekeeper tales. He seems to treat the little grocery store as a man's vital center, almost like his spouse. When the store goes, the man goes too, or is permanently injured by the loss. *The Assistant* and some of the stories in *The Magic Barrel* illustrate this, and in *Idiots First* the idea is repeated in **"The Cost of Living."** "Sam and Sura closed the store and moved away. So long as he lived he would not return to the old neighborhood, afraid his store was standing empty, and he dreaded to look through the window."

But Malamud's reconstructionist view of society and 'poisoned world' prospect do not tell the whole story. The gray despair, the pogrom-colored chronicles of defeat are abated somewhat by another motif, generally presented in a deceptively oblique manner so that it seems almost to reinforce the destruction it is apparently designed to mitigate. This is the "new life" theme, representing the transformation psychology Malamud makes use of to give his down-and-outers a second chance, another "go." Even though the "new life" sometimes overlaps and seals the earlier, doomed life (**"The Jewbird"**), it is in this (occasionally muted) sanction of hope that Malamud's compassion, his almost undetectable optimism are to be found. And perhaps what has made Malamud's work stand out at a time when such alchemists of grace and love as Flannery O'Connor and George P. Elliott have written at length on the redemption of the lost is that Malamud's transformations generally demand less credulity on the reader's part, less acceptance of a specific religious dogma to account for the changes. Although Malamud does occasionally invoke the supernatural, his new lives have an inner consistency that does not embarrass the reader who is unwilling to accept suddenly an alien body of religious tradition (Frank Alpine's circumcision may possibly be an exception). If Malamud's ghetto tales of suffering and turning over a new leaf do not make kinsmen of us all, do not exactly represent emblems of the modern psyche, at least they strike a very sympathetic chord, and this is a sufficient achievement in its own right.

On the opening page of *Idiots First* Malamud has placed a quotation: "Women and children first. *Old Saying.*" Taking this in conjunction with the book title and the title story, it appears that Malamud is suggesting "new life" transformation possibilities for the traditional helpless ones: women, children, idiots. In **"Idiots First"** the moribund father Mendel engages in what seems like mortal combat with the Angel of Death, who is unwilling to extend Mendel's deadline; suddenly there is Divine intervention, and Mendel is at last able to assure his idiot boy a new life, in California. "Mendel found Isaac a coach seat and hastily embraced him. 'Help Uncle Leo, Isaakil. Also remember your father and mother.' " There is a slight

touch of Faulkner in all this. Aside from Faulkner's penchant for idiots, *The Hamlet* contains a scene in which Flem Snopes has the upper hand over the devil. And there is a touch of Malamud's own *A New Life*, in which another New York misfit will be reborn on the Pacific coast. In **"Still Life"** a new life is killed at the outset because the attitude of reverence that actuates Mendel is not felt by the parent. Fidelman's prostitute-landlady, as she confesses to him, took her uncle as her lover, became pregnant, and when the baby was born, threw it into the river. " 'I was afraid it was an idiot.' "

Occasionally the "new life" brings disappointment and death, or a new kind of misery, as in **"The German Refugee," "The Maid's Shoes,"** and **"Life Is Better Than Death."** In the first, Mrs. Gassner is reborn as a Jew, and immediately killed by the Nazis; her husband, realizing the failure of his "new life" in America without her, at once takes his own life. The last two stories concern hopeless, drab Italian women who take lovers—thereby transforming their empty widowed existences—but remain in a limbo state of squalor and alienation. Ironically, it is the "new life" in **"Life Is Better Than Death"** that proves the female agonist's undoing: learning from the lonely widow whom he has seduced that she is now carrying his child, Cesare flees, depriving her of the one satisfaction that made her early life supportable, fidelity to her faithless husband. In the dramatic sketch, **"Suppose A Wedding,"** a young engaged woman is on the threshold of forsaking her store-owner fiancé for a poor writer who seems capable of opening up a new world to her. To be sure, women, children, and idiots may be first, but all of Malamud's agonists are *theoretically* eligible for "new life" salvation. In **"Black Is My Favorite Color"** the liquor store owner is desperately trying to achieve it—through union with Negroes—but he cannot break through. The two antagonistic clothier's assistants in **"The Death of Me"** stubbornly refuse the new life (of amity and peaceful coexistence) that their employer urges upon them, and through their refusal cause his death. In the two Fidelman stories, **"Still Life"** and **"Naked Nude,"** the art student in Italy finally achieves a temporary love-union with the prostitute of his dreams, and realizes at last his long-dormant artistic powers, at the same time outwitting the brothel-keepers who have enslaved him and forced him to copy a masterpiece. But "new life" salvation in Malamud is generally a strictly academic affair.

Where does Malamud obtain the material for his fictions? The "Jewish mystique" theory by means of which reviewers have pampered, imprisoned, and dematurated Malamud (what might be considered a literary analogue of Betty Friedan's "feminine mystique" process which men have employed to keep women from achieving adulthood) would have it that he is bringing the riches of classic Yiddish literature, modernized somewhat, to our present-day "lonely crowd" society in which Jews are indistinguishable from Gentiles. Alfred Kazin, for example, in his 1958 review of *The Magic Barrel,* says that reading certain passages in Malamud, "I get something of the same deep satisfaction that I do from the great realistic masters of Yiddish literature."

Malamud, apparently, derives certain of his story lines from a great variety of sources other than the classic Yiddish writers. As most commentators are aware, his first novel, *The Natural,* is quite unlike his later work and derives quite obviously from Jesse Weston's recension of the Arthurian legend, *From Ritual to Romance. A New Life* recasts Joyce's Leopold Bloom as Seymour Levin. Malamud's Italian stories appear to owe much to Henry James. **"Naked Nude"** is a clever retelling of the basic idea he conveyed in "The Real Thing": the spurious becomes more genuine than the original. **"Life Is Better Than Death"** is a humanized treatment of James's ridiculously unreal graveyard lovers in "The Altar of the Dead." **"Still Life"** with its striking sketch (executed by Fidelman) of the Italian woman and her long-dead child, is a reconstruction, in part, of James's "The Madonna of the Future." **"The Maid's Shoes,"** with its familiar Malamudian theme of incommunicability ("Only two souls in the whole apartment, you would think they would want to talk to each other once in a while."), reads like a rewrite of James by Alberto Moravia. **"The Jewbird"** seems to hark back to Poe's "The Raven." **"Idiots First"** with its Angel of Death and midnight-deadline, is based on an ancient folktale; many years ago the essential idea was adapted by Al Capp for a "L'il Abner" strip. The "poor little grocery store" theme of **"The Cost of Living"** is a fragment of *The Assistant,* as are three of the stories in *The Magic Barrel* (**"The Bill," "The Prison," "Take Pity"**). Malamud has borrowed from himself also in **"A Choice of Profession,"** which is simply a de-Judaized version of a portion of *A New Life.*

The question of literary origins in Malamud is well worth raising, because his work—hypnotically compelling on different levels though it may be—is not without its chunks of poorly-digested derived material. To cite one more example . . . One of his most striking images, the beggar Susskind in **"The Last Mohican"** ("like a cigar store Indian about to burst into flight"), seems very much like a literary changeling. Susskind, in this tale which appeared in *Partisan Review* in the Spring, 1958 issue, may be considered the last honest man, honest to art and to conscience, that is. His Jewishness—and he is a refugee *from Israel in Italy*—heightens his uniqueness: Hitler has just killed six million Jews, and the survivors are fast losing their Jewish identity. An impressive picture. But in the Spring, 1955 issue of *Antioch Review* Samuel Yellen's story, "Reginald Pomfret Skelton," which deals with a lonely, fearful Jewish refugee professor at a midwestern university, describes the exile figure in this manner: "He himself, however, belonged to the Lost Tribe, those scholars cut off, alien, adrift, growing fewer month by month, a vanishing race like the early American Indian."

But Malamud's talent is enormous, and if his underlying symbolizations of a reconstructed society, a poisoned world, and a new life are not immediately clear to the general or the critical reader, there is still enough left in his haunting stories to cause the reader to brood for a long time after the stories have been read and reread. Who is strong in this life, Malamud asks, the unchallengeable Angel of Death whose "no" means *"no,"* or a weak, dying Job with a human millstone around his neck? Who knows

his rightful place, a wiseguy salesman kicking out a smelly old *schnorrer* of a Jewbird, or the intruder himself, who (like the "loathsome hag" in Chaucer or the frog prince) may be all the more worthy because he is so hard to put up with? The real question, Malamud makes clear, is who will give a little? 'Don't you understand what it means human?' shouts Mendel, choking the Angel of Death, in a Malamudian gesture protesting a blighted universe. 'Don't you know what it means peace, acceptance, humanity?' shout Malamud's characters mutely as they feel the corrosive rejection of their fellows. Love maybe is a lot to ask, but at least attachment or respect? Adele in **"Suppose A Wedding"** enters the room and discovers her parents in each other's arms. "Ah, you've been fighting again," she says sadly. And before that they have betrayed each other, again and again, just as Malamud's other story characters have repeatedly betrayed or been betrayed. But, Malamud shouts out to us, Mendel won *his* battle!

It would be well, though, if Malamud changed his pace and his style somewhat, perhaps even his subject matter. Not in the direction of his early baseball novel, *The Natural,* however; ever since that work he has managed a fairly tight control over his materials, except in the long academic novel, *A New Life.* It is just that his imagination of disaster is becoming a commonplace with the reader as it has already become a commonplace with the critics. " 'If a chain store grocery comes in you're finished,' " Kaufman tells Sam (**"The Cost of Living"**). " 'Get out of here before the birds pick the meat out of your bones.' " We can imagine what will happen here. And the disaster stories for which we can't write our own Malamudian ending after we've read the first few pages (**"The Jewbird"** perhaps, or **"Naked Nude"**) are all too few. Perhaps the forthcoming Fidelman tales which Malamud has promised us will give him the new scope he needs to utilize his fragile storytelling gifts. More than any other Malamudian character Fidelman is constantly growing, realizing himself, transforming his unsatisfactory old life into a more satisfactory new one. As for what Malamud must guard against, as he splices rhythms and catchphrases from any number of dialects to develop his future materials, he has

---

Theodore Solotaroff on Malamud's characters:

Malamud's figures have, or gain, an expert knowledge of suffering, whether in the flesh from poverty and illness, or in the mind from frustration and remorse. Their character is almost invariably formed by hunger, and they are connected to each other not by normal social ties but by a common fate of error and ill-luck and sorrow, of having lost much by their sins and gained little by their virtues. But their lives are suffused with an earnestness of feeling and are directed by an assurance of moral order which enables them to be cast whole and to restore the drama of conscience to fiction.

Theodore Solotaroff, in his "Bernard Malamud: The Old Life and the New," in his The Red Hot Vacuum, and Other Pieces on the Writing of the Sixties, *Atheneum, 1970.*

already sounded the warning himself. The narrator in **"The German Refugee,"** in observing the European exiles and their peculiar problem with English, remarks: "To many of these people, articulate as they were, the great loss was the loss of language—that they could not say what was in them to say. You have some subtle thought and it comes out like a piece of broken bottle. They could, of course, manage to communicate but just to communicate was frustrating."

Samuel Irving Bellman, "Women, Children, and Idiots First: The Transformation Psychology of Bernard Malamud," in Critique: Studies in Modern Fiction, *Vol. VII, No. 2, Winter, 1964-65, pp. 123-38.*

Lionel Trilling   (essay date 1967)

[*An American critic and literary historian, Trilling was also an essayist, editor, novelist, and short story writer. In the following essay, which was originally published in 1967 as a preface to "The Magic Barrel" in his anthology* The Experience of Literature, *he analyzes the symbolic meaning of the rendezvous between Leo and Stella in "The Magic Barrel."*]

Much of the curious power and charm of **"The Magic Barrel"** is surely to be accounted for by the extraordinary visual intensity of a single paragraph, the last but one, which describes the rendezvous of Leo Finkle and Stella Salzman. The glare of the street lamp under which Stella stands, her white dress and red shoes, and also the red dress and white shoes that Leo had expected her to wear (for this too is envisioned), the bouquet of violets and rosebuds that Leo carries as he runs toward her—these elements of light and color make a scene which is pictorial rather than (in the literal sense of the word) dramatic. Nothing is *said* by the lovers, the whole meaning of the moment lies in what is *seen*. Indeed, had a single word been uttered, the effect of the strange and touching tableau would have been much diminished. In their silence, the lovers exist only in the instant of their first sight of each other, without past or future, unhampered by those inner conditions which we call personality. They transcend personality; they exist in their essence as lovers, as images of loving. And our sense of their transcendence is strengthened by those "violins and lit candles" that revolve in the sky, as if the rendezvous were taking place not in the ordinary world but in a world of emblems, of metaphors made actual.

This concluding scene is striking not only in itself but in the retroactive effect that it has upon the whole story. The anterior episodes take on new meaning when we perceive that they have issued in this moment, with its dignity of pictorial silence, its dreamlike massiveness of significance. The absurd transaction between Salzman and Leo Finkle, Salzman's elaboration of deceit, the dismal comedy of Leo's walk on Riverside Drive with Lily Hirschorn, the odd speech, habits, and manners of the characters—all these sordid or funny actualities of life are transmuted by the rapturous intensity and the almost mystical abstractness of the climactic rendezvous.

The intense pictorial quality of this last scene is of course a reminiscence of the iconography of a particular painter. Whoever knows the work of Marc Chagall will recognize in "the violins and lit candles [that] revolved in the sky" a reference to the pictures of this modern master, in which fantasy suspends the laws that govern the behavior of solid bodies, giving to familiar objects—violins and candles are among his favorites—a magical and emblematic life of their own. Married love is one of Chagall's subjects; many of his paintings represent bride and bridegroom or husband and wife in a moment of confrontation at once rapturous and fearful. Even the kind of bouquet that Leo carries is characteristic of Chagall—James Johnson Sweeney, in his book about the artist, tells us that "flowers, especially mixed bouquets of tiny blossoms," held for Chagall a peculiar interest at one period of his life; they charmed him visually and also by the sentiments they implied.

The knowledge of Malamud's direct reference to Chagall is helpful in understanding the story. For Chagall is the great celebrator of the religious culture of the Jews of Eastern Europe. It is this culture, now virtually gone, having been systematically destroyed by the Germans and Russians, that poor Salzman represents in a sad, attenuated, transplanted form, and that has put its mark on Leo, who regards it with ambivalence, and on Stella, who has rejected it. It was a culture based upon a devotion to strict religious observance, of which the highest expression was the study of God's Law contained in the Bible and in the vast body of commentary that had accumulated through the ages. Assiduity in study and distinction in learning made the ground not only of piety but of prestige—to rear a learned son or to acquire a learned son-in-law was the ambition of every family concerned with its social standing.

The American reader can comprehend something of the quality of this life by bringing to mind what he knows of the towns of Puritan New England in the seventeenth century. The two theocratic cultures were alike in the intensity of their faith, in the omnipresence of religion in daily life, in the pre-eminence given to intellectual activity both as an evidence of faith and as the source of authority and status—if one recalls the veneration given to Mr. Dimmesdale, the learned young minister of Hawthorne's *The Scarlet Letter,* one has a fair notion of how the rabbi of an orthodox Jewish community was regarded. The two societies are also alike in the harsh and difficult view they took of life, in their belief that life is to be lived under the control of the sterner virtues. Neither can properly be called ascetic, for both—and perhaps especially the Jewish—held marriage in high esteem. But in both societies devotion to the Word of God implied a considerable denigration of the charms and graces of life and a strict limitation upon the passions.

The artist who portrays a culture of this kind will in all probability be concerned with the elements of feeling that it represses or denies; his partisanship will be with the graces of life and the passions of human desire. *The Scarlet Letter* is a case in point—Hawthorne directs all our sympathy to the doomed love of Arthur Dimmesdale and Hester Prynne rather than to the Puritan godliness that chastises it. Chagall depicts with affectionate reverence the religious life he knew in his childhood in the little Russian city of Vitebsk, but his representation of love is marked not only by the joy that is natural to it but also by the joy of its liberation from the piety that had held it in check.

The rapture of Leo's rendezvous with Stella [in "The Magic Barrel"] is not merely that of a young man's erotic urgency. It has something of the ecstasy of religious crisis—Leo is experiencing the hope of what he calls his "redemption." His crisis is the more portentous because he believes that his redemption will come to him through sin.

—Lionel Trilling

It is a great advantage to art to be able to assert its partisanship with passion as against piety and godliness; in the exercise of this preference the artist is necessarily dealing with a situation charged with high feelings. The passions of human desire probably gain in intensity, and they certainly gain in interest, when they meet with adversity. The love that proclaims itself in the face of strict prohibition has more significance for us than a love that is permitted and encouraged. And of the several kinds of illicitness in love, that which is prohibited by religion and called sin is likely to seem the most intense and interesting of all—it borrows something of the grandeur and absoluteness of the power that forbids it. The rapture of Leo's rendezvous with Stella is not merely that of a young man's erotic urgency. It has something of the ecstasy of religious crisis—Leo is experiencing the hope of what he calls his "redemption." His crisis is the more portentous because he believes that his redemption will come to him through sin.

For that Stella is sinful, that she is sin itself, is the judgment passed upon her by her father's tradition. Her father curses her, although he loves her, and he mourns her as dead because she is unchaste. He speaks of her as "wild," "without shame," "like an animal," even "like a dog." And the young man, bred to the old tradition, is no less ready to recognize her sinfulness, although his image of sin is not repellent but attractive: he eagerly anticipates Stella's appearance in a red dress, red being the color of an open and shameless avowal of sexuality. Red may be the color of sin in general, as when the prophet Isaiah says, "Though your sins be scarlet, they shall be white as snow," but more commonly it represents sexual sin in particular—one of the synonyms the dictionary gives for *scarlet* is *whorish*.

The reader, of course, is not under the necessity of believing that Stella is what her father makes her out to be—possibly her sexual life is marked merely by a freedom of the kind that now morality scarcely reproves. Her dress

is in fact not red but white, the virginal color; only her shoes are red. And in her eyes, we are told, there is a "desperate innocence." We see her not as Sin but as what William Blake called Experience, by which he meant the moral state of those who have known the passions and have been marked, and beautified, by the pain which that knowledge inflicts. This is the condition to which Leo Finkle aspires and which he calls his redemption. His meeting is with life itself, and the moment of the encounter achieves an ultimate rapture because of the awareness it brings him, like an illumination, that the joy and pain he had longed to embrace, and had been willing to embrace as sin, need not be condemned.

Lionel Trilling, "Bernard Malamud: 'The Magic Barrel'," in his Prefaces to The Experience of Literature, *Harcourt Brace Jovanovich, 1979, pp. 170-74.*

Ruth R. Wisse   (essay date 1971)

[*Wisse is a Rumanian-born educator and critic. In the following excerpt from her* The Schlemiel as Modern Hero, *she surveys Malamud's depiction of the* schlemiel *in* Pictures of Fidelman, *arguing that the character-type as well as Malamud's portrayal of it have become increasingly less effective.*]

The progress of the schlemiel as a literary hero was . . . seriously deflected by mounting opposition in the dominant culture, beginning in the mid-1960s, to liberal resignation. Ironic accommodationism, which was intellectually respectable a decade earlier, was denounced as a liberal plot to speed the advent of a fascist state. The Vietnam war, the most persistent war in American history, could not be stopped or contained by those who called it stupid, nor by those who called it tragic, nor even by those who called it genocide. Noam Chomsky and Arthur Schlesinger arguing in the editorial columns of *Commentary* over the meaning of the war seemed, for all their obvious sincerity and information, to be merely an updated version of the Tuneyadevke bathhouse philosophers. As debates lengthened and the war with them, impotence no longer served as proper comic material. The concomitant polarization of left and right in politics and the righteous anger of formerly pacific groups like the blacks and high school students and women, brought on a period of alignment, even a return to ideology. And all activism dismisses the schlemiel. Single-minded—not to say simple-minded—dedication to a particular cause or specific goal cannot tolerate a character whose perception of reality is essentially dualistic. The schlemiel, on his part, is too skeptical of visionary schemes to follow a messianic movement like Marxism and too wary of gloom to accept a fatalistic call like that of the black extremists who declare it is better to die on your feet than live on your knees. One European rabbi is said to have worn a coat with contradictory quotations sewn into the lining of his two pockets. On one side the quotation read: "The world was created for your sake"; on the other, "You are but dust and ashes." Out of the ability to sustain this paradoxical position and to wear such a coat, the irony of East European Jewry grew. But the lifeblood of irony coagulates when a society becomes either wholly optimistic or wholly pessimistic about human potential or God's.

We see the demise of irony reflected in the very literature that gave it such forceful expression. Consciously, or despite their actual intentions, American Jewish writers recreate the familiar character only to prove that he no longer serves.

One sad requiem for the schlemiel is composed by Bernard Malamud, in the six episodes that comprise **Pictures of Fidelman.** In much of his writing, Malamud has been attracted to the weak character for both his comic and tragic qualities. Levin begins *A New Life* when he is pissed on by an aggressive child, and his first lecture is marked by the unusual attention accorded to one who has forgotten to zip up his fly. Yakov Bok, whose surname means goat, is the tragic equivalent of Levin. In *The Fixer,* Malamud has dramatized the most classic case of victimization in recent Jewish history to prove the liberating effects of imprisonment.

Malamud's interest in the Jewish character has not been sociologically determined. Alone among American writers he has fixed on the Jew as representative man—and on the schlemiel as representative Jew. His Jewish Everyman is an isolated, displaced loner, American in Italy, Easterner in the West, German refugee in America, bird among bipeds. Though they sometimes speak with a Yiddish intonation, his heroes bear little actual resemblance to their coreligionists. Malamud's failing shopkeepers and starving boarders appear in contemporary fiction as a kind of anachronism; in the works of his contemporaries, like Wallace Markfield, Mordecai Richler, Herbert Gold, such characters are already subjects of nostalgia.

Malamud sees the schlemiel condition as the clearest alternative to the still-dominant religion of success. "The Morris Bobers and S. Levins in Malamud's fictional world succeed as men only by virtue of their failures in society" [Sidney Richman, *Bernard Malamud,* 1966]. There is, of course, nothing new about this opposition to success in American fiction. Anti-heroes from the pens of Henry James through James T. Farrell have reached the point of no return by climbing to the doom at the top. But some moderns, Malamud especially, have stated the case positively, for the failures, rather than negatively, against the successes. In Malamud's stories, the protagonist usually has the raw potential for becoming a schlemiel, that is, the potential for suffering, submitting to loss, pain, humiliation, for recognizing himself as, alas, only himself. This potential is sometimes realized, sometimes not. The hero of *A New Life,* S. Levin, wins what the title promises because he takes burdens on himself and follows the bungling path of the loser. A relative, H. Levin, in a story called **"The Lady of the Lake,"** changes his name and, as he hopes, his status to Freeman, but ends as a slave to his own deception, embracing "only moonlit stone," the symbol of deception. The character courageous enough to accept his ignominy without being crushed by it is the true hero of Malamud's opus, while the man playing the Western hero without admitting to his real identity—Jewish, fearful, suffering, loving, unheroic—is the absolute loser.

Pictures of Fidelman, studies of one more such protagonist, appeared between 1958 and 1969, a span of eleven years. At the beginning of the series of stories, the main character is another of Malamud's protests against what he calls "the colossally deceitful devaluation of man in this day." By the end, both character and author are dispirited, possibly because of an overly lengthy association, but more probably as a result of the growing difficulties in the culture of keeping such a character alive.

In the first episode, which reads like a Jewish parody of *The Aspern Papers,* one Arthur Fidelman, "self-confessed failure as a painter," turns up in Rome on a carefully planned and budgeted trip to prepare a study of Giotto. Fidelman has the good fortune to meet his "Vergil," a moral guide in the form of Shimon Susskind, who is "a Jewish refugee from Israel no less." The author's selectivity is nowhere more apparent than in this deliberate distinction between the Jewish type that interests him ("I'm always running") and the Israeli heroism which does not ("the desert air makes me constipated").

Alone among American writers Malamud has fixed on the Jew as representative man—and on the schlemiel as representative Jew. His Jewish Everyman is an isolated, displaced loner, American in Italy, Easterner in the West, German refugee in America, bird among bipeds.

—*Ruth R. Wisse*

Susskind leads Fidelman to a true understanding of his own schlemielhood, which is also the process whereby a man becomes a *mentsh,* as Hassan has so quotably put it. The unredeemed Fidelman's crime is his refusal to part with his suit. As he justifiably explains to the schnorrer, Susskind, "All I have is a change from the one you now see me wearing." Though Fidelman's crime is mere parsimony, and though he does give up five banknotes in his eagerness to rid himself of Susskind, the acts of withholding and of giving only under duress, confirm that Fidelman is unsatisfactory in human responses. He is too measured, both in taking and giving. He is even afraid of his passion for history: "This kind of excitement was all right up to a point, perfect maybe for a creative artist, but less so for a critic. A critic, he thought, should live on beans." Susskind takes it upon himself to be the visiting American's "guide."

Cruel to be kind, Susskind steals the budding scholar's opening chapter on Giotto, and as we later learn, consigns it to the flames. The disorientation Fidelman experiences after the loss of his chapter is the first hopeful sign of his development; his quest for the manuscript, orderly at first, then increasingly frantic, is accompanied by the disintegration of his former self. He cannot go on with the meticulous note-taking; he rearranges his studied schedule of travel, this time improvising; he frequents movie houses instead of museums, sees the prostitutes in the street, not merely those on canvas; and, eventually, tracking Susskind down, he is exposed to misery in a form and degree unknown to him before. Slowly, he learns.

The redemption is not complete until after a visit to Susskind's room, a visit from which "he never fully recovered." Fidelman brings Susskind the suit he has so consistently denied him. But Fidelman has yet to grasp the full interconnection between life and art. In return for his suit, Susskind returns the empty briefcase, revealing that its content, the Giotto chapter, has been destroyed.

"I did you a favor," says Susskind, "The words were there but the spirit was missing."

Vergilio Susskind thus leads Fidelman into the final humiliating perception of the failure of all he had previously aspired to as success. The acceptance of failure is the crucial moment of initiation, as when Yakov Bok accepts his imprisonment, or when Frankie Alpine accepts himself as Jew. Now, reconciled to failure, Fidelman can proceed to live out his comic humanity.

This first episode, called **"The Last Mohican,"** tells a fairly standard story, and we are all antipriggish enough to appreciate a bit of *Pull Down Vanity* [a short story collection by Leslie Fiedler]. A repressed American critic in ox-blood shoes with a neat schedule of inquiry is itching to be reformed, and nothing in the denouement is surprising or displeasing. But when Fidelman next turns up as an inferior painter, paying, like Gimpel the Fool, far more than he should for the privilege of loving an Italian *pittrice,* the theme of failure intensifies. Malamud challenges the last remnant of the hero-myth in Western culture, the myth of the artist as the final embodiment of that noble quest for purity and truth. Fidelman is not fearlessly independent but the enslaved toilet cleaner and copyist for a pair of small-time art thieves. Fidelman is not perfect in his moral radiance but a cheap procurer, and a not-too-successful one at that. Above all, Fidelman is a bad artist, as inferior a craftsman as the Bratslaver's simple man was a bad shoemaker. No matter how intimate his knowledge of life or how edifying his many adventures of body and soul, his art never improves. He works among compromises, with dictated subjects, tools, circumstances. This is a generalized portrait of the artist as schlemiel, a man drawn on the same scale as other men, small and silly, but involved in a recognizably human enterprise.

The adventures of Fidelman become increasingly zany, keeping pace with the subject's experiments in painting and the author's growing ambivalence about his character. By the penultimate episode, from which the book's title is taken, the frenetic, staccato pace gives the uncomfortable impression that Fidelman's time has run out, like a wound-up doll that is stumbling to a halt after a lengthy dance. The "pictures" are hurried impressions of the subject in real and imagined poses. While Fidelman does not seem appreciably different, the cost of his style of living has risen so sharply that the gentle ironies have worn thin, revealing much harsher ones: "Fidelman pissing in muddy waters discovers water over his head." Language, imag-

ery, and the hero, have lost the innocence of earlier episodes. The quick impression of church art, as summarized by Fidelman, is a house of horrors:

> Lives of the Saints. S. Sebastian, arrow collector, swimming in bloody sewer. Pictured transfixed with arrows. S. Denis, decapitated. Pictured holding his head. S. Agatha, breasts shorn clean running enflamed. Painted carrying both bloody breasts in white salver. S. Stephen crowned with rocks. Shown stoned. S. Lucy tearing out eyes for suitor smitten by same. Portrayed bearing two-eyed omelet on dish . . .

The artist's vision runs amok. Withdrawing completely from representational art, and from human life, Fidelman tries digging perfect holes, travelling from place to place with his mobile exhibition. The holes are graves, the death of expression. Fidelman's soul is in obvious danger, and as in the opening story, Susskind appears as savior. There, events were plotted realistically, and if certain images rose to the level of symbols, they were still embedded in the actual events of the story. But by this point the lines between realism and symbolism have disappeared, as in the mind of one who can no longer accurately distinguish between fact and fancy. Susskind is Sussking, the reincarnated Christ, preaching the new gospel. "Tell the truth. Don't cheat. If its easy it don't mean its good. Be kind, specially to those that they got less than you." Fidelman in this frame is the guilt-ridden Judas who sells his redeemer for thirty-nine pieces of silver and "runneth out to buy paints, brushes, canvas." The morality of the artist is the betrayal of goodness. The final "picture" has Fidelman as "the painter in the cave," an artistic Plato, trying to capture pure ideas in pure geometric designs. Susskind reappears in the cave of shadows as the source of light—a one-hundred-watt light bulb. The bulb is the Hebraic light giving out its moral message to the Hellenized painter, telling him to go upstairs to "say hello to your poor sister who hasn't seen you in years." Bessie, his source of support over the years, is dying, and it would make her so happy to see her brother Arthur again. At first Fidelman insists on staying put and painting out his perfect truths on the walls of the cave, but eventually he gives up his "graven images" long enough to fulfill his obligation, to go upstairs and say his last goodbye. "Bessie died and rose to heaven, holding in her heart her brother's hello." The standard bedside leave-taking, although here in a parodistic form, does not entirely cancel out the underlying seriousness of Fidelman's decision. The closing line is "natura, morta. Still life," echo of a previous motif, the counterpoint of dead nature, yet still, life.

Because he is a human animal, the artist dare not deal in Platonic purities; there is someone dying in the room upstairs to whom he is accountable and whose imperfections he shares. To live within the comedy of human limitation, while striving to create the aesthetic verities in some eternal form—that is the artistic equivalent to the schlemiel's suspension between despair and hope. Between the house of horrors that opens the story—art like Francis Bacon's that lingers over the brutal and the grotesque—and the escape from reality, represented by the empty holes and geometric forms to which Fidelman turns for solace, lies the real task of art, the confrontation with Bessie. From her Fidelman first escaped to Rome, and it is to her, to the "too complicated" (repeated three times) past that she represents that he returns. But the prolonged unwillingness of Fidelman to leave his purities, and the tortured difficulties of the style, point strongly to the increasing difficulty of maintaining schlemiel irony. In fact, the concluding episode called **"Glass Blower of Venice,"** is a labored story, dragging its sad weight along much as its hero drags his customers piggyback across the flooded piazza.

Fidelman enters his final metamorphosis, as craftsman and bisexual lover. Not finding everything he seeks in the mythical Margherita, he is taken over by her husband, Beppo. "Fidelman had never in his life said 'I love you' without reservation to anyone. He said it to Beppo. If that's the way it works, that's the way it works. Better love than no love. If you sneeze at life it backs off and instead of fruits you're holding a bone." A homosexual with hemorrhoids is the contemporary candidate for the role of victimized male, seeing that representations of the cuckold and rejected suitor are outworn. By taking upon himself the burden of this unsanctioned love, Fidelman becomes a still more faithful human adventurer, for only the man with the heaviest load is, according to Malamud's perception, the realized being.

What distinguishes this story from earlier ones is its utterly cheerless tone, and its fatal self-consciousness. As if holding the bone were insufficient, Fidelman learns to love his man as he learns to blow glass. The two are one, and the paragraph describing this double education ends with the prescription: "If you knew how, you could blow anything," the author blowing up his own metaphor with a rude bray. Beppo slashes up all Fidelman's canvases on the theory that no art is better than bad art, and by accepting this harsh judgment the painter is supposed to prove his mastery over a bad fate. Beppo, like Susskind, teaches the gospel of failure as the beginning of wisdom.

Fidelman, now the wiser adventurer, returns home where, we are told, "he worked as a craftsman in glass and loved men and women." Yet this time the internal evidence of the story is unconvincing, and it contains nothing to warrant our faith in the upbeat conclusion. The life of Fidelman has grown as heavy as the punning. Humor has descended to scatology, from heart to rectum. The author repeats a process he has already described, but without conviction. Final pictures of Fidelman are of a comic strip caricature, a poor stumblebum whose failures remain unmitigated. The price of failure hardly seems worth the prize.

> *Ruth R. Wisse, "Requiem in Several Voices," in her* The Schlemiel as Modern Hero, *1971. Reprint by The University of Chicago Press, 1980, pp. 108-24.*

Christof Wegelin (essay date 1973)

[*Wegelin is a Swiss-born American educator and critic. In the essay below, he compares Malamud's treatment of such themes as life, art, and the American in Europe with Henry James's treatment of similar themes.*]

"What is an American?" The question asked by the French immigrant Hector St. John de Crèvecoeur even before the Revolutionary War was at an end has haunted many Americans down to our own time. Our colonial beginnings left us with the task of defining our national identity, and from the same source came the habit of defining it in terms of our deviation from European patterns—social, political, moral, cultural patterns—a habit reinforced by later waves of immigration. All white Americans, after all, have European ancestors. This is why until recently most of our major novelists sooner or later felt they had to come to terms with the Old World and why many of them have explored their relationship to it by writing "international" stories and novels in which Americans are brought in contact and conflict with Europeans and European ways of life.

One element is universal in this literature throughout the nineteenth century, whether we think of travel essay or fiction and whether the focus be aesthetic or social or political: the contrast between a new Western world where, to paraphrase Henry James, the forms of human life are being forged in a deafening daily present, and on the other hand, a Europe where the past lingers over the present like a dream made visible. The American view of this contrast has tended to have a strong moral flavor derived from the seventeenth-century Edenic vision of the early settlers. In the late nineteenth century, when more and more Americans travelled in Europe and their social adventures were recorded in the burgeoning genre of the "international novel," ignorance of the world and artless manners on their part were therefore given great moral value. But this view went under with other optimisms in 1914 in the cataclysm of what used to be called The Great War.

After 1918 the fiction in which Americans recorded their experience of Europe changed. The country-houses and genteel drawing-rooms of the pre-war decades, the realm of social conquest and of marriage between European nobility and American wealth—these were replaced by cafés, studios, fiestas, with their less eminent, more casual alignments. In the "century of the common man," private scenes gave way to public at the same time that relation-

---

Malamud on Fidelman and the schlemiel:

[Stern]: *Fidelman is characterized by some critics as a schlemiel.*

[Malamud]: Not accurately. Peter Schlemiel lost his shadow and suffered the consequences for all time. Not Fidelman. He does better. He escapes his worst fate. I dislike the schlemiel characterization as a taxonomical device. I said somewhere that it reduces to stereotypes people of complex motivations and fates. One can often behave like a schlemiel without being one.

> *Bernard Malamud with Daniel Stern, in "The Art of Fiction: Bernard Malamud," in* Conversations with Malamud, *edited by Lawrence M. Lasher, University Press of Mississippi, 1991.*

ships and roles lost their official and representative functions. The young American women of Howells and James, with their bright spiritual spontaneity, turned into the sophisticated, rootless, and sometimes deadly heroines of Edith Wharton and Scott Fitzgerald; tycoons and their wives were displaced by journalists and artists. The genteel society and the American innocence of former years still haunted a number of lesser novels often imitative of James, but the more prominent, the more original and more representative authors projected other scenes, other social elements and other themes.

Now, forty years later, we are even further along the road of historical change. Another world war, political and technological revolutions, and the cultural enrichment of the American scene have transformed the nature of transatlantic confrontation. In 1955 one of our leading quarterlies initiated a symposium to assess the state of American culture. The question of the American relation to Europe arose repeatedly, but the only thing that seemed certain was that transatlantic cultural relations were not what they used to be. Mid-twentieth-century America seemed less culturally deprived than the America of Hawthorne or James, Europe less compelling.

Fiction translates this general cultural view into dramatic and psychological terms. In the relations between Americans and Europeans contrast now is minimized. No longer is the American in Europe an innocent abroad. Having participated in wars and revolutions which have naturalized violence and cruelty, he has become an equal among the knowing, the corrupt. In this respect the difference between what followed the first world war and what followed the second is slight. The new relationship is documented by the fiction of Hemingway, Dos Passos, McAlmon in the twenties and thirties, by Hawkes, Styron, and others in the forties, fifties and sixties. The search of black Americans for their cultural roots poses a special problem, which may well help us to realize that the old transatlantic perspective is becoming less pertinent to the assessment of the American place in the world. But this loss of pertinence is implicit in much of the international fiction since World War I: generally speaking, the white American in this fiction is no longer in conflict with the European but at one with him in cruelty, anxiety, need.

In a moral sense, then, this late stage in the history of the American relation to Europe as recorded by the novelists may be described as a return from the western paradise to the world. If in the white man's version this history began in the seventeenth-century with the escape of the Pilgrims from the bondage of the Old World into a new Canaan and later into the moral health of Jeffersonian society, the return movement too began very early—first to the mementos and monuments of the American past in Europe (for example, in Irving), then to the social complexities and the intellectual and artistic resources our ancestors had abandoned (in Cooper, James, and others). And now, finally, it has come to the darkening condition of the human community independent of national variants. This last is frequently the subject of our contemporaries, even when they write about Americans in Europe.

Bernard Malamud is an interesting case in point. He is a sophisticated artist aware of his literary antecedents. Titles like *A New Life,* **"The Last Mohican," "Lady of the Lake"** may suggest this. His Italian stories contain numerous Jamesian motifs, sometimes in strangely Kafkaesque distortion, as in **"Behold the Key,"** where Rome remains as impenetrable to the American visitor as Kafka's castle is to K. **"Lady of the Lake,"** another of his Italian stories, stays even closer to James though demonstrating clearly the change a century has brought in the American consciousness. Like Christopher Newman, a representative American from James's early work, Malamud's Henry R. Freeman is abroad in search of romance. But whereas James's Newman lives up to the large implications of his name, Freeman is not really Freeman but Henry Levin, a floorwalker at Macy's department store. And his hope for a romantic marriage to nobility collapses, not because the lady he courts turns out to be only the caretaker's daughter, not because she is less than he imagined, but because she treasures what she has suffered for in Buchenwald, treasures, that is, the very Jewish solidarity which he has denied by changing his name. **"Lady of the Lake"** plays a variation on the traditional contest between natural and artificial aristocracy which James's Newman, one of Nature's noblemen, wins hands down. In Malamud, the lady's title may be spurious, but her innate nobility has been certified in experience; it is Freeman who turns out to be sham. The basic pattern of the story—the American's quest for romance and his discovery of reality—is traditional, but innocence has ceased to be the American's distinguishing mark.

Malamud's most extended and most interesting treatment of the American in Europe is contained in *Pictures of Fidelman* (1969), which unites three earlier stories of Arthur Fidelman, an American in Italy, with three recent additions to round out his career in what may be called an episodic novel. Some of the chapters again invite comparison with James's treatment of similar themes and in fact become more meaningful when the reader is aware of the parallels. But the moral ambience of the older writer is changed almost beyond recognition, indeed is changed so much that at first glance it may seem frivolous to try and fit Malamud's schlemiel into the traditional pattern. But when the attempt is made, the parallels and incongruities between Malamud and James reveal that the Fidelman cycle traces the very curve of the American's emancipation from his earlier roles on the international scene.

The search for romance, in life and in the stores of European art, and the discovery of reality, particularly the reality of the quester's own true nature and condition, are again at the thematic core. But Fidelman is an artist manqué and the particular form his search takes is determined by his bungling efforts to find his true vocation, his proper relation to the artistic life. As the epigraph from Yeats says,

> The intellect of man is forced to choose
> Perfection of the life, or of the work. . . .

But Fidelman wants both. And his story consists of a series of picaresque adventures in Rome, Milan, Florence and Venice, in which he tries to find his way between the demands of his intellectual and physical needs at the same time that a series of confrontations with various Old-

World characters leads him to self-realization—as Jew, as lover, as artist. Italy supplies the traditional locale of the artistic quest. But the divergences between Fidelman's experiences and those of his predecessors become increasingly emphatic from story to story; the tone increasingly ribald, Fidelman's adventures more and more indecorous, extravagant. His career is a burlesque of the earlier patterns of transatlantic discovery and can in fact be summed up as the transformation of a nineteenth-century American cultural pilgrim into a twentieth-century man stripped of genteel pretensions and *thereby* achieving the harmony of life and work.

We first meet him in **"Last Mohican"** in front of the railway station of Rome "absorbed in his first sight of the Eternal City." Although he is equipped in the best twentieth-century fashion with tweed suit and Dacron shirt his stance is old-fashioned, that of the innocent from the New World (perhaps the western barbarian or noble savage ironically suggested by the title) before the wonders of an old civilization. The concluding lines of the first paragraph make this clear: Fidelman "was conscious of a certain exaltation that devolved on him after he had discovered directly across the many-vehicled piazza stood the remains of the Baths of Diocletian. Fidelman remembered having read that Michelangelo had helped in converting the baths into a church and convent, the latter ultimately changed into the museum that presently was there. 'Imagine,' he muttered. 'Imagine all that history.'" The opening passage represents an American archetype and may remind us, for instance, of Hawthorne's sense a century earlier that in Rome all ages are simultaneously present. Fidelman is conscious of an exaltation and a role inherited from earlier Americans; the role has *devolved* on him. Malamud's choice of the verb is precise though quiet. That the role of representing the New World, the role of the Mohican, is played by the Jew, gazing in innocent wonder at a civilization after all younger than his own, gives the portrait added ironic point and helps to set the comic tone which is to dominate the book.

Fidelman's representative quality is underlined by his mission. Feeling that he has failed as a painter, he has turned to art history and come to Italy to write a critical study of Giotto. But the present will not let him indulge his essentially sentimental vision of the past. Almost at once he is pursued by Susskind, a mysterious refugee from Germany, Hungary, Poland, even from Israel, a Wandering Jew and incarnation of the reality of poverty and want. Susskind keeps demanding that Fidelman give him one of his two suits, a demand Fidelman refuses: "All I have is a change from the one you now see me wearing. Don't get the wrong idea about me, Mr. Susskind. I'm not rich," he says reasonably and truthfully. But Susskind keeps up the pressure and ultimately, in a dream revealing himself as the Virgil to Fidelman's Dante, teaches him that his study of the past has been an escape from responsibility, that the knowledge of the past must prove itself in the present. Fidelman has failed as art critic; his indifference to the refugee's need shows that he has not understood the lesson in charity taught by Giotto's Saint Francis, who gives his golden robe to a poor old knight.

This lesson is the first of many suggesting the interdependence of the two perfections, of the life and the work. It causes Fidelman to shed the inherited pilgrim's role. Other lessons follow until in the end he finds his own proper mode of existence and returns home.

> Fidelman's career is a burlesque of earlier patterns of transatlantic discovery and can in fact be summed up as the transformation of a nineteenth-century American cultural pilgrim into a twentieth-century man stripped of genteel pretensions and *thereby* achieving the harmony of life and work.
>
> —*Christof Wegelin*

In **"Still Life,"** the second story, he has gone back to painting; the investigation of history has given way to the creative exploration of his own experience. Still in Rome, he rents a corner in the studio of a young woman painter, and the story traces his progress as painter and lover. Landlady and canvas are equally resistant until one day, when Fidelman gazes down on the rooftops and monuments of Rome, still feeling a stranger to its elusive spirit, a thought strikes him: "if you could paint this sight, give it its quality in yours, the spirit belonged to you. History become aesthetic!" And if history, why not Annamaria, his landlady? "What more intimate possession of a woman!" But only when he remembers the lesson of the great masters and paints her as "Virgin with Child" does he succeed. Then he catches an immediate likeness, then he penetrates to the mystery of her soul: for she too has had a child, incestuously conceived and murdered in a moment of terror. With the aid of the traditional archetype, the Madonna and Child, the artist's imagination has discovered not only her beauty but also the guilt which she has never dared tell the priest. In a sense Fidelman has become her confessor. In a final tableau the physical and moral mingle grotesquely. He has dressed up to paint himself as priest, and seeing him thus, the woman is moved to pour out her guilt and demand that he impose penance; much, much more than prayers, she demands. "In that case," says Fidelman, "better undress." "Only . . . if you keep your vestments on," she insists. The cassock is too clumsy, but he agrees to the biretta, which must do for the Jewish skull cap. In the final act it is the Jew who possesses her, the Jew represented from the start by the emblematic Star of David concealed in his pictures possessing the Catholic Annamaria represented by an emblematic black cross always concealed in hers. "Annamaria undressed in a swoop," the story concludes. "Her body was extraordinarily lovely, the flesh glowing. In her bed they tightly embraced. She clasped his buttocks, he cupped hers. Pumping slowly he nailed her to her cross." The image, boldly merging crucifixion and fornication, represents his discovery of the Roman sense of guilt and of his own different nature. The story, it must be added, is, like the whole book, a masterpiece of tonal variations and atonal combinations—solemn, crass, ironic and mocking and always intriguing—which may puzzle us at times but which underline the change a century has brought about in the American exploration of Europe—in the nature of the quester and of his quest.

In the rest of the "pictures" of Fidelman the development begun in **"Still Life"** continues. Generally he grows in self-knowledge and courage as he declines in respectability. In **"Naked Nude"** he is held captive in a hotel run for the convenience of prostitutes by a brace of strong men, lovers, since in this modern and democratic seraglio the safety of the eunuch of old has been replaced by that of the homosexual. The price of his freedom is that he help them steal Titian's great picture of the Venus of Urbino from a nearby museum by painting a copy which they will substitute for the original. Fidelman does not like to steal from another painter, but his captors assure him that it is the way of art as it is the way of the world: "Tiziano will forgive you. Didn't he steal the figure of the Urbino from Giorgione? Didn't Rubens steal the Andrian Nude from Tiziano? Art steals and so does everybody." But Fidelman wants to be honest, at least to himself, and what follows is a variation on the theme of the vital relation between life and art. He tries innumerable schemes for producing the copy—painting over photographic reproductions, studying models of every kind—all without success until one day he accidentally sees one of the ladies of the house naked. The sight fires his memory and imagination and he paints every nude he has ever seen into his picture, every woman he has ever dreamed of or lusted after. Ultimately it is the life urge, including the knowledge that if he does not produce the gangsters will do away with him, which brings success in the artistic task. The nude he paints is "naked," as the title of the story proclaims, because it represents his own life, himself: "The Venus of Urbino, c'est moi!"

The liberation of the creative flow initiates the liberation of the man. First the gangsters give him his passport back, the official token of his identity. When the theft of the Titian is accomplished he is to receive his stipulated pay, the return fare to America. But the master stroke of the author and his creature is yet to come. At the last moment, in the dark museum, when the original has been taken off the wall and is standing next to the copy on the floor, Fidelman rehangs the Titian and steals his own copy. At this moment, he becomes superior to the accompanying gangster, knocks him unconscious and, sacrificing the promised reward, achieves his freedom—from more than his jailers. For by choosing his own creation he has chosen himself. The story ends, as many of Malamud's stories do, in a suggestive tableau: after the escape Fidelman unwraps the Venus in the pitch black night and "by the light of numerous matches adores his handiwork." This proud obeisance distinguishes him radically from his earlier self, the cultural pilgrim and art historian of his first entry on the European stage.

For five years **"Naked Nude"** (1963) seemed to record the triumphal end of the saga of Fidelman. Then Malamud took his burlesque odyssey up again, ultimately to bring him home, from Europe as well as from the existential solitude. **"A Pimp's Revenge"** finds Fidelman in Florence in need of further liberation, this time from apron strings, another tie to the past. If his struggle with Titian led him to an almost Emersonian declaration of independence from the courtly muses of Europe, his struggle with a childhood photograph of himself with his mother teaches him a lesser dimension of his nature. He is engaged in a dual struggle: trying to paint his masterpiece, a "Mother and Son," and finding the right relation with Esmeralda, a young prostitute he has taken from the street and set up housekeeping with. He takes a rather high tone with Esmeralda's former pimp. But as he finds it more and more difficult to live by his art, he himself assumes the pimp's role, condoning in himself what earlier he had condemned in the other. In all other respects, he settles into a comfortable bourgeois existence, summed up in a telling image: a checking account with the Banco di Santo Spirito, where Esmeralda's earnings are deposited. But while Fidelman the man may take his ease, the artist struggles. His attempt at the "Mother and Son" remains frustrated. Only when Esmeralda burns the fatal photograph and thus stops him from trying to paint himself back into his mother's arms, as she puts it, only then is the artist in him liberated. Then he paints with confidence, amusement, a sense of discovery. For almost imperceptibly his subject changes: "Mother and Son" turns into "Sister and Brother" and finally into "Prostitute and Procurer." In the course of these transmutations the face of the female figure changes too: first it was his mother's taken from the snapshot, then his sister's from memory, finally Esmeralda's from life. But the face of the male figure remains his own. And though he considers substituting that of the pimp, "the magnificent thing," Malamud tells us, "was that in the end he kept himself in." If the artist has again grown in self-realization, however, the man cannot live with his discovery, and the story ends in a macabre catastrophe. Goaded by the subtle poison of the pimp's faint praise, Fidelman ruins the painting by trying to improve it. The rest is one quick rush of destruction. When he discovers what he has done he smears a tube of black all over the canvas; Esmeralda, shouting "murderer," dashes at him with the bread knife; he twists it out of her grasp and in despair lifts the blade "into his gut." Esmeralda's *former* pimp reaps satisfaction from this revenge, but it is the act of Fidelman's own self-abused spirit.

Rehabilitation comes in the concluding story, **"Glass Blower of Venice,"** in which we find him recovered or resurrected but at any rate reduced to humble service as a kind of St. Christopher, carrying passengers piggy-back through the flooded squares of Venice. This useful function initiates his incorporation into the human community. He establishes "the first long liaison of his life" with one of his passengers, the wife of Beppo the glass blower. It is a relation of sexual convenience but in time accompanied by a friendship with the husband, which grows and grows until, in a scene of wild grotesquery, Beppo slips into his wife's place and he and Fidelman become *real* lovers. Never before has Fidelman loved anyone without reservation; now he loves Beppo. Beppo leads him to his real self, the place where perfection of life and work is one. He strips him of past artistic pretension, then proceeds to teach him the rites of love and the art of blowing glass. The two merge on the level of broad pun and of theme. In a page or two of descriptive legerdemain devoted to their work with the hot molten glass, every move they make is in essence sexual, "a marvelous interaction," Malamud tells us. For the first time in his life Fidelman works instructed by love in a medium which is his very own. The cant of theory and the false starts derived from imitation are left behind. Now he creates beauty not out of despair or desperation but out of joy. His education finally completed and partly in deference to the duty which Beppo owes his family, the American sails home, where, his story concludes, "He worked as a craftsman in glass and loved men and women."

In large outline the story of Fidelman conforms to the basic plot of international fiction in which the American goes to Europe, where he is tried and where his identity is defined. Not surprisingly, as a number of critics have noted, Malamud intones some Jamesian motifs. Doubtless he knows his James well. But *Pictures of Fidelman* is a portrait of the American specifically as artist, and the treatment of a similar theme in "The Madonna of the Future," one of James's very early stories, seems to have haunted Malamud. A comparison, therefore, may point up how the intervening century has modified the American relation to Europe.

James's concern with the nature of art is dramatized in the contrast between two artists in Florence, an American and an Italian. The American, an unworldly idealist who has Raphael's brain but not his hand, aspires to paint a "résumé" of all the Italian Madonnas, but dreams away his life in front of an empty canvas; the Italian meanwhile employs his manual aptitude in turning out unbreakable but suggestive and therefore marketable figurines of cats and monkeys illustrating the various combinations of "the amorous advance and the amorous alarm." Both artists get their inspiration from the same woman—the American in pure contemplation of an idealized image unchanged by time, the Italian in domestic intercourse with a mistress visibly coarsened by life. A similar triangle is at the center of Malamud's **"Still Life."** In each story, moreover, the woman, a "maiden mother" who has lost her child, represents a mundane version of the painter's holy subject. And the contrast between sacred and profane in each story bears on the central problem of artistic creation. James's American is incapable of realizing his idea in shape and color on canvas because in ecstasy before the magic of the old masters he has lost his eye for life; the Fidelman of **"Still Life"** from a similar preoccupation with the great images of art escapes into abstraction—until he realizes with what seems a side-glance at James's story that the "furthest abstraction . . . is the blank canvas," a dead end: "If painting shows who you are why should not painting?" It is only when the imagination and life interbreed, as in the portrait of Annamaria as an archetypal "Mother and Child," that painting succeeds, that is, that it moves by revealing truth.

If all this suggests that James and Malamud both see art as closely related to life, a theme we shall return to pres-

ently, their portrayals of the international scene differ profoundly: the moral distance between American and Italian has shrunk. And **"A Pimp's Revenge,"** in which the same triangle of characters recurs, demonstrates the loss of the dear old American innocence even more explicitly. Now Fidelman, like James's visionary, is in Florence, set on painting a Madonna but somehow incapable. The psychological action of the story traces his and our discovery of his true nature and condition in the evolution of his painting. And the macabre end of the process expresses his despair at finding that he has become morally indistinguishable from the Italian pimp, in fact his double. Even as artist he now combines the roles James assigned to his American and Italian separately. While he wrestles with his lofty subject, the natural demands of the body cause him to produce small carved Madonnas for the tourist trade. Unlike James's Italian, he keeps his commercial art respectable. But when machine-made products drive his from the market and to make a living he turns pimp, he more than matches James's Italian pornographer. Prurience now enters his artistic activities and the parallel with James's story becomes so specific that it is difficult to imagine Malamud unconscious of it. While Esmeralda is on her job Fidelman sits nearby, ready to protect her from unruly customers, meantime appropriately occupied with a sketching pad in which, Malamud tells us, "he sometimes finds himself drawing dirty pictures: men and women, women and women, men and men." James's practical Italian described his "dirty" figurines in an impertinent murmur, repeated as the final phrase of the story: "Cats and monkeys, monkeys and cats; all human life is there!" The reappearance of the cadence in Malamud's description of Fidelman's sketches underlines how far the American artist has travelled from his splendid vision. There are other moments when something close to a verbal echo accentuates the divergence. James said of his exemplary American idealist:

> A creature more unsullied by the world it is impossible to conceive, and I often thought it a flaw in his artistic character that he hadn't a harmless vice or two. It amused me vastly at times to think that he was of our shrewd Yankee race; but, after all, there could be no better token of his American origin than this high aesthetic fever. The very heat of his devotion was a sign of conversion; those born to European opportunity manage better to reconcile enthusiasm with comfort.

A century later esthetic and other fevers, allied in Fidelman, seem to have abated. Frustrated in artistic ambition Fidelman feels he "could stand a little sexual comfort"; and once he has settled down with Esmeralda, his whole existence is a picture of middle-class ease recalling the tableaux of James's Italian artist and model united suggestively at dinner or a late breakfast. "Shopping for food's a blessing," Fidelman thinks: "you get down to brass tacks. It makes a lot of life seem less important, for instance painting a masterwork." Though not born to the manner, he has learnt "to reconcile enthusiasm with comfort" like any European.

The contrast with James's story of almost a century before

draws our attention not only to the changed moral ambience and the shrinking of transatlantic differences but also to Malamud's concern with the relation of art and life, to Fidelman's refusal to choose between the two perfections. As we have seen, the question of their relationship concerns him in all his adventures; but only in the last one in Venice does he achieve their reconciliation when both are energized by love, and ambition and talent are one. Between the Florentine quest and the Venetian fulfillment, however, Malamud has interposed a fifth chapter, fittingly entitled **"Pictures of the Artist."** Unlike the other chapters, it is a surrealistic dream sequence, filled with allusions to historical painters, candid snapshots or jaundiced sketches of the artists ("I paint with my prick. Renoir. I paint with my ulcer. Soutine. I paint with my paint. Fidelman . . . Painting is nothing more than the art of expressing the invisible through the visible. Fromentin . . . ") There are allusions also to a multitude of paintings—a whole catalogue of saints, for instance— and to literary works, above all the *Chants de Maldoror* by that forerunner of the surrealists, Ducasse alias Lautréamont, with which this chapter shares the abandonment to the inner vision, to memory and fantasy. And finally, there are allusions to the other chapters in the book, more probably than he who reads and runs is likely to realize. One hesitates to speak with much assurance of the meaning of a piece as dense and in part obscure as this tour de force, but so much is clear: in all its variety of tones and modes it elaborates the central theme of the Fidelman story—the question of the relation of art to life. Let a single illustration suffice.

In a moment of frustration in an earlier chapter, Fidelman exclaims: "That's my trouble, everything's been done or is otherwise out of style—cubism, surrealism, action painting. If I could only guess what's next." Now, in Chapter Five, he has invented what's next. In his frantic search for originality he has taken to digging "spontaneously placed holes" in the ground which, when seen together, constitute "a sculpture." He exhibits them for a fee and proudly advertises them as "new in the history of Art." But when called on to explain himself, all he has is theoretical claptrap:

> Primus, although the sculpture is more or less invisible it is a sculpture nevertheless. Because you can't see it doesn't mean it isn't there. . . . Secundus, you must keep in mind that any sculpture is a form existing at a point radiating in all directions, therefore since it is dug into the Italian earth the sculpture vibrates overtones of Italy's Art, history, politics, religion; even nature as one experiences it in this country. There is also a metaphysic in relation of down to up, and vice versa . . .

Fidelman's listener, a poor young man who has spent his last ten lire to buy an admission instead of bread for his hungry babes, disagrees but is sent packing—only to return not long afterwards, transformed into a mysterious and threatening stranger. Now *he* initiates a metaphysical discussion of Fidelman's holes but without Fidelman's ostentation: "To me if you'll pardon me, is a hole nothing"; and he proceeds to prove his point by throwing an apple

core. "If not for this could be empty the hole. If empty would be there nothing." The Yiddish plainness underlines the contrast with Fidelman's vacuity. But Fidelman persists: "Form may be and often is the content of Art." Malamud himself begs to differ. Like James, he thinks of fiction as closely related to life and history. After Dachau and the Moscow trials, after Pearl Harbor, Hiroshima, Korea, Dallas, and Vietnam, "who runs from content?" he asked when he accepted the National Book Award for *The Fixer* in 1967. The rejection of "signification" in the novel, he suggested, would lead to its death: "To preserve itself [art] must, in a variety of subtle ways, conserve the artist through sanctifying human life." And while as a writer he welcomed "the invention of new forms that may bring the novel to greater power," he repudiated a theory which "ultimately diminishes the value of a writer's experience, historical and personal, by limiting its use in fiction." Content, in a word, "cannot be disinvented." Fidelman's mysterious stranger argues more palpably: "You have not yet learned what is the difference between something and nothing," he says. Then, administering to the horrified Fidelman a resounding blow with the shovel, he topples him into the larger of the two holes and fills it up with earth, thus extinguishing both sculptor and sculpture. "So it's a grave. . . . So now we got form but we also got content." And so, we may add, life and art are inextricably fused. It is the lesson Fidelman has to learn. And after the grotesque flashes of merriment and the methodical madness of Chapter Five, Beppo the Glass Blower teaches it in the positive way of love to a once more resurrected Fidelman in the last chapter.

His final adventure in Venice, as we have seen, leads this schlemiel abroad to the recognition of who he is: not the critic of Giotto, not the painter of traditional subjects or abstractions, nor the extravagant inventor of a totally new form, but the craftsman whose art is the product of the spontaneous response to life, and who is thereby enabled to bridge Yeat's division and achieve "perfection" in life and work. The quotation marks have become necessary, however, for the meaning of "perfection," along with much else, has changed since James, the imperative of self-fulfillment having at least in part replaced that of principle. In a general sense, Italy has served Fidelman as Europe has served Americans before him. But Fidelman's self-discovery is distinguished from those earlier ones in two important ways. For one thing, it is private instead of generic; it has nothing to do with the difference between American and European systems of government or society; it involves no international contrast. Fidelman has discovered himself as individual, not as American or democrat or natural nobleman. Nor is he distinguished by moral superiority, as the American heroes and heroines in James and Howells, for instance, frequently are. Far from staying aloof in critical detachment or native innocence, he meets his European counterparts on their own level. He picks pockets, makes love to bony chambermaids, pimps for his young whore, cuckolds Beppo and then becomes his lover. And he takes to the ways of this world he has entered like a fish to water, for it reveals to him what has been in him from childhood. "I am what I became from a young age," he says when he contemplates his self-portrait of the artist as pimp. Not that he judges himself, however. The very idea of moral judgment is foreign to this American in Europe. And this—that moral judgment is simply not in it—more than anything else characterizes the change from the earlier treatments of transatlantic confrontation. Fidelman's self-portrait is both example and symbol of this change. In the hands of James's American visionary the image of purity, the Madonna, had turned into the ultimate abstraction of the blank canvas; now it turns into the all too earthly-concrete "Prostitute and Procurer." To Fidelman the modern pair is no less sacred than the "Mother and Son" out of which they evolve:

> This woman and man together, prostitute and procurer. She was a girl with fear in both black eyes, a vulnerable if stately neck, and a steely small mouth; he was a boy with tight insides, on the verge of crying. The presence of each protected the other. A Holy Sacrament.

The change which has come over the treatment of the American experience of Europe expresses itself finally in a tone which frequently jolts the reader by the deadpan treatment of melodramatic or grotesque situations, the matter-of-fact coarseness which may sometimes tempt him to question the author's taste. At times one feels that Malamud is playing rather frivolously, not to say contemptuously, with his antecedents and with his audience. The defense that comes to mind immediately is that this dancing on graves, this affront of the reader's sensibilities, underlines the studied rejection of the idealism which characterized former American champions in the international contest and seals the loss of innocence.

> Christof Wegelin, "The American Schlemiel Abroad: Malamud's Italian Stories and the End of American Innocence," in Twentieth Century Literature, Vol. 19, No. 2, April, 1973, pp. 77-88.

Bernard Malamud with Leslie Field and Joyce Field (interview date 1973)

[*Leslie Field is a Canadian-born American educator and critic. Joyce Field is an American educator and critic. They have coedited two essay collections on Malamud:* Bernard Malamud and the Critics *(1970) and* Bernard Malamud: A Collection of Critical Essays *(1975). In the following excerpt from an interview which was conducted in 1973 and published in 1975, Malamud comments on some of his fictional characters and some of the major themes in his works.*]

[The Fields]: *I. B. Singer has said he writes about devils, sprites, and evil spirits—about the supernatural in general—because he believes in the supernatural. Much earlier, Hawthorne explained that he wanted to find some "neutral ground" for his fiction. Your use of the supernatural has been compared to that of Singer and Hawthorne. Do you believe in the supernatural? Do you look for a "neutral ground" in your fiction as you order your supernatural or fantastic worlds? Or do some other explanations apply to this world of your fiction?*

[Malamud] I don't believe in the supernatural except as I can invent it. Nor do I look for a "neutral ground" for

my fiction. I write fantasy because when I do I am imaginative and funny and having a good time.

In one of your early, infrequent interviews, we believe you said the Kafka was one of the modern authors who had influenced you. How?

He writes well. He moves me. He makes me want to write well and move my readers. Other writers have had a similar effect. I guess what I'm trying to say is that I am influenced by literature.

There has been much critical commentary concerning a statement you are alleged to have made: "All men are Jews." Did you ever actually make this statement? Do you believe it is true? It is, of course, a view one cannot take literally. In any event, would you elaborate on the "All men are Jews" statement?

I think I said "All men are Jews except they don't know it." I doubt I expected anyone to take the statement literally. But I think it's an understandable statement and a metaphoric way of indicating how history, sooner or later, treats all men.

Some have seen parallels between your work and painting, especially the spiral, mystical works of Chagall. This has been observed, for instance, in your short story "The Magic Barrel." *Elsewhere readers have remarked on your concern with the plastic arts in general—in* Pictures of Fidelman, *for example. What influence has painting had on your fiction? Have you consciously tried to fuse one art form with another?*

It's true that I did make use of what might be called Chagallean imagery in **"The Magic Barrel."** I did so intentionally in that story, but I've not done it again in any other piece of fiction, and I feel that some critics make too much of Chagall as an image maker in my work. Chagall, as a painter, doesn't mean as much to me as Matisse, for instance. Painting helps me to see with greater clarity the multifarious world and to depict it simply.

Saul Bellow, Philip Roth, Bruce J. Friedman, and other contemporary American novelists have rejected the label "Jewish-American Writer." In one way or another you have also. Nevertheless, you, the other writers mentioned—and one could bring in additional writers such as Chaim Potok and Herbert Gold—are still being classified as Jewish-American writers by many scholars, critics, and readers. It is our impression that the responsible people who place you and others in this category do not intend to reduce your stature or disregard the universalism they see in your work. They have simply categorized or schematicized as scholars are prone to do, much as one labels Faulkner a Southern-American writer because the spirit of place (the South) imbues his work or Graham Greene an Anglo-Catholic writer because a certain spirit of a specific religion permeates much of his significant work. How do you respond to this categorizing of you and your work? Would you reject the term Jewish-American writer categorically?

The term is schematic and reductive. If the scholar needs the term he can have it, but it won't be doing him any good if he limits his interpretation of a writer to fit a label he applies.

Bellow pokes fun at this sort of thing by calling "Bellow-Malamud-Roth" the Hart, Schaffner and Marx of Jewish-American literature.

Whether or not you accept the label of Jewish-American writer, would you not agree that your writing reveals a special sense of a people's destiny that more often than not cannot be fully grasped in all its nuances and vibrations by those who are not fully sensitized to that people or its destiny? On one level, for example, it has been said that one must be a Russian in order to respond completely to the nineteenth-century notion of salvation through suffering that is dramatized so well by Dostoevsky. Or that only blacks can truly appreciate the plight of black America. Could one not also say that only those who understand the Yiddishkeit *of the characters or the Yiddish milieu are able to respond fully to the silent communication between a Morris Bober and a Brietbart or between a Yakov Bok and his father-in-law, and so on?*

I'm sensitive to Jews and Jewish life but so far as literature is concerned I can't say that I approve of your thesis: that one has to be of a certain nationality or color to "fully grasp" the "nuances and vibrations" of its fiction. I write on the assumption that any one sensitive to fiction can understand my work and *feel* it.

Much has been made of the prison motif in your work. Do you see the prison metaphor as one that aptly describes the dilemma of modern man? If so, could you elaborate on this?

It's a metaphor for the dilemma of all men throughout history. Necessity is the primary prison, though the bars are not visible to all. Then there are the man-made prisons of social injustice, apathy, ignorance. There are others, tight or loose, visible or invisible, according to one's predilection or vulnerability. Therefore our most extraordinary invention is human freedom.

It has been noted that if one is to interpret your work correctly, one must not weigh Judaic interpretations too heavily. One must rather look to the Christian symbolism or perhaps the Judaic-Christian. How do you respond to this?

I don't know whether there is a "correct" interpretation of my work. I hope not.

You yourself have said that in your fiction you are concerned with humanity, man's humanism. Could you explore this notion somewhat?

I don't think I ought to. People can read; they can read what I say. That's a lot more interesting than reading what I say I say. . . .

The tension between life and art seems to be a major concern in your fiction. One could see it in some of your early work. And as recently as The Tenants *and* **Rembrandt's Hat** *it is obvious that this tension is still a significant part of your fiction. Of course* **Pictures of Fidelman** *is introduced by the epigraphs taken from Rilke and Yeats, and is followed by A. Fidelman's terse conclusion. Many would agree that life versus art is central to the Fidelman stories. Do you concur? Can you perhaps now probe in a bit more detail the life versus art theme as you see it?*

It isn't life versus art necessarily; it's life *and* art. On Fidelman's tombstone read: "I kept my finger in art." The point is I don't have large thoughts of life versus art; I try to deepen any given situation. . . .

At one time you mentioned that even though a number of years separate your first Fidelman story from the last one, when you initially created Arthur Fidelman you had plans that went beyond **"The Last Mohican."** *Can you explain why it was that they became a series of separate stories ultimately woven into a novel rather than a novel more in the form of* The Assistant *or* The Tenants? *Also, the name Fidelman. Some critics have played around with the name as symbol. Few, however, have noted that it is also your mother's maiden name. Was this choice significant or incidental?*

Right after I wrote **"The Last Mohican"** in Rome in 1957, I worked out an outline of other Fidelman stories, the whole to develop one theme in the form of a picaresque novel. Why do it the same way all the time?

I used my mother's maiden name because I needed a name I liked.

Has your wife's Italian background contributed to your "Italian" stories in the same way that your Jewish background has contributed to your "Jewish" stories? We are talking here more of an Italian and Jewish context, characterization, and rhythm of place rather than simply settings and people that happen to be Italian and Jewish.

Yes. I met Italians in America through my wife before and after we were married, and because she had been to Italy and could speak Italian like a native, we decided to live in Rome with our children in 1956-7. Through her relatives and acquaintances I was almost at once *into* Italian life and got the feel of their speech, modes of behavior, style. When I go abroad I like to stay in one place as long as possible until I can define its quality.

Do you read much of the criticism of your fiction? How do you respond to literary criticism in general?

I read here and there in criticism about my work when it hits the eye. I don't go looking for it. I like imaginative interpretations of my books, whether I agree with them or not. I enjoy criticism that views the work in ways I haven't anticipated—that surprises me. I dislike crap—criticism, favorable or unfavorable, that really doesn't understand what the books are about. I do take seriously insightful criticism of individual works that affirm judgments, negative or positive, of my own.

Does teaching interfere with your writing of fiction or does it help and complement in some ways?

I devote little time to teaching now—a quarter of a program, one class in the spring. Teaching "interferes" only in cutting down writing time. On a day I teach I can't write. But teaching helps more than it hinders. It gets me out of my study and puts me in touch with people. And I like reading, and talking about books.

I'm not arguing that the academic life is the life for a writer—often it restricts experience and homogenizes it; but I am grateful that when I was earning little or nothing as a writer, because of teaching, when I wrote I wrote only what I wanted to write. . . .

Are you very concerned with drawing prototypes and archetypes in your fiction as opposed to depicting realistic human beings? In other words, do you find yourself deliberately flattening out some of your characters much as a Stephen Crane would do or as a Cézanne would do in painting because you are at times much more interested in something beyond the depiction of a recognizable three-dimensional character?

I would never deliberately flatten a character to create a stereotype. Again—I'm not much one for preconceptions, theories—even E. M. Forster's "flats and rounds." Most of all I'm out to create real and passionate human beings. I do as much as I can with a character. I may not show him in full blast every moment, but before the end of a fiction he has had a chance to dance his dance. . . .

Would you agree that yours is basically a comic vision of life?

There is comedy in my vision of life. To live sanely one must discover—or invent it. Consider the lilies of the field; consider the Jewish lily that toils and spins.

Do you see a major shift in the point of view of your recent short stories collected in **Rembrandt's Hat** *as opposed to views you may have held when you wrote* **The Magic Barrel** *and* **Idiots First**? *There is still, of course, the concern with humanity or* menschlechkeit. *Is there more stoic acceptance in these stories?*

They're the stories of an older man than the one who wrote **The Magic Barrel** and **Idiots First,** possibly a man who knows more than he did ten or fifteen years ago.

Do you read more fiction or nonfiction these days? At any rate, could you give us some notion of your current reading?

I read a good deal of biography. I like some of the Latin American novelists I've been reading lately. I read too much half-ass American fiction and not enough good poetry. At the moment I'm rereading *Walden*. I'm also reading Jane Goodall's study of chimps, *In the Shadow of Man.* More than half of my reading centers around what I may need to know for my own writing.

> Bernard Malamud, Leslie Field, and Joyce Field, in an interview in Bernard Malamud: A Collection of Critical Essays, *edited by Leslie Field and Joyce Field, Prentice-Hall, Inc., 1975, pp. 8-17.*

Bernard Malamud with Curt Leviant   (interview date 1974)

[*In the following excerpt from an interview, Malamud discusses his early life, literary influences, and approach to writing fiction.*]

[Leviant]: *What sort of Jewish education did you get?*

[Malamud]: First let me give you some background on my parents. They were born in Russia, the Ukraine—in small towns—and came to the United States between 1905 and

> The Malamud canon is filled with . . . schlemiels, from the early stories of *The Magic Barrel* to his most recent novel, *The Fixer.* I suspect the most damning thing one can say about Malamud's development is that he has done little more than rewrite "The Magic Barrel" for the past fifteen years.
>
> —*Sanford Pinsker, in his "The Schlemiel as Moral Bungler: Bernard Malamud's Ironic Heroes," in his* The Schlemiel as Metaphor: Studies in the Yiddish and American Jewish Novel, *1971.*

1910. My father became a grocer and my mother helped him. Because of poor *parnosse* (livelihood) they stayed late in the store—

Like Bober in The Assistant?

Yes . . . My home life, then, was meager. I saw little of them in a family context, even though I helped out in the store when I was in high school. My parents, though sensitive people, were not well educated.

But like all Jewish parents they wanted their son to have an education.

Of course. There were Yiddish books at home which I was unable to read, and I regret this. In a way I feel I was gypped, just as I was when I didn't have the opportunity of learning music. But my parents did take me to the Yiddish theater. As a child I saw the plays of Sholom Aleichem and Peretz, as well as certain melodramas.

There was also a link between our family and the Yiddish stage. My mother's brother was a *soufflyor* for the Yiddish theater—one who prompts the actors from a booth at the front of the stage—and he managed a Yiddish theatrical troupe, Samuel Goldberg's, when it was on tour in Argentina. My mother also had a cousin, Isador Cashier, a well-known Yiddish actor, who performed in the original production of I. J. Singer's *Yoshe Kalb.*

My father was mildly socialistic and not religious. Usually, there were no synagogues around. So, then, as a combination of these factors, I received little in the way of a Jewish education.

Then you never went to heder *or Talmud Torah?*

No. I did go to *shul* with friends, but I was unable to read Hebrew. I was also never taught to read Yiddish.

But do you understand Yiddish? Can you speak it?

I can get along in Yiddish. If in Israel a lady asked me for directions, I could reply, but I can't make my way with more intellectual material. Once, when I was a student at City College, I wanted to go to a Yiddish club to learn Yiddish, but I was talked out of it. I was told to study Hebrew instead.

Did you speak Yiddish with your parents?

Yes. . . .

Have you done any reading in classical Hebrew or Yiddish literature in translation?

I've read Mendele Mokher Seforim, Sholom Aleichem, Peretz, Sholem Asch and one or two others.

Have you read Isaac Bashevis Singer's works?

Quite a few books. I came to him rather late.

And of Hebrew?

I've read Agnon and some of the modern Israeli writers including Mati Megged and Aharon Megged. I've also read Amos Oz.

Have you been to Israel? Have you thought of setting a story there?

I have visited Israel, but I can't set a story there because I spent only two weeks in Israel.

I assume you've been to Russia, because **"Man in the Drawer"** [*about a half-Jewish Russian writer*] *takes place there.*

Yes, I have. And look what I found in Moscow, a volume of Jewish stories in English by Ivan Olbracht.

Do you feel that you are part of a literary tradition? If so, is it American, Jewish, Western, or a fusion of all of these?

A fusion. I've read in all these literatures. A large part of my background is American literature. I've been "influenced" by Hawthorne, Melville, Henry James, Faulkner, Sherwood Anderson, Hemingway, and others whose works I've read with great care and interest. What I mean is that literature in general has influenced me, but American literature in particular. I also know something of the literature of England, France, Italy and Germany, and as I've said, I have read Yiddish literature and seen Yiddish drama.

What role does the Jewish tradition play in your work? I note, for instance, that your novel The Tenants *concludes with the Yiddish phrase* "hob rahmones," *followed by many lines of the word* "mercy."

I would say that my subject matter mixes the universal and the particularly Jewish. Some borderline figures in my work act under the influence of their Jewish background. I write about Jews because I know them. I'm comfortable with them. The interest in ethicality by the Jews has always excited me. The struggle against self is a basic struggle. Almost anything one reads touches on this. Also, the history of the Jews is a great drama. Obviously, it's not one of pure darkness. I also like Jewish history as a metaphor for the fate of all men.

There are times when I write about Jews but not about Jewish concerns. I'm interested in literature, profoundly moved by it. I've dedicated my life to it. I am a writer and I write what I know. I write what I have to write. A writer must be free to choose any subject matter.

But choosing any subject matter depends on time and cir-

cumstances. *Abraham Cahan, editor of the* Yiddish Daily Forward, *couldn't get his Jewish-themed work accepted by an American publisher late in the nineteenth century, despite intervention by one of the most influential American writers at the time, William Dean Howells. At that period, publishers simply wouldn't publish a work on a Jewish theme, about Jewish immigrants in New York City.*

I'm not talking about publication. I'm talking about writing. There are hundreds of Russian writers who write what they please, but only for the drawer. . . .

What besides their names and milieu makes your characters Jewish?

Their Jewish qualities, the breadth of their vision, their kind of fate, their morality, their life, their awareness, responsibility, intellectuality, and ethicality. Their love of people and God. Someone said recently that my characters are God-haunted.

God-haunted? I had supposed man-haunted was more accurate.

There are some characters who strongly believe in God. And let me add that I don't feel inhibited in inventing God-haunted characters, which has nothing to do with whether I am or am not religious.

Would you like to speak on how one of your stories came to be written? For instance, **"The First Seven Years,"** *or* **"The Jewbird,"** *or* **"Man in the Drawer?"**

I don't like to explain my stories, and as a rule I won't comment on interpretations of my fiction, so that students will feel free to interpret it as they please. I like imaginative interpretations of my books whether I agree with them or not, so long as they are consistent and make sense.

If the characters in **"Talking Horse"** *had had general American or, let's say, Irish names, would you have had a different tale?*

Yes, but I still might have had a Jewish story. Richard Fein, the critic, once wrote that there are three ingredients to a Jewish story. It has to have a horse, a victim, and loose technique. Since **"Talking Horse"** has all of these, I suppose it may be defined as a Jewish story. However, I don't think that's very important.

Why, then, did you choose to make the heroes of **"Talking Horse"** *Jews?*

Because I write easily of Jews. Of course, **"Talking Horse"** has some relationship to the Book of Jonah, and also to the Old Testament beyond the Book of Jonah. Incidentally, **"Jewbird"** [*about a talking Jewish bird named Schwartz*] led to **"Talking Horse,"** and I plan to do a third story with a talking animal, probably a short novel.

Could you categorize your stories as falling into any of these groups: stories from real life, stories spurred by other fiction, stories purely imaginative?

A combination of these.

There is obviously much blending, but could you give an example from your writing of any of these categories? For instance, I have in mind **"Silver Crown,"** *in your latest book* of stories, **Rembrandt's Hat.** *Wasn't that story based on a news item, late in 1972, I believe, that two hasidic faith healers had been arrested in the Bronx for conning Jews out of their money with false promises of miracles?*

Yes, it was taken from *The New York Times.* However, all the characters are mine.

In one of Hawthorne's prefaces, he defines romance as "a neutral territory somewhere between the real world and the fairyland, where the actual and the imaginary meet." Elsewhere, he states that romance is a piece of writing "wherein the author mingles the marvelous rather as a slight, delicate evanescent flavor. . . in which there is some legendary mist which the reader may either disregard . . . or allow it to float imperceptibly for the sake of picturesque effect." Can this version of romance as a genre of fiction be applied to your stories?

I believe that the link with Hawthorne exists, and so does one with Henry James, which critics recently commented on.

What foreign authors do you like?

Borges, Marquez, Böll, Gunter Grass, some of Solzhenitsyn, some of Jean Genet.

Do you do much rewriting, as Isaac Babel is said to have done: fifty versions of one short story, each version getting progressively shorter. Or do you work like Joyce Carol Oates, who conceives a work of fiction, then types it up rapidly without changing a word?

I am a rewriter. I rewrite a number of times. Imaginative richness is born in rewriting.

Thomas Mann and Shmuel Yosef Agnon set rigorous writing schedules for themselves. Of Agnon it was known in Israel that one dare not call him in the morning, because he did not like to be disturbed during his morning writing. Do you have a vigorous schedule of this sort? I recall reading years ago in The New York Post—*I think this was when you were at the University of Oregon—that you taught three days a week and wrote three days a week.*

Yes, I write mostly in the morning. I used to teach half a week and write half a week but now I write six out of seven days.

Have your stories been translated widely?

Into twenty-one languages in all, including a story into Chinese.

Nationalist Chinese or Communist Chinese?

Taiwan. I'm also translated and footnoted in Japanese. In one footnote, the translation of *Gottenyu* [dear God] came out as "God damn you!"

When did you first begin to write? Where were you first published?

I began writing when I was a kid in grammar school in Brooklyn. My first commercially published story appeared in *Harper's Bazaar* in 1950. . . .

Some of your magnificent end-lines sound as though they might have been the spurs to the entire story. (For example,

the first epigraph in **Rembrandt's Hat:** *"And an old white horse galloped away in the meadow" is by T. S. Eliot.) Have you ever constructed a story from an end-line?*

Yes, I have had experience of this sort. However, I reread the line from Eliot's "Journey of the Magi" after **"Talking Horse"** had been written.

Have you ever used your own fiction in your classes?

Never. And I have no intention of doing so.

Which is your favorite work among your own fiction?

I really have none, although there is some tendency to favor one's early work.

Do you see an inner cohesiveness, a miniature world, in your works—as for instance the world of Faulkner, or the world of Sholom Aleichem—with an ethos all its own?

I like to be told that I've created a world.

> *Bernard Malamud and Curt Leviant, in an interview in* Hadassah Magazine, *Vol. 55, June 1974, pp. 18-19.*

Lois S. Lamdin on the protagonists of Malamud's short fiction:

The heroes of Malamud's short stories serve as a convenient point of departure for understanding his use of the schlemiel, for Malamud's short fiction is of a piece with his novels, suggesting in miniature the motifs and themes which the novels, with their fuller orchestration, will develop in detail. The central figures of these stories are always men. (In Malamud's fiction women may attend the men in their sufferings, but they are peripheral figures who, although they may share in or even precipitate the catastrophe, stand in no essential relationship to it.) These men may be broadly categorized as of two types—those of limited perceptions and horizons who cannot articulate nor fully comprehend their state of being; and those of quickened intellectual powers and keen vision who, despite their acute understanding, nevertheless are trapped in their eternal victimhood.

> Lois S. Lamdin, in her *"Malamud's Schlemiels,"* in A Modern Miscellany, *Carnegie-Mellon University, 1970.*

Leslie Field   (essay date 1975)

[*In the excerpt below, Field examines the* schlemiel *as a character-type in Malamud's fiction and discusses the theme of growth through loss in* Pictures of Fidelman.]

From Roy Hobbs of *The Natural* and Frank Alpine of *The Assistant,* through Seymour Levin of *A New Life,* Yakov Bok of *The Fixer,* Harry Lesser of *The Tenants,* and on through many of the short-story characters—especially Arthur Fidelman, who came to rest in **Pictures of Fidelman**—one sees the Malamud *schlemiel* used to realize a variety of themes and motifs.

One continues to see the *schlemiel* in the recent stories collected in **Rembrandt's Hat.** In **"The Silver Crown,"** for example, a young biology teacher purchases a silver crown from a wonder rabbi for $986, ostensibly to cure his father of cancer. The father dies. In **"Man in the Drawer"** Howard Harvitz, a writer, leaves America to forget his troubles, and with all the great expanse of Russia, he is the one (selected?) to stumble on a Jewish taxi driver/author who pushes a forbidden manuscript on to him, one which can land the American in trouble much more serious than that he had originally tried to escape if he agrees to smuggle it out of the country. And in the story which gives the collection its name we have a final scene showing Rubin, the *schlemiel,* in the men's room "regarding himself in the mirror in his white cap, the one that seemed to resemble Rembrandt's Hat. He wore it like a crown of failure and hope." But of all the Malamud characters, early and late, one must return to Arthur Fidelman as the Malamud *schlemiel par excellence.*

Through the pages of various standard dictionaries one looks in vain for a workable definition of the *schlemiel,* that character who has become the beloved creature of Yiddish comic fiction. However, three recent books—two of them scholarly, and one a rollicking dictionary runthrough of Yiddish terms—do supply us with what the dictionaries, to their detriment, have failed to provide.

Ruth Wisse has written a compact, scholarly little book [*The Schlemiel as Modern Hero,* 1971] which may be subtitled "the birth and death of the *schlemiel.*" She traces the *schlemiel*-type of character in literature back to its East European origins, placing it in a socio-historical context, and then brings it up to date in the post-Holocaust literature of the Jewish-American writers, where, apparently, it had a brief flurry of popularity, reached a zenith in Saul Bellow's *Herzog,* and then died quickly with Bernard Malamud's ***Pictures of Fidelman,*** Philip Roth's *Portnoy's Complaint,* and the nonfictional *Making It* by Norman Podhoretz.

The *schlemiel,* she says, "is a character of folklore and fiction," but he differs from the usual non-Yiddish comic or humorous or even antihero character. Wisse analyzes the *schlemiel's* character in terms of several different categories. The "political *schlemiel,*" for example, is one who is always completely apart from or "out of step with the actual march of events." As far back as the Middle Ages the Jew was the actual or "potential victim" in a hostile society. In part, his vulnerability was used as a humorous shield to soften the brutality of an alien world. Wisse probes "the historical irony," "the fools of folklore," "the social *schlemiel,*" and the type known as the "Hassidic fool." For Wisse a folkloristic anti-intellectualism becomes the hallmark of the *schlemiel.* Humor emerges, for instance, when we have tales of fools in early Yiddish literature in which faith displaces reason. In hopeless situations for marginal peoples antirationalism becomes a sort of salvation. In effect, the *schlemiel* defines his own world, which bears no relationship to the world others know. Thus emerges a comic figure who seems to be a victim, but who, because he redefines his world, wins out in the end.

Both Wisse and Sanford Pinsker [in his *The Schlemiel as Metaphor: Studies in the Yiddish and American Jewish Novel,* 1971] see one strong double source for the Mala-

mud *schlemiel*—the nineteenth-century Yiddish writers Mendel Mocher Seforim and Sholom Aleichem. Why was the humorous figure of the East-European Yiddish *schlemiel* brought over to America? Wisse asks. Moreover, how did he manage to survive in an American fiction and consciousness in which the down-to-earth American hero from Davy Crockett to Hemingway was deeply ingrained? One answer, Wisse believes, is that World War II was America's last large engagement in which it emerged as a clear-cut "winner." The years following were far less decisive. Increasingly, America appeared in a complex, confused, and shadowy light. More and more it took on the image of a "loser." Thus the rejection in American life and letters of the Hemingway heroes. The ground for a short while became fertile for the re-appearance of the Yiddish *schlemiel* à la Malamud and Bellow.

Wisse believes that the heyday for the *schlemiel* in Jewish-American fiction was the fifties and sixties and that the chief practitioners were Malamud, Bellow, Isaac Bashevis Singer, and Bruce Jay Friedman. But she further believes that we reach a pinnacle in Bellow's Moses Herzog, whom she considers the most excellent example of a *schlemiel* as a "liberal humanist"—and then we go downhill.

When we reach America of the Vietnam War, racial strife, and violence, losing becomes too stark, too concrete, and the two-decade flirtation with the *schlemiel*-figure is terminated. Moreover, in the last third of twentieth-century America, it is no longer impossible for the Jew to succeed within the framework of the larger society. Humorous, passive figures must disappear in an active society. Thus does Wisse see Malamud's Fidelman, Roth's Portnoy, and even the real-life Podhoretz of *Making It* as sounding a death knell for the *schlemiel* in modern American literature and life. There is, however, some evidence to suggest that Wisse may be premature in any funeral arrangements she may contemplate for the *schlemiel.* For example, even as Wisse formulated her concluding statements, Bellow and Malamud continued to hone their *schlemiels*—as Harry Lesser of *The Tenants* took on Willie Spearmint and Artur Sammler of *Mr. Sammler's Planet* confronted his black pickpocket and exhibitionist.

Pinsker, in *The Schlemiel as Metaphor,* covers some of the same ground as does Wisse, especially when he discusses "the *schlemiel* family tree." However, he often sees the *schlemiel* as an important part of Yiddish folk humor, which in itself is an offshoot of the Hassidic movement of Eastern Europe of the eighteenth century, a movement characterized by joyous, popularized didacticism.

Pinsker and Wisse seem to agree that the *schlemiel* is an Old World phenomenon, and an uneasy immigrant once he appears in America. After all, they point out, failure was a way of life for the oppressed Jew in the Old Country. In America he could succeed. Thus all logic would indicate that the *schlemiel* on Main Street would be an anachronism unless he adopted a new style, which, according to Pinsker, must be an "ironic posture."

For Pinsker, the Malamud *schlemiel* can be seen as "moral bungler" or "ironic hero." The typical Malamud *schlemiel,* in Pinsker's view, is "a moral bungler, a character whose estimate of the situation, coupled with an overriding desire for 'commitment,' invariably caused comic defeats of one sort or another." And from **"The Magic Barrel"** with Leo Finkle through Frank Alpine of *The Assistant,* Seymour Levin of *A New Life,* and finally Yakov Bok of *The Fixer,* Pinsker detects the many nuances of the Malamud *schlemiel.* Pinsker sees Malamud refining his various *schlemiels,* his "moral bunglers," who move "haphazardly toward redemption." Redemption, however, Pinsker believes, is elusive for Malamud's *schlemiels* until it is achieved by Yakov Bok.

It is perhaps left for Leo Rosten in *The Joys of Yiddish* to balance the scholarly treatments given by Pinsker and Wisse. What or who is a *schlemiel?* he asks. One of his simple definitions is that the *schlemiel* is a foolish person, a simpleton. Or a consistently unlucky or unfortunate person; a fall guy, a hard-luck type, a born loser, a victim. Rosten recites a Yiddish proverb to illustrate: "The *schlemiel* falls on his back and breaks his nose." Or one sees a *schlemiel* as a clumsy, butterfingered, gauche type. He could be considered a social misfit, a naïve, trusting, gullible customer.

In Yiddish humor one often hears the words *schlemiel, schlimazl,* and *nebbish* used interchangeably. Rosten tries to set the record straight: "The classic attempt to discriminate between the [first] two types runs: 'a *schlemiel* is a man who is always spilling his soup—down the neck of a *schlimazl.*'" Or, to make a triple distinction: "The *schlemiel* trips, and knocks down the *schlimazl;* and the *nebbish* repairs the *schlimazl's* glasses."

A fairly common view is that the most comprehensive definition of the *schlemiel* has come from Golda Meir, the Prime Minister of Israel, when, not too long ago, she whimsically traversed time and space to encompass a whole people as *schlemiel.* Half in jest, Mrs. Meir observed that most of the world's oil was "in the wrong places." She said that "Moses led the Israelites through the desert for 40 years and ended in the one place in the Middle East with no oil."

When one listens to Golda Meir, Leo Rosten, Ruth Wisse, Sanford Pinsker, and many others too numerous to mention, one cannot fail to recognize one significant comic vein that Malamud mined through his novels and short stories. And this comic vein is Arthur Fidelman's heritage.

In addition to those of Pinsker and Wisse, one should consider four other full-scale essays on Malamud's *schlemiels.* The first, by Lois S. Lamdin ["Malamud's *Schlemiels,*" *A Modern Miscellany,* 1970], gives a general run-through of the *schlemiels* she finds in Malamud's work. "They are fit protagonists in a fiction whose central motif is the omnipresence of suffering, for they are born to suffering, conditioned by it, and ultimately find the meaning of their lives in learning to deal with it. As sufferers they serve as root symbols for the condition of man." Lamdin joins other critics in seeing the Malamud *schlemiel* as a victim, who "if he can learn through his suffering to accept the burden of his humanity, can achieve redemption." She concludes by saying that the major Malamud *schlemiels* "have used

their membership in the brotherhood of *schlemiels* as a passport to a higher order of humanity."

The other three essays deal almost exclusively with *Pictures of Fidelman.* Barbara F. Lefcowitz says [in "The Hybris of Neurosis: Malamud's *Pictures of Fidelman,*" *Literature and Psychology* (1970)] that "Malamud both depicts and parodies neurosis by juxtaposing two sets of values, the first composed of the private world of Fidelman as victim and obsessional neurotic, and the second of the socio-historical world of Fidelman as a victimizer."

[In "Structure and Content in Malamud's *Pictures of Fidelman,*" *Connecticut Review* (October 1971)] Robert Ducharme does more to place Malamud's book into perspective than any other critic. He sees "the themes of the book . . . as fresh restatements of the author's consistent humanism." But Ducharme devotes most of his essay to the form of *Pictures of Fidelman.* He describes the book as a "picaresque chronicle" or "a novel in the broad sense of Sherwood Anderson's *Winesburg, Ohio.*" Ducharme claims that the parts of Malamud's book "may stand as independent stories, but there is a definite sense in which they belong together . . . to form a self-contained narrative." He further points out that "the book is like a series of pictorial tableaux, each story an image of Arthur Fidelman." Ducharme concludes that "throughout *Pictures of Fidelman* the ideas of suffering and responsibility have played a subtle and important thematic counterpoint to the central character's overriding quest for success in life and art. These themes and the character of Fidelman himself have drawn these six stories together into a loose novelistic unity they would not otherwise have."

Christof Wegelin in his opening lines re-asks the question "What is an American?" posed early in our history by Crèvecoeur. It was raised then in the context of Old World vs. New World standards, and as Wegelin points out [in "The American *Schlemiel* Abroad: Malamud's Italian Stories and the End of American Innocence," *Twentieth-Century Literature* (April 1973)], major American writers from Henry James through Scott Fitzgerald have used that same context. But there has been a change. A change from the innocent abroad to parity abroad. "Generally speaking, the White American in this fiction is no longer in conflict with the European but at one with him in cruelty, anxiety, need." Wegelin goes on to use Fidelman as his "case in point."

The collection of six stories called *Pictures of Fidelman* appeared in 1969, but the first of these, **"The Last Mohican,"** dates back to 1958. Two others were included in Malamud's second collection. Two of the final three were printed later in magazines, and then all were brought together in a somewhat revised form as *Pictures of Fidelman: An Exhibition.*

We have in this collection or novel Malamud's antihero—Arthur Fidelman—conceived about fifteen years ago in **"The Last Mohican"** as a young Jewish-American art critic in Rome, who continued his adolescence as a would-be artist in Rome and Milan in **"Still Life"** and **"Naked Nude,"** achieved *schlemieldom's* young manhood—still as artist—in other Italian cities (in **"A Pimp's Revenge"** and

"Pictures of the Artist") and, finally, emerged as an adult artist-*schlemiel* in Venice. This was in the last story, **"Glass Blower of Venice,"** where, ostensibly, our *schlemiel* discovers life and the true meaning of love, gives up art *per se,* and goes back to America to become a *mentsch* or human being.

So ends the sage of Arthur Fidelman—or is it only the beginning of an understanding not only of this book, but of much of the rest of Malamud?

Had Malamud simply given us the Yiddish figure of the *schlemiel,* we might have ended with farce or slapstick. However, in this story sequence, as in the novels, Malamud seems intent on unfolding his themes bit by bit as he reveals character. Fidelman's habitual pattern is that of apprenticeship or education. And the subgenre he is part of falls into that category which has been distinguished, by German criticism at least, as the *Bildungsroman.*

We are in effect dealing with a sequence of stories or a novel focusing on development of character. When this development is confined to the professional sphere of the developing novelist or artist—the story tracing the growth of a hero as creative man—we have a *Kunstlerroman.* The more common term is *Bildungsroman.* The term applies to **Pictures of Fidelman** as it does to James Joyce's *A Portrait of the Artist as a Young Man* and Thomas Wolfe's *Look Homeward, Angel,* even though Fidelman's destination is not that of Stephen Dedalus or Eugene Gant.

The form of **Pictures of Fidelman** may be closer to that of Mark Twain's *Huck Finn* in that we have a combination of two subgenres: the *Picaresque* and *Bildungsroman:* i.e., the one portraying the episodic, seemingly indiscriminate movement of a character from place to place, and the other showing the growth of a central character amidst swirls of experience. In Malamud all is infused with the comic tone—the Jewish-American *schlemiel* in Italy working out and having his destiny worked out for him as he moves to ultimate discovery of self—and possibly salvation. Perhaps Arthur Fidelman is really not Huck Finn at all but rather Don Quixote. Or a Sholom Aleichem character. Or a younger Reb Yudel of S. Y. Agnon's *The Bridal Canopy.*

Pictures of Fidelman is introduced by three epigraphs, the first by Rilke: "*Not to Understand.* Yes, that was my whole occupation during those years—I can assure you, it was not an easy one." The second is from Yeats: "The Intellect of man is forced to choose Perfection of the life, or of the work . . ." And the third is the terse utterance from Fidelman himself: "Both."

If we trace our *schlemiel*-hero through the various stories we can see him as through a prism: many different reflections. The six stories are six episodes or pictures, which taken together form a portrait.

The first picture [**"The Last Mohican"**] is taken in Rome. Young Fidelman, the would-be art critic, has written the first chapter on his book on the painter Giotto. His manuscript is stolen by a *luftmentsch,* a vagrant—a Jewish nuisance named Shimon Susskind, a refugee from Israel. Susskind chases Fidelman all over Rome, and then be-

comes the pursued. Fidelman catches up with him, retrieves the now empty briefcase which had housed his papers, but is told by Susskind that the manuscript has been burned. "I did you a favor," he says. "The words were there but the spirit was missing." Or as Shlomo Carlebach, the great Hassidic folk-singing rabbi would put it, the words are simply "the black letters on a white background. Since both are from God, we have Black Fire on White Fire. What is Black Fire? Words. Nothing more. But the White Fire! That is the Spirit, the magic of the universe, the Holy Flame which makes us see all and one another and pulls us close together—as brothers."

The title of Picture Number Two is **"Still Life."** Locale—Rome once again. Instead of nuisance Susskind, Fidelman has Annamaria. He rents part of the studio from her, moves in, and they both paint. But Fidelman spends more time pursuing the woman than his art. What follows is a series of eccentric misadventures. Ultimately he fumbles his way into the young woman's heart by clothing himself as a priest. In this guise he attempts a self-portrait "of the artist as priest." In a flash Annamaria confesses *to* him ("Forgive me, Father, for I have sinned . . . "), undresses *for* him, and is bedded *by* him.

In Picture Number Three [**"Naked Nude"**] the scene changes to Milan. Here Fidelman is a penniless artist, a petty thief, until he is seized by two Mafia-like creatures (Angelo and Scarpio) and forced by them to slave away in a Milanese brothel. The gangsters concoct a Damon Runyan-like plan to steal a Titian nude and replace it with a Fidelman forgery. Fidelman must do the forging and stealing—if he wants his freedom. He does. But in the process he falls in love with his own work, the forgery, steals it, and escapes. Before the denouement the antihero suffers the usual humiliations reserved for all well-placed *schlemiels.* Fidelman, slapped around by his captors and harried by the harpies in the whorehouse, cannot concentrate on the painting he must duplicate. He needs a live model. In a passage that reminds us of *Catch-22,* we have the following:

> In desperation, on the verge of panic because time is going so fast, he thinks of Teresa, the chambermaid. She is a poor specimen of feminine beauty but the imagination can enhance anything. Fidelman asks her to pose for him, and Teresa, after a shy laugh, consents.

> "I will if you promise not to tell anybody."

> Fidelman promises.

> She undresses, a meager, bony girl, breathing heavily, and he draws her with flat chest, distended belly, thin hips and hairy legs, unable to alter a single detail. Van Eyck would have loved her. When Teresa sees the drawing she weeps profusely.

> "I thought you would make me beautiful."

> "I had that in mind."

> "Then why didn't you?"

> "It's hard to say," says Fidelman.

"I'm not in the least bit sexy," Teresa weeps.

Considering her body with half-closed eyes, Fidelman tells her to go borrow a long slip.

"Get one from one of the girls and I'll draw you sexy."

She returns in a frilly white slip and looks so attractive that instead of painting her, Fidelman, with a lump in his throat, gets her to lie down with him on a dusty mattress in the room. Clasping her slip-encased form, the copyist shuts both eyes and concentrates on his elusive Venus. He feels about to recapture a rapturous experience and is looking forward to it but at the last minute it turns into a limerick he didn't know he knew:

"Whilst Titian was mixing rose madder,
His model was crouched on a ladder;
Her position to Titian suggested coition,
So he stopped mixing madder and had'er."

Angelo, entering the storeroom just then, lets out a bellow. He fires Teresa on her naked knees pleading with him not to, and Fidelman has to go back to latrine duty the rest of the day.

The setting for Picture Four ["**A Pimp's Revenge**"] is Florence. First Fidelman sculpts sorry-looking Madonnas, which he sells for a pittance to enable him to paint his masterpiece. One day he meets and takes as mistress Esmeralda, the prostitute. Meanwhile Fidelman struggles with his great painting. At first it is "Mother and Son." Then it becomes "Brother and Sister." And finally he calls it "Prostitute and Procurer"—the last after he gives up his hack-sculpting for the more lucrative and less tiring position of panderer to Esmeralda. At last he completes the painting. A masterpiece for certain. Both he and Esmeralda agree ecstatically. But Fidelman (or "F" as he is called in this story) can't let well enough alone. In the middle of the night he has the urge to rework the painting, and during the evening he succeeds in destroying that which was to have been the culmination of his five years' struggle.

Fidelman is a wanderer in Picture Five ["**Pictures of the Artist**"]. He moves around Italy kaleidoscopically. It is all episodic, fragmented. A psychedelic mosaic. In one sequence he sculpts perfect holes in the ground which he then tries to exhibit—for a price. In true *schlemiel* fashion someone smacks him silly with his own shovel.

The final picture of Fidelman ["**Glass Blower of Venice**"] is taken in Venice. Here Fidelman finally stops painting and lives by doing menial work. Then one day he seduces Margheretta, the wife of Beppo, a glass blower. Naturally, the husband discovers his adulterous wife in bed with Fidelman. But all works out well because it turns out that the glass blower is a homosexual, who takes on Fidelman as lover and apprentice.

Beppo teaches Fidelman a craft, and instructs him in the arts of art, and love, and life. He destroys all of Fidelman's paintings because they are so bad. "Don't waste your life doing what you can't do. . . . After twenty years if the rooster hasn't crowed she should know she's a hen." And finally it is Beppo who directs Fidelman towards the future—"If you can't invent art, invent life." Fidelman gives

Beppo back to his wife and in the last lines of the story we are told that "Fidelman sailed from Venice on a Portuguese freighter" and that "in America he worked as a craftsman and loved men and women."

So the artist as *schlemiel* ends his journey, gives up his artistic ambitions, and returns home. What has happened to him in the process? In one sense we can see Fidelman in terms of gain and loss. That is, in the six stories he loses "something valuable in order to gain a truth or further understanding" [Martin Tucker, *"Pictures of Fidelman,"* *Commonweal* (June 27, 1969)]. What he loses almost always turns out to be something that he could well do without anyway—that which proves an obstacle to insight. Many perceive this "loss" as a controlling theme in Malamud's fiction. Some have seen it as a Henry Jamesian innocents-abroad theme. Others have called it Malamud's "addiction to failure." A *schlemiel* must fail, must fumble, must lose things, but in the end *may* somehow achieve a goal more meaningful than mere winning.

A few examples suffice: In "**Last Mohican**" Fidelman loses his manuscript, but as we saw, he finds out that Susskind really did him a favor after all: "The words were there but the spirit was missing." In "**Still Life**" Fidelman loses pride in himself but gains a mistress, whom he loves. In the succeeding stories he continues to lose—his sister's photo, his masterpiece, old values—as he moves closer to an understanding of himself. In the last story he loses everything in rapid succession—his mistress, her husband, all his paintings—but finally learns (so we are told) that he can regain his home and his somewhat ambiguous future.

Looked at another way, Fidelman may be understood in terms of the prison motif or metaphor. In this respect he parallels the host of other Malamud *schlemiels* to whom everything happens. In *The Assistant* Frank Alpine is imprisoned in Moris Bober's dreary grocery store; *The Fixer's* Yakov Bok, the epitome of the uninvolved man, is "seized by history" and literally thrown into a Russian prison, where he is degraded and humiliated by his vicious anti-Jewish guards. Even as recently as *The Tenants* we have Harry Lesser and his self-imposed prison in a tenement scheduled for demolition as Harry tries day by day to complete the novel that refuses to be written. Fidelman is often his *own* prisoner also as a result of his bungling, his lust, his misdirection, and sheer chance. In "**Naked Nude**" he comes closer to Yakov Bok's situation in that he is actually held prisoner in a house of prostitution by the two gangsters. It may be that "the prison, like the *schlemiel* who is usually its chief inmate, is Malamud's way of suggesting that to be fully a man is to accept the most painful limitations" [Robert Alter, "Jewishness as Metaphor," in *Bernard Malamud and the Critics*].

Often in the nick of time one's nemesis seems to change to guardian angel. Note again Susskind, who says after he steals the manuscript, "I did you a favor. . . . " Susskind's message to Fidelman over and over seems obvious: "You are not a critic! You are not an artist! Be yourself!" Thus did Susskind save Fidelman from himself in order to help him see within himself. And Fidelman, who all along spurned Susskind and begrudged him a suit of clothes, shouts, "Susskind come back . . . the suit is yours. All is forgiven." One small step toward salvation.

Self-centered and ambivalent Fidelman rejected his family and left America for his new life in Italy. Then, toward the end of his Italian journey, in a disjointed, partially escha-tological section, he moves still closer to salvation by con-juring up his sister Bessie, who is on her deathbed in New York. He is able to offer her a final "hello" before she dies. The bond of blood holds fast. "It's as though you were try-ing to paint yourself into your mother's arms," said Es-meralda. Indeed, Fidelman, turn his back as he will, al-ways seems to resurrect Bessie and their dear, dead moth-er. She may inhabit a Susskind or a Beppo—but as guiding shade she hovers and persists. A brief movement from fic-tion to life and one finds that the senior Mrs. Malamud's maiden name is in fact—Fidelman. Is Arthur Fidelman's darting about, then, a groping for his source? A movement toward reciprocation of maternal love? Elsewhere, we have seen, he offers love to Esmeralda, Teresa, Anna-maria, Beppo's wife, and, finally, Beppo himself.

Put another way one can say that *Pictures of Fidelman,* a *Picaresque Bildungsroman,* "is an allegory of the artistic and moral life" [Robert Scholes, "Portrait of the Artist as 'Escape Goat,' " *Saturday Review* (May 10, 1969)], with the protagonist as bungler, scapegoat, sufferer, cad, pre-tender, loser, prisoner, innocent abroad—or *schlemiel.* He is a Leopold Bloom of many false starts, beset by many pit-falls, a man who is hit not only by the garbage but the gar-bage can as well—yet one who seems to win through and *may* gain salvation in the end by giving rather than taking, by rejecting lust for love, by abandoning the pretenses of art for the honesty of craftsmanship.

Thus we return to the opening epigraphs: Rilke's *"Not to Understand"* is the starting place for the *schlemiel.* Then Yeats's "Perfection of the life, or of the work . . . " occu-pies a central position for the questing protagonist. But in the end for Fidelman the age-old talmudic principle is op-erative: *"Ein Brere*—I can do no other. There is no choice. I must reject *both* Rilke and Yeats so that I can under-stand, and then accept *both* life and art." What happens when life pits itself against art or art pits itself against life is grotesquely demonstrated in the later book, *The Ten-ants.* In one sense Willie Spearmint represents life, raw force, black rage. And Harry Lesser, humane though he is, seems to be a manifestation of art, the esthetic principle. When their final, inevitable confrontation comes, they singlemindedly, monomaniacally dismember each other, oblivious to landlord Levenspiel's anguished refrain of *Rachmones, Hab Rachmones, Mercy, Have Mercy.* Fortu-nately, Arthur Fidelman is spared the horrible fate of Wil-lie Spearmint and Harry Lesser. Fidelman has learned his painful lesson as they, apparently, have not. One must ac-cept both life and art. *Ein Brere. No Choice.* It can't be ei-ther/or. It must be—*Both.*

> *Leslie Field, "Portrait of the Artist as 'Schle-miel (Pictures of Fidelman)',"* in *Bernard Malamud: A Collection of Critical Essays, ed-ited by Leslie Field and Joyce Field, Prentice-Hall, Inc., 1975, pp. 117-29.*

Marcia B. Gealy   (essay date 1979)

[*In the essay below, Gealy highlights elements of Hasidic folklore and teachings in Malamud's short stories.*]

In his book, *World Of Our Fathers,* Irving Howe calls Ber-nard Malamud "the most enigmatic, even mysterious of American Jewish writers" and "a grandson without visi-ble line of descent—of the best Yiddish writers." He con-cludes that Malamud's use of motifs of the past probably "came to him (as Yiddish critics like to say) 'through the air,' particles of culture floating about, still charged with meaning and potent enough to be reshaped in American fiction."

These "particles of culture" which characterize Mala-mud's best writing, particularly some of his finest short stories, I would identify with Hasidism, a Jewish religious movement founded shortly before the middle of the eigh-teenth century by the East European saint and mystic, Is-rael ben Eliezer, the Baal Shem Tov. Some of the major teachings of Hasidism, a transformation or reinterpreta-tion of an older Jewish mysticism which made it accessible to the masses of the people, are the need to journey inward to achieve salvation, the importance of identification with a holy man or teacher, the primacy of love, and the reality of evil. In addition, the Hasidic belief in the sanctity of the tale, the notion that a story could have potency to effect change, led to the development of a vast and rich folklore. Hasidic tales permeated the culture of the East European *shtetl* until its destruction in the twentieth century and di-rectly, or indirectly, have influenced the thinking of East European Jews and their descendants. If Malamud recalls for us the humor of Sholom Aleichem and, more signifi-cantly, the irony of I. L. Peretz, if his tales infuse us with the same sense of mystery that we find in the recreated Ha-sidic tales of Martin Buber, it is because he shares a com-mon past with all of these writers.

Among his finest short stories, there are five which partic-ularly illustrate Malamud's use of Hasidic themes: **"The Last Mohican," "The Magic Barrel," "Idiots First," "The Jewbird,"** and **"The Silver Crown."** All of them deal with old-world Jews, displaced or in tension with the world around them; there is a *schnorrer* (beggar), a *shad-chan* (matchmaker), even the suggestion of a wonder-working rabbi. From Yiddish folklore the author draws on a talking bird and the angel of death, and each of these figures takes on special significance within the Hasidic tra-dition. To understand the Hasidic elements in these short stories is to enrich our appreciation of some of Malamud's most creative work.

The motif of the journey as a means to the discovery of self, an inward journey that promises salvation, is em-ployed most successfully in **"The Last Mohican."** Arthur Fidelman, a "self confessed failure as a painter," goes to Italy to become an art critic and learns, instead, to become a *mensch.* Fidelman's mentor in Rome is Shimon Susskind, refugee from Israel, a combination *schnorrer,* wandering Jew, and Virgil. Fidelman, like most of Mala-mud's young Jewish intellectuals, is out of touch with his past and reluctant to give of himself. He comes to Italy with an intense passion for Italian history and to study

Giotto. When Susskind asks Fidelman for his suit, the student reacts with annoyance; he is, after all, supporting himself with hard-earned money and has only two suits. Pursued by Susskind through the streets of Rome, Fidelman turns into a pursuer when he suspects the beggar has stolen his briefcase. His search for Susskind leads him to a Sephardic synagogue, a Jewish cemetery, and, ultimately, the beggar's meager hovel. Confronted with the realization of his own people's history, but more with the knowledge of Susskind's particular suffering, Fidelman is finally able to identify with the beggar and gives him the suit. Even when he realizes that Susskind has burned his manuscript (probably for fuel), Fidelman finally has the insight to forgive everything. After all, as Susskind had noted, "The words were there but the spirit was missing."

Fidelman's identification with Susskind starts early. As he departs from the railway station in Rome he has a vision of himself, an "unexpectedly intense sense of his being" that has been stimulated by the appearance of Susskind, a man of about his own height, who, in spite of his emaciated frame and bizarre dress, somehow suggests Fidelman. The student protests against this identification, wanting to give Susskind only token recognition at best, for he has come to Italy to know Giotto. But Susskind, in hounding Fidelman, is suggesting that he will never know the Italians until he knows himself. The student does not start to suspect this truth until his pursuit of Susskind compels him to face the refugee's suffering. As his understanding grows, even his dress changes, for he puts on the beret and pointed shoes that link him with the refugee. But it is only when he decides to stay in Rome, more to find Susskind in order "to know man" than to hope for the recovery of his manuscript, that we can be sure that Fidelman is on the way to salvation. When he dreams of Giotto's fresco of St. Francis giving a cloak to a poor knight and is able to identify himself with St. Francis, and Susskind with the knight, he can do so because he has first recognized Susskind as a fellow Jew, a man for whom he is responsible.

As a Jewish Virgil, Susskind leads his initiate on a journey through Hell that promises transformation. But, unlike Dante's Virgil, Susskind is no exemplar of cool and dispassionate reason. On the contrary, he has all the bravado, all the *huzpah* (arrogance), associated with the common beggar or *schnorrer* of East European *shtetl* society. Because he is a product of this society, Susskind knows that as a beggar he is an occasion for *mizvos* (good deeds) and, thus, an instrument of grace. If he feels himself at an advantage, if he does not hesitate to demand his due, it is because he realizes that the more fortunate need him as an object of charity. In the culture of the *shtetl* it is the *schnorrer* who opens "the portals of heaven" for the more fortunate man. The Hasidim emphasize this belief with the words of Rabbi Shmelke:

> The poor man gives the rich man more than the
> rich gives the poor. More than the poor needs
> the rich man, the rich is in need of the poor.

Like most *schnorrers,* Susskind is also a *luftmensch,* who lives on air, and is usually on the run. But there is also a sense of mystery about him; he is, after all, a refugee from Israel, homeless even in the homeland, destined, it seems, to keep on running. In the final analysis, the power of "**The Last Mohican**" can be attributed to Shimon Susskind who, with all his grotesque humor, can be identified with the wandering beggars and fools of Hasidic folklore. Like them, he is an enigmatic mixture of the commonplace and mysterious, the saintly and demonic; like them, he makes people dream and leads them to themselves.

"**The Magic Barrel,**" the title story of Malamud's first collection, is probably the best one that he has written to date. Like so many of Malamud's better stories, which suspend us between the real and the supernatural, "**The Magic Barrel**" also contains within it an artful fusion of Hasidism's basic teachings. Leo Finkle, a young rabbinical student, must learn the lesson of the heart over the head. He does so from Pinye Salzman, a questionable mentor, who leads him on a tortuous journey and through an experience of evil. Only by identifying with, and embracing, this evil can Leo find himself and the love that he so desperately seeks.

As a tormented yeshivah student in search of a wife because "he might find it easier to win himself a congregation if he were married," Leo is more concerned with the law than with its spirit. Even his coming to a marriage broker, an "ancient and honorable" profession in the Jewish community, is more the result of his fear of looking for a bride for himself than of his respect for Jewish tradition. Because of his desperation, he lets himself be manipulated into a meeting with Lily Hirschorn, an old maid school teacher, but his experience with Lily, who in her poignant honesty sparks Leo's own, reveals to him a terrifying insight: he had come to God not because he loved Him, but because he did not. Once he is confronted with the knowledge of his own unworthiness and terrorized by what he feels is an inability to love, Leo suffers mightily. But he accepts his suffering with some consolation; "perhaps with this new knowledge of himself he would be more successful than in the past." The proof of this success is his attraction to Stella, the matchmaker's renegade daughter, in whom Leo sees a suggestion of evil. That Leo can identify with evil and say "It is thus with us all" is the mark of his maturity and his ultimate redemption.

As an old-world *shadchan,* Pinye Salzman represents a classic type in Jewish folklore. Noted for a tendency toward humbug and a genius for euphemistically glossing over the defects of clients, the *shadchan* is not without a comic pathos. As the guide who shows to one who is lost the way through the mysterious maze of love and redemption, Salzman is reminiscent, in some ways, of Shimon Susskind of "**The Last Mohican.**" Slightly built to the point of wasting away, in ill-fitting clothes and smelling of fish, Salzman, like the refugee from Israel, is comic and grotesque, yet not without a sad dignity. If there is a suggestion of the demonic about Susskind, it also clings to Salzman, for Leo sees him as a "commercial cupid" and a "cloven-hoofed Pan." To trust in Salzman, the yeshivah student must suspend his rationality. Also, like Susskind, Salzman is a *luftmensch* who lives on air as well as in his socks, the implication being that he lives on hopes and miracles. Finally, as with Susskind, there is an air of mystery surrounding him. Does his magic barrel exist or is it a "figment of imagination"? Did he plant his daughter Stella's picture in the envelope to entice Leo or was it just an accident? In the world of the Hasidim, what the imagination creates has its own kind of truth, and, as the Baal Shem Tov has taught, "there are no accidents." Thus, the whole tenor of the story suggests that Salzman planned the final meeting between the student and his daughter for their mutual benefit, and if, at the end, he chants the prayers for the dead, he does so within the context of a culture where death is but the first step in the process of transformation. [In a footnote, Gealy adds that in " 'The Magic Barrel': Pinye Salzman's Kadish," in *Studies in Short Fiction* (Winter 1973) "Richard Reynolds notes that the prayer for the dead, the *Kadish,* is closely associated with 'Messianic times when resurrection will take place' so that Salzman's final prayer is for effecting Stella's resurrection"].

As the embodiment of evil ("she should burn in hell" Salzman says of her), yet with eyes that suggest a "desperate innocence," Stella incorporates that wonderful mixture of experience and innocence that we associate with a Malamud heroine like Helen Bober in *The Assistant*. Stella is not a realized character, of course; we never hear her speak and we see her only in picture, first in the photograph that Leo finds in Salzman's envelope and, finally, in the stunning tableau that Malamud presents at the end of his tale. In the photograph that first captivates Leo, Stella is hauntingly familiar yet absolutely strange; her face reflects deep suffering and somehow gives an impression of evil. Yet Leo sees in her "his own redemption," for, as the matchmaker put it, "If you can love her, then you can love anybody." Stella is, in other words, like Helen Bober, a combination Lilith-*Shekhinah* or destroyer-preserver figure who tests the hero and offers pain, judgment, and ultimate insight. The female in that role, as demon and godly presence, is an interesting aspect of Jewish mysticism and Hasidic folklore. In the Kabbalah, the demonic is seen as the offspring of the feminine sphere and, in Kabbalah symbolism, woman represents the quality of stern judgment. Nevertheless, as Gershom Scholem points out [in *Major Trends in Jewish Mysticisms,* 1961], this is not a negation of womanhood because of the paradoxical Kabbalistic conception of the *Shekhinah,* the feminine element in God. The *Shekhinah* or Divine Presence of God is thought of as the queen or mother of the world of sanctity, just as Lilith, the "harlot, the wicked or the black" is thought of as the queen or mother of the realm of evil. Nevertheless, we must keep in mind the Hasidic insistence on the unity of all things, on the acceptance of evil for "if there were no evil, there would be no good, for good is the counterpart of evil." Finally, dressed in red and white, the traditional colors of sin and purity, Stella waits for Leo at the end of his quest, an emblem of the good and evil that the hero must embrace as a seal of his redemption.

The final tableau—Leo running toward Stella with violets and rosebuds, while violins and lit candles revolve in the sky—transports us into a dream world where anything is possible. Many critics, writing of this scene, have remarked on its affinity with the paintings of Marc Chagall,

and, not surprisingly, for Malamud's world, like Chagall's, is the visionary world of Hasidism where all of God's creation, good and evil, death and life, swirl together in a unified whole.

The Hasidic belief in inner salvation, an important theme in Malamud's early stories, is not as prevalent in his later work, where other Hasidic teachings, such as the potency of love (or hate) and the terrors of evil (both, of course, associated with the process of transformation in the earlier work) are more prevalent. Three stories which skillfully demonstrate these themes are **"Idiots First"** and **"The Jewbird"** (in *Idiots First*) and **"The Silver Crown"** (in *Rembrandt's Hat*).

"Idiots First," is based on a common motif in folk literature: the confrontation of a mortal with the Angel of Death. In Jewish legends "some exceptional act of piety or benevolence" can often prevail against death, as is seen in the folk exegesis on Proverbs: 10:2; 11:4—"Charity delivers from Death." In the culture of the Hasidim, though death is accepted, even embraced, there are times when death is postponed because of special circumstances. The tale is told of the Baal Shem Tov who, wanting the recovery of Rabbi Leibush, "scolds" the Angel of Death and causes him to run away. There is also the story of Rabbi Levi Yitzhak who prays for a four day extension to his life so that he might accomplish certain tasks and, as the tale goes, it was so.

Within the same tradition, Malamud weaves a story of old Mendel and his idiot son, Isaac, and Mendel's attempt to forestall the Angel of Death until he can safeguard Isaac's passage on a train to California. Desperately in need of thirty-five dollars to complete the purchase of Isaac's ticket before midnight, Mendel visits a pawnbroker, a Jewish philanthropist who gives "only to institutions," and a poverty-stricken rabbi who, despite the screams of his wife, tosses Mendel his new fur-lined caftan. During the length of his quest, Mendel is pursued by Ginzburg, "a bearded man with hairy nostrils and a fishy smell," the East European Jewish version of the Angel of Death. Finally, with enough money in hand to purchase the train ticket, Mendel is stopped by the ticket collector—Ginzburg in uniform—and is told that his time is up. He pleads for a short extension to put Isaac on the train and when Ginzburg will not relent, lunges at him crying, "You bastard, don't you understand what it means human?" Wrestling nose to nose, Mendel sees reflected in Ginzburg's eyes the depths of his terror, but Ginzburg sees in Mendel's eyes the extent of his own wrath. Utterly astounded, Ginzburg relents and allows Mendel the extra time to put Isaac on the train. Afterwards, Mendel returns, seeking Ginzburg.

The power of **"Idiots First"** lies in its masterful tension between terror and hope and the artfulness with which we are suspended between the real and the supernatural. Death is a messenger who croaks *"Gut yontif"* (Good holiday), an omnipresent force that talks of "cosmic universal law," but who picks his teeth with a matchstick. If Ginzburg is, on the one hand, inexorable, he is, on the other, able to reflect on himself. We see here Malamud's gift in creating a dream-like landscape, for, while the setting is New York, the deserted streets and the reappearance of the bearded stranger transport us to somewhere beyond. Finally, there is Malamud's special way of combining affirmation with a suggestive, mocking irony. Mendel has conquered death but only for a few minutes; Isaac, a half-wit, will go to California, but to the care of an eighty-one year old uncle, and how long will Uncle Leo live? In the context of both the story and the Hasidic tradition, however, neither such qualifications nor such questions ultimately matter. As an idiot, Isaac is an example of the world's unfortunates, but the blessed of God. If Mendel forestalls Death for only a little while to perform a good deed, Hasidic holy men have prayed for the same favor. Finally, Death is not the ultimate enemy but a friend to be embraced when the right time comes. Thus, Mendel ascends the stairs to seek out Ginzburg.

"The Jewbird," a combination of beast fable and parable, emphasizes the Hasidic teaching of the reality of evil. If a man will not accept evil as part of himself, if he cannot say with the Hasidic rebbe, "I experience it [evil] when I meet myself," if he is determined only to project it on to another, then evil has the power to destroy that man rather than to lead him on the pathway to good. Malamud incorporates this teaching in his story of the Cohen family and their encounter with a talking bird—a "skinny . . . frazzled . . . black-type longbeaked bird"—who flies into their New York apartment one day and announces 'I'm a Jewbird.' "

According to Samuel Bellman [in "Women, Children, and Idiots First: The Transformation Psychology of Bernard Malamud" in *Bernard Malamud and the Critics,* 1970], the Jewbird as a talking "crow" seems to hark back to Poe's "The Raven," but it would seem to me more appropriate to place it within the context of Jewish tradition. Talking animals are common in Jewish folklore and are distinctive for the ways in which they take over Jewish mannerisms and modes of speech. Malamud's Jewbird, Schwartz, who smells of herring and speaks with a Yiddish accent, is an obvious product of the East European *shtetl.* In addition, there is the Hasidic belief that, under special circumstances, a man can be turned into an animal. The tale is told of the Baal Shem Tov's encounter with a man who has been turned into a horse for neglecting to pay a debt. [In a footnote, Gealy refers the reader to "Malamud's tale **'Talking Horse'** in *Rembrandt's Hat,* for a delightful Jewish version of the birth of a centaur"]. Mrs. Cohen wonders if Schwartz "might be an old Jew changed into a bird by somebody." Schwartz's answer to the supposition is simply "Who knows? Does God tell us everything?"

But the story may be related to Hasidic teaching in a more profound way, for Harry Cohen could be any man who rejects evil as part of himself, who projects it on to another, and destroys the other without realizing that the other is part of himself. When Schwartz flies into Cohen's apartment asking for sanctuary, he says he is fleeing from "Anti-semeetes," but Cohen's fear and persecution of Schwartz make him the anti-Semite who does Schwartz the most harm.

Cohen can't stand Schwartz's eating habits, his bedraggled appearance, his bad smell; he even suspects that Schwartz might be some kind of "devil." But Cohen's wife and child beg that the bird be allowed to stay and soon Schwartz becomes a tutor to the son. Though the boy's grades improve, the elder Cohen is simply resentful and wants Schwartz to keep on migrating. One night, when his wife and son are out of the apartment, Cohen attacks the Jewbird, whirls him round and round his head—in the way that the scapegoat fowl is whirled round the head of the penitent on the eve of Yom Kippur—and tosses him into the night. Cohen destroys the Jewbird for what he thinks is the bird's offensiveness; actually, as the Hasidim would see it, he is destroying that frightening part of himself which is necessary for his completion.

The terror and pessimism of **"The Jewbird"** are lightened, at least until the end, by Malamud's use of whimsical fantasy. The bird's fractured English, his preference for "matjes" over "schmaltz" herring, his request for the *Jewish Morning Journal* all add an element of humor to an otherwise grim story. The final effect is melancholy, however; as the ancient tradition teaches and as Hasidic story confirms, a Jew (man) can be his own worst enemy.

In an even more somber tone, **"The Silver Crown,"** the opening story of *Rembrandt's Hat,* is also concerned with the reality of evil; in particular, the terrors of repressed hatred. Interestingly enough, Malamud has said that the story is based on a *New York Times* story of the arrest of two Hasidic faith healers in the Bronx, but that the characters are his own creation.

Albert Gans, a high school biology teacher, desperately seeks aid from a wonder-working rabbi to heal his dying father, who suffers from a mysterious ailment. Cancer "of the heart" the old man calls it. The young Gans, "naturally empiric and objective—you might say non-mystical," goes to the faith healer against his better judgment; it is his last attempt to "repay" his father for his generosity towards him. The faith-healer, Rabbi Lifshitz, though not specifically identified as one, is almost certainly a Hasid. He studies a mystical book "like the Kabbalah" and seems to have inherited the power of healing from his father and grandfather. He insists that his idiot daughter, Rifkele, is in the reflection of God, for it is love, not reason or faith, that puts us in closest touch with Divine Grace. The rabbi says that it is Albert's love that will heal his father, but he charges a fee to construct a sign of this love, a silver crown. Though Albert reluctantly agrees to purchase the crown—the biggest, most expensive one to accomplish the miracle—his pride in rationality and his doubts about the rabbi so overwhelm him that he returns the next day to demand his money back. In the final confrontation, as the rabbi pleads with Albert to think of his father, the young Gans, in his fury at what he thinks has been a deception, unmasks his own feelings and wishes his father dead. Calling him a "murderer," the rabbi rushes into his daughter's arms; fleeing from the revelation of his own feelings, Albert rushes down the stairs. An hour later, the elder Gans expires.

The conflict in **"The Silver Crown"** is not so much between doubt and faith as between love and hate. In the rabbi's words:

Doubts we all got. We doubt God and God doubts us. This is natural on account of the nature of existence. Of this kind doubts I am not afraid so long as you love your father.

Twice the rabbi asks Albert if he loves his father and both times Albert avoids answering the question directly. If Albert wants to save his father it is from a sense of gratitude and from a concern that his own "conscience be in the clear." But Albert's initial unwillingness to face his repressed hatred for his father and his closing cry of "He hates me, the son-of-a-bitch, I hope he croaks" suggest that the final unmasking will leave him with a lifetime of regret. When he runs down the stairs with a "spike-ridden headache," he is fleeing from a terrifying recognition of self that his pride cannot accept.

The power of **"The Silver Crown"** comes from the tension that it evokes between the mysterious and the commonplace, and from the artistry with which it explores the complexities of human nature. Is the rabbi a "clever confidence man" or a genuine magician like the Baal Shem Tov? Did Gans "murder" his father, as the rabbi claims, or did the old man die of natural causes? As in so many of Malamud's tales, the answers to such questions do not ultimately matter. What does matter is that Gans, in his unwillingness to face his feelings, has denied both his father and himself. That the elder Gans had sensed his son's true feelings is implied in his cancer "of the heart." If hate is to be turned into love, a man must first accept it as his own. Albert is ensnared in "the conceit born of self-deception," a sin that, to a Hasid, weighs more than "all the sins in the world." Though there is some question about Rabbi Lifshitz's authenticity in **"The Silver Crown,"** there is no doubt that the arch-deceiver of the story is Albert Gans himself.

In many ways **"The Silver Crown"** is a recreation of characters and themes that Malamud has shown us before. The Bronx biology teacher is another of Malamud's young intellectuals, skeptical to the bone and reluctant to love. His quest for his father is ultimately tied to his knowledge of self, a knowledge that he would deny rather than face. Rabbi Lifschitz is another of Malamud's enigmatic holy men, ready to lead the young man into an experience with evil, the instrument for grace or damnation as the hero would choose. The notable difference between **"The Silver Crown"** and the earlier tales which resemble it, is the pessimism which prevails here. Albert Gans, unlike Arthur Fidelman or Leo Finkle, does not achieve salvation. Yet this tale, like **"The Jewbird,"** while it does not evoke the delight of the earlier stories of transformation, nevertheless may be seen within the framework of Hasidism. Though its teaching emphasizes inner salvation and joy in all that is, it does not deny the dark side of life and man's freedom of will. In some Hasidic stories, a man chooses Hell; in Bernard Malamud's fiction he sometimes makes the same choice.

Looking back on Malamud's short stories, we see a reflection of the same concerns that are found in his novels. The quest for salvation, when achieved, is ultimately tied to the acceptance of self. If a man fails another, he has first failed himself. Yet, I think that none of the novels can match his

short stories, perhaps because, as Philip Roth has written [in "Imagining Jews," in *The New York Review of Books* (October 1974)], Malamud's imagination is "essentially folkoric and didactic," and such an imagination lends itself more readily to the terseness associated with the traditional tale. Remarking on Malamud's relation to the tradition of Yiddish tale telling, Earl Rovit says [in "The Jewish Literary Tradition," in *Bernard Malamud and the Critics*] that

> though Malamud captures elusive tones and shadows of the traditional Yiddish tale, he is not at all a teller of tales in the traditional manner. He is an extremely self-conscious short story writer, keenly sensitive to the formal demands of the short story. . . .

It is here that Rovit's judgments must be qualified, for it seems clear to me that Malamud, in the twentieth century, is doing with the Yiddish tale what Peretz did with it in the nineteenth. Peretz, a reworker of Hasidic folk materials and one of the founding fathers of modern Yiddish literature, is certainly one of its most conscious stylists. His concept of tradition is a dynamic one. Thus, he starts his essay, "What Our Literature Needs," with the phrase: "First of all, tradition." But not long afterward he adds, "Let there be no misunderstanding. I am not proposing that we lock ourselves in a spiritual ghetto. We must leave it—but with our own soul, our own spiritual wealth. We must make exchanges." It is in this context that Peretz, who himself broke away from traditional Judaism, puts his own stamp on Hasidic tales. What he does, especially in his later and stronger stories, is to rework folk and Hasidic materials "in a way that appears to be folklike but is actually the product of a sophisticated literary intellect" [Irving Howe and Eliezer Greenberg, eds. "Introduction," *Selected Stories: I. L. Peretz* (1974)]. Or, to put it another way, what Peretz accomplishes through his sense of distance, his use of irony, his control of tragic vision is, in the words of the Yiddish poet, Jacob Glatstein, "to give the agnostic legitimacy" and "to preserve Jewish life for him."

Robert Alter on Malamud and Jewish folk culture:

Malamud is, to the best of my knowledge, the first important American writer to shape out of his early experiences in the immigrant milieu a whole distinctive style of imagination and, to a lesser degree, a distinctive technique of fiction as well. He is by no means a "folk" artist, but his ear for the rhythms of speech and the tonalities of implication, his eye for the shadings of attitude and feeling, of Jewish folk culture, have helped make the fictional world he has created uniquely his own. Though such influences are hard to prove, I suspect that the piquant juxtaposition in his fiction of tough, ground-gripping realism and high-flying fantasy ultimately derives from the paradoxical conjoining of those same qualities that has often characterized Jewish folklore.

Robert Alter, in his "Bernard Malamud: Jewishness as Metaphor," in his After the Tradition: Essays on Modern Jewish Writing, *E. P. Dutton & Co., 1969.*

Malamud's reworking of Hasidic themes is not unlike Peretz's; there is the same controlled tension between skepticism and wonder, the same juxtaposition of sacred and profane, the same fusion of Jewish past and present. But, in the best sense of the tradition, Malamud, too, has broken away and found his own distinctive voice. While both writers excel in a kind of bittersweet irony, while both can be ambivalent, even sour in tone, there is often a warmth and humor to Malamud which is more difficult to find in Peretz. Nevertheless, each writer at his best proves the sanctity of the Hasidic tale, for each, by reminding man of his kinship with the past, suggests the possibilities of transformation.

> *Marcia B. Gealy, "Malamud's Short Stories: A Reshaping of Hasidic Tradition," in* Judaism, *Vol. 28, No. 1, Winter, 1979, pp. 51-61.*

J. Gerald Kennedy (essay date 1980)

[*Kennedy is an American educator and critic. In the excerpt below, he argues that "The Jewbird" is a parody of Edgar Allan Poe's "The Raven."*]

Unlike other literary modes, parody describes not an intrinsic structure or quality in a work but rather a condition of relationship to another text or set of texts. Parody creates a theoretical juxtaposition in which the more recent work ironically re-presents selected elements of its antecedent, usually through mocking exaggeration. As Jonathan Culler has noted [in his *Structuralist Poetics,* 1975], parody typically places in tension two authorial perspectives: "the order of the original and the point of view which undermines it." This subversive process resists easy explanation, however, since it resides in the play of differences and similarities between texts. In order for parody to occur, there must be a patent resemblance—usually in style or theme—between the second text and the first. Yet the element of parody emerges only when we perceive the disparities lodged in this network of correspondences: the verbal deviations, contextual changes, and transformations of familiar narrative patterns. Though parody typically employs overt distortion (and can be said to fail when its target is not immediately recognizable), it may, like other forms of irony, possess a complexity of purpose and implication. In a single work, the parodist may undertake to satirize the content of an earlier text, the affectations of its author, the formal conventions he utilized, or the cultural values projected in his writing. The parodist may (like Jane Austen in *Northanger Abbey*) aim to lampoon a specific genre or aesthetic tradition. Or he may be engaged in a more private enterprise: to exorcise a secret demon and thus rid himself of an earlier writer's perplexing and undesired influence.

Among the multiple uses of parody, this last strategy seems both more interesting and, because it involves an esoteric intention, less susceptible to analysis. An initial clarification comes, however, from Proust, who in acknowledging the entrancing effect of Flaubert's writing declared:

> Concerning Flaubertian intoxication, I wouldn't know how to recommend too highly to writers the purgative, exorcising force of parody. When one has just finished a book, he not only wishes to continue to live with its characters, . . . but also our inner voice, which has been conditioned during the entire reading to follow the rhythm of a Balzac or a Flaubert, wants to continue to speak like them. One must let it have its way a moment, let the pedal prolong the sound; that is, create a deliberate parody, so that afterward one can again recover his originality and not create involuntary parody all of his life.

Proust suggests that this method of regaining one's authorial voice entails a willful, temporary surrender to the language of the earlier text. By sustaining the sound of this "rhythme obsesseur," the writer frees himself from the repetition mechanism which produces inadvertent parody. Proust's formulation describes a purgative impulse present to some extent, perhaps, in all parody, since mockery tacitly expresses (as Harold Bloom might say) an anxiety about the influence of an earlier work and a desire to break its hold. Yet it seems equally apparent that self-conscious exorcism must produce a form of parody unlike the transparent derision of Fielding's *Shamela* or Hemingway's *The Torrents of Spring*. The difference will be one of kind rather than degree, inasmuch as the Proustian "pastiche volontaire" develops not from a sense of the foolishness of the earlier work but rather from an awareness of its haunting insistence. Since in this scheme ironic emulation reflects both the avowal and displacement of an influence, we should anticipate in literary exorcism a quality antithetical to conventional parody: ambivalence.

This is precisely the condition which obscures the filiation between Bernard Malamud's story **"The Jewbird"** (from **The Magic Barrel**) and Poe's famous poem, "The Raven." To gain further insight into the phenomenon Proust has adumbrated, I wish to treat these works as a provisional model of the complex linkage produced by exorcism. I assume at the outset that a parodic relationship exists; that the purpose of this ironic re-presentation is unclear; and that this ambiguity signals the unfolding of an exorcistic project. To explain: it seems almost self-evident that Malamud's tale consciously exploits the dramatic situation of "The Raven," for in both works a black bird of mysterious origin and seemingly magical intelligence flies in an open window and takes up residence in the protagonist's apartment. We see both birds perched above a doorway, uttering words that torment the human listener; gradually we realize that the bird objectifies some aspect of the protagonist's experience with which he has failed to come to terms. The man is oppressed by the bird's presence and tries to learn its ultimate purpose, but failing to do so, he implores the bird to leave. Presented so starkly, these parallels seem obvious, and it is a matter of some astonishment that critics have barely mentioned the connection. Yet this neglect illustrates one of the odd features of exorcistic parody: it is simultaneously overt and discreet, unmistakably present yet playfully elusive.

Of course thematic parallels do not in themselves constitute parody; the effect of sly imitation emerges rather through the comic variations worked upon "The Raven." Such disparities lend ironic resonance to verbal echoes:

Poe's persona commands the bird, "Tell me what thy lord-ly name is on the Night's Plutonian shore!" But Mala-mud's Harry Cohen, a frozen food salesman, snarls less poetically: "So what's your name, if you don't mind say-ing?" Poe's speaker expresses his fears about the raven's hellish origins: " 'Prophet!' said I, 'thing of evil!—prophet still if bird or devil!—' " The same uncertainty afflicts Cohen, who asks the Jewbird, "You sure you're not some kind of ghost or dybbuk?" Later he repeats the question, using the exact contraries of Poe's speaker: "But how do I know you're a bird and not some kind of a goddamn devil?" The vulgarity epitomizes Malamud's transforma-tion of the Poe material; Cohen's modern slang and the banal details of his world create an indirect contrast to the formal elegance of "The Raven."

Closer attention to dramatic parallels further sharpens our sense of potential parody in **"The Jewbird."** The initiatory event in each work is the appearance of a mysterious bird, and in "The Raven" this moment suggests the advent of nobility: "In there stepped a stately Raven of the saintly days of yore; / Not the least obeisance made he; not a min-ute stopped or stayed he; / But, with mien of lord or lady, perched above my chamber door." When the Jewbird ar-rives, however, there is a conspicuous lack of decorum: "The bird wearily flapped through the open kitchen win-dow of Harry Cohen's top-floor apartment on First Ave-nue near the lower East River. . . . This black-type long-beaked bird—its ruffled head and dull eyes, crossed a lit-tle, making it look like a dissipated crow—landed if not smack on Cohen's thick lamb chop, at least on the table, close by." After Cohen takes a swat at him, the Jewbird shifts to a more familiar position: "The bird cawed hoarse-ly and with a flap of its bedraggled wings—feathers tufted this way and that—rose heavily to the top of the open kitchen door, where it perched staring down." Malamud's caricature of Poe's raven possesses some critical justifica-tion: we recall that the bird initially provokes a smile from Poe's narrator; that its crest is "shorn and shaven"; that its appearance is laughably described as "grim, ungainly, ghastly, gaunt." Malamud further distorts these qualities to make the Jewbird "bedraggled," "scrawny," and mal-odorous; at one point Cohen explodes, "For Christ sake, why don't you wash yourself sometimes? Why must you always stink like a dead fish?"

Whether ominous or merely offensive, the bird's presence at last becomes so aggravating that the protagonist com-mands his visitor to leave. Poe's persona beseeches the raven: "Get thee back into the tempest and the Night's Plutonian shore!" Less grandiosely Cohen warns the Jew-bird, "Time to hit flyways. . . . Now scat or it's open war." Here, however, Malamud's story departs from its analogical relationship to the poem. Whereas Poe's char-acter ultimately realizes that he will never escape from the raven's influence, Cohen indeed declares war on Schwartz the Jewbird; reversing the nemesis relationship, he buys a cat and permits it to stalk the feathered intruder. Hence near the end of the tale we see Schwartz perching "terror-stricken closer to the ceiling than the floor, as the cat, his tail flicking, endlessly watched him."

But despite these entertaining parallels, made to seem all

the more glaring by selective emphasis, Malamud's evoca-tion of "The Raven" does not produce the effect of con-ventional parody—mockery through distortion. Indeed, although he appropriates Poe's central concept (a visita-tion by a mysterious talking bird), reduces it to comic terms, and develops a set of verbal and dramatic similari-ties laced with ironic disparities, Malamud refrains from anything like overt ridicule of Poe's poem. Instead, he sub-merges the parody and directs his satire at an aspect of the Americanized Jew personified by Cohen: a contempt for the customs and manners of Old-World Jews. As Robert Alter has pointed out, these traditional ways are embodied in Schwartz, the wandering Jewbird, whose chutzpah and fondness for herring and schnapps disgust the "assimilat-ed" Cohen. As Alter explains [in "Jewish Humor and the Domestication of Myth," in *Veins of Humor,* edited by Harry Levin, 1972], the bird represents for Cohen "the stigmatized stereotype of a kind of Jew that he emphatical-ly wants to leave behind. Cohen is really attacking part of himself in his hostility toward Schwartz." The essential truth about the frozen-food salesman emerges at the story's end when Cohen's son finds the remains of Schwartz's body and asks who killed him; his mother an-swers, "Anti-Semeets." In this sense, the tale dramatizes a familiar theme in recent Jewish fiction: the Jew's compli-cated and sometimes scornful attitude about his own cul-tural roots.

Understandably, critical attention to **"The Jewbird"** has dealt almost exclusively with this issue; in satirizing Jew-ish anti-Semitism, Malamud attacks a problem of social, ethnic, and political significance. His decision not to lam-poon "The Raven" seems therefore understandable, since blatant parody would have compromised the satirical as-sault and diminished its effect. Yet the verbal echoes and dramatic parallels remain; the poem lingers as an ironic, ghostly presence in **"The Jewbird,"** seemingly unrelated to the surface narrative and its satirical objectives. What do these traces then signify? It would be possible to argue that Malamud conjures up elements of the poem to re-mind us of Poe's notorious anti-Semitism; however, this reading depends more upon external information about Poe than upon textual evidence. One could also argue that the bluntness of Cohen's language and the banality of his ordeal are designed to mock through parodic inversion the ornate rhetoric and Romantic melancholy upon which the effect of "The Raven" depends; but this analysis seems tenuous at best, since **"The Jewbird"** displays neither ex-plicit scorn for the poem nor visible hostility toward the Romantic sensibility.

And so we return to the original paradox: the poem ob-trudes as a palpable yet phantasmic influence, which dom-inates the foreground of **"The Jewbird"** while remaining nearly invisible—a kind of purloined letter. And the more intently we seek the function of this allusion/illusion along the plane of satirical meaning (in relation to the at-tack on Jewish anti-Semitism), the less certain we become of its instrumentality. Aside from the curious fact that, as in "The Raven," the appearance of the Jewbird coincides with the death of a woman (here, Cohen's mother), the overlapping between the two texts seems almost gratu-itous. But it does not occur by chance: at the very least, these parallels imply a sustained imaginative engagement with the poem. And if we are willing to move from the level of overt satire to consider Cohen's struggle with Schwartz figuratively, as the reflection of Malamud's reflection on "The Raven"—that is, as metaphor—quite a different understanding of the action emerges. From this perspective, the relationship between Cohen and the bird seems analogically to represent the author's effort to free himself from the persistent, improbable influence of "The Raven." Ludicrous but inescapable, the bird (poem) torments Cohen (Malamud) by insinuating itself into his private world. For a time, Cohen accepts its presence and allows it to have its way, but to reassert his authority, he finally attacks the bird and flings it out the window. Thus the literal events mirror the key stages in Malamud's presumed ordeal with the poem; the narrative becomes a metatext on its own composition. This oblique view of **"The Jewbird"** also reveals an absolute disjunction—perhaps symptomatic of literary exorcism—between public and private implication. Cohen's final gesture (the destruction of Schwartz) clarifies the incommensurability of satirical and parodic meaning: while on one level this pogrom illustrates the shameful anti-Semitism that Malamud obviously disparages, on another it conversely represents a necessary, purgative process—the writer's effort to cast out a literary bête noire, the influence of "The Raven."

Such a theory of composition enables us to come to terms with the ambiguous evocation of Poe which informs **"The Jewbird."** Apparently "The Raven" epitomized those aspects of Poe's writing which constituted for Malamud its imaginative contagion; to break its hold, Malamud indulged in authorial play, allowing the idea of the poem to express itself in idiomatic Yiddish humor, in a comic form possessing its own integrity and purpose. While Harry Cohen is said to receive a "permanent scar" from his bout with the Jewbird, the evidence of Malamud's fiction seems to indicate that through this ironic transformation of "The Raven," he effectually liberated his work from Poe's influence. Despite his fascination with magic and the supernatural, for example, Malamud appears not to have drawn upon the Gothic fantasies of his predecessor; as Professor Alter has shown [in "Bernard Malamud: Jewishness as Metaphor," in his *After the Tradition,* 1969], he derives this occult interest principally from the motifs of Jewish folklore. Yet critical emphasis on ethnic, Jewish elements in his fiction has perhaps obscured Malamud's response to goyish American literature. That this dimension will assume greater interpretive importance seems inevitable in the wake of *Dubin's Lives,* a 1979 novel depicting the troubled love life of a Jewish biographer whose literary obsessions include Thoreau, Emerson, and Twain. A passing reference to "the miserable youth of Edgar Allan Poe" reminds us of the obsession Malamud had already displaced in writing **"The Jewbird."** . . .

By its nature, all parody involves a systematic play of similarity and difference; but in literary exorcism this process functions as a kind of therapeutic game, a conscious and controlled manipulation of those elements in another author's writing which have exerted a persistent and perhaps inexplicable effect. By appropriating and transforming these materials, by marking them as his own and subordinating them to his own imaginative ends, the parodist effects a psychological release and completes the demystification (or detoxication) of the prior text. Restraint governs the procedure; while the transposition of borrowed elements to a new environment produces ironic overtones and implications, the earlier text never becomes the explicit object of ridicule: the name of the demon cannot be spoken. Indeed, as we discover in **"The Jewbird,"** these transposed elements are sometimes so fully subsumed by the narrative in which they occur that they acquire a phantasmic quality. This paradoxical phenomenon of visibility/invisibility can thus be understood finally as a function of the contradictory process described by Proust as exorcism. One regains his authorial voice by losing it: the obsessive material assumes a tangible form as the parodist allows it to have its way for a while; yet the whole enterprise depends upon his ability to reassert control, to subordinate this material to his own creative purposes, and at last to slide it beneath the surface of the liberating text. Only through this arcane ritual, it would seem, can he free himself from the literary influence which haunts him like an ominous bird of yore.

J. Gerald Kennedy, "Parody as Exorcism: 'The Raven' and 'The Jewbird'," in Genre, *Vol. 13, No. 2, Summer, 1980, pp. 161-69.*

Sheldon J. Hershinow   (essay date 1980)

[*In the following excerpt, Hershinow comments on Malamud's concern with human nature's ambivalence and his stylistic technic of combining fantasy and realism.*]

The principal subject of Malamud's short stories is the ambivalence of human nature. **"The Bill"** (1951), for example, emphasizes the duality of human nature in which compassion wars with self-interest, conscience with greed. A tenement janitor, Willy Schlegel, takes advantage of a neighborly grocer, Mr. Panessa, by running up a bill of eighty-three dollars and then switching to a nearby self-service market. Obsessed by guilt, he develops a hatred for the elderly Panessa. When he receives a letter from Mrs. Panessa pleading for ten dollars for her sick husband, Willy hides in the cellar, but the next day he pawns his overcoat and runs back with the money—only to discover the grocer being carried off in a coffin. Willy's sinking heart becomes "a black painted window. . . . And the bill was never paid." The ending of the story makes clear to the reader that Willy has turned Mr. Panessa's gift into an emotional debt that he can never repay, although it remains uncertain whether Willy himself shares the insight.

In this early story Malamud has the kindly Mr. Panessa express a sentiment that can serve as a metaphor for Malamud's persistently expressed view of humans as sentient beings who need compassion and communion in the face of an often oppressive existence. Although on the edge of bankruptcy, the grocer extends credit to a poverty-stricken customer, saying that being human meant "you give credit to somebody else and he gave credit to you." To fail to give "credit" to another human being—even when you know the credit is undeserved—is to deny the humanity in yourself, to extinguish within your own being the light that has been given to you.

Malamud depicts down-and-out characters who try to salvage small victories from large defeats. Using ingenious symbols, and picturesque or grotesque characters, he ends his short stories with quick, mildly shocking conclusions: two men kissing, death chants for the living, reversals of victor and victim, the ascendence of a black Jewish angel, flashes of self-revelation. These frozen tableaux leave the reader slightly dazzled and bewildered. The apparent simplicity of Malamud's plots and the obviousness of his subject matter combine with the sophisticated techniques of the modern short-story writer to create a tension—an intricate interplay of form and content—that captures, when successful, a strangely haunting segment of human experience. In his parables of pain, suffering, and the possibility of moral growth, Malamud is able to touch the conscience and excite the visual imagination.

In **"The Mourners"** (1955), Kessler, a retired egg candler, lives as a recluse in "a cheap flat on the top floor of a decrepit tenement on the East Side," having long ago abandoned his wife and children. After an argument with the janitor over the disposal of the garbage, Kessler is given notice, but he refuses to leave. With the compassionate help of his neighbors, who are aroused by his suffering and loneliness, Kessler manages to cling to his "home." The landlord, Gruber, threatens Kessler with dispossession. Kessler responds by barricading himself inside his flat.

One day, overcome by apprehension at his tenant's silence, Gruber climbs the four flights of stairs to Kessler's apartment. Despite pangs of guilt, he plans to increase the rent after Kessler's eviction. When his loud knocking brings no response, Gruber nervously lets himself in with a passkey. He discovers Kessler sitting on the floor (a sign of mourning in Jewish tradition), "rocking back and forth," moaning and tearing at his flesh. Kessler is mourning for himself, his past misdeeds, his abandoned wife and children. But Gruber, "sweating brutally," suddenly conceives the notion that Kessler mourns for him, his dead spirit of humanity. He becomes filled with remorse for all the pain he has inflicted. "With a cry of shame he tore the sheet off Kessler's bed, and wrapping it around his bulk, sank heavily to the floor and became a mourner."

Within nine pages Malamud creates a strangely moving experience. The bleak setting of crumbling tenements and stinking apartments serves as an appropriate backdrop for Kessler's life of self-imposed loneliness and isolation. The conditions of his apartment parallel the rotting, disordered, aimless wreckage of his life. He is a grotesque character leading a grotesque life. And yet, by the end of the story Kessler arrives at a moral insight—and what is more, causes another, Gruber, to have a shock of ironic self-recognition.

Some critics have complained that the spectacular epiphany in which the two men join together in their repentance is too abrupt and weighted with meaning to be supported by such two-dimensional, grotesque characters. The criticism is certainly just. Here, even more than in his novels, Malamud strains the plot line in the direction of symbolic

meanings. Nonetheless, **"The Mourners"** produces a haunting, disquieting reaction that stays with the reader long after the story is put aside. Malamud uses a spare, symbolic design that moves Kessler and Gruber from caricature to moral allegory. In the process he somehow creates a surprisingly full experience.

Several techniques of style contribute to this accomplishment. Gruber's speech is laced with colorful expressions that nicely capture his put-upon air of imposed burdens, as when he implores his janitor, "Don't monkey with my blood pressure." Malamud underscores Gruber's exaggerated air of suffering by using the language of hyperbole. When he receives bad news while eating dinner, "The food turned to lumps in his throat." When Gruber enters Kessler's apartment and sees him engaged in his act of mourning, he "gazed around the room, it was clean, drenched in daylight and fragrance." Bypassing realism, Malamud is better able to capture the moment of moral crisis, when Kessler and Gruber transcend their suffering by remembering (or discovering) their common humanity. Yet, ironically, Gruber's genuine and moving self-recognition comes from the mistaken impression that Kessler is mourning for him, when in fact Kessler mourns only his own past misdeeds. It is a moment of double self-discovery mixed with misapprehension, a powerful statement in irony that creates a bittersweet moment of pained possibility.

"Angel Levine" (1955) is less somber and more fantastic. Manischevitz, a poor Jewish tailor, undergoes Job-like "reverses and indignities." He has lost everything, business, son, daughter; he has a wife who is hopelessly ill and Manischevitz is himself too sick to work more than a few hours a day to maintain their bare existence. In answer to his prayers, Levine arrives, a black Jewish angel who is "in a condition of probation" until he can earn his wings through inspiring the tailor's faith. Unable to accept the idea of a Jewish angel being black, Manischevitz rejects him, and both fall into deep despair. Finally, continued suffering causes the tailor to acknowledge Levine as "an angel from God," whereupon Levine soars off to heaven on "a pair of magnificent black wings" and Manischevitz's troubles miraculously cease. "A wonderful thing . . . ," he tells his suddenly healthy wife, "Believe me, there are Jews everywhere."

In this story Malamud uses fantasy as a unifying frame for a mixture of the comic and the serious. The reader must accept the story on three levels simultaneously—the real, the supernatural, and the allegorical. The matter-of-fact language has a rough-hewn simplicity that convinces one of the reality of Manischevitz's suffering:

> Fanny [his wife] lay at death's door. Through shrunken lips she muttered concerning her childhood, the sorrows of the marriage bed, the loss of her children, yet wept to live. Manischevitz tried not to listen, but even without ears he would have heard.

Although Levine claims to be an angel, he is described in the language of everyday reality, so that the reader, like Manischevitz, wonders how a spiritual being could appear in such an earthy, slightly disheveled form. Levine is a realistic angel, but he also has the symbolic and allegorical function of a conscience figure who provides Manischevitz with a test of faith. In this way the story becomes a comic parable leading to a moment of self-recognition for Manischevitz and moral awareness for the reader.

After first meeting Levine, Manischevitz wonders, "so if God sends me an angel, why a black?" He becomes convinced of Levine's legitimacy when he dreams of the black "standing before a faded mirror preening small decaying opalescent wings." He passes his test of faith by accepting Levine as a humane, compassionate, and possibly supernatural being and arrives at the insight that shows the point of the parable—"there are Jews everywhere." In other words, all men suffer, but we can transcend our suffering if we recognize and have faith in our common humanity.

Some commentators have maintained that the story is too fanciful and fantastic to be taken seriously. True, the presence of the supernatural is likely to puzzle the reader, but Malamud creates confusion deliberately for comic and thematic effect. For example, the final line about Jews being everywhere serves not only as an ironic, slightly enigmatic statement weighted with moral meaning, but also as a comic punchline that satirizes the myth of the Jews holding the patent on suffering. In addition, the fantastic comedy of the story implies the existence of a spiritual dimension in life without commiting Malamud to a specific faith, dogma, or theology.

"The Jewbird" (1963) is an even more bizarre fantasy, but in this case the central character fails his test of faith. Harry Cohen, a frozen-food salesman, unconsciously wishes to escape his Jewishness and become a fully assimilated American. His latent hatred of Jewishness becomes aroused when a talking bird—a Yiddish-speaking Jewbird called Mr. Schwartz—flies into his kitchen. Asking only for a place to stay, a little herring, maybe a glass of schnapps, Schwartz in return helps Harry's son with his schoolwork. In time, with his Yiddish speech and old-country ways Schwartz becomes a haunting reminder of Harry's immigrant experience. Harry becomes increasingly hostile to Schwartz and eventually throws him out the window into the winter snow, apparently killing him.

Clearly Schwartz serves as a symbolic character, a subconscious double who represents that part of Cohen, his Jewish identity, that he wishes to deny. Harry is a trapped and tortured character; his failure to accept the Jewbird represents a rejection of himself. **"The Jewbird,"** like **"Angel Levine,"** is an anecdote whose punchline provides the point of the comic parable: "Who did it to you, Mr. Schwartz?" asks the weeping son upon finding the frozen, mangled corpse. "Anti-Semeets," Mrs. Cohen says later. If **"Angel Levine"** suggests that Jews (metaphorically) are everywhere, **"The Jewbird"** demonstrates the opposite, that anti-Semites are everywhere; even a Jew can become one by denying a part of himself and losing his sense of humanity.

The story succeeds because of the matter-of-fact style with which Malamud treats the fantastic. "The window was open so the skinny bird flew in. Flappity-flap with its fraz-zled black wings. That's how it goes. It's open, you're in. Closed, you're out and that's your fate." The idiom is a terse, rapid vernacular that captures the rhythms of Yiddish combined with an ironic understatement. In addition, the differing speech patterns of Harry Cohen and Jewbird Schwartz reveal the central conflict between Jewish heritage and assimilationist ambition. Speaking of Cohen's son, Schwartz says, in Yiddish-English, "He's a good boy—you don't have to worry. He won't be a schicker [drunk] or a wifebeater, God forbid, but a scholar he'll never be, if you know what I mean, although maybe a good mechanic. It's no disgrace in these times." Harry replies in colloquial American, "If I were you . . . I'd keep my big snoot out of other people's private business." As Harry's antagonism climaxes, the two engage in a farcical wrestling match in which Schwartz catches Harry's nose in his beak and Harry punches the bird with his fist. If the style were more elaborate, the whole thing would be only a gag using the comic technique of incongruous juxtaposition. By maintaining the contrast between the matter-of-fact, earthy language and the fantastic events, Malamud creates a comic parable whose silliness turns serious at the end. The reader, by virtue of Cohen's failure to accept his own buried genuine self, is given a glimpse of moral insight into the painful duality of human nature.

In **"Idiots First"** (1963), the Angel of Death materializes as an arrogant, bulky figure named Ginzburg, "with hairy nostrils and a fishy smell," who pursues a dying Jew named Mendel. The action turns on Mendel's desperate determination to fend off his pursuer until he can get his grown imbecile son, Isaac, on a train to a California kinsman. His frantic efforts to raise money for Isaac's fare culminate in violence when Ginzburg, reappearing as the station ticket collector, informs the pleading father he has missed the train, which Mendel can plainly see waiting at the platform. "What will happen happens," Ginzburg smirks. "This isn't my responsibility. . . . I ain't in the anthropomorphic business." Nor, he adds, is pity his "commodity." "The law is the law . . . the cosmic universal law." Shouting, "You bastard, don't you know what it means human?" Mendel seizes the collector by the throat, and, despite the freezing cold that invades his body, refuses to release his grip. As the gasping father clings to Ginzburg, he sees in the collector's eyes "the depth of his [own] terror." But Mendel sees also that Ginzburg, staring into his eyes, has glimpsed in them the depth of his own "awful wrath." Angel or not, the collector beholds darkness and "a shimmering, starry, blinding light" that astounds and shames him. "Who me?" Ginzburg asks and relinquishes his grip. Isaac is free to go.

The story is a virtual mini-drama of Malamud's themes of compassion, charity, and sacrifice. Mendel's outraged cry, "Don't you know what it means human?" protests a blighted universe, but nonetheless his demonstration of love does make a difference, and in the end neither the Angel of Death nor his "cosmic law" has proved a match for a dying father's love. This bizarre story suggests that humans can defy inevitability; even fate may be humanized and life snatched (if briefly) from death.

"Idiots First" succeeds because of Malamud's skillful

blending of reality and dream, natural and supernatural. From the opening lines, when Mendel draws on his "cold embittered clothing," reality becomes shaped by human feeling. As Mendel scurries about frantically trying to raise the train fare, the reality of the New York City setting on a bleak November night slowly slips away and becomes transformed into a vaguely surrealistic dream landscape of dark, deserted streets. At one point Mendel enters a strange park with leafless trees and a mournful wind, where he encounters a mysterious stranger whom he perceives to be Ginzburg. Unlike **"The Mourners,"** in which Malamud puts a grotesque character into a realistic setting, in **"Idiots First"** he places comparatively real characters into a grotesque setting. The effect produces a disquieting blurring of the line between reality and fantasy. We do not know how much of the action "really" happens and how much exists in Mendel's desperately fearful imagination. The epiphany produces a shock that slowly turns to admiration as we realize we have before us a seriocomic parable of human pain and possibility.

In Malamud's most well known and perhaps best story, **"The Magic Barrel"** (1954), Leo Finkle, an ascetic, scholarly rabbinical student nearing graduation, decides to acquire a wife. He calls in a marriage broker, Pinye Salzman, who promises the timid Leo results from the photographs and information cards kept in a barrel. One prospect, Lily Hirschorn, asks how he became "enamored of God," and the potential rabbi unconsciously blurts, "I came to God not because I loved Him, but because I did not." This brief encounter proves to be a soul-shattering experience, as Leo comes to the unexpected realization that he cannot

Caricature drawing of Malamud, by David Levine. Reprinted with permission from The New York Review of Books. *Copyright (c) 1973 Nyrev, Inc.*

love God because he does not love humanity. However, he guiltily consoles himself that "he was a Jew and a Jew suffered"—and if he is imperfect, his ideal is not. He feels that this new self-knowledge will help him find a bride.

His hopes quickly fade; most of Pinye's photographed faces bear the marks of defeat. Yet the final one, a girl whose face seems to reflect both youth and age, innocence and experience, touches his heart. If Pinye is delighted at the prospect of a commission, he is horrified at Leo's choice. Her picture was a mistake, he protests. The girl is Pinye's own daughter, Stella, "a wild one." "To me she is dead now," Pinye declares. But Leo insists. This girl will understand him—perhaps even love him. "He . . . concluded to convert her to goodness, himself to God." Yet when the old man finally agrees, Leo suspects a well-laid trap. Stella awaits him under a street lamp wearing a white dress and red shoes. As Leo rushes toward her, he notes that her eyes are "filled with desperate innocence," and he pictures in her "his own redemption." Around the corner the old marriage broker leans against the wall chanting prayers for the dead.

The events of the story force Leo to realize that his years of isolated study have served largely as an escape from life. His attraction to Stella derives from his belief that she has lived, has experienced the pain of life and yet has retained a kind of innocence. When he meets her she wears scarlet for prostitution and white for purity. The ambiguous concluding tableau does not reveal whether Leo has headed towards salvation or destruction.

Speaking a colorful Yiddishized English and reeking of fish, Pinye Salzman is half con-man and half spiritual exemplar. Each of the marital candidates sounds like a used car for which Pinye makes a "pitch." When Leo meets Lily Hirschorn, he realizes that both of them have been "sold a bill of goods." She is older than he thought; he is not the "wonder rabbi" she had expected. Yet, as Lily's questions force him to a moment of profound self-illumination, Leo has the strange sense that Pinye lurks nearby, "perhaps in a tree . . . , flashing the lady signals with a pocket mirror." After he has fallen in love with Stella from her picture, Leo is "afflicted by a tormenting suspicion that Salzman had planned it all to happen this way." The reader, like Leo, is left wondering whether Pinye is merely a clever con-man or a spiritual teacher.

Pinye's earthy speech and high-pressure sale's techniques create a comic contrast to Leo's learning and innocence. Pinye also contrasts in another way—he serves as a representative of the traditional, old-country way of life, an ethos that is fast disappearing in modern America. The old man is astonished to hear the young rabbinical student from Cleveland launch into a learned discourse on the time-honored institution of the arranged marriage. However, Leo reveals his true feelings when he rejects Pinye's final, and most attractive, candidate: " 'Ruth K. Nineteen years. Honor student. Father offers thirteen thousand cash to the right bridegroom. He is a medical doctor. Stomach specialist with marvelous practice. Brother in law owns garment business. Particular people.' . . . 'But don't you think this young girl believes in love?' " A fear of life and love, not a pious sense of tradition has led Leo to the old matchmaker. Yet Pinye serves as counterpart as well as contrast to Leo. He is a subconscious double who represents a submerged part of Leo's soul that he cannot ignore. Dogged by the wily old man, Leo learns that life consists of more than book learning. In this way Pinye serves as the catalyst for Leo to gain insight into himself.

In a nearly perfect union of form and content, Malamud uses fantasy and the changing of the seasons to create a unifying frame for this comic parable of denial of life and the hope of regeneration. Malamud structures the actions of the story around the symbolic association of spring with hope and regeneration. Leo's pain and isolation occur in winter; with spring comes the incident with Lily and the possibility of a new life. Leo's painful self-insight amounts to the labor pains of his emotional rebirth.

More remarkable is the language through which Malamud infuses the story with fantasy. At the moment of Leo's insight into his lack of love, he looks at the sky and sees "a profusion of loaves of bread go flying like ducks over his head." Malamud captures Pinye's plaintive frustration at Leo's indecisiveness by describing him as "a skeleton with haunted eyes"; hurt by Leo's rejection of him "Salzman's face went dead white, the world had snowed on him." When Leo meets Stella, Malamud writes, "he pictured, in her, his own redemption. Violins and lit candles revolved in the sky." The careful phrasing of the first of these two sentences makes clear that the optimism belongs to Leo and may or may not be shared by Malamud; the second sentence contains no definite indication whether the vision of violins and candles in the sky exists only in Leo's mind; this ambiguity causes a blurring of the lines between fact and fantasy.

The concluding picture of Pinye chanting the prayer for the dead (kaddish) uses realistic language but occurs within the context of fantasy. The effect is to produce a striking but deliberately ambiguous ending. In Jewish tradition a man may chant kaddish for a living relative as a means of symbolically disowning that person. In a general sense, kaddish may simply suggest great sorrow. Does Pinye mourn simply because his daughter is dead to him? Or does he mourn for himself because of his complicity in bringing Leo and Stella together? Or, perhaps, for Leo's loss of innocence? Or Stella's sinful ways? All (and more) are possible. The ironic juxtaposition of hopeful optimism with unexpected sorrow, all within a context of fantasy, suggests the inappropriateness of a literal interpretation. The reader is left with the illogical, vaguely unsettling but deeply moving impression that Pinye's mournful chant somehow captures the pain, suffering, and loneliness of life while also welcoming the possibility of spiritual growth.

> *Sheldon J. Hershinow, in his* Bernard Malamud, *Frederick Ungar Publishing Co., 1980, 165 p.*

Iska Alter (essay date 1981)

[*In the following excerpt, Alter addresses issues of black-white race relations in Malamud's "Angel Levine" and "Black Is My Favorite Color."*]

A short story is a way of indicating the complexity of life in a few pages, producing the surprise and effect of a profound knowledge in a short time. There's, among other things, a drama, a resonance, of the reconciliation of opposites: much to say, a little time to say it, something like the effect of a poem.

—*Bernard Malamud, in Daniel Stern's "The Art of Fiction: Bernard Malamud," in* Conversations with Malamud, *edited by Lawrence M. Lasher, 1991.*

[The] respective fates of Jews and blacks have been linked since Noah and his sons Ham, Shem, and Japheth built the Ark. But it is only in America that the Jew's fortunes have been so wedded to the black experience, at once so like and yet so unlike his own.

By characterizing the Jew, representing the powers of the intellect, and the black, embodying the threat of violent sexuality, as the villainous participants in the archetypal struggle between evil and good, white Christian America thrust upon them an unexpected, uneasy alliance as perennial outsiders and strangers. "The Jew was seen as the usurer, the castrator, the bad father, the abuser of the intelligence, the icy realist, the cold crafty figure of vengefulness, the anarchist, and the revolutionary. The Negro was perceived as a simple-minded child, as a primitive, a rapist, a brute, a murderer, a symbol of unbridled emotions" [Lenora Berson, *The Negroes and the Jews,* 1971]. Though both the Jew and the black have internalized facets of these externally imposed stereotypes in defining themselves and the other, the Jew could always regard himself as a member of the chosen people, hence superior to any local environment he might temporarily inhabit. However, the black stereotype, rooted as it is in a stigmatized color permanent and ineradicable, is a degrading and debasing one. So the union, tenuous at best, began to disintegrate even as it was forming.

As the Jew became assimilated into a society whose concept of caste was based on color rather than creed, he moved further and further from a tradition of suffering and exile, and he looked to the black as a way of relieving the guilt created by abandoning his past.

> And so, as the WASP used the Jew so the Jew uses the Negro as a symbol of his own lost misery. This empathy with the wretched of the earth, this transference of sorrow, this unease at a certain comfort, all translate themselves into a feeling of guilt and obligation which have led to the close identification of many Jews with the Negro. For the Jew, the Black man has become a kind of stand-in for himself. [Berson]

The black man, whose enslaved ancestors identified with the suffering and persecuted Hebrews, increasingly rejects these Jewish protestations of sympathy, understanding, and innocence because of the role the Jew has come to play in the economic life of the ghetto. To poor blacks, the Jewish shopkeeper, landlord, pawnbroker, welfare investigator, teacher is "the Man," the visible force of the oppressing "Mr. Charlie." This perception of the Jewish role in the black ghetto has been described by James Baldwin, remembering his own experiences [in his *Notes of a Native Son,* 1957]:

> Jews in Harlem are small tradesmen, rent collectors, real estate agents, and pawnbrokers; they operate in accordance with the American business tradition of exploiting Negroes, and they are therefore identified with oppression and hated for it. I remember meeting no Negro in the years of my growing up, in my family or out of it, who would really ever trust a Jew, and few who did not, indeed, exhibit for them the blackest contempt.

It is the writers, Mailer, Bellow, and Malamud, who have charted the shifting ambiguities inherent in this symbiotic dependency. Indeed, [in his *Waiting for the End,* 1965] Leslie Fiedler has noted about the Jewish-American novelist "that at the same moment the Jew whom his Gentile fellow-citizen emulates may himself be in the process of becoming an imaginary Negro." We can trace the extent to which the Jewish psyche has been absorbed by the riddle of black identity by examining varying depictions of this association in Malamud's **"Angel Levine"** [and] **"Black Is My Favorite Color."** . . . It is this area of Malamud's social criticism that has been most clearly affected by rapidly changing contemporary events.

"Angel Levine" was published during the bland, self-satisfied decade of the fifties when few Americans were even capable of acknowledging the depth of Negro discontent. The injustice done the Negro (not yet metamorphosed into the black) had not yet been recognized as an issue of sufficient political importance at a time when the Cold War seemed to foreshadow Armageddon, nor had civil rights seized the public imagination as the testing ground for this society's oft-stated belief in equality. Malamud's short story is a fifties parable, suffused with the admirable but optimistic innocence that characterized the liberalism of that good grey era. This hopefulness, based, perhaps, on naive assumptions about what constituted black attitudes toward white society, is concerned with the degree to which a simple verbal commitment to the ideal of brotherhood can effect extensive and permanent changes in the conditions of urban blacks.

The protagonist of this brief fable is a poor, prematurely old Jew, Manischevitz by name. His poverty places him on the same economic level as the blacks whom he must learn to accept; his wife Fanny even takes in laundry, the characteristic occupation of black women. His age and his religion place him within a tradition that fears the stranger, especially the dark stranger. His afflictions are Job's:

> Although Manischevitz was insured against fire, damage suits by two customers who had been hurt in the flames deprived him of every penny he had collected. At almost the same time, his son, of much promise, was killed in the war, and his daughter, without so much as a word of warning, married a lout and disappeared with him as off the face of the earth. Thereafter Manischevitz was victimized by excruciating backaches and found himself unable to work even as presser. . . . His Fanny, a good wife and mother . . . began before his eyes to waste away.

Manischevitz's suffering has been adequately generalized (note especially that the daughter runs away with a lout, not necessarily a Christian) to make him an emblem for stricken, victimized, and fearful humanity.

To alleviate Manischevitz's, and therefore humanity's pain, God sends a black Jewish angel. But Manischevitz is initially too suspicious to honor this historically threatening and alien figure as a savior. Necessity, however, drives him out of his narrow definition of the human family to seek Alexander Levine in Harlem. There he discovers a new, but not unfamiliar world, that is in some ways a black replica of his own. The first person he speaks to is a tailor, a shadowy mirror of himself, "an old skinny Negro . . . sitting cross-legged on his work-bench . . . Manischevitz admiring the tailor's deft, thimbled fingerwork." On a second journey into Harlem, a mysterious congregation of black Jews, inhabiting what was previously a cabaret, reveals through the words of a young boy the eternal wisdom, "God put the spirit in all things. . . . He put it in the green leaves and the yellow flowers. He put it with the gold in the fishes and the blue in the sky. That's how it came to us." As an act of faith in this newly acquired credo, Manischevitz sees through to the essential Levine and accepts him as a Jew, hence a redeemed member of humanity, in spite of his sharp, new unangelic clothes and the "drunken look [that] had settled upon his formerly dignified face." This gesture, incorporating the black angel into the race of man, assures humanity's renewal. He returns to Fanny, miraculously resurrected, and well at last, saying "A wonderful thing Fanny. . . . Believe me, there are Jews everywhere."

Although there is much sympathy evident in the story, I wish to suggest an alternative, albeit somewhat controversial, reading of **"Angel Levine,"** one that seems to advance a more equivocal doctrine. It is, perhaps, an uncomfortable assertion of Judaic moral dominance and white humanitarianism, rather than a completely triumphant paean to universal brotherhood, which ultimately subsumes Alexander Levine's blackness into a concept of mankind that would erase ethnic and racial differences. Although Malamud attempts to impose the quality of shared experience by creating a common economic status for Manischevitz and Levine, there is a dramatic difference. In America, where caste is chiefly a racial phenomenon, the Jew is less threatened by the prejudices of society. His position is less precarious because his skin will always be white, insuring the possibility of assimilation. The black, however, is ineradicably black. Therefore his situation is, for the most part, an inescapable factor of his birth.

On a deeper level, however, Manischevitz is a singularly inappropriate metaphor for suffering humanity. He is very much a Jew who accepts the concept of Jewish exclusivity, instead of the belief in the brotherhood of man. Even to consider the idea of a black Jew threatens that insular cohesiveness that permitted Jewish survival. Confronted by the actual probability of a black Jewish angel, Manischevitz regards it as a cruel and bitter joke on a man whose identity has been defined by references to Jewish religious practice: "What sort of mockery was it . . . of a faithful servant who had from childhood lived in the synagogues, always concerned with the word of God?" His name is even the brand name of a line of products made specifically for the kosher home.

While his two uncertain journeys to Harlem widen a restricted environment, they are in fact rejections of that black world. Manischevitz is appalled by the raucous sensuality inherent in the aspects of black life he witnesses, "whitefaced," through the window of Bella's nightclub. And he is horrified by what has happened to Alexander Levine, losing his Jewishness as he has descended into what Manischevitz regards as the essence of blackness. But these rejections are reciprocal. Not only is Manischevitz repelled by the black vision of existence, but also the inhabitants of Harlem do not welcome the intrusion of his white Jewishness: "Beat it, pale puss." "Exit, Yankel, Semitic trash." Manischevitz recognizes only Levine's religion, not his color, nor his significance for the human community. The black feather that falls from his wings as he ascends to heaven turns white before it dissolves and disappears into the imagination.

It is particularly interesting to observe in this context what happens to the figure of Alexander Levine, black, Jewish, and "a bona fide angel of God within prescribed limitations." It is his Jewish identity, rather than his black self, that seems to endow Levine with his essential uniqueness. And when this is denied him by Manischevitz's suspicion and prejudice, Alexander Levine declines into a vicious parody of what white society assumes the black man is. His language disintegrates into black patois, his face loses its dignity, he consorts with whores.

After his initial rebuff, Levine's appearance and angelic ethics deteriorate; and this visible decay disappoints Manischevitz:

> His derby was dented and had a gray smudge on the side. His ill-fitting suit was shabbier, as if he had been sleeping in it. His shoes and trouser cuffs were muddy, and his face was covered with an impenetrable stubble the color of licorice. . . . A big-breasted Negress in a purple evening gown appeared before Levine's table, and . . . broke into a vigorous shimmy. . . . As Bella's gyrations continued, Levine rose, his eyes lit in excitement. She embraced him with vigor . . . and they tangoed together across the floor, loudly applauded by the noisy customers.

A second refusal sends the angel deeper into this negative stereotype, complete with that most Jewish of fears—drunkenness:

> He [Levine] was sitting loose-lipped at Bella's side table. They were tippling from an almost empty whiskey fifth. Levine had shed his old clothes, wore a shiny new checkered suit, a pearl-gray derby, cigar, and big, two-tone button shoes. To the tailor's dismay, a drunken look had settled upon his formerly dignified face. He

leaned toward Bella, tickled her ear lobe with his pinky, while whispering words that sent her into gales of raucous laughter. She fondled his knee.

And when he is finally acknowledged as an angel, he discards his "nigger" costume and returns to his old clothes, calling the transformation "freshening up." If he cannot be Jewish, apparently his only other choice is to become the white man's version of "the nigger." If there might exist a more positive black identity, it is not considered.

The humane and redemptive elements of **"Angel Levine"** are undeniable. That Manischevitz is meant to be an example of suffering mankind rather than simply a Jew *sui generis* is clear, but not entirely convincing. As Robert Alter asserts [in "Bernard Malamud: Jewishness as Metaphor," in *After the Tradition*, 1969], "the Jew as Everyman is a kind of literary symbol that is likely to wear thin very quickly," because as he further points out, to universalize the unique history of the Jews can be both an insulting and a sentimental vulgarization of their tragic past. And if such a metaphor might violate the particular Jewish experience, surely it does an equal injustice to the black traditions presented in the story. It would appear then, that some of the unconscious assumptions that control the dynamics of **"Angel Levine"** serve to undercut the ideal of the brotherhood of man. It is the Jew, identified as such, who is made the moral paradigm with which the black man must identify. And that such an identification is desirable goes without saying. When we examine **"Black Is My Favorite Color,"** we can see the further disintegration of traditional egalitarianism in the face of history.

The idealism concerning the possibilities of racial harmony that dominates the surface of **"Angel Levine"** is the motive force behind the civil rights movement of the early nineteen sixties. Blacks and whites together ("We shall not be moved") integrated lunch counters, picketed Woolworth's, rode freedom buses South, desegregated schools, were bombed, hosed, bitten by dogs, jailed, beaten, sometimes murdered. Under pressure exerted by both races, the institutions of government and society seemed increasingly responsive to the demands for justice, ready to redeem the pledges of the American Revolution owed to its black citizens. On a hot, steamy day in August, 1963, Martin Luther King told a rainbow gathering of honorable, optimistic people massed before the Lincoln Memorial of a dream as old as hope. And "We Shall Overcome" became the nation's new anthem.

Given this atmosphere, the pessimism of **"Black Is My Favorite Color"** strikes with the uncommon force of prophecy. It is the story of the sweet-sour existence of the aptly named Nat Lime as he unsuccessfully attempts to counter through love the deepening hostility of blacks to all manifestations of white domination. He is a man who inhabits a black society in which the most preliminary human overtures are often seen as a purposeful extension of the white man's power. However, this unhappy portrait may be regarded as an overt extension of the underlying pressures noted in **"Angel Levine."** It is also worth observing at this point that while **"Angel Levine"** is a fantasy whose very form accentuates the implausible but humane conclusion, **"Black Is My Favorite Color"** is quintessential realism, thereby reinforcing the truth of its unhappy ending.

The title itself does not seem to imply the unconscious sense of Jewish moral superiority of **"Angel Levine,"** but rather a capacity to accept and love human difference. "I got an eye for color. I appreciate. Who wants," says Nat Lime, "everybody to be the same?" But **"Black Is My Favorite Color"** as a title serves, in fact, to emphasize the ironic discrepancy between desire and reality that so dominates a story which opens in an environment of willed isolation and deliberately blurred identities: "Charity Sweetness sits in the toilet eating her two hardboiled eggs while I'm having my ham sandwich and coffee in the kitchen. That's how it goes only don't get the idea of ghettoes. If there's a ghetto I'm the one that's in it." And it is the black maid who rejects the idea of community in the ritual act of breaking bread, sensing perhaps not the impulse to equality but the patronizing white employer, for whom she does housework: "The first time Charity Sweetness came in to clean . . . I made the mistake to ask her to sit down at the kitchen table with me and eat her lunch. . . . So she cooked up her two hardboiled eggs and sat down and took a small bite out of one of them. But after a minute she stopped chewing and she got up and carried the eggs in a cup in the bathroom and since then she eats there." Nat Lime's bewildered readiness to accept "colored people" makes this intentional segregation an understandable gesture.

In **"Angel Levine,"** the author tries to establish at least the appearance of brotherhood by creating a similarity of class. Nat Lime in **"Black Is My Favorite Color"** is clearly an exploitative presence in Harlem, no longer a replica of the white milieu, but hostile territory. He is a Jewish liquor dealer feeding off the need to dream, the desire to escape, a man who gives discounts to his better customers, thereby keeping them sedated and desensitized. In describing the problems caused by the liquor traffic in the ghetto, Lenora Berson says: "Of all the enterprises that have exploited the poor, none has encouraged more atrocious social fallout than the liquor trade, which includes alcoholism, sexual promiscuity, family instability, violence, brutality and the improvident use of limited funds." And though Nat asserts that "personally for me there's only one human color and that's the color of blood," his vocabulary throughout the story reveals a preoccupation with the divisions that race creates.

Blackness has always represented for Nat Lime the extremes of experience unavailable to a nice Jewish boy who at the age of forty was still dutifully living with his mother, and who can innocently claim "I'm the kind of man when I think of love I'm thinking of marriage." Black lives, in both social and psychic terms, express the limits to which the human spirit can be stretched and still survive:

> Any Negro who wishes to live must live with danger from his first day, and no experience can ever be casual to him . . . knowing in the cells of his existence that life was war, nothing but war, . . . could rarely afford the sophisticated inhibitions of civilization and so he kept for his survival the art of the primitive, he lived in the enormous present. . . . Hated from the outside

and therefore hating himself, the Negro was forced into exploring all those moral wildernesses of civilized life. . . . The Negro chose to move instead in that other direction where all situations are equally valid, and in the worst of perversion, promiscuity, pimpery, drug addiction, rape, razor-slash, bottle-break . . . the Negro discovered and elaborated a morality of the bottom. [Norman Mailer, "The White Negro," in his *Advertisements for Myself,* 1960]

Although this is surely Norman Mailer's fantasy about black existence, as James Baldwin points out, it is nonetheless significant that it is precisely this rhetorical stance that becomes part of revolutionary black nationalism as it evolves in the late sixties and early seventies. Eldridge Cleaver put it succinctly [in his *Soul on Ice,* 1968]: "The term *outlaw* appealed to me. . . . I was an 'outlaw.' I had stepped outside of the white man's law, which I repudiated with scorn and self-satisfaction, I became a law unto myself. . . . "

As a child, Nat Lime was poor in a marginal white neighborhood, but the blacks were poorer still, their environment a perpetual reminder of the constancy of death: "the Negro houses looked to me like they had been born and died there, dead not long after the beginning of the world." And Nat is fully aware of the edge his whiteness confers, feeling a prick of conscience that must eventually be acknowledged: "In those days though I had little myself I was old enough to know who was better off, and the whole block of colored houses made me feel bad in the daylight." Black existence defines the complexity of human experience, providing for Nat a sense of what life is really like: "brother, if there can be like this, what can't there be?" This assumption naively and unwittingly exhibits that inherited sense of superiority to *their* poverty, coupled with a fear of the excesses of that black world. But Nat is also admitting an attraction to a world pulsating with vitality, a confession, perhaps, of an absent element in his own personality, a revelation seen by one of life's voyeurs: "Sometimes I was afraid to walk by the houses when they were dark and quiet. . . . I liked it better when they had parties at night and everybody had a good time. The musicians played their banjos and saxophones and the houses shook with the music and laughing."

Violence, so integral to the black milieu he observes and an inevitable component of behavior under conditions of internal and external stress, horrifies Nat to the point of denying its necessary presence: "I was frightened by the blood and wanted to pour it back in the man who was bleeding. . . . I personally couldn't stand it, I was scared of the human race." Yet for the young Nat Lime, it is Buster Wilson's self-containment, his ability to confront his world of blood and to remain apparently untouched by its pain, that is an ineluctable part of his fascination: "but I remember Buster watching without any expression in his eyes."

Blackness also represents the seductiveness of open sensuality, "the young girls, with their pretty dresses and ribbons . . . caught me in my throat when I saw them through the windows." It is therefore not surprising that it is only a black woman who excites Nat, saying of Ornita

Harris' obvious sexual attractiveness and exoticism: "She was a slim woman, dark but not the most dark, about thirty years . . . also well built, with a combination nice legs and a good-size bosom that I like. Her face was pretty, with big eyes and high cheek bones, but lips a little thick. . . . That was the night she wore a purple dress and I thought to myself, my God, what colors. Who paints that picture paints a masterpiece. Everybody looked at us but I had pleasure." Yet the physical presence of her sexuality is described as white: "Under her purple dress she wore a black slip, and when she took that off she had white underwear. When she took off the white underwear she was black again. But I know where the next white was . . . ."

Given Nat Lime's complex but ambiguous responses, it is not surprising that his efforts to establish actual relationships with blacks fail, leaving the human contract unfulfilled. His putative friendship with Buster is part envy, part guilt, an effort that barely recognizes Buster as a human being. He envies Buster's independence, "I liked his type. Buster did everything alone." Nat Lime's underlying attitudes at this point, and through the entire story, resemble those which Norman Podhoretz described in his famous essay, "My Negro Problem—And Ours":

> What counted for me about Negro kids of my own age was that they were "bad boys." There were plenty of bad boys among the whites . . . but the Negroes were *really* bad, bad in a way that beckoned to one, and made one feel inadequate. *We* all went home every day for a lunch of spinach-and-potatoes; *they* roamed around during lunch hour, munching on candy bars. . . . *We* rarely played hookey, or got into serious trouble in school, for all our streetcorner bravado; *they* were defiant, forever staying out (to do what delicious things?), forever making disturbances in class and in the halls, forever being sent to the principal and returning uncowed. But most important of all, they were tough; beautifully, enviably tough, not giving a damn for anyone or anything. . . . To hell with the whole of the adult world that held *us* in its grip and that we never had the courage to rebel against. . . .
>
> This is what I saw and envied and feared in the Negro. . . .

Nat is ashamed of his whiteness, the sign of his responsibility for the conditions which determine the contours of Buster's life. But when Buster invites him into his home, Nat only wishes to escape the impoverished reality of what he sees there, "it smelled so heavy, so impossible, I died till I got out of there. What I saw in the way of furniture I won't mention—the best was falling apart in pieces." So Nat mitigates his guilt by giving Buster those fragments of whiteness he can afford to part with, assuming, of course, that Buster wants those emblems of conscience: "I stole an extra fifteen cents from my mother's pocketbook and I ran back and asked Buster if he wanted to go to the movies . . . which includes my invitations to go with me, my (poor mother's) movie money, Hershey chocolate bars, watermelon slices, even my best Nick Carter and

Merriwell books that I spent hours picking up in junk shops, and that he never gave me back."

His affair with Ornita Harris, however, seems an honest attempt to accept her blackness and to love at last. Yet strain and ambivalence are always present. His initial rebellion is a pallid one, minimizing risk and courting safety. On their first date, he takes her to Greenwich Village, a bohemian environment which willingly tolerates interracialism. He will not take her home to meet his dying mother—that is too great a chance to take. They have their first sexual encounter in a rented room. Only when his mother and the tradition she embodies ("Nathan," she said, "if you ever forget you are a Jew a goy will remind you") is dead, can his rebellion become more overt and seek society: he sells his mother's bed; he invites Ornita into his home; he takes her to meet carefully chosen, *liberal* friends; he proposes marriage.

But this time it is the black community that will not sanction such a union because it is a relationship that seems to reenact the sexual pattern of slavery: the black woman considered only as an object to be manipulated by the white man's lust, no matter how strong are Nat's protestations of love and affection. Significantly, it is at this juncture that the young black men, serving as the active agents of community disapproval, choose to remind Nat of his position as economic exploiter:

> "You talk like a Jew landlord," said the green hat. "Fifty a week for a single room."
>
> "No charge fo' the rats," said the half-inch brim.

In this atmosphere, shaped by overt hostility, unspoken anger, and unconscious ambivalence, the reassuring notion that love can solve all problems seems unworkable.

Nat is incapable of understanding the continued refusals his giving impulse has met with, because he is trapped by the complicated ambiguities of his own responses. He cannot see that to be defined solely in terms of the experiences inaccessible to the white man, to be wanted only as the complement to an incomplete self, is sufficient cause for rejection. Nor is he conscious of his social and political situation in an environment that regards him as the enemy, where even a blind man senses his whiteness and spurns his help. Nat Lime is finally left in his bewilderment to confront a locked door behind which Charity Sweetness sits in splendid isolation. Indeed the world has become a series of locked doors through which love cannot enter, for "the language of the heart either is a dead language or else nobody understands the way you speak it."

> *Iska Alter, "The Broader Canvas: Malamud, the Blacks, and the Jews," in his* The Good Man's Dilemma: Social Criticism in the Fiction of Bernard Malamud, *AMS Press, Inc., 1981, pp. 62-82.*

Dorothy Seidman Bilik   (essay date 1981)

[*In the following excerpt, Bilik examines Malamud's depiction of immigrants and survivors and his use of language, setting, and character to describe Jewish culture.*]

No contemporary American writer has written about immigrants and survivors more frequently or more imaginatively than has Bernard Malamud. His fictional world is peopled with Diasporans of all kinds but, unlike Cahan's assimilated Levinsky, Malamud's characters embody significant fragments of the Jewish past. Most frequently Malamud portrays remnants of the earlier generation of immigrants, unwilling refugees from American Jewish affluence, survivors of an older Jewish community who retain unassimilated Jewish values and who do not relinquish their accents and their anachronistic occupations. Although Malamud includes some survivors of the Holocaust in his fictional Ellis Island, he has not yet directly portrayed a survivor as central figure. . . .

Nevertheless, Malamud's immigrant characters, even when they are not survivors, frequently have the insubstantiality of remnants or of dream figures. Insofar as they embody the modern sense of dream-made-real, Malamud's immigrants resemble the European survivors discussed by Lawrence Langer [in *The Holocaust and the Literary Imagination*, 1975]. However, only in *The Fixer*, where the dream is a nightmare indeed, does Malamud's world contain the horrors that Langer includes in the aesthetics of atrocity. In Malamud's other fictions the grotesque elements are countered with the possibility of realizing the Diaspora dream of earthly redemption. In addition, Malamud's modern adaptation of the traditionally ironic tone of the Yiddish story teller distances and ameliorates some of the grimmer implications of his fiction.

The dreamlike insubstantiality, the redemptive vision, and the irony are frequently manifested in Malamud's modern counterparts to the East European Hasidic *rebes* and *tsadikim*. Malamud's modern *tsadikim* are considerably less saintly than their historic predecessors, but their very susceptibility to the modern world allows them to be more effective as teachers—the essential task of a *rebe*. Fictional antecedents for Malamud's *rebes* are Henry Roth's Reb Yidel Pankower and Isaac Rosenfeld's Reb Feldman. In Rosenfeld's novel the relationship of the *rebe* to the young seeker is shown as anachronistic. In the writings of Malamud, the teacher is both more ambiguous and more effective, yet the ancient Jewish paradigm is discernible. The pupil-teacher relationship may be of a younger, assimilated Jew to an older, more traditional Jew; sometimes the relationship is between Jew and gentile; usually the relationship is between a more callow seeker and one more experienced in suffering. Frequently Malamud develops the quester and the teacher as dual protagonists or *Doppelgänger* (*The Assistant*, "**The Magic Barrel**," "**The Last Mohican**"). The immigrant figure is the keeper of the Jewish past, a past that is transmitted in much the same way that the Hasidic masters passed on wisdom and lore to their pupils. Indirectly by means of parable, sometimes fragmentarily, sometimes inadvertently, unlikely modern Hasidim like Morris Bober, Pinye Salzman, Shimen Susskind, and others pass on meaningful fragments of Jewish ethics and collective Jewish history to questers and novices who are even more unlikely and unaware than their teachers.

The Malamud novice or quester is frequently in error at the beginning of his quest. Sometimes he attempts to make a new life free of his past (*Pictures of Fidelman,* "**Lady of the Lake**") or attempts to live a life in terms of false goals (*The Assistant,* "**The Magic Barrel**"). Through his encounter with an immigrant or exile, the quester once more confronts his own historic past or reforms his goals and sometimes, in classic style, achieves recognition and reversal. The contact between quester and immigrant *Doppelgänger* at times results in the quester's seeming to incorporate the older figure. The older figure may wane, even die, but some of his spirit or knowledge lives on in the now-changed quester. Three of Malamud's most widely known works are examples of this pattern—the novel *The Assistant* and the short stories "**The Magic Barrel**" and "**The Last Mohican**." . . .

[Pinye Salzman, the matchmaker of the title story in the collection *The Magic Barrel*,] is even more a survivor of the earlier pre-Holocaust European culture [than Morris Bober, the grocer from Malamud's novel *The Assistant*]: as a matchmaker his occupation is more anachronistic than that of the "Ma and Pa" grocery store owner. Yet because of Pinye, whether by intention or not, Leo Finkle changes his quest from an opportunistic search for a proper bride for a rabbi to a spiritual journey in search of redemption for himself and for Pinye's wayward daughter. The matchmaker appears and disappears like some orthodox-unorthodox fairy godfather; but he is a materialist nonetheless. Leo's oxymoron for him is "commercial cupid."

Pinye is literally a *luftmentsh* [a contemplative, impractical person]; his wife says his office is "in the air" and "in his socks." Pinye's measure of a successful match is the traditional one: it should join piety and learning to money and status. Leo at first is as practical as Pinye: he seeks a bride to acquire a congregation. Of course, Leo's learning and piety are shown to be shallow and his eventual bride may be nothing but a poor prostitute. In the end Pinye remains with feet in both worlds, while Leo has perceived that he can now love everyone and that redemption can come through love and suffering. In the final tableau Leo, with flowers in outstretched arms, runs to meet his love, who stands under a street lamp, smoking. Pinye waits around the corner, chanting the prayer for the dead. Leo has already been "afflicted by the tormenting suspicion that Salzman had planned it all to happen this way." But what of the reader's suspicions? For whom, ask critic and reader, does Pinye pray? Sidney Richman, who describes Pinye [in his *Bernard Malamud*, 1966] as half criminal, half messenger of God, offers a range of possibilities:

> It is impossible to tell for whom Pinye chants— for himself and his guilt . . . for Finkle's past or Finkle's future, or for all these reasons. . . . that Salzman chants for everything seems only proper; for if Leo has graduated into saint and rabbi, it is only by succumbing to the terrors which the role prescribes. What better reason to chant when to win means to lose.

In the Malamudian world the "evil" of an orthodox rabbi married to a reformed prostitute would only be mourned by a practical *luftmentsh* like Salzman. It is surely too cynical and literal to suggest that Pinye is mourning his matchmaking fee, yet it is not too far-fetched to feel that he may be mourning his own loss of integrity or Leo's loss of success. The reversal has taken place: Pinye, now ascetic, dignified, and orthodox, stands motionless while a flower-bedecked Leo runs, lured by visions of violins and lighted candles. No explication suffices or seems really called for—it is a bravely ambiguous ending. Pinye now shares with Leo the suffering his daughter has previously inflicted on him alone. Malamud's critics may not have recognized his unique brand of negative capability.

Malamud exhibits courage in the ease with which he treats sacrosanct subjects in his fictional use of holocaust survivors. Few of his contemporaries have been so casual or so comic, although Wallant and I. B. Singer have presented unpleasant and opportunistic Holocaust survivors. But only Malamud, with his fabulist's license, has created such a comic survivor as the artful Susskind of **"The Last Mohican."**

Susskind, the quintessential *shnorer* ('clever beggar'), can also be a teacher, even a Virgilian spiritual leader. He is truly a remnant of remnants, a survivor of survivors, and the last of his tribe. He has survived the death camps and is a "refugee" from Israel. His reasons for leaving Israel are an indication of his incorrigible marginality: " 'Too much heavy labor for a man of my modest health. Also I couldn't stand the suspense'." So this remnant looks for shady deals, quick profits, and Jews to sponge on in Rome. Fidelman is the comic Dante to Susskind's Virgil.

Fidelman, at the beginning, is involved in a pretentious and alien occupation, that of academic art critic writing a study of the fourteenth-century Florentine artist Giotto, a painter of Christian subjects. In one of the most patent of Malamudian rebirths, Fidelman is literally led through his Jewish past in a search for Susskind, who has stolen the first and only chapter of the manuscript. Significantly on a Friday night, Fidelman goes from synagogue to ghetto, symbolically traversing two thousand years of Jewish history in Europe, a history that culminates for him in the old Jewish cemetery with its memorial to Auschwitz. Previously Italian Renaissance history, aesthetic and Christian, had "exalted" him; European-Jewish history oppressed him, attached him to a past he had tried to ignore, "although, he joked to himself, it added years to his life."

The usual reversal completes the story. Fidelman, now resembling his shabby quarry, sees Susskind engaged in what appears to be an alien occupation, that of selling beads and rosaries in front of the Vatican. Malamud has done his ironic homework, for the selling of Christian religious objects has long been a traditional occupation among Rome's Jews. Even in this, the surface *shnorer* Susskind has more integrity than the secret *shnorer* Fidelman. But Fidelman is worthy of regeneration, for he has a moment of "triumphant insight" in which he recognizes that Susskind was right to burn Fidelman's Giotto chapter. Susskind has said that "the words were there but the spirit was missing." What endows the unlikely Susskind with exemplary artistic integrity in a world of pretentious sham is his superiority in suffering, his experience of Jewish history. And what finally gives the pretender, Fidelman, his insight is his own condensed, removed recapitu-

lation of that experience heightened by his own sense of loss. For Fidelman has been the parasite—living off his sister and, as dilettante, poaching on Roman history, Italian art, and Christian subject matter. In a dream Susskind asks Fidelman if he has read Tolstoy, and then enquires, " 'Why is art?' " The morality is Tolstoyan. Art must illuminate the human; the human takes precedence over the aesthetic. The human is the way toward the aesthetic.

The Magic Barrel contains other stories of survivors and immigrants. Frequently Malamud presents a learning situation. In **"The First Seven Years"** the immigrant Feld learns from his younger helper, Sobel. Sobel's superiority in suffering, his experience as a survivor, give him the moral advantage and it is Feld who ends with material aspirations subsumed by insight. The dreary setting is alleviated not only by the book culture that surrounds Sobel but also by the biblical overtones that Malamud invokes. Sobel has labored for five years for his modern Laban; but he must "pound leather for his love" for two years more to conform to the biblical seven. One can only hope that the title does not suggest that Sobel, like Jacob, will have to labor an additional seven years for his Rachel.

Two more stories, **"Take Pity"** and **"The Loan,"** directly involve immigrants and survivors and in neither story is there redemption or resurrection. Eva, the refugee widow of **"Take Pity,"** has learned only one thing, to refuse pity, and has gained in fierce pride. This bleak tale pits Rosen's need to give against Eva's inability to take. Not all the characters in Malamud's universe are capable of transcending suffering: the sufferer is not necessarily ennobled.

In **"The Loan,"** however, Malamud's imaginative boldness asserts itself. The immigrant baker Lieb (from the verb "to love") sells the "bread of affliction," which is the designation for the unleavened bread of the Passover service. Lieb's bread is leavened with his own tears. It is extremely popular; all come to buy where the body of the world's ills is shared as in communion. An old friend appears in the bakery to request a loan. Lieb's second wife, suspicious, possessive, self-conscious of her status as second wife, refuses to leave them alone, yet by the pervasive Malamudian pattern of reversal—epiphanylike in this story—Bessie is seen as the superior sufferer despite her apparent selfishness and lack of charity. Kobotsky, the friend, despite his Job-like afflictions (he even suffers from boils), is not as pitiable. He appears to have been Lieb's betrayer, and he is self-pitying. Yet, honorably, he is seeking money to buy a headstone for his wife's grave, and his tale makes even Bessie weep.

Kobotsky's sad tale is given perspective by the weight of Bessie's suffering. Her recital of twentieth-century Jewish woes is authorially and soberly presented:

> But Bessie, though weeping, shook her head and before they could guess what, had blurted out the story of her afflictions: how the Bolsheviki came . . . and dragged her beloved father into snowy fields without his shoes; the shots scattered the blackbirds in the trees and the snow oozed blood; . . . how she, . . . years later found sanctuary in the home of an older brother in Germany, who sacrificed his own chances to

send her, before the war, to America, and himself ended, with wife and daughter, in one of Hitler's incinerators.

The passage has dignity, yet in the placement of modifiers (before the war, himself ended) there is a foreshadowing of Bessie's own voice, which speaks out in the subsequent paragraph:

> "Working day and night, I fixed up for him his piece of business and we make now, after twelve years, a little living. But Lieb is not a healthy man, also with his eyes that he needs an operation, and this is not yet everything."

The differences in tone and diction are obvious, but even more striking are the similarities in rhythm and structure. And, in Malamud's story, "this is not yet everything." For, during Bessie's dramatic recital, Lieb's tear-moistened loaves are burning. The unmarked grave of Kobotsky's wife is seen in the context of millions of unmarked graves: "The loaves in the trays were blackened bricks—charred corpses." The diction is deliberate and the parallels point to no easy morality. It would be beyond the boundaries of this study to analyze all Malamud's short stories in which immigrant characters figure. It should be noted, however, that of the thirteen stories in the 1958 collection, *The Magic Barrel,* seven directly focus on immigrants and an eighth has a Holocaust survivor as heroine.

In *Idiots First,* Malamud continues to write about the lives of European-born Jews. In one story in the collection, **"The German Refugee,"** he depicts an actual refugee. Malamud here writes of an educated immigrant like the secular and intellectual Jews favored in the fiction of Bellow. The narrator is a "dangling man" who teaches English to refugees. It is 1939 and the narrator says, " 'Here I was palpitating to get going, and across the ocean Adolf Hitler, in black boots and a square mustache, was tearing up and spitting out all the flowers.' " The irony, the innocence, and the brutality are American.

The story gives Malamud the opportunity to use accent in varying ways. The refugee, Oskar Gassner, despondent over his lack of progress, asks his tutor, " 'do you sink I will succezz?' " and immediately the stage German is followed by a sensitive analysis of what loss of language means for the refugee. Here were cultivated European intellectuals who felt "you had some subtle thought and it comes out like a piece of broken bottle," who expressed their loss of linguistic identity with despair: " 'What I know, indeed, what I am, becomes to me a burden. My tongue hangs useless.' " In contrast to the articulate older exile, Oskar is comic but moving: " 'If I do not this legture prepare, I will take my life.' "

But, for all the pity Oskar evokes, he is in error and must learn a bitter lesson. He is self-concerned and, like Kobotsky, self-pitying. He does not listen to news broadcasts. Instead, "in tormented English he conveyed his intense and everlasting hatred of the Nazis for destroying his career, uprooting his life after half a century, and flinging him like a piece of bleeding meat to the hawks." Oskar is shown as insufficiently compassionate, despite his suffering. Thus, after twenty-seven years of marriage and de-

spite her protestations of faithfulness, he left his gentile wife behind in Germany.

Oskar does not think about his wife. Indeed it is despair about his lecture that causes him to attempt suicide. Finally, with the narrator's help, he prepares his lecture on Whitman. He shows that the Whitmanesque idea of brotherhood influenced German poets but, he adds ironically, not for long. Yet a greater irony is revealed in the dénouement: the idea of brotherhood survived in Oskar's abandoned wife who converted to Judaism in outrage and despair after he left Germany. For this romantic gesture she is arrested, "she is shot in the head and topples into an open tank ditch, with the naked Jewish men, their wives and children, some Polish soldiers and a handful of Gypsies." When Oskar learns of his wife's death, he once more attempts suicide and this time succeeds. . . .

Malamud transmits past history and traditional values by his bold use of idiosyncratic language. It is language that creates discomfort given the seriousness of Malamud's subject matter, and it has discomfited a number of critics. Alfred Kazin feels [in "Fantasist of the Ordinary," in *Commentary* (July 1957)] that "Malamud's problem is to form a creative synthesis out of the Yiddish world of his childhood and his natural sophistication and heretical training as a modern writer." [In "Bernard Malamud," in *New Statesman* (30 March 1962)] Frank Kermode sees the problem of synthesis slightly differently and calls Malamud a writer of alien sensibility: "You have to know whether the occasional corruptness of style and invention is there because a dream is out of control or as a justifiable complexity of tone." Neither Kazin nor Kermode has expanded his comments about Malamud's language. But the reader is aware of the conscious incongruity that Kermode stresses and that makes Kazin uneasy.

Malamud does not fuse his styles, he deliberately contains them. His bits and pieces of dialogue are startling, designed to pull the reader's attention to the incongruence of the language. He draws attention to comic possibilities in moments of pathos and tragedy, not with the intention of melding language, but rather with the idea of encapsulating these unassimilated, unmeltable, and unadaptable bits. These are remnants that correspond to the survivor aspects of the characters themselves. Failure to recognize [the] unhomogenized "bone in the throat" quality of much of Malamud's language causes critical problems in analysis.

In discussing Pinye Salzman [from **"The Magic Barrel"**], one critic stresses the correlation between language and character, as evidenced in the following passage: " 'In what else will you be interested,' Salzman went on, 'if you not interested in this fine girl that she speaks four languages and has personally in the bank ten thousand dollars? Also her father guarantees further twelve thousand.' " It has been suggested that the passage presents in inferior language similarly inferior Jewish values (money, status) as though they were the ultimate goods in marriage. Yet it is the inferior Pinye who makes possible Leo's spiritual renewal, that same Pinye who conveys somber dignity in the final scene of the story. . . .

Malamud does not transcribe language as Henry Roth attempted to do in *Call It Sleep*. Morris Bober [from *The Assistant*] neither drops his final "g's" nor turns them into "k's." He does not mispronounce "th" or "w." But the rhythms of "Yinglish" are captured to assert that marginal *luftmentshn* like Pinye and Susskind, and the dull and plodding, like Morris, remain in some ways attached to other values. Although they are speaking an adopted language, their native language colors and conditions their speech. Aspects of language, like values from an older culture, stubbornly persist as anomalous remnants despite changes in time and circumstance. The language also establishes an incongruence between what is said and the way it is said. Truth, integrity, and feelings for the past are represented by uneducated, indecorous, and unintentionally (on the part of the speaker) comic speech. Other twentieth-century writers, among them John Steinbeck, William Faulkner, and Ralph Ellison, have attempted to show that speakers of regional dialects are worthy of serious attention. But Malamud uses dialect and accent unrealistically to deliberately startle and unnerve.

In **"Angel Levine"** values are expressed by an unlikely black Jewish angel (a bizarrely modern Elijah) and a comic Job named Manischevitz. The point of view is that of the immigrant Manischevitz but the conversion pattern is the same. Manischevitz's imaginative act of faith, his belief in the black Jewish angel, redeems Levine and, at least temporarily, saves Manischevitz's wife. Manischevitz speaks to God both in his own words and through the narrator:

> Throughout his trials Manischevitz had remained somewhat stoic, almost unbelieving that all this had descended upon his head, as if it were happening, let us say, to an acquaintance or some distant relative; it was in sheer quantity of woe incomprehensible. It was ridiculous, unjust, and because he had always been a religious man, it was in a way an affront to God. . . . When his burden had grown too crushingly heavy to be borne he prayed in his chair with shut hollow eyes. "My dear God, sweetheart, did I deserve that this should happen to me?" Then recognizing the worthlessness of it, he put aside the complaint and prayed dumbly for assistance: "Give Fanny back her health, and to me myself that I shouldn't feel pain in every step. Help now or tomorrow is too late. This I don't have to tell you." And Manischevitz wept.

And what of the reader? Does he weep? The echoes from the Book of Job and the sober but ironic narrative tone mitigate the bathetic end of the prayer. Manischevitz retains his dignity, and his intimate relationship with God is manifest. Perhaps out of context the "Yinglish" might cause one to laugh, but in Malamud's work the laugh is a lament.

Critics have been aware of the complex and paradoxical effects of Malamud's style. Kazin calls it "tense expressiveness." Hassan detects "a Hemingway cleanness in this dialogue, a kind of humility and courage, but also a softness Hemingway never strove to communicate" ["The Qualified Encounter," in his *Radical Innocence: Studies in the Contemporary American Novel*, 1961]. The almost con-

tradictory quality of the commentary suggests the uncertainty and tension that the style conveys. The style is unsynthesized and uneasy, like the lives of the characters. Perhaps the model is not Hemingway but rather the Joycean style in *Dubliners* (1916), which conveys tension and ambiguity with admirable economy. In *Dubliners* what is expressed is stasis and paralysis. Malamud's characters, Diaspora Men, are not static. Leo Finkle moves toward his ambiguous love while Pinye oddly chants; Fidelman, with newly acquired insight, runs toward a disappearing Susskind. . . .

In Malamud's fictional world, with its emphasis on the unexpected, Jewish characters do not enjoy an innate moral superiority. . . . But history, economics, circumstances, and the unsought experience of suffering are what define the Malamudian teachers and *tsadikim,* and Malamud's Jews qualify. Even among the less admirable, . . . there is a potentiality for moral growth. The reader is induced to see embodied in the most unlikely spirit a spark of righteousness. Only the ambitious accountants and lawyers, those who follow the American Dream of worldly success, are refused Malamud's mercy and are denied possibilities for moral development.

The prime rhetorical manifestations of the potential for moral development lie in unexpected turns of inappropriate language and in unexpected, non-self-serving gestures like Susskind's theft of the manuscript, Pinye's recitation of the *Kaddish,* and, in **"The Mourners,"** the landlord's joining his pariah tenant in lamentation. In one of the bleakest of Malamud's novels, *The Tenants,* the stereotypical figure of the Jewish slum landlord is endowed with moral consciousness. He is the one who begs for mutual pity from the embattled Negro and Jew. What is stressed is not the integration of language and personality but rather the anomalous, the infinite variety of the good, the difficulty of rendering judgment on human character, the error of basing judgment on outward appearance and speech.

Malamud's use of dialect is varied. In **"Angel Levine,"** for example, he uses Negro minstrel dialect in a passage that satirizes Jewish talmudic disputation. His disregard for verisimilitude also gives him the freedom to use immigrant dialect where those who speak are not immigrants, for example, in the speech of Frank in *The Assistant* and of the protagonist in *The Fixer*. . . .

Like the language that conveys the sound and feeling of Yiddish-American but is not meant to be realistic, . . . [Malamud's] works include much that is fantastic. The title story of the collection *Idiots First* demonstrates a virtuoso use of idiosyncratic language and fantasy. Mendel is the dying father of Isaac, a thirty-nine-year-old idiot. Mendel hopes to get Isaac off to California before Ginzburg, the absurdly named Angel of Death, "gets" Mendel. [**"Idiots First"**] is anthropomorphic from the beginning as Mendel draws on "cold, embittered clothing." When Mendel speaks of his death he does so in accents that would be comic in another context: " 'Look me in my face,' said Mendel, 'and tell me if I got time till tomorrow morning?' " " 'For what I got chicken won't cure it.' "

But the climax of the story is Mendel's debate with Ginzburg, now disguised as a ticket collector. The metaphysical discussion sounds like a vaudeville routine. Mendel wants Ginzburg to allow him to put Isaac on the train to California. He asks Ginzburg what his duties are and Ginzburg responds like a typical employer: " 'To create conditions. To make happen what happens. I ain't in the anthropomorphic business.' " Mendel's reply suggests that he does not know the meaning of "anthropomorphic": " 'Whatever business you in, where is your pity?' " Ginzburg lowers his diction although his manner has never been elegant. " 'This ain't my commodity. The law is the law.' " (Note lower case.) Despite Mendel's pleading, Ginzburg, embodying the "cosmic universal law," is obdurate. Mendel tells of his wretched life and begs:

> "Now I ask you a small favor. Be so kind, Mr. Ginzburg."
>
> The ticket collector was picking his teeth with a match stick. "You ain't the only one, my friend, some got it worse than you. That's how it goes in this country."
>
> "You dog you." Mendel lunged at Ginzburg's throat. . . .
>
> "You bastard, don't you understand what it means human?"

Mendel's question is as absurd as his attempt to murder the Angel of Death. But Mendel is also heroic because he is incapable of recognizing the inhuman even in the nonhuman. And the biblical tale of Abraham, Isaac, and a less colloquial Angel of Death adds another dimension to Mendel's struggle. The battle continues: "They struggled nose to nose, Ginzburg, though his astonished eyes bulged, began to laugh. 'You pipsqueak nothing. I'll freeze you to pieces.' His eyes lit in rage. . . ." Now Ginzburg makes a discovery; indeed, he is in "the anthropomorphic business":

> Clinging to Ginzburg in his last agony, Mendel saw reflected in the ticket collector's eyes the depth of his terror. But he saw that Ginzburg, staring at himself in Mendel's eyes, saw mirrored in them the extent of his own awful wrath. He beheld a shimmering starry, blinding light that produced darkness.
>
> Ginzburg looked astonished. "Who me?"
>
> His grip on the squirming old man slowly loosened, and Mendel, his heart barely beating, slumped to the ground. "Go." Ginzburg muttered, "Take him to the train."

If there is terror and wrath why not pity as well? All are part of "what it means human" and even the Angel of Death is not excluded from the human. That all this superhuman effort is expended to send a thirty-nine-year-old idiot to his eighty-one-year-old uncle in California only emphasizes Malamud's stubborn insistence on salvation and survival, no matter how absurd.

Fittingly, unlike Abraham Cahan and Henry Roth, Malamud does not place his fabulous characters in a realistic urban setting. Unlike his contemporaries Bellow, Wallant,

and I. B. Singer, he does not emphasize the concrete urban matrix, the subway station, the West Side cafeteria. Malamud's remnants are isolated among isolates, separated even from experiencing the city as wasteland, always unrooted, always threatening to move on.

Robert Alter, among others, complains of Malamud [in "Bernard Malamud: Jewishness as Metaphor," in his *After the Tradition,* 1969] "that nowhere does he attempt to represent a Jewish milieu, that a Jewish community never enters into his books except as the shadow of a vestige of a specter." Clearly it is not because Malamud cannot write realistic, socially and historically rooted fiction. *The Tenants, The Fixer,* and *A New Life* are all strongly rooted in history, event, and social milieu. But in the immigrant stories the particular strength of these Diaspora Men resides in their not being rooted in space, in their unassimilated, alien transcendence of milieu. Unlike the prewar immigrant, Malamud's Jews do not perceive of America as a "promised land." [In "Bernard Malamud: The Magic and the Dread," in his *Contemporaries,* 1962] Alfred Kazin complains of Malamud's "abstractness" and contrasts him to the Yiddish masters who "gave the earth of Russia, the old village, a solid reality, as if it were all the world they had to cherish." But Malamud, although close to them in spirit according to Kazin, does not show "the world, but the spectral Jew in his beggarly clothes—always ready to take flight." Is this not precisely what Malamud intends? The setting, like the language, attempts to capture that which is essential, that which can be distilled into something ultimately portable.

Malamud is not, as Kazin avers, abstract out of despair; rather, he attempts in language, setting, and character to preserve what is most ephemeral and yet what can best be preserved. That which an immigrant can carry with him may be nonmaterial, may suffer a sea change, may even be debased, but it is transmittable, capable of living under the most adverse conditions, and hence the only heritage worthy of transmission. It is ambiguously compounded of common suffering, common humanity, common responsibility, and common peril. And how well Kazin (still carping) sees what Malamud is trying to do with his surreal language: "He makes you think not that Jews really talk

---

Sandy Cohen on *Pictures of Fidelman:*

In *Pictures of Fidelman* Malamud portrays the selfishness of *eros* in part as the manifestation of various forms of neuroses. Fidelman's private neuroses are often symptomatic of more broadly social problems. For example, Fidelman's treatment of Susskind is symbolic of America's treatment of other countries, Italy especially. But Fidelman's treatment of Susskind is also symbolic of Everyman and his moral-ethical responsibilities as well as the relationship between ego and alter-ego. *Eros* is portrayed in great part as Fidelman's compulsion for perfection, a compulsion that often leads to tragic results.

Sandy Cohen, in Bernard Malamud and the Trial by Love, *Rodopi, 1974.*

that way but how violent, fear fraught, always on edge, Jewish talk can be."

Dorothy Seidman Bilik, "Malamud's Secular Saints and Comic Jobs," in her Immigrant-Survivors: Post-Holocaust Consciousness in Recent Jewish American Fiction, *Wesleyan University Press, 1981, pp. 53-80.*

Mark Shechner   (essay date 1984)

[*Shechner is an American educator and critic. In the following review of* The Stories of Bernard Malamud, *he comments on the appeal, style, and themes of Malamud's short fiction, noting that his stories share an overriding tone of mourning.*]

Any doubts we may have had about Bernard Malamud's stature as a modern master should be dispelled by [*The Stories of Bernard Malamud*]. This personal selection of twenty-five stories presents Malamud at his best—as a writer of eloquent and poignant vignettes. Though Malamud has published seven novels, each one touched with his distinctive laconic grace, the short story remains the purest distillation of his abiding leitmotif: the still, sad music of humanity. Typically, the Malamud story is an epiphany of disappointment and failure, a document of the half-life—the shabby region of mediocre existence just a notch above pure disaster—bathed in the melodies of despair, in the taut, concise adagios of woe. By and large, however, Malamud's range of characters and situations has been too narrow to sustain longer constructions. Lacking variety and any feel for the architecture of sustained fiction, his novels hold the note of sorrow too long, until what had begun as a lamentation ends as a *kvetch*. But in the short story, Malamud achieves an almost psalmlike compression. He has been called the Jewish Hawthorne, but he might just as well be thought a Jewish Chopin, a prose composer of preludes and nocturnes.

The Malamud character is one we've long since come to recognize: the underground man transposed into a small merchant or retiree or pensioner. He is commonly alone, or beset by family, creditors, or customers (he seldom has friends). He runs a grocery, a deli, a candy store where the cash register is always empty and the accounts receivable book full. His sons, if he has sons, avoid him; his daughters, like Lear's, are ungrateful, and there is no Cordelia to love him in spite of himself. He may have a heart condition, like Mendel in **"Idiot's First,"** or Marcus the tailor in **"The Death of Me,"** or Mr. Panessa in **"The Loan,"** or he may take his own life, like Rosen the ex-coffee salesman in **"Take Pity,"** or Oskar Gassner in **"The Jewish Refugee."** At his most wretched he is a Jewbird, black as a caftan, fishy as a herring, and cursed/blessed with the powers of flight, though he longs only for the comforts of a home. With few exceptions, he is miserable, without hope, and waiting for death. Indeed, not only does the typical Malamud story end with death, but the keynote story in this collection, **"Take Pity,"** begins with death, one that releases the character into a chamber of heaven that looks remarkably like a furnished room. Even death, it seems, brings no elevation.

This makes for anything but happy reading, and we might well ask why anyone would bother with a writer so insistently depressive, who peoples his stories with characters who exist for most of us only in memory and nightmare. That is not a simple question to answer, but we might begin with Malamud's own words. In one of the stories in this collection, **"Man in the Drawer,"** Levitansky, a Russian-Jewish writer whose work cannot be published in the Soviet Union, entices an American journalist, Howard Harvitz, who is touring Russia, to read some of his stories. Harvitz, after much shilly-shallying, reads them and renders an approving judgment: "I like the primary, close-to-the-bone quality of the writing. The stories impress me as strong if simply wrought; I appreciate your feeling for the people and at the same time the objectivity with which you render them. It's sort of Chekhovian in quality, but more compressed, sinewy, direct, if you know what I mean." Levitansky, it appears, is a portrait of what Malamud himself might have been and have suffered had fate seen fit to send his grandparents east to Russia rather than west to America, and these terms of praise are Malamud's own terms for what is strong in his art.

Sinewy, direct, simply wrought, close to the bone—Malamud's writing is all that, but an appreciation of his simplicity takes us only so far toward a definition of his appeal, which has, I think, two other sources: an apprehension that touches some core of panic in all of us and his music. **"Man in the Drawer"** exhibits a dimension of the Malamud world that powerfully draws us in. Levitansky is the nightmare Jew, but he is also Harvitz's semblable, his alter ego, the victim who, but for an accident of fortune, might be himself. Plainly, he is *our* other self. Malamud's tenement Jews, his Russian-Jewish writers, his lonely pensioners, his forsaken fathers and embittered children are all stained by that tincture of possibility. Even in the midst of plenty, in this best of all possible diasporas, a portion of every Jew stands poised for flight and expecting the worst. It is Malamud, more than any other Jewish writer, who retains that imagination of disaster and speaks the old dialects of loneliness, confinement, and exile.

The music of Malamud's writing is a curious one—dark and brooding but not overly abundant or reliably melodic. One comes repeatedly upon passages that are just plain clumsy, as though Malamud had forgotten the syntax of English or pieced together his own upon Yiddish syntactical patterns. He is no Bellow or Roth or Updike with an endless fund of bright phrases at his elbow; his idiom is a limited one that has not noticeably grown in the thirty-four years he has been writing. He writes in what might be called basic English, now lyrical, now stumbling, reminding us more than a little of Isaac Babel in his regard for simple truths and his studied neglect of ornamentation.

Within that limited budget of words, however, Malamud achieves in his stories a *Kleine Nachtmusik,* a simple melodic weariness that envelops his characters like a syrup.

> Davidov, the Census-taker, opened the door without knocking, limped into the room, and sat wearily down. Out came his notebook and he was on the job. Rosen, the ex-coffee salesman, wasted, eyes despairing, sat motionless, cross-

legged, on his cot. The square, clean but cold room, lit by a dim globe, was sparsely furnished: the cot, a folding chair, small table, old unpainted chests—no closets but who needed them?—and a small sink with a rough piece of green, institutional soap on its holder—you could smell it across the room. The worn black shade over the single narrow window was drawn to the ledge, surprising Davidov.

It takes us a while to comprehend that Rosen is dead and that death is no release, just a pane of one-way glass between himself and the living. The green institutional soap, the worn shade, the cot are the furniture of his life and of his heart, which has all the color and warmth of a cold-water flat. Alfred Kazin speaks of Malamud's poverty as "an aesthetic medium . . . coloring everything with its woebegone utensils, its stubborn immigrant English, its all-circulating despair." One might want to say that defeat, not just poverty, is the enveloping medium, but Kazin's general point stands: some depletion of the spirit—call it poverty, call it defeat—not only commands the situation but choreographs every act, every speech, every word on the page. Through seas of sadness, Malamud's characters swim like fish.

The initial impression Malamud gave in the 1950s, with his early stories in **The Magic Barrel** and the novels *The Natural* and *The Assistant,* was that of being a purveyor of Jewish admonitions. The novels in particular cast long, didactic shadows and ask us to judge some of their characters as deserving of their trials. Moreover, *The Natural* and *The Assistant,* as well as stories like **"The Lady of the Lake," "Girl of My Dreams,"** and **"The Magic Barrel,"** broadcast suggestions of a sexual moralism as well, though its exact nature is never spelled out. The sexual moralist in Malamud has been largely excluded from this collection, and where sex turns up in a moral equation, as it does in **"God's Wrath"** and **"The Magic Barrel,"** it posits mysteries rather than precepts.

And yet Malamud *is* a moralist and an insistent one, though the law to which he binds his characters has little in it of noticeably Jewish content. It is the law of simple charity and compassion. Most of his characters either earn their misery through hardheartedness or are the victims of others'. Kessler, the former egg candler of **"The Mourners,"** is quarrelsome and a troublemaker and is self-isolated in his tenement apartment. Rosen, the ex-coffee salesman in **"Take Pity,"** has been driven to the grave by a widow who, out of misplaced pride, rejects his charity. Glasser, the retired shamus in **"God's Wrath,"** has had poor luck with his children, and we may guess without being told that they had had no better luck with him. In story after story coldness is returned for love, a warm heart is battered by a cold one. The word "no" is the most powerful and bitter word in all of Malamud.

Malamud is quintessentially a Jewish writer, though there is nothing of religious belief and only the shards of ritual to be found in his writing and only *shmatas* of Jewish culture or history. Yet, for all that, his writing is so impregnated with Jewishness—as distinct from Judaism—that there can be no mistaking it. Sometimes it is the spectral Jewishness of Singer and Chagall, but more commonly it

is the melancholy Jewishness of Roman Vishniac's photos of the old country in its last hours. In his modest and laconic style of narrative, Malamud has found the exact prose equivalent of the dull light and gray tones of Vishniac's world, a world exhausted by siege and conscious of its defeat.

Perhaps Malamud's Jewishness is best understood in terms of Matthew Arnold's definition of Hebraism, "strictness of conscience." By such a definition, Malamud is our leading Hebraist of letters, for strictness of conscience is as much his abiding theme as sorrow is his abiding disposition. But though Malamud treats it as a requirement of civilized existence, he often renders it as a curse, a habit of withholding that interdicts the normal flow of human feelings. Many of Malamud's characters treat others with a rabbinical harshness, though one detached from any conception of a sacramental life or, for that matter, a clear moral intention. They habitually ward off intimacy and often give the appearance of performing archaic rites that they have long since ceased to understand. A textbook approach to their "problem" might call them compulsive-neurotics, for they are case studies of conscience gone haywire.

In a Malamud story, conscience beyond an individual's need or capacity or right to do good propels the argument. In **"Take Pity,"** Rosen recites to a census-taker in heaven the tale of his failures at charity toward the wife of a grocery store owner. She would not heed his advice to liquidate the store; she refused his offer of a place to stay when the store went bankrupt; she recoiled at his proposal of marriage; she returned money anonymously given, knowing it was from Rosen. But, determined Rosen, *"I will give."*

> "I went then to my lawyer and we made out a will that everything I had—all my investments, my two houses that I owned, also furniture, my car, the checking account—every cent would go to her, and when she died, the rest would be left for the two girls. The same with my insurance. They would be my beneficiaries. Then I signed and went home. In the kitchen I turned on the gas and put my head in the stove."
>
> "Let her say no now."

This is charity unto death. By what right does Rosen impose these unwanted gifts upon the unwilling widow? And by what law of self-reliance does she so obdurately decline what is offered her solely out of love? Both Rosen and the Widow Kalish are stark examples of a Hebraism so advanced, so unleavened by reflection or sweetness and light as to be the literal death of one and the spiritual death of the other.

> Davidov, scratching his stubbled cheek, nodded. . . . He got up and, before Rosen could cry no, idly raised the window shade.
>
> It was twilight in space but a woman stood before the window.
>
> Rosen with a bound was off his cot to see.

It was Eva, staring at him with haunted beseeching eyes. She raised her arms to him.

Infuriated, the ex-salesman shook his fist.

"Whore, bastard, bitch," he shouted at her. "Go 'way from here. Go home to your children."

Davidov made no move to hinder him as Rosen rammed down the window shade.

Strictness of conscience has proven to be a moral cul-de-sac for both. Malamud's Jewish characters, one often feels, are automatons of conscience and fanatics. It is a commonplace of criticism that they are ruined by circumstance, but it is less often observed that those circumstances are helped along by their own narrowness and rigidity.

So deeply ingrained is this woe that it seems virtually biological—a mourning bound in helixes within every cell. But in the first postwar decade, it had the full sanction of the times and was well-nigh universal among Jewish writers and intellectuals. The sorrow that penetrates to the bone in Malamud was the mood of a generation of Jewish writers who had been raised on immigrant poverty and worldwide depression and brought abruptly to adulthood by the holocaust. Low spirits came as naturally to them as hunger or ambition or breath.

But for some of those writers sorrow was a transient mood and a burden, and they were glad to be relieved of it in the 1950s when the prevailing conditions of life would no longer sustain their Dostoevskian migraines. As a character in an unfinished novel by Saul Bellow announced in 1950, "You heard me tell my old aunt a while back when she asked me what I wanted, that I didn't want to be sad any more." Bellow, his stethoscope pressed to the bosom of the *zeitgeist,* had uttered that sentence on behalf of a new mood which held that "being sad is being disfigured," and while in 1950 he was still tentative enough to put those sentiments in the mouth of a mental patient in a novel he could not complete, three years later he would confirm them in a full-blown festival of high spirits, *The Adventures of Augie March.*

Throughout the fifties and the sixties, Malamud stood aside from the cavalcade of cheerfulness and let it pass unapplauded. Though he *would* take detours into sunnier climes and endeavor to compose in a more robust key, most notably in **Pictures of Fidelman,** he never strayed far from his sorrow. Throughout the fifties, while other writers in the *Partisan Review* orbit were spreading the good news about "Our Country and Our Culture," Malamud was prowling the tenements of the imagination for vistas of misfortune, scenes of Old World pathos in New World ghettos. His major novel of that decade was *The Assistant,* his story of Jewish and Italian self-immolation in a failing grocery store. If the Kennedy era and the years of the counter-cultural revolution made any impression on his mood, it is not visible in his stories of the sixties. One single note sounds long and uninterrupted through the stories of three decades: the note of mourning.

Collected Stories is a book of mourning, an anthology, one might say, of elegies. Even where there is no death,

characters cloak themselves in talliths and recite Kaddishes for the living, as Salzman the matchmaker does for his client, Leo Finkle, in **"The Magic Barrel"** and Kessler the egg candler and Gruber the landlord do for themselves at the end of **"The Mourners."** Malamud has written stories of other kinds but has selected these for reissue, as if to honor that region of his imagination that is most accustomed to grief. The singularity of this grieving marks the book as a testament, a memorial, we may suppose, to the world that disappeared into the crematoria of Auschwitz, the memory hole of Russia, the suburbs of America. This book, then, is an act of Yiskor, an admonition to remember.

But such a reading leaves certain things unexplained: the broken bonds between children and parents and the resounding NO that frustrates every desire, every generous act. This sorrow, appended to history though it may be, is also unmistakably personal and was planted in the heart before it ever found its image in the world; we may be certain of that. But this heartache, whatever the source, has led Malamud to a deep identification with the tears of the Jewish past and an affection, to the point of love, for a world that his father's generation fled as best it could: the tenement, the candy store, the hand-to-mouth hardships of immigrant life. All Jewish writers respond in some degree to this undertow of ghetto misery—but only Malamud has canonized it.

This steady allegiance to a single grief, despite all the vicissitudes of personal fortune and historical change, calls to mind Isaac Rosenfeld's words about Abraham Cahan's David Levinsky, a man who in *The Rise of David Levinsky* courts a singular aridity of spirit that he himself does not comprehend.

> Because hunger is strong in him, he must always strive to relieve it; but precisely because it is strong, it has to be preserved. It owes its strength to the fact that for so many years everything that influenced Levinsky most deeply—say, piety and mother love—was inseparable from it. For hunger, in this broader, rather metaphysical sense of the term that I have been using, is not only the state of tension out of which the desires for relief and betterment spring; precisely because the desires are formed under its sign, they become assimilated to it, and convert it into the prime source of all value, so that the man, in his pursuit of whatever he considers pleasurable and good, seeks to return to his yearning as much as he does to escape it.

Like Levinsky, Malamud's characters preserve the hunger and court the downside of life out of hidden motives that they mistake for principles. They reach for their cup of sorrow.

I'm told by Japanese friends that Malamud translates better than other Jewish writers and has a larger audience in Japan than Bellow. I can't testify to the truth of that but I think it plausible. So much of Bellow's power springs from his linguistic virtuosity, whereas Malamud's is rather subterranean and prelinguistic and pressed into images rather than words, Jewbirds rather than Herzogs. As that suggests, these stories are, at their best, symbols of hidden things which have the power, much like myth, to spread wide ripples from very small disturbances. To paraphrase Gide, we should not understand them too quickly.

Mark Shechner, "Sad Music," in Partisan Review, *Vol. LI, No. 3, 1984, pp. 451-58.*

Jeffrey Helterman   (essay date 1985)

[*Helterman is an American educator, novelist, and critic. In the following excerpt, he provides a thematic overview of Malamud's short fiction.*]

The surprising thing about Malamud's short fiction is that we recognize ourselves in his characters. None of us are like them; we are not that wretched, and we have more style—at least, we have some style. The recognition is not like that felt when we read Philip Roth who seems to have met our uncles and our teachers and our army sergeants and our college roommates and has gotten down their gestures and voices and attitudes perfectly. Nor is the recognition like that felt (at least by intellectuals or those with pretensions toward intellect) when reading Saul Bellow, whose characters, whether quiz show contestants or gangsters, seem to have struggled with every intellectual problem ever faced by thinking man. The ideas are familiar, even if the solutions are new. We don't get that sense of familiarity in Malamud. We've never met his characters before, and yet the shock of recognition is much deeper. They are us. The reader's moment of recognition in reading Malamud is the same as that of the well-dressed banker who looks at one of Rouault's tragic clowns and wonders how the painter could know so much about the banker's inner self; it is like the moment when a well-trained athlete looks at Modigliani's gaunt, skeletal men and sees his true self, weak and frightened, which he has hidden under all his painstakingly built musculature. The characters in Malamud's short fiction are recognizable because they show us ourselves an inch below the skin. What is recognizable is our most essential passions: we are that wretched. We give ourselves over to love or hate or fear so elemental that no external value matters—not the manners limned so accurately by Roth or the ideas traced so complexly by Bellow. Though almost all the characters in the short stories are Jewish, perhaps of the three writers, it is least essential to be Jewish in order to recognize oneself in the characters of Malamud.

In his short stories, Malamud keeps the reader on the cutting edge of emotion through the intensity of his characters, all of whom have occupations, but rarely have functions other than their relations with another person. The characters are seldom seen working at their jobs (though almost all work very hard), and when they are seen working, their work becomes a metaphor for their emotion or sometimes the emotion itself. Malamud's characters will make shoes because of love, press pants out of hate, or paint pictures to combat loneliness or guilt. All of their energies are directed toward their emotions, yet their tales are told in such spare, ironic prose that they rarely become sentimental. Sentimentality is also avoided because opposing kinds of emotional energy are often seen to be twin aspects of the same elemental force. Thus love and hate are almost always conjoined, and charity is never so tender as when it is most ferocious. This is no matter of Freudian sublimation in which the repression of some emotion becomes another, but rather a recognition of the duality of human nature—that the greatest pride is often found in obstinate humility and that the most religious men are usually not those who seek God or the spirit, but those who look to understand themselves or to help their fellow man.

Pascal says man has developed the need for *divertissement* ("diversion") to keep him from the most frightening of all activities: contemplation of his own condition. There is no *divertissement* in Malamud's short fiction. His characters do not play, they do not worry about the latest styles or the newest cars or contemporary politics. Instead they constantly have to face the fearsomeness of their own nature. This lack of diversion does not always lead to pessimism as might be expected. Rather single-mindedness taken to an extreme often uncovers resources the characters never knew they possessed—and the reader shares this knowledge with the characters.

Malamud's characters also take the reader into other realms unexplored by most of his contemporaries. His characters often find the mystical when they least expect it. The world of the spirit is wonderfully accessible in Malamud's short stories because mystic creatures manifest themselves in the most ordinary forms without losing their power to amaze. The Angel of Death *must* look like the hard-hearted Ginzburg in **"Idiots First."** After we read Malamud we realize we have met this creature before: we have seen that strange gaunt face on the edge of our consciousness. He is no longer a vague concept, but a real being, and his reality is responsible for the way that Malamud's fiction haunts us. The *dybbuks* (evil spirits or the souls of dead men in living bodies), like Susskind in **"The Last Mohican,"** who haunt Malamud's heroes are also typical of how familiar the supernatural is in his fiction. Susskind appears to be an ordinary man, a presumptuous beggar at most, yet he has the power to lead Fidelman in and out of dreams and then out of himself and toward God. And the reader does not say, "How absurd!" but, "Yes! it is possible and besides, I think I once ran into a man like that and if I had only . . . " In reading Malamud, it is not so much a question of suspending one's disbelief, but of doing just the opposite, allowing that belief that has been repressed since the Age of Reason to resurface.

Malamud's spirituality convinces us because he is able to put the mystical in the most mundane settings and then have us believe in both. With a perfect sense of timing, he gradually reveals that two men speaking to each other in **"Take Pity"** are a dead man and the angel sent to record the dead man's charity. The reader has just begun to wonder what language, older than Hebrew, one of the men is writing, when he realizes with a shiver that the other is about to tell how he took his own life trying to be charitable to a woman. This shiver is nothing to the one felt when the room in which the two are conversing turns out to be the grave, and the dead man looks out a window and sees the woman, still alive, trying to apologize for being too proud to accept the man's charity when he was alive.

Malamud does this again and again. By the time the mystical is upon us, it is just ordinary enough for us to accept it. Often this is because Malamud's characters accept it first. When a loving father in **"Idiots First"** races to put his idiot son on the day's last train to California, it slowly dawns on the father that the man trying to stop him is no bill collector or social worker, but the Angel of Death. Once the reader accepts this, he is awed but not surprised when the father bests the angel in a struggle which is literally beyond life and death. The reader is in Grand Central Station and in the realm of the spirit at the same time.

At this point, metaphors resonate into something larger: in **"The Loan,"** burnt loaves in a baker's oven no longer *resemble* the corpses in Hitler's incinerators; they are the corpses in Hitler's incinerators. A **"Talking Horse"** is not, as the reader first suspects, a man in a horse costume, but a real talking horse. Just when the reader has convinced himself that this makes sense, Malamud turns him again and reveals that the talking horse is really a centaur who has been mysteriously locked into the flesh-and-blood upper half of a horse—a costume, but one unlike any ever seen before. The reader is surprised, but acquiesces; this, too, makes sense. Malamud has worked his magic, and the last wave of the wand reveals that this centaur is in many ways ordinary enough to face the same human problems as the reader.

Malamud can make anyone human. When a Jewish bird helps junior with his homework, it is not surprising because the bird sounds exactly like a helpful **"Jewbird."** He *kvetches* ("whines"), mooches, spouts homely wisdom, worries about the availability of herring, and fears anti-Semitism from one of its most dangerous sources—Jews who have forgotten what Judaism means. That the fate of this upstart crow is felt as tragedy is a further tribute to Malamud's genius for merging the miraculous with the ordinary.

The short stories of Malamud (now collected in one volume) originally appeared in three collections, *The Magic Barrel, Idiots First,* and *Rembrandt's Hat.* Almost all are tight, spare stories that revolve around the relations of two, sometimes three, characters. The themes are freedom, commitment, responsibility, and the bonds of love and hate that link man to man. Most have Jews as their central characters, though sometimes, these Jews take surprising forms: there is a black guardian angel in **"Angel Levine,"** an intrusive bird in **"The Jewbird,"** and Jewish centaur in **"Talking Horse."** Though most of the stories take place in urban Jewish settings, there is a large fraction of Malamud's short fiction set in Italy (where he lived in 1956). Even among these, the main characters are often Jewish, and a group of the Italian stories has been regathered into a picaresque novel, *Pictures of Fidelman.*

"Man in a Drawer," the longest of Malamud's short stories, brings together many of the themes that are found in his short fiction. The hero, Howard Harvitz, is totally uncommitted as the story begins. He has put his plans to remarry his first wife on hold, he knows he is a hack as a free-lance writer, he considers himself a marginal Jew, and he has decided to visit Russia as an "intellectual" tourist (the kind who visits the Chekhov and Dostoevsky museums). His only recent act of commitment is a nominal one: he has changed his last name back from Harris to Harvitz. When he suddenly has responsibility thrust upon him, Harvitz will test the right to his true name.

Harvitz is approached by Levitansky, a Russian writer who is also a marginal Jew, and asked to smuggle Levitansky's stories out of the USSR. Levitansky has been denied publication in Russia, an act which puts both him and his work "in the drawer." Harvitz's cooperation might mean imprisonment for the American tourist who would prefer not to get involved. Such unwanted responsibility is the typical burden for Malamud's heroes. Harvitz has many good reasons for not risking his freedom for this stranger, but in the end he takes the chance. This heroic act pushes him to the center of all areas in which he was marginal. He is moved to commit himself after reading four of the stories, all of which show the small but terrifying suffering caused by one man's not taking responsibility for another. That the stories are Jewish in subject matter also influences Harvitz to aid a fellow Jew, and take responsibility for him, and helps Harvitz to earn the Jewish name he has already taken back. He also demonstrates the courage once part of the phrase "free lance" (of a knight errant) by risking his freedom for the work of a fellow writer, but most importantly, he demonstrates his commitment to mankind by getting involved in the life of a stranger.

This kind of courage is not always so easily forthcoming. Another margin dweller, Henry Levin, a floorwalker in the book department of Macy's, gives up his Jewish name [in **"The Lady of the Lake"**] and christens himself Henry Freeman. As Freeman, he falls in love with the aristocratic Lady of the Lake, and, believing that her questions about his religion are caused by her anti-Semitic prejudice, he denies that he is Jewish. To his chagrin, he discovers that she is a Buchenwald survivor, looking for someone to share her race's suffering and her own. Instead of freeing himself, Freeman only frees himself from his roots and his humanity. Instead of embracing his lady, he finds himself clutching a bloodless stone statue. The former book salesman finds himself in a land of imagination far beyond his own petty daydreams.

Freeman's lack of commitment is shared by Cronin in **"A Choice of Profession"** and Gans in **"A Silver Crown."** Both men are teachers, but are also men who are afraid of love. Both see commitment as something interesting to contemplate for the future, but both are afraid to give themselves entirely to a relationship. Cronin, who has just become a teacher, takes up with a woman whose past, he discovers, includes both incest and prostitution. Though he judges her entitled to her past mistakes, he not only gives her up, but he informs on her to a man he thinks has become her lover. Cronin, like most of Malamud's moral cowards, gives himself the best of motives for betraying the woman's trust. Though his real reason is jealousy, he convinces himself that he betrays her secret to protect her new lover, a family man. He also finds nothing wrong in setting himself up in judgment on the woman. He does feel some moral compunction and is uneasy enough about this incident to give up his newly chosen profession of teaching.

Gans, on the other hand, fails, even as he goes through the motions of total commitment. With his father dying of "cancer of the heart" and all medical alternatives exhausted, Gans sacrifices his rational principles and 986 dollars to buy a silver "healing crown" from a faith-healer. Though it would appear that Gans has done all he can to save his father, he has, in fact, done nothing more than buy off his guilt for not loving the old man. He questions the faith-healer minutely about the powers of the crown, but, as is usual in Malamud's short fiction, the answer is so simple that wise men overlook it (Gans is a high school biology teacher, but his name means "goose" or "fool"). The crown depends not on faith in it or in Judaism or even in God. Nothing else matters so long as Gans loves his father. When Gans admits he hates his father, the old man dies. In Malamud, even taking responsibility is not enough. It must be done without qualification, the moment a man looks for good reasons to do a good deed, the deed ceases to be good.

> **In Malamud, even taking responsibility is not enough. It must be done without qualification, the moment a man looks for good reasons to do a good deed, the deed ceases to be good.**
>
> *—Jeffrey Helterman*

Two characters who ask no questions about love are Sobel, a shoemaker's apprentice in **"The First Seven Years"** and Finkle in **"The Magic Barrel."** In each case, they are faced by fathers who have idealistic expectations for marriage. Feld, the shoemaker, has dreams of an ideal match for his daughter and cannot believe that she would prefer his immigrant apprentice to a promising assimilated Jew. The choices for the daughter, like many in Malamud, are defined clearly between the material world and the spiritual. Her father's choice is a business student who reads only his texts, while Sobel reads for no other reason than to read. Feld cannot understand a man who reads when he has no desire to advance himself. After firing Sobel to get him away from his daughter, Feld suffers a heart attack (most illnesses, especially heart attacks and headaches, are more moral than medical in Malamud). When Sobel goes back to work for him, Feld realizes that the purity of his love has been refined in the suffering of the concentration camps and allows him to finish his seven-year apprenticeship in both the shop and in his daughter's heart.

Salzman, a *schadchen* ("marriage broker"), dreams of finding the perfect mate, not for his daughter, but for his customer Finkle. Finkle is a rabbinical student, and Salzman wants only the best for him. He claims to keep his files in a barrel whose magic assures happiness. Though the barrel and, in fact, his office are frauds, Salzman believes in the efficacy of his craft and is appalled when Finkle chooses Salzman's own daughter, who is a prostitute. Finkle, unlike Cronin in **"A Choice of Profession,"** truly does not judge when he falls in love and comes fully alive when he offers flowers to Stella Salzman who is standing under a lamppost. Salzman, refusing to accept the magic of his own profession, chants the prayer for the dead signifying that the rabbinical student is lost to the faith. Almost certainly the reverse is true, by trusting in his love for another human being, Finkle has become ready to love God and man, and, therefore, will be worthy to be called rabbi at just the moment that Salzman stops thinking of him as a rabbi.

Sometimes the act of faith is a small gesture that points an uncommitted man toward commitment. In **"A Summer's Reading,"** the hero claims falsely that he is not wasting his summer, but is spending it reading one hundred books. When a neighbor, Mr. Cattaranza, spreads the news of this virtuous act, the whole neighborhood begins to look on the boy as a hero. The boy brazens out his lie until Cattaranza discovers the lie, but does not betray him. This trust is enough to change the boy's life, and he finally sits down and begins to read. The same kind of faith is exhibited in **"The German Refugee"** where a refugee intellectual is encouraged by a young American student to give a lecture in English. The young man's faith in the refugee is enough to overcome his personal diffidence in his ability to handle English and the lecture succeeds. Such personal faith is not enough to sustain the refugee in a world gone mad, and he commits suicide by gassing himself after he learns that his gentile wife had converted and then had been murdered by the Nazis.

A more positive conclusion to this kind of exhibition of faith occurs in **"Rembrandt's Hat"** in which an art teacher, Arkin, casually mentions to a colleague, a failed sculptor named Rubin, that his hat looks like a hat Rembrandt was wearing in a self-portrait. Rubin takes this pleasantry for an insult, though Arkin cannot understand why. Eventually, the two men arrange their lives—from when they eat, to what exhibitions they visit, to their office hours—around the simple object of avoiding each other. It is not until Arkin takes the time to put himself in Rubin's place that he can see how the comparison with a great artist might humiliate one of little talent. When Arkin looks at slides of the Rembrandt portrait, he discovers that he was even wrong about what the hat looked like, making the original remark seem even more like a gratuitous insult. Though the point of contention is a small one, Arkin humbly admits his error, and this admission is enough to break down the wall that the two colleagues have built up. The center of this story is Arkin's compassion, the ability to put himself in another's place and to suffer with him. Compassion is the emotional act that compares to the intellectual act of commitment.

Compassion and commitment are not one-sided affairs. The mutuality of responsibility is seen in two stories, **"Take Pity"** and **"Angel Levine,"** in which the recipients of mercy have trouble accepting the love proffered by another human being. In **"Take Pity,"** Davidov, the recording Angel comes to Rosen to take account of his good deeds. Rosen tells how he tried to offer charity to a poor widow who, in her pride, kept refusing to accept it. Eventually, Rosen willed everything he owned to her and put his head in the oven and turned on the gas. When the anguished widow appears at the window looking in at the dead man, Rosen calls her a whore and closes the shade on her. Because she refused to take (accept) pity, Rosen has no deeds of charity to show the recording angel. Every act in Malamud is mutual in this way. There are always two people involved, and if either fails, both fail.

Manischevitz in **"Angel Levine"** also has trouble accepting proffered grace, but more out of despair than pride. He has grown so used to suffering that he cannot believe God cares about him or would send an angel to cure his sick wife. When the angel turns out to be a hip-talking Negro, Manischevitz believes even less, and yet, because it involves his wife, he is willing to go to Harlem to remove the last doubt that he is making a mistake. Though Levine dressed in a checked suit and pearl gray derby in Harlem looks even less like an angel than he did before, Manischevitz becomes convinced by the very absurdity of the situation that Levine must be what he says he is. Belief, after all, is accepting the impossible as true; it takes no faith to believe in the rational. When Manischevitz believes in Levine, that is, accepts the love that is offered him, the black angel literally earns his wings. Manischevitz returns home to find his wife is already up and cleaning the furniture. He regales her with the news that no reader of Malamud finds surprising, "there are Jews everywhere."

Though the bond between these two "men" is gentle, a number of the stories deal with the seemingly inescapable ties that join one human being with another. Often the bonds of hate or fear are just as powerful as those of love. The most straightforward demonstration of this is in **"The Death of Me"** where two tailor's assistants live only to torment each other. Their lives are defined and energized by a hatred whose origins are beyond reason. When the tailor separates the two so that they cannot expend their rage on each other, their productivity declines as does their interest in life itself. Only a return to the near-murderous rage stirs them back to life.

Though **"The Death of Me"** goes no further than to establish this connection, several other stories examine its consequences. The **"Talking Horse,"** Abramowitz, finds himself inextricably bound with his master, a mute clown named Goldberg. Though powerful enough to escape from Goldberg, Abramowitz stays, hoping to coax out of his master the secret of his own strange condition—what it is that gives him yearnings beyond those of an ordinary talking horse. Abramowitz puts up with endless abuse, but when he discovers that Goldberg has been lying to him, he goads his master into a tremendous struggle that makes Goldberg tear off Abramowitz's upper half, revealing him to be a centaur. Malamud makes it clear that without the struggle, Abramowitz would never know who he was and would be condemned to think of himself as a freak instead of a miracle. By working his character out through the struggle with another, Abramowitz is no longer trapped

as a circus entertainer and is free to roam the prairies with the power of a beast and the intellect of a man.

Sometimes this link of hatred grows poisonous as in **"The Bill"** where Schlegel buys from the Panessa Grocery on credit and then comes to hate Panessa for trusting him. As his bill gets larger, Schlegel sees the grocer growing uglier until his stooped back seems to be hunched. Eventually this breach of trust grows so great that Panessa dies of it, and Schlegel, trying to say the right thing, finds that his "tongue hung in his mouth like dead fruit on a tree."

The link of hate can also be redemptive as in **"The Mourners,"** where a landlord grows to hate one of his obnoxious tenants to the point where his obsession is to get the man evicted from the building. When, at last, it seems the landlord has triumphed, he finds his tenant sitting *shiva* ("the formal act of mourning"). The landlord suddenly realizes that the mourning is for him, that his hatred has made him a dead man, and he covers his head and joins his tenant in mourning the inhumanity of the human race.

Most of Malamud's urban stories have the quality of still lives. The characters only occasionally go anywhere, they rarely move more than enough to survive, and they often end up in frozen attitudes like the mourners. Malamud's Italian stories, on the other hand, move at a much faster pace. The heroes of these stories, usually Jewish-Americans, are in a rush to get somewhere, but this haste gets entangled in a world of smouldering Italian passion and/or intrigue. The hero of **"Behold the Key,"** an American student of Italian history, is led by his Italian guide on a wild goose chase in an effort to find an apartment. Ultimately the guide promises him one that was kept by a countess for her lover. After many comic disappointments and a few well-placed bribes, the apartment and its key are found, but when the apartment is opened all the furniture has been slashed by the spurned lover. In addition to jealousy, the lover's motive for vandalizing the apartment includes his hatred for the guide. Though the American has been a student of Italian history, this scene tells him more about the passionate spirit of the Italian people than all the books he has studied. The lover throws the key at the student leaving a permanent scar on his forehead. The student will be forever branded with this knowledge that comes from experience rather than study.

The same frenzied pace is found in the Fidelman stories (**"Last Mohican," "Still Life,"** and **"Naked Nude"**). Malamud uses Fidelman to develop Henry James's favorite theme of the American innocent abroad, but in a most un-Jamesian manner. Fidelman is in constant motion as an array of charlatans, con men, obsessed women, and thieves test and change his American moral values. Fidelman keeps trying new kinds of art to relate to the Italians, but he is always one step behind. He also seeks, and occasionally participates in, a richness of passion not typical of Malamud's urban heroes.

Malamud's Italian stories cover thematically much the same ground as his urban Jewish ones, but the landscapes are much richer, filled with the antiquity of the country and the warmth of the Mediterranean skies. They tend to celebrate passion in a way that only a few of the urban stories do. **"Life Is Better than Death"** begins with the kind of mourning found in **"The Mourners"** or **"The Bill,"** but ends with the heroine, a widow pregnant and deserted by a man she met in the cemetery, vowing never to mourn again. Though fully aware of death, she has committed herself to life.

> *Jeffrey Helterman, in his* Understanding Bernard Malamud, *University of South Carolina Press, 1985, 153 p.*

Joel Salzberg   (essay date 1986)

[*In the following essay, Salzberg interprets Malamud's story "Take Pity" as an allegory concerning the mystery and unrelenting nature of human suffering.*]

Among the most successful stories in **The Magic Barrel** blending realism and fantasy, **"Take Pity"** has never been particularly troubling to critics. [In a footnote, Salzberg states: "Both the title of the story and its conclusion are ambiguous and may be variously interpreted. The title may be read as Rosen's plea to Eva to accept his pity or as his plea to Eva to pity him by accepting his aid. It may also be taken as Eva's plea to Rosen to be left alone. Eva's appearance at the conclusion with 'haunted, beseeching eyes' and arms extended is, perhaps, an entreaty for understanding and forgiveness. Conversely, this final confrontation with Rosen may suggest some inherent resistance in Eva to accept charity at any price."] Those few who have discussed it have assumed the following thematic scheme to be at the center of the story, and the casual acceptance of that scheme has resulted in the neglect of other issues critical to a fuller appreciation of this work. When Axel Kalish, the owner of a failing grocery store, suddenly dies, Rosen the coffee salesman attempts to give his widow Eva both advice and direct aid. In Eva's refusal to accept Rosen's repeated benevolent offers, and in Rosen's increasingly persistent efforts to extend them, each one insults and injures the other. So fierce is Rosen's determination to aid Eva that the coffee salesman commits suicide in order to leave his money and property to her and her children. Equally determined to respond to this act of ultimate charity, either by rejecting it, or pleading for understanding and forgiveness for her past behavior, Eva also commits suicide and, at the end of the story, stands before Rosen in Malamud's version of limbo in a poignant gesture of appeal. [In a footnote, Salzberg adds: "Malamud's supernatural setting may evoke associations with the Old Testament Sheol, a kind of Hades, in its shadowy, somnambulistic character. Whether it is a final destination or a purgatorial half-way house for Rosen and Eva, Malamud is silent. He also remains aloof from the moral implications of the double suicide."] Thematically, critics have generally read **"Take Pity"** as an illustration of the excesses to which pride and stubbornness can lead.

This reading of Malamud's bitter comedy rings true within certain limits of characterization and character interaction. Although Malamud does not place the action within a clearly defined time period, two intersecting historical contexts—the Nazi destruction of European Jewry and the poverty associated with the 1930's Depression—

obliquely influence the meaning of this tightly structured narrative, taking it beyond a grimly humorous study of mutually violated pride. These contexts of misery, while only allusive in the story, are ultimately responsible for producing in Eva the suffering that is central to her identity. I believe that Eva's suffering, like that of Bartleby's in Melville's story "Bartleby the Scrivener," is not only irremediable, and the basis for her intransigent behavior, but also a cosmic mystery that defies both human and nonhuman comprehension. Moreover, Malamud's brilliance in **"Take Pity"** lies in his ability to create from the bitter domestic warfare of Eva and Rosen—" 'I felt like to pick up a chair and break her head' "—an allegory on that mystery and on the unrelenting nature of all human suffering. [In a footnote, Salzberg adds: "Eva's name is altogether appropriate for Malamud's story in its allusion to the exile and suffering of her namesake, Eve, the mother of mankind."]

When Rosen relates his chronicle of pain to the interrogating but noncommittal bureaucratic angel Davidov, we learn that Eva and Axel Kalish have virtually escaped from the dead. Although Eva and Axel are not specifically represented as immigrant survivors, Axel is identified by Rosen as a recent refugee from Poland. Rosen's passing comment on the husband's background seems to take for granted that she too has shared it, insofar as Eva has no private history apart from Axel's. Responding to Rosen's plea that she run away from the graveyard grocery store and go to relatives, Eva replies bitterly: " 'My relatives Hitler took away from me.' " If Eva herself is not an actual Holocaust survivor, she has indeed lived in the shadow of Holocaust suffering. In America, Eva's experiences become for her a recreation of the mute but painful environment of her European past. Rosen tells Davidov, " 'I met her where she always was—in the back room there in that hole in the wall,' " and he periodically refers to the grocery store as a "grave" and its general location "a dead neighborhood." As a woman utterly victimized and degraded by her past and her present, Eva has lost the capacity to hope. There is no haven to which she can flee, either because her relatives have been killed in the Holocaust or because Axel's are nonexistent.

Since Rosen is himself financially secure, because of his properties and investments, and is also sensitive to human misery—" 'I have a heart and I am human' "—he naively assumes that he can help Eva escape her old life and attain a new one. But Eva's reply to Rosen's offer of aid only elicits from her the central leitmotif of her existence, her sense of futility. " 'Where will I go, where . . . ,' " she laments. Rosen's inability to understand Eva is less a matter of his own insensitivity than it is of the geographical and emotional distance from sufferings of which he is ignorant. Like Eva he has also been an immigrant to America, but he has preceded her by over three decades—" 'After thirty-five years' experience I know a graveyard when I smell it.' " While Rosen has been around poverty and suffering in America, he has nevertheless acquired an American optimism that encourages action and hope. The coffee salesman, however, is a stranger to Eva's Eastern European sense of fatality, and the inevitable clash of these personalities is the result of their radically opposed visions of life.

Rosen finally grasps that Eva has formed an intense personal dislike of him, but while his capacity for sympathy is large, his knowledge of human nature is limited. Thus he fails to grasp that Eva has come to feel predestined to suffer. Despite a brief moment of optimism about the future (which is, in all likelihood, a ploy to deter Rosen's benevolent overtures), Eva has already capitulated to fate. Experience has taught her that her future will be no different from her past: " 'In my whole life I never had anything. In my whole life I always suffered. I don't expect better. This is my life.' " Both her European past and American present converge to create a woman who sees herself as an outcast and beyond salvation. Inevitably Rosen's penetration into Eva's sphere of suffering only brings him intellectual and moral darkness, as the end of the story amply suggests.

[In "A Note on 'Take Pity,' " *Studies in Short Fiction* (1969)] Sanford Pinsker has faulted Rosen for a boorishness and vulgarity reflected in his insistent benevolent gestures of charity. Such a reading of Rosen's character magnifies his abrasiveness out of all proportion and may cause us to lose sight of Eva and the dynamics of her interaction with Rosen. It is implicit in the story that Eva is filled with bitterness before it is directed at Rosen. Indeed, her own husband is not exempt from her scorn in that his death is experienced as abandonment: " 'Where will I go, where with my two orphans that their father left them to starve?' " At yet another point in her exchanges with Rosen, when he makes his economically expedient offer of marriage, revealing that he has a mortal illness, Eva's reference to her husband underscores the bleakness of her married life: " 'I had enough with sick men.' " Eva's increasing dislike of the coffee salesman must be understood in the context of her European past and American present, for her experiences with death and sickness, suddenly mirrored in Rosen, have been a familiarity that now breeds contempt. He becomes an unwelcome *memento mori* of her suffering, and his charitable intentions not only act like salt in her old psychic wounds but also awaken in her a new sense of degradation.

The coffee salesman, considering his background and lack of education, quickly says what he feels, but he is not entirely without tact or delicacy. Those qualities are soon worn thin by Eva's dogmatic refusals of aid which violate both Rosen's sense of humanity and the very life of her children, Fega and Surale. In an allegorical sense, Rosen comes to the defense of the human as represented by those children. In speaking of Fega and Surale to Davidov, the census-taker, he reveals the main source of his motivation throughout the story: " 'I didn't want them to suffer,' " he explains. If expressions of suffering and futility are the leitmotifs of Eva's existence, the desire to alleviate suffering serves as the leitmotif of Rosen's existence and is typified by his bewildered question: " 'Why should somebody that her two children were starving always say no to a man that he wanted to help her?' " As Rosen's helplessness and frustration increase, his benevolence toward the intractable Eva becomes an angry obsession: " '*But I will give*,' " he adamantly asserts. Bad form is surely less of a sin in Malamud's world than it is in the fiction of Henry James. If Rosen is excessive, his excesses are those of an overly

sympathetic heart, which in Malamud's fiction is almost a moral imperative, even though the sympathetic heart may be treated ironically as in *A New Life*. The substance of Rosen's offers are not in themselves inherently insulting. On the contrary, they are in keeping with the highest expressions of the Mishneh Torah:

> There are eight degrees of charity. The highest is to give assistance to a neighbor who has fallen on hard times by making him self-supporting through a gift, a loan, by making him a partner, or by finding him a job.
>
> . . . . .
>
> Third is when the giver knows who receives his charity, but the receiver does not know from whom the aid came. [Harry Gersh, *The Sacred Books of the Jews*, 1968]

Rosen extends credit to Eva's failing grocery store and secretly pays the company for which he works. He later attempts to avoid embarrassing Eva with a direct gift of money by using a go-between as a pretended friend of her husband who is desirous of paying back an old debt. While such acts of secret charity are third in the hierarchy of charitable principles set forth in the Mishneh Torah, Rosen's first direct attempt to aid Eva involves making her self-supporting. He offers her a rent-free apartment and payment to a neighbor for the care of her child so that she can find employment and save her money.

One should note that Eva does not despise Rosen at the outset. His plea that she avoid wasting her life initially elicits from her an explanation rather than scorn. She declares to Rosen the grim but undisputable facts of her life: that she has "nobody" and " 'no place to go.' " The demeaning word "charity" is used by Eva herself only later as the verbal sparring intensifies. Rosen then argues that his offers are made not out of charity but as her husband's friend; her reply, however, is part of a verbal fortress that she erects in order to maintain an imperviousness against any form of sympathetic human intervention, although Rosen is the immediate source: " 'Mr. Rosen, my husband didn't have no friends.' " [In a footnote, Salzberg states: "The reader should recall that Rosen recommends credit for Axel's grocery store against his better judgment; moreover, Axel is apparently about to take Rosen's advice just before he dies. ' "Be a painter, a janitor, a junk man, but get out of here before everybody is a skeleton." ' "] If life has brutalized Eva, the result seems to be a loss of her own humanity. As a consequence, she refuses to allow her children to take food from Rosen, and their gradual starvation abets her own Medea-like impulse toward their immolation and her own.

The basic stuctural device of Malamud's story, the interrogation of Rosen by Davidov, the census-taker, on the incidents leading to Rosen's arrival, has a two-fold purpose. The information which Davidov receives advances the plot of the story. At the same time the omissions in Rosen's account concerning the reasons for Eva's behavior contribute to one of Malamud's major themes, the failure of either human or angelic intelligence to comprehend human suffering. In his attempt to relate to Davidov the manner of Axel Kalish's death, Rosen can only resort to a tautology. " 'Broke what breaks,' " he explains. His circular answer suggests the futility of attempting to describe the mystery of the mortal condition. Indeed, knowledge is as limited in Malamud's conception of divine space as it is on earth, and this fact seems to be supported by the meagre resources allotted to Davidov: a "pencil stub," "a cracked razor blade," and "an old-fashioned language that they don't use it nowadays," which appears to be incomprehensible. Divine indifference is also suggested by Davidov's own boredom and lack of curiosity. When Davidov asks Rosen to begin his account, Rosen's sarcastic reply is the only weapon he can use to indict the apparent incompetence of the authorities in charge. " 'Who knows where to begin? . . . Do they know where to begin?' " he asks of the census-taker.

Rosen's desire to remain in darkness may be an appropriate reflection of the spiritual and psychological void in which he exists, but the drawn shade at his window, as we soon discover, is intended as a possible barrier against Eva, whom Rosen had come to dread: He "blurt[s] out her name" when he arrives and also " . . . seemed to be listening for something." More unbearable than even her stubbornness is the terrifying revelation of irremediable suffering her life has come to symbolize for the well-intentioned and previously optimistic Rosen. Moreover, Eva's appearance in Malamud's netherworld with "haunted, beseeching eyes" and out-stretched arms moves Rosen to moral horror and outrage, granting even her possible need to seek forgiveness from him, for her presence suggests the abandonment of her children. Thus Rosen's terms of opprobrium—"whore, bastard, bitch,"—are figuratively appropriate references for her in their allusion to her unnaturalness, particularly as a mother. In his confrontation with Eva, Rosen, like Mendel the protective father in **"Idiots First,"** has wrestled with someone who seems other than human. But unlike Mendel, who in the strength and ardor of his own humanity briefly humanizes Ginzburg, an angel of death, Rosen fails in his struggle to humanize the implacable widow. Eva and Davidov become, in their own way, morally repulsive to Rosen in their indifference to and detachment from human sympathies. And the question Rosen's own benevolent efforts pose to them, "Don't you

understand what it means human?", remains disturbingly unanswered, foreshadowing such later works as *The Tenants* and *God's Grace*.

Joel Salzberg, "Irremediable Suffering: A Reading of Malamud's 'Take Pity',", in Studies in Short Fiction, *Vol. 23, No. 1, Winter, 1986, pp. 19-24.*

Irving Halperin   (essay date 1987)

[*An American educator and critic, Halperin has written widely on Jewish literature. In the following excerpt, he examines the theme of responsibility in "The Mourners."*]

What, briefly, are some elements of [Malamud's] legacy? For one, much can be learned from his uses of the moral imagination. Throughout his literary career, he was engaged in a religious-like enterprise to dramatize the importance of heartfelt moral values. Not that he was a "messages-lessons" writer; for as he himself once stated in an interview, "The best art contains a marvelous combination of the esthetic with the moral." And he added:

> It means a great deal to me to be able to invent what one would call a life that is valued. And to do it in such a way that it is not a preachment of any kind, but rather a form of esthetic—that it becomes an esthetic in itself. In other words, one creates beauty and feeling at the same time he creates value, that value which we call morality . . . Morality, obviously, is not effective without feeling. Where I feel myself gifted is to feel the moral act and to be moved by the moral imagination.

Another element of Malamud's legacy is that his work encompasses both ethnic and universal concerns. He wrote about Jews because, in his own words, he was "comfortable with them," because he admired their "awareness, responsibility, intellectuality." Ultimately, his subject matter may be perceived as a mix of Jewish particularism and nondenominationalism; indeed, he saw Jewish history as a metaphor for the fate of all men. Hence the epigraph in *Idiots First:* "All men are Jews." Or, as he stated this belief differently in an interview:

> I try to see the Jew as universal man. Every man is a Jew though he may not know it. Jewish drama is prototypically a symbol of the fight for existence in the highest possible human terms.

What I especially value is Malamud's treatment of the theme of responsibility; that is, the moral imperative for a person to respond responsibly to the humanity in another. Of course this familiar theme appears in innumerable novels and short stories by other authors, but in Malamud's fiction it takes on a distinctive radiance. And nowhere else in his work is this subject matter more powerfully rendered than in one of his finest stories, **"The Mourners,"** a work that Malamud himself must have thought well of because he chose it alone to read for a Library of Congress recording. . . .

The essential method of **"The Mourners"** is a process

Leslie Field on Malamud as a Jewish writer:

Malamud is a Jewish-American writer within the loose tradition of that special breed of hyphenated Jewish writer. He is a brother to the many intellectual and literary Jews who years ago left the *shtetl* and traditional Judaism to reach out into the world. They rejected the confines of their past as they accepted "enlightenment." In so doing they as people and the characters they gave us all took on the qualities of marginality as these writers ignored, skirted, homogenized, or rejected important concerns of the Jewish people.

Leslie Field, in his "Bernard Malamud and the Marginal Jew," in The Fiction of Bernard Malamud, *edited by Richard Astro and Jackson J. Benson, Oregon State University Press, 1977.*

whereby the two protagonists are led to a spiritual trans-formation. The story gets underway in typically taut, un-encumbered Malamudian prose. We quickly learn, as early as the first paragraph, that Kessler, a retired egg can-dler, had abandoned his young wife and three children some thirty years before, and that since then he has not attempted to contact them, or even to learn whether they are alive. For ten years he has occupied a small, dismal flat on the fifth floor of a decrepit tenement on the East Side of New York. Difficult and quarrelsome, he keeps apart from his neighbors who, in turn, shun him. It seems that he has a filthy, smelly flat, and this condition so vexes the tenement's janitor that he complains to Gruber, the land-lord, who then orders his janitor to give Kessler notice. Gruber (the name evokes the Yiddish term for coarse, *grubber yung*) does not feel that he is under any obligation to his elderly tenant, even though the latter has resided in the building for ten years. Kessler "makes dirt" and, con-sequently, threatens Gruber's monetary investment. Moreover, Gruber has in mind that, with the departure of this tenant, the flat can be rented out for five dollars more than Kessler is paying. Clearly, the landlord is indifferent to the traditional principle that all Jews are responsible for one another. It is ironic, we realize, that Gruber is so con-cerned with *shmuts* (dirt) when he himself is a fat man who wears yards of baggy clothes and mops himself with a perspiration-stained handkerchief—baggy clothes, yel-lowish handkerchief, precise and palpable details, the life-blood of good fiction.

Representative of Malamud's ear for immigrant English is the janitor's ultimatum to Kessler: "Mr. Gruber says to give notice. We don't want you around here. Your dirt stinks the whole house." In depicting Kessler's response, Malamud leaves out what a second-rate writer might well have put in, an obvious explanatory statement to the effect that Kessler is terrified. How, then, is this moment ren-dered? We see that Kessler looks "like a corpse adjusting his coffin lid." And on the heels of this disquieting image, when the old man begins shouting imprecations at the jan-itor, we are informed that Kessler's eyes were "reddened, his cheeks sunken, and his wisp of beard moved agitatedly. He seemed to be losing weight as he shouted." Rather than have the narrator explicitly tell us about Kessler's inner state, it is much better conveyed from the outside, through specification of the tenant's physiognomy. "He seemed to be losing weight as he shouted." A sentence which bodies forth Malamud's idiosyncratic angle of vi-sion, a most informative vision because it acquaints us with people who are markedly different from ourselves; a vision which has produced some of the most original American fiction in the last three decades.

Much of the story's most effective dialogue—dialogue which may be paraphrased only at the risk of erosion—occurs after Kessler refuses to leave and barricades his door, and then Gruber, still indifferent to the old man's pain, storms into his tenant's flat, shouting, "I want you to scram outa here. Move out or I'll telephone the city marshal." When Kessler starts to reply, the other cuts him short: "Don't bother me with your lousy excuses, just beat it." Surveying the dimly-lit flat, the landlord says, "It looks like a junk shop and it smells like a toilet." To which

affront Kessler pleads. "The smell is only cabbage that I am cooking for my supper. Wait, I'll open a window and it will go away." "When you go away, it'll go away," Gru-ber says, in what sounds to this reader like Talmudic sing-song, probably intentional on Malamud's part. Kessler's cry, "I didn't do nothing, and I will stay here," elicits Gru-ber's threat: "If you're not out by the fifteenth, I will per-sonally throw you out on your bony ass." The deft use of the adjective "bony" to reveal further Gruber's vulgarity supports Mark Twain's inimitable declaration that "the difference between the almost right word and the right one is the difference between a lightning bug and lightning."

A few days later, the marshal and his assistants, holding the old man by his "skinny legs" (the adjective here sug-gests not only Kessler's helplessness but also Malamud's empathy for his character's ordeal), remove the old man and deposit him and his furniture on the sidewalk before the tenement. There, while it rains and then snows, Kess-ler sits, looking like—and here an appropriate simile brackets this recluse's misery—"a piece of dispossessed goods." Precisely at this juncture there is a turning point in Kessler's situation. It occurs after he is involuntarily prodded to take an initial step toward what eventually will be his inner transformation. But for the reader this unex-pected development is not readily discernible. By not dis-closing what he knows of the emergent change in Kessler, the narrator piques our curiosity. In any event, the old man probably would have continued to sit there had it not been for the intervention of an elderly Italian woman whose flat adjoins Kessler's. Outraged, perhaps seeing herself as a potential victim of Gruber's, she keeps shriek-ing until finally her two sons and another neighbor carry Kessler and his belongings back up to the evicted man's flat, where the old man sits on his bed and weeps. Then the Italian woman, in a gesture of nurturing, makes her devastated neighbor a plate of hot macaroni, which subse-quently is described as "stiffened," probably to suggest Kessler's death-in-life existence.

Furious at this defiant action by his tenants, Gruber again barges into Kessler's flat and threatens the old man with arrest. Weeping bitterly and hitting his chest with his fist, Kessler bursts out, "What did I do to you? Who throws out of his house a man that he lived there ten years and pays every month on time his rent? What did I do, tell me? Who hurts a man without a reason? Are you a Hitler or a Jew?" A cry that, in another context, evokes one of the most memorable scenes in *The Assistant:* when Morris Bober, whose life exemplifies the Jewish ethic of *mentshlekhkayt,* says to his employee, Frank Alpine: "Our life is hard enough. Why should we hurt somebody else? For everybody should be the best, not only for you or me. We ain't animals."

Kessler's question, "Are you a Hitler or a Jew?", under-scores the story's theme: Gruber can continue to be a tor-mentor or he can assume responsibility for his tenant. But the landlord does not respond to this question and leaves the flat in anger. Still, Kessler's agony has finally, albeit only partially, reached Gruber. We surmise this through some clues that the narrator gives us: specifically, when Kessler is weeping and striking his chest, Gruber removes his hat and listens "carefully" to the other's plaint; also, the next morning he decides to speak to Kessler again and offer to get him into a public home.

A master of building narrative tension, Malamud heightens the conflict between the two men when, on the next morning, Gruber, this time prepared to take a conciliatory stance, reenters Kessler's flat to find the old man sitting, without shoes, on the bedroom floor. "There he sat, white from fasting, rocking back and forth, his beard dwindled to a shade of itself." Why the *shiva* position? the reader, abruptly thrown off balance, wonders.

Here the narrator enters directly into Kessler's mind, and we learn that the latter is feeling excruciating remorse for having abandoned his family. "How, in so short a life, could a man do so much wrong? This thought smote him to the heart and he recalled the past without end and moaned and tore at his flesh with his fingernails." Now the narrator informs us, in a succinct sentence, that Kessler first began to feel remorseful when, after his eviction, he was sitting on the sidewalk. In presenting this picture of Kessler's anguish, the narrator avoids being explicit—the kind of explicitness which is anathema to fiction—about why this change of heart has occurred now; the explanation is left to the reader's intelligence, and we deduce that what long had been repressed and frozen in Kessler has been penetrated by his neighbors' humane act.

Troubled, frightened, Gruber at first does not know what to make of Kessler's behavior. He considers leaving, escaping from the oppressive sight of the old man. But then all at once he is struck with the recognition that "the mourner was mourning him; it was *he* who was dead." Meaning, the narrator compels us to recognize, spiritually dead. Now it is Gruber's turn to be in pain. "Sweating brutally, he felt an enormous weight in him that slowly forced itself up, until his head was at the point of bursting. For a full minute he awaited a stroke; but the feeling painfully passed, leaving him miserable."

Presently looking around the room, Gruber suddenly—curiously, at first the reader thinks—experiences it as "clean, drenched in daylight and fragrance." How can this be, since until then the flat had been depicted as badly lit and malodorous? The explanation points up the magic of Malamud's artistry, the kind of magic that sustains the passion of reading: the words "daylight" and "fragrance" can be seen as objective correlatives for Gruber's transformation. Now, in the story's last sentence, Gruber, feeling intense shame for his treatment of his tenant, snatches the sheet from Kessler's bed and, as though wrapping himself in sackcloth, wraps it around his body, sinks to the floor and becomes a mourner. Which is to say, he becomes a *mentsh.*

From the vantage point of this conclusive ending, we can retrospectively see how the story has travelled, how its narrative structure has been formed by the movement of the landlord and his tenant toward a spiritual transformation. The awakened conscience of Kessler and Gruber binds them to Jewish tradition and, by extension, to mankind, as implied by the epigraph of *Idiots First*: "All men are Jews." Finally, **"The Mourners"** is a convincing dem-

onstration of Malamud's assertion that the "best art contains a marvelous combination of the esthetic with the moral."

> *Irving Halperin, "The Theme of Responsibility in Bernard Malamud's 'The Mourners',"* in Judaism, *Vol. 36, No. 4, Fall, 1987, pp. 460-65.*

Lawrence Jay Dessner   (essay date 1988)

[*In the following essay, Dessner discusses Malamud's self-conscious blending of fairy tale and realistic elements in "The Magic Barrel" and the story's resultant ambiguity.*]

Although Bernard Malamud's **"The Magic Barrel"** has already been granted that intimation of immortality which derives from frequent reprinting in anthologies designed for college undergraduates and their mentors, criticism has yet to do the story the justice of explicating its ambiguities or attending to the ironic playfulness which is their ground. From the first, a symptom of critical unease, caused by the story's inconsistent allegiance to the conventions, or clichés, of literary genre, has been a concern for its apparent or potential sentimentality: "There is a sentimentality to these tales [in ***The Magic Barrel***], as well as a condescending cuteness which mars them seriously. . . . Except for their settings . . . they might have been published in one of the women's magazines, so sentimental, so treacle-laden are they. In short, they are emotional clichés" [Richard Shickel, "Decline of the Short Story," *The Progressive* (1958)].

This is the extreme position, but even his admirers have felt that Malamud was playing dangerously close to the edge of bathos: "He is saved [from sentimentality] . . . by a certain irreducible sourness in most of his characters and by the intransigence of the circumstances he has created" [Henry Popkin, "Jewish Stories," *Kenyon Review* (1958)]. And again: "One reason why I salute Mr. Malamud is that in ***The Magic Barrel*** he keeps right off the hokum-schmokum, I-should-drop-dead folksy kind of Jewish story for which, I am sure, we would have been all too pathetically grateful" [Keith Waterhouse, "New Short Stories," *New Statesman* (1960)]. Despite the story's recalling, if avoiding, the genre of the "hokum-schmokum," Alfred Kazin thought it a "little masterpiece," although he noted a limit in Malamud's range because of the extremes to which he seemed forced to go "to outwit his own possible sentimentality" [*Contemporaries: From the 19th Century to the Present,* 1982]. *The Spectator*'s reviewer [Ronald Bryden] found that Malamud skirted sentimentality, that seductive patch of quicksand often lurking in the "slightly hackneyed field of New York Jewish humor." He "has a trick," wrote this critic, "of leading his simple O. Henry anecdotes to suddenly complex, reverberant endings."

The complex ending of **"The Magic Barrel,"** in particular, has become a focus of debate. It presents us with Leo Finkle, a rabbinical student whose pursuit of a bride acceptable to a congregation precipitates a crisis of confidence and then a passionate desire for a young woman whose father had disowned her because of her sins. "A wild one—wild without shame. . . . Like an animal. Like a dog," is the way the distraught father, Pinye Salzman, the matchmaker, describes her. When **"The Magic Barrel"** reaches its conclusion, the rabbi-to-be approaches the girl in the character of her suitor, while her father, who had at Leo's desperate urging brought the two together, "chanted prayers for the dead." Like the conventional prostitute, "Stella stood by the lamp post, smoking," but she is wearing white as well as red and Leo "pictured in her his own redemption." As if in celebration of their nuptials, "Violins and lit candles revolved in the sky." This ending has raised more questions than it has settled and it has not, as endings often do, answered questions that had arisen earlier: Did the matchmaker manipulate Leo so as to cause or prompt him to fall in love with Stella? Is he using Leo to get his despised daughter off his hands or does he believe in the possibility of her salvation, and of Leo's, through hers? What is the moral of the piece, its tone and intention? What is the author's attitude to his story, which is to say, what is its genre?

To these and related questions a disconcertingly wide variety of answers have been offered. Some readers, seeming to be making a virtue of necessity, evidently believe "that to reduce the story to specific meaning is to do the author an injustice" [Richard Reynolds, " 'The Magic Barrel,' " *Studies in Short Fiction* (1973)]. On the other hand, a critic insists that those who find the story ambiguous are also those who "actually *believe* that breaking all the rules and sleeping with a prostitute is a maturational experience" [Bates Hoffer, "The Magic in Malamud's Barrel," *Linguistics in Literature* (1977)]. It is evidently possible to admire the story greatly without understanding the motivations of one of its central characters and so without understanding its narrator's moral attitude toward the story as a whole. A critic argues that "**'The Magic Barrel'** is not only the finest piece in the collection . . . it is perhaps one of the finest stories of recent years." Yet, this critic goes on to say that "it is impossible to tell for whom Pinye chants—for himself and his guilt, . . . for Finkle's past or Finkle's future, or for all these reasons. . . . What better reason to chant when to win means to lose" [Sidney Richman, "The Stories," in *Bernard Malamud and the Critics*, 1970]. The story's reputed sentimentality, its "effort to induce an emotional response disproportionate to the situation, and thus to substitute heightened and generally unthinking feeling for normal ethical and intellectual judgment," may have spread to the critic who reached this conclusion: "The reader is left with the illogical, vaguely unsettling but deeply moving impression that Pinye's mourning chant somehow captures the pain, suffering, and loneliness of life while also welcoming the possibility of spiritual growth" [Sheldon Hershinow, *Bernard Malamud*, 1980].

Crucial to the tonal ambiguity of the story's ending, and therefore to questions of its sentimentality, is the problem of Salzman's motivation. To some readers, this problem is without a solution: "The reader, like Leo, is left wondering whether Pinye is merely a clever con-man or a spiritual teacher" [Hershinow]. To others, the solution is quite clear: Salzman is an "imposter" "who has neither office

nor magic barrel filled with dossiers of choice brides." His prayer for the dead "signifies that the rabbinical student is lost to the faith" [Jeffrey Helterman, *Understanding Bernard Malamud,* 1985]. Still others have found that Salzman's prayer mourns "the death of the old Leo who was incapable of love," and "celebrat[es] his birth into a new life." In this view, Salzman "engages in a ruse" to teach Leo that "love is existential" [Theodore Miller, "The Minister and the Whore," *Studies in the Humanities* (1972)]. But an equally confident reader speaks of "an ending of powerful affirmation [in which] the student, rejecting all of Salzman's goods, fastens upon the broker's own daughter, a girl who is clearly marked as bad luck" [Charles Alva Hoyt, "The New Romanticism," in *Bernard Malamud and the Critics*]. The implication here is that Salzman sought unsuccessfully to lure Leo into an unexceptional but morally deleterious match with one of his aging or otherwise poorly qualified clients. Leo's preference for the tainted daughter affirms then the Nietzschean virtues of the self-destructive personality. Elsewhere, evidence that would dissolve the story's seeming "paradox" has been found in parallels of varying explicitness between Salzman and the goat-god Pan, and there is a critic who concludes that Malamud's ending is "a kind of Joycean epiphany" which makes the story "a consciously ironic parable and not an escape from tragedy" [Mark Goldman, "Comic Vision and the Theme of Identity," in *Bernard Malamud and the Critics*].

The difficulties we have been reviewing arise not from any essential obscurity in the story, but from its author's and its narrators' unrelenting and exhilarating playfulness and from the failure on the part of critics to attend to that playfulness, to let themselves see that this serious story is awash in jokes about the literary genres to which **"The Magic Barrel"** belongs or alludes. (It may be to easy to forget that Matthew Arnold's own attack on the bleak, even dingy, tone of the middle-class heroes of Victorian Hebraic moral seriousness was itself often made with Hellenic sprightliness.) The literary games being so vigorously played on the field of **"The Magic Barrel"** are not ends in themselves but means of expressing the moral dichotomies which can be derived from the fundamentally contradictory meanings of the word "magic." The word refers equally well to the clever tricks of the stage magician as to the miracles performed by the God-obsessed prophet or by a supernatural power itself. The word invokes the actions of the trickster which are so complex as to appear, but only to *appear,* to be beyond rational, logical, explanation or cause as well as those God-like actions which are by definition uncaused, beyond the explanations of reason. By playing on this doubleness of meaning, **"The Magic Barrel"** asks about the kind of magic which is at work in the universe it imagines. Are the wonders of this universe explicable, subject to rational analysis, or are they beyond reason's power and understanding? That the story does not answer this question of questions does not mean that it is an ambiguous work. The story's point is that the universe the story imagines—a convenient stand-in for the one we inhabit—is ambiguous, indecipherable, suffused with uncertainty about its relationship, if any, to Deity, if any. This radical doubt is not presented as a cause for heavy-headed dismay. Here, as in much of Malamud's fiction, radical skepticism is not burdensome but a provocation to delight.

The joyful playfulness at the heart of **"The Magic Barrel,"** thwarting and perplexing some of its best readers, is voiced through an incessant irony. Often obvious, often subtle, irony permeates **"The Magic Barrel"** as much as the shadow of sentimentality does. In suggesting now that its universe is mundane, now that it is miraculous, it takes away with one hand what it gives with the other while pretending, straight-faced, to be unaware of this duplicity. Or rather it pretends to pretend to be so unaware. It says things it only wishes to be true, unsaying them at the very instant of their utterance. Sentimentality is undercut by rude skepticism, faith by naturalistic doubt, but then that doubt is questioned by the manifestation of the supernatural, that skepticism by the advent, sentimental or otherwise, of hope.

The oscillation of the implied author's faith is constantly figured in his wavering loyalty to the conventions of literary genre, which in turn determines the narrator's style of self-presentation, the descriptions of natural phenomena, the problematic character of Pinye Salzman, and the basis of the obsession which so suddenly and insistently draws the rabbinical student to the prostitute.

The agent of the story's irony, the narrator, is himself a figure of irreducible contradiction. His speech, the essence of his action as narrator, is not that of a native speaker of English, at least as the story begins: "Not long ago, there lived in uptown New York, in a small, almost meager room, though crowded with books, Leo Finkle, a rabbinical student in the Yeshivah University." The inclusion of the definite article before the identifying name of the university marks the sentence off from the received standard English of educated discourse. Both "in the University" and "in University" have the flavor of the British upper classes. "At the University" and "at Yeshivah University" are unexceptional American idiomatic forms. Our narrator sidesteps these possibilities for a Yiddish-flavored alternative. And there is something elusively but surely not "right" either about "though crowded with books." We understand that the relative abundance of books is judged by our narrator to stand in a compensating relationship to the shortcomings of the apartment, and it is heartening to hear that commonplace in whatever dialect, but our narrator is imperfectly sensitive to the nuances of standard idiom. If we recast the phrase we hear that "In a small, almost meager room which was, however, crowded with books," while not without its awkwardness, is in its sound and syntax as surely native as the original version is not.

But no sooner have we adjusted our expectations to the peculiarities of this narrator's voice and to his chosen genre then both the dialect and the fairy tale ambience, the vagueness of placement in time and space—"Not long ago" is a variant of "Once upon a time," "in uptown New York" a version of "somewhere west of Laramie" or a seacoast in Bohemia—vanish without either warning or trace:

> Finkle, after six years of study, was to be ordained in June and had been advised by an acquaintance that he might find it easier to win

himself a congregation if he were married. Since he had no present prospects of marriage, after two tormented days of turning it over in his mind, he called in Pinye Salzman, a marriage broker whose two-line advertisement he had read in the *Forward*.

Vagueness has given way to exactness of reference—"six," "June," "two," "two"—and the narrator's language has become elegantly correct. We notice the gracefully rhythmic alliteration of: "advised by an acquaintance," and "after two tormented days of turning it over." There is the tactfully and delicately-expressed prudence and its correctly accompanying subjunctive: "he might find," "if he were married." The verb in "Win himself a congregation" is precisely the right one, not indeed as formal as our narrator himself might choose, too flippant in its metaphor's suggestion of play or deceit to suit Leo himself, but certainly the very one Leo's acquaintance, who is tacitly quoted here, found comfortably appropriate. Notice the dignity suggested by that "present" before "prospects," that insinuated assurance that we are among men of the world here, upper lips stiff, for whom even an emotional crisis will be taken in stride. True, Finkle is "tormented," but for two "days" instead of the expected "nights," and his "turning . . . over" occurs in the decorous safety of "his mind" rather than bodily on a bed of pain.

The narrator, that voice that effortlessly slides from the untutored dialect of the foreign born to the eloquent precision of the highly educated writer, will in due course be seen to be at his ease recording references to Salzman's colorful dialect and Yiddish ("Yiddishe kinder"), yet knowledgeable with regard to French tags ("au courant," "petite") and classical mythology ("a cloven-hoofed Pan"). The volatile instability of the narrator's identity is integral to the shifting of his story's genre from speech-oriented folk or fairy tale or parable of wisdom to highly literate, even bookish, modern skeptical realism. Playfully, as if to celebrate by making unmistakably obvious his own remarkable range of cultural reference and the story's dazzling inconsistencies, the narrator enters Leo's consciousness at a moment when the language and special knowledge of both Jewish and Christian orthodoxy are placed in ludicrous juxtaposition in a single consciousness: "He had lived without knowledge of himself, and never in the Five Books and all the Commentaries—mea culpa— had the truth been revealed to him."

Here and at other points in the story when what is at hand is not the abstract or symbolic pain of fairy tale but realism's implacable and concrete anguish, the narrator drops his Yiddish-flavored dialect and his playful use of the fairy tale's magical, that is, supernatural, conventions. But such reversions to sober seriousness of content and presentation are always short-lived, soon interrupted or concluded when the merciful spirit of play reasserts itself. In the midst of Leo's agony, for instance, the narrator refers to it with a folkloric, non-realistic image: "His beard darkened." The result of such narrative maneuvers is delighted surprise, comic relief, and a distancing reminder that Leo is nothing more than a character in what is not only a fiction but a fairy tale. Suddenly, he becomes a flat rather than a round character, and we may laugh at him and his plight, knowing that the genre of which we have just been reminded will not permit him to suffer too deeply, too long, or without due recompense.

The narrator's playfulness with the conventions of genre is not limited, however, to the psychological effect of transmuting the reader's pain to pleasure. His failures of consistency announce and enforce an agnostic's freedom from dogma, a joyously playful willingness *not* to know more about the moral universe but that it is eternally and provocatively not to be known.

The literary games being so vigorously played on the field of "The Magic Barrel" are not ends in themselves but means of expressing the moral dichotomies which can be derived from the fundamentally contradictory meanings of the word "magic."

—*Lawrence Jay Dessner*

The second paragraph of our story initiates what will become an elaborate play with the tantalizing but incomplete evidence of the metaphysical status of Pinye Salzman. He "appeared one night out of the dark fourth-floor hallway." The aura of the supernatural that the title and opening words of **"The Magic Barrel"** have let out of the bag, as it were, tempts us to imagine the matchmaker literally "appearing," that is materializing out of spirit into the semblance of flesh, literally extruding himself "out" of the smoky gloom of the poorly lit hallway. Repeatedly, Salzman is said to "appear," "reappear," and "disappear" "as if on the wings of the wind." The cumulative suggestion is that he materializes rather than merely moves from place to place. Often his appearance comes at the most opportune time, as far as his prospects go of making a customer out of Leo. On one occasion, for instance, Leo dismisses Salzman in exasperation, but no sooner does Leo's anger leave him than "almost at once there came a knock on the door" and Salzman "was standing in the room." It is not clear whether Salzman walked into the room or beamed himself down in it.

The second part of the sentence which introduces Salzman reins us in. The man, if man he be, is "grasping a black, strapped portfolio that had been worn thin with use." His "overcoat [is] too short and tight for him." With this and what immediately follows, the spell of the folk or fairy tale is weakened. Salzman has become no more than a long-suffering, hard-working mortal. The narrator, expressing sympathy for his humble, arduous, and unremunerative calling, briefly drops down into the matchmaker's own dialect: "Salzman, who had been long in the business. . . ." (Standard English for that would be, "Salzman, who had been in the business a long time. . . .") His clothes are poor, he is missing some teeth, and he "smelled, frankly, of fish, which he loved to eat." But despite these unpromising attributes, Salzman still may be some sort of spirit, goblin, phantom, in deep disguise, for "his presence [as in the "presence" of royalty, perhaps] was not displeasing [our narrator has resumed his impeccably correct British English with its habitual litotes], because of an amiable manner curiously contrasted with mournful eyes." Notice the elegant play of m's and c's in that phrase, and, on the vowel side, of the a's of "because of an amiable manner." Except for the missing teeth, Salzman's eyes are the first of his facial features to be noticed. (They will prove to be of primary importance before long.) Then comes his aesthete's "wisp of beard" and "bony fingers." Then the eyes again, "mild blue eyes [which] revealed a depth of sadness." And it is this "characteristic," the narrator tells us, which first appealed to Leo, putting him "a little at ease."

When the matchmaker and his client settle down to business, they do so "at a table near a window that overlooked the lamp-lit city." Like the opening words, "Not long ago," "lamp-lit" carries a hint of the days before electric light, of gas, even of oil. But, typically for this story, the question is complicated by the facts that the post which supports modern electric street lighting is still called a "lamppost" and modern electrical fixtures are commonly called "lamps." Suggestive as it may be, "the lamp-lit city" is not a reliable index to the story's historical period. Similarly, as suggestive as Salzman's eyes, beard, hands, and entrance may be, they tell us nothing for certain about his metaphysical status. And complementing and echoing these ambiguities is the narrator himself, about whose ethnic origins and loyalties, as expressed in his habits of speech, we will be in a state of bemused ignorance until it dawns upon us that he is himself a notable aspect of the comedy of ambiguity he is presenting to us.

Some will need only the next page or so before such dawning, for when the very sensitive Leo, distressed by Salzman's way of flipping through the cards on which his female offerings are described, looks away from him, "He now observed the round white moon, moving high in the sky through a cloud menagerie, and watched with half-open mouth as it penetrated a huge hen, and dropped out of her like an egg laying itself." This is the first of five scenes in **"The Magic Barrel"** which have reminded readers of the painter Marc Chagall. [In an endnote, Dessner states: "The others are: Salzman 'hiding . . . in a tree, . . . or perhaps a cloven-hoofed Pan,' 'a profusion of loaves of bread . . . flying like ducks over his head,' Leo's years of study seen as 'pages torn from a book, strewn over the city,' and 'Violins and lit candles revolved in the sky.' "] Indeed, Chagall's paintings are known for the way figures, animate and inanimate, appear floating high in the sky. Both artists seem to use a similar method to testify to the presence of the supernatural in the realm of nature. As Sandy Cohen says [in *Bernard Malamud and the Trial by Love*, 1974], "Chagall suspends the laws of physics to portray the parallels and the harmony between this world and the next—between the physical and the spiritual. . . . " Unlike Chagall's paintings, however, Malamud's linear art permits him to have it more than one way. Not only do his enchanted skyscapes, unlike Chagall's, vanish as suddenly as they materialize, but they are embedded in the context of the story's characters and train of events. There is more than one way then to understand the significance of this and of the story's other instances of unusual objects floating in defiance of gravity. My analysis of this one should provide a pattern pertinent to those other scenes as well.

Clouds do indeed float in the sky, taking all sorts of shapes, including those reminiscent of the shapes of animals. The fastidious Leo, distressed by the way his search for a wife has led him into embarrassing and uncomfortably intimate discussions with the crude matchmaker, distressed too by his increasing awareness of his own ominous moral and even spiritual inadequacies, has turned away from Salzman. He "pretended not to see" Salzman flipping through his "much-handled" index cards on which are written the vital statistics of his marriage-minded offerings and instead "gazed steadfastly out the window." Faced for the first time with the practical aspects of courtship and with the probability of his own impending marriage, Leo's mind and heart are in a tumult. At this moment, the narrator reminds us that Leo's upheaval about love and sex involves the eternal cycle of natural rebirth: "Although it was still February, winter was on its last legs, signs of which he had for the first time in years begun to notice." Leo had told Salzman that he had for the past "six years devoted himself almost entirely to his studies" so that he knew little of "the company of women." But in the spring a young man's fancy lightly turns to thoughts of love, so, like a patient being tested with Rorschach ink blots, Leo projects his immediate obsessions out onto the canvas of the sky and interprets one of the cloud shapes as a female doing what females as females do, laying an egg. The roughly egg-shaped moon passes behind the translucent clouds among which is one which roughly resembles and readily brings to Leo's recently sensitized mind the idea of a hen. This isn't simply fantasy or fairy tale in the manner of Chagall, an index to this world's essential spirituality; it is psychological realism in the manner of Freud. Indeed, before that hen gives birth, it is said to have been "penetrated." No wonder Leo watches "with half-open mouth" in awe and astonishment.

This comic, psychological interpretation of the episode, however, ignores the use of the moon in its ancient role in the iconography of love. It ignores the charming touch of the fairy-tale imagination which pictures "winter" as a worn-out old man "on his last legs," and it ignores that conventional association of romance which requires the progress of the seasons to correspond to the progress of the protagonist. The peak of Leo's sexual expressiveness will occur, of course, at the end of the story on a "spring night." The glowing February moon, like the entire skyscape, is not only symbolic. Both "round" and "white," as our narrator describes it, the moon is an index to Leo's susceptibility to feminine voluptuousness.

This discussion of the play of genres would not be complete without our noting that here, as repeatedly in **"The Magic Barrel,"** the psychological drama of the young male's belated entrance into social, sexual, and ethical maturity appropriates the conventions, not of dramatic real-

ism, but of farce. Take for instance Leo's repeatedly embarrassing encounters with his landlady. Her love-obsessed boarder, who has just walked out of a cafeteria without paying, fails to recognize her as she saunters past him in the street. When Leo, "sensing his own disagree-ableness," apologizes to her for this and other lapses, he does so so "abjectly" that the poor woman "ran away from him." This slap-stick sequence is a parody of Leo's serious problems. He has a lot to learn about women and about himself. But serious as his plight presents itself to him, its farcical elements and the narrator's handling of the telling of it assures the reader, for the moment at least, that a happy ending rather than a life in therapy, or with a wife in therapy, or some even worse fate will be Leo's portion. Later, when Leo is faced with the most difficult crisis life has thus far offered him, he "hurried up to bed and hid under the covers." In farce such behavior assures escaping the worst. Here, at an early stage of his search for a wife, staring out the window at those remarkable clouds, Leo is presented as the conventionally comic, sex-crazed adolescent. He is sweating in anguish behind as dignified a front as he can manage, and we are all amused. The more he suffers, the more we laugh.

Between the story's conventional situation of the sexually innocent male's confrontation with the experienced female and the narrator's agile, tongue-in-cheek transformations of both the story's genre and the narrator's tone and manner, the story hovers at the edge of hilarity. At the same time, the pathos of Leo's plight and the implicit promise of his escape from it hover at the edge of sentimentality. And yet also at the same time, the "shame and fear" that "possessed" Leo when he told Lily H., one of Salzman's prospects, "that I came to God not because I loved Him, but because I did not," that "he did not love God so well as he might, because he had not loved man," have the seriousness and dignity associated with tragedy. And yet at this moment, when his "terrifying insight" "brought him to the point of panic" and Leo "covered his face with his hands and cried," Malamud's complex and ironic juggling of generic conventions dissolves the boundaries between fairy tale, moral fable, psychological realism, sentimental hokum, and farce.

In the midst of Leo's absorption with the hen in the sky, the narrator wipes away the trace of a smile that was making itself more and more discernible and replaces it with a poker player's face from which issue these sober tones:

> Salzman, though pretending through eyeglasses he had just slipped on, to be engaged in scanning the writing on the cards, stole occasional glances at the young man's distinguished face, noting with pleasure the long, severe scholar's nose, brown eyes heavy with learning, sensitive yet ascetic lips, and a certain, almost a hollow quality of the dark cheeks. He gazed around at shelves upon shelves of books and let out a soft, contented sigh.

Where has our overage trouble-prone comic adolescent gone? Where our narrator's accent and fairy-tale practices? And perhaps the most arresting questions arise here: is Pinye Salzman, who speaks of his eligible women as merchandise and lies freely both to them and to Leo, merely the insensitive, materialistic matchmaker he appears to be? Is his sigh the traditional humble Jew's appreciation of learning or the greedy tradesman's gloating over his prey? Or, in keeping with fairy-tale convention and with the suggestions of supernatural powers that often accompany him, is Salzman some sort of ministering angel or fairy godfather, chuckling to himself about his projected course of action, his strategy for redeeming the strayed man of God? Or is Salzman closer to the Satanic model, leading Leo to destruction either for the ordinary devilish reasons or merely in hopes of saving, or at least providing for, his own daughter? Much of the story is concerned with the oxymoronic and impenetrable epithet the narrator applies to Salzman in passing, "commercial cupid," businessman divinity.

Avid to meet the girl whose photograph has so appealed to him, Leo travels by subway to Salzman's Bronx address but finds him not at home. His wife says that his office is "in the air," an allusion to the Yiddish tradition of the *luftmensch,* as well as yet another suggestion of Salzman's supernatural status. [In an endnote, Dessner comments on the definition of *luftmensch:* "Literally, a man of the air. In *The Joys of Yiddish,* 1968, Leo Rosten's definitions include 'an impractical fellow, but optimistic,' and 'One without an occupation, who lives or works *ad libitum.*' Rosten captures the spirit of the type by recalling Israel Zangwill's fictional luftmensch whose business cards read 'Dentist and Restaurateur.' "] Leo returns directly to his apartment and is "astounded" to find the matchmaker there waiting for him. Since Leo travelled by subway, it does not seem possible that, short of flying, Salzman could have reached Leo's apartment ahead of him unless Salzman had started for his apartment before Leo had left word for him and that explanation, which would involve a remarkable coincidence or Salzman's ability to know what Leo was thinking, seems equally improbable. Leo's question, "How did you get here before me?" confronts Salzman with the issue of his essential nature, but Salzman parries Leo's question by an answer of enigmatic curtness, "I rushed." It is a stylistic hallmark of the story that Salzman, Leo, and the narrator are capable of similarly terse and abrupt comic deflections. When Lily H. learns that Leo is not "enamored of God" in the way she had hoped, the narrator sums up her disappointment—and undercuts the pathos of it—by the comic, summary sentence, rhyming, balanced in structure, and intricately alliterative, "Lily wilted." When Leo catches Salzman in his salesman's exuberance representing one of his clients to be "Age twenty-nine," three years younger than she had earlier been said to be, it is Leo's turn for the memorably terse, comic rejoinder, "Reduced from thirty-two?" It is as if Leo, Salzman, and the narrator, despite their great differences in role and in manner, were co-conspirators in the story's generation of comic ambiguities. After Salzman's explanation which explains nothing, Leo lets the matter drop, joining the conspiracy *not* to pursue the question of Salzman's nature to a conclusion.

Another question with far-reaching ramifications for our understanding of Salzman and the story is that of the "magic" barrel itself. Boasting to Leo about the large number of his clients, Salzman says his drawers are filled with index cards and so "I keep them now in a barrel." Whether or not Pinye Salzman literally possesses such a barrel—"magic" or otherwise—we are, however, debarred from knowing. One would think that the barrel is merely Salzman's metaphor, and Leo, seeing no sign of it in Salzman's apartment, tells himself that it is "probably also a figment of the imagination." But Malamud doesn't even let this detail escape his veil of ambiguity. The narrator tells us that a curtain divided Salzman's one-room apartment and that the curtain was "half-open." Leo's search then was necessarily limited. We have been at this impasse before, but perhaps we can move past it by considering the nature and result of Salzman's ministrations, whether plotted or inadvertent, that is, Leo's sudden yet lasting infatuation, if the word does not prejudge the analysis, with Stella. What can we make of that infatuation?

As with other aspects of **"The Magic Barrel,"** analysis of its central event, Leo's sudden, strong attraction to Stella, leads toward contradictory results and these in turn toward differing ideas of the story's overall tendency. In fact, the nature of Leo's reaction to the snapshot of Salzman's daughter is the story's determining question. Salzman may be nothing more than a shallow and greedy salesman, a cynical peddler of damaged and discounted goods, and yet the world in which he plies his trade may be thought to be redeemed by Leo's response to his daughter's photograph: "He gazed at it a moment and let out a cry." Considerations of career, propriety, and self, are cast aside in an instant:

> Her face deeply moved him. Why, he could not at first say. It gave him the impression of youth—spring flowers, yet age—a sense of having been used to the bone, wasted; this came from the eyes, which were hauntingly familiar, yet absolutely strange. He had a vivid impression that he had met her before, but try as he might he could not place her. . . . It was not, he affirmed, that she had an extraordinary beauty—no, though her face was attractive enough; it was that *something* about her moved him. Feature for feature, even some of the ladies of the photographs could do better; but she leaped forth to his heart—had *lived,* or wanted to— more than just wanted, perhaps regretted how she had lived—had somehow deeply suffered; it could be seen in the depths of those reluctant eyes. . . . Her he desired. His head ached and eyes narrowed with the intensity of his gazing, then as if an obscure fog had blown up in the mind, he experienced fear of her and was aware that he had received an impression, somehow, of evil.

The initial shock is expressed in a wordless "cry." Then Leo, by instinct as well as training an inveterate analyst, seeks an explanation for what has happened to him. He identifies as possible causes the paradox of Stella's aura which combines both youth and age and the paradox of strangeness and familiarity. He assures himself that his experience is not one of mere sexual arousal: Stella is not "an extraordinary beauty." He returns to his initial formulation, the combination of youth and age, innocence and experience, attraction and repulsion. Then Leo drops his inconclusive and half-hearted analysis. Readers of **"The**

Magic Barrel," however, will want to stay with the analysis longer in hopes that doing so will clarify the story's ambiguities of genre and intention.

Leo himself seems to think that Stella's having "deeply suffered" is paramount. He speaks repeatedly of being "of service" to her and of finding "redemption" in so doing. We recall his earlier self-diagnosis and understand that Leo hopes to love God better through loving mankind better. That Stella has made herself ineligible for ordinary love only raises the stakes toward Dostoevskian heights.

Leo is unaware of the farcical and sentimental aspects of his program and not concerned to try to understand the genesis of his sudden passion for Stella which engendered this drama, or melodrama, of redemption through suffering. Having fallen in love, he knows what he wants to do about it but has no interest in discovering why and how his passion was aroused. Indeed, his offering no explanation of that allows the implication that there *is* no explanation, that his falling in love, in that it passeth understanding, was an intrusion of the irrational, that is, of the uncaused, into an otherwise rational universe. This is an essentially religious, albeit unorthodox view, at least as consonant with Christianity as with some forms of contemporary Judaism. Not through reason and a knowledge of "the Five Books and all the Commentaries," but through the magical allure of Salzman's fallen daughter, has Leo learned to serve his fellow mortals and so come, as Lily put it, "to be enamored of God."

This interpretation of the events is so lacking in Malamud's usual playfulness and yet so mined with submerged ironies that one is tempted to say that only a Leo could believe it. Unlike Leo, readers of the story are not likely to forget the other possibilities that Leo himself had repeatedly raised. Soon after being smitten by Stella, he obtains her father's agreement to arrange a meeting with her and is then "afflicted by a tormenting suspicion that Salzman had planned it all to happen this way." This is a resurgence of earlier fears that he was being manipulated by Salzman, even that Salzman had supernatural means of doing so. In the aftermath of his troubling meeting with Lily, "he would not put past Salzman's machinations" the fact that "it snowed." For Salzman to have planned Leo's falling in love with Stella, Salzman would have had to slip her picture in with the others left with Leo.

But this would only insure Leo's seeing the photograph. To insure Leo's falling in love because of it would require Salzman to have and to employ superhuman powers. The idea that Leo's love for Stella was beyond reason meshes with the story's fairy-tale ambience, with its surrealistic skyscapes, and with those miraculous aspects of Salzman's powers. The happy coherence of these motifs and the overall interpretation they point to is undercut, however, by the equally coherent view that whatever magic we find in **"The Magic Barrel"** is of the sleight-of-hand variety, the gods having departed. In this view, Leo's distress about his sexual and theological identity is nothing more than a mask for what is biological and psychological, another rather elementary instance, like the "penetrated" hen in the clouds, of Freudian sublimation. Since he is by training a man of the cloth, his choice of explication and justifi-

cation of the events is made for him. The theme of redemption through a fallen woman is a fanciful piece of self-deception, a mere conventional cover for what is apparent to all disinterested—and thoroughly amused—observers. Leo has hidden his sexual passions under a cloak of mystery and charity and the old chestnut about the prostitute with a heart of gold: "What's a nice girl like you doing in a place like this?" How effectively that conventional question preempts inquiry about the nice boy's motives for being in the same place!

The cynical view that love can be understood as an expression of rational functioning of biological and psychological mechanisms gains support by a discovery Leo himself makes. At the critical instant of the critical moment, with Stella before him in her ambiguously suggestive red and white, Leo has an insight that resolves his conflict and sends him forth "with flowers outthrust" and which cues another celebration, or psychological projection, in the heavens: "Violins and lit candles revolved in the sky." Leo hesitates no longer: "He pictured, in her, his own redemption." The critical discovery that comes to Leo at this moment is that Stella's eyes, "filled with desperate innocence," "were clearly her father's." No wonder he was so intrigued when he first saw her picture. Her eyes *were* both "hauntingly familiar, yet absolutely strange." The mystery of Leo's fascination with Stella is then no mystery at all, not the consequence of a manifestation of spiritual or supernatural "magic" in the mundane world. What has happened has been the result of the biological probability that Stella's eyes would resemble her father's.

Malamud's narrator has been reminding us of Salzman's eyes and of Leo's responsiveness to them from the very beginning. However crass Salzman's behavior, those "mournful" eyes are more than compensation to Leo. They "revealed a depth of sadness"; they are "melancholy eyes" and "haunted eyes." Leo's sense that Stella has suffered, "been used to the bone, wasted," and been sanctified by that suffering, "came from the eyes." One could say that Leo is responding to more than the unaccountable familiarity of the eyes in Stella's picture, that he senses in them her father's sensivity to and experience of redemptive suffering.

Malamud's text also sanctions a comic complication of this already deeply ironic interpretation. Leo's discovery of Stella's resemblance to her father, as it happens, is not his first such discovery of her inherited traits. Having fallen in love with Stella through her photograph, Leo rushes to Salzman's apartment. After all, her picture was among those Salzman left for him. His first response to the "thin, gray-haired woman, in felt slippers" who opens the door is this: "He could have sworn he had seen her, too, before but knew it was an illusion." Even though Leo says this resemblance is "an illusion," readers need not be misled by this ironic narrative ruse into believing that Stella resembles her father but not her mother. While alert readers of **"The Magic Barrel"** sense that the link between Stella and her mother will involve a link between Stella and her father, Leo himself is unaware of this so that we have the delicious dramatic irony of his continuing to run "around in the woods."

In the end, despite his daring decision to pursue it differently, love has come to Leo Finkle after all in the time-honored way both Salzman and Leo's tradition recommend, "as a by-product of living and worship." His intercourse with Salzman, his exposure to the matchmaker's vivacious energy, his "amiable manner," and his notably solemn eyes have produced, as a by-product, the rabbinical student's infatuation with the older man. This "love" makes itself known to us, but surely not to Leo, in the younger man's adoption of the older's mannerisms of speech and salient characteristics of appearance. Leo thinks he loves Stella, but when he finds Salzman in a cafeteria, "Leo had grown a pointed beard and his eyes were weighted with widsom." He has become a novice in the service of Pinye Salzman. His speech, too, formally so impeccably "Americanized" (Salzman's word in boasting about Lily's qualifications, now sounds like this: "It is not impossible," and "Just her I want." Of course Leo cannot marry Salzman, who among other things is already married, nor can he admit to himself his predilection. Fortunately, fortuitously, Stella comes along. Leo transfers his passion to her, concocts, subconsciously, his highly acceptable if sentimental rationale for his unusual marital choice, and down comes the curtain on the play. It has been a fairy tale, or a farce, except we have been deeply touched by the characters as individuals and by the seriousness of their plights. It has been a work of psychological realism, except that the tongue in cheek has too prominently bulged. It has been a moral fable, except for the indeterminacy of its moral grounds and for the inconsistency of its generic conventions. Whatever Salzman's magic is, Malamud's art is much more than what is implied by "a trick," or even a bag of tricks. Now, a barrel? That's another story altogether.

"Leaning against a wall," which cannot but allude to the ancient wailing wall in the old city of Jerusalem, "Salzman chanted prayers for the dead." It is reasonable to expect that a story that offers and then undercuts diverse interpretations about so much should encourage conflicting views about all its parts. But the only "dead" person in **"The Magic Barrel"** is, or was, Stella. "This is why to me she is dead now," cried her father, grieving over her moral failure, her fate worse than death. (As if to clarify the matter, Malamud added "to me" after the *Partisan Review* publication.) Stella's father, seeing his daughter on the road to salvation, or on the road to easy street, or at last off his hands and off his mind, or even about to make a connection with the rabbinical student for whom he himself harbors warm feelings, prays. The Jewish prayers for the dead, the Kaddish, do not mention death. "They are praises to God." However Pinye Salzman understands the event, he has good reason to praise God in thanksgiving. In whatever diverse ways we choose to read its genres, to play the game of **"The Magic Barrel,"** or by extension to accept our endlessly enigmatic universe, we may all join in its praise.

Lawrence Jay Dessner, "The Playfulness of Bernard Malamud's 'The Magic Barrel'," in Essays in Literature, *Vol. 15, No. 1, Spring, 1988, pp. 87-101.*

Irving Howe   (essay date 1989)

[*In the following excerpt from a review of* The People, and Uncollected Stories, *Howe argues that the stories in the collection are flat and dispirited.*]

Of the 16 uncollected stories in [**The People, and Uncollected Stories**], about half constitute apprentice work, written mostly in the 1940s. These stories already bear Malamud's personal stamp: they are morally earnest, compassionate, and nicely put together. Yet I think I know why he decided not to publish them. They droop with a dispirited realism, a flatness of voice. They start and end with suffering, something that is always at the heart of Malamud's work, but they fail to reach that moment of surprise or illumination that lifts the best of his later stories.

One early story, **"The Grocery Store,"** I found moving, perhaps because its setting, the poor immigrant Jewish streets, is one I shared in my youth with Malamud. A decent piece of work, **"The Grocery Store"** remains no more than a faithful picture of remembered life, without that touch of "invention" Malamud would always try for. If you compare this story with a somewhat later one, **"The Loan,"** you can see how Malamud succeeded in getting past the sluggishness of an honorable realism while still, even in his freest fables, retaining a fundament of realistic notation. **"The Loan"** ends with a bit of action—two poor Jews embrace and sigh over their lost youth: "They pressed mouths together and parted forever." That must seem implausible to anyone familiar with the life Malamud drew upon: immigrant Jewish men didn't press mouths together. Yet in the story itself, this works beautifully, providing a moment of intense elevation, a compact in defeat.

About the later stories, mostly published in the 1980s, though perhaps written somewhat earlier, there is not much to say. They are diverse in subject, competent enough, and rather dull. Two of them, fictional mini-biographies of Virginia Woolf and Alma Mahler, were experiments that might have led to something fresh if Malamud had had more time. As it is, these two experimental pieces seem unfinished: there is something flat and toneless, something unprovisioned, about them. Malamud was obviously groping toward a new mode. The stories reveal little, however, about the two fascinating women he chose as his subjects or about what he was trying to do as a writer.

What these later stories show is a writer struggling with the exhaustion of his subject. "I may have done as much as I can with the sort of short story I have been writing so long—the somewhat mythological, biblically oriented tales," Malamud wrote to himself in 1983-84. The struggle of an aging writer to find a second voice can be terribly painful. The fact that in his last sustained piece [**The People**] Malamud did find that voice should bring joy to all his admirers. If only fate had given him a few more months.

Still, power to **The People!**

Irving Howe, "Paleface and Redskin," in The

New Republic, *Vol. 19, No. 3903, November 6, 1989, pp. 116-18.*

Bette Pesetsky   (review date 1989)

[*Pesetsky is an American short story writer, novelist, and critic. In the following excerpt from a review of* The People, and Uncollected Stories, *she comments favorably on several of the stories.*]

The burdens of conscientious literary executors are great. What should they permit to be published? And how will the author's reputation withstand the examination of work never finished? Bernard Malamud left the responsibility for such decisions to Robert Giroux, Timothy Seldes and Daniel Stern. The result was the publication of this intriguing posthumous book, which consists of an unfinished novel and 16 short stories. Fortunately, *The People, and Uncollected Stories* proves that Bernard Malamud's reputation has been left in good hands.

Of the 16 stories also collected in this book, six have never been previously published. Although the stories, which are dated between 1940 and 1984, are uneven in quality, they mark the steps in the development of a distinctive literary voice. Bernard Malamud was one of those rare writers whose earliest stories display an astonishing mastery of technique and form. These works presage both the themes of his novels and those of his later stories. They take place in the land of his archetypal Jewish immigrant—where old men sit, their dreams of success in America vanquished, their defeat a certainty.

The store becomes the principal setting for tests of humanity in two of the previously unpublished stories. In **"The Grocery Store,"** written in 1943, a shopkeeper named Sam sits and remembers: "Nineteen impoverished years in the grocery business to this end. Nineteen years of standing on his feet for endless hours until the blue veins bulged out of his legs and grew hard and stiff so that every step he took was a step of pain." Sam tries to kill himself, but fails. He is not yet ready for rebirth and redemption.

In **"Riding Pants,"** written in 1953, a widowed butcher lives with his son, Herm, above his store, a failing shop whose condition parallels his diminished life. Herm seeks to escape by constantly wearing riding pants, garb for a fabled escape. But reality overwhelms his father and he destroys the pants. After an attempt at revenge fails, Herm accidentally locks himself in the store's walk-in icebox. "He might have cried," Malamud writes, "but the tears were frozen in, and he began to wonder from afar if there was some quicker way to die. By now the icebox had filled with white mist, and from the distance, through the haze, a winged black horse moved toward him." The story ends with a tightly wrought epiphany in which Herm sees his father humiliated by a customer and recognizes the degree of the old man's pain; in a gesture that opens him to understanding, Herm puts on a blood-smeared butcher's apron.

Malamud's stories seem to have a built-in past; they evoke memories in the reader. In **"Spring Rain,"** a lonely man who is alienated from his wife and daughter finds companionship with his daughter's suitor. In **"An Exorcism,"** an older writer finds that he has created a monster in a younger writer who records his own life as it happens. Less successful is **"The Literary Life of Laban Goldman,"** a tale in which the publication of an immigrant's letters in a newspaper leads to night-school fame and a brief, aborted romantic meeting with a fellow student.

The last two pieces in this book, written in 1984, represented a new direction for Malamud. He termed these stories, which take the facts of life and make them seem a fantasy, "fictive biographies." In **"In Kew Gardens,"** we move swiftly through Virginia Woolf's life; in **"Alma Redeemed,"** Alma Mahler survives her famous husbands.

Bernard Malamud was a writer whose long career was properly studded with the rewards of achievement—two National Book Awards, the Pulitzer Prize and the Gold Medal for Fiction from the American Academy and Institute of Arts and Letters. But Malamud was far more than the sum of his prizes. He was a natural storyteller who seduced us with fable and myth and folklore and affirmed our astonishment at the possibilities of life.

Bette Pesetsky, "Schlemiel of the Golden West," in The New York Times Book Review, November 19, 1989, p. 7.

Lawrence M. Lasher   (essay date 1990)

[*In the essay below, Lasher analyzes the style and themes of "The German Refugee," noting the link Malamud dramatizes between individual morality and history.*]

Bernard Malamud's **"The German Refugee,"** first published in 1963 and collected in *Idiots First,* has attracted relatively little critical attention. Reviews and discussions of *Idiots First* tend to focus on the more immediately striking title story, the experimental **"The Jewbird,"** or the two Fidelman stories. On the other hand, **"The German Refugee"** is particularly interesting from several points of view. It is one of only a few stories in which Malamud makes extended use of the limited first-person point of view; it signals a clear turning toward political and public themes and anticipates *The Fixer* in its attempt to define the connection between private morality and public events; it is the only place in the canon where Malamud allows the Holocaust to emerge from the generalized background of his characters' lives into vivid and compelling imagery.

What has gone unremarked is the way in which the story exposes Malamud's growing preoccupation with the relationship of art—in this instance, narrative art—to reality. At the center of the story is Malamud's attempt to define the ground from which narrative art such as his own springs, and its uses in a world in which history seems to produce only suffering. The story can be read as an exploration of the relationship between history and narrative as Malamud invites the reader to be witness at the birth of the artist, as personal experience embedded in the web of history becomes moral understanding which is communicated, finally, through aesthetic form. Despite Malamud's efforts to clarify this complex relationship in the more richly textured later works—*Pictures of Fidelman, The Tenants,* and *Dubin's Lives*—**"The German Refugee,"** despite its brevity, remains his most lucid and powerful comment on this complex and dynamic process.

Set in the hot Manhattan summer of 1939, the story relates the efforts of Oskar Gassner, a refugee from Berlin and the Weimar Republic, to learn English and to write and deliver an introductory lecture as a prelude to a series of lectures and, later, to a course on the literature of Weimar. Oskar has left Germany under pressure and, ostensibly because she was anti-Semitic, has left behind his wife of twenty-seven years. Under the tutelage of Martin Goldberg, a twenty-year-old college student and the first-person narrator, Oskar, throughout the summer and through cycles of hope and despair, struggles to write his lecture on the subject of Whitman's influence on German poetry. Suffering from a kind of writer's block, he is unable to write the lecture until Martin, for whom Oskar's struggle takes on a personal importance, provides the catalyst in a series of notes he has prepared for Oskar's use. The lecture, which argues that the notion of "brudersmensch" is Whitman's central influence on German poetry, is written and, with Martin's help, is delivered at the Institute for Public Studies. Two days later, Martin discovers that Oskar has committed suicide and subsequently discovers a letter from his mother-in-law which informs Oskar that his deserted, "anti-Semitic" wife was converted to Judaism and shortly afterward was arrested and murdered by the Nazis in a Polish forest.

Of primary interest here is the complex narrative structure beneath the conventional first-person narration in which the major action of the story is told. The events of the summer are related by the youthful Martin Goldberg as he struggles to keep Gassner alive—to assist him in his desperate attempt to escape from his damaging past and into a possible future. But just beneath the surface of this primary action is an older Martin Goldberg, the mature narrator who writes from some unspecified point in the future. This narrator is the authentic writer who, having been forced to see the necessary relationship between private acts and history, has been transformed from the brash, bookish, young American of the opening of the story, and, playing a kind of Ishmael to Oskar's Ahab, has survived to tell us. A primary strategy of the story is to make the reader witness to the transformation of the naive, first-person Martin into the familiar Malamudian third-person, omniscient voice, which, unlike the characters it describes, suffers from no mistaken notions about the terms of human experience and is deceived by no rational or romantic illusions. Thus, by the end of the story, the ironic tension between narrator and authorial view is resolved as the young narrator gives way to the authorial vision articulated by a mature sensibility. The experience of Gassner's history, together with the unfolding horror in Europe, transforms the youngster's sensibility and makes possible the artist whose voice we hear both at the end of the story and in its opening sentences. It seems clear that in Martin's transformation Malamud reflects something of his own formative experience at the time of the outbreak of the war. As Joel Salzberg has astutely observed [in his Introduction to *Critical Essays on Bernard Malamud,* 1987], "for all his cautioning . . . Malamud appears to be a self-referential writer—especially in his treatment of the artist manque. . . . "

Part One introduces Martin as naif, as a "skinny, life-hungry kid" who "would brashly attempt to teach anybody anything for a buck an hour," and Oskar as one of Malamud's victims who "sags," breathes "as though he were fighting a battle," and drops his hand to his side "like a dead duck." The teaching contract is established and in Part Two Martin begins his efforts, in that "sticky, hot July," to help Oskar with his English. The rejection of German and the attempt to learn English takes on symbolic suggestion as Oskar, with Martin's help, tries to escape from the ruins of his past and into an ordered and meaningful future. Under the influence of Martin's increasingly intense commitment to him, the German's mood begins to lighten, but he slips back into depression and despite Martin's increasingly strenuous efforts "to get Oskar into production . . . the lecture refused to move past page one." The opening of Part Three is placed precisely on "the seventeenth of July" as Malamud paints Oskar's ongoing agony and Martin's increasing disquiet against the backdrop of the events in Poland that fateful summer. Three weeks after their initial meeting, Oskar's attempts to write the lecture are still unproductive.

> **"The German Refugee" can be read as an exploration of the relationship between history and narrative as Malamud invites the reader to be witness at the birth of the artist.**
>
> —*Lawrence M. Lasher*

At this point Malamud explores Oskar's private preoccupation with the wife he left behind in Germany. The complex interdependence of Oskar's individual moral failing and the larger public stage of the story is one key to the story's meaning and to the transformation of Martin. The enlightened Weimar intellectual, the child of the liberal, modern values of the best that Europe had to offer, will be revealed to himself and to his American "son" as complicit in the fascist horror which is in the process of engulfing Europe. It will be that awful revelation which will produce Oskar's suicide and will undercut the theme of Oskar's lecture—Whitman's "brudersmensch"—and the naive American optimism which Martin had carried up the steps to Oskar's hotel room a few weeks earlier.

The gradual revelation of the terms of Oskar's abandonment of his wife to the Holocaust cuts very close to the bone of Malamud's moral vision. The moral failure which grows out of self-deception and unresolved narcissism produces a failure of love, helping to create or sustain a world built on anti-human behavior. What makes this story unusual in the canon is that the moral drama is witnessed by the first-person narrator, adding another step in the working out of Malamud's vision and connecting it to his understanding of the way in which the writer employs and extends that moral vision.

Malamud's revelation of the terms of Oskar's abandonment of his wife leaves little doubt that he intends that the reader—and Martin—will see clearly the truth of Oskar's behavior. Oskar's rationale for the desertion is doubly qualified: "I feel certain that my wife, in her heart, was a Jew hater." His subjective judgment—"I feel certain"—about her subjective feelings—"in her heart"—turns Oskar's self-justification into a strained rationalization for what seems more likely to have been an opportunistic grasp at freedom from what "wasn't a very happy marriage. She had turned into a sickly woman, physically unable to have children."

This careful undercutting of the justification for Oskar's behavior is first reinforced by Martin's discovery of the wife's stark assertion of her faithfulness in a letter to Oskar; "Ich bin dir siebenundzwanzig Jahre true gewesen," and later by the revelation of her conversion to Judaism. Eventually Martin will be unable to resist the truth of the victimization of the wife and its connection to the rising tide of inhumanity in Europe in the late summer and early fall of 1939.

As the story moves toward its climactic conclusion, the narrative attention shifts increasingly to Martin's sensibility as Malamud moves the focus of the story closer to its thematic center. As Oskar is playing out a variation of Malamud's familiar theme—the destructive force of self-seeking at the expense of love and duty—it is Martin's observation of Oskar and the effect of Oskar's despair and death on the artist as a young man which becomes the real subject of the story. Martin is falling victim to a despair of his own: "I was sometimes afraid I was myself becoming melancholy, a new talent, call it, of taking less pleasure in my little pleasures." Like Oskar, Martin feels "defeated"; although it is Oskar's sobs he hears on his way down the stairs from Oskar's apartment, he is well on his way to his own version of the racking despair which Oskar confronts. "I will quit this," he decides, for "it has gotten to be too much for me, I can't drown with him." And the next day he stays at home "tasting a new kind of private misery too old for somebody my age. . . ."

The lecture is completed and translated during the first week of September; again, the event in the narrative foreground is played out against the political background, in this case the invasion of Poland. Malamud means the reader to understand the nature of the self-deception going on here, for while Oskar and Martin "are greatly troubled, there was some sense of release [that the invasion of Poland had finally taken place]; maybe the brave Poles would beat them." The mistaken romantic idealism of the poetry is matched by the naiveté of the political analysis. With Martin's help, Oskar has struggled not toward a new future but back to the illusions of his former life and, by implication, back into the rational/romantic false assurances of the premodern world. For the moment illusion produces a sense of possibility: the weather changes for the better and Oskar's "unfocused quality" is corrected. "His

blue eyes returned to life and he walked with quick steps. . . ."

In the course of the successful lecture, Malamud brings the irony of the situation to a climax when Oskar reads from Part Five of "Song of Myself"—the central mystical assertion of the poem embodied in the joining of the soul and body followed by Whitman's most ringing assertion of the central transcendental vision:

> And I know the spirit of God is the brother of
> my own,
> And that all the men ever born are also my
> brothers, and the women my sisters and lov-
> ers,
> And that the Kelson of the creation is love, . . .

In the teeth of the invasion of Poland and the fall of Warsaw, the terrible prelude to chaos, Oskar and Martin manage the Whitmanic assertion to a "crowded auditorium" which includes "prominent people. . . . Two reporters . . . [and a] lady photographer." It is as though the central vision of nineteenth-century romantic idealism—the core of the transcendental vision of value—is here stubbornly and desperately reasserted in the face of a reality which is the absolute denial of the assertion. "Oskar read it as though he believed it," but again the narrative expands momentarily to drive the irony home for the reader who knows the fate of Poland and most of Europe: "Warsaw had fallen but the verses were somehow protective." The ironies here are direct and multi-layered, for the public occasion of the lecture seems to suggest something of the collective refusal of the West to recognize the full implications of the Hitlerian threat in the late thirties and right up to the outbreak of the war. The assertion of value embodied in the passage quoted by Oskar may have been psychologically protective for the West but it was politically disastrous for the world. It is not Whitman's poetry, nor Oskar's journalism and public lectures, which will stand against the beast. "Brudersmensch" as poetry, as intellectual formulation and aesthetic form, may seem somehow protective, but as always in Malamud, it is action in the world—or the failure of action in the world—which creates history. For Martin Goldberg—and for Bernard Malamud in his early twenties—the easy, romantic assertions of the nineteenth century must be measured against the encroaching realities of the mid-twentieth century. Martin's—and Malamud's—"ignorance, limitations and obsessions" must be expunged if the authentic narrator is to emerge at the end of the story.

Part Six ends with the illusion of victory completed: Martin feels "pride . . . in the job he had done," and Oskar has escaped from his heavy, hot German clothing into a "blue suit"; his English is much improved, the weather has improved, and he has been able to "hide the deepest wounds." The principals have been permitted the maximum extension of illusion as the war begins and the mass murder in Poland starts the process which will lead to the death camps. The reversal is swift and complete.

Two days after the lecture (now the end of September) Martin climbs the stairs to Oskar's apartment to discover that Oskar has committed suicide. Oskar's death precipitates the final movement of the story: with an extraordinary economy of means Malamud brings together the various threads of the story—the drama of Oskar and his wife, Martin's discovery of the truth beyond Oskar's representation of it, and the powerful revelation to Martin of the truth of what is occurring in Europe and what the future there is likely to bring. At the same time Malamud will extend his theme(s) to include a penetrating insight into the nature of the relationship of narrative art and the artist to reality. The process involves the protagonist's confrontation with reality, as illusion and self-deception are swept away in an epiphanic moment. The new vision transforms Martin from the limited, first-person narrator, locked into a completed past, into the omniscient narrator who "sees" through to the truth and speaks in an on-going present tense.

Martin's first shocked response to Oskar's corpse is denial. His verbal reaction is "No, oh, no," as language is invoked to deny the reality of what he is seeing. While it was possible for Oskar to deceive himself and Martin about the real terms of his behavior toward his wife, and while it may have been possible to deny the implications of the fall of Warsaw at a remove of five thousand miles and in the presence of the "comforting" assertions of Whitman, there is no denying the reality of Oskar's body on the kitchen floor—the face "beet-red" and the "lips bluish, a trace of froth in the corners of the mouth." Oskar's body will permit only the devastating truth that Martin is made to confront in the traumatic moment: "I said no but it was unchangeably yes." Martin's confrontation with the truth of Oskar's corpse precipitates a symbolic death and rebirth. As Martin enters the apartment a policeman asks him who he is, "and I couldn't answer." This refusal of his earlier identity is completed a few sentences later when he is named for the first time in the story. Significantly, he is named by Oskar in the note in which Oskar "left Martin Goldberg all his possessions." It is at this point that we hear clearly the voice of the mature narrator speaking from some unspecified point beyond the ending of the temporal frame of the story. In the present tense and with a rhetorical assertiveness, the narrator declares "I am Martin Goldberg." The Martin Goldberg who has spoken from within the temporal limits of the first-person narration and who has accepted and supported Oskar's self-delusion and made it his own is effaced and replaced by the mature Martin Goldberg, the narrator who will impose a larger meaning on the story as the events are penetrated by the omniscient eye of the artist.

In addition to providing the final revelation which solves the "mystery" of Oskar's suicide, the last two paragraphs make literary use of the iconography of the Holocaust as it is used nowhere else by Malamud. Further, the conclusion completes the important shift in the form of the narrative as Malamud replaces the naïf as narrator with the mature artist and connects the ending and opening sentences of the story in a circular structure which defines the larger meaning of the story.

A week passes between Oskar's death and Martin's return to the apartment "to inherit or investigate . . . to look through his things." He has been sick for a week and the Martin Goldberg who comes to seek understanding is not the same nameless, brash student of a few months earlier. The young Martin—full of pride, hope, illusion, and ambition—had died his symbolic death a week earlier in Oskar's kitchen amidst the acrid smell of the suicide gas. Martin sinks into "the depths of Oskar's armchair" where he will spend the morning trying to read the journalist's correspondence. Oskar's heir in more than the material realm, Martin is about to look out from the depths of the chair into a reality unmediated at the political level by false hopes and consequent illusions about who Hitler is and what his intentions are, and at the domestic level by Oskar's egocentric self-delusions and rationalizations. Interestingly, that "new" reality takes the form of a text—the antithesis of the Whitman text—in a letter from Frau Gassner's mother reporting the conversion, arrest, and murder of Oskar's wife by the Nazis.

At the most immediate level, the revelation that Frau Gassner has been murdered by the Nazis connects Oskar's domestic experience and personal moral failure with the central and defining event of the mid-century. Thus one strategy of the story, to dramatize the connection between personal morality and history, is accomplished in a seamless fusion in the final images of the story. It takes Martin "hours to decipher" the "tight script" of the letter which is written in German, the language of the past which Oskar and Martin have been working so hard to replace with English during the summer. But the past will not be effaced, and the symbolism of the passage insists upon the archetypal nature of the moment as the youthful seeker after truth, his illusions dispelled and on the edge of understanding, confronts the real terms of the human experience as they arise out of a physical text.

Never bound by the conventions of realistic narrative, Malamud, in the long, last paragraph of the story, makes an abrupt and unexplained shift in narrative voice and tense from the conventionally limited first-person voice speaking in the narrative past, to a more-or-less omniscient third person which uses an intrusive and startling present tense:

> She writes in a tight script it takes me hours to decipher, that her daughter, after Oskar abandons her, against her own mother's fervent pleas and anguish, is converted to Judaism by a vengeful rabbi. One night the Brown Shirts appear, and though the mother wildly waves her bronze crucifix in their faces, they drag Frau Gassner, together with the other Jews, out of the apartment house, and transport them in lorries to a small border town in conquered Poland. There, it is rumored, she is shot in the head and topples into an open tank ditch, with the naked Jewish men, their wives and children, some Polish soldiers, and a handful of gypsies.

The Martin Goldberg who announced himself in the previous paragraph takes control of the narrative as the youthful participant-narrator is effaced from the text. The final paragraph is a new text, the work of the mature narrator who transforms the "facts" of history and human experience into significant form and meaning. The ego-centered "me" of the opening sentence gives way to the poet-narrator; the voice which relates the horrifying details of the wife's experience is the characteristic Malamudian third-person narrator who subjects reality to the artist's penetrating vision. The narrative technique of the paragraph is familiar to any reader of Malamud's stories: the restrained and calculated selection of detail, together with a rhetorical heightening through poetic diction and device, and the powerful irony of the controlled understatement of the last sentence. Illusion, pretension, self-absorption all give way as reality is subjected to the penetrating vision of the artist's eye.

As Malamud allows the narrator-artist to take over the text from the narrator-adolescent, there is an abrupt shift from the conventional narrative past tense to a sharply intrusive present. The effect is extraordinary as the description of the murder in Poland overwhelms our notion of a past, completed event and leaps into an on-going, eternally reiterated active present. This bold manipulation of tense, together with the specification of the event through detail, insists upon the overwhelming reality of this event, on the notion that the Holocaust is never over and that we live always at risk given the weakness of "civilized" human beings like Gassner, and the collapse of the rational/romantic vision which has sustained us into the wasteland of the modern. The denial of the Whitmanic vision is implicit and complete as the transcendental text is replaced by the modern text—Martin's version of the letter—the searing vision of the final paragraph of the story.

But the ending of the story is not the end—for the end is in the beginning. The essential truth of the story rises out of the same perception which will generate the vision underlying *The Fixer*—that is, the ineluctable causative link between individual morality and history. The extraordinary power of the story depends upon the connection Malamud makes between the closing and opening paragraphs. The form of the opening sentences of the story is initially puzzling, for the opening, which provides our first view of Oskar, rests beyond the limited vision of the first-person narrator and is written in the present tense through an omniscient eye: "Oskar Gassner sits in his cotton-mesh undershirt and summer bathrobe at the window of his stuffy, hot, dark hotel room on West Tenth Street while I cautiously knock. Outside, across the sky, a late-June green twilight fades in darkness. The refugee fumbles for the light and stares at me, hiding despair but not pain."

Oskar is "seen" here not by the youthful, untransformed Martin but rather by the omniscient narrator: the artist's eye sees the truth of Oskar's existence before he opens the door to the young Martin, the "I" who enters the narrative at the end of the first sentence of the story just as he will leave it finally in the "me" of the last paragraph. The limited, egocentric, first-person narrator is framed by and contained within the omniscient voice of the opening and closing sentences of the story.

The circular narrative form of the story brings us back to the beginning, where Oskar is fixed in a timeless present—an everyman who, having lost his humanity, can do no more than stare out of his hot window as a perpetual twilight fades into perpetual darkness. Oskar is eternal witness to the appalling vision of the result of his own inhumanity so piercingly evoked by the narrator-artist in the final sentences of the story. Oskar and the reader are left to contemplate the results of the failure of love, most immediately in the awful death of Frau Gassner and, in the context of history, in the advent of the Holocaust. As always in Malamud, the emphasis is on the individual and the personal, for it is here that evil and good find their sources.

What is finally placed in the balance against the weight of the destructive forces inherent in the human experience is the insight into those forces, an understanding that is appalling in its clear-eyed vision of the Holocaust which is always potential in private and public human history—a vision which resists self-serving and destructive illusion and which shapes reality into significant form that carries with it, after all, the implication of control. We share with Martin his understanding of the appalling facts, and as we enter into the narrator-reader relationship with him, we become the initiates; we are brought to an emotive understanding available only through art. This is as much as Malamud can give us.

> Lawrence M. Lasher, "Narrative Strategy in Malamud's 'The German Refugee'," in Studies in American Jewish Literature, *Vol. 9, No. 1, Spring, 1990, pp. 73-83.*

Joel Salzberg   (essay date 1993)

[*In the essay below, Salzberg identifies several levels of parody in Malamud's short story "The Girl of My Dreams."*]

Dismissed with faint praise in the 1960s by such otherwise sympathetic Malamud critics as Sidney Richman and Sam Bluefarb, **"The Girl of My Dreams"** (1953) might be likened to Malamud's own characters in suffering the fate of being virtually unknown and unloved. [In his *Bernard Malamud,* 1966] Richman observes that "the story remains, at best, only interesting" and too reliant on "satire and farcical symbolism"; Bluefarb, after severely condensing its plot and themes, refers to it [in "The Scope of Caricature," in *Bernard Malamud and the Critics,* 1970] as an example of Malamud's exceptional handling of caricatures. "[Malamud's] puppets, unlike O. Henry's, draw real blood," he observes ". . . when they are cut by the jagged edges of life." In a seminal essay, "Malamud's Use of the Quest Romance" [*Genre* (1968)], which explores the "loathly lady" motif from *The Natural* through *The Fixer,* Edwin Eigner omits even the most perfunctory comment on Malamud's comically inventive handling of this romance motif in his story.

For nearly 30 years, then, Richman and Bluefarb's initial observations on **"The Girl of My Dreams,"** followed up only by the brief comments of Sandy Cohen [in *Bernard Malamud and the Trial by Love*] and Iska Alter [in *The Good Man's Dilemma: Social Criticism in the Fiction of Bernard Malamud*] in the 1970s and 1980s, respectively, comprise the baseline criticism on this story, thus inadvertently consigning it to a premature literary burial. When measured against **"The Magic Barrel"** (1954), a text recently prized by Lawrence J. Dessner [in "The Playfulness of Bernard Malamud's 'The Magic Barrel,'" *Essays in*

Literature (1988)] for its engaging ironic play with language and genres, **"The Girl of My Dreams"** must appear both rhetorically and verbally thin, or too farcical in relation to the later, and in no small measure, revisionary text. Is this story no more than an apprentice piece appropriately interred in a Malamudian fictional mausoleum, along with other of his unread fictional artifacts, or has the comic art of this fiction suffered from benign neglect? I submit that to read Mrs. Lutz's harassing courtship of the resisting Mitka merely at the level of domestic farce, resolved affirmatively in an epithalamial fantasy, is to miss the richness of Malamud's parodic play with his own life, with literary and painterly conventions, and with his own humanist vision.

Pirjo Ahokas in *Forging a New Self* has perceptively noted that parody was not merely a fashionable postmodern digression for Malamud resulting in such experimental works as **Pictures of Fidelman** (1969) and *The Tenants* (1971), but rather a literary tendency reflected in his very first novel, *The Natural* (1952). Her recent reexamination of Malamud's novels has relevance not only to one of Malamud's earliest stories but also to a consideration of the biographical context of a writer whose life was occasionally a resource for self-parody. In his autobiographical memoir, *Long Work, Short Life,* Malamud reveals that he was employed as a clerk in the Census Bureau in Washington, DC, and wrote short stories surreptitiously on the job and obsessively at night in his rooming house: "Although my writing seemed less than inspiring to me," Malamud reflects, "I stayed with it and tried to breathe into it fresh life and beauty, hoping that the gift was still in my possession, if by some magic act I could see life whole. And though I was often lonely, I stayed in the rooming house night after night trying to invent stories I needn't be ashamed of." Malamud follows these remarks with this self-reflection: "I was spending too much time being in love, as an uneasy way of feeling good when I wasn't writing." These self-perceptions were to become the germs for Malamud's Mitka, as well as an evolving conception for writers and artists who fail at both art and life.

As an aspiring Jewish writer starting out in the eve of the second world war, Malamud was to enact his own version of the quest romance, undergoing trials that tested his ability to achieve literary authority. In retrospect, his aspirations to become a writer must have appeared to him, at times, as bordering on perversity. In his memoir, Malamud recalls the loneliness and frustration of those apprenticeship years and describes finding comfort in the sardonic voice of his literary double, Franz Kafka: "I'm reminded of Kafka's remark in his mid-twenties: 'God doesn't want me to write, but I must write.'" This compulsion was to occupy Malamud as a theme in his fiction from the very beginning to the very end of his career and was inseparable from his own self-consciousness as author. In **"The Girl of My Dreams,"** three decades before these autobiographical reminiscences, Malamud playfully embroidered the established conventions of the medieval quest romance and Chagall's tableau of marital unions with his own earlier quests for success in art and love.

As Linda Hutcheon points out [in *A Theory of Parody: The*

Teaching of Twentieth-Century Art Forms, 1991], the motives for parody may be various, but Malamud's practice reflects the two common denominators fundamental to the mode: filial respect and filial rejection, both of which govern his treatment of these romantic conventions. Thus both in its emulation and deflation of respected literary and painterly works, **"The Girl of My Dreams"** served those psychological and literary ends by which Malamud, as an apprentice writer, might authorize himself into existence. In this connection, Gerald Kennedy has demonstrated in his intertextual study of Poe's "The Raven" and Malamud's **"The Jewbird"** ["Parody as Exorcism," *Genre* (1980)] that such parody became for Malamud a literary ritual—indeed, the equivalent of an invocation to the Muse.

In "Malamud's Use of the Quest Romance," Eigner, although he does not address Malamud's irreverent treatment, identifies a significant paradigm informing the author's early fiction. The paradigm typically involves a quest hero who becomes the object of the amorous attentions of a beautiful temptress possessed of supernatural powers and unlimited resources. According to Lucy Allen Paton, one of Eigner's sources, "In the fairy mythology of romance the law is invariable, that for the mortal who once has experienced the fairy control there is no true release, and the fay is never to be thwarted in her plans to win the hero whose love she seeks" [*Studies in the Fairy Mythology of Arthurian Romance,* 1960]. One variant of the beautiful fairy mistress is the "loathly lady," who may appear as a woman of unsurpassed beauty or alternately as a hag, as in the case of Malamud's treatment of the more-than-homely Mrs. Lutz. No fetching Lady of the Lake, the landlady, with her Yiddish-inflected voice, is the very antidote to romance. Gray-haired, overweight, draped in a flannel bathrobe, and scorned by Mitka, Malamud's "loathly landlady," like her literary ancestors in Arthurian romance, must come to be loved, despite her grotesqueness, before the hero can experience his own redemption. To that end, moreover, the depth of Mitka's emotional need and the prompting of his mythopoeic imagination conspire to make him vulnerable to the loving harassment of the devious Mrs. Lutz.

If sorcery, shapeshifting, and temptation are attributes of the "loathly lady" in Arthurian convention, the first two of these powers are playfully insinuated into Malamud's "loathly landlady," while the third is unambiguously ascribed to her. Indeed, in Malamud's stark and unaccommodating world, Mrs. Lutz's human ingenuity is a virtual necessity, and her eventual success is as transformative as a supernatural spell in a fairy tale. Mrs. Lutz, as the narrator observes, "tried all sorts of baits and schemes to lure him [Mitka] forth"; and, portentously, as if to signal a conspiratorial hand abetting the destruction of "the proud ideas he had given his book," it is the landlady's dusty trash can in which "Mitka had burned the manuscript of his heart-broken novel." [In a footnote, Salzberg adds: "The autobiographical germ for both Mitka's artistic self-contempt and the burning of his manuscript is, in all likelihood, anchored in Malamud's account of a similar occurrence in his own life before he wrote **"The Girl of My Dreams,"** which he recalls in *Long Work, Short Life:* 'A novel I had started while I was teaching in Erasmus Hall Evening High School, in Brooklyn, was called *The Light Sleeper.* It was completed but not sold. I burned it one night in Oregon because I felt I could do better. My son, who was about four at the time, watched me burning the book. As we looked at the sparks fly upward I was telling him about death; but he denied the concept.' With slight variation, the destruction of a manuscript is a recurring Malamudian motif that appears in *Pictures of Fidelman* and *The Tenants.*"] This seemingly innocuous vehicle of the ordinary—a kind of inanimate sorceress's apprentice—is to appear once more in a dream of literary self-immolation sponsored by the dissembling Madeline/Olga, Mitka's unseen but as yet seductive literary double. Through his own initial experience of literary self-immolation, which he imaginatively merges with Madeline's, Mitka eventually undergoes a series of other purgatorial trials orchestrated by a plot circuitously coaxing him to an inspired vision of marital union.

As in the Arthurian stories involving a supernatural Lady of the Lake or a loathly lady, temptations and lures are tests that the quester must overcome before he can achieve his elevated vision of love and his vocation as lover. In Mitka's world, these temptations reside in food, as well as transient images of female beauty, and are closely observed by an author-narrator who alternates between innocently neutral description and ethnically tinged sarcasm. Empowered in the arts of home and hearth, Mrs. Lutz offers a variety of enticements to Mitka, the last of which becomes the catalyst for his quest beyond the rooming house for the girl of his dreams: "She left a tray in the hall—a bowl of hot soup whose odor nearly drove him mad, two folded sheets, pillow case, fresh towels, and a copy of that morning's *Globe.*" The "loathly landlady," like other residents in a Malamudian world, must somehow be Houdini-like in order to transcend her own human limitations. When Mitka proves impervious to the lures of Mrs. Lutz's creature comforts, the lovelorn landlady next becomes the agent of coincidence, initiating Mitka's romantic quest and her own transformation into a bride. In finding a copy of the *Globe* left at his door by Mrs. Lutz, Mitka is narcissistically drawn to a feminine image inscribed in the literary section of the paper and idealized by his own imagination.

A more detailed elaboration of the plot illustrates the scope of Malamud's parodic play with Mitka's romantic destiny. In Mitka's reading of the column called the "Open Globe," the writer is awakened to feelings of love and pity by the Madeline Thorne's autobiographical narrative. Although her story falls within the boundaries of what passes for Malamudian realism, the account, as it relates to Mitka's own story, is dreamlike in its displacement of the scene describing Mitka's own literary apocalypse with Madeline Thorne's. In her fictitious story, the hand of another well-meaning landlady is now a direct cause for the destruction of a manuscript. To Madeline's question as to the fate of her typewritten pages, the "other" landlady innocently replies: "I burned them in the barrel this morning." For Mitka the imagined literary destruction of this manuscript, in his tormenting dream of the burning

barrel, centers the story once again in sinister images redolent of sorcery:

> So he lay on the bed and whether awake or asleep dreamed the recurrent dream of the burning barrel (in it their books commingled), suffering her agony as well as her own. The barrel, a symbol he had not conceived before, belched flame, shot wordsparks, poured smoke as thick as oil. It turned red hot, a sickly yellow, black—loaded high with the ashes of human bones—guess whose.

Mitka's dream of literary extinction, replete with charnel house imagery, both repeats and intensifies his earlier purgatorial experience: "The sparks, as he stirred, flew to the apples, the withered fruit representing not only creation gone for nothing (three long years), but all his hopes, and the proud ideas he had given his book." As the failed writer/lover is conned into transitory moments of hope, he becomes increasingly apocalyptic and funereal as hope turns into disappointment. Inevitably, he is made vulnerable to the earthly delights of Olga's food preparatory to receiving the earthly Mrs. Lutz arrayed—in his imagination—for a bridal.

Malamud establishes "the loathly landlady" as an overpowering maternal figure whose resources seem limitless—indeed a Jewish mother surrogate—to whom Mitka relinquishes his life. If, as Lucy Allen Paton observes, the fay of Arthurian romance "has complete foreknowledge, and . . . has guarded from infancy the mortal whom she finally takes to the other world as her beloved," then Mrs. Lutz, in her ascension to Mitka's imaginary bride, serves as a parodic counterpoint to her literary ancestor. As a prelude to the fateful coincidences or strategies embedded in the plot, Mrs. Lutz "masterfully sniffed [the fact]" that Mitka is a writer, and later spies on him, prostrate in bed, through the keyhole of a closed door, just as Salzman [in **"The Magic Barrel"**] surreptitiously studies the face of Leo Finkle. And like Salzman, who annoyingly persists in addressing Leo Finkle by the titles of "Rabbi" or "Doctor Finkle," Mrs. Lutz irritates Mitka by her proud and possessive reference to him among her roomers as "My writer upstairs." After Mitka resists the temptations of food, she tries to lure him from behind his locked door by conjuring up, as it were, a new guest in her establishment, a character existing in the story only through the odor of her perfume and Mrs. Lutz's impromptu and resourceful passing reference: "Beatrice—a real beauty . . . and a writer too." But before the still invisible Beatrice can guide Mitka to heaven, Mrs. Lutz informs him that Beatrice's writing is in advertising, not literature; his idealized vision transformed into the mundane, he returns to his despondency and Beatrice to the proverbial hat. The following morning he awakens to find a copy of the *Globe* at his door deposited by Mrs. Lutz, and his quest for the girl of his dreams is revived by the yet unseen Madeline Thorne, whom Mitka imagines as "maybe twenty-three, slim yet soft bodied, the face whiplashed with understanding." If Mitka's spirits are at first buoyed by the discovery of and identification with a female version of himself who has suffered for art, he is once again deflated when Madeline Thorne informs him that the story of her incinerated manuscript was merely an invention.

While Mrs. Lutz does not, in the older tradition of the supernatural, visibly transform herself into another identity, her felt presence offstage, as she is gradually insinuated into Mitka's imagination within the plot, has the force of authorial premeditation. The artful landlady, as both a visible and invisible character, is the writer's faithful familiar in the first half of the story, and is always available in the rooming house to perform a service, if it will bring Mitka into her company: "The old tease coyly knocked . . . Gurgling, 'For you, Mitka darling,' [as] she at last slipped it [the letter from Madeline Thorne] under the door—her favorite pastime." Hoping that the imagined Madeline Thorne will at least provide him with romantic solace as compensation for his failure as a writer, Mitka persuades the now reticent voice on the phone to a rendezvous. In having Madeline identify herself as a woman who will "be wearing a sort of reddish babushka," Malamud evokes Hawthorne's *The Scarlet Letter* (as he does when Leo Finkle meets the fallen Stella, wearing red shoes, at the conclusion of **"The Magic Barrel"**), and thus expands his range of parodic literary play. Predictably, Madeline's "sort of reddish babushka" is transformed into a most unscarlet "sickly running orange," as the ideally imagined Madeline materializes into Olga, "hefty . . . eyeglassed, and marvelously plain." Again, Mitka's expectations are plunged into the depths, shortly before he meditates on Mrs. Lutz as his bride, when Olga reveals that her beautiful daughter "died at twenty—at the fount of life." If narrative insinuation operates as a mysteriously teasing hieroglyph in Malamud's plot, Mitka's lamentation virtually decodes authorial intent, suggesting that more is going on behind the scenes than actually meets the reader's eye:' "Ah, colossal trickery—was ever a man so cruelly defrauded?"

No sooner do Mitka and Olga face each other across a table at a bar than Madeline/Olga tries to alter her all too depressing image through more verbal allusions that turn out to be essentially illusions: "You'd have liked me when I was young, Mitka. I had a sylphlike figure and glorious hair. I was much sought after by men. I was not what you would call sexy but they knew I had it." The palpable woman cannot deflect Mitka's restlessness, and she produces yet another potentially distracting shape for Mitka's imagination, that of her daughter, who "had flowing hair and a sweet hourglass figure. Her nature was beyond compare." But whatever shards of Mitka's romantic aspirations still remain, they vanish when Madeline/Olga reveals: "She died at twenty—at the fount of life." Suggesting to Mitka that what he sees is not an altogether accurate reading of the text, Madeline/Olga deconstructs herself, as it were, into variations of a young fairy mistress as a way of romantically and erotically adorning the trap to which the conspiratorial elements of the plot inevitably lead. When Mitka discovers that he is on a fool's errand, that there is no end to the shapeshifting of Madeline/Olga as womanly text, he eventually submits to powers beyond his control, the unavoidable fate of the quest hero under the spell of the fairy mistress.

Whether Mrs. Lutz, who remains absent from the plot in the second half of the story, indeed serves as the inscrutable power behind Mitka's romantic misadventures is a teasing mystery that both beckons to and distances readers, flirtatiously mocking their desire to know. Mrs. Lutz, however, continually hovers within Mitka's consciousness, as much as in the reader's. "Another Landlady," he exclaims, finally succumbing to the temptation of food—"He ate, grateful she had provided an occupation." Thus Mitka's encounter with Olga, in its repetition of his earlier encounters with Mrs. Lutz, superimposes on the naturalism of the plot a sense of the surreal, if not the supernatural: both women reminisce over their lost youth, complain of sad lives with missing husbands, and are unpublished writers who freely give writerly advice to another failed writer, adding (premeditated?) insult to injury. Finally, the narrator's reference in the library to Madeline/Olga as "the old girl" is, a few pages later, used once again in Mitka's reflection on Mrs. Lutz: "He thought of the old girl." Within the formulation of a plot that, with a sly knowingness, mocks the very design of its own coincidences, Mrs. Lutz and Olga suggest something more than the same generic landlady.

Like Alfred Hitchcock, Malamud, on occasion, seems to have enjoyed catching glimpses of his own image in the text, but for Malamud such exhibitionism is clearly in keeping with the author's irrepressible urge to self-parody. In **"The Girl of My Dreams"** the preoccupations of Malamud's own life and art are projected through the mask of Madeline/Olga, who paraphrases the author's more sober thoughts on the art of fiction, subsequently recorded in an interview with Daniel Stern ["The Art of Fiction: Bernard Malamud," in *Conversations with Bernard Malamud,* 1991] and restated in other interviews. Madeline/Olga instructs Mitka on how to survive as a writer: "After you've been writing so long as I you'll learn a system to keep yourself going. It depends on your view of life. If you're mature you'll find out how to work." And to Mitka's self-deprecating comment on his writer's block, Olga replies: "You'll invent your way out . . . if you only keep trying." In the Stern interview, question and answer touch on the same issue of artistic self-discipline that governed Malamud's own writing habits, which he mocks under the cover of fiction:

> **Interviewer:** What about work habits? Some writers, especially at the beginning, have problems settling how to do it.
>
> **Malamud:** There's no particular time or place—you suit yourself, your nature. . . . How one works, assuming he's disciplined, doesn't matter. The real mystery to crack is you.

Malamud's own theories on writing become self-parody in the voice of Madeline/Olga and serve a fictional design, the intent of which is to play off the ideal against the real, deflation against elevation. Early in the story, for example, Mitka recalls, both with mixed pride and self-mockery, a more creative moment in his life, when he was "Mitka the Magician," but, at the conclusion, after he has assuaged his pangs of physical hunger, Mitka's sense of the ludicrous calls forth a new self-definition, "Mitka, the

Camel." Now deprived of both artistic success and romantic solace by Mrs. Lutz's surrogate, Mitka is now ready to resign himself to the "loathly landlady" because, through his own despair, he has ostensibly acquired the necessary Malamudian sympathy for those who suffer. In a tone of classic Yiddish resignation: "He pitied [Olga], her daughter, the world. Who not?" Malamud, however, was capable of kidding his own lines in **"The Girl of My Dreams"** and the Fidelman stories, even when they are imbued with the kind of humanistic generosity for which he has been identified in such works as *The Assistant* (1957), **"Take Pity"** (1956), or **"Idiots First"** (1961).

While the endings of both **"The Girl of My Dreams"** and **"The Magic Barrel"** are tangibly influenced by the levitating brides and bridegrooms illustrated in such paintings as Chagall's *The Three Candles* (1938-40), *The Tree of Life* (1948), and, possibly, *Night* (1953), it is important to distinguish the tonal and thematic differences between the two stories. Unlike the primarily romantic and lyrical Chagallian unions that bring **"The Magic Barrel"** to its conclusion, the abrasive language and tone of **"The Girl of My Dreams"** collide with its Chagallian subject matter: "He thought of the old girl. He'd go home now and drape her from head to foot in flowing white. They would jounce together up the stairs, then (strictly a one-marriage man) he would swing her across the threshold where the fat overflowed her corset as they waltzed around his writing chamber." These double-edged lines carry an undercurrent of black humor just beneath the surface of wedded joy, and through them Malamud seems to deflate the Chagallian vision of marital union through his own brand of fantasy, which is more sour than sweet.

Making the following grudging confession to Leslie and Joyce Field [in "An Interview with Bernard Malamud," in *Conversations with Bernard Malamud,* 1991], Malamud observed: "It's true that I did make use of what might be called Chagallian imagery in **'The Magic Barrel.'** I did so intentionally in that story, but I've not done it again in any other piece of fiction, and I feel that some critics make too much of Chagall as an image maker in my work." Malamud's pronouncements on what he did, and did not borrow, from Chagall should be taken with caution, for the author was apparently self-conscious about acknowledging his indebtedness to what he considered to be Chagall's sentimental vision. Through his parodic response, Malamud tried to overcome the anxiety of the Chagallian influence. Indeed, Malamud pointedly observed to Daniel Stern that Chagall "rides his nostalgic nag to death." It should be recalled that two of the Chagall paintings I have referred to, *The Three Candles* and *The Tree of Life,* were completed several years before Malamud published **"The Girl of My Dreams"** in *American Mercury* (76 [1953]: 62-71). *Night* was finished in 1953, the year Malamud's story first appeared. In the note to *The Tree of Life* in *Chagall,* Susan Compton's comments suggest specific points of contact between **"The Girl of My Dreams"** and *The Tree of Life:*

> The picture is no doubt a reference to his [Chagall's] own wedding with Bella and it includes a reminder of the same story from her memoirs quoted in the catalogue entry for *The Wedding.*

Earlier in the account, Bella had described the bride: "What did she look like? / A bride was first and foremost a long white dress that trailed along the ground like something living, the whole covered by an airy veil."

In his essay, "Chagall 'over the Roofs of the World,' " Norbert Lynton observes, moreover, that "in Russian 'Chagall' suggests striding along, taking great steps." Intentionally punning on Chagall's name or invoking it by coincidence, Malamud represents the "jouncing" couple as the visual expression of what Chagall's name means in Russian.

In his comically grotesque rendering of the "jouncing" bride and bridegroom, Malamud seems to convert what Iska Alter perceives as a traditional "hymeneal dance" into a ritual of despair. The more optimistic reading of the story may force one to confuse Mitka's repressed anger for the emotion, as well as the physical motion, of Hasidic joy. As we have seen a bit earlier in the text, it is with the grimmest funereal tone that Mitka is forced to return to Mrs. Lutz and her boarding house, now inclusively referred to as "home." The juxtaposed visual perspectives that begin and end the last page carry, in their sense of contradiction, the tension and impact of an oxymoron. On this last page, just after Olga has revealed that her daughter Madeline is dead, Mitka is described as "a man in mourning." And in the concluding passage of the story, Mitka reemerges in an image of celebration, as he "jounces" with Mrs. Lutz as his bride over the threshold of his room.

In summary, Malamud's various levels of parodic play may well be taken as the overlooked purloined letter of the story, especially when that story is embedded within a collection, *The Magic Barrel* (1958), whose humanistic themes have preempted the attention of his readers for over 30 years. Reread in the light of such play, **"The Girl of My Dreams"** becomes charged with a new literary authority.

> *Joel Salzberg, "The 'Loathly Landlady', Chagallian Unions, and Malamudian Parody: 'The Girl of My Dreams' Revisited," in* Studies in Short Fiction, *Vol. 30, No. 4, Fall, 1993, pp. 543-54.*

FURTHER READING

Bibliography

Salzberg, Joel. *Bernard Malamud: A Reference Guide.* Boston: G. K. Hall & Co., 1985, 211 p.
    Annotated and chronological list of writings about Malamud from 1952 to 1983.

Criticism

Adler, Brian. "*Akedah* and Community in 'The Magic Barrel'." *Studies in American Jewish Literature* 10, No. 2 (Fall 1991): 188-96.

Contends that the relationship between Salzman and Finkle in "The Magic Barrel" is one of symbolic father to symbolic son in which Salzman assists Finkle's reintegration "into the emotional and spiritual wellsprings of his community."

Ashmead, John. "Bernard Malamud." In *American Writing Today,* edited by Richard Kostelanetz, pp. 155-65. Troy, N.Y.: The Whitston Publishing Co., 1991.

Overview of Malamud's works which Ashmead interprets in relation to Western humanism and mythology, Jewish-American and Yiddish culture, and nineteenth-century American Romanticism.

Astro, Richard, and Benson, Jackson J., eds. *The Fiction of Bernard Malamud.* Corvallis: Oregon State University Press, 1977, 190 p.

Collection of essays covering various aspects of Malamud's career and works.

Bryant, Earle V. "The Tree-Clock in Bernard Malamud's 'Idiots First'." *Studies in Short Fiction* 20, No. 1 (Winter 1983): 52-4.

Comments on the scene in which the branches of a tree reverse position in "Idiots First."

Ducharme, Robert. "Structure and Content in Malamud's *Pictures of Fidelman.*" *Connecticut Review* 5, No. 1 (October 1971): 26-36.

Contends that *Pictures of Fidelman* "marks a structural departure for Malamud," although the character-type of the protagonist and the themes of the six stories are consistent with his previous work.

Field, Leslie A., and Field, Joyce W. *Bernard Malamud and the Critics.* New York: New York University Press, 1970, 353 p.

Collection of essays covering various aspects of Malamud's career, including his short fiction.

——. *Bernard Malamud: A Collection of Critical Essays.* Englewood Cliffs, N.J.: Prentice-Hall, 1975, 179 p.

Contains several essays that focus on Malamud's short fiction.

Lefcowitz, Barbara F. "The *Hybris* of Neurosis: Malamud's *Pictures of Fidelman.*" *Literature and Psychology* XX, No. 3 (1970): 115-20.

Describes Fidelman as a neurotic character through whom Malamud "depicts and parodies neurosis by juxtaposing two sets of values, . . . the private world of Fidelman as victim and obsessional neurotic, and the second of the socio-historical world of Fidelman as victimizer."

Malin, Irving. "Portrait of the Artist in Slapstick: Malamud's *Pictures of Fidelman.*" *The Literary Review* 24, No. 1 (Fall 1980): 121-38.

Argues that Malamud confronts the problems of the artist in *Pictures of Fidelman* and "asserts, through slapstick, bedroom farce, and fantastic adventures, the seriousness of art and life."

May, Charles E. "Something Fishy in 'The Magic Barrel'." *Studies in American Fiction* 14, No. 1 (Spring 1986): 93-8.

Identifies the marriage broker and his daughter Stella as archetypes of sexual desire and argues that the focus of "The Magic Barrel" is on the rabbinical student's developing awareness of his sexuality.

Mesher, David R. "The Remembrance of Things Unknown: Malamud's 'The Last Mohican'." *Studies in Short Fiction* XII, No. 4 (Fall 1975): 397-404.

Analyzes "The Last Mohican" which, Mesher contends, occupies a central place in Malamud's fiction because the technique of the double and the motif of a stolen manuscript appear in many of his novels and short stories.

O'Keefe, Richard R. "Coitus as Crucifixion: An Intertextual Note on Bernard Malamud and John Malcolm Brinnin." *Studies in Short Fiction* 27, No. 3 (Summer 1990): 405-08.

Compares the metaphor depicted in the concluding lines of Malamud's "Still Life" with the last stanza of Brinnin's 1951 poem "The Double Crucifixion."

Richman, Sidney. "The Stories," in his *Bernard Malamud,* pp. 98-139. New York: Twayne Publishers, 1966.

Examines the stories in *The Magic Barrel* and *Idiots First.*

Salzberg, Joel. *Critical Essays on Bernard Malamud.* Boston: G. K. Hall & Co., 1987, 229 p.

Contains reviews of Malamud's novels and short story collections as well as several essays addressing his short fiction.

——. "Of 'Autobiographical Essence' and Self-Parody: Malamud on 'Exhibition' in *Pictures of Fidelman.*" *Genre* XXIV, No. 3 (Fall 1991): 271-95.

Examines the autobiographical elements in *Pictures of Fidelman,* noting that Malamud used the stories "as a vehicle for narrative experiments and as a mask for self-contemplation."

Solotaroff, Robert. *Bernard Malamud: A Study of the Short Fiction.* Boston: Twayne Publishers, 1989, 200 p.

Covers Malamud's collected and uncollected short fiction, noting the thematic and technical continuities, variations, and experiments of his short works as well as the interconnections between Malamud's life and his fiction.

Storey, Michael L. "Pinye Salzman, Pan, and 'The Magic Barrel'." *Studies in Short Fiction* 18, No. 2 (Spring 1981): 180-83.

Notes parallels between the marriage broker from "The Magic Barrel" and Pan—a half-goat, half-human god from Greek mythology.

Studies in American Jewish Literature, Bernard Malamud: In Memoriam 7, No. 2 (Fall 1988): 134-250.

Contains essays addressing various aspects of Malamud's career as well as an interview and a bibliographical essay.

Interview

Lasher, Lawrence M., ed. *Conversations with Bernard Malamud.* Jackson, Miss.: University Press of Mississippi, 1991, 156 p.

Collects previously published interviews with Malamud that were conducted from 1958 through 1986.

Additional coverage of Malamud's life and career is contained in the following sources published by Gale Research: *Concise Dictionary of American Literary Biography 1941-1968; Contemporary Authors,* Vols. 5-8, rev. ed., 118 [obituary]; *Contemporary Authors Bibliographical Series,* Vol. 1; *Contemporary Authors New Revision Series,* Vol. 28; *Contemporary Literary Criticism,* Vols. 1, 2, 3, 5, 8, 9, 11, 18, 27, 44, 78; *Dictionary of Literary Biography,* Vols. 2, 28; *Dictionary of Literary Biography Yearbook: 1980* and *1986; DISCovering Authors; Major 20th-Century Writers;* and *World Literature Criticism.*

John O'Hara

1905-1970

(Full name John Henry O'Hara; also wrote under the pseudonym Franey Delaney) American short story writer, novelist, playwright, and essayist.

INTRODUCTION

O'Hara was a prolific and popular fiction writer whose works generally focus on upper middle-class social life in the United States during the first half of the twentieth century. In such novels as *Appointment in Samarra* and *Butterfield 8,* and in his numerous short story collections, O'Hara examined the status-conscious social order of affluent Easterners, the destructive power of lust in human relationships, and the often paradoxical disparity between the public and private behavior of individuals. O'Hara achieved an immense readership and financial success during his lifetime, yet critics were largely unsympathetic in their appraisals of his works, citing among his chief faults an overabundance of insignificant detail, a lack of coherent action, and a realistic style that had come to seem anachronistic after World War II.

Biographical Information

O'Hara was the eldest of eight children born to a prosperous, hard-working physician in Pottsville, a small town in the coal-mining region of eastern Pennsylvania. Although as Irish Catholics the O'Haras remained outside of Pottsville's most elite Protestant social circles, his father's wealth did afford O'Hara the opportunity to closely observe the status symbols and behavioral code that defined social class. O'Hara was an unsuccessful student who was dismissed from prep school due to a drunken spree; nevertheless, he hoped to enter Yale University in 1925. His plans changed when his father died suddenly, leaving the family without financial means. O'Hara embarked on a series of odd jobs and continued to drink heavily, but during this time he started to publish some of his short stories in the *New Yorker* magazine. Encouraged by this modest achievement, O'Hara completed in 1934 his first novel, *Appointment in Samarra,* which brought him immediate renown. With the publication the following year of his novel *Butterfield 8* and *The Doctor's Son, and Other Stories,* a compilation of his *New Yorker* stories, O'Hara's reputation as a writer was firmly established. He worked as a scriptwriter in Hollywood beginning in the mid-1930s, and his screenplay *Moontide* contributed to the success of that film, which was nominated for an Academy Award in 1942. While O'Hara continued to write prolifically—working most nights from midnight to dawn—he

discontinued writing short stories after a falling out with the *New Yorker* in the late 1940s. When he began writing short fiction again in the 1960s, O'Hara issued nearly a collection a year until his death in 1970.

Major Works

O'Hara's short fiction generally concerns social life in the three settings he knew best: Pottsville and the surrounding coal region, Hollywood film society, and the social milieu of wealthy New York City. While the settings varied, the subjects and themes of the stories remained relatively constant throughout O'Hara's more than 400 stories. He typically examined significant incidents in the lives of average individuals, focusing on the conflict between personal urges and social codes of conduct, the destructive potential of sexual promiscuity and infidelity, the ruthlessness of social snobbery, the cruel machinations of fate, and the struggle of individuals to overcome loneliness and find a place in society. Many stories reveal a pessimistic outlook, depicting wasted lives or resolving in violence. In other works protagonists achieve a measure of happiness but usually outside—or at least out of view—of the social milieu that gives rise to the conflict. Utilizing an objective viewpoint, accurate dialogue, and realistic depiction of scene, O'Hara's style has been termed journalistic and identified with the realist/naturalist tradition in modern literature. He stated that his foremost concern as a writer was "to get it all down on paper. . . . The United States in this century is what I know, and it is my business to write about it to the best of my ability, with the sometimes special knowledge that I have. The Twenties, the Thirties, and the Forties are already history, but I cannot be content to leave their story in the hands of the historians and the editors of picture books. I want to record the way people talked and thought and felt, and do it all with complete honesty and variety."

Critical Reception

While reviewers often praised such aspects of O'Hara's stories as narrative irony, colloquial dialogue, or insightful presentation of character, the critical consensus about O'Hara's prolific output was unfavorable. Critics principally fault O'Hara for lacking discipline in indiscriminately assembling detail upon detail and mixing the meaningful with the insignificant, thereby undermining relevance and coherence in his works. O'Hara and his supporters countered that reality itself displays little "discipline" or "coherence." However, even his detractors judged his short fiction superior to his monolithic novels. For all the negative criticism of O'Hara's writings he was among the most popular authors of his era, and biographer Matthew J. Bruccoli has expressed the opinion of many readers in his evaluation of O'Hara as "one of our best novelists, our best novella-ist, and our greatest writer of short stories."

PRINCIPAL WORKS

SHORT FICTION

The Doctor's Son, and Other Stories   1935
Files on Parade   1939
Pal Joey   1940
Pipe Night   1945
Hellbox   1947
A Family Party   1956
Sermons and Soda-Water   1960
Assembly   1961
The Cape Cod Lighter   1962
The Hat on the Bed   1963
The Horse Knows the Way   1964
Waiting for Winter   1966
And Other Stories   1968
The Time Element, and Other Stories   1972
Good Samaritan, and Other Stories   1974

OTHER MAJOR WORKS

Appointment in Samarra   (novel)   1934
Butterfield 8   (novel)   1935
Hope of Heaven   (novel)   1938
Moontide   (screenplay)   1942
A Rage to Live   (novel)   1949
The Farmers Hotel   (novel)   1951
Pal Joey   (libretto)   1952
Sweet and Sour   (essays)   1954
Ten North Frederick   (novel)   1955
From the Terrace   (novel)   1958
Ourselves to Know   (novel)   1960
Five Plays   (dramas)   1961
The Big Laugh   (novel)   1962
Elizabeth Appleton   (novel)   1963
The Lockwood Concern   (novel)   1965
My Turn   (essays)   1966
The Instrument   (novel)   1967
Lovey Childs: A Philadelphian's Story   (novel)   1969
The Ewings   (novel)   1972

*This work comprises an adaptation of the short story collection of the same name.

CRITICISM

William Rose Benét   (essay date 1935)

[*In the following review of* The Doctor's Son, and Other Stories, *Benét praises O'Hara's understanding of human nature.*]

Mr. O'Hara's novel, *Appointment in Samarra,* was one of the sensations of last season. Ernest Hemingway approved it, Dorothy Parker was enthusiastic about it. It bore the *imprimatur* and the *nihil obstat* of the smartest minds. It started the town talking.

To my mind he has written about more significant people in his present book of short stories, a good many of which have appeared in *The New Yorker.* The long title story ["**The Doctor's Son**"] is new and excellent. It is drawn from those youthful impressions that are the most indelible. The Pennsylvania Country Club people of *Appointment in Samarra,* many of them almost unbelievably cheap, were observed and depicted from impressions of a later date. In spite of Mrs. Parker's opinion, it seems to me that they were mercilessly depicted. Naturalism could go no further. No one can quarrel with that attitude on the part of the author; but one may wonder why so brilliant a talent was expended on this particular material. The material in the present book of short stories interests me more, though it may not be such a smack in the eye.

There have been many stories told from the viewpoint of shrewdly innocent and but half-developed youth. Ernest Hemingway has done some good ones. But Mr. O'Hara's story, **"The Doctor's Son,"** owes practically nothing to

Hemingway in manner, and the *milieu* is entirely the author's own. It is impressive.

I would criticize the other stories in general terms only on the basis that a few of them seem to me to fail in bringing out the significance Mr. O'Hara evidently feels to be latent in them. I've read **"New Day"** three times and I still can't see much reason for its being, except as the beginning of something. Just as you get interested in **"Mrs. Brown"** the story is over. **"Mort and Mary"** is a good picture of a certain kind of Catholic man, and so what? Mere portraits of futility do not seem to me interesting enough. On the other hand, take the exceedingly brief **"Early Afternoon."** It has the bite of acid. Its ending is perfect. Take the next story, **"Pleasure"**; Stephen Crane would have admired it. **"Alone"** impresses me. **"On His Hands"** is a good presentation of a young rotter. **"It Wouldn't Break Your Arm"** handles its situation well, and **"Mr. Cass and the Ten Thousand Dollars"** is a true tragedy of the trivial. I found **"Mrs. Galt and Edwin"** and **"Hotel Kid"** and **"In the Morning Sun"** examples of the considerable range of observation possessed by this writer. **"Back in New Haven"** impales adolescence with mimetic art, **"Straight Pool"** is finely sardonic and **"All the Girls He Wanted"** good irony. And then, for a tough story, there's the grimness of **"Sportsmanship"**; and, for ironic humor, there's **"The Public Career of Mr. Seymour Harrisburg."**

Yes, there's a lot in this book and *multum in parvo*. The *New Yorker* story is typically a vignette, so many of these are vignettes; but Mr. O'Hara understands how and why people tick, and is sensitively aware of what apparently trivial actions imply. This book is one of the best short-story collections of the year although the tales are not of the usual magazine length or general type; perhaps *because* of that fact. At all events, Mr. O'Hara has an independence that is admirable and knows human nature quite remarkably well. You feel that almost any manifestation of life is fascinating to him. That is why he is able to make it fascinating to the reader.

> *William Rose Benét, "O'Hara's Short Stories," in* The Saturday Review of Literature, *Vol. XI, No. 33, March 2, 1935, p. 517.*

Lionel Trilling   (essay date 1945)

[*Trilling was one of the twentieth century's most significant and influential American literary and social critics, and he is often called the single most important American critic to apply Freudian psychological theories to literature. In the following review, Trilling favorably appraises* Pipe Night.]

John O'Hara occupies a unique position in our contemporary literature. He stands alone not by reason of his literary skill, although that is considerable, but by reason of his subject—he is at present the only American writer to whom America presents itself as a social scene in the way it once presented itself to Howells or Edith Wharton, or in the way that England presented itself to Henry James, or France to Proust.

More than anyone now writing, O'Hara understands the complex, contradictory, asymmetrical society in which we live. He has the most precise knowledge of the content of our subtlest snobberies, of our points of social honor and idiosyncrasies of personal prestige. He knows, and persuades us to believe, that life's deepest intentions may be expressed by the angle at which a hat is worn, the pattern of a necktie, the size of a monogram, the pitch of a voice, the turn of a phrase of slang, a gesture of courtesy and the way it is received. "Cigarettes, there in the white pigskin box," says one of his cinema queens, and by that excess of specification we know the room and the mind and the culture in which the box has its existence.

Our Latin teachers used to take pleasure in explaining that the word *mores* meant not only morals but customs, and not only customs but manners. O'Hara works with the consciousness of this identity of meaning. For him customs and manners are morals.

In this he is of course no different in intention from the social novelists of twenty years ago. But writers like Dreiser or Sinclair Lewis, concerned as they were with Philistinism in the gross, were inclined to see society as a solid, undifferentiated front of respectability against which free spirits beat and bruised their wings. They did not permit themselves to see the details, the infinitely various ways in which the same thing is expressed, the tangle of antagonistic manners of which the social fact is composed; and they always assumed that poor people or really good people lived outside the world of social desires. Dreiser was notoriously unperceptive, even absurd, in his portrayal of manners. Even Sinclair Lewis, for all his great comic success with Babbitt in the bathroom and at the club, did not have an eye for the truths of the social shadings.

A few contemporary novelists have had some measure of O'Hara's gift of observation. Dos Passos, for example, has drawn on a kindred sensibility for some of his best effects. Edmund Wilson's interesting novel, *I Thought of Daisy,* is full of sharp social perception, and George Weller's two works of fiction were most promising in this respect. And of course there was Fitzgerald, who in many ways is O'Hara's master. But at the present time O'Hara stands pretty much alone in his devotion to the precise social fact, and at his best he has a great deal to tell us.

He is not always at his best. Of the thirty-one stories of *Pipe Night,* the new collection, a few—such as **"Now We Know," "Free," "Nothing Missing," "Too Young"**—fall into the pit of easy and all too well known sentiment. A larger group takes what value it has—considerable but not finally impressive—from its anthropological accuracy and from a quality of grim, humorous social notation in the good tradition of Petronius. But no less than seven of the new stories, and that makes a fair proportion, are first-rate.

These seven stories—**"Summer's Day," "The King of the Desert," "Bread Alone," "A Respectable Place," "Graven Image," "Revenge"** and **"Lieutenant"**—are remarkable if only because they so brilliantly transcend their form. For the very short story, with its well-taken bitter or pathetic point, is getting more and more tiresome, what with its situation so briskly set up and its insight so neatly given and the author skipping so nimbly out of the way, leaving the reader with the emotion on his hands to do with it what he can. Katherine Mansfield bastardized the great Chekhov to create this genre and we have all admired it for two decades while secretly we have been bored with it. O'Hara works more and more in this form, but he does not get easily trapped by the clichés it is likely to generate; he is saved by his passionate social curiosity and his remarkable social intelligence.

O'Hara's insatiable curiosity provides him with the actuality that fleshes his stories and keeps them from being what examples of this genre too often are, stories of pathetic sensibility. His intelligence has taught him how intense and how deep are the emotions which social considerations call forth. He has always been aware, to take but a single and obvious example of his perception, of how secretly profound is the feeling which many modern Americans have about their college lives; it seems to me that no other writer could have projected the story **"Graven Image"** in which the New Deal bigwig, even at the moment of his greatest power, cannot forget or forgive his exclusion from the Harvard Club he had wanted to make. (It is worth noting, by the way, that O'Hara is the first writer—and even he is a little late—to deal fictionally with the social and emotional possibilities of the New Deal dignitaries.)

Edmund Wilson has referred to O'Hara's sensitivity to social differences as "half-snobbish," and perhaps any close observer of social values must in this sense be a little ambiguous. But O'Hara knows that social judgments of a strict kind are not confined to the upper classes. They are as frequent in the poolroom as in the club lounge. And he knows that in the poolroom as elsewhere they are deeply involved with other vital considerations; in **"Lieutenant"** dim class loyalties are mixed up with intense feelings about age and virility to make one of the best comments we have yet had on the social changes the war is bringing.

An emphasis on the accuracy of O'Hara's social sense may seem to imply that a very subtle reporting is the best it can give us. But the accuracy of O'Hara's observation exists for more than its own sake. It allows him to deal with emotion in a specially effective way. Thus the grief of T. K. Attrell in **"Summer's Day"** is conveyed by a variety of literary devices, but its special poignancy appears through the particular quality of the social intercourse at the fashionable beach, and its hopeless isolation is made manifest by Attrell overhearing a group of half-grown boys speaking with vulgar contempt of his age and of his suicide daughter. That boys might indeed happen to talk with such spiteful cruelty is the kind of thing O'Hara would know.

Again, **"Bread Alone"** is—after Gertrude Stein's "Melanchta"—the best story that I know about a Negro because the Negro is so precisely seen in all his particularity as a Negro that he wonderfully emerges, by one of the paradoxes of art, as a man and a father.

Yet again, in a writer of the liberal persuasion it required not only a clean conscience on anti-Semitism but also the perfect innocence which knowledge can give, to draw the issue, in **"King of the Desert,"** between two clever Jewish writers from Hollywood and a simple rancher, to show the writers' expert kidding to be ambivalent between affection and malice, to show the rancher's pride in his New England ancestry as a rather nice thing in him, and at last to disclose fully and disagreeably the writers' unpleasant impulse; literature has of late grown very pious and it is a relief to see O'Hara's intelligence being perfectly clear that the particular relates to the general but is not to be confused with it.

O'Hara's stories are getting neater, tighter and more economical in their form, and this, I suppose, constitutes an increase in expertness. But I cannot observe the development with pleasure, not merely because the span, tempo and rhythm of the stories in **Pipe Night** need to be varied to avoid monotony, nor because I have a taste for a more relaxed kind of writer such as O'Hara himself gave us in **The Doctor's Son,** but because this increasing virtuosity of brevity seems to tend away from the novel and it seems to me that for O'Hara's talents the novel is the proper form. There is perhaps a specific short story talent which, for those who have it, makes the novel an impossible form. O'Hara may be a writer of such a talent; if he is, then what he can accomplish in the short story is a sufficient justification of his gifts. Still, no one who has recently reread *Appointment in Samarra* can help thinking of O'Hara as a novelist.

Even the incoherence of *Butterfield 8* and the flippant treatment of the almost interesting idea of *Hope of Heaven* do not discourage the promise of *Appointment in Samarra.* That first novel was not a great book, nor even a perfect book, but it was an organized book—it organized not only its material but also its author's talents. The quality of the two later novels seemed almost to suggest that the intensity of the vision of explosive doom of *Appointment in Samarra* had damaged O'Hara's ability to think in terms of coherence—that he could handle only the quick, isolated, discontinuous insights of the short stories.

To be sure, the stories taken together are not without their coherence; they relate to each other and add to each other's meaning. But the novel was invented, one might say, to deal with just the matter that O'Hara loves. Snobbery, vulgarity, the shades of social status and pretension, the addiction to objects of luxury, the innumerable social uncertainties, the comic juxtaposition of social assumptions—the novel thrives on them, and best knows how to deal with them.

But it is one of criticism's unpleasant traits to ask for what it thinks we should have instead of finding pleasure in what we do have. And what we have from O'Hara when he is at his best is very good indeed.

> *Lionel Trilling, "John O'Hara Observes Our Mores," in* The New York Times Book Review, *March 18, 1945, pp. 1, 29.*

John Woodburn   (essay date 1947)

[*In the following review, Woodburn discusses O'Hara's strengths and weaknesses in* Hellbox.]

Most of the twenty-six stories which comprise *Hellbox* have appeared in *The New Yorker.* Written in the abrupt, bony, close-mouthed prose with which O'Hara muffles his social comment, they foregather a little uncomfortably in book form. An O'Hara story has a way of standing out like tattooing in Harold Ross's magazine, and a quick glance at a swatch of dialogue any place on the page is usually enough to identify one of his stories, without looking at the end for his name. Taken one by one, with a week or two in between, they seem to me to be at their best, but I have had, and still have, the feeling that O'Hara's stories don't bind well. When they are lined up, as they are here, the pattern begins to show a little, the diameter appears not so great as you thought you remembered, and the impact of the stories, almost always at the end, sets up a bumpy rhythm.

I don't think *Hellbox* stands up well beside *Pipe Night,* and there are stories in both books which I like very much, and some which I don't like at all. Anyway, whatever I say, he is a damned interesting writer, and more. As Lionel Trilling has said:

> He knows, and persuades us to believe, that life's deepest intentions may be expressed by the angle at which a hat is worn, the pattern of a necktie, the size of a monogram, the pitch of a voice, the turn of a phrase of slang, a gesture of courtesy and the way it is received.

I copied that from the jacket of *Hellbox* and it is true of O'Hara's writing and he owes a great deal, almost all that is good in his writing, to that especial ability. But sometimes he gives you that especial ability and not a hell of a lot else. His ear is matchless; I don't know of a better, he has a merciless, absolutely thorough eye, and a way of making you feel you know him through his stories, without ever barging in on them. When he is good, which he is very often, he is superb; he hits you where you live, and makes the story stay with you. But when he is not, when most of the work is left up to his eye and ear, and he tries to parlay them into a story, he can be as bad as he can be good. Sometimes he overestimates the ductile strength of a situation and it breaks before it threads, and then you have all that wonderful fidelity of dialogue and highly selective, evocative detail piled on something which buckles beneath it. At least that's the way I felt about **"Like Old Times,"** in which two people sit in a night-club and speculate about five other people at another table in the same club, and **"Conversation in the Atomic Age,"** in which a Los Angeles society woman chatters vicious gossip to a bored man, other than the reader. I don't know what would have happened to that story if the title hadn't stuck by it through thin and thin.

O'Hara can do stories which are essentially portraits and do them beautifully—and I am thinking of some right now, in *Hellbox:* **"Common Sense Should Tell You,"** of a Hollywood Big Shot whose compulsive hedonism is destroying him and he knows it; and **"Pardner"**—a marvelous picture of a cynical adolescent who wants to be a cowboy (I am asking Santa Claus for **"Pardner"** for Christmas); and **"The Decision,"** about an immobilized doctor, and **"Drawing Room B,"** a non-publicity picture of a fall-

ing movie star. These, and a few others, I like a great deal. To show you, for instance, how O'Hara can light up a scene with a single, simple word, read this: "The radio was tuned in to an all-night recorded program, and the man at the good upright piano was playing the tunes that were being broadcast." Now read that again and leave "good" out. All through his writing O'Hara does things like this—a word or a phrase will turn the light on, so that you know almost immediately what is going on, because you have been given the precise, economical information. This is what he can do better than anyone else around now, and when the material lives up to it, as it does in the best of his stories, and there are some in *Hellbox,* his importance becomes so clear, his comment so admirable and unanswerable, that you find yourself arrogantly asking, insisting, that he never do less than his best.

> *John Woodburn, "Tattooed Portraits," in* The Saturday Review, *New York, Vol. XXX, No. 32, August 9, 1947, p. 10.*

Harry T. Moore (essay date 1960)

[In the following review, Moore praises characterization in Sermons and Soda-Water.*]*

In the preface to this collection of three short novels John O'Hara says that "the Twenties, the Thirties and the Forties are already history, but I cannot be content to leave their story in the hands of the historians or the editors of picture books." In this statement, besides admitting that he is deliberately writing the social-history type of fiction, he shows that he is aware how effectively this kind of literature can get under the skin of every-day reality. And doesn't a tipsy O'Hara debutante in an eastern Pennsylvania country club usually reveal more about certain phases of American life of thirty years ago than a stack of reports and statistics?

Old O'Hara hands will welcome his rather emphatic but, as he says, temporary return to shorter fiction after his decade of turning out lengthy best sellers such as *Ten North Frederick* and *From the Terrace.* Those volumes appealed mostly to the reading group he now speaks of as "the non-professional public . . . whose first test of a book is its avoirdupois." Even if O'Hara hasn't quite mastered the technique of the middle-size story, his characterizations in this new trio are more sharply defined than in his stretched-out novels. They offer some of his choicest portraits of inhabitants of the Volstead and New Deal eras.

The best organized of these three novellas is *Imagine Kissing Pete*—despite the author's tendency in it to digress rather than dramatize. *We're Friends Again* and *The Girl on the Baggage Truck* begin as obituary reflections and then, working into the past, thin out into chronological summaries. The human mind, which in following a narrative expects something that resembles an ending, gets one in *Imagine Kissing Pete;* the narrator is aware of it to the extent of calling it a happy ending. He knuckles sentimental tears out of his eyes at the conclusion of this grimly detailed account of a small-city marriage that, after years of antagonism complicated by the couple's social decline, has finally reached a state of limited contentment.

The kissings of Pete by various women, at the last by his wife exclusively, are staged in the O'Hara country around Gibbsville (translated from Pottsville), Pa., and this tale of "the losing, not the lost, generation" is told by a character long identified with this author: James Malloy, the doctor's son, who once again leaves Gibbsville to become a writer in New York. Other O'Hara old-timers also reappear, among them Julian English of *Appointment in Samarra,* who in an offstage bit once again keeps that appointment.

Malloy, who is likewise the narrator of the other two stories, is in all three of them more than a mere observer; his erotic entanglements of one kind or another with leading female characters keep him closely involved in the action. The settings of both *We're Friends Again* and *The Girl on the Baggage Truck* are for the most part the other O'Hara country, New York bars and hotels, and the second of these novellas contains a shrewdly recorded Prohibition-age party on a Long Island estate. However, in spite of lively episodes in these two stories, the action in each of them is too scattered to provide the cumulative force needed for a fully successful short novel.

We're Friends Again, extending from the Nineteen Thirties through World War II, has some interesting sequences devoted to two of Malloy's unsuccessful love affairs. *The Girl on the Baggage Truck* is about a film star who is first seen posing for a cheesecake shot after arriving at Grand Central. In all three stories O'Hara projects with skill the behavior and idiom of his characters, which range from Boston clubmen to Pennsylvania Dutch bartenders, all of whom capture the accent and excitement of the America he knows so expertly.

> *Harry T. Moore, "The Losing Generation," in*
> The New York Times Book Review, *November 27, 1960, p. 6.*

O'Hara on *Sermons and Soda-Water*:

[These] are three stories of men and women who were a bit too young to have been disillusioned by World War One. Everybody can understand a war. But it is not so easy to understand an economic revolution; even the experts continue to be baffled by it; and the people of my time never know what hit them or why. When some semblance of order was restored to the domestic economy, we looked about us and the world was already in cataclysm, not much easier to understand than the economic bafflement and over-simplified by the twin villains, Hitler and Mussolini, somewhat complicated by our convenient courtesy to the third villain, Stalin. It is not my intent and not by job to analyze these factors in *Sermons and Soda Water* but only to look at some of the people who were affected by them, in the Twenties, Thirties and Forties.

> *Quoted by Matthew J. Bruccoli in* The O'Hara Concern, *Random House, 1975.*

Granville Hicks   (essay date 1961)

[In the following review, Hicks discusses subject and technique in Assembly.]

In the past year the work of John O'Hara has been appearing in *The New Yorker* after a considerable absence, and it has been pleasant to find it there. As I remarked in reviewing his collection of novellas, *Sermons and Soda-Water* [*Saturday Review,* 10 December 1960] the shorter O'Hara is usually the better O'Hara.

Assembly contains twenty-six stories, ten of which were published in the *New Yorker.* "All but three or four of these stories," O'Hara says in the foreword, "were written during the summer of 1960 . . . and it was some of the most joyful writing I have ever done. The pleasure was in finding that after eleven years of not writing short stories, I could begin again and do it better." He has reason to be happy, for the best of the stories are as good as anything he has written.

The collection is nicely varied. Two of the stories are long enough to be called novellas, and others are only a few pages. One or two—*e.g.,* **"You Can Always Tell Newark"**—are so tightly plotted that they approach slickness, but these are exceptional. The tone is mostly quiet, though **"In a Grove"** bursts into melodramatic violence. Several of the stories are laid in the Pennsylvania city O'Hara calls Gibbsville, scene of *Appointment in Samarra* and *Ten North Frederick.* Others deal with characters from Broadway or Hollywood, and others with the well-to-do of the Atlantic seaboard.

O'Hara is, as he has called himself, an old pro, and he never botches a story. On the other hand, I don't think, as he seems to, that it is technical mastery that gives his work its distinction. In the foreword he says, "There may be as many as a dozen persons in the world who are able to detect the techniques employed." He underestimates the growth of literary sophistication in recent decades. There are dozens of writers in the United States who know quite as much about technique as John O'Hara, and not a few of them are his superiors. He is good, but he doesn't stand, as he seems to think, on a lonely pinnacle.

He also, I feel, exaggerates the importance of his researches in social history. His later novels have been too heavily documented, and even in the shorter works his devotion to the precise fact is sometimes excessive. His accuracy is often a comfort. When he has a character reading Dreiser's *The Genius* in 1916, you can be sure that the book had been published by that date. If he writes about the dance bands of the Twenties, you can rely on what he says. But precision of this kind is at best a minor virtue. In his foreword he writes, "If you are an author, and not just a writer, you keep learning all the time. Today, for instance, I was thinking about dialog, listening to dialog of some characters in my mind's ear, and I learned for the first time in my life that almost no woman who has gone beyond the eighth grade ever calls a fifty-cent piece a half-a-dollar." This may be true, but when O'Hara states that a careless author might spoil a characterization through ignorance of this fact, he is talking through his hat.

O'Hara's great strength is his curiosity about people, about what they do and why they do it. I have an impression that O'Hara doesn't like people, most people, very much, and he shows little compassion in his writings, but it does seem true that nothing human bores him. His sympathy has a limited range, but his interest is unbounded.

He is, of course, particularly interested in what people do about their sexual urges. When *A Rage to Live* appeared soon after the Kinsey Report, someone compared O'Hara's attitude to Dr. Kinsey's, and with justice. He has the same all-embracing curiosity and the same determination to refrain from moral judgments. If he isn't perfectly objective, neither was Kinsey.

One great difference is that O'Hara makes a place for romantic love, as several stories in *Assembly* show. In **"The Man with the Broken Arm"** the hero remains romantically attached to an actress who has treated him shamefully. **"The Lighter When Needed"** portrays a man and woman who have been devoted to one another, outside of marriage, for more than thirty years. **"The High Point," "A Cold Calculating Thing,"** and **"The Properties of Love"** all deal with love that has endured for a long time, though in each instance the lovers are not married. Not all the affairs in the book, of course, are romantic. In **"Mary and Norma,"** for instance, we have a pair of sisters-in-law who rush from infidelity to infidelity. There are some happy marriages but more unhappy ones. Sexual aberrations are touched upon. But romantic love obviously seems to O'Hara one of the observable facts of human experience.

Another theme that concerns O'Hara, and here more than ever before, is the approach of old age. **"The Trip"** is a beautifully done story of the way death becomes a reality to a man who has led an easy life. **"Call Me, Call Me"** is a sympathetic portrait of an actress who is passing her prime. In **"Mrs. Stratton of Oak Knoll"** a painter, getting on in years, says, "I've always been interested in the near-misses. Understandably. I'm one myself." As he moves towards sixty, O'Hara finds new phenomena with which to occupy himself.

At the end of his last story in the book, **"A Case History,"** a Gibbsville lawyer named Arthur McHenry speaks angrily of a novel by one James Malloy, a character who has often served as O'Hara's *alter ego.* Dr. Drummond says he can't understand what people were so sore about. "He gave the town a black eye, that's why," the lawyer replies. "And not one damn thing he wrote about actually happened." Dr. Drummond counters: "That's what I said. But you as a lawyer, and I as a physician, we know that things *like* them happened." "Oh, hell," says McHenry, "as far as that goes, I know some things that if young Malloy ever heard about them . . ." He breaks off, and Drummond says, "So do I, Arthur."

This is nicely ironic in the context of the story, but it may also be interpreted as O'Hara's justification of his practices. He has never copied life, he is saying, but he has always sought to be lifelike. In a period in which symbolism and fantasy have become more and more important, in which any beginner can talk about levels of meaning, he has come as close to pure realism as a serious writer can.

His devotion to the observed fact, though sometimes a liability, has saved his work from a certain sort of triviality. Much of what O'Hara tells us in the long novels isn't important, but that doesn't mean that none of it is. If he has been principally preoccupied with the surfaces of life, at least he has taken a hard, practiced look at those.

> *Granville Hicks, "A Deep Look at the Surface," in* The Saturday Review, *New York, Vol. XLIV, No. 47, November 25, 1961, p. 21.*

Edward Russell Carson   (essay date 1961)

[*In the following essay, Carson surveys prominent subjects and themes in O'Hara's short fiction.*]

Lionel Trilling declares in an Introduction to [*The Selected Short Stories of John O'Hara,* 1957] that it is only on the basis of the author's "passionate commitment to verisimilitude . . . " of social distinctions that O'Hara stands or falls as a generist in the short story medium. While it is only too easy to point to a great many of these stories as being expressive of the doctrine of a certain kind of social naturalism, it has until now remained a sadly neglected phase of scholarship and criticism that O'Hara's theme often consists of considerably more than such alone. This is to say that many of the better stories (especially those contained in the Trilling collection) express a vision of reality which at times makes the social temper of certain of these appear trivial by way of comparison. The best (and the longest) of these stories embody a vision of the futility of human effort in the face not only of the hostility of social demand, but, beyond this, the ineffably dark and unknowable forces of a universe itself even more violent in its capacity to defeat the luckiest of us. In such fine stories as **"Summer's Day," "The Doctor's Son," "Over the River and Through the Wood," "The Decision,"** O'Hara begins with the realities—and impossibilities—of class mobility—but *finishes,* after exploiting to the utmost their maximal pungence of verisimilitude, by presenting us with his tragic sense of the meanness of reality itself. It is also not of minor importance that O'Hara has cast his characters in these better stories as being from the uppermost ranges of the social compost heap. It is O'Hara's intention (not only as an inversion of his personal sadism) to demonstrate to his readers that even the Very Rich must suffer undue punishment at the hands of unmanageable destiny. O'Hara is always bringing to bear the overwhelming intensity of his focus upon the periphery of the wall of our isolation, which only takes the most elemental form as it reveals itself in mannerisms, affectations and habits. Among these are the judgments of one's intellect. True, O'Hara as a social commentator whose " . . . characteristic way of representing the elemental [in human nature] is through its modification by social circumstance . . . " is the typical outlook on the part of most of the discerning critical intelligentsia. At least, such has been the tendency of Charles Poor, Lionel Trilling, Edmund Wilson and John Woodburn. Only a varied amount of positive criticism (and this dedicated to the novels alone) extrapolates from this basic groundwork toward any realization of a more cosmic ideal in O'Hara as a short-story writer.

In fact, it is during O'Hara's moments of indulgence of the superfices of social realism that his work degenerates into a series of vignettes of the life of the characters being described, puny in view of their insignificance of any "theme." This theme may often amount to little more than the conclusion that a man's wife is chronically unfaithful—as in **"Saffercisco,"** or that it will only be **"Days"** before two people will commit adultery in a suburban setting. Such stories have their start and finish in the tiny bit of reality which they set out to describe but never lead to more than a manner of word-picture as their subject material. It is during such exercises as **"Pershing or Ten Eyck, Ten Eyck or Pershing," "Back in New Haven,"** or **"Invite"**—all written in the first person as, respectively, a speech to a certain Delphian society, a diary entry, or a letter—that O'Hara's journalistic inclination is diverted into the medium of reportage for its own sake rather than reportage used in an effort to exceed itself in the interest of grave and poignant human document. The best of O'Hara's stories are laden with such exempla. However, they will usually contain, incidentally speaking, any number of them, all of which may be summated into a series of concretions which underlie the essential meaning of a story. They represent the social circumstance alone, rather than how this circumstance may be seen to combine with several others of its own kind in modifying any representation of the elemental. Consider again Trilling's pursuit of this train of reasoning, as it applies to the story **"Summer's Day."** This is a story dealing with the reactions of an older man toward the suicide of his daughter.

> . . . The story proceeds on a series of small observations which include the protocol of an exclusive beach club and the question of who is sitting on whose bench; the social position of Catholics; the importance of election to a Yale senior society; the kind of epicene gossip that well-brought-up adolescents might take pleasure in. And the elemental fact which we confront when the story comes to its end is a good deal more than what we blandly call bereavement, it yields an emotion much more terrible than grief—the father's knowledge that he has reached the end of manhood and that the nothingness of life has overtaken him.

As these items accumulate, the sum total of their occurrence—proliferatively—makes for the story's final conviction of the belief expressed by Mr. Attrell that " . . . there was really nothing to face, really nothing." As DeFoe anchors the gradual trend of Moll Flanders toward middle-class respectability in the bedrock of monetary substance, so does O'Hara allow each moment of depiction of the class-standing of every personage to eventuate in the final predicament of such as Attrell. The greatest moments in all of O'Hara's literary output occur as a result of his fusion of the graphic details in these short stories into the symbols which they collectively embody of a manner of despair common to every man. What therefore matters in the treatment of each story followed below is, primarily, the specific nature of the tragic emotion pointed out; and secondarily, O'Hara's use of the concrete and graphic indices of descriptive technique in rendering apparent this tragic realization.

"Over the River and Through the Wood" proceeds along a surface of indices toward the final realization that a man named Mr. Winfield has grown old, and do what he may, grown ugly for no reason of his own. As in these other stories, the issue of aloneness finally pervades. The nursery-song title ironically applies to a sleigh-ride through Connecticut, at the end of which Mr. Winfield does little more than surprise one of the young ladies at her bath in the family manse.

It is only because Mr. Winfield performs an accident that he is defeated. This defeat consists of aggravating the already-present awareness of his personal unwantedness. Mr. Winfield and the reader cannot help but notice that his inclusion in the sleighing party is due only to an act of etiquette. It is never shown that anyone—neither Sheila, his granddaughter, nor her friends, nor even Ula, the maid—positively desires his presence for reasons of companionship or even amusement. "So it was sit outside and freeze or sit on the little seat inside." Not even when Mr. Winfield leaves a window open in the sleigh, while seated on the strapontin and creating an uncomfortable draft, do the girls immediately notice this physical discomfort. Sheila "closed the windows, not even acknowledging Mr. Winfield's shamed apologies." Upon arriving at the home, there is an omen cleverly revealed of what is to follow as "he went out to the darkened hall and Ula, the maid, jumped in fright. 'Ugh. Oh. It's you, Mr. Winfield. You like to scare me.' "

The only sense of happiness contrived by Mr. Winfield is during his isolation within his bedroom. Here, at least, he is free to reflect, as he sits like Joe Chapin in his den, "humming old songs, sipping watered whiskey and reviewing his life." Mr. Winfield is alone, and for the time being at least, is able to see his way of life as offering little better than this recollective sense of mentally re-ordering the memories of his situation. This, and the sense of physical well-being which he enjoys partaking of: "Little touches, ashtrays, flowers . . . ," the chocolate he drinks, which "made him a little thirsty, but it was good and warming, and Mary was right; it was better than a drink." But even this cannot last. O'Hara now takes us into a reportorial exegesis of the condition of Mr. Winfield's family home. His daughter's husband has bought the house, and Mr. Winfield, no longer wealthy, has had to give in. The dimension of O'Hara's social-class depiction is enacted in the humiliation Mr. Winfield must acknowledge, as it is specified in monetary terms, as frigidly impersonal as in the very legal contract itself. His son-in-law has told him, "I'll pay the delinquent taxes myself and give you a hundred and fifty thousand dollars for the house and grounds." In other words, Mr. Winfield " . . . was 'protecting' them all over again, by selling his house so that he would not become a family charge—protecting the very same people from the embarrassment of a poor relation." Mr. Winfield has been deserted by all those who might have been close to him at one time, and even before his catastrophic *faux pas,* would be only too happy to live out the rest of his years in this at least physically comfortable interior, remote from the intervention of unfeeling humanity and nature itself.

It is purely by circumstance that Mr. Winfield's mishap takes shape. Ula, the maid, has left two cups upon a tray for Mr. Winfield's chocolate. During the ride, Mr. Winfield has listened with some intensity to the conversation of his daughter and her friends. One of them is Kay Farnsworth. Mr. Winfield suddenly realizes that she is the most interesting person he has met in many dull years. On the basis of the overheard conversation, he decides that "It would be fun to talk to her, to sound her out and see how far she had progressed toward, say, ambition or disillusionment." If for this once only, he feels that he must invite her to have cocoa with him, "As former master of this house."

By accident the maid has left an extra cup on the tray. And it is by accident, more likely than not the result of deafness brought on by his own senility, that Mr. Winfield mistakes the girl's "In a minute" for "come in." He opens the door to discover her practically naked. "There was cold murder in the girl's eyes, and loathing and contempt and the promise of the thought his name forever would evoke. She spoke to him: 'Get out of here, you dirty old man.' " Insult is added to the already standing injury long inimical to Mr. Winfield's pride. **"Over the River and Through the Wood,"** besides being as descriptive as it is of Mr. Winfield's introspective solitude, is thus a statement of how an ordinary—and by the less socially exalted of us, forgivably trivial—mistake can be to one's undoing. As at Joe Chapin's funeral, " . . . Friends [could] bore you as much as enemies, and the ones quickly became the other over nothing more important than a near-sighted revoke at bridge. . . . " Mr. Winfield has been driven back into the confinement which he has had no desire to partake of, by behaving naively. All during the story, every person has behaved supremely in accordance with the code of his class—either as master or servant. It is a petty and self-righteous caste of society which Kay Farnsworth represents, in view of her total lack of deference in the presence of an older gentleman. Mr. Winfield can now do little better than face the realization that "there was all the time in the world, too much of it, for him. He knew it would be hours before he would begin to hate himself. For a while he would just sit there and plan his own terror."

"Decision" is a story prelusive of the thesis stated by Higgins in *Ourselves to Know,* that isolation from society is the ultimate fate of any of us who will stand face to face with our own essence—social forces can affect us up to a point (particularly in view of O'Hara's emphasis upon the aspects of vertical mobility)—but once we become inured to their operation beyond ourselves, we are forced into the contemplation of why we behave as we do—in regard to these elements. This is why O'Hara can say with utmost certitude that "my characters have two patterns. One is superficial . . . the other is psychological." In **"Decision,"** the social forces of family censure force Francis Townsend into the remoteness of his home, never to travel outside of Gibbsville, never to marry, and never to practice medicine. His uncle, upon Townsend's graduation from medical school, informs him that because his parents both died in mental institutions, he may neither practice nor marry. His uncle says to him, " 'You won't have to worry about money. I've fixed that at the bank. Give yourself plenty of

time to pick and choose. You'll decide on something.' . . . 'Oh, very likely I will,' Francis said. 'I won't just stay on here in the village.' But that, it turned out, was what he did decide to do." Francis Townsend is rendered the victim of a now outmoded system of psychology. While it may be generally regarded today that insanity need not be considered transmissible by heredity, the uncle of Francis Townsend stands for those forces of social reaction, one step away from superstition in their dogma. Although from a distinguished background, Townsend cannot accept his position in such a milieu without being forced into the concomitant resignation to the demands of outer authority that he submit or suffer an even worse fate than to be an M.D. without a practice.

"Decision" gives one a sense of material gratification—in regard to the sensate objects depicted by O'Hara—especially the interior furnishings of Francis Townsend's abode—which is made that much more instrumental to the purpose of the story by the feeling they create of their unvarying mundaneness. Every material detail is rendered as poignant—that is, as unpoignant—as Townsend's own fate. The lifelessness of these objects presents a humble and somber backdrop to the everyday rounds of Francis Townsend as he spends his day from getting out of bed at 6:30, to taking his walk, to going to his place at the village bar, until he returns home that night, to read from the 19th-century novels in his library—"till it was time to bank the kitchen fire for the next morning and finish off the last of the wrapped bottle of rye." The sturdy and well-finished physical objects stand by impersonally while Townsend lives on. "The home of Francis Townsend could have been taken for the birthplace of a nineteenth-century American poet, one of those little white houses by the side of the road that are regarded by the interested as national shrines. . . . " It is the feeling of unvarying habit, created by O'Hara's command of interior genre, which provides insight into the blankness of Townsend's existence. As in a Dutch interior, all the objects in the central still-life composition which stand in the middle of the home being described, stand out in their objective arrangement—artificial but nevertheless there—while through the window or doorway can be seen the vacant and airy nothingness of exterior reality. Such is Townsend's given condition—to live amid these physical realities and see in their enduring solidarity the contrast to so ephemeral a manner of suffering as his own. Townsend will at any rate accept his defeat bravely, and with grace.

"The Chink in the Armor" is a study in snobbery and the life of those who perpetually practice this vice. However, even Chauncy Wayne is not safe. This is because even though he may appear safe from censure from any person beneath his exalted social station, it is within his own stratum that he must expect and be on guard against the nemesis of social disapproval. No one is safe from snobbery—not even those at the very apex of the social-class pyramid. Mr. Wayne lives on an income in a private apartment in New York which is furnished with ancestral portraits and even with family armor. Nevertheless, the armor may impress many but not those members of Mr. Wayne's coterie who know one of his innermost personal secrets. Metaphorically, this is the chink in the armor—a silver cigarette box, the existence of which renders the armor a thing of solely antiquarian value, incapable any longer of being of practical use to Mr. Wayne in New York in the 1950's. To those of tantamount arrangement in the social hierarchy as Mr. Wayne (not to mention those even higher), Wayne is merely one-of-a-kind—no better, no worse.

The story involves Chauncy Wayne's hour of moral triumph. For once, anyway, he feels that he has "the edge" over a contemporary. This is a young man, the son of another who knows that Wayne has bought and presented himself with a silver cigarette box, inscribed with the names of the members of a billiard team. The father of Ted Crow is anathema to Wayne because of his knowledge of the latter's indulgence of his own vanity. In **"The Chink in the Armor"** (as in many others), the issue of personal vengeance looms large in the motivation of Chauncy Wayne. He invites Crow to his apartment to warn him against dropping out of an exclusive Manhattan Club. It is because, however, of Wayne's exaltedness of breeding and complete confidence in the unalterable status of his position, that he can advise Crow for his own good. To hold a grudge against Ted Crow because of his father's knowledge would be the epitome of debasement to the same moral (and speaking in terms of minute gradations), social, level of conduct. Wayne's effort at magnanimity in advising the younger man is one of O'Hara's most significant ventures into the depiction of social snobbery. Not only is **"The Chink in the Armor"** documentary of the variety of life among the Very Rich to be lived while poised on razor's edge while in fear of discovery of the family "skeleton in the closet." It is also demonstrative of a kind of snobbery particular to a given, if rarefied, section of the *haute monde.* Such is not the case in another *Hellbox* story, **"Other Women's Households."** Here, a young married couple bitterly acknowledge their submission to the principal stockholder of the town bank who refuses to see the wife on the grounds of her flaunting of the mores of the local bourgeoisie. Such is no less the case with Julian English, still so uncertain of his place in society that he must condescend to throw a drink in the face of an upstart. **"The Chink in the Armor"** presents a more subtle embodification of the snobbery not of a man who is on the move but one who is already there. Mr. Wayne's form of condescension is the product of unnumbered generations. Mr. Wayne can consider impersonally the issue of social derogation as a thing of will. He knows by his middle age (regardless of his former days at Princeton, when Crow's father "was the dirt under his feet, especially during Bicker Week") that to snub another human is to his own moral discredit, and not to that of the snubbed. O'Hara presents the social difference between the two generations as being simply this—one takes the issue of personal vengeance seriously enough to advise his son somehow to remind Wayne of his previous malfeasance—the other remains far above such rancor. It is, to Mr. Wayne, meretricious of the best possibilities in a man. Even so, he will devour his Christmas pudding and enjoy it as well. Mr. Wayne lectures Ted Crow tactfully on the topic of his adulterous relations with the wife of a fellow club member. It becomes subtly apparent that Mr. Wayne is enough Crow's superior as regards age as well as social standing to do so with authority and impunity. As the story comes to a finish,

Mr. Wayne shows Crow around the apartment. The two approach Mr. Wayne's dressing room, in which is located the ominous silver cigarette box. " . . . Mr. Wayne did not lead the way into the room. 'That about does it,' he said. He was obviously trying to guess whether Ted had seen the silver box, and if so, whether the box meant anything to him. He held out his hand and adroitly led Ted to the hall door. . . . " Mr. Wayne has had his moment of revenge through his own magnanimous and efficacious handling of the situation.

This same recurrent motif of the resolution of the desire for personal revenge appears thematically in many of the short stories. Notable examples are **"The Chink in the Armor," "Someone to Trust," "All the Girls He Wanted,"** and **"Price's Always Open."** In each of these stories, O'Hara makes the very most of the score that must be settled. Regardless of life's essential meaninglessness, the protagonist must be able to retain the sense of his own potency over and against those who would deny him such in the interests of his indignity. Doubtless, psychologically speaking, O'Hara's millionaires satisfy the same need for the author to attain this sense of power, if without the activation to stoop to a fisticuffs or telling another person to his face that his is a gratuitous existence. Life, because it is difficult for any personage created by O'Hara, has only these two ephemeral sources of reward: the gratification of tactile or gustatory stimulus by physical well-being (as in **"Decision"**), or the sense of temporary moral victory over an adversary, of getting the edge. **"Someone to Trust,"** for example, is a story dealing with an out-of-work entertainer on the hideout from a criminal mob. His former mistress is by now about to marry another man as soon as Tommy Welting arrives in New York. He manages to take refuge in her apartment and then burns a photograph of the girl's new lover. Against the imperturbable forces of his own misfortune, Welting is somehow able to enjoy the intense if fleeting joy of his satisfaction of revenge. In keeping with O'Hara's contention that since life's rewards are all of little endurance, one can at least enjoy the temporary moral satisfaction of getting the edge on one's tormentors. It is purely a question of time before the evil ones finally and completely win out. In a matter of months, Tommy Welting may be dead at the hands of hired murderers. He can meanwhile recoup the belief in his own pride. " 'A man could stay here forever, if he had to,' he told himself."

"All the Girls He Wanted," in like manner, is a study in a woman's recollections of a young man with whom she at one time commenced to have an affair, then after reneging, learns that her best friend has taken up where she herself left off. Her moment of triumph occurs after learning that the young man, Cliff Kizer, has been brutally mangled to death in an auto wreck. The woman begins by reflecting upon the grotesque nature of his death. " . . . They had taken life out of him and left him in a car that did not catch fire. They—God—had not even burned him up with fire, but had left his terrible broken body for anyone to see. Frances hugged herself. . . . " **"All the Girls He Wanted"** also uses a device of allowing Frances' speculations on Kizer—before and after his death—to succeed each other as they occur in the mind of this woman, irre-

O'Hara in 1966.

spective of objective chronological sequence. This is why, at the end of the story, Frances' learning that her friend has been deceived into having her affair by Kizer, now dead after the most painful manner of infliction, only can make her extremely happy to have been able to picture him lying dead. The bestial in Frances, as in all of us, makes for the story's climax on a note of optimism. She, too, has gained the upper hand for a moment. The story ends as Frances is able to say to herself that she is a "lucky, lucky girl."

Edmund Wilson refers to **"Price's Always Open"** as the one story in which "the forces of democracy finally win out." Which is to say that it is a story of social class conflict. It nevertheless has in common with many of the other stories this vengeance motif, if placed in a social setting. By means of threatening the summer crowd (after he has knocked a man unconscious), Price is able to get the better of a social superior. This same young man has kicked a man knocked down in a fight, and sees fit to do the same to Price's summer counterman, a student at Holy Cross. The story very effectively achieves its sense of justice along with whatever elements of vengeance O'Hara wishes to characterize in Mr. Price. One wonders, however, in doing justice to Wilson's statement, whether, as is usual to O'Hara, Price emerges victorious, in view of the

story's ending as follows: " . . . thinking it over, Mr. Price agreed with himself that those would be the last sounds he ever expected to hear from the summer crowd."

"The Doctor's Son" is the first in a series of several stories (and two novels, *Butterfield 8* and *Hope of Heaven*) which employ as their protagonist James Malloy, son of a Gibbsville doctor. Throughout the development of O'Hara's fictional style, Jim Malloy, like no other major character, serves as the personification of the author himself. Other O'Hara heroes—Julian English, Sidney Tate, Joe Chapin, and so on—represent less an embodiment of Hara's own person—autobiographically presented—than they do the result of O'Hara's observation of them from without, controlled and modified by the intensity of O'Hara's moral judgment. O'Hara has chosen these characters for the depiction of them much as F. Scott Fitzgerald might be described in the words of Malcolm Cowley, "as if at the same time he stood outside the ballroom, the little midwestern boy with his nose to the glass, wondering how much the tickets cost and who paid for the music." He writes of such people in the knowledge that his social and aesthetic distance from them enables rather than hinders a sense of objectivity as the result of remoteness. Malloy, on the other hand, is shown to be from Northeastern Pennsylvania, the son of well-to-do (if not munificent) parents. As the stories continually reappear, he is shown as not going to college (O'Hara's regret at not attending Yale is by now the salient feature of most biographers' squibs which refer to his life before the publication of *Appointment in Samarra*), working as a reporter, and finally as a script-writer in Hollywood. There could be no more directly autobiographic redaction of O'Hara's own exposure to the horror of death by disease in Gibbsville during an epidemic of influenza to those in the mining section and to the father of Malloy's girl. This is followed by Malloy's learning of the scandal of adultery between her mother and the substitute doctor. Malloy is able to avoid the injury of class-snobbery throughout his life.

> . . . What I want to say, what I started out to explain was why I said, "you people, you members of the upper crust," and so on, implying that I am not a member of it. Well, I'm *not* a member of it. . . .

His only canon for social standing lies in the middle-class standard of ability which particularly—as in *Hope of Heaven*—is reflected by means of monetary earning power. This is why Malloy writes for the films. More important, however, this emphasis upon cold cash as the sole agent of purchase of the symbols of wealth—the deliberate insistence upon Malloy's immediately acknowledging to himself that recently acquired wealth, not inherited, makes for a social difference—is the essential undercurrent in **"Transaction,"** a story in the ***Hellbox*** series. Malloy recognizes that social classes will and must exist in society. He is the spokesman for O'Hara's stoically conservative—and what any number of critics will doubtless refer to as snobbishly reactionary—stand in favor of class distinction as being revelatory of the best in humankind, even while O'Hara's other protagonists, as they appear in his novels, can be seen to embody and bring out the worst. Malloy can choose his friends and mistresses as he sees fit, on the basis of their personal attractiveness, exclusive of their parents' or their own Dun and Bradstreet rating. Such is the case with the women presented in *Butterfield 8* and *Hope of Heaven*. Malloy remains on the periphery of society at all elevations—much like Pal Joey, that "night-creature" so described by Lionel Trilling—always observing, never forgetful, but impervious to what can affect others less worldly (and less flush) than himself.

"The Doctor's Son" reminds one almost immediately of Hemingway's Nick Adams stories, particularly "Indian Camp." In both, a boy accompanies an older person to a treatment of patients in squalid surroundings. Jim Malloy and Nick Adams thus undergo their first eyewitness contact with death by unnatural causes. There is also an interesting parallel between Malloy's recollection that after losing his girl, he "never can remember her married name" and Adams' suddenly remembering, also at the end of the story, that "his heart was not broken" in "Ten Indians." Both boys have experienced much by their early teens, but have emerged whole in spite of it. For O'Hara, however, **"The Doctor's Son"** involves the transplantation of Nick Adams' Michigan countryside into Gibbsville. Its chief appeal as a story lies in its Gibbsvillian topography which O'Hara makes one with the main item of Jim Malloy's maturity, so suddenly enforced upon him. Malloy has discov-

ered that death can occur in a distasteful fashion—and even to those one is intimately concerned for. Not only this, but that same Mr. Evans has been the object of his wife's unfaithfulness. The impact of these events so overwhelms and innures Malloy, that the issue of his girl's departure recedes only too obviously before these shocks. Malloy has suddenly become an adult. He is "only surprised [but not overwhelmed]" when Edith Evans elopes.

"The Doctor's Son" is actually a story more given to tactile and graphic attention to its setting than many of the later stories. There is nevertheless in the story **"Transaction"** an insight into the mature Malloy, now become a successful script writer after *Hope of Heaven,* who is in Cambridge to pay for a Duesenberg limousine. His meeting with the married couple makes for a study in depiction of the minutiae of class difference and the stand Malloy takes in regard to it.

Much of **"Transaction"** consists of description for its own intrinsic interest of the details of the interior of the home lived in by the couple, as well as their habits, mannerisms, artifacts. These are the Van Burens. The wife

> . . . straightened her back, after the manner, possibly, of a dowager aunt. This girl, Malloy knew, was a lady. She was nearly a generation away from certain friends of his, but he was sure that if he started the do-you-know game there would be a tumbling forth of names—aunts and uncles, cousins and parents of her friends. . . .

As Charles Van Buren, the husband, comes in to find Malloy and his wife talking together, he says to both of them

> . . . trying to be jovial [that they are] "drinking their heads off, bag packed, I suppose I'll find a note on the pillow." . . . "Yes and look at the bag. Louis Vuitton," she said. . . . "Naturally it'd be a man with money," said Van Buren. There was no bitterness in the way he said it, but it was not the thing to say, and they all knew it. . . .

Then, as Malloy presents Van Buren with the check, Malloy notices that the car now has a spotlight which he insists upon paying for. This is the most important point in the story (occurring as it does in most of O'Hara's), near the end. He writes out another check for seventy-five dollars, and the transaction is concluded. Malloy sees the Duesenberg as a symbol of the life he wishes to become accustomed to. More than this, however, he would rather pay cold cash for the extra fixture because he is not ashamed to admit to the Van Burens that his intimacy with the mechanical and economic fixtures of a Duesenberg is something which he owns up to and will not avoid merely for the sake of social courtesy. Malloy sees an expensive Duesenberg as a symbol, but also as a reality. He is never afraid to point out to others, as O'Hara himself does, if less explicitly in his fiction, that it is not enough only to dress and talk in a cherished manner. To do so by itself is a form of grossest hypocrisy. Money must remain the responsible agent, even for Van Buren, whose "buttoned-down collar of his shirt was a little frayed, as though he had done an imcomplete job with nail scissors." It will likewise remain so for Malloy himself, who may one day marry and rear a son who is elected to a Yale senior society.

"Miss W." follows **"Transaction"** in the *Hellbox* collection. The story concerns Miss Woodberry, who teaches at a girls' junior college and at the time of the story is signing in girls back from weekend vacation. One of them is late and has not reported back. She finally is returned by Malloy in the same Duesenberg. The girl has been in a slight accident. Miss Woodberry is surprised to meet Malloy, who is an old friend. Again, one gets the feeling that Malloy's entire life consists of driving about the countryside near exclusive schools and colleges in his Duesenberg, secure in the knowledge that his earning power has enabled him to do so. His performance of the slight favor is part of the magnanimity due to such a station. It is "For old times' sake," as he explains to Miss Woodberry, who gives Malloy a free meal. The final moment of triumph is Malloy's. He is only too happy to recollect and review his former days, as he sits in Miss Woodberry's study. She notes,

> . . . "Here we sit, fat and middle-aged, me chewing on one side of my mouth because I'm afraid of losing a filling. . . . It's not too bad." Malloy says nothing. "Well, at least we can pretend it isn't." "Right," he said.

Malloy wants only to enjoy his series of remembrances, although there is a hint in his final reply, of still dormant sexual attraction.

Following **"Miss W."** is the last story in *Hellbox*, **"Conversation in the Atomic Age."** Seen superficially, it is a deft and satiric record of nothing more than a lunchtime conversation between Malloy and a Los Angeles society woman, set in Hollywood. Its location in *Hellbox* may be seen as a coda to the depiction of O'Hara–Malloy. While the woman, Mrs. Schmidt, does most of the talking, it is Malloy, who, secure in view of his social position because he has "paid his way" as a successful screen-writer, can talk to her exactly as he pleases. However, he realizes that to remind her of her inanity would only be to touch on too sensitive a spot. Malloy is only too interested in watching Mrs. Schmidt give herself away; by the end of the story it even is conceivable that Malloy is using her as material for another film. He may be slightly flip, but never rude or even in earnest. This would be to curtail Malloy's own contemplation. Finally, Malloy looks across at another table to notice the wife of a good friend at lunch with another man. Malloy can only respond by taking home his luncheon guest. He has seen all that he might want to see that afternoon, or any other afternoon. He is shown as avoiding any form of positive participation which might affect the purity of his vision, even in the interests of a good friend. He may write it out of his system, but he will not consider willful action.

As a stylist in the short story medium, John O'Hara at times comes close to a more poignant and literal command of his material than in even the best of his novels. O'Hara's most outstanding defect—artistically speaking, his most flagrant sin of commission—is his tendency never to know when to stop, particularly in his tactile and visual descriptions of social class insignia. There are times *A Rage to Live* offers the most compelling instance of this—at which

the subtle and intricate psychological motivation of a character becomes overshadowed by O'Hara's equally attentive reaction of what he or she has eaten for breakfast or the details of one's living-room interior. In the short stories, however, the reader is never aware of such excesses. Every one of the descriptions of such similar items (*vide* **"A Summer's Day"**) adds somewhat, if only minutely, to the gradual accumulation of the realm of the major theme. "Just what is the purpose of these extraneous diversions?" asks Edmund Wilson, writing seven years after the appearance of *Appointment in Samarra*. Not so, as regards the finer short stories of O'Hara. These more capably allow O'Hara himself more efficaciously to sublimate his at times insatiable urge in the direction of description for its own sake into meaningful symbolism, valuable as much for its quaintness of sociological insight as for the light it sheds on a story's final statement of any character's predicament. Thus, such particulars gradually snowball into a total impression created by the realization of a major chord. That "the description is never gratuitous or for its own sake" can hardly be denied the stories, even though one often demands this same of the longer ventures into prose fiction.

If there are any salient and always predictable qualities to the fiction of John O'Hara, one of these would have to consist of his pessimistic awareness of the helpless despair of the sensitive individual in the face of a hierarchic social system. Trilling compares O'Hara to Kafka, insofar as both writers recognize that it is always easy to make the one fatal mistake in one's everyday life which will set into motion against himself the mechanism of the social machinery which impersonally is responsible for that individual's survival but could, in such cases, be as equally effective in sealing his doom. This, plus the theory, somewhat existentialist in its own way, of the "Hellbox" or private suffering of each of us, regardless of his social attitudes, resulting from the conflict between individual nature, or idiosyncrasy, and the inhibitions enacted by the hostility of reality itself. Every man has to suffer, O'Hara is continually implying; yet this must be in his own way and by himself. No other party can share in the privateness of this hell. Every man is an island.

The stories, at their best, convey O'Hara's conviction of pessimism in a direct and, unlike the novels, condensed, manner of statement. At their worst, they appear purely anecdotal beside O'Hara's more serious examples, only as vignettes or individual monologues. But O'Hara is never so much in command of the situation as when he can, like a Flemish miniaturist, present a household interior in all its graphically precise realism, in the midst of which a man or woman sits alone with his or her memories and sensations, ultimately impervious either to these tactile realities or even to whatever other persons may be sharing this reality being set down. A good example would be the story **"The Cold House."** While it may lack the conviction of **"The Decision"** or any of the stories described above, this story's greatest merit inheres in its capacity to suggest visually to its reader that this home is Mrs. Carnavon's private inferno, as real as any of the objects with which she feels herself immured. Near the very end, "She saw herself . . . how to love." **"The Cold House"** exemplifies well O'Hara's concern with the description of the "crypt of useless things"—and the knowledge that these useless things will never assuage the death of a son.

> *Edward Russell Carson, in his* The Fiction of John O'Hara, *University of Pittsburgh Press, 1961, 73 p.*

David Boroff (essay date 1963)

[*In the following review of* The Hat on the Bed, *Boroff commends O'Hara's portrayal of American life.*]

John O'Hara continues to astound us not only with his productivity, but with his range of characters, the profusion of incident, the indomitable curiosity, the calm omniscience. But John O'Hara is a major American writer who has been little honored. His chief rewards have been a tight grip on a popular audience and considerable financial success.

He has been accused of being retrograde as a literary artist, holding to an outmoded social realism. (But we have come to realize that there are few viable alternatives; the novel of sensibility seems more and more strained and irrelevant.) He has been charged with sexual obsessiveness, but he is continually eclipsed by a zealous brigade of pornographers. It is said that his canvas is too straitened, that he writes only about the upper class. But that is not so; in the present collection, for example, at least one-third of the stories deal with the middle class, the lower class and the declassed. And there are those who sneer that he writes too much, too hastily and to little purpose.

In literature, as in the social sciences, a significant difference in degree brings about a difference in kind. The sheer weight of O'Hara's work, his obstinate persistence, confer on the author a certain dignity and worth. (To be sure, it is not the multiplication of his sins that turns the trick but the expanding mass of what is enduring and worthwhile.) And O'Hara's is not an artistic achievement alone. Like some other artists—Dreiser, Joyce and James come to mind—his triumph is one of character. He has stuck to his guns, and it is my conviction that time will vindicate him. In terms of what he sets out to do—to create a portrait of the America he knows—O'Hara is one of the great writers of our time.

His new collection of short stories, **The Hat on the Bed,** consists of 24 stories of varied length, density and significance. A few are mere transcripts of conversation, flat, toneless, sometimes desultory. (They almost justify the strictures O'Hara's critics direct against him.) But this book also contains masterpieces of compression and revelation—an incredible amount of life packed into a few pages. A few are longer stories—novellas really—turned out with stunning authority, written by a man whose capacity for recall and invention is indefatigable.

One of these longer stories is **Ninety Minutes Away,** an unsentimental, shrewdly accurate account of a Philadelphia tart. O'Hara knows low-life, and he approaches it neither with beatnik adoration nor psychological moralizing. He accepts the world of drifters and prostitutes and seedy reporters and is able to make us see it from the in-

side. A second novella, **Yucca Knolls,** is a brilliant portrait of Hollywood—of Cissie Brandon, a dignified woman who made her living performing in a ghastly but profitable series of folksy movies, and Earl Evans, who violates the Hollywood mores of subservience and is ultimately broken by the town. The author's strengths are very much in evidence here. Evans is like something out of Genet—a street fighter, a lady's man, a homosexual, a criminal. Yet there is never an implausible note in O'Hara's prose, as there is in so much Hollywood fiction. He is forever the imperturbable police reporter. He has seen a lot, and he understands a lot. His confidence and poise are not easily threatened.

The shorter pieces move freely through O'Hara terrain. There is the inevitable story about a chauffeur who, it turns out, had intimidated his mistress for years by being "a perfect servant." There is the aging lady in a hotel apartment who is engaged in a tug-of-war with a maid she wants to dominate. There is the lower-class woman having an affair with her dead sister's husband under the guise of looking after their children. And there is John Barton Rosedale, the aging actors' actor, who moves with a kind of bitter elegance at his club and glowers at the new people from Madison Avenue.

All this is familiar O'Hara. A new note—similar to the mood of gentle reconciliation to be found in *Elizabeth Appleton,* his latest novel—is sounded in **"The Man on the Tractor"** in which "the fabulous Denisons" return for a brief visit to the Gibbsville from which they came, after years in New York and Europe. In a real sense, this story is a valedictory to the world O'Hara knew. Their old friends are either dead or in A.A., the Denisons discover, and the town itself is going fast.

"We're losing population, a thousand a year," a local banker reports. "The town is back to where it was in the 1910 census, and no new industries coming in. These people that are buying your land, they'll put up a supermarket and a big parking lot, but sure as hell that's going to be the end of some more of the smaller stores. . . . Banking isn't much fun any more, the hard luck stories I have to listen to. . . . It's the fast buck, the quick turnover, build as cheaply as possible, take your profit and get out."

John O'Hara's work will be a memorial to that dead and dying world.

> *David Boroff, "A Portrait of America," in* The New York Times Book Review, *December 8, 1963, p. 6.*

Gore Vidal (essay date 1964)

[*Vidal is an American novelist, essayist, and playwright who is particularly noted for his historical novels and iconoclastic essays. His work in all genres is marked by his urbane wit and brilliant technique. In the following excerpt, originally published in 1964, Vidal negatively assesses O'Hara's fiction.*]

In 1938, writing to a friend, George Santayana described his first (and presumably last) encounter with the writing of Somerset Maugham. "I could read these [stories], enticed by the familiarity he shows with Spain, and with Spanish Americans, in whose moral complexion I feel a certain interest; but on the whole I felt . . . wonder at anybody wishing to write such stories. They are not pleasing, they are not pertinent to one's real interests, they are not true: they are simply graphic or plausible, like a bit of a dream that one might drop into in an afternoon nap. Why record it? I suppose it is to make money, because writing stories is a profession . . . " In just such a way, the Greek philosophers condemned the novels of the Milesian school. Unpleasing, impertinent, untruthful, what else can one say about these fictions? except to speculate idly on why grown men see fit to write them. Money? There seems nothing more to be said.

Yet there is at least one good reason for a serious consideration of popular writing. "When you are criticising the Philosophy of an epoch," wrote Alfred Whitehead in *Adventures of Ideas,* "do not chiefly direct your attention to those intellectual positions which its exponents feel it necessary to defend. There will be some fundamental assumptions which adherents of all the various systems within the epoch unconsciously presuppose." Writers of fiction, even more than systematic philosophers, tend to reveal unconscious presuppositions. One might even say that those writers who are the most popular are the ones who share the largest number of common assumptions with their audience, reflecting, subliminally, as it were, prejudices and aspirations so obvious that they are never stated and, never stated, never precisely understood or even recognized. John O'Hara is an excellent example of this kind of writer, and useful to any examination of what we are.

Over the last three decades, Mr. O'Hara has published close to thirty volumes of stories, plays, essays, novels. Since 1955 he has had a remarkable burst of activity: twelve books. His most recent novel, *Elizabeth Appleton,* was written in 1960 but kept off the market until 1963 while five other books were published. His latest collection of short stories, **The Hat on the Bed,** is currently a best seller and apparently gives pleasure to the public. In many ways, O'Hara's writing is precisely the sort Santayana condemned: graphic and plausible, impertinent and untrue. But one must disagree with Santayana as to *why* this sort of work is done (an irrelevant speculation, in any case). Money is hardly the motive. No man who devotes a lifetime to writing can ever be entirely cynical if only because no one could sustain for a lifetime the pose of being other than himself. Either the self changes or the writing changes. One cannot have it both ways. O'Hara uses himself quite as fully and obsessively as William Faulkner. The difference between them lies in capacity, and the specific use each makes of a common obsession to tell what it is like to be alive. But where Faulkner recreated his society through a gifted imagination, O'Hara reflects his, making him, of the two, rather more interesting for our immediate purpose, which is to examine through his books the way we live now.

O'Hara's work is in the naturalistic tradition. "I want to get it all down on paper while I can. The U.S. in this century, what I know, and it is my business to write about it to the best of my ability with the sometimes special knowl-

edge that I have." He also wants "to record the way people talked and thought and felt, and to do it with complete honesty and variety." In this, he echoes Sinclair Lewis, Emile Zola, and (rather dangerously) the brothers Goncourt.

The Hat on the Bed is a collection of twenty-four short stories. They are much like O'Hara's other short stories, although admirers seem to prefer them to earlier collections. Right off, one is aware of a passionate interest in social distinctions. Invariably we are told not only what university a character attended but also what prep school. Clothes, houses, luggage (by Vuitton), prestigious restaurants are all carefully noted, including brand-names. With the zest of an Internal Revenue man examining deductions for entertainment, O'Hara investigates the subtle difference between the spending of old middle-class money and new middle-class money. Of course, social distinctions have always been an important aspect of the traditional novel, but what disturbs one in reading O'Hara is that he does so little with these details once he has noted them. If a writer goes to the trouble to say that someone went to St. Paul's and to Yale and played squash, then surely there is something about St. Paul's and Yale and squash which would make him into a certain kind of person so that, given a few more details, the reader is then able to make up his mind as to just what that triad of experience means, and why it is different from Exeter-Harvard-lacrosse. But O'Hara is content merely to list schools and sports and the makes of cars and the labels on clothes and he fails to do his own job in his own terms, which is to show us *why* a character who went to Andover is not like one who went to Groton, and how the two schools, in some way, contributed to the difference. O'Hara is excited by fashionable schools in much the same way that Balzac was by money, and perhaps for the same reason, a cruel deprivation. Ernest Hemingway (whose malice was always profound) once announced that he intended to take up a collection to send John O'Hara through Yale. In his own defense, O'Hara has said that his generation did care passionately about colleges. Granting him this, one must then note that the children and grandchildren of his contemporaries do not care in the same way, a fact he seems unaware of, and one which undermines his claim to be putting it all down just the way it is.

The technique of the short stories does not vary much. The prose is plain and rather garrulous; the dialogue tends to run on, and he writes most of his stories and novels in dialogue because not only is that the easiest kind of writing to read but the easiest to do. In a short story like **"The Mayor,"** one sees his technique at its barest. Two characters meet after three pages of setting up the scene (describing a hangout for the town's politicians and setting up the personality of the mayor, who often drops in). Then two characters start to talk about a third character (the mayor) and his relationship with a fourth, and after some four pages of dialogue—and one small uninteresting revelation—the story is over; in Santayana's image, a daydream. One has learned nothing. Felt nothing. Why record it?

Another short story, **"How Can I Tell You?,"** is purest

reverie. We are shown a car salesman who by all worldly standards is a success; he even gets on well with his wife. All things conspire to make him happy. But he suffers from *accidie,* as the Latins say. The story begins *in medias res.* He is making an important sale. The woman buying the car talks to him at great length about this and that. Nothing particularly relevant to the story is said. The dialogue wanders aimlessly in imitation of actual speech as it sounds to Mr. O'Hara's ear, which is good but unselective, with a tendency to use arcane slang ("plenty of glue") and phonetic spellings ("wuddia"). Yet despite this long conversation, the two characters remain vague and undefined. Incidentally, Mr. O'Hara almost never gives a physical description of his characters, a startling continence for a naturalistic writer, and more to be admired than not.

The woman departs. The salesman goes to a bar where the bartender immediately senses that "You got sumpn eatin' you, boy." The salesman then goes home. He looks at his sleeping wife who wakes up and wants to know if something is wrong. "How the hell can I tell you when I don't know myself?" he says. She goes back to sleep. He takes down his gun. He seems about to kill himself when his wife joins him and says, "Don't, please?" and he says, "I won't." And there the story ends. What has gone wrong is that one could not care less about this Richard Cory (at least we were told that the original was full of light and that people envied him), because O'Hara's creation has no face; no history. What the author has shown us is not a character but an event, and though a certain kind of writing can be most successful dealing only with events, this particular story required character shown from the inside, not a situation described from the outside, through dialogue . . .

Perhaps the most remarkable thing about O'Hara is that for one who is in many ways a typical American writer, both in his virtues and faults, he has practically no sense of humor, the one gift our culture most liberally bestows on its sons. He is never anything but dead-serious about his adulterers and their schools and their clubs and their cars. Now one does not mind the absence of wit in his writing. He is not that sort of writer. Yet accepting him for what he is, a reliable recorder, one still longs for a flash of humor, of irony, of the sense that the preoccupations of his characters (and himself) might just possibly be absurd if only in the sight of eternity.

To be effective, naturalistic detail must be not only accurate but relevant. This is a tiresomely obvious thing to say but repetition does not seem to spoil the novelty of it as criticism. Each small fact must be fitted to the overall pattern as tightly as mosaic. Yet the temptation to add more details than are needed is irresistible. And O'Hara seldom resists. His recent work is over-loaded with names, places, prices, brand-names, reflecting his own pleasure in getting them down simply for their own sake. If he can come up with the exact name of the jazz singer who sang in a certain club of a certain city in a particular year he seems to feel that his work as recorder has been justified. This might do for a social historian or magazine profile writer, but in a novelist it is a deadly preoccupation which, para-

doxically, can make for great popularity, and that brings us to the audience and its unconscious presuppositions.

Right off, one is struck by the collective narcissism of his readers. Until our day, popular writers wrote of kings and queens, of exotic countries and desperate adventures, of worlds totally unlike the common experience. No longer. Today's reader wants to look at himself, to find out who *he* is, with an occasional glimpse of his next door neighbor. Now, at best, fiction is an extension of actual life, an alternative world in which a reader may find out things he did not know before and live in imagination a life he may not live in fact. But I suggest that never before has the alternative world been so close to the actual one as it is in the novels of John O'Hara and his fellow commercialities. Journalism and popular fiction have merged, and the graphic and the plausible have become an end in themselves. The contemporary public prefers mirrors to windows.

The second unconscious presupposition O'Hara reveals is the matter of boredom. Most of the people he describes are bored to death with their lives and one another. Yet they never question this boredom, nor does their author show any great awareness of it. He just puts it all down. Like his peers, he reflects the *tedium vitae* without seeming to notice it. Yet it lurks continually beneath the surface, much the way a fear of syphilis haunted popular writing in the nineteenth century. One can read O'Hara by the yard without encountering a single character capable of taking pleasure in anything. His creatures are joyless. Neither art nor mind ever impinges on their garrulous absorption in themselves. If they read books, the books are by writers like O'Hara, locked with them in their terrible self-regard. They show little curiosity about other people, which is odd since the convention of each story is almost always someone telling someone else about so-and-so.

Finally, there is the matter of death. A recent survey among young people showed that since almost none believed in the continuation of personality after death, each felt, quite logically, that if this life is all there is, to lose it is the worst that can happen to anyone. Consequently, none was able to think of a single "idea," political or moral, whose defense might justify no longer existing. This, to put it baldly, is to me the central underlying assumption of our society and one which makes us different from our predecessors. As a result, much of the glumness in our popular writers is that of a first generation set free from an attitude toward death which was as comforting as it was constraining. At his level, O'Hara reflects the fear that death is extinction, particularly in a short story, **"The Trip,"** from the collection ***Assembly.*** Here the method is flawless. An elderly New York clubman is looking forward to a boat trip to England, the scene of many pleasures in his youth (the Kit Kat Club with the Prince of Wales at the drums, etc.). He discusses the trip with his bridge partners, a contented foursome of old men, their pleasant lives shadowed only by the knowledge of death. An original member of the foursome died some years earlier, and there had been some criticism of him for he had collapsed "and died while playing a hand. The criticism was mild enough, but it was voiced, one player to another; it was simply that Charley has been told by his doctor not to play bridge, but he had insisted on playing, with the inevitable, extremely disturbing result." But there were those who said how much better it was that Charley was able to die among friends rather than in public, with "policemen going through his pockets to find some identification. Taxi drivers pointing to him. Look a dead man." Skillfully O'Hara weaves his nightmare. Shortly before the ship is to sail for England, one of the foursome misses the afternoon game. Then it is learned that he has died in a taxi cab. Once again the "inevitable, extremely disturbing" thing has happened. The trip is called off because " 'I'd be such a damn nuisance if I checked out in a London cab.' " This particular story is beautifully made, and completely effective. Yet Boccaccio would have found it unfathomable: isn't death everywhere? and shouldn't we crowd all that we can into the moment and hope for Grace? But in O'Hara's contemporary mirror, there is neither Grace nor God. And despite our society's nervous, intermittent religiosity, death has been accepted not only as man's inevitable end, but as the one "extremely disturbing" fact.

In his way, O'Hara reflects our society's self-regard, boredom, terror of not being. Why our proud Affluency is the way it is does not concern us here. Enough to say that O'Hara, inadvertently, is a reliable witness. Also, he has many virtues. For one thing he possesses the narrative gift, without which nothing. He has complete integrity. What he says he sees he sees. Though his concern with sex has troubled many of the Good Gray Geese of the press, it is a legitimate concern. Also, his treatment of sexual matters is seldom irrelevant, though touchingly old-fashioned by today's standards, proving once again how dangerous it is for a writer to rely too heavily on contemporary sexual *mores* for his effects. When those *mores* change, his moments of high drama become absurd. "Would you marry me if I weren't a virgin?" asks a girl in one of the early books. "I don't know. I honestly don't know," is the man's agonized response, neither suspecting that even as they suffer, in literature's womb Genet and Nabokov, William Burroughs and Mary McCarthy are stirring to be born. But O'Hara, with his passionate desire to show things as they are, is necessarily limited by the things he must look at. Lacking a moral imagination and not interested in the exercise of mind or in the exploration of what really goes on beneath that Harris tweed suit from J. Press, he is doomed to go on being a writer of gossip who is read with the same mechanical attention any newspaper column of familiar or near-familiar names and places is apt to evoke. His work, finally, cannot be taken seriously as literature, but as an unconscious record of the superstitions and assumptions of his time, his writing is "pertinent," in Santayana's sense, and even "true."

Gore Vidal, "John O'Hara," in his Homage to Daniel Shays: Collected Essays 1952-1972, *1972, Reprint by Vintage Books, 1973, pp. 164-73.*

Stanley Kauffmann   (essay date 1964)

[*In the following excerpt, Kauffmann offers an ambiva-*

lent review of The Horse Knows the Way *and notes a lack of development in O'Hara's work.*]

[*The Horse Knows the Way*] is a collection of twenty-eight stories. In his Foreword [O'Hara] warns us that this may be his last book of stories for a while, assures us that he makes a nice income from stories, reminds us (reviewers particularly?) that he has the Award of Merit from the American Academy of Arts and Letters, avers that he will push on. "I have work to do, and I am not afraid to do it."

The Foreword is, like most of O'Hara's personal statements, insufferable. The stories are, like most of O'Hara's stories, very easily read, even when they are vacuous. After I finished the present volume, I re-read a couple of stories from his 1945 collection, *Pipe Night,* and it was like watching an early James Stewart film on the Late Show. You realize that, essentially, nothing at all has changed. The years have done nothing but age him; what was good remains good, what was bad remains bad. There has not even been deterioration, let alone development.

O'Hara is the last of the prominent Hemingway offspring and certainly the most successful. He has carried a stenographic method to the degree where one can enjoy it as such, just as one can—for a time, at least—enjoy soundtapes of almost any party conversation simply because it *is* recorded and shares the peculiar mystique of any record, sound or photographic. But his arrogance about his naturalistic methods, his reluctance to use other techniques that could condense and heighten, sometimes leads him to exposition of facts in dialogue that betrays the very naturalism itself:

> " . . . that's as much as any other man in town gets, unless he graduated from P.C.P. But they start higher, the P.C.P. graduates."

> "But you have your license, Philadelphia College of Pharmacy or no Philadelphia College of Pharmacy."

That unlikely mouthful of reply, by a wife to a husband, would have been unnecessary if the author himself had been willing to tell us succinctly what P.C.P. means.

O'Hara's stories are set principally in the three areas he has previously staked out: Gibbsville, Pa., New York, and Hollywood. There are character sketches, so cleverly done that their emptiness is doubly disappointing: for instance, **"The Answer Depends."** Some stories are muted melodrama, like **"The Madeline Wherry Case,"** whose only real asset is its reticence. Some, like **"In the Mist,"** are views of a decadent world from within, or hint at a mystery that lacks content, like **"The Gun."** Saul Bellow wrote of O'Hara: "Certain of his stories run like little trolleys, bright and glittering, but without a passenger."

There are a few, however, with passengers. Two, in particular: **"Can I Stay Here?"** is a telling encounter between an aging actress and a former beau's daughter. **"School,"** about a father visiting the prep-school son who has snitched to the mother about the father's affair, builds a tension between well-realized characters that creates drama and a corner of society.

But in all the stories, even the best, there is a taint of one-upmanship, the strain to be an insider. This, too, is O'Hara's inheritance from Hemingway. Where the latter titillated us stay-at-homes with travel-snobbism about France and Spain and Cuba, O'Hara is a class or genre snob. When he writes about rich New York society or Pennsylvania Dutch society or low Hollywood "high" society, his teeming minutiae, used with a kind of nervous relentless casualness, connote a sophomoric pride that he has been there and that his reader probably has not. It gives his work an air of a Leonard Lyons column. Even without the foreword, his book seems to combine the values of the social climber and the lodge member. This book and his whole body of work are proof that skills, sometimes dazzling skills, are not enough.

Stanley Kauffmann, "O'Hara and Others," in The New York Review of Books, Vol. III, No. 9, December 17, 1964, pp. 21-2.

Creating the *Pal Joey* stories:

O'Hara achieved one of his greatest public successes through writing stories about a man who seemed to personify his cynical view of humanity. These stories take the form of letters written by an amoral nightclub singer in the Middle West called Pal Joey, who is always in search of a pretty "mouse" to sleep with and who will use anyone, including his girls, to further his career. The first of these stories was written in 1938 just after the O'Haras returned from Europe and were in need of money. Having completed *Hope of Heaven* at the Ben Franklin Hotel in Philadelphia, O'Hara told [his wife] that he would go there again to work on a few stories for the *New Yorker*. Leaving her at her mother's apartment at Ninety-third and Fifth Avenue, he took a taxi south to Penn Station. He was suffering from a hangover, so on the way downtown he decided to get out and buy himself a restorative at the bar of the Pierre Hotel. After a couple of drinks, he decided it would be just as easy to stay at the Pierre as go to Philadelphia, so he checked into a room. That was the beginning of a two-day bender. On the morning of the third day, as he later recounted, he woke up and found that instead of completed stories, all he had "was the typewriter, some blank paper and a lot of empty bottles." Then the remorse set in: He asked himself, "What kind of god damn heel am I? I must be worse'n anybody in the world." Then he thought a minute: "No, there must be somebody worse than me—but who? Al Capone, maybe. Then I got it—maybe some nightclub masters of ceremony I know."

Frank MacShane, in his The Life of John O'Hara, E. P. Dutton, 1980.

Sheldon Norman Grebstein (essay date 1966)

[*In the following excerpt, Grebstein surveys O'Hara's short fiction from* The Doctor's Son, and Other Stories *(1935) to* Hellbox *(1947) in terms of the stories' various ironies.*]

Almost without exception the stories in **The Doctor's Son** are sensibility stories. Following the example of Chekhov,

who has been the greatest single influence upon the course of the modern short story (although O'Hara himself need not have read Chekhov directly, since the same influence was at work upon such writers as Katherine Mansfield, Joyce, and Hemingway), O'Hara's works here depend almost entirely upon character and situation rather than upon plot and action. In fact, many of them are plotless; almost nothing happens. The "action" consists of an entirely different process than that usually denoted by the word. In the sensibility story the action is largely psychological; it arises out of the interplay of the personalities and characters of the story's people. Its climax ordinarily depends far less upon circumstance or other material cause than upon the sudden realization, either by the protagonist or by the audience, of some hitherto unknown or hidden aspect of human nature, more often than not an ugly or unpleasant aspect. This moment of truth, or moment of confrontation of the truth, Joyce called an "epiphany." Likewise, O'Hara's stories often create the effect of what might be called "perceptual distance," or the difference between reality as the story's protagonist views it (or once viewed it) and as the reader, from his superior vantage place and with his superior information, knows it actually to be. The mood or response created by this distance is that of irony, and irony is indeed the effect of virtually every story in **The Doctor's Son,** as it is also generally characteristic of the sensibility story.

This irony may function in two ways. In its most familiar application O'Hara operates as a comic writer and a satirist by aligning himself with the reader and with commonly accepted standards *against* the fictional character; he thus makes the character and his behavior the objects of ridicule and punishment. What O'Hara aims at in such stories have traditionally been the targets for the satirist's shafts: snobbery, viciousness, ostentation, self-importance, conformity; and it is to O'Hara's credit that he riddles human follies and pretensions with savage effectiveness. If O'Hara's satirical stories are not his most profound work—although they lack nothing in cleverness and subtlety—the fault is less O'Hara's than that of satire itself. By its very nature satire forestalls profundity because profundity inhibits the immediate response which satire wishes to arouse.

The first kind of irony, the satirical form, characterizes the majority of stories in **The Doctor's Son,** as it is also prevalent in O'Hara's short fiction written during the 1930's and 1940's. Inveterately, O'Hara's aim is to demonstrate that men are not so good as they think themselves, or that their true motives are quite other than those they confess. Such pieces as **"Ella and the Chinee," "On His Hands,"** and **"The Girl Who Had Been Presented"** set forth savagely comic satirical portraits of egotists who sacrifice others to their own supposedly superior selves, but in truth they are inferior to those they reject or despise.

Other stories, for example **"It Wouldn't Break Your Arm,"** present strikingly accurate satirical likenesses of certain types, in this case the vindictive ex-wife who under the guise of friendship conveys a disturbing piece of information to her recently divorced husband. Occasionally O'Hara plays a variation upon his satirical technique, es-

pecially in the monologue, by presenting in an inflated eu-
logistic style the lives of nonentities whom the eulogist
wishes to exalt to heroic stature. This is a type of hyperbole, a mock hyperbole: the trivial and mundane rendered
even more trivial by the attempt to dignify and elevate it.
Such tales, **"Walter T. Carriman"** and **"Mrs. Whitman"**
in *Pipe Night,* are especially notable for what they suggest
of the tensions, failures, and defeats which the eulogists attempt to gloss over. Once more the result is comic irony,
particularly poignant and subtle because it is double-
edged in its exposure of both the eulogized and the eulo-
gizer.

There is a sub-species of O'Hara's work in this ironic vein
which one hesitates to call "satire" because the comic element has vanished. This species might be labeled "Portraits of Heels," although the word "heel" fails to properly
convey the relentless thoroughness of O'Hara's depiction.
Such portraits are most common in O'Hara's Broadway-
Hollywood fiction, but are by no means limited to it. For
example, two of the best stories in *Hellbox* depict superficially different but fundamentally similar men. **"Someone
to Trust"** concerns a small-time mobster, in hiding from
his former associates, who bends a trusting ex-girl friend
to his purposes by expertly and coldbloodedly playing
upon her generosity and sentimentality. **"Wise Guy"** is a
skillful constructed tale wherein the narrator incriminates
himself by both word and deed. Separated from his son by
divorce, he first forgets and then violates an occasion of
reunion with the boy in order to keep a date with one of
his female chums. Any concern with the child's feelings
occurs to the father only as an irritation.

A female of this same species appears in **"Olive"** (*Files on
Parade*)**,** a sardonic tale about a hotel switchboard operator whose built-in sense of social inferiority expresses itself
in the deliberate destruction of a budding and tender relationship between a spinster and an elderly man. These despicable characters all have reason for what they do, but
there is a surplus of savagery in them, a gratuitous viciousness not explicable as an outcome of their need to survive;
and this sort of malice O'Hara hates and makes his object.
Whatever one may call these stories, "satire" no longer
seems the proper name.

Actually, the portraits of heels occupy a transitional position between O'Hara's two basic modes of irony. The second kind, the irony inherent in the nature of human nature
or the conditions of life or the workings of fate, functions
in fewer stories of *The Doctor's Son* and the other collections; but such stories are the more serious and memorable. While in the satiric tales the reader aligned himself
with the world against the fictional character, in the stories concerned with irony of character and circumstance
the writer wishes to disclose some hard truth about the
way things are, to lay bare some secret we once knew but
have almost managed to forget, to bring to light some buried facet of character. In these stories the fundamental
irony is that inherent in the human condition, the irony
of sensitive creatures with ideals and illusions existing in
a universe in which the ideal appears only accidentally, if
at all, and never for very long. But O'Hara is not at any
point "philosophical" or "cosmic"; he avoids such ab-

stractions. Always he works with people, and only with
people.

To come to cases, in **"The Doctor's Son,"** the first and longest story in O'Hara's earliest collection, there are two
ironic developments: first, that disease kills haphazardly,
so that the good often die while the evil flourish; second,
that the pressures which ought to stimulate the growth of
love often stifle it instead. These developments illustrate
both the irony of fate acting as a capricious force, and the
irony of fate as it alters character. Another story communicating the same sort of irony is **"All the Girls He Wanted."** In it a young married woman, expecting to be con-
soled by her best friend about the death of a man she secretly loves, is herself called upon to supply the consolation to the best friend—whom she learns was the dead
man's mistress. Yet another is **"Straight Pool,"** wherein
a good but insensitive man, distraught by his marital problems, confesses his troubles to the very fellow responsible
for them.

Two stories which graphically demonstrate what might be
termed the irony of character, that which stems from mis-
judging or misunderstanding others or one's self being
misunderstood, are **"Sportsmanship"** and **"Over the
River and Through the Wood."** These, with a few others,
are the worthiest stories in the volume and, in general, rep-

O'Hara at the time of Pipe Night.

resent the kinds of O'Hara short fiction which will endure. **"Sportsmanship"** chillingly demonstrates that the quality of mercy does not reside in every human breast: a young man tries to make restitution to his former employer, owner of a poolroom, by returning to work off his debt for money he has stolen; he does fulfill his promise, serving faithfully until the entire sum has been paid back, only to be mutilated for his unforgiven crime.

"Over the River and Through the Wood," another story reflecting unquestionable artistry (how have anthologists missed it?), unforgettably portrays the final defeat of a now aging and almost broken but once rich, attractive, and important man. His defeat stems from his gesture of friendship toward a beautiful, arrogant young woman, a gesture which she in part misconstrues and attributes to his depravity, and a gesture whose motive the reader himself must ponder. In any case, her contemptuous rejection of him annihilates what little remains of his dignity and self-respect.

Failure, defeat, loss, pain, misfortune, cruelty are the themes dominant in O'Hara's better stories. Occasionally one finds such a tale as **"I Never Seen Anything Like It"** (in which a speakeasy proprietor recounts how his place was burglarized, marveling all the while at the superb smoothness and efficiency of the hoodlums) that is rich with comic humor. And, as has been seen, humor is rarely absent from the satirical portraits and sketches so prominent in O'Hara's early work, although the comic and satiric stories do not lodge most firmly in the memory. The others—those dealing with the terrors of aging, or the conflict between the old and the young, with the tribulations of love, with the lot of the lonely, the outcast, and the suffering—are the tales which affect the reader most deeply.

Representative of this latter group is the strongly autobiographical **"The Doctor's Son,"** already mentioned above, which invites comparison to such early Hemingway pieces as "Indian Camp." Not only is the style Hemingwayesque—its terse sentences indited by the youthful narrator who speaks as if through clenched teeth—but also the theme: a boy's initiation into life and his forced recognition of its agonies. During the influenza epidemic in which Jimmy Malloy acts as a driver both for his overworked doctor-father and for a medical student brought in to assist in this emergency, he learns about disease, death, and deceit. Although as a physician's son in a mining community young Malloy is not unused to death and sickness, the amount here overwhelms him. The atmosphere of disease and unpredictable disaster is further accentuated by what he observes of man's inner corruption, especially the conduct of Mrs. Evans with the young man who has come in to heal and save. Against this background the story poses an ironic counterpoint, that between "Love" (both Mrs. Evans' adulterous love for Dr. Meyers and Jimmy's own pure love for Edith Evans) and Death, which seems to prefer as its victims the good, the strong, the innocent, and the gentle. As a final irony it seems that love, both pure and depraved, is a graveyard flower best nourished by disease and death. Hardly a cheerful or uplifting story, this, but there is nothing trivial about it.

In accord with the predominantly ironic view of his earlier story collections, O'Hara's inquiries into human nature are more likely to sadden than exhilarate. Most frequently he uncovers some wickedness, some depravity, some buried sin, often where one least expects it. A number of stories in *Pipe Night* are among many that could be cited in support of this conclusion. In **"On Time"** Laura, the story's protagonist, thought a model of virtue and dependability by her friends, regains her lost pride by cruelly lying to her former lover about the circumstances of a crucial rendezvous. Likewise, Kathy in **"Too Young,"** betrays the adoration of her young admirer when he learns that she is cheap enough to take her pleasure with a tough motorcycle cop. Nor is there anything especially admirable about either partner of the decaying marriage portrayed in **"Radio."** The wife who has deceived her husband invites no more disdain than the nasty-mouthed and petty man she has cuckolded. But no matter how disenchanted O'Hara's perspective in these stories, one never infers misanthropy. There is too much regard for what people suffer. No one who reads such a story as **"Now We Know,"** with its poignant portrayal of a doomed-from-the-start love between a Jewish bus driver and his Irish passenger, a receptionist, could ever suspect O'Hara of the callousness and contempt for humans which is essential to misanthropy. O'Hara is simply a Realist.

Although irony pervades the best stories among those published during the first two decades of O'Hara's career, *The Doctor's Son, Files on Parade, Pipe Night,* and *Hellbox* are all softened and illuminated by a compassion which tempers the irony, keeping it from nihilism and despair. In such pieces as **"The Man Who Had to Talk to Somebody," "Alone," "Hotel Kid,"** and **"In the Morning Sun"** (all from *The Doctor's Son*), O'Hara reveals his sympathy with the lonely, the outcast, and the suffering: a man who has lost his family and status because of imprisonment for a bad check and yet who does not seek pity, only someone to listen to him when he is compelled to air his misery; a recently widowed husband about to attend burial services for his wife, who has drowned; an intelligent and forelorn little boy who spends his childhood in hotel corridors while his mother, a high-class prostitute, travels from city to city in search of big money; a man of once-compelling mind and personality, exhausted before he is thirty, afflicted by some incalculable and inexpressible inner torment—these are some of the characters and situations which evoke O'Hara's compassionate response. Furthermore, O'Hara's affection and admiration for certain kinds of people stand out in such stories as **"Pleasure,"** in which O'Hara delineates the stern self-discipline of a working girl whose life is lived so close to the bone that her concept of pleasure is to smoke an entire cigarette.

Files on Parade, a collection generally not complimentary to O'Hara because so much of it consists of mere sketches, anecdotes, and vignettes, nevertheless contains two stories which show both O'Hara's compassion and his deep knowledge of human behavior. **"The Cold House"** is a delicate and moving tale about a woman who travels to her summer house in the attempt to recapture the memory of her son, buried not long before. However, she realizes that if she makes an altar of her grief and a museum of her dead son's possessions, she will soil and pervert her true feelings for him, and so she returns to her own life in the city. A few lines from this story demand citation for what they illustrate of the tautness of O'Hara's prose and the discipline with which he handles emotion:

> She could see clearly, like watching a motion picture of herself, what she would have done, what she had been in terrible danger of doing: next August, next September, a year from next August and a year from next July, she would have come up here, unlocked the door, come in this room and stood. She saw herself, a woman in white, trying to squeeze out a tear at the sight of these things of wood and brass and paper and glass—and all the while distracted by the sounds of passing cars, the children next door, the telephone downstairs, the whirring vacuum cleaner. And she even knew the end of this motion picture: she would end by hating a memory that she only knew how to love.

O'Hara's extraordinary insight into the thoughts and emotions of the old extends as well to his treatment of the minds and hearts of the young. **"Do You Like It Here?"** deals with the persecution of a new boy at a fashionable prep school by one of the school's resident instructors. The master accuses the student of stealing, a gambit which is but the beginning of a whole process of terrorization which will destroy the boy's life at the school. And because he is the son of divorced parents and has moved from place to place, he lacks the stability of background and record which would make him invulnerable to persecution. An even more ominous undertone sounds if one infers, as the story suggests, that there has been no theft at all and that a sadistic instructor torments his chosen victim for his own perverse pleasure. Yet what could have been a bitter, dead-end tale is made deeply affecting because of O'Hara's involvement in the destiny of his protagonist.

Virtually all of O'Hara's basic techniques of short fiction are exhibited in *The Doctor's Son* and in the other collections between 1935 and 1947. In *The Doctor's Son,* as elsewhere, almost every tale is related by a speaking voice. Sometimes it is the single voice of the story's central character cast in the form of satirical monologue. Sometimes the voice is that of the first-person narrator who may be merely the source of information about the story's protagonist (the "I as Witness" approach) as in **"The Man Who Had to Talk to Somebody"** and **"Hotel Kid"**; or the narrator may himself be the central character (the "I as Protagonist"), as in **"The Doctor's Son"** and in **"It Must Have Been Spring."** Sometimes one overhears the voice of the protagonist speaking to himself (the interior monologue), as in **"It Wouldn't Break Your Arm," "Back in New Haven,"** and **"All the Girls He Wanted."** Or O'Hara may combine two points of view, opening in the conventional manner of the editorial omniscient to establish setting and cast, and then subtly shifting into the interior monologue as in **"Mrs. Galt and Edwin"** and in **"In the Morning Sun"**—or into dialogue which constitutes the remainder of the story as in **"The Girl Who Had Been Presented"** and in **"On His Hands."**

Even when O'Hara employs, as he often does, the editorial omniscient, one has the sense of *listening* to a story rather than seeing it on the page. Description and narration are at a minimum; dialogue is virtually all. Thus, O'Hara's method is the dramatic rather than the panoramic. What we learn from these stories we learn as in life: by watching people behave and listening to them speak. Further, O'Hara has the marvelous gift of constructing exactly the sort of dramatic scene, of catching precisely the tones and shadings and inflections which enable, indeed which require, the reader to grasp the truth. At his best he gives us an unsurpassed sense of reality, of life happening *now,* as if spontaneously.

Another of O'Hara's fundamental and characteristic methods, undoubtedly developed in the short story before being employed in the novels, is that already seen elsewhere: the delayed revelation. In the stories O'Hara makes it serve as the uncovering, usually at the last moment, of some essential fact or happening (often in the character's past) which completes the reader's knowledge of the protagonist and permits him to distinguish between the character's version of reality and reality itself. We watch and listen, learning as the story (and the speaking voice) proceed. We suspect, conjecture, infer until at last we *know.* To O'Hara's credit this delayed revelation is rarely of the sort still employed in the well-made story as it was perfected by O. Henry; that is, it does not ordinarily involve some new development or unforeseen twist of circumstance. Rather, it is the final and culminating piece of information which impels the reader to complete his conjectures and suspicions, and from them to draw illuminating conclusions.

By this method O'Hara also achieves many of his ironic effects. For example, in **"Mary,"** the story of a beautiful but unlettered Polish girl who rises in the world by dint of her charms and their shrewd dispensation, we perceive what Mary really is (despite her lavish apartment, fashionable address, and imposing manners) in the story's concluding lines: "One night I called her and she had nothing to do, so I went to see her. I was very careful of my behavior, never batting an eye when she said 'eyether,' and drinking my highball in a chair that was a room's width away from her. The telephone rang. She answered it and made a date with the voice at the other end of the wire. She hung up and smiled at me. 'That was Ted Frisbee, the polo-player,' she said. 'I'm awf'ly fond of him. He has such a nice sense of yoomer.' "

As in the passage above, the effect may be satirical, in this case gently and comically so. Elsewhere the revelation may be far more somber, opening up to the reader a vista of anguish already suffered and more pain yet to come. In **"In the Morning Sun"** a mother watches her twenty-seven year old son who has already been through a destructive divorce, a serious illness, and other possible disasters. As in other such instances of the delayed revelation, this entire story pivots upon a slight action and a few whispered words: "She stood up again and looked out at Sam. He was not reading, he did not look as though he cared or knew whether there was anyone else in the world. When she first looked, he was leaning forward and his hands covered his forehead and temples and eyes, and then his head went back and his tired face faced the sky, and she could almost hear him saying it: 'Oh. Oh.' And his mother shivered, for there was nothing she could do.''

From these examples it should be apparent that, while the delayed revelation is essentially a technique, a mode of construction, it also connotes the writer's world-view. Given thematic application and interpretation, the delayed revelation states O'Hara's belief that human beings always retain some mystery concealed to even their most intimate associates, and that the dullest and seemingly most predictable is a creature of infinite variety. Whether or not this is the ultimate truth about people, once the reader enters O'Hara's imagined world, he convinces us that it is so. No mere hack could accomplish this sort of persuasion.

Since O'Hara's expertise as a writer of short stories has often been admired but rarely discussed in detail and almost never subjected to close analysis, a careful study of two representative stories should serve to support some of the conclusions advanced above and to convey a more precise understanding of O'Hara's method. **"Radio"** (*Pipe Night*) and **"Horizon"** (*Hellbox*) are characteristic pieces. Both are relatively short, tightly written, and quietly effective; and, although one might hesitate to call them the best of O'Hara, they are certainly typical of the good O'Hara. Both also illustrate the pervasive irony of O'Hara's earlier stories.

"Horizon" employs that point-of-view which O'Hara does peculiarly well: the editorial omniscient which merges into the interior monologue. While the surface of the story remains consistently third person, with O'Hara and the reader seemingly viewing the characters from outside, with the characters referred to by name or third-person pronoun, and with verbs cast in the past tense, actually O'Hara works much of the time from inside the protagonist's mind to apprise the reader of hidden truths no observer could know. As a result, the reader—without realizing just how and when—moves from the vantage place of third person to first person, from outside to inside.

Strictly speaking, this is not interior monologue of the Proustian or Joycean sort because one does not get the complete impression of participating in thoughts at the very instant of their formulation, of being borne on a stream of sensual responses, of hearing the inchoate and incessant flow of silent speech uttered in the brain. O'Hara can achieve this impression also, and he does employ the classic interior monologue on occasion, as in the story **"Alone"** (*The Doctor's Son*); but, much more characteristically, he conjoins the finished and conclusive effect derived from the objective mode with the immediate and concrete effect of the subjective.

A citation from **"Horizon"** should illustrate how observations which could come only from the outside are intermingled with those which could only be originated by the protagonist. Although I have italicized only those few lines which O'Hara casts strictly in the form of interior monologue, in actuality it would be extraordinarily difficult for the reader to distinguish between what the charac-

ter is thinking and what the author is observing. Shortly after the story begins, its protagonist—McGuire, a longtime newspaperman—gazes out his office window and meditates upon his past:

> For eighteen years this side of the state capitol had been his horizon. *Well, that was not precisely true.* He had only been sitting at a desk facing the city room, and beyond it, this side of the capitol ten years—about ten years. There had been the times he had sat in on the night desk, when his horizon was the mailboxes and newspaper files. *You could take those times out of the eighteen years. You could also take out the four months* when he had undergone a miserable self-imposed exile as managing editor of the *Beacon.* The *Beacon* being on Front Street, he hadn't even seen the capitol dome. At the *Beacon* his horizon had been Holzheimer's Storage Warehouse—Long Distance Moving. But anyway, to all intents and purposes he was now looking at what had been his horizon for either ten or eighteen years. *Either way it was no good, and eighteen was only a little worse than ten. You didn't get used to hanging if you hung long enough.* With some bitterness McGuire reflected that hoodlums could have painted dirty words on the other side of the state capitol, or a strange art commission could have painted it with pink and blue diagonal stripes, and he wouldn't have known about it. Oh, he'd have *heard* about it [O'Hara's italics], and most likely in the case of a story as important as that he would have done the rewrite job on it. But in the ordinary course of his life, he would not have seen the words or the stripes.

By such simple yet expert methods does O'Hara attain the effect of simultaneity and depth.

The passage above contains yet other evidence of the subtlety of O'Hara's approach. This excerpt from the second paragraph of the story already conveys something of the desolation, loneliness, and emotional poverty of McGuire's life. That is the very crux of the story, as well as its ironic point, for McGuire invites comparison with such other tormented souls as Melville's Bartleby. Indeed, McGuire with his fixed view of the wall of the state capitol, with his profession as a kind of scrivener, and with his inability to engage in deeply meaningful interchange with other humans reminds the reader of Bartleby; but McGuire is a more verbal and familiar figure. If O'Hara hardly equals Melville's enormous genius, his more limited aims are admirably executed. Suspicious of metaphor and not a symbolist in any wide sense of the term, O'Hara does capably employ emblems to underscore his meaning. Thus in the passage just cited there are a series of ironic wordplays and cunning juxtapositions which underlie O'Hara's seemingly transparent prose and intensify the story's theme and impact.

The first and most obvious of the ironic devices is the wordplay involved in the contrast between the word "horizon"—the leitmotif of the passage and the title of the story, with all it suggests of distance, vastness, hope, possibility—and such other words as "desk," "city room" (in itself an ironic combination), "mailboxes," "files," *Front*

Street" (my italics), and "storage warehouse." A second ironic implication is the notion that such a man as Mc-Guire once managed a newspaper called the *Beacon,* with all it connotes of illumination, freedom, inquiry, idealism; and, even more ironic, McGuire found his employment there "a miserable self-imposed exile."

A third ironic device is O'Hara's contrast of McGuire's present existence with the two buildings whose exteriors McGuire knows better than any others and whose walls he has come to think of as a sort of prison, the state capitol and the storage warehouse. Although much that goes on in a state capitol is dull, much of it is also momentous, involving decisions and crises affecting multitudes of people. Similarly, a storage warehouse does not on first thought seem a very stimulating place; but, when one realizes that this is the warehouse of a long-distance moving company and that the objects it contains have been heaped up by the constant flux and change which are the backwash of modern life, one sees again demonstrated that lack of imagination, that unwillingness or inability to unleash the heart and mind which are precisely McGuire's defects and which in fact constitute his "self-imposed exile."

Further, in his visualization of such events as the deface-ment of the state capitol by "hoodlums" or its adornment by a "strange art commission" one perceives McGuire's conceptualization of any lapse from the routine as dis-tasteful. These thoughts are a final insight into McGuire's mental patterns. But what prevents him from simply walking around to look at the other side of the state capi-tol, or from taking a different and longer way to work? McGuire could supply no answers to such questions, other than that it never occurred to him to do so, or that it was too much trouble. Only chance or some special as-signment could propel him out of his customary path. Be-cause the reader knows this, because O'Hara has made him know it, he realizes that McGuire will never carry out his sudden impulse to quit his job and strike out for new horizons. One realizes, too, that McGuire's greatest ad-venture will be the mere contemplation of the idea of quit-ting, of shattering the mold. In this fashion O'Hara com-bines in **"Horizon"** ironic technique with irony of theme. Withal, the story leaves no corrosive taste upon the read-er's palate because O'Hara not only presents McGuire but also *judges* him with mercy and concern.

Like many O'Hara stories, **"Radio"** is written in the edito-rial omniscient mode, but most of the tale actually consists of dialogue. All narration and description are kept at an absolute minimum. The work opens with three short ex-pository sentences setting the scene and identifying the main characters, and from time to time there are other ex-tremely brief narrative passages, stage directions really, interposed to provide continuity. In fact, because all but a hundred words of the story are dialogue, it could with very little revision be staged as an exceedingly compact but complete one-act play.

Since the dialogue must carry such heavy weight, taking upon itself the burdens usually borne by narration, de-scription, and exposition, it must be totally convincing and representative of its speakers; and it is. The speakers are a badly educated man and wife of lower middle class.

However, they are neither obtuse nor grossly ignorant. They have that hard practical intelligence, that keen func-tional awareness, that capacity for double-meanings, in-sinuations, and repartee which is true both of a particular kind of person and of one type of standard O'Hara charac-ter. In any case, the writer, who depicts them with unchal-lengeable fidelity, discerns just the right grammatical er-rors, slang and catch-phrases, constructions and locu-tions, to set them perfectly as to class and background. More profoundly, he conveys that mixture of ignorance and knowledge, that pretense of sophisticated cynicism adopted in order to disguise basic confusion, which char-acterize an intellect in quasi-developed condition. For ex-ample, there is this discussion of popularity polls:

> She rubbed her lower lip. "I wonder who they call up and ask them what they're listening to. They never asked me. I don't even know any-body they ever asked."
>
> "That's not the way they do it anymore. They have another way of doing it nowadays."
>
> "How do they, then?" she said.
>
> "Well, they still use the phone in some cases. In certain cases they call up and ask you what pro-gram are you listening to, but then they have other ways too."
>
> "*What* other ways?"
>
> "Why, they take some kind of a cross section of the public—what income bracket you're in, how many cars do you own, how many radios and so on, and they figure out how many people are lis-tening to such-and-such a program."
>
> "How could they figure it out if they didn't ask you?"
>
> "They don't have to ask each individual party. They have their own way of doping it out from some kind of a formula. Naturally they don't go around blabbing what the formula is, or other-wise why couldn't I steal the formula and go into business for myself with their idea?"
>
> "In other words, you don't know."
>
> "Of course I don't know. I never pretended as if I did know."
>
> "Oh, no, certainly not. If I wouldn't of asked you a simple question like how did they figure it out you would of gone on all night talking like a big authority on the subject, and wouldn't that be typical."

Such painfully comic and superbly accurate rendition of marital bickering comprises most of the story, and from this sample one can understand why certain critics have claimed that O'Hara could not write his dialogue but must catch it instead on some recording device. But there is an-other than linguistic dimension. The passage just cited also transmits something of the motivation, of the very quality, of each of the marital partners. He is pompous and verbally self-assertive as a cover for his essential sense of inferiority. She is wholly pragmatic, impressed only by demonstrated results. One suspects that she continually leads her husband into such traps precisely so as to gain further opportunities to undercut him—opportunities she would never bypass. Deeper yet, it is likely that her husband's bluster but fundamental ineffectuality as a man (an ineffectuality she promulgates by her castration techniques) have allowed her, perhaps even impelled her, to seek gratification outside of marriage with a man formerly their friend, a man we also infer has the charm and daring her husband lacks.

However, the wife's adultery is not revealed until the last twenty lines of the story; and once revealed, the couple's irritability with one another, the sarcastic edge of each remark, and the tangible atmosphere of tension and hostility suddenly leap into new and sharper perspective. The reader had attributed the bickering to the kind of incompatibility, the contempt bred by familiarity, the consistent mediocrity common to many (the cynic would say *most*) marriages. The husband's role becomes especially coherent, for he has learned of his wife's misbehavior without her awareness of his special knowledge. This knowledge has given him the upper hand in the marriage, for the first time one suspects; and, ironically true to his wife's conception of him, his new role only intensifies his arrogance. Yet, to her surprise, his arrogance is now no longer mere bluster. With the realization that he has been cuckolded, Klauser becomes a man—or, more accurately, a male. If this is not to say he becomes a whole human being, at least he discovers enough nerve in his sense of his wife's vulnerability to take command of the cave, for the present. And so the story ends, as Klauser confronts his wife with her misdeed and simultaneously assumes mastery:

> He got up and went to her. "Thinking of the children all of a sudden, eh? How about at Rockaway, those times you and Harry—I guess you were thinking about the children then? And a couple of other times I could mention I'm not suppose to know about." He slapped her hard across the face. "You bitch."
>
> "Don't you hit me again," she said.
>
> "Sure I will," he said, and did. "As much as I want to, because, Baby, you're stuck." He walked to a taboret where he kept his rye. He took out a pint bottle and held it up to the light. He began to sing softly: "Da-da de da-da de da. 'Don't get around much any more.' Baby, are you stuck!"
>
> She nodded. "Uh-huh," she said. "I'm stuck."

With this exchange of sarcasms, as each character makes his separate plans for the future and the reader enjoys a multiple awareness of the ironic possibilities inherent in the situation, O'Hara wins through to one of his most admirable effects: a sense of the ongoing current of existence. Whatever happens between Klauser and his wife, their lives can never be as they were. The ultimate irony is that each is "stuck" with the other; that, if Klauser continues to play the overlord, he will lose all remaining chances for serenity. So, too, the wife must realize that she can neither go back to her former status as loyal spouse nor on to other lovers without surrendering the shards of her self-respect.

These ironies of characterization and theme are emphasized and counterpointed by the story's deployment of language. The entire conversation which ends in the revelation and crisis stems from the song "Don't Get Around Much Any More," broadcast over the radio in what at first appears to be a cosy domestic scene. The husband hears the song, comments upon it, one remark engenders another, until finally the words of the refrain, "don't get around much any more," are turned back upon the wife in Klauser's exposure of her infidelity. There is yet other ironic wordplay. Throughout the story we note the stress upon and repetition of such words as "funny" and "laugh," underscoring this hardly humorous situation. The word "radio" also recurs, signifying the dehumanized quality of the couple's relationship. Perhaps the most telling technique of all, which cannot be fully described but only named, is O'Hara's skill in arranging all the seemingly random, disjointed, and offhand remarks of this apparently routine marital bickering into a subtle and tightly woven pattern delineating the texture of two lives. With all its swerves, irrelevancies, and circumlocutions, the dialogue drives swiftly and powerfully to its intended goal. It recalls similar treatments by Chekhov of the dreariness of many common lives.

Sheldon Norman Grebstein, in his John O'Hara, *Twayne Publishers, Inc., 1966, 175 p.*

Charles Child Walcutt (essay date 1969)

[*In the following excerpt from his study* John O'Hara, *Walcutt discusses* Pipe Night *and* Sermons and Soda-Water.]

Pipe Night is [a collection of stories and sketches that display familiar O'Hara characteristics] bordering on reportage, glimpses of all sorts of American people caught with their blinds down and their frailties glaring. Thirty-one sketches in a small volume concentrate on showing literally just *how* people talk, try to communicate, and usually fail because they do not have the language or the manners and knowledge of manners that would enable them to think below the surface of the clichés among which they live. They are epiphanies of the moral and cultural underworld that prevails in our time. Brittle tableaux of empty people. Voices perfectly heard and reproduced, echoing emptinesses. Here there are no rich, yearning, inarticulate inner selves striving to communicate, but rather the jangling, brassy notes of cheap instruments that have never been tuned toward gentleness or understanding.

The range and accuracy of O'Hara's observation compensate richly for the bleak deprivations of spirit upon which his eye consistently lights. Their qualities can be felt if we review several of them. **"Walter T. Carriman"** is a verbose, fatuous "tribute" by a friend, whose prose style is represented by the following sentence: "Not having been surrounded in his childhood by great riches, which have been known to disappear overnight, leaving their possessors with memories to dwell upon to the boredom of less comfortably placed friends of later years, Walter, on the other hand, was not raised in poverty and squalor, the details of which can, in their recital save in the hands of a

Dickens or an equally great artist, prove equally boresome." The peaks of eulogizing rhetoric are regularly separated by valleys (if not crevasses) of qualification. Walter was fond of sports in the required American fashion until the high-school "training rules proved irksome to a lad of Walter's spirit and he dropped the sport in freshman year. (The truth is that Walter took his first cigarette at the age of fourteen and from then on was a rather heavy smoker.)" The resonating pomposities carry Walter from theater usher to classified-ad taker ("a post requiring infinite patience, a good ear, a cheery speaking voice, and a legible hand, the last, by the way, an accomplishment of Walter's which I seem to have overlooked in my 'roundup' of the man's numerous good points") to food checker to freight clerk, after which "Walter next returned to the transportation field, serving briefly as a conductor on the street railways of Asbury Park . . ."; thence to night clerk in a hotel and so on to obesity and an early death by heart failure. The banality of the life glows in the falsity of the tribute, and the two combine to convey a sense of barrenness that would be hard to exceed.

Until we move on to the following sketches. **"Now We Know"** is the brief exchange between a bus driver and a girl who gets on his bus first, at the end of the line, every morning. He makes jokes like not opening the door till she bangs on it, conversations follow, and presently he declares his love along with the news that he has asked for a transfer to another line. He has a wife and children that he cannot leave, but he can think of nothing but the new girl. So now they know. The moment of anguished confession escapes from the life sealed in the quiet desperation of routine. **"Free"** tells of a lady from Pasadena arriving at her hotel in New York for an annual three-day shopping spree. With plenty of money, her family left behind but safe, she takes a hot bath and plans her day with a daydream: she will exchange warm looks with a handsome man in the street, and then she will pass on without encouraging him further. She'd like to, but she will not, although she is "free." In **"Can You Carry Me"** a vulgar motion-picture actress abuses the editor of a magazine that has published an unfriendly article. Over drinks, she tells him that she is suing his magazine for a million dollars—until they get pretty drunk and go to bed together.

"A Purchase of Some Golf Clubs" gets its interest from what is unsaid. A girl sits in a bar drinking; a mechanic off duty talks to her, discovers that she is trying to sell an elegant set of golf clubs, with a leather bag, for twenty-five dollars. She has to have the money to retain a lawyer because her husband is in jail for hitting a man with his car while drunk. So the fellow takes the clubs, although he never plays golf, and the girl says she wishes he didn't drink so much. All this amounts to is the briefest encounter between people from (apparently) very different ways of life. The boy in **"Too Young"** is a high-school sophomore infatuated with a college girl at the beach club, who discovers that she is having an affair with a motorcycle cop. He thought her sublimely untouchable; she was using the cop, cynically, to satisfy her physical needs. In **"Summer's Day"** the ubiquitous theme of status cuts across the pathos of age. A very old couple—but he is wearing the hatband of a Yale club—accept the homage of a rising

Irishman who did not make any club at Yale. In the bathhouse the old man overhears teen-agers talking about what a pitiful old pair he and his wife are, hears the Irishman smack one of them briskly for his bad manners, and wonders how he will ever again be able to face the Irishman or his wife, "But then of course he realized that there was really nothing to face, really nothing." In **"Radio"** a couple trade abuse and insults over one Harry, who owes money to the husband and has had an affair with the wife. One gathers that this Harry so impressed the husband that he was putty in Harry's hands, and now the husband strikes his wife some hard blows in the face and tells her that she is "stuck" with him for good. The cruel, stupid dialogue seems unsurpassably authentic. In **"Nothing Missing"** a fellow fresh from a year in prison stops in a small-town gift and book shop, talks to the apprehensive girl in charge, stares at her—and stares (not having seen a girl for a year)—then leaves dispiritedly. Again, no communication.

A couple of hard, smart guys from Hollywood make fun of **"The King of the Desert,"** a dude rancher, needling and subtly mocking, until one of them gets careless and says to the other, " 'What'd I tell you? A bit of a jerk' "—and lands on the floor, out cold, from the rancher's punch. Significantly, it is status again—the rancher's admission that he feels a bit superior because he comes from *Mayflower* stock—that precipitates the explosion. A tavern owner running **"A Respectable Place"** makes the mistake of letting the Patrolmen's Benevolent Fund pay the damage when a drunken cop shoots up his bar. He makes no complaint, just lets them take care of the damage; but the cops harass him with contrived summonses, and he soon has to close his place. In another story Laura meets by chance the man she loved passionately and planned to run away with ten years ago. She was **"On Time,"** but he did not appear, and so she went back to her husband. Now she learns from him that he was hit by a taxi and broke a leg on that critical day. Relief from her humiliation flows over her like balm. To set the score straight, however, she tells him that, after all, she had changed her mind and did not come to their meeting place. In **"Graven Image"** a gentleman named Browning meets an Under Secretary, who is clearly not a gentleman, for dinner in a Washington hotel. Browning, an old-line conservative, wants a job in the war machine from his successful friend. They define their status-gap when the Under Secretary notices that Browning, wearing a wristwatch, does not show his Porcellian emblem on a chain, and the latter tells Joe that if he had made the exclusive club at Harvard he might not have had the resentful drive that had carried him to the top. Mollified, the Under Secretary promises the job; Browning is so pleased that he orders a celebrative drink—and then makes his fatal error in a passage that must be quoted. Notice how Browning reveals the arrogance of class, the arrogance that cannot feel what it is like to be on the outside looking hungrily in, the arrogance that is, finally, unforgivable. Browning says:

> "But as to you, Joe, you're the best. I drink to you." The two men drank, the Under Secretary sipping at his, Browning taking half of his. Browning looked at the drink in his hand. "You

know, I was a little afraid. That other stuff, the club stuff.''

"Yes," said the Under Secretary.

"I don't know why fellows like you—you never would have made it in a thousand years, but"—then, without looking up, he knew everything had collapsed—"but I've said exactly the wrong thing, haven't I?"

"That's right, Browning," said the Under Secretary. "You've said exactly the wrong thing. I've got to be going."

The reversal in this story is very neat: one's sympathy must be with the gentleman Browning at first, for the Under Secretary demonstrates an uncouth arrogance of power as well as bad manners; but Browning is destroyed at the end by a deeper and blinder arrogance.

The catalogue of exhibits continues with a drunken movie star, a middle-aged stockbroker unaccountably in love with a charming teen-ager, a civilian having an affair with a navy wife and suffering in a mixture of passion, subterfuge, and disloyalty, and a dozen more. Always the ear is perfect, the setting quickly and deftly established, the marks of conflicting status delineated. A night-club girl talking to a sailor says, " 'Also I was with a unit we entertained for the sailors a couple places.' " He explains somewhat illiterately that he is getting training in diesels and saving his money. She thinks he is a hick, but she would like to be considered as a person by him. He thinks she is an "actress" with vast experience—and ends by calling her "hustler" when she rebuffs him. Thus two on approximately the same level cannot penetrate their own stereotypes. Their misadventure is balanced by a hilarious conversation in which a punchy fighter tries to bribe an ethical editor to buy some stories about the ring.

O'Hara has made his own little genre in these sketches. It's a world of snobs and misfits where the elements of culture and status do not cohere into any approach to the good life. The people are crude, or trapped, or hateful, or greedy, or arrogant. They are edgy and suspicious, feeling their ways among the shadows of ignorance, fear, and mistrust. Swagger, cruelty, wealth, success do not finally enable them to escape from the prison of self.

From the Gibbsville base and the theater-world side, we move to the other side: New York-Philadelphia-Washington business and society, which completes the triangle of O'Hara subjects. Of course the three areas overlap, in the person of their narrator.

Sermons and Soda Water is composed of three novellas related by one Jim Malloy, the writer who has been the O'Hara persona since *Appointment in Samarra*. Malloy had not made the social grade in Gibbsville, being Catholic and new there. But now he has risen so high that he hardly thinks about old Gibbsville. He has rubbed elbows with movie stars and shared pillows with Long Island socialites from old, old families. These stories are presented as insightful (if condescending) anecdotes on How It Is by one who knows all the postures of American status. One look and Malloy can tell how much class is present. Classy people cannot be known by their conduct—for they are

capable of everything—unless it is viewed by an expert. He places them accurately whether they do anything or not. The rich and well-born are freer than their simpler compatriots; they suffer extremes of privilege and frustration; their class is to be known by nuances of speech and attitude that are not always visible to the common reader; if they have a quality in common that Malloy seems to admire, perhaps it is guts—or a certain aplomb in coming to terms with what happens to them.

These novellas are distinguished by an unusual manner and tone. The narrator tells them as the events appeared to *him,* so that in effect each story is an incident of autobiography. There are the characters, and then there is the way they appeared or related to Malloy. He sees them at intervals and is brought up-to-date on events. He can record his conversations with them, or he can tell us how they seemed to him or how he felt about them after a time. So he lives among them not as a character but as an autobiographical representative of the author. The effect is unusual and interesting; it is as if the reader were privileged to spend a long night with O'Hara in his study while he chatted easily and discursively about his recollections, assuming that his friendly companion was more interested in the storyteller than in the people he told about—although of course the story was fascinating because of the intimate and casual manner in which it was told.

The Girl on the Baggage Truck (the first novella) is about Charlotte Sears, a movie actress who almost makes a tremendous marriage—but the man kills himself and disfigures her in an automobile accident. Ironically, it transpires that he was a crook about to be indicted, and she was just passing her prime as an actress. The story takes Jim Malloy into Long Island society, but not until he has talked about Charlotte's enormous Hollywood contract, got into bed with her, and divined that her rich lover is a phony. Out among the blooded millionaires, Jim is so "in" that he can discuss matters of status with friends there who would never dream of speaking on such topics to *hoi polloi.* For example, he's talking with Charley Ellis, heir to millions, about the millionaires at a party. Junior Williamson, Charley explains, is one of the royalty, " 'and the others are the nobility, the peerage.' " There are no commoners. Can one get in? asks Malloy. " 'What if I married Polly Williamson?' " She is Junior's wife, and both have enormous fortunes. " 'Well, you wouldn't marry her unless you were in love with her and she was in love with you, and we'd know that. You'd get credit for marrying her in spite of her dough and not because of it. But you could never look at another woman, not even flirt a little. You couldn't start spending her money on yourself. You'd have to get something to do that her money wouldn't help you with. *And* if Polly had an affair with another guy, you'd take the rap. . . .' " Presently Malloy goes over to Polly Williamson, whom he has scarcely met, and says, " 'I have to tell you this. It may be the wrong time, Mrs. Williamson, and it may not last, and I know I'll never see you again. But I love you, and whenever I think of you I'll love you.' " She replies, " 'I know, I know. Thank you for saying it. It was dear of you.' "

This exchange is the heart of the story. Malloy knows *real* class when he sees it. And real class responds to his tribute as only it can. Charley says, " 'Oh, that was a damn nice thing to do, to make her feel love again. The existence of it, the urgency of it, and the niceness.' " On the heels of this triumph, bad temper characteristically flares up: Jim tells the crook he is a crook.

The second novella, ***Imagine Kissing Pete,*** is about a spirited girl with class who marries an oaf. The marriage goes bad for three reasons, any one of which could make a story. First, there is the fact that Bobbie married Pete not only on the rebound but also to spite the fellow who jilted her. Second, there is the Depression, and Pete loses his job and sits around glum and drinking. Third, Pete, who was a prudish virgin, goes wild at the discovery of sex and chases wives so outrageously that he and Bobbie are excluded from their former social life. The data outrun the needs of the story, but again the real transaction here is between the reader and Jim Malloy, whose relaxed reportage is at the focus of attention. There is time for Jim to dig around in Gibbsville gossip and expose the depravities of Prohibition, time for a remarkable display of the abrasions among and within married couples of the younger set, time for a fight after a Country Club dance. Bobbie and Pete, who reappear after some time, go far down till they hit bottom and start back up. Bobbie, from Lantenengo Street, becomes the (respectable) belle of a tavern near the factories. But somehow they weather the storm, rediscover some affection, and raise a child who graduates from Princeton with the top prizes. The whole story seems obscurely to hint that class will win out, but it does not say so. Perhaps the happy ending is pure luck. O'Hara does not try to suggest a meaning in his account of how it was. The most reliable inferences that we can make have to do with people's immediate reactions to situations.

We're Friends Again (the third novella) moves back to the Long Island people of ***The Girl on the Baggage Truck.*** Jim has a long evening with a pair of socialites, after which he drops (rather drunk) into bed with a Broadway actress (also rather drunk, but an old friend). In the morning they worry about whether they were noticed by the columnists. How can the "beautiful young actress" and the "sensational young novelist" fail to have been noticed at the 21 and El Morocco? They can't—but this prelude serves to float us into the social world where Jim Malloy can relate to the richest of them. This is Polly Williamson, so splendid and beautiful and classy that he loved her at first glance two novellas back. Now she is his fan, reads his novels, and even shows up in Boston to see his play because she fears that it may not make it to Broadway. She is the ultimate American woman; he is her culture hero. The point of the story is that this Polly Williamson, heiress to millions, is married to a bone-crushing woman-chasing multimillionaire who resembles no one so much as Tom Buchanan of *The Great Gatsby.* She seems to be a nobly suffering, utterly proper aristocrat; but it transpires that for years she has been having an affair with a quiet Boston aristocrat, which almost nobody suspected, and she marries him later. And so again we find that we just don't know what goes on under the surface, although it is almost sure to be more sex than we suspect. Malloy is delighted to discover that Polly's "real" marriage is with the quiet

Bostonian. "It is always a pleasure to discover that someone you like and have underestimated on the side of simplicity turns out to be intricate and therefore worthy of your original interest," he says. The bulk of the story is *discussion,* in the Shavian sense—information about how it was that comes out after the fact as people chat over lunch or a drink. It is very interesting. The simplicity of the prose, the bits of information about millionaires, society, the War Office, and sex may make up for the fact that the people are not deeply known. Yet their conversations are absorbing. On the last page of the third novella, Jim Malloy discovers that his old and very good friend Charley Ellis was deeply in love with his wife, who told nasty tales about Polly and her Boston man and was an America-Firster. Jim concludes, "I realized that until then I had not known him at all. It was not a discovery to cause me dismay. What did he know about me? What, really, can any of us know about any of us, and why must we make such a thing of loneliness when it is the final condition of us all?" The special quality of O'Hara is that he can be so interesting in describing the glittering surface of How It Was with respect to status, money, drinking, and sex.

There are gross lapses of taste in these tales, where the axes of realism, sex, and status cross. It's all right for Jim Malloy to explain that Nancy Preswell, who is going to marry Charley Ellis, is a bitch, but one may doubt the taste of his telling the actress with whom he spent the previous night that he can take her out for a snack after her play and still—if she refuses to go to bed with him again—pick up a girl at one of the night clubs. The ploy succeeds, and Julie re-embarks on their affair for some months. It goes on until one day they have a halfhearted discussion about whether they should marry. She decides against it because they are both very bad Catholics, but still Catholics, and a marriage between them would have to be permanent. She has had a couple of abortions, she says, but if she becomes pregnant by Jim she will tell him and hope he will marry her. But it isn't really love, and a paragraph later she drops into his apartment for her things, because the man she had been planning to marry when Jim showed up again has come back. So they go to bed for a last turn, the details of which are vivid but not significant except to show that conventional ideas about how people feel and relate do not correspond to what takes place in the jungle they inhabit. Love and sex don't often go together. Women love one man but desire another and marry a third because he is rich. Or they marry one and immediately discover the need for an affair. Human relations are almost never *right,* and it is plain that nobody knows where he stands. People are drained of the capacity for love or belief or idealism—even though they have very strong opinions on many subjects and will, over the second drink, fight anybody over them. The disillusion lends no tone of bitterness or despair to the stories. The facts are recited with detachment, candor, and gusto. And the aristocrats continually surprise us by being more brave, intelligent, honorable, intricate, faithful, and idealistic than anybody supposed. It is a puzzling world, and nobody has caught its gleam and movement so well as O'Hara.

Charles Child Walcutt, in his John O'Hara, *University of Minnesota Press, 1969, 48 p.*

O'Hara on the value of creative writing courses:

Creative writing, or literature, comes from all sorts of people and all sorts of places; so I do not rule out the possibility that it may come from a creative writing course. But there really is no shortcut to good writing, and no way to learn it except to write. If my daughter, now fifteen, should want to write, I would urge her not to take a creative writing course. The time would be better spent in Latin or Greek, French or Russian; or in history or physics or in political economy or in philosophy.

The word *creative* seems to contradict the idea of writing as a teachable art. The word *valid* . . . also disturbs me. Valid is one of the most misused words in modern jargon. It is an egghead favorite and almost never correctly used. It is one of those words like *dichotomy, denigration, ambivalence,* and God knows how many others that I consider show-off words. Instead of trying to teach "creative" writing, students should be taught how to spell and to respect the language. How many creative writing students can use *who* and *whom* correctly? . . .

Most students who want to be writers are looking for a life of undisciplined ease, and the product of creative writing courses proves it. If you're going to write, nothing will stop you, but writing is strictly a do-it-yourself enterprise.

In his "An Artist Is His Own Fault," edited by Matthew J. Bruccoli, Southern Illinois University Press, 1977.

Charles W. Bassett   (essay date 1982)

[*In the following essay, Bassett examines O'Hara's accomplishment in "Alone."*]

As regularly as John O'Hara's novels were savaged by literary critics as prolix, disunified, and just plain dull, his short stories were just as regularly lauded—and often by the very same critics. Certainly O'Hara's principal literary analysts, the authors of extended critical studies of his work, admire his accomplishment in short fiction. Comparing O'Hara to Chekhov and Katherine Mansfield, C. C. Walcutt asserts that "the American short story may well be our best literary achievement in prose—and O'Hara stands close to the top." Sheldon Grebstein feels that O'Hara's achievements in the short story form are "profound, serious, and artistically accomplished." Matthew Bruccoli calls O'Hara "our greatest writer of short stories," and Frank MacShane praises "thirty or forty short stories and novellas, for their artistic delicacy and a psychological astuteness unsurpassed in American literature."

During his long career, John O'Hara published 402 short stories, an absolutely prodigious number for a "serious" American writer. In such an abundance, quality is bound to range from the sublime to the trivial. Nevertheless, O'Hara is always a "pro," a sure-handed and careful craftsman. What his critics object to, however, is monotony. O'Hara once claimed that "I had an apparently unexhaustible urge to express an unlimited supply of short story ideas." That O'Hara's ideas seem less than consis-

tently different to his detractors is demonstrated by this typical review in *Time* [27 November 1964]: "These stories, taken by themselves, have the sting of fresh work by a fine author. But [O'Hara] has written so many stories that his fresh, vigorous writing is debased by the illusion of sameness."

Of course animadversions like *Time's* are not unexpected in light of O'Hara's record of fecundity. Beginning in 1935 with his first collection of short fiction, *The Doctor's Son and Other Stories,* and concluding in 1974 with the last (and posthumous) collection, *Good Samaritan & Other Stories,* O'Hara produced fifteen volumes of short stories and three more of novellas. In the 1960's alone, O'Hara brought out six big collections containing 134 stories. His Random House editor, Albert Erskine, estimates that O'Hara wrote "slightly more than one a month for the last ten years of his life, and a great number of them belong among his or anyone's best."

Given this combination of massive productivity and relative critical cordiality, John O'Hara's reputation as a master of the American short story should have been established beyond doubt. That this is not the case must-in part be attributed to O'Hara's own touchiness. As Bruccoli has pointed out, O'Hara's rank in the pantheon of American short story writers depends upon whether his work is anthologized and taught in schools and colleges. However with only one exception, O'Hara refused permission to reprint his short fiction in "best stories" volumes or in American literature textbooks from 1937 until his death. Reputedly O'Hara abhorred the selection process and felt further that inclusion somehow diminished the market value of his work. Whatever the reason, O'Hara's shortsighted refusals to reprint must share some of the blame for his modest contemporary stature as a short story writer and for the fact that almost all of those many, many short stories are out of print.

Despite the smug "I told you so" response of some of his critical detractors, the loss of O'Hara's accomplishments in short fiction is a severe one for students of the genre. Only those willing to seek O'Hara's stories out will be able to appreciate the careful and precise economy with which he depicts so many meaningful crises in the lives of his stories' protagonists. O'Hara's short fiction—from first to last—deals expertly with elemental concerns: inferiority, shame, pride, viciousness, guilt, resentment, parental neglect, violence, passionate sexual impulse, love and death. In the stories of the 1930's and 1940's, he most often reveals these themes through ironic (sometimes satiric) monologues and dialogues, establishing the "perceptual distance" that is one of the trademarks of an early O'Hara story. Author and reader share a cool remoteness from the reality that the central character understands, and the effect can be comic, biting, or savage. As O'Hara's life and career progress, his narrative technique becomes less dramatic, his intrusions more ruminative, and his attitudes more compassionate. For all of the softening of mood and tone in many of these later stories of the 1960's, O'Hara never writes with philosophical serenity; to the end, an O'Hara story is most often a chronicle of the bleak emptiness of human life.

O'Hara with Senator John F. Kennedy and W. H. Auden at the 1956 National Book Awards ceremony.

Nevertheless, readers have two different models to choose from as typically vintage O'Hara short stories: the terse, heavily ironic, and often brutal early portrayals of weaklings, boors, and poseurs; and the later and longer contemplations of aging, past mistakes, loneliness, and approaching death. Preference will vary with the reader, but critical consensus would seem to point to the earlier stories as more aesthetically balanced and more psychologically acute—indeed, as more characteristic of John O'Hara.

An outstanding example of O'Hara at his early best is **"Alone,"** a short story originally published in *Scribner's Magazine* in December 1931 and reprinted in **The Doctor's Son and Other Stories** (1935). O'Hara was hardly an unknown writer when *Scribner's* editor Kyle Crichton bought **"Alone"** for $75 (some 73 O'Hara stories had already appeared in *The New Yorker,* beginning in May 1928). Still, O'Hara believed that his career began broadening out with the *Scribner's* acceptance. M. J. Bruccoli contends that **"Alone"** does not "represent any departure from O'Hara's other work at that time," and even though O'Hara inundated Crichton with additional stories, *Scribner's* bought just one O'Hara story (**"Early Afternoon,"** July 1932) in the early Thirties and only one more during the rest of the decade. O'Hara had to continue to rely on

The New Yorker as the principal outlet for his short stories.

As a matter of fact, **"Alone"** is one of very few O'Hara stories to employ a modified stream-of-consciousness narrative technique, or what Grebstein has called "the classic interior monologue." Normally, O'Hara's stories feature a distinctive combination of editorial omniscient narrative combined with "inside" portrayals of some of the character's thoughts, thus welding the objectivity of realism with the subjectivity of modernism. In **"Alone,"** however, despite O'Hara's use of the third-person singular throughout (Hague, the protagonist, never refers to himself as "I," not even in his thoughts), the action takes place almost entirely within the consciousness of the central character. Consequently, **"Alone"** is technically different from "O'Hara's other work at that time"; the point of view is more personal, the flow of thoughts more inchoate, and the sense of reader identification more immediate.

For all that, **"Alone"** is still one of O'Hara's classic "sensibility" stories, its action psychological and its chief purpose to generate empathetic understanding. Such "plot" as the story has is rudimentary: in his boyhood bedroom, the widowed Hague awaits burial services for Nora, his recently drowned wife. Nothing really "happens" in the story, if by "nothing" the reader means immediate, material, and physical circumstances effecting a significant change in the protagonist's life. Yet in the 1500 words of **"Alone,"** we join Hague (we never learn his given name) in confronting the terribly empty facts of death, loneliness, and despair. Plotless though the story might be in a traditional sense, it is almost Joycean in its evocation of an "epiphany"—our realization of the meaning of **"Alone."**

At the same time, O'Hara remains the realist throughout this short story, as he does in all his published work. Hague is a demonstrably "ordinary" person, the kind of character—abounding in O'Hara's fiction—who is both intellectually and morally unequipped to cope with disaster. Because Hague seems so ineluctably shallow and his thoughts so quotidian, the unwary reader could dismiss him and his plight as simply pathetic. However, lurking just beneath the unremarkable surface of **"Alone"** are the themes that O'Hara made it his job to explore in story, novel, and play for forty years: family relationships, guilt, sex, and death.

Moreover, O'Hara's unerring sensitivity to the social locus of his character, to the paraphernalia of Hague's bourgeois existence, ground these thematic abstractions in a solidly explicit milieu. The limits of the short story form itself force O'Hara to suggest rather than enumerate the components of social place—a concision that critics find wanting in his novels—but Hague is certifiably of this time, of that place.

We know Hague's middle-class background (and therefore some of his characteristic modes of reaction) because O'Hara includes just enough significant detail to allow us to infer it. Hague has always had his own bedroom in a surburban house (he remembers a backyard tent and a stable-garage). He has won a tennis trophy (now tarnished by age) at camp. Hague is a college man (he handles a tobacco pipe with an inlaid silver "C"—Cornell? Colgate?) and has married Vassar-graduate Nora. Hague's family is traditionally Protestant (his sister had been kept from marrying a Catholic), and we expect his wife's funeral services to be held in Hague's family's church (her parents are dead, hence the ceremonies become Hague's responsibility). His job in a city office is important enough that he can expect a two-month leave of absence because of his bereavement. Finally, Hague seems to earn an adequate though not munificent salary (a trip to Bermuda to forget "wouldn't cost much"), and Nora had had the twenty thousand dollars (now, guiltily, Hague's) which her father had left her.

All in all, then, in **"Alone"** O'Hara focuses on a thoroughly conventional young man whose life has been unalterably affected by the accidental drowning of his wife. Most of John O'Hara's fiction is consistently haunted by at least a soupcon of cosmic irony—the inexplicable and unfair disastrousness of fate. At the same time, O'Hara is less interested in the operations of a cosmic nemesis than in the emotional ramifications of catastrophe, both in its effects on the ill-equipped human psyche and in the possible implications of character with fate. O'Hara's Hague is a victim of calamity—though obviously poor, drowned Nora

is unluckier even than he—but **"Alone"** is best understood as a study in deep-seated anxiety, in sexual guilt, and in dependency.

Nora's death has forced Hague out of the routines of his "adult" life and transmitted him back to his childhood—his mother, his family house, his past. O'Hara's recreation of Hague's patterns of thought shows us that Hague has never really broken free from his mother, indeed, that despite several abortive attempts to revolt against his mother, Hague's marriage itself is a repetition of the guilty dependency of his earlier maternal relationship. Archetypically Hague has feared abandonment by the maternal figure, and with Nora's drowning, that fear has come true.

Consciously, Hague has attempted to establish himself as an independent individual: in the face of maternal disapproval, Hague has married Nora, thus "breaking" the Oedipal pattern. However, the seat of Hague's mother's objection to the marriage—that Nora is older than Hague—only accentuates the Freudian conflict here: Hague's mother fears her displacement by Nora, a mother-surrogate, and Nora gets both child and lover in the younger Hague. Either way, the "revolt" of Hague is doomed from the onset, if indeed his conduct can be considered a revolt at all. More probable is the hypothesis that Hague simply craves maternal security.

Nevertheless, Hague cannot admit his dependence, least of all to himself, and he uses sexual activity to demonstrate his autonomy. In defiance of his mother's restrictiveness, he had lived with Nora before their marriage, and, ultimately, legitimized his defiance: "He knew now that that was as close as his mother dared come to telling him not to marry Nora. Well, he had married her, God damn it, and he had been happy." On the other hand, Hague is not content with "maternal" domination by Nora either; he carries on semiserious flirtations with other women after his marriage: "He remembered a night when he had kissed a girl Phil had brought to their apartment." Consequently, Hague at once cherishes the safety of maternal oversight, but he also establishes a habit of sexual assertion in his effort to "be a man."

O'Hara uses Hague's boyhood tennis trophy to suggest the ambivalence of these contradictory impulses. Hague has won the trophy, a now-tarnished cup, in "manly" competition with his peers, hence establishing his prowess. But this cup, an age-old symbol of the female, is obsolete, tarnished, soiled, empty. "Winning" the prize, in sexual as well as athletic competition, has proven to be hollow for Hague, the insubstantiality of his victories ultimately as meaningless as his putative revolts.

Despite the despair implicit in this insight, Hague is too committed to ingrained patterns of experience to understand the origins of his ambivalence. Not a particularly insightful or introspective man, Hague has simply lived with his women, expecting them to indulge his expectations, nurturative or carnal, as need be. He has not understood the contradictions inherent in this mother-mate combination; consequently, he feels, but does not comprehend, the guilt that the contradiction generates. O'Hara introduces more than a trace of the incest taboo in Hague's musings over his mother's "predatory" struggles to maintain control of her son and over his sister's virginity. However, Hague needs conventional authority figures, helpmates without sexual allure, so that he can be punished for his unnatural desires.

Hague's guilt is exacerbated by his knowledge that Nora was pregnant when she drowned. He has a vision of himself as "the father of two children and the husband of a healthy girl," but he does little to convince us of his mature understanding of the paternal role. Given his generally childish egocentricity, we are led to believe that Hague might well have considered his offspring more a rival than a charge. Accordingly, that the unborn child dies with Nora can be considered another victory, but one achieved with even more enormous costs in guilt.

Hague's competitive nature and his consequent suspicion of potential rivals becomes even clearer in his thoughts about Phil Casey, his and Nora's closest friend. Hague would prefer to believe that Casey "liked Nora so much because he was so fond of Hague," but he cannot be sure. The only other person save the physician to know of Nora's pregnancy, Casey has been too close to the Hagues' sexual life to be entirely trustworthy. So Casey's consolation after Nora's death must also be rejected as "unbearable, unbearable."

Ultimately Hague emerges as a paradigm of self-pity. Although he may be more sinned against than sinning, he hugs his grief solipsistically and indulges his tears. (Hague weeps three times in **"Alone,"** but more for himself than for Nora.) Doubtless he "loved" Nora in his own way, but inescapably he loves himself more. After all, Nora left him alone, and Hague cannot entirely forgive her for that.

When his mother finally appears to call him to the services, Hague is characteristically riven by assertiveness and guilt. He is brutal to his timid mother, reducing her to tears in which he is only too eager to join. "He put his arms around her, and he knew that in all the world there was nothing he wanted but to hold her like that. He didn't care what she said as long as she wept for him."

Thus O'Hara ends this very effective and affecting story with our understanding of the protagonist's genuinely doleful situation tempered by our insight into his neurotic failings. O'Hara's approach to Hague's loss and grief is compassionate, but the story also graphically demonstrates that true compassion involves forgiveness for the unworthy, for the weakling, for the self-pitying. Irony, therefore, leavens compassion in **"Alone,"** and the result is a truly outstanding early example of John O'Hara's mastery of the short story. If he did as well in other stories, he rarely surpassed **"Alone."** We can only lament the fact that most modern readers will never be able to appreciate his achievement.

Charles W. Bassett, "John O'Hara's 'Alone': Preview of Coming Attractions," in John O'Hara Journal, *Vol. 5, Nos. 1 & 2, Winter, 1982-83, pp. 18-24.*

Edgar McD. Shawen   (essay date 1982)

[*In the following essay, Shawen discusses the thematic relevance of the title* Waiting for Winter *to the stories included in that collection.*]

Since John O'Hara rarely commented on the titles of his short story collections, an occasion when he did do so is of some interest. I refer to the "Author's Note" prefixed to **Waiting for Winter.** It begins: "The title of this collection is like any other title; it could have been something else. And yet it is as apt as a title ever need be." After pointing out that titles are often changed in translation, citing the French translation of *Butterfield 8*—entitled *Gloria*—as an example, O'Hara explains that the title **Waiting for Winter** derives from his preference for cold weather for writing novels and his consequent use of the summer months for writing short stories while waiting for "long-writing weather." The preface concludes: "Of course it [the title] has other implications as well." This concluding remark comprises the entire final paragraph.

What these implications of his title are, O'Hara never spells out. However, an examination of the stories in the collection reveals in many of them a common thematic concern which can be expressed metaphorically by the title phrase, "waiting for winter." As often happens in O'Hara, conflict between the desires and aspirations of the individual, and the limitations imposed by the social order and the conditions of one's life, is central to most of the stories. Here, that conflict is most often resolved by individual self-assertion in an escape from the social order or in the creation of a quietly unconventional life style within the social order. A few stories are concerned with the failure of self-assertion. The sense that self-assertion makes the individual's future secure is especially strong; characters appear to be figuratively waiting—and preparing—for their own winters.

An example is in order. **"The General,"** one of the longer stories in the collection, relates in almost tedious detail the life of a retired general, Dixon L. Hightower, and his wife. General Hightower is a middle-aged man of quiet elegance whose life is defined by his infallible routine of daily visits to his tobacconist, his broker, and his club; his wife gardens. As a former high military officer, General Hightower is a pillar of the community; each year he gives the local Memorial Day address and presents high school American history awards, and he is welcome at his broker's office despite his modest trading because "he added tone to the place and Westmore & Company knew it and he knew it." He values security and stability so much that he and his wife have continued to live in her ancestral home although the neighborhood around them has so deteriorated that their friends will no longer visit them.

Only at the end of the story do we learn the secret foundation of the Hightowers' domestic bliss and tranquillity: General Dixon L. Hightower is a transvestite, with his wife's approval and participation. The latter part of the story reviews their rather coldblooded courtship and their difficult sexual adjustment to married life. But after an episode, following a separation, of unusual passion and intensity General Hightower dressed in his wife's evening dress, necklace, and scarf. Her reaction was one of surprise, but not of offense or ridicule, and after a calm and practical discussion of how they might conduct their role reversal, they agreed on the moral and social status of their shared secret:

> " . . . It's just for the fun of it, you and I. Neither one of us would ever think of telling anyone else."
>
> "All right, now please come back to bed."
>
> "I will if you undress me," he said.
>
> "You mean as if I were a man?"
>
> "There's nothing wrong in it, Sophie. I don't see anything wrong. We're husband and wife."
>
> "Yes," she said.

His transvestism becomes a regular part of their relationship, although she eventually stops dressing as a man. Despite their unusual nocturnal activities, their daily routine and the correctness and sedateness of their demeanor do not change. By day the clothes are carefully put away and never referred to.

Yet this secret life, in violation of community standards and of the image the Hightowers present to the world, is the basis of their happiness. It satisfies the inner needs of the outwardly staid general and is a large part of his wife's attraction to him: "At breakfast he would read his newspaper and make his comments on the events of the outside world. He was the same man, because she knew him to be, and as she said about once a year, if other people knew him as she did they would realize that he was one of the most fascinating men you could ever hope to meet." The Hightowers have achieved a viable compromise between the mores of the community and their personal drives and needs. They have neither openly defied social standards nor sacrificed themselves to them. But the necessary impetus to this happy equilibrium has been in the direction of individual self-assertion. Compliance and dissatisfaction precede innovation and fulfilment. It is a recurrent pattern in *Waiting for Winter.* Indeed, in **"The General"** the pattern is reinforced for the reader by O'Hara's reversal of time: the portrayal of the Hightowers' staid diurnal life precedes the account of the first transvestite episode—an episode which was actually the prelude to that life—and the shock of revelation and then clarity for the reader resembles Sophie's reaction.

The establishment of unconventional personal relationships that satisfy the needs of lonely or frustrated or insecure people occurs in various other stories in *Waiting for Winter.* In **"Afternoon Waltz"** a young man and an older married woman become lovers. John Evans is shy, studious, the orphaned son of austerely religious parents. He is becoming blind, and is totally blind by the end of the story. Harriet Shields is lively and social, a wealthy woman who practices "scandalmongering as an art." She is attractive but not flirtatious, but her husband is an aging drunkard whom she regards bitterly as a "toothless baby." Between these two people—Harriet says they are both "afraid of tenderness"—arises a bond which survives his eventual blindness and her eventual widowhood, though they do not marry. As they dance to her record player on warm afternoons, the sound of the music is "not loud enough to disturb anyone." The relationship is discreet, but it is not quite clandestine. O'Hara emphasizes the presence of an inquiring community by stressing certain character traits and narrative techniques. First, gossiping is a primary activity of Harriet and of John's middle-aged housekeeper, and an active concern with the business of others is widespread in the Gibbsville of the story. Second, at the beginning of the story O'Hara presents descriptions as they would appear to an imaginary observer on the street: "A few [of the houses on the block] were constructed to have the front parlor half a story above the street level, so that not even a very tall passer-by could see in the parlor windows. Where the front parlor was on street level, the passer-by's curiosity was frustrated by curtains of heavy lace and lowered window-shades." The reader becomes that curious observer, peering vainly like a nosy Gibbsvillian into the private lives of houses designed expressly to frustrate him. Between poles of individual privacy and public inquisitiveness John Wesley Evans and Harriet Shields fulfill themselves with each other.

Hollywood is a frequent setting in *Waiting for Winter* for stories which depict unusual but satisfying relationships. O'Hara's Hollywood is in many ways the Tinseltown of tradition—a jungle of lost and rootless people with false names and false personalities, people who live by playing roles and forget who they are. But where Jacquelyn Susann converts this world into *roman a clef* and Nathanael West into apocalyptic symbol, O'Hara treats it as a community much like any other. O'Hara almost always presents the Hollywood of the Thirties and Forties, when a handful of powerful studios held stars in check through airtight contracts with frequent options and severe morals clauses. The combination of economic hierarchy and restraint of individual conduct gives this world surprising similarity to Gibbsville. But Hollywood lacks the stability, the sense of place and history, and the basic moral consensus that endow even the most rebellious Gibbsvillian with a personal identity. It is not surprising, then, that the Hollywood stories in *Waiting for Winter* deal with the search for belonging or that their characters must find it in unusual ways.

Sally Standish in **"The Way to Majorca"** is typical of the protagonists of such stories. At twenty-seven she is typecast in undemanding roles, and she fears that her next option may not be picked up. Her natural concern for economic security is sharpened by her nomadic background: alcoholic parents, now dead, and a marriage at eighteen to a vaudeville actor who put her on the train back to New York after only two months. Sally finds her solution in an alliance with Meredith Manners, an aging homosexual screenwriter who longs to retire in comfort to Majorca. Neither individually has the wealth or leverage to break free of the studio that owns their contracts, but together they do. At Manners' suggestion, they marry and use the threat of unfavorable publicity (since Manners is homosexual), and the awkwardness for the studio of using the morals clause (since their offense is marriage), to force the studio to pay them for the remainder of their contracts while they relax on the Mediterranean.

This happy ending comes about because of Sally's willingness to commit her future to a most unlikely person, Manners. Her past makes her self-reliant and wary yet also creates a need: "Advice, that's what I need. Somebody that I can honestly trust to give me the right advice." Ironically, it is Manners' lack of sexual interest in her that insures his objectivity, that makes him the right man. Yet their conversations consistently reveal a mutual respect that promises stability in their friendship and their unorthodox marriage. Sally's trust in Manners is revealed in their climactic meeting with the studio boss, Sol Hamper. Instructed by Manners to say nothing, "not even hello," Sally says exactly two words, "no" and "goodbye." The last lines of the story make her almost a comic puppet:

> "Look at her. Tell her it's all right to smile, will you?"
>
> "Smile for the man, Sally."
>
> She smiled.

Yet their strange misalliance allows Sally Standish and Meredith Manners to defeat the system, achieve freedom, and reach their Shangri-la.

In the novella *Natica Jackson*, another young actress finds refuge and stability in an unusual relationship. Natica Jackson is younger than Sally Standish, on her way up where Sally may be on her way down, but she occupies the same position of economic vulnerability and has suffered from the same lack of effective parental authority. Natica's parents have long been separated; her mother whines about her arthritis and begs for work as a film extra. But at a major crisis in Natica's career, surrogate parents come to the rescue, Morris and Ernestine King, the couple who serve jointly as her agents.

From the beginning the story hints that the Kings, who are apparently childless, have parental feelings toward Natica:

> Morris thought he saw through Ernestine's interest in Natica Jackson. "She's a little like you, Teeny," he said. "If you had a daughter that's what she'd be like. She even resembles you facially."

As the story develops, the Kings, especially Ernestine, manage every detail of Natica's career and life, even to the point of choosing her a boyfriend, the jaded bisexual writer Alan Hildred (a character very similar to Meredith Manners). Morris says of Ernestine: "If you got one real friend in this business, it's Ernestine. So don't go antagonizing her too far. Everybody has to have one real friend in this business." And Ernestine says of Morris: "Tough. Shrewd. He'll murder you in a business deal. He'll have the gold out of your teeth before you open your mouth. But if he likes you, once he gets to liking you, you never saw such real, genuine loyalty. And he likes you, Natica." Natica pursues on her own her affair with a married chemist, Hal Graham, despite the Kings' warnings. Yet when Graham's wife kills the couple's children, and Natica faces the end of her career if her involvement with Graham is publicized, the Kings work out a plot to silence the only other person (a private detective) who knows Gra-

ham is her lover. Natica simply hands them the problem; as she says, "I felt panicky till you and Morris got here." And as Morris leaves for the crucial meeting with the detective, she concludes the story: "I can wait . . . I have complete confidence in Morris." Despite the insecurity of life in Hollywood and the inadequacy of her real parents, Natica has found friends who can be relied on in a crisis, and that friendship gives her confidence and a sense of belonging.

A final example of this type of Hollywood story in *Waiting for Winter* is **"James Francis and the Star."** This story describes the friendship of a writer, James Francis Hatter, and a famous actor, Rod Fulton. Their friendship survives a variety of strains. While Hatter's career stagnates, Fulton advances from a parking-lot attendant to one of Hollywood's biggest stars. Fulton spends several years overseas during World War II. Fulton's first wife, Angela, has an affair with Hatter; his second wife, Melina, detests Hatter and bars him from her house. The two men have arguments and misunderstandings. Yet the friendship, falsely suspected by Angela of homosexual overtones, continues, a sort of anchor in Fulton's chaotic life. Each respects and helps the other. Hatter deals with the fatal shooting of one of Angela's lovers in a way that spares Fulton pain and publicity. Fulton arranges purchases of Hatter's stories, and his lavish party for Hatter's fiftieth birthday is the climax of the story. As the two approach middle age, their easy camaraderie, while not the central fact in either's life, is something to rely on.

Other stories in *Waiting for Winter* depict characters who are able to create new ways of living in breaking away from a drab or limiting past. **"The Tackle"** tells of a college football hero who refuses to let other people's memories of his athletic glory prevent him from building a new life outside sports as a successful financier and husband. While Hugo Rainsford says of football that "I loved it, and I still do," he follows it less closely as time passes and considers himself "the victim of bores who wanted to talk about something he had graduated from." In **"Leonard,"** an elderly man is told that he is no longer welcome at the bar where he spends his afternoons and evenings. So he marries a much younger woman who is also a regular patron of the bar, and they begin their new life together with a honeymoon trip to Mexico City. In **"The Jama"** a widower who lives on his boat keeps as his crew a young couple—even though he fears they will kill him for the boat—simply because "I'm all alone in the world." And in **"Yostie"** another elderly man, Irwin Yost, is awakened to the femininity of a young woman who works for him, and to his own capacity for responsiveness, through the casual attention paid her by a drifter. When Mildred Kunkel, despite the social awkwardness and taciturnity she shares with Yost, welcomes Yost's interest, their future together as they wait for the winter of their lives seems assured.

There are twenty-one stories in *Waiting for Winter*. Among those not discussed above, some develop along the lines I have presented as typical for the collection. Others, more consistent with the bulk of O'Hara's work, depict characters unable to break away successfully from an unsatisfying rut. In **"A Good Location"** and **"Late, Late**

Show" fantasies of radical change are not pursued. In **"A Good Location"** partners in a struggling gas station dream of the success they would find in a new station at a more accessible site but lack the daring for an actual move. A retired advertising executive, in the latter story, remembers a dilettantish former associate who drifted from career to career, temporarily successful in each but unable to commit himself. **"Fatimas and Kisses"** and **"The Neighborhood"** portray men who can escape from drab and loveless marriages only by the murder of their wives, desperate acts of violence which destroy whatever future these men might have found. In **"The Assistant"** and **"The Skeletons"** characters sink into stagnation and pointlessness. Helen, the band singer in **"The Assistant,"** moves from one superficial sexual relationship to another, using alcohol as her "assistant" or crutch; that she has memorized her lawyer's telephone number says much about her life. The members of the Roach family, in **"The Skeletons,"** lack real involvement with each other, lack any meaningful employment or activity, and are in danger of becoming public laughingstocks through their eccentricity; while at the end of the story one daughter has found commitment through an impulsive marriage, and the other daughter is starting to form friendships, the parents remain mired in trivial conversation, moral naivete, and excessive leisure time. All these stories comment by their very presence on those I have discussed earlier: while the struggle to establish a new and satisfying life may succeed, its success is not assured, and individuals whose struggles fail face disappointment and bitterness.

It is impossible to leave *Waiting for Winter* without some mention of **"Flight,"** perhaps the strangest and most memorable short story O'Hara ever wrote and the only one in this collection to employ prominently winter as a symbolic season. The story line is simple. A retired playwright, Charles Kinsmith, takes a bad fall on an icy road while out for a walk. He returns home to a hot bath, two drinks, and a long conversation with his wife about their life together and about their son Rex, killed twenty years earlier as a fighter pilot. After a period of dream-filled sleep, presented as an interior monologue extending the earlier dialogue with his wife, he awakes to find himself paralyzed and dies quietly in his wife's arms. O'Hara's achievement is to invest Charles Kinsmith's death with the sense that it is a fitting and symmetrical end to a worthwhile life and at the same time, through symbols of flight, to convey the mystery and the fellowship of death as an experience.

Charles' lengthy, and technically daring, review of his life is a prelude to death, a summing-up. And Emily Kinsmith's closing words express both the ultimate incomprehensibility of death and her willingness, at the end of a long and happy married life, to face it: " 'I wonder what's next,' she said. 'You know, Charles. What's next?' " But the story's examination of death is best held together by the recurrent metaphor of flight and fall from flight. Rex's death was a fatal fall, in the prime of youth and strength, that prevented his ever declining from the glory of that prime. Charles' fall is a momentary exhilaration—"I was given the gift of flight. . . . I had the experience of being air-borne"—but he hits the ground "with a jolting, humil-

iating abruptness" before regaining his balance and composure. For each, the temporary soaring, the escape from earth and gravity, is followed by the plunge back to earth. It is in Emily's mind as she speaks to the doctor near the end of the story that these two falls are brought together and seen as figures for the ineffable: "Hello? Yes, is this you, Jimmy? It's Charles. He just went down in flames. He was flying like a bird, and he went down in flames." Such a death is not to be feared, and Emily longs to be taken with Charles, not because she cannot face life but because death is at once a reunion with her husband and son and the natural culmination of her and Charles' life together. Death as flight or as winter is final, but it has been prepared for by a full life of love and of fidelity to what one truly values. **"Flight"** thus epitomizes the collection in which it appears.

John O'Hara is best known for the depiction of a fictional world in which the matrix of social and economic relations becomes an almost Aeschylean web circumscribing the individual's freedom and determining his fate. Even for the seemingly powerful rich, writes Matthew Bruccoli, "their possessions—the things they spend their money and mortality on—are the symbols of their bondage to deterministic forces." Caught in the toils of a system that denies him freedom in any area of life, even the freedom to flee, the individual sinks into "helpless despair" and some form of self-destruction; we think of Julian English's suicide by asphyxiation (the method is symbolically significant even if based on historical events) in *Appointment in Samarra,* or of Joe Chapin's slow, quiet destruction by alcoholism in *Ten North Frederick.* The pessimism of such a pattern makes O'Hara often depressing even when he is technically most admirable—depressing because he never achieves genuine catharsis. But in *Waiting for Winter* we see another side of O'Hara. The individual may face a hostile and restricting reality, whether social, economic, or (in the case of **"Flight"**) metaphysical, and he may not be able to change or destroy it; but he finds a compromise with reality. He finds in human contact, in some form of human love, a way either to escape out of the given reality into a new and self-constructed reality or to establish within the social order a small oasis of happiness and fulfilment. Where discipline and courage meet imagination, he can win what he wants.

Edgar McD. Shawen, "The Unity of John O'Hara's 'Waiting for Winter'," in John O'Hara Journal, *Vol. 5, Nos. 1 & 2, Winter, 1982-83, pp. 25-32.*

Robert Emmet Long (essay date 1983)

[*In the following essay, Long surveys O'Hara's later short fiction—from* Assembly *(1961) to the posthumously published* Good Samaritan, and Other Stories *(1974).*]

In 1961 O'Hara published his first volume of new stories since 1947. Entitled *Assembly,* it contained twenty-six stories, most of them written during the previous summer at Quogue. *Assembly* initiates the later phase of O'Hara's career in the short story, a period of great productivity and achievement. O'Hara himself, in his introduction to the volume, has recorded the sense of exhilaration he experienced in returning to write short stories after a long absence from the form. "It was the most joyful writing I have ever done," he remarked. "The pleasure was in finding that after eleven years of not writing short stories, I could begin again and do it better; and the joy was in discovering that at fifty-five . . . I had an apparently inexhaustible urge to express an unlimited supply of short story ideas."

The stories in *Assembly* are noticeably longer than the early ones, with two of them, **"Mrs. Stratton of Oak Knoll"** and **"A Case History,"** nearly the length of nouvelles. The pace of the stories is also more leisurely, revealing an interest in the finely observed textures of social experience. Some of the tales have a sinuous movement and edge their way with an inviting indirectness toward their denouement. The narrator's voice often suggests urbanity—a large acquaintance with the world and the nuances of human behavior. The stories are of widely varied kinds. James Malloy is reintroduced, having grown more suave in the course of time, and in several stories the reader is taken back to Gibbsville after World War I. Aging actors and actresses appear in sophisticated settings, and hard-boiled characters meet in pool halls and bars. A number of the tales are set in the suburbs of New York, and often have a married couple as their principal characters. Characteristically, these suburban couples are fairly affluent and older than O'Hara's early short story protagonists. They have good manners and vote the Republican ticket. Aging is a prominent theme in the tales; some of them, like **"The Trip,"** are shadowed with a consciousness of approaching death.

"The Pioneer Hep-Cat" is one of the volume's more lacerating stories, but in many respects it reads like one of O'Hara's early pieces, since it is told in monologue form by a local newspaper editor as he speaks to an audience of high school students in a small Pennsylvania town. He would like to tell them about a General Corrigan who was born in the town, but he has been told that they want to hear about a Jazz Age musician named Reds Watson, who grew up there. Reluctantly, with obvious discomfiture, he informs them of Reds's life—a case of "great talent wasted." It is somewhat improbable that he would allow himself to go into the unpleasant story before the students, but allowing that he does, the tale gains by being related by such a man as the narrator. The old-fashioned normative and local values that O'Hara has insinuated into his voice authenticate that Reds's life belongs to actual fact, has not been "made up."

At the age of thirteen, according to the editor's account, Reds had one of his arms amputated. As a child amputee, he had a paper route and delivered papers to the town's various saloons, where the patrons insisted that he sing— and drink with them. He drank to take his mind off the pain in his arm stump, and by the time he was twenty, he drank heavily. His face purpled from drink, he became sullen, bitter, and hostile. When not performing as a singer with touring dance bands, he dosed himself with alcohol. Eventually he lost his jobs with the bands, and every remnant of respectability. At the age of twenty-five he was

found dead on the bandstand of the Alhambra dance hall in Scranton. The dance hall had been closed for the summer, and as the narrator remarks in the last sentence, "the watchman had no idea what Reds had gone there for."

This great, understated last line evokes a whole world of maiming and isolation. Although Reds's life is an extreme case, one is swayed to give it credence by the reliability of the narrator, who also serves to create internal tensions within the story. He is frankly embarrassed by the account he relates, and seems to discourage the idea that Reds's life was at all representative of the town. He had wished to speak of General Corrigan, a better reflection of community values. In other words, he attempts to cover up, but in the course of the story is forced to reveal a buried truth of the life of the community—the horrible maiming and alienation that existed within its normality.

"The Sharks" is perhaps more characteristic of the volume in its concern with the manners of older, affluent characters. In **"The Sharks,"** the Dennings are curious about a stranger who, at the beginning of the summer, acquires a house in their coastal community. He is an older, well-to-do homosexual, and the Dennings fear that he may attract a colony of homosexuals and that the old-fashioned nature of the place will change. Later in the summer, they learn that the man has just been murdered by a young gas-station attendant he had brought home with him one night. But the Dennings' anxieties are not allayed, for soon, like "sharks," other men of the same background, attracted with an almost dreamlike perversity to the notoriety of the incident, come looking for houses too. The seemingly "safe" world of the Dennings is broken in upon by the strangeness of the world without.

"Sterling Silver," one of the collection's best stories, deals with a middle-aged couple who stay at a fashionable California watering place. Their neighbors in Cabaña 18 are Norman and Irma Borse, a nouveau riche couple who have arrived from Los Angeles in their Rolls-Royce. They are inevitably brought into contact with the Borses, and on several afternoons the narrator and Norman Borse are golf partners. Borse is a developer in Santa Ana, his wife, the former Irma Hopwood, was the "beret girl" pictured on the cover of *Life* magazine and on countless highway billboards across the country as part of an advertising promotion for a product. . . .

One of the striking features of the story is the manner of Borse's speech, which O'Hara has rendered vividly:

> "It's an advantage when the wife has money of her own," he said. "I got one of my brothers that everybody knows the only reason why his wife is sticking to him is the money. We weren't always millionaires, the Borse brothers. Al married very young and she'd of been all right for like if he'd of stayed where he was, making a nice living but never very big. He had a used-car lot on Cahuenga, and a nice home in the Brentwood section. But he came in with my older brother and I and inside of three years if you wanted to find her she'd be in Bullock's-Wilshire or I. Magnin's, spending. Which was all right, understand. A man makes a lot of money, his wife is entitled. But she got so she hated him. The

more he made, the more he gave her, the more she hated him."

Soon afterward, however, the narrator's wife tells him that Irma Borse sleeps with waiters while her husband is playing golf, is "a sterling silver bitch" he "stole from a billboard" and has to live up to. Everything now falls into place with an expertness that distinguishes the whole narration.

In two other deftly handled stories—**"The Girl from California"** and **"Mary and Norma"**—O'Hara varies the setting and social level of his characters. In **"The Girl from California,"** Vincent Merino and his wife, the movie actress Barbara Wade, are in New York from the West Coast. While they are staying in the city they go over to Trenton in a chauffeur-driven limousine to see the Merino parents. The old Italian neighborhood is revisited, complete with the appearance there of State Senator Appolino, who would like to exploit the occasion of their visit politically by having some of his constituents come to meet them. Inside the family house, Merino's middle-aged father speaks of his hernia and of his having been "operated," and advises his son, if he wants his marriage to succeed, to "start a baby right away." His own marriage, however, has sagged into futility and boredom. Vincent and Barbara have dinner at the house, but find themselves feeling uncomfortable and out of place. On the way back to New York, after leaving early, they realize that the family has hated them for their success, mobility, and freedom.

The failure of families also enters into **"Mary and Norma,"** a story about two sisters-in-law. At the end of the story, they talk together in Norma's house, and it comes out that they are both cheating on their husbands, for whom they have no respect or love, and from whom they have received none. Scrupulously observed, vulgar and powerful, **"Mary and Norma"** is a controlled study in disintegrating relationships that, at the end of the piece, uses the house, stark and bare on the eve of moving, in a suggestive, quasi-symbolic way, just as the Italian house in **"The Girl from California"** has also been used to provide a focus for the failure of the familial bond.

In other stories O'Hara plays variations on the theme of aging. **"Reassurance"** examines the lives of an older couple, the Rainsfords, now retired in Virginia and living away from their former friends in New York. When they are visited by a couple they have known for years, Mary and Henry Roberts, they talk chiefly about friends of their own age, a number of whom have died. After the couple leave, Henry Roberts has a heart attack at the wheel of his car, and the Rainsfords are summoned to join Mary Roberts at the hospital. When they return home, after Henry Roberts's death, they settle back into the little comforts of their life, the little reassurances that everything is normal—while they try not to ask themselves how much time they may have left. The emphasis of this understated tale is on the consciousness of the aging characters, as it is in another story, **"The Trip."** In **"The Trip,"** an older man plans a journey to London, and has begun to look forward to it. But when friends at his club begin dying suddenly of heart attacks, one in a taxi on his way to the club, he decides to cancel his vacation. His vision of his dying alone in a taxi in a far-off city where no one knows him becomes fixed in his mind, and after the story ends it lingers in the reader's mind as well.

Assembly, with its medley of voices and finely attuned moods, was followed annually for the next several years by a new story collection. *The Cape Cod Lighter* (1962), published the next year, does not contain as many memorable stories as does *Assembly,* but was O'Hara's most popular short story collection and attracted a new audience for his short fiction. The title of the volume (some people bought the book, it was said, to find out what the title meant) refers to a device for starting fires in fireplaces, and hints at human fires ignited by an outside agency. But, in fact, the tales contain no extraordinary conflagrations. They are on the whole rather quiet, understated rather than overstated. A number of the tales have a sketchiness about them, as if O'Hara were content to create an atmosphere, a situation, and allow the reader to imagine the rest. In certain cases, however, as in **"The Bucket of Blood,"** these stories that read like sketches are actually carefully worked out conceptions.

"The Bucket of Blood," set back in time in Gibbsville, recounts the appearance in the town of Jay Detweiler, and his rise from transient to elevator operator to manager of a pool hall to owner of a saloon known as the Bucket of Blood. Nothing of a startling nature happens to Jay, but in the course of the story one comes to see his life—the shady policemen whose good will he has had to "buy," the whorehouses located within the same two-block area as his saloon, the thin line between financial security, even if of a rough and dubious kind, and the underworld of the dispossessed. The story has a downbeat ending, and seems to have no great point. Against certain odds, Jay Detweiler has managed to become the owner of a saloon.

"The Bucket of Blood," in other words, reads very much like a vignette. One of the finest features of the tale is simply the richness of its texture, the low-life world O'Hara creates that is absolutely convincing and real. But it is also a story that requires the reader to do some of the work of "imagining," and the hand of the craftsman can be noted in it. O'Hara's description of Jay when he arrives in Gibbsville in his mid-thirties is so brief that it might be overlooked, but it is revealing. He remarks that "already the upper half of his thin little face was shaded blue and his eyes were teary." The description makes him seem unwholesomely starved and desolate. What is striking about him at the end, after having accommodated his sexual needs with prostitutes, and with one in particular, is that he is still unmarried, and most of all, is singularly alone.

The reader's sense of Jay at the end is affected, too, by the time frame that O'Hara has used. The tale opens in the past, but at a "present" point in the past, and then sweeps back to an earlier time and forward again toward the opening. The opening description of the Bucket of Blood may be almost forgotten at the end, but it is relevant. O'Hara remarks, in this opening, that "Jay had an alarm clock on the back bar and on the wall a large Pennsylvania Railroad calendar, showing a passenger train coming out of the Horseshoe Curve. Otherwise the saloon was devoid of decoration." This is Jay's life—stark, ugly, devoid of anything that might enhance it humanly, stripped down to clocks and calendars that mark the passing of time before Jay dies alone and enters the grave.

Two other effectively rendered stories concerned with characters who do not belong to polite society are **"The Sun-Dodgers,"** a raw, suspenseful, and ultimately humorous tale about Broadway "night people" of the thirties—journalists, bookmakers, and mobsters who gather in speakeasies; and **"The Butterfly,"** about a young woman who, to the dismay of her half-respectable mother, goes off with a not-at-all respectable steeplejack. Yet O'Hara is able to move with ease from one social level to another. **"Sunday Morning"** takes place essentially within the mind of a solidly middle-class suburban housewife, Marge Fairbanks. As the story opens she has lingered over coffee and cigarettes in town on a Sunday morning, before driving back home; but en route her car stalls, and she is enclosed again within her thoughts. What she thinks is that she does not really want to return home. The children are up by now and messing about, and her husband of twelve years is sleeping with his arms around a pillow. Suddenly she asks herself a question: Who is she? Why is she living? O'Hara steals into this woman's consciousness as if it were his own; and the same stealthy probing of women's minds is witnessed in two other tales, **"The Women of Madison Avenue"** and **"The Nothing Machine."** In these stories O'Hara "impersonates" women, enters into their intimate thoughts and inmost natures as only another woman, seemingly, would be able to do.

At the same time O'Hara begins to make exploratory probes of homosexuality. **"Jurge Dulrumple,"** set in Gibbsville during an earlier time, concerns two women, Miss Ivy Heinz and Miss Muriel Hamilton, who as the account opens sing "two-part harmony" while they travel along a road in a motor car. They laugh as they recall their earlier experience with George Dalrymple ("Jurge Dulrumple," jestfully, to them), a serious, sheltered young bank clerk who is inept with women, and had proposed to both of them within a month's time. The word "lesbian" is never used in the story, but the obvious lack of interest in men of one of them, and their close association like that of a married couple, intimate a lesbianism that makes the courtship of both by the sexually inexperienced Dalrymple doubly amusing.

Another tale with a homosexual implication is **"Pat Collins,"** a long story that begins in the present and moves back into the past. The device O'Hara uses in the story is the same one that he used in *Ten North Frederick,* in which an opening situation is presented before the narrative drops back into the past to bring out its significance. The situation at the opening of **"Pat Collins"** is that two men, Whit Hofman and Pat Collins, once close friends, now merely nod and pass on when they encounter each other on the street. When O'Hara reverts to the past of the late 1920s, it is brought out that Hofman, a social leader of Gibbsville, had befriended Collins when he opened his new garage and helped to have him admitted to the Lantenengo Country Club. This act, which ought to have brought them even closer together, has the reverse effect.

On their first night at the country club, Collins's wife Madge drinks too much, embarrassing her husband before his friend and his wife. Moreover, almost on sight, Kitty Hofman takes a deep and lasting dislike to Madge, and from that point onward the men are divided by the antagonism that exists between their wives.

As the story proceeds, Pat Collins's situation becomes increasingly painful. To put it very simply, Madge Collins is a woman who has designs on her husband's friend. Kitty Hofman is aware of it, and the complication produces difficulties in the Hofman marriage. They take a world cruise, but instead of mending their differences it merely divides the Hofmans further. Kitty has an affair abroad, and after their return to Gibbsville their marriage is never again very sound. Whit Hofman, emotionally estranged from his wife, has an affair with Madge Collins, and Pat is cut off from the man toward whom he has felt a kind of love.

Although muted, it seems a kind of love. Even Madge, reflecting on Pat's feeling for Whit, asks herself: "did he not all but love Whit too?" Madge has sexual relations with her husband and also with Whit, giving them an odd kind of intimacy, although a very wounding one for Pat. He soon begins to drink at Dick Boylan's speakeasy, and allows his business to go to pieces; and when Boylan observes Pat's troubled state of mind he concludes that it must have to do with either money or a woman. O'Hara comments that it "never occurred to Dick Boylan—or, for that matter, to Pat Collins—that Pat's problem was the loss of a friend." Skillfully insinuated, this undercurrent in Pat's feeling for Whit affects the reader's sense of him at the end. By then, Pat seems bereft of close human ties of any kind. He spends most of his time at his garage, which is open twenty-four hours a day; he is cut off emotionally from his wife and he has no male companions. Each time he passes Whit on the street it is a mocking reminder of the scarring deprivations Pat has suffered.

Unlike *The Cape Cod Lighter,* with its many themes, *The Hat on the Bed* (1963) concentrates upon a single one, that of aging. The manner of the stories, however, is often light, even at times wryly amused. A good example would be **"The Glendale People,"** about an aging film actor who lives alone in a Florida cottage overlooking the Gulf of Mexico, with his souvenirs and framed photographs of movie actors and actresses. He is at first said to be a bachelor, but it later comes out that he is the veteran of five unsuccessful marriages. He is attempting to adjust to associating with rather dowdy, older couples whose circumstances, like his own, are a little pinched, and whom, in his earlier Hollywood days, he avoided and referred to as "Glendale people." Near the end, the New York publisher Carson Burroughs visits him, asking how he is progressing with his memoirs, for which he has given him an advance. At the end it comes out that the poor man, after five years of sharpening pencils and sitting down to write, still cannot begin to put his life down on paper. Comically, he is revealed as a man who, at every stage of his career, has been at sea.

"Agatha" is a gemlike story about a fairly well-to-do older woman who has had three husbands and now lives in an apartment building in New York, where she has a maid whom she shares with another East Side family. Her name, revealingly, is Mrs. Child. Mrs. Child is a trifle lightheaded or absent-minded, and she has in the past had some incidents in which a cigarette left carelessly burning had started a small fire. She knows that she should be more careful, and could even be asked to leave her building as an undesirable tenant. In fact, as the story opens, she has just burned a small hole in the carpet with a cigarette, and is trying to cover it up so that the maid will not know. When the maid appears, Mrs. Child explains hastily that one of her dogs has chewed a hole in the carpet, and that she must have the carpet man come by the next day to look at it. Flushed, she then tells the maid that she will be going out to buy another coat. "Do you think I'm mad, Mary?" she says suddenly, in a remarkable last line. "I *am* a little mad, aren't I?"

Many of the stories in *The Hat on the Bed* are filled with fine "effects," and some conclude with one. **"The Windowpane Check"** seems close to perfection in its plotting and in the sheerness of its ending. One day on a train an older man notices another man wearing a jacket that seems identical to the one, specially made for him by a Scottish tailor, that he had given to a church auction after his wife's death. As they talk, he learns that it *is* the same jacket, and that he and the other man have much in common as widowers who have tried to divest themselves of painful reminders of their happier pasts. At the end, they become one, in their bereavement and barrenness of their present lives. The elegant craftsmanship of **"The Glendale People,"** **"Agatha,"** and **"The Windowpane Check"** is also seen in other tales in the volume—in **"The Manager"** (a collector's item among O'Hara's stories), and **"The Man on the Tractor."** In **"The Man on the Tractor,"** the Denisons, Pam and George, once, according to Gibbsville legend, thought to have inspired characters in F. Scott Fitzgerald, return to the town later in life, sobered and chastened, to find their romantic past vanished and their contemporaries dead or dying. The story is strongly reminiscent of Fitzgerald's "Babylon Revisited." However, it is not Paris, but Gibbsville—now losing population and its large estates reduced to small parcels of land—that is the scene of the Denisons' reckoning.

The theme of time and aging that is prominent in *The Hat on the Bed* recedes, however, in the volume of short stories *The Horse Knows the Way* (1964), which was published just before *The Lockwood Concern* and reflects at least one of its concerns—that of the character who is cut off from others. O'Hara's orchestration of this theme is accomplished in many different ways, sometimes through characters who suffer a grotesque isolation, or are involved in actual violence. In **"The Madeline Wherry Case,"** a woman driven to the breaking point shoots her husband; and in **"The Jet Set,"** another woman, corrupted by her involvement with a set of sophisticated people, leaps to her death. In other stories, such as **"The Bonfire"** and **"Can I Stay Here?,"** the isolation theme is treated without recourse to outward violence. In **"The Bonfire,"** a recent widow, a young mother whose husband has committed suicide as the story opens, approaches a group of friends who are having a beach picnic by a bonfire, only to run

from the bonfire, suddenly stricken with the sense that she no longer has any "place." **"Can I Stay Here?"** deals with a teen-aged girl belonging to a well-to-do East Side family, who has become disoriented. O'Hara shifts at the end of the story to the consciousness of the girl, a postponed revelation that has the effect of unsettling eeriness.

O'Hara varies his theme by focusing upon characters who belong to different social strata, and is often most successful in stories whose characters are below the level of respectability. **"I Spend My Days in Longing"** deals with a transient musician who has fallen into a state of malaise, and eventually commits suicide. **"The Law Breaker,"** one of the best stories, is about a young man of good family who becomes a rum runner in the coastal waters of Florida. The story has an episodic movement, and is notable for its raw atmosphere and tough-guy characters. The slowly gathering implications of the story come together only at the end, when various narrative patterns converge—the protagonist's exclusion first by his parents, then by his lady friend, and finally by the mob.

The writing of *The Lockwood Concern* appears to have energized O'Hara's imagination, for the story collection that follows it, *Waiting for Winter* (1966), is one of his finest and most versatile. In *The Hat on the Bed* and *The Horse Knows the Way*, a dominant theme emerges, but in *Waiting for Winter* many strong themes compete for attention. Not only some but most of the stories in the volume represent O'Hara at his best, and they are of very diverse kinds, taking place in both the past and present and on all levels of society. In these tales, O'Hara uses different types of narration, including the "life chronicle" in capsule, returns to explore Hollywood with greater compassion than before, and brings the formerly marginal figure of the homosexual into closer relation to the mainstream of human experience.

A number of the tales in *Waiting for Winter* are set in Gibbsville at the end of the 1920s. In **"Yostie,"** a widower past middle age operates a bathhouse and refreshment stand at a boating place not far from Gibbsville. To this place comes a sinister stranger who calls himself Mr. Smith. "Smith" is the kind of figure O'Hara does to perfection. He is somehow "dangerous," and has about him a kind of leering sexuality. Yostie, the refreshment stand proprietor, is repelled and yet almost hypnotized by this drifter. By the time he breaks free of him and Smith leaves, however, Yostie has been awakened to the sexual desire he has suppressed, and begins to think of marrying Mildred the waitress by the summer's end. The workmanship of the story is more sophisticated than it might seem. The setting of the story, for example, at a distance from the community but connected to it tenuously by a trolley line, has been used by O'Hara to emphasize Yostie's situation. His encounter with Smith, moreover, reveals a mythic pattern in the tale—a Jungian descent into the unconscious, confrontation with an "outlaw" self, and reintegration of personality.

In each of his Gibbsville stories, O'Hara employs a different method or narrative strategy. In **"The Skeletons,"** he uses an omniscient narrator; but in **"Fatimas and Kisses,"** the story is told in the first person by James Malloy, whose point of view is restricted. Malloy, then working as a cub reporter for a Gibbsville newspaper after the death of his doctor father, enters only marginally into the action—although far enough to bring him face to face with a brutal tragedy within a family. The story has the disturbing power of déclassé realism, and it might be inferred that such harsh realism is O'Hara's real form. Yet in another fine tale, **"Afternoon Waltz,"** O'Hara deals with upper middle class Lantenengo Street lives in a way that involves an element of delicate fantasy. **"Afternoon Waltz"** is about a young man who has been settled with an inheritance but goes blind; in the course of the story of an older woman, a widow who lives next door, teaches him to dance, and they thereafter have an affair. The music of a Victrola waltz can be heard from her living room window at the end, as deprivation and pleasure mingle—with a strangely evocative effect that lingers in the reader's imagination.

Other stories in *Waiting for Winter,* forming a group by themselves, are concerned with Hollywood, but they are rather different from O'Hara's early Hollywood stories. For one thing, their pace is more leisurely, with two of them—**"James Francis and the Star"** and *Natica Jackson*—the length of nouvelles. For another, O'Hara's hostility toward show business people in the early stories has given way to a more complicated or problematic attitude. While the characters are still limited in various ways, they are now capable of a fuller range of emotions.

"The Way to Majorca" is a comic tale about an actress, Sally Standish, who appears in commercially successful Grade B movies. Before long, however, she will be too old for such roles, and has become concerned about her future. In this, she is similar to Meredith Manners, who has written a number of her films and now plans a retirement in Majorca, where he can live inexpensively on what he has been able to save. Together, pooling their savings, they could live in Majorca very comfortably. Meredith Manners is a man in his forties who, because he has fallen arches, moves very slowly; he dresses in tweeds, smokes a pipe, and is a homosexual. Their elopement makes the Los Angeles papers, which print an account of Sally Standish's former romantic attachments and describe Manners sardonically as "a confirmed bachelor." Side by side with a photographic layout of stills from Sally's films, they print a group photograph of Manners with his friends, who include a hair stylist and an elderly tennis player.

The studio head, the delightful Sol Hamper, is shaken by the marriage and by Sally's breaking her contract with the studio. Yet in the end their marriage and retirement to Majorca, where they will join a colony of Meredith's friends, seems no more odd or grotesque than the film world they are anxious to leave. Even Sol Hamper, admitting that he, too, would like to get out of show business, asks about Majorca as a retirement place. "How are they toward Jews, do you happen to know?" he asks. One of the fine things about the story is the generous quality of its satire. Sally Standish and Meredith Manners are treated humorously, of course, but their working out an improbable *modus vivendi* for their lives is made to seem un-

O'Hara in his study.

derstandable, and they are even accorded a certain respect.

Sol Hamper, who enlivens the story toward the end, also shows O'Hara imagining new character types in the later stories and expanding upon them. **"The Portly Gentleman,"** another Hollywood story having an element of grotesqueness, deals principally with a stout actor named Don Tally, but the character who is captured best is his agent Miles Mosk. Midway through the story he points out to Tally that he is not dependent upon him for a livelihood, having already provided well for himself and Mrs. Mosk, who owns a "mutation" mink. O'Hara is particularly effective in rendering Mosk's strange speech:

> Mr. Don Tally, I got a nice home in Great Neck, a boy serving his internship at Mount Sinai Hospital, another boy studding law his second year at Columbia Law School. And I got annuities besides, to take care of Mrs. Mosk and I the rest of our natural lives. This I got from my ten percent of you and many's another talented artist I kept working steady. A person willing to work steady, I had the experience and the know-how and the numerous personal contacts whereby I pick up the long distance telephone and inside of three-four minutes I got a deal.

In *Natica Jackson,* the Sol Hamper-Miles Mosk figure appears as the agent Morris King who, in this case, has brought his wife Ernestine into the business with him. Morris and Ernestine are brought to life immediately through their speech, which comments fully on the nature of their experience in Hollywood, which has hardened them without depriving them of their humanity.

Natica Jackson, a long story, does many things at once. It creates the studio world of Hollywood, and it examines the thin line separating this professional world of illusion-making and the real world without. In this tale it is, again, or at least partly, grotesqueness that fascinates O'Hara. The story begins with a small whim that makes the actress Natica Jackson take a slightly different route home from the studio. Her turning down an unfamiliar street results in a minor auto mishap and in Natica's finding a lover, a married man with a conventional middle-class background. Yet by the end the most unforeseeable consequences ensue, for the man's "normal" background is not all that it seems. His wife is quite mad (in a startling passage O'Hara actually looks into the madness of her mind), and with a Medea-like vengeance upon her husband and his lover, whose identity she does not know, she drowns her two small children. Strangely, irrationality breaks out not in the illusion industry but in the colorless, repressed world of the middle class. But what is most notable of all in the story is that Natica Jackson, the actress, is treated not as a type, or even more particularly as a Hollywood type, but as a fully dimensional woman.

"James Francis and the Star," a companion story, works with a large span of time, and illustrates the new method O'Hara sometimes employs in the later period. Rather than focusing upon a decisive moment in a character's life, he looks for a pattern in a lifetime's experience—as Fitzgerald had done in his story "The Rich Boy." The story treats the lives of two characters—James Francis Hatter, a Hollywood writer, and Rod Fulton, his actor friend. The vicissitudes of their careers and personal relationship are brought out—their periods of obscurity and success, Fulton's wives (one of whom is shared by James Hatter), the scandal that affects them both, their partial reconciliation later in their lives.

At the end, a question is raised that was broached at the beginning: To what extent has the bond between them had a homosexual basis? Even they are unsure, although the womanizing but still unmarried James Hatter is willing to concede that there may always have been some on his part. The story unfolds through ever more elaborate turns of plot, but what is ultimately of interest is the relationship of the two male friends. The story suggests throughout a fluid sexuality, in which there may be crossings over from heterosexuality into homosexuality—as in the case of two female characters in the tale. And although James Hatter and Rod Fulton have no sexual contact, their sharing of the same woman, and the shifting dominator-and-dominated tensions between them do suggest a sexual undercurrent in their friendship. On the other hand, the story is not merely about their problematic bonding; in a larger sense, it is about the lack of real fulfillment in the lives of even the most outwardly successful. Both Rod Fulton and James Hatter have had some success, and Fulton has had a good deal of it. But the truth of their lives is that they have both suffered disappointment, are not particularly happy, and give the sense of being essentially alone at the end. The undercurrent of sexual attraction between them emphasizes a longed-for closeness that is always to be unfulfilled.

Apart from the Gibbsville and Hollywood tales, *Waiting for Winter* contains other stories that deal with diverse subjects and are of different kinds. They include a number of superior stories—the realistic, haunted **"Flight,"** in which an older playwright, past the peak of his career, dies after a fall on the ice; and **"Andrea,"** about a young woman who, in the course of a marriage and many affairs is unable to find herself, and whose suicide at the end has the weird effect of an optical illusion. **"Andrea"** encompasses a long period of time, but **"Assistant"** takes place in the early hours of a single morning. Maggie Muldoon, a much-married nightclub singer on her way down awakens early in her New York apartment and in the sequence that follows, through her recall of the past, her background is filled out, leading to the expected arrival in an hour of Jimmy Rhodes. Rhodes is a man-about-town who has no taste and is "all wrong," but will provide her with a desperately needed anchorage. Maggie, whose morning vodkas are her "assistant" to get her through her day, remembers Rhodes's having brought her home the night before and, in a fogged way, his having said he would come back the next morning at seven. So she remembers, but when she goes into the living room and switches on the light she finds Rhodes dead on the couch. Dressed in a frilly shirt and tasseled shoes, he is still seated, staring straight ahead, as if waiting to be called into her bedroom. "The worst," O'Hara remarks in the final sentence, "was the eyes, seen through thick lenses."

O'Hara's versatility in *Waiting for Winter* may be illustrated by two final stories that are in every way different yet are both the work of a master—**"The Jama"** and **"The General."** **"The Jama"** is a suspenseful story about a widower who owns a yacht and has a man and woman on board who work for him and with whom he drinks—both hardened types, the woman flashily cheap. On shore, a man named Blair observes the yacht through a pair of binoculars and then goes out to the yacht to talk to the owner. The atmosphere on board is disturbing, and more disturbing still is Blair's final recognition that the owner may well be done away with by his employees before reaching his Florida destination. At the end, **"The Jama"** becomes another of O'Hara's imaginings of isolation.

One of the pleasures of **"The Jama"** is its carefully controlled and very gradual revelation of the yacht owner's frightening situation. **"The General,"** on the other hand, is a smilingly ironic tale, told in a leisurely fashion and having no sense of peril whatever. O'Hara's manner could not be more urbane. This urbanity involves a continual play of irony over the principal figure, Dixon Hightower. Hightower is nominally a general, but this title has come to him through his belonging to the National Guard, following his service in World War I, where he never saw action. He married a wealthy woman, relieving him of the need to work; and as the story opens his life is made up of a ritual of small routines—mailing a letter at the post office, spending the afternoon at his club. Hightower is a man, like Robert Millhouser in *Ourselves to Know,* whom life has passed by.

One smiles at the futility of his life, his rather timidly respectful devotion to outward forms and social rituals. Later one smiles when, in the privacy of his bedroom, Hightower is revealed as a transvestite. His wearing of female garments to stimulate him into sexual relations with his wife is an amusingly fanciful idea, and yet is made to seem plausible by the lonely and bloodless nature of his life. The success of the story is in the manner of its handling—O'Hara's superbly wry humor, the deftness of his treatment of the general and his sheltered, innocently compliant wife. O'Hara gives the impression that he knows the couple to the life—the genteel forms they observe, the halts in their speech, the way they think, what they say to each other in the bedroom. **"The General"** is the last word in virtuosity in a story collection that reveals it at every point.

And Other Stories (1968), a slighter volume than *Waiting for Winter,* is the last collection of short stories that O'Hara published during his lifetime. It contains twelve stories, seven of which are set in "the Region," including one, **"A Few Trips and Some Poetry,"** that is a hundred and twenty pages long—approximately a third of the book. Much the best of the grittily realistic tales is **"The Gunboat and Madge,"** the narrative of which moves back and forth in time, beginning with the appearance in Gibbsville of Jay Fitzpatrick, a small-time prizefighter known as "the Gunboat." In the second round of a fixed fight the Gunboat is stretched on the canvas by the local boy, Kid Flynn; afterward, the two go out together to drink and visit the local "hoors." But it turns out that Jay is more fortunate than Kid Flynn who, late that night, has his throat slashed by "a fat and solemn Negro" in Collieryville. Jay becomes a bartender and bouncer at Bressler's saloon, where he steals steadily from his employer until, on Bressler's death, he buys the establishment from his widow.

The Gunboat's consort in Gibbsville is a woman named Madge who, after stealing from her employer, opens the La France Beauty Salon. Both dress flashily and frequent speakeasies; but although the Gunboat dreams of someday becoming "big," it is obvious that he and Madge have gone as far in life as they can go. At the end, the narrative leaps forward to the present as the Gunboat and Madge, now retired, celebrate their fortieth wedding anniversary in Florida, where they live. The Gunboat uses a cane, but is in fairly good health. Madge likes to sunbathe, wearing large sunglasses with rhinestones studding the rims. Her hair is dyed blue. O'Hara is present in this story in all his strength—in his earthy realism, his sly drollery, and the grotesqueness he brings to his characters' lives.

A striking feature of *And Other Stories* is the unusual degree of interest O'Hara shows in lesbianism—"a perplexing aspect," as Matthew Bruccoli has remarked, "of O'Hara's last phase." This concern appears in several of the stories, obliquely in **"We'll Have Fun,"** and directly in the sophisticated and psychologically suspenseful **"The Broken Giraffe."** But it is treated most fully in the nouvelle-length story **"A Few Trips and Some Poetry."** The story is narrated by James Malloy, beginning at the time of his youth in Gibbsville and his romantic interest in Isabel Barley, a young Wellesley graduate living in nearby Turnersville. At one point they have sexual relations and know that they are not in love but, as Malloy says, "would be loving each other" for the rest of their lives.

"A Few Trips and Some Poetry" is a "life chronicle" that recounts, over a period of many years, the stages of their relationship and various reunions, of Isabel's two marriages, and her eventual adoption of a lesbian life. At the end, when both of them are a good deal older, Malloy calls on Isabel at her country house, shared with a younger woman with whom she has had a placid relationship and found a kind of peace. The younger woman, whom Malloy finds that he likes, idolizes Isabel. Isabel has not as yet told her, however, although she does tell Malloy when they talk together alone, that she has cancer, "is riddled with it." The ending, which has the form of a farewell, requires the most delicate handling, and is given it by O'Hara. He manages to create the mood of an idyll at the end, as love is approached but love-and-division becomes the final statement O'Hara has to make about life.

After O'Hara's death, fifty additional, uncollected stories were found among his papers at "Linebrook." Thirty-two of them were collected in *The Time Element and Other Stories* (1972), but this volume is made up entirely of stories from O'Hara's earlier period, almost all of them having been written in the 1940s. *Good Samaritan and Other Stories* (1974) is a slender volume containing fourteen stories written in the 1960s, twelve of them previously unpublished. Several of the stories in the volume compare with O'Hara's best. These include the title story, **"Good Samaritan"**; **"The Gentry,"** a slowly paced, atmospheric tale set in a small Pennsylvania town; and **"A Man to be Trusted,"** in which James Malloy, making his final appearance, recounts his relationship as a boy, and then later in life, with an attractive, older, married woman.

In this way, O'Hara's stories conclude as they began, with James Malloy, depicted as an adolescent in **"The Doctor's Son,"** a young reporter in *Butterfield 8,* a middle-aged man in later stories, a widower, and then a still older man who witnesses the death of his friends. In **"A Man to be Trusted,"** in his last appearance, he is an adolescent again as the story opens, involved marginally with an older woman, but in such a way as to make the relationship impossible. An early sexual experience, followed by a sense of guilt, and the threat of reprisal (figured in the husband and the gun he carries) make the tale similar to O'Hara's first story, **"The Doctor's Son,"** which is filled with sexual guilt and a projected sense of punishment. The first and last Malloy tales thus encompass much of O'Hara's other fiction, in which sex, guilt, punishment, and the burden of isolation are prominent themes.

Taken as a group, the later stories reveal a new richness and expansion of O'Hara's art. O'Hara is able to relax, as he previously could not, into the pleasures of extended observation, and as a psychologist of his characters' lives he has never been more acute or written with such grace. O'Hara is unapologetically graceful in these stories, capable of extraordinary delicacy of handling. At the same time he enlarges upon his themes—creates the life of modern suburbanites, of America's affluent class, of older characters who have to confront death, to surrender the last of their illusions. He is a raw realist, an elegant humorist, an ironist, an elegist, a virtuoso who has gained in confidence and poise. But what one notices most of all about these stories is that O'Hara has learned compassion, has treated his sufferers with generosity, and as equals with himself.

Robert Emmet Long, in his John O'Hara, *Frederick Ungar Publishing Co., 1983, 197 p.*

O'Hara assessing his popularity in 1967:

[My] books have sold something like 15 million copies, and I could not have attained that circulation if I had not been readable. . . . I still manage to find my books on the current best-seller lists. And do you know why? Because I give them what *I* want. Not what *they* want. The author who believes he is going to *give them what they want* is making a great, great mistake, for the truth is that they don't know what they want. And for an author to attempt to anticipate what they want is an act of dishonesty.

Quoted by Matthew J. Bruccoli in The O'Hara Concern, *Random House, 1975.*

Francis C. Molloy   (essay date 1984)

[*In the following essay, Molloy discusses O'Hara's stories of the 1960s that incorporate suburban settings.*]

Critics of John O'Hara traditionally have classified the settings of his works according to three social and geographical divisions. New York, Hollywood, and the small Pennsylvania city of Gibbsville, modeled after his home town of Pottsville. While most of O'Hara's fiction does indeed fall into these divisions, critics have overlooked a series of stories from his later collections that cannot be placed in the New York/Hollywood/Gibbsville categories. Where O'Hara had tended to write, in earlier stories, about characters in relatively specialized and removed worlds—Hollywood actors and actresses, smalltime hoods moving in their own moral framework, aristocrats imprisoned in the protected shell of the past—the stories discussed here, those set in post–World War II suburbs, reflect O'Hara's movement beyond the concerns associated with the major settings of his earlier fiction.

All of O'Hara's suburban stories deal, to some extent, with the tension between day-to-day "normality" and the intrusion of emotions and events that conflict with the *status quo*. The setting of these stories reinforces that conflict for O'Hara's depiction of suburbia ties in with his protagonists' attempt to maintain a façade that belies a deeper unrest. Within this general area of concern, the stories fall into several groupings that show O'Hara gradually adapting his earlier approaches to more modern material and themes. Additionally, they reveal his ability to universalize the suburban experience without falling into the easy trap of stereotyping it.

Most of O'Hara's suburban fiction appeared in the 1960's,

for several probable reasons. In addition to the fact that the suburbs were themselves coming into prominence during the decades following World War II, O'Hara had moved to a suburban residence near Princeton in 1957. Also, according to his preface to *Assembly* (1961), he had written almost no short fiction between 1949, when he broke with *The New Yorker* over Brendan Gill's negative review of *A Rage to Live,* and 1961. Returning to the short story after this hiatus, O'Hara approached the form with new vigor.

This new period, in turn, brought with it several shifts in the author's approach to the short story. Changes in both technique and, to a greater extent, tone between O'Hara's earlier and later work have been noted. The later stories gain in length and complexity while still retaining the economy that characterizes O'Hara's short fiction. Overshadowing the irony and satire of his earlier work is a more compassionate tone, one that remains realistic rather than sentimental but that reflects O'Hara's greater empathy with the mature characters who populate his later work.

The first group of stories to be discussed recalls O'Hara's earlier, more naturalistic work and reflects fairly strongly the popular image of suburbia at the time he was writing, in the early 1960's. In **"The Twinkle in His Eye," "Justice," "The Jet Set,"** and **"The Madeline Wherry Case,"** O'Hara brings to the suburban setting his career-long concern with secrets that build up over time toward irreversible, and often fatal, emotional and physical violence. The length and complexity of these pieces also lend them a "case history" flavor, as does the omniscient narrative point of view that probes the characters' intricate psychological motivations. These stories reflect a writer in transition, taking a traditional approach to contemporary material.

The melodramatic quality of these stories about suburban violence also derives from their overwhelming atmosphere of seemingly preordained corruption. O'Hara gives credence to the power of social codes, both internally and externally imposed, yet invests the neatly structured suburban world with an undercurrent of more turbulent, less easily codified passions. In **"Justice,"** for example, the protagonist Norman Daniels is exiled by the community after his lover is murdered by her jealous husband. The complex issue of Daniels' guilt is sustained by the first-person narrative viewpoint. He tries to explain and justify his role in the scandal, and it quickly becomes clear that Daniels "doth protest too much": he both deceives himself about the extent of his involvement and fails to convince the reader of his moral superiority. Having confused *de jure* innocence with *de facto* innocence and unable to comprehend why his public image cannot exculpate him, he sinks into moral limbo.

In a similar act of self-deception, Gordon Whittier, of **"The Twinkle in His Eye"** harbors a passionate hatred of his wife, a hatred founded on small incidents that, unknown to her, have built up his resentment over the years. His hatred comes into conflict, however, with his equal passion for maintaining a respectable façade. Hence, he remains imprisoned in a state of permanent mediocrity, unable to act upon the emotions that obsess him. Characters like Daniels and Whittier, who rationalize their own weaknesses by pleading the need to protect a public image, quickly reveal themselves as hypocrites—not only in our eyes but in the eyes of their communities as well.

"The Jet Set" and **"The Madeline Wherry Case"** also use violent death to dramatize the question of moral responsibility. In the first story, a man's knowledge of a dark secret in a woman's past eventually drives her to suicide. Lawrence Graybill's culpability, O'Hara suggests, is shared by the community at large; these suburbanites, banded together by their "passion for competitiveness," choose toughness over compassion. The story points toward one inescapable clause in the moral contract, that of accepting responsibility for one's actions and of refraining from the disabuse of powers over others.

The question of victimization by the community also arises in the second story, which recounts the events that drive an adultress, Madeline Wherry, to murder her husband. By tracing Madeline's actions before the murder, O'Hara builds up the contrast between her vital relationship with her lover and her stifling marriage to a husband who has himself been unfaithful. Here again the protagonist is caught between two worlds, that of an external social code and a more powerful one of private emotions. As in the other stories of destruction, O'Hara hints at no reprieve for Madeline Wherry: just as surely as she will be punished for her crime of passion, her life with Bud Wherry would have constituted a more subtle but equally dehumanizing punishment. While Lawrence Graybill and Madeline Wherry arrive at greater self-knowledge than do Whittier and Daniels, they attain it too late to act positively on it.

This first group of stories, then, contains O'Hara's most disparaging view of suburban life, one in which emotional and physical violence are as much a part of the landscape as are the country club and the commuter train. In one sense, he seems merely to filter stereotypes of suburban corruption through the lens of melodrama. Despite their violent and somewhat sensationalist nature, however, these stories do not limit themselves entirely to expose tactics or a fatalistic condemnation of suburban life. Although both adultery and violent death are consummate within the pages of **"Justice," "The Jet Set,"** and **"The Madeline Wherry Case,"** O'Hara handles the baser details of such acts off-stage, so to speak, leading us to look for the story's focus beyond the obvious sources of drama in its plot.

If we follow this lead, we discover a more complex vision than might be immediately apparent. In several cases, it is not the victim of the violence who gains our interest but, instead, a protagonist who has had a relationship with that victim. O'Hara draws a direct correlation between the protagonist's self-knowledge and his freedom to act, and this theme is intimately related to the suburban setting. In all of the stories, we encounter characters whose self-knowledge has been clouded and distorted by their acquiescence to the suburban social structure.

O'Hara's point is that while suburbia may seem to be the villain in these stories, this is not entirely so. The suburbs in these stories, like their inhabitants, exhibit varying degrees of morality. The protagonists within them all fail to meet the same challenge: that of recognizing the point where the community can no longer define their moral code and where they must begin defining it themselves. Norman Daniels and Gordon Whittier never achieve the ability to control their own actions; Lawrence Graybill and Madeline Wherry achieve it, but too late.

A pattern that recurs in a second group of suburban stories involves a more subtle kind of disruption, an outsider's intrusion into a protagonist's calm existence. The conflict in this set of stories, like that in the first, lies in the disparity between acceptable morality and behavior and violations of that code. While in the stories just discussed this conflict manifests itself in irreversible consequences, in this second group of tales O'Hara remains more ambivalent about the possibility of balancing the *status quo* and the inner life. The protagonists of these stories begin with the assumption that, by obeying outward signs of social and moral propriety, they are operating under a self-sustaining philosophy of life. An interruption of the external routine, however, forces the central character to the point of greater self-awareness.

The intrusion of such an outsider forms the basis for **"Saturday Lunch,"** in which two suburban housewives suddenly realize that they have both been sexually propositioned by the same man, a seemingly harmless real-estate man named Duncan Ebberly. As the disrupter of their world, Ebberly embodies the ugliness that lies just beneath the calm surface of suburban existence. Carol Ferguson and Alice Reeves' encounters with him open their eyes to that sordid dimension of life which their society denies simply by ignoring its existence.

Although much of this narrative recounts the incident during which Ebberly approaches Carol, the real revelation O'Hara is aiming for has more to do with Carol and Alice's relationships with their husbands. Even more disturbing than Ebberly's advances is the distance between Jud Ferguson and Joe Reeves' images of their wives and the private ordeal that these women have sustained. O'Hara implies that even apparently "normal" suburbanites have secrets that are belied by the appearances they maintain, just as Ebberly appears to be no more than a harmless, stammering, middle-aged bachelor. The author makes this point subtly, through interchanges such as this one between Jud and Joe, remarking on their wives' sensitivity to the weather:

> "Is anybody cold here?" said Carol Ferguson. "Jud, will you go back and see if that kitchen door blew open?"
>
> "I wasn't going to say anything," said Alice Reeves. "But I think there must be a door open somewhere."
>
> "So delicate," said her husband.
>
> "Christ, aren't they?" said Jud Ferguson.

Both husbands display a protective, slightly patronizing attitude toward their spouses, absurd in light of what the reader has learned about the women. In surburbia, the same reliance on appearances that allows Ebberly to prey on women also prevents his victims from retaliating.

A similar lack of communication—a problem that lies at the heart of many marriages in O'Hara's suburbs—is revealed in **"The Clear Track."** Although composed of eight pages of almost straight dialogue, this story really concerns the Loxley's inability to talk to one another about the problems at the crux of their marriage. Their respective affairs with others are discussed only by accident, in the course of conversations about other things, and neither partner has the courage or the energy to follow through on them. As a result, each gives the other the "clear track" to pursue infidelity, even though both immediately realize that it is not the direction they want to take.

O'Hara's method in this story reinforces his message: by focusing on "the numerous small transactions that are the formalities of a marriage during trying times," he shows the Loxleys relegating their marital problems to the same level of small talk with which they discuss interior decorators and other instances of "how things will look." By the end of the story the reader feels the same sense of frustration that informs the couple's relationship, for the barrier of triviality surrounding their marriage prevents either confrontation or resolution. Just as the dialogue in **"Saturday Lunch"** and **"The Clear Track"** leaves the most important things unsaid, so their characters' hesitancy to ruffle the smooth surface of their existence prevents them from getting to deeper issues.

Chance encounters with outsiders also figure in **"The Time Element"** and **"Sunday Morning."** The irony of the first story derives from the reversal in the circumstances of Rob Wilson and Kit Dunbar, two former lovers who meet after nearly a decade. Their conversation reveals, subtly, that her life has steadily improved in an almost inverse pattern to his inward demise. Despite their superficial similarities—both have several children and are in the same social class (Wilson has learned about Kit's life in Chicago because his wife "gets the Junior League magazine")—telling changes have upset the balance of power between them. Kit, Wilson notices immediately, is more beautiful at thirty-five than when he jilted and deceived her nine years before; she vetoes sitting in a bar because, she says, "I don't want a drink and I'd rather you didn't too"; she has given up smoking ("I suppose I ought to," he replies) and is clearly in control of the interview: "I can ask questions, and you can't. I didn't ask to see you, you know." Although their conversation is short and mainly factual, it is filled with the undertones of Kit's disgust toward Wilson and her anxiousness to end the meeting.

By the end of their interview, Wilson understands the nature of the "simple mysterious thing," the indefinable malaise that has been bothering him: reminded of how he betrayed Kit, he realizes how his dishonesty has affected his own marriage. The narrator suggests that Wilson's former self-deceit will be replaced not by optimism but by the middle ground of realism: "He would be late for dinner, but not very late." O'Hara's understated handling of the story's end, like that of **"Saturday Lunch"** and **"The Clear Track,"** complements his subject: the sense of a confining

existence that, by relying more on form than on content, leaves its inhabitants in a paralyzed, static state that must be resisted.

Similarly, **"Sunday Morning"** takes its protagonist to the point of revelation but leaves her just short of transcending her ennui. The action consists of Marge Fairbanks' brief trip into town for the Sunday papers. Within this apparently simple story, O'Hara relates a series of small events from Marge's point of view, leaving the reader with a full sense not only of her daily life but also of her frustration with it. Her "independence" is measured by small acts of defiance and attempts to break out of the routine existence she has fallen into.

Her sojourn into town exposes her, and the reader, to small reminders of the pettiness and hypocrisy of her fellow suburbanites: she sees, on their way to Mass, a couple who were too drunk to drive the night before; she is greeted rudely by the drugstore proprietor; most disturbingly, a neighbor sounds her out on the possibility of having an affair. Her exchange with Ralph Shipstead reveals her own ambivalent feelings and the fortuitous set of values by which she lives. She brushes him off abruptly; but then, driving home, her thoughts go back to their meeting. She finds him a "loathesome man"—ostentatious, unrespectable, overconfident—but still, "he wanted her, and it excited her to think that in her present frame of mind he could almost have her. Almost."

Marge's conflicting emotions range from sarcastic thoughts about her neighbors ("Would anyone be interested to learn that Nannie Martin was thinking of changing to Presbyterian? Would the *Herald Tribune* send a reporter to interview Dixie Green if they knew that Dixie had once had a date with a gentleman who now sat in the White House?") to a dread, all the more disturbing for its vagueness, of returning home to her mundane family life. Her exact problem lies in the mediocrity of her situation, for she is defined only by her position as a wife, a mother, a potential partner in adultery:

> But what was *she*, Marge Fairbanks? A secure wife, yes and a conscientious mother, yes. But what else? But she, she, she? What was she, apart from husband and children, apart from Ralph Shipstead's mechanical lechery for her? And worst of all, what did she want, what could she be, other than what she had and what she was? Was this all? Was it worth it?

Marge Fairbanks' malaise, then, is brought on not by the presence of any definable qualities in her life but rather by the absence of those qualities. From an outsider's perspective, she really has nothing to complain about: her life, like her husband's lovemaking, is "usually all right." The seriousness of her situation is not revealed until the end of the story, when the car, out of gas, stalls on the road to her home, and she sits there in reverie:

> The drizzle on the windshield reminded her of tears, and she waited for the thought to bring the tears, but they did not come. She was not even that unhappy . . .

> She put the keys in her pocket and got out of the

car, and as she began the homeward walk she kicked the front tire. It hurt her toe, and now she could cry, a little.

This final scene, which shows her need for an external reason to cry and to release her emotions, suggests that she is just beginning to attain a tentative self-knowledge. Although able to ask herself some crucial questions, she remains nonetheless unable to answer them because the apparently "all right" nature of her suburban life prevents her from seeing beyond its, and her own, surface.

Although less overtly dramatic than the tales of physical violence discussed above, this second group of stories nevertheless contains disturbing elements. Their lack of catharsis and their overwhelming tone of anticlimax and stasis are in their own way as pessimistic as the destructive outcome of a story like "The Madeline Wherry Case." In these stories we are more likely to perceive the suburbs as a place of potential psychological entrapment; for while the characters in the first group do achieve a kind of dismal escape through adultery and violence, characters like the Loxleys and Marge Fairbanks may be doomed to repeat the present.

A final group of stories offers O'Hara's strongest suggestion of an alternative to the violence seen in the first group of stories and the ennui portrayed in the second. O'Hara never goes so far as to suggest that life in the suburbs can be idyllic; his characters all, invariably, face threats to that illusion. What he offers as a means of coping, in its place, are a willingness to compromise and, more important, a sense of compassion. In keeping with the technique used in the second set of stories, O'Hara uses the pattern of an epiphany effected by an outsider or an unexpected incident. The characters in this final group of stories, however, unlike those in the first two, seem able to incorporate their new knowledge into their suburban existence.

Several of these stories revolve around domestic scenes including not only a husband and wife but also their children. O'Hara thereby suggests that encounters between parents and children are one way of investing values and ideals with new vitality. In "The Father," "The Lesson," "Appearances," and "Family Evening," O'Hara examines the difficulties and rewards of achieving understanding through such encounters. For example, Miles Berry in "The Father" undergoes a change when his sister sends him an old photograph of his wife, a newspaper clipping that shows Vilma as a young, single woman of seventeen at a Frank Sinatra concert in 1945. His shock of recognition at this evidence of her once-vital spirit comes amidst the banality of their current life, placing the present in sharp relief against the past. The photo is a reminder of Vilma's and, by extension, his own lost youth and romanticism.

Fortunately, the contrast is strong enough to show Berry how precious that romanticism is, and he is able to translate his awareness into a new sensitivity toward his daughter, Ava. The final implication is that Berry will alter his habit of taking his wife and daughter's emotions, as well as his own, for granted, and of subordinating the sentimental to the pragmatic (O'Hara—not accidentally, it would seem—assigns Berry the occupation of a mechan-

ic). The structure of this story reinforces its theme, the ability of small, seemingly unassociated incidents to evoke strong memories and emotions and to provide everyday reminders of age and mortality. Consistent with O'Hara's overall treatment of suburbia, the protagonist's revelation comes in an almost accidental way. Its effect is no less profound, however, for its understated quality.

In a similar way, the daughter in "The Lesson" must bridge the gap of years and emotions between her divorced parents. Having grown up with her mother, the daughter learns from her father that, prior to the divorce, both parents had been involved in a series of affairs. Unexpectedly, this insight gives both father and daughter new knowledge and respect for one another. Mimi, now married and about to have her own child, must reassess her mother's version of her father—"She's made you sound like such an awful son of a bitch that you couldn't possibly live up to it." But she has also built up an image of him, through pictures, as a football hero in his college days. She learns from their meeting that neither of these black-and-white extremes is accurate.

The father, in turn, is equally surprised by his daughter's mature ability to accept the past without condemning him. While Mimi's insight is accompanied by a slight edge of cynicism, she gains in perception what she loses in idealism. Like Miles Berry, both Mimi and her father must acknowledge shortcomings in their own assumptions before they can connect with other people. Again, the changes in them are more subtle, internal ones, unlikely to change the outward patterns of their lives but certain to transform their private visions.

"Appearances" reverses the roles of parent and child somewhat: in this story the daughter's affair has broken up her marriage. By building the story's structure around three separate conversations—between father and mother, father and daughter, and mother and daughter—O'Hara delineates the different degrees of communication among these three family members. Once more, he focuses on the need to temper an adherence to the *status quo* with an acceptance of weaknesses in oneself and others, and again he reinforces that theme through a series of understated events that culminate in a subtle but transforming revelation.

The three conversations in "Appearances" lend several levels of meaning to the title. Following a talk with his daughter Amy, Howard Ambrie believes he has had a breakthrough in communication with her, though actually he has barely scratched the surface of the truth concerning her marriage and divorce. Amy appears to have been "a hell of a nice girl," but the history of her marriage indicates otherwise. Only the mother, Lois, who regards her daughter first as a woman and only then as her child, is able to act as Amy's *confidante*. Like Mimi in "The Lesson," Lois Ambrie transcends the expected behavior associated with her family role and, hence, brings honesty and compassion to her dealings with Amy.

The potential for maturity in a parent-child relationship also forms the subject of "Family Evening." Like "Appearances," this story comments on the bond between mother and daughter; like **"The Father,"** it suggests the positive power of the past. Bob Martin, the guest whom Norman and Libby James invite to dinner, belongs to what their daughter Rosie jokingly refers to as the "B.D.'s"—Better Deads—a categorical term for anyone over thirty. As the evening evolves, it gradually becomes clear that Martin was once Libby's old flame. The subtle humor derives from Rosie's viewpoint as the youthful chaperone of the group and her clear disapproval of her mother's sudden gaiety.

After dinner, alone with Rosie for a few minutes in her room, Libby wants to suggest that they all "step out." During a poignant moment, Libby studies herself in the mirror and asks her daughter how she "really" looks:

> "You look fine," said Rosie.
>
> "No, I don't," said her mother. She turned away from the mirror. "Do me a favor, Rosie. You suggest it."
>
> "Me! . . . All right, if you stop feeling sorry for yourself all of a sudden. You and the rest of the B.D.'s."
>
> Her mother smiled. "Dear Rosie. It hurt, but it worked." She got up and followed Rosie down the hall, humming "Do It Again," a danceable number of 1922.

The reversal of roles here, with Rosie assuming the task of being the "sensible" member of the group, demands that she suspend her youthful disapproval of her mother's frivolity. In addition, she foregoes an after-dinner outing with her own friends in order to give her mother a chance to "step out." By doing so, she earns her mother's gratitude and willingness to confide in her as well as a new degree of maturity.

Two final stories in this third group show how compromise tempered with compassion can rescue individuals from seemingly hopeless situations. In both stories, O'Hara returns to the paradox explored in **"The Twinkle in His Eye"** and **"The Time Element"**: that of a materially successful man who nevertheless feels despair. Unlike the more fatalistically inclined characters in those stories, though, the protagonists of **"How Can I Tell You?"** and **"The Pig"** are saved by their ability to connect with other human beings.

In **"How Can I Tell You?"** O'Hara recounts a day in the life of Mark McGranville and creates a disturbing portrait of alienation and confusion. Each event that should, theoretically, raise McGranville's spirits—a highly profitable afternoon in his job as a car salesman, a leisurely drink after work—leaves him not merely depressed but in an even worse state, that of an undefinable neutrality and emptiness.

When, in their bedroom, his wife Jean tentatively asks him what's wrong, he replies, "How the hell can I tell you when I don't know myself?" After she falls asleep, and after he himself has slept for an hour, he quietly slips back out to the living room and tries to analyze his feelings:

> He was thirty years old, a good father, a good husband . . . His sister had a good job, and his

mother was taken care of. On the sales blackboard at the garage his name was always first or second, in two years had not been down to third. Nevertheless he went to the hall closet and got out his 20-gauge and broke it open and inserted a shell.

As he sits in semi-darkness smoking a cigarette he hears his wife:

> Her voice came softly. "Mark," she said.
>
> He looked at the carpet. "What?" he said.
>
> "Don't. Please?"
>
> "I won't, he said.

These final lines, while hardly optimistic, suggest an affirmative vision. O'Hara emphasizes Jean's intuitive quality as Mark watches her sleeping, "making the musical notes of her regular breathing, but the slight frown revealing that her mind was at work . . . in ways that would always be kept secret from him, possibly even from herself." In contrast, Mark's own sleep is so "busy, busy, busy" with mental activity that he does not even realize he has been asleep until he looks at the clock.

By juxtaposing their two ways of sleeping, O'Hara underscores the contrast between their reactions to Mark's despair. Each of their reactions is, in its own way, extreme. Mark's of course, because of the irreversibility of the act that he contemplates; Jean's because of its understated quality. Yet the gentleness of her request is precisely what reveals her understanding of her husband. While not the "logical" approach to the situation, Jean's is, intuitively, the right complement to Mark's failure to find rational sources for his ennui. It also allows him to change the course of his actions while saving face: his wife, by recognizing her husband's isolation and expressing her need for him, provides him with the crucial human connection that breaks through his emotional barrier.

Lawrence Chandler, the protagonist of **"The Pig,"** also contemplates suicide, but for a reason more definable than Mark McGranville's: Chandler has just learned that he has terminal cancer. On the way home that evening on the commuter train, he confides in his friend and business associate, Mike Post. Chandler's alternative plan to committing suicide is to postpone telling his wife, Ruth, of his impending death. He fears that Ruth, because of the lingering nature of his disease, will eventually wish that he would stop "hanging on." Post understands but tries to persuade him otherwise.

To make his point, Post relates a parable about Pig Pignelli, a soldier who served under him in World War II. "Before we were shipped overseas he was hopeless. Always out of uniform, buttons undone, hat on crooked, dirty equipment," he tells Chandler. "But once we got overseas . . . he became the most reliable soldier I had." The Pig volunteered for what was essentially a suicide mission, an act that cost him his life. What this proved to Post was that "people you count on want to be counted on. The Pig knew perfectly well that I was going to have to ask him to volunteer, and while I was figuring out how to say it, he saved me the trouble." To give Ruth the same opportunity to help him through this crisis, Post tells Chandler, would be "The highest compliment you could ever pay her. . . . That you need her, and need her so much that you had to tell her right away." Like Mark Mc-Granville, Lawrence Chandler must adjust his own assumptions about the limits of his wife's strength in order to be worthy of her compassion. The end of the story indicates that he will follow this course.

Although O'Hara did not turn to the suburban setting until relatively later in his career, his treatment of it reflects both concerns carried over from his earlier fiction and concerns particular to the suburban setting itself. Thematically, the tension common to these stories involves the disparity between appearance and truth—a theme integral to the suburban way of life, defined as it is in his stories by the sometimes overwhelming control of the *status quo* over his characters. His perceptive portrayal of the dynamics of marriage, particularly the problems of adultery, reflects a commitment to the belief that "ordinary" people harbor ideas and emotions that, if explored, are intrinsically interesting enough to merit a realistic treatment.

In terms of style and tone, his frequent reliance on dialogue, understatement, and reportage are consistent with his preference for indirect rather than explicit moral statements. In turn, his application of these techniques to the stories set in suburbia enhances their artistry. For, while much of his non-suburban fiction concentrates on portraying aristocratic, or, at the opposite end, lower-class characters, in these stories his goal is the evocation of lives that are, like his craft, filled with everyday detail, casual conversations, and apparently insignificant events.

This is not to underestimate his skill at portraying the world of Gibbsville or of pre–World War II Hollywood and New York; O'Hara displayed his intimate knowledge of these times and places as well until the end of his career. What we get in the suburban stories that is missing in much of his earlier work, however, is a sense of form reinforcing content: O'Hara's suburban stories frequently offer us a fragmented view of reality, a momentary inkling of truth, a glance at the inner life of a character—subjects that demand a more understated treatment.

These stories, then, shed additional light on the integrity of his fiction, a body of work which is due for the same careful re-evaluation that his biography has received over the past decade. They reveal that his writing was not as restricted to the traditionally recognized settings in his canon as his critics have assumed and show his ability to distill the essence of a setting that was developing contemporaneous to his writing about it. To paraphrase the title of Don Schanke's interview with him ["John O'Hara Is Alive and Well in the First Half of the 20th Century," *Esquire,* August 1969], John O'Hara is alive and well in the *second* half of the twentieth century, too.

> *Francis C. Molloy, "The Suburban Vision in John O'Hara's Short Stories," in* Critique: Studies in Modern Fiction, *Vol. XXV, No. 2, Winter, 1984, pp. 101-13.*

George Monteiro   (essay date 1987)

[*In the following essay, Monteiro examines narrative irony in* A Family Party.]

Those contemporary reviewers who liked John O'Hara's *A Family Party* (1956) described it as "warm-hearted" and "mellow." Most of the subsequent criticism has sounded a similar note. The story has been called "a sentimental portrait of a doctor who devoted himself to the well-being of a town," and the author's "tribute to his father and to Dr. O'Hara's profession," one in which the "author's motivations"—"kindness and 'respect' "—are perfectly clear. O'Hara himself insisted that it was a "simple, honest story." Only Robert Emmet Long has acknowledged the subtlety of the story. It is "one of O'Hara's cruelly ironic monologues," he concludes, in which the narrator "unwillingly" reveals that "the honored guest's life has been lonely and anguished."

Long's comments on *A Family Party,* though brief, are the most useful to date. It is true that while the author intends to pay loving homage to his anguished father-physician, he does such a good job of undermining the narrator whose testimonial monologue constitutes the story we have that his speaker, who embodies and expresses the values of the town, becomes, in this respect, as important to the narrative as is the guest of honor. What he chooses to say and how he says it tell us volumes about the ethos of the town of Lyons, Pennsylvania. It is clear that the author's attitude toward the speaker (and by extension toward the entire town) is at best sardonic, that the speaker's (and the town's) attitude toward the doctor who is being honored is both sentimental and profoundly mendacious, and that the author's attitude toward the doctor is compassionate and considerate.

A Family Party opens with a short section, printed in italics to set it apart from the rest of the tale, that tells of the circumstances surrounding the principal narrative that follows and explaining that that narrative is a stenographic report of an address given by the main speaker at a dinner honoring a small-town physician on the occasion of his retirement from the profession after forty years of practice. This "report" on the stenographic report that constitutes the "story" told in *A Family Party* identifies the speaker and the honoree, gives the date of the dinner and its location, lists the organizations sponsoring the affair, names the clergymen who have official duties, and nods in the direction of the high school orchestra performing under its female leader. In short, this note presents the information more or less that a newspaper reader would have every right to expect in a headnote preceding the printing of the speech itself. Its prose is plain in style, neutral in tone, and consciously workmanlike. As such, it contrasts distinctly with the style, tone, and authorial intention of the address by "Mr. Albert W. Shoemaker, president of the Shoemaker Printing Company and former editor and publisher of the Lyons *Republican,* at a dinner in honor of Dr. Samuel G. Merritt."

"Bert" Shoemaker's tone is breezy and marked by studied conviviality. His diction is informal, the syntax of his sentences folksy. The speech is "marred" as prose by repetitions and awkward self-interruptions, not to mention the coy references to things he will not talk about (because to do so would be indiscreet, by the standards of others, or by the speaker's own). Here is the first paragraph (following the obligatory words of address to the dignitaries and guests), which is typical enough in tone and style to stand for those aspects of the speech as a whole:

> Back in February of this year, when a few of us old-timers accidentally discovered that we had in our midst a man who had held the same job for close on to forty years, that seemed such a remarkable accomplishment in these days that a few of us decided we ought to do something about it. This town of ours used to be an important railroad center, before they put in the buses and before the business of mining coal was all shot to—well, a certain place that I understand they have all the coal they need, if the reverend clergy will pardon me.

To be singled out are such folksy and colloquial examples of speech as "us old-timers," "close on to forty years" and "this town of ours." We can almost hear the knowing wink when he makes his little joke about the place he will not name but which rhymes with the "well" that usurps its position.

The purpose of the speech is to honor the town's retiring physician. Dr. Merritt is too-obviously well-named for he has manifested, according to all the evidence, the qualities that the townspeople are now called upon to admire and reward: selflessness, sacrifice, professional competence, and civic-mindedness. The speaker asserts as much and in every instance tells an illustrative anecdote: the doctor's handling of injuries at a train wreck, his easy way with those patients in his debt, and his fund-raising for the creation of a hospital that at the last moment he decides altruistically to allow others to build in (and credit to) a nearby town. To round out his account of the doctor's character, moreover, the speaker lets it be known (as he must) that he is privy to some of the doctor's secrets of character and motivation (the doctor and his family, he reveals, put up $30,000 of their own money to prime the fund-raising pump for the town's proposed hospital). The doctor has his foibles, though. He chews tobacco, if only a few people know it, and he plays poker, so badly though that his card-playing poses no danger to his standing as a Methodist.

All this "Bert" Shoemaker handles with confidence and obvious aplomb. He is clearly a man comfortable among fellow townspeople at this "family party." Effortlessly in this unwritten speech—he has only a few jottings on crib-cards ("Family" and "Hobbies," for example) that he sometimes anticipates—he reaches the last phase of his performance. It is the most difficult thing he has to do, it turns out, for it involves bringing up the large unspoken matter in the town, so far unmentioned: the madness and continued confinement of the doctor's wife. The speaker tackles this dreaded subject by telling a lightly sentimental story of adolescent courtship, deferred marriage, two pregnancies and the death of the babies, and depression that deepened into permanent madness. At first the speaker appears to be dwelling unduly on the matter. But, as it turns out, the story is fully appropriate to the occasion, for

the prize the townspeople have for their doctor is a check for $20,000 on a silver platter engraved:

> *Presented to*
> *Samuel G. Merritt, M.D.,*
> *at a Family Party in Honor of*
> *His First Forty Years of Service*
> *To His Community.*

The money is intended for the maternity ward of the Johnsville Hospital, to be known—in honor of the doctor's wife—as the "Alice C. Merritt Ward."

This evening's "family party" culminates in this showing of communal appreciation. Even the reference to the "first" forty years is intended only as a well-meaning joke. But this aura of well-being, orchestrated skillfully by the town's spokesman, may not be entirely warranted. There are indications to the contrary. Early in his speech "Bert" Shoemaker refers to the ancient practice among railroaders for bestowing a gold watch upon an employee at his retirement. The check for charity and the engraved silver platter are the townspeople's equivalent of the railroader's watch. And they are, in their own way, as inadequate to compensate for a life of service as the watch is to compensate the worker for his labor on the railroad's behalf. And yet, the speaker's tone is nothing if not smug and self-satisfied. The question, all but asked, is how *can* this town adequately thank this man whose rewards have been to be taken (patients who could pay for his services do not do so), hated (when during the strike he will not return the townspeople's contributions to the hospital fund), and even robbed (his shotgun is stolen from his car while he ministers to the victims of the train disaster). Yet, the speaker's "mister-smooth-it-all-away" tone would persuade us that the equation has been given and at the last everything is all right. But it is not, and the point should be put clearly. *A Family Party* is not the heart-warming story about a doctor's dedication to his patients and their expression of gratitude for his forty years of service that *Collier's* paid for and published. Rather it is the story of the town of Lyons, which, in turn, is the story of the American small town that invariably "uses" its benefactors, scraping up its thankfulness at the last in one showy gesture. An evening of gratitude, it is expected, will even things out. They have chosen their spokesman well ("Bert, you're it," they tell him) not only because he is the doctor's best friend but because, as O'Hara makes deftly clear, he is the self-satisfied, self-congratulatory, self-deceiving voice of the suggestively named town of Lyons. What should be recognized is the subtlety of O'Hara's execution of his decision to tell his "small-town story" as a poker-faced parody, drawing upon the familiar form of the honoring speech at a retirement dinner. Entirely in the hands of a "heart-warming," not entirely reliable narrator, *A Family Party* offers his readers a special instance of O'Hara's narrative virtuosity and, perhaps, his feelings as a doctor's son.

George Monteiro, "All in the Family: John O'Hara's Story of a Doctor's Life," in Studies in Short Fiction, *Vol. 24, No. 3, Summer, 1987, pp. 305-08.*

FURTHER READING

Biography

Bruccoli, Matthew J. *The O'Hara Concern: A Biography of John O'Hara.* New York: Random House, 1975, 417 p.

Critical biography. According to Bruccoli: "*The O'Hara Concern* is intentionally biased by my conviction that John O'Hara was a major writer who was underrated by the critical-academic axis sometimes called The Literary Establishment. We never have so many great writers that we can discard one because his aims and standards are unfashionable."

Gibbs, Wolcott. "Watch Out for Mr. O'Hara." In *The "Saturday Review" Gallery,* edited by Jerome Beatty, Jr., and the Editors of the *Saturday Review,* pp. 276-82. New York: Simon and Schuster, 1959.

Personal reminiscence written in 1938.

MacShane, Frank. *The Life of John O'Hara.* New York: E. P. Dutton, 1980, 274 p.

Concludes that "O'Hara's industry—his obsession with writing—was a curse as well as a blessing, for he wrote too much and the quantity of his work confused his public and caused him to be undervalued. . . . By now, however, it is clear what his best work consists of—thirty or forty short stories and novellas, for their artistic delicacy and a psychological acuteness unsurpassed in American literature."

Criticism

Boroff, David. "Chapters of America." *The New York Times Book Review* (26 November 1961): 4-5, 44.

Positive review of *Assembly,* concluding that the collection offers "a renewed reminder that O'Hara is one of the country's most distinguished authors."

Donohue, H. E. F. "Steering Clear of Green Pastures." *Book Week,* New York (6 December 1964): 5, 41.

Review of *The Horse Knows the Way.* According to Gold, "these stories enhance the staggering fact that O'Hara's range is ever widening, deepening, showing a sensibility that makes much of what we read from other authors seem like advertising slogans."

Hicks, Granville. "The Shorter, Short Novels." *Saturday Review,* New York, XLIII, No. 50 (30 December 1960): 18.

Reviews *Sermons and Soda-Water.* In Hicks's view, "The great value of the [novella] form for O'Hara lies in the fact that it compels him to omit most of the documentation that is his pride and the despair of many of his critics. . . . Here, as in some of his early work, he makes a little count for a lot."

McCormick, Bernard. "A John O'Hara Geography." *Journal of Modern Literature* 1, No. 2 (second issue 1970-71): 151-68.

Reprints an article from *Philadelphia Magazine* (November 1969) tracing similarities between Schuylkill County, Pennsylvania, and the fictional region surrounding "Gibbsville" in O'Hara's works.

Peden, William. "*Vanity Fair* Updated." *Saturday Review,* New York, XLVI, No. 1 (5 January 1963): 39.

Favorable review of *The Cape Cod Lighter,* noting that "in spite of occasional prolixity, irrelevance, and repetition, [O'Hara] is still one of the best short fiction writers banging around in this corner of the world, and *The Cape Cod Lighter* is a book to be reckoned with."

Rogers, Thomas. "Money Talks." *Book Week,* New York (27 November 1966): 4, 27.

Negative assessment of *Waiting for Winter.*

Rosenfeld, Isaac. "Racket or Tragedy." *The New Republic* 112, No. 20 (14 May 1945): 681-82.

Reviews *Pipe Night* and William Sansom's *Fireman Flower, and Other Stories.* Of O'Hara's collection, Rosenfeld states, "*Pipe Night* is so much a book of the times that it is at least fifty years out of date. . . . [There] is nothing new, unique or particularly revealing in O'Hara's insight, for all the importance he attaches to what he sees, hears and understands; nothing that does not go back at least to the reporter's sketch-pad of the twenties, if not straight to O. Henry."

Sandberg, Peter L. "Conflicting Passions in Gibbsville, Pa." *Saturday Review,* New York, LI, No. 48 (30 November 1968): 43, 58-9.

Review of *And Other Stories* identifying "A Few Trips and Some Poetry" as "by far the best piece in the book."

Sigelman, Lee. "Politics and the Social Order in the Work of John O'Hara." *Journal of American Studies* 20, No. 2 (August 1986): 233-57.

Focuses on "the understanding of politics and the social order presented in the fiction of John O'Hara, a popular American novelist who has never been considered a political writer but who . . . formulated a highly sophisticated interpretation of the interplay between political and social forces."

Sullivan, Richard. "O'Hara's Short Stories: Bright, Bitter, 'Moral'." *The New York Times Book Review* (17 August 1947): 5.

Assesses the strengths and weaknesses of *Hellbox.*

Walton, Edith H. "Mr. O'Hara's Stories." *The New York Times Book Review* (24 February 1935): 7.

Reviews *The Doctor's Son, and Other Stories,* distinguishing the title story as "not only . . . excellent reporting, but it is less slick than most of John O'Hara's work, and has a quality of honest emotion."

Wilson, Edmund. "The Boys in the Back Room: James M. Cain and John O'Hara." *The New Republic* 103, No. 20 (11 November 1940): 665-66.

Appraises O'Hara's work to date, finding that "the short stories have distinctly improved while the long stories have distinctly deteriorated."

Additional coverage of O'Hara's life and career is contained in the following sources published by Gale Research: *Concise Dictionary of American Literary Biography 1929-1941; Contemporary Authors,* Vols. 5-8, rev. ed., 25-28, rev. ed.; *Contemporary Authors New Revision Series,* Vol. 31; *Contemporary Literary Criticism,* Vols. 1, 2, 3, 6, 11, 42; *Dictionary of Literary Biography,* Vols. 9, 86; *Dictionary of Literary Biography Documentary Series,* Vol. 2; and *Major 20th-Century Writers.*

Cynthia Ozick

1928-

American short story writer, novelist, essayist, poet, and translator.

INTRODUCTION

In her short fiction, on which her esteemed reputation largely rests, Ozick repeatedly addresses the difficulty of sustaining a Jewish identity and heritage in a predominantly secular and assimilationist society. As well, she commonly examines the calling and accountability of the artist, especially within the context of the Jewish moral code.

Biographical Information

Born in New York City and educated at New York University and Ohio State University, Ozick published her first book, a novel, in 1966. *Trust,* the story of a young woman's search for identity, was written over the course of six years. The work received only lukewarm critical and commercial reception, and Ozick turned to writing short stories and novellas, which were published in magazines such as *Commentary, Esquire,* and *The New Yorker.* Short fiction subsequently became the basis for Ozick's literary reputation. Ozick has explained that one of her reasons for using the novella form is that she no longer has the ambition to write anything as long as *Trust.* Ozick is also a noted critic, particularly of Jewish–American literature, and has conceived of New Yiddish, which would be comprehensible to speakers of English yet preserve the inflections and tone of the waning Jewish language.

Major Works

In most of Ozick's short fiction, the plot revolves around the dilemma of being Jewish in modern Western society, particularly the United States. In "Levitation," a couple in a mixed Jewish and Christian marriage fail to understand each other's priorities due to the basic incompatibility of their worldviews. Ozick sees American culture as predominantly pagan, concerned with nature and the physical realm of existence, and therefore inherently in conflict with the worship of the noncorporeal God of Judaism. For example, in "The Pagan Rabbi," the title character is torn between love of religion and scholarship on the one hand and attraction to nature and magic on the other. Ozick is also concerned with the idea that the production of art and literature is blasphemous, believing that

it puts the artist in direct competition with God as creator. A recurring theme of her work, present in "Usurpation (Other People's Stories)" and in others, is that every writer borrows material from other writers and, more importantly, "usurps" God's domain by attempting to replicate or transform reality through fiction. The idea of a person taking on the role of a godlike creator is given a humorous twist in "Puttermesser and Xanthippe," in which Ruth Puttermesser creates a female golem to help with her housework. The creature is useful at first, but begins to run amok, forcing her creator to destroy her. A similar religious offense is treated in Ozick's story "The Shawl" and its sequel, "Rosa." The focus of the narratives is a woman who idolatrously worships the memory of her infant daughter, who was murdered in a Nazi death camp.

Critical Reception

Ozick's short fiction has always been extremely well-received by critics. The stories are free, many commentators have said, of the opaque language that made *Trust* so difficult to read. In work subsequent to the novel, Ozick controls her treatment of language so that, while sophisticated and erudite prose remains a hallmark of her writing style, complicated diction does not impede her narratives. Reviewers have generally recognized Ozick's strengths to be her challenging ideas and evocative style, while noting weaknesses in her characterization and emotive qualities. The accessibility of Ozick's fiction to average readers has been questioned by some critics who find her style overly pedantic and parochial, with its strong emphasis on Jewish concerns. In response to this objection, Victor Strandberg has commented: "What matters in the end is the imaginative power to elevate local materials toward universal and timeless significance. By that standard, I judge Ozick's work to be memorably successful."

PRINCIPAL WORKS

SHORT FICTION

The Pagan Rabbi, and Other Stories   1971
Bloodshed and Three Novellas   1976
Levitation: Five Fictions   1982
The Shawl: A Story and a Novella   1989

OTHER MAJOR WORKS

Trust   (novel)   1966
Art and Ardor   (essays)   1983
The Cannibal Galaxy   (novel)   1983
The Messiah of Stockholm   (novel)   1987
Metaphor and Memory   (essays)   1989

CRITICISM

Johanna Kaplan   (essay date 1971)

[*Kaplan is an American critic, novelist, and short story writer whose fiction explores the Jewish experience in America. In the following excerpt, she lavishly praises* The Pagan Rabbi, and Other Stories, *and perceives the collection as addressing the search of individuals for transcendent meaning in life.*]

[In *The Pagan Rabbi, and Other Stories*] all that was best in the novel [*Trust*]—that relentless, passionate, discovering and uncovering intelligence—is present and instantly recognizable, but there is now a difference in the prose. It is sharpened, clarified, controlled and above all beautifully, unceasingly welcoming.

From the very first opening sentences, we are immediately drawn in. "When I heard that Isaac Kornfeld, a man of piety and brains, had hanged himself in the public park, I put a token in the subway stile and journeyed out to see the tree." Who is this man? Quick! We have to know: in one sentence alone, we are at the end of a life and in the middle of a world—a world, as it happens (because it is Cynthia Ozick's), about which all our guesses, as rapidly as they come, will be wrong.

Or the beginning of **"Envy"**: "Edelshtein, an American for forty years, was a ravenous reader of novels by writers 'of'—he said this with a snarl—'Jewish extraction.' He found them puerile, vicious, pitiable, contemptible, above all stupid. . . . Also, many of them were still young, and had black eyes, black hair, and red beards. A few were blue-eyed like the *cheder-yinglach* of his youth. Schoolboys. He was certain that he did not envy them, but he read them like a sickness."

Instantaneously, we are right in the center of a mind, in the swirl of a world. *People* live here, and people with ideas: who they are, how they think, what they do, matter. Accomplices, voyeurs, we quickly want to draw up the shades and find out.

What we find out is that these people live as much in a real country, a real place (the brilliantly evoked smells and textures of streets in Manhattan, of a rich man's house in Kiev in **"Envy,"** of a close, muggy summer night in a suburban town in **"The Doctor's Wife"**) as much as in a confused and adamantly uncompromising country of the spirit. They puzzle how to live not only within the confines of daily life as it's given to all of us, but with the gnawing agony of the unsleeping, merciless past that carries them into no country that exists: the supernatural.

It is not the familiar science-fiction, super-technology land that they are teased into inhabiting. Rather, because America—what Edelshtein, the embittered, untranslated Yiddish poet calls "America the bride, under her fancy gown nothing"—is so severe a disappointment to them, a lie they cannot forge a compromise with, they push out the boundaries of their imaginations and reach into territories that they know in their hearts, in their history, are forbidden. They cannot make peace with or take part in human life as it goes on: husbands, wives, babies, are so much endless, purposeless repetition seen as ugliness, a species of unalterable decay, sickness and stupidity. What comes upon them—they are forced to it, it's not within their control—is a lust for the supernatural, for God's earthly form in fantastic, inadmissible, demonic creatures. This lust, torturously pursued and grappled with, blinds them, overwhelms them; in frenzy and passion, they feel themselves freed, and at the very same time know that their punishment is not concealed, but in fact embedded in their ecstatic, maddened liberation.

Miss Ozick seems to be constantly struggling with this theme, which is of course a variant of the question: what is holy? Is it the extraordinary, that which is beyond possible human experience—dryads (**"The Pagan Rabbi"**) or sea-nymphs (**"The Dock-Witch"**)? Or is the holiness in life to be discovered, to be seen in what is ordinarily, blindly, unthinkingly discounted? "The disciples of Reb Moshe of Kobryn . . . disregarded feats in opposition to nature—they had no awe for their master when he hung in air, but when he slept—the miracle of his lung, his breath, his heartbeat!"

This tension runs through all the stories and all the characters. Yet they are never characters who, as in some fiction, exist primarily to represent attitudes. From their smallest idiosyncratic gestures—their ways of eating, dressing, moving and arguing—to their largest concerns, they are people whom one knows, and not because we have met them before, but because we are meeting them, getting to know them *now.*

Cynthia Ozick is a kind of narrative hypnotist. Her range is extraordinary; there is seemingly nothing she cannot do. Her stories contain passages of intense lyricism and brilliant, hilarious, uncontainable inventiveness—jokes, lists, letters, poems, parodies, satires. In the last story, **"Virility,"** a young, immigrant, would-be poet tries to learn English and write poetry at the same time by scrawling his poems on the torn-out pages of a dictionary. When asked why he doesn't use "regular paper," he says, "I like words . . . I wouldn't get that just from a blank sheet."

This book has no blank sheets. It reminds us that literature is not a luxury or diversion or anachronism, but an awakening and a restorative for the center of our lives.

> Johanna Kaplan, *"A Lust for God's Earthly Forms,"* in The New York Times Book Review, *June 13, 1971, p. 7.*

Josephine Z. Knopp   (essay date 1975)

[*Knopp is an American educator, critic, and the author of* The Trial of Judaism in Contemporary Jewish Writing *(1974). In the following essay, originally published in 1975, she praises* The Pagan Rabbi, and Other Stories *for the insights it provides into Jewish heritage and contemporary Jewish life.*]

Jewishness and Judaism are among Cynthia Ozick's central concerns as a writer. One is struck, for example, by her recent piece in *Esquire,* "All the World Wants the Jews Dead." It is not merely the title that is striking; Ozick is genuinely concerned with "the precariousness of Jewish survival." She goes on, "If I say *Jewish* and not *Israeli,* it is because they are one and the same thing, and no one, in or out of Israel, ought to pretend differently anymore. . . . It is no good for anti-Semites to pretend anymore that they are 'anti-Zionist' but not 'anti-Jewish,' or that the two notions can be kept separate."

These remarks, certain to offend, perhaps outrage, many liberals (to say nothing of the radical left), are characteristic of much of Ozick's work. As creator of fiction, as political commentator, as literary critic, she does not shrink from taking risks, when that furthers the dissemination of her unique vision of the truth.

Another example is furnished by the *Midstream* article, "Literary Blacks and Jews," in which Ozick discusses Bernard Malamud's *The Tenants* and the relationship of that novel to the Ralph Ellison–Irving Howe controversy which began eight years before its publication. Her discussion is incisive, shedding new light both on the controversy and the novel, which, as she puts it, "Together . . . make a bemusing artifact in reverse archaeology. Dig them up and discover, in genteel form, the savage future." What seems most important, finally, is her view of the savage present. Willie, the black writer/protagonist of *The Tenants,* is talented, but brutish, a stereotype, prefabricated (to use Ellison's word). On this point Ozick comments,

"But the real question is: who cast this die, who prefabricated Willie? . . . Malamud did not make Willie. He borrowed him—he mimicked him—from the literature and politics of the black movement. Willie is the black dream that is current in our world. Blacks made him." Deeply pessimistic, she concludes that "black militancy, in and out of print, has now come to define itself if not largely then centrally through classical anti-Semitism," and of *The Tenants* she draws the related inference that "its theme is pogrom."

In the collection *The Pagan Rabbi and Other Stories,* published in 1971, Ozick's fictional concerns are largely consonant with the point of view she establishes in her essays. The collection contains seven stories, of which three—the title story, **"Envy; or, Yiddish in America,"** and **"The Suitcase"**—may, without excessive theorizing, be denoted "Jewish." Several others are at least arguably so. One of these, surely, is **"The Butterfly and the Traffic Light,"** a brief and curious work, the earliest story of the collection. The principal character, Fishbein, an intellectual and a Jew, is somehow at odds with the society in which he moves. For Fishbein the midwestern university town that is now his home "was an imitation of a city," and America itself is a place "where everything was illusion and all illusion led to disillusion." He prefers the capitals of Europe with their active public life, whose streets were "employed" by "beggars and derelicts" and by "crowds assembled for riot or amusement or politics."

Fishbein expresses strong opinions in religious matters as well. He is convinced that " 'It's as foolish to be fixed on one God as it is to be on one idea . . . The index of advancement is flexibility.' " In his view the traditional Jewish insistence on a "rigid unitarian God" has been "unfortunate for history," leading, for example, to the—in his opinion unnecessary—Maccabean War, when there should have been "room for Zeus *and* God under one roof."

If Fishbein's attraction to the multiplicity of gods in classical Greece and Rome anticipates the theme of **"The Pagan Rabbi,"** his unease within American society foreshadows the main concerns of **"Envy; or Yiddish in America,"** which expresses the strains of the Jewish immigrant experience in America by mourning the death of Yiddish, which "was lost, murdered. The language—a museum." The fate of Yiddish is no mere abstraction here; it is given substance through the sufferings of the sixty-seven year old Yiddish poet, Hershel Edelshtein, whose works have no audience, either in his adopted New York City or in Tel Aviv. Regardless of the quality of his poetry, Edelshtein can have no audience without first acquiring a translator. His own English is too poor, despite his forty years in America, to carry out the translations himself.

Edelshtein and his fellow suffering Yiddish poet, Baumzweig, turn their frustrations to a shared hatred of Yankel Ostrover, a writer of Yiddish stories: "They hated him for the amazing thing that had happened to him—his fame." Remindful of a quite familiar and important current figure on the New York Jewish literary scene, Ostrover had begun as "a columnist for one of the Yiddish dailies," but now has an international reputation. He is considered a "modern"; he is "free of the prison of Yiddish," his every new story immediately translated for publication in English.

Ostrover has a variety of translators, one of them "a spinster hack" to whom Edelshtein writes in the hope of getting his four volumes of poetry translated into English. Her refusal is also an act of confession as she explains why she continues to translate for Ostrover, despite his abuse. It is not money or a belief in Ostrover's talent that motivates her, but rather the need to define herself: "I'm 'Ostrover's translator.' You think that's nothing? It's an entrance into *them*. I'm invited everywhere." Asserting that the quality of Ostrover's Yiddish is irrelevant ("Whatever's in Yiddish doesn't matter"), she reveals that "Transformation [into English] is all he cares for."

The driving force of Edelshtein's continuing search for translation is more complex. In part it is envy of Ostrover and the desire for fame of his own. Childless, he fears a death that will leave no trace of his presence on the earth. Like Ostrover, Edelshtein seeks immortality, but an immortality more universal, encompassing a genuine desire to save from extinction the Yiddish language, and with it the work of the great Yiddish writers of the past. "Whoever forgets Yiddish," he writes, "courts amnesia of history. . . . A thousand years of our travail forgotten." And he tells a skeptical Ostrover, " 'In Talmud if you save a single life it's as if you saved the world. And if you save a language? Worlds maybe. Galaxies. The whole universe.' " Ostrover's reply: " 'Hersheleh, the God of the Jews made a mistake when he didn't have a son, it would be a good occupation for you.' "

There are ironic reverberations, therefore, in Edelshtein's interchange with Hannah, a young and intelligent Jewish girl, born in America but fluent in Yiddish, a rarity presenting the poet with a golden opportunity he is quick to seize upon. Though Hannah can recite Edelshtein's Yiddish verses from memory, to her Ostrover is in the mainstream of literature, a "contemporary," who "speaks for everybody," while Edelshtein, Baumzweig and their fellows represent only literary "puddles." She rejects Edelshtein's claims upon immortality, refusing his request for translation because, as she says, " 'You don't interest me.' " Without mercy, she ignores Edelshtein's pleas both for himself (" 'Animate me! Without you I'm a clay pot!' ") and for the future of the language (" 'You'll save Yiddish,' . . . 'you'll be like a Messiah to a whole generation, a whole literature.' "). Like Frankie Alpine of Malamud's *The Assistant*, she repudiates Jewish suffering as unnecessary, as somehow willful: " 'All you people want to suffer.' " With references to "you people" and "you Jews," Hannah separates herself from Jewish history in an act which is a reversal of Alpine's conversion to Judaism. Despite her unusual background, like other Jews she has joined "them," America, the world-at-large.

Thus, though the action of **"Envy"** is confined almost exclusively to Jewish—one should say Yiddish—New York, its conflicts internal ones, the story is nevertheless suffused by the kind of tension that can be generated only at the interfaces of distinct cultures. The larger society is present, if only by implication, impinging upon and affecting the interactions of those on the inside. In the story's final pages—Edelshtein's exchange of clichés and epithets with an anti-Semite—we do at last hear the voice of a Gentile, if only by telephone. This conversation is uproariously funny, yet deadly serious at the same time, as becomes clear with Edelshtein's final sally: " 'On account of you children become corrupted! . . . On account of you I have no translator!' " Though one may be inclined at first to dismiss this as an absurd attempt by a desperate Edelshtein to assign blame for his failures, upon reflection it seems otherwise. Both the "spinster hack" and Hannah have been corrupted, that is to say diverted from the true service of the Yiddish language and—in Edelshtein's view—of the Jewish people, by the conflicting claims and opportunities of the surrounding culture.

By contrast, the setting of **"The Suitcase"** is the art world of the larger New York society; its sole Jew is Genevieve Levin, mistress of aspiring artist Gottfried Hencke. Sophisticated and intelligent ("Smith, '48, *summa cum laude,* Phi Beta Kappa"), Genevieve has helped Gottfried arrange a showing of his works and a lecture on Hencke's art by a famous critic. The story concerns the interplay between Genevieve and the only other truly substantial figure in the story, Gottfried's father, who was born in Germany, but no longer thinks of himself as German, after many years of life as an architect in America.

Genevieve is hard on the Germans, "the sort who, twenty years after Hitler's war, would not buy a Volkswagen." Intentionally provoking Gottfried's father, only half-joking, she compares the crowd at the opening to inmates of a concentration camp and refers to Gottfried's paintings as "shredded swastikas." Mr. Hencke, immediately grasping her intention, understood that "she thought him a Nazi sympathizer even now, an anti-Semite, an Eichmann." His unspoken defense constitutes a retreat to the safety of a Hellenistic conception of history: "Who could be blamed for History?" he thinks, "It did not take a philosopher . . . to see that History was Force-in-Itself, like Evolution." With Genevieve continuing the pursuit, blaming Jung for the murder of the Jewish psychologists under the Nazis, Mr. Hencke is driven to an open defense as well: " 'In sixty-eight years . . . I have harmed no one. I have built towers . . . I have never destroyed.' "

After a lecture in which the literary critic contrasts Gottfried's paintings, as "The art of Fulfillment," with Melville's *Moby-Dick* (the art, presumably, of Yearning), a lecture which parodies itself, describing Hencke's art as " 'an art not of hunger, not of frustration, but of satiation. An art, so to speak, for fat men,' " Genevieve renews the attack with a reference to Mr. Hencke's brother-in-law, a shampoo manufacturer in Cologne: " 'Confide in me the nature of the shampoo. What did he make it out of? Not now. I mean during the war. . . . Whose human fat? What Jewish lard?' " Despite the torment Genevieve causes him, Mr. Hencke keeps his composure, enjoying her wit and quick intelligence; he thinks of her as "a superior woman," and, partly perhaps from guilt, he generalizes to " 'A superior race, I've always thought that. Imaginative.' " But his composure does not last long, as, triggered by a remark Mr. Hencke makes about his boyhood in Germany, Genevieve explodes, " 'Don't speak to me about German chimneys,' . . . 'I know what kind of smoke came out of those damn German chimneys.' " At this, "His eyes wept, his throat wept . . . she was merciless."

Genevieve is cast here in the familiar role of the Jew as prophet, as moral *nudnick,* chosen, perhaps choosing, to spread the gospel of truth and *mentshlekhkayt,* humaneness and compassion among the Gentiles. That Mr. Hencke was born German is really beside the point, merely a convenience for Genevieve to work into her message: all are guilty. But Genevieve too is guilty. Indeed Leslie Fiedler's comments on Bellow's *The Victim* apply to **"The Suitcase"** as well: "Bellow . . . has had the imagination and sheer nerve to portray the Jew, the Little Jew, as victimizer as well as victim." Genevieve as Jew is a victim, but in the story it is Mr. Hencke who is victimized, reduced from strength and self-assurance to uncertainty and tearful guilt. Admitting to Genevieve that he really has come to New York to leave for Europe the next morning rather than exclusively to attend the opening, as he has led his son and daughter-in-law to believe, he feels constrained to assure her that he is not going to Germany: " 'Not Germany, Sweden. The Swedes were innocent in the war, they saved so many Jews. I swear it, not Germany.' "

The plight of the Jews in Nazi Germany somehow gets confused in Mr. Hencke's mind with Genevieve's discovery that her pocketbook is missing, stolen during the opening. His denials of wrongdoing in the matter of Jews mingle with a wholly unexpected and unnecessary claim of innocence in the theft, and in an act of self-mortification he throws his suitcase open to prove that it does not contain the missing pocketbook. Thus, humiliated, guilty for reasons which are at best obscure, he may be considered a victim of Jewish revenge, a revenge that brings an unwelcome awareness of his implication, the implication of the world, in distant atrocities, and an awareness too that Genevieve, though a victim herself, "was not innocent."

Genevieve's sphere of action is the larger American society but, like Fishbein, she is uncomfortable there, alienated, unwilling to accept its standards and premises. By contrast, in the story **"Virility,"** Edmund Gate (born Elia Gatoff), a young Jewish immigrant from Czarist Russia by way of Liverpool, wasting no time on alienation, plunges directly into American society. He comes to America with no money, hardly any English, and no apparent talent, yet, believing in the efficacy of hard work and in the opportunities of the New World, he strives to be a poet—in English. After several years of work on a newspaper and no success as a poet, his poetry suddenly—as it seems, miraculously—improves beyond recognition, catches on, is published in the best magazines, and receives great and deserved critical acclaim. He has five volumes of poetry published under the title *Virility* and he lectures all over the world to the praise, the frenzied adulation, of audiences three times as big as Caruso's. Of Gate's poetry it is said, "If Teddy Roosevelt's Rough Riders had been poets, they would have written poems like that. If Genghis Khan and Napoleon had been poets, they

would have written poems like that. They were masculine poems . . . full of passion and ennui."

If Ozick, as writer, is a feminist anywhere it is in this story. For it develops that the miraculous change in Gate's poetry has a simple explanation—plagiarism. The poetry is not that of Edmund Gate at all, but in fact written by his mother's spinster aunt, Tante Rivka of Liverpool, who has been steadily sending Gate poetry in her frequent (and unanswered) letters. Three years after her death Gate has enough material left for just one more book of poetry, originally to be published as *Virility VI.* He confesses the hoax however, and the book appears under the name *Flowers from Liverpool,* the pretty cover, "the color of a daisy's petal," containing a picture of Tante Rivka as a young woman in Russia. Though the collection by chance comprises the best of all of Tante Rivka's poetry, "the crest of the poet's vitality," "the reviewers are unenthusiastic, unimpressed." Where *Virility* was greeted by " 'Seminal and hard.' 'Robust, lusty, male.' 'Erotic,' " *Flowers from Liverpool* is merely " 'Thin feminine art,' 'Limited. . . . A spinster's one-dimensional vision.' " If Edmund Gate's poetry had " 'The quality, in little, of the very greatest novels,' " Tante Rivka shows " 'The typical unimaginativeness of her sex,' 'Distaff talent, secondary by nature.' " At best hers is a " 'Lovely girlish voice reflecting a fragile girlish soul: a lace valentine.' " So much for literary criticism and male superiority.

But if there is bitterness here, there is also humor. Ozick demolishes the male supremacists with the same hilarious derision that she employs against the anti-Semites in **"Envy."** Thus, Gate's last words, uttered to the narrator while gripping himself between the legs—presumably for verification—are "I am a man." He is wasted away, drunk and bitter, blaming his aunt for, as he puts it, running out on him. His death follows shortly thereafter, at the age of twenty-six, in a drunken suicide leap from a bridge.

Tante Rivka's death, by contrast, occurs not out of desperation, but with dignity, as a result of pride in self-sufficiency. Having grown too old and feeble to work, she allows herself to starve to death rather than ask for help in her time of need. Tante Rivka's lifelong employment in a millinery shop sewing on veils brings to mind Edelshtein's observation in **"Envy"** that the Jewish poets "are a mob of working people, laborers, hewers of wood, . . . our chief poet . . . a house painter."

In a strange and intriguing epilogue it is suggested that Gate did not die—his body was never recovered from the river—but lived on past the age of one hundred, in misery, doubting his manhood, uncertain of his gender. This unusual twist is but one example of Ozick's penchant for the unexpected and bizarre, which is evident in several of her stories, notably **"The Doctor's Wife,"** a tragedy of emasculation and frustrated ambition with a Jewish cast of characters, and in the two tales **"The Dock-Witch"** and **"The Pagan Rabbi,"** in which the bizarre turns to the supernatural.

Like **"Envy"** and in contrast to **"The Suitcase," "The Pagan Rabbi"** is a story set within the Jewish community, a tale of Jews acting among Jews. Yet—and again as in

"Envy"—the pressures of the external world exact their toll, in this case upon Rabbi Isaac Kornfeld, a pious and learned man, Professor of Mishnaic History, who, in an act totally inimical to his practice of Orthodox Judaism, hangs himself from a tree with his own prayer shawl. If in **"Envy"** the struggle with the world at large is one to maintain uniqueness, cultural "Jewishness," the conflict in **"The Pagan Rabbi"** is that of opposing theologies. Here it is not the Jewish community which is challenged, but Judaism itself, tested against the lure of classical paganism.

The story is constructed as an enlargement upon a working out, of its own epigraph, the following passage from the Mishnaic *The Ethics of the Fathers:*

> Rabbi Jacob said: "He who is walking along and studying, but then breaks off to remark, 'How lovely is that tree!' or 'How beautiful is that fallow field!'—Scripture regards such a one as having hurt his own being."

Such a one is Isaac Kornfeld, who, even as a young student, was fascinated by the philosophy of the ancient Greeks, to the dismay of his father, for whom philosophy was an abomination, the corridor to idolatry. Isaac studies not only Saadia Gaon and Yehudah Halevi, but Dostoyevski, Thomas Mann, Hegel, and Nietzsche as well. Marrying Sheindel, Isaac predictably continues his Talmudic studies in the seminary and launches a brilliant academic career, but he also develops an unexpected—and at first unexplained—passion for nature and the outdoors. The aberration grows in him to the point that he spends every night in the park, returning home only at six or seven in the morning. The letter—Sheindel refers to it as a love letter—found in his pocket after the suicide explains the rabbi's metamorphosis, his deep involvement in paganism and his love affair (there is no other way to describe it) with a dryad, the "free soul" of a young oak tree.

According to the carefully argued discussion of Isaac's letter, man's soul is "indwelling," trapped inside the body, while plants, animals, stones, rivers, all other things of nature, have souls free to roam outside the body. Isaac has an ingenious explanation why Moses, knowing all, failed to speak of the free souls to the ancient Hebrews enslaved in Egypt. And he believes that "To see one's soul is to know all, to know all is to own the peace our philosophies futilely envisage." Accordingly, "an extraordinary thought emerged" in him, the desire to couple with one of the free souls, in the hope that "the strength of the connection would . . . wrest my own soul from my body . . . draw it out . . . to its own freedom." Not surprisingly, he is able to justify his desire on the basis of innumerable precedents from mythology, and by reference to Genesis and Job.

Successful in calling forth the tree nymph and entering into a liaison which grows more passionate nightly, the rabbi ultimately succeeds in freeing his soul, which appears in the form of an old studious Jew, with beard and prayer shawl, carrying a bag stuffed with books. As the old Jew walks he studies a Tractate of the Mishnah, indifferent to the glories of nature by which he is surrounded. The dryad despises the rabbi's soul because, as she puts it, "It

conjures against me. It denies me, it denies every spirit and all my sisters . . . it denies our multiplicity." Ignoring his pleas, she leaves Isaac—from her point of view he has "spoiled himself with confusions"—whereupon the rabbi seizes his soul's prayer shawl and hangs himself with it from his beloved's body, the young oak tree.

Though Ozick is capable of trenchant humor and despite the fact that the subject of **"The Pagan Rabbi"** would lend itself to a humorous treatment, at least in part, the story, in contrast to a number of others in the collection, in fact provides very little occasion for mirth. It is clear that the author is in deadly earnest about the theological conflicts and ultimate transformation that take place within Isaac. Thus, it is not by chance that she has chosen the separation of body and soul as the primary object of Isaac's quest. For, in sharp distinction to the classical view of man's nature, Judaism has traditionally held that body and soul, the mundane and the transcendent, are inseparable elements of a single being, with man's essence determined by both. In actively working against this basic tenet of Judaism Isaac has committed a transgression comparable in seriousness to his eventual suicide.

Isaac's internal struggle brings to mind I. B. Singer's Yasha Mazur, the magician of Lublin, who is a "soul searcher, prone to fantasy and strange conjecture." Like Isaac, Yasha is deeply moved by the order and beauty in nature, but with the fundamental difference that despite a deep-seated religious skepticism he sees the hand of God in evidence everywhere, as the causal agent in all natural phenomena: "Oh, God Almighty, You are the magician, not I! . . . To bring out plants, flowers and colors from a bit of black soil!" At times flirting with paganism himself, Yasha nevertheless retains the basic framework of Judaism—God as creator of nature in contrast to God within nature—and thus his ultimate fate stands in stark contrast to that of Isaac. Inverting Isaac's transformation, Yasha, the life-long doubter, becomes a man of piety, studying Talmud, and advising his fellow Jews in their times of trouble. An important clue to the differences between the two men is furnished by Sheindel: " 'The more piety, the more skepticism. A religious man comprehends this.' " Though both men are subject to the temptations and pressures inherent in the external society, a healthy skepticism has freed Yasha to turn to God in his maturity, whereas Isaac's demise stands as a rebuke to the life of studious piety unleavened by the perspective achieved in entertaining radical doubt. The condition of Isaac's soul reveals that the excursion into paganism has been contrary to his own essential nature, which remains that of the pious and scholarly Jew, that he has indeed "spoiled himself with confusion."

If Ozick's Rabbi Isaac Kornfeld resembles Singer's Yasha Mazur, her interest in the supernatural is reminiscent of Singer as well. Like Singer she employs the supernatural as she does the natural; both are admitted as causal factors in the explanation of events. Comparisons may be drawn with other Jewish writers as well. Her character Edelshtein, for example, is as memorable, on a smaller scale, of course, as is Sammler, displaying a similar sense of history and comparable intellectual powers.

With Bellow, Ozick shares a talent for illuminating distinctions as well as a feeling for the Jewish immigrant experience in America, and with Roth a keen, at times withering, humor capable of exposing the foibles of Jewish life in the diaspora. As with other Jewish-American writers who merit serious attention, Ozick's work displays an acute historical consciousness, an understanding of the role of Judaism in world history. Her Jewish stories earn that designation by virtue of a perspective shaped by the author's sense of Jewish history. They succeed in placing contemporary Jewish problems within their historical framework, thus illuminating the anomalies of modern Jewish life while at the same time revealing the significance for the present of the link with the Jewish past.

> *Josephine Z. Knopp, "Ozick's Jewish Stories,"*
> in Cynthia Ozick, *edited by Harold Bloom,*
> *Chelsea House Publishers, 1986, pp. 21-9.*

On Ozick's writing style:

Cynthia Ozick has the enviable knack of moving, with impressive speed, in opposite directions at the same time; her specialities are prose poetry, intellectual slapstick, meticulous detail, and wild rhetorical fantasy. The result at its best is an audacious and unorthodox balancing of forces, both within the story and within the sentence. Within the story, there is tension between a carefully rendered milieu and the wildly elaborated fantasy which arrives to transform it. Within the sentence, there is a running battle between a realism that describes things as they are, and a rhetoric that takes constant liberties with the appearances.

Adam Mars-Jones, in his "Fantastic Flushes," The Times Literary Supplement, *April 23, 1982.*

Thomas R. Edwards (essay date 1976)

[*Edwards is an American critic and educator. In the following essay, he praises Ozick's collection* Bloodshed *as a whole, while faulting the story "Usurpation" as self-conscious and esoteric.*]

Cynthia Ozick is never in danger of saying too little as a writer. She confesses to a fondness for the novella, and there's no doubt that she needs space for her fiction, which is episodic, anecdotal, informed by a sensibility that feeds on words but also on anxieties about words, doubts (as she explains in a personal and chatty preface [to *Bloodshed and Three Novellas*]) about the rightness of telling stories at all, especially if the writer is Jewish.

When these anxieties are in the foreground, as they are in **"Usurpation,"** subtitled "Other People's Stories," I have my doubts about her work. A Jewish woman writer, unable to write a story about magical silver crowns because Bernard Malamud has already written one like it, encounters an unpleasant but ambitious young student writer who hustles her into reading an unpublished story of his own. His story is terrible, but its subject—a young writer being advised by an eminent older one to overcome his

envy—so intrigues her that she begins to tell it herself, but with improvements and amplifications. In her version, the old writer tricks the younger one into putting on a magical silver crown which makes him instantly successful and famous, as well as old and diseased. Unable to remove his crown, he soon dies.

Having told her story, the woman writer seeks out the student whose story she's usurped and Malamudized, so to speak. She finds him in an abandoned tenement in Brooklyn, where she meets his cousin, the wife of a self-styled rabbi who's in jail for selling silver crowns under false pretenses, as in Malamud's story. She puts on one of the crowns, and then reads the rabbi's ill-written but powerfully embittered manuscript about an indifferent God's refusal to work miracles on behalf of his people, such as stopping the Holocaust.

Even this inadequate summary—I've had to leave out the ghost of Tchernikhovsky and a good deal more—would have been impossible for me without the aid of Ozick's preface, in which she explains this parable about the "anxiety of influence." She says it expresses the fear she feels, as a Jewish writer working in a language not of her own people, that art is a magical act which, though sanctioned by pagan and Christian traditions, is a blasphemy against the God of Israel, who has forbidden idolatry and magic:

> **"Usurpation"** is about the dread of Moloch, the dread of lyrical faith, the dread of metaphysics, the dread of "theology," the dread of fantasy and fancy, of god and Muse; above all the dread of idols; the dread of the magic that kills. The dread of imagination.

Even a skeptical gentile can find this dread impressive. And Ozick's anxiety about being a writer while writing a story about that anxiety is fascinating. But the unnamed critic whom Ozick mildly rebukes was not far from the mark in charging her story with mystification. Certainly her gloss on **"Usurpation"** is more coherent and moving than the story itself.

The other stories in **Bloodshed** seemed to me much better than this one. **"An Education,"** about a guileless young archaeologist being morally cannibalized by a pretentious pair of intellectual frauds, is more a product of ironic sophistication than of human understanding, but it is full of splendidly malicious jokes ("Rosalie was one of those serious blue-eyed fat girls, very short-fingered, who seem to have arrived out of their mothers' wombs with ten years' experience at social work"). **"Bloodshed,"** about a moment of bitter conflict between a Hassidic rabbi and a skeptical outsider who turns out to be carrying a gun, is, like **"Usurpation,"** hard for a goy to make out, but it proceeds with intensity and economy.

The best thing here is the marvelous novella **"A Mercenary,"** a tale of impersonations and identity changes set in the world of international diplomacy. Stanislav Lushinski, a Polish Jew who represents a tiny new African state at the United Nations, is a popular TV talk-show personality, but never goes without a briefcase full of false passports in case a quick getaway is called for. He is a richer figure than most of Ozick's other characters, less constrained by some governing idea. His troubled assistant, Morris Ngambe, an Oxford man who remembers participating in the ritual eating of his mother by all her loving kin, is simpler but equally engaging in his efforts to cope with the violence of life in primitive places (he's been snubbed by Puerto Ricans, mugged by blacks, and bitten by a chow dog who perhaps represents the Oriental component of this dangerous melting pot)—" 'New York is just what they say of it—a wilderness, a jungle.' "

Morris is bemused by Lushinski's complete and sincere assimilation into his own Africa while he, Morris, must uneasily remain in "a city of Jews" which ought to be but isn't the place for a Lushinski; and it is Morris who comes closest to uttering the story's hidden motto:

> It may be that every man at length becomes what he wishes to victimize.
>
> It may be that every man needs to impersonate what he first must kill.

Lushinski, at home again in the Africa he loves differently but not less well than its "natives" do, can dismiss Morris's speculations as "a lumpy parroting of *Reading Gaol*" with perhaps some Fanon or Genet thrown in: "Like everyone the British had once blessed with Empire, Morris was a Victorian. He was a gentleman. He believed in civilizing influences; even more in civility. He was besotted by style. If he thought of knives, it was for buttering scones." He himself remembers other uses of knives, fighting for survival in the forests of occupied Poland whose horrors he has been trying to put behind him all his life, and he resents the charge that he's an impersonator, a fake, a Jew after all.

But this splendid serio-comic tale finally brings both Lushinski the mercenary and Morris the imperialist together in a single focus, showing the ironies and the pathos of assimilation as a common ground between their very unlike histories. The "magic" which Cynthia Ozick elsewhere fears works wonderfully in this nearly perfect long short story which, she tells us, was first conceived as a novel. It shows that, after all, a story told in the right way is just long enough, whatever its size.

> *Thomas R. Edwards, "The Short View," in*
> The New York Review of Books, *Vol. XXIII, No. 5, April 1, 1976, pp. 34-7.*

Ruth R. Wisse (essay date 1976)

[*Wisse is a Rumanian-born Canadian educator, translator, and the author of* The Schlemiel as Modern Hero *(1970). In the following excerpt, first published as "American Jewish Writing, Act II," in* Commentary, *June 1976, she analyzes Ozick's stories as an attempt to begin a new Jewish literature.*]

The career of American Jewish literature would seem to have reached a turning point. Over the past three decades, Jewish writers have made their way into the mainstream of American fiction, and have now been canonized in university curricula. A swell of anthologies, secondary studies, and courses is evidence of a success achieved and acknowledged—a success not only of individual writers

admired for their particular talents, but of what is generally seen as an entire cultural movement or school. Despite an occasional objection (like that of the late Philip Rahv) to "the ignorant and even malicious idea that such a school exists," no one would seriously deny that the years since the end of World War II have been fat ones for American Jewish writing, and few would any longer deny that those years seem to be coming to an end. But where some critics see an imminent decline of the genre as a whole, others anticipate spirited new developments.

Certainly a case can be made for the exhaustion of an "American Jewish" approach or an "American Jewish" subject matter. The twin themes of marginality and victimization, which have come to be associated in Western literature with the Jew, have been brought to maturity in this country in the work of Saul Bellow, Bernard Malamud, and Philip Roth, and it is questionable how much longer they can profitably serve. The Jewish male as son and would-be lover has become a stock literary fixture—John Updike's parody of the type in *Bech* is a gentle hint that even the *goy* has the formula, so enough already. Where it once required an act of courage for a serious Jewish writer to risk parochialism by creating a distinctively Jewish character, the fact that Jewishness is now in literary fashion means that anyone can invoke it as a shorthand for signification, what Marcus Klein calls "a kind of strawberry mark, something that must mean something because it is celebrated in literature."

The attenuated Jewishness that has begun showing up in literature has its obvious source in the culture at large. As American Jews exhibit fewer identifying characteristics, the novelist of manners finds it harder to establish that bit of ethnic specificity, of local color, that will distinguish his work. Echoes of Yiddish grow fainter as actual speakers of the language withdraw into old age or hasidic ghettos. It was once possible for a Jewish writer to write a "Jewish" book simply as a result of having lived in certain sections of Chicago or New York. One had inherited, as the novelist Norma Rosen has put it, a trust fund: "Without even trying, one had certain speech rhythms . . . , colloquialisms that were inherently funny, relationships always good for cutting down by wit." Nowadays, there is nothing much in the speech or appearance of the average Jew to distinguish him from any other American, and fewer of those cultural features which critics have grown accustomed to identifying as "Jewish."

The combined effect of literary saturation and a diluted Jewish culture has prompted some critics to prophesy the end of the Jewish movement in American writing. American Jewish literature, they say, derives its strength from the peculiar tension of the Jew who is native to two cultures while fully at home in neither; hence, the more fully the Jew becomes integrated into the larger culture, the less the tension and the fewer the creative energies generated by it. Jews, of course, will continue to write, but they will have lost the cutting edge of their hyphenated identity. . . .

Having no longer to defend themselves from real or imagined charges of parochialism, the new Jewish writers of the 70's are freer to explore the "tribal" and particularistic aspects of Judaism, and even, turning the tables, to speculate on the restrictive limits of English as a literary language. Here the ethnic label fits more comfortably, for these are writers who self-consciously define themselves as Jews and attempt to express their artistic vision in Jewish terms. Their interest is not in the sociological or even the psychological legacy of a Jewish background, but in the national design and religious destiny of Judaism, in its workable myths. No longer content "to draw on the interest of what was put into the bank long ago by others" (to quote Norma Rosen again), they attempt to draw directly from Jewish sources and out of Jewish culture an image of an alternative civilization.

The self-styled spokesman and most audacious writer of this movement is Cynthia Ozick, who first presented her program at the America-Israel Dialogue of 1970, announcing that American Jewry was moving "Toward Yavneh," that is to say, toward the creation of an indigenously Jewish culture in the English language. Despite an almost complete lack of supportive evidence, Miss Ozick foretold the emergence of a new kind of literature as part of this general cultural renaissance: "A liturgical literature [which] has the configuration of the ram's horn: you give your strength to the inch-hole and the splendor spreads wide." The image of the *shofar,* or ram's horn, redolent of biblical history and the most awesome moments of the High Holy Days, was meant to discredit all those universalist Jews who had been blowing into the wrong end: George Steiner for glorifying the Exile as "an arena for humankind's finest perceptions"; Philip Roth for his protest, "I am not a Jewish writer; I am a writer who is a Jew"; Allen Ginsberg with his loud persuasion that religions are "allee samee." As against these, Miss Ozick argued that nothing produced by Jews in the Diaspora had lasted except that which was "centrally Jewish," particularistic and narrow in creative inception; and only that would survive which was written in a Jewish tongue. Her most highly charged—and correspondingly imprecise—remarks concerned the emergence in America of just such a new language, a Judeo-English, or "New Yiddish," the beginnings of which, she said, literate Jews were speaking and writing even now. The holy sparks struck in this new tongue would be the American Jewish literature of lasting merit.

The poetic sweep of these comments was more in the nature of visionary prophecy than of critical analysis, but the fiction produced by Cynthia Ozick in the intervening years provides more substantial evidence for her claims. Her most effective stories and novellas are not only steeped in internal Jewish life and lore to a degree that sets them apart from the work of her contemporaries and predecessors; they are actually Jewish assaults on fields of Gentile influence.

In the title story of her first collection, *The Pagan Rabbi,* a brilliant talmudist falls in love with the world of nature, and, feeling the agony of separation so acutely, he hangs himself to effect a pantheistic reunion. The notes and letter that he leaves behind offer eloquent testimony to the pagan ideal of freedom and passionately declare the pleasures of natural loveliness, but the story is on the side of his pious widow who damns them utterly with the biblical term, "abominations." Into the mouth of the errant rabbi the author has put part of her own aestheticist longing, raising worship of the beautiful to the highest philosophic and religious pitch, but only to oppose it finally, almost pitilessly, in the name of religious values.

The story, though written in English, bears significantly on Jewish literature in both Yiddish and Hebrew. One of the most pervasive subjects of the modern Yiddish and Hebrew literary tradition is the rediscovery of those natural human instincts which would free the dust-choked ghetto Jew from the stifling repressions of *halakhah* and religious inhibitions. In the works of Mendele, Sholem Aleichem, Peretz, Bialik, Feierberg, and Tchernikhovsky, the physical world of sun, storm, trees, and rivers provides a model of freedom counterposed to the self-denial of *shtetl* culture. The pagan rabbi of Miss Ozick's story, shaped by that same talmudic culture but inhabiting the contemporary world, sees in nature not a necessary corrective but a competing force that commands an allegiance as fierce as God's. Her story unmasks the ideal of beauty and shows it to be, for the Jew, a force as destructive as any the "Gentile" world can offer.

Jewish vulnerability to Gentile standards is also the subject of a second story, **"Envy; or, Yiddish in America,"** a masterpiece of contemporary fiction. Through the frustrations of an aging Yiddish poet, the story details the humiliating effect of America and American values on a once-fertile culture. The English language, by bestowing fame on some (through translation), and oblivion on others, decrees who shall live and who shall die. The Yiddish writer, forever doomed to servitude amid plenty, is frozen in an attitude of envy toward those who, through the magic of translation, achieve success in an alien world. Although the story's detailed description of the Yiddish literary milieu is as authentic as gossip, its subject is the dead-serious one of a culture that must pay constant tribute to English hegemony or lose its children and all its future.

The struggle against the assaults and seductions of the Gentile world continues to absorb Cynthia Ozick in her latest collection of fiction, *Bloodshed and Three Novellas.* Three of the four novellas here are directly about that confrontation, and though free of the actual "bloodshed" promised by the book's title, do throb with ominous intensity.

The first story, **"A Mercenary,"** introduces Lushinski, a Polish Jew by birth, now a citizen and the UN representative of a tiny African nation, and a permanent resident of New York. Lushinski's prodigious services and warm attachments to other cultures, African and American, are stimulated by the stark fear of his own Jewish identity, but his mistress, whom he calls a German countess, and his UN assistant, a true African by the name of Morris Ngambe, have little difficulty penetrating the ironic mask of the intellectual and exposing the vulnerable Jew, the potential victim, beneath. In the title story, **"Bloodshed,"** a Jewish fund-raiser visits his distant relative in a newly established hasidic community outside New York. Suspicious of fraudulence in others, he is forced, during the course of an interview with the *rebbe,* to acknowledge his own deceit and his own demonic capacities. **"An Education,"** the earliest and the least successful of the four novellas, is a heavily ironic treatment of a prize student who tries, and fails, to understand life by the same ideal systems of grammar and definition that can be used in Latin declension. In the last novella, **"Usurpation,"** the protagonist-narrator is a Jewish writer identifiable with the author herself. With disturbing unreserve, the writer-narrator covets, appropriates, and then corrupts the work of others in her own need to make a perfect story and to win the "magic crown" of fame and immortality.

The unsettling effect of both action and style in this last story is deliberate. The novella blurs the normal lines of demarcation between fact and fiction: the narrator tells us that she attended a public reading by a famous author and heard him read a story that she felt to be "hers"; then gives us the plot of a recently published story by Bernard Malamud that the knowledgeable reader would recognize as *his*; then changes the ending of the Malamud story and proceeds to find the "real persons" on whom the story was presumably based, as well as the unpublished manuscripts of its main character. In questionable taste, Miss Ozick also incorporates into her novella another story, which she uses as a literary foil, an actual work that she had seen in manuscript (it was subsequently published in *Response* magazine) by a young writer with a less secure reputation than Malamud's. On this story too she builds her own, in a candid act of plagiarism.

The novella, which freely reworks and passes comment on the works of other writers, is intended to undermine the act of fiction as process and as product. To deflate the mystique of the artist, Miss Ozick presents "herself" as a selfish and somewhat nasty finagler. In place of the grand notions of creativity, she gives us the petty emotions and treacherous techniques, the false bottoms and promises that produce the illusion of fictional magic.

But this act, the "Usurpation" of "Other Peoples' Stories," to use the double title of the novella, is only the lower manifestation of a higher, more significant act of false appropriation to which Miss Ozick wishes to draw attention. The thoroughly Jewish concern of this work is the writing of fiction itself, in Miss Ozick's view an inheritance from the Gentiles and by nature an idolatrous activity. Art—in the Western tradition of truth to fiction as its own end—is against the Second Commandment, she says, and anti-Jewish in its very impulse. As a Jewish artist, Miss Ozick undertakes to subvert the aesthetic ideal by demonstrating its corrupting and arrogant presumption to truth. Thus, the Hebrew poet Saul Tchernikhovsky, one of those who worshipped at the shrine of pagan freedom and natural beauty, finds himself, at the end of the novella, caged in Paradise before a motto that teaches: "All that is not Law is levity." Like the pious widow who hardened her heart against the pagan rabbi, the Jewish artist must refuse and denounce the allure of art.

It is not unusual in modern fiction for a story or novel to question its premises without giving them up. *Bloodshed,* however, commits an act of self-destruction. Like a prizefighter who cannot stop punching at the signal of the bell, Miss Ozick adds a preface to her four novellas to push her

meaning home. It is she herself who "explains" her final story, reducing it like a tendentious reviewer to a moral function:

> **"Usurpation"** is a story written against story-writing; against the Muse-goddesses; against Apollo. It is against magic and mystification, against sham and "miracle," and, going deeper into the dark, against idolatry. It is an invention directed against inventing—the point being that the story-making faculty itself can be a corridor to the corruptions and abominations of idol-worship, of the adoration of magical event.

The preface tells us when the stories were written, why they have been included here, what they are about. This is not footnoting, like Eliot's notes to *The Waste Land* to which the author ingenuously compares it, but self-justification and special pleading.

The preface betrays the insecurities of both the artist and the Jew. Though she admires the transforming, magical kind of art, Miss Ozick is, in fact, an intellectual writer whose works are the fictional realization of ideas. Her reader is expected, at the conclusion of her stories, to have an insight, to understand the point of events rather than to respond to their affective power. Miss Ozick has publicly regretted this quality of hers, and accused herself of lacking what George Eliot calls "truth of feeling." It is true that, marvelously imaginative as she is with words and ideas, Miss Ozick is not on the whole successful at creating autonomous characters whose destiny will tantalize or move the reader.

Because she is a Jewish writer who prides herself on the "centrally Jewish" quality of her work, Miss Ozick has hit a curious snag here. The writer who can achieve "truth of feeling" produces universal art whatever the ethnic stuff of his subject, but a writer of ideas requires a community of knowledge and shared cultural assumptions. In her preface, Miss Ozick says she has to explain the meaning of **"Usurpation"** because a certain non-Jewish critic had failed to understand it. This failure she attributes not to the story's possible artistic shortcomings, but to its Jewish specificity, which puts it outside the critic's cultural range: "I had written 'Usurpation' in the language of a civilization that cannot understand its thesis." As the prophet of an indigenous Jewish culture in the English language, she might have been expected to hail the critic's failure to understand as a milestone—an authentic breakthrough in the creation of a distinctive Jewish literature. Instead, determined to have both the cake and the eating of it, she anxiously becomes her own translator, explaining Tchernikhovsky, Torah, the large ideas as well as the factual underpinnings of her work. If her kind of art is not inherently universal, she is apparently prepared to provide "art with an explanation" in order to spread the splendor wide.

Saving herself from a lonely ethnic fate, Miss Ozick appears in the preface not simply as an author but as cultural impresario of a new Jewish literature in America. Elsewhere, in book reviews, letters-to-the-editor, and public appearances like the America-Israel Dialogue of 1970, she has launched a veritable campaign to promote the idea of a Jewish literary community with meaningful ties to the past, to Israel, and to Jewish literature in Jewish languages. The thrust of this campaign is the Judaization of English, not only for the small community of Jews but for the wider world, so that Jewish writers may create their own literature and still hope to overcome the natural barriers of distinctiveness and particularism.

Aside from the difficulty of knowing, at this point in its development, just what, specifically, a "Jewish" literature in English would look like, one may ask why *any* Jewish writer with access to English should want to risk a parochial fate when even Miss Ozick, keeping an anxious eye on the reviewers, has shown herself to have second thoughts on the subject. Nor is her fortification of art by advertising a reassuring sign of confidence in her project. Still, the reach of Jewish literature in English in the direction she proposes, though modest, has been noticeable in recent years. . . .

To distinguish between a kind of American Jewish writing that may be on its way out, and one that may be on its way in, is not to make any statement of relative value, but simply to point out the difference between writers who have all along insisted they belong to the Anglo-American tradition, though their heritage be Jewish, and writers who self-consciously place themselves within a Jewish cultural sphere, though their language is English. Perhaps a modest example can illustrate the point.

Cynthia Ozick's title story, **"Bloodshed,"** bears a remarkable resemblance to Philip Roth's "Eli, the Fanatic," the most "Jewish" story in his 1959 collection, *Goodbye, Columbus.* In both of these fictional confrontations between a secularized American Jew and an old-country believer, the moral scales are tipped in favor of the latter, not merely for his wry intelligence and personal courage, but also for his having survived the Holocaust. In both works the protagonist capitulates to this superior moral force, admits the relative hollowness of his own comfortable existence, and recognizes, even if he cannot accept, the elevated spiritual situation of the other.

The differences between Roth and Ozick start in their choice of locale. Roth's Eli Peck is a young lawyer in Woodenton, an American suburb where Jews are resolutely, though not yet comfortably, indistinguishable from their Gentile neighbors; into this suburb Rabbi Tsuref comes as a stranger to remind its Jews of something valuable they have lost. Cynthia Ozick's Bleilip, on the other hand, also a lawyer, takes a Greyhound bus out of New York to reach his destination, a small, self-contained hasidic community where *he* is the only stranger. Through this artificial device (there is no practical reason for Bleilip to have made the trip), Miss Ozick transports her character into a traditional Jewish environment which then authorizes, and, in fact, demands ongoing references to an internal Jewish world in which the Americanized Bleilip is at a cultural disadvantage. As against Roth's use of the shorthand symbol of a secure religious tradition to expose the social and psychological insecurity of a modern Jewish community, Miss Ozick portrays a real-life situation in which issues of faith and doubt, foreign to the skeptical Bleilip, are taken seriously and are seen to have consequences.

Paradoxically, however, it is Philip Roth and not Cynthia Ozick, or Hugh Nissenson, who can best afford to write about the American Jewish reality. For American Jews today in their numbers live not on Nissenson's Lower East Side or in Ozick's hasidic *shtetl*, but in "Woodenton," the home of Eli Peck. With no desire (to put it mildly) to do "public relations" for Judaism or the Jews, Philip Roth has been free to draw from his observation and experience whatever they may yield. For those, by contrast, who take Judaism seriously as a cultural alternative, and wish to weave new brilliant cloth from its ancient threads, the sociological reality of the present-day American Jewish community would seem to present an almost insurmountable obstacle. Writers like Ozick and Nissenson, who feel the historic, moral, and religious weight of Judaism, and want to represent it in literature, have had to ship their characters out of town by Greyhound or magic carpet, to an unlikely *shtetl*, to Israel (the scene of many of Nissenson's stories in his previous collections), to other times and other climes, in search of pan-Jewish fictional atmospheres. In the meantime the actual world of American Jews has lent itself to the production of satire, but not so far to any nobler art.

Ruth R. Wisse, "Ozick as American Jewish Writer," in Cynthia Ozick, *edited by Harold Bloom, Chelsea House Publishers, 1986, pp. 35-45.*

Leslie Epstein (essay date 1982)

[*Epstein is an American educator, novelist, and short story writer, perhaps best known for the novel* King of the Jews: A Novel of the Holocaust *(1979). In the following review of the collection* Levitation, *he finds Ozick's work to be hampered by her ideology.*]

The prospect of reviewing a new book by Cynthia Ozick gave me great pleasure, since I believe her two previous collections—**The Pagan Rabbi and Other Stories** and **Bloodshed and Three Novellas**—to be perhaps the finest work in short fiction by a contemporary writer; certainly it is the work in that genre that has most appealed to me. Then the bound galleys of **Levitation** arrived, subtitled *Five Fictions.* Immediately a voice whispered, "On guard! Why *fictions*? Why not stories, why not novellas, as the subtitles of the two earlier volumes plainly declared their contents to be? What is a *fiction,* anyway? A quick glance through the galleys provided a calming, commonsensical answer. Some of these five pieces seemed to be stories, while others, although made up and works of the imagination, were not what we think of as tales. But a closer reading has proved unsettling. *Each* of these works, however dazzling, original and even beauteous, does shy crucially from the kind of resolution we rightly demand from imaginative fiction. I'll attempt, in what follows, to explain.

The two works in the middle of the book are the furthest from story form. **"From a Refugee's Notebook"** consists of two fragments supposedly left in a rented room by a European or South American refugee. The first is a meditation on the subject of Freud's room, the burden of which seems to be that Freud, in his attraction to the cauldron of the unconscious, to the irrational, wished to become a god. The argument is fairly irrational itself:

> The dreams that rise up from couch and armchair mix and braid in the air: the patient recounts her dream of a cat, signifying the grimness of a bad mother, and behind this dream, lurking in the doctor, is the doctor's dream. The gods walking over the long-fringed table shawl have chosen their king.

The second fragment discusses the fad of Sewing Harems "on the planet Acirema." These were women who sewed up their vaginas but occasionally managed to conceive anyway when they rented themselves out, en masse, for the pleasure of wealthy businessmen. Most of this Swiftian exercise focuses upon the unfortunate children, who band together in Momist sects, produce offspring of their own and in time come to spread their totems, "great stone vulvae," over the surface of the globe. This "fiction" is less sterile and recondite than it is private—by which I mean it reveals nothing of the personality or situation of the refugee, its putative author. We are refused entrance to a fictional world.

I lump, perhaps mistakenly, the brief story **"Shots"** with **"From a Refugee's Notebook."** Here the narrator does not hide. She is a 36-year-old professional photographer, and she has a story to tell: how she falls in love with Sam, a scholarly expert on South America whose life seems devoted to hatred of his wife, Verity. The curious thing about this piece is that the affect is not in these relationships. The narrator's infatuation and Sam's loathing are described in such a heap of images ("Verity was the Cupid of the thing, Verity's confidence the iron arrow that dragged me down. She had her big foot on her sour catch.") that we have to take them on faith. Indeed, the very demands of storytelling are dealt with as a kind of annoyance ("How to give over these middle parts?"). What remains, the point of the passion, is a fascination with caducity and the relationship of photography to it. In part we are dealing with nothing more than that chestnut, the camera as a weapon that is aimed and shot. In one scene, in fact, a translator is shot with bullets at the very instant the narrator shoots him on film. In larger measure, however, photography is art (literature, fiction) and the writer another sort of simultaneous translator who fears—hence the turning away from elements of story—being gunned down.

What, then, of the title story, which seems a straightforward tale? **"Levitation"** is about a mixed marriage between Feingold, a Jew, and his convert wife, Lucy. Both are minor writers ("anonymous mediocrities"); each has left his or her tradition by marrying the other; and both, in their imaginative impotence, are seduced by status, gossip and power. There is much that is fine and amusing in this double portrait—especially in the oddly appealing scenes of the happy couple in bed discussing their novels or issues of style: "bald man, bald prose," says Lucy, feeling pity for any writers who have not married their own kind. Of course Lucy and Feingold are *not* the same kind, a fact which becomes apparent at the end of a party they throw in their apartment. Among the many nobodies present are two types of Jew: the humorists, the humanists,

who are described as going "off to studio showings of *Screw on Screen* on the eve of the Day of Atonement; and the fanatics, among them Feingold, who are obsessed with Jewish history, that is, with atrocity, abominations and the Holocaust. What happens is that as these last subjects are discussed the religious Jews begin to levitate, rising higher and higher, into the "glory of their martyrdom." If the common reader—probably a humanist, if not a nibbler of bacon—finds this hard to take, consider what happens to Lucy. She is suddenly illuminated by, glorified by, a vision of her own pagan roots: ". . . before the Madonna there was Venus; before Venus, Aphrodite; before Aphrodite, Astarte." And there is more—seething dancers, gross sexual symbols, Jesus in flesh. My point is not that the dice are loaded against this character, the deck so patently stacked. It is that the game is no longer being played by the rules of fiction. Probability, necessity, recognizable human feeling are replaced by the laws of what can only be called mystical vision.

Which brings us to the last two works, one short, one long, which together make up a good deal more than half this volume. Both **"Puttermesser: Her Work History, Her Ancestry, Her Afterlife"** and the novella-sized **"Puttermesser and Xanthippe"** are concerned with the same character, a not-so-young lawyer and municipal servant, Ruth Puttermesser. The two stories are the best in the book—often humorous, wonderfully quirky and possessed of a Dickensian delight in depicting the cracks and crannies in the Municipal Building and the Kabbala. And yet, I fear, my thesis holds. For example, the finest moment in the first Puttermesser story occurs when she travels to the run-down flat of her Uncle Zindel for a Hebrew lesson. Here is a character! Here is a voice!

> First see how a *gimel* and which way a *zayen*. Twins, but one kicks a leg left, one right. You got to practice the difference. If legs don't work, think pregnant bellies. Mrs. *Zayen* pregnant in one direction, Mrs. *Gimel* in the other. Together they give birth to *gez*, which means what you cut off.

Yet no sooner does Uncle Zindel take shape before us than he is vaporized. "Stop, stop! Puttermesser's biographer, stop!" In that halt we are told the old man has been dead for decades, the lesson never happened, the meeting never occurred. Could there be a plainer instance of how our text, our "biographer," quails before the demands of, the power of, imagination? Let us put it another way: Puttermesser is not to be examined as an artifact but as an essence. No wonder the ending is but a cry for help: "Hey! Puttermesser's biographer! What will you do with her now?"

"Puttermesser and Xanthippe" is meant to be an answer. Here our civil servant creates, half inadvertently, a golem, Xanthippe, one of a long series of such creatures—half Frankenstein's monster, half Captain Marvel—designed by rabbis to get Jews out of a jam. Puttermesser uses hers—the first lady golem, by the by—initially to cook and clean, then to get herself elected mayor ("The Honorable Ruth Puttermesser") and finally to turn New York City into a *gan eydn*, a paradise on earth. It is a marvelous conceit, wittily, charmingly conducted. The undoing of the dream, when the sexually crazed Xanthippe runs amok, is less successful; even in a world run by mystical lore, the denouement seems arbitrary and unconvincing. But the deepest flaw in **"Puttermesser and Xanthippe"** is the absence of an Uncle Zindel—of a fully human, fully feeling voice. Indeed, the only really touching moment occurs at the end, when Xanthippe is being destroyed. She opens her eyes. She sees Puttermesser circling counterclockwise around her, according to the method of the Great Rabbi Judah Loew: "O my mother," the golem cries, "why are you walking around me like that?" Which is to say, the most moving human cry comes from a nonhuman creature, already half turned back into dust.

It is time to call a halt, time to determine—perhaps we can only speculate—what is going on. The clue to this turn in Cynthia Ozick's work is her concentration upon language, upon sheer words—lists, syllables, names, letters. There is hardly a page of this book not, to one degree or another, obsessed by the magical power of writing. The golem is assembled after Puttermesser has held the Sunday Times (a world of woe in print) in her arms, just as Feingold and friends began to levitate only after the same edition of the paper had been burnt in the fireplace. Every golem is made of holy syllables, and some from 221 alphabetical combinations; each may be undone by reciting the same formula backwards; Xanthippe is killed outright by scraping the letter *aleph* from her forehead. In broad terms, I think the issue here is again one of translation—how to turn our secular language into holy script; how, in a sense, Puttermesser's list of Russian bureaucrats (who hinder Jewish emigration) or former mayors can be simultaneously translated into, let us say, Hebrew incantations or the names of the Rabbis of Baghdad, of Prague, of Worms. There is great danger for a writer here. At the end of the list is the Name of Names, which of course is ineffable, which is silence.

Our author knows her dilemma and has addressed it before. In her preface to ***Bloodshed*** she speaks of her frustration at not being able to write in a Jewish language instead of profane, biased English. And more: in that preface, as well as in a remarkable essay, she writes of the blasphemy of the imagination as if the impulse to create were a violation of the Second Commandment, "as if ink were blood," as if her stories were the hated idols themselves. So there ought to be no doubt what the golem (like the camera, like the shabby novels of the Feingolds, and perhaps even Freud's cauldron) represents. It is her art, by which we may be purified and saved; by which we may be engulfed and even destroyed. It is awesome to watch this great and generous talent turn with such intensity upon itself. One longs, in spite of the impertinence, in spite of the risk of blasphemy, to cry out! Cynthia Ozick! Walk counterclockwise! Make seven circles! Undo what you are doing! God is—as one of your own characters tells us—in details.

> Leslie Epstein, "Stories and Something Else," in The New York Times Book Review, February 14, 1982, pp. 11, 25.

On Ozick's narrative voice:

Beneath the texture of Ozick's seemingly improvised prose can be sensed something like an Emersonian Over-Soul, something we might refer to as One Voice. This Voice can only be evoked in human language; it cannot be uttered, though it informs all language. This One Voice is like the biblical God, "a principle which it is blasphemy to visualize." Like God, this Voice is Reality, its manifestations in human language comprise actuality. Though it always speaks to us through language, we never hear it directly. It is the grain or idiom of all narrative. Since it is the origin of all language, there are no original stories: "All stories are rip-offs. . . . Whatever looks like invention is theft"; there are no original thoughts: "We are not willing to admit that we do not generate our own thoughts, but that, on the contrary, they appear to be generated *for us,* as if by a transcendent engine that connects the process of mind to some outward source"; there are no original words: "The house of the word is where one learns how the word is superfluous."

> *Catherine Rainwater and William J. Scheik in their*
> " 'Some Godlike Grammar': An Introduction to the
> Writings of Hazzard, Ozick, and Redmon,"
> Texas Studies in Literature and Language 25,
> No. 2 (Summer, 1983).

Cynthia Ozick with Catherine Rainwater and William J. Scheick   (interview date 1982)

[*Rainwater and Scheick are American critics and educators. Scheick has written book-length studies of H. G. Wells, Ralph Waldo Emerson, Edward Taylor, and Jonathan Edwards. In the following excerpted interview, which was conducted in 1982, Ozick discusses several subjects, including her literary theory, preferences for the novella form, and the significance of Judaism in her writing.*]

[Rainwater and Scheick]: *Your writings are expressed in very original voices, but we wonder who, of the authors of fiction which has engaged you, has been most influential on you at different stages of your progress as a writer?*

[Ozick]: At various stages, intimately and obsessively, the following: E. M. Forster, Henry James, Chekhov, Conrad, Hardy, George Eliot, and Tolstoy are on the periphery—not "models," but awesome presences. I suppose it ought to bother me a bit that these names are so typical, accessible, classical—"everybody's" list, in fact. But for a long while they were inescapable; I madly read and reread. I will shamefacedly admit that I am currently in *Middlemarch* again. Yet I seem to be free now of the need to hear a Voice in my head.

Literary influence might be construed as a life-giving as much as a life-taking act. Do you think of your work as regenerative, as recreating older patterns?

"Influence" is nourishing, yes. It warms hope; simply, it inspires. Though sometimes I find myself wishing I could write a contemporary *Middlemarch,* I know it is impossible to "recreate patterns." Perhaps influence *can't* be "regenerative." I think it is a question of love and gratitude and moral pleasure one feels after reading the great literary humanists. There's a lyrical paragraph in the second chapter of *Brideshead Revisited* that sends me spinning into pure language-joy—but what else can one do with it other than gape in bliss?

Are there in your opinion only "the same old forms, conventions" ["Envy"] or is there in any sense progress *in literary art?*

Oh yes, there *is* progress in literary art. My good friend Lore Segal (author of *Lucinella,* an instance of such progress) and I often talk about how the old way of saying "She thought," followed by "thought" in the form of orderly declarative sentences, has had to be reconstituted through the evolution of new conventions. Joyce's way, for instance, is itself by now a too-familiar convention, though often ravishing; so are the Joycean dialogue-dashes in Gaddis' *The Recognitions.* The burgeoning of new forms is the glory of art, and the form innovators, like Barthelme, have plenty to teach their own generation. Form innovators appear rarely, and don't grow on trees. They both create the *Zeitgeist* and are conceived in the womb of the *Zeitgeist:* you can't imagine John Lyly writing *Euphues* in the 1980s, and you can't imagine Donald Barthelme writing quirky idiosyncratic nihilistic parodies in the sixteenth century.

Do you think of the literary act as process, *something always in medias res?*

No. As discovery, rather. If you believe you will discover something, then you have also committed yourself to the belief that there is something preexistent, waiting to be discovered. It seems to me the Story is already *there,* and it is my task to go and catch it. This is different from feeling you must *make* a story, which act would be as you describe it: "the literary act as process."

Do you find yourself excessively attentive to the beginning and ending of a story while you are writing it?

I am never attentive to the end, at least not until I get there, because I trust the end to be implicit in the beginning. The beginning is very hard, because one must listen to it exactly, in order to hear two things: first, the voice that will carry the tale; and second, the assurance that you are not being misled, that you have in fact found your way, that you are grabbing onto the right tale. Being in possession of the first is usually a strong support for the second.

But all this sounds a lot more confident than the experience itself, which is tentative, hesitant, terrifically unsure of itself, and often profoundly panicked. I sometimes (in the scary difficulty of trying to begin) recite Gertrude Stein: "The way to begin is to begin." Often it takes weeks for me to "find" the story. At this very moment I am in that stew. . . .

In your preference for the novella over the novel and the short story, you seem to envince a distinct attitude toward fictional technique and form. Beyond what you intimate in the Preface to **Bloodshed,** *how do you define a novella?*

The "preference" for the novella is in reality the consequence of two accidents.

The first is a life accident: the fact that *Trust* took so long (six and a half years), and was preceded by seven apprentice years, when I was at work on an ambitious "philosophical" (so I privately thought it) novel called *Mercy, Pity, Peace, and Love.* (The title of the latter, over such a long span, became abbreviated, moving from M. P. P. L. to Mippel. An endless suck on that Mippel. When I deserted it to begin *Trust,* which I conceived of as a novella that would take six weeks, I had already written three hundred thousand words.) When I finally finished *Trust* (on the day John F. Kennedy was assassinated), I realized that I never again wanted to engage myself in something so long. After such an extended immolation, I needed (it seemed to me then) frequent quick spurts of immediacy—that is, short stories which could get published right away. As it turned out, the stories too took years and years to find publication and some recognition. . . .

The second point is that I don't, I'm afraid, write novellas on purpose. Each novella was begun with the intention of writing a short story, but there is something in me that "writes long," and since I have been in ongoing fear of the endless dark that haunted the writing of *Trust,* what has emerged, willy-nilly, is the novella length. I never sought it out, as James did, because I thought it "blest."

The Preface to **Bloodshed** is a piece of fiction like any other. "Preface" is the title of the fiction.

Is the novella, in your terms, defined by any formal attributes?

The novella, it seems to me, is a long short story. Like a short story, and unlike a novel, it is characterized by a single trajectory. It is less complex than a novel, but more intense.

The force of your style, its charge of vitality, conveys an impression of improvisation, as if in defiance of containment by any form. How do you consider your style in relation to your sense of the novella?

Ouch. Your questions are getting harder and harder. This is probably one I can't attempt to deal with, because I am myself not aware of "an impression of improvisation." In fact, my habit is not to go on to the next sentence until I have perfected the one before it; isn't that the opposite of ad hoc "improvisation"? On the other hand, the inflexible principle of never turning back to revise or in any way fiddle with what I've already finished (in the sense also of having given it "finish," that is, burnishing), often enough gets me into a pickle. Rather than go back, I accept the fix I'm in, and accommodate the future to the immovable past. This offers a sensation akin, perhaps, to Houdini's. I'm locked in and have to figure out how to escape. I weave loopholes; I unriddle; I decipher. Is this what you mean by "an impression of improvisation"? If so, it is related to the principle of nonrevision rather than to the nature of the novella.

Actually you evince several styles in your work. Has any pattern of development emerged in your experiments with style over the years?

I am trying to give myself the freedom to be free—to do whatever I damn please, however I damn please. This is not so free as it sounds! It is a way of running scared. What I *don't* approve of is ventriloquism in style, however skilled. I have a secret disdain for writers in whom one can read their stylistic admirations and enthusiasms (though this is charming in child writers who are, still, more readers than they are writers), or in whose style one can smell *only* the shallow lesson of Now.

I ought to add also that I haven't been conscious of "experimenting." Things come out as they come out.

Concern with style is, finally, concern with authorial management of narrative voice. Your stories seem to speak in different narrative voices—what figures in your thoughts when you decide on the tone of voice of a story you are writing?

Small hints I get from what it is I may be about to discover. For instance, Lewis Carroll had no business letting *Alice in Wonderland* end in the revelation—with Alice's sister turning up, unwanted, unneeded, out of the blue—that it was all a dream. The tone of "You're nothing but a pack of cards!" is brilliant, but it shatters everything Alice, in her sober, logical, flat, antilyrical, pragmatic-phlegmatic voice, has been teaching us all along. We've *known,* all along, that we were in another order of things, and to tell us that it was all a "curious dream" is to tell us we weren't inside a reality; but we were. The narrative voice must never betray its own discoveries and perceptions, as Lewis Carroll forces Alice to do, miserably and unluckily, on the next-to-last page. We can forgive him because the betrayal is late and brief, and because Alice's true voice all through her book has given us the power to forgive her creator's having let her down.

The "tone of voice of a story you are writing" must be allowed to rule—to rule absolutely, without authorial interference, manipulation, desire, or will. In short, there *may* not be "authorial management of narrative voice," and in this I suppose I am expressing disagreement with the question's premise. For me, "concern with style" means authorial hands off.

Is it accurate to say that behind your various narrative voices the reader should "hear" (in some profound sense) one Voice?

No, I think the opposite, if the capital V of Voice suggests the Creator of the Universe. The writer of fiction is really a kind of idolator, or, worse, divinity-seizer. The writer of fiction intends to become a small-scale god, a creator, setting herself or himself in competition with the Creator. That, after all, is the warning inherent in the Second Commandment. Whoever sets up an image-making shop is in competition with the Maker of the world.

When I spoke in the Preface to **Bloodshed and Three Novellas** of "the cannibal touch of story-making," what I had in mind was not influence (that is, cannibalization of older works), but something rawer and closer to the ground of the mind than that. "Canaanite babies were regularly sacrificed to fanciful clay forms," I wrote. Fiction is one of the fanciful forms. Aesthetics tears away from humanity: the commonest illustration is the playing of Mozart at the gates of Auschwitz. "The old cannibal-gods still inhabit the earth," I wrote. "The deep pity of the Second Commandment is treated as null and void. Human sacrifice to this and that fantasy continues to teem on the planet." It is true that to write a story is not to become a cannibal and eat your neighbor; but there is in every act of creation the faint shadow of idol-making, and in every idol there is an invitation to cannibalism. Hubris is the opposite of piety; and Art is hubris. Pagans excel at Art; Hebrews (as Matthew Arnold and George Eliot understood) engage themselves in Deed. (It seems to me oftener and oftener nowadays that the humblest aide in a hospital who carries bedpans is a higher human being than any writer of stories.) The Second Commandment says: Succor your fellow-beings. But artists play with clay, and then ask that the clay be honored.

In your remarks about Voice you appear to be returning to the subject of influence and tradition. Your work is obviously imbued with Jewish culture; would you agree that chiefly the mystical traditions of this culture most appeal to you?

Jewish mystical traditions have appealed to me as succulent matter for the magic making of fiction; but outside of fiction—that is, intellectually—I feel a strong hostility to all mysticism as smacking of antinomianism and pantheism. (Which is to say, Grace sans Deed, and a confusion of Creator with created.) And since both antinomianism and pantheism are, it seems to me, versions of idolatry, I tend to think that antiidolatrous, antiantinomian Judaism is at its heart antagonistic to mysticism. Surely rabbinic Judaism (that is, since the opening of the Talmudic era) is essentially rationalist. I feel much more at home with the mainstream rationalist line of Jews (called *mitnagdim,* meaning protestant, alluding to their opposition to pneumatism), from which, both temperamentally and ancestrally, I stem.

Fiction, however, is the playground of mysticism and magical notions.

Do you feel that your works present Judaism as more universal or inclusive than some people consider it to be?

How can monotheism not be universal or inclusive? And what else is Judaism if not, first and foremost, monotheism?

I am not much impressed by what "some people consider" Judaism to be. A misconstruction, not to say a maligning, of Judaism is the cornerstone of the Christian Gospels: it is no wonder that "some people consider" Judaism to be what it is not. I am nonplused when I am told that Jews worship "a God of Wrath." It is not Judaism that invented hell. I am even more nonplused when I am told that Jewish religious sensibility is "material," as opposed to the Christian "spiritual." It is Christianity, never Judaism, that adheres at its foundation to the notion of materiality—it is Christianity, never Judaism, that turns spirit to matter in Incarnation and Eucharist.

But perhaps these observations are not responsive to the intent of the question. As far as I know, I do not, as a writer of fiction, "present Judaism." It seems to me that I do what other fiction writers do: present stories.

Do you think your wish to "present stories" is impeded by

*the fact that the Jewish materials used in your stories are sometimes inaccessible or maybe even alienating to many potential readers? We are thinking, for instance, of a remark in **"Usurpation"** concerning how "people hate to read foreign words."*

I wonder about the premises of the question itself. Think: would this question be addressed to Mark Twain, Faulkner, Tolstoy, Thomas Hardy, George Eliot, or Conrad? If not, why not?

After all, it can sometimes become a small hardship to read passages of James, who dots his prose with French, if you have no French. (I don't know any French.) Yet James isn't inaccessible or alienating.

I have no access to Southern life or dialect; yet Faulkner and Mark Twain aren't inaccessible or alienating. At least I've not yet heard them characterized as such.

I have no access to the culture or rural speech patterns of the English countryside a century ago; yet Thomas Hardy and George Eliot aren't inaccessible or alienating.

I have no access to the oligarchy of nineteenth-century Russia; yet Tolstoy isn't inaccessible or alienating.

I have no access to sailing ships, their technology, or the specialized language of their technology; yet Conrad isn't inaccessible or alienating.

Far from impeding or alienating, literature universalizes, familiarizes, connects, makes intimate, draws near, creates jubilant sympathies.

*Do you sometimes write with a special audience in mind, perhaps even to the degree implied by a statement by Goethe cited in your **"The Suitcase"**: "For the people gay pictures, for the cognoscenti, the mystery behind"?*

I write with the hope of engaging my own interest. (Think of Jane Austen and Emily Dickinson, doing nothing else!) It is astonishing to discover that what attracts one mind sometimes attracts another.

Nowadays, I am afraid, the attraction is limited perforce to the "special audience" that can read serious writing. The decline of literacy erodes expectations. Recently I looked into a quite ordinary nineteenth-century periodical and realized the kind of substantially difficult, even elevated, language a plain citizen had to be in control of then, just to read a daily newspaper; this explains how a serious literary writer—for instance, Dickens—could also have been a popular one. Today strong language control is uncommon among "average" readers, so that serious writers, by default, appear to write "for the cognoscenti."

But surely one doesn't set out to weave a veil "for the mystery behind." Speaking for myself, I want to reveal, not conceal!

What obligations does an author have to her readers?

To be (and here is a word in urgent need of rehabilitation) *interesting.*

What do you most want readers to receive from your fiction?

Intellectual and emotional recognition *and* surprise, simultaneously.

*In **The Pagan Rabbi** a character observes that "instinct is a higher . . . thing." Do you intend for readers to discover the "truth" of your narratives primarily through thought or through feeling?*

I am convinced—at least so I experience it in myself—that thought *is* feeling; and that there is no feeling that cannot be formulated (or even felt) as a thought.

Instinct *isn't* a "higher thing," it seems to me; a tragic thing, rather, from the human point of view, in that instinct cannot be individually arrived at. It is a group convenience, a mob contrivance.

Your interest, as one of your voices says, in "metaphysical speculation" ["Usurpation"], in mystical truths, seems to evoke an allegorical manner in some of your writing. Do you consider some of your works to be allegorical?

Two stories—"The Pagan Rabbi" and "Usurpation"—intend to be representative of certain ideas; but I think of them rather as parables than allegories. In an allegory, the story *stands for* an idea, and the idea can be stated entirely apart from the story; in a parable, story and idea are so inextricably fused that they cannot be torn free of each other. In this sense, I hope I've written an occasional parable. But I would never seek out allegory, which strikes me as a low form.

*A voice in **"Usurpation"** seems to repudiate some allegorical techniques when it complains, "I am against all these masks and tricks of metaphor and fable. That is why I am attracted to magical tales: they mean what they say; in them miracles are not symbols, they are probabilities." That voice might or might not speak for you, of course. What is wrong with metaphor, and do you downplay metaphor in your own work?*

That is a character's voice. For me, metaphor is everything—no, almost everything. Metaphor and irony are, worked together, very nearly art's everything.

Is it that metaphor can transubstantiate or convey a leap of faith?

Yes. That is why it is so dangerous.

Is the trouble with metaphor related to the limits of language generally?

The trouble with metaphor is that it relates to the *lack* of limits of language generally. Metaphor can kill. "Root out this cancer from our society" more often than not means, and is the means of, murder. Language can brilliantly clarify; it can also create, just as brilliantly, the Big Lie. Metaphor is one of the most powerful ways we can tell the truth; it is also one of the most powerful ways we can lie. In fiction—which is a lie that tells the truth—it can do both. . . .

Does your own fascination with the dialectic between laughter and silence influence your manner of fictional characterization? We note, for instance, what appears to be your preference for caricature rather than for mimetic charac-

terization to convey, as a voice in **"Envy"** *remarks, a "reality beyond realism."*

I wish I could answer this interesting question. I am ashamed to say that I have not been aware of a "preference for caricature," and I am perplexed by my inability to think myself into the idea of a "dialectic between laughter and silence." The truth is that in writing fiction I really don't know *what* I am doing: sooner or later I *will* find out, but by then it is too late for a metaphysics of Fiction!

Is your method of characterization designed to reflect some authorial sense of human "fate" or "destiny"?

Hardy-fashion, do you mean? No. Character is almost always fate, I think. We do what is inherent in us to do. But this is not a matter of predetermination, since character is subject to repair and renewal. If I have an "authorial sense," I think it has to do with the idea of personal redemption: whether missed, dismissed, or seized.

> Cynthia Ozick, Catherine Rainwater and William J. Scheick, in an interview in Texas Studies in Literature and Language, *Vol. XXV, No. 2, Summer, 1983, pp. 255-65.*

Victor Strandberg (essay date 1983)

[*Strandberg is an American critic and educator. In the following excerpt, he provides an overview of Ozick's stories, particularly focusing on such themes as Jewish identity, the temptation of paganism, and the vocation of the artist.*]

Compared with the immense scope and baroque complexity of *Trust,* Ozick's tales may seem an anticlimax, as the author herself implies in her recent statement, "I care more for *Trust* than for anything else I have written." The tales, however, have been the basis of her reputation—doubtless in part because *Trust* has been out of print—and as the many admiring reviews indicate, they constitute an important achievement in their own right. In her stories Ozick makes a transition from being an "American novelist" to being one of our foremost Jewish American storytellers.

Obviously a collection of short stories cannot be expected to display the coherence or unified focus which we expect to find in a novel. In her three collections Ozick gathers a rather disparate group of writings, ranging from brief sketches to novella-length narratives, in which her literary modes vary from conventional realism to parable and fantasy. To a surprising degree, nonetheless, she imposes a web of coherence upon the stories through her continuous process of "reinvigorating" (a favorite word in her literary criticism) her central themes and obsessions. By imagining radically new sets of characters and dramatic situations and by employing fresh ways of approaching her material—especially in the comic/ironic mood—she extends and deepens her ground themes rather than merely repeats them from one book to another. In the ensuing discourse I hope to trace these thematic patterns through their various artistic mutations, touching lightly on those stories I consider fairly transparent or relatively less important

while devoting stronger emphasis to the more substantial or difficult pieces.

The predominant themes in her three later books are familiar to readers of *Trust,* but their interaction now assumes an altogether different profile. The Pan-versus-Moses theme continues to sustain a *basso continuo* presence in the time frame that stretches from **"The Pagan Rabbi"** (1966) through the Puttermesser-Xanthippe stories of *Levitation* (1982), but this central theme of *Trust* gradually loses importance to two themes which were subordinate in the novel: problems of the artist, particularly the Jewish or female artist; and the exigencies of Jewish identity. This latter theme, relegated to Enoch in *Trust,* eventually emerges as the transcendent issue of the story collections, evoking the author's deepest emotional and artistic power.

Illustrating the new balance among her triad of ground themes is a brief quantification: of the seven stories in *The Pagan Rabbi,* only two make the Pan/Moses dichotomy their central theme, while two others touch on the issue. By comparison, five of the tales focus upon the figure of the artist, and six of the seven amplify the theme of Jewish identity, leaving only **"The Dock-Witch"** to carry forward the Gentile cultural ambience of *Trust.*

Although the pantheistic element thus seems downgraded from its paramount status in *Trust,* it still rates enough importance to justify making **"The Pagan Rabbi"** the title story for the whole volume. In this tale the Pan/Moses conflict attains a new intensity, in part because the story is a more concentrated form than the novel, but equally because the adversary ideologies are more clearly drawn: not Tilbeck versus the general modern malaise, but Pan versus orthodox Judaism. Moreover, the conflict now occurs within a single individual, the learned rabbi whose suicide occasions the story.

> **To a surprising degree, Ozick imposes a web of coherence upon the stories through her continuous process of "reinvigorating" her central themes and obsessions.**
>
> **—*Victor Strandberg***

As in *Trust,* a vital symbol in **"The Pagan Rabbi"** is the tree which functions as both totem (for Hellenic nature worship) and taboo (for Hebraic forbidden knowledge). Sex and death, the two modes of forbidden knowledge associated with the Semitic myth of The Fall, do in fact pertain to the rabbi's tree: sex, when he couples with the tree's dryad; and death, when he hangs himself from its branches. Yet it is Pan who prevails over Moses in this encounter. Death here becomes (as Walt Whitman called it) a promotion rather than a punishment in the light of the rabbi's pantheistic insight: "The molecules dance inside all forms, and within the molecules dance the atoms, and within the atoms dance still profounder sources of divine vitality.

There is nothing that is Dead." From this Spinozan heresy—Spinoza is cited by name by the dryad—arise two intolerable consequences for traditional Judaism. First, the Second Commandment is nullified by the immersion of the Creator in his creation: "Holy life subsists even in the stone, even in the bones of dead dogs and dead men. Hence in God's fecundating Creation there is no possibility of Idolatry." And second, as a final outrage against the Hebraic ethos, the concept of holiness, of being separate from the unclean, becomes meaningless. Even more than Town Island in *Trust,* the setting of **"The Pagan Rabbi"** is thus befouled with corruption, so that the rabbi's ecstatic sexual union occurs in an environment of "wind-lifted farts" and "civic excrement" created by the city's sewage polluting the nearby seashore. Even so, the vitality of Nature overrides the authority of the Torah. When the Law undertakes direct competition with the senses, claiming to sound "more beautiful than the crickets," to smell "more radiant than the moss," to taste better than clear water, the rabbi on the instant chooses to join his dryad lover, hanging himself from the tree with his prayer shawl.

Because the narrator of **"The Dock-Witch"** is a Gentile, neither the Jewish horror of idolatry nor the ideal of holiness stands in opposition to his pantheistic enticement. So the protagonist, originally a midwestern churchgoer, yields immediately and guiltlessly to the impulse which brings him to New York to live within sight of the East River. Here the pagan goddess of Nature is connected, like Tilbeck in *Trust,* with the sea and pagan Norsemen (her final metamorphosis puts her on the prow of a Viking ship) as well as with the original Canaanite seagoers, the Phoenicians whose tongue she speaks. Between seeing off a shipload of Greeks to their homeland and another vessel packed with orthodox Jews to theirs, the Dock-Witch so affects the narrator's view of nature that even a pair of penguin-sized rats on the dock appear "sacerdotal" to him, "like a pair of priests late for divine service." And as with Tilbeck and the Pagan Rabbi, the speaker's immersion in nature is consummated in a sexual union of insatiable magnitude—"she made me a galley slave, my oar was a log flung into the sea of her."

The hunger for the world's beauty that underlies these extraordinary sexual encounters relates the tales of Pan-worship; to both the theme of Jewish identity and that of the portrait of the artist. An engaging example of all three themes working in concert is **"The Butterfly and the Traffic Light,"** which is not really a tale but a sketch of the artist toying creatively with his (her) material. Here the thematic triad begins to form when a character named Fishbein talks with a young woman about the "insistent sense of recognition" that can attach to so mundane a thing as a street in their small city: "Big Road was different by day and by night, weekday and weekend. Daylight, sunlight, and even rainlight gave everything its shadow, winter and summer, so that every person and every object had its Doppelgänger, persistent and hopeless. There was a kind of doubleness that clung to the street, as though one remembered having seen this and this and this before." To see this doubleness is the beginning of metaphor, so that an unneeded traffic light over Big Road becomes, for the young woman, "some sort of religious icon with a red eye

and a green eye," and this in turn becomes a new version of the Hellenism/Hebraism dichotomy:

> "No, no," he objected, " . . . A traffic light could never be anything but a traffic light. —What kind of religion would it be which had only one version of its deity—a whole row of identical icons in every city?"
>
> She considered rapidly. "An advanced religion. I mean a monotheistic one."
>
> "And what makes you certain that monotheism is 'advanced'? On the contrary, little dear! . . . The Greeks and Romans had a god for every personality, the way the Church has a saint for every mood. Savages, Hindus, and Roman Catholics understand all that. Its only the Jews and their imitators who insist on a rigid unitarian God. . . . A little breadth of vision, you see, a little imagination, a little *flexibility,* I mean—there ought to be room for Zeus *and* God under one roof. . . . That's why traffic lights won't do for icons! They haven't been conceived in a pluralistic spirit, they're all exactly alike."

Two other metaphors give this sketch a behind-the-scenes candor, the impression of the author's mind disclosing the way it works. One is the butterfly of the title (a metaphor of the finished art work), prettier but less significant than the caterpillar (art in the process of creation): "The caterpillar is uglier, but in him we can regard the better joy of becoming." The other metaphor is that of the immortal city—like Jerusalem, Baghdad, or Athens—mythologized by millennia beyond any sense of utility. America, in this sense, has no cities; and that, we may surmise, is why Town Island is the crucial setting in *Trust:* it had been hopefully christened Dorp Island a mere three hundred years ago, like Gatsby's Manhattan, by Dutch sailors.

Whereas **"The Butterfly and the Traffic Light"** creates a positive impression of artistic creativity, two other sketches of the artist render a feminist protest in one instance and a nightmare vision of failure in the other. The feminist satire is **"Virility,"** an attack against male supremacy in art that correlates largely with Ozick's ridicule of "The Testicular Theory of Literature" in her essay, "Women and Creativity: The Demise of the Dancing Dog." So manly has the poet Edmund Gates become, after his meteoric rise to success in **"Virility,"** that his very shape now resembles a "giant lingam," and his reviewers search for appropriate imagery to describe his verses: "The Masculine Principle personified," "Robust, lusty, male," "Seminal and hard." When it turns out that an elderly aunt had actually written the poems, the praises turn to abuse ("Thin feminine art," "A spinster's one-dimensional vision"), and Edmund Gates does penance for his impersonation by spending his remaining half century going in drag.

If such artistic fraudulence is contemptible, there is one thing even worse: having talent without the strength of character to realize it. In **"The Doctor's Wife,"** Doctor Silver's failure to realize his talent resembles that of Hemingway's persona in "The Snows of Kilimanjaro": "he thought how imperceptibly, how inexorably, temporary accommodation becomes permanence, and one by one he counted his omissions, his cowardices, each of which had fixed him like an invisible cement. . . . At twenty he had endured the stunned emotion of one who senses that he has been singled out for aspiration, for beauty, for awe, for some particularity not yet disclosed. . . . At forty he was still without a history." Apart from Hemingway and the later Henry James, who feared a wasted life ("The Beast in the Jungle" is especially relevant here), one other favorite writer of Ozick's makes a curiously negative contribution to **"The Doctor's Wife."** The success of Anton Chekhov, another bachelor-doctor-artist like Doctor Silver, stands as a reproach to the latter's arrested development while at the same time it represents something like Harold Bloom's "Anxiety of Influence" thesis. In fact, the story is a perfectly Chekhovian paradigm of waste and futility, vividly illustrating the banality of marriage (a theme carried over from *Trust*), the illusiveness of happiness, and the human incapacity to achieve or even to formulate a meaningful purpose in life. The Chekhovian tone is especially strong concerning this last motif: "his life now was only a temporary accommodation, he was young, he was preparing for the future, he would beget progeny, he would discover a useful medical instrument, he would succor the oppressed, . . . he would be saved."

In the end Doctor Silver preserves not a scrap of his life in art—in fact he has not lived—nor does he even manage to define what mode of art might suit his need. Bewildered by the chaos of it all, he leaves the capturing of his own time to his brother-in-law, a commercial photographer, while he finds his secret vision of beauty, ironically, in a photograph of the young Chekhov standing near a woman who becomes Silver's imaginary wife, in a final Chekhovian lapse into protective illusion.

The remaining two tales in *The Pagan Rabbi* also portray artistic failure, but their ultimate concern is Jewish identity. Both **"The Suitcase"** and **"Envy; or, Yiddish in America"** define the Jewish ethos by contriving a memorable confrontation between Jew and Gentile. In **"The Suitcase,"** the adversaries at first seem totally assimilated into the larger American society. The Gentile, formerly a pilot in the Kaiser's air force, has lived in America so long that he "no longer thought of himself as German." Apart from naming his son Gottfried—he later wishes it were John—his only connection to his native land has been a sister whose eleven-year-old daughter died in the bombing of Cologne. The Jew is Genevieve, a brilliant woman who has become mentor and mistress to the German's son, though both lovers are married to others. She too has become assimilated, preferring the art world of New York to her dull Jewish husband (a C.P.A.) and four daughters back in Indianapolis. For her Gentile lover, a painter, she has even culled through German literature, selecting comments from Beethoven, Mann, and Goethe for Gottfried's exhibition program. (The program features a talk by one "Creighton MacDougal" of *The Partisan Review,* a pretentious fraud who gives Ozick occasion for some wicked satire concerning a certain prominent critic.)

When these two characters meet—the painter's father and mistress—their layers of assimilation rapidly peel away, exposing the ethnic granite at the core of each personality. Her innate Jewishness rises to the mention of Carl Gustav

Jung as "some famous Jewish psychiatrist," to which she replies "He isn't a Jew. . . . That's why he went on staying alive." The father's ethnicity thereupon reacts in a surge of defensiveness: "He knew what she meant him to see: she scorned Germans, she thought him a Nazi sympathizer even now, an anti-Semite, an Eichmann. She was the sort who, twenty years after Hitler's war, would not buy a Volkswagen. . . . Who could be blamed for History? It did not take a philosopher . . . to see that History was a Force-in-Itself, like Evolution."

Of course he is not a bad fellow. All he wants, as a German, is to forget history, which is exactly what she, as a Jew, cannot permit. Ostensibly he gets the best of her by breaking up the miscegenetic dalliance and sending Genevieve back to her Jewish family. But the final victory is hers. At the end of the tale, when Genevieve's purse is reported stolen, he compulsively proves himself innocent by opening his suitcase and demanding that she search it. It is a paradigm of his much larger and unanswerable need for innocence, brought to exposure by his remark that tomorrow he sails abroad:

> "To Germany?"
>
> "Not Germany. Sweden. I admire Scandinavia. . . ."
>
> "I bet you say Sweden to mislead. I bet you're going to Germany, why shouldn't you? I don't say there's anything wrong with it, why shouldn't you go to Germany?"
>
> "Not Germany, Sweden. The Swedes were innocent in the war, they saved so many Jews. I swear it, not Germany. It was the truckmen [who stole your purse], I swear it."

A similar confrontation of Jew versus Gentile concludes **"Envy; or, Yiddish in America,"** where the aging Yiddish poet Edelshtein gathers together the familiar thematic triad: problems of the artist, Jewish identity, and the pagan enticement. What defeats the artist in this story is not lack of will or talent but entrapment within a minority culture which is dying from worldwide loss of interest within modern Jewry. Edelshtein has found that even the nation of Israel has no use for "the language of the bad little interval between Canaan and now," and with Yiddish eradicated from Europe by the Holocaust, there remains only America as a site where the Yiddish culture might survive. Here, however, to his dismay, the younger generation of American Jews actually refers to its elders as "you Jews" while disdaining the Jewish obsession with history as "a waste." Meanwhile, America interprets Jewish culture through novelists who were "spawned in America, pogroms a rumor, . . . history a vacuum. . . . They were reviewed and praised, and were considered Jews, and knew nothing."

Yet Edelshtein himself exhibits telltale signs of cultural betrayal. Emanating from the same reflex which makes him envy "natural religion, stones, stars, body," his dream life hovers about Canaanite temptations, including homoerotic feelings for Alexei, a friend of his boyhood, and similar lads spotted in the subway: "The love of a man for a boy. Why not confess it? Is it against the nature of man to rejoice in beauty?" And his lapse into wishing "he had been born a Gentile" must mitigate the acculturation he finds blameworthy in others. Moreover, the Gentile/pagan preference for flesh over spirit—"Our books are holy, to them their bodies are holy," **"The Pagan Rabbi"** had said—gains new appeal when measured against the decrepitude of the Yiddish speakers. Between them, Edelshtein and Baumzweig constitute a catalog of decay featuring a dripping nose, a urine-stained fly "now and then seeping," "Mucus the sheen of the sea," "thighs . . . full of picked sores," and a recurrent "vomitous belch."

The status of Yiddish in America seems analogous to this decrepit condition, but in the end it is not Yiddish so much as Jewish history which Edelshtein struggles to preserve from oblivion. Like the face-off between Jew and German in **"The Suitcase,"** Edelshtein's confrontation with the Christian evangelist focuses upon a vein of history that the Gentile prefers to dismiss. To Edelshtein's list of historic villains—"Pharoah, Queen Isabella [who expelled the Jews from Spain], Haman, that pogromchick King Louis that they call in history Saint, Hitler, Stalin"—the evangelist responds with the sort of fancy that Leo Baeck classified as Romantic Religion: "You're a Jew? . . . Accept Jesus as your Saviour and you shall have Jerusalem restored." As in **"The Suitcase,"** the thrust and parry of dialogue quickly strikes ethnic bedrock, Edelshtein placing his adversary among his list of villains—"Amalekite! Titus! Nazi!"—when the majority culture bares its teeth in familiar fashion: "You people are cowards, you never even tried to defend yourselves. . . . When you were in Europe every nation despised you. When you moved to take over the Middle East the Arab Nation, spic faces like your own, your very own blood-kin, began to hate you. . . . You kike, you Yid."

By way of transition to the next book, it should be noted that Edelshtein's closing outcry, "On account of you I have no translator!" obscures a fundamental precept stated earlier in the story: that Yiddish is untranslatable. Even without the indifference of young Jews and the contempt of Gentiles to contend with, Edelshtein's poetry would remain hopelessly incommunicative to a non-Yiddish readership:

> The gait—the prance, the hobble—of Yiddish is not the same as the gait of English. . . . *Mamaloshen* doesn't produce *Wastelands*. No alienation, no nihilism, no dadaism. With all the suffering, no smashing! NO INCOHERENCE! . . . The same biblical figure, with exactly the same history, once he puts on a name from King James, COMES OUT A DIFFERENT PERSON!

In her preface to **Bloodshed,** Ozick amplifies this statement with an exposition of her own problems with the English language: "A language, like a people, has a history of ideas. . . . English is a Christian language. When I write English, I live in Christendom. But if my postulates are not Christian postulates, what then?" The specific story to which she relates this problem is the next one we shall consider, **"Usurpation (Other People's Stories)"** in **Bloodshed.** Having written this Preface, she says, solely

from frustration over a critic's comment that this story is unintelligible, she explains why it may have seemed so: "There is no way to hear the oceanic amplitudes of the Jewish Idea in any English word or phrase. 'Judaism' is a Christian term. . . . English . . . cannot be expected to naturalize the life-giving grandeur of the Hebrew word—yet how much more than word it is!—'Torah.' . . . So it came to me what the difficulty was: I had written '**Usurpation**' in the language of a civilization that cannot imagine its thesis."

As these fragments of the Preface indicate, **Bloodshed** is the book in which Ozick most markedly stakes her claim to being a Jewish author—more profoundly Jewish, I should say, than the more celebrated names like Saul Bellow and Philip Roth. All four of the stories in **Bloodshed** take as their governing theme the betrayal of Jewish identity. Her thematic triad remains intact, however, in that the appeal of paganism and the portrayal of the artist maintain substantial importance as ancillary issues.

With its artist-persona and its renewal of the Pan-versus-Moses conflict, **"Usurpation (Other People's Stories)"** is the entry in **Bloodshed** that best illustrates this continuing thematic interplay. Subserving this portrait of the artist mired in self-conflict are two issues the author discussed at length in her essay "Judaism & Harold Bloom": Bloom's "anxiety of influence" thesis, here taking the form of writer's envy; and the conflict between Judaism—specifically the Second Commandment—and art. This latter question evokes the most forgivable and yet—to the author—the most worrisome instance of cultural subversion in the volume. As her Preface states: "the worry is this: whether Jews ought to be story-tellers! . . . There is one God, and the Muses are not Jewish but Greek. . . . Does the Commandment against idols warn us even against ink?"

In the light of this question, the narrator's usurpation of other people's stories—here referring to Bernard Malamud's "The Silver Crown"—shortly becomes a minor issue. In this most openly confessional of Ozick's stories, the essential usurpation encompasses a much larger prize: the appropriation of an alien culture, which alone can make storytelling permissible: "Magic—I admit it—is what I lust after. . . . I am drawn not to the symbol, but to the absolute magic act. I am drawn to what is forbidden." Because "the Jews have no magic," she goes on, "I long to be one of the ordinary peoples. . . . oh, why can we not have a magic God like other peoples?"

The answer to that question comes through another usurpation, borrowed from a would-be artist's manuscript. In it the narrator finds the concept of the writer as "self-idolator, . . . so audacious and yet so ingenious that you will fool God and live." The writer who has done this is Tchernikhovsky, a Jew who has lapsed into "pantheism and earth-worship . . . pursuit of the old gods of Canaan." Despite this apostasy, which culminates in his "most famous poem, the one to the god Apollo," he ascends after death into the Jewish paradise, where the narrator glimpses Tchernikhovsky wickedly at ease in Zion, hobnobbing with his pagan gods, savoring his faunlike pleasures, and ignoring with impunity his Jewish obligations of worship: "Tchernikhovsky eats nude at the table of the nude gods, clean-shaven now, his limbs radiant, his youth restored, his sex splendidly erect . . . ; he eats without self-restraint from the celestial menu, and when the Sabbath comes . . . as usual he avoids the congregation of the faithful before the Footstool and the Throne." The story's last sentence, however, makes it clear that though he could fool the Jewish God, neither he nor any other Jew can ever fool the gods of that alien culture in praise of which he had written his poetry. They will always know he is not one of theirs: "Then the taciturn little Canaanite idols call him, in the language of the spheres, kike."

If **"Usurpation"** portrays the least blameworthy betrayal of the Jewish heritage, **"An Education"** treats the most blameworthy, which may explain why it emanates the most sardonic tone of these four stories and is the most immediately comprehensible. Written about the time *Trust* was completed, it extends several of the novel's themes, as is evident in the heroine's (Una's) initial interest in the classics (she earns two graduate degrees) and her ultimate disinterest in marriage (she refuses to marry her lover). In the opening scene, a Latin class, Una is called to explain the genitive case—a term that becomes a key to the story, both as a description of marriage and as a foreshadowing of Una's total possession by a singularly irresponsible married couple.

That married couple, in turn, illustrates the central theme of the story, the cultural vacuum which ensues when they try to integrate themselves within the Gentile majority. Having changed their name from Chaims ("But isn't that Jewish?") to Chimes ("Like what a bell does"), they further de-Judaize themselves by eating ham, naming their daughter "Christina," and making a joke of a Holy Ghost/Holocaust pun. The retaliation for this betrayal of their heritage comes when Clement Chimes, a would-be artist, is unable to progress beyond the title page of his masterwork, "Social Cancer/A Diagnosis in Verse/And Anger." Leaving aside his lack of talent, we may read this story as the obverse of **"Envy; or Yiddish in America."** Contrary to Edelshtein, who fails because his art is rooted in a dying minority culture, Chimes fails because, having renounced his Jewish birthright, he faces the dilemma of trying to write literature without any cultural roots whatever.

Whereas **"An Education"** presents an essentially comic view of Jewish deracination, **"A Mercenary"** projects a tragic instance of this governing theme—tragic in the old sense of portraying grievous waste. Beginning rather shockingly with an epigraph from Joseph Goebbels ("Today we are all expressionists—men who want to make the world outside themselves take the form of their lives within themselves"), this tale applies Goebbels's remark to three characters representing the civilizations of three different continents. The two main characters have in some sense exchanged birthrights: Lushinski, a native of Poland, by becoming the United Nations representative of a small black African country; Morris, his assistant, by submerging his African past under a European veneer acquired at the University of Oxford. A third character,

Louisa, Lushinski's mistress in New York, is American and hence too innocent either to require or to comprehend a multiple identity; but she, like the others, follows Goebbels's expressionist standard insofar as she prefers her innocent inner picture of the world to the reality defined by actual history.

Lushinski is the "Mercenary" of the title, an eloquent "Paid Mouthpiece" for his African dictator both at the U. N. and in television talk shows featuring "false 'hosts' contriving false conversation." In his latter role he makes a televised confession of murder, but he never tells anyone who his victim was—not even Morris or Louisa. Instead he tells his audience of other violence: how the Germans took Warsaw on his sixth birthday, causing his wealthy parents to buy him a place with a peasant family, after which the parents, though Aryan in looks and manners, were identified as Jews and shot. It is not very entertaining material, commercially speaking, and after a commercial break, the mercenary in the man rises to meet the mercenary medium; he makes his tale out to be a jest, a fabrication to entertain his listeners: "All this was comedy: Marx Brothers, . . . the audience is elated by its own disbelief. . . . Lushinski is only a story-teller."

In thus making a travesty of his tragic past, Lushinski is not solely interested in commercial advantage; he mainly wants to exorcise the self he was, the child who "had survived the peasants who baited and blistered and beat and hunted him. One of them had hanged him from the rafter of a shed by the wrists. He was four sticks hanging." Telling Louisa he is "the century's one free man," he explains: "every survivor is free. . . . The future can invent nothing worse." Having chosen to use his freedom to establish a new identity, he has largely succeeded. Though "born to a flag-stoned Warsaw garden," he now feels himself "native to these mammalian perfumes" of African flowers, in token of which he long ago immersed his being in this culture's pagan hedonism ("these round brown mounds of the girls he pressed down under the trees"). To underscore further his freedom from that Jewish child in his past, he has taken a crypto-German mistress in America: "They spoke of her as a German countess—her last name was preceded by a 'von' . . . though her accent had a fake melody either Irish or Swedish." At the same time he has done all in his power to offend Jews everywhere: "Always he was cold to Jews. . . . In the Assembly he turned his back on the ambassador from Israel. . . . All New York Jews in the gallery."

Yet the Jewish child is not wholly expungeable. For all his sophistication, words like "peasant" and "Jew" evoke visible fear in Lushinski; and most important, he reveals that telltale sign of Jewish identity, a passion for Jewish history. The history in question—Raoul Hilberg's monumental work, *The Destruction of the European Jews*—opens a breach between Lushinski and his mistress, who sees no purpose in this masochistic morbidity:

> "Death," she said. "Death, death, death. What do you care? You came out alive." "I care about the record," he insisted. . . . He crashed down beside her an enormous volume: it was called *The Destruction*. She opened it and saw tables

and figures and asterisks; she saw train-schedules. It was all dry, dry.

Paradoxically, his affinity for Jewish history has only strengthened his need for exorcism, as his Gentile mistress correctly infers: "You hate being part of the Jews. You hate that. . . . Practically nobody knows you're a Jew. . . . *I* never think of it."

In the remainder of the tale, Lushinski accelerates his flight from his Jewish past by becoming "a dervish of travel" as he speaks about Africa on the television and lecture circuit and by cementing his ties to his African "homeland." Morris, the real African, meanwhile moves in a direction exactly opposite to that of Lushinski, gradually shedding his European veneer so as to recover his tribal birthright: "the dear land itself, the customs, the rites, the cousins, the sense of family." Pushed in this direction by his revulsion against the Tarzan movies—"Was he [Morris] no better than that lout Tarzan, investing himself with a chatter not his own? How long could the ingested, the invented, the foreignness endure"—Morris tries to push Lushinski likewise. From New York, "a city of Jews," he sends a letter to the seacoast villa in Africa where Lushinski is enjoying his employer's gratitude. The letter describes a Japanese terrorist, jailed for slaughtering Jews in an air terminal, who in his prison has converted to Judaism. Lushinski reads the message as an unmasking: "It meant a severing. Morris saw him as an impersonator. . . . Morris had called him Jew."

Thus a familiar pattern recurs: a Jew who tries mightily to be assimilated is in the end forced back into his native Jewishness. Like Tchernikhovsky in **"Usurpation,"** whom the Canaanite gods called kike though he had fooled the God of the Jews, Lushinski will finally be pronounced Jew no matter how far he might flee into the hinterland. As the tale ends, the word *Jew*—abetted by the memory-evoking colors of his surroundings—thrusts him away from the pleasures of his new country and toward the land of his birth; and thence to a closing revelation: the name, in the last two lines, of the man Lushinski had killed and buried in Warsaw:

> And in Africa, in a white villa on the blue coast, the Prime Minister's gaudy pet, on a blue sofa . . . smoking and smoking, under the breath of the scented trees, under the shadow of the bluish snow, under the blue-black pillars of the Polish woods, . . . under the rafters, under the stone-white hanging stars of Poland—Lushinski.
>
> Against the stones and under the snow.

Up to this point the stories in ***Bloodshed*** have portrayed the deracination of Jewish identity in terms of art (**"Usurpation"**), sociology (**"An Education"**), and politics (**"A Mercenary"**). In her title story, **"Bloodshed"**—and doubtless this is why it *is* the title story—Ozick brings forward her most momentous mode of deracination: the theological. In this instance the theology does not involve a conflict between Judaism and some alien system (e.g., Pan versus Moses); rather, its focus lies wholly within a Jewish matrix. Cleared thus of goys and pagans, the narrative measures a New Yorker named Bleilip, a middling

sort of Jewish American, against "the town of the hasidim," an Orthodox village within range of Bleilip's neighborhood that is inhabited almost entirely by survivors or children of survivors of the death camps. Ostensibly, he has come hither to visit his cousin, but in reality he is in flight from a despair so deep that he has been toying with the idea of suicide—toying, literally, in that he carries in one pocket a toy gun ("to get used to it. The feel of the thing") and in another pocket a real pistol. Thus possessed by the Sickness unto Death, Bleilip has undertaken this sojourn among the faithful as a last feeble grasp for beliefs by which to live.

Fundamentally, the issue in **"Bloodshed"** is the most crucial dichotomy within the Judaic ethos: the contradiction between sustaining unbearable suffering, as predicated by Jewish history, and the "L'Chaim" or "To Life!" principle, which holds that life is always worthful. The cause of Bleilip's despair is his enclosure within the far side of this contradiction, so that his religious belief fails in the face of recent Jewish history—the bloodshed of the story's title. Regarding the Holocaust, even the Orthodox rebbe, a survivor of Buchenwald, apparently shares Bleilip's sick-soul condition. At worship he describes the appalling transference wrought by that monstrous event upon the ancient idea of the scapegoat: "For animals we in our day substitute men. . . . [W]e have the red cord around our throats, we were in villages, they drove us into camps, we were in trains, they drove us into showers of poison. . . . [E]veryone on earth became a goat or a bullock, . . . all our prayers are bleats and neighs on the way to a forsaken altar. . . . Little fathers! How is it possible to live?" Now when it most seems that the rebbe is Bleilip's alter ego, he turns on Bleilip: "Who are you?" To Bleilip's answer—"A Jew. Like yourselves. One of you"—the rebbe retorts: "Presumption! Atheist, devourer! For us there is the Most High, joy, life. . . . But you! A moment ago I spoke your own heart for you, *emes* [true]? . . . You believe the world is in vain, *emes*?" This exchange leads to the rebbe's final divination: "Empty your pockets!" Even before the guns come to view, the rebbe—a death camp survivor speaking to a New York intellectual—says the key sentence: "Despair must be earned."

Other Jewish writers have threaded forth a similar response to the Suffering/L'Chaim dichotomy—Saul Bellow's *Herzog* is a masterly example—but Ozick remains distinctive for her theological rather than philosophical orientation. In **"Bloodshed"** her confrontation of Jewish opposites concludes in a kind of theological dialectic. Bleilip, the hater of bloodshed, admits he once used the pistol to kill a pigeon. The rebbe, defender of the faith, admits that "it is characteristic of believers sometimes not to believe." What they hold in common, as Jews, at last takes precedence: first, a belief, if only "now and then," in "the Holy One. . . . Even you [Bleilip] now and then apprehend the Most High?"; and second, the blood-kinship, including the most dreadful meanings of the term, that the Most High has seen fit to impose upon His people. The rebbe's last words, "Then you are as bloody as anyone," become Bleilip's final badge of Jewish identity in this most severely Jewish of the book's four tales. They also make a convenient bridge from this title story of ***Blood-***

shed to the title story of *Levitation,* where Jewish history again transforms bloodshed into a singular mark of Jewish identity.

Levitation: Five Fictions is a collection which ventures into fantasy, fable, and allegory. Beneath these novel tactics, however, Ozick's earlier triad of ground themes continues to inform the new book. Behind her fresh slate of characters facing new dramatic situations in widely different settings, the essential issues remain the familiar concerns with Jewish identity (**"Levitation"**), the pagan enticement (**"Freud's Room,"** the Puttermesser-Xanthippe stories), and the struggles of the artist (**"Shots"**).

In her title story, Ozick tries a new tactic: adopting the point of view of a Christian minister's daughter. Ozick's task is eased, however, by the woman's desire to marry "Out of [her] tradition," which makes her eligible for marriage to Feingold, a Jew who "had always known he did not want a Jewish wife." A Psalm her father recites from the pulpit leads her to settle the issue: she will become "an Ancient Hebrew."

After her conversion, the marriage seems unusually companionable; they are both novelists, as well as "Hebrews," and they love their professional intimacy: "Sometimes . . . it seemed to them that they were literary friends and lovers, like George Eliot and George Henry Lewes." As writers, they share a view of literature that makes them feel "lucky in each other. . . . Lucy said, 'At least we have the same premises.' " The central point of **"Levitation,"** however, is that they do not have the same premises—as Hebrews. Whereas her concept of "Ancient Hebrew" leads inevitably to Jesus as her stopping point, his concept of "Hebrew" begins in the Middle Ages and ends in World War II: which is to say, Feingold is a Jew, not a Hebrew. As such, he is obsessed with Jewish, not biblical, history: "Feingold's novel—the one he was writing now—was about [the] survivor of a massacre of Jews in the town of Estella in Spain in 1328. From morning to midnight he hid under a pile of corpses, until a 'compassionate knight' (this was the language of the history Feingold relied on) plucked him out and took him home to tend his wounds."

When they throw a party to advance their professional interests, this dichotomy between "Jew" and "Hebrew" widens to Grand Canyon proportions. To Lucy's dismay, her husband insists upon pouring out his obsessions upon the company: "Feingold wanted to talk about . . . the crime of the French nobleman Draconet, a proud Crusader, who in the . . . year 1247 arrested all the Jews of the province of Vienne, castrated the men, and tore off the breasts of the women." Eventually, she is driven to cut him off: "There he was, telling about . . . how in London, in 1279, Jews were torn to pieces by horses. . . . How in 1285, in Munich, a mob burned down a synagogue. . . . Lucy stuck a square of chocolate cake in his mouth to shut him up."

There is one guest, however, who does not want Feingold to shut up: a man who updates Jewish history. A Holocaust survivor, he describes in a whisper the slaughter at (apparently) Babi Yar, gripping the other listening Jews with hypnotic power but leaving Lucy alone and bewildered: "Horror; sadism; corpses. As if . . . hundreds of Crucifixions were all happening at once . . . bulldozers shoveling those same sticks of skeletons." As the whisper rasped on, the "room began to lift. It ascended . . . levitating on the little grains of the refugee's whisper. . . . They were being kidnapped, these Jews, by a messenger from the land of the dead." Eventually, they levitate beyond her range of hearing, rapt in their necrotic visions; and she is free at last to define her revulsion: "A morbid cud-chewing. Death and death and death. . . . 'Holocaust,' someone caws dimly from above; she knows it must be Feingold. . . . Lucy decides it is possible to become jaded by atrocity. She is bored by the shootings and the gas and the camps. . . . They are tiresome as prayer."

As the Jews soar up and away, she comes to a realization. Essentially she is not Jewish nor Ancient Hebrew nor Christian: she is a pagan, a believer in the Dionysian gods of the earth. What evokes this insight is her recollection of Italian peasants dancing, shouting "Old Hellenic syllables," and ringing bells like those "the priests used to beat in the temple of Minerva." In this scene "she sees what is eternal: before there was the Madonna there was Venus, Aphrodite . . . Astarte. . . . [T]he dances are seething. . . . Nature is their pulse. . . . Lucy sees how she has abandoned nature, how she lost the true religion on account of the God of the Jews."

Of the three recurring themes in **"Levitation,"** two—paganism and Jewish identity—are treated seriously, and one—the Feingolds as artists—is handled with *levity.* (An additional pun underscores the priestly tribe of Levi in old Israel.) In **"Shots,"** the portrayal of the artist is the central theme, calling up Ozick's most serious intentions. The art form in **"Shots"** is photography—a subject she has touched upon with great sensitivity elsewhere (see her "Edith Wharton" essay, e.g.)—but it shortly becomes an analogue for her own calling, a fable of the writer. The fable ranges into allegory along the way, but with the saving virtue of being meaningful both on a symbolic plane and on the level of immediate realism. The allegory begins with the motif of infatuation, initially with the art form itself. What the camera (or literature) offers its devotee is the power to raise the dead ("Call it necrophilia. . . . Dead faces draw me"), to preserve youth ("time as stasis . . . the time . . . of Keats's Grecian Urn"), to touch eternity. For the camerawoman/narrator of **"Shots,"** these powers are summed up in two images. One, from her childhood, is an ancient photo of "the Brown Girl," showing the face in youth of a patient at the nearby Home for the Elderly Ill—which face has since become one with the institution's "brainless ancients, rattling their china teeth and . . . rolling . . . their mad old eyes inside nearly visible crania." The other image is her own handiwork, a happenstantial filming of an assassination that blinks from life to death: "I calculated my aim, . . . shot once, shot again, and was amazed to see blood spring out of a hole in his neck."

But the infatuation grows beyond her embrace of a magic box. While on assignment to cover a public symposium, she becomes enthralled by one of its speakers, a professor of South American history. If Ozick's mode in this story were realism, doubtless the subject would be Jewish history; for her portrayal of the artist, it does not matter. What does matter is the photographer's compulsive immersion in the professor's subject, which brings her into open rivalry with his wife, Verity. Though she is a perfect wife, a paradigm of multiple abilities, "He didn't like her. . . . His whole life was wrong. He was a dead man . . . ten times deader than [the assassin's victim]."

Here the symbolism becomes complicated. If Verity (Conventional Realism) is unable to bring her husband out of a condition similar to rigor mortis, she nonetheless has little to fear from her photographer-rival, who has her own handicaps. Though she gets deeply into Sam's sphere (as Verity cannot), and though she does revitalize him, hers must at best be a partial claim on his favor: she (Art, Imagination) may be History's off-hours paramour; Verity is his lawful and permanent companion. For all their affinities, the ways of Art and History are not finally compatible. "You really have to *wait*," she tells him; "What's important is the waiting." But her mode of perception is untranslatable: "I wanted to explain to him, how, between the exposure and the solution, history comes into being, but telling that would make me bleed, like a bullet in the neck" (the assassin's victim had been a "simultaneous translator").

Like so many other Ozick tales, **"Shots"** ends in a flare of combat. Verity and her historian-husband, for their part, overcome the narrator by dressing her in archaic brown clothes, making her a "Period piece" (in Verity's phrasing). The period piece cannot resist this inevitability; eventually even the artist must submit to time and history. "I am already thirty-six years old, and tomorrow I will be forty-eight," she says, and thereby completes a circle: "I'm the Brown Girl in the pocket of my blouse. I reek of history." But still she registers a final dominance of art over history. With all the intensity of the sex drive, she captures the image of her adversary for eternity: "I catch up my camera . . . my ambassador of desire, my secret house with its single shutter, my chaste aperture. . . . I shoot into their heads, the white harp behind. Now they are exposed. Now they will stick forever."

Apart from **"Freud's Room,"** a speculation about the "hundreds of those strange little gods" that Freud collected, the remainder of *Levitation* is mostly fantasy in the comic/satiric mode. Over half the book traces the adventures of an urbanite named Ruth Puttermesser—fortyish, single, possessing "one of those Jewish faces with a vaguely Oriental cast," devoutly loyal to New York, victim of job discrimination, and so hungrily intellectual that her dream of Eden is an eternal reading binge: "She reads anthropology, zoology, physical chemistry, philosophy, . . . about quarks, about primate sign language, . . . what Stonehenge meant. Puttermesser . . . will read at last . . . all of Balzac, all of Dickens, all of Turgenev and Dostoevski, . . . and the whole *Faerie Queene* and every line of *The Ring and the Book* . . . at last, at last!"

Clearly Puttermesser is in some ways an alter ego of her maker, a role she expands upon in the dozen sections making up the **"Puttermesser and Xanthippe"** narrative. This sustained excursion into fantasy describes Puttermesser's creation of her own alter ego, the golem Xanthippe. This delightful creature, made of earth and breathed into life through the speaking of the Name, has to be dissolved into the earth again in the end because of her uncontrollable sexual hunger. Wearing a toga, or a "sari brilliant with woven flowers," Xanthippe the Jewish golem elides into a Greek sex goddess risen from earth; as such, she gives a new twist to Ozick's old Hellenism/Hebraism dichotomy. Here our female Pan and Moses work in harmony, as it were, with Puttermesser using the golem's magic to effect a Mosaic transformation of New York City. Elected mayor, she rids the city of its crime, ugliness, and debt: "Everyone is at work. Lovers apply to the City Clerk for marriage licenses. The Bureau of Venereal Disease Control has closed down. The ex-pimps are learning computer skills. . . . The City is at peace," But predictably, the harmony of Jewish and Greek gods is short-lived. Succumbing to the unruliest of gods ("Eros had entered Gracie Mansion," Xanthippe becomes Puttermesser's adversary, consuming the mayor's entire slate of city officers in her sexual fire; and when the golem returns to the earth, her magic goes with her, leaving the city in its normal ruined condition. With Puttermesser's closing outcry—"O lost New York! . . . O lost Xanthippe!"—the book as a whole attains a circular structure: it began with a levitation and ends with a collapse back to ordinary reality.

In concluding this essay, my chief regret is that even in so generous an allotment of pages as I have had here, it has not been possible to render any proper appreciation to the continuous execution of Ozick's art—the line by line, scene by scene, page by page vivacity of imagination and vigor of style. If we postulate that the "scene" in fiction corresponds to the image in poetry, we may say that Ozick's interplay of fictional devices consistently develops scenes answering to Ezra Pound's Imagist Manifesto of 1913: they "transmit an intellectual and emotional complex in an instant of time." . . .[The] Pagan Rabbi's breathtaking consummation of love with the dryad; Puttermesser chanting her beloved golem back to a pile of mud; Tchernikhovsky insolently at ease in Zion; Lushinski in Africa contemplating his buried self in Warsaw; the many dramatic verbal battles rendered with a perfect ear for speech patterns: Edelshtein versus the evangelist, Bleilip versus the rebbe, German versus Jew in **"The Suitcase"**—such scenes bespeak a gift of the first order of talent. Even if not outstandingly abundant in the fashion of Joyce Carol Oates or Saul Bellow, Ozick's stream of creativity has been outstandingly pure.

Although her ensconcement within a minority subculture may initially seem to limit her appeal to a larger audience, I (though not Jewish) have found that the obstacles to understanding her work have little to do with her Jewish materials. They result, rather, from her willful adherence to basic aesthetic principles. A holdover from the Modern Period—the Age of Eliot, Faulkner, Joyce—she is no more inclined to simplify her complex art, so as to ease her reader's task, than she is to falsify her view of reality, so as to thrive in the marketplace. Her Jewish heritage, for the most part, is not more constrictive than Hawthorne's or Faulkner's regionalism.

What matters in the end is the imaginative power to elevate local materials toward universal and timeless significance. By that standard, I judge Ozick's work to be memorably successful. Her variety and consistent mastery of styles; her lengthening caravan of original and unforgettably individualized characters; her eloquent dramatization through these characters of significant themes and issues; her absorbing command of dialogue and narrative structure; her penetrating and independent intellect undergirding all she writes—these characteristics of her art perform a unique service for her subject matter, extracting from her Jewish heritage a vital significance unlike that transmitted by any other writer. In the American tradition, Cynthia Ozick significantly enhances our national literature by so rendering her Jewish culture.

> *Victor Strandberg, "The Art of Cynthia Ozick," in* Texas Studies in Literature and Language, *Vol. 25, No. 2, Summer, 1983, pp. 266-312.*

Ellen Pifer   (essay date 1985)

[*Pifer is an American critic and educator. In the following essay, she studies the symbolism in "Puttermesser: Her Work History, Her Ancestry, Her Afterlife," and "Puttermesser and Xanthippe."*]

The narrative features of Cynthia Ozick's fiction, her use of self-referential devices and fantastic events, clearly place it within the development of postmodernist or antirealist literature. The philosophical and technical self-consciousness of postmodernism—the way it calls attention to the process and problems of its own narration, for example—has made contemporary fiction a predominantly ironic and parodistic literary mode. What sets Ozick's work apart from that of her postmodernist contemporaries is the orthodox vision conveyed through her sophisticated and playful narrative techniques: a vision of moral and spiritual truth rooted in the Old Testament and its Ten Commandments. Inspired by the ancient wisdom of Mosaic law, Ozick's consciousness as a writer has been forged by the history and traditions, as well as by the suffering, of the Jewish people. Far from creating orthodox or didactic effects, however, her fiction is often irreverent, startling, even grotesque. Subject to unexpected twists and sudden disasters, the universe of Ozick's two novels, various novellas, and numerous short stories is frequently visited by magic and the demonic. Irradiating the quotidian landscape, elements of the fantastic cast a symbolic light on local characters and conditions. Drawing upon the traditions and lore of Judaism, Ozick conjures her Jewish magic to illuminate the moral dimensions of both fiction and contemporary reality.

Two recent and related works by Ozick brilliantly reveal the paradoxical originality and orthodoxy of her fiction: the short story, **"Puttermesser: Her Work History, Her Ancestry, Her Afterlife,"** and the subsequent novella, **"Puttermesser and Xanthippe."** Their eponymous heroine, Ruth Puttermesser, is a New York City lawyer struggling against the forces of discrimination and corruption in this world while dreaming of a better one to come. As

her author demonstrates, Puttermesser's eventual attempt to institute a reign of reason in her city does even greater violence to the human condition than does the villainy ravaging it from within. To explore the implications of this paradox, Ozick employs a self-conscious narrative persona who alternately serves as guide, watchdog, and goad to her unwary readers. Calling attention to the literary status of the text, the narrating persona deliberately reveals Puttermesser's author to be a fallible mortal, not an omniscient god. By qualifying even the author's power to create images, Ozick's self-conscious narrative techniques illuminate and underscore her central theme: the dangers of idolatry.

A characteristic example of narrative reflexivity occurs midway through the short story when the narrating persona pauses to address the reader in a few short paragraphs that signal a fork in the road of Puttermesser's biography: "Now if this were an optimistic portrait," she says, "exactly here is where Puttermesser's emotional life would begin to grind itself into evidence." Ozick's readers must not expect such conventional satisfactions, however; a romantic denouement "is not to be." The narrator declares that Ruth Puttermesser, already past thirty, "will not marry," though she may involve herself in "a long-term affair"—though again, "perhaps not." By drawing attention to Puttermesser's fate, the narrator warns us that certain tried and true narrative conventions—the assurance of a "happy ending," for example—have no place in this story. And while the author's intentions appear to be clear—for she has "authority" over the fiction—some of the doubt riddling problematic human existence is also reflected in the text. Certain details of Puttermesser's existence, such as a possible long-term affair, have yet to be determined; the narrator, and perhaps even the author, is privileged but hardly omnipotent.

Shortly after the passage cited above, there follows an extended account of Puttermesser's visit to her Uncle Zindel, who appears to live among the "Spanish-speaking blacks" of New York City and to teach his niece Hebrew twice a week. Initially Puttermesser's visit, and the loving instruction in the mysteries of the Hebrew alphabet that she receives from her uncle, are vividly rendered. But just as Puttermesser, with bent head, begins to trace "the bellies of the holy letters," the narrator calls a halt to the proceedings. "Stop, stop!" she cries, rhetorically waving an invisible hand at the author. "Disengage, please. Though it is true that biographies are invented, not recorded, here you invent too much. A symbol is allowed, but not a whole scene: do not accommodate too obsequiously to Puttermesser's romance. . . . Uncle Zindel lies under the earth of Staten Island. Puttermesser has never had a conversation with him; he died four years after her birth." By admonishing Puttermesser's author-"biographer" in front of the reader, as it were, the narrator succeeds in demoting the authorial presence from remote god to simple human being. Puttermesser's "biographer" is, by virtue of being a mere mortal, an impressionable author in danger of indulging her own, as well as her protagonist's, romantic longings. Though the powers of creation may bestow apparently godlike authority on an author or biographer, each is only human. This truth, as we shall see, has the gravest implications for Puttermesser herself; in the subsequent novella, **"Puttermesser and Xanthippe,"** she will assume, with disastrous consequences, some godlike powers of her own.

Inspired by the ancient wisdom of Mosaic law, Ozick's consciousness as a writer has been forged by the history and traditions, as well as the suffering, of the Jewish people.

—*Ellen Pifer*

When the narrator beseeches Puttermesser's author to "disengage, please," she is diplomatically, if somewhat stagily, suggesting that the reader perform a similar mental operation. To disengage may also mean, in the business of reading, to engage more closely with the text at hand. One might even take time to leaf back to the page on which the scene with Uncle Zindel began—the scene, that is, which did not actually occur. There the reader notes with reawakened attention the deceptively innocent phrase, enclosed in parentheses, that might have been overlooked initially: "Twice a week, at night (it seemed), she went to Uncle Zindel for a lesson." *Seeming* belongs, of course, to the world of appearances. This innocent phrase, tucked within parentheses, opens a chink in the surface of reality and alerts us to the ironies that lie coiled beneath like springs—or, to borrow a later metaphor, like a snake. Early in Puttermesser's "life history," Ozick warns her readers to approach this story with a certain wariness. Both reader and author, after all, are fallible mortals subject to the tendency to identify with and therefore to indulge the desires of a fictional character. As Ozick later makes clear [in **"Puttermesser and Xanthippe"**], self-indulgence puts us in danger of complying with Puttermesser's own folly—her belief in "the uses of fantasy" and the idolatrous practices to which such faith inevitably leads. Lest we unwittingly succumb to idolatry—by exalting our own powers of creation—Ozick delineates the moral limits to which even poetic license is subject. Hence the narrator admonishes us, along with the author-biographer, not to "invent too much": "do not accommodate too obsequiously to Puttermesser's romance." According to Ozick's moral vision, fiction has as deep an obligation to truth-telling as any work of history—though it must be admitted that invention inheres in both forms of narrative.

Her skillful handling of the narrating persona allows Ozick to draw attention to the presence of symbol and invention in her narrative while simultaneously invoking its claims to truth. She manages this effect primarily by suggesting that all biographers are authors of fiction, the case of Puttermesser's "biographer" being a pointed example. While Puttermesser's "biography" has, therefore, the truth of history about it—being the record, after all, of a life—every biography, no matter the subject, is "invented,

not recorded." Both the biographer and the storyteller bestow shape, definition, and meaning on their subject by employing the patterns of art and imaginative invention. Elsewhere, in a published essay, Ozick elaborates upon this analogy: "A good biography," she says, "is itself a kind of novel. Like the classic novel, a biography believes in the notion of 'a life'—a life as a triumphal or tragic story with a shape, a story that begins at birth, moves on to a middle part, and ends with the death of the protagonist." It is the shape and notion of "a life" that this miniature "biography" of Puttermesser—spanning her "ancestry," "work history," and "afterlife"—both invokes and parodies. From the title's peculiar suggestion of an afterlife to the narrator's stagy interruptions, this biography playfully exposes its inherent contradictions. Ozick's narrative techniques are not the product of mere aesthetic gamesmanship, however. Puttermesser's life history is a parody, first and foremost, because she has no history. Though she longs to "claim an ancestor," her only meeting with Uncle Zindel is a fantasy. "She demands connection—surely a Jew must own a past. Poor Puttermesser has found herself in the world without a past."

The playful sabotage of Uncle Zindel's existence within the narrative is only one example of the way in which Ozick uses parody to expose a profoundly serious, if not tragic, historical dilemma that permeates her fiction: the destruction of Jewish identity by the forces of deracination, from the obliterating horrors of the Holocaust to the less obvious perils of contemporary assimilation. Unmoored in the New World from Judaic tradition and fidelity to Mosaic law, Ruth Puttermesser, the descendant of immigrants, can in effect claim neither a Yankee nor a Jewish heritage. Her dispossession is satirically underscored by the narrator's description of Puttermesser's immigrant "grandfather in his captain's hat." This forefather, whom Puttermesser knows only by his photograph, was merely a counterfeit captain—his hat a replica of the ones he sold as "a hat-and-neckwear peddler to Yankees." Pointing up the irony of the grandfather's Yankee pose, Ozick's narrator informs us that Puttermesser's grandfather "gave up peddling to captain a dry-goods store in Providence, Rhode Island." In this wry sentence, the reappearance of the captain's hat in verbal form suggests that Puttermesser's grandfather clung to his Yankee guise even after he had peddled his last hat. Puttermesser's father, the son of this counterfeit captain, evidently furthered the process of cultural dispossession. His daughter Ruth, we are told, "began life as the child of an anti-Semite. Her father would not eat kosher meat—it was, he said, too tough. He had no superstitions." And while great-uncle Zindel is her mother's relative, "Puttermesser's mother does not remember him." He is only "a name in the dead grandmother's mouth." To his name and legend, nonetheless, "Puttermesser clings. America is a blank, and Uncle Zindel is all her ancestry."

History, as the protagonist of [**"Envy; or, Yiddish in America"**] says, has become "a vacuum." New York City teems with the uprooted offspring of mutually hostile races and forgotten cultures. The dream of a regenerated New World lies in ruins—the wilderness of a hundred clashing "life-styles" replacing memory in "America's blank." Symptomatic of this dispossession, Puttermesser's younger sister has married "a Parsee chemist" and gone to live with her Indian husband in Calcutta: "Already the sister had four children and seven saris of various fabrics." Here Ozick's laconic syntax satirically equates the children with the saris, as bizarre manifestations of cultural rootlessness. Within two generations the Yankee captain's hat has been replaced by seven saris; the ease with which cultures are abandoned and adopted suggests not tolerance among peoples but their mutual deprivation.

Like "America's blank," Puttermesser's "work history" invokes its opposite: discontinuity rather than progression. In recognition of this discontinuity, Ozick's narrator interjects further apparently casual remarks that satirically expose the social injustice that operates in an alleged democratic society. Once again she employs deliberately reductive syntax to underscore the dehumanizing forces against which Puttermesser struggles. Despite her academic honors, her position as editor of the *Yale Law Review* and her "standardized" English pronunciation—drilled into her by fanatical teachers, elocutionary missionaries hired out of the Midwest by Puttermesser's prize high school—Puttermesser's work history is a story of defeat. True assimilation into the cultural mainstream proves impossible. Immediately upon graduation from law school she is hired, "for her brains and ingratiating (read: immigrant-like) industry," by "a blue-blood Wall Street firm." Here the narrator's apparently casual comment, enclosed within another set of parentheses, suggests the disconcerting reality behind the mask of social propriety. The dedicated industry by which Puttermesser hopes to gain a foothold in the social establishment only confirms, to her blueblood employers, her essential identity as a futilely aspiring immigrant. This sense of futility is reaffirmed in a later sentence, informing us that routinely "three Jews a year joined the back precincts" of "Midland, Reid & Cockleberry" and "three Jews a year left—not the same three," however. By syntactically reducing them to interchangeable entities, Ozick suggests that these young Jews, while certainly usable to the elite Wall Street firm, are as expendable, culturally speaking, as the seven saris of Puttermesser's sister on her grandfather's Yankee captain's hat.

Weary of being patronized, Puttermesser eventually finds a new job in the city Department of Receipts and Disbursements, where she is "not even a curiosity." Here those who share her title of assistant corporation counsel are mostly "Italians and Jews"—though, again, Puttermesser bears the distinction of being the only woman. The department soon emerges as a microcosm of the chaotic, anonymous, and brutal world of the urban melting pot. Here there are "no ceremonies and no manners," only "gross shouts, ignorant clerks, slovenliness, [and] litter on the floor." The ladies' room reeks of urine, the departments of corruption. Heads of departments are "all political appointees—scavengers after spoils." Puttermesser, the highly motivated, scholastically brilliant granddaughter of an immigrant peddler, has climbed the American ladder of success only to discover the ignominy of existence among scavengers and thieves. Her response to this ignominy is, once again, to indulge in fantasy, as evinced by her nightmarish vision of the Municipal Building where she works: "It was a monstrous place, gray everywhere, abundantly tunneled, with multitudes of corridors and stairs and shafts, a kind of swollen doom through which the bickering of small-voiced officials whinnied." The building is likened at once to an underground maze for rats and to a permanent psychotic condition—where oppression and doom swell to organic life, crushing all that is human. In Puttermesser's mind, the American dream has become a Kafkaesque nightmare. And from this hellish nightmare of the present the dreamer seeks escape, through "the uses of fantasy," to a better "World to Come." As though compensating for her failure to recover her lost ancestry as a Jew, Puttermesser drifts into daydreams of a future paradise.

The "dream of *gan eydn*—a term and notion handed on from her great-uncle Zindel"—is what links Puttermesser's unrequited longing for a past, or ancestry, to her utopian fantasies of a "World to Come." To "postulate an afterlife" is, like the fantasized visit to Uncle Zindel, "a game in the head not unlike melting a fudge cube held against the upper palate." This implied comparison between Puttermesser's delectable fantasies of heaven and the rich pleasures of eating chocolate fudge is sustained by other images throughout the narrative. Derived from both Hebraic Eden and the pagan world of nature, Puttermesser's dream of paradise is also an intellectual's garden of rational delights. For Puttermesser, it is in "the green air of heaven [that] Kant and Nietzsche together fall into crystal splinters" like some radiant philosophical manna. Her Eden, summoned in the language of "old green book-[s]," is both a philosopher's and a child's paradise, offering "perfection of desire upon perfection of contemplation" along with an unstinting supply of delicious fudge. Conveniently enough, and in keeping with the nature of romantic fantasy, "in Eden there was no tooth decay" [**"Puttermesser and Xanthippe"**]. Fed by the radiant waters of "Intellect and Knowledge," Puttermesser's "luxuriant dream" [in **"Puttermesser and Xanthippe"**] betrays an escapist's indulgence. Like her weakness for fudge, her dream expresses a naive longing for the sweet life.

By carefully arranging the elements of her narrative [in **"Puttermesser: Her Work History, Her Ancestry, Her Afterlife"**], Ozick creates the startling suggestion that Puttermesser's dream of paradise is allied to her nightmarish fantasies of hell. Not coincidentally, Puttermesser's luxuriant dream of a new Garden of Eden—where it is "green, green, green everywhere, green above and green below"—suggests the same verdant growth as the Municipal Building's monstrous "vegetable organism." In Puttermesser's view, this "building and its workers were together some inexorable vegetable organism with its own laws of subsistence. The civil servants were grass. Nothing destroyed them, they were stronger than the pavement, they were stronger than time." Like some hideous dragon crouched in the underworld, "the organism breathed, it comprehended itself." Verdant nature is, of course, a traditional aspect of biblical Eden as it is of the pastoral idyll. In Puttermesser's fantasies, however, the repeated emphasis on green nature and its organic potency begins to sound a warning note. That Puttermesser's dream of heaven contains the seeds of its own monstrous hell is a prophecy subsequently fulfilled by the creation, and destruction, of the golem.

The appearance of the golem in the novella ["**Puttermesser and Xanthippe**"] graphically demonstrates Puttermesser's enchantment with the uses of fantasy. By introducing this magical event into an otherwise familiar urban environment, Ozick dramatizes the dangerous power of the human mind, dabbling in creation, to unleash lethal forces in the concrete world. Yet the opening pages of the novella hardly prepare the reader for such extraordinary developments. Here we find Puttermesser, at the age of forty-six, entrenched in the vicissitudes of quotidian existence—further than ever, it would appear, from the realization of her dreams. Whether or not her love of fudge has persisted, Puttermesser is by no means in heaven. Unprotected by any celestial immunity to tooth decay, she has developed "peridontal disease" involving "sixty percent bone loss." Her "gums were puffy, her teeth in peril of uprooting. It was as if, in the dread underworld below the visible gums, a volcano lay watching for its moment of release." Yet despite—or because of—the disappointments of actual life and the forces of deracination threatening even her teeth, she has not ceased to believe in the uses of fantasy. The pressure of these fantasies will, in fact, unleash the dread volcano lying in wait. Through the power of her "unironic, unimaginative, her plain but stringent mind," Puttermesser activates forces dangerous to herself, to others, and to the city she so fervently desires to save.

Puttermesser's predilection for fantasy, Ozick makes clear, might not be attributable to an excess of poetic imagination. Though idealist and dreamer, she is an intellectual and rationalist for whom Plato is favorite bedtime reading. (Her lover, who tires of waiting for her to finish the *Theaetetus,* finally abandons her.) Like other literal-minded idealists who are determined to realize their vision, Puttermesser is compelled not to invention but to implementation. Still employed at the Department of Receipts and Disbursements, she is more beguiled by the uses of fantasy than any poet to whom Plato might accusingly point, for she attempts to realize her ideals in action rather than in words. Out of the degenerate and disorderly universe of New York City she seeks to create a new world, an earthly paradise. Longing for social redemption, worshipping "this god of the ideal" [a phrase used by Ozick in her preface to **Bloodshed and Three Novellas**], Puttermesser sets a minor miracle in motion. Out of her "desires as strong and strange as powers" there springs a golem. Apparently validating Puttermesser's faith in "the uses of fantasy," the golem vows to her maker: "You made me. I will be of use to you." Puttermesser's ambition to construct an ideal city thus begins to materialize; the idealist becomes a social engineer.

Ozick's own use of fantasy, the literary invention of a golem, is a form of narrative reflexivity that serves both to distance the reader from depicted events and to suggest latent ironies and complexities of meaning. Just before the golem appears, Puttermesser, alone in her apartment, carries the Sunday *New York Times,* "as heavy as if she car-

ried a dead child," to her bed. Already her active mind anticipates the impact of those scenes—of murder, larceny and rape—that inevitably blare from a metropolitan newspaper's pages. Instead of these images, however, Puttermesser confronts "a naked girl [who] lay in [her] bed. She looked dead—she was all white, bloodless." Noting the grittiness of the creature's skin, Puttermesser shudders at the thought that some "filthy junkie or prostitute" has crawled into her bed. The narration of Puttermesser's discovery emphasizes rather than resolves the incongruity between the magical nature of the golem and the laws of ordinary reality. No sooner does Puttermesser assume a plausible social identity for the naked creature—an identity continuous with the urban reality trumpeted from the pages of the *Times*—than she perceives her to be an unfinished work of creation. Without hesitation, Puttermesser "reach[es] out a correcting hand" and begins to pinch and mold the creature's unfinished nose and mouth. Then, like a sculptor at work on a clay model, she focuses her attention on perfecting its features by lengthening a forefinger that strikes her as too short: "It slid as if boneless, like taffy, cold but not sticky, and thrillingly pliable. Still, without its nail a finger can shock." Here again the description emphasizes the incongruous nature of Puttermesser's response. Impressed by the golem's unfinished finger, Puttermesser immediately accepts the magical manifestation; she is even thrilled by the golem's pliability. To Puttermesser, moreover, "the body had a look of perpetuity about it, as if it had always been reclining there, in her bed." Her reaction hints at Puttermesser's emotional and psychological *readiness* for the appearance of this "child" in her bed. Meanwhile the narrator plays up the ironic contrast between this filthy creature of clay and the pristine bed in which she appears: "such a civilized bed, the home of Plato and other high-minded readings." The suggested link between these superficially disparate phenomena—the lofty realm of "Intellect and Knowledge" and the chthonic origins of the golem—will gradually be made clear.

The narrator of "**Puttermesser and Xanthippe**" functions in much the same way as her counterpart in the earlier "biography." Although she now refrains from overtly addressing the author, her controlling presence and occasional, ironic asides arouse critical awareness and thus effect our continued disengagement from "Puttermesser's romance." In the earlier short story, the narrating persona predicted that Puttermesser would not marry. In the subsequent novella Ozick confirms the reliability of the persona's detached perspective by demonstrating the truth of her prediction. Now forty-six, Puttermesser herself recognizes "that she would never marry," "would never give birth." She is not yet reconciled to childlessness, however, and "sometimes the thought that she would never give birth tore her heart." As she carries the *Times,* as heavy as a dead child, to the bed in which she will abruptly discover the golem, Puttermesser laments that unborn child. Recalling Goethe's poem *Der Erlkönig,* she romantically envisions a parent's tragic loss: "The child was dead. In its father's arms the child was dead." Without repeating a previous warning—that we not "accommodate too obsequiously to Puttermesser's romance"—the narrator transmits a similar, if more obliquely stated, message: Puttermesser "imagined daughters. It was self-love; all these daughters were Puttermesser as a child." Egoistic self-love apparently fuels both Puttermesser's desire for a daughter and her predilection for fantasy: "She believed in the uses of fantasy. 'A person should see himself or herself everywhere,' [Puttermesser] said. 'All things manifest us.' " By juxtaposing Puttermesser's ardent longing for a daughter with the sudden appearance of a "child" in her bed, Ozick suggests the source of the golem's creation: the potent magic of human desire. By giving reign to her fantasies, moreover, Puttermesser unwittingly attempts to usurp the supreme role of God the Creator—envisioning a world that in "all things manifest[s]" her rather than Him. Between her faith in a monotheistic God and her belief in the uses of fantasy springs a contradiction that is gradually writ large in the text of Puttermesser's existence.

This contradiction is complicated by the fact that Puttermesser employs traditional Jewish magic to summon the golem to life, just as she will later use magic to destroy her. Reading the "single primeval Hebrew word, shimmering with its lightning holiness" on the golem's forehead, Puttermesser utters "the Name of Names" aloud—whereupon "the inert creature, as if drilled through by electricity," leaps "straight from the bed" into life. This symbolic electrical force may emanate from the same source that galvanized, in a lightning flash, Dr. Frankenstein's monster: the heavens. Yet despite the evidence that a creative force beyond her own—in this case, the power summoned by invoking God's holy name—is needed to jolt matter into life, Puttermesser unconsciously begins to assume the role of ultimate creator. It later "disturbs her that she did not recall making [the golem]"—but as Puttermesser gazes upon her "handiwork," the narrator's language parodistically echoes the biblical account of creation: "She looked at the [golem's] mouth; she saw what she had made."

An extension of Puttermesser's "desires as strong and strange as powers," the golem declares to her "maker": "I know everything you know. I am made of earth but also I am made out of your mind." She adds, "I express you. I copy and record you." Yet the golem proves to have a mind of her own—and, as a logical consequence of her origins, a mind that seeks to manifest itself everywhere. "Use me in the wide world," she instructs Puttermesser; yet subservience to her creator contradicts the willfulness of the mind the golem manifests. As soon as she springs to life, therefore, the creature challenges Puttermesser's will and intentions. To begin with, she rejects the Hebrew name that Puttermesser, who has "always imagined a daughter named Leah," bestows on her; the golem insists on being called by the pagan Greek name of Xanthippe. To no avail, Puttermesser voices her objection, saying, "Xanthippe was a shrew. Xanthippe was Socrates' wife." Thus indirectly Ozick reinforces the connection, suggested earlier, between the golem's recalcitrant nature and the high-minded realm of Plato and rational ideas. Like Socrates' infamous wife, Puttermesser's surrogate daughter will prove a scourge rather than a helpmate.

The unlikely relation of rational ideas to Jewish magic is a theme Ozick develops by means of a major self-conscious narrative device: the interpolation of other texts within the writer's own, which inevitably draws attention to the literary artifice. The interpolation of sources of golem history throughout the ages also emphasizes Ozick's contemporary reworking of a traditional theme. Not only does Puttermesser's author update the ancient theme by providing an urban American setting for the golem; she reverses the tradition established since biblical times by making the golem female. Formed in the image of her female creator, Xanthippe envinces the new power of women in contemporary Western society. Only those who have experienced some degree of social and intellectual authority are likely, it would seem, to nurture the ambitions of a golem maker. A "classical feminist" deeply committed to the social, political and intellectual equality of women, Ozick does not present Puttermesser's golem making as a glorious matriarchal feat overturning male-centered religious tradition. Rather, through the analogies established between Puttermesser and her male predecessors, Ozick suggests that her heroine falls prey to the same overweening ambition indulged, for millennia, by male dreamers and intellectuals.

The interpolated sources on the golem, it quickly becomes clear, establish Puttermesser's unambiguous affinity with her male counterparts. They also provide Ozick's less well informed readers with a brief but necessary introduction, spanning six pages of an eighty-page text, to the long history of the golem in Jewish lore. The immediate occasion for this helpful summary is Puttermesser's pressing curiosity to understand what she, the golem maker, has wrought. While she knows "the noble Dr. Gershom Scholem's bountiful essay 'The Idea of the Golem' virtually by heart," she traces "the history of the genus golem" in numerous other sources as well. Originating, as Scholem points out, in a Hebrew word in the Bible, then evolving through medieval cabalistic texts and legends, the permutations of golem history culminate in the nineteenth century, although they may also be found in modern literary fables and tales.

By reading up on "the genus golem," Puttermesser seeks to discover why she—avowedly "no mystic, enthusiast, pneumaticist, ecstatic, kabbalist"—has been visited by this magical manifestation. Following the process of Puttermesser's inquiry, Ozick's readers benefit from the information she gains but through her narrative strategies are able to arrive at their own significantly different conclusions. What strikes Puttermesser as she reads is "the kind of intellect (immensely sober, pragmatic, unfanciful, rationalist like her own) to which a golem ordinarily occurred." The "Great Rabbi Judah Loew, circa 1520-1609," for example, was "a solid scholar, a pragmatic leader" who fashioned a golem out of clay in an attempt to save the Jews of Prague. Whether the foregoing parenthetical remark on the nature of Puttermesser's sober intellect is registered in her own consciousness or provided for the reader's benefit by the narrator, who has made several previous parenthetical appearances, remains ambiguous. In any event alerted to possible parallels, Ozick's readers begin to discern further analogies between Puttermesser and her precursors. We learn, for example, that Rabbi Loew was moved to create a golem when, as they had for Puttermesser, "the scurrilous politics of his city" had "gone too far." And when told that the great rabbi "entered a dream of Heaven" in order to discover the secret of golem making, readers are likely to recognize Puttermesser's own heavenly dream as having similarly paved the way.

Puttermesser's "sober, pragmatic, unfanciful, rationalist" intellect is in marked contrast to the traditional stereotype of the female mind as being weak, irrational, fickle. The traditional stereotype might help, in fact, to account for the consistently male identity of the golem maker and his golem in Jewish lore throughout the ages. Overturning this tradition as well as the stereotype, Ozick's account neither exalts nor deprecates Puttermesser's sober intellect. Committed to the principle of sexual equality, Ozick portrays Puttermesser as neither inferior nor superior to her male counterparts. Possessed of formidable rational powers long thought to belong solely to men, Puttermesser is shown to incur the same risks that attend the male golem maker's intellectual ambition. Both the interpolated sources, as they are arranged in the narrative, and the narrator's parenthetical asides alert the reader to the morally problematic nature of Puttermesser's enterprise. Yet Puttermesser herself, because of her unqualified trust in the methods of the "reasoner" and the "refinements of . . . analysis," remains blind to the danger. Reading about the original golem makers' attempts to imitate creation by activating matter, she quickly perceives that they are "the plausible forerunners" of contemporary "physicists, biologists, or logical positivists." Mistakenly vindicated by what she perceives as having "nothing irrational in it," Puttermesser concludes that "she would not be ashamed of what she herself had concocted."

By fashioning her minihistory of the genus golem a-chronologically, Ozick ensures that her readers will not remain so complacently unaware. After providing the high-minded example of Rabbi Judah Loew in the sixteenth century, the narrator introduces various accounts going back to the time of the prophets Jeremiah and Daniel. "Even before that [time]," she continues, "thieves among the wicked generation that built the Tower of Babel swiped some of the contractor's materials to fashion idols, which were made to walk by having the Name shoved into their mouths; then they were taken for gods." The achronological account of the history of the golem thus hints at the possible deterioration of the golem maker's idealistic intentions, like those of Rabbi Loew, into sheer will for power. The narrative handling of the interpolated texts ultimately serves to underscore the protagonist's own moral decline: the golem Xanthippe signals Puttermesser's descent from dreaming idealist to practical politician, culminating in her eventual declaration, "I have to be Caesar."

In the name of rational idealism, Puttermesser brings the golem to life and justifies her creation, unaware that she has released telluric forces that will not respond to the appeal of reason. In this way she indeed resembles her "scientific" precursors, whose initial enthusiasm for the pragmatic uses of the golem she also rehearses. The tasks she assigns Xanthippe quickly escalate from the traditional duties of servant and housekeeper to the implementation of a PLAN by which New York City can be rehabilitated and redeemed. With the golem's assistance she campaigns throughout the city for the office of mayor. Her party, "Independents for Socratic and Prophetic Idealism—ISPI for short," promises "to transform the City of New York into Paradise." Here again, the arrangement of narrative details comments ironically on Puttermesser's ambitions. In the acronym of the party's name as well as in its campaign poster, the snake of irony hisses audibly—the asp in ISPI—at Puttermesser's Edenic dream. The poster "shows an apple tree with a serpent in it. The S in ISPI is the serpent. Puttermesser . . . has promised to cast out the serpent." Despite such a promise, the serpent lies dramatically coiled, as letter, sign, and symbol, within the text of the narrative. Symbolizing Adam and Eve's defiance of God's law in their temptation to acquire absolute knowledge and power, the serpent indicates the inherent flaw in Puttermesser's dream of Eden. She too will grow infatuated with power and dream of making "an entire legion of golems"—"herself the creator down to the last molecule of [their] ear-wax."

Embedded in Ozick's narrative, as it is in the name and poster representing Puttermesser's political party, the serpent is a potent sign that draws the reader's attention to unseen forces ready to spring into action like the volcano, "in the dread underworld" of Puttermesser's infected gums, "waiting for its moment of release." Arresting the reader's attention, these patterns and images tend to slow the momentum of the plot. Calling attention to this effect, Ozick's narrator slyly remarks on the reader's probable inertia: "All this must be recorded as lightly and swiftly as possible; a dry patch to be gotten through, perhaps via a doze or a skip." As Puttermesser is progressively more caught up in her luxuriant dream—earnestly believing she can apply her material magic to remaking reality into "a rational daylight place [that] has shut out the portals of night"—careless readers may tend to go along with the delusion. By dozing and skipping over the bright surface of visible reality, they will have submitted to some rather potent local magic: the illusions of art. The spell of the narrative, its stream of successive events, is itself a kind of luxuriant dream that catches the passive dreamer in its coils.

To break this spell, as we have seen, Ozick employs a variety of self-conscious devices, including the narrative persona who needles the reader into critical awareness and moral attention. As a further strategy Ozick divides **"Puttermesser and Xanthippe"** into twelve sections or chapters, each preceded by a Roman numeral and a descriptive title or heading. These headings frame the action while they distance the reader from its immediate effects—so that the often ironic relation between incident and meaning gradually emerges. One heading, for example, is entitled "Puttermesser's Fall, and the History of the Genus Golem." The fall recounted in the narrated events, however, is hardly a moral one. Ostensibly the title refers to Puttermesser's losing her job at the Department of Receipts and Disbursements. In this instance, she is merely the victim of a corrupt system of spoils. What the heading obliquely suggests, on the other hand, is a possible connection between the appearance of the golem and some moral blunder or fall on Puttermesser's part.

The title of a later chapter, "The Golem Destroys Her Maker," is also superficially misleading: Puttermesser is not literally destroyed, but later the golem is. The title is a comment, not on these literal events, but on Puttermesser's shaky status as idol maker: "The coming of the golem animated the salvation of the City, yes—but who, Puttermesser sometimes wonders, is the true golem? . . . Xanthippe did not exist before Puttermesser made her . . . [but] Xanthippe made Puttermesser Mayor, and Puttermesser sees that she is the golem's golem." Having unleashed, with her material magic, the forces of nature, Puttermesser cannot control what she has wrought. Xanthippe daily grows larger, and her capacity to carry out Mayor Puttermesser's will is more than matched by her own monstrous will, size, and appetite. When the golem, whose "blood is hot," tries to slake her mounting lust on the city officials, they are quickly exhausted and finally ruined in the process. Of the "broad green City" she helps transform into a temporary Eden, Xanthippe has said earlier, "I can tear it all down." Now the golem begins to fulfill her prophecy.

Like the insatiably lustful pagan goddess in Ozick's story **"The Dock-Witch,"** Xanthippe embodies the destructive potency of organic nature. That telluric forces can wreak havoc when human consciousness—pagan, romantic, or "scientific"—exalts them is a pervasive theme in Ozick's fiction. Fashioning a clay idol by means of her own Jewish magic, Puttermesser has entered into this dangerous worship. So instead of slaying the dragon—the fearful "organism" that "breathes and comprehends itself"—Puttermesser has roused it in another form. Like all idolators, she is enslaved by the very powers she has sought to placate. Having unleashed those forces in order to perfect the material order, she becomes "the golem's golem." Now as the city grows "diseased with the golem's urge," Puttermesser's career as mayor is clearly over. In this sense destroyed, she must destroy the golem before riot and rage demolish what is left of the city.

Traditional tales of the fantastic, Tzvetan Todorov has pointed out, describe the conflict between reason and the "mirror" world of magic and distorted perception. Ozick significantly inverts these conventions to create a parable for our time, suggesting that reason may detonate its own fatal magic. The golem is created, then justified by her maker's worship of "Intellect and Knowledge"; yet Puttermesser loves her creation as her "own shadow," an extension of her (godlike) self. In a similar act of self-love, the male protagonist of Ozick's book [*The Cannibal Galaxy*] exalts the educator's power "to seize in the hand new mind, fresh clay, early intellect," and mold it like a "monarch" in his image. The sinister irony is, of course, that one act of usurpation follows another. By exalting his own powers of creation over any other and declaring himself the highest law and authority, the usurper is in danger of creating his own alter ego. Summoned like Xanthippe by the usurper's magic, such a creature is likely, as a mirror of his creator's will, to defy the very power that made him.

Puttermesser's matriarchal urges are not depicted as mor-

ally superior to her male counterpart's patriarchal drives. Her overweening fantasies are, moreover, an extension of rational idealism rather than poetic imagination. Ozick is not suggesting, however, that rationalists are the only dreamers susceptible to forms of idolatry. As a writer who by her own statement "lust[s] after stories more and more," she also detects the whiff of idolatry permeating the rituals of art. Fashioning images that stun and captivate, inciting the beholder to wonder—and perhaps worship—at the altar of art, the artist is implicated in the idol making that preoccupies Ozick everywhere in her writing. This concern is voiced most directly in **"Usurpation (Other People's Stories),"** a novella that, by Ozick's testimony, suggests how "the story-making faculty itself can be a corridor to the corruptions and abominations of idol-worship, of the adoration of magical event." For Ozick, "belief in idols is belief in magic. And storytelling, as every writer knows, is a kind of magic act" [Preface, *Bloodshed and Three Novellas*]. Because, like Puttermesser, "artists play with clay and then ask that the clay be honored," there is "in every act of creation the faint shadow of idol-making" [Catherine Rainwater and William J. Scheick," "An Interview with Cynthia Ozick (Summer 1982)," *Texas Studies in Literature and Language* 25 (Summer 1983)].

Readers of the Puttermesser stories might well assume that the self-conscious narrative devices that Ozick employs are themselves symptomatic of their creator's idolatrous self-love. They are, it might be said, the author's way of arranging her fictional universe so that "all things manifest her." Victor Strandberg has said, with some justification, that Ruth Puttermesser "is in some ways an alter ego of her maker" ["The Art of Cynthia Ozick," *Texas Studies in Literature and Language* 25 (Summer 1983)]. Sharing much of her author's experience and many of her avowed interests—especially in the pursuit of "Knowledge and Intellect"—Puttermesser, it might then be suggested, is a kind of golem herself, forged by Ozick's own, highly original Jewish magic. When subjected to careful analysis, however, Ozick's self-conscious narrative techniques prove to work in quite the opposite way: even her most overt authorial ploys are ranged against the idol-making tendencies of art itself.

A conclusive example of this countering effect occurs in the final paragraph of [**"Puttermesser: Her Work History, Her Ancestry, Her Afterlife"**]. Here, directly addressing the reader, the narrator says: "The scene with Uncle Zindel . . . could not occur because, though Puttermesser dares to posit an ancestry, we may not. Puttermesser is not to be examined as an artifact but as an essence. . . . Puttermesser is henceforth [in the subsequent novella, that is] to be presented as a given." Adopting the first person plural "we," the narrator appears to be speaking now on behalf of the author-biographer as well as herself. Obliquely she alludes to some operating principle—moral, aesthetic, perhaps both—that prohibits author and narrator from indulging the kind of fantasy in which Puttermesser "dares" to engage. Acknowledging their mortal limits, they apparently do not aim to usurp the role of ultimate Creator, the source of that human essence of which Puttermesser, though a fictional character, partakes. In other words,

Puttermesser is not simply presented as the author's artifact but as a representative of the race descended from Adam and Eve. She is not the author's golem or clay idol, fashioned for the uses of fantasy by an arbitrary set of signs and symbols. As the image of a human being, her origins and her essence are ultimately a given of Creation—God-given, that is—even while she is conjured, shaped, and manipulated by the author. While the first half of this assertion underscores the moral and metaphysical basis of Ozick's art, the latter half recognizes the temporary and local powers of the artist. As Vladimir Nabokov once put it, in a now familiar phrase, an author "may impersonate an anthropomorphic deity" within the world of his fiction, but his godlike authority does not extend beyond the page.

Having alerted us to Puttermesser's ineffable essence, Ozick redirects attention to the playfully staged dialogue between the narrator and Puttermesser's silent biographer. The first Puttermesser story ends as the narrating persona calls out to the silent author: "Hey! Puttermesser's biographer! What will you do with her now?" To pose such a question in the concluding line of a story is, quite obviously, to flaunt the conditions of artifice. Yet Ozick remains true to her character's essence by offering an answer to this apparently rhetorical question—couched in the form of yet another fiction, published five years later. **"Puttermesser and Xanthippe,"** the overt creation of self-conscious artifice, nonetheless testifies to Ozick's profoundly moral commitment as an artist. Like most of her other fiction, both the Puttermesser stories employ postmodernist narrative techniques to convey a deeply orthodox vision of reality. One of Ozick's abiding concerns, as I have demonstrated, is the multivalent forms of idolatry that have proliferated in our era—an era not merely secular in nature but one that exalts usurpation in every conceivable arena of life: practical and political, philosophical and artistic. In all spheres of social and cultural activity idols to which are attributed absolute power and authority are eagerly embraced: the glorified state, the arm of technology and progress, the "final solution," the mythical promise of artificial intelligence or simply those old and familiar gods, Moloch and Mammon. Among artists and literary scholars the ideal, or idol, of usurpation is no less evident. Among Ozick's contemporaries, the prominent Yale critic, Harold Bloom, for example, unambiguously exalts the usurper at the heart of all literary endeavor: "We read," Bloom says, "to usurp, just as the poet writes to usurp. Usurp what? A place, a stance, a fullness, an illusion of identification or possession; something we can call our own or even ourselves." But to Cynthia Ozick this fullness, presence, essence, or identity is already ours—the given of Creation it is the artist's responsibility to fulfill rather than merely invent. To the testimony of this presence, as witness rather than usurper, she dedicates the narrative magic of her art.

Ellen Pifer, "Cynthia Ozick: Invention & Orthodoxy," in Contemporary American Women Writers: Narrative Strategies, *edited by Catherine Rainwater and William J. Scheick, The University Press of Kentucky, 1985, pp. 89-109.*

Ursula Hegi   (essay date 1989)

[*Hegi is a German-born American educator and novelist. In the following essay, she praises* The Shawl *for its emotional intensity.*]

Devastating and exquisite, Cynthia Ozick's ninth book, **The Shawl,** carries the emotional impact of a much longer work. In only 56 pages that contain a short story, **"The Shawl,"** and a novella, **"Rosa,"** Ozick creates a world that reaches beyond words, beyond pages, a world that evokes nightmares contained between the lines and leaves us mute.

The short story is set in a concentration camp where Rosa hides her daughter in a shawl she has tied to herself. Nursing her daughter, she is a "walking cradle . . . a floating angel," and the 15-month-old Magda is "a squirrel in a nest, safe." But the safety is deceptive as the child sucks on her mother's dry breast and then on the shawl, "flooding the threads with wetness. The shawl's good flavor, milk of linen."

Rosa knows her daughter cannot live for long, and that awareness cuts through every moment. This child who looks "Aryan" and quite likely is the consequence of Rosa's rape by a German soldier, needs to be protected from her cousin, Stella, a starving 14-year-old who surely would devour her.

In a scene unequaled in contemporary literature, the child who has been "buried away deep inside the magic shawl, mistaken there for the shivering mount of Rosa's breasts," is thrown at an electric fence by a concentration-camp guard. But even here, Ozick's language transcends the gruesome facts of Magda's death as the child swims "through the air . . . like a butterfly touching a silver vine." Yet, her language does not diminish the horror but rather intensifies it. To protect herself with silence, Rosa is left drinking the shawl.

This shawl is the connecting force between the story and the novella, **"Rosa."** Although the novella does not vibrate with the taut power of the story, it rounds out the pattern of Rosa's life 30 years later as she tries to resist the impact of her daughter's death. Here, too, the language fits the situation—it is immediate and reveals in the first line that Rosa is "a madwoman and scavenger."

Rosa resists the label "survivor" that society has applied to her and others who got out from concentration camps. "It used to be refuge, but now there was no such creature, no more refugees, only survivors, a name like a number . . . blue digits on the arm."

She protects herself with many small obsessions. Her life is fragmented—fantasy, memory and reality blending in an ever-shifting pattern. Destructive and self-destructive, Rosa isolates herself within a tight circle of habits. After demolishing her antique shop back East, she moves into a dingy hotel for the elderly in Florida. "The whole peninsula of Florida was weighted down with regret. Everyone had left behind a real life."

Rosa's daughter has not stayed for her at the age she died, but has grown, taking on a history of her own, a ghost nourished by Rosa's intricate fantasies. "Magda, a beautiful young woman of thirty, thirty-one: a doctor married to a doctor; large house in Mamaroneck, New York; two medical offices, one on the first floor, one in the finished basement."

Rosa's most significant communications lie in the countless letters she writes to Magda, who can change from a doctor to a teen-ager to a professor of Greek philosophy at Columbia. Her niece, Stella, who sends her monthly checks, keeps reminding her that Magda is dead. To avoid conflict, Rosa pretends she believes her. This deception forms an even stronger bond between her and the adult daughter of her fantasies.

She sees herself as a woman who does not have a life. Her worry about misplaced underpants turns into an obsession that blots out the horror of Magda's death, a horror always ready to envelop her again if she isn't careful. She begins to suspect Simon Persky, a retired man who tries to court her, of stealing the pants. The imagined theft leaves her feeling humiliated, anxious as she searches for the pants in the streets.

She feels superior to Simon as she recalls the Warsaw of her childhood, her privileges and education that set her apart even in the ghetto. "Imagine confining us with teeming Mockowiczes and Rabinowiczes and Perskys and Finkelsteins, with all their bad-smelling grandfathers and their hordes of feeble children . . . we were furious . . . "

When her niece honors her request and sends her Magda's shawl, Rosa feels disappointed because it does not "instantly restore Magda, as usually happened . . . The shawl had a faint saliva smell, but it was more nearly imagined than smelled." Yet, when her daughter finally materializes, she displaces reality, taking on more specific traits than most of the live characters.

Cynthia Ozick's *The Shawl* is brilliant, moving, and chilling as it attempts to convey a terror so immense that it overwhelms the characters and renders them speechless. To build any language out of this inability to articulate seems impossible; yet, Ozick does it in such a way that we, as readers, share the characters' powerlessness to give words to their innermost experiences and, therefore, are forced to relive them.

Ozick as a literary technician:

Cynthia Ozick is a carver, a stylist in the best and most complete sense: in language, in wit, in her apprehension of reality and her curious, crooked flights of imagination. . . . [She] has the poet's perfectionist habit of mind and obsession with language, as though one word out of place would undo the whole fabric.

A. Alvarez, in "Flushed with Ideas: 'Levitation'" Cynthia Ozick, edited by Harold Bloom. New York: Chelsea House, 1986.

Ursula Hegi, "A Frail, Connecting Thread," in Los Angeles Times Book Review, *October 8, 1989, p. 2.*

Hans Borchers (essay date 1991)

[*In the following essay, Borchers analyzes Ozick's portrayal of German characters and, by implication, Germany in "The Suitcase" and "The Mercenary."*]

Mr. Hencke, the father of the artist, was a German, an architect, and a traveler—not particularly in that order of importance. He had flown a Fokker for the Kaiser, but there was little of the pilot left in him: he had a rather commonplace military-like snap to his shoulders, especially when he was about to meet someone new. This was not because he had been in the fierce and rigid Air Force, but because he was clandestinely shy. His long grim face, with the mouth running across its lower hem like a slipped thread in a linen sack, was pitted as a battlefield. Under the magnifying glass his skin would have shown moon-craters. As a boy he had the smallpox. He lived in a big yellow-brick house in Virginia, and no longer thought of himself as a German. He did not have German thoughts, except in a certain recurring dream, in which he always rode naked on a saddleless horse, holding on to its black moist mane and crying "*Schneller, schneller.*" With the slowness of anguish they glided over a meadow he remembered from child-hood, past the millhouse, into a green endlessness hazy with buttercups. Sometimes the horse, which he knew was a stallion, nevertheless seemed to be his wife, who was dead.

These are the beginning lines of Cynthia Ozick's short story **"The Suitcase"** published in 1971 in *The Pagan Rabbi and Other Stories,* the first of Ozick's three collections of short fiction. Quite obviously, we are looking at a text which takes us right to the center of our concern with the significance of Germany in Ozick's work. Mr. Gottfried Hencke, who is one of the two principal characters in **"The Suitcase,"** is not only summarily identified as a German, the narrator also takes care to round out the image of Mr. Hencke by elaborating on his personal history and his physical appearance; we are even granted access to his dream life. Three items stand out in the portrait: the contrast between Mr. Hencke's German background and his present situation and station in life, the imagery used to describe his face, and, most importantly, the recurring dream which is referred to as his only German thought.

As for the contrast between past and present, it is noteworthy that the story's first sentence introduces Mr. Hencke as a German, although, as we find out a little further down in the quoted passage, he no longer thinks of himself as such but rather, so we assume, as an American. The reason for his changed perception of his national allegiance is his life history. Mr. Hencke is sixty-eight years old at the time of the story's action, which takes place in 1965. As we gather from other information in the story, he emigrated to the United States sometime between his service as a German Air Force pilot in the First World War and the outbreak of the Second World War. In America he pursued a distinguished career as an architect of high-rises, a builder of towers, becoming, to all intents and purposes, a respected American citizen. In spite of this personal history, which is, above all, singularly free of any overt implication in Germany's Nazi period, the story emphasizes Mr. Hencke's German background and identity. The two images which Ozick employs to depict Mr. Hencke's face are unequivocal. His mouth is likened to "a slipped thread in a linen sack," a comparison suggesting the idea of a sudden, if unintentional, loss of control in an otherwise orderly design. The smallpox-scarred complexion on Mr. Hencke's "long grim face" elicits the connotations of moon-craters and a battlefield. Both images—along with his name, a near homophone of the German word for "hangman"—serve to mark this character, if not, in a traditional sense, as the story's villain, then at least as a not-to-be-trusted and potentially violent person. What is perhaps not so traditional about **"The Suitcase"** is the fact that although Mr. Hencke does evidently not bear the accoutrements of the hero, he is nevertheless the story's center of consciousness. It is through *his* eyes that we observe both the other characters and the progress of the action; throughout the story we are given privileged access to *his* feelings and intimate thoughts.

We are even let into his dream world, a specifically German dream world, we are told. Apart from the above-mentioned night dream about Mr. Hencke's riding in the nude on a saddle-less horse into a meadow full of buttercups that he remembered from his childhood in Germany, we are also presented, as the story unfolds, with two split-second flashes of memory which are actually variants of the same daydream—presumably about another, but very similar, scene from Mr. Hencke's German childhood.

Before commenting on this daydream and his dreaming in general, a brief outline of the story's fairly straightforward plot structure is in order. The setting is an art gallery on New York City's West Fifty-Third Street, and the overall sequence of events may be summarized as a vernissage. The artist whose paintings are being presented to the public for the first time is Mr. Hencke's son, the American-born and Yale-educated Gottfried Hencke, Jr. We are witnessing the progress of the vernissage from the arrival of the first visitors, through the opening speech of the famous critic, who had been hired to embellish with his intellectual brilliance the exhibit of a basically mediocre painter, to the festive conclusion of the occasion involving some modest drinking and dancing. This is only the backdrop, however, for what turns out to be the story's center of interest: the encounter and the emotionally charged exchanges between the artist's father and the artist's mistress, Genevieve. Like Mr. Hencke, Genevieve Lewin, a married Jewish woman from Indianapolis, had come to New York City to be present at the opening of Gottfried's exhibit; and again like Mr. Hencke, who at the outset of the vernissage had deposited a small suitcase—the suitcase of the title—at the foot of a chair, Genevieve, wishing to be unencumbered by her pocket book for the duration of the party, had put it on the very same chair. The story's finale is triggered by the theft of Genevieve's pocketbook. Although she has lost all her money and her airline ticket, Genevieve declines to stay overnight at the Henckes. Accepting a check from her lover's wife, she dashes to the air-

port to return to her Jewish husband and her four daughters in Indianapolis, disgusted by the loss of her belongings, but even more by the encounter with the artist's father.

It is the encounter, or maybe we should say, the confrontation of an American of Jewish descent with an American of German descent. The animosity that is generated in the course of this confrontation is due to Genevieve's insistence on her Jewish identity and to Mr. Hencke's obtuse refusal to scratch at the veneer of his secure American citizenship. Mr. Hencke fails to see any relationship whatsoever between his own almost-forgotten German background and the murdering of the Jews during Germany's Nazi period. The theoretical framework for this denial of any kind of moral implication in the Holocaust is his perception of history as an impersonal, anonymous force. When Genevieve provokes him by the statement that his son's abstract paintings reminded her of "shredded swastikas," Mr. Hencke has the following thoughts:

> He knew what she meant him to see: she scorned Germans, she thought him a Nazi sympathizer even now, an anti-Semite, an Eichmann. She was the sort who, twenty years after Hitler's war, would not buy a Volkswagen. She was full of detestable moral gestures, and against what? Who could be blamed for History? It did not take a philosopher (though he himself inclined toward Schopenhauer) to see that History was a Force-in-Itself, like Evolution. There he was, comfortable in America, only a little sugar rationed, and buying War Bonds like every other citizen, while his sister, an innocent woman, an intellectual, a loyal lover of Heine who could recite by heart *Der Apollogott* and *Zwei Ritter* and *König David* and ten or twelve others, lost her home and a daughter of eleven in an RAF raid on Köln.

Mr. Hencke's ostensible urge to deny any kind of moral responsibility in the face of Genevieve's relentless insistence on his connectedness with twentieth-century German history takes an absurd turn at the end of the story. Subsequent to the disappearance of Genevieve's pocketbook, an atmosphere of general suspicion develops at the vernissage party. It is in this atmosphere of distrust that Mr. Hencke nervously volunteers to open his suitcase. He wishes to prove his innocence by letting Genevieve have a look at the suitcase's contents:

> "Now just look, look through everything, nothing here but my own, here are my shirts, . . . my new underwear. Only socks, see? Socks, socks, shorts, shorts, shorts, all new, I like to travel with everything new and clean, undershirt, undershirt, shaving cream, razor, deodorant, more underwear, toothpaste, you see this, Genevieve?"

We are tempted to take this final tableau of the story—Mr. Hencke's embarrassed fingering of his new and clean underwear under the scrutiny of Genevieve's eyes—as the answer to our probing into Ozick's fictional representation of a German character in her short story **"The Suitcase."** He is depicted as someone who rejects his implication in history, who has sloughed off his former identities, who now lives, as we learned in the initial quotation, in Virginia, the state whose very name connotes innocence, and who, when confronted with the assertion of his moral accountability, points to a suitcase full of spotless underwear.

But the story offers an additional level of meaning. The key to this other level is Mr. Hencke's dreaming. There are two occasions in the story when the two adversaries are at least socially close, so close, in fact, that Genevieve is moved to quickly embrace the father of her lover. In both instances the physical contact with Genevieve conjures up in Mr. Hencke's mind the fleeting daydream of a childhood scene quite similar to the one that had become an integral part of his recurring night dream, particularly in terms of the predominance of the color yellow. Here is the first of the two instances:

> [Genevieve] embraced the father of the artist. The very slight fragrance of the pumpernickel crumbs on the underpart of her chin . . . made a flowery gash in his vision. Some inward gate opened. He remembered still another field, this one furry with kümmel, a hairy yellow shoulder of a field shrugging in the wind.

In the second instance the connection between Genevieve as the catalyst of the flashback and the memory flashback itself is stressed even more, as Genevieve leans over to Mr. Hencke to kiss him: "She kissed the father of the artist. The hairy kümmel valley was photographed by flash bulb on the flank of his pancreas."

Given this textual evidence, it is probably no exaggeration to speak of the story's preoccupation with Mr. Hencke's dreams and dreamlike memories from childhood. At the very end of the text, in the next to the last paragraph, his mental obsession is brought to a climax as he watches Genevieve, check in hand, leave for the airport:

> In his tenuously barbule soul . . . the father of the artist burned in the foam of so much kümmel, so many buttercups, so much lustrous yellow, and the horse's mane so confusing in his eyes like a grid, and why does the horse not go faster, faster?

One need not be much of a Freudian to recognize in Mr. Hencke's fixation on the yellow meadows of his German childhood and on the horse that does not run fast enough—not fast enough, apparently, to traverse an anxiety-laden region of his mind—a subconscious obsession with guilt. The fact that this guilt complex is twice brought to the threshold of his consciousness by the embrace of his antagonist, the Jewish woman Genevieve, and that it is furthermore emphatically associated with yellow star-shaped flowers—an icon that nobody who is minimally aware of the precarious relationship between Germans and Jews in the twentieth century is likely to misunderstand—points to the source of Mr. Hencke's vague, dreamlike feelings of guilt. Underneath the workings of his conscious mind, which vigorously rejects Genevieve's overt accusations, there is a strong countercurrent of largely unconscious sensations of guilt. One way to accommodate this apparent contradiction, to account for Mr. Hencke's ambivalent state of mind, would be indeed

to refer to the Freudian concept of the return of the repressed.

Our reading of **"The Suitcase"** has netted the general insight that the topic of Germany features prominently in Ozick's story. It is noteworthy, however, that the Germany which kindles the author's imagination is not the Federal Republic of the present time, but the Germany of the Nazi period and the Holocaust. Given this preoccupation with Nazi Germany, it is somewhat surprising that the character who represents the idea of Germany in **"The Suitcase"** is not a German closely linked to the Nazi period (nor is he a citizen of the Federal Republic), but an American of German descent who did not even live in Germany during the Hitler years. This strategy in the casting of her principal character is a narrative device which allows Ozick to abstract from the period of Nazi Germany—or any other period in German history, for that matter—and to operate with a historically indefinite concept of Germany. It is a strategy which reminds us of a recent article on "Stereotypes of Germans in American Culture" in which Paul Monaco has commented on a tendency prevalent in the United States to understand Nazism as the necessary end result of a German culture that extends far back into the past and, by extension, to link the image of Germany almost exclusively to the political triumph of Nazism and its consequences:

> The point is that, in essence, Hitler and Nazism are represented, in even the best [American] writing and teaching on the subject, as the end product of patterns in *German* thought, *German* culture, and *German* society.

Even though Cynthia Ozick's story **"The Suitcase"** may be looked upon as an example of this penchant to mistake the stereotypical abbreviation, i.e. Nazi Germany, for German history and culture as a whole and in general, we have to relativize such a finding by pointing to the complexity with which Cynthia Ozick constructs the fictional representation of her prototypical German in **"The Suitcase."** Mr. Hencke is not a one-dimensional character. His indignation at Genevieve's insinuations and open accusations is put into perspective, if not openly challenged, by the repeated injection of dream material and memory flashbacks into his stream of consciousness. Although he feels victimized and unjustly categorized by the vengeful concept of a German national character implied in Genevieve's aggressive remarks, it seems that Gottfried Hencke subliminally, i.e. through his dream activity and his memory flashbacks, accepts such a categorization, and that there is even a strong undercurrent of guilt in the makeup of his psyche.

It is an ambiguous message, then, that **"The Suitcase"** contains in terms of the treatment of the theme of Germany. Although set in 1965 and published in 1971, the story is not about Germany in the 1960s or 1970s, but about an earlier period, Germany's Nazi past. The principal device for establishing this particular period as the story's center of interest is the confrontation between Mr. Hencke and Genevieve: the confrontation between an American architect who is passed off as the cliché German—complete with smallpox-scarred face, military deportment and arrogant demeanor—and his Jewish antagonist, who aims at tearing the mask of an American complacency from his face in order to reveal the unreformed Nazi underneath. Read along these lines, **"The Suitcase"** could indeed be understood as a fictional confirmation of Paul Monaco's observation about the confusion of Germany with Nazi Germany "in even the best [American] writing and teaching on the subject."

Such a reading does not do the story full justice, however. We are reminded of a similar issue in Saul Bellow's early novel *The Victim,* which also moves beyond the topic of anti-semitism to explore, through the confrontation of a Jew and a Gentile, the intricate problem of victimization. Josephine Z. Knopp elaborates on the analogy between Bellow's novel and Ozick's story in her article on "Ozick's Jewish Stories" [*Studies in American Jewish Fiction* 1, No. 1 (Spring 1975)], and she asserts that "Genevieve as Jew is a victim, but in the story it is Mr. Hencke who is victimized, reduced from strength and self-assurance to uncertainty and tearful guilt." Seen in this light, **"The Suitcase"** may not be classified simply as another example of the notoriously anachronistic American image of Germany, an image which reduces Germany to an extension of Nazism. Indeed, what makes us suspicious of such a reading right at the outset of Ozick's story is the fact that the confrontation is rendered from Mr. Hencke's point-of-view. Given access to his thoughts and feelings about Genevieve's accusations and, more importantly, to his subconscious fixation on a cluster of images suggesting guilt and the urge to overcome it, we are gradually made to change our perception of a character who, at the beginning of the story, is clearly earmarked as the story's villain. As the antagonism between Genevieve and Mr. Hencke builds up—with the former's shrill insistence on the latter's implication in the crimes committed by Nazi Germany—we cannot help but sympathize with Mr. Hencke. His seemingly secure self-image as an American architect and his blatant denial of any responsibility notwithstanding, Gottfried Hencke is on quite another level revealed as a complex personality of considerable moral sensitivity.

Since our interest is in Ozick's treatment of Germany in her work in its entirety, we now, after a close reading of one of her short stories, need to raise a few questions of a more general nature. How significant is the topic of Germany in her writings? Could it possibly be a leitmotif, a concern that features prominently in all of her work? If so, do we find the same ambivalence towards the topic that we came across in **"The Suitcase"** in her other writings as well? Or is **"The Suitcase"** an exception, is the foregrounding of Germany, German characters, and "German thoughts" (a phrase Ozick uses in **"The Suitcase"**) peripheral to other more central concerns in her work, and, if this is the case, what are those more central concerns, and how do they relate to the idea of Germany? To deal with these questions somewhat systematically, we first of all have to briefly describe her place in the contemporary literary scene in the United States.

Despite the wide appeal of Ozick's multi-faceted work, there is probably no other area of present-day American literature to which it has more immediate relevance than Jewish-American fiction. Reviewing the scholarship devoted to post-World War II Jewish-American fiction, we can make two general observations: that it has been voluminous and of a very diverse nature, but that, by and large, it has been informed by the basic assumption that this literature, in authorial intention as well as in content and meaning, has a universalistic orientation rather than a parochial one. Consequently, critics have emphasized the affinity between Jewish-American fiction and the mainstream, rather than postulating the ethnic particularity of this fiction. To give just one example from a broad range of writing including the works of Saul Bellow, Bernard Malamud, and Philip Roth, we may refer to Roth's bestseller of 1969, *Portnoy's Complaint,* a novel which by common critical consent demotes the classic Jewish protagonist, thereby dealing the death-blow to an identifiable Jewish-American writing. Congruence between Jewish-American and mainstream fiction has in this view finally been achieved. Compared to Roth, who is five years younger, but who gained prominence in American letters already at the end of the fifties, Ozick is a latecomer to Jewish-American literature. When, soon after the publication of Roth's notorious novel, she made her breakthrough on the coattails of her collection *The Pagan Rabbi and Other Stories,* another critical consensus was reached to the effect that hers was a fresh and hitherto unheard voice in Jewish-American fiction.

This critical reaction was triggered as much by the aesthetic merits of the collection as by some of the provocative statements she had made in her essays. Among these, the essay "Toward a New Yiddish," published in *Judaism* in 1970 and reprinted in Ozick's first essay collection *Art and Ardor* (1983), probably contains the most forceful and revealing commentary on the status quo of Jewish-American writing and on its future. Ozick premises her argument on the axiom that Jewish culture and literature in America exist in "Diaspora" [her capitalization], and that in order to survive they have to resist even the minutest compromise with the surrounding host culture. Interestingly, she singles out Philip Roth as her point of reference in Jewish-American literature—and as the example to avoid:

> . . . if Philip Roth still wants to say "I am not a Jewish writer; I am a writer who is a Jew," the distinction turns out to be wind; it is precisely those who make this distinction whom Diaspora most determinedly wipes out.

Elaborating on the antagonism between the Diaspora culture and a genuinely Jewish literature, she has the following to say:

> The fact is that nothing thought or written in Diaspora has ever been able to last unless it has been centrally Jewish. If it is centrally Jewish it will last for Jews. If it is not centrally Jewish it will last neither for Jews nor for the host nations. . . . By "centrally Jewish" I mean, for literature, whatever touches on the liturgical. . . . In all of history the literature that has lasted for Jews has been liturgical. The secular Jew is a figment; when a Jew becomes a secular person he is no longer a Jew. . . . If we blow into the nar-

row end of the *shofar,* we will be heard far. But if we choose to be Mankind rather than Jewish and blow into the wider part, we will not be heard at all; for us America will have been in vain.

The allegory at the end of the preceding quote makes it clear why Ozick's passionate plea for a liturgical literature startled critics into the realization that they were dealing with a new kind of Jewish writer—one who went against the grain of a Jewish-American literature that makes it its task to address mankind. Thus, Alfred Marcus in 1973 hailed Ozick as the precursor of a "new" Jewish-American literature "which may, let us face it, have only a limited audience, and which will probably not reach the best-seller lists" ["From Bereshit to Shmot: The Making of a New Jewish Literature," *Response* 7]. And it was Ruth R. Wisse, in "American Jewish Writing, Act II," a landmark article published in the June 1976 issue of *Commentary,* who identified Ozick as the leader of a new movement or, as she phrases it, a second act in Jewish-American writing. Here is how Wisse outlines the salient characteristics of this second act:

> Having no longer to defend themselves from real or imagined charges of parochialism, the new Jewish writers of the 70's are freer to explore the "tribal" and particularistic aspects of Judaism, and even, turning the tables, to speculate on the restrictive limits of English as a literary language. Here the ethnic label fits more comfortably, for these are writers who self-consciously define themselves as Jews and attempt to express their artistic vision in Jewish terms. Their interest is not in the sociological or even the psychological legacy of a Jewish background, but in the national design and religious destiny of Judaism, in its workable myths. No longer content "to draw on the interest of what was put into the bank long ago by others" (to quote Norma Rosen again), they attempt to draw directly from Jewish sources and out of Jewish culture an image of an alternative civilization.

Fourteen years after the publication of this perspicacious assessment of a movement towards re-ethnization in Jewish-American literature, Ozick's centrality to this movement has been generally recognized, not only because of the uninterrupted stream of publications flowing from her typewriter, both fiction and essays, but also because of her continued partisanship for a literature derived from a specifically Jewish tradition that deliberately takes the Torah, the Talmud and the mystic sources of the Cabala into account—as opposed to a literature, to paraphrase Ozick's diagnosis of the work of universalists like Roth or Bellow, that exploits Jewish marginality in the American host culture with the aim of transforming this material into images of the essential alienation of mankind.

Returning to our concern with Ozick's perception of Germany and the Germans from the vantage point of this brief synopsis of her position in the debate about Jewish-American literature, we begin to realize that there really cannot be much space in her fiction for an extensive interest in the theme of Germany. What is important to her is the imaginative exploration of Jewish particularity—in terms of religion, philosophy, myths, and cultural traditions in general. Given the fact that Ozick expressly declines to deal in her fiction with gentile America, even as it intersects with the Jewish ethnic group in the United States, it should not come as a surprise that another, even more distant gentile country, Germany, and its people do not feature prominently in her work.

But then Germany is not just any other country, certainly not for a Jewish writer working in the post-Holocaust period. In the sense that the Holocaust cannot be thought of without reference to Germany, Germany does of course feature in Ozick's writings, and **"The Suitcase"** is a case in point. In his study of the Holocaust in American Jewish fiction [*Crisis and Covenant,* 1986], Alan L. Berger observes "that Holocaust centrality is a touchstone of authentic Jewish writing." Cynthia Ozick, who, as we have seen, has made authentic Jewish writing into her program, lives up to Berger's criterion for authenticity by repeatedly returning to the Holocaust in her fiction. Looking at her work in its entirety, we can even assert that, in contrast to the general reluctance of Jewish-American literature to approach this highly problematic subject, Ozick has made the Holocaust into one of the most central concerns of her fictional imagination. Each one of her three novels, *Trust* (1966), *The Cannibal Galaxy* (1984), and *The Messiah of Stockholm* (1987), at least touches upon the subject, and more than half of her published short stories either explicitly deal with the Nazi crimes committed against European Jewry or else transform the Holocaust into an obsession, a sort of nightmarish incubus in the psyche of her characters.

The Holocaust is thus unquestionably a major thematic preoccupation in her work, and it is in keeping with her self-image as a Jewish writer that this should be so. Germany and the Germans, on the other hand, inextricably bound up in this theme as they are, cannot be said to inform her fiction in the same way as, for example, they inform a novel like Walter Abish's *How German Is It* (1980) in which "the new Germany" is represented in great detail—even though, as Joseph C. Schöpp has argued, the purpose is not realistic illusion but the fabrication of a postmodern textual design. We may even contend that Germany is a concept much too distant and foreign to Ozick's imagination as a writer to warrant a substantial inclusion in her fiction. This view is actually corroborated by a programmatic statement Ozick recently made about her thoughts and feelings with regard to the Federal Republic of Germany. It was published in *The Quarterly* in the Winter issue of 1988 and reprinted in *Harper's Magazine* of February 1989 under the title "Why I Won't Go to Germany." The statement turns out to be a letter Ozick wrote to a Jewish-American professor who had invited her to come to Germany and to participate in a conference on current "German-Jewish relations"; the text is quite plainly not a piece of fiction, but a document actually mailed and subsequently submitted for publication, in the form of an open, if anonymized, letter, to *The Quarterly* (the quote is from *Harper's Magazine*):

> Dear Professor X:
>
> Thank you for your letter inviting me to Germa-

ny to participate in a conference on current "German-Jewish relations" in the aftermath of the Holocaust, initiated and organized by distinguished Jewish Americans, yourself among them, and joined on your letterhead by other Americans of distinction and by prominent Germans of good will. It is very kind of you to have had me in mind; I am touched by your generosity and trust. I wish my response could be simpler than it is destined to be. . . .

Professor X, I am a Jew who does not, will not, cannot, set foot in Germany. This is a private moral imperative; I don't think of it as a "rule," and I don't apply it to everyone, particularly not to German-born Jews, who as refugees or survivors have urgencies and exigencies different from my own. Not setting foot in Germany is for me, and I think for many garden-variety Jewish Americans like myself, one of the few possible memorials; . . .

But there is another point of view as well, one that may be more relevant here. Yours is the fourth invitation I have had to go to Germany. Each was issued with the best will in the world: a German hand reaching out in peace from a democratic German polity—a remembering hand, never a forgetful one. The hand of the "new generation." The more that hand reaches out in its remembering remorsefulness, in its hopeful good will, the more resistant my heart becomes.

Here is why. I believe that all this—the conscientious memorializing of what happened four and five decades ago to the Jewish citizens of Germany and of Europe—is in the nature of things an insular and parochial German task. It is something for the Germans to do, independently, in the absence of Jews—the absence of Jews in contemporary Germany being precisely the point. The German task is, after all, a kind of "liberation" (of conscience into history), or emancipation, and the only genuine emancipation—as we know from many other national, social, and cultural contexts—is autoemancipation. So when Germans want to reflect on German-Jewish "reconciliation," or—skirting that loaded word—"German-Jewish relations," it seems to me they are obligated to do it on their own. . . . Europe no longer has what it used to call its "Jewish problem," the Germans having solved it with finality. But there remains now a German problem—the ongoing, perhaps infinitely protracted, problem of the German national conscience—and its gravamen is that the Jews aren't there.

This letter amply explains why it is important for Germans of good will to take up an expression from the passage just quoted, to explore the representation of Germany and the Germans in Ozick's writings. Without wanting to question the personal decision she has made and without drawing into doubt the respect that we owe her position, we come to realize that Ozick has resolved to avoid any contact with present-day Germany, thereby depriving herself of one of the primary sources of inspiration for a writer of fiction: immediate sense impressions. In Alain Resnais's film *Mon Oncle d'Amerique* we come across the phrase "America does not exist. I know 'cause I've been there." It is a phrase which teaches us a lot about the problem of images we carry around in our minds about another country. One reading of the dictum would be that the other country remains a fictitious concept unless we go there and see for ourselves. Since Cynthia Ozick refuses on principle to come and see, it seems plausible to assume that her notion of Germany is made up of preconceived ideas and projections—just as the image of America prevalent in the minds of Europeans has traditionally been made up of projections of a similar order.

The purpose of this essay, however, is not to censure Ozick for what could be seen as a heavily biased and anachronistic image of Germany, but to identify this image and to account for it. What we have established so far is that Ozick's idea of Germany does not derive from an exposure to contemporary Germany, which she even deliberately avoids, but that her ardent engagement in the task of revitalizing Jewish history through the means of imaginative fiction and her corresponding obsession with the Holocaust are at the root of whatever images of Germany and the Germans her fiction comes up with. Following our discussion of the short story **"The Suitcase,"** it remains for us to evaluate a little further the results and implications of a fictional strategy that closely correlates Germany and the Holocaust.

In her study *By Words Alone: The Holocaust in Literature* (1980) Sidra Dekoven Ezrahi makes the systematic distinction between two varieties of Holocaust literature: documentary literature which attempts to rescue from oblivion the entire range of historical facts—at the expense of artistic imagination—on the one hand, and on the other, a mythologizing and aesthetic transformation of the actual events at the cost of historical precision. Ozick, in a 1969 review of Elie Wiesel's *Legends of Our Time,* comes out unmistakably in favor of documentarism; she forcefully argues for a literature of meticulous bookkeeping, a literature which provides its readers with a complete protocol of the atrocities committed against the Jews by Nazi Germany:

> The task . . . is to retrieve the Holocaust freight car by freight car, town by town, road by road, document by document. The task is to save it from becoming literature.

Interestingly enough, the issue of the alternative between documentary literature and a literature that allows free rein to the writer's imagination is taken up in Ozick's short story **"A Mercenary"** from her second collection, ***Bloodshed and Three Novellas*** (1976). The mercenary of the title is a forty-six-year-old diplomat by the name of Stanislav Lushinski, who acts as the representative of a small African country at the United Nations in New York City. Born in central Europe and during the war handed over by his parents to a Polish farmer and his wife to be hidden away from the marauding German soldiers, Lushinski looks back at a life of adventure and peregrinations, a life which resulted in a chameleon-like personality and, more significantly, in the loss of his Jewish identity. It does not take much more than this brief character outline to classify **"The Mercenary"** as one of several satires Ozick has written on the assimilated and rootless Jew who denies or rejects his Jewish identity. More important in our present context, however, is Lushinski's mistress, Louisa, who is not only totally devoted to him, but who is also a German:

> They spoke of her as a German countess—her last name was preceded by a "von"—but she seemed altogether American, though her accent had a fake melody either Irish or Swedish. She claimed she had once run a famous chemical corporation in California, and truly she seemed as worldly as that, an executive, with her sudden jagged gestures, her large hands all alertness, her curious attentiveness to her own voice, her lips painted orange as fire. But with Lushinski she could be very quiet. . . . She mothered him and made him eat. If he ate corn she would slice the kernels off the cob and warn him about his stomach.

Quite clearly, this is a far cry from the pock-marked physical appearance of Mr. Hencke. What is more relevant than Louisa's looks, however, is her relationship to Lushinski. Ironically, the task to permanently remind this identity-less Jew of his roots falls to Lulu, as he calls his German mistress. When one evening Lushinski finds her moved to tears over the book *Night,* Elie Wiesel's personal memoir of his time in a concentration camp, he encourages her to read instead a documentation of the Holocaust replete with data and statistics about the trains and the number of people and the gas chambers. The title of the documentation, *The Destruction,* is representative of the dry universality of its message. Louisa cannot accept this seemingly objective, but inhuman, attempt to deal with the murder of men and women. And she specifically protests against the book's title, *The Destruction:*

> She read a little in the enormous book. The title irritated her. It was a lie. "It isn't as if the whole *world* was wiped out. It wasn't like the Flood. It wasn't *mankind,* after all, it was only one population. The Jews aren't the whole world, they aren't mankind, are they?" She caught in his face a prolonged strangeness: he was new to her, like someone she had never looked at before. "What's the matter, Stasek?" But all at once she saw: she had said he was not mankind.

Even though Louisa's remark could be misconstrued as a cynical observation diminishing the enormity of the Holocaust, such a reading would go against the story's principal concern, which we can identify as an extended indictment of Lushinski's urge to universalize his own experience of persecution. Using the rhetorical strategies of satire, the story builds a strong case against this urge, and it is in particular Louisa's mission to remind Lushinski of his failure to identify and to prod him into an acceptance of his Jewishness. Siding quite obviously with Louisa on the issue of Jewish authenticity versus universality, Ozick also seems to share her character's preference for artistic imagination over documentarism in dealing with the Holocaust. **"The Mercenary"** suggests that it is fiction, and not the cold compilation of facts, which has the power to move people and to make them emotionally aware of the

terrible truths that the Holocaust has in store for us. It is revealing that this message is in contradiction to what Ozick had announced in her above-quoted review of Elie Wiesel's book. Harold Bloom, in his introduction to the collection of essays on Ozick [*Cynthia Ozick,* 1986], finds her "critical speculations" often "contradicted by her narrative art," and here we certainly have an instance which confirms this observation. The final assessment of her protagonist's lover, the German countess Louisa, follows a similar line of argument. In terms of our interest in Ozick's image of Germany and the Germans, it is remarkable that the task of criticizing Lushinski for his apostasy and of constantly reminding him of his Jewishness—in accord with Ozick's most highly valued principles—should be given to, of all people, a German. If we take Ozick's letter to Professor X as a theoretical statement disclosing her emotions about Germany as well as the intellectual constructions she arrives at as a consequence of these emotions, we have to conclude that **"The Mercenary,"** in a manner very similar to **"The Suitcase,"** points to a discrepancy between discursive theory and narrative practice.

Generalizing from our observations on Ozick's fictional treatment of German characters and her non-fictional pronouncements on Germany we may say, first of all, that the subject, perhaps a little surprisingly, is not very prominent in her writings. At the same time, we sense that it does occupy a very special place in her mental geography and that her thinking about Germany is indeed emotionally highly charged. The few times that she expressly takes it up in her writings, she approaches it from the perspective of her two principal concerns: Jewish identity in a diaspora surrounding and the Holocaust. Given her conviction that the writing of American Jews should be committed to the exploration of the Jewish tradition and that it should shun the cultural encounter with the gentile world, be it an American or a German world, both the Holocaust perspective she uses for the delineation of her German characters and the relative lack of such characters are understandable. If understandable within her system of feeling and thinking about Germany, such a perception is also very likely to generate atrocious anachronisms. Artists, so we assume, have the responsibility to eschew, not to perpetuate or multiply, such misrepresentations. They carry the burden of dissipating and transcending our stereotypes in the act of creation. It follows that an artist whose view of another country and its people denies the idea of historical progress and deliberately suppresses all intellectual curiosity about this other country except for a specific period in the past, is working with a serious handicap and may be in danger of becoming self-serving and parochial.

Ozick's letter to Professor X ends with a paragraph which indicates that the danger is very real in her case. In this letter, Ozick cites and discusses her correspondence with a young German woman who, at the time, was writing a Ph.D. dissertation on Ozick's work. She had written Ozick from her German university, speaking in the letter of her earnest interest in American-Jewish fiction and asking her for information and support. By way of describing her own background, this young woman—so Ozick continues to paraphrase the letter she received—had mentioned that her grandfather, even though a theologian of the Protestant church and critical of the National Socialists, had, out of a feeling of patriotism, sent four sons into the war, three of whom were killed in action. Ozick uses the remaining lines of her essay to comment on the grandfather's understanding of patriotism and to make it clear how much she disapproves of the family background that this young German Ph.D. candidate had volunteered to share with her. Although she recognizes her correspondent's sincerity ("My correspondent is clearly engaged, from her point of view, in an intellectual project of remorse and restitution . . . "), she ends her reproachful commentary with the intransigent remark: "It would be better all around if she would neglect the study of 'American Jewish fiction' and begin a cultural meditation on her grandfather's mind."

Our close readings of **"The Suitcase"** and **"The Mercenary"** have demonstrated that Ozick is capable of handling her fictional Germans with a larger degree of empathy than she managed to muster for this real-life German correspondent. It is obvious that in her stories she avoids the role which she tends to assume in her non-fiction, i.e. the role of the self-appointed propagandist whose uncompromising statements about Germany or, for that matter, about the Palestinians in their precarious relationship with the state of Israel have become well-known. Gottfried Hencke, tinged as he is by Ozick's exclusionary views on Germany, does certainly not come across as the purveyor of a heavy-handed political or moral message, nor does Louisa in **"The Mercenary."** On the contrary, both characters are aesthetically compelling representations of human beings with all their complexities and contradictions. This is especially true of Gottfried Hencke. It may be a measure of the success with which Ozick renders this character that Gottfried Hencke transcends the stereotype of a post-World War II generation of Germans characterized by moral obtuseness and the inability to mourn. Gottfried Hencke is certainly not a mourner, but Cynthia Ozick has also revealed to us the night side of his personality.

> *Hans Borchers, "Of Suitcases and Other Burdens: The Ambiguities of Cynthia Ozick's Image of Germany," in* The Centennial Review, *Vol. XXXV, No. 3, Fall, 1991, pp. 607-24.*

Ruth Rosenberg (essay date 1991)

[*In the following essay, Rosenberg perceives "The Pagan Rabbi" as an example of a modern "aggada," or Jewish parable.*]

Erich Auerbach's acclaimed critical work, *Mimesis,* opens with an interpretation of Odysseus's scar. Its precisely rendered visibility is what makes it typical of Homeric narrative strategy, as Auerbach notes. A consideration of the distinction between Odysseus's scar and the scar of the widow Sheindel in Cynthia Ozick's **"The Pagan Rabbi"** helps to illuminate the differences between the Hellenic and the Hebraic narrative traditions, and indicates the

context within which Ozick has adapted the ghost story genre to Jewish themes and concerns.

According to Auerbach, "The Homeric style knows only a foreground, only a uniformly illuminated, uniformly objective present." In Hellenic epic, he observes, "everything is visible," everything is "clearly outlined" and "totally foregrounded." The Hebraic style is profoundly different. Instead of a clearly delineated and brightly illuminated scene, it presents only heard voices. Auerbach notes that the sacrifice of Isaac opens with God calling Abraham: "We only hear His voice, and that utters nothing but a name . . . and of Abraham too nothing is made perceptible except the words in which he answers." Nothing is described. Nothing is located in time or space. Everything is so indeterminate, so obscure and enigmatic, that it places great demands upon the reader. The biblical epic, like the mark on Sheindel's cheek in the Ozick story, must be interpreted in terms of history. Its narrative style is "fraught with background." Its hidden depths insist upon interpretation. The Greek epic, in its lavish descriptions, sought only to give pleasure. The Hebrew epic, lacking even in adjectives, seeks to impose truth: "The Bible's claim to truth is not only far more urgent than Homer's, it is tyrannical—it excludes all other claims."

The clash of these two cultures has been a persistent theme of Cynthia Ozick's fiction, and nowhere more so than in **"The Pagan Rabbi."** The narrator of the story has heard of the suicide by hanging of his old friend, Rabbi Isaac Kornfeld, and has gone first to see the tree where Isaac was found and then to visit Isaac's widow, Sheindel, with some hope of marrying her himself. The fathers of both the narrator and Isaac were distinguished rabbis who "vied with one another in demonstrations of charitableness, in the captious glitter of their scholia, in the number of their adherents." The only issue on which they agree is that Greek thought is "an abomination." Vehemently, they both condemn pagan idolatry. Yet both rabbinic dynasties are doomed to be lost. Of the two sons, who had been classmates in the seminary, one, from overmuch reading of philosophy, became an atheist and withdrew from the study of the Law; the other, from too much reading of Romantic poetry, became a pagan and hanged himself from a tree in a public park. What led to Rabbi Isaac Kornfeld's suicide is interpreted by the narrator from two documents removed from the dead man's pockets and given to Sheindel, Isaac's widow. One is a small notebook, containing entries in Greek, Hebrew, and English. The other Sheindel angrily describes as a "love letter"; it records Isaac's conversion to animism, his copulation with a dryad, and his confrontation with his newly "liberated" soul, figured as an old man with a pack of books on his back. To the narrator's horror, Sheindel condemns him bitterly: "I think he was never a Jew."

If the unnamed fathers, the anonymous narrator, the unspecified locale, the indeterminate time, and the invisibility of the characters were not enough to mark this narrative as Hebraic, the overheard voices that substitute for description should do so. For example, we know that Sheindel has beautiful hair only because the narrator's "Puritan" ex-wife remarked upon it at Sheindel's wedding. For the most part, characters are defined by their moral positions, and this strategy is centrally Jewish. An ethical posture takes the place of a physical appearance. In contrast, as Auerbach notes, Homeric narrative "delights in physical existence" and by making that perceptible, "bewitches, ingratiates, and ensnares us into sharing that reality." That reality "conceals nothing, contains no teaching, has no secret second meaning." The Hebraic mode, in contrast, "does not court our favor by pleasing us"; rather, it demands that we subordinate our reality to its absolute demand for priority.

Lest we miss this claim, Ozick has pointed to it in her epigraph. Prefacing her story is a lesson from "The Ethics of the Fathers," insisting that scripture takes precedence over nature: "Rabbi Jacob said: 'He who is walking along and studying, but then breaks off to remark, "How lovely is that tree!" or "How beautiful is that fallow field!"—Scripture regards such a one as having hurt his own being.' " Ozick's parable contemporizes this description. A Talmudic scholar is deluded into addressing a young oak tree as "Loveliness." The concluding episode dramatizes how deeply this interruption of his study by the beauties of nature has hurt his being. He not only fails to recognize but vehemently repudiates his emanation, his soul, which appears to him as a spectral figure studying Scripture as it walks along a dusty road. At the same instant that he disavows his soul, his body shrivels like a withered leaf. He is already dead, has already separated soul from body.

In rewriting "The Ethics of the Fathers" for a contemporary audience as an encounter with a ghostly double, Ozick is simultaneously revoicing yet revising her literary "fathers." For thirteen years she was haunted by the "master," Henry James. From the age of twenty-two to the age of thirty-five, she was held in thrall by James, having first succumbed to his spell when, as a graduate student, she wrote her thesis on him. So absolute was her apprenticeship that she felt herself becoming transformed into "the elderly bald-headed Henry James." She wrote, in "The Lesson of the Master": "You could see the light glancing off my pate; you could see my heavy chin, my watch chain, my walking stick, my tender paunch." Under his domination she determined to craft a Jamesian masterpiece. Her immense novel, *Trust,* which ran more than eight hundred manuscript pages, was begun in 1957 and finally finished in 1963. To her disappointment, it "did not speak to the Gentiles, for whom it had been begun, nor to the Jews, for whom it had been finished." Significantly, what "judaized" her style was thinking through the novel's only Jewish character. By formulating the question, "What is it to think as a Jew?," she succeeded in freeing herself from her long indenture to the "religion of art." The offerings laid on its altar began to seem increasingly idolatrous to her in the light of the second commandment, and she began to think of that prohibition as requiring a perceptual shift. Were her essays indexed, the longest entry would no doubt appear under the term "idolatry." The Mosaic injunction against images freed Ozick from the Jamesian stress on a visual center of consciousness that sees all, the perceiving eye upon which nothing is lost.

Ozick has often mentioned that Judaism begins with the "Shema," meaning "hear." The devout Jew listens to the word of God. Jean-François Lyotard writes [in his essay "Jewish Oedipus"] "In Hebraic ethics, representation is forbidden; the eye closes; the ear opens." To underscore Rabbi Kornfeld's transgression, [Ozick] literally underlined his narcissistic wish: "To *see* the soul, to confront it—that is divine wisdom." When his blasphemous desire is granted and his soul, disengaged from his body, faces him, he rejects it. "Didn't you wish to see me with your own eyes?" it asks. Rabbi Kornfeld's body shrieks, "It is not mine!" This scenario may be a conscious reworking of Edith Wharton's famous story, "The Eyes," in which a man is periodically confronted with a pair of supernatural eyes that reflect his own dissolution but which he does not identify as his own. As in Ozick's story, a supernatural apparition dramatizes the extreme state of the viewer's soul, but the rabbi sees not what he has become but what he has lost.

The loss is rendered, however, in aural, not visual, terms, specifically Jewish terms. The soul tells him, "If you had not contrived to be rid of me, I would have stayed with you till the end . . . In your grave beside you, I would have sung you David's songs, I would have moaned Solomon's voice to your last grain of bone. But you expelled me." Rabbi Kornfeld could have been comforted throughout eternity by the Psalms and the Song of Songs. Instead, through his own insistence on specular reflection, he will be deaf to the Word of the invisible God who manifests Himself only as a voice and has banned the making of images. Having carefully laid the ground that, for the pious, the truth is heard, Ozick shows the extent of his breach of the Covenant by depriving the Rabbi of the participation in the communal "Hear O Israel."

For Ozick, finding an authentically Jewish narrative strategy that encompassed this shift of emphasis from the eye to the ear liberated her from James's influence and allowed her to serve as a cultural ambassador in her own right. Invited to speak in Israel in 1970, she advocated a turning away from the "aestheticized, paganized, parodistic forms of fiction" toward a "centrally Jewish" genre.

What Ozick proposed specifically was a return to parable, in Hebrew "Aggada," rabbinic narrative. Aggada comprises one-quarter of the Talmud; the rest is called "Halacha," and consists of legal material. According to Susan Handelman, these narratives are so highly regarded that "a lesson derived from a story where the principle was applied has greater substantiality than a direct statement of the principle!" Furthermore, she continues, "a law derived from a *story* in the Talmud has greater validity than a law directly stated in the Talmud." So Aggada was valued over Halacha. Ozick urged other American-Jewish writers to experiment with the form "utilizing every innovative device," every possible linguistic technique, every available authorial strategy, even those developed by Romantic aestheticism, so long as they were adapted to the Jewish worldview. Such aggadic fictions could prove, in her words, "significant literature capable of every conceivable resonance."

Because aggadic fiction conveys its meaning implicitly,

however, rather than didactically, those who miss the generic clues will misunderstand. Two examples from critics who misread **"The Pagan Rabbi"** by misunderstanding its genre illustrate such skewed responses. Catherine Rainwater and William Scheick read the story within the genre conventions of "popular romance" and find it to be "about metamorphosis and enchantment." Victor Strandberg approaches it from the conventions of Frazer's *The Golden Bough* and finds it to be an instance of ritual magic in the sacred grove, going so far as to assert: "It is Pan who prevails over Moses in this encounter. Death here becomes (as Walt Whitman called it) a promotion rather than a punishment." Both responses miss the story's parabolic nature, overlooking the epigraph and the significance of its echo in the climax, when the pagan rabbi confronts his soul.

An even more egregious example of misreading is Ruth Wisse's. Wisse ignores all of Ozick's denunciations of "aestheticism" and reads **"The Pagan Rabbi"** as the externalization of an inner, suppressed "aestheticist longing." To compound this misattribution, the critic then categorizes it as sentimental ghetto fiction.

> Into the mouth of the errant rabbi the author has put part of her own aestheticist longings, raising worship of the beautiful to the highest philosophic and religious pitch, but only to oppose it finally, almost pitilessly, in the name of religious values . . . One of the most pervasive subjects of the modern Yiddish and Hebrew literary tradition is the rediscovery of those natural human instincts which would free the dust-choked ghetto Jew from the stifling repression of "halakhah" and religious inhibitions. In the works of Mendele, Sholem Aleichem, Peretz, Bialik, Feierberg, and Tchernikovsky, the physical world of sun, storm, trees, and rivers provides a model of freedom counterposed to the self-denial of shtetl culture.

Yet Ozick goes out of her way to make Rabbi Kornfeld's "aestheticist longings" appear ludicrous, utterly unfounded on reality. He has gone from park to park, looking for the right setting in which to contemplate the beauties of nature. What he finds is a waste land, as the narrator describes it: "The tree was almost alone in a long rough meadow, which sloped down to a bay filled with sickly clams and a bad smell. The place was called Trilham's Inlet, and I knew what the smell meant: that cold brown water covered half the city's turds." Where is that lyrically evoked world of sunshine? The weather in Ozick's text is "bleary with fog," a beating rain falls, flattening decaying leaves. Where are the fresh air and the green grass luring scholars away from the ghetto? Ozick shows us an abandoned plastic wreath on the "rusting grasses" and bulldozers biting "into the park" where "the rolled carcasses of trees" are stacked. Far from an enticement, the landscape emits "a stench of sewage." No fresh breezes blow, only "a wind blowing out a braid of excremental malodor into the heated air." By relying upon the eyes that feed his "aestheticist longings," Rabbi Kornfeld is duped into seeing what is not there.

The point being illuminated in the parable could not have

been more tellingly made than by these critical commentaries. One's expectations are conditioned by what one has read. If one comes to a tale of oreads, nymphs, and dryads from a familiarity with Ovid's *Metamorphoses,* one will see it as an example of romance. If one approaches it from the perspective of the ritual slaughter of the king, then one focuses on the archetypal tree. If one's frame of reference is the shtetl culture, then one ignores all the cues that invalidate its appropriation into that tradition. The details fail to fall into place until the appropriate schema has been selected.

The danger, as the epigraph suggests, lies in lifting one's eyes from the appropriate book. The claim being made in this passage from "The Ethics of the Fathers" is that study of the Halacha has absolute priority. This is borne out by a pun. The Hebrew word derives from a root meaning "to walk" or "the way." Talmudic scholars studying Halacha as they walk figure prominently in the prefatory opening and in the closure of the story. Therefore, to interrupt one's concentration on scripture is to lose one's way. Furthermore, implicit in the epigraph are the defenses against so going astray. In the same tractate of the Mishnah as the quotation from Rabbi Jacob are the discussions of the "Fences around the Law." These safeguards against transgressions are called "takkanot" (enactments) and "gezerot" (decrees) in "The Ethics of the Fathers."

To guard against being misled and losing the path, all the characters allude frequently to these fences. The most tragic such allusion is tattooed on Sheindel's cheek. The barb of the electrified fence around the concentration camp where she had been born and orphaned cut an asterisk-shaped scar into her face. Only seventeen when she married Isaac, the widow who bore him seven daughters asked why God had spared her from the Holocaust only to let her wed a transgressor: "I was that man's wife, he scaled the Fence of the Law. For this God preserved me from the electric fence." More than a visual detail, Sheindel's scar carries the symbolic weight of individual and cultural history.

The secularized narrator, who has become a bookseller and therefore a reader of and trafficker in the wrong books, reads Sheindel's scar accordingly, as an "asterisk" that pointed to "certain dry footnotes," namely, that for a woman, she is "astonishingly learned." Thus even with the help of footnotes he cannot interpret the meaning of Rabbi Kornfeld's death or the rage and bitterness of his widow. The narrator further demonstrates his own lack of midrashic exegesis by his inability to interpret Isaac's notebook. He has lost the rabbinic method for making inferences from conjoined passages or "smuchin." The juxtaposed Greek, Hebrew, and English verses are dismissed by him as meaningless; but to the pious widow, they record her husband's growing paganism. She taunts the narrator for his incomprehension by telling him he "can't follow."

Scornfully, Sheindel begins to read him the letter in which her husband had argued that animism had a "continuous, but covert expression, even within the Fence of the Law." Shortly afterward, the narrator reads Rabbi Kornfeld's account of an incident in which he saw a ghostly figure save his daughter from drowning. Sheindel "maliciously" accuses her husband of going out of his way to find "proofs" for what he saw, in other words, of attempting to alter the shape of the Fence of the Law to suit his convenience. When the narrator wonders at such skepticism in a woman so pious, Sheindel tells him: "Only an atheist could ask such a question." She continues: "The more piety, the more skepticism. A religious man comprehends this. Superfluity, excess of custom, and superstition would climb like a choking vine on the Fence of the Law if skepticism did not continually hack them away to make freedom for purity." Adherence to the Law does not imply blindness but rather a reasoned observation from the perspective of the Law, from within the Fence of the Law.

Since Ozick has characterized herself repeatedly as a rationalist, Sheindel's defense of her skepticism might well denote her status as authorial persona. To one interviewer, Ozick said: "I myself am hostile to the whole mystical enterprise. I'm a rationalist, and I'm a skeptic" [Eve Ottenberg, "The Rich Visions of Cynthia Ozick," *New York Times Magazine,* April 10, 1983]. To another she said: "Ancestrally, I stem from the Mitnagged tradition, which is superrational and super-skeptical. That's the part of me that writes the essays and has no patience with anything mystical" [Patricia Blake, "A New Triumph for Idiosyncrasy," *Time,* September 5, 1983].

This last comment suggests that the traditions of Judaism are multiple and distinct. On the basis of an onomastic link between Rabbi Kornfeld's legal wife and his illicit consort, one could argue a connection between the normative and covert traditions of Judaism. The spirit with whom Isaac coupled is repeatedly addressed by him as "Loveliness." The Yiddish word for "Loveliness" is "Sheindel." This would suggest that the Rabbi's nocturnal search for manifestations of animism, or the secrets of the Zohar and of other "hidden" texts that had been suppressed in the interests of normative Judaism, was an effort to recover those censored heresies that ran counter to the official religion. In short, he was turning from the embraces of legitimate Judaism to embrace its forbidden doctrines. Gershom Scholem, whom Ozick visited in Israel, had made the recovery of this suppressed religion his lifelong project. In "The Magisterial Reach of Gershom Scholem," Ozick described his search as having sprung from a desire to revitalize religion for assimilated German-Jewish intellectuals like his friend, Walter Benjamin.

The counterargument to legitimizing Kabbala, however, is the most compellingly significant way of regarding Sheindel's scar. It gathers resonance when one weighs all the accumulated references to the Fence of the Law. If the mark of the Holocaust on Sheindel's cheek is taken as a sign that only a remnant of European Jewry escaped the furnaces, then the issue being raised in Ozick's parable is the survival of Judaism itself. Against the six million slaughtered and the thousands assimilated in the diaspora, where are those to inherit and to transmit the Covenant?

The story privileges Sheindel's survival, and indicates that hers is the appropriate form of "loveliness"—the beauty of the Law, the mark of which she carries on her cheek. Yet in linguistic citations, an asterisk denotes an anomalous form. Such an unattested entity is a pious and learned woman in the eyes of a patriarchal religion. Better qualified by virtue of her understanding than either of the former rabbinical students to transmit the Law, she cannot. And the narrator proposes to perpetuate her limited role as wife and mother by marrying her after a suitable period has elapsed. Yet the scar and the learning it represents to him make her inaccessible to him. Her command of the intricacies of the Law is a wasted resource to an orthodox community where women are consigned, in the synagogue, to a place behind the curtain. Therefore, the narrator's dilemma comes to stand for a historical impasse. The very intellectual gifts that render her incomprehensible to Gentiles are, by virtue of her gender, unavailable to those most urgently in need of them. This situation acquires further resonance against suggestions that she is the authorial persona.

An exploration of the layers of possible meaning for Sheindel's scar is typical of the reading required by Hebraic narrative. Robert Alter has said of Talmudic scholarship: "Meaning was conceived as a *process,* requiring continual revision—both in the ordinary sense and in the etymological sense of seeing-again—continual suspension of judgment, weighing of multiple possibilities, brooding over gaps in the information provided." Alter's visual metaphor interrogates Rabbi Kornfeld's scholarly credentials; unlike the skeptical Sheindel, he does not question what he sees. He is not sufficiently critical. To the extent to which he is pursuing a hidden or suppressed truth, however, Rabbi Kornfeld is another Talmudic exegete in pursuit of endlessly deferred meanings. His quest is paralleled by that of the narrator, who is looking for the meaning of the rabbi's death but frustrated by the complexities of the meanings he encounters.

A further footnote to which Sheindel's scar may allude would involve Ozick's views of the Romantics, especially Wordsworth. Lionel Trilling asserted in "Wordsworth and the Rabbis" that Rabbi Jacob's warnings against nature implied four latent affinities between "the Law, as the Rabbis understood it, and Nature, as Wordsworth understood that." Ozick's indignation at this equation spilled out in fiery polemics in three essays published in *Art and Ardor.* She considers "Tintern Abbey" a step away from the Nazi furnaces. The rationale for this denunciation derives from the view that nature-worship is idolatrous, a pantheism that assaults monotheism. The very worship of inert matter, for which Trilling had praised Wordsworth—"when sentience was like a rock or a stone or a tree . . . then existence was blessed" [**"The Pagan Rabbi"**]—makes the poet blasphemous. And all Romantic quests for the muses in bushes or brooks are similar violations. For Ozick, such mystical impulses are sinister, decadent, diabolical, insidious, demonic, destructive forces. She condemns magic as the dark death-drive, as the "yetzer ha-ra" (evil impulse). To her, Wordsworth's contemplation of his own mind as it reflected back to him from a benign landscape is a profanity in its narcissistic, self-reflexive deification of his own creativity.

The author's attitudes, made so explicit in her essays, align her stance to the moral posture assumed by her fictive counterpart, Sheindel. They both depict themselves as wielding pruning shears, or sheathed in heavy garden gloves, tearing away the choking vines that are "excrescences" on the Fence. Their vehement energy scarcely enables them to keep pace with the unhealthy growths choking its "purity." It consumes all their strength to rip away these weeds that sprout up and strangle. They hack, and slash, and rip out, and still the Fence is entangled. The task Ozick set herself in her aggadic fiction is to represent this struggle with every literary device available. The olfactory imagery alone should have indicated her attitude toward nature-worship. But for those readers who, because of their own preoccupations, missed the fetid stench, the ghost is there to remind them that reality resides only in the text from out of which the universe was created. "To understand creation, one looks, *not to nature,* but to the Torah," [Susan A. Handelman writes in *The Slayers of Moses: The Emergence of Rabbinic Interpretation in Modern Literary Theory,* 1982]. The possibilities of the ghost story form, a form favored by Ozick's old master Henry James, to warn against the purely visual by exploiting the visual supernatural were recognized by Ozick in **"The Pagan Rabbi."**

The centrality of the Torah is lyrically envisioned in the epiphanic ending of Ozick's aggadic rendition of "The Ethics of the Fathers." Isaac Kornfeld beholds his soul as "a dusty old man" with "a matted beard" who is "walking on the road" and "reading as he goes." He "reads the Law" and "passes indifferent through the beauty of the field"; "his nostrils sniff his book as it flowers lay on the clotted page": " 'I will walk here alone always, in my garden'—he scratched his page—'with my precious birds'—he scratched at the letters—'and my darling trees'—he scratched at the tall side-column of commentary. . . . 'The sound of the Law,' he said, 'is more beautiful than the crickets. The smell of the Law is more radiant than the moss. The taste of the Law exceeds clear water.' "

> *Ruth Rosenberg, "The Ghost Story as Aggada: Cynthia Ozick's 'The Pagan Rabbi' and Sheindel's Scar," in* Haunting the House of Fiction: Feminist Perspectives on Ghost Stories by American Women, *edited by Lynette Carpenter and Wendy K. Kolmar, The University of Tennessee Press, Knoxville, 1991, pp. 215-28.*

FURTHER READING

Bibliography

Chenoweth, Mary J. "Bibliographical Essay: Cynthia Ozick." *Studies in American Jewish Literature* 6 (Fall 1987): 147-63.
> Lists works by and about Ozick. Chenoweth also comments on the works cited and offers biographical information.

Currier, Susan, and Cahill, Daniel J. "A Bibliography of Writings by Cynthia Ozick." In *Contemporary American Women Writers,* edited by Catherine Rainwater and William J. Scheick, pp. 89-116. Lexington: The University Press of Kentucky, 1985.
> Includes listings of Ozick's fiction and nonfiction writings.

Criticism

Hadas, Rachel. "Text and Stories." *Partisan Review* LVIII, No. 3 (Summer 1991): 579-85.
> Reviews *The Shawl* and compares it to Umberto Eco's novel *Foucault's Pendulum.*

Halperin, Irving. "Rosa's Story." *Commonweal* CXVI, No. 22 (15 December 1989): 711-12.
> Generally favorable review of *The Shawl.*

Kauvar, Elaine M. "Cynthia Ozick's Book of Creation: 'Puttermesser and Xanthippe'." *Contemporary Literature* 26, No. 1 (Spring 1985): 40-54.
> Analyzes the themes and symbols in "Puttermesser and Xanthippe."

Prose, Francine. "Idolatry in Miami." *The New York Times Book Review* (10 September 1989): 1, 39.
> Favorable review of *The Shawl.*

Rainwater, Catherine, and Scheick, William J. " 'Some Godlike Grammar': An Introduction to the Writings of Hazzard, Ozick, and Redmon." *Texas Studies in Literature and Language* 25, No. 2 (Summer 1983): 181-211.
> Compares Ozick's fiction with that of Shirley Hazzard and Anne Redmon for its concern with the "ordered and meaningful exploration of chaos" and emphasis on memory, free will, language, and art.

Trapido, Barbara. "Champagne." *Spectator* 248, No. 8020 (27 March 1982): 25.
> Brief review of *Levitation: Five Fictions.* Trapido states: "Cynthia Ozick's 'fictions' are characterized by a bizarre, edgy brilliance and fantastical imagination."

Wilner, Arlene Fish. "The Jewish-American Woman as Artist: Cynthia Ozick and the 'Paleface' Tradition." *College Literature* 20, No. 2 (June 1993): 119-32.
> Places Ozick in the tradition of "paleface" American writers, who focus on the intellectual aspects of life, as opposed to the "redskin" school of American fiction, which emphasizes experience and emotion.

Interviews

Kauvar, Elaine M. "An Interview with Cynthia Ozick." *Contemporary Literature* 26, No. 4 (Winter 1985): 375-401.
> Ozick discusses several topics, including her ideas on art as a form of idolatry and Judaism as a basis for Western thought and culture.

———. "An Interview with Cynthia Ozick." *Contemporary Literature* 34, No. 3 (Fall 1993): 359-94.
> Ozick comments on a wide range of subjects, including the Jewish experience in America, Judaism and feminism, and her conception of authentic Jewish literature.

Teicholz, Tom. "The Art of Fiction XCV: Cynthia Ozick." *The Paris Review* 29, No. 102 (Spring 1987): 155-90.
> Ozick discusses the writing process, the concept of New Yiddish, and the influence of Judaism on her life and writing.

Additional coverage of Ozick's life and career is contained in the following sources published by Gale Research: *Contemporary Authors,* Vols. 17-20, rev. ed.; *Contemporary Authors New Revision Series,* Vol. 23; *Contemporary Literary Criticism,* Vols. 3, 7, 28, 62; *Dictionary of Literary Biography,* Vol. 28; *Dictionary of Literary Biography Yearbook: 1982;* and *Major 20th-Century Writers.*

Arthur Schnitzler

1862-1931

Austrian short story writer, playwright, novelist, and autobiographer.

INTRODUCTION

Schnitzler is known primarily for his psychological analysis of the decadent culture of pre–World War I Vienna. In his works he examined the subconscious motivations and longings of his characters, giving literary expression to Sigmund Freud's discoveries in depth psychology. Schnitzler's short fiction often explores the neurotic sex-obsession of the Viennese aristocracy and the inseparableness of illusion and reality. A stylistic experimenter in both drama and prose, Schnitzler introduced the Viennese dialect to the Austrian stage and was one of the first practitioners of the stream-of-consciousness technique.

Biographical Information

Schnitzler was born in Vienna into a cultivated, upper-middle-class, Jewish family. His father, a prominent physician, disapproved of his son's literary aspirations and persuaded him to study medicine instead. Schnitzler remained, however, deeply interested in drama and literature, and rose to the forefront of a literary movement known as "Young Vienna," which opposed the naturalism sweeping Germany and the classicism of Franz Grillparzer. The principles of the emerging field of psychiatry, to which he was exposed through his medical studies, profoundly affected Schnitzler's philosophy and techniques as a writer. Although he never completely abandoned his medical practice, Schnitzler became increasingly absorbed in his literary career. He died in 1931.

Major Works

In his short fiction Schnitzler combined clinical objectivity with dramatic situations and plot reversals similar to those in his highly successful theatrical works. He often employed innovative narrative techniques, particularly the interior monologue, which anticipated the work of more famous writers, including James Joyce. Considered one of the first masterpieces in the stream-of-consciousness mode in European literature, the novella *Leutnant Gustl* (*None But the Brave*) typifies Schnitzler's short fiction in its psychological analysis of a military officer who believes he must commit suicide when his honor is compromised. After spending a sleepless night contemplating his own

death, Gustl learns that the offense to his honor was unobserved and that the man who insulted him has died during the night; with no witnesses to his disgrace Gustl is freed from the honor code that required his suicide. The novella *Fräulein Else*, parts of which critics have interpreted as a consideration of the "Oedipus complex" identified by Freud, comprises the thoughts of a teenage girl who is offered money to resolve her father's debts if she will appear naked before a wealthy, older acquaintance. A later novella, *Flucht in die Finsternis* (*Flight into Darkness*), presents a grim, clinical examination of a man's descent into madness. In his other short works Schnitzler considered subjects and themes that offered further opportunities to present psychological portraits of individuals in crisis, often depicting marital infidelity, the sexual activities of upper-class Viennese society, the isolation of the individual, and changing perceptions of illusion and reality.

Critical Reception

Schnitzler's work was extremely popular in the years before the First World War, but he was always a controversial figure. His mordant depiction in *None But the Brave* of the fatuous lieutenant and the ridiculous intricacies of the military honor code raised such a furor upon publication that he was compelled to resign his position in the army medical reserve. Other works, namely *Casanovas Heimfahrt* (*Casanova's Homecoming*) and the drama *Reigen* (*Hands Around*), were subject to obscenity trials in the United States. In general critics have praised his subtle evocation of mood, deft characterization, witty dialogue, and craftmanship, but have faulted the narrowness of his subject matter—Vienna and the wealthy Viennese—as well as his preoccupation with erotic themes and what some commentators consider the passionless remoteness of his prose. The anti-Semitic attacks that plagued him throughout his career culminated in the banning of his work by the nazis. While both the controversial nature and the popularity of Schnitzler's works have diminished, he is nonetheless remembered for his wistful, yet penetrating, portrayal of a dying age.

PRINCIPAL WORKS

SHORT FICTION

Sterben 1895
  ["Dying," in *The Little Comedy, and Other Stories,* 1977]
Leutnant Gustl 1901
  [*None But the Brave,* 1926; also published as *Lieutenant Gustl,* in *Arthur Schnitzler: Plays and Stories,* 1982]
Frau Beate und ihr Sohn 1913
  [*Beatrice,* 1926]
Casanovas Heimfahrt 1918
  [*Casanova's Homecoming,* 1923]
Fräulein Else 1924
  [*Fräulein Else,* 1925]
Die Frau des Richters 1925
  ["The Judge's Wife," in *The Little Comedy, and Other Stories,* 1977]
Traumnovelle 1926
  [*Rhapsody: A Dream Novel,* 1927]
Spiel im Morgengrauen 1927
  [*Daybreak,* 1927]
Flucht in die Finsternis 1931
  [*Flight into Darkness,* 1931]

OTHER MAJOR WORKS

Das Abenteuer seines Lebens (drama) 1891
Anatol (drama) 1893
  [*Anatol,* 1911]
Das Märchen (drama) 1893
Liebelei (drama) 1895
  [*The Reckoning,* 1907; also published as *Light-o'-Love,* 1912; and *Playing with Love,* 1914]
Der grüne Kakadu (drama) 1899

[*The Duke and the Actress,* 1910; also published as *The Green Cockatoo,* 1913]
Der Schleier der Beatrice (drama) 1900
Reigen (drama) 1903
  [*Hands Around,* 1920; also published as *La Ronde,* in *Arthur Schnitzler: Plays and Stories,* 1982; and *The Round Dance,* 1982]
Der einsame Weg (drama) 1904
  [*The Lonely Way,* 1904]
Zwischenspiel (drama) 1905
  [*Intermezzo,* 1915]
Der Weg ins Freie (novel) 1908
  [*The Road to the Open,* 1932]
Der junge Medardus (drama) 1910
Das weite Land (drama) 1911
  [*The Vast Domain,* 1923; also published as *Undiscovered Country,* 1980]
Professor Bernhardi (drama) 1912
  [*Professor Bernhardi,* 1927]
Therese (novel) 1928
  [*Theresa,* 1928]
Jugend in Wien (autobiography) 1968
  [*My Youth in Vienna,* 1970]

CRITICISM

The Times Literary Supplement (essay date 1929)

[*In the following review of* Little Novels, *the critic finds the stories skillfully written but artificial.*]

Little Novels consists of ten of Arthur Schnitzler's short stories, all written between 1900 and 1910. Most of the ten are studies in feminine psychology, accomplished, clever, surprising, but rather on the romantic side of things. Love, it seems, was a desperate business in the Vienna of a generation ago; passion played fast and loose with the commonplaces of existence, and the happiest of husbands and wives were those whose infidelities were not discovered. Herr Schnitzler has generally written in restrained and refreshingly straightforward language, but he has also shown a marked liking for pathological types and emotional aberrations and enigmatic feminine passions and so on. The result is that his stories, although they are contrived with great skill and although they display a remarkable power of analysis, seldom strike the reader—the English reader more particularly—as being quite real.

There is, indeed, an element of artificiality in every story in this volume. The first, **"The Stranger,"** is the tale of a woman of inscrutable impulses who fascinated a great number of men. One of them, a sober, conventional official, fell madly in love with her, saw that she was queer, and married her, determined to commit suicide on the day she left him. She departed one morning after a honeymoon lasting a fortnight; and the husband thereupon went out to shoot himself at about the same moment that his wife, for some reason beyond human fathoming, was betraying him with a stranger. **"The Fate of the Freiherr von Leisenbohg"** is a little less mysterious. He fell deeply in love with another temperamental woman, an opera singer, who rejected his advances, but who retained his affection during all the years in which she took one lover after another, and who finally yielded to him for one night for no more worthy purpose than to expiate the curse of the last and most jealous of her lovers. The story has an extraordinarily deft ending, but it is obvious that the whole thing was written round the surprise which is sprung on the reader in the last couple of pages. Equally effective in its slightly artificial way is **"The Greek Dancing Girl,"** which tells of a woman who died because she no longer had the peculiar strength of mind which enabled her to disbelieve in her husband's infidelities. **"The Death of a Bachelor,"** which is again a masterly piece of construction, asks the reader to believe that a dying man would occupy the last few moments of his life in writing a letter to his friends for the purpose of informing them that he had seduced each of their wives in turn.

Psychological experiments in this manner are put to greater artistic advantage in the stories of the occult. **"The Prophecy,"** for instance, tells of a man whose fortune was told to him by a Jewish conjurer (who gave the name of Marco Polo), and whose destiny was consummated during the performance of a play in which the dramatist had visualized every detail of the conjurer's prophecy. Unreal as the stories are in fact, they are the work of a story-teller who has never had much to learn in the way of craftsmanship. Mr. Eric Sutton's translations have the directness and the finish which Schnitzler requires in English.

A review of "Little Novels," in The Times Literary Supplement, *No. 1437, August 15, 1929, p. 635.*

Babette Deutsch   (essay date 1929)

[*Deutsch was an acclaimed poet, novelist, critic, and translator of numerous volumes of German and Russian verse. In the following excerpt, she reviews* Little Novels.]

Most of the ten stories that make up [*Little Novels*] very clearly "date." It is not only because of the style of the ladies' coiffures, nor yet the fact that they drive to the ball in carriages rather than motors. Nor is it owing to the leading themes: the frailty of women, the headlong passion of men—themes which were a commonplace when Cleopatra flourished and a familiar jest to Potiphar's servants. These tales date because of the viewpoint that is implicit in them and that seems somehow as remote as the waltzes of Strauss, the warm-skinned luscious models of Stuck, the fabulous gayety of pre-war Vienna.

To describe the viewpoint in two words would be to call it sophisticated romanticism. Sex is the guiding force in the lives of the quite trivial people with whom the story-teller concerns himself, but though they commit murder and shoot themselves because one woman is more fascinating or one man more attractive than another, the thing that drives them lacks the terrible significance that it has for a writer like D. H. Lawrence, and one feels that all

these bullets and all this blood are like the cigarettes that used to be manufactured for ladies—disguised by a faint flavor of violets. There is nothing here of elemental fury, of animal urgency.

Not that the stories are lacking in the the creatures and the victims of their little lusts, people who are relieved from the pressure of economic necessity to no purpose. But whereas Hemingway's characters are sick with the knowledge of their own frustrated existence and his tales vivid with disgust, Schnitzler's characters live in an atmosphere perversely enticing as the taint in gamy meat.

But if there is something old-fashioned, and so slightly unreal, about most of these stories, all of them are skillfully written and are as easy to read as Viennese coffee is to drink. Several touch upon the supernatural and handle this unlikely motif in a felicitous and thrilling fashion. Schnitzler does masterly work when he treads the borderline between truth and fantasy: the reader is no less exhilarated than confused by being made to breathe alternate gusts of air from two alien universes.

The finest piece in the collection is [**"Blind Geronimo and His Brother"**] a story about a blind beggar and his brother that, except for its happy conclusion, might have come from the pen of Maupassant, and that stands quite apart from the rest of the volume. Carlo, an Italian peasant boy, accidentally blinded his brother Geronimo with his airgun when both were small, and ever he imagines, is now thinking him a common thief, though the idea of rifling the pockets of strangers is scarcely as nasty as the thought that Carlo has robbed his blind brother. It will be impossible to explain the theft to the magistrate: the actual motivation is too plausible. Just when Carlo's wretchedness seems as impenetrably black as the darkness in which Geronimo walks the blind man drops the guitar, stretches out his arms and kisses Carlo on the mouth. That moment sets back the clock for poor Carlo; the world becomes a place in which, jail or no jail, blind beggar or no such thing, one can live with courage and contentment. His brother is restored to him, his lifelong sacrifice recompensed, his peace made whole. In spite of the fact that Geronimo's thought processes are not made as clear as is desirable, the tale is a lovely fabrication, deeply moving and full of vigor and tenderness. It is the one story in the book that deals with common folk, and, curiously enough, the author makes them more credible and certainly much more touching figures than any of his passion-ridden barons, sculptors and barristers. However seductive the world in which those gentlemen so gracefully move, however rough and dismal the world of blind Geronimo, one is grateful for the glimpse into that more honest place.

Babette Deutsch, "Sophisticated Romantics," in New York Herald Tribune, *August 25, 1929, p. 7.*

The New York Times Book Review   (essay date 1931)

[*In the following review of* Flight into Darkness, *the critic observes the "scientific remoteness" with which the story is presented.*]

The last novel to come from the pen of Arthur Schnitzler was named, in a moment of prophecy, *Flight Into Darkness.* His life and his work, always intimately connected, had completed a full cycle. Toward the end, he withdrew from the gayety of Vienna and lived in solitude, probably deeply affected by the suicide of his daughter. His art, the art of the novelle, he had brought to a perfection long lost to Continental literature. Recently he sought to conquer new worlds with *Theresa,* a long novel commendable only for Schnitzler's precision of detail. His literary career had come to a natural standstill, and he seemed prepared, mentally and spiritually, for death. He had passed from the gay and turbulent emotions of youth through a period of gloomy passion and bitterness to a serene and intellectual naturalism. What he feared most was the flight into darkness, the destruction of his beautifully ordered cosmos by madness. To this theme his last book is devoted.

It is a principle of modern theorists (Schnitzler was a doctor) that an obsessive idea, unless destroyed at an early stage, will project itself into reality. The Robert of this book, because of some twist in his strong affection for his brother Otto, feared that somehow he must die by his brother's hand. With bold strokes, without extraneous incident yet with a medical exactness of detail, Schnitzler develops this premonition into a persecution mania. Indeed, in the staccato intensity of this development a superficial but significant reason for the brevity of all his novelle can be found.

Psychologically, the first incident in the story was probably some youthful jealousy between the brothers. But Schnitzler does not show the kernel of insanity at its inception. Adhering to his strict rule of compactness, he begins with the first external manifestation of abnormality in Robert's mind. One morning as he is about to go to work, he notices that his left eye-lid hangs lower than his right. This sets him to brooding morbidly on paralysis and mental decay. He recalls the time when his friend Höhnberg went mad, as a result of which he had asked Otto, under the authority of a doctor, to put him to death should he show similar signs of madness. His life, then, is in Otto's hands. And what if Otto should go mad? What if the rest of the world went mad? Thus fear is born, the terrible fear that grows and grows until it occupies the whole of Robert's being. Good friends, strangers, and harmless incidents are all found to be dangerous by the distorted logic of his mind. Most tragic is the brief period in which he is aware of his insanity and tries to control it; but that soon ends as he is pushed further and further toward destruction. The end comes, of course, with the final and terrible realization of the obsessive idea.

Schnitzler's technical perfection obtains for him the inevitability of great drama. While he applied his technique to sex complexes his stories were full-blooded and vital. But all his craft does not seem able to enrich his story when he deals with a theme that is more impersonal and abstract, such as a persecution mania. *Flight Into Darkness* is a skillful book, but it is not a moving book. It suffers from a coldness, a lack of compassion, a scientific remoteness which compares but poorly with the rich intensity, be it gay or tragic, of *Fräulein Else, Beatrice* and *Rhapsody.*

"Schnitzler's Last," in The New York Times Book Review, *November 15, 1931, p. 7.*

Richard Plant (essay date 1950)

[*In the following excerpt, Plant comments on literary technique in Schnitzler's short fiction.*]

It is . . . the vast domain of the soul which unceasingly occupied Arthur Schnitzler, a panorama that can never be charted completely. Never weary, he plumbed the depths of the human psyche, tracing its aberrations, soarings, downfalls, and duplicities. In his stories, he usually opens up the soul of one single person, registers every change and development of emotions, moods, fears, hopes, associating one with the other and using a palette of the finest shading. Thus even those Novellen which are recounted from several points of view can be called multiple "Ich-Novellen," since the workings of different characters are laid bare with equal omniscience. The plays, though by necessity not as much seen from within as the prose pieces, often reveal in their basic technique such striking similarities to the stories that they could be rewritten as such. Quite frequently, Schnitzler indeed started an idea as a story, then recast it as a drama, or vice versa, altering and eliminating as he went along.

And there is one element which plays and stories have in common, which, as effective on the stage as in a narrative, seems to me a primary element of Schnitzler's writings. It is, in a way, an instrument of technique, used so often that one might call it a signature of the author's productions. It is not the characters—they are not the central point of interest for the author because they repeat themselves too constantly: the aging Anatols, the cuckolded but forgiving husbands, the sensitive egotists, the brutal esthetes, the dilettantes obsessed by their passion for erotic adventure, the women on the verge of awakening or of resignation. The central point is, rather, a constellation of two or a few characters, an initial relationship, almost abstract, which is then wheeled around, switched back, turned in an unexpected direction until it is almost reversed.

In the sketch **"Der Wittwer,"** for example, a man whose wife has just died, finds among her papers a letter from his best friend, Richard. Apparently, Richard was her lover. The husband's anger slowly changes to resignation: perhaps his wife had needed more tenderness. On Richard's arrival, however, he learns that his friend has been engaged to another girl for quite some time, which means that he had tricked the dead woman in a much more infamous way. Furious, he calls Richard a scoundrel. This "turnabout"—that the friend has deceived the wife, too— is worked out further in the dramatic version of the same plot, in *Die Gefährtin.* After the widower has accused his assistant and friend of duplicity, emphasizing that the engagement to the girl constitutes a much worse deception than the initial adultery, he learns from an old friend that his wife had long known about the engagement and approved of it. This second turn, a sort of double twist, is a typical sample of Schnitzler's dramatic and narrative plot technique. The case of **"Der Wittwer"** and *Die Gefährtin* proves so fruitful because here the same material is used for short story and drama, with the one-act-play adding one more "turnabout." This chain of cautiously calculated turnabouts we also find in one of Schnitzler's most moving, perhaps one of his best stories, **"Der blinde Geronimo."** Here the blind Geronimo begins to doubt his brother Carlo's loyalty when a traveler makes him believe that Carlo has embezzled a twenty-franc gold piece. In order to regain his brother's affection, Carlo actually steals twenty francs from guests at the inn. But precisely the fact that he then hands over the gold piece to Geronimo turns the blind man against him. Only at the end, as the gendarme arrests Carlo for having stolen the money from the guests, does Geronimo realize that Carlo has sacrificed himself to keep Geronimo's love. Perhaps the reader senses even in this comparatively simple turnabout structure the intelligence of an engineer, of a mathematician rather than of an orthodox impressionist or lyricist. . . .

Schnitzler is a juggler of psychological situations which he wheels around and around, and in which usually someone's attempt to achieve a certain aim brings, ironically, the opposite result. Quite often, perhaps too often, the author uses erotic constellations as basic structures. However, he records mainly the dynamics of love, the eternally changing aspects of an affair, the self-deception and the deception of others, the shock of recognition of one's own possibilities and dangers. He has fashioned many of his plots as erotic puzzles to which he supplies surprising (or if one has come to know him, not so surprising) answers. He is lucid even when presenting chaos and turmoil, and his dramatic use of the *Umbruch* distinguishes, him from the archimpressionists, from Herman Bang, Jens Peter Jacobsen, or Maurice Maeterlinck.

In **"Die Toten schweigen,"** the decisive twist occurs toward the end, within the heroine's soul. The story starts with an almost conventionally dramatic occurrence: Emma, the wife of a professor, has an affair with a young man, Franz. During a night ride in a carriage, the drunken coachman loses control, the carriage keels over, Emma and Franz are thrown into a country road. Emma is unhurt; Franz seems to be dead. Instead of calling for help she runs away in a panic. While running, she begins to doubt whether Franz is really dead—a sort of first "turn." But her fear of what people will say is stronger: she hurries home, changes clothes and, strangely enough is perfectly calm when confronting her husband. (Another slight twist, since we were led to expect her to be hysterical.) After a while, however, as she looks into the understanding eyes of her husband and listens to his soothing words, she undoes what she has attempted and—last turn—decides to confess everything.

In Schnitzler's two monologue stories, **Leutnant Gustl** and **Fräulein Else,** these *Umbrüche* happen so frequently that it becomes impossible to count them. **Leutnant Gustl,** one of Schnitzler's most acid and most successful humorous stories, centers around the insult of a fat baker to what the young lieutenant considers his honor. First Gustl decides to commit suicide: even though no one may have heard the insult, it is enough that he himself knows of it.

> **Schnitzler is a juggler of pyschological situations which he wheels around and around, and in which usually someone's attempt to achieve a certain aim brings, ironically, the opposite result.**
>
> —*Richard Plant*

From then on, Gustl changes his decisions from page to page. One chain of associations drives him away from suicide, another drives him toward it. Conveniently, Schnitzler mercilessly exposes the shallow and cold character of his slightly oversexed hero. As a matter of fact, the virtuoso technique of interlinked chains with which Schnitzler manages to convey Gustl's whole world might easily obscure the fact that the basic idea is again a reversal. On the morning of the planned suicide, Gustl learns that the baker has had a stroke. Although by then Gustl was ready to kill himself because he could never lead an honorable existence with the memory of the insult, he now happily decides to live on, and orders more breakfast. It could be shown that this technique of to-and-fro has been perfected in the less ironical, much more forceful story of *Fräulein Else* (she must show herself in the nude, she must not; she will do it alone, before Paul and Cissy, before the whole hotel, etc.), but this would lead us too far into a discussion of the monologue Novelle as Schnitzler fashioned it.

That the basic blueprint of this *Liebesdenkspieler,* this mathematician of love, does not change from 1894 to the works of his later years can be most clearly illustrated by *Spiel im Morgengrauen,* published in 1926. Not only does Kasda constantly win and lose during the card games, whereby the perspectives of his future life are opened and closed in rapid succession, but after he has killed himself, the very uncle who had refused to advance the necessary money, rushes to the scene with the needed sum. The money was lent to his uncle by the woman who seemingly refused to pay Kasda and who has made him feel ashamed of himself. The speed of these reversals lends the story something mechanical, as though the characters were puppets. Schnitzler, if he was conscious of the puppet quality inherent in many of his works, must have been unable to change this pattern. Thus, in *Der große Wurstl* he drives this calculus of love and death to a point where it becomes a parody of itself. . . .

A similar abundance of mechanics can be found in many of his longer stories. Fortunately, what the playwright presented as action or in self-analytical dialogues or monologues, the prose writer can develop cautiously in the "Ich-Novelle" with its interlocking links of associations. A peculiar brand of betrayal, a rather singular series of psychological equations, is revealed in *Frau Beate und ihr Sohn,* a much maligned story. . . . Beate, widow of the famous actor Ferdinand, mother of an adolescent boy, Hugo, has succumbed to the advances of her son's friend, Fritz. It was the first time since her husband's death, and with something like a shock she discovers that the realm of the erotic has begun to mean much too much to her. The real shock, however, comes when, almost against her wish, she overhears young Fritz telling his friends about his affair with her, using the uncouth expressions of a boasting adolescent. Fritz has betrayed her confidence. What should have been their secret he laughingly makes public, humiliating her and also making her realize how far she has lost herself. As her guilt feelings mount, she begins to feel responsible for her boy's strained love affair with the much older Baroness Fortunata. Very discreetly, Schnitzler makes us aware of the interchangeability of his figures. As to Beate herself, we guess that in young Fritz she has loved only her son Hugo: Schnitzler does not make it too explicit but the story's end, I think, hardly leaves any doubt. Hugo, in turn, stands for her actor husband Ferdinand, whose erratic nature had always confused and fascinated her. In addition, she is now certain that Ferdinand deceived her with many women, that he found in her only consolation, peace, protection against himself.

But Schnitzler does not stop here. Ferdinand was not simply one person with fixed qualities. A true actor, he was Hamlet, Don Carlos, Richard III, presenting a different face, a different character every night. Every night she found, so to speak, another person and thus deceived her husband with the characters he had himself created. To the outside world, she was a devoted wife, but in reality she fulfilled her dangerous longings for adventure. Now, as the betrayal of Fritz fills her with guilt, as her son's love affair throws her into a deep turmoil, the chaos within her becomes too strong. She drowns in the arms of her son who—Schnitzler leaves this open—may have known about her dangerous love all along.

Characteristically, two main facts that Ferdinand was really Hamlet, Richard III, etc., and that he had many flirtations are furnished by Beate's memory. Since the entire story is seen through one person's eyes and could almost be called a monologue story, like *Fräulein Else,* the remembered incidents appear, in the chains of associations, as powerful as the present ones. The remembered deception thus brings about another mental turn, because the entire relationship between Beate and Ferdinand is revealed in a new light. But in a masterful manner, Schnitzler conveys to us that, of course, Beate is not quite sure of her suspicions: memory is most unreliable, as irresponsible as hope and wish. . . .

With everything enclosed within the sensibility of a single personality, *Beate* depicts the dialectics of the soul, with one *Umbruch* after another to propel the plot forward. The psychological equations are worked out intricately, but not to such a degree as to turn the figures into mere puppets. *Betrug*—actual, remembered, direct or oblique— causes the turnabouts which lead the psyche into a realization of its own abyss.

This examination of *Beate* can by no means be called exhaustive. As in numerous other Schnitzler creations, there exist in this Novelle problems still waiting for extensive analysis. We touched on the relationship of past and present while discussing how Beate's remembrance of Ferdinand influenced her actual behavior. That Schnitzler was fascinated by the peculiar magic of memory and anticipa-

tion and their relation to the present, is shown by a superficial inspection of his work, from the early Anatol playlets to the late *Der Gang zum Weiher.* In similar fashion, a wish, even if not quite conscious, may assume the importance of something real: the entire behavior pattern of *Therese* is based on her *idée fixe* that her death wish has thwarted her unwanted child's mentality. Truth and fiction, too, are quite closely related, and the author presents this relationship again and again with particular enjoyment. We have room here for only one example. In *Die große Szene,* the famous actor Konrad Herbot, during a dispute with the deceived fiancé of a girl he once loved, stylizes this discussion in such an elegant manner, using it as a sort of springboard for all sorts of theatrical effects, that his wife, listening in the next room, realizes with horror how Konrad embellishes the facts, how incapable he is of separating them from fiction. The wish and the event which follows it, the past love and the present, are perhaps parts of a larger duality, that of appearance and reality, which Schnitzler is constantly fusing. Not only in what may be called trick stories like **"Das Tagebuch der Redegonda," "Das Schicksal des Freiherrn von Leisenbohg,"** or in the plays within plays (*Der grüne Kakadu, Die letzten Masken,* and others) can this shifting from reality and unreality be found, but in an amazingly large number of his other productions as well.

How this further ties in with his intrinsic impressionism, with the "Ich-Novelle," with our pattern of turnabout and *Betrug,* with his irony as well as his style, this paper can not attempt to show. Perhaps the publication of Schnitzler's correspondence will facilitate the task of future students. This paper only intended to isolate the *Umbruch* in its manifold variations, to investigate the rich manifestations of infidelity, deceit, and betrayal. It seemed necessary to reinterpret the *Liebesdenkspieler,* the engineer of psychological equations, whose constructions, though solidly built and firmly soldered, are easily overlooked, because Arthur Schnitzler has hidden them, obscured them by his stream-of-consciousness method. And it is this method with which he has brought the impressionist German short story to perfection while at the same time transcending it.

Richard Plant, "Notes on Arthur Schnitzler's Literary Technique," in The Germanic Review, Vol. XXV, No. 1, February, 1950, pp. 13-25.

Victor A. Oswald, Jr., and Veronica Pinter Mindess (essay date 1951)

[*In the following essay, Oswald and Mindess present a psychoanalytic interpretation of the central character in* Fräulein Else.]

It is astonishing how little exact knowledge we have had about the relationship between Schnitzler and Freud and about the much-mooted question of the influence of psychoanalysis on Schnitzler's work. In his published writings Freud mentions Schnitzler only *en passant.* Schnitzler's journals, in which there is frequent mention of psychoanalysis, cannot be published for years to come. [The critic adds in a footnote: "By the terms of Schnitzler's will his journals cannot be published before the fortieth anniversary of his death, October 21, 1971. The autobiography, which ends with the eighties of the last century, can be published after the twentieth anniversary of his death in 1951."] Apparently no one ever troubled to inquire whether Freud and Schnitzler exchanged letters, probably on the assumption that there was not likely to be correspondence between two men who spent most of their lives in the same city.

Ignorance, unfortunately, has not deterred critics and even scholars from making assumptions, chief among them that Freud and Schnitzler were lifelong friends and, as a corollary, that Schnitzler owed much of his command of depth psychology to this friendship. Joseph Körner set the pattern by flatly labeling Schnitzler a pupil of Freud's, and the perpetuation of the label can be seen, for instance, in Oberholzer's casual characterization of Schnitzler as one "especially trained in psychology through early [*sic*] contact with the leader of the Viennese school of psychoanalysis, Sigmund Freud."

At long last, however, there have turned up among Schnitzler's posthumous papers no less than nine letters to him from Freud. The earliest of them (May 8, 1906) establishes the fact that from the outset Schnitzler was, in Freud's own eyes, a pioneer in depth psychology. Freud goes so far as to say that he envies Schnitzler's intuitive perception. Another letter, the third in chronological sequence, dated May 14, 1922, establishes two further facts: that even at that late date in their lives Schnitzler and Freud were only on a footing of mutual admiration and had never conversed with each other; and that Freud had come to consider Schnitzler not merely his peer as a master of depth psychology but almost his alter ego.

The two men were peers. Each of them was, in his own way, both artist and scientist. The essential difference is this: Freud's work was that of analysis, Schnitzler's that of synthesis. Freud, through the objective study of men and women, arrived at a re-evaluation of human behavior. Schnitzler, through intuition—or, as Freud suggests, through self-observation—created men and women whose behavior is as humanly real as that of the subjects of Freud's scientific study.

We should now be able to take a firm stand. On Freud's own authority we must regard Schnitzler as an independent master of depth psychology, and it should henceforth be indisputable that an understanding of depth psychology is requisite to any complete interpretation of the men and women who people Schnitzler's work.

Fräulein Else is a case in point. For example, Max Krell's treatment of her as a sort of Austrian Gibson Girl, achieves, through over-simplification, only a monstrosity of distortion:

> Fräulein Else, a nineteen-year-old slip of a girl, cultured, rather unspoiled and artless, has retained her cheerfulness amid all worries up to the moment of supreme crisis. A letter from her mother confronts her with the task of appealing to a wealthy elderly man in behalf of her father,

who is threatened with arrest and imprisonment—whereby sexual complications are broached and developed *in extenso*. She makes a sacrifice that goes beyond her powers, but which simultaneously makes manifest her naïveté and purity. . . . To be sure, Fräulein Else strikes us today [1925] as a bit dated . . . a creature . . . who has none of the acerbity of the modern girl, given to dallying with the idle dreams to which a frivolous society educated her only to demand of her, all unprepared, a greatness and a nobility not to be expected from this education.

[Josef] Körner, who goes into greater detail in his analysis of the story, evaluates it from the same point of view. He recognizes Else's sense of isolation, but ascribes it solely to the discord of her family life. He derives her preoccupation with thoughts of suicide from the same source, with the reminder that she bears the burden of a hereditary taint—an uncle had committed suicide at the age of fifteen. He ascribes her prevailing sense of guilt to "a few dissolute wishes and dreams"—which is a fantastic understatement. And his conception of Else is that of a chaste and fragile young thing who cannot face the ugliness of life:

> She, a girl whose woman's honor has never been offended, is confronted with the demand that she permit herself to be seen nude as the price of monetary aid [for her father] . . . even so slight a violation of her chastity causes her to collapse, she falls into madness and commits suicide.

Richard Plant [formerly Richard Plaut], to be sure, has a genuine understanding of Else. It is he who uses the term "narcissistic" to describe her personality. It is he who points out that Dorsday's stipulation coincides with her own tendency towards exhibitionism, and that she is driven to catastrophe by her subconscious drives. But he does not investigate the nature of her hysterical seizures—he calls the seizure after her exhibition a fainting spell; he overlooks the indication of the one deeply repressed drive that is the ultimate determinant; and he reverts to surface interpretation in accounting for her suicide: "She hears how everyone turns from her. She takes veronal because there is no road back to everyday life. She is too deeply in pawn to middle-class existence."

What no one has pointed out is the fact that Else has all the symptoms of the hysterical neurotic and that Schnitzler has throughout the story supplied all the indicia requisite to understand that this is not a matter of outraged honor but a case of pathology. Let us see whether it will not reward us to penetrate as deeply as we can into the structure of Else's personality.

It is clear from the very outset that Else's ego adjustment is narcissistic. First of all, she is dependent for her self-esteem on the reactions of the people with whom she comes into contact, intimately or casually. She is painfully self-conscious at every encounter:

> That was rather a good exit. Here's hoping Paul and Cissy don't think me jealous. Why are those two young people greeting me? I don't know

them. . . . Did I nod back ungraciously or haughtily? I didn't mean to act that way.

The narcissistic adjustment is, obviously, a precarious one. If the ego is deprived of approval and admiration, what Freud calls "narcissistic supplies," it will fall prey to depression and despair.

Equally characteristic of narcissism is the exhibitionist nature of Else's sexual fantasies: ". . . or perhaps it would be pleasant to marry an American, and then live in Europe. A villa with marble steps going into the sea. I'll be lying naked on the marble." Exhibitionism, along with its counterpart scoptophilia—the sexualization of the sensation of looking—are considered by Freud to have a common precursor in the sexual aim of looking at oneself. Let me quote [Otto] Fenichel to demonstrate further the connection with the narcissistic adjustment:

> Due to this origin, exhibitionism remains more narcissistic than any other partial instinct. Its erogenous pleasure is always connected with an increase in self-esteem, anticipated or actually gained through the fact that others look at the subject.

Moreover, this introversion of Else's libido results in an incapacity for object-relationships. People are merely possible sources of gratification. A mature feeling of love is beyond her ken, and the sexual relationship, robbed of all affective elements, represents something that is inexplicably repulsive, though desired. She thinks only of selling herself or having innumerable lovers:

> I'm not in love and I never have been. . . . I think that I just can't fall in love with anyone. That's really remarkable, for I'm certainly a sensualist.

> [Thinking about Cissy and Paul] I wonder whether Cissy leaves her door open at night, or does she only open it after he knocks. . . . And then they lie in bed together. Nasty! I won't share my bedroom with my husband and my thousand lovers.

> Paul, if you give me thirty thousand you may have anything of me that your heart desires. . . . No, Paul, you can't have me even for thirty thousand. But for a million? . . . If I marry some day I'll probably do it cheaper.

Finally, death-wishes are part of the pattern of insufficiency, though they are also closely associated with a fundamental repression the consideration of which we shall postpone:

> I wonder where I'll be at forty-five. Possibly dead.—I hope so.

> It's almost dark now. Night. Deathly night. Oh, I wish I were dead.

As Reik has pointed out, to the neurotic personality death may represent both liberation from psychic conflicts and atonement for death-wishes against others. In Else's case there is also an unmistakable libidinous association which is revealed as the narrative proceeds. As Fenichel puts it: ". . . suicide is carried out because hopes and illusions

of a relaxing gratification are connected with the idea of suicide. Actually analyses of attempts at suicide frequently show that the idea of being dead or of dying has become connected with hopeful and pleasurable fantasies."

All the indicia we have examined thus far are taken from the *status quo ante,* most of them from the stage prior to the receipt of the letter from her mother. Else is obviously not prepared to adjust herself to any disturbance of her precarious equilibrium. She is ill-equipped to cope with the news that her father, a lawyer who plunges in the stock market, has embezzled trust funds to cover losses, to say nothing of coping with her father's request, conveyed by her mother, that she appeal to fellow-resort-guest Dorsday, a family acquaintance, to provide—with no just expectation of restitution—the thirty thousand gulden required to save her father from prison. Least of all is she equipped to react unequivocally to Dorsday's stipulation: he will comply with the request at the price of seeing her *au naturel* either in his rooms or in a starlit clearing in the forest.

Under the impact of these blows Else's feeble controls abdicate. Her sexual fantasies proliferate and grow more and more lurid, culminating in the idea that she will display herself to everyone:

> How would you like it, Father, if I auctioned myself off this evening just to save you from prison. It would make a sensation—!

> I'd like to lie alone by the sea on the marble steps and wait, and at last a man would come, or several men, and I'd choose one, and the others whom I'd reject would throw themselves despairingly into the sea. Or they'd have to be patient, until the next day.

> Must it be Herr von Dorsday? If one sees me, others shall see me. Yes. Wonderful idea. Everybody shall see me. The whole world shall see me—and then comes the veronal.

Simultaneously there is an increase in the attraction of death, associated with ideas of revenge and of liberation. It is important to remember that she prepares the dose of veronal before she sets out for the social rooms to give her ekdysiastic performance:

> It's a shameless life. It would be best to jump from that cliff and have it over with. It would serve everyone right.

> Who'll cry when I'm dead. Oh, how beautiful it would be to be dead.

Above all, as the narrative unfolds we become aware of two facts: that Dorsday constitutes a father-image for Else and that there is something remarkably askew about her feelings toward her "Papa." At first we see only affection for her father not unmingled with contempt; but the ambivalence widens, from the time she receives her letter, to embrace the extremes of love and hate. Her mind becomes fixed upon the idea that he will prefer suicide to prison:

> I'm a snob. Father knows it and always laughs at me. Oh, dear Father, you worry me a great deal. I wonder whether he has ever deceived

Mother. *Has* he? Of course he has. Often. Mother's rather stupid.

[From her Mother's letter] " . . . he came home quite in despair. . . . " [Else's comment] Can Father ever be in despair? . . . [From the letter] "Father came home at one o'clock and now it is four o'clock in the morning. He's sleeping at last, thank God." [Else's comment]—It might be best for him if he never woke up.

I'm sitting quietly on the window sill, and Father is to be locked up. No, never, never! It mustn't be! I'll save him! Yes, Father, I'll save you!

I'm living here as a smart, elegant young woman, while Father is back there in Vienna with one foot in the grave—or rather in jail. [Note the symptomatic slip of the tongue.] If Father runs away to America I'll go with him. I feel all confused.

During the course of her conversation with Dorsday, these death-wishes are linked with her recurrent fantasies of her own death:

Let Father kill himself. I'll kill myself, too.

Kill yourself, Father!

There's nothing left to do, Father. You'll have to kill yourself.

Finally, when Dorsday leaves her alone in the garden she falls briefly into a hysterical dream state and we are able at last to penetrate—though only momentarily—the depths of her subconscious mind.

We cannot pause to examine this dream in detail, but we must emphasize two elements of it that are of vital pertinence to this study and which foreshadow the ultimate revelations of Else's subconscious after she has drunk the veronal. One is the unmistakable representation of the fact that Dorsday is a father-surrogate; the other is Else's hidden libidinous aim connected with the idea of death.

She dreams that she is dead, lying in state in the family drawing room. Her father is in prison. Dorsday comes to pay his respects: "At whom is he waving that handkerchief? Mother comes down the steps and kisses his hand. Ugh! How nasty! Now they whisper to each other."

Later she dreams of getting up and looking out of the window at a regatta, finally of setting out to walk to the cemetery for her own burial:

I'm going so quickly that no one follows me. Oh, how fast I can go. They're all still standing in the streets marveling . . . I'd rather go across the field. . . . The naval officers stand with swords at present-arms. Good morning, gentlemen. Open the gate, Sir Matador. Don't you recognize me? I'm the girl that just died. But you mustn't kiss my hand. . . . Where's my grave? Is that embezzled, too? Thank God, it's not the cemetery at all. It's the park in Mentone. Father'll be glad that I'm not buried. I'm not afraid of snakes. If only my foot isn't bitten by one. Oh, dear!

Surely no comment is required on the symbolical significance of snakes, nor on the sexual connotation of the two occurrences of hand-kissing. And I suppose we need only a brief reminder that rapid walking and running represent the sensation of sexual experience, as do, especially, climbing and flying. As for the general purport of the dream, let me quote Fenichel again:

Hysterical dream states are closely related to [hysterical] seizures. As in seizures, the daydreams, which represent derivatives of the repressed, involuntarily take possession of the personality, but here the pantomimic discharge is lacking. The day-dream, an outgrowth of Oedipus fancies, breaks through as such, removing the patient from reality. Sometimes the sexual meaning of this absence is directly apparent in a voluptuous pleasure the patient obtains from it. More often the affect, too, is repressed, and the new wave of repression against the mobilized derivatives keeps them so remote from awareness that the patient himself is unable to give any account of what he has experienced and is aware only of a gap in his consciousness.

When Else awakes from her dream, the only element that she can at first recall is the figure of the matador: "What could I have been dreaming about? About a matador? What sort of matador was he?"

And she reverts to the enigma before abandoning it: "How pleasant it was a little while ago on the bench—When I was already dead. Matador.—If only I could remember what it was.—It was a regatta.—Right.—And I was watching it from the window. But who was the matador?—"

She cannot, of course, undo the secondary repression. The matador is not unmasked until her subconscious is liberated by the dose of veronal. We know only that he is someone she seeks libidinously in death, presumably because this libidinous association would be impossible in life.

Fräulein Else reveals one of Schnitzler's strongest assets as a writer: his unusual and penetrating understanding of the female psyche. His women are generally more interesting and more alive than his men.

—*Claude Hill, in his "The Stature of Arthur Schnitzler,"* **Modern Drama**, *May 1961.*

She later associates the idea of seeking and never finding with Dorsday, as she starts to look for him in the social room of the hotel: "Herr von Dorsday isn't here. Victory! Saved! But how so? I must look further. I'm condemned to look for Herr von Dorsday till the end of my life."

Though I am sure I need not plead that Dorsday is *not* the

matador, I want to link this seeking association with the idea of Dorsday as a father-surrogate. He has all the requisites. He is a friend of Else's father's about her father's age. Her mother's letter reminds her, "He always liked you particularly," and she herself recalls: "He stroked my cheek when I was twelve or thirteen years old." Moreover, Dorsday is now in a position of power. He has money, and money is for Else *the* value. His power is, in fact, so great that it momentarily approaches omnipotence. The fate of the whole family is in his hands. He is, so to speak, an ideal surrogate to replace the discredited parent proper. In Else's dream he *has* replaced her father. And this idea is reverted to in her last unconscious fantasy: "Go and catch Dorsday. There he goes. Don't you see him. There he jumps over the pond. He's killed Father. . . . "

Remember, above all, that her first reactions toward him display a characteristic ambivalence:

> He still looks rather well with his grayish Van Dyke beard. But I can't feel at all attracted to him.

> [Just before the tête-à-tête] What is he [Paul] saying? He can go to the devil. Why do I smile at him so coquettishly? I don't mean it for him at all. Dorsday's leering at me. Where am I? Where am I?

> [At the start of the conversation with Dorsday] It would be fun if he suddenly proposed to me.

> [A moment later] Why do I look at him so coquettishly? He's already smiling knowingly. Oh, how stupid men are.

Let us now re-evaluate the central conflict. Else is impelled, in effect at her father's behest, to commit an act which to her fundamentally connotes sexual satisfaction. The concomitant circumstances fulfill her notion of the conditions for surrender of chastity—she is to sell herself at a price. Actually, she is as eager to be seen as Dorsday is to see her. If only—she thinks—it were not Dorsday with whom the scene must be played. And her fantasy dwells repeatedly on Paul, but particularly on "the *filou*," a Lothario-Casanova type who had previously been a guest at the resort:

> Oh, if it only were somebody else. Anybody else. He could have everything he wanted tonight. But not Dorsday!

> No more time to lose. Don't become cowardly again. Off with the dress. Who'll be the first? Will it be you, cousin Paul? Your luck that the Roman head [the *filou*] isn't here any more.

Now Dorsday is about as repulsive a scoptophiliac as we are likely to meet. But we must not overlook the fact that there is another man of her acquaintance—one sole other man, to be exact, and at that a young one—to whom she would be equally loath to display herself:

> Fred. I mean Herr Friedrich Wenkheim. Incidentally, the only decent person I ever knew in my life. The only one I could have loved—if he hadn't been such a decent person.

> I'm a hussy. They all know it. . . . Only Fred

doesn't know it, the stupid fellow. That's why he loves me. But I'd rather not be naked in front of him. I wouldn't have any pleasure from it at all. I'd be ashamed. But in front of the *filou* with the Roman head—how gladly!

> I'll consult Fred. He's the only one who really cares for me.

Here we must juxtapose two further passages of interior monologue:

> Mother's rather stupid. She hasn't the vaguest notion of what I'm like. Neither do other people. As for Fred—well, yes, but only a vague notion.

> You're all to blame that I've become what I am. . . . What I feel—the things stirring and trembling in me—have you ever cared? Sometimes there was a look in Father's eyes as though he had a vague notion, but it quickly passed away.

Need I belabor the point that Fred—decent, reliable, understanding Fred—is another father-surrogate, though an entirely different sort? Clearly the taboo that Else dreads to transgress has incestuous implications, and, like all taboos, combines insidiously motives of attraction and repulsion. It is on this dilemma that Else is impaled.

Else's controls collapse completely after she awakes from her day-dream and goes back to the hotel. She strips, puts on only shoes and a cloak and then goes down to the social rooms of the hotel literally at the command of the drives of every passing moment. She finally comes upon Dorsday—and, fatally, the *filou*—drops her cloak, and then falls into a hysterical seizure. The nature of this seizure is most illustrative. It is a hysterical disturbance, a motor paralysis with an inhibition of one sense only, the sense of sight; and the magical connotations of Else's inability to see are not merely implicit, but explicit in her interior monologue: "My eyes are closed. No one can see me."

She is carried to her room, recovers command of herself for one brief moment to the extent that she can drain the glass of veronal, falls back into her hysterical seizure and lapses into oblivion.

Even before she is carried up to her room the figure of the matador comes floating up from her unconscious: "Why are they all whispering. It's like a death chamber. The stretcher will be here at once. Open the gate, Sir Matador."

And he reappears in the ultimate revelation of her unconscious in a context that unmasks him, that reveals who it really is that tries to "kiss her hand," with whom in her subconscious mind she longs to "fly."

> Look, they're all marching in convicts' clothes, and singing. Open the gate, Sir Matador! It's all just a dream. What have you brought along for me, Father? Thirty thousand dolls. I'll need a separate house for them. [Dolls are, of course, symbols for children. That Else should want her father to provide a house of her own needs no elaboration.] What's that? A whole chorus? And an organ, too? . . . Never have I heard anything so beautiful. . . . Give me your hand, Father.

We'll fly together. The world is so beautiful
when you can fly. Don't kiss my hand. I'm your
child, Father.

I should not wish to leave the impression that I think this
psychoanalysis of Else tells the whole tale. I think it is obvious that the analysis is requisite to a complete understanding of her attitudes and her actions. But I am fully
aware that *Fräulein Else* is also a story about a family,
about a society, and even about a civilization. It is, by implication, a scathing denunciation of the values by which
so many men have lived, and not only in Vienna!—money,
the appurtenances of society life, and the pursuit of *Liebelei*. It is the tragedy, not merely of a girl impoverished
of love, but of a way of life impoverished of all significance.

> *Victor A. Oswald, Jr., and Veronica Pinter
> Mindess, "Schnitzler's 'Fräulein Else' and the
> Psychoanalytic Theory of Neuroses," in* The
> Germanic Review, *Vol. XXVI, No. 4, Decem-
> ber, 1951, pp. 279-88.*

Heinz Politzer   (essay date 1963)

[*Politzer was an Austrian-born American critic, translator, and editor who wrote extensively on German literature. In the following excerpt, he discusses Schnitzler's
short fiction in a consideration of the dual nature—both
poetic and scientific—of Schnitzler's literary art.*]

On May 15, 1922, Arthur Schnitzler received a letter written for the occasion of his sixtieth birthday. The letter-
writer greeted Schnitzler with unqualified approval as "an
explorer of psychological depths, as honestly impartial
and undaunted as anyone has ever been." Appraising the
achievements of the sexagenarian in scope and depth with
rare perception, the well-wishing critic mentioned in particular "your determinism as well as your skepticism—
what people call pessimism—your preoccupation with the
truths of the unconscious and of the instinctual drives in
man, your dissection of the cultural conventions of our society, the dwelling of your thoughts on the polarity of love
and death." The letterwriter was both literally and figuratively a compatriot of Schnitzler; he came from a similar
background and had experienced similar disappointments. Thus he felt compelled to conclude his congratulations in a somewhat resigned mood. "If you had not been
so constituted," he said "your artistic abilities, your gift
for language, and your creative power would have had free
rein and made you into a writer of greater appeal to the
taste of the masses."

To be recognized and commended in this fashion by the
creator of psychoanalysis must have been one of the most
valuable birthday gifts Arthur Schnitzler received that
day. . . .

A tribute to Schnitzler could not begin from a more suitable vantage point than Freud's appraisal of the writer as
a psychologist. By rounding out this image with a sketch
of Schnitzler the poet, we may gain something like a
bird's-eye view of the border area which extends between
poetry and psychology.

In his commendation Freud gave top priority to Schnitzler's determinism. Indeed, determinism formed a link between the doctor and the writer; it stemmed, at least partly, from the scientific training both men had undergone.
Schnitzler was destined by his father, a renowned physician, to study medicine, and he started his career as a general practitioner. Even after he had left the medical profession and established himself as a writer, he continued to
consider himself a scientist. Since, during his formative
years, Schnitzler served as an assistant in the clinic of
Freud's teacher, Meynert, he could not help accepting the
prevalent view that the human will was utterly subservient
to the limitations imposed upon it by man's body. Thus
it sounded like a declaration of principles when Schnitzler
ended one of his early stories, **"Der Sohn" ("The Son")**
(1892), with the statement that it has not become at all
clear to us "how little we are allowed, and how much we
are compelled, to want" (. . . "wie wenig wir wollen dür-
fen und wie viel wir müssen.")

Yet having been born two years after Schopenhauer's
death, he was no longer concerned so much with the world
as will and representation as with the Ego as the sum total
of instincts and illusions. The interest in hypnotic techniques which he shared with the young Freud, led him inevitably from the exploration of broad philosophical concepts like Schopenhauer's pessimism to the more detailed
and better accountable investigations of the human psyche. "An experience," he was to write as late as 1927,
"may be superficially done away with—it will remain
present as long as we have not completely understood it.
Only when it has lost its secret for us do we have the right
to call it past." This was a poet's variation on the psychologist's theme. Though Schnitzler decided at one point to
become a poet, he became and remained for the rest of his
life a *doctor poeta*. . . .

Schnitzler directed the sobering light of his wide-awake
mind upon the souls of his characters. This is what Freud
meant when he called him an explorer of psychological
depths, impartial and undaunted. He was never more sci-
entifically impartial and poetically undaunted than when
he wrote, in 1900, the first radical interior monologue in
the German language, *Leutnant Gustl*. The title of the English translation, *None but the Brave*, is misleading: ridi-
culing the hero, it pronounces an ironical value judgment
on his ordeal, an attitude Schnitzler is most anxious to
avoid in the story itself.

For the sake of scientific objectivity Schnitzler dismisses
here almost completely the narrator, that is: himself. The
author no longer accompanies his figure, nor does he describe him in his own words. Instead, Gustl's thoughts
and emotions, his reactions and conclusions are allowed
to present themselves in their raw, natural, state. The designation "stream of consciousness" story does not apply
here either, for Schnitzler succeeds in penetrating the lieutenant's consciousness and in opening up the sphere of his
pre-conscious. Snippets of thought and shreds of sentiments are shown floating and bubbling, ostensibly without
any sense or reason. The author observes this amorphous
mass of associations from the outside, registering its fluc-
tuations and vacillations as if he were looking into a witch-

es' cauldron. It is no witches' cauldron, however, it is a very modern soul.

To perform this experiment Schnitzler has chosen the most neutral, most average object available to him at that time. Traditionally a young Austrian lieutenant around the turn of the century was a nondescript man, a "Mann ohne Eigenschaften." He was distinguished neither by material riches nor intellectual gifts. The routine of peacetime service had left his inner life as blank as an empty mirror. At the same time he played a representative rôle in the society of his day. On him and his like rested the security of the empire. He was both smiled at and pampered like a pet. By taking this pet seriously for the short hours of one night, Schnitzler exposed the inner weakness of this guarantor of Austria's security. His experiment with Leutnant Gustl's soul touched a traumatic spot in the political unconscious of his fatherland. Schnitzler was punished accordingly by being demoted from his officer's rank. Moreover, the very plot of his story was an indictment of the obsolete code of honor which prevailed in Austrian society. Thus he challenged the archaic structure of the Habsburg empire. All this Schnitzler achieved simply by setting up optimal conditions for his experiment.

The lieutenant has picked a quarrel with a civilian; since this civilian is an academician, a *Doktor,* he is allowed to face Gustl in a duel. On the eve of the combat Gustl is insulted by a middle-class baker; the offence, although it is negligible, can only be remedied by another duel. But Habetswallner, the baker, is by his social status, rather, by the lack of it, barred from the honor of meeting the lieutenant with his weapon in the hand. Since Gustl lacks courage and presence of mind to strike the baker down on the spot, he himself is disgraced, and can no longer "hack the doctor to mincemeat," as he was resolved to do. He has to choose between quitting the army and committing suicide. He decides for the latter and thereby enters the experimental situation prepared for him by his scientist-author. This is the lieutenant's whole story, or almost the whole of it. Taken by itself, it exposes to ridicule the prejudices of society.

Gustl, on the other hand, experiences the night before his death. He is a young man, and the night is a spring night, enlivened by bells telling the hours which still separate him from his death. The problem is formulated now: How does man react in the imminence of his death? (In this respect *Leutnant Gustl* is a companion piece to *Reigen* where Schnitzler studied man under the impact of the love act.) Does Gustl, in the extremeity of his situation, gain new insights? Is he led to extraordinary decisions by the inescapability of his death? Does the specific weight of his human nature change? What appears before the eyes of a drowning man during the last seconds of his existence unfolds before the observer's glance in the carefully registered convulsions of Gustl's psyche.

Although the lieutenant occasionally comes close to a better understanding of himself, he fails to learn from his experience, let alone to change. Ironically, he is allowed to save face by a stroke the baker suffers during the night of the experiment. Habetswallner's death is the ultimate test devised by the experimenter, who thus assumes the part

of destiny, of the *deus ex machina.* But even when it is released from excruciating suspense, Gustl's soul remains unaffected. Displaying the vitality of a cork tumbler, the lieutenant re-emerges as little scarred as he is bettered. His aggressiveness, his wantonness, his sluggishness of heart have successfully resisted the anguish, the proximity of death, and even the judgment of God, to which the experiment had exposed him. A hollow man has demonstrated his hollowness. Leutnant Gustl remains Leutnant Gustl. *Quod erat demonstrandum.*

With the restraint that befits a scientist, Schnitzler avoided asking for sympathy for his object by allowing Gustl to die. (The lieutenant's death would have been more than easy to achieve in view of the structure of his character and the plot of the story.) Instead, Schnitzler silently condemns him to life, to a mediocre existence composed of petty adventures and facile frustrations. This is, of course, the unspoken moral of a psychoanalytical parable. It is also a diagnosis. In Leutnant Gustl's mind Schnitzler read the pathological condition in which Austria, and perhaps Europe, found herself around the *fin de siècle.* And just as a correct diagnosis contains, to a certain degree, the prognosis, and anticipates the course the malady will take if it remains unchecked, so we are able to gather from Gustl's aimless and confused musings a warning of the catastrophe which was to befall the continent in 1914, fourteen years after the story was published. We discover in the young lieutenant's psyche an aggressiveness which drove him and his generation to the battlefields of the first world war. How typical Gustl was for Austria's state of mind we can see from Karl Kraus's monumental war tragedy, *The Last Days of Mankind* (1919). The lieutenants Nowotny, Pokorny, and Powolny who haunt the pages of Karl Kraus's satire as leitmotives are Leutnant Gustl's comrades. . . .

In the story *Casanovas Heimfahrt* (*Casanova's Homecoming*) of 1918 the theme of the duel is most revealingly connected with the motif of the aging lover. The argument over life and death is won by a Casanova whose energies are already waning. At the same time, the duel is no longer used to express Schnitzler's abhorrence of petrified social customs. It has ceased to be a fatally ridiculous relic of a barbaric past. Much rather it is shown as an elementary constellation of human destinies, man fighting man for the possession of woman, age fighting youth because it refuses to abdicate. A stark naked Casanova faces his young, boisterous and boastful adversary, likewise naked, on a dew-sprinkled meadow. An almost mythical encounter takes place; in a heroic setting—a landscape which could have been painted by Poussin—decline and ascent face each other for the decisive combat. Sword in hand, Casanova asks: "Am I not a god? Are we not both gods?" and again: "(Is this) a fight? No," he answers himself, "it is a tournament (*ein Tournier*)." This duel is a game royal and an ordeal, a challenge to fate and the gods to whom the fighter has likened himself, a battle between the life forces of Fall and Spring.

Ironically, Fall wins out and Spring succumbs. Casanova, who measures the strength and skill of his arm against those of a physically superior opponent, remains the master of the battlefield. And yet, to top irony with irony, the answer he receives from fate is highly unsatisfactory. He is only saved to spend the rest of his life in the ignominy of his decline. As was the case in *Leutnant Gustl* life becomes the suspension of a death sentence. From now on Casanova's existence will be self-destruction on the instalment plan. Fate is a very witty puppeteer and its final joke consists in severing all the strings by which it had led its marionettes. This is indeed what "The Great Unknown" does in the grotesque puppet play *Zum grossen Wurstel* (*The Great Clown Show*) of 1904. He accompanies this act of ultimate alienation with the words: "Am I a God? . . . a fool? . . . Am I like you? / Am I myself—or nothing but a symbol?" The question put to fate elicits nothing but a question as a reply. . . .

Schnitzler, the literary scientist, was a radical experimenter as well as a traditional artist. His treatment of the dream, for instance, is both novel in a psychoanalytic way, and conventional in the dream images chosen and in the use made of them as dramatic and, to a lesser degree, epic devices. In *Der Schleier der Beatrice* (*The Veil of Beatrice*) the poet Filippo Loschi dismisses his beloved because she has seen herself in a dream as Duke Bentivoglio's consort. In a famous tirade the poet defines dreams as "desires devoid of courage . . . insolent wishes chased back by the light of day into the corners of our soul whence they dare to creep out only by night." Calling Beatrice the "whore of (her) dream," the poet packs into an aphoristic nutshell Freud's *Interpretation of Dreams* which, incidentally, was to be published only one year after *Beatrice,* in 1900. He also anticipates W. B. Yeat's dictum, "In dreams begin responsibilities" by more than a decade. . . . While Schnitzler seems to agree to the principles Freud had developed for analyzing the processes of dream production, the *Traumarbeit,* he uses dreams as a poetic device very much in the way Shakespeare, Calderon, and Grillparzer used them on the European stage.

In the late story *Traumnovelle* of 1926, unaccountably translated into English as *Rhapsody,* Fridolin, the physician, is allowed to act out in a turbulent and disturbed night the libidinous drives dormant in his soul. His wife, Albertine, projects during the same night her unfulfilled desires and frustrated agressions onto the screen of a dream. The parallelism of the man's actual escapade and his wife's dream adventure are set in the relation of a counterpoint leading, with great compository skill, to climax and catharsis. The formal use made of psychopathological material elevates the story from the level of a clinical study to that of a novella—masterfully executed in a very traditional way. Again Schnitzler reveals his proximity to psychoanalysis by uncovering the unconscious of his figures, and using clinical material to suit his literary ends. But Fridolin's adventure at a masked ball—the face masks turn out to be the only pieces of costume worn for this occasion—and the symbolism of Albertine's dream are not just Freudian; they are also quite theatrical. If the *Traumnovelle* is a psychoanalytic study of the interpenetration of day and dream, and love and death, it also treats the Freudian themes in a highly stylized and, one is tempted to say: operatic, way. Above all, Schnitzler does not seem to be interested so much in the presentation of the libidi-

Schnitzler in later years.

nous drives and urges of his figures, their repressions and sublimations, as he is in what he himself calls man's exposure to "the incomprehensible wind of destiny." His approach to destiny may have been Freudian, but his awareness of fate's incomprehensibility certainly was not, and this last phrase "the incomprehensible wind of destiny," could easily have been coined, three hundred years before Schnitzler and Freud, by one of the great poets of the Baroque. . . .

When Fridolin in the *Traumnovelle* contemplates the process of decomposition in the body of a woman he had desired only the night before, Schnitzler merely adds physiological detail to the metaphysical horror of a genuinely baroque vision:

> He saw a yellowish, wrinkled neck, he saw two small and yet somewhat deflated girl's breasts between which the breastbone was outlined under the pale skin with cruel precision so as if the process of putrefaction had been anticipated there, he saw the rounding of the dull-brown underbelly, he saw beautifully shaped thighs opening indifferently around a dark shade which had lost now all secret and all sense, he saw the knee arches turned gently outwards, the sharp edges of the shin-bones and the slender feet with the toes bent inward . . . Instinctively and almost

as if he had been forced and guided by an invisible power, Fridolin touched with both hands the forehead, the cheeks, the shoulders, the arms of the dead woman; then he intertwined his fingers with those of the dead as if it were a game of love, and although her fingers were stiff it seemed to him that they tried to move and to respond to his; moreover it was as if from under her half-closed eyelids a distant and colorless glance was straying to meet his eye, and he bent down as if he had been attracted by magic.

Unaccountably, this passage is missing from the American edition of *Rhapsody.*

Until his end Schnitzler prided himself on being a *Naturforscher,* an explorer of the naturally given. And the passage just quoted proves that he knew how to use anatomical data to best literary advantage. He was a psychologist, and there is no doubt that he succeeded in this love scene between a living man and a dead woman in exposing the romantic motif of death-in-love and love-in-death to the sober light of neuro-pathology. Personally, I am most fascinated by the use he makes of two hidden half-phrases. Fridolin, Schnitzler remarks, acted "as if he had been forced and guided by an invisible power," and again, "as if he had been attracted by magic." He chooses a contrary to fact condition, an "as if" clause, to guard against the invasion of his scientific world by a power beyond his control. If we are willing to take a writer's words seriously then we perceive behind these precautionary measures, these "as ifs," Schnitzler's feeling for the eternal and the mysterious. It is this feeling that unites him with the literary tradition which survived in him. He was able to gain from a ghastly morgue scene the pathos of a genuine *memento mori.* More generally speaking: the flight from death into dance, from perdition into embrace, the anxiety stirred up in free-wheeling souls by the passing of time are in Schnitzler's world the psychological variations of a profoundly baroque theme.

Biographically speaking, Schnitzler's own conflicts may have been aggravated by his insistence on the mysterious element in his art. In terms of literary criticism, however, we cannot help seeing in this blend of the analytical with the traditional Schnitzler's lasting contribution to European letters. He refused to disentangle the woof of destiny from the warp of human character. This prevented him from creating a true tragedy as well as a true comedy, although his friends expected him to produce at least the latter. Instead he excelled in what he called the tragicomic mood. . . .

Tragicomedy was the artistic means which Schnitzler selected to work out an acceptable approach to human affairs. For the sake of humanity he advocated as perfect as possible an understanding between man and man. But, for the sake of his art, he would not carry his rationality so far as Freud did. A moralist in a minor key, Schnitzler was occasionally heard to cry out against "this hodgepodge of restraint and insolence, of cowardly jealousy and fake equanimity—of raging passion and empty voluptuousness," which he saw around himself and projected onto the stage. It is no accident that this diagnosis is made by a physician and that it occurs toward the end of a play,

Das weite Land, which Schnitzler specifically called a tragicomedy. But not only is Doctor Mauer the only decent human being in this drama, he is also the least interesting. In Schnitzler's work, the scientist, the doctor, the psychologist takes at best the place occupied by the chorus in the drama of the Greeks: he serves as the knowing witness of an inexorably absurd fate. This is even and especially true when the doctor turns dramatic hero and comments on the scene from the center of the stage, as is the case in the grim comedy *Professor Bernhardi* of 1912.

The poet Arthur Schnitzler was a wise doctor. Relentlessly he diagnosed the human absurdity in the tragicomedies that fill his books. He analyzed the psyche of a moribund society because he foresaw and dreaded the epidemic character of the neuroses that were bred and spread by it. But unlike his successors in the field of modern tragicomedy—from Jean Cocteau to Tennessee Williams and Samuel Beckett and beyond—he did not look down on the figures he had created. He lingered among them and suffered with them. He knew about their ultimate secret, and, knowingly, kept it.

Heinz Politzer, "Arthur Schnitzler: The Poetry of Psychology," in Modern Language Notes, *Vol. 78, No. 4, October, 1963, pp. 353-72.*

Ursula Mahlendorf (essay date 1977)

[*Mahlendorf is a German-born American educator, novelist, and critic. In the essay below, she offers a close examination of "The Last Letter of a Litterateur."*]

Austrian, German, and Swiss writers of the period between 1890 and 1960 express in their treatment of the artist as a literary character a repeated complaint in work after work: the artist hero cannot feel. If he could overcome his emotional sterility, if he could only love, so their plaint and perplexity goes, he would create better works and feel fulfilled. The reasons for his plight and the degree of insight into it that he shows vary, and it is this variation which gives dignity, weight, and interest to the problem. The artist's inability to feel makes his work sterile, without passion, form without life, "cool, smooth, and insolent." The artist who suffers from "the impotence of the heart" recurs as a serious or comic figure throughout the works of Heinrich and Thomas Mann, Musil, Kafka, Werfel, minor and major Expressionists, and even such post WW II authors as Günter Grass and Max Frisch.

At the core of all "impotence of the heart" treatments there is a fantasy of an oedipal drama whose *dramatis personae* easily can be separated from their various disguises. The youthful artist protagonist is a son figure with a mission to redeem humanity through his art. His mistress and muse spurs him on to fulfill his role as redeemer. In all the permutations in which she appears (from mother to homoerotic love object) she is passive, ill, weak, in need of rescue, the alluring but always remote goal of his quest. The antagonist is an older male, an authority figure who stands in the way of the hero's mission. He may be the woman's father, husband, or professional protector (lawyer, physician etc.). The resolutions to the triangle situation differ as do the disguises of the *dramatis personae.* All writers of the period, however, relate artistic achievement or failure to the way in which the oedipal conflict is resolved.

Arthur Schnitzler's novella **"The Last Letter of a Litterateur"** (written from 1910 to 1917 and published posthumously) shows a wider and deeper understanding of the problem of the artist than most portrayals of the artist during this period, although it is quite a short work. Schnitzler reveals the developmental psychic roots of dilemmas that confront the impotent artist, he uncovers the conscious and unconcious meanings of this artist's quest, and explores the different functions of artistic work in the artist's life.

Schnitzler was, of course, exceptionally well qualified to deal with these questions. Besides being a trained physician, he was also a literary man who recognized this particular artistic problem in himself. He had the honesty (and the strength) to portray in this story an aspect of himself as the litterateur, an aspect of his own physician father as the doctor, the litterateur's antagonist, and an aspect of his mother as the litterateur's mistress.

As a moralist, Schnitzler was interested in the ethical factors involved in the psychology of this artistic type. But he also had the knowledge and the intuitive grasp of interpersonal and intrapersonal psychology to see through the ramifications of the problem. Schnitzler's acquaintance with Freud and his theories, his friendship and discussions with members of the Vienna psychoanalytical circle such as Ernest Jones and Theodor Reik, sharpened his psychological knowledge. His own medical-psychiatric training, practice, and interest, and his study of human psychology as a moralist and dramatist often led him into (what I believe to have been) seeming disagreements with Freud and his circle. It will be my task in this study to understand Schnitzler's contribution to the artist problem in his work (as exemplified by **"Last Letter"**) and in his theory (as exemplified in essays and aphorisms). Through my treatment of the artist problem in Schnitzler's work and theory, I hope to shed some light on his relationship to Freud and his circle. Moreover, the artist problem in Schnitzler needs to be evaluated against the background of the cultural crisis which affected Austria during the first decades of this century, a crisis faced by other countries and their writers later in the century. Through an analysis of Schnitzler's artist figures, we can arrive at an understanding of the problematic personal and cultural situation of the twentieth century artist in general.

FORM AND PLOT

The novella is written in the form of two letters of unequal length, the first a suicide note and the second a comment upon it. The first letter-writer is a dramatist, the second a physician who attends the dramatist's mistress and his former tutor. Four lines of impersonal editorial explanation separate the two letters from each other, balance the two points of view, and provide the perspective for both letters. The four editorial lines state that, at the time the two letters are being read, both writers are dead.

In the lengthy introduction to his letter (one sixth of the entire story), the dramatist weighs the reasons for wishing to commit suicide precisely at the moment of his mistress'

death and he deliberates on explanations why he is writing to this physician of all people. As answer to the questions he has raised in this section of his letter, the dramatist launches into the background of his wish to die. He organizes the second part of his letter in such a manner that it suggests a series of dramatic-novellistic scenes, each of which contains three major characters and a different place and time of action. The three characters are the dramatist, his mistress, and four different, but basically similar physicians representing authority. In the course of an elopement from Vienna the places of action change to Naples, Rome, Florence, the Alps, and a northern Italian lakeside villa, the journey suggesting a quest. The name of the final destination, the villa Conte Bardi, evokes the realm of death and transforms the dramatist into an Orpheus claiming his Eurydice from the shores of death. The time of action spans a season from early spring to late fall and suggests a nine months' gestation.

The first scene of this epistolary drama opens on a dance festivity just after the writer, who feels that his present art lacks "depth and passion," has completed a comedy and a love affair with one of its actresses. The first glance he and Maria exchange draws them to each other irresistibly as if they were in a dream. He emphasizes his sense of fatality at their meeting by saying "our fate was sealed for all time." The lovers meet in the midst of the dance of life for what turns out to be a dance of death. After they have danced only a few steps, Maria faints. She awakens from her faint as her mother rushes up and attempts to explain away her indisposition. The writer, in a visionlike flash of inspiration, arrives at a diagnosis of Maria's faint (it is due to the overexertion of her diseased heart) and comes to a decision about his life. He envisions that Maria, despite her heart condition and at the risk of her life, will become his mistress and that therefore she will die. Being left to experience his first great sorrow, he will become a great artist. He foresees that her physicians and her mother will oppose their marriage and that Maria will submit to his wishes in defiance of them. At this point, he recognizes the mother and daughter as former old acquaintances and finds it easy to renew their friendship.

The scene shifts to a few days later when he visits Maria and her mother and begins his courtship. In daily converse with her, his forebodings disappear and he looks forward to a happy life with her. He asks for her hand in marriage. Her mother defers her decision until the family physician has been consulted. The physician advises against marriage because Maria's "diseased heart is not at all equal . . . to the excitement of a passionate relationship." For the sake of his art, the writer decides to take upon himself "crime and punishment" and asks Maria to elope with him to Italy.

The next scene opens in Florence after an uninterrupted journey of several months, during which Maria has "become ever freer and more cheerful." It is now high summer and Maria experiences recurrences of her fainting spells. Her lover calls for the help of a physician only after he finds her unconscious one day on returning from a walk. In a confidential talk, the doctor confirms the earlier prognosis that Maria will die and advises the writer to move with her to a cool mountain location.

The next scene sees the couple in a mountain resort where Maria has renewed fainting spells and where her lover spends his days roaming the countryside and contemplating "what I had envisioned earlier as my mission and what I now recognized to be a necessity, namely the *work of art*." At a noon hour on a mountain meadow, the writer has another visionary experience during which he comes to realize his actual alienation from his mistress and hence the vanity of his hope for his art. Filled with guilt because of his murderous design on the life of his beloved, he wishes to punish himself with a death that is reserved to great criminals, a fall from a precipice. He desists with the thought that his death would hurt Maria (he does not think that the strain might kill her). Beginning to hope that her condition might not be serious after all, he decides to seek another medical opinion. "By chance" he meets a world famous heart specialist, who confirms the earlier prognosis and who advises him to live with her as a brother and to seek, with approaching fall, a gentler climate.

The last scene of the writer's letter is set at the villa Conte Bardi. For a few days Maria seems to improve. The couple spend their days drifting on the waters of the lake and hardly paying attention to each other. In his ennui, the writer begins to suspect that after her death he will resume his former frivolous and ordinary existence. One day, however, the lovers exchange a glance as they did on the evening of their first meeting; their love reawakens and, after an embrace, he thinks he wants to die after she does. At this point, she needs relief from medication and he sends for another, last physician. The doctor, the writer of the second note, gives Maria only a few days to live and, in addition to the relief of morphia, provides her with a nurse. The arrival of the doctor weakens the writer's resolve to die. Finally, he decides to kill himself just at the moment of Maria's death. His letter ends with the words, "And I would create the work without equal, the work which would justify me before God, myself, and the world. And that may not be. That must not be. Maria is worth a greater sacrifice than has ever been brought to a mortal. I shall obliterate myself before I have achieved my consummation. Therefore I have made up my mind . . . "

The letter which follows the four lines of editorial comment gives the doctor's report of the suicide and of Maria's simultaneous death. The doctor clarifies his relationship to the writer and to the nurse whom he left with Maria and to whom the writer felt attracted, even while composing his suicide note. The doctor disparages the writer as an immoral weakling incapable of creating a great work, because "without true morality there is no genius." He adds that he gave to charity the money the writer left him. He deals the writer some more blows by remarking that he married the nurse the writer coveted, that they, on their honeymoon, saw the performance of a play of the writer's, which they found embarrassingly poor, and that now, ten years after the writer's death, all his plays are forgotten while he, the doctor, happily survives with a flourishing practice, a wife, and three children. To add insult to injury, the doctor signs his name to the letter (the writer failed to sign his and the doctor withholds it): Anton Vollbringer. It is a name which draws the reader's attention to the fact that the doctor is a man who completes his missions, the feat the writer seemed unable to accomplish.

The novella contains a veritable storehouse of Schnitzler stock motifs, characters, and situations, from his earliest works on up to 1917. It is a characteristically Schnitzlerian statement of the artist problem.

WISHFULFILLMENT AND OMNIPOTENCE OF THOUGHT IN RELATIONSHIP TO THE MOTHER FIGURE

Schnitzler gives to the writer a tone that is at times ironic, at times exalted and melodramatic (e.g., "only now . . . the mysterious meaning of the fate which joined us and transcended me and our love became clear"). The feelings and actions he reports in his relationships to Maria suggest soap opera. For example, the dramatist knows at once after their "first decisive glance" that they are "destined" for each other; she follows him "like a sleepwalker." In fact, if Schnitzler made his writer talk in this style consistently and if it had no function beyond itself, the reader would dismiss the work as "kitsch." Schnitzler counteracts the occasional melodrama by endowing the writer with cunning, acid wit, and with some insight into himself and his relationships. For example, the *literateur* suspects that his vision of his murder of Maria is a literary day dream and that he is unable to tell the difference between fact and fiction: "How often in the manner of poets and fools had I not entertained evil, criminal, devilish or noble and self-sacrificing thoughts."

The melodramatic tone has the function of indicating to the reader that the writer lives a fantasy of omnipotence. At first reading, the epistolary form masks the degree of the writer's projection and wishfulfillment, because we expect a letter writer to be subjective and personal. A second look at the exaggerations, inconsistencies, and repetitions reveals that the writer does everything in his power to keep himself, Maria, and the reader from noticing that he lives in a world of fantasy. Thus, once he has projected his wishes upon Maria, he perceives only those of her reactions to him which confirm his fantasy of her and he minimizes other impressions. Hence she appears to him (and to the unsuspecting reader) a victim whom he totally controls. He never asks her what she feels about him. In fact, their silences are remarkable; all their important communications are by *chance* eye contact. He does not notice her several fainting spells and many "other painful symptoms." He deceives her about her condition. He spends many hours, indeed entire days, away from her. Yet despite these obviously unloving actions, he asserts again and again "my passion was capable of . . . enrapturing her"; "we had become inseparable, truly one"; "and only now there was happiness." The repetitious assurances of his love and union with her show that he does not feel what he says, that he needs to reassure himself by his words that he felt any love for her. The lovers' avoidance of close contact with each other, their restless journey in Italy, their social isolation and solitude, their costly and remote residences at the Villa Bardi serve the purpose of evading the test of reality and of maintaining the fantasy of love.

The woman whom he chooses as a target for his omnipotence fantasy qualifies for the role of motherly muse and virginal victim by her very name: Maria. Because she and her mother are old acquaintances of the writer's, we may assume that the writer knows of her circumstances and of her illness. If he admitted such prior knowledge before giving the reader his premonitions, it would detract from the ominous character of their meeting and therefore lessen his sense of omnipotence. Therefore, with an offhand remark, he minimizes the extent of his information about her. Moreover, it is convenient that Maria is a malleable, inexperienced woman who is not particularly beautiful and who has no unusual prospects for marriage because she is an orphan, in poor health, and without much of a dowry. Living in semi-retirement with her mother, young and eager to live (as testified by her coming to the ball though not able to participate in the dancing) she is an ideal candidate for seduction and the kind of adventure the litterateur wants.

A host of details support the interpretation that Maria is, for the writer, a symbolic mother figure. Just after exchanging his first glance with her, the writer remarks, "I loved her. She was the first woman whom I loved." The tense he chooses for his statement appears odd in German as well as in English. By using the past tense rather than the pluperfect and an adverb (e.g., whom I had ever loved), the writer indicates that he is not thinking of the particular woman whom he came to love but rather of the creature whom he loved with his first glance, namely his mother.

The clearest indication that Maria is a mother figure appears in the repeated prohibitions against approaching her sexually. The first of the physicians who treats her, "an elderly gentleman" advises with some "embarrassment" against a marriage, especially against a marriage based on sexual attraction. His prohibition only increases the lovers' desire and they embark on their journey. The Florentine physician whom the couple consult does not specifically impose a sexual tabu; but his recommendation to remove Maria from the inclement heat of Florence, like the third physician's advice to seek a milder climate, hints at the sexual prohibition. The third physician moreover strengthens his point by admonishing the writer to live with Maria as "brother and sister." The fourth physician, by stationing a nurse at Maria's bedside puts a definite end to all thoughts of love making with her.

The prohibitions are seemingly made because of Maria's heart condition. As a physician Schnitzler of course knew that a woman who can stand such extensive travel as Maria does need not refrain from sexual relations. On the symbolical level, her weak heart expresses her inability to love. She can neither give, nor respond to, nor accept love. She dies of a failure of love, his as much as hers. The writer questions the physician's prohibitions from the beginning of their relationship ("the passion of our relations had a favorable influence upon Maria's heart condition") and he believes the doctor who forbade their marriage to have been "ignorant, malevolently foolish, or jealous." In all

the scenes of the story, a reference to love, kisses, union, passion is immediately followed by the appearance of a father figure who prohibits them.

It is a telling feature that the writer wishes to be inspired to feeling by a woman who, from the symbolism associated with her, cannot (because of her heart condition) and must not feel (because of the incest tabu). We should expect that her incapacity to respond would generate anger and frustration in the writer. That this is indeed the case (despite the writer's avowal of love all through the story) appears nowhere more clearly than in their first meeting and is well symbolized by their first dance and her faint. Upon coming into contact with him, she faints, being thus totally accessible to him physically, a passive object dependent upon him, but entirely inaccessible to him as a feeling and responding subject. Precisely at this point he has his fantasy of becoming her murderer through his love of her. He does not acknowledge his anger (and that is what the murderous fantasy signifies). Rather he converts the unacknowledged feeling of anger into a project that will produce sorrow in him and out of his sorrow and love he will create a great work. The feelings of love and sorrow however, remain a plan for the future and meanwhile his unacknowledged anger, expressing itself as neglect, as abuse and as unresponsiveness to her needs, destroys her. What Maria dies of is in the final analysis of little concern. That she dies is decisive. Insofar as Maria is a human being who is more than his projections, a human being who has needs and wishes of her own, the relationship with her poses some important ethical problems. In tracing the intrapsychic aspects of the litterateur's relationship to Maria and in making them understandable, Schnitzler does not excuse or condone any of his actions or neglect the ethical dimensions of the interpersonal relationship.

The litterateur never acknowledges, never allows himself to feel, his anger at the mother figure and hence it remains undifferentiated from the love and guilt feelings he professes. The denial of feeling, the lack of emotional differentiation affects his entire emotional life and makes it flat, superficial, unconvincing, and confused. This superficiality in turn affects his art and this he is conscious of and wishes to remedy. He speaks and thinks about emotion in very curious language indeed. For instance, at the death of his beloved, he plans to feel sorrow, anticipates pain, indeed envisages "unimaginable new experiences never felt by anyone before." He speaks in this manner because his emotional life has remained project, fantasy, an experience anticipated in the future. And in his striving for omnipotence, he does all he can to keep actual persons and actual feelings at bay. Future feelings and anticipations, however, never yield satisfaction or fulfillment in the present. As a consequence, he must repeat his actions of conquest (and Maria is not the first) and his assurance of love. Yet he is condemned to never believe himself and to remain in a circle of emotional sterility. The dilemma of emptiness appears most clearly in his vision on the mountain meadow. Because his feeling for Maria is so confused and not rooted in a tangible social world, it may vanish suddenly, leave him empty, in despair, and terrified of death. Indeed he is so terrified of emptiness that in "self-preservation" he wants to rush into suicide. He finally resolves his fear by rushing to rescue Maria, and the circle of empty activity continues.

The hero's situation with Maria reflects his developmental situation with his mother as a child. His present relationship with Maria shows that she must have been an unresponsive and withholding mother, a mother unaccepting of the child's anger. In addition, she must have been available to the child physically, in fact, even seductive. Maria demonstrates such seductiveness after her faint by her play with her fan. The mother must have bound the child in a continual cycle of promise and frustration. Ungiving, the mother figure ultimately represents death and emptiness. The desire to murder her is the desire to punish her for her seductive withholding and to wrest feeling from her. Ironically, feeling is precisely what she does not have. Bound as he is, however, the child continues to struggle for her feeling. By following Maria into death with his suicide, the writer merely continues the struggle for feeling beyond life. His words, "to die after her . . . was a form nothing more" reflect this conviction. But even these words and the very struggle for feeling have no other function than to shield him from actually feeling in the present. The unfeeling mother thus appears to be at the heart of the writer's quest into death.

PROVOCATION AND MANIPULATION IN HIS RELATIONSHIP TO THE FATHER

Since he does not feel and cannot wrest feeling from Maria, is the litterateur merely locked with her in a repetitive, mutually frustrating, destructive, senseless embrace? In a way this is indeed so. We would need to look no further if the novella ended with the death of the lovers. Schnitzler ends, however, with the note by one of the father figures. We therefore must pay more attention to the father figures than we have. We have seen that a series of symbolic father figures prohibits and blames the *Literat* for his sexual relations with the woman. Their disapproval, however, is mild, distant, and ineffective and does not keep him from breaking the incest tabu but rather spurs him on by adding the zest of forbidden fruit ("my guilt . . . had to increase my passion monstrously." His many conscious allegations to the contrary the litterateur is not really concerned with the woman. The woman is rather a means to affect and to anger the father. I believe that the litterateur's relationship with the maternal Maria, his art, which includes his suicide note as a last and final sample, and his suicide are attempts to win the father's recognition. Let us look at the kind of note the litterateur writes to gain insight into what it reveals about the father-son relationship, what his art consists of and what function it has.

A suicide note can have a serious effect on its recipient only if its writer actually dies. The writer who has paid for his audience with his life blood therefore has the advantage over the recipient, who must listen to him, a fact the litterateur points out to the doctor, "it is easy for me to ask for I am dead." But the writer must make sure that the note will be found and read. The litterateur thus produces a dramatic context in which the doctor cannot help but find the note. "With a well aimed shot in the temple" the litterateur is found in his desk chair with the open and unfinished note before him. However, once he has given the dramatic pointer to the physician, the writer hedges. He begins his note as if it were a story, "Night rests over the lake." The doctor who finds the note with the body must assume that it is a suicide note and begin reading it—especially as it is not addressed to anyone in particular. After reading the second sentence ("The mountains tower silently and black in the distance") he might pause in his reading and assume that this is not a suicide note afterall but a story—only to find himself addressed in the third sentence, and addressed in a manner as if the dead man had caught him prying: "But read on, my friend, this is indeed a letter." The *mis en scène* which invites perusal, the actual wording of the first two sentences which seem to ward it off, the third sentence which confirms the *mis en scène* but which teases the doctor for having actually followed its directions, set up a characteristic pattern between the writer and the doctor. The writer raises expectations in his reader and then punishes him for having had them.

The fourth sentence of the introduction appears to elaborate on the nature description given in the first and second sentences, "On the opposite shore there is the glitter of the sidewalk lights which I shall not see being extinguished." By calmly continuing the nature description of the beginning of his letter the writer acts as if, in his suicide note, he had nothing better to do than to note his romantic surroundings. The fact that he is going to die is worth only an indirect statement in a subordinate clause. To minimize even that, he casts doubt on its validity by adding, "Or shall I, after all?" The reader's response to these deliberations might be one of wonder if the suicide is really as calm as he claims to be. The writer anticipates him in his response by his next sentence, "If I were really convinced in my inmost being that this letter really is my last, and that everything will be over for me in a few hours, would I order my words so matter-of-factly, indeed even with some care? And why not?" Now that the reader is in the grip of speculations as to why the writer appears so composed, he is offered a partial explanation, a generalization of an impersonal nature concerning suicide: "But it is, afterall, calming to know that one has *decided* and is not *condemned* to die. That one does not *have to* do something, makes everything easier, even dying." The reader might make all kinds of responses to his assertion (from believing it to be rationalization to thinking it is resignation). The writer, however, expects derision from the doctor and forestalls it with, "You make a wry face, my dear fellow." He continues with a prediction of the doctor's further response, "but you read on. That I am dead puts you into a more benevolent, or at least curious, mood." The prediction is designed to insult the doctor (you feel benevolent because I am dead) and to stimulate guilt (you wished me dead). As if to forestall the possibility that the doctor might discontinue reading the note right then and there, the writer provokes him by a direct question: "But I ask you—as you doubtless ask yourself—why do I write this letter just to you . . . ?" Once again the writer uses the technique of engaging the other's attention (I ask you) and predicting his response (as you ask yourself). Before the doctor has even had a chance to clarify his response (why me?), the writer in his continuation of the question punishes him by attributing revulsion and incomprehension to him " . . . to you, for whom all I say and shall say, must be, has to be, both revolting and profoundly incomprehensible." Yet, even in the insult (you are too pure and stupid to understand me) there is contained the plea and admonition to the doctor to try to understand.

The letter writer exploits the advantage of writing a last letter to attract the other's attention. By predicting the doctor's responses, he directs and controls them. But he also punishes or condescendingly rewards them. And into each punishment or reward he builds a new provocation. There is no direct communication between the two men, as witnessed by the absence of salutation to the doctor. Instead the writer engages the doctor in an emotional push and pull of indirect manipulation and teasing. The writer thus controls the doctor's every move and, in addition, emotionally punishes him for making the move. How effective the writer's technique of indirection, control of response and punishment is appears from the doctor's reply ten years later. In addition, the writer uses his letter to evade the necessity of facing his situation as he is dying and a feeling response to it. He hides from the realization of his condition by generalization (*one* dies, not I die); by the very act of writing instead of being with Maria ("she yearned to breathe her last in my arms"); and by projection (it is the doctor who is hostile not he, Maria who is sick not he).

The writer uses the first four pages of the twenty-three page letter to establish a network of claims upon the doctor as his enemy from childhood, as an heir to his last will and testament, as a father confessor to a confession of crime and punishment, and as a co-conspirator on the woman's life (by imputing that the doctor might have given Maria too much morphium). He casts aspersions on the doctor's honesty, his professional ethics, and his personal worth and self-esteem. Needless to say, he makes none of these claims outright. Rather by insinuation he attempts to bind the doctor in a bond of ambivalent dependency. In the entire section the writer does not answer the central question which presumably prompted him to write his letter, namely what is the meaning of his relationship to Maria and the doctor and why does he commit suicide. The function of this part of the letter is therefore to establish claims upon the doctor's attention and to engage him in an emotional relationship even while denying that this is what he is doing.

The writer begins the next section with a shift away from provocation by a question of how he might tell his story most effectively ("Where do I begin?"), a question which he, skilled manipulator of the reader that he has proved himself to be, certainly need not ask. Once he has drawn attention to matters of form, and avoided the issue as to why he is writing, he chooses a dramalike novellistic form of narration. Instead of addressing the doctor, he now involves him in the action, at first by getting him to identify with the other physicians (whose judgment and values he shares) and later by making him an actor in the lovers' life. The dramalike narration thus continues and intensifies the claims upon the doctor. The dramatist in this way demonstrates by means of his suicide note that his art can estab-

lish a common ground between father and son on which they can explore their relationships to each other (with the son calling all the shots). The psychological dynamics underlying both parts of the letter are those of a quest for the father, just as the journey and affair with Maria was a quest for the mother.

If we see the narration, the act of writing, as a quest for the father, the writer's contacts with the different father figures appear in a new light. The symbolic meaning of their profession designates all of them as nurturing parental figures. He hears of the father figures at the time he meets Maria because when she faints "there were calls for a doctor." When he experiences his first vision of their love and her death, he immediately anticipates that "the doctors will advise against or even prohibit marriage." The doctor/father figure hence appears from first mention in the double role of helper/prohibitor. The first physician seeks the writer out with the actual prohibition, appeals first to his tact, insight and affection for the woman and then resorts to the threat that the breaking of the tabu will have serious consequences, namely "most serious guilt and pangs of conscience." The elopement with Maria is at first a successful rebellion, the dire predictions are not realized. The writer only turns for help to the next doctor when he can no longer overlook the fact that the breaking of the tabu has had results after all. His callousness in overlooking Maria's faints and discomforts derives at least in part from his hesitation in approaching the father after breaking the tabu. This second physician tells him that Maria will die and that she can only be given relief for her symptoms. The breaking of the tabu has thus led to the originally desired result—it has impregnated Maria not with life but with death (hence the nine months from first meeting to death). The writer now follows the doctor's prescriptions "to offer Maria relief." After his vision and despair in the mountains and the first inkling of the danger to his own life, he seeks out another doctor in what is an attempt to undo what he has done. By his choice of a world famous heart specialist, he wants to prove the other doctors (and himself) wrong. The hopes he fastens on this third doctor border on a belief in miracles, hence he experiences the doctor's arrival in their resort "as if fate wanted to assure me of its benevolence." The attempt to reverse the course of events ends with this doctor's "one first glance" diagnosis of her condition as hopeless. The fourth and final physician is a figure familiar from childhood; angry, unable to cure but a provider of relief through drugs. In the meetings with the doctors, in the writer's quest, there is a progression from first hearing a doctor called to the final recognition of the doctor's indubitable and "inextinguishable hatred."

After fall and expulsion, the usual quest hero in his encounters gains new insight, knowledge and relationships; he overcomes enemies, and arrives at a goal and reconciliation. The writer meets the same father figure time and again. He cannot ask for a meeting with this father for his own sake but meets the father only through the mother. All their encounters and all their communications remain indirect. The distance between father and son in this relationship is so great that the son can reach the father only by his death (the son must kill himself before the father will read the note), can affect him only by breaking the incest tabu and by his "murder" of the mother. At the core of each father figure, the litterateur experiences rejection and anger. In the last figure these crystallize into a figure of unforgiving rage.

The doctor-tutor represents the introject of the bad father, the father whose glance the litterateur-son repeatedly calls "hostile" or "malicious." As he appears from his letter, he is a man well defended against making contact. He is exact, with a keen sense of order (it is he who mentions all the dates, he who is impressed by the well-aimed shot). He believes himself objective, referring to himself as "the signer of this letter." He moralizes (no genius without morality) and expends his sarcasm on the dead man. He hides his hatred by partial admissions such as that of "a certain antipathy to the writer" which, he insinuates to the reader, the reader could not help but share. He condescendingly offers his blessing to the dead man ("May he rest in peace").

We are now in a position to understand the meaning of Vollbringer's concluding words and to appreciate Schnitzler's intent behind the sequence of the letters. Written ten years after the writer's death, the doctor's comment shows that it was indeed difficult to reach the father; it takes him ten years to respond and even then he does not do so openly. The comment shows that the litterateur has succeeded in affecting the father, has held him under a ten year spell of outrage, and has provoked him to an anger which erases the writer's very memory: "I deem it appropriate to withhold his name." But precisely by his ten year grudge and by the force of his angry attempt at extermination, Vollbringer confirms the writer's influence, hence power, and the success of his artistry. He feels no love, no concern, and no regret for the dead man but he cannot let go of him. Even after ten years he must "correct some misconceptions" of a dead man who has left no witnesses but himself. He is bound to the dead man as much as the dead man was bound to him.

Schnitzler relates the inspiration and the driving force of the litterateur's writing to his need to communicate with the father. The cleverness of his technique and the masking of intents, motives and feelings derives from the danger inherent in the communication with this kind of father. We now recognize why the writer's plays must needs be "cool, smooth, and insolent." The decisive fact in his lack of feeling in his art is not that he has no feeling, as he believes, but that he must hide it, cannot express it forthrightly and hence gets neither relief, nor reward, nor punishment for it. The father, appearing as he does as the nurturing parent, invites his approach and promises to satisfy it. But because he is so forbidding, the son is caught in an approach-avoidance dilemma from which there is no release. The writer's art does not help him to break through the dilemma. It is merely a technique of remaining in it ever more smoothly.

The developmental situation reflected in the *Literat's* relationship to the father figures is thus quite similar to his relationship with Maria, the mother figure. While the mother is promising but withholding love, the father is distant and angry but promises nurture. The love which the mother promises but withholds causes the child to turn for nurture to the father. But the father is difficult to reach and accessible only through the mother (through breaking the incest tabu at the price of her death and the son's guilt). In the father, if he comes too close, he encounters an annihilating rage. He is caught, with each parent, in an approach-avoidance dilemma. He moves back and forth between the two approach-avoidance dilemmas, using the approach-avoidance dilemma with his mother as material to manage his dilemma with the father and thereby increasing the dilemma with him. He has developed techniques (and that is what his art is) to provoke the father in an effort to get him to respond even while protecting himself against his rage by evasion. His art has become a habit which protects him from insight and maintains both dilemmas.

With Maria's death, the writer stands to lose not only the fantasy of love that she constitutes and to encounter the emptiness he fears but he also stands to lose his access to the father figures (with the mother dead, there is no need for the father-physician's attendance). And with both removed, he loses his motivation to pursue his art, hence the comfort of the habit which allowed him the illusion of control. It is for this reason that, at the point of Maria's death, he needs to carefully engineer the sequence of events. To avoid the terror of emptiness on all three losses and to maintain control, he must kill himself exactly at the moment when Maria dies, thus maintaining his illusion of his hold on her. He must further write exactly up to the moment of his and her death, thus holding on to his art. For this reason, his suicide note is long and repetitious. In fact, he has stated the issues in the first section of his note; the rest is dramatic repetition. He must further leave a work which is both sufficiently provocative and incomplete so that the doctor is forced to write, upon his instigation, a reply and conclusion. The doctor's name *Vollbringer* now takes on a different meaning. The father finishes the task the son has set him. [The critic adds in a footnote: "Cf. *vollbringen* has the meaning of completing a task. There are, in the name also biblical connotations, cf. Christ's last words, 'Es ist vollbracht,' John 19: 30, connotations which strengthen the artist-saviour theme."] The function of art for this artist is therefore the control and manipulation of parental figures (the audiences of his life and work) beyond his death. His art is a tool of attack and defense, a technique of "survival," which assures him immortality at the price of his life.

In the exploration of his relationship to the father as well as to the mother figure the litterateur discovers emptiness, anger, destruction, and death. The destructiveness of these parental introjections destroys him and the partners of his interpersonal relationships, Maria and Vollbringer. His responsibility for Maria's death is clear and obvious. His part in Vollbringer's is not. The author-editor, by implying his death in the editorial comment, establishes a connection between their deaths as well as between their lives. The litterateur's story is a horrifying vision of an artist's dilemma. There is no way out of it for the litterateur. He is totally caught in the dilemma, hence determined by it. The situation of the litterateur, however, is not the situation of the editor or of Schnitzler. Let us see what Schnitzler accomplishes by his fiction of two letters and comment and of an editor.

THE FUNCTION OF THE FICTIONAL LETTER AND OF THE EDITOR

The litterateur does not resolve his dilemma by his art and his letter remains incomplete. Schnitzler completed his story, though with some difficulties, thus showing that he could in fact let go of his characters and that he resolved his problem with them. The fiction of the letters allows the two characters to speak for themselves. The reader of the **"Last Letter"** thus begins his perusal of the story in somewhat the same position as the doctor who finds the note. Over the first few pages, he differentiates himself from the finder of the note and begins to ask questions about the litterateur's relationship to the doctor and to the woman. The reader's main identification during his first reading of the litterateur's letter remains with the litterateur's point of view and Schnitzler makes sure that he does not get an entirely negative impression. Insofar as the reader shares some of the illusions and fantasies of the litterateur, the reader identifies with him.

The counterpoint view in the doctor's letter causes the reader to reevaluate his impression of the litterateur. The reader might be tempted to remain at the level of seeing him with the doctor's eyes if it were not for the editorial comment which draws his attention to the fact that (as far as the editor is concerned) both letters writers are equal. Hence at a second reading of the story, the reader reads with a very different orientation. He begins to compare statement against statement and to look at the two positions critically. This critical distance helps the reader to come to an understanding of the interpersonal dynamics which underlie the relationship between the two men and the woman. For example, the reader might suspect from the litterateur's exaggerations and repetitions that the litterateur's fantasy at times runs away with him. But then the litterateur also points out to him that this might be the case. The editorial comment and the doctor's answer, however, do allow the reader to sort out what is fantasy and what is real event and what fantasies led to what real results (e.g. Is Maria under his power from his first glance at her? Why? With what consequences?). The very presence of an editor provides a base from which to begin to decode the meanings of the symbolism of name, place, persons, actions, and events. And we are led into the kind of analysis I have given. In addition, the fiction of the letter form suggests that the author does not wish to take sides and to influence the reader, being therefore very different from the litterateur who wishes to manipulate his.

The reader begins with sympathy for the characters and gradually discovers in critical understanding the deeper meanings of the characters' relationships to each other. Moreover, in so far as the reader shares the characters' problems, the process of insight initiated by the editor's sequence can help him to understand them and himself. From all this we gather that Schnitzler's art is therapeutic in aim because it evokes the characters as an emotional reality, makes conscious in the reader what is unconscious to the characters and finally leaves the reader free to make his own choices about his life, based on the insights he has gained from an understanding of the characters. Schnitzler arrived at the identical aims for his psychological art as Freud did for his psychoanalytic practice.

In the editorial comment, Schnitzler goes a step further in the criticism of the doctor's position. The editor indicates in his four lines that he received both letters from "the estate" of the doctor. He does not say when or how the doctor died nor what happened to the wife and children of whom he spoke with such pride. Nor does the editor indicate his own relationship to the dead men. The very fact that a stranger edits the letters means a number of things. He makes that which was private public, thus giving the personal relationship a wider social significance. He passes judgement on the doctor as well as the litterateur. The doctor's order of things (his detachment, seeming objectivity, hypocrisy, malice) has come to an end. The father who tutored such a son has lost all his children. The past which shaped this destructive artist is erased with both figures.

The litterateur wished to manipulate and to destroy directly by his art. Art, for Schnitzler, is a process of symbolic destruction. But it is not that alone. In the editor Schnitzler hints at a new kind of artist: one who provides a perspective for his reader and gives him a tool by which to analyze the destructive artist and his psychology. He is a humbler artist who is a stranger to the savior pose of the litterateur.

In the story, Schnitzler does not tell us how he arrived at his and the editor's positions. Schnitzler did identify with the litterateur and the doctor and needed to liberate himself from the threat which the litterateur constituted for him and for his art. To understand more fully how Schnitzler freed himself from the litterateur and the bad father and mother introjections we must turn to Schnitzler's theory of art, his life, and his occupation with ethics and psychology.

NEGATIVE (LITTERATEUR) AND POSITIVE (DICHTER-POET) TYPES AND NEGATIVE AND POSITIVE FUNCTIONS OF ART.

In **"The Last Letter,"** Schnitzler portrayed a negative type of artist (the *Literat*) whose very existence implies a positive counter type (a *Dichter*). During the years when he was working on the novella (1910-17) he was also occupied with a theoretical formulation of the artist problem in a larger framework, a theory which he finished in 1923 and published in 1927 as *The Human Mind in Word and Deed* (*Der Geist im Wort und der Geist in der Tat*). The distinction between *Literat* and *Dichter* reflects a basic antithesis between the negative (that is destructive) and the positive (that is life-giving) direction of the mind in all human endeavor, whether it be in word or in deed. Among the representatives of the positive state of mind in the sphere of the word are prophet, historian, philosopher, poet, priest, statesman; in the sphere of action they are leader, explorer, builder, scientist, physician, and hero. Their negative equivalents are idolater, pulpiteer, politician, litterateur, journalist, sophist, adventurer, dictator, swindler, quack, and speculator. The professions and talents he mentions are only specific vocations in which the various states of mind operate. Moreover, a person could very well be both a man of the word and a man of action. A poet could also be a scientist, or a statesman could be a poet and a leader as well. The essential difference for Schnitzler is that the disposition of the mind is either innately positive or negative; there is "no transition from the positive to the negative type."

To return to the specific examples of the positive and negative types in the **"Last Letter"**: although the gulf between poet and litterateur is unbridgeable, the two types are related by many correspondences. It is often hard to distinguish between them because their works and their lifestyles may be almost identical. On the whole, the positive type lives in the realm of truth. The ethical attitudes which are characteristic of him are altruism, *agape,* depth of feeling, commitment, loyality, humor, matter-of-factness, confidence and responsibility. The negative type lives in the realm of deception. The attitudes which are characteristic of him are self-centeredness, insensitivity, sensationalism, success, irony, opportunism, arrogance, and frivolity. Even when he is in error, the positive type is fruitful "for . . . there is the truth of his person." Both types produce what is conventionally called art. Both influence their contemporaries, the negative type often more strongly than the positive type. Only the positive type, however, produces what is life giving and lasting while the negative type is destructive, produces what is death giving and, fortunately, not lasting.

What Schnitzler describes in static terms in his essays appears as dynamic interaction in **"The Last Letter."** In the interaction of Schnitzler as author and fictional editor with the characters and the reader, we can discern the origins of the positive type. What drives the litterateur to his creation (the suicide note) and to his personal death is the *fear* of a loss of control, the fear of emptiness and death. And according to Schnitzler's theoretical statements all artists derive their motivation for creation from "a traumatic neurosis, from a drive to escape the dread of transitoriness and death (*dem Grauen der Vergänglichkeit*). Art wants to conserve; only secondarily does the artist wish to form. Some artists escape into the creation of character and others into play." The litterateur shields himself from the fear of death in ways different from the poet's. The litterateur converts into symptom, denies, substitutes, splits, projects, provokes, deceives, taunts, and by these strategies he controls and manipulates. The *Dichter* Schnitzler transforms his fear into exploration and clarification of emotion. And he uses the insights he has gained in his exploration to set values. Let us explore further the contrasting *ways* in which *Literat* and *Dichter* use their fear.

DENIAL / EXPLORATION OF FEELING AND PSYCHOLOGY AND LITERATURE

For Schnitzler, the artist is primarily a creator of character. The raw material of his art is available to all humans, as it is life itself and human dreams. In their dreams, "all humans have fantasy" and create characters. For Schnitzler as much as for Freud, uncontrolled fantasy is pathological. The *Literat* cannot control his fantasy as he kills himself for the sake of his fantasied omnipotence. The *Dichter* is able to integrate fantasy into his conscious life. The

Dichter uses the world as material for his art. "The line of his life and his creation are the same," and he "gives of himself." This does not mean that he is identical with his characters or uses his characters as mouthpieces. Rather he gives of himself in his empathic understanding of his characters, in his feeling and insight about himself and them. Because he gives of himself, his characters, once he has begun to create them, have an effect back on him and continue growing as much as he himself grows with them. The entire creative undertaking thus is an exploration and adventure in which the poet does not foresee every move. The *litterateur* as we have seen, manipulates the world as his material and he foresees exactly where his figures will move. He calculates his moves mathematically.

The most important tool in the artist's creation of character is psychological insight into intra and inter-psychic process, "a fact which the great writers of all ages knew: that the psyche basically is not easy to know, . . . that aside from consciousness the psyche has unconscious contents and these contents produce effects." Intrapsychic knowledge by itself does not suffice for Schnitzler, "it means little to know men; the most essential thing is to have insight into human relationships. And these too deceive, are pretense or mask to the point of being impenetrable. You know an individual only when you can see him in all his relationships." The writer's imagination penetrates through deception and guise. The writer is sensitive to and knows how to decipher the underlying messages and meanings of the human conduct and interpersonal behavior which he observes and participates in. And he can encode into his work the detail of description, action, or expression which will mediate to the reader the underlying meaning of his character's interactions, plans, goals and ideals. In gathering his materials the writer practices in art what [Theodor] Reik came to call "listening with the third ear." In getting his reader to decode the implications of the detail of descriptions (e.g., such detail as the meaning of the seasons, the Villa Conte Bardi, the *Literat*'s exaggerations etc.), the psychological writer teaches his reader to listen with the third ear.

The writer needs not only insight into common sorrows and joys of man but also patience and tolerance for the more exotic or despised varieties of experience. Schnitzler gives as an example the writer's need to have empathy for a character's sorrow at not being able to enjoy oysters or caviar. All psychological insight, however, is dependent on the writer's capacity (and willingness) to feel. The writer's concern with psychology is not a matter of systematic and intellectual insight alone. Systematizers, like some Freudians, he felt, neglected "the fluctuating borderland between consciousness and the unconscious. The unconscious does not," so he continued his criticism "begin as soon as some people seem to believe out of laziness (an error the psychoanalysts do not always avoid). The art of the poet consists above all in drawing the lines between what is conscious, half conscious and unconscious as sharply as possible." Schnitzler agreed with the Freudians on the importance of early relationships for a person's life. "In the life of every human being, the same types which only belong to his particular history ever recur in ever different forms: Father, mother, friend (male, female); betrayer, and beloved. There is perhaps nowhere a stronger endorsement of Freud than in the following aphorism: "The secret of human relationships lies in something deeper than the character traits of people . . . even deeper than personality: . . . the secret lies alone in Eros (not in the erotic) which therefore must be the most important and far reaching concept."

We are now in a better position to understand the difference between Schnitzler as author/editor and the litterateur as artist. The litterateur, to be sure, attempts to explore his relationship to Maria and the doctor, but he does so only to manipulate them. What limited insight he has, he uses only for manipulation. He consciously makes an attempt to get out of his unfeeling position. But, and here is the rub and that is why the disposition to a negative or a positive direction of the human spirit must have appeared inborn and unchangable to Schnitzler: a man cannot plan to feel and he cannot simply decide to feel. The emotional life upon which art and the artist depend is not a matter of freedom of choice. A man feels or he does not. In our earlier account of the writer's present relationships with Maria and Vollbringer we retraced those early parental relationships which shape his present. And these are unchangable, they would need to be modified so that the litterateur could feel. Schnitzler was not a therapist or was too much of a pessimist to believe that a person of negative disposition might have the chance of a transforming therapeutic experience: "the negative type may have an innate yearning for the essence of the positive type"; "the litterateur under the influence of a strong personal experience may seem, in one of his works, like a poet. But such deception does not last." There is no change and there is no second chance for the litterateur.

Because he has shut himself off from others, walled himself off by projection and denial, the litterateur can neither gain clarity about himself and others, nor can he grow. He remains unconvinced by his professions of love for Maria which he needs to repeat and exaggerate, the less he feels and believes them. He remains as unaware of the degree of his repetitiveness as he is of the significance of his repetitions, exaggerations, and the discrepancies between his words and his acts. The insights which we, his readers, have gained into the meaning of his relationships are those which Schnitzler mediates to us. The litterateur remains totally unconscious of them. All experiences and encounters remain external to him. He does not know the extent of his anger toward Maria nor does he recognize the degree of his spite and rage at Vollbringer. Consequently, the anger, the rage and the spite rule him and drive him on to his manipulations. He is condemned to remain a manipulator.

POSITIVE AND NEGATIVE TYPES, MANIPULATION AND ETHICS

The manipulative type became for Schnitzler a wider social and cultural problem with which he occupied himself ever more urgently. As a manipulator, the litterateur resembles other Schnitzler heroes who experiment with human beings, such as Paracelsus (1897), the puppeteer George Merklin in *Marionettes* (1903), the writer von Sala

in *The Lonely Way* (1903), Marco Polo in *The Prophecy* (1904), Hofreiter in *The Wide Domain* (1910), or Falkenir and Doehl in *Comedy of Seduction* (completed 1914). All these exploiters derive their power from their greater insight into the psychological mechanisms, the weaknesses and blindness of their victims. The need of the manipulators to explore, exploit, and control stems from their actual or imagined impotence and is a defense against it. All of them are willing to stake their lives on defending their real or imagined position of power. The effect of their manipulations on and power confrontations with their usually unsuspecting victims is almost always destructive to their victims and often to themselves. By inclination all of the manipulators are, or tend toward, the negative types Schnitzler was to describe in *The Mind in Word and Deed*. Their professions are those he associates with the negative type: e.g. litterateur-journalist (Doehl), scientist-quack (Paracelsus), adventurer-conjurer (Marco Polo). In his earlier work, Schnitzler does not see the artist figures among them as critically (e.g. Sala or Merklin) as he does the litterateur of the **"Last Letter,"** who stands at the end of the sequence of exploiters. In his earlier work, Schnitzler endows the manipulator with more insight into himself and with a more poignant need to exploit. With regard to the explorer-exploiter-artist we can perceive a definite development in Schnitzler's thought. He moved from a fascination with the psychological dynamics of the figure and the ramifications of manipulation to an ethical evaluation and final condemnation of the figure. **"The Last Letter"** has a central position in this development. In it, Schnitzler came to see through the type and to take a stand on him. In works following, Schnitzler relegated the manipulator type into the background (*cf.* the musician lover of *Therese,* 1928; the swindler father of **Fräulein Else,** 1924), or moved on to other problems.

Several critics have noted the change in Schnitzler's work after WWI. Reinhard Urbach relates it to an acceptance on Schnitzler's part of aging and death. Harry Slochower relates it to the impact on Schnitzler of the actual disintegration of the Austro-Hungarian Empire. Both factors play a role. By gaining an increasingly deeper understanding of the manipulator's psychology, an understanding sharpened by his observation of the political-journalistic manipulations during the war, and by seeing the manipulator's effect on others and on the disintegration of the culture as a whole, Schnitzler was enabled to take an ethical stand on him. This stand appears to have given him the strength to accept for himself the powerlessness which his manipulators are not able to accept and to renounce for himself, in so far as he identified with the manipulative artist-leader, the fascination with this artist type. Schnitzler anticipates the critique of, and in **"The Last Letter"** resolves the claims of, the manipulative artist-leader. During the twenties and into the forties these figures were to be given a much more extensive treatment and analysis by Thomas Mann as Cipolla (*Mario and the Magician,* 1929) or as Adrian Leverkühn (*Doctor Faustus,* 1948). Simultaneously with Schnitzler's portrayal, the exploitative leader type also made its appearance in Freud's *Group Psychology and the Analysis of the Ego* (1921).

In his theoretical writings of this period from the turn of

the century into the early twenties, Schnitzler dealt with the existential problem of power and powerlessness, power play and manipulation in regard to the artist in terms of the philosophical-ethical issues of freedom, chance, and determinism. In various forms, these particular problems occupied, of course, all of his Viennese and German speaking contemporaries. None of them found (nor could find, of course) a philosophical answer to the philosophical paradox. Yet each of Schnitzler's contemporaries found a different solution to it on the existential grounds of their particular life situation, their backgrounds and their needs. Schnitzler conceived of the problem in terms of his needs as a practicing playwright and novelist. The problem presented itself to him in terms of his background as a physician who was influenced by nineteenth century biological, physiological, cultural determinism, and by Mauthner's and Mach's scepticism.

> Without our belief in free will the world would not only be the stage of the most terrifying meaninglessness but also of the most unbearable boredom. Irresponsibility eliminates any ethical demand even as it becomes conscious; the ego without responsibility would no longer be ego, the world no stage of tragedy or comedy, which take place between individuals but would rather be a boring or sad farce between drives which manifest themselves by chance in this or that individual.

The fear which haunted Schnitzler in thinking about an either deterministic or irrational world with puppet-like humans was that in such a world dramatic art could not exist (it did not matter if men were puppets manipulated by unconscious or mindless impulse or by mechanistic biological, physiological and cultural determinants extrinsic of or intrinsic to the individual). In such a world, all arts along with all human activity lose their meaning and function. Art works become reducible either to a catalogue of fortuitous and random impulses made by an artist automaton of unknowable construction or to a catalogue of totally necessary and predictable mechanisms made by an artist mechanism. The fear of psychological reductionism which has haunted literary scholarship in its attitudes to Freud's theories of unconscious determinism is similiar to Schnitzler's fear of determinism.

Schnitzler confronted the deterministic and irrational positions by taking an existential stand for which he gave a psychological justification. The stand he took was a matter of belief (Glauben), a leap into ethics, so to speak. His justification was that without such a belief there was no possibility for man to develop ego functions, consciousness, culture, and art, all of which constituted for him a meaningful personal and social life. Schnitzler's stand runs parallel to Freud's as expressed in his ego psychology of the early twenties, with the decisive difference that Freud was never troubled about the determinist position and never thought that such a position excluded an ethical point of view. On the contrary, he found it acceptable to derive ethics and cultural achievement from the ego ideal as shaped by the paternal image and by the culture.

Why the difference between Freud and Schnitzler? After all, they both turned to questions of man in relationship to his society in a response to WWI and the disintegration of their culture in the collapse of Austria. Freud did so with the conviction that the continuance of a social order (though increasingly threatened during the twenties) was assured by the cultural transmission of values from a basically benevolent father to a receptive son. By an understanding of the mechanisms of transmission, Freud hoped to allay the excessive control of the superego and to free and strengthen the ego so that the person could choose from among the values of the ego ideal. Freud could trust in the goodness of his paternal image and culture to provide, with some modifications, life sustaining and meaningful values. Not so Schnitzler. The negative image of his father and his different position in Viennese society led to a much deeper pessimism.

THE FATHER IMAGE AND THE LITTERATEUR IN SCHNITZLER'S LIFE

The doctor in **"The Last Letter"** resembles Schnitzler's own father. Like the doctor, Father Schnitzler came to Vienna as a tutor. Like the doctor he gradually worked his way up. While the doctor is presented as a foreigner in Milano, Schnitzler's father was a foreigner in Vienna. Both men married women of good local families. Schnitzler's father had resigned his youthful ambition to become a Hungarian Shakespeare in favor of a very successful medical practice. A well known laryngologist and art lover, he was consulted by the artists of the Viennese stage and opera. Having had to make his own way, Father Schnitzler did not regard his son's early and continued literary efforts "with undivided joy." He wanted his son to become a capable physician and considered his artistic endeavors a waste of time. Repeatedly, Father Schnitzler sought the advice of artist patients about his son's literary efforts. Such continual distrust of his capabilities, which extended to most of young Schnitzler's activities, resulted in lifelong weak self-esteem as a writer and a physician. Just as decisive as the criticism was a lack of feeling, an emotional distance, a lack of involvement of both parents in the child's life, which was all the more damaging as it was coupled with a compensatory concern, even an indulgence on the part of his mother, for his physical welfare.

The father, although not denying his Jewish descent, attempted to fit into Viennese society by making a success of his career as a physician and in so doing neglected other values. Like many of his 19th century rationalist-materialist contemporaries, he did not transmit to his son a religious or cultural value orientation. His mother's side of the family compensated to some extent for this lack of a valid cultural identification. Hence, removed from a strong Jewish identity by one generation, burdened with a weak and ambivalent father identification, not quite at home in Viennese society, Schnitzler was more critical of the culture as a whole than Freud. He was excessively sensitive to its lack of sustaining values and finely attuned to the dangers inherent in its disintegration. Moreover, the anger, competitiveness, and frustration between Schnitzler and his father could never be worked out. Their distance to each other did not allow them to come close enough to each other either in love or in hatred to resolve the oedipal relationship. Much like the litterateur, the

Schnitzlers were much too busy and escaped into activity as a substitute for emotional contact. As a consequence, whatever paternal values Schnitzler held unconsciously were negative and not very trustworthy because they were contaminated by unresolved anger.

The litterateur represents that part of Schnitzler as an artist in which he embodied his own most negative and destructive side, the part of him that was the true son of the bad father. Like the litterateur, the youthful Schnitzler, as he tells us in his autobiography, liked to identify with, even though he could not quite play, the roles of the passionate lover, of the promising, misunderstood poet and of the dandy about town in search of erotic adventure. He remarks about his earlier childish manipulative role playing and adolescent playacting that they may have been "as responsible for my early poetic productions as an inborn poetic drive." The emotional distance and the apparent lack of feeling, the restlessness as a way of avoiding both closeness with others and reflection, all these Schnitzler attributes to himself.

His insight into the litterateur's unfeelingness, alienation, confusion, manipulativeness and underlying rage derive from personal experience. The image of the negative father and the negative son left Schnitzler with the conviction that if such a father totally determined his son, the son could not help but be inescapably bound to him and to the core of his deadly anger. Values and ethics derived from a relationship with such a father could not but lead to death and disintegration. Moreover, if the son is thus determined, he cannot engage emotionally with the father, never come to a confrontation, and never resolve the anger. Thus father and son remain locked into an unredeemable vicious cycle until they are both destroyed. We should remember that the negative type, though possessing a yearning for the positive type's attributes of honesty and truth, is incapable of changing from his position of negation. He is innately negative and a person is either a negative or a positive type. To get out of the position of the litterateur, there was for Schnitzler no other way but to assume the creation of new values, values free of the destructive father image. Hence, what I have called his leap into ethics. Needless to say, Schnitzler did have enough of an identification with good parental images (especially from his mother's family) so that he was not identical with his litterateur. It was these identifications which made possible the leap into ethics.

Moreover, through the practice of his art over the years, in his constant evocation of the manipulative type, his fears, his oedipal constellation, his destructiveness, Schnitzler gathered ever more strength against the type, and finally freed himself from him. His art thus helped in his salvation. But in his mind it could have this effect only because he had taken a stand. Art was and remained unredemptive for the litterateur.

CONCLUSION

In the neo-romantic and expressionist movements of Schnitzler's age from about 1890 to 1930, many writers identified with the unfeeling artist, the poet who suffers from the impotence of the heart with whom we began our

essay. None of them saw as clearly as Schnitzler his deadly potential. The destructive artist whose portrayal begins to dominate Austrian and German literature at this time in various variations differs from his romantic predecessors in several respects. The artist hero of Hoffmann or Mörike, for example, challenges the father figure but he uses his art to transform his challenge into a literary symbol. He gives his work of art to the father as the representative of society in restitution for the challenge. He may fail and destroy himself but he does not deliberately use his art against others. The artist figure of the turn of the century almost seems to be a new breed. The father-son relationship which shapes the artist has become more distant, complex, angrier. The artist-son is more repressed than his predecessor. He is more alienated from himself and from others. He is more pretentious. He directs his challenge against the father figure or his surrogate indirectly and surreptitiously, with much spite and venom. He deflects some of his anger against the woman in the triangle and, like the litterateur, he may be freer in expressing his murderous impulses against her. His art is a tool in manipulation and control and ultimately a weapon designed to destroy others. As a comic figure in the works of the period, he remains ignorant of all his designs (e. g. Detlev Spinell in Mann's *Tristan,* 1903); as a tragic figure he may be granted a measure of insight into his plight and accept some responsibility for it (e. g. Adrian Leverkühn in Mann's *Doctor Faustus,* 1948).

Schnitzler's portrayal of the destructive type is an early example of the figure. Schnitzler understood the type more clearly than his contemporaries did and he assigned him a larger role in his cultural scheme. He foreshadows the writer become politician. The editor (and author) as counter types break through and break down by analysis the omnipotence fantasy of the destructive type. But the device of introducing an editor does not strike me as quite powerful enough. He is developed too little to carry effectively the heavy burden of putting the reader into an analytical frame of mind and of destroying the litterateur and all he stands for. Schnitzler probably kept the editor (and thus himself) in the background because in rejecting the manipulative artist-saviour he did not want to create a new saviour.

Schnitzler took seven years to complete the tale. He identified long and closely with its characters and found it hard to resolve the emotional problem they represented. Only by his leap into ethics and by his continued artistic work was he able to resolve the dilemma they posed, the private and personal dilemma as much as the cultural one. He may not have published the tale because he felt that the problem was too personal, the social message not strong enough, and the objectifying device of the editor too weak to assure audience understanding. He was after all one of the first to create such an artist figure and to see through it dispassionately, a feat Thomas Mann was not able to do until *Mario and the Magician* (1929). His expressionist contemporaries were not capable of understanding their artist figures, much less of differentiating themselves from them or of showing their readers how to differentiate themselves and free themselves from their influence. They and Mann remained puzzled by the destructive artist's paradoxes, spell-bound by his saviour stance and explored the figure until he became a commonplace. Schnitzler, having faced the problem of the destructive artist sooner and at greater depth than his contemporaries, overcame it sooner than they did and was left free, in his last works, to explore other and, as in [*Rhapsody: A Dream Novel*], more humane and optimistic concerns.

> Ursula Mahlendorf, "Arthur Schnitzler's 'The Last Letter of a Litterateur': The Artist as Destroyer," *in* American Imago, *Vol. 34, No. 3, Fall, 1977, pp. 238-76.*

Frederick J. Beharriell   (essay date 1977)

[*In the following excerpt, Beharriell traces elements of "autobiography and realistic portraiture" in* Fräulein Else.]

Fräulein Else is thought by some to be [Schnitzler's] most impressive fictional achievement. At the same time, consisting as it does of an inner monologue of a nineteen-year-old girl written when Schnitzler was sixty, it has seemed to represent a *tour de force* of sheer imaginative creativity. In February 1925, Schnitzler wrote to a former fellow student, a G. Nobl, who had apparently inquired as to the real-life model for the fictional Else:

> Now, concerning your specific question, "Fräulein Else," as I pictured her, never lived, and the incident I related is completely freely invented. Naturally, one will find traits of "Fräulein Else" duplicated in many a girl one has known, and I myself could name more than one female from whom I, partly consciously and partly unconsciously, borrowed for the figure of Else. Certain events that occur in Else's family took place, as you probably know, in my circle of relatives, and the young daughter of the unfortunate lawyer, my cousin who died so young, was actually named Else. There is absolutely nothing else in my story that has any connection with reality in the narrower sense of the word.

[Schnitzler's autobiography, *Jugend in Wien,* published in 1968], however, shows that the central plot situation of *Fräulein Else,* the dilemma of an attractive girl who is forced to approach a lecherous older man for a large loan, was not invented, but is based on a real-life experience. The story of Schnitzler's maternal uncle, Edmund Markbreiter, runs through the autobiography like a melancholy refrain. Like Else's fictional father, Uncle Edmund was a famous attorney whose extravagance and irresponsibility brought him repeatedly in peril of public scandal and imprisonment. He it was who had, as Schnitzler notes, a daughter Else, "clever, pretty, and tart," of around Schnitzler's own age, and who, like Fräulein Else, died young. The autobiography shows that in the summer of 1887 Schnitzler had to accompany Edmund's young and attractive sister-in-law, Dora Kohnberger, on a "painful visit" to a "family friend" to plead for a large loan in order once again to rescue Uncle Edmund. This family friend, like Dorsday in the *Novelle,* was a bachelor, a wealthy art dealer, and an unsuccessful wooer of Dora. In the long, embarrassing interview, Schnitzler reports, the wealthy

admirer, like Dorsday, conducted himself toward the attractive suppliant "with something less than good taste."

A second real-life source was the notorious Veith affair in 1908. The fictional Else, it will be recalled, is at least in certain moods, sometimes consciously and sometimes unconsciously, convinced that her father foresaw and counted on the probability that Dorsday would demand sexual favors in return for the loan. "Otherwise he could have telegraphed or come himself." This striking motif of the upper-class father who "sells" his daughter's favors parallels the Veith scandal. A *comes romanus,* "Conte" Veith, had over a period of years procured the favors of his own daughter, known in society as "Komtesse Mizzi," for cash, to numerous Viennese aristocrats. The father, in fact, always waited below to collect the money, of which he kept careful records. For years the Viennese police condoned the arrangement because, according to one report, the customers were all "highly placed cavaliers." When the matter finally became a public scandal, Komtesse Mizzi, like Else, killed herself, though by "going into the Danube," rather than with Veronal. The scandal was discussed at length in the press, and was such common knowledge that Otto Brahm could refer to the "Conte Veith" without further explanation in a letter to Schnitzler of July 3, 1909.

It is, however, not only the central plot idea and situation that are thus rooted in actual events. The characters, too, prove to be based, in their salient qualities, on clearly iden-

Schnitzler circa 1894.

tifiable models. Else's father, for example, though he never actually appears in the *Novelle,* is a vividly realized, indeed a memorable personality. A gifted and renowned lawyer, he is described by colleagues as "a genius." His grace and charm are strangely conjoined with a child-like irresponsibility that keeps him constantly on the brink of bankruptcy, and which leads him to the fatal embezzlement that precipitates the story's crisis. For this unusual combination of traits Schnitzler clearly drew not only upon the model of his uncle, already noted, but upon that of his gifted maternal grandfather, Philipp Markbreiter, a medical doctor, doctor of philosophy, and founder and editor of a medical journal. Grandfather Markbreiter had inexorably succumbed to an all-consuming gambling mania, recklessly squandering his substance in stock market and lottery. Among the shocking examples of his grandfather's frequent crises, Schnitzler relates how Dr. Markbreiter, immediately after the wedding, borrowed back the dowry he had just paid to his daughter's new husband, as he needed the money to pay a gambling debt: the dowry was never restored. Even late in his seventies Dr. Markbreiter, who still possessed his "sophisticated charm," travelled each winter to the gaming tables of Monte Carlo, "and the family was regularly forced to send him—usually more than once—the money for his return ticket, since he consistently lost all available cash at the roulette tables." There is thus a component of painful personal experience in the figure of Else's gifted but feckless father, and later in the powerful *Spiel im Morgengrauen,* where Schnitzler traced in detail the tragic psychology of the gambling neurosis.

Philipp Markbreiter's son, Edmund, in what Schnitzler saw as a hereditary decline of the family line, had reproduced in even more extreme forms the personality flaws of his father. He too, though a famed attorney, was in Schnitzler's words "an incorrigible spendthrift and stock-market gambler," constantly facing scandal, financial ruin, and prison. The whole circle of relatives and friends were repeatedly called upon to give or lend in order to rescue him. Another uncle, Anton (Toni) Schey, had had to come to Edmund's rescue so frequently that his contributions eventually amounted to nearly a quarter-million gulden. And just as Else's father, after repeated borrowings, was forced to sign a humiliating undertaking that he would never again approach the relatives, "especially Uncle Bernhard," so in real life Schnitzler's Uncle Toni had finally, on a certain date, made in his account book the eloquent entry, "To the good-for-nothing scoundrel (*Haderlump*) E. M. (Edmund Markbreiter) for absolutely the last time, two hundred thousand gulden, under the condition that he never dares come into my sight again." From that time on Uncle Toni seized every opportunity to show this entry to relatives and acquaintances.

When Else reflects in wonderment on her parents' extravagant life-style, and in particular on the gala New Year's Eve banquet for fourteen which they gave in spite of their near bankruptcy, it is clear that the novella is recalling the lavish gatherings attended by the young Schnitzler at Uncle Edmund's home, "where the food, the drinks, and the cigars were excellent—at the expense, it's true, of the creditors." Yet another uncle, the husband of Schnitzler's aunt Johanna, was an unsuccessful businessman who also had to be rescued more than once from the courts, and who finally did in fact end in bankruptcy. And when Else speculates that her father may be forced to "flee to America," the story is echoing the fact that a friend of the author's, a cousin of his teen-age sweetheart Fännchen, had committed forgery and was in fact forced to escape to the United States; so that the young Schnitzler could, as he puts it, "boast, among other dubious specimens in my gallery, of a friend who was under warrant of arrest." A cousin, Raoul Markbreiter, had likewise gone to America after committing embezzlements.

The figure of Else's father seems to owe little to Schnitzler's own father, a strong and successful man who, in spite of an unhappy experience when he lost his savings in the great crash of Black Friday in May 1873, normally played the role of rescuer of "defrauding and bankrupt relatives." One aspect of the Schnitzler family climate does, however, anticipate the story. Johann Schnitzler, the father, "was so full of himself," and the mother "had so completely and to the point of self-renunciation subordinated herself to her husband" that both parents—in spite of their unquestioned love—took less part in the inner development of their children, and "brought to this development far less genuine and encouraging understanding than they ever could have admitted." Later when discussing, significantly, his own eighteenth year (Fräulein Else is nineteen) Schnitzler stresses again this inability of his parents to establish genuine rapport and sympathy with their children; and of his relationship with his brother Julius he writes that it was more hearty (*herzlich*) than intimate (*innig*). In all this there is an obvious model for Else's complaint that no one, and especially not her father or her mother, understands her: "Mama is rather stupid. She knows nothing about me at all"; "in our house everything is passed off with a joke, though nobody really feels like laughing. Everyone is afraid of the others, and everyone is alone."

Nor does Schnitzler, in the autobiography, spare his parents from the charge of materialism and greed, a theme which echoes through *Fräulein Else* in the recurring motif of the "buying and selling" of women. Else mentally accuses her father of offering her favors to Dorsday, and cries out against a world where every girl is raised to "sell herself." This selling may be as a prostitute; or, as her friend Bertha has done, to further a career; but it is seen most often in the socially approved *mariage de convenance* of her class, like that of her friend Fanny who has married a wealthy man she detests. Else recalls with bitterness that her own parents have already attempted to pander her in marriage—her word is *verkuppeln*—to the wealthy, fifty-year-old Dr. Wilomitzer: "They only educated me in order to sell myself one way or another."

The autobiography makes clear that this bitter criticism stems from first-hand experience. Schnitzler's own parents, for example, had strongly opposed their daughter's engagement to the impecunious young doctor she loved, and whom she later married. His own father, Schnitzler says, "would sooner have married his daughter to an unloved, but rich man than to the excellent suitor she did love." Johann Schnitzler also let his unwilling son know unmistakably that the daughter of a certain wealthy stockbroker would be a most desirable match. Nor had Schnitzler forgotten that his young cousin Mathilde had been married by her parents to an older relative whose weak heart held prospects of an early death. This latter gentleman, an antique dealer with a Hungarian name and a habit of flaunting his wealth, may well, incidentally, have contributed additional inspiration for the creation of the art dealer, Dorsday. A similar incident that remained long in the author's memory was his being forbidden entry to the home of his early sweetheart Fännchen Reich, praised by Schnitzler in youthful poems, plays, and fiction: her parents saw in him a threat to their plan to marry her to a rich banker twice her age.

Thus, without questioning in any sense the elements of rational planning and of sheer creative imagination that have long been praised in Schnitzler's work, it is now possible, thanks to the biographical revelations of the last decade, to document an additional important element of personal experience and confession. It may be, also, that "reality" has some light to throw on the great unsolved problem in *Fräulein Else* criticism. For it is a curious fact that although Schnitzler's unparalleled skill in the interior monologue technique permits the reader to share the heroine's every thought, emotion, memory, and unconscious wish, with the result that Else's is perhaps the most accessible and fully revealed personality in all German literature, there nevertheless has never been any consensus on the most challenging question concerning this personality. The conflicting views in their extreme forms are, on the one hand, that Else's was, even before the Dorsday incident, a fatally morbid personality, doomed to suicide one way or another in any case. The other view sees her as a normal, even a superior person for whose immaturity, however, and puritanical Victorian training, the sudden, humiliating ordeal of public self-exhibition is an understandably fatal blow.

Of the latter school, for example, were Jonas Lesser, Max Krell, Sidney Shultz, Hans Brandenburg, *The Times Literary Supplement,* and the anonymous reviewer of the film version in *Die Literatur,* all of whom apparently consider Else completely normal. Others, like the reviewer for the *Zeitschrift für künstlerische Kultur* (March 1925), P. C. Kennedy, R. Ellis Roberts, and Edwin Muir, speak of hysteria, morbid psychology, and "neurosis ending in madness;" the most frequently recurring term in these interpretations is "pathological." In an early psychoanalytically-informed study, Victor Oswald pointed to Else's hysteria, narcissism, "seizures," exhibitionism, and death-wish, and concluded that her tragedy is a result, not of "outraged honor," but of "pathology"; Robert Bareikis's thorough and expert psychoanalytic study similarly pronounces the heroine a neurotic woman, "victim of a repressed Oedipus Complex which was never resolved in a normal manner," a product of "a disturbed childhood." Klaus D. Hoppe of the Hacker Clinic, Beverly Hills, on the other hand, analyzed Else and found no pathology more serious than "inner directedness." Robert O. Weiss, in a non-school-oriented psychological study based on Edward Strecker's pragmatic diagnostic system, concludes that before her final mental collapse Else was "a

schizoid personality, pre-psychotic," with "insoluble conflicts" and "anxiety and guilt neuroses." In what is easily the best appreciation of the story as an artistic whole, William H. Rey, while singling out Else's brief narcissistic episode at the mirror as "not normal," attributes it entirely to her harrowing predicament of the moment and insists repeatedly on her basic normality: "Else has unhealthy traits *as has every person* but she is not on that account a pathological figure. . . . Rather she is one of the most touching and noblest girl-characters in Schnitzler's late prose works . . . *a whole person* . . . by no means a narcissistic introvert . . . definitely not psychopathic, but characterized by a psychological wholeness (*seelische Ganzheit*)." The most recent study of *Fräulein Else,* a Marxist reading by Manfred Diersch, seeks to explain the "pathological" in Else's personality as the inevitable product of the sickness of "late-bourgeois" society, but it founders on the paradox of a heroine described as a pathological deviation from normality, but at the same time as a symbol of the normal, healthy citizen in a "meaningless" society: clearly Else may be called normal or pathological, but not, as Diersch seeks to do, both.

This question of the normality or psychopathy of the heroine in what is, after all, essentially a psychological study, concerns not only the central theme of the work, but the important question of whether this heroine is intended as a universal human symbol or, like the unhappy protagonist of *Flucht in die Finsternis,* an isolated pathological case. The wide differences of critical opinion certainly reflect in part the continuing highly imperfect state of the psychiatric art. It may be that we have here a question which science itself cannot answer. Even so, it may be possible to arrive at something like consensus as to the author's intent, the nature of Schnitzler's own concept of his heroine.

The first note of the idea for *Fräulein Else* in Schnitzler's posthumous papers reads (typed):

> A young girl enters the dining room of the mountain hotel naked. She says she was robbed. Motive: She does it to test the men who are wooing her. Better stylized.

There follow these notes pencilled in Schnitzler's difficult hand:

> She wants to see their expressions . . . Until . . . when she was in the meadow she took the side-road. . . . threw off her clothes . . . I want to see you naked. Maybe she'll grant my wish But she may enjoy it too —(illegible). Her father ruined. She learns of it in the mountain hotel, goes to the old friend. She can save him. She loved him a little . . . Meanwhile news that her father has hanged himself.

A third, typed preliminary sketch of six pages is much closer in essentials to the final version, and reads, after the key interview with Dorsday:

> She stays behind, not with hate only. Dorsday is a scoundrel and yet not only a scoundrel. He is repugnant to her and yet not only that. Certainly he'd be discreet. What is it in her that resists it? Shame? She knew that she wasn't bash-

ful. She remembered a vacation experience four years before . . .

This vacation experience is the incident when Else, knowing she was observed by two men, stood unclothed on a balcony. Obviously she wants, yet does not want to comply with Dorsday's demand: "Such a sacrifice. Is it really a sacrifice?"

It is clear from these notes that Schnitzler's original plot idea concerned a normal girl. Her appearing naked in public was to be of her own volition, a deliberate trick to "test" the reactions of her suitors. The second, pencilled version has transferred the initiative to Dorsday, a man attractive to the girl, and Schnitzler's interest has focused on the ambivalence of her reaction: she has an urge toward exhibitionism and "loved him (Dorsday) a little." In the third, typed preliminary sketch, Else's ambivalence—shame plus exhibitionism—emerges even more clearly as the center of interest.

As to the heroine's narcissism, there is nothing in Schnitzler's notes, nor in Freud's 1914 essay "On Narcissism" which Schnitzler had certainly read, to suggest that she is in any way abnormal. To the contrary, Freud writes,

> The comparison of man and woman shows that there are fundamental differences between the two in respect of the type of object choice. . . . A different course is followed in the type most frequently met with in women, which is probably the purest and truest feminine type. With the development of puberty the maturing of the female sexual organs, which up till then have been in a condition of latency, seems to bring about an intensification of the original narcissism, and this is unfavorable to the development of a true object-love . . . there arises in the woman a certain self-sufficiency (especially when there is a ripening into beauty) which compensates her for the social restrictions upon her object-choice. Strictly speaking such women love only themselves. . . . Such women have the greatest fascination for men . . . as a rule they are the most beautiful . . .

Yet these earliest working sketches did not include, either, any thought of the heroine's suicide. At some point in the working out of the story, Schnitzler decided that Else would, as a result of the crisis, take her own life. That in Schnitzler's view this new development also implied a hereditary pathological taint is clear from a typical passage in the autobiography. One of Schnitzler's aunts had lost four children to early deaths, two dying of diphtheria within a period of a few days, whereupon the mother fell into a deep melancholy, "such as can occur," writes Schnitzler, surprisingly, "even after such a shocking event, *only in an already hereditarily predisposed* [*belastet*] *mind*, a mind which under other circumstances would perhaps never have felt or even suspected the danger of such a misfortune" (emphasis added). Others might see this mother's melancholy as a natural aftermath of such a tragic loss. That Schnitzler is at pains to emphasize that it betrays "an already pathologically predisposed mind" reminds us of the author's almost life-long preoccupation with the question of pathological mental heredity. Indeed

one of the most striking features of the autobiography is its concern with this idea. Hartmut Scheible, after a close study of the diaries has pointed to Schnitzler's suppression of his own "fears of mental illness" and of "the dangers by which he saw himself threatened." Schnitzler reports repeatedly on what he believed was a "hereditary decline" in his mother's family. Relating that her youngest brother, Julius, had shot himself at the age of seventeen, Schnitzler observes that in this tragedy "mental illness appeared with tragic clarity in the Markbreiter family for the first time." He considered his mother's sister, Irene, tainted (*belastet*). He attached perhaps undue significance to the fact that, of the children of her youngest sister, Pauline, two daughters died young, and reports that in the fates of the other three "the decline of the family continued and continues with tragic regularity." The only son, "seemingly untainted," also died young. The mother developed "nervous disorders, particularly agoraphobia." Yet another daughter, still living when Schnitzler wrote the autobiography, committed suicide in 1923, just two years before the writing of *Fräulein Else.* The fecklessness of his maternal grandfather and of his maternal uncle, Edmund, already noted, only foreshadowed the fact, according to Schnitzler, that all of Edmund's children "were living examples of the inexorably advancing hereditary decay in our family." One of these had to flee to America to escape arrest, and another, Else, died young of tuberculosis. And this seemingly exaggerated awareness of possible hereditary dangers was not confined to his own family, but extended even to actual and prospective sweethearts. When Schnitzler was twenty-three, for example, he was strongly attracted to an unusually beautiful girl of a respected and well-to-do family, "without doubt the loveliest and most maidenly of all the girls who had ever interested me and returned my interest." Yet, though she clearly preferred him to her other suitors, he was eventually and definitively put off by what he describes as "a certain fickleness and absent-mindedness (*Fahrigkeit und Zerstreutheit*)" in which he suspected something "pathological."

In the literary works the reflection of this special concern with hereditary taint can be seen from the beginning. An unpublished 103-page *Novelle* written when Schnitzler was twenty-four and entitled *Belastet* illustrates this preoccupation. The hero is a melancholy youth who feels himself too soft and sensitive for a medical career. His natural father, a "neuropathically tainted" poet with an "infinitely delicate and sensitive nervous system," comes of families on both parental sides which have already produced many cases of insanity, melancholia, and nervous illness. The hero's mother, Ella, shows an equally tainted ancestry. A doctor, a family friend, had striven unsuccessfully to prevent this tragic marriage, from which he foresaw future generations of insane descendants. At the twenty-fifth anniversary celebration of the hero's adoptive father, a prince, incurable insanity breaks out in the young man in accordance, as the story says, "with the melancholy laws of heredity."

In his autobiography Schnitzler points with some pride to the fact that this early work "treats the problem of pathological heredity in a rationalistic-romantic way before Ibsen had become known in Germany." He does not mention the obvious autobiographical significance of the father-prince's twenty-fifth anniversary jubilee, a fictional celebration which is, in fact, quite irrelevant to, and indeed distracts from the story's central theme. The personal roots of "Belastet" become clear when it is recalled that, at that same time, Schnitzler was composing a *Festspiel* for the twenty-fifth jubilee celebration of his own father's graduation and assumption of the editorship of the *Wiener Medizinische Presse*. The elder Schnitzler arranged that this occasion should be observed with elaborate ceremony, including newspaper reporters, official speeches, and an evening performance, before a highly distinguished audience, of young Arthur's specially composed playlet. In the *Festspiel* Schnitzler pictured his father's career, culminating in the jubilee ceremony itself. The autobiography observes cryptically that this *Festspiel*, like "Belastet," "is connected with the problem of hereditary taint, though, it is true, in a lighter and quite unconscious way." There is thus both internal and external evidence that Schnitzler's concern with pathological heredity had a highly personal component. Striking evidence of the unusual role played in his work by this problem has been assembled in compelling form by Robert O. Weiss. As late as 1928, in *Therese*, and 1930, in *Abenteurernovelle*, Schnitzler was writing of hereditary insanity, and his last work, ***Flucht in die Finsternis***, is a study of paranoid schizophrenia.

In the light of all this evidence, certain clues in ***Fräulein Else*** take on a new significance and pattern. Just as the autobiography's revelation of Schnitzler's long-standing special fear of venereal disease illuminates certain brief references in *Reigen* and other works, so what might well seem fleeting fancies or spur-of-the-moment exaggerations in Else's thought process are now seen to be fraught with ominous significance. Like Schnitzler, Else believes her family is *"belastet"*: "the best thing for our family would be for it to die out." The possibility that her father might kill himself comes easily to her thoughts. Her brother Rudi shows signs of instability, and seems destined to become a gambler, a libertine, or a criminal. Her father's youngest brother had shot himself at the age of fifteen, "no one knows why," and Else strikingly resembles him. She herself had frequently told Fred that she would someday take her own life: "I've known for a long time I'd end up that way. . . . it makes no difference whether at nineteen or twenty-one." As Else is nineteen, this thought clearly implies that she contemplates the probability of suicide in the foreseeable future even should the present crisis be resolved.

In light of this pattern, her thoughts of self-destruction, long antedating the current crisis, are seen to have been intended by Schnitzler to betray an innately morbid personality. Well before opening her mother's first letter, Else thinks spontaneously of her own death, speculating that even if accidental it would be generally believed to be suicide. Here again, what could be taken at first reading as frivolous or humorous fancy is seen in retrospect to be part of the morbid pattern. In the very next paragraph, still before reading the letter, her mother's intrinsically harmless words, "Don't be angry with us," are enough to cause the thought of a double parental suicide to flash through Else's mind.

A seemingly conclusive piece of evidence became known only in 1976. It concerns a significant difference between Schnitzler's concept of the Oedipus complex and the official Freudian view. There can of course be no question but that the Oedipus constellation lies at the root of Else's personality. While her stream of consciousness contains much else, the enigmas, such as the true meaning of the *Filou*, the matador, the ensign, and the Dorsday figures, and the meanings of her dreams, are as Rey has best shown, solved by the Oedipus concept. It is, then, of definitive importance that in 1926, just two years after writing the story, Schnitzler recorded his belief that the Oedipus complex is not a universal human phenomenon but is found only in sick minds. This observation was a part of his decades-long study of psychoanalysis, a study on which he kept critical notes: "It [psychoanalysis] proclaims complexes, not only the Oedipus complex, but now especially the castration complex, as a normal, regular fact of the unconscious mental life, whereas both complexes, if indeed they have any significance at all, should be considered only as pathological conditions." This opinion is, of course, at variance with Freud's, and establishes that Schnitzler conceived of Else as a pathological personality.

Thus the autobiography not only provides new evidence of the role of what Schnitzler himself called "reality in the narrower sense," but with its revelation of a personal concern with pathological heredity leads to corroboration in published and unpublished works, and finally to a solution of the central problem of the novella itself.

Additional evidence of the extent to which Schnitzler's art was rooted in personal experience is found in the extracts from published and unpublished diaries and letters located by Reinhard Urbach and published in his *Schnitzler-Kommentar*. *Doktor Gräsler, Badearzt*, for example, has its roots in a diary entry of 22 November 1908 describing a visit from a doctor who had long spent his winters in Assuan. The fifty-five-year-old man spoke movingly of his loneliness and showed letters and pictures of a forester's twenty-year-old daughter, who was eager to go with him to Egypt in spite of his own doubts of the wisdom of such an adventure. ***Flucht in die Finsternis*** incorporates not only Schnitzler's personal anxiety feelings and "hallucinations," but much from the relationship with the tragic Peter Altenberg. The exterior stimulus for *Das Vermächtnis* was the sudden death, in a fall from a horse, of a young man who lived in the same Praterstrasse building as one of Schnitzler's aunts; this building is the setting of the play. *Die letzten Masken* immortalizes an incident when a high school friend he had not seen in fifteen years rudely sneered at Schnitzler's literary fame, insulted him, and challenged, "make a play out of me: I'm crazy."

To recognise this element in Schnitzler's art is not to suggest that it is the whole, or indeed even the essence of that art. Schnitzler himself, who reflected much on the nature of the creative process, reminds us in a striking passage of the infinite complexity of the literary work:

> When a subject begins to ripen in an author's heart, this process is comparable to the expansion of a cell, whose walls gradually become thinner and porous and acquire so to speak a

thousand, a hundred thousand mouths. Everything that comes near a cell that has changed in this way can, indeed must become nourishment for it. It excludes or quickly rejects anything unsuitable; but it devours, digests, and assimilates whatever might be advantageous to it. And just as such a cell absorbs everything that can further its nourishment, its development, its completion, so does that literary subject absorb into itself everything from the poet's experiences and emotions that may be useful to it; it rejects what is unusable, expels it, and gradually spreads wider and wider, so that it finally seems to encompass the total content of the poet's soul, and indeed the poet's soul itself seems assimilated into the subject.

It is now clear that in the case of Schnitzler's art this creative process involved the absorbing of a greater component of actual experience, personal emotion, and hidden confession than had been known. This fact makes possible an answer to the question of Else's normality or psychopathy. Our study has also shown again that the often maligned biographical approach, while it can never do justice to a work as an aesthetic whole, can sometimes, as in *Fräulein Else,* solve problems of meaning and of author's intent.

> Frederick J. Beharriell, "Schnitzler's 'Fräulein Else', 'Reality' and Invention,'" in Modern Austrian Literature, *Vol. 10, Nos. 3-4, 1977, pp. 247-64.*

Paul Schlueter　(essay date 1979)

[*Schlueter is an American educator and critic whose books include* The Novels of Doris Lessing (1973) *and* Shirley Ann Grau (1981). *In his criticism he is "particularly interested in the relationship between the arts (especially literature) and religious faith (especially Christianity)." In the following review, he briefly considers the stories collected in* The Little Comedy, and Other Stories.]

It is almost a commonplace that Arthur Schnitzler (1862-1931) and Sigmund Freud—almost exact contemporaries, both physicians, both living in Vienna at the same time, the same circle of acquaintances—never happened to meet. This is especially surprising when one realizes the degree to which intuitive "Freudianism" can be found in Schnitzler's drama, notably such plays as *Reigen* (1897; translated as *Hands Around* and *The Merry-Go-Round,* and filmed as *La Ronde,* 1950), and *Professor Bernhardi* (1912), and in a variety of long and short fiction, of which *Casanova's Homecoming* (1921, seized by the New York Society for the Suppression of Vice) may be the most famous. In these and in a host of other works, Schnitzler explored bypaths of human psychology, especially those darker recesses of behavior made so emphatic when illustrated in the lives of fashionable Viennese living in the last days of the Habsburg empire. His less-than-enthusiastic evaluation of the world-weary poseurs of society are thus as valid today as when he produced the first continental version of the interior monologue at the turn of the century. Indeed, it is surprising that the five excellent tales in

[*The Little Comedy, and Other Stories*] have never previously been available in English, because they reinforce Schnitzler's place as the definitive chronicler of the excesses prevalent at the end of an era.

The five stories are all radically different—and the translations just as varied in English that ranges from stilted to fluent. The title story is about a game of deception in which a fashionable Viennese couple individually pretend to be humble, poor folk, only to acknowledge their "true" selves at the same moment and, presumably, live "happily ever after." **"Riches"** is an allegorical account of a painter who wins great wealth by gambling, who hides the money and for twenty years cannot recall where, and who, on his deathbed, remembers the location in time to tell his son; the son, also an aspiring artist, has been forced, like his father before him, to do more mundane kinds of painting to survive. The neat conclusion in which the son prodigally loses his fortune in the presence of the same jaded millionaire who was responsible for the father's getting it in the first place is both predictable and yet affecting, not just in the sense that history repeats itself on a humble scale, but even more in the way in which two lives are utterly ruined by the love of money, one by not having it, the other by having it for only a moment.

The other three stories are more substantial than these first two. **"The Son"** is a brief account of a mother's compensation for a wastrel son's abuse, and is saturated with a sense of needless guilt. **"The Judge's Wife,"** also somewhat allegorical or at least on the fairy-tale level, tells of a dedicated judge who has to sentence a life-long friend to prison; the judge makes the sentence more severe than necessary because of his duke's presence in the courtroom, but he discovers not only that the duke reverses the sentence, but also that he gains the judge's wife as a mistress. Whether or not the story, as the book's jacket states, "strikes a blow for feminine liberation," is problematic; more likely, it merely suggests that not one of the principals in the story knows how to relate openly and candidly with another, except for the duke, and as a consequence all have their lives affected adversely.

The final story, **"Dying,"** is by far the best—and longest. It is also the one with the greatest psychological depth and perplexity. A young man, knowing he is gradually dying, attempts by travel and other means to dramatize his plight; his fiancée, who has sworn that she will die with him, accompanies him in a fruitless effort to find a peace other-wise denied him. Filmed for television (according to the book's jacket), and clearly anticipating *Love Story,* **"Dying"** captures remarkably well the self-induced despair and pity present in a man who cannot accept either his impending death or his unfulfilled life. The love the couple had shared thus becomes a form of mutual contempt. In all respects, the story is well told—and well translated by Harry Zohn.

Schnitzler, a very wise man, not only captured the moment of jaded, morbid self-defeat in his work, he also was able to embue this feeling with a sardonic, melancholic sense of pointless introspection. These five stories are a fine tribute to his talent.

Paul Schlueter, in a review of "The Little Comedy and Other Stories'," in Studies in Short Fiction, *Vol. 16, No. 3, Summer, 1979, pp. 244-46.*

Lee B. Jennings   (essay date 1981)

[*Jennings is an American educator and critic who has written extensively on myth, archetype, and the grotesque in German literature. In the following essay, he considers decadent aspects of* Traumnovelle.]

The term 'decadent' as applied to Schnitzler's work serves one useful purpose: it relates this work to the socio-historical background out of which it grew and to the trends of thought prevailing at that time and place. Yet the term has its drawbacks.

First, the concept of 'decadence' usually applied is a narrow one, developed by literary scholars (largely on the basis of Schnitzler's work, a dubiously circular procedure) and perpetuating itself within their circles. The features it comprises—epigonal 'lateness,' effeteness, enervation, *carpe diem* sensualism, unreality feelings, and the 'all-the-world's-a-stage' syndrome—are ones with which we have no quarrel; but much is hereby excluded which belongs not only to the general understanding of the term but also to its usage in the study of world literature. This is a tame decadence, without diabolism, horror, depravity, untrammeled hedonism, overriding aesthetic elitism, or even a serious questioning (as opposed to discreet circumvention) of traditional mores. It is a decadence more of attitude than of practice, one with which one can live comfortably.

Secondly, the term implies a socio-historical relevance which it may not actually have. It has recently been suggested that the 'decadent' *Weltanschauung* of Schnitzler and his Viennese contemporaries was not so much a true mirroring of the condition of the Austro-Hungarian Empire, which was not in a recognizable state of decline in the heyday of 'decadence,' as it was a fashion adopted by politically disenfranchised intellectuals.

Thirdly, 'decadence,' like 'Biedermeier,' is one of those unfortunate terms that carry some ineradicable residue of opprobrium. Its introduction into literary considerations is of necessity accompanied by apologies and defences, as if some charge of dissoluteness and moribundity were being made. As a result, melioristic tendencies are mobilized, the basic wholesomeness of Schnitzler's works is inappropriately stressed, and the reading of a work may be distorted.

Traumnovelle contains one of Schnitzler's bolder scenes—a dance at which all the women are nude. This surely smacks of decadence, and one suspects that the secondary literature has been at pains to stress the basic non-decadence of the work as a result of this. It thus becomes important to examine the author's standpoint here, in so far as it is determinable. Is he advocating, condemning, or merely recording the sexual permissiveness here embodied, or is this a false issue? No clear answer may be found, but it is hoped that posing the question may clear the air and further a more objective appreciation of the work.

Traumnovelle ends on an 'upbeat' note: the sanctity of marriage and of the family is hinted at, and, as one interpreter has claimed, the humanistic tradition is upheld [William H. Rey]. Whether this is a virtue or a flaw can be argued. An 'upbeat' ending of a 'downbeat' work can be regarded as a structural inconsistency, and we have surely progressed beyond the belief that a work of art must be overtly edifying.

The lack of a clear standpoint on the part of an author may serve an artistic or even (paradoxically) a didactic purpose. Brecht's 'epic theater' is a case in point, as is Kleist's posing of moral dilemmas or Kafka's cultivation of dreamlike incongruity. An author's ambiguity may indicate that he is attempting to work out his own perplexities and to pose questions that have no ready answer, in which case his perplexities and those of the reader may enter into a captivating resonance. Or, if his attitude is more sovereign, self-assured, or condescending, he may feign perplexity in order to induce the reader to arrive at conclusions that are already clear in his (the author's) own mind.

Schnitzler's ambiguity does not fit easily into these categories. He is nothing if not sophisticated and knowing, and he is hardly an author we should expect to involve the reader in his own metaphysical gropings and existential quests. There are, however, unanswered questions in his work that tend to be masked by the air of sly omniscience and professional aplomb projected by his narrators.

We should like to know, for instance, how Fridolin's peevishness is supposed to be taken by the reader when he (Fridolin) finds out that his wife harbours adulterous lusts not unlike his own. Are we supposed to chuckle at the naïve outrage of a male chauvinist given a dose of his own medicine, or is the author naïvely underwriting a double standard? We are similarly baffled by Fridolin's resentment at the hostility implicit in Albertine's dream of laughing at his execution while she herself (in the dream) is engaged in a prototypal 'love-in.'

At this point we face the question of Schnitzler's psychological insight, a matter which has been considerably contaminated by our knowledge that Schnitzler was in some way acquainted with Freud's work, or thought along lines similar to those of Freud, or at least lived in the same city. An imaginative author may anticipate a psychological doctrine, especially if it is a valid one—but he does not usually formulate it. To imply, as some seem to do, that Schnitzler might have brought forth the doctrines of psychoanalysis if he had but cared to do so is fatuous, and Freud's polite homage to Schnitzler must be understood in this light.

Fridolin may be justified, in the author's eyes, in believing that his wife is responsible for her dreams. If he realizes this, however, he is not quite the *naïf* he otherwise appears to be. Perhaps we are supposed to marvel at the hidden truth in his own dim and palpably inequitable opinion that the dream reveals something amiss in his relationship with his wife. There remains a nagging suspicion, however, that we are not supposed to marvel at Fridolin's psychological intuition at all, but rather to laugh at his irrational belief that persons can be held responsible for their dreams.

Like many persons before and since Freud, Schnitzler is depth-psychologist enough to believe that dreams may be symbolic expressions of deep feelings and repressed thoughts. What bearing these feelings and thoughts have on our waking lives, however, is not at all clear. It is doubtful, for instance, if Schnitzler shares Freud's estimation of the degree of suppressed hostility present, or inherent, in most close personal relationships. If he does approximate Freud's thought in this respect, then Albertine's dream, being a quite normal phenomenon, reveals no particular crisis and is no cause for alarm. If there is no approximation to Freud's dream theory at all, then Fridolin's alarm is likewise uncalled for. Most probably Schnitzler is treading some middle ground of dream theory, so that author, reader, and Fridolin are equally in the dark about the importance to be attached to Albertine's dream. The symmetry of the work may demand that Albertine's subjective experience of largely uncontrollable fantasies be set equal to Fridolin's escapade in their marriage-threatening potential; but neither common sense nor Freudian doctrine supports this view.

The general impression we get of Fridolin is that of a beloved rascal used to getting his own way, or a more emancipated version of the fairy-tale fool who blunders into demonic perils but is ultimately saved by his basic innocence. We may tend to overlook the fact that his innocence, much more so than that of his wife, is the result of chance circumstance. There is little reason to think that he would avoid an extramarital liaison if he were not continually thwarted in his efforts to have one, or that he will avoid any in the future; nor do we know whether the author disapproves of such behaviour or perhaps considers it permissible and non-threatening within the existing social code. As a result, we cannot judge whether the renewed marital harmony indicated at the end represents any clear progress. The story has the air of a fable without a moral, yet it is not clearly a cynical anti-fable bearing out the perplexity of modern man adrift among changing values. Schnitzler, while faithfully recording a collison of mores, not only declines to take sides but apparently fails to notice that side-taking is something that might be expected of him.

Fridolin does have a basic problem, the elaboration of which could be a valid implicit aim of the author: his schizoid lack of self. Here we might glimpse a timely problem intuitively grasped but as yet unsolved. The very constitution of the story defeats this view, however. The stress on dream (in Albertine's case) and on a dreamlike real experience (in Fridolin's case) detracts somewhat from any implied statement by the author on the relative chaos of raw existence as a fitting environment for psychic fragmentation. The transition to a dream world in Fridolin's nocturnal wanderings, especially in the too-striking coincidence of the secret society's password, 'Dänemark' (a country which was the scene of the couple's previous near-indiscretions), is made too plain for this. Life does not simply become dreamlike here; it arouses suspicion of being

or approaching an actual dream or illusion, subject to its own laws, defying logic but symbolically congruent, telling, however, little about the hero's normal waking experience or his reactions to it.

Fridolin wavers from moment to moment between love and hostility, familial devotion and unencumbered pleasure-seeking, professional dedication and vagabondism—a legitimate standpoint for a fictional hero, except that it seems to be unattended by any indication on the part of character or author that this veritable oscillation of personalities is taking place or that there is anything unusual or ominous about it.

Fridolin returns home, after repeated mindless gallivanting in search of he knows not what, to find that his straying, which may or may not be his natural right, may have been forgiven, providing that there was anything to forgive. Although in the final conversation between husband and wife it is suggested that the two have finally 'awakened' to a more responsible and conscious form of existence, there is really no assurance that things will not get dreamlike and uncertain again, nor is there any real conviction that this would be a bad thing, since the dreamlike condition was not all that unpleasant. By putting Fridolin's mask, which she has found, beside herself in bed, Albertine may be forgiving him (as he thinks), but she may also be accusing him. Perhaps she is making a symbolic point: that he has only personae, but no real self.

There are unanswered questions about Fridolin's nocturnal escapade, assuming that we are to understand it as real, not imaginary. Commentators are accustomed to refer to the arcane doings he worms his way into as an 'orgy,' yet it is a curiously restrained one. The women at the dance are nude—but why are the men fully clothed? Why do the participants show up dressed as monks and nuns, and why is church music played? Why is it all so grimly solemn, and why is the violation of secrecy subject to such draconian punitive measures? One can understand that the celebrants would not like word of their apparently aristocratic conclave to filter down to the masses, but they even seek, unrealistically, to conceal their identity from each other. It seems unlikely that their indiscretion, if found out, would have resulted in anything so drastic as public prosecution or serious ostracism by their peers, the elaborate mechanism of discretion being what it was.

When the Unknown Woman 'sacrifices' herself to protect Fridolin (one gathers, by submitting to the sexual advances of the men present), why does she feel sufficiently disgraced to commit suicide (as it is later suggested that she has done)? At an orgy one would expect less rigid standards of respectability to prevail. It seems doubtful, in fact, that this is an orgy at all. The Unknown Woman reproaches Fridolin for his levity in thinking that there might be side rooms to which couples might slip off to be together. Whatever sexuality is present seems curiously displaced; it is not the real reason everyone is there.

Some have found an air of the ludicrous, perhaps of the satiric, about the activities of the secret society. It has been suggested that its gothic rigmarole may represent some misguided, reactionary attempt at élitism on the part of the common crowd. From what we can learn about the identity of the members, however, they may actually be aristocrats, not bourgeois poseurs. The idea of a group of confused burghers seeking status by way of an arcane mélange of sexual emancipation, ultramontanism, and proto-fascism has intriguing farcical possibilities, but it is not the more genteel brand of lunacy that we expect of Schnitzler.

Similarly, Fridolin's bumbling efforts to break into the group have been seen to represent the prototypal predicament of the disenfranchised outsider trying to get into the inner circles. Fridolin, like other less enlightened bourgeois types in Schnitzler's works, affects an aristocratic-military hauteur in his attempts to extricate himself, but a penchant for social climbing was not what brought him there. He is frustrated in his attempt to inject a chivalric rationale into the absurdity surrounding him; whether the cavaliers are real or would-be aristocrats, these are not the rules by which they are playing now. One of them tells him: 'Es handelt sich hier nicht um Genugtuung, . . . sondern um Sühne.'

Schnitzler's dramatic method is the intellectualization, the refinement of the Viennese waltz. . . . His power lies chiefly in the creation of an atmosphere—a dim twilight atmosphere as of autumn evenings crowded with reminiscence.

—*Ashley Dukes, in his introduction to "Reigen," "The Affairs of Antol," and Other Plays, by Arthur Schnitzler, translated by Marya Mannes and Grace Isabel Colbron, 1917.*

It is difficult to know when Schnitzler is being ironic—possibly he did not always know himself—but this description does not seem to have been written with tongue in cheek. There is too much grimness, poignancy, and true horror about the passage, and the air of erotic fascination, though somewhat overwrought, rings true, as it would not if a parody were intended.

There is a curious ritualistic air about the proceedings. The religious garb and music can only be understood as blasphemous, and it seems clear that Fridolin has stumbled onto a society of Satanists. This may explain the extreme secrecy measures; at least it provides a more compelling reason than does discreet lasciviousness. To be sure, the usual rituals of Satanists, as described, for example, in the black mass chapter (XIX) of Huysmans's *Là-bas,* are imperfectly represented—though there are faint resemblances, as in the arrival by cab at a secluded estate in a dimly lighted suburb.

The 'sacrifice' of the Unknown Woman may actually represent her serving as the human altar in a black mass. To be sure, this leaves her trepidations unexplained, unless it

was understood that she was to be ritually murdered afterward. Her apparent suicide by poisoning falls out of this pattern, though on the other hand poisoning was much favoured by the French Satanists. The aromatic Mediterranean scent noticed by Fridolin may be nothing but incense, and it is certainly quite different from the stench of burning atropine-bearing herbs mentioned by Huysmans.

Thus, while Schnitzler cannot be said faithfully to depict a Satanistic ritual, neither can he be said not to depict one at all. His intent is probably to create an enigma, to confront his hubris-ridden hero with a situation that wholly eludes his categories of experience while appearing to be compatible with them. The result is to enhance the life-is-a-dream theme; reality does resemble a dream when its sense-giving pattern becomes less discoverable. At the same time, Fridolin is confronted with a situation that bears out the fragmentation of his own personality. His reactions fluctuate wildly between indignant bravado and amused contempt, as his interpretation of the data before him oscillates. His quest for adventure has led him to the outer limits of his ken, and even his viewing of the body in the morgue leaves him baffled. He is in danger of casting aside what ego he has left to enter into the realm of raw, unordered experience, a danger that the founders of Christianity may have had in mind when they said that this world is of the devil.

While it is tempting to find a link between Schnitzler's allusion to Satanic rituals and the decadent writers of the past, it is still true that *Traumnovelle* is a predominantly anti-decadent work. The dance ritual is not made to look particularly attractive, and we note in Fridolin only idle curiosity and titillation, not the mingled ecstasy and abhorrence of the true decadent. Schnitzler does appear to have drawn upon the decadent tradition, however, to insert into his work an oblique but pointed warning about the dangerous path being tread by his unwittingly impressionistic hero.

The self-sacrifice of the Unknown Woman, and Fridolin's attempt to defend her, have been regarded as a touching emergence of altruism in a hedonistic milieu—but toward what end? Neither she nor Fridolin have ever seen each other before, and their infatuation with each other scarcely seems a sufficient reason to place their lives at stake. One has to assume overpowering mindless devotion to an attractive intruder on her part, and a reflexive defence of honour, coupled with the hope of an amatory conquest, on his part. To say that this is all symbolic is to beg the question, since in a work that implies some claim to realism successful symbols must first be successful as representations of real things. Is it perhaps Schnitzler's intent to make a mockery of altruism? In this case he would emerge as an anti-altruist, in itself a tenable standpoint. But the care with which he arranges to have the motif of self-sacrifice appear also in Albertine's dream makes it seem that he attaches some positive importance to it, and this detracts again from any claim to productive cynicism that might be made for him in this instance. Likewise, when Schnitzler appears to sanctify domesticity at the end of his tale, this occurs at the expense of his role as a chronicler of existential confusion.

In the realm of decadence one man's poison is another man's meat. What to one may presage Vandals at the gates may appear to another as a healthy loosening of pointless traditional strictures. Now, as in Schnitzler's day, more may be revealed about the critics's preconceptions than about the author's work when such matters are discussed—especially if the author was as skilled a 'shadow-boxer' as Schnitzler. Our present reflections indicate that Schnitzler's humanistic meat was tainted, his cynical poison detoxified.

It would take considerable sociological expertise to determine what was considered permissible and impermissible, and by whom, in Schnitzler's milieu as compared to that of the current reader. It has been pointed out that the gap between public and private behaviour was somewhat larger in earlier times, and this may help to explain Schnitzler's apparent lack of shock at what went on behind closed doors. One gets the impression upon reading this work, however, that Schnitzler's standpoint—though his taciturnity may evoke an unjustified impression of sophistication and modernity—was approximately that of a somewhat conservative person with liberal leanings in our own day. We surmise that he considered public nudity and sexual promiscuity shocking, that beneath his compassion for woman's plight lies a belief that philandering is a man's privilege, that his respect for the institution of marriage is tempered by considerable scepticism about it. Bourgeois mores may elsewhere be controverted in the name of humanitarianism, as appears to be the case in *Fräulein Else,* but their basic validity is the presupposition for the story's effect. When Schnitzler depicts moral relativism, amorality, or (as some would say) emancipation in his characters, his attitude towards them remains unclear. A desire to shock or titillate can never quite be ruled out. Probably his conviction as to the sanctity or viability of bourgeois and idealistic traditions wavered as much as do those of many present-day authors. In his confusion, at least, he was ahead of his time.

It can be questioned, of course, whether Schnitzler's personal views have any bearing on the appreciation of his literary works. It is indeed possible to regard him solely as an aesthetic artificer or as a chronicler of his milieu. If we do admit, however, that the author's cultural or ideological orientation, either implicit or explicit, plays a role in the understanding of his work, then our task is theoretically twofold. We must first establish the socio-historical milieu of the author, with its permissions and its taboos, and then we must take account of this knowledge in evaluating our own reaction to the work. There are hopeful signs that steps are being taken in this direction in Schnitzler's case.

The term 'decadence' seems at first glance to provide a point of reference whereby Schnitzler's work can be understood in its proper ambience; but on closer examination it proves to undermine this purpose. The term inevitably implies an affinity between the describer and the thing described which runs counter to Schnitzler's studied aloofness. Also, while seeming to further historical objectivity, the term tends to be contaminated by present-day, ideologically tinged and idiosyncratic notions of what is wholesome. Further, it has a way of evoking inappropriate

efforts to 'rescue' the author from charges of subverting such idealistic constructs as the *Humanitätsideal.*

We cannot, of course, employ the confused mores of our own day in attempting to re-examine the moral or behavioural implications of Schnitzler's work. It seems unlikely, however, that the boundary of the permissible has shifted so radically as to affect the interpretation of *Traumnovelle.* The work still emerges as a moral conundrum, carefully engineered so as neither to yield a solution nor to provide any clues as to why no solution is forthcoming. If Schnitzler has a message, it is that the reader is a fool for seeking messages. This seems a tenable, even cheering standpoint—until the suspicion begins to grow in the reader that, in subscribing to it, he is a greater fool.

> Lee B. Jennings, "Schnitzler's 'Traumnovelle'—Meat or Poison,'" in Seminar, *Vol. XVII, No. 1, February, 1981, pp. 73-82.*

Stanley Elkin (essay date 1982)

[*An American novelist, short story writer, and essayist, Elkin is renowned for the poetic vigor and comic ingenuity of his prose, which has prompted critics to regard him as one of the most entertaining stylists in contemporary American literature. In the following excerpt, which was originally included in Elkin's foreword to Schnitzler's* Plays and Stories *(1982), he comments on* Lieutenant Gustl *and* Casanova's Homecoming.]

Schnitzler's use of stream-of-consciousness in *Lieutenant Gustl,* though certainly innovative, is, on the face of it, clumsy, his use of the "I" in his silly, blustering young officer's interior monologue unfortunate, probably impossible (rather like trying to sustain in even so short a piece of fiction as the short story the second person point-of-view).

> How much longer is this thing going to last? Let's see what time it is . . . perhaps I shouldn't look at my watch at a serious concert like this. But no one will see me. If anyone does, I'll know he's paying just as little attention as I am. In that case I certainly won't be embarrassed. . . . Only quarter to ten? . . . I feel as though I'd been here for hours. I'm just not used to going to concerts. . . . What's that they're playing? I'll have a look at the program. . . . Yes that's what it is: an oratorio. Thought it was a mass. That sort of thing belongs in church.

People do not think to themselves syntactically; they don't remind themselves—"That was funny a week ago when she was at the Gartenbeau Café with him, and I was sitting opposite Kopetzky; she kept winking at me"—of what they already know. The effect is not only unnatural, it is insane, as talking to oneself is supposed to be insane. Yet in Schnitzler's remarkable novella all sense of the innate falseness of the point-of-view drops almost immediately away, and it is as if the author had invented for this particular character in this particular situation a diction and tense and viewpoint entirely, and distinctively, and perfectly, his own, as if Schnitzler were taking the affidavit of Lieutenant Gustl's soul. Indeed, that seems to be precisely what he's doing, giving the reader privileged information to another man's character. The effect is extraordinary and very powerful, for Gustl, with his straight, humorless failure of perception and highfalutin' notions of himself, makes a terrible witness and becomes, before our eyes, a sort of witless, unforgivable Falstaff, unregenerate and unforgettable. That this is a consequence of the very clumsiness of the point-of-view in hand-glove relation with Gustl's measly character is almost certainly the case, granting the reader not only his inside information about Gustl (and advancing, incidentally, the difficult technique of the "unreliable narrator") but a kind of licensed omniscience, and not only creating, within the small compass of a brief book, a memorable character but turning his voice into what is possibly a unique trope in literature.

Schnitzler's Casanova, in *Casanova's Homecoming,* is an even greater achievement, if for no other reason than that he has a more interesting mind than Gustl and finds himself in a more interesting situation, Casanova's problems being "real," while Gustl's are only made up, self-inflicted, the product of a locked-in imagination engined by an unrelenting egoism. But there *are* other reasons.

The character of a great man, now aging, whose deeds are "by degrees passing into oblivion" is not an unfamiliar one. Movies have rendered him for years: broken-down sheriffs and old gunfighters, all the worn-out spies come in from the cold, all the drunk docs called to draw upon depleted skills in times of crisis, have become stock stick figures in the literature. What Schnitzler has going for him in *Casanova's Homecoming* is the conception of using a legendary character—though this isn't new either; Shaw had recycled Don Juan; Joyce Odysseus—with whom we're already familiar, so that neither the protagonist nor the other characters have constantly to remind us how the mighty are fallen. We know because he is in our heads. What he has going for him further is that Casanova *isn't* called upon in emergency and, further still, that his particular depleted skills are only personal, and that all Casanova wants is to have a last fling and go home. The "only personal" is, of course, the best and most difficult situation of all, not more valuable to literature than its great other half—going home, coming to terms, resignation and acceptance—not more valuable because, finally, they are the same.

If the cliché about novelists not making good playwrights is true, as I think it is in the case of Arthur Schnitzler, it isn't because talent lapses or undergoes some radical seachange as the writer turns his attention from one form to the other but because of something in the nature of the forms themselves—that, broadly and vastly oversimplified, theater is public and political—an actor's lines are even *called* "speeches"—an occasion, while fiction, with its disregard for time—or at least length—and its concomitant gifts of extension and an almost holographic ability to project in the round, is essentially private and personal, an occasion, too, of sorts, but lonelier, no occasion at all, really.

Stanley Elkin, "Foreword to 'Plays and Stories'," in his Pieces of Soap, *Simon & Schuster, 1992, pp. 207-14.*

Paul F. Dvorak   (essay date 1986)

[In the following excerpt, Dvorak offers introductory commentary on some of Schnitzler's best-known short stories.]

["The Widower ("Der Wittwer," 1894) is] a tale in which marital infidelity ignites a confrontation between friends. Richard, a well-to-do middle-aged man, has just lost his younger wife to illness and on the evening of the day of the funeral contemplates their life together in their summer home where so much of their life was shared. Richard also laments the fact that his best friend Hugo, "the one he most wanted to see," was not at the funeral, because like many others he had traveled off to the North Sea for the summer vacation. As his wife's possessions bring back memories, Richard fatefully uncovers a stack of letters from Hugo to his wife. Like a bolt of lightning the experiences of the past flash before him and he understands all too clearly what has happened. Richard awaits Hugo's arrival and reflects on how he will greet him; his rational decision to show understanding struggles with his desire for revenge. The story takes its final twist as Hugo reports that he is engaged to another woman and wants Richard to join him during his period of bereavement. At this point Richard's emotions gain the upper hand; he pulls Hugo to the letters lying on the piano and vents his anger, not at the infidelity to him but to his wife's memory.

[As in many of his works] Schnitzler has intertwined a moral dilemma within the framework of love and marriage. One central event, the death of Richard's wife, has precipitated the psychological wrestling match within human beings. The conflict worked out in the protagonist's mind is between understanding and the emotional reaction which Richard himself has trouble controlling. Just as Hugo's passion for Richard's wife was apparently involuntary, so too are Richard's feelings for revenge. Alongside Hugo's obvious culpability, Schnitzler allows the possibility for another interpretation, for despite his submission to passion, Hugo was in fact acting in Richard's and his wife's best interests by becoming engaged to someone else. What appears to be a very banal plot is nevertheless a very complicated interplay of the psychological forces which determine human action. Apparent melodrama reveals deeper psychological forces. Just as the initial precipitator of the plot, the sudden, unexpected death of his wife, occurred like a thunderbolt, so too did his final reaction to Hugo.

"The Dead are Silent ("Die Toten schweigen," 1897) is one of Schnitzler's best known stories in the English-speaking world. It has gone through a dozen English publications and reprintings and has been included in such anthologies as *The Smart Set* (1913) and *The Bachelor's Companion* (1944). Predictably, the plot develops from a case of marital infidelity. Emma, a young married woman, has gone off to meet her lover Franz for a secret rendezvous, while her older husband is attending an evening faculty meeting. As Emma and Franz are riding along a dark road outside of Vienna, the drunken driver loses control of the horses, the carriage topples, and Franz is thrown out and killed.

Using stream-of-consciousness and interior monologue

techniques, Schnitzler examines Emma's psychological state of mind as she contemplates how she should act. Her intuitive inclination to protect herself and her family's reputation wins out over her feelings of love for Franz and her sense of moral responsibility. She convinces herself that Franz is truly dead and rationalizes that remaining at the scene of the accident would serve no useful purpose. It would only bring needless shame upon her. Franz, she rationalizes, would have expected her to act this way, since there is nothing else she can do for him. Emma flees the scene and rushes home on foot, while the coachman is off looking for help. Having overcome several obstacles which would have given her away, Emma nevertheless cannot conceal the evening's events from the husband she has deceived for years. The dead may be silent, but the living bear the psychological burdens of guilt, which become too much for Emma. In a twist of fate she confesses her whole affair with Franz to her husband. The relief of being freed from her feelings of guilt joins with the hope that "everything will be all right again," and gives the story a positive ending.

"Blind Geronimo and His Brother" ("Der blinde Geronimo und sein Bruder," 1900) is an anomaly in the work of Arthur Schnitzler in that there is an apparent happy ending to the story. What continues to join it to the other works is the recurring theme of appearance and reality. What separates it as well is the fortuitous resolution of the conflict between Geronimo and his brother Carlo. Geronimo's blindness, psychologically speaking, is lifted as he finally realizes and accepts his brother's love for him, as he perceives in a flash the genuineness of his brother's actions. There is a contrast here between this flash of recognition and that in **"The Widower"** where a life-long relationship of trust between friends is destroyed by the realization that Hugo has been having an affair with Richard's wife. Just as all of Hugo's actions suddenly become clear to Richard, so too does Geronimo understand the meaning of his brother's actions: the words, the deeds take on new meaning. What Schnitzler has again developed is the concept of dualistic reality. The same actions and appearances can be interpreted in contradictory ways. In the case of Richard, there was irrefutable evidence, the letters from Hugo to Richard's wife, that past actions were in need of reinterpretation. In the case of Geronimo it is only inner, intangible evidence, faith and belief, which changes how he views the past.

"Blind Geronimo" is the story of two brothers who earn their living by singing and playing guitar and begging for handouts from the travelers through the Alpine passes between Austria and Italy. Geronimo has been blind for years; he lost his sight when a stone shot from his brother's slingshot struck him in the eye. Through the years Carlo has tried to repay his brother by caring for him and dedicating his life to him. Yet the remorse and guilt Carlo feels cannot endear him totally to his brother, who feels both love and hate for him. When a young traveler maliciously misleads Geronimo into thinking he has given Carlo a twenty-franc coin, Geronimo will not believe his brother's explanation that he received nothing. Carlo finally decides to steal a gold coin from one of the overnight guests at the inn to quell his brother's suspicions and anger. But Carlo

is no thief at heart or in practice. He is caught by the police and, in the moment of truth, Geronimo realizes his brother has stolen for him and finally recognizes his love.

Schnitzler's story is reminiscent of other writings of this time. Joseph Roth's novel *Job* (*Hiob*) is one more example of the Schlemihl who finally finds happiness after a life of hardship. Compacted into a short story, Schnitzler's work reveals the same positive qualities. Geronimo's and Carlo's lives will not change externally and they will continue to beg for a living. What has changed is the acceptance of their condition and of each other. Though living a simple life, they are happy, something which money, position, and wealth cannot buy. Geronimo sees the light, though he remains physically blind.

In **"The Last Letter of an Artist" ("Der letzte Brief eines Literaten,"** 1932) Schnitzler employs an ambiguous narrator, but removes the letter one step further from the reader by involving a doctor-friend of the artist who has found the letter and appends his own commentary to it. Self-irony plays an important role as the narrator analyzes himself and proceeds with the story of his love for Maria. The ostensibly correct and counter-opposed interpretation of Dr. Vollbringer, whose name implies "achiever" or "accomplisher," is contrasted with that of the effete artist, whose social position and roots in "the real world" are less firmly established. [In his *Arthur Schnitzler: A Critical Study,* 1971, Martin] Swales skillfully discusses the interplay of narrative technique Schnitzler employs in unfolding his characters' psychological states of mind and their moral position. The situation here is similar to that in **"Andreas Thameyer's Last Letter" ("Andreas Thameyers letzter Brief ")** where letter-form is used to show the characters' states of mind, but ambiguously as Swales describes. It is also similar to **"The Little Comedy" ("Die kleine Komödie")** where the two main characters independently chronicle their relationship to each other in letters to separate friends.

As he waits in the adjoining room for the death of his beloved, the artist tells the story of their love. Maria suffers from a weak heart, which the passionate romance places in even greater jeopardy. In stylized, inflated language, interspersed with statements of clear reflection, the writer comments on himself as well. The fact that the writer is attracted to the nurse as well is an indication of his fickleness, insincerity, and impressionistic being. Both characters, the artist and Vollbringer, attempt to justify their positions. In doing so the two of them reveal the shallowness and inadequacy of their respective attitudes.

"The Second" ("Der Sekundant," 1932) blends reality and dream once again. Narrated in the first person, the story tells of a young man's experiences during and after a duel. Loiberger, a well-to-do, adventuresome type, is killed by his opponent. The narrator has accepted the responsibility to inform Loiberger's young wife of what has happened. Having occasionally been a guest at Loiberger's villa, the narrator reflects on his encounters with Agathe, and upon his arrival at the villa finds himself swept away into a world of dreams and fantasies that are periodically interrupted by the reality of his assumed mission. The narrator cannot bring himself to explain the true purpose of his visit as his own repressed feelings for Agathe surface. Finally, Dr. Mülling, the narrator's associate at the duel, arrives to set matters straight. The narration then jumps to a point some years later when the narrator and Agathe, now remarried, meet again at a party. Her look merges into his "so purely, so forgetfully, so guiltlessly" with no apparent recollection of the afternoon they spent together when both of them struggled with their emotions. Dream and reality become so closely aligned that one is led to doubt even the most apparently genuine of experiences.

> *Paul F. Dvorak, in an introduction to* Illusion and Reality: Plays and Stories of Arthur Schnitzler *by Arthur Schnitzler, translated by Paul F. Dvorak, Peter Lang, 1986, pp. vii-xxviii.*

Kenneth Segar   (essay date 1988)

[*In the following excerpt, Segar examines the narrative perspective of* Flucht in die Finsternis *and interprets the story as a conflict between rationality and irrationality.*]

The story of *Flucht in die Finsternis* has been recounted in the following manner:

> Robert, a widowed *Sektionsrat* in the Austrian Ministry of Education, has had a 'nervous breakdown' and is just returning to Vienna from a long vacation which he has taken for the sake of his health. At first, the reader is led to believe that the extended leave of absence has fulfilled its purpose, that, substantially, Robert has recovered. One receives the first suspicion that all is not well yet from the multitude of minor deviations from normal thought patterns. Any one of these slight abnormalities could be regarded without great alarm, but in aggregate they appear somewhat suspicious: Robert shows evidence of hypochondriasis, forgetfulness, irritability, hypersensitivity, feelings of unreality, and compulsive thinking at the outset. There is only one physical symptom: a hysteric ptosis of the left eyelid.
>
> Gradually, as the symptomatology is augmented, the picture grows more serious. Robert develops an obsessive idea to the effect that during one of his memory lapses he might have killed his ex-paramour Alberta, as well as his wife Brigitte—Alberta from jealousy, Brigitte to regain his freedom. Nevertheless, he still has the faculty of returning to reality, to recognise these thoughts as phantasies. A euphoric period during which he rationalizes his illness is followed by more paranoid thinking and emotional depression.
>
> In Vienna his brother Otto, a prominent psychiatrist, succeeds for a time in putting Robert at his ease, and a relatively long interval of remission ensues, as the sick man regains pleasure and satisfaction in his work and resumes social contacts, but then any hopes for a permanent recovery vanish. Robert has a relapse: projecting his own guilt feelings upon his friend, Dr. Leinbach, he causes an embarrassing scene in a café house [sic]. Even though he can still control his overt

> behavior most of the time, the schizophrenic pattern becomes more and more evident in his thoughts and attitudes. Simultaneously, the paranoid symptoms increase in severity and frequency. He lives now in almost constant fear of his brother from whom he had once extracted the promise to kill him if he should ever become hopelessly insane. Characteristically, he now suspects Otto of being on the verge of insanity and interprets all of his brother's words and actions as indicative of the latter's fratricidal intentions. Cunningly he lays plans to induce Otto to return his written permission to administer euthanasia, but his suspicions merely deepen when his brother gladly complies with the request.
>
> New delusional material is added: he believes that Otto has warned other people about him, that he is being watched, that everyone is talking about him, and that Alberta's American fiancé intends to kill him. His overt behavior becomes noticeably bizarre, and in order to outsmart his brother, he intends to stage a double suicide of himself and Paula Rolf, to whom he had become engaged during his remission. In a confused state he goes to Paula's home and makes her promise to follow him to a secret place of refuge. This flight is necessary, he explains, because Alberta's mad American might do them both harm if they stayed on in Vienna. He actually leaves the capital, and while waiting for Paula's arrival, he writes an autobiographical sketch, expressing his conviction that Otto will eventually become the instrument of his destruction. Even at this point, however, the ambivalence of his life-long love-hatred for his brother remains operative as he admits his feelings of love for Otto and expresses his hope for the latter's mental recovery.
>
> Since Paula neither arrives as arranged nor sends a message, Robert is now convinced that she has betrayed him and his hiding place to Otto. The latter actually comes to investigate Robert's sudden disappearance, but the psychotic is certain that his life is in acute danger. When Otto embraces him affectionately, Robert, in a trance-like state of extreme terror, shoots his brother through the heart. Completely disturbed and frightened he flees into the open country. He is found thirty miles away, dead of exposure and the injuries contracted in his panicky flight. [R. O. Weiss, 'A study of the psychiatric elements in Schnitzler's "Flucht in die Finsternis"',' *The Germanic Review* (1958)]

The detailed analysis of the text so narrated can serve to give body to only one perspective, namely that of a fictive clinical case. The natural history of a degenerative disease is shown to rest on a complete symptomatology, a conjectural aetiology and differential diagnosis offered by the material of the text. And, indeed, the text does appear to contain descriptions which read almost as definitions of the symptoms enumerated. Take, for example, the following statement, used to document 'affective ambivalence', the condition in which otherwise mutually exclusive contrasts exist side by side in the psyche: 'Was er jetzt in sich erlebte, war nur ein Beispiel mehr für das unheimliche Auf und Nieder seiner Empfindungen, die demselben Menschen gegenüber von opferbereiter Zärtlichkeit und verzehrender Leidenschaft bis zur Abneigung, Widerwillen, Grimm, Wut und Todeswünschen zu schwanken vermochten'. In fact, this analysis convincingly documents the whole range of symptoms cited: 'flattening of emotions', 'withdrawal symptoms', 'distractability', 'flight of ideas', 'feelings of unreality', 'hallucinations' 'delusive material', 'compulsive material' and so on.

Now whilst Schnitzler clearly knows that he has produced a psychopathological study, his own description of the work does not contain so clear-cut a clinical determinism as appears in the above analysis. Thus, Schnitzler writes in a letter to Clara Katharina Pollaczek: 'Ueber die Diagnose werden wir noch sprechen. Gewiss ist die Komödianterei ein wesentliches Element in Roberts Seelenzustand, aber die Zwangsläufigkeit der Gedanken ein zweifellos pathologisches Element, das zur wirklichen Geisteskrankheit wird, sobald die Fähigkeit der Correctur wegfällt'. The 'Diagnose' and 'pathologisches Element' are countered by the capacities of a human subject, who indulges in 'Komödianterei' and has a certain 'Fähigkeit der Correctur'. And if we look back to early days of the genesis of the work, we find Schnitzler writing in his diary of 28 November 1913: '—Das rein pathologische ist nun einmal für die Kunst verloren; so rett ich mich, resp. den Helden in einen Grenzzustand, einen Kampf, in dem er unterliegt.—' And, indeed, Schnitzler's art precisely offsets his pointillistically presented case-book material, the protagonist as clinical object, by a simultaneous and pervasive narrative mode in which the protagonist is experienced as a suffering yet embattled subject. From this perspective we are dealing not with a patient in the later stages of mental disturbance but with a human being struggling not to go mad.

The author of the clinical analysis, Robert O. Weiss, states that he wishes simply to make explicit what Schnitzler has surreptitiously integrated into his text, to show that Schnitzler 'was far ahead of his time in his understanding of the dynamics of mental disease'. But, of course, his account of the story, which we have quoted in full, actually destroys the narrative strategy of the author. For, although this clinical material is indeed subtly integrated into the story-telling voice, the more palpable aspect of the narrative mode, from the first page to within lines of the end of the work, is 'hero viewpoint': the reader's awareness is essentially limited to the perceptions and experience of the protagonist. Our imaginative transference to his mind is then sustained by constant use of indirect speech or reported thought, inner monologue, 'erlebte Rede'. Of all the facets of 'hero viewpoint', it is without doubt 'erlebte Rede', the protagonist's consciousness within the authorial mode (third-person past tense), which sustains our empathetic involvement in Robert's struggle not to succumb to his mental disturbance. For example: 'Von seinem eigenen Leben gleichsam im Stich gelassen, im innersten leer geworden, hatte er allzu willig, ja, mit einer gewissen Selbstgefälligkeit eine Art Rolle für sich zu spielen begonnen, die wachsende Gewalt über ihn erlangt und allmählich gedroht hatte, sein innerstes Wesen zu verstören. Nun aber reckte er die Stirn hervor wie aus gefähr-

lichem Nebeldunst und er fühlte den Willen und die Kraft in sich, wieder gesund und—endlich wahr zu werden'.

Now this passage may be deeply ironic, both because the Novelle is structured to deny the protagonist the possibility of becoming 'wieder gesund' and because being 'endlich wahr' (as I show in my next section) means the diametric opposite of recovery. However, if the language of 'Willen' and 'wahr' and the tone of conviction are Robert's (the emphatic 'ja' his attempt at self-persuasion), the third-person past-tense narration is still also the authorial voice, here conniving at the reader's acceptance of the protagonist's sense of responsibility for his condition, and acceptance of its eradication as a genuine moral possibility. Thus 'erlebte Rede' powerfully underpins the protagonist's viewpoint, and constantly sustains our empathy.

A second method of sustaining empathy is provided by the protagonist's *remission from and insight into* his pathological condition. Both aspects of Robert's behaviour—again ironically, because from a clinical perspective they are known symptoms of 'schizophrenia, paranoid type'—help to retain the sense of the protagonist's being not unlike the 'normal' reader. Thus, during the period of remission from his worst symptoms, Robert again takes an interest in life and work, and indeed contrives to become engaged to Paula Rolf. As for 'insight' into his own pathology, Robert, on occasions throughout the work, shows himself to be aware of the absurdity of his thoughts and reactions.

Schnitzler in 1925.

Momentarily imagining that a figure standing opposite the entrance to his brother's house is a policeman come to arrest him for the murder of Alberta, he quickly corrects his bizarre view: 'Sind wir so weit? dachte er flüchtig. Dann aber lachte er. Es wäre das Neueste, sagte er vor sich hin, wegen einer Wahnidee verhaftet und zur Rechenschaft gezogen zu werden. Denn dass es nur eine törichte Einbildung gewesen war, die ihn früher überfallen, dessen war er jetzt wieder ganz gewiss'. Again in Chapter VI:

> Was für eine Tollheit, dachte er, mir einzubilden, dass ich Brigitte vergiftet habe . . . Erzählte ich, dachte er weiter, meinem Freunde Leinbach von den Gespenstern dieser Nacht, was fände er mir zu erwidern? Vor allem wohl, dass er für seinen Teil von den meisten verstorbenen Menschen seiner Bekanntschaft sich zuweilen einbilde, sie umgebracht zu haben,— ferner dass es am Ende keinen besonderen Unterschied bedeute, philosophisch betrachtet, ob man jemand wirklich töte oder ihm nur den Tod wünsche;—endlich, dass wir eigentlich alle mehr oder weniger Mordgesellen seien; und dass er von seinem Standpunkt es mir auch gar nicht übelnähme, wenn ich sowohl Alberta als auch Brigitte wirklich umgebracht hätte. Kenne ich dich, Freund Leinbach?

Albeit, in both examples, the very next sentences reveal Robert's ever-present paranoia, it is difficult to read particularly the above inner monologue, characterised by insight into his own pathology as well as by witty parody of his friend's 'philosophical' manner, and subscribe to a purely clinical account of the protagonist. The reader is manipulated into considering the possibility that the lighter realms of consciousness yet have healing power. Insight occurs as late as Chapter XIII: 'Sofort aber erkannte Robert diese Auslegung, die er eine Sekunde lang einem nichtsbedeutenden Mienenspiel zu geben bereit war, als das letzte Aufflackern einer lächerlichen, längst abgetanen Wahnidee'. Of course, such insight diminishes with the progression of Robert's condition and finally vanishes. But its presence helps to maintain our transference into the mind of the struggling protagonist long after we might otherwise have been repelled by the psychosis, and the reader is thus able to suffer with Robert in his oppressed humanity rather than merely observe and diagnose his clinical collapse.

Thirdly, in the face of Robert's increasingly abnormal behaviour, Otto (the 'Nervenarzt') suggests that his brother may be suffering from some kind of emotional disturbance but that, in his view, he is not insane and must therefore take charge of his life. Otto offers a diagnostic view of Robert's condition:

> Gewiss kommt es darauf an, mein Lieber, ob eine sogenannte Zwangsvorstellung zu weitern Konsequenzen führt, insbesondere, ob sie sich in Zwangshandlungen umsetzt oder ob sie rechtzeitig korrigiert wird. Solange man in der Lage ist, eine seelische Störung in dem Augenblick abzustellen, wo es bedenklich wäre, ihre logischen Konsequenzen zu ziehen, so lange, due entschuldigst schon, habe ich keinen rechten Respekt vor ihr. . . .

And furthermore, Otto sees in such 'Verrücktheiten':

> eine Neigung zur Verspieltheit, zur Unwahrheit, zur Komödianterei, kurz, ein unanständiges Bestreben, vom wirklichen Ernst des Lebens abzurücken und unbequeme Verantwortlichkeiten abzulehnen. Ein solches Bestreben hat ja natürlich, wenn du willst, auch etwas Krankhaftes, aber mit Wahnsinn hat es gewiss nicht das geringste zu tun.

To Robert's worried question: 'Und bist du auch sicher, die Grenze immer bestimmen zu können?', Otto replies: 'Gewiss bin ich das, sonst hätte ich meinen Beruf längst aufgegeben'.

Although the statement in which the above quotation occurs is made to Robert, and could be viewed simply as a means of allaying his fears, it is sufficiently long and detailed to form a profession of medical belief by Otto. Schnitzler's own 'Fähigkeit der Correctur' is to be found here, and it may not surprise us that in the 1920s Schnitzler had penned a medical note to the effect that the line between 'wirkliche Geisteskrankheit' and its 'verblasstes Abbild beim Psychastheniker', between 'fixe Idee' and 'Zwangsvorstellung', between 'Melancholie' and 'Verstimmung' can and must be drawn: it is 'eine *scharf gezogene Grenze*' and 'sie heisst Krankheitseinsicht'; similarly, he avers, for the dividing line (and here he admits the much greater difficulty) 'zwischen bewusst und unbewusst, verantwortlich und unverantwortlich'. Otto and Schnitzler, then, adduce an argument for Robert to see himself, just as the reader is encouraged to see him, as responsible for his future development.

Thus, the various narrative techniques of hero-viewpoint, the choice of a particular mental illness with its misleading rationalities, the attitude of the psychiatric expert, all these things tend to present the protagonist as the responsible subject of his actions. Indeed, we are made to empathise with a mind felt to be oppressed but essentially like our own. It is not until the last pages of the work that the author cares to spell out the solipsistic vision of his protagonist, as when we read of Paula: 'Sie stand vor ihm, totenblass und mit einem verzerrten Lächeln. Aber er merkte nicht, dass ihre Züge sich so seltsam verändert hatten'. And it is only within lines of the end of the work that the reader is bidden to step finally outside the consciousness of the protagonist, when Schnitzler offers an authorial statement which is the antithesis of the protagonist's: 'Und die Worte versagten ihm [Otto]. In seinen Augen war Angst, Mitleid und Liebe ohne Mass. Doch dem Bruder bedeutete der feuchte Glanz dieses Blickes Tücke, Drohung und Tod'. Here, the authorial 'Doch' separates the sane from the insane vision.

What then are the implications of such a dual narrative perspective, in which we have on the one hand a natural history of disease, on the other an embattled subject, whose responsibility for his mental condition we are encouraged not to exclude from consideration until we reach the above words? The immediate suggestion is: if 'normality' is the sphere of human freedom, and 'abnormality' that of domination by the impersonal mechanisms of the psyche, then the reader (who experiences Robert as an embattled subject for well nigh the entire work) is challenged to put his or her finger on the precise point in the narrative where the protagonist has irrevocably moved from freedom into unfreedom. Can one—the narrative structure seems to ask—draw Otto's precise line between the two spheres? Or again, is Robert in fact insane at the outset? and if not, is this outcome irresistible? By manipulating our empathy well beyond the point where we might be repulsed by the psychotic material, the author has in effect undermined our ability to know where we are in the presence of relative moral freedom and where in that of clinically determined behaviour.

This interrogation of psychological determinism—'unheilbarem Wahnsinn verfallen'—and moral responsibility—'Ich bin ja frei . . . Ich habe die Wahl'—had been one of Schnitzler's major preoccupations throughout his literary career. Here he engages more powerfully than ever before, not least because he has chosen as his image of unfreedom the massive personality disruption of psychosis. The author has moved beyond the sphere of neurotic material—his and Freud's habitual space—to treat a mental disorder which calls into question the victim's very status as a creature of reason. Here the problem of freedom of the will undermined by pervasive psychical mechanisms is posed in its extremest form.

Unquestionably, the Novelle reflects a highly personal crisis of the period in which the first full draft was completed. Schnitzler's diary reveals deep depression associated with disharmony in his marriage, with his sense of being a dilettante compared to the social worth of his surgeon brother (and to no small extent with increasing deafness and noises in the head). But it was clearly the chaos of a world in the throes of the 1914-18 War which produced his profoundest distress and finds emblematic treatment in the drastic image of psychosis. Here, in the apparently ineluctable derangement of the protagonist, is the 'Wahnsinn', 'Sinnlosigkeit', 'Grauen', 'Schwachsinn, ganz in der pathologischen Bedeutung des Wortes', which are Schnitzler's key terms in his commentary on the War. Appropriately the early version of *Flucht* is referred to in the diaries as 'Wahnsinnsnovelle' and 'Wahnsinn', and the MS title is 'Wahn'. But if the War is a general madness, what of the justifications of it as 'historische Notwendigkeit' and 'Schicksalsnotwendigkeit', which human decision is powerless to alter? By shaping the Novelle as the natural history of a degenerative disease, thus confirming the protagonist's anxiety that he will cease to have reason and choice, that he will be reduced to the status of a 'willenlosen Sklaven des Schicksals', Schnitzler examines his contemporaries' fateful sense of 'Notwendigkeit' from the empirical perspective of clinical medicine. What he offers us from here is a bleak account of his protagonist's (and our own) limited moral freedom. This aspect of the text is the fictional projection of the author's war-time depressive obsession with unfreedom.

However, Schnitzler's agonised personal diary on the War, published posthumously as *Ueber Krieg und Frieden*, reveals not only the depressive bemoaning of 'Grauen' and 'Sinnlosigkeit' but equally the rationalist's continual objection to the mindless idea of historical ne-

cessity. Against this idea, Schnitzler stresses how humankind must take charge of its destiny. To take one example, he writes in 1915 that it is a nonsense to state 'dass der Krieg eine Notwendigkeit sei und man sich daher nicht gegen ihn auflehnen dürfe. Auch Pest und Cholera sind Notwendigkeiten. Erst dass wir uns gegen angebliche Notwendigkeiten auflehnen, macht uns ja zu Menschen'. The cries of the embattled moralist find expression in the text in all those narrative elements which, as we have seen, affirm Robert's rational capacities and responsibility for his condition, and so salvage him as moral agent.

One function of all the narrative elements of heroviewpoint is, we have seen, to tie Robert to our world, the rational order of 'Normalmenschen' and so give his battle the kind of human substance Schnitzler is suggesting for the struggle against plague, cholera, War. But the other function is to allow the author to suggest that if Robert's mind can for so long appear to be essentially like our own, *it is surely not impossible for our minds to follow the path of his mind into collapse.* Through the reader's inability not to inhabit the 'abnormal' mind the author is able to suggest the ever-present threat to our own rationality. We are thus forced to recognise that the would-be rational author is giving full rein to his sense of the dark reality evinced by the irrationality of the War. The pressure of his war-time perplexity and distress transforms the narrative structure of clinical determinism countered by, but ultimately superior to, ethical voluntarism into a pessimistic statement of the failure of rationality as organising capacity of the psyche, a vision of humankind's unequal struggle to master the chaos of the Id. . . .

> By manipulating our empathy well beyond the point where we might be repulsed by the psychotic material in *Flucht in die Finsternis,* Schnitzler has in effect undermined our ability to know where we are in the presence of relative moral freedom and where in that of clinically determined behaviour.
>
> —*Kenneth Segar*

During the period of the writing of *Flucht,* so-called phenomenological and existential psychology was being promoted in an attempt not to use the abstractions of clinical categories to discuss psychopathology, but rather to try to understand the patient as *subject* of his or her experience. The new psychology sought to counter the 'genetic' approach of (by the second decade of the century) now classical psychoanalysis, with its emphasis on a deterministic past, and to present a future-oriented view of pathological (as of all other human) behaviour. But if the subject's relationship to time was central to their perspective, these new psychologists also demanded examination of the subject's relationship to the extensive world. By such consideration of temporality and spatiality, phenomenological and existential analysis hoped to establish not symptomatology, but the subject's state of consciousness and, ultimately, mode of being-in-the-world. The technique is not unlike the imaginative writer's creation of a character with whom the reader can empathise; and in *Flucht* Schnitzler powerfully challenges our reading of an 'objective' case-book in the context of Robert's peculiar experience of space (essentially as darkness) and time (stasis, circularity).

Thus, there are constant descriptions of enveloping darkness—welling up from the bowl of the arena, closing round the train as it deserts the sunlit sea-shore to enter a long tunnel followed by a twilit landscape, engulfing Robert suddenly on the stairs of his hotel as an automatic lightswitch extinguishes the stair-lights, and so on through the text until Robert has murdered his brother and rushes 'durch den dunklen Gang, die Treppe hinab' into 'eine klingende blaue Nacht, die niemals für ihn enden durfte'. What we are given here is the protagonist's dominant mode of being-in-the-world. Eugene Minkowski (influenced by Bergson's notion of 'élan vital') writes: 'Pour vivre, nous avons besoin d'étendue, de perspective. L'espace est aussi indispensable à l'épanouissement de la vie que le temps.' And: 'Il y a toujours devant moi comme de *l'espace libre* dans lequel peuvent, sans encombre, s'épanouir mon activité et ma vie. Je me sens à *l'aise*, je me sens libre dans cet espace que j'ai devant moi'. For the normal subject, 'la clarté de cet espace visuel' is in fact the sense of 'l'ampleur de la vie'. However, the other side of the coin, of 'l'espace clair' is the morbidity of 'l'espace noir', of 'la nuit obscure . . . un brouillard opaque qui nous enveloppe comme l'obscurité, nous isole et nous pénètre jusqu'au fond de notre être'. Such then, in the terms of existential psychology, are the two modes of experiencing space: on the one hand, the socialised mode, in which one's activity finds its appropriate place in extension and amplitude; on the other hand, the isolating mode of envelopment and constriction which denies all purposeful activity. Writing of the sense of being-in-the-world of the schizophrenic, Minkowski concludes: 'Nous pouvons dire maintenant que le *monde morbide de notre malade est constitué sur le mode de l'espace noir'*.

From this interpretative perspective, the component of time is equally significant in Schnitzler's fictional construction. He shows that the protagonist cannot use time creatively, and the sense of a meaningless circularity always threatens. Thus, there are what Minkowski terms *'actes sans lendemain'*: 'und konnte sich bei all dem niemals vorstellen, dass sein ganzes Unternehmen ernst gemeint sei und zu einem bestimmten Ziel führen sollte'. Robert's actions can seem to him 'zwecklos und lächerlich' and his thoughts 'ohne Sinn und Zweck'. This can lead to that most degrading of senses of time, meaningless repetition, circularity—what Minkowski describes as *'actes figés'*: 'da man ja alles unendliche Male zu durchleben verdammt war'. This latter aspect of Robert's fruitless relationship to time is most pointedly revealed in his compulsive repetitions of the actions of his friend of younger days, Höhnburg, whose inexorable decline into insanity prefigures Robert's own collapse.

What the final image of *Flucht* does is bring these spatial and temporal components of Robert's experience together to assert that their modalities are the essence of his being-in-the-world, the truth of his selfhood. Thus, he rushes out into 'eine klingende blaue Nacht, die niemals für ihn enden durfte. Und er wusste, dass er diesen gleichen Weg schon tausende Male dahingerast und dass es ihm bestimmt war, ihn noch *tausende* Male bis in alle Ewigkeit durch klingende blaue Nächte hinzufliehen'. Robert is at the last, as always, compulsively fleeing in the face of reality. His repeated experience of 'dark space' is here conflated with 'une *dislocation très profonde du phénomène du temps avec une prévalence du passé qui représente . . .* l'aspect le plus statique du temps vécu'. It is, of course, the triumphant ring of this final experience (the 'klingende blaue Nacht' is both protagonist's viewpoint and authorial description-cum-connivance) which offers the ultimate justification of a phenomenological and existential reading of the text: in the face of this image, there is something inappropriate in wanting to reduce that experience to the final phase of a clinically documented dementia. In living out the modality *'d'actes sans lendemain, d'actes figés, d'actes à court-circuit, d'actes ne cherchant point à aboutir'*—which is all that 'dark space' and 'static time' with their constant deprivation of extension, amplitude and vitality can permit,—Robert must flee into a darkness he has always known, has 'improperly' and hopelessly tried to shun, and has in a heightened state now made fully his own. Appalling, destructive and self-destructive the last acts of the protagonist may be, but they are the truth of his being: he has, desperately, found himself.

By salvaging the protagonist's relationship to the world he inhabits as something comprehensible to us, Schnitzler is not only creating empathy with an abnormal mental condition, he is again reflecting a problem magnified by psychopathology back on to the life of the reader. Experiencing the external world as dark and nightmarishly static is not merely the truth of Robert's inner state, but becomes symbolic of that irrationality on which all our lives may founder. Indeed, Schnitzler underpins this perspective by creating from Robert's experience of external reality archetypal patterns of human experience: *the decline of the year, the labyrinth, the oracle.*

Thus, Robert's fate is played out in terms of light and darkness, of summer sun and winter ice. A summer convalescence is concluded in 'Spätoktobertagen', whose mild air 'mit sommerlicher Wärme schmeichelte'; later, Robert walks with Paula in the park 'im lauen Nebel eines windstillen Novembertags'; soon, 'der erste Schnee dieses Winters fiel leise, und ein graues Dämmern sank in die kleinen, ärmlichen, entlaubten Gärten'; rapidly, the year approaches its end, with the 'Dämmer eines frühen Dezembernachmittags'. The final chapter opens with the words: 'An diesem grauumzogenen Dezembertage dunkelte es früh'; and finally Robert's corpse is discovered 'an einem steinigen Abhang, der zu der fast vereisten Ache hinabführte'. So, a pathological decline which is also the shape of all our lives.

Equally, the text bristles with images of encroaching darkness, constricting or descending paths, culminating in the depiction of Robert's arrival at the fateful 'Gasthaus' where he will murder his brother. Here is the most powerful presentation of external reality as baleful symbolic landscape. Certainly, the description has reference to Robert's inner state of emotional emptiness, and so underpins the clinical aspect of the work, yet it also contains in an uncanny way the terrible presence of an as yet unrealised catastrophe:

> Nun, da er das langgestreckte Dorf, das er sich auch auf der Herreise immer nur im frischen Grün und in Sommerfarben vorzustellen vermocht hatte, winterlich verschneit vor sich liegen sah, war ihm, als empfange ihn eine ganz andere, eine fremde, nie vorher geschaute Gegend. Er überliess einem Lohndiener seine Tasche und folgte ihm über eine Brücke, unter der die Ache rauschte, durch eine längs des Wassers hinführende Allee, deren er sich aus jenem Sommer wie eines hohen, schützenden Baumganges erinnerte, endlich durch einen Torbogen, unter dem aus einer schmiedeeisernen Laterne ein mattes, gelblichrotes Licht schimmerté, auf den verlassenen Hauptplatz mit dem schweigenden Brunnen, zum Gasthof hin.

The atmosphere of this 'Gegend' in its change from leafy summer to bleak winter is 'strange' with Robert's self-alienation; but the silent and deserted scene affects the reader with a wider sense of disquiet. The 'gelblichrotes Licht'—which later becomes 'gelblichtrüb'—acts as a portent of danger; and the words 'zum Gasthof hin', long delayed in this long-drawn period, fall as after an ominous drum roll. It is as though Robert, by following the porter over the bridge, along the 'Allee' and through the archway to the empty square and silent fountain, has been forced to tread the path into some ghastly labyrinth from which he will never escape alive. The literal depiction of Robert's external and internal situations is again transcended by what emerge as symbols reverberating with our sense of the irrational in life. Here, the declining year and fateful labyrinth combine to persuade the reader of the hidden forces which threaten the frail structure of our rational order.

The last, and perhaps the most startling symbol in this poetic vehicle of inevitability, is the strange letter in which Robert asks his brother to perform euthanasia if ever he detects signs in him of incurable insanity. Placed in Otto's hands years before the events here described, the letter (written after Robert's deep shock at the relentless decline into insanity of his young friend Höhnburg) comes into central focus in the course of the story as the object around which all Robert's anxieties crystallise. Robert is at one point thankful that Paula knows 'nichts von dem Brief, der in meines Bruders Händen ist, von dem furchtbaren Brief, der ihm Gewalt über mein Leben gibt'. And later: 'Er erbebte. Plötzlich wieder war er sich der Gefahr bewusst geworden, die ihn bedrohte. Der Brief! Otto hatte den Brief in Händen, an dem Roberts Schicksal und Leben hing'. Whilst at once clinical sign and motor-force of Robert's disturbance, the letter—'dieses unglückselige Schriftstück'—allows us to sense beyond its pathological implications a force for destruction. It comes to have the potency of an oracle, whose prophecy Robert is powerless

to resist: the title of the work *Flucht in die Finsternis* thus has psychological but also mythic status—Oedipus rushes headlong into the danger he seeks to flee. The pattern is, as for the previous symbolic material, archetypal, helping to give Robert's predicament representative human status. The decline of the year, entering the labyrinth, the fulfilment of the oracle—these motifs retain for us their connexions with larger human experience, and Robert's fate thereby reflects back on all our lives.

In an important sense, the letter as oracle is the key to Schnitzler's dark presentiment: for Robert is the helpless victim of *what he has himself decreed*. By asking his brother to perform the act of euthanasia should he be threatened by insanity, he has himself set up the determining force to which he must succumb. Seen thus, the narrative closure, which is darkness and destruction, is even more sinister than suggested in our initial argument about the failure of freedom and reason in the face of all the impersonal (irrational) determining forces of the psyche. Robert as human subject capable of acquiring representative status by means of a symbolic narrative structure becomes the bearer of a more intolerable message: for does not the symbolic motif of the self-dictated oracle suggest that what we call 'will' is nothing other than the *necessary* expression of the beings we are? Robert's dark space and fruitless acts as symbolic motifs are in fact what we all 'wollen müssen'. Thus, for example, there lurks the horrible possibility that Europe, humanity, 'wills' the irrationality of 1914, that the War *is* 'notwendig' in an existential sense. Perhaps this is the purport of Schnitzler's anxious question about the 'Sinnlosigkeit' of the War: 'Oder sollte es doch einen Sinn haben? Dann müsste man erst recht verrückt werden. What if unreason, not reason, 'macht uns ja zu Menschen'? . . .

Rationality and irrationality confront one another most substantially in the structured dualism at the heart of the work, namely in the relationship of the two brothers. The relationship occupies us from the very first pages of the Novelle, where we are apprised of the inseparable bond which Robert feels exists between himself and Otto. They might lose touch with each other for days and weeks at a time, 'es kam doch immer wieder ein Ereignis, das . . . sie beide ihre Zusammengehörigkeit als unzweifelhaft und unauflöslich empfinden liess'. Indeed, the work would seem to bear this judgment out: the brothers are bound together in the most powerful (and destructive) way by the letter as oracle, which gives Robert's life into Otto's hands and thereby takes Otto's life. If Otto is the embodiment of reason, called to sit in judgment on (diagnose) unreason, then Robert is unreason, become so virulent as to destroy reason and itself.

It is in the relationship of the two brothers that Schnitzler's ambivalence regarding the supremacy of rationality or irrationality reveals, in the first instance, the most *personal* aspect of his anguish: the problematic relationship to his own brother, Julius. In his medical notes, his war diary, his collections of 'Sprüche', in his art—'Willkür im Leben, Gesetz in der Kunst'—he is on the side of the rationalist Otto. But in his increasing emotional disturbance, in his sense of being a dilettante compared to the sterling worth of his brother Julius—'Ich empfinde das Gemisch von pathologischem-künstlerischem-dilettantischem in meinem Wesen'—he is clearly to be identified with the protagonist. It is, after all, Robert's inner complexity (artistic personality dressed as bureaucrat, inveterate egoist with introjected yearnings for his brother's security and normality) and his threatened being that Schnitzler delineates with such understanding. Schnitzler writes in his diary: 'Umarmung der Brüder—ich identifizire [sic] mich mit dem Helden,—den Bruder mit Julius . . . ' His own love-hatred must be exorcised by the fictive killing of his real-life brother.

At an *intellectual* level, the problematic fraternal relationship suggests, of course, that very crisis of rationalism that has been in large part the substance of this analysis. When we read of Otto that 'ihm die Kugel mitten ins Herz gedrungen, und er sank lautlos auf den Boden hin', we know that we have witnessed the covert ('lautlos') murder of Reason; when we reach the final image of Robert fleeing into 'eine klingende blaue Nacht, die niemals für ihn enden durfte', we know that this is the necessary self-destruction perpetrated by a homicidal and suicidal Unreason. Schnitzler is here the rationalist and moralist whose confidence in rationalism as a conceptual framework for understanding and control has, as for so many others in this period, been increasingly shaken. It is his sense of the lurking danger in this state of affairs which is also powerfully shaped by the final images of the work.

Finally, those self-same images give the crisis of rationalism a *social and political* dimension. If, as we have seen, the 1914-18 War gives Schnitzler's personal and intellectual concerns much more disturbing contemporary substance, how much more chilling for us to think of those final images concluding a work published in 1931, when an increasingly irrational Europe had begun its new flight into aggression and self-destruction. A postscript to Schnitzler's pessimism may appropriately be taken from the closing words of the contemporary work *Das Unbehagen in der Kultur* (1930): despite its 'Kulturentwicklung', Freud writes, humankind now has the technical capacity to destroy itself, hence its 'Angststimmung'; and the fateful question is whether the 'Aggressions- und Selbstvernichtungstrieb' will be vanquished by 'der ewige Eros'. It is surely significant that future weal or woe depends simply on the outcome of a struggle between two instincts, and that rationality and freedom play no part in Freud's (unwittingly pessimistic?) assessment of civilisation. 'Aber wer kann den Erfolg und Ausgang voraussehen?' he asks, with the rational detachment appropriate to the psychopathologist. Schnitzler, himself somehow holding on to rationality through his objective presentation of the protagonist's irrationality, has nonetheless created as the reader's abiding sense of the work a symbolic vehicle of inevitability and a narrative closure of darkness and destruction. Clearly, he is not so sanguine as Freud, and (aside from the historical resonances: personal, intellectual and sociopolitical) the narrative strategy of **Flucht** has taught the reader not to be so either.

Kenneth Segar, "The Death of Reason: Narrative Strategy and Resonance in Schnitzler's

'Flucht in die Finsternis', " in Oxford German Studies, Vol. 17, 1988, pp. 97-117.*

FURTHER READING

Alexander, Theodor W., and Alexander, Beatrice W. "Schnitzler's *Leutnant Gustl* and Dujardin's *Les lauriers sont coupés.*" *Modern Austrian Literature* 2, No. 2 (Summer 1969): 7-15.
Traces the extent of Schnitzler's acknowledged indebtedness in *Leutnant Gustl* to Edouard Dujardin's *Les lauriers sont coupés* for the form of the interior monologue.

————. "A Possible Model for Schnitzler's *Fräulein Else.*" *Modern Austrian Literature* 19, Nos. 3-4 (1986): 49-61.
Draws parallels between *Fräulein Else* and the *Tagebuch eines halbwüchsigen Mädchens,* the diary of a Viennese teenager published in 1919.

Apsler, Alfred. "A Sociological View of Arthur Schnitzler." *Germanic Review* XVIII, No. 2 (April 1943): 90-106.
Concludes that "Schnitzler was really a tragic personality. A great poet who, with his talents, could have easily become a spiritual leader, a figure of national and international importance. Yet he kept away from the people who needed his insight and guidance. Through difficulties in social adjustment he became an extreme individualist, but he was always aware of the hopeless aspects of individual isolation."

Lederer, Herbert. "Arthur Schnitzler: A Chronicle of Loneliness." *German Quarterly* XXX, No. 2 (March 1957): 82-94.
Examines the "problem of loneliness" in Schnitzler's fiction and drama.

Liptzin, Sol. *Arthur Schnitzler.* New York: Prentice Hall, 1932, 275 p.
Appreciative, thematic study of Schnitzler's career.

Madland, Helga Stipa. "Baroja's *Camino de perfección* and Schnitzler's *Leutnant Gustl:* Fin de Siècle Madrid and Vienna." *Comparative Literature Studies* 21, No. 3 (Fall 1984): 306-22.
Compares *Leutnant Gustl* and Pío Baroja's *Camino de perfección,* concluding that "while the accent of Schnitzler's and Baroja's social and political criticism differs and there also exist differences in the structure of the works, their content, and the personalities of the protagonists, both Gustl and Fernando are representative of the fin de siècle cultural crisis facing all of Europe."

Maurer, K. W. "Some Reflections on Arthur Schnitzler." *German Life and Letters* 2, No. 3 (April 1949): 214-21.
Summarizes "Dead Men Tell No Tales" in a consideration of major subjects and themes in Schnitzler's work.

Slochower, Harry. Review of *Flight into Darkness,* by Arthur Schnitzler. *New Republic* LXIX, No. 885 (18 November 1931): 22-3.
Discusses Schnitzler in the context of Viennese culture of the pre–World War I period, concluding that "his work is the final charming embodiment of a culture,

sweet, feminine and tired; it is the tactful expression of an age that is not unmourned."

Swales, Martin. *Arthur Schnitzler: A Critical Study.* Oxford: Oxford University Press, 1971, 289 p.
  Contains analysis of several works of short fiction by Schnitzler.

Weiss, Robert O. "A Study of the Psychiatric Elements in Schnitzler's *Flucht in die Finsternis.*" *Germanic Review* XXXIII, No. 4 (February 1958): 251-75.
  Clinical analysis of Robert in *Flight into Darkness.* Weiss concludes that the novella portrays a case-history in paranoid schizophrenia.

Additional coverage of Schnitzler's life and career is contained in the following sources published by Gale Research: *Contemporary Authors,* Vol. 104; *Dictionary of Literary Biography,* Vols. 81, 118; and *Twentieth-Century Literary Criticism,* Vol. 4.

Mikhail Zoshchenko

1895-1958

(Born Mikhail Mikhailovich Zoshchenko; also transliterated as Mixail and Michael; also Zoščenko and Zostchenko) Russian short story writer, novelist, essayist, playwright, and autobiographer.

INTRODUCTION

Zoshchenko was the most popular satirist in the Soviet Union from the early 1920s until 1946, when his works incurred official disfavor. During this period, Zoshchenko examined the confusion that resulted from the social programs of the new Soviet state and the ways that ignorance and greed could be masked by propaganda and government policies. To accomplish this, he utilized a distinctive vehicle for his trenchant satires: a traditional Russian literary technique, known as *skaz,* which establishes a narrator, usually a comic character, who is distinct from the author. The language of Zoshchenko's *skaz* narrators—a unique blend of colloquialisms, the specialized jargon of numerous professions, half-assimilated Party slogans, and malapropisms—is one of the most notable features of his work.

Biographical Information

Zoshchenko's father was a painter and small landowner in the Ukraine who, though not wealthy, was able to send his son to study law at the University of St. Petersburg. At the beginning of World War I, Zoshchenko abandoned his studies and joined the Imperial Army, where he became a lieutenant in the grenadiers. During the war he suffered gas poisoning, which left him in chronic ill health and which biographers believe may have caused the heart disease from which he eventually died. After the Russian Revolution Zoshchenko joined the Red Army, though he never joined the Communist Party and in fact remained politically uncommitted throughout his life. Between his two periods of military service, Zoshchenko held a number of disparate jobs—including postmaster, cobbler, poultry breeder, and border patrolman—which would work their way into the satiric situations of his later fiction. He began writing humorous sketches for newspapers primarily to earn a living, and quickly became known for his work satirizing the everyday hardships faced by the Soviet citizen. In 1946 Andrei Zhdanov, the Secretary of the Central Committee of the Soviet Communist Party and formulator of the official guidelines for Soviet media, attacked Zoshchenko and his work in a speech, condemning him as a "vulgar Philistine" and his works as "rotten, vulgar, and empty." Although Zoshchenko continued to

write and to publish sporadically thereafter, his career as a satirist essentially ended. In place of the witty characterizations and lively storylines that had marked his earlier fiction, Zoshchenko's subsequent works followed the imperative of Socialist Realism that dictated a writer must celebrate the glory of the Soviet state.

Major Works

With the publication of his first volume of short stories, *Rasskazy Nazara Il'icha gospodina Sinebryukhova,* Zoshchenko was established as Russia's most popular humorist. During the four years from 1922 to 1926, he published more than twenty collections of humorous stories that together sold millions of copies. In a typical Zoshchenko story of this period mass confusion results when sincere but muddled citizens attempt to implement government directives with no clear idea of what is expected of them. Zoshchenko also found a rich vein of humor in contrasting the ideal of life in the Soviet Union with the reality of the situation and in showing how removed some government programs were from the needs and desires of the people. In "The Woman Who Could Not Read," for example, nationwide efforts to eradicate illiteracy fail to move a woman to learn to read—until she finds a scented letter in her husband's pocket. Zoshchenko published similar short humorous stories for more than two decades, and had ventured into the production of longer and more serious works near the end of his career.

Critical Reception

Critics have found Zoshchenko's short stories to be masterful descriptions of the vagaries and inconsistencies of human nature, as well as heartbreakingly humorous depictions of human foibles and sufferings. His *skaz* technique is often discussed, and commentators have maintained that Zoshchenko's use of comic narrators allowed him greater freedom of expression than might otherwise be advisable. Despite official censure in 1946, Zoshchenko's works remained popular with the reading public; after his death Zoshchenko was "rehabilitated" and collections of his stories, carefully edited to expunge any unorthodoxies, were republished. More than any other writer, Zoshchenko provided an accurate and intimate portrait of daily life in the Soviet Union in the mid-twentieth century.

PRINCIPAL WORKS

SHORT FICTION

Rasskazy Nazara Il'icha gospodina Sinebryukhova 1922
Nyervnyie Lyudi 1925
Urazhayemye grazhdanye 1926
Sentimental 'nyie povesti 1927
Golubaya kniga 1935
Russia Laughs 1935
Rasskazy o Lenine 1940
The Woman Who Could Not Read, and Other Tales 1940
Povesti i rasskazy 1952
Rasskazy, fel'etony, povesti 1952
Scenes from the Bathhouse, and Other Stories of Communist Russia 1961
Nervous People, and Other Satires 1963

OTHER MAJOR WORKS

Svadba (drama) 1922
Prestupleniye i nakazaniye (drama) 1932
Vozvrashchyonnaya molodost' (novel) 1933
Pered voskhodom solntsa (autobiography); published in journal *Oktyabr'*, 1943
Parusinovyi portfel' (drama) 1944
Povest 'o Razume (autobiography); published in journal *Zvezda*, 1972

*These two works were translated and published together as *Before Sunrise* in 1974.

CRITICISM

Elizabeth Hart   (review date 1935)

[In the following review, Hart praises the humor and likeable characters in Russia Laughs.*]*

Those who read "Story in America; 1934-1935," will probably remember **"What the Nightingale Sang,"** though they may have forgotten that the author was Mikhail Zostchenko. In an anthology unusually well supplied with arresting short stories, this one stood out for two reasons: the tart, provocative, oddly delightful flavor of its humor and the fact that it was written by a citizen in good standing of the U. S. S. R., a country that American readers do not generally associate with humorists—most certainly not with humorists like Zostchenko.

> **Zostchenko extracts every drop of satirical comedy from the blunders and peccadillos of his characters, but his laughter has tolerance and a rather wry understanding.**
>
> **—Elizabeth Hart**

This story heads a translated collection of forty-nine called **Russia Laughs,** and while I am not certain that it is the best of the lot, I believe that it is the best key stone to Zostchenko. It contains the essence of a viewpoint that the rest of the book rounds out and confirms. "Without fear of appearing a ridiculous being from some other century" (or of sticking out a nimble tongue at the pompous circles likely to make this accusation), this writer's primary concern is with individuals. Bylinkin and Triodin, Egorka Bassoff and Boris Ivanovitch Kotofoyeff are themselves first, and only secondarily government clerks of the seventh class, unliquidated priest, hereditary priest and musician in a State Orchestra. Furthermore, they are presented in relation to present-day conditions, not to the beautiful future life which Zostchenko contemplates, "without the slightest guaranty of ever attaining it." Perhaps when the Perfect State has liquidated selfish and mercenary motives, human love will be purged of its absurd and ignoble elements and become an emotion worthy only of the highest and most serious poetry.

Meanwhile, Lizochka and Bylinkin come to grief over a chest of drawers; Zabyeshkin desperately courts a fat and aging widow for the sake of her snug cottage and milk goat; another man's idyll is blighted because he cannot afford to indulge his lady love's passion for cream tarts and operatic performances. Three hundred years hence, when everything is given away free, there will be no stealing. But today the great cities of the Soviet are very merry places, "as long as you have money. Without money however" . . . Hence we get youths like Maxim. And in the simple countryside we get the imaginative and resourceful horse thief, Grischka Zhigan.

Zostchenko extracts every drop of satirical comedy from the blunders and peccadillos of his characters, but his laughter has tolerance and a rather wry understanding. It is not only by his easy conversational style and his racy colloquialisms that he manages to associate himself with the people he writes of. He frequently has a quiet way of turning the hatpin and the slapstick (he is adept in the use of both) inward.

And, on the whole, his bedraggled heroes and heroines are a likeable lot. They are also curiously familiar to an American reader. It must not be thought, however, that because Zostchenko draws deeply on the failings that flourish everywhere on the globe, he ever neglects those peculiar to his own corner. Some of his sharpest and funniest attacks are leveled at Soviet cant, Soviet dogmatism and the sort of intellectual Boy Scoutism that hangs depressingly about so much Soviet writing and speaking for mass consumption. **"A Slight Mistake"** and **"Social Cares"** are particularly good examples of his skill along this line. Some of his most ludicrous situations could never have been imagined by a writer living outside the boundaries of the U. S. S. R., as for instance the one in that uproarious tale, **"The Troublesome Grandfather."** He makes the housing problem more uncomfortably, almost painfully, vivid than any foreign critic I ever read in **"The Bath"** and **"Family Vitriol."** In fact, a great deal of his fun-poking would probably be furiously resented by Communist critics here if he happened to be French or English or American.

How these critics will receive **Russia Laughs** is a matter of uncertain conjecture. Last year there appeared in *The New Masses* a series of articles on contemporary Soviet literature. The writer was inclined to view with disapproval, if not with positive alarm, the effect of certain books like Ilf and Petrov's *The Little Golden Calf* on Communists and potential converts to communism outside Russia. I confess that his uneasiness seems to me without foundation. Surely the already converted can be trusted with an intimation or two that all is not yet quite perfect in their Promised Land. As to the others, the ones still outside the pale, I cannot believe that it is the Ilfs and Petrovs and Zostchenkos that will prevent them from entering. All these men are enormously popular with Russian readers. And most of us will incline to agree with Whit Burnett's prefaced opinion to this book that it is a sign of health and a good thing "that Russia can laugh when the gadfly stings."

Elizabeth Hart, in a review of "Russia Laughs," in New York Herald Tribune Books, *September 1, 1935, p. 14.*

V. S. Pritchett (review date 1940)

[*Pritchett is a highly esteemed English novelist, short story writer, and critic. He is considered one of the modern masters of the short story as well as one of the world's most respected and well-read literary critics. Pritchett writes in the conversational tone of the familiar essay, a method by which he approaches literature from the viewpoint of a lettered but not overly scholarly reader. A twentieth-century successor to such early nineteenth-century essayist-critics as William Hazlitt and Charles Lamb, Pritchett employs much the same critical methods: his own experience, judgment, and sense of literary art are emphasized, rather than a codified critical doctrine derived from a school of psychological or philosophical speculation. His criticism is often described as fair, reliable, and insightful. In the following excerpt, Pritchett discusses the intimacy and depth of Zoshchenko's portrayal of ordinary Russians, a depth he finds lacking in English short fiction of the same period.*]

The English are not a nation of good storytellers. Listen on a bus, in the train, in the pubs, cafés and sitting-rooms; it is rare to hear a story well told, neighbours vividly described, dialogue dramatically reported. Go to Wales, Ireland, the Steppes, and every sentence spoken sounds like the opening line of a tale. We lack the naivety or the detachment which turns ourselves or our friends into a living folklore or newspaper. Middle-class life is not to blame entirely, for the same condition is found among workers. Possibly we had that naivety before the Reformation, but I fancy that the general attitude to our own lives has always been ruminative, sentimental and moralistic. We have little experimental curiosity about our life stories, despite our tobacco-clouded introspections and those sudden gulfs of insight, which occur chiefly—unless I misread W. H. Auden—as we lean over the wash-basin. Worry about events and people, and not the events and people themselves is our instinctive interest. I think any short-story writer must have felt this when, eyes open and ears cocked, he snoops about in search of those Jamesian "germs, inveterately minute." The English simply present their lives baldly, are half-submerged by them anyway, and think it rather immoral to present them well.

A collection of Michael Zoshchenko's short stories, **The Woman Who Could Not Read,** translated with a pleasant air of naturalness by Elisaveta Fen, shows up our short-story writing badly. We have had many writers who could turn a triviality fancifully round their pen-nibs. But they leave it still a triviality. The Russian writers—and Zoshchenko is the heir of a tradition—are realistic about their trivialities; they make them not into fanciful elaborations, but into homely illustrations of our greater cares. A peasant urgently goes in search of a wife:

> Well, I harnessed the nag, put my new trousers on, washed my feet and drove off.

"Washed my feet"! A whole life springs up, a man who has been a mere mind suddenly has a body. It is the only description of him in the story, but its visual effect is enormous. It is Tchekov's trick of describing the moonlight by the glint on a broken bottle. But it is not chiefly in the detail of a story that the English short-story writer fails. He has no idea of the art of brevity. In fifteen hundred words Zoshchenko can do almost anything. The English writer of brief stories is limited over and over again either to mere whimsicality, or especially to the lyrical description of an emotional state, a piece of landscape. By this, of course, he gives voice to that meditative, ruminative romanticism of our natures. But we feel that the author, having no invention, has made the best of a bad job; he had no point of view about other people, because he had never got beyond that literary adolescence which has a point of view about itself only. Zoshchenko's stories have none of this poetical priggishness. Brief as they are, they are full of people and incident, frequently have "a plot" and they have also that suggestive quality, a hint dropped here and there, which opens up worlds for the mind to wander in a long time afterwards. And although his stories are written in conversational style, the talk is without those studied buttonholings or breezy non-intimacies of our conversational manner—what Mr. Cyril Connolly has called the "you-man" style. Zoshchenko may talk, for all one knows, as all Russians talk, and certainly as they often do in Tchekov; he talks like an ordinary man without the ordinary man's pomposity and self-consciousness; we recognise the talk, however, because it is like what we say, not indeed to each other, but to ourselves:

> The country air, they say, is very good for you. The air of pine forests, especially, is said to be wholesome for the lungs. So the doctors say. As to myself, I don't really know. I rather doubt it. . . . Though the country air may do you good in the end, you're sure to catch some infection on the way there.

It is easy to overrate—and also underrate—Zoshchenko's sketches. Their subjects are familiar: the farces of the housing situation in Moscow, the digs at a State which makes five-year plans but can't produce electric-light meters, the eternal Russian foolery at the expense of bureaucrats. Some readers are surprised that Zoshchenko's cynicism and satire are permitted and widely enjoyed in Russia. Miss Fen, the translator, says that the greater and better part of his work belongs to the collectivisation period, when there was more freedom for writers than there is now. To-day (she says) he is obliged to add cautions and morals to his stories. Certainly the title story, which describes how a woman decided to learn to read and write—and thereby liquidate national illiteracy—because she discovered a perfumed letter in her husband's coat, looks as if it had been tampered with and neutralised. There is no means of knowing how Zoshchenko is affected; but English short-story writers have their own difficulties, too, with the unofficial censorship of the magazines. Direct political censorship is probably less harmful to imaginative writers than the business man's indirect censorship. For censors are usually stupid or venal. They strain at gnats and swallow camels: the wise writer soon learns to give them gnats to strain at. Censorship, after its first stone-walling phase has passed, may be a stimulus. It encourages subtlety. A hint, an insinuation, the click of the tongue in the cheek, are often more effective in a story than the sullen verbosity of free protest. I assume in reading Zoshchenko's stories that the Soviet censor was wise enough to let well alone when he discovered that Zoshchenko was

writing on what must be a major spiritual problem in Russia: the nostalgia for personal life. But whether the censor was indulgent, subversive, officially wily or blind, Zoshchenko is the gainer by the ever possible threat. He slips his theme across nonchalantly by pretending to be silly, a harmless, clever crank or buffoon, who always skids on the banana-skin or, by advocating with exaggeration the correct point of view:

> To have your own private flat is, no doubt, a sign of petty bourgeois mentality.

> It is better to live as one large friendly communal family than to shut yourself inside your domestic fortifications.

> You ought to live in communal flats. There everything is public. There's always someone to talk to, to ask advice from. And to have a fight with, too, if you feel inclined.

Zoshchenko gets away with anything by farcical advocacy, and by presenting himself as the idiotic enthusiast.

It is interesting to look at the Zoshchenko technique in what I think is the best story in the book, the one entitled **"A Mistake,"** which was published in this paper some time ago. This is a story which lasts in the mind because it lives on many levels and is related to a whole world of fundamental ideas; yet it is a ridiculous, cruel story. The scene is in a crowded train travelling into the country. I have already quoted the opening passage about country air, and that is all the description there is in the tale. There is an old woman with a basket. She is merely "any ordinary old woman." She is followed by a bullying man described in one line as "somewhat of a dandy, quite smartly dressed and with a little moustache." The central situation is established at once. The man is cursing the woman, the passengers are indignant with him. Because he is attacking a woman? No. Zoshchenko chooses the public, the social side of our nature, and it is this that gives both novelty and individuality to his people. They are indignant because he is attacking "an old domestic worker . . . humiliating her proletarian dignity." One of the passengers—"a rather excitable fellow," is all we are told—begins to lead the protest. He is so furious, he grabs the dandy by the coat. Climax. Then the anti-climax: the dandy reveals the old lady is not "an old domestic worker," she is his mother. The excitable fellow backs away, apologetically—and this is good observation—he does not apologise fully until he has justified himself:

> You ought to have declared this as soon as you got in. Otherwise how the devil are we to know. She carries no label on her.

Then everyone apologises. It was only the dandy's mother. This is the-collapse-of-old-gentleman phase in the *Punch* anecdotes, but the story is more than that. There the incident could have ended, starkly. But Zoshchenko never depends mechanically on merely trick endings and stings-in-the-tail. He ends with character, not incident, a character which has developed and conveyed the whole incident to an even more sardonic plane of satire: blowing himself up, the dandy becomes sarcastic:

> As to the Labour Code regulations, p'rhaps I

know them better than anyone else here. P'rhaps I am an old revolutionary who's been living in Leningrad since 1917. . . .

The story begins in one mood, a lackadaisical one, and grows into a totally different one quite naturally. That seems to me one of the signs of mastery in a short story.

It is easy to trace Zoshchenko's ancestry of satirical extravagance and farce in Russian literature. Every Russian writer has written something funny about teeth and preposterous about Government officials from Gogol onwards. Outside Russia, Zoshchenko seems to have affinities with the American, Wm. Saroyan, who, in the same disarming way, has picked up the man in the street and treated him naively, farcically, mystically. He and Zoshchenko are a pair of innocent hopefuls, a Laurel and Hardy, who can't stop talking. Zoshchenko, of course, is never mystical. His optimism comes in mad moments, as in the story where he goes off on a disastrous bicycle ride and is arrested. Saroyan and Zoshchenko are the two sides of the medal of writing about the people; Zoshchenko the harder, more ingenious, older lag. Saroyan urges the ordinary man into the earthly paradise with the humility of faith in man; Zoshchenko urges him on with the comic staggers of perpetual over-reaching. The same zest for the future is in both.

> *V. S. Pritchett, in a review of "The Woman Who Could Not Read," in* The New Statesman & Nation, *Vol. XX, No. 510, November 30, 1940, p. 542.*

Elisaveta Fen   (essay date 1942)

[*Fen has translated several volumes of Zoshchenko's short stories into English, including* The Woman Who Could Not Read, and Other Tales *and* The Wonderful Dog, and Other Tales. *In her foreword to* The Wonderful Dog, *written in 1941 and excerpted below, Fen observes that Zoshchenko's humor derives from the incongruity in everyday life "between the ideal and its realization."*]

I believe it would hardly be an exaggeration to say that the work of Michael Zoshchenko was virtually unknown in this country until, in the spring of 1938, *The New Statesman and Nation* began to print the writer's translations of his stories. Since then, several other papers, such as *The Spectator, Lilliput* and the *News Chronicle* have found room for them in their pages, and a collection of them was published by Methuen & Co., Ltd., under the title **The Woman Who Could Not Read And Other Tales,** in 1940.

The publication of the second volume by the same firm can be presumed to speak for itself. It indicates that the kind of humour in which Zoshchenko excels appeals to a certain type of English reader, and that the appeal is, most likely, on a deeper level than mere preparedness to be amused. One is tempted to interpret it as a proof that a greater affinity exists between the English and the Russian sense of humour than is probably possible between any other two peoples.

Mr. H. E. Bates, I believe, laid his finger on the right spot

when he wrote in *The Spectator* that the chief characteristic of this kind of humour was the ability 'to squeeze fun out of what are essentially situations of pain.' Both the Russians and the English, although maybe for different causes inherent in their mentality, use laughter as a protective device: they 'laugh so that they do not weep'. Both peoples, faced with a *fait accompli,* are capable of accepting it with a philosophical stoicism; when they are placed in a situation where open fight is impossible, they react by a grin of challenge rather than by tears of despair.

The characteristic situation which moves Michael Zoshchenko to a display of humour is generally a situation of incongruity—admittedly the most common source of fun. These incongruities appear to be presented on a superficial plane, but are in fact related, on a deeper level, to the universal, age-long incongruity—the discrepancy between the ideal and its realization.

No matter where you open this book, or which story you begin to read, in every one of them the scene is set for this discouraging, yet stimulating contrast—between what is and what may have, or should have been. A man is taking a girl home, and talks to her of his exceptional love, offering to throw himself into the icy river to prove it. A burglar emerges from a dark alley; and the young hero meekly allows himself to be stripped, protesting merely that the girl should be treated likewise—for the sake of justice. A woman leaves her husband after a quarrel—she is free to do so under the Soviet law—but has to return ignominiously, after a day's tramp in the streets, for there is not a room, not even a corner of one in the whole of the old capital, in which she might set up an independent home. Men and women live in communal flats; the opportunity for mutual aid is unequalled, for all the necessities of life are scarce. Firewood is particularly precious in winter, but—it is stacked outside in the communal yard, and the members of the commune steal assiduously from one another, so that a clever device of detection has to be thought out by a resourceful lad. A young police officer is placed in a position of responsibility in a small provincial town; he is proud of it, but—power intoxicates. So when he comes across a pig wandering in the streets he is ready to shoot it as a disturber of public order, and in the end arrests his own wife, who tries to stop him. A group of young people, roused by a discussion of international affairs, decide to ring up the Kremlin and ask the opinion of a People's Commissar on the subject which interests them. But— when the call is answered, they lose heart, and none of them dares to declare his identity. They are terrified of speaking to their own leaders! The propaganda for electrification is carried on apace, but—when a man has electricity put in at last, he must redecorate the whole of his room, for he cannot bear the spectacle of its pitiful dilapidation, revealed by the brighter light. And finally, his efforts are all wasted, because his landlady cuts the electric wires: she has no money for redecoration, and would rather not know how dreadful her own rooms look when lit by electricity.

One could continue indefinitely multiplying examples; some stories stress an obvious contrast, in others it is more subtle, almost concealed. They represent a series of illustrations of a universal human fallacy, the fallacy of assuming that human beings can be transformed by didactic measures alone, by government decrees, proclamations and sermons. The fact that human beings have a way of transforming the measures imposed upon them from outside, in a most profound and subtle way, always escapes the rationalist. And Russia throughout her history had, in her immensity, provided the most tempting experimental field for adventurous rationalists, of whom Peter the Great was neither the first, nor the only one. At one time, since the establishment of Bolshevism, small groups of rationalists were given free rein. Experimentation proceeded apace: measures and reforms were introduced on paper where there were no means of carrying them into practice; people were instructed in revolutionary virtues where their past had failed to prepare them for the present; and many of the reforms were destined to remain a dead letter, with the consequent rich harvest of incongruities.

From this befogged atmosphere of ideological conflicts and practical muddles, emerges the Man-in-the-street with a grin on his face. He is the animal on whom the experiment is being performed. He is an ox, if you like, who pulls the heavy chariot of a Totalitarian State, as he had for centuries pulled the tottering vehicle of the ineffective Monarchy. He is patient and mostly good-humoured, but he is by no means dumb. The old régime had ill-used him as a beast of burden, the new régime has added a restricting harness to his load. He has become a circus ox: he has to keep to a certain, very intricate 'line' of politically orthodox behaviour. Knowing the price he will have to pay if he stumbles, he grins and picks his way with great caution. But he gets some of his own back by muttering comments on his drivers and himself.

Zoshchenko's Man-in-the-street is not a thoroughbred creature with centuries of training in his blood. In the pre-revolutionary past he had little opportunity for learning, and since then, his more sophisticated brothers had been slaughtered on the altar of the Mass god. Sometimes he finds it convenient to pretend that he is more ignorant than he really is—another device of self-protection. But frequently he is genuinely ignorant, and his vocabulary is that of a child of four. Yet, with all that, he is clearly aware of the gap existing in his environment, in his mind even, between what really is and what is desirable; he has an insatiable hankering after a 'better life', which had been promised to him so often by the visionaries and the demagogues.

Will the time ever come? In one of his stories Zoshchenko makes his Man indulge in a fantasy of a wonderful scientific invention. 'Some day, may be, they'll invent some quite incredible and fantastic apparatus, perhaps a little machine called "Three Wishes". Anyone would be able to turn a little lever, and his three wishes would come true.'

'But,' he wonders a little later, 'might it not turn out to be not an undisguised blessing, after all? Might not some people turn the lever in order to grab more money, prizes, honours and respect for themselves?'

And he shrinks away from the dangerous dream into

which his unsatisfied desires have led him. 'It's best not to look too far forward,' he concludes.

One wonders, if this dream of a miraculous invention had become a reality, what would be the three secret wishes for which Zoshchenko's Man-in-the-street would turn the handle? I venture to guess that one of them, perhaps even the first, would be the one most common and natural—the wish for freedom.

> *Elisaveta Fen, in a preface to* The Wonderful Dog, and Other Tales *by Michael Zoshchenko, translated by Elisaveta Fen, 1942. Reprint by Hyperion Press, Inc., 1973, pp. v-ix.*

Rebecca A. Domar   (essay date 1953)

[*In the following excerpt, Domar describes the critical reaction to Zoshchenko's short fiction, examining the controversy surrounding the short story "Adventures of a Monkey."*]

On August 14, 1946, the Central Committee of the Soviet Communist Party, in a public statement, severely reprimanded the editorial boards of the literary journals *Star* (*Zvezda*) and *Leningrad* for publishing certain works of Zoshchenko and Akhmatova, ordered the *Star* to print no more of Zoshchenko's works, appointed A. M. Egolin as chief editor of the *Star* while retaining him as assistant director of the Board of Propaganda of the Central Committee, and abolished *Leningrad* on the ground that at that time there did not seem to be enough artistic literary works to fill the pages of two journals in the city of Leningrad.

Later that month, in his report at meetings of the active Party members and of writers of Leningrad, A. A. Zhdanov, Secretary of the Central Committee of the Communist Party, enlarged upon the Resolution.

At its meeting on September 4, the Presidium of the Board of the Union of Soviet Writers resolved, among other things, to expel Zoshchenko and Akhmatova from the Union, on the ground that only those writers can belong to the Union who "stand on the platform of Soviet power and participate in socialist construction."

In regard to Zoshchenko, the publication of his story **"Adventures of a Monkey" ("Prikliucheniia obez'iany")** by the *Star* in its May–June issue of 1946 was given as the immediate reason for these drastic decisions of the Central Committee and of the Union of Soviet Writers. At the same time it was made clear that Zoshchenko's previous writings and his past in general were not without blemish. Particular attention was drawn to his autobiographical story *Before Sunrise,* which had been published three years earlier. Finally, Zoshchenko was accused of having done nothing during the war to help his country and his people.

In the resolution of the Central Committee and in Zhdanov's report Zoshchenko's works and ideas were described as "shallow, insipid, and cheap," "encouraging a putrid ideological neutrality, crassness, and an apolitical attitude, intended to disorient our youth and poison its mind," "sinking to the lowest moral and political depths"—"a crude lampoon on Soviet life," "filth and obscenity." Zoshchenko himself was referred to as "a philistine," "a vulgarian," "a vile mind," "an unprincipled literary hooligan," "the dregs of literature."

These epithets and accusations were hurled at a writer who for the last quarter of a century had been extremely popular among Soviet readers, who had been regarded as an outstanding, if not the leading, Soviet satirist and humorist, who had often been elected by his fellow writers to positions of responsibility, who in 1939 had received the medal of the Red Labor Banner "for outstanding progress and achievements in the development of Soviet belles-lettres," and who as late as April, 1946, had been awarded a medal for his "valiant work during the Great Patriotic War of 1941-45." Zhdanov himself testified to Zoshchenko's popularity and high position in the Soviet literary world when he said in his report that the journals *Star* and *Leningrad* had been very willing to publish his works, that theaters had been "readily and gladly" placed at his disposal for the reading of his works, and that the story **"Adventures of a Monkey"** had been read in a great number of them in Leningrad.

> Moreover, he was permitted to take a leading part in the Leningrad branch of the Union of Writers and to play an active role in the literary affairs of Leningrad. . . . Zoshchenko almost became a coryphaeus of literature in Leningrad. . . . He is extolled on the Leningrad Parnassus.

In its resolution on Zoshchenko, the Union of Soviet Writers pointed out with great indignation that in 1946 a collection of Zoshchenko's stories, including **"Adventures of a Monkey,"** had been published by both the Leningrad branch of the State Publishing House and a Moscow organization ("Biblioteka Ogonëk"), in a large number of copies. The very magnitude of the storm indicates Zoshchenko's importance in the Soviet literary world and his popularity among the people.

It is difficult to reconcile the vilification of Zoshchenko as "the dregs of literature" with the familiar assertion that the tremendous progress of the Soviet people in the realm of culture has made them far superior to the peoples of the Western world, that their highly developed literary tastes clamor for the very best which Soviet and world literatures can offer them. How, then, could "the dregs of literature" have been so popular among such people? Why have they been so badly mistaken during a quarter of a century as to be unable, without the aid of the central organ of the ruling Party, to perceive the real nature of the writer? This contradiction is merely sharpened by investigation of the immediate complaints against Zoshchenko by the Central Committee and Zhdanov.

"Adventures of a Monkey," published by the *Star* in its section "New Stories for Children," was evidently intended as a tale for children, in a humorous, jocular tone. The following is a summary of the story:

> In a southern city of the USSR during the War, a little monkey, a marmoset, escapes from its cage when a bomb explodes in the zoo. Not see-

ing any use remaining in a town under bombardment, the monkey runs off into the countryside, climbs a tree, and falls asleep. A passing military man sees the monkey. Fearing that it will starve to death in these parts, he takes pity on it and carries it off to a town where he has friends who will take care of the little animal. On the way to his friends, he stops off on some business. The unguarded monkey escapes and walks along the streets of the town until it becomes hungry. Now, where can a monkey get food in a town? It cannot go to a restaurant. It cannot buy anything in a store because it has neither money nor a ration card. While passing by a cooperative food store, the monkey sees fresh vegetables on the counter. There are people standing in line, and the saleswoman is selling them food. But what does a monkey know about waiting in line, buying, selling, paying? The animal is hungry and sees food: there is no reason why it should go on being hungry while there is food. So the monkey runs over the heads of the customers to the counter, grabs a bunch of carrots, and dashes out of the store.

One can easily imagine what happens next. A whole crowd, preceded by a dog, joins the chase: first, the street boys, then a great number of adults, and after them a militiaman with his whistle. While trying to escape from this crowd, the little monkey says to itself that it should never have left the zoo: after all, it could breathe more freely in a cage than here in the street. Finally, the monkey climbs a fence, jumps into a backyard, and there is found by a boy who takes it home and feeds it. While they are having tea, the boy's grandmother puts her piece of candy on her saucer, and the monkey snatches the candy. Of course, a monkey is not like a human being: the latter would not take anybody's candy when that person could see him doing it. But the grandmother grows very angry and says that she does not want to share her house with a monkey. One of them will have to go to the zoo. The boy assures his grandmother that he will train the monkey and that she will have nothing to worry about.

Next day, when the boy is at school, the monkey gets out of the house through an open window. In the street, the animal is caught by an old man who is on his way to the bathhouse. It occurs to the old man that he can sell the monkey in the market and buy himself a few drinks for the money. But since he does not feel like returning home, he takes the monkey along to the bathhouse and starts to wash the animal there, saying to himself that he can get more money for a clean monkey than for a dirty one. At first the monkey likes the warm water and the heat in the room, but when soap gets into its eyes, it bites the old man's finger and rushes out of the bathhouse.

And, of course, there is another chase in the street. But it so happens that the boy who had kept the monkey in his home is returning from school and sees the chase. The military man who brought the monkey to the town is also passing by, as the old man comes running from the bathhouse with his boots in his hands. The boy takes the monkey in his arms and says that it is his. But the old man also claims it, and, as proof that the monkey belongs to him, shows his bitten finger. But the military man declares that he was the first master of the monkey and that he wants to give it to the boy because the boy is kind to it. The boy takes the monkey home and cares for it. He trains the little animal in such a way that the monkey learns very good manners. Children and many adults can learn their manners from the monkey.

Analysis of this story led the Central Committee of the Communist Party to the following conclusion in its decree:

> **"Adventures of a Monkey"** . . . is a vulgar lampoon on Soviet life and on Soviet people. Zoshchenko disfigures and caricatures Soviet customs and Soviet people, slanderously portraying Soviet people as primitive, uncultured, stupid, with philistine tastes and customs. Zoshchenko's malicious, hooligan-like depiction of our way of life is accompanied by anti-Soviet attacks.

Zhdanov added in his report:

> The meaning of this "work" by Zoshchenko is that he portrays Soviet people as idlers and monsters, stupid and primitive. . . .
>
> If you read the story **"Adventures of a Monkey"** very carefully and think about it, you will see that Zoshchenko bestows on the monkey the role of a supreme judge of our social customs and makes it teach the Soviet people a moral lesson. The monkey is presented as an intelligent being with the right to appraise the conduct of people. Of necessity, Zoshchenko had to give a monstrous, caricatured, and vulgar portrayal of the life of the Soviet people in order to make the monkey utter the foul, poisonous, anti-Soviet quip that it is better to live in the zoo than outside it, that one can breathe more freely in a cage than among Soviet people.
>
> Is it possible to sink any lower morally and politically? And how can the people of Leningrad tolerate such filth and obscenity on the pages of their journals?

The story is a humorous portrayal not of the Soviet people, but of mankind in general—a type of writing hardly consistent with the official conception of socialist realism. There are no specifically Soviet elements in it. The Soviet Union has no monopoly on zoological gardens, cooperative food stores, and public bathhouses: such establishments exist in many other countries as well. During the War there was rationing in many countries, and people often had to stand in line. Stupidity and alcoholism are universal evils, and not peculiarly Soviet traits. There is not one country on our planet where the manners of children and of many adults could not be improved. The only Russian element in the story consists in the proper names. The action could take place in any country of the "capitalist" world, including prerevolutionary Russia. Of all the characters in the story, only the old man is drawn as a complete fool. The grandmother, the salesgirl in the store, and the cashier in the bathhouse are treated with good-natured humor, as is the crowd which chased the monkey down the street. The boy who took care of the monkey and the military man who saved it are portrayed as kind, intelligent, and sympathetic. The only custom mentioned in the story is that of going to the public bathhouse, the sole personal "taste" or habit that of having a piece of candy with one's tea; and Zoshchenko does not make fun of them. The monkey regretted leaving the zoo, where it could breathe more freely in its cage, only while being pursued down the street by a dog and a crowd of people. The charge that Zoshchenko's story is a lampoon slandering Soviet life is an absurdity. It conveys the idea that life in the so-called "civilized" world has become rather complicated and that there are people, both children and adults, who are not perfect. There is nothing new or outrageous in this idea except that it is not treated by the one method prescribed for Soviet literature: socialist realism.

As unfounded as the criticism of **"Adventures of a Monkey"** is that given by the Central Committee, in the same vituperative terms, to Zoshchenko's story *Before Sunrise* (1943), although, it is true, some objections on the grounds of taste may be raised in this case.

The Party branded Zoshchenko as unpatriotic by its charge that, safe in his refuge at Alma-Ata, he had done nothing during the War to help the Soviet people in their struggle against the Germans. In sober fact, Zoshchenko, at the age of forty-six, suffering from a bad heart and shattered nervous system ever since he was wounded and gassed in the First World War, would have been a liability in besieged Leningrad or at the front. He was one of a considerable number of writers who found refuge in Central Asia, where the state of his health would not handicap his work. After about a year and a half there, he returned to the West. Occasional mention of Zoshchenko in the *Literary Gazette* and *Literature and Art* indicates that he was quite active during the war period, that his work was praised several times, and that in April, 1946, four months before the "storm," he received the medal for his work in the War.

Zoshchenko's expulsion from Soviet literature cannot be explained on the basis of the reasons given in the Resolution of the Central Committee and in Zhdanov's report. The real motives must be sought in the nature of his work in general and in the relations between him and the Communist Party, or what may be considered its official literary critics, from the very beginning of his career up to 1946.

Mikhail Zoshchenko was born in Petersburg in 1895. His father was Ukrainian, a painter, and his mother a Russian actress. The family belonged to the gentry. After graduating from a *gymnasium* (secondary school) in 1913, Zoshchenko entered the faculty of law of Petersburg University. Two years later he volunteered for military service and was sent to the front as an officer. From 1917 to 1921, after the combat injuries which left him in poor health for the remainder of his life, he tried a number of occupations, including voluntary service in the Red Army. In 1921 he began to write.

Zoshchenko made his appearance on the literary scene in that year as a member of the Serapion Brothers. The well-known manifesto of this early Soviet literary organization, written by Lev Lunts, was accompanied by short autobiographies of most of the "Brothers." Zoshchenko's, entitled "About Myself, about Ideology, and about One or Two Other Things," was particularly frank and irreverent. Twenty-five years later this piece was quoted by Zhdanov as a proof of Zoshchenko's "hooliganism" and "complete lack of moral principles." In spite of the frivolous and joking tone, this early autobiographical note reveals a political and ideological position in regard to Communism and the Bolsheviks which appears to have changed very little over the years. Zoshchenko wrote that he did not attach much importance to political ideology and that his own consisted in the lack of hatred for anyone. He could not have any "exact ideology," as demanded by the critics, because no political party satisfied him entirely. Still, he stood closer to the Bolsheviks than to any other party, and he was willing to go along with them. But he himself was not a Communist or a Marxist, and he doubted that he would ever be.

The manifesto and Zoshchenko's "confession" aroused strong criticism. On the whole, the critics recognized the talents of the Serapion Brothers, and some commended them for not running away from the Revolution. But the critics objected to what they considered the "incorrect" approach of the Brothers to the Revolution: they wrote in a detached manner not about this great event itself, but about petty occurrences of everyday life. One critic predicted a short life for this literary movement, while another declared the movement already dead.

Zoshchenko very soon became a favorite of Soviet readers. If the popularity of a writer can be measured by the size of the editions of his books, then during 1917-27 Zoshchenko shared second place with Gorky and Neverov (about one million copies each), after Dem'ian Bednyi (over two million copies). If, like the others, Zoshchenko had been publishing throughout the entire period, instead of during the second half only, he might well have reached the top of the list.

The works which made Zoshchenko so popular at the beginning of his literary career were, first of all, his numerous satirical short stories. In them he describes everyday incidents which take place in an overcrowded community apartment, in the street, public garden, or park, restaurant, cinema, theater, store, tavern, street car, office, village—wherever there are people. The characters are ordinary human beings drawn from all walks of life. They see the Revolution not as a great event which marked the beginning of a new and better life for Soviet citizens, but simply as a change of conditions necessitating readjustment on the part of the individual. One has to fight in order to keep or to regain one's place in life, especially one's material well-being, and, whenever possible, one may even use the new conditions to gain new advantages. Some of Zoshchenko's characters have managed to find a comfortable and warm place under the new regime, while others have difficulty in adapting themselves.

Human foibles of all kinds are the object of Zoshchenko's satire: ignorance, stupidity, cruelty, pettiness, greed, bad manners, rudeness, selfishness, narrow interests, lack of culture—in short, everything which now comes under the convenient and all-embracing titles of philistinism (*meshchanstvo*) and crassness (*poshlost'*). Zoshchenko sometimes ridicules certain defects of Soviet life, such as the housing shortage, poverty and dirt in the community apartments, the penchant for changing names and titles, incessant meetings and conferences, and what he considers the excessive concern of literature with such problems as the "liquidation" of illiteracy and the fight against alcoholism. Almost all of these early stories are told by a narrator, who speaks the language of people with little education and culture. It is full of peculiar expressions, slang, bookish and scholarly words used out of place, high-sounding slogans applied to petty occurrences of everyday life. This inimitable style—remarkable for its cleverness, wit, pointed phrases, for all shades of irony from the utterly frank to the most subtle, and sometimes very skillfully blended with lyricism—was probably one of the main reasons for Zoshchenko's great popularity; he had numerous imitators, but no successful rival.

In the few longer tales written during this period, again as satirist and humorist, Zoshchenko is content to treat only the "negative" sides of human nature and life, here mainly in members of the intelligentsia. He does not think highly of human beings in general: in his ironical prefaces, digressions, and asides, he often complains about their imperfections, both physical and mental, of their insignificance, of the mercenary motives hidden behind even their most ordinary civilities. He asserts that he does not exaggerate, that he lives in the midst of the people whom he portrays and sees them in their true colors. In his depiction, human foibles (or, let us say, "philistinism" and "crassness") are not confined to any one social class of Soviet society. From former aristocrat to poor peasant, Zoshchenko finds these traits in almost every human being, regardless of social class. And he believes that there will be enough of these topics to last him for the rest of his life. The idea that life in the future will be good and that people will live well and happily he views with frank irony. For him, "philistinism" and "crassness" are everywhere, and, what is more, they are here to stay.

By implication, then, if not by outright declaration, Zoshchenko was convinced at the beginning of his literary activity that human nature could not be changed by a revolution and a different form of government and that, consequently, the efforts and the promises of the Communist Party to reeducate the people and to create superior men and women were doomed to failure. To prove his point, of the ubiquitousness and persistence of the unregenerate homunculus, Zoshchenko drew from the life around him and from the newspapers (which often supplied him with topics for his stories) enough material for the several hundred satirical short stories and *feuilletons* which he wrote during the 1920s. Their tremendous popularity can hardly be explained by the excellence of his style alone: the wry realism of his stories must also have appealed strongly to Soviet readers, who found in them a reflection of the life they lived and saw around themselves, without the usual tiresome emphasis on official ideology and strident propaganda motives.

For this very reason, critics were placed in a peculiarly difficult dilemma in dealing with Zoshchenko, and tended to shy away from discussion of this nonconformist author whom the Soviet public read with conspicuous delight. Throughout the twenties the amount of critical attention given to a writer with such a large and enthusiastic following was disproportionately small. This neglect could be partly justified by the fact that most of his writing fell into the category which he himself ironically called "the disrespected small form," the form of the very short story, or sketch, and of the *feuilleton,* which the critics considered unworthy of their notice. They were inclined to regard him, according to Zoshchenko himself, as a mere newspaper reporter.

His longer stories, however, received more attention. (In this respect, Zoshchenko's experience paralleled that of Chekhov, between whose early work and that of Zoshchenko there is a certain similarity.) Some acclaim greeted Zoshchenko's first published pieces, the **Stories of Sinebriukhov** (1922), a series of tales told by a hapless braggart who, intent on easy pickings and the saving of his own skin, survived the horrors and absurdities of war and civil war only to find that the incomprehensible new society had no place for him. In the several long stories collected under the title **Sentimental Tales** (1927), there is a steady undercurrent of tragedy in the comic and farcical lives of the misfits and derelicts from the intelligentsia who are the heroes. At this time, before the entrenchment of the dogma that pity toward the new Soviet man was misplaced and unnecessary, critics pointed out as a virtue the sadness, sympathy, gentleness, and lyricism in Zoshchenko's narration of these stories. Other critics voiced various degrees of indignation at his "incorrect" approach to the Revolution and to Soviet life. They objected to the fact that Zoshchenko wrote not of the Revolution itself, but only of its "backyard": the trifling little incidents, the anecdotes, the man-in-the-street to whom the Revolution meant nothing but a change of government. One decrier hinted that Zoshchenko himself was no better than the heroes of his stories. And the writer was warned that, without that "complete and lofty" ideology which he had mentioned slightingly in his works, he would soon lose his place in Soviet literature.

Slyly and adroitly, Zoshchenko parried the criticism directed at him, through the fictitious narrator whom he employs in most of his work during the late twenties—a half-educated, ostensibly naive observer who, passively accepting the new order while betraying his nostalgia for the less strenuous days of the past, describes the current scene in the slang and political catchwords of the hour. In **"Hidden Treasure,"** he ridicules the new literary imperative that every piece of writing, no matter how short and insignificant, must have an ideological basis. In another story Zoshchenko's habitual mouthpiece regards with considerable irony the very idea of his writing, as the Communist critics recommended, on the subjects of the Revolution, the civil war, the changes in human life, the heroism of the people or of individuals, and the other "great" issues. He refers in the same tone of banter to the argument that belles-lettres should aid in solving problems of the day, such as a shortage of packing material, the building of silos, or the organization of collective farms. He himself did not refuse to write about such topics, but he intimated that their only proper place was in the newspaper *feuille-*

ton or the satirical sketch. In the long story **"What the Nightingale Sang About"** (1927), his narrator protests against the "materialistic" view of love he sees as prevalent among Party members, who are generally inclined to disparage this emotion. Zoshchenko's "author" cannot possibly agree with their opinion. He is loath to reveal intimate facts of his past life to unkind critics, but he remembers from his youthful days a young girl with a pathetic, silly little white face, before whom, transported by joy and all sorts of noble emotions, he would fall to his knees and kiss the ground "like a fool."

> Now, when fifteen years have passed and the author's hair is turning a little gray from various ailments and the shocks and worries of life, when the author simply does not wish to tell lies and has no reason to tell them, when, finally, the author desires to perceive life as it is without any falsehood or embellishment, he still maintains, without fear of appearing a ridiculous creature out of the past century, that scholars and politicians are very much mistaken about this matter [of love].

He deplores the concept of a human being as "out of tune" with the times and therefore to be denied a place on earth, and pleads: "Let me talk, comrades! Let a man express his idea at least for the purpose of discussion!" In response to the critical imperative that the works of Soviet writers should be optimistic and cheerful, Zoshchenko describes in **"A Gay Adventure"** the most "cheerful" occurrence he can recall, an episode reminiscent of Dostoyevsky's *Crime and Punishment* and intended as a parody on the forced optimism ground out at Party behest. He does not spare Party members his direct satire. . . .

In general, Zoshchenko's extremely subtle irony, his trick of not meaning what he says and not saying what he means created many pitfalls for the unwary critic. Several made fools of themselves by treating a satirical piece seriously. The most vociferous of Zoshchenko's critics fulminated from the tribunal of the official newspaper of the Soviet government. While recognizing Zoshchenko's talent and popularity, this critic charged him with having no love for mankind and no faith in its future, with being himself "a low, crude man-in-the-street, who with a kind of malicious joy rummages around in human refuse." The success of Zoshchenko's works ("vile anecdotes and utter slander against man") was explained by the fact that his portrayal of the contemptible little human being created by tsarist Russia and, in the author's eyes, unchanged by the Revolution, provided for some readers "a blissful escape from the loud slogans of the Revolution."

That Zoshchenko was able to publish his work in spite of the castigation by such a spokesman exemplifies the comparative freedom which Soviet writers then enjoyed. Obviously, there was much that invited satire in the tenacious residue of the old order left in the minds of the people, and in the incongruities created by the New Economic Policy in a country striving toward socialism. Throughout the twenties such material was recognized as fair game for the satirists. A license could always be revoked, however, as offenders were warned who grew careless in the vicinity of a Party preserve. In 1928, despite the warning of the preceding year, it was still possible to publish a ninety-page book devoted exclusively to critical analyses of Zoshchenko's work from the point of view of literary form, and not of political ideology. The several contributors to the volume, including the famous Shklovskii and Vinogradov, attributed Zoshchenko's distinction not to the superficial comic element and other "disrespected" features usually singled out by critics, but to his literary merits: good construction, the device of telling a story on two planes (that of the narrator and of the hero), his deft and ingenious language, deceptively simple in appearance, but actually exceedingly complex.

Again, in a foreword to the book, Zoshchenko seizes the opportunity to retort to his critics: "In literature there is a so-called 'social command.' As I see it, this command is at present erroneously formulated." What is called for is not a red Leo Tolstoy, as is demanded by the injudicious, but something like his own "disrespected" small form, associated in the past at least with the very worst literary traditions. This is the social command he obeys.

> I'm not trying to sneak into "high" literature. There are already enough writers in "high" literature as it is. . . .
>
> The thing is, I am a proletarian writer. Rather, I am parodying that imaginary, but genuine, proletarian writer who might exist in the present conditions of life and in the present milieu. Of course, such a writer cannot exist, for the time at least.
>
> I am only parodying. Temporarily I am pinch-hitting for the proletarian writer. For this reason the themes of my stories are shot through with the naive philosophy which is cut to measure for my readers.

In his longer pieces he is also parodying; in this case he is "pinch-hitting" for the writer from among the intelligentsia who perhaps does not exist at the moment, but who would have to exist if he were to fulfill the social command actually given by public opinion.

A few years later one of Zoshchenko's most sympathetic critics found the "positive" value of his work to lie in these longer pieces, where "the outlook of the intelligentsia [understood here as the former privileged classes in general] is exposed with exceeding fullness and clarity, almost with declarative statement." In this respect the novelettes are the key to his work:

> Zoshchenko takes to pieces fiber by fiber the psychology of the person of the old world: . . . the combination of crassness, mercenary calculation, profit-motive, all this pillar of bourgeois society, based on private property, with an elaborate system of "elevated" ethical and esthetic standards.
>
> The man of the bourgeois world, caught in the vicious circle of its inconsistencies, cannot accede to the Revolution, which strips away all masks and exposes all contradictions. He is doomed to complete disorientation . . . and to moral destruction.

At the end of this first period of Zoshchenko's career, the writer himself answers point-blank the importunate question put to him by the critics from the beginning, the question of his work as a social factor in socialist reconstruction:

> In our time, is the role of an exposer and satirist like Zoshchenko adequate if the writer wishes to be in reality a writer of his epoch?
>
> [It has been shown] what forces the work of Zoshchenko disposes of and destroys. What forces, then, does he . . . affirm in his work? What is contrasted to that twisted metaphysical system of the philistine outlook which he has exposed? . . .
>
> This question was put to Zoshchenko in one of his talks with beginning writers. "You boldly satirize our social deficiencies. Why do you not unite these deficiencies with achievements? Will you be able to work in this way?" To this question Zoshchenko answered: "The thing is that my genre, that is the genre of the humorist, is incompatible with description of achievements. That is the concern of writers of another genre. To each his own way: the tragic actor plays in *Hamlet*; the comic actor plays in *Revizor*. It seems to me that each one must proceed according to his own bent."

> *Rebecca A. Domar, "The Tragedy of a Soviet Satirist: The Case of Zoshchenko," in* Through the Glass of Soviet Literature: Views of Russian Society, *edited by Ernest J. Simmons, Columbia University Press, 1953, pp. 201-43.*

Zoshchenko, circa 1923.

Sidney Monas (essay date 1961)

[*In the following excerpt from his introduction to* Scenes from the Bathhouse, and Other Stories of Communist Russia, *Monas provides an overview of the structure and themes of Zoshchenko's short fiction.*]

Mikhail Zoshchenko was born in 1895. His father was an artist, a nobleman, and a bit of a philanderer. His mother was a woman who demanded much and received little. Distressed by her son's behavior, she accused him of being like his father—"a solitary" and "a frozen heart." It wasn't exactly a happy family, but intellectually cultivated and financially comfortable.

He grew up in St. Petersburg, that "unreal city" of fogs and floods, the capital of a decadent empire, and the source of a great literary mythology that expressed the alienation of man from nature and from his own humanity. As a writer Zoshchenko remained fairly immune to the power of this myth. His positivist bent was too strong. He wrote as a detached observer of the street and the everyday, of manners rather than morals, of the commonplace, rather than of the phantasmagoria of Gogol and Bely, the writers of the myth. As a personality, however, he was a true alienated product of the "artificial" city and, like many great comedians, a morose, melancholic, estranged man, driven to humor and "play" as his only means of handling a gross and cacophonous world.

He was a strange, frail, sensitive, detached, proud, and rather difficult child. He read a great deal, especially in the biologic sciences, which caught his interest at an early age. He undoubtedly read Gogol and Leskov. His independent spirit made school uncomfortable for him, and he did not do well there. He found it difficult to forgive a schoolmaster who commented "Rubbish!" on one of his early compositions.

World War I broke out while Zoshchenko was still enrolled as a student at the University of St. Petersburg, and he hastened to volunteer. He was several times wounded, several times decorated, and promoted rapidly to the rank of major. He suffered not only the hardships of war and the responsibilities of command, but the vagaries of his own temperament—by no means a heroic one.

In the summer of 1916 he was gassed, and his health went to pieces. Then, assigned by the Kerensky government to administer a military post office in Archangel at the time of the Allied occupation of that port, he rejected an opportunity he had there—proffered by an attractive Frenchwoman—of emigrating to Paris. Soon after that, he volunteered for the Red Army and saw action again in Lithuania, but his health forced him to retire within six months.

Zoshchenko's early melancholy persisted and drove him to take on a series of bizarre jobs. He worked as an instructor in poultry husbandry on an experimental collective farm; he was a detective, a professional gambler, a telephone operator for the border guard, and (for him, perhaps the most bizarre job of all) a clerk-typist. On the whole, he preferred nonclerical, nonintellectual work; no job, however, held him for long. In 1921 he was back in his native Petrograd, discovering his real and permanent profession—that of a writer.

In the early twenties Zoshchenko was associated with a group of young writers who called themselves the Serapion Brethren after the hermit Serapion as he is portrayed in a tale by E. T. A. Hoffmann, a writer they admired. These young men were what Trotsky called "fellow travelers." They were willing to go along with the Bolsheviks but were eager to maintain a certain independence of outlook and to avoid party discipline. In response to the enthusiasm of party literati for using the arts as effective propaganda, Victor Shklovsky, a talented critic and a Serapion Brother, posed a question: "Can you drive nails with a samovar?" He answered: "Yes, you can. But that is not what it is for."

The Serapion Brethren did not favor "art for art's sake." Their preoccupation with style was of a very different kind from that of the symbolists. They abhorred the mystique of inspiration and the cult of art. They were not religious. Symbolism tasted stale to them. The Brethren preferred to think of themselves as craftsmen rather than geniuses. They tried for a fresh language based on popular usage, on the vocabulary and syntax of the street and countryside. What they had over reality was not so much a firm grip as a light touch.

These men were vivid and original experimenters, and Russian literature of the twenties owes much to them. Their independence of spirit was not so deep, however, as to involve them in tragic consequences when the relative freedom of the twenties came to an end. They did not struggle too hard when independence had to be abandoned. Of the prose writers of the group, Zoshchenko alone continued to write in much the same vein in the thirties as he had in the twenties. He was still not a hero, but he had a certain Schweikian talent for personal survival and for survival as a writer.

Zoshchenko is a very funny writer: that much needs no arguing. He is funnier to Russians than he is to those who see his stories at a considerable distance from the situations they describe and from the language that is so peculiarly appropriate to them. Yet, he is as far from being a local folk-humorist as he is from being a conventional, "classical" satirist. If he is a satirist at all, it is in the more ancient, original sense of the term—a writer of satyr plays. His theme is not the corruption of morals, but brute energy and animal desire which burn through manners as through a cardboard grate.

The theme which runs through all of Zoshchenko's works is the fiery resistance nature offers to history. He himself is a detached observer, neither on one side nor the other. He has been burned by both.

Zoshchenko's technique is that of the *skaz*, the oral tale. The tale is supposed to have a moral, instructional point, to illustrate something; that is the excuse for telling and listening. But the point gets lost on the way: the storyteller is caught up in the story itself or simply succumbs to the delight of having an audience. It is himself he expresses, and not the moral. Either he loses it completely and arrives at a conclusion as unexpected for him as it is for his audience, or he tacks it on by *force majeure*, exposing either his own clay feet or the insubstantiality of all conclusions, or both. In Russian literature it was Leskov who first developed this technique, derived from popular story-telling. The narrator is himself a character, whom we come to understand through the words and expressions he uses and misuses, his repetitions, digressions, the things he chooses to talk about, and the things we know are there between the lines but which he is clearly incapable of expressing. The difference between the *skaz* and the ordinary "point-of-view" story or novel is, first of all, its oral quality—the sound of the spoken voice—and, secondly, the untutored, "primitive" nature of the narrator, his unself-consciousness. Among American writers, Ring Lardner uses this technique in a number of places—in his baseball stories, and most successfully in the story called "Haircut." However, Lardner was much more of a moralist than either Leskov or Zoshchenko. He used the technique to condemn the narrator or to induce the reader to feel sorry for him. Leskov and Zoshchenko do this to a far lesser degree. As in Lardner, the narrator inadvertently expresses his own *poshlost*—his vulgarity, his trashiness, the cheap fake of his pretensions—but this is less important than the sheer absurdity of the tricks nature plays with him. Leskov was capable of sustaining this kind of interest over considerable length. Zoshchenko, like most moderns, is shorter-winded, but the brevity of his stories is part of their effect.

They are composed with care, with attention to details of diction, inflection, and rhythm. This is by no means obvious, and, indeed, the effect would be lost if it were. The materials are so primitive that the reader would instantly resent any kind of obvious manipulation on Zoshchenko's part as grossly unfair. The effects of spontaneity and immediacy, of the candid photograph, the sketch made hastily on the spot exactly as observed, the tape recording, are all indispensable to Zoshchenko's art.

Zoshchenko is, obviously, a very funny writer. Nevertheless, the over-all effect of his work is anything but funny. He leaves one with the sense of a dreary, depressing, mournful, almost intolerable world.

—Sidney Monas

The situations that provide the material for his stories are the most common and ordinary details of everyday Soviet reality, familiar not only to the average Soviet citizen but even to the casual tourist: the housing shortage, the scarcity of consumers' goods and the inefficiency of consumers' services, bad roads, bureaucracy and red tape, the ferocious juxtapositions of backwardness and material progress. These things are not merely the background for the stories: they determine motives, they shape or obliterate intentions, they conceal, they expose, they frustrate, they assume a shape and a character of their own, and they are felt as a natural force almost as intractable and indifferent to human concern as the desert or the sea. They may be

tricked or circumvented, but they cannot be made to care; moreover, they will inevitably leave their stamp on the trickers and circumventers. A person may resemble the desert; the desert is never like a man.

Personal problems and private griefs, fine feelings and an aesthetic sense, are reduced, against this desert, to the scale of absurdity. It isn't fidelity or infidelity in marriage that counts; it's the availability of an apartment. People will, of course, attempt to inflate their feelings in talk, but they are betrayed by the language they use. The desert is not only around them, it is in them.

Zoshchenko uses careless language carefully. His narrators are not illiterate peasants, but they are usually not far removed from that condition. Their talk is anything but folksy. It is a weird mixture of peasant idiom, misunderstood highfalutin phrases, rhetorical flourishes, explanatory asides that are anything but explanatory, repetitions, omissions, propaganda jargon absurdly adapted to homey usage, instructional pseudoscientific words, foreign phrases, and proverbial clichés joined to the latest party slogans. For his diction and syntax, even more than for the situations in which they occur, Zoshchenko was charged with "caricature." In his autobiography, however, Zoshchenko insists that he merely records the language of the streets, arranging and selecting, it is true, but not exaggerating.

The struggle between nature and history, backwardness and revolution, produces the kind of anomalous situation that Zoshchenko delights in, and he swoops like a hawk on those peculiarities of the Russian language and its usage which reflect that struggle. His verbal "soup," the words he chooses for his palette, are often themselves the product of the kind of situation he is writing about. Take the story **"Kochergà"**: here, the action centers entirely on the peculiarities of this everyday word.

Kochergà means "a poker," and nothing could be more ordinary. However, its associations are with dark little houses heated by wood stoves around which bearded faces nod. It is out of place in the office building of a modern bureaucracy. Because of the shortage of space, a new state institution is housed in an old building that has no central heating and is kept warm by means of six wood stoves located in different parts of the building. The old stoker tends these, mumbling into his beard as he carries his *kochergà* from one to the other. When an employee who accidentally bumps into him has her hand burned by the poker, the old peasant shows himself surprisingly on the side of history and suggests to the manager of the establishment a rationalization of his work. If there were a poker by each stove, the risk of singeing employees could be avoided. All the manager has to do is order five more pokers from the warehouse, but here the manager comes to grief.

Although it is a perfectly common word, *kochergà* is of Tartar origin (another aspect of its dark association) and has grammatical peculiarities. In Russian, the number five takes the genitive plural of the noun—but what is the genitive plural of *kochergà*? Nobody knows. The manager is a bureaucrat; he cannot afford to consult other institutions, such as the Academy of Sciences; it wouldn't do for his dignity and career. He exhausts all intellectual resources within his own establishment. In desperation he even calls on the stoker—he may be a peasant but he *is* a specialist in stoves—"been around them all his life." The stoker responds, using, naturally, the diminutive form so dear to peasant speech. For dignity, that won't do either: the manager doesn't want to be taken for a peasant. Finally, he attempts to resolve his dilemma by calling in a member of his legal staff to draft an order which will obtain the "five pokers" without having to refer to them directly. The resulting document is a masterpiece, but it comes to nothing. There is a shortage; there *aren't* any pokers. The warehouse answers using the diminutive form.

Zoshchenko's longer stories, which he calls novelle, are literary parodies. They are what happens when *poshlost* claims for itself not the intelligence but the sentiment of genius. **"Michel Siniagin"** is a parody of the literary memoirs that appeared with such frequency both in Russia and abroad in the ten years or so following the Revolution, written by men of the symbolist generation who had met Tolstoi or seen Blok disappearing around the corner. **"Love"** is a parody of the gnomic wisdom-literature *à la* Rozanov, dear to the apocalyptic generation of the Russian intelligentsia. Zoshchenko never forgave the schoolmaster and the editors who wanted him to "write like a classic." He takes the pretension to style and the pretension to fine feeling into the world of the housing shortage. It bounces like an oversized lead balloon.

The lead balloon is one kind of literary parody Zoshchenko uses; there is another, which he uses much more subtly, which we might call the cork anchor. In the story called **"An Amusing Adventure,"** Zoshchenko adapts the traditional form of bourgeois bedroom farce to his own abbreviated story form and to the "new class" of the Soviet overprivileged. It would be a mistake, however, to see this as a satire on "new class" morality. Zoshchenko does not seem to have anything against the privileged status of his protagonists, nor does he seem to have anything against their marital infidelity. True, he makes fun of their lies and deceptions; he doesn't like lies. But who does? The story is, in fact, completely lacking in moral bite. The point, if we must have a point beyond the *brio* of the story itself, is that nature is still with us, even in the socialist society; that having a bedroom at all is often more important than who sleeps in it; that rationality is a convention like marriage, and a pretty frail one; and that contrary to the usual ending of bourgeois farce, bedroom tangles do not lend themselves easily to rational solution, but only to further bedroom tangles—if one has a bedroom, that is.

In the story called *"Liaisons Dangereuses,"* the parody, this time of Choderlos de Laclos' great psychological novel, is even more subtle. In the French novel, the supremely intelligent and self-conscious hero has succeeded in mastering his animal nature and completely subordinating it to his will and intellect, which are committed to power—that is, to asserting his superiority over other human beings. His greatest "success" is his own self-destruction. Unlike the other works which Zoshchenko parodies, *"Liaisons Dangereuses"* is a model of brevity and lucidity of style. But Zoshchenko's very stupid hero

manages to achieve the same result by the opposite means in much briefer compass!

It should be abundantly clear by now that Zoshchenko was not a typical satirist of the period of the New Economic Policy (the NEP, 1921-28) like Ilf and Petrov. That period was, nevertheless, peculiarly congenial to him. Not only was it a period of vigorous experimentation in all fields—especially the arts—during which his stories could pass as *"samo-kritika"* ("self-criticism," dear to the Bolsheviks, in which everything can be taken for a ride except the big boys on top and the policy they make), but the NEP itself created a rather obvious Zoshchenko-like world. It was a period during which a prominent Bolshevik (Bukharin) put on the mask of Guizot to urge the still uncollectivized Russian peasants to "enrich themselves." It was a period during which free enterprise was considered embarrassing but necessary, and during which the new socialist society suffered all the ills its leaders attributed to capitalism—unemployment, graft, exploitation—but during which it was still relatively free and uncoerced. The interaction of the old and the new, the ideal and the real, the brilliant and the backward, in the landscape of an underdeveloped and rather primitive economy, produced Zoshchenko types and Zoshchenko situations with a profusion that even the talented Ukrainian writer from Leningrad could not take full advantage of.

From the time of the Five-Year plans, Zoshchenko's life as a writer became increasingly hazardous. In 1946 he was singled out, along with Anna Akhmatova, for particularly violent attack by no less a party figure than Zhdanov, a pseudo critic, who called him a "pseudo writer." The story Zhdanov attacked most particularly and crudely was the curiously innocent little parable, **"The Adventures of an Ape."** From that time on, Zoshchenko published little—a few stories, a few articles. In the early days of the thaw, he wrote a few sketches on writing and writers which appeared in the humor magazine *Krokodil*—mildly courageous pieces, not uninteresting but undistinguished. In general, his stories after 1946, though not different in substance from his earlier work, lack the force and fun of the real Zoshchenko.

He died in 1958 at what, for him, was a fairly ripe old age. An edition of his collected stories appeared shortly after his death and was quickly sold out. He seems to have left behind no imitators (with the possible exception of K. himself) and no disciples, and his name no longer appears in print in the Soviet Union, even for attack.

For the nontotalitarian reader it is at first a little difficult to understand the violence of Zhdanov's obliterating speech. It is true that Zoshchenko makes bureaucrats look absurd, that he exposes the inefficiencies and incompatibilities of daily life in the Soviet Union, and that he is more than a little wistful about the goods famine. But these things are well within the pale of *samokritika*. One can find their equivalents in almost any issue of *Pravda* or *Krokodil*. What, then, was the real reason?

A "pseudo writer": an interesting expression. It is a little like calling Harry Truman a "pseudo politician." The point is that Zoshchenko was a real writer and nothing but a writer, and that in spite of a few deliberately disconcerting gestures to the contrary, he never tried to drive nails with a samovar. In a totalitarian society, that is reason enough to blast away. However, there were even better ones.

Reading one or a few stories of Zoshchenko is not the same as reading him in bulk. He is, obviously, a very funny writer. Nevertheless, the over-all effect of his work is anything but funny. He leaves one with the sense of a dreary, depressing, mournful, almost intolerable world. One might well exclaim, as Pushkin was supposed to on reading Gogol: "How sad is our Russia!" Moreover, Zoshchenko's "objective correlatives" are very much more obviously *there,* in the real world, than Gogol's were. It is not so much a question of his violation of this or that canon of socialist realism, of his remaining inside or outside the bounds of *samo-kritika,* as of the total effect of his work. Altogether, one can hardly claim that Zoshchenko's stories would bolster the mandatory optimism of a Soviet citizen.

There is a short preface appended to one of the hospital stories. In it Zoshchenko states that *Krokodil* had entrusted him with a number of letters to the editor complaining of treatment in Soviet hospitals and had commissioned him to write either a conventional article, in the *samo-kritika* vein, or a sketch. He claims that he decided, after deliberation, on the latter; but we cannot believe for a moment that he deliberated at all. Any or even all of the details might appear in a conventional Soviet article; however, the hospital we see is a Zoshchenko hospital, and surely he could have created no other. It is the essence of everything that is wrong with hospitals at their worst, where science (which Zoshchenko respects almost as Gogol respected religion) goes astray in the hands of a contemptuous, case-hardened bureaucracy.

Again, Zoshchenko has never created a single "positive hero" (a *must,* for Soviet writers)—one that Zhdanov could look on with approval. Few of the stories are without some human pathos, and some (like **"The Crisis,"** one of his funniest) actually approach the humor of Charlie Chaplin; unlike Chaplin's films, however, Zoshchenko's "little fellows" rarely came out on top.

For the most part, his protagonists are fools, knaves, charlatans, fakes, poseurs, reeking of *poshlost.* There are some exceptions. Nazar Ilich Sinebriukhov (the hero of **"Victoria Kazimirovna"**), although vamped by a false ideal, has heroic traits. So does the protagonist of **"My Professions."** However, most of his people are victims—either of themselves, or of history, or of nature, or of all three.

Let us examine more closely what happens when Zoshchenko takes nature to the bathhouse. You can't do without a public bathhouse when there's an acute housing shortage. There is something elemental and at the same time microcosmic about this locale, and Zoshchenko returns to it obsessively. There are three bathhouse stories in this collection, written about twenty years apart. The first is by far the funniest and makes the most vivid impression, and the other two depend on one's having read the first for their effect. For one thing, all three stories take

place in the *same* bathhouse. By taking a good look at the décor, by noting how the arrangements change, and by listening to the quality of the talk, one can learn something of what the Five-Year plans have done, and what they have not done.

The first story is Chaplinesque. The "little fellow" is frustrated by the crude and irrational arrangements at every turn. He needs tickets to get his clothes back. "But where is a naked man going to put tickets?" He can't get himself clean because the other bathers, scrubbing out their dirty laundry, keep splashing him. He is denied even the elementary pleasure of hearing the soap squeak as he washes himself. Frustration at every point.

In the second story, conditions have improved considerably. Manners are more civilized—but only on the surface. Clothes are stolen. The manager who barges in when the theft is reported turns out to be a woman who embarrasses everyone in the men's dressing room. The "little fellow" who had his clothes stolen turns out, after some administrative confusion, to have been a thief himself. The problems here are already a little more complex.

The third story is scarcely funny at all. It is a "symbolic" story, not the sort of thing Zoshchenko does best. It ends on a note of real gloom, which Zoshchenko's attempt to modify by rather mechanical means does little to attenuate. The bathhouse by this time is everything a public bathhouse should be. The bathers are decorous and civilized. The manager is still a woman, the same woman, but elderly now and with some respect for the dignity of her male customers. Yet, something is wrong, in a deeper and far more complicated way. There is a malady.

One of the attendants is a bright-eyed young lad from the country. What is he doing, working at a job like this? He has ambition but no imagination. One of the customers is a stuffy, unpleasant, moralistic papa, who keeps lecturing his snively little boy (his name, shades of Gogol, is Icarus!) on public behavior. Another is an even more unpleasant, and even sinister, buttinsky who can't wait to denounce someone to the police. The central figure is an elderly mechanic who has earned a Soviet fortune by working for years at bonus wages in the Far East, for a motive that has now become irrelevant, and who carries his wealth as though it were an albatross. He cannot spend it; he cannot give it away; he is not a miser and takes no joy in keeping it for its own sake. "It's only money." However, in this case it is symbolic money. The old mechanic has won out against nature, but in the winning he has had to make himself the kind of man for whom the victory is useless. He leaves the bathhouse in deep melancholy. Zoshchenko doesn't bring this one off too well. This bathhouse is almost bathos; but against the background of the two other stories it is not without a certain power.

The cumulative effect of Zoshchenko's stories is, as I have noted, a depressing one. His work is poor in positive figures and entirely lacking in heroes of the imperative never-never-land type that socialist realism requires. In this struggle with nature, there are moments of real pathos and occasional little victories, but no triumphs. If orthodox Soviet critics try to palm off Gogol's nightmare world as "the Russia of his time," they would like to pass off Zoshchenko's Russia as a misfit "pseudo writer's" nightmare, or still better, ignore it entirely.

One aspect of Zoshchenko's work is depressing in a different sense: his curious lack of development as a writer. The third bathhouse story, it is true, involves a far more complex situation than the first; but Zoshchenko's means are not up to it. His successful pieces, in spite of their enormous range of incidents and their variety of observed detail, have a curious sameness. Nor is this a function of their brevity alone. (One has only to compare an early Chekhov story with a later one to grasp what a writer's development means.) Nor is it the limitation of his talent. At least there are a few striking indications that this is not the case.

"Victoria Kazimirovna," one of his very early stories, written in 1917 and published in his first volume, is of a quite different dimension than the rest of his work. The gallows humor, the crude and yet complex cogitations of Nazar Il'ich Sinebriukhov, his peasant's way of looking out for himself, knowing his life isn't worth much but that he has no other, his infatuation with the strumpet-aristocrat, Victoria Kazimirovna—these have a depth and a resonance and a poignance that is lacking elsewhere: "Only I remembered then just how that crow had flown over me . . . Och, I pulled myself together." That crow is Sinebriukhov's vision of his own death. Isaac Babel might have been glad to have written this story.

> *Sidney Monas, in an introduction to* Scenes from the Bathhouse, and Other Stories of Communist Russia *by Mikhail Zoshchenko, edited by Marc Slonim, translated by Sidney Monas, The University of Michigan Press, 1961, pp. v-xvii.*

Hugh McLean   (essay date 1963)

[*In the following excerpt from his introduction to* Nervous People, and Other Satires, *McLean discusses the role of narrator in Zoshchenko's trademark satirical short stories.*]

One of the paradoxes of post-Revolutionary Russian literature has been the remarkable vitality of comedy and satire. After all, revolution is a grim and bloody business, and its aftermath is often grimmer and bloodier than the revolution itself, as totalitarian fanaticism with its program of planned happiness and its machinery of planned terror undertakes the task of compressing a nation's life into a predetermined mold. The consequences are material hardship, social dislocation, and omnipresent fear—all of which have been features of Russian life since 1917. Whatever the economic, social, and military achievements of the Soviet regime, it is hard to see how its subjects have found much in it to laugh at. Indeed, it would almost seem as if laughter were forbidden them altogether—public, literary laughter at any rate. Most laughter is by nature irreverent, and irreverence is by definition subversive: it is "unfear" (*in-re-vereri*). If fear is the chief emotional instrument of rule, then laughter becomes a danger to the state. What the Soviet regime has therefore sought from its literary servants has been not laughter but reverent, "epic" celebrations of its own greatness, choruses of everlasting yeas.

But the nay-saying strain in human nature is a strong one, and somehow laughter manages to survive a surprising amount of prohibiting pressure. In any event, it is a fact that some of the greatest comic works of modern times have been written by Soviet Russians: the two satirical plays by Vladimir Mayakovsky, the two picaresque novels *The Twelve Chairs* and *The Golden Calf,* as well as the short stories and *feuilletons* by Ilya Ilf and Evgeny Petrov, and the stories, tales, and sketches of Mikhail Zoshchenko.

Since it extends all the way from the Revolution to 1958, Zoshchenko's literary career offers a vivid illustration of the vicissitudes of a Soviet humorist during those forty turbulent years. He was born in 1895, in the Ukrainian town of Poltava, but spent most of his life in St. Petersburg. His Ukrainian father was a mediocre painter of historical subjects. His mother, a Great Russian, had been an actress. The family appears to have been comfortably off, distinctly upper-class in mores and tastes. Zoshchenko attended a good Gymnasium and later enrolled in the Faculty of Law at Petersburg University, but did not complete the course. In 1914 he volunteered for military service and after a special indoctrination course was commissioned a sub-lieutenant and shipped off to the front. He saw a great deal of action, was wounded several times and also gassed—an experience which left him with permanent damage to his heart and liver.

Doubtless the satirist's mocking, derisive, generally negative view of human beings and their pretensions was already ingrained in Zoshchenko by the time of the Revolution. It showed itself partly in the extreme restlessness which led him through an extraordinary series of jobs and occupations during the revolutionary period, and it was probably a factor in his decision to side with the Reds in the Civil War. He joined the Red Army in 1918, more from negative than from positive motives, as he later confessed: "I am not a Communist, and I entered the Red Army to fight against the nobility and the landlords, a milieu I know quite well enough." Because of his war injuries he was released from the Red Army as physically unfit for service and spent the next few years acquiring a varied storehouse of potential literary material. "In three years I changed cities twelve times and professions ten. I was a policeman, a bookkeeper, a cobbler, an instructor in aviculture, a telephone operator for the border patrol, a detective, a court secretary, and a government chief clerk."

But during this kaleidoscopic succession of experiences Zoshchenko was clearly preparing himself for his true calling, literature. He began writing professionally in 1921, and his first volume of collected stories appeared in 1922. It was an immediate success with the reading public—a success Zoshchenko was to repeat and maintain for many years to come, in fact for as long as he was allowed to publish. During the twenties and thirties he was, next to Gorky, the most popular living Russian writer. Huge editions of his works were reprinted again and again, and the name Zoshchenko became a household word among persons who could hardly have mentioned another contemporary writer. At the same time, this mass popularity was not purchased at the price of any loss of artistic integrity or even of the esteem of the literati; indeed, Zoshchenko is one of the few writers of modern times who have successfully bridged the gap between the elite and the average reader. The most astute and discriminating critics, like Viktor Shklovsky and Viktor Vinogradov, were as entranced by his stories as any philistine in the street.

From the very beginning of his literary career Zoshchenko showed an unusual independence and boldness of attitude—a sturdy refusal to see the world through any glasses but his own. In the early 1920's he was associated with a remarkable group of young writers who called themselves the "Serapion Brothers," taking their name from the hermit hero of one of E. T. A. Hoffman's stories. Despite their vast differences over literary principles, forms, and subjects, the group shared a common conviction that art should maintain its independence from politics and its freedom to follow its own devices. It was for a collection of autobiographical pieces, *The Serapion Brothers About Themselves,* that Zoshchenko wrote his own manifesto of independence. This was an unusually bold piece even for such a bold company, but the boldness was ostensibly tempered by the offhand tone of sly banter which was to become Zoshchenko's trademark:

> . . . Being a writer is sort of hard . . . Take ideology—these days a writer has got to have ideology.
>
> Here's Voronsky now (a good man) who writes: "It is necessary that writers should have a more precise ideology." Now that's downright disagreeable! Tell me, how can I have a "precise ideology" when not a single party among them all appeals to me?
>
> I don't hate anybody—that's *my* precise ideology.
>
> Still more precise, if you please. Well, in their general swing the Bolsheviks are closer to me than anybody else. And so I'm willing to bolshevik around with them . . . But I'm not a Communist (or rather, not a Marxist), and I think I never will be.

Needless to say, this damaging document was unearthed by heresy-hunting literary detectives of later years and hurled back at Zoshchenko with the customary cries of outraged admonition, and it was to constitute one of the main points in the bill of particulars against Zoshchenko drawn up by Comrade Zhdanov in 1946. By that time such a pledge of qualified allegiance sounded as seditious as a bomb hurled at the Kremlin walls.

During the relatively liberal twenties and even later Zoshchenko somehow managed to get away with his irreverences. To be sure, there were warnings—rumbles, snarls, and even an occasional nip—from the regime's literary watchdogs, but as yet no all-out assault. No doubt Zoshchenko's persistence in the face of these repeated danger signals was a demonstration of his determination and courage. But that he succeeded for so long in displaying his boldness in print was one of the advantages of his peculiar artistic method—a combination of irony, ambiguity, and camouflage which for many years bewildered his censors. It was discouragingly hard to pin him down.

Zoshchenko's method of artistic camouflage was not actually invented by him, but rather adapted from certain nineteenth-century Russian writers who had faced similar problems in evading the Czarist censorship, particularly Gogol and Leskov. The basic ruse is to create uncertainty in the reader's mind about the author's relation to his work and in particular about his emotional attitude toward the events and characters presented. One way of doing this is to interpose a narrator between the author and the story, preferably a narrator sharply distinguished in some way—origin, status, education, or sex—from the author himself. The author then ostensibly figures merely as a transmitting agent and presumably cannot be held responsible for the narrator's statements. If the narrator expresses heretical ideas or reprehensible attitudes, they cannot be charged to the author; indeed, if the narrator is presented in a negative or satirical manner, the author may well maintain that his own position is diametrically opposed.

From the artistic point of view the important thing in "camouflage" narrative of this kind is to establish the distinction between author and narrator, not merely by stating it explicitly, but by embedding it in the texture of the story itself. In other words, the narrator must be set apart from the author not only socially and morally, but also stylistically. This is easiest to do, even in Soviet Russia, if the author and narrator belong to different social classes. Clearly, for speakers of a given language, geographical region and class constitute the chief social determinants of linguistic behavior; and for purposes like Zoshchenko's, class is the more satisfactory basis for "motivating" a stylistic distinction between author and narrator. Two individuals who come from the same region but belong to different classes will share many of the same experiences but see them from different points of view and, most important, express their views in different natural styles. The satirist can then provide, so to speak, a simultaneous double commentary on the events presented: one, the narrator's, explicit, and the other, his own, implicit. Of course, this distinction in styles may have artistic functions other than camouflage. The mode of narration is an effective means of characterizing the narrator himself, who is frequently a prominent actor in his own tale; and often the narrator's style, if colorful enough, has artistic value in its own right, a diverting display of picturesque linguistic behavior.

In a series of stories written in the early twenties, Zoshchenko used a narrator very close to the Leskovian archetype: Gospodin Sinebryukhov (Mr. Bluebelly), an ex-peasant and ex-sergeant in the Czar's army, who regales us with tales of his experiences in the war and its aftermath. These experiences are varied and entertaining enough, but Bluebelly's greatest artistic distinction lies in his use of language, which is somehow symbolic of the whole disrupted era of war and revolution. Though fundamentally a "dumb" peasant, he has become semiliterate during his years in the army and has picked up bits and pieces of linguistic "civilization," rather poorly assimilated, in the form of newspaper jargon, foreign words, often distorted and imperfectly understood, and "officialese." This peasant in a state of transition toward urban mass culture is a pathetic and often ludicrous creature, and the incongruous hodgepodge of his language is intrinsically funny. And of course, in this bizarre language Bluebelly can make all sorts of dubious judgments about the world he lives in without anyone's dreaming of attributing these views to Mikhail Zoshchenko.

Before long, Zoshchenko found less obvious stylistic masks than Bluebelly. In most of the stories written after the mid-twenties Zoshchenko took a somewhat better educated narrator than Sinebryukhov, though one still socially and intellectually distant from the author. The language of this new narrator approaches normal Russian, though not normal literary Russian. It is highly colloquial in tone and often in vocabulary, and its forays into literariness are usually tinged with parody, mostly unconscious. It represents the language of the urban man-in-the-street, the semi-educated mass man. This language is distinguished from Zoshchenko's own not so much by obvious grotesqueries like Sinebryukhov's—though there are some of these—as by its sheer colloquial informality, its deviation from accepted norms of literary discourse. Reading it, we inevitably conclude that a person who speaks this way must belong to the lower orders of society; he could not have passed through the taboo-imposing experiences of a traditional Gymnasium and university education. Further, this informality of language symbolizes and blends with the ideas and sentiments it communicates— "everyman's" reflections, sometimes apt, often ignorant, almost always naïve, on life and the world around him. "Debased" language combined with naïveté of thought implies that the author's attitude toward his apparent spokesman is tinged with irony, and we naturally conclude that the narrator's ideas are to be regarded with skepticism. But we cannot always be sure. Sometimes "naïve" remarks, like the child's observation about the emperor's clothes, have a way of striking taboo targets. The reader's uncertainty—is the author being serious or not?—proved extremely useful to Zoshchenko throughout his entire career.

Besides his value as a mask for a censor-shy author, this man-in-the-street narrator with a taste for armchair philosophizing is a remarkably vital creation in his own right. There is a satisfying, down-to-earth humanness about him, a kind of philistine vigor which helps us to see things in their proper proportions. He is the voice of the philistine in all of us. In an era of ringing words and cataclysmic events, when empires are toppling and the advent of a new epoch in human history is being proclaimed, he asserts the eternal verities of what the Russians call *byt,* a rather pejorative term for the mundane aspects of everyday life. Socialism, communism, world revolution, the end of the exploitation of man by man, the five-year plan in four years—all this is very well, Zoshchenko's hero seems to say, I'm for it and take pride in it, and so forth. But our real lives are not lived on this plane. Striped socks, sausages, sofas, bedbugs, bathrooms, and sex: these are the things that really stir our souls. There is more human pas-

sion in some housewives' squabble in a communal kitchen or in a bridegroom's quest for a second-hand armoire than in a hundred *Pravda* pep talks.

In a collection of novelettes called **Sentimental Tales** which he published in 1929 Zoshchenko "lays bare," to use a favorite term of the Russian formalists, the ambiguous relationship between himself and his narrator; he calls attention to it, makes it explicit. The book has three prefaces, supposedly to three successive editions. The first two are signed by the putative author, one I. V. Kolenkorov (the name comes from the Russian word for "calico," a cheap, mass-produced material doubtless symbolic of Kolenkorov's social and cultural standing). In both his prefaces Kolenkorov expresses his gratitude to "the well-known writer Mikhail Zoshchenko" for his kind assistance in putting the tales into publishable form. In the third preface this well-known assistant comes out from behind the scenes and speaks in his own name:

> In view of previous misunderstandings, the author informs his critics that the person who tells these stories is, so to speak, an imaginary figure. He is the middling type of intellectual who happened to live on the border line between two epochs. We were forced to endow this upstart of ours, I. V. Kolenkorov, with such things as neurasthenia, ideological waverings, gross contradictions, and melancholy. The author himself, M. M. Zoshchenko, the writer, is, it is true, the son and brother of such unhealthy people, but he has long since surmounted all that. At the present time he has no contradictions. If he may occasionally lack complete peace of mind, it is for entirely different reasons, which the author will tell about sometime later. In this instance it is a literary device. And the author implores his esteemed critics to remember this particular fact before they open fire on a defenseless writer.

Of course, such ostensible revelations of the author's true face are in fact only sleight-of-hand tricks with the "calico" mask. The "true" author, though he calls himself M. M. Zoshchenko, proves to be almost as questionable a figure as Kolenkorov, whose "son and brother" he admits he is. The tongue-in-cheek claim to freedom from "contradictions" is proof enough in itself. If more were needed, there is evidence enough, in *Before Sunrise* and elsewhere, that the real Zoshchenko had more than his share of unsurmounted "contradictions," including ideological waverings and especially melancholy. But the bantering, "naïve" philosopher who appears as the "author" in many of Zoshchenko's stories is in fact another mask behind which the true Zoshchenko can only be glimpsed darkly.

In the late twenties and for a time thereafter this system of ironic camouflage worked quite well. Some critics threatened Zoshchenko, urging him to declare himself unequivocally for the regime and to give up his irritating ambiguity, which was misleading the masses. But for the most part Zoshchenko only smiled and quickened the conjuror's patter that accompanied his tricks. During the thirties, however, he seems to have thought it politic to throw the critics a bone in the form of a few irreproachably "correct" Soviet stories. For once he laid aside his mask of irony and wrote like the serious, dedicated servant of the communist ideal that the regime expected its "engineers of human souls" to be. In 1934 he did his stint for a particularly unpleasant propaganda volume entitled *The White Sea—Baltic Canal,* edited by the former literary *Gauleiter* Leopold Averbakh (later purged). This work was designed to show that the Soviet forced labor camps, far from being a brutal travesty of the regime's "socialist" ideals, were actually beneficent institutions, something like psychological blacksmith shops, where convicts engaged in digging the White Sea—Baltic Canal under the fatherly supervision of the NKVD were "reforged" into useful Soviet citizens. Zoshchenko's piece, "The Story of One Reforging," purports to be a truthful record of one of these spiritual metamorphoses. It is entirely serious in tone and lacks any of the familiar Zoshchenko flavor. It also lacks any literary value. Other "bones" were a satirical biography of Alexander Kerensky and a saccharine series of *Stories About Lenin* written for children.

Having thus openly rendered unto Caesar, Zoshchenko apparently felt that he had won the right to pursue his own artistic bents. First, he continued to produce regularly works in his "trade-mark" genre, the short-short story or sketch, only two or three pages long, which he had made peculiarly his own. These little satires, which often made their first appearance in newspapers, were largely responsible for Zoshchenko's enormous popularity. They seemed to strike a responsive chord in the hearts of Russians of every description. Seemingly innocuous anecdotes illustrating what used to be called "defects in the mechanism," that is, disparities between official mythology and the stubborn facts of everyday life, they appealed to people as an expression of their irrepressible, unofficial human needs. No matter how unabated his Communist enthusiasm, no one could deny that for most Russians life was pretty hard; and to laugh about hardship made it easier to bear. Zoshchenko had a keen eye for the comic incongruities that cropped up constantly to bedevil people's lives. For instance, at one time in the thirties it was apparently impossible to find any but very high-powered light bulbs in Soviet stores. A trivial circumstance, no doubt, but one of the many small annoyances that caused so much human wear and tear for ordinary Russians. Zoshchenko transforms irritation into comedy in **"A Clever Little Trick,"** as his hero complains to the meter reader, who has commented on what a lot of current he is using, that he cannot summon courage to venture into a bathroom illuminated by a dazzling 500-candlepower bulb.

The building of the Soviet Utopia required not only a complete change in the economic and social conditions of life, but also a basic transformation in the behavior patterns of its citizens. To be sure, according to the Marxist formula, "being determines consciousness"; fundamental changes in the economic and class structure of society will in time automatically produce changed human beings. But this process takes time, and in the meantime the majority of Russians had been psychologically shaped under capitalism and carried with them into the new society obnoxious "capitalist survivals in the human consciousness." Official critics friendly to Zoshchenko interpreted his satires as directed against these "capitalist survivals"; he was thus playing a historically progressive role in helping the new Soviet man to throw off these unwanted relics of the past. Zoshchenko never openly objected to this useful interpretation, but one cannot escape the impression after reading many of his stories that he hardly shared it; he did not believe that all the antisocial tendencies of Soviet citizens were attributable to capitalism. Human nature, Zoshchenko seems to be saying, is much more intractable than the Utopians think.

For instance, one of the attributes of the new socialist man was supposed to be a sense of collective responsibility. The new society was no longer the capitalist jungle where men fought one another for the necessities of life, but a co-operative enterprise where all strove together for a common goal. Zoshchenko displays his skepticism in an anecdote called **"The Bottle."** A young man accidentally drops a bottle on the sidewalk and walks away in disgust, making no effort to pick up the pieces of broken glass. Other passers-by likewise fail to take any socially responsible action against this dangerous hazard. The narrator, who is watching these events while sitting on the opposite curb, bemoans such appalling evidence of bourgeois-individualistic survivals in the popular mind:

> What do I see? I see people walk on the broken glass. They curse, but still they walk. What lack of culture! There's not a single person who will fulfill his social obligations. . . . No, my friends! I think. We do not yet understand our social responsibilities. We traipse along over broken glass.

The narrator, of course, accepts the "capitalist survivals" theory. But does Zoshchenko?

With his elusive, innocent manner Zoshchenko got away with themes few other writers would have dared to touch; he even skirted some of the really forbidden topics of Soviet literature, such as the Party purges. One unsettling phenomenon of Soviet life in the thirties (and also recently) was the rapid changes in the names of institutions, streets, and whole cities as the stars of leading Party personalities rose or set. In **"An Incident on the Volga"** Zoshchenko succeeded in making this ominous feature of the permanent purge petty and ridiculous. During a single excursion trip on the Volga a steamer's name is changed, much to the confusion of its passengers, from *Comrade Penkin* to *Storm* to *Korolenko.* The name *Korolenko* was likely to last, the narrator observes, " . . . since Korolenko was dead. Whereas Penkin was alive. And this was his basic shortcoming, which led to his name's being replaced."

In most of these stories Zoshchenko's method might be called "reverse idealization": he debases, degrades, vulgarizes, trivializes the material. Nothing is too sacred for his mocking irony. In **"Poverty"** even Lenin's far-sighted program for the electrification of Russia, which had inspired so many poets to write hymns to planning and progress, is brought down to the setting of a petty-bourgeois bedroom, now lit up by electricity for the first time:

> You couldn't see much by kerosene light. But now that we're all lit up, what do we see? Over there, someone's torn slipper lying around; in another place the wallpaper is ripped off and

hangs in tatters; here a bedbug races along, running away from the light; or you see some indescribable rag, a gob of spittle, a cigarette butt, and a flea capers about . . .

The reason these irreverences were tolerated as long as they were lay partly in the magic word "petty bourgeois." The petty bourgeoisie was the repository of capitalist survivals in their most squalid form. The aristocracy and big bourgeoisie had been scattered by the Revolution to the four corners of the earth, but the artisans, the petty tradespeople, the minor civil servants and clerks had mostly stayed on, adapting themselves as best they could and carrying on their vulgar and materialistic existence in the midst of Soviet cities. As a class the petty bourgeoisie was doomed by history: it would either be cast aside or else be transformed and transfigured by society's victorious march toward socialism. Therefore, if Zoshchenko's satires were aimed at the petty bourgeoisie, so much the better, ran one official interpretation. But even in the writings of official Soviet critics the term "petty bourgeois" is sometimes used as if it describes, not a concrete sociological category, but an attribute of human nature—the petty, self-seeking, vulgar, and mundane element in everyone. But of course, "we are overcoming these things," and in the future Communist society there will be no room for them. In Zoshchenko, however, belief in the universality of petty-bourgeoisdom is often quite explicit, and only slightly less so are his doubts about the possibility of overcoming "these things."

> There exists an opinion [he wrote in an appendix to *Youth Restored*] that I write about the petty bourgeoisie. However, people often say to me, "Isn't there some mistake in your work? With us the petty bourgeoisie does not exist as a separate class. That mournful category of people is not characteristic of our country. For what purpose do you depict the petty bourgeoisie and lag behind the types and tempos of contemporary life?" . . . There is no mistake [Zoshchenko replies]. I do write about the petty bourgeoisie . . . For the most part I create a synthetic type. In all of us there are certain traits of the petty bourgeois, the property owner, the money grubber. I write about the petty bourgeoisie, and I suppose I have enough material to last me the rest of my life.

> *Hugh McLean, in an introduction to* Nervous People, and Other Satires *by Mikhail Zoshchenko, edited by Hugh McLean, translated by Maria Gordon and Hugh McLean, Pantheon Books, 1963, pp. vii-xxviii.*

Isaac Bashevis Singer   (essay date 1963)

[*Singer was a Polish-born American novelist and short story writer. Awarding Singer the Novel Prize for Literature in 1978, the Swedish Academy cited him for "his impassioned narrative art which, with roots in a Polish-Jewish cultural tradition, brings universal human conditions to life." Among his best-known works are the novels* The Slave (1962) *and* Shosha (1978). *In the following review of* Nervous People, and Other Satires, *Singer ap-plauds Zoshchenko's realistic portrayal of Soviet life under Joseph Stalin.*]

Mikhail Zoshchenko has been compared by some critics to Chekhov, Leskov, and even to Gogol, but these comparisons seem to me highly exaggerated.

Zoshchenko possessed the honesty of the great Russian literary masters, but lacked their power of characterization. He did not try, perhaps was not able, to depict human individuality, and his talent expressed itself mainly in dramatizing the comic and tragicomic situations created by the Communist revolution.

For example, there is in [*Nervous People, and Other Satires*] the story of the the vacationers who take a pleasure trip on the Volga in a ship called "Comrade Penkin." Returning to the dock after a few days in Samara, the tourists discover that their ship has left, with their baggage. After much consternation and bewilderment, they learn that the ship is still there but that the real Comrade Penkin has just been purged and the ship named after him given a new name.

In a time when almost all Soviet writers indulged in singing praises to the regime, Zoshchenko had the courage to convey in simple language the troubles and anxieties of the average citizen. He described these human tribulations without accusations or bitterness, and with that characteristic fatalism, which is supposed to be a part of every Russian's soul, whatever his aims and convictions.

Born in the Ukraine in 1895, Zoshchenko served as an officer in the Czar's army, was wounded in the World War I, and in 1918 volunteered for the Red Army. He died in Russia in 1958. Since his childhood, Zoshchenko had an inclination towards melancholy, from which his genre of humor derives. There is a deep sadness and a mood of futility in Zoshchenko's works. The reader hears the author say: no system can change man's fate; no wisdom and cunning can do away with man's foolishness and his will to wrong himself and others.

Zoshchenko began his literary career with longer stories or novellas, but his real achievement is in his very short stories or *feuilletons,* pieces of two or three pages. Written in a style without literary ornament, with a quiet humor and a rare frankness, these stories are full of information about everyday life in the Soviet cities. Not long before he was purged, Zoshchenko published *Before Sunrise,* a kind of autobiography which is composed of very short episodes. This unfinished work, more than anything else Zoshchenko wrote, reveals his compassionate nature. Only a part of the book is printed in this collection.

I doubt if Zoshchenko should be viewed primarily as a creative artist. He was, rather, a social writer, a journalist on a grand scale, not unlike the famous Doroshevich who wrote about exiles in Siberia at the beginning of the century. Many of Zoshchenko's stories concern actual events either witnessed by him or told to him by readers. Most of his short stories are really case histories of the entanglements of red tape and the planned economy in the Soviet Union.

Zoshchenko, neither Communist nor anti-Communist,

performed the miracle of remaining for decades the most severe and most popular critic of the Soviet system. True, the purge did not omit him, and Zhdanov finally declared him an enemy of the people and a hoodlum. His works were banned and he was expelled from the Union of Soviet Writers. But the fact that Zoshchenko survived as long as he did is remarkable, and probably a result of his resigned view of life. Reading Zoshchenko, even the severe Communist censor had to smile and to forgive. Now that Zhdanov has been liquidated and Stalin is dead, Zoshchenko's works are again published in the Soviet Union.

For the student of Russian life under Communism, the book is most valuable. Those who are concerned with Russian literature will also find *Nervous People* highly interesting, for although Zoshchenko is not a writer on the level of Chekhov, he manages in his own terms to evoke for the reader Chekhov's melancholy vision of Russia and his quiet despair of the human race.

> Isaac Bashevis Singer, "Russian Anxiety," in
> Books, *August 25, 1963, p. 6.*

Michael Frayn (essay date 1964)

[*Frayn is an English novelist, dramatist, editor, and translator. In the following essay, he evaluates Zoshchenko's proficiency as a satirist.*]

"The great 20th-century satirist," it calls Zoshchenko on the jacket. Well, is he? I feel as if I'd been asked to write a security testimonial for an old friend, and suddenly realised I'd no idea what his politics were. I've been reading Zoshchenko's stories with pleasure ever since I knew enough Russian to make sense of the vulgar colloquialisms in which they are written. When I was an undergraduate I tried to copy his deceptively simple throwaway style—even to the point of imitating the rhythm of his prose, sawing my sentences off short and filleting them of all unnecessary pronouns and articles. (Was chic. I thought. Others—not. "What's this," they said, "for Christ's sake? The Chinese water torture?") But in all that time I never really stopped to consider what attitudes or intentions lay behind his humour. No doubt Zoshchenko left them ambiguous partly for political reasons. All the same, after the sheer grinding boredom of what passes for satire these days, I'm beginning to think that humour, like the humorist, is not necessarily the better for having the bones that support the body visibly sticking through the skin.

I just thought Zoshchenko was funny. In this I was not alone; he was more popular in Russia between the wars than any living author apart from Maxim Gorky. He was born in 1895 into a genteel artistic family, brought up in St. Petersburg, and saw a good deal of action during the Great War as an officer in the Tsar's army. But in 1918 he threw in his lot with the Bolsheviks (though he seems never to have become one), and joined the Red Army, after which he became, among other things a policeman, a book-keeper, a cobbler, an aviculture instructor, a telephone operator for the border police, a detective, a court secretary, and a government clerk. When he began to write his success was immediate, and endured until 1946, when he was attacked by Zhdanov for "cheap hee-hawing

at Soviet reality," and proscribed. In 1956, two years before his death, he was republished, presumably rehabilitated. All the same, when I was in Leningrad in 1956 and asked if I could meet him, I stirred up such marshes of steaming abuse that I thought it might be best not to press the matter, and to spare him the embarrassment of a Western visitor. Even radically Leninist friends assured me that he was an obscene and worthless writer.

Zoshchenko's technique is in essence the technique of Wodehouse or Damon Runyon—a particular colloquial speech-pattern stylised to the point of self-parody. The colloquial idiom he starts with is what one might call working-class Sovietese. He cuts it like a clown's suit, at once too short and too baggy—monosyllabic where it ought to be expansive ("And on the way the general overate, and died of dysentery"), heavily padded with euphemisms and so-to-speaks where it should be terse ("On the one hand, sometimes it would seem more advantageous for us not to be alive. But on the other hand, so to speak, no, thank you very much"). He exaggerates that curious Russian obliquity and inconsequentiality which lend such an indissoluble air of Russianness to even the best translations of Russian novels, and he laces the mixture with misapplied scientific terminology and plonking Party clichés. Armed with this superbly inappropriate piece of linguistic equipment he sets out to describe love, birth, and death, and to elucidate the finer points of Soviet manners. It's like a clown performing a surgical operation with a giant collapsible rubber knife and fork, and a lot of the pleasure comes from watching the delicacy and ingenuity with which he wields his preposterous instruments.

Is he a satirist, though? Well, he makes fun of the shortcomings in Soviet bath-house administration and the supply of electric light bulbs. So do the writers in *Krokodil*. The staff of *Krokodil* do it because they want inefficient bath-house personnel to mend their ways. Zoshchenko does it because he thinks it's funny that human beings who aspire to run an ideal state cannot even run a bath-house properly. Again and again he slyly measures the grandiose pretensions of political optimism against the scale of man—and a small man at that. In all his stories he reminds us that men are moved by greed, hampered by idleness and fate, bound by the squalor of their circumstances, preoccupied with the trivia of daily living. He remarks on these things ostensibly to help bring reality into line with the ideal, in fact to cut the ideal down to the size of reality. His superficial ambiguity is both part of his comic technique and his political protection. In the long run, of course, it was not ambiguous at all, and he was silenced.

I don't know whether telling in jest truths that may not be told in seriousness is to be a satirist. I suppose you might say his stories are all in a sense satires on the tone of official Soviet attitudes. But I can imagine people saying that anyway he wasn't a *real* satirist—he didn't mimic Stalin's accent, or call Beria an old fool, or write skits on the purges or the labour camps. (Though as a matter of fact, back in 1924 when more things were possible he did write a brilliant parable—called **"Dog Scent"**—on the secret police.) At this point, clearly, in the context of a totalitarian state, the quest for "real satire" becomes purely metaphysical. And quite apart from that, to dismiss Zo-shchenko for saying nothing about the concentration camps is reasonable only if you are also prepared to dismiss, say, Pope for saying nothing about the misery of the London poor.

Still, for the English reader Zoshchenko's stories must stand or fall by their funniness. Unfortunately no humorist who depends as heavily as Zoshchenko does on the comicality of his style can really survive translation. (Imagine *The Code of the Woosters* in Russian.) But the translators have produced a very readable version [in *Nervous People, and Other Satires*], and to wring even readable English out of Zoshchenko's Russian is a considerable achievement.

> Michael Frayn, "Satire and Melancholy," in Encounter, *Vol. XXII, No. 1, January, 1964, pp. 70-2.*

Zoshchenko's narrative style:

For people who cannot read Russian, it is difficult to appreciate the enormous impact that Mikhail Zoshchenko's stories had on early Soviet readers. His style has been compared to that of Damon Runyon, but a more apt comparison would be to the American television characters Archie Bunker, George Jefferson, and Fred Sanford (of "Sanford and Son"). It is not so much the plot of a Zoshchenko story or the characterization that sets it apart, but instead the way in which a character or narrator becomes entangled in and betrayed by his idiosyncratic use of language.

Tom J. Lewis, in a review of A Man is Not a Flea, World Literature Today, *1990.*

Linda H. Scatton   (essay date 1987)

[*In the following essay, Scatton examines the themes of Zoshchenko's "Lenin stories" and compares them to hagiographic literature.*]

In much the same way that American children are regaled with tales of the honesty, bravery and resourcefulness of our founding fathers, Soviet children learn of the saint-like qualities of Vladimir Il'ič Lenin. Mixail Zoščenko published a total of eighteen children's stories about Vladimir Il'ič Lenin, all of which appeared in 1939 and 1940, a period rich in Lenin stories. Three collections by different authors entitled *Tales of Lenin* were published in 1939 alone. Zoščenko's first collection was among these in 1939 (Moscow-Leningrad, Detizdat), and was republished the following year by Učpedgiz in Leningrad. A second collection, which included some new stories, was published by Pravda in Moscow in 1941. All but two of the Lenin stories appeared in *The Star.* Critical response to these pieces was generally favorable; given the nature and stature of their subject, this was to be expected. The critics did find fault, however, with the means by which Zoščenko sought to portray Lenin, especially in the second group of stories. In order to make Lenin look more like a hero of irre-

proachable ethics, they claimed, Zoščenko had lowered the moral level of the characters surrounding him. For example, when Lenin exhibits what can only be termed common courtesy in the stories, he is held up as a model of new socialist morals and wisdom, while others in the stories are portrayed as Philistines. However these objections are really beside the point, since the genre to which the Lenin stories belong numbers this device among its most basic.

Zoščenko's stories belong to the general category of hagiographic literature about Lenin and to the specific subclass of works about Lenin for children. The *Tales of Lenin* present the following composite portrait of Lenin: he is truthful (**"The Carafe"**), fearless (**"The Little Gray Goat"**), brilliant, well-disciplined in mind and body (**"How Lenin Studied"**), iron-willed and selfless (**"How Lenin Quit Smoking"**), clever (**"How Lenin Outsmarted the Police"**), resourceful (**"Sometimes It's OK to Eat Inkwells"**), generous (**"How Lenin Bought a Boy a Toy"**), modest and self-effacing (**"At the Barber's"** and **"How Auntie Fedos'ja Chatted with Lenin"**), brave, considerate and solicitous of others (**"An Attack on Lenin"**), law-abiding and unpretentious (**"Lenin and the Sentry"**), forgiving (**"Lenin and the Stovemaker"**), self-critical (**"A Mistake"**), observant (**"The Bees"**), and sensitive to beauty (**"Hunting"**).

Although only two of the tales concern Lenin as a child (**"The Carafe"** and **"The Little Gray Goat"**), the stories are all couched in the simplest language possible, in order to make them easily accessible to a young audience. The narration proceeds in slow motion, using almost none of the colloquial language which was the well-known Zoščenko trademark. (On the rare occasions when such language is used, it appears in the direct speech of one or more of the characters.) The paragraphs, uniformly short, as remains typical for Zoščenko, start repeatedly with "and," thus lending the narration almost a Biblical air. Many of the stories either begin or end with the moral or point stated directly, in a fashion reminiscent of eighteenth-century fables by Krylov. Unlike Zoščenko's more famous works, these stories exhibit little or no humor or irony. In fact, on the few occasions when these elements were present, they were termed inappropriate by Zoščenko's critics and they were removed from later editions: "Although Lenin's hunter-like turns of phrase show that Comrade Zoščenko intended to write a humorous story, they are hardly acceptable as a device for revealing Lenin's character."

The first group of Zoščenko's Lenin stories appeared in *The Star,* No. 1, 1940: **"Lenin and the Stovemaker," "An Attack on Lenin," "How Lenin Quit Smoking," "How Lenin Bought a Boy a Toy," "How Lenin Studied," "At the Barber's," "The Carafe," "Sometimes It's OK to Eat Inkwells," "The Bees," "Hunting."** The second group, published in Numbers 7, 8-9 of 1940, includes **"Lenin and the Sentry," "Lenin and the Firewood," "How Lenin Was Given a Fish," "A Mistake," "How Auntie Fedos'ja Chatted with Lenin."** (Two other stories which belong to this series were published separately: **"At Age Forty-seven"** appeared in *Red Army Soldier,* No. 1, 1941, and **"The Little Gray Goat"** was included in the 1939 volume of *Tales*

Dust jackets of three collections of Zoshchenko's stories.

of Lenin.) When the critics who attacked the second group of stories accused Zoščenko of lowering the moral qualities of Soviet citizens in order to make Lenin look better by comparison, they did not seem to realize that the writer had few other avenues of portrayal open to him. By depicting Lenin in the execution of his official duties as head of state, Zoščenko placed him in a context fraught with danger for the creative artist. Certainly, there is a mystique about Lenin which the portrayal of him within such a day-to-day context might easily dispel.

Two important factors inherent in the structure and realization of these stories combined to shape a dangerous stumbling block for Zoščenko. The first of these is the character of hagiographic literature itself: it is, by nature, a genre built on contrasts. No person may be made to seem extraordinary without the ordinary as background. The stronger the intended contrast, the greater must be the distance between the exception and the rule. Any subject endowed with superhuman, divine qualities must be seen against the background of the mere mortals among whom he moves. This is the stuff of which high drama is made; Russian *Saints' Lives* are filled with examples. One need only recall the saint who, as a mere infant, refused to suckle at his mother's breast during a fasting period; another who cried out three times in church while still in his mother's womb, ran away from home to join a monastery at age ten, and later lived an ascetic existence in the wilderness,

refusing all luxuries and honors offered to him. Indeed, there are many instances in Zoščenko's Lenin stories where the hero fulfills the kenotic ideal, one of the most basic traditions of the Russian saints. He humiliates himself before a sentry; he wears plain and undistinguished clothing so that people do not recognize him as a person of special import; he disciplines his body, does manual labor and scorns all luxuries (e.g., the smoked fish proffered to him in **"A Mistake"**); he forgives the chronically rude and ill-tempered stovemaker; he "suffers for the faith" in a tsarist prison and as the object of an assassination attempt; he is at one with nature and incapable of destroying any part of it (e.g., **"The Bees"** and **"Hunting"**). As a young boy, Lenin shows signs of his future greatness when he reveals his fearlessness in **"The Little Gray Goat"** and his honesty in **"The Carafe."** At the risk of carrying this series of analogies too far, one might even point to the story **"At The Barber's"** as Zoščenko's version of the Tonsure.

As similar to the spirit of hagiography as many of these Lenin stories may be, they still necessarily lack the one element which, in religious literature, distinguishes the saint from other men: the divine, the supernatural. With the religious impetus absent, and the need, nevertheless, to create a saint-like *persona*, Zoščenko was left with only the background, the context. Since the miraculous was inadmissible evidence, it was necessary to show Lenin as more kind, more humane, more honest, more self-sacrificing, more brave than other men, i.e., to readjust the context in order to accommodate the non-miraculous hero who is its subject. One sure way to do this was to alter the context itself, to make the people surrounding the hero less brave than he. As the critics Martynov and Goffenšefer noted in their reviews of the Lenin stories, Zoščenko did just this.

The second factor, which is closely related to the first, concerns Zoščenko's artistic method as such. It was his habit and his *forte* to pit the negative against the positive in his works, frequently blackening the negative excessively in order to make the contrast more striking. For his short stories, he had created a "collective type" of Soviet Philistine, one whose portrayal included the most compromising traits of Zoščenko's contemporaries. In these early stories, the attention is focused on the negative, with the positive assumed and never explicitly stated. In the Lenin stories, however, the attention is set on the positive. Although the basis here is still contained in contrast, the real problem for Zoščenko, as always, was to find a way to convey the positive. He uses the sole method with which he has had success earlier: he blackens the negative to heighten the contrast, although here the negative is at backdrop rather than center stage. This device is one of the few left to him, since it was unacceptable to portray Lenin speaking in the familiar Zoščenkovian style or evincing even the slightest hint of humor. All of Lenin's utterances are marked by gravity, seriousness and completely bland, standard language. The few times that the narrator alludes to the behavioral gulf which lies between Lenin and other Soviet citizens ("Another person, in Lenin's place, would probably have . . . ") and, consequently, when he uses language which is more colorful, he comes under attack.

It is sobering to note that just these sections have been eliminated from the later editions of the Lenin stories.

When Lenin appears as a child in the stories, his speech is standard, correct, listless and colorless: "But why is he afraid? I don't want him to cry and be afraid. Children should be brave." (**"The Little Gray Goat"**). Lenin as an adult is a model of correct behavior and normative language. In a word, he is dull. Zoščenko's attempts at least to make interesting the background against which he functions proved dangerous for him both artistically and politically.

In her second volume of *Notes about Anna Axmatova* (Paris, 1980), Lidija Čukovskaja relates a conversation with Zoščenko in which he lays the blame for his political misfortune of 1946 squarely on the shoulders of a secondary character in his story, **"Lenin and the Sentry."** The tale describes how a Red Army guard at first refuses Lenin permission to enter the Smol'-nyj Institute because the sentry does not recognize the leader. It is the person who berates the guard for his ignorance (in spite of the fact that Lenin praises him for doing his duty) whom Zoščenko came to view as the root of all his troubles. In the original version of the story, this person sported a mustache and a goatee. Zoščenko's editor claimed that this description bore too close a resemblance to Kalinin and advised the writer to get rid of the beard: "M. M. agreed: he crossed out the goatee. The mustache and rudeness remained. Stalin imagined that he was the one being described."

Zoščenko's attempt at secular hagiography in the *Tales of Lenin* ultimately fails for the reasons outlined above. Both his creative method and the contrastive nature of the genre were inimical to a successful portrayal of Lenin as a man among men. That a writer of Zoščenko's talents and bent tried his hand at this portrayal at all tells us perhaps more about the political realities of the late thirties/early forties than about the artistic evolution of the writer.

> Linda H. Scatton, "Zoščenko's Lenin Stories: The Pitfalls of Hagiography in a Secular Context," *in* New Studies in Russian Language and Literature, *edited by Anna Lisa Crone and Catherine V. Chvany, Slavica Publishers, Inc., 1987, pp. 253-57.

> **Whether we blame Zoshchenko's own limitations or those imposed on him, the fact remains that at least three-fourths of what he wrote is crud, and the fourth part, while brilliant and witty, lacks the philosophical, psychological and social depth of great literature.**
>
> —*Gary Kern, in* World Literature Today, *1977.*

J. Patrick Polley   (essay date 1987)

[*In the following excerpt, Polley analyzes Zoshchenko's "bathhouse stories" within the context of political oppression in the Soviet Union.*]

The year 1925 saw the infant Union of Soviet Socialist Republics embarking on the fourth year of the New Economic Policy (NEP), an attempt to resuscitate the shattered economy after the ravages of the Civil War. The end of the war had brought relief from the excesses of War Communism, while the NEP reinstituted the motive of personal incentive into the economic life of the country. The task of building the socialist state was to proceed, but some time was allowed for the reeducation of the masses who were to be weaned away from their pre-October world outlooks.

During the years from 1923 to 1929, literature flourished. Soviet drama and literature turned from the symbolists, and became concerned with the life of the proletarians and the peasantry. The writings of this period are from the point of view of the workers and peasants, and they are about the ideals and lives of everyday people. The authors Mikhail Zoshchenko and Vladimir Mayakovsky highlighted ordinary people and their language by having them talk about themselves and to each other in their own patios. An element of everyday life that both authors incorporated into their satirical works was the public bathhouse. The bathhouse was not merely a public place used as a setting, but a metaphor of the Soviet state. . . .

Zoshchenko's **"Banya"** is the tale of a fellow who goes to a public bathhouse for his wash-up, but is unable to get his bath. First, he has no place to put the checks he received for his clothes. Then he can't find a bucket to wash with, and has an unsuccessful run-in with a man hoarding three buckets before he swipes one from a befuddled old man. Even though he now has a bucket, he can't wash because there is no place to sit. When he finally finds a seat, he is splattered by citizens doing their laundry. The final indignity comes when he discovers that he has lost one of the clothes checks, and he must accept someone else's trousers from the attendants. Throughout this short work, Zoshchenko's characters speak in an amalgam of current Party slogans, bits of Communist doctrine, and Russian proverbs. Our luckless and nameless narrator introduces each new inconvenience with "That's the only trouble". The dialogue between the characters is marked constantly by the admonition "You're not in a theater," which is meant to remind their fellow proletarians of the serious nature of their dealings. Zoshchenko uses the pomposity and false urgency of the standard Communist literature as a foil in his satire. He shows how such grandiloquent language becomes inappropriate in the common run of things, and thus invites the reader to wonder if such language has any appropriate context at all, or if it is just bluff and bluster.

But Zoshchenko doesn't confine his examination of the new regime to its use of language and the vulgarization of Communist rhetoric. The bathhouse is itself a metaphor of the new collectivism. It is difficult to maintain a sense of individuality or privacy while scrubbing one's body in full view of one's neighbors. To stand in a room full of one's comrades, all wearing the clothes they were born in, has a negative effect on one's opinion of life in the worker's paradise. The presence of so many bolsheviks in the buff increases the urban worker's sense of alienation, as when the narrator muses that all these launderers take the joy, the quiet joy, out of bathing. **"Banya"** has the appearance of a work poking fun at the bureaucracy of state institutions, but the quiet acceptance of this inefficiency and the expectation by the narrator that things will always be slightly askew lends a sombre note to this story. The worker's revolution has altered the society, but it has not yet perfected it, nor is there much hope that it will greatly better the plight of people. . . .

Zoshchenko published his second bathhouse story, **"Bathhouse and People"**, the same year [as Mayakovsky's "Banya"]; and there is a subtle difference between the two stories. His 1925 piece was a lighter, funnier work that commented on the minor frustrations of life. In the second work, the author takes a more open political stand. The story is no longer told in the first person, but is a recounting of a tale told to the author. In the tale, a technician, or spetsy, goes to a bathhouse where his clothes are stolen while he is bathing. He becomes bewildered, addresses his comrades by the prerevolutionary form gospodin (gentlemen), and generally loses his bearings. When the manager is summoned, a woman appears. This further disorients the man, who calls her a Kursk anomaly. She bristles, informing him that women are appointed bathhouse managers because male managers used to drop in too often in the women's section. The poor cowed technician finally leaves after being lent some pants by the bath attendant, but he forgets his vest. The people at the bathhouse think that the thief dropped it, so they call the militia. Arriving at an address found in the vest, they discover it is the technician's vest, but they also discover cloth that he has swiped from the tailor shop where he works. The technician is arrested, and Zoshchenko ends the story on an admonitory note, writing that both bathhouses and their patrons could stand some straightening up.

This story is weaker in style than the first. The vernacular used is far blander, for the technician is the only individual whose language is developed with any sense of artistry. And that development is done only to stigmatize him by showing that he still has a pre-October mentality. This mentality and his thievery are presented together as being characteristic of the technicians, who were also guilty of the epidemic of "wrecking" in the Soviet economy. This change of style and attitude may be ascribed to the increased repression of dissent that accompanied Stalin's rise. On August 17, 1933, Zoshchenko travelled with a group of writers to the newly finished White Sea canal, where they interviewed the prisoners, many of them engineers and technicians, on the effects of corrective-labor camps. All discussions took place between the writers who were on a boat, and the prisoners who were on shore, accompanied by prison trusties and guards. The prisoners revelled in the joy of the reeducation they had received through the medium of manual labor, a joy duly noted in the volume commemorating this feat of Soviet engineering and penology. However, the circumstances of the interview and the condition of the inmates could not have es-

caped Zoshchenko's notice. He did not know that 100,000 prisoners died in 18 months building that canal, but he must have known that something terrible had happened, that his country was travelling into a dark and frightening place, where a few incautious words could cost a life. Zoshchenko listened, fenced in his writing, and lived. His satire softened and stagnated. His 1943 novella, *Before the Sun Rises,* was attacked in *Bolshevik* as being overly self-centered, and only three installments were published. He was villified in 1946, along with Anna Akmatova, by the Leningrad Party boss Zhdanov, and wrote little more before his death in 1958. In the course of his speech, Zhdanov said regarding Zoshchenko that

> He who is afraid of criticism of his work is unworthy of the respect of the people. (Tumultuous applause).

A point well taken, and one that both Zoshchenko and Mayakovsky would have endorsed.

The bathhouse stories of Zoshchenko, together with Mayakovsky's play, clearly show the choking off of dissent and criticism that accompanied Stalin's rise. There was no room for Zoshchenko's humorous pessimism, or for Mayakovsky's revolutionary idealism. When these writers were repressed, not only their political voice but also their literary voice was stifled, and sensitivity to language and style was lost. For both writers the bathhouse served as a model of collective cleanliness. By the '30s, both men realized that some stains can't be washed out. They saw the stain of depotism had marred their new society for good and adjusted to it accordingly, Mayakovsky with a dramatic exit, Zoshchenko with resignation.

> *J. Patrick Polley, "When Cleanliness Was Next to Godlessness: The Proletarian Bathhouse," in* From the Bard to Broadway, Vol. VII, *edited by Karelisa V. Hartigan, University Press of America, 1987, pp. 167-76.*

FURTHER READING

Criticism

Cook, Bruce A. "The Humanity of a Russian Humorist." *The Commonweal* LXXV, No. 13 (22 December 1961): 344-45.

> Mixed review of *Scenes from the Bathhouse, and Other Stories of Communist Russia.* Cook asserts that "Zoshchenko's Russians are nothing less than human—and that is the chief virtue of this uneven and unusual collection of pieces: its intense humanity."

Cournos, John. "Stories by a Russian Humorist." *The New York Times Book Review* (13 October 1935): 8, 26.

> Hails Zoshchenko's short story collection *Russia Laughs* as a new kind of Russian humor, and compares it with the work of the classic Russian satirist Nikolai Gogol.

Kern, Gary. Review of *Neizdannyj Zoščenko,* by Mikhail Zoshchenko. *World Literature Today* 51, No. 3 (Summer 1977): 459-60.

Review of a collection of previously unpublished short works by Zoshchenko. Kern writes that with nearly all of Zoshchenko's works now available it may be time to assess his place in Russian literature, concluding that the author was original but not profound.

Lewis, Tom J. Review of *A Man Is Not a Flea,* by Mikhail Zoshchenko. *World Literature Today* 64, No. 4 (Autumn 1990): 662.

Asserts that "it is not so much the plot of a Zoshchenko story or the characterization that sets it apart, but instead the way in which a character or narrator becomes entangled in and betrayed by his idiosyncratic use of language."

Lowery, Burling. "The Common Man of the Kremlin." *The Saturday Review* XLVI, No. 39 (28 September 1963): 54.

Discusses language and point of view in Zoshchenko's *Nervous People, and Other Satires.*

Murphy, A. B. *Mikhail Zoshchenko: A Literary Profile.* Oxford: Willem A. Meeuws, 1981, 163 p.

First book-length study of Zoshchenko in English. Murphy surveys Zoshchenko's life, career, and critical reception, providing English translations of major Russian criticism.

Scatton, Linda Hart. *Mikhail Zoshchenko: Evolution of a Writer.* New York: Cambridge University Press, 1993, 296 p.

Full-length study of Zoshchenko's career. Scatton identifies stylistic and thematic unities in his short fiction, and describes the critical reassessment of Zoshchenko's work from 1978 to 1993.

Simmons, Ernest J. "It Was No Longer Good Form to Laugh." *The New York Times Book Review* (26 November 1961): 4, 44.

Positive review of *Scenes from the Bathhouse, and Other Stories of Communist Russia.*

Additional coverage of Zoshchenko's life and career is contained in the following sources published by Gale Research: *Contemporary Authors,* Vol. 115 and *Twentieth-Century Literary Criticism,* Vol. 15.

Appendix:

Select Bibliography of General Sources on Short Fiction

BOOKS OF CRITICISM

Allen, Walter. *The Short Story in English.* New York: Oxford University Press, 1981, 413 p.

Aycock, Wendell M., ed. *The Teller and the Tale: Aspects of the Short Story* (Proceedings of the Comparative Literature Symposium, Texas Tech University, Volume XIII). Lubbock: Texas Tech Press, 1982, 156 p.

Averill, Deborah. *The Irish Short Story from George Moore to Frank O'Connor.* Washington, D.C.: University Press of America, 1982, 329 p.

Bates, H. E. *The Modern Short Story: A Critical Survey.* Boston: Writer, 1941, 231 p.

Bayley, John. *The Short Story: Henry James to Elizabeth Bowen.* Great Britain: The Harvester Press Limited, 1988, 197 p.

Bennett, E. K. *A History of the German Novelle: From Goethe to Thomas Mann.* Cambridge: At the University Press, 1934, 296 p.

Bone, Robert. *Down Home: A History of Afro-American Short Fiction from Its Beginning to the End of the Harlem Renaissance.* Rev. ed. New York: Columbia University Press, 1988, 350 p.

Bruck, Peter. *The Black American Short Story in the Twentieth Century: A Collection of Critical Essays.* Amsterdam: B. R. Grüner Publishing Co., 1977, 209 p.

Burnett, Whit, and Burnett, Hallie. *The Modern Short Story in the Making.* New York: Hawthorn Books, 1964, 405 p.

Canby, Henry Seidel. *The Short Story in English.* New York: Henry Holt and Co., 1909, 386 p.

Current-García, Eugene. *The American Short Story before 1850: A Critical History.* Twayne's Critical History of the Short Story, edited by William Peden. Boston: Twayne Publishers, 1985, 168 p.

Flora, Joseph M., ed. *The English Short Story, 1880-1945: A Critical History.* Twayne's Critical History of the Short Story, edited by William Peden. Boston: Twayne Publishers, 1985, 215 p.

Foster, David William. *Studies in the Contemporary Spanish-American Short Story.* Columbia, Mo.: University of Missouri Press, 1979, 126 p.

George, Albert J. *Short Fiction in France, 1800-1850.* Syracuse, N.Y.: Syracuse University Press, 1964, 245 p.

Gerlach, John. *Toward an End: Closure and Structure in the American Short Story.* University, Ala.: The University of Alabama Press, 1985, 193 p.

Hankin, Cherry, ed. *Critical Essays on the New Zealand Short Story.* Auckland: Heinemann Publishers, 1982, 186 p.

Hanson, Clare, ed. *Re-Reading the Short Story.* London: MacMillan Press, 1989, 137 p.

Harris, Wendell V. *British Short Fiction in the Nineteenth Century.* Detroit: Wayne State University Press, 1979, 209 p.

Huntington, John. *Rationalizing Genius: Idealogical Strategies in the Classic American Science Fiction Short Story.* New Brunswick: Rutgers University Press, 1989, 216 p.

Kilroy, James F., ed. *The Irish Short Story: A Critical History.* Twayne's Critical History of the Short Story, edited by William Peden. Boston: Twayne Publishers, 1984, 251 p.

Lee, A. Robert. *The Nineteenth-Century American Short Story.* Totowa, N. J.: Vision / Barnes & Noble, 1986, 196 p.

Leibowitz, Judith. *Narrative Purpose in the Novella.* The Hague: Mouton, 1974, 137 p.

Lohafer, Susan. *Coming to Terms with the Short Story.* Baton Rouge: Louisiana State University Press, 1983, 171 p.

Lohafer, Susan, and Clarey, Jo Ellyn. *Short Story Theory at a Crossroads.* Baton Rouge: Louisiana State University Press, 1989, 352 p.

Mann, Susan Garland. *The Short Story Cycle: A Genre Companion and Reference Guide.* New York: Greenwood Press, 1989, 228 p.

Matthews, Brander. *The Philosophy of the Short Story.* New York: Longmans, Green and Co., 1901, 83 p.

May, Charles E., ed. *Short Story Theories.* Athens, Oh.: Ohio University Press, 1976, 251 p.

McClave, Heather, ed. *Women Writers of the Short Story: A Collection of Critical Essays.* Englewood Cliffs, N. J.: Prentice-Hall, 1980, 171 p.

Moser, Charles, ed. *The Russian Short Story: A Critical History.* Twayne's Critical History of the Short Story, edited by William Peden. Boston: Twayne Publishers, 1986, 232 p.

New, W. H. *Dreams of Speech and Violence: The Art of the Short Story in Canada and New Zealand.* Toronto: The University of Toronto Press, 1987, 302 p.

Newman, Frances. *The Short Story's Mutations: From Petronius to Paul Morand.* New York: B. W. Huebsch, 1925, 332 p.

O'Connor, Frank. *The Lonely Voice: A Study of the Short Story.* Cleveland: World Publishing Co., 1963, 220 p.

O'Faolain, Sean. *The Short Story.* New York: Devin-Adair Co., 1951, 370 p.

Orel, Harold. *The Victorian Short Story: Development and Triumph of a Literary Genre.* Cambridge: Cambridge University Press, 1986, 213 p.

O'Toole, L. Michael. *Structure, Style and Interpretation in the Russian Short Story.* New Haven: Yale University Press, 1982, 272 p.

Pattee, Fred Lewis. *The Development of the American Short Story: An Historical Survey.* New York: Harper and Brothers Publishers, 1923, 388 p.

Peden, Margaret Sayers, ed. *The Latin American Short Story: A Critical History.* Twayne's Critical History of the Short Story, edited by William Peden. Boston: Twayne Publishers, 1983, 160 p.

Peden, William. *The American Short Story: Continuity and Change, 1940-1975.* Rev. ed. Boston: Houghton Mifflin Co., 1975, 215 p.

Reid, Ian. *The Short Story.* The Critical Idiom, edited by John D. Jump. London: Methuen and Co., 1977, 76 p.

Rhode, Robert D. *Setting in the American Short Story of Local Color, 1865-1900.* The Hague: Mouton, 1975, 189 p.

Rohrberger, Mary. *Hawthorne and the Modern Short Story: A Study in Genre.* The Hague: Mouton and Co., 1966, 148 p.

Shaw, Valerie, *The Short Story: A Critical Introduction.* London: Longman, 1983, 294 p.

Stephens, Michael. *The Dramaturgy of Style: Voice in Short Fiction.* Carbondale, Ill.: Southern Illinois University Press, 1986, 281 p.

Stevick, Philip, ed. *The American Short Story, 1900-1945: A Critical History.* Twayne's Critical History of the Short Story, edited by William Peden, Boston: Twayne Publishers, 1984, 209 p.

Summers, Hollis, ed. *Discussion of the Short Story.* Boston: D. C. Heath and Co., 1963, 118 p.

Vannatta, Dennis, ed. *The English Short Story, 1945-1980: A Critical History.* Twayne's Critical History of the Short Story, edited by William Peden. Boston: Twayne Publishers, 1985, 206 p.

Voss, Arthur. *The American Short Story: A Critical Survey.* Norman, Okla.: University of Oklahoma Press, 1973, 399 p.

Walker, Warren S. *Twentieth-Century Short Story Explication: New Series, Vol. 1: 1989-1990.* Hamden, Conn.: Shoe String, 1993, 366 p.

Ward, Alfred C. *Aspects of the Modern Short Story: English and American.* London: University of London Press, 1924, 307 p.

Weaver, Gordon, ed. *The American Short Story, 1945-1980: A Critical History.* Twayne's Critical History of the Short Story, edited by William Peden. Boston: Twayne Publishers, 1983, 150 p.

West, Ray B., Jr. *The Short Story in America, 1900-1950.* Chicago: Henry Regnery Co., 1952, 147 p.

Williams, Blanche Colton. *Our Short Story Writers.* New York: Moffat, Yard and Co., 1920, 357 p.

Wright, Austin McGiffert. *The American Short Story in the Twenties.* Chicago: University of Chicago Press, 1961, 425 p.

CRITICAL ANTHOLOGIES

Atkinson, W. Patterson, ed. *The Short-Story.* Boston: Allyn and Bacon, 1923, 317 p.

Baldwin, Charles Sears, ed. *American Short Stories.* New York: Longmans, Green and Co., 1904, 333 p.

Charters, Ann, ed. *The Story and Its Writer: An Introduction to Short Fiction.* New York: St. Martin's Press, 1983, 1239 p.

Current-García, Eugene, and Patrick, Walton R., eds. *American Short Stories: 1820 to the Present.* Key Editions, edited by John C. Gerber. Chicago: Scott, Foresman and Co., 1952, 633 p.

Fagin, N. Bryllion, ed. *America through the Short Story.* Boston: Little, Brown, and Co., 1936, 508 p.

Frakes, James R., and Traschen, Isadore, eds. *Short Fiction: A Critical Collection.* Prentice-Hall English Literature Series, edited by Maynard Mack. Englewood Cliffs, N.J.: Prentice-Hall, 1959, 459 p.

Gifford, Douglas, ed. *Scottish Short Stories, 1800-1900.* The Scottish Library, edited by Alexander Scott. London: Calder and Boyars, 1971, 350 p.

Gordon, Caroline, and Tate, Allen, eds. *The House of Fiction: An Anthology of the Short Story with Commentary.* Rev. ed. New York: Charles Scribner's Sons, 1960, 469 p.

Greet, T. Y., et. al. *The Worlds of Fiction: Stories in Context.* Boston: Houghton Mifflin Co., 1964, 429 p.

Gullason, Thomas A., and Caspar, Leonard, eds. *The World of Short Fiction: An International Collection.* New York: Harper and Row, 1962, 548 p.

Havighurst, Walter, ed. *Masters of the Modern Short Story.* New York: Harcourt, Brace and Co., 1945, 538 p.

Litz, A. Walton, ed. *Major American Short Stories.* New York: Oxford University Press, 1975, 823 p.

Matthews, Brander, ed. *The Short-Story: Specimens Illustrating Its Development.* New York: American Book Co., 1907, 399 p.

Menton, Seymour, ed. *The Spanish American Short Story: A Critical Anthology.* Berkeley and Los Angeles: University of California Press, 1980, 496 p.

Mzamane, Mbulelo Vizikhungo, ed. *Hungry Flames, and Other Black South African Short Stories.* Longman African Classics. Essex: Longman, 1986, 162 p.

Schorer, Mark, ed. *The Short Story: A Critical Anthology.* Rev. ed. Prentice-Hall English Literature Series, edited by Maynard Mack. Englewood Cliffs, N. J.: Prentice-Hall, 1967, 459 p.

Simpson, Claude M., ed. *The Local Colorists: American Short Stories, 1857-1900.* New York: Harper and Brothers Publishers, 1960, 340 p.

Stanton, Robert, ed. *The Short Story and the Reader.* New York: Henry Holt and Co., 1960, 557 p.

West, Ray B., Jr., ed. *American Short Stories.* New York: Thomas Y. Crowell Co., 1959, 267 p.

Short Story Criticism Indexes

Literary Criticism Series
Cumulative Author Index

SSC Cumulative Nationality Index
SSC Cumulative Title Index

How to Use This Index

The main references

```
Calvino, Italo
   1923-1985.....CLC 5, 8, 11, 22, 33, 39,
                                73; SSC 3
```

list all author entries in the following Gale Literary Criticism series:

BLC = *Black Literature Criticism*
CLC = *Contemporary Literary Criticism*
CLR = *Children's Literature Review*
CMLC = *Classical and Medieval Literature Criticism*
DA = *DISCovering Authors*
DC = *Drama Criticism*
HLC = *Hispanic Literature Criticism*
LC = *Literature Criticism from 1400 to 1800*
NCLC = *Nineteenth-Century Literature Criticism*
PC = *Poetry Criticism*
SSC = *Short Story Criticism*
TCLC = *Twentieth-Century Literary Criticism*
WLC = *World Literature Criticism, 1500 to the Present*

The cross-references

```
See also CANR 23; CA 85-88;
   obituary CA 116
```

list all author entries in the following Gale biographical and literary sources:

AAYA = *Authors & Artists for Young Adults*
AITN = *Authors in the News*
BEST = *Bestsellers*
BW = *Black Writers*
CA = *Contemporary Authors*
CAAS = *Contemporary Authors Autobiography Series*
CABS = *Contemporary Authors Bibliographical Series*
CANR = *Contemporary Authors New Revision Series*
CAP = *Contemporary Authors Permanent Series*
CDALB = *Concise Dictionary of American Literary Biography*
CDBLB = *Concise Dictionary of British Literary Biography*
DLB = *Dictionary of Literary Biography*
DLBD = *Dictionary of Literary Biography Documentary Series*
DLBY = *Dictionary of Literary Biography Yearbook*
HW = *Hispanic Writers*
JRDA = *Junior DISCovering Authors*
MAICYA = *Major Authors and Illustrators for Children and Young Adults*
MTCW = *Major 20th-Century Writers*
SAAS = *Something about the Author Autobiography Series*
SATA = *Something about the Author*
YABC = *Yesterday's Authors of Books for Children*

Literary Criticism Series
Cumulative Author Index

Baroja (y Nessi), Pio
1872-1956 .... **TCLC 8; HLC**
See also CA 104

Baron, David
See Pinter, Harold

Baron Corvo
See Rolfe, Frederick (William Serafino
Austin Lewis Mary)

Barondess, Sue K(aufman)
1926-1977 .... **CLC 8**
See also Kaufman, Sue
See also CA 1-4R; 69-72; CANR 1

Baron de Teive
See Pessoa, Fernando (Antonio Nogueira)

Barres, Maurice 1862-1923 .... **TCLC 47**
See also DLB 123

Barreto, Afonso Henrique de Lima
See Lima Barreto, Afonso Henrique de

Barrett, (Roger) Syd 1946- .... **CLC 35**
See also Pink Floyd

Barrett, William (Christopher)
1913-1992 .... **CLC 27**
See also CA 13-16R; 139; CANR 11

Barrie, J(ames) M(atthew)
1860-1937 .... **TCLC 2**
See also CA 104; 136; CDBLB 1890-1914;
CLR 16; DLB 10; MAICYA; YABC 1

Barrington, Michael
See Moorcock, Michael (John)

Barrol, Grady
See Bograd, Larry

Barry, Mike
See Malzberg, Barry N(athaniel)

Barry, Philip 1896-1949 .... **TCLC 11**
See also CA 109; DLB 7

Bart, Andre Schwarz
See Schwarz-Bart, Andre

Barth, John (Simmons)
1930- ...... **CLC 1, 2, 3, 5, 7, 9, 10, 14,
27, 51; SSC 10**
See also AITN 1, 2; CA 1-4R; CABS 1;
CANR 5, 23; DLB 2; MTCW

Barthelme, Donald
1931-1989 ...... **CLC 1, 2, 3, 5, 6, 8, 13,
23, 46, 59; SSC 2**
See also CA 21-24R; 129; CANR 20;
DLB 2; DLBY 80, 89; MTCW; SATA 7,
62

Barthelme, Frederick 1943- .... **CLC 36**
See also CA 114; 122; DLBY 85

Barthes, Roland (Gerard)
1915-1980 .... **CLC 24**
See also CA 130; 97-100; MTCW

Barzun, Jacques (Martin) 1907- .... **CLC 51**
See also CA 61-64; CANR 22

Bashevis, Isaac
See Singer, Isaac Bashevis

Bashkirtseff, Marie 1859-1884 ... **NCLC 27**

Basho
See Matsuo Basho

Bass, Kingsley B., Jr.
See Bullins, Ed

Bass, Rick 1958- .... **CLC 79**
See also CA 126

Bassani, Giorgio 1916- .... **CLC 9**
See also CA 65-68; CANR 33; DLB 128;
MTCW

Bastos, Augusto (Antonio) Roa
See Roa Bastos, Augusto (Antonio)

Bataille, Georges 1897-1962 .... **CLC 29**
See also CA 101; 89-92

Bates, H(erbert) E(rnest)
1905-1974 .... **CLC 46; SSC 10**
See also CA 93-96; 45-48; CANR 34;
MTCW

Bauchart
See Camus, Albert

Baudelaire, Charles
1821-1867 ..... **NCLC 6, 29; DA; PC 1;
WLC**

Baudrillard, Jean 1929- .... **CLC 60**

Baum, L(yman) Frank 1856-1919 ... **TCLC 7**
See also CA 108; 133; CLR 15; DLB 22;
JRDA; MAICYA; MTCW; SATA 18

Baum, Louis F.
See Baum, L(yman) Frank

Baumbach, Jonathan 1933- ...... **CLC 6, 23**
See also CA 13-16R; CAAS 5; CANR 12;
DLBY 80; MTCW

Bausch, Richard (Carl) 1945- ...... **CLC 51**
See also CA 101; CAAS 14; CANR 43;
DLB 130

Baxter, Charles 1947- .... **CLC 45, 78**
See also CA 57-60; CANR 40; DLB 130

Baxter, George Owen
See Faust, Frederick (Schiller)

Baxter, James K(eir) 1926-1972 .... **CLC 14**
See also CA 77-80

Baxter, John
See Hunt, E(verette) Howard, Jr.

Bayer, Sylvia
See Glassco, John

Beagle, Peter S(oyer) 1939- .... **CLC 7**
See also CA 9-12R; CANR 4; DLBY 80;
SATA 60

Bean, Normal
See Burroughs, Edgar Rice

Beard, Charles A(ustin)
1874-1948 .... **TCLC 15**
See also CA 115; DLB 17; SATA 18

Beardsley, Aubrey 1872-1898 ..... **NCLC 6**

Beattie, Ann
1947- .... **CLC 8, 13, 18, 40, 63; SSC 11**
See also BEST 90:2; CA 81-84; DLBY 82;
MTCW

Beattie, James 1735-1803 .... **NCLC 25**
See also DLB 109

Beauchamp, Kathleen Mansfield 1888-1923
See Mansfield, Katherine
See also CA 104; 134; DA

Beaumarchais, Pierre-Augustin Caron de
1732-1799 .... **DC 4**

**Beauvoir, Simone (Lucie Ernestine Marie
Bertrand) de**
1908-1986 .... **CLC 1, 2, 4, 8, 14, 31, 44,
50, 71; DA; WLC**
See also CA 9-12R; 118; CANR 28;
DLB 72; DLBY 86; MTCW

Becker, Jurek 1937- .... **CLC 7, 19**
See also CA 85-88; DLB 75

Becker, Walter 1950- .... **CLC 26**

Beckett, Samuel (Barclay)
1906-1989 ...... **CLC 1, 2, 3, 4, 6, 9, 10,
11, 14, 18, 29, 57, 59; DA; WLC**
See also CA 5-8R; 130; CANR 33;
CDBLB 1945-1960; DLB 13, 15;
DLBY 90; MTCW

Beckford, William 1760-1844 .... **NCLC 16**
See also DLB 39

Beckman, Gunnel 1910- .... **CLC 26**
See also CA 33-36R; CANR 15; CLR 25;
MAICYA; SAAS 9; SATA 6

Becque, Henri 1837-1899 .... **NCLC 3**

Beddoes, Thomas Lovell
1803-1849 .... **NCLC 3**
See also DLB 96

Bedford, Donald F.
See Fearing, Kenneth (Flexner)

Beecher, Catharine Esther
1800-1878 .... **NCLC 30**
See also DLB 1

Beecher, John 1904-1980 .... **CLC 6**
See also AITN 1; CA 5-8R; 105; CANR 8

Beer, Johann 1655-1700 .... **LC 5**

Beer, Patricia 1924- .... **CLC 58**
See also CA 61-64; CANR 13; DLB 40

Beerbohm, Henry Maximilian
1872-1956 .... **TCLC 1, 24**
See also CA 104; DLB 34, 100

Begiebing, Robert J(ohn) 1946- ..... **CLC 70**
See also CA 122; CANR 40

Behan, Brendan
1923-1964 .... **CLC 1, 8, 11, 15, 79**
See also CA 73-76; CANR 33;
CDBLB 1945-1960; DLB 13; MTCW

Behn, Aphra
1640(?)-1689 .... **LC 1; DA; DC 4; WLC**
See also DLB 39, 80, 131

Behrman, S(amuel) N(athaniel)
1893-1973 .... **CLC 40**
See also CA 13-16; 45-48; CAP 1; DLB 7,
44

Belasco, David 1853-1931 .... **TCLC 3**
See also CA 104; DLB 7

Belcheva, Elisaveta 1893- .... **CLC 10**

Beldone, Phil "Cheech"
See Ellison, Harlan

Beleno
See Azuela, Mariano

Belinski, Vissarion Grigoryevich
1811-1848 .... **NCLC 5**

Belitt, Ben 1911- .... **CLC 22**
See also CA 13-16R; CAAS 4; CANR 7;
DLB 5

Bell, James Madison
1826-1902 .... **TCLC 43; BLC**
See also BW; CA 122; 124; DLB 50

Bell, Madison (Smartt) 1957- ...... **CLC 41**
See also CA 111; CANR 28

Bell, Marvin (Hartley) 1937- ..... **CLC 8, 31**
See also CA 21-24R; CAAS 14; DLB 5;
MTCW

Bell, W. L. D.
See Mencken, H(enry) L(ouis)

Bellamy, Atwood C.
See Mencken, H(enry) L(ouis)

Bellamy, Edward 1850-1898 ...... **NCLC 4**
See also DLB 12

Bellin, Edward J.
See Kuttner, Henry

Belloc, (Joseph) Hilaire (Pierre)
1870-1953 .... **TCLC 7, 18**
See also CA 106; DLB 19, 100; YABC 1

Belloc, Joseph Peter Rene Hilaire
See Belloc, (Joseph) Hilaire (Pierre)

Belloc, Joseph Pierre Hilaire
See Belloc, (Joseph) Hilaire (Pierre)

Belloc, M. A.
See Lowndes, Marie Adelaide (Belloc)

Bellow, Saul
1915- ...... **CLC 1, 2, 3, 6, 8, 10, 13, 15,**
25, 33, 34, 63, 79; DA; SSC 14; WLC
See also AITN 2; BEST 89:3; CA 5-8R;
CABS 1; CANR 29; CDALB 1941-1968;
DLB 2, 28; DLBD 3; DLBY 82; MTCW

Belser, Reimond Karel Maria de
1929- .... **CLC 14**

Bely, Andrey .... **TCLC 7**
See also Bugayev, Boris Nikolayevich

Benary, Margot
See Benary-Isbert, Margot

Benary-Isbert, Margot 1889-1979... **CLC 12**
See also CA 5-8R; 89-92; CANR 4;
CLR 12; MAICYA; SATA 2, 21

Benavente (y Martinez), Jacinto
1866-1954 .... **TCLC 3**
See also CA 106; 131; HW; MTCW

Benchley, Peter (Bradford)
1940- .... **CLC 4, 8**
See also AITN 2; CA 17-20R; CANR 12,
35; MTCW; SATA 3

Benchley, Robert (Charles)
1889-1945 .... **TCLC 1**
See also CA 105; DLB 11

Benedikt, Michael 1935- .... **CLC 4, 14**
See also CA 13-16R; CANR 7; DLB 5

Benet, Juan 1927-................. **CLC 28**
See also CA 143

Benet, Stephen Vincent
1898-1943 .... **TCLC 7; SSC 10**
See also CA 104; DLB 4, 48, 102; YABC 1

Benet, William Rose 1886-1950 ... **TCLC 28**
See also CA 118; DLB 45

Benford, Gregory (Albert) 1941-.... **CLC 52**
See also CA 69-72; CANR 12, 24;
DLBY 82

Bengtsson, Frans (Gunnar)
1894-1954 .... **TCLC 48**

Benjamin, David
See Slavitt, David R(ytman)

Benjamin, Lois
See Gould, Lois

Benjamin, Walter 1892-1940 ..... **TCLC 39**

Benn, Gottfried 1886-1956........ **TCLC 3**
See also CA 106; DLB 56

Bennett, Alan 1934- .... **CLC 45, 77**
See also CA 103; CANR 35; MTCW

Bennett, (Enoch) Arnold
1867-1931 .... **TCLC 5, 20**
See also CA 106; CDBLB 1890-1914;
DLB 10, 34, 98

Bennett, Elizabeth
See Mitchell, Margaret (Munnerlyn)

Bennett, George Harold 1930-
See Bennett, Hal
See also BW; CA 97-100

Bennett, Hal .... **CLC 5**
See also Bennett, George Harold
See also DLB 33

Bennett, Jay 1912-............... **CLC 35**
See also AAYA 10; CA 69-72; CANR 11,
42; JRDA; SAAS 4; SATA 27, 41

Bennett, Louise (Simone)
1919- .... **CLC 28; BLC**
See also DLB 117

Benson, E(dward) F(rederic)
1867-1940 .... **TCLC 27**
See also CA 114; DLB 135

Benson, Jackson J. 1930-......... **CLC 34**
See also CA 25-28R; DLB 111

Benson, Sally 1900-1972 .... **CLC 17**
See also CA 19-20; 37-40R; CAP 1;
SATA 1, 27, 35

Benson, Stella 1892-1933........ **TCLC 17**
See also CA 117; DLB 36

Bentham, Jeremy 1748-1832 ..... **NCLC 38**
See also DLB 107

Bentley, E(dmund) C(lerihew)
1875-1956 .... **TCLC 12**
See also CA 108; DLB 70

Bentley, Eric (Russell) 1916-...... **CLC 24**
See also CA 5-8R; CANR 6

Beranger, Pierre Jean de
1780-1857 .... **NCLC 34**

Berger, Colonel
See Malraux, (Georges-)Andre

Berger, John (Peter) 1926- ...... **CLC 2, 19**
See also CA 81-84; DLB 14

Berger, Melvin H. 1927- .... **CLC 12**
See also CA 5-8R; CANR 4; CLR 32;
SAAS 2; SATA 5

Berger, Thomas (Louis)
1924- ...... **CLC 3, 5, 8, 11, 18, 38**
See also CA 1-4R; CANR 5, 28; DLB 2;
DLBY 80; MTCW

Bergman, (Ernst) Ingmar
1918- .... **CLC 16, 72**
See also CA 81-84; CANR 33

Bergson, Henri 1859-1941 .... **TCLC 32**

Bergstein, Eleanor 1938- .... **CLC 4**
See also CA 53-56; CANR 5

Berkoff, Steven 1937-............ **CLC 56**
See also CA 104

Bermant, Chaim (Icyk) 1929- ...... **CLC 40**
See also CA 57-60; CANR 6, 31

Bern, Victoria
See Fisher, M(ary) F(rances) K(ennedy)

Bernanos, (Paul Louis) Georges
1888-1948 .... **TCLC 3**
See also CA 104; 130; DLB 72

Bernard, April 1956- .... **CLC 59**
See also CA 131

Bernhard, Thomas
1931-1989 .... **CLC 3, 32, 61**
See also CA 85-88; 127; CANR 32;
DLB 85, 124; MTCW

Berrigan, Daniel 1921-............. **CLC 4**
See also CA 33-36R; CAAS 1; CANR 11,
43; DLB 5

Berrigan, Edmund Joseph Michael, Jr.
1934-1983
See Berrigan, Ted
See also CA 61-64; 110; CANR 14

Berrigan, Ted.................... **CLC 37**
See also Berrigan, Edmund Joseph Michael,
Jr.
See also DLB 5

Berry, Charles Edward Anderson 1931-
See Berry, Chuck
See also CA 115

Berry, Chuck .... **CLC 17**
See also Berry, Charles Edward Anderson

Berry, Jonas
See Ashbery, John (Lawrence)

Berry, Wendell (Erdman)
1934- .... **CLC 4, 6, 8, 27, 46**
See also AITN 1; CA 73-76; DLB 5, 6

Berryman, John
1914-1972 ...... **CLC 1, 2, 3, 4, 6, 8, 10,**
13, 25, 62
See also CA 13-16; 33-36R; CABS 2;
CANR 35; CAP 1; CDALB 1941-1968;
DLB 48; MTCW

Bertolucci, Bernardo 1940- .... **CLC 16**
See also CA 106

Bertrand, Aloysius 1807-1841 .... **NCLC 31**

Bertran de Born c. 1140-1215 ..... **CMLC 5**

Besant, Annie (Wood) 1847-1933 ... **TCLC 9**
See also CA 105

Bessie, Alvah 1904-1985.......... **CLC 23**
See also CA 5-8R; 116; CANR 2; DLB 26

Bethlen, T. D.
See Silverberg, Robert

Beti, Mongo................. **CLC 27; BLC**
See also Biyidi, Alexandre

Betjeman, John
1906-1984 .... **CLC 2, 6, 10, 34, 43**
See also CA 9-12R; 112; CANR 33;
CDBLB 1945-1960; DLB 20; DLBY 84;
MTCW

Bettelheim, Bruno 1903-1990 ...... **CLC 79**
See also CA 81-84; 131; CANR 23; MTCW

Betti, Ugo 1892-1953 .... **TCLC 5**
See also CA 104

Betts, Doris (Waugh) 1932-.... **CLC 3, 6, 28**
See also CA 13-16R; CANR 9; DLBY 82

Bevan, Alistair
See Roberts, Keith (John Kingston)

Beynon, John
See Harris, John (Wyndham Parkes Lucas)
Beynon

Bialik, Chaim Nachman
1873-1934 .... **TCLC 25**

Bickerstaff, Isaac
See Swift, Jonathan

Bidart, Frank 1939- .... **CLC 33**
See also CA 140

Bienek, Horst 1930- .... **CLC 7, 11**
See also CA 73-76; DLB 75

Bierce, Ambrose (Gwinett)
1842-1914(?) ...... **TCLC 1, 7, 44; DA;
SSC 9; WLC**
See also CA 104; 139; CDALB 1865-1917;
DLB 11, 12, 23, 71, 74

Billings, Josh
See Shaw, Henry Wheeler

Billington, Rachel 1942- .... **CLC 43**
See also AITN 2; CA 33-36R

Binyon, T(imothy) J(ohn) 1936- .... **CLC 34**
See also CA 111; CANR 28

Bioy Casares, Adolfo
1914- .... **CLC 4, 8, 13; HLC**
See also CA 29-32R; CANR 19, 43;
DLB 113; HW; MTCW

Bird, C.
See Ellison, Harlan

Bird, Cordwainer
See Ellison, Harlan

Bird, Robert Montgomery
1806-1854 .... **NCLC 1**

Birney, (Alfred) Earle
1904- .... **CLC 1, 4, 6, 11**
See also CA 1-4R; CANR 5, 20; DLB 88;
MTCW

Bishop, Elizabeth
1911-1979 ...... **CLC 1, 4, 9, 13, 15, 32;
DA; PC 3**
See also CA 5-8R; 89-92; CABS 2;
CANR 26; CDALB 1968-1988; DLB 5;
MTCW; SATA 24

Bishop, John 1935- .... **CLC 10**
See also CA 105

Bissett, Bill 1939- .... **CLC 18**
See also CA 69-72; CANR 15; DLB 53;
MTCW

Bitov, Andrei (Georgievich) 1937- ... **CLC 57**
See also CA 142

Biyidi, Alexandre 1932-
See Beti, Mongo
See also BW; CA 114; 124; MTCW

Bjarme, Brynjolf
See Ibsen, Henrik (Johan)

Bjornson, Bjornstjerne (Martinius)
1832-1910 .... **TCLC 7, 37**
See also CA 104

Black, Robert
See Holdstock, Robert P.

Blackburn, Paul 1926-1971 ...... **CLC 9, 43**
See also CA 81-84; 33-36R; CANR 34;
DLB 16; DLBY 81

Black Elk 1863-1950 .... **TCLC 33**

Black Hobart
See Sanders, (James) Ed(ward)

Blacklin, Malcolm
See Chambers, Aidan

Blackmore, R(ichard) D(oddridge)
1825-1900 .... **TCLC 27**
See also CA 120; DLB 18

Blackmur, R(ichard) P(almer)
1904-1965 .... **CLC 2, 24**
See also CA 11-12; 25-28R; CAP 1; DLB 63

Black Tarantula, The
See Acker, Kathy

Blackwood, Algernon (Henry)
1869-1951 .... **TCLC 5**
See also CA 105

Blackwood, Caroline 1931- .... **CLC 6, 9**
See also CA 85-88; CANR 32; DLB 14;
MTCW

Blade, Alexander
See Hamilton, Edmond; Silverberg, Robert

Blaga, Lucian 1895-1961 .... **CLC 75**

Blair, Eric (Arthur) 1903-1950
See Orwell, George
See also CA 104; 132; DA; MTCW;
SATA 29

Blais, Marie-Claire
1939- .... **CLC 2, 4, 6, 13, 22**
See also CA 21-24R; CAAS 4; CANR 38;
DLB 53; MTCW

Blaise, Clark 1940- .... **CLC 29**
See also AITN 2; CA 53-56; CAAS 3;
CANR 5; DLB 53

Blake, Nicholas
See Day Lewis, C(ecil)
See also DLB 77

Blake, William
1757-1827 ..... **NCLC 13, 37; DA; WLC**
See also CDBLB 1789-1832; DLB 93;
MAICYA; SATA 30

Blasco Ibanez, Vicente
1867-1928 .... **TCLC 12**
See also CA 110; 131; HW; MTCW

Blatty, William Peter 1928- .... **CLC 2**
See also CA 5-8R; CANR 9

Bleeck, Oliver
See Thomas, Ross (Elmore)

Blessing, Lee 1949- .... **CLC 54**

Blish, James (Benjamin)
1921-1975 .... **CLC 14**
See also CA 1-4R; 57-60; CANR 3; DLB 8;
MTCW; SATA 66

Bliss, Reginald
See Wells, H(erbert) G(eorge)

Blixen, Karen (Christentze Dinesen)
1885-1962
See Dinesen, Isak
See also CA 25-28; CANR 22; CAP 2;
MTCW; SATA 44

Bloch, Robert (Albert) 1917- .... **CLC 33**
See also CA 5-8R; CANR 5; DLB 44;
SATA 12

Blok, Alexander (Alexandrovich)
1880-1921 .... **TCLC 5**
See also CA 104

Blom, Jan
See Breytenbach, Breyten

Bloom, Harold 1930- .... **CLC 24**
See also CA 13-16R; CANR 39; DLB 67

Bloomfield, Aurelius
See Bourne, Randolph S(illiman)

Blount, Roy (Alton), Jr. 1941- ..... **CLC 38**
See also CA 53-56; CANR 10, 28; MTCW

Bloy, Leon 1846-1917........... **TCLC 22**
See also CA 121; DLB 123

Blume, Judy (Sussman) 1938-... **CLC 12, 30**
See also AAYA 3; CA 29-32R; CANR 13,
37; CLR 2, 15; DLB 52; JRDA;
MAICYA; MTCW; SATA 2, 31

Blunden, Edmund (Charles)
1896-1974 .... **CLC 2, 56**
See also CA 17-18; 45-48; CAP 2; DLB 20,
100; MTCW

Bly, Robert (Elwood)
1926- .... **CLC 1, 2, 5, 10, 15, 38**
See also CA 5-8R; CANR 41; DLB 5;
MTCW

Bobette
See Simenon, Georges (Jacques Christian)

Boccaccio, Giovanni 1313-1375
See also SSC 10

Bochco, Steven 1943-............. **CLC 35**
See also CA 124; 138

Bodenheim, Maxwell 1892-1954 ... **TCLC 44**
See also CA 110; DLB 9, 45

Bodker, Cecil 1927- .... **CLC 21**
See also CA 73-76; CANR 13; CLR 23;
MAICYA; SATA 14

Boell, Heinrich (Theodor) 1917-1985
See Boll, Heinrich (Theodor)
See also CA 21-24R; 116; CANR 24; DA;
DLB 69; DLBY 85; MTCW

Boerne, Alfred
See Doeblin, Alfred

Bogan, Louise 1897-1970..... **CLC 4, 39, 46**
See also CA 73-76; 25-28R; CANR 33;
DLB 45; MTCW

Bogarde, Dirk .... **CLC 19**
See also Van Den Bogarde, Derek Jules
Gaspard Ulric Niven
See also DLB 14

Bogosian, Eric 1953- .... **CLC 45**
See also CA 138

Bograd, Larry 1953-.............. **CLC 35**
See also CA 93-96; SATA 33

Boiardo, Matteo Maria 1441-1494 .... **LC 6**

Boileau-Despreaux, Nicolas
1636-1711 .... **LC 3**

Boland, Eavan (Aisling) 1944-... **CLC 40, 67**
See also CA 143; DLB 40

Boll, Heinrich (Theodor)
1917-1985 .... **CLC 2, 3, 6, 9, 11, 15, 27,
39, 72; WLC**
See also Boell, Heinrich (Theodor)
See also DLB 69; DLBY 85

Bolt, Lee
See Faust, Frederick (Schiller)

Bolt, Robert (Oxton) 1924- .... **CLC 14**
See also CA 17-20R; CANR 35; DLB 13;
MTCW

Bomkauf
See Kaufman, Bob (Garnell)

Buchheim, Lothar-Guenther 1918- . . . **CLC 6**
See also CA 85-88

Buchner, (Karl) Georg
1813-1837 . . . . **NCLC 26**

Buchwald, Art(hur) 1925- . . . . **CLC 33**
See also AITN 1; CA 5-8R; CANR 21;
MTCW; SATA 10

Buck, Pearl S(ydenstricker)
1892-1973 . . . . **CLC 7, 11, 18; DA**
See also AITN 1; CA 1-4R; 41-44R;
CANR 1, 34; DLB 9, 102; MTCW;
SATA 1, 25

Buckler, Ernest 1908-1984. . . . . **CLC 13**
See also CA 11-12; 114; CAP 1; DLB 68;
SATA 47

Buckley, Vincent (Thomas)
1925-1988 . . . . **CLC 57**
See also CA 101

Buckley, William F(rank), Jr.
1925- . . . . **CLC 7, 18, 37**
See also AITN 1; CA 1-4R; CANR 1, 24;
DLBY 80; MTCW

Buechner, (Carl) Frederick
1926- . . . . **CLC 2, 4, 6, 9**
See also CA 13-16R; CANR 11, 39;
DLBY 80; MTCW

Buell, John (Edward) 1927- . . . . **CLC 10**
See also CA 1-4R; DLB 53

Buero Vallejo, Antonio 1916- . . . **CLC 15, 46**
See also CA 106; CANR 24; HW; MTCW

Bufalino, Gesualdo 1920(?)- . . . . **CLC 74**

Bugayev, Boris Nikolayevich 1880-1934
See Bely, Andrey
See also CA 104

Bukowski, Charles
1920-1994 . . . . **CLC 2, 5, 9, 41, 82**
See also CA 17-20R; CANR 40; DLB 5,
130; MTCW

Bulgakov, Mikhail (Afanas'evich)
1891-1940 . . . . **TCLC 2, 16**
See also CA 105

Bulgya, Alexander Alexandrovich
1901-1956 . . . . **TCLC 53**
See also Fadeyev, Alexander
See also CA 117

Bullins, Ed 1935- . . . . **CLC 1, 5, 7; BLC**
See also BW; CA 49-52; CAAS 16;
CANR 24; DLB 7, 38; MTCW

Bulwer-Lytton, Edward (George Earle Lytton)
1803-1873 . . . . **NCLC 1**
See also DLB 21

Bunin, Ivan Alexeyevich
1870-1953 . . . . **TCLC 6; SSC 5**
See also CA 104

Bunting, Basil 1900-1985. . . . **CLC 10, 39, 47**
See also CA 53-56; 115; CANR 7; DLB 20

Bunuel, Luis 1900-1983 . . **CLC 16, 80; HLC**
See also CA 101; 110; CANR 32; HW

Bunyan, John 1628-1688 . . **LC 4; DA; WLC**
See also CDBLB 1660-1789; DLB 39

Burford, Eleanor
See Hibbert, Eleanor Alice Burford

Burgess, Anthony
. **CLC 1, 2, 4, 5, 8, 10, 13, 15, 22, 40, 62,
81**
See also Wilson, John (Anthony) Burgess
See also AITN 1; CDBLB 1960 to Present;
DLB 14

Burke, Edmund
1729(?)-1797 . . . . **LC 7; DA; WLC**
See also DLB 104

Burke, Kenneth (Duva)
1897-1993 . . . . **CLC 2, 24**
See also CA 5-8R; 143; CANR 39; DLB 45,
63; MTCW

Burke, Leda
See Garnett, David

Burke, Ralph
See Silverberg, Robert

Burney, Fanny 1752-1840 . . . . . . **NCLC 12**
See also DLB 39

Burns, Robert
1759-1796 . . . . . . **LC 3; DA; PC 6; WLC**
See also CDBLB 1789-1832; DLB 109

Burns, Tex
See L'Amour, Louis (Dearborn)

Burnshaw, Stanley 1906- . . . . . **CLC 3, 13, 44**
See also CA 9-12R; DLB 48

Burr, Anne 1937- . . . . **CLC 6**
See also CA 25-28R

Burroughs, Edgar Rice
1875-1950 . . . . **TCLC 2, 32**
See also CA 104; 132; DLB 8; MTCW;
SATA 41

Burroughs, William S(eward)
1914- . . . . **CLC 1, 2, 5, 15, 22, 42, 75;
DA; WLC**
See also AITN 2; CA 9-12R; CANR 20;
DLB 2, 8, 16; DLBY 81; MTCW

Burton, Richard F. 1821-1890. . . . **NCLC 42**
See also DLB 55

Busch, Frederick 1941- . . . **CLC 7, 10, 18, 47**
See also CA 33-36R; CAAS 1; DLB 6

Bush, Ronald 1946- . . . . **CLC 34**
See also CA 136

Bustos, F(rancisco)
See Borges, Jorge Luis

Bustos Domecq, H(onorio)
See Bioy Casares, Adolfo; Borges, Jorge
Luis

Butler, Octavia E(stelle) 1947- . . . . . **CLC 38**
See also BW; CA 73-76; CANR 12, 24, 38;
DLB 33; MTCW

Butler, Robert Olen (Jr.) 1945- . . . . . **CLC 81**
See also CA 112

Butler, Samuel 1612-1680 . . . . **LC 16**
See also DLB 101, 126

Butler, Samuel
1835-1902 . . . . . . **TCLC 1, 33; DA; WLC**
See also CA 104; CDBLB 1890-1914;
DLB 18, 57

Butler, Walter C.
See Faust, Frederick (Schiller)

Butor, Michel (Marie Francois)
1926- . . . . **CLC 1, 3, 8, 11, 15**
See also CA 9-12R; CANR 33; DLB 83;
MTCW

Buzo, Alexander (John) 1944- . . . . . . **CLC 61**
See also CA 97-100; CANR 17, 39

Buzzati, Dino 1906-1972 . . . . **CLC 36**
See also CA 33-36R

Byars, Betsy (Cromer) 1928- . . . . **CLC 35**
See also CA 33-36R; CANR 18, 36; CLR 1,
16; DLB 52; JRDA; MAICYA; MTCW;
SAAS 1; SATA 4, 46

Byatt, A(ntonia) S(usan Drabble)
1936- . . . . **CLC 19, 65**
See also CA 13-16R; CANR 13, 33;
DLB 14; MTCW

Byrne, David 1952- . . . . **CLC 26**
See also CA 127

Byrne, John Keyes 1926- . . . . **CLC 19**
See also Leonard, Hugh
See also CA 102

Byron, George Gordon (Noel)
1788-1824 . . . . . . **NCLC 2, 12; DA; WLC**
See also CDBLB 1789-1832; DLB 96, 110

C.3.3.
See Wilde, Oscar (Fingal O'Flahertie Wills)

Caballero, Fernan 1796-1877 . . . . . **NCLC 10**

Cabell, James Branch 1879-1958 . . . **TCLC 6**
See also CA 105; DLB 9, 78

Cable, George Washington
1844-1925 . . . . **TCLC 4; SSC 4**
See also CA 104; DLB 12, 74

Cabral de Melo Neto, Joao 1920- . . . **CLC 76**

Cabrera Infante, G(uillermo)
1929- . . . . **CLC 5, 25, 45; HLC**
See also CA 85-88; CANR 29; DLB 113;
HW; MTCW

Cade, Toni
See Bambara, Toni Cade

Cadmus
See Buchan, John

Caedmon fl. 658-680 . . . . **CMLC 7**

Caeiro, Alberto
See Pessoa, Fernando (Antonio Nogueira)

Cage, John (Milton, Jr.) 1912- . . . . . **CLC 41**
See also CA 13-16R; CANR 9

Cain, G.
See Cabrera Infante, G(uillermo)

Cain, Guillermo
See Cabrera Infante, G(uillermo)

Cain, James M(allahan)
1892-1977 . . . . **CLC 3, 11, 28**
See also AITN 1; CA 17-20R; 73-76;
CANR 8, 34; MTCW

Caine, Mark
See Raphael, Frederic (Michael)

Calasso, Roberto 1941- . . . . **CLC 81**
See also CA 143

Calderon de la Barca, Pedro
1600-1681 . . . . **LC 23; DC 3**

Caldwell, Erskine (Preston)
1903-1987 . . . . **CLC 1, 8, 14, 50, 60**
See also AITN 1; CA 1-4R; 121; CAAS 1;
CANR 2, 33; DLB 9, 86; MTCW

Caldwell, (Janet Miriam) Taylor (Holland)
1900-1985 . . . . **CLC 2, 28, 39**
See also CA 5-8R; 116; CANR 5

Ch'ien Chung-shu 1910- . . . . **CLC 22**
See also CA 130; MTCW

Child, L. Maria
See Child, Lydia Maria

Child, Lydia Maria 1802-1880 . . . . **NCLC 6**
See also DLB 1, 74; SATA 67

Child, Mrs.
See Child, Lydia Maria

Child, Philip 1898-1978 . . . . **CLC 19, 68**
See also CA 13-14; CAP 1; SATA 47

Childress, Alice
1920- . . . . **CLC 12, 15; BLC; DC 4**
See also AAYA 8; BW; CA 45-48;
CANR 3, 27; CLR 14; DLB 7, 38; JRDA;
MAICYA; MTCW; SATA 7, 48

Chislett, (Margaret) Anne 1943- . . . . **CLC 34**

Chitty, Thomas Willes 1926- . . . . **CLC 11**
See also Hinde, Thomas
See also CA 5-8R

Chomette, Rene Lucien 1898-1981 . . **CLC 20**
See also Clair, Rene
See also CA 103

Chopin, Kate . . . . **TCLC 5, 14; DA; SSC 8**
See also Chopin, Katherine
See also CDALB 1865-1917; DLB 12, 78

Chopin, Katherine 1851-1904
See Chopin, Kate
See also CA 104; 122

Chretien de Troyes
c. 12th cent. - . . . . **CMLC 10**

Christie
See Ichikawa, Kon

Christie, Agatha (Mary Clarissa)
1890-1976 . . . . . . **CLC 1, 6, 8, 12, 39, 48**
See also AAYA 9; AITN 1, 2; CA 17-20R;
61-64; CANR 10, 37; CDBLB 1914-1945;
DLB 13, 77; MTCW; SATA 36

Christie, (Ann) Philippa
See Pearce, Philippa
See also CA 5-8R; CANR 4

Christine de Pizan 1365(?)-1431(?) . . . . **LC 9**

Chubb, Elmer
See Masters, Edgar Lee

Chulkov, Mikhail Dmitrievich
1743-1792 . . . . **LC 2**

Churchill, Caryl 1938- . . . . **CLC 31, 55**
See also CA 102; CANR 22; DLB 13;
MTCW

Churchill, Charles 1731-1764 . . . . **LC 3**
See also DLB 109

Chute, Carolyn 1947- . . . . **CLC 39**
See also CA 123

Ciardi, John (Anthony)
1916-1986 . . . . **CLC 10, 40, 44**
See also CA 5-8R; 118; CAAS 2; CANR 5,
33; CLR 19; DLB 5; DLBY 86;
MAICYA; MTCW; SATA 1, 46, 65

Cicero, Marcus Tullius
106B.C.-43B.C. . . . . **CMLC 3**

Cimino, Michael 1943- . . . . **CLC 16**
See also CA 105

Cioran, E(mil) M. 1911- . . . . **CLC 64**
See also CA 25-28R

Cisneros, Sandra 1954- . . . . . . **CLC 69; HLC**
See also AAYA 9; CA 131; DLB 122; HW

Clair, Rene . . . . **CLC 20**
See also Chomette, Rene Lucien

Clampitt, Amy 1920- . . . . **CLC 32**
See also CA 110; CANR 29; DLB 105

Clancy, Thomas L., Jr. 1947-
See Clancy, Tom
See also CA 125; 131; MTCW

Clancy, Tom . . . . **CLC 45**
See also Clancy, Thomas L., Jr.
See also AAYA 9; BEST 89:1, 90:1

Clare, John 1793-1864 . . . . **NCLC 9**
See also DLB 55, 96

Clarin
See Alas (y Urena), Leopoldo (Enrique
Garcia)

Clark, Al C.
See Goines, Donald

Clark, (Robert) Brian 1932- . . . . **CLC 29**
See also CA 41-44R

Clark, Eleanor 1913- . . . . **CLC 5, 19**
See also CA 9-12R; CANR 41; DLB 6

Clark, J. P.
See Clark, John Pepper
See also DLB 117

Clark, John Pepper 1935- . . . . **CLC 38; BLC**
See also Clark, J. P.
See also BW; CA 65-68; CANR 16

Clark, M. R.
See Clark, Mavis Thorpe

Clark, Mavis Thorpe 1909- . . . . **CLC 12**
See also CA 57-60; CANR 8, 37; CLR 30;
MAICYA; SAAS 5; SATA 8, 74

Clark, Walter Van Tilburg
1909-1971 . . . . **CLC 28**
See also CA 9-12R; 33-36R; DLB 9;
SATA 8

Clarke, Arthur C(harles)
1917- . . . . . . **CLC 1, 4, 13, 18, 35; SSC 3**
See also AAYA 4; CA 1-4R; CANR 2, 28;
JRDA; MAICYA; MTCW; SATA 13, 70

Clarke, Austin 1896-1974 . . . . **CLC 6, 9**
See also CA 29-32; 49-52; CAP 2; DLB 10,
20

Clarke, Austin C(hesterfield)
1934- . . . . **CLC 8, 53; BLC**
See also BW; CA 25-28R; CAAS 16;
CANR 14, 32; DLB 53, 125

Clarke, Gillian 1937- . . . . **CLC 61**
See also CA 106; DLB 40

Clarke, Marcus (Andrew Hislop)
1846-1881 . . . . **NCLC 19**

Clarke, Shirley 1925- . . . . **CLC 16**

Clash, The . . . . **CLC 30**
See also Headon, (Nicky) Topper; Jones,
Mick; Simonon, Paul; Strummer, Joe

Claudel, Paul (Louis Charles Marie)
1868-1955 . . . . **TCLC 2, 10**
See also CA 104

Clavell, James (duMaresq)
1925- . . . . **CLC 6, 25**
See also CA 25-28R; CANR 26; MTCW

Cleaver, (Leroy) Eldridge
1935- . . . . **CLC 30; BLC**
See also BW; CA 21-24R; CANR 16

Cleese, John (Marwood) 1939- . . . . . **CLC 21**
See also Monty Python
See also CA 112; 116; CANR 35; MTCW

Cleishbotham, Jebediah
See Scott, Walter

Cleland, John 1710-1789 . . . . **LC 2**
See also DLB 39

Clemens, Samuel Langhorne 1835-1910
See Twain, Mark
See also CA 104; 135; CDALB 1865-1917;
DA; DLB 11, 12, 23, 64, 74; JRDA;
MAICYA; YABC 2

Cleophil
See Congreve, William

Clerihew, E.
See Bentley, E(dmund) C(lerihew)

Clerk, N. W.
See Lewis, C(live) S(taples)

Cliff, Jimmy . . . . **CLC 21**
See also Chambers, James

Clifton, (Thelma) Lucille
1936- . . . . **CLC 19, 66; BLC**
See also BW; CA 49-52; CANR 2, 24, 42;
CLR 5; DLB 5, 41; MAICYA; MTCW;
SATA 20, 69

Clinton, Dirk
See Silverberg, Robert

Clough, Arthur Hugh 1819-1861 . . **NCLC 27**
See also DLB 32

Clutha, Janet Paterson Frame 1924-
See Frame, Janet
See also CA 1-4R; CANR 2, 36; MTCW

Clyne, Terence
See Blatty, William Peter

Cobalt, Martin
See Mayne, William (James Carter)

Coburn, D(onald) L(ee) 1938- . . . . . . **CLC 10**
See also CA 89-92

Cocteau, Jean (Maurice Eugene Clement)
1889-1963 . . . . **CLC 1, 8, 15, 16, 43; DA;**
WLC
See also CA 25-28; CANR 40; CAP 2;
DLB 65; MTCW

Codrescu, Andrei 1946- . . . . **CLC 46**
See also CA 33-36R; CANR 13, 34

Coe, Max
See Bourne, Randolph S(illiman)

Coe, Tucker
See Westlake, Donald E(dwin)

Coetzee, J(ohn) M(ichael)
1940- . . . . **CLC 23, 33, 66**
See also CA 77-80; CANR 41; MTCW

Coffey, Brian
See Koontz, Dean R(ay)

Cohen, Arthur A(llen)
1928-1986 . . . . **CLC 7, 31**
See also CA 1-4R; 120; CANR 1, 17, 42;
DLB 28

Cohen, Leonard (Norman)
1934- . . . . **CLC 3, 38**
See also CA 21-24R; CANR 14; DLB 53;
MTCW

Couch, Arthur Thomas Quiller
See Quiller-Couch, Arthur Thomas

Coulton, James
See Hansen, Joseph

Couperus, Louis (Marie Anne)
1863-1923 .... **TCLC 15**
See also CA 115

Court, Wesli
See Turco, Lewis (Putnam)

Courtenay, Bryce 1933- .... **CLC 59**
See also CA 138

Courtney, Robert
See Ellison, Harlan

Cousteau, Jacques-Yves 1910- ...... **CLC 30**
See also CA 65-68; CANR 15; MTCW;
SATA 38

Coward, Noel (Peirce)
1899-1973 .... **CLC 1, 9, 29, 51**
See also AITN 1; CA 17-18; 41-44R;
CANR 35; CAP 2; CDBLB 1914-1945;
DLB 10; MTCW

Cowley, Malcolm 1898-1989 .... **CLC 39**
See also CA 5-8R; 128; CANR 3; DLB 4,
48; DLBY 81, 89; MTCW

Cowper, William 1731-1800 ...... **NCLC 8**
See also DLB 104, 109

Cox, William Trevor 1928- ... **CLC 9, 14, 71**
See also Trevor, William
See also CA 9-12R; CANR 4, 37; DLB 14;
MTCW

Cozzens, James Gould
1903-1978 .... **CLC 1, 4, 11**
See also CA 9-12R; 81-84; CANR 19;
CDALB 1941-1968; DLB 9; DLBD 2;
DLBY 84; MTCW

Crabbe, George 1754-1832 .... **NCLC 26**
See also DLB 93

Craig, A. A.
See Anderson, Poul (William)

Craik, Dinah Maria (Mulock)
1826-1887 .... **NCLC 38**
See also DLB 35; MAICYA; SATA 34

Cram, Ralph Adams 1863-1942 .... **TCLC 45**

Crane, (Harold) Hart
1899-1932 .... **TCLC 2, 5; DA; PC 3;
WLC**
See also CA 104; 127; CDALB 1917-1929;
DLB 4, 48; MTCW

Crane, R(onald) S(almon)
1886-1967 .... **CLC 27**
See also CA 85-88; DLB 63

Crane, Stephen (Townley)
1871-1900 .... **TCLC 11, 17, 32; DA;
SSC 7; WLC**
See also CA 109; 140; CDALB 1865-1917;
DLB 12, 54, 78; YABC 2

Crase, Douglas 1944- .... **CLC 58**
See also CA 106

Crashaw, Richard 1612(?)-1649 ...... **LC 24**
See also DLB 126

Craven, Margaret 1901-1980 .... **CLC 17**
See also CA 103

Crawford, F(rancis) Marion
1854-1909 .... **TCLC 10**
See also CA 107; DLB 71

Crawford, Isabella Valancy
1850-1887 .... **NCLC 12**
See also DLB 92

Crayon, Geoffrey
See Irving, Washington

Creasey, John 1908-1973 .... **CLC 11**
See also CA 5-8R; 41-44R; CANR 8;
DLB 77; MTCW

Crebillon, Claude Prosper Jolyot de (fils)
1707-1777 .... **LC 1**

Credo
See Creasey, John

Creeley, Robert (White)
1926- ..... **CLC 1, 2, 4, 8, 11, 15, 36, 78**
See also CA 1-4R; CAAS 10; CANR 23, 43;
DLB 5, 16; MTCW

Crews, Harry (Eugene)
1935- .... **CLC 6, 23, 49**
See also AITN 1; CA 25-28R; CANR 20;
DLB 6; MTCW

Crichton, (John) Michael
1942- .... **CLC 2, 6, 54**
See also AAYA 10; AITN 2; CA 25-28R;
CANR 13, 40; DLBY 81; JRDA;
MTCW; SATA 9

Crispin, Edmund .... **CLC 22**
See also Montgomery, (Robert) Bruce
See also DLB 87

Cristofer, Michael 1945(?)- .... **CLC 28**
See also CA 110; DLB 7

Croce, Benedetto 1866-1952 ...... **TCLC 37**
See also CA 120

Crockett, David 1786-1836 .... **NCLC 8**
See also DLB 3, 11

Crockett, Davy
See Crockett, David

Croker, John Wilson 1780-1857 .. **NCLC 10**
See also DLB 110

Crommelynck, Fernand 1885-1970 .. **CLC 75**
See also CA 89-92

Cronin, A(rchibald) J(oseph)
1896-1981 .... **CLC 32**
See also CA 1-4R; 102; CANR 5; SATA 25,
47

Cross, Amanda
See Heilbrun, Carolyn G(old)

Crothers, Rachel 1878(?)-1958 ..... **TCLC 19**
See also CA 113; DLB 7

Croves, Hal
See Traven, B.

Crowfield, Christopher
See Stowe, Harriet (Elizabeth) Beecher

Crowley, Aleister .... **TCLC 7**
See also Crowley, Edward Alexander

Crowley, Edward Alexander 1875-1947
See Crowley, Aleister
See also CA 104

Crowley, John 1942- .... **CLC 57**
See also CA 61-64; CANR 43; DLBY 82;
SATA 65

Crud
See Crumb, R(obert)

Crumarums
See Crumb, R(obert)

Crumb, R(obert) 1943- .... **CLC 17**
See also CA 106

Crumbum
See Crumb, R(obert)

Crumski
See Crumb, R(obert)

Crum the Bum
See Crumb, R(obert)

Crunk
See Crumb, R(obert)

Crustt
See Crumb, R(obert)

Cryer, Gretchen (Kiger) 1935- ...... **CLC 21**
See also CA 114; 123

Csath, Geza 1887-1919 .... **TCLC 13**
See also CA 111

Cudlip, David 1933- .... **CLC 34**

Cullen, Countee
1903-1946 ...... **TCLC 4, 37; BLC; DA**
See also BW; CA 108; 124;
CDALB 1917-1929; DLB 4, 48, 51;
MTCW; SATA 18

Cum, R.
See Crumb, R(obert)

Cummings, Bruce F(rederick) 1889-1919
See Barbellion, W. N. P.
See also CA 123

Cummings, E(dward) E(stlin)
1894-1962 ...... **CLC 1, 3, 8, 12, 15, 68;
DA; PC 5; WLC 2**
See also CA 73-76; CANR 31;
CDALB 1929-1941; DLB 4, 48; MTCW

Cunha, Euclides (Rodrigues Pimenta) da
1866-1909 .... **TCLC 24**
See also CA 123

Cunningham, E. V.
See Fast, Howard (Melvin)

Cunningham, J(ames) V(incent)
1911-1985 .... **CLC 3, 31**
See also CA 1-4R; 115; CANR 1; DLB 5

Cunningham, Julia (Woolfolk)
1916- .... **CLC 12**
See also CA 9-12R; CANR 4, 19, 36;
JRDA; MAICYA; SAAS 2; SATA 1, 26

Cunningham, Michael 1952- .... **CLC 34**
See also CA 136

Cunninghame Graham, R(obert) B(ontine)
1852-1936 .... **TCLC 19**
See also Graham, R(obert) B(ontine)
Cunninghame
See also CA 119; DLB 98

Currie, Ellen 19(?)- .... **CLC 44**

Curtin, Philip
See Lowndes, Marie Adelaide (Belloc)

Curtis, Price
See Ellison, Harlan

Cutrate, Joe
See Spiegelman, Art

Czaczkes, Shmuel Yosef
See Agnon, S(hmuel) Y(osef Halevi)

D. P.
See Wells, H(erbert) G(eorge)

de la Roche, Mazo 1879-1961 . . . . . . **CLC 14**
See also CA 85-88; CANR 30; DLB 68;
SATA 64

Delbanco, Nicholas (Franklin)
1942- . . . . **CLC 6, 13**
See also CA 17-20R; CAAS 2; CANR 29;
DLB 6

del Castillo, Michel 1933- . . . . **CLC 38**
See also CA 109

Deledda, Grazia (Cosima)
1875(?)-1936 . . . . **TCLC 23**
See also CA 123

Delibes, Miguel . . . . **CLC 8, 18**
See also Delibes Setien, Miguel

Delibes Setien, Miguel 1920-
See Delibes, Miguel
See also CA 45-48; CANR 1, 32; HW;
MTCW

DeLillo, Don
1936- . . . . . **CLC 8, 10, 13, 27, 39, 54, 76**
See also BEST 89:1; CA 81-84; CANR 21;
DLB 6; MTCW

de Lisser, H. G.
See De Lisser, Herbert George
See also DLB 117

De Lisser, Herbert George
1878-1944 . . . . **TCLC 12**
See also de Lisser, H. G.
See also CA 109

Deloria, Vine (Victor), Jr. 1933- . . . **CLC 21**
See also CA 53-56; CANR 5, 20; MTCW;
SATA 21

Del Vecchio, John M(ichael)
1947- . . . . **CLC 29**
See also CA 110; DLBD 9

de Man, Paul (Adolph Michel)
1919-1983 . . . . **CLC 55**
See also CA 128; 111; DLB 67; MTCW

De Marinis, Rick 1934- . . . . **CLC 54**
See also CA 57-60; CANR 9, 25

Demby, William 1922- . . . . . . **CLC 53; BLC**
See also BW; CA 81-84; DLB 33

Demijohn, Thom
See Disch, Thomas M(ichael)

de Montherlant, Henry (Milon)
See Montherlant, Henry (Milon) de

de Natale, Francine
See Malzberg, Barry N(athaniel)

Denby, Edwin (Orr) 1903-1983 . . . . . **CLC 48**
See also CA 138; 110

Denis, Julio
See Cortazar, Julio

Denmark, Harrison
See Zelazny, Roger (Joseph)

Dennis, John 1658-1734 . . . . **LC 11**
See also DLB 101

Dennis, Nigel (Forbes) 1912-1989 . . . . **CLC 8**
See also CA 25-28R; 129; DLB 13, 15;
MTCW

De Palma, Brian (Russell) 1940- . . . . **CLC 20**
See also CA 109

De Quincey, Thomas 1785-1859 . . . **NCLC 4**
See also CDBLB 1789-1832; DLB 110

Deren, Eleanora 1908(?)-1961
See Deren, Maya
See also CA 111

Deren, Maya . . . . **CLC 16**
See also Deren, Eleanora

Derleth, August (William)
1909-1971 . . . . **CLC 31**
See also CA 1-4R; 29-32R; CANR 4;
DLB 9; SATA 5

de Routisie, Albert
See Aragon, Louis

Derrida, Jacques 1930- . . . . **CLC 24**
See also CA 124; 127

Derry Down Derry
See Lear, Edward

Dersonnes, Jacques
See Simenon, Georges (Jacques Christian)

Desai, Anita 1937- . . . . **CLC 19, 37**
See also CA 81-84; CANR 33; MTCW;
SATA 63

de Saint-Luc, Jean
See Glassco, John

de Saint Roman, Arnaud
See Aragon, Louis

Descartes, Rene 1596-1650 . . . . **LC 20**

De Sica, Vittorio 1901(?)-1974 . . . . . **CLC 20**
See also CA 117

Desnos, Robert 1900-1945 . . . . **TCLC 22**
See also CA 121

Destouches, Louis-Ferdinand
1894-1961 . . . . **CLC 9, 15**
See also Celine, Louis-Ferdinand
See also CA 85-88; CANR 28; MTCW

Deutsch, Babette 1895-1982 . . . . **CLC 18**
See also CA 1-4R; 108; CANR 4; DLB 45;
SATA 1, 33

Devenant, William 1606-1649 . . . . **LC 13**

Devkota, Laxmiprasad
1909-1959 . . . . **TCLC 23**
See also CA 123

De Voto, Bernard (Augustine)
1897-1955 . . . . **TCLC 29**
See also CA 113; DLB 9

De Vries, Peter
1910-1993 . . . . **CLC 1, 2, 3, 7, 10, 28, 46**
See also CA 17-20R; 142; CANR 41;
DLB 6; DLBY 82; MTCW

Dexter, Martin
See Faust, Frederick (Schiller)

Dexter, Pete 1943- . . . . **CLC 34, 55**
See also BEST 89:2; CA 127; 131; MTCW

Diamano, Silmang
See Senghor, Leopold Sedar

Diamond, Neil 1941- . . . . **CLC 30**
See also CA 108

di Bassetto, Corno
See Shaw, George Bernard

Dick, Philip K(indred)
1928-1982 . . . . **CLC 10, 30, 72**
See also CA 49-52; 106; CANR 2, 16;
DLB 8; MTCW

Dickens, Charles (John Huffam)
1812-1870 . . . . . **NCLC 3, 8, 18, 26; DA;**
WLC
See also CDBLB 1832-1890; DLB 21, 55,
70; JRDA; MAICYA; SATA 15

Dickey, James (Lafayette)
1923- . . . . **CLC 1, 2, 4, 7, 10, 15, 47**
See also AITN 1, 2; CA 9-12R; CABS 2;
CANR 10; CDALB 1968-1988; DLB 5;
DLBD 7; DLBY 82; MTCW

Dickey, William 1928- . . . . **CLC 3, 28**
See also CA 9-12R; CANR 24; DLB 5

Dickinson, Charles 1951- . . . . **CLC 49**
See also CA 128

Dickinson, Emily (Elizabeth)
1830-1886 . . **NCLC 21; DA; PC 1; WLC**
See also CDALB 1865-1917; DLB 1;
SATA 29

Dickinson, Peter (Malcolm)
1927- . . . . **CLC 12, 35**
See also AAYA 9; CA 41-44R; CANR 31;
CLR 29; DLB 87; JRDA; MAICYA;
SATA 5, 62

Dickson, Carr
See Carr, John Dickson

Dickson, Carter
See Carr, John Dickson

Didion, Joan 1934- . . . . . **CLC 1, 3, 8, 14, 32**
See also AITN 1; CA 5-8R; CANR 14;
CDALB 1968-1988; DLB 2; DLBY 81,
86; MTCW

Dietrich, Robert
See Hunt, E(verette) Howard, Jr.

Dillard, Annie 1945- . . . . **CLC 9, 60**
See also AAYA 6; CA 49-52; CANR 3, 43;
DLBY 80; MTCW; SATA 10

Dillard, R(ichard) H(enry) W(ilde)
1937- . . . . **CLC 5**
See also CA 21-24R; CAAS 7; CANR 10;
DLB 5

Dillon, Eilis 1920- . . . . **CLC 17**
See also CA 9-12R; CAAS 3; CANR 4, 38;
CLR 26; MAICYA; SATA 2, 74

Dimont, Penelope
See Mortimer, Penelope (Ruth)

Dinesen, Isak . . . . **CLC 10, 29; SSC 7**
See also Blixen, Karen (Christentze
Dinesen)

Ding Ling . . . . **CLC 68**
See also Chiang Pin-chin

Disch, Thomas M(ichael) 1940- . . . **CLC 7, 36**
See also CA 21-24R; CAAS 4; CANR 17,
36; CLR 18; DLB 8; MAICYA; MTCW;
SAAS 15; SATA 54

Disch, Tom
See Disch, Thomas M(ichael)

d'Isly, Georges
See Simenon, Georges (Jacques Christian)

Disraeli, Benjamin 1804-1881 . . **NCLC 2, 39**
See also DLB 21, 55

Ditcum, Steve
See Crumb, R(obert)

Dixon, Paige
See Corcoran, Barbara

Dixon, Stephen 1936-............. **CLC 52**
See also CA 89-92; CANR 17, 40; DLB 130

Dobell, Sydney Thompson
1824-1874 .... **NCLC 43**
See also DLB 32

Doblin, Alfred .... **TCLC 13**
See also Doeblin, Alfred

Dobrolyubov, Nikolai Alexandrovich
1836-1861 .... **NCLC 5**

Dobyns, Stephen 1941-............ **CLC 37**
See also CA 45-48; CANR 2, 18

Doctorow, E(dgar) L(aurence)
1931- ..... **CLC 6, 11, 15, 18, 37, 44, 65**
See also AITN 2; BEST 89:3; CA 45-48;
CANR 2, 33; CDALB 1968-1988; DLB 2,
28; DLBY 80; MTCW

Dodgson, Charles Lutwidge 1832-1898
See Carroll, Lewis
See also CLR 2; DA; MAICYA; YABC 2

Dodson, Owen (Vincent)
1914-1983 .... **CLC 79; BLC**
See also BW; CA 65-68; 110; CANR 24;
DLB 76

Doeblin, Alfred 1878-1957....... **TCLC 13**
See also Doblin, Alfred
See also CA 110; 141; DLB 66

Doerr, Harriet 1910- .... **CLC 34**
See also CA 117; 122

Domecq, H(onorio) Bustos
See Bioy Casares, Adolfo; Borges, Jorge
Luis

Domini, Rey
See Lorde, Audre (Geraldine)

Dominique
See Proust, (Valentin-Louis-George-Eugene-)
Marcel

Don, A
See Stephen, Leslie

Donaldson, Stephen R. 1947-....... **CLC 46**
See also CA 89-92; CANR 13

Donleavy, J(ames) P(atrick)
1926- .... **CLC 1, 4, 6, 10, 45**
See also AITN 2; CA 9-12R; CANR 24;
DLB 6; MTCW

Donne, John
1572-1631 .... **LC 10, 24; DA; PC 1**
See also CDBLB Before 1660; DLB 121

Donnell, David 1939(?)-........... **CLC 34**

Donoso (Yanez), Jose
1924- .... **CLC 4, 8, 11, 32; HLC**
See also CA 81-84; CANR 32; DLB 113;
HW; MTCW

Donovan, John 1928-1992 .... **CLC 35**
See also CA 97-100; 137; CLR 3;
MAICYA; SATA 29

Don Roberto
See Cunninghame Graham, R(obert)
B(ontine)

Doolittle, Hilda
1886-1961 ..... **CLC 3, 8, 14, 31, 34, 73;
DA; PC 5; WLC**
See also H. D.
See also CA 97-100; CANR 35; DLB 4, 45;
MTCW

Dorfman, Ariel 1942-.... **CLC 48, 77; HLC**
See also CA 124; 130; HW

Dorn, Edward (Merton) 1929-... **CLC 10, 18**
See also CA 93-96; CANR 42; DLB 5

Dorsan, Luc
See Simenon, Georges (Jacques Christian)

Dorsange, Jean
See Simenon, Georges (Jacques Christian)

Dos Passos, John (Roderigo)
1896-1970 ...... **CLC 1, 4, 8, 11, 15, 25,
34, 82; DA; WLC**
See also CA 1-4R; 29-32R; CANR 3;
CDALB 1929-1941; DLB 4, 9; DLBD 1;
MTCW

Dossage, Jean
See Simenon, Georges (Jacques Christian)

Dostoevsky, Fedor Mikhailovich
1821-1881 ...... **NCLC 2, 7, 21, 33, 43;
DA; SSC 2; WLC**

Doughty, Charles M(ontagu)
1843-1926 .... **TCLC 27**
See also CA 115; DLB 19, 57

Douglas, Ellen
See Haxton, Josephine Ayres

Douglas, Gavin 1475(?)-1522........ **LC 20**

Douglas, Keith 1920-1944 .... **TCLC 40**
See also DLB 27

Douglas, Leonard
See Bradbury, Ray (Douglas)

Douglas, Michael
See Crichton, (John) Michael

Douglass, Frederick
1817(?)-1895 .... **NCLC 7; BLC; DA;
WLC**
See also CDALB 1640-1865; DLB 1, 43, 50,
79; SATA 29

Dourado, (Waldomiro Freitas) Autran
1926- .... **CLC 23, 60**
See also CA 25-28R; CANR 34

Dourado, Waldomiro Autran
See Dourado, (Waldomiro Freitas) Autran

Dove, Rita (Frances)
1952- .... **CLC 50, 81; PC 6**
See also BW; CA 109; CANR 27, 42;
DLB 120

Dowell, Coleman 1925-1985....... **CLC 60**
See also CA 25-28R; 117; CANR 10;
DLB 130

Dowson, Ernest Christopher
1867-1900 .... **TCLC 4**
See also CA 105; DLB 19, 135

Doyle, A. Conan
See Doyle, Arthur Conan

Doyle, Arthur Conan
1859-1930 .... **TCLC 7; DA; SSC 12;
WLC**
See also CA 104; 122; CDBLB 1890-1914;
DLB 18, 70; MTCW; SATA 24

Doyle, Conan 1859-1930
See Doyle, Arthur Conan

Doyle, John
See Graves, Robert (von Ranke)

Doyle, Roddy 1958(?)-........... **CLC 81**
See also CA 143

Doyle, Sir A. Conan
See Doyle, Arthur Conan

Doyle, Sir Arthur Conan
See Doyle, Arthur Conan

Dr. A
See Asimov, Isaac; Silverstein, Alvin

Drabble, Margaret
1939- .... **CLC 2, 3, 5, 8, 10, 22, 53**
See also CA 13-16R; CANR 18, 35;
CDBLB 1960 to Present; DLB 14;
MTCW; SATA 48

Drapier, M. B.
See Swift, Jonathan

Drayham, James
See Mencken, H(enry) L(ouis)

Drayton, Michael 1563-1631........ **LC 8**

Dreadstone, Carl
See Campbell, (John) Ramsey

Dreiser, Theodore (Herman Albert)
1871-1945 .... **TCLC 10, 18, 35; DA;
WLC**
See also CA 106; 132; CDALB 1865-1917;
DLB 9, 12, 102; DLBD 1; MTCW

Drexler, Rosalyn 1926- .... **CLC 2, 6**
See also CA 81-84

Dreyer, Carl Theodor 1889-1968.... **CLC 16**
See also CA 116

Drieu la Rochelle, Pierre(-Eugene)
1893-1945 .... **TCLC 21**
See also CA 117; DLB 72

Drop Shot
See Cable, George Washington

Droste-Hulshoff, Annette Freiin von
1797-1848 .... **NCLC 3**
See also DLB 133

Drummond, Walter
See Silverberg, Robert

Drummond, William Henry
1854-1907 .... **TCLC 25**
See also DLB 92

Drummond de Andrade, Carlos
1902-1987 .... **CLC 18**
See also Andrade, Carlos Drummond de
See also CA 132; 123

Drury, Allen (Stuart) 1918-........ **CLC 37**
See also CA 57-60; CANR 18

Dryden, John
1631-1700 ... **LC 3, 21; DA; DC 3; WLC**
See also CDBLB 1660-1789; DLB 80, 101,
131

Duberman, Martin 1930-........... **CLC 8**
See also CA 1-4R; CANR 2

Dubie, Norman (Evans) 1945-...... **CLC 36**
See also CA 69-72; CANR 12; DLB 120

Du Bois, W(illiam) E(dward) B(urghardt)
1868-1963 ...... **CLC 1, 2, 13, 64; BLC;
DA; WLC**
See also BW; CA 85-88; CANR 34;
CDALB 1865-1917; DLB 47, 50, 91;
MTCW; SATA 42

Dubus, Andre 1936-... **CLC 13, 36; SSC 15**
See also CA 21-24R; CANR 17; DLB 130

Duca Minimo
See D'Annunzio, Gabriele

Ducharme, Rejean 1941- .... **CLC 74**
See also DLB 60

Duclos, Charles Pinot 1704-1772 ..... **LC 1**

Dudek, Louis 1918- .... **CLC 11, 19**
See also CA 45-48; CAAS 14; CANR 1;
DLB 88

Duerrenmatt, Friedrich
.... **CLC 1, 4, 8, 11, 15, 43**
See also Duerrenmatt, Friedrich
See also DLB 69, 124

Duerrenmatt, Friedrich
1921-1990 ...... **CLC 1, 4, 8, 11, 15, 43**
See also Duerrenmatt, Friedrich
See also CA 17-20R; CANR 33; DLB 69,
124; MTCW

Duffy, Bruce (?)- .... **CLC 50**

Duffy, Maureen 1933- .... **CLC 37**
See also CA 25-28R; CANR 33; DLB 14;
MTCW

Dugan, Alan 1923- .... **CLC 2, 6**
See also CA 81-84; DLB 5

du Gard, Roger Martin
See Martin du Gard, Roger

Duhamel, Georges 1884-1966 .... **CLC 8**
See also CA 81-84; 25-28R; CANR 35;
DLB 65; MTCW

Dujardin, Edouard (Emile Louis)
1861-1949 .... **TCLC 13**
See also CA 109; DLB 123

Dumas, Alexandre (Davy de la Pailleterie)
1802-1870 .... **NCLC 11; DA; WLC**
See also DLB 119; SATA 18

Dumas, Alexandre
1824-1895 .... **NCLC 9; DC 1**

Dumas, Claudine
See Malzberg, Barry N(athaniel)

Dumas, Henry L. 1934-1968 ..... **CLC 6, 62**
See also BW; CA 85-88; DLB 41

du Maurier, Daphne
1907-1989 .... **CLC 6, 11, 59**
See also CA 5-8R; 128; CANR 6; MTCW;
SATA 27, 60

Dunbar, Paul Laurence
1872-1906 ...... **TCLC 2, 12; BLC; DA;**
          PC 5; SSC 8; WLC
See also BW; CA 104; 124;
CDALB 1865-1917; DLB 50, 54, 78;
SATA 34

Dunbar, William 1460(?)-1530(?) .... **LC 20**

Duncan, Lois 1934- .... **CLC 26**
See also AAYA 4; CA 1-4R; CANR 2, 23,
36; CLR 29; JRDA; MAICYA; SAAS 2;
SATA 1, 36, 75

Duncan, Robert (Edward)
1919-1988 .... **CLC 1, 2, 4, 7, 15, 41, 55;**
                PC 2
See also CA 9-12R; 124; CANR 28; DLB 5,
16; MTCW

Dunlap, William 1766-1839 .... **NCLC 2**
See also DLB 30, 37, 59

Dunn, Douglas (Eaglesham)
1942- .... **CLC 6, 40**
See also CA 45-48; CANR 2, 33; DLB 40;
MTCW

Dunn, Katherine (Karen) 1945- ..... **CLC 71**
See also CA 33-36R

Dunn, Stephen 1939- .... **CLC 36**
See also CA 33-36R; CANR 12; DLB 105

Dunne, Finley Peter 1867-1936.... **TCLC 28**
See also CA 108; DLB 11, 23

Dunne, John Gregory 1932- .... **CLC 28**
See also CA 25-28R; CANR 14; DLBY 80

Dunsany, Edward John Moreton Drax
  Plunkett 1878-1957
See Dunsany, Lord; Lord Dunsany
See also CA 104; DLB 10

Dunsany, Lord .... **TCLC 2**
See also Dunsany, Edward John Moreton
Drax Plunkett
See also DLB 77

du Perry, Jean
See Simenon, Georges (Jacques Christian)

Durang, Christopher (Ferdinand)
1949- .... **CLC 27, 38**
See also CA 105

Duras, Marguerite
1914- ...... **CLC 3, 6, 11, 20, 34, 40, 68**
See also CA 25-28R; DLB 83; MTCW

Durban, (Rosa) Pam 1947- .... **CLC 39**
See also CA 123

Durcan, Paul 1944- .... **CLC 43, 70**
See also CA 134

Durrell, Lawrence (George)
1912-1990 .... **CLC 1, 4, 6, 8, 13, 27, 41**
See also CA 9-12R; 132; CANR 40;
CDBLB 1945-1960; DLB 15, 27;
DLBY 90; MTCW

Dutt, Toru 1856-1877.......... **NCLC 29**

Dwight, Timothy 1752-1817...... **NCLC 13**
See also DLB 37

Dworkin, Andrea 1946- .... **CLC 43**
See also CA 77-80; CANR 16, 39; MTCW

Dwyer, Deanna
See Koontz, Dean R(ay)

Dwyer, K. R.
See Koontz, Dean R(ay)

Dylan, Bob 1941- ...... **CLC 3, 4, 6, 12, 77**
See also CA 41-44R; DLB 16

Eagleton, Terence (Francis) 1943-
See Eagleton, Terry
See also CA 57-60; CANR 7, 23; MTCW

Eagleton, Terry .... **CLC 63**
See also Eagleton, Terence (Francis)

Early, Jack
See Scoppettone, Sandra

East, Michael
See West, Morris L(anglo)

Eastaway, Edward
See Thomas, (Philip) Edward

Eastlake, William (Derry) 1917- ..... **CLC 8**
See also CA 5-8R; CAAS 1; CANR 5;
DLB 6

Eberhart, Richard (Ghormley)
1904- .... **CLC 3, 11, 19, 56**
See also CA 1-4R; CANR 2;
CDALB 1941-1968; DLB 48; MTCW

Eberstadt, Fernanda 1960- .... **CLC 39**
See also CA 136

Echegaray (y Eizaguirre), Jose (Maria Waldo)
1832-1916 .... **TCLC 4**
See also CA 104; CANR 32; HW; MTCW

Echeverria, (Jose) Esteban (Antonino)
1805-1851 .... **NCLC 18**

Echo
See Proust, (Valentin-Louis-George-Eugene-)
Marcel

Eckert, Allan W. 1931- .... **CLC 17**
See also CA 13-16R; CANR 14; SATA 27,
29

Eckhart, Meister 1260(?)-1328(?) .. **CMLC 9**
See also DLB 115

Eckmar, F. R.
See de Hartog, Jan

Eco, Umberto 1932- .... **CLC 28, 60**
See also BEST 90:1; CA 77-80; CANR 12,
33; MTCW

Eddison, E(ric) R(ucker)
1882-1945 .... **TCLC 15**
See also CA 109

Edel, (Joseph) Leon 1907- ...... **CLC 29, 34**
See also CA 1-4R; CANR 1, 22; DLB 103

Eden, Emily 1797-1869 .... **NCLC 10**

Edgar, David 1948- .... **CLC 42**
See also CA 57-60; CANR 12; DLB 13;
MTCW

Edgerton, Clyde (Carlyle) 1944- .... **CLC 39**
See also CA 118; 134

Edgeworth, Maria 1767-1849...... **NCLC 1**
See also DLB 116; SATA 21

Edmonds, Paul
See Kuttner, Henry

Edmonds, Walter D(umaux) 1903- .. **CLC 35**
See also CA 5-8R; CANR 2; DLB 9;
MAICYA; SAAS 4; SATA 1, 27

Edmondson, Wallace
See Ellison, Harlan

Edson, Russell .... **CLC 13**
See also CA 33-36R

Edwards, G(erald) B(asil)
1899-1976 .... **CLC 25**
See also CA 110

Edwards, Gus 1939- .... **CLC 43**
See also CA 108

Edwards, Jonathan 1703-1758.... **LC 7; DA**
See also DLB 24

Efron, Marina Ivanovna Tsvetaeva
See Tsvetaeva (Efron), Marina (Ivanovna)

Ehle, John (Marsden, Jr.) 1925- .... **CLC 27**
See also CA 9-12R

Ehrenbourg, Ilya (Grigoryevich)
See Ehrenburg, Ilya (Grigoryevich)

Ehrenburg, Ilya (Grigoryevich)
1891-1967 .... **CLC 18, 34, 62**
See also CA 102; 25-28R

Ehrenburg, Ilyo (Grigoryevich)
See Ehrenburg, Ilya (Grigoryevich)

Eich, Guenter 1907-1972 .... **CLC 15**
See also CA 111; 93-96; DLB 69, 124

Eichendorff, Joseph Freiherr von
1788-1857 .... **NCLC 8**
See also DLB 90

Evan, Evin
See Faust, Frederick (Schiller)

Evans, Evan
See Faust, Frederick (Schiller)

Evans, Marian
See Eliot, George

Evans, Mary Ann
See Eliot, George

Evarts, Esther
See Benson, Sally

Everett, Percival
See Everett, Percival L.

Everett, Percival L. 1956- .... **CLC 57**
See also CA 129

Everson, R(onald) G(ilmour)
1903- .... **CLC 27**
See also CA 17-20R; DLB 88

Everson, William (Oliver)
1912- .... **CLC 1, 5, 14**
See also CA 9-12R; CANR 20; DLB 5, 16;
MTCW

Evtushenko, Evgenii Aleksandrovich
See Yevtushenko, Yevgeny (Alexandrovich)

Ewart, Gavin (Buchanan)
1916- .... **CLC 13, 46**
See also CA 89-92; CANR 17; DLB 40;
MTCW

Ewers, Hanns Heinz 1871-1943 ... **TCLC 12**
See also CA 109

Ewing, Frederick R.
See Sturgeon, Theodore (Hamilton)

Exley, Frederick (Earl)
1929-1992 .... **CLC 6, 11**
See also AITN 2; CA 81-84; 138; DLBY 81

Eynhardt, Guillermo
See Quiroga, Horacio (Sylvestre)

Ezekiel, Nissim 1924- .... **CLC 61**
See also CA 61-64

Ezekiel, Tish O'Dowd 1943- .... **CLC 34**
See also CA 129

Fadeyev, A.
See Bulgya, Alexander Alexandrovich

Fadeyev, Alexander .... **TCLC 53**
See also Bulgya, Alexander Alexandrovich

Fagen, Donald 1948- .... **CLC 26**

Fainzilberg, Ilya Arnoldovich 1897-1937
See Ilf, Ilya
See also CA 120

Fair, Ronald L. 1932- .... **CLC 18**
See also BW; CA 69-72; CANR 25; DLB 33

Fairbairns, Zoe (Ann) 1948- .... **CLC 32**
See also CA 103; CANR 21

Falco, Gian
See Papini, Giovanni

Falconer, James
See Kirkup, James

Falconer, Kenneth
See Kornbluth, C(yril) M.

Falkland, Samuel
See Heijermans, Herman

Fallaci, Oriana 1930- .... **CLC 11**
See also CA 77-80; CANR 15; MTCW

Faludy, George 1913- .... **CLC 42**
See also CA 21-24R

Faludy, Gyoergy
See Faludy, George

Fanon, Frantz 1925-1961 ..... **CLC 74; BLC**
See also BW; CA 116; 89-92

Fanshawe, Ann .... **LC 11**

Fante, John (Thomas) 1911-1983 ... **CLC 60**
See also CA 69-72; 109; CANR 23;
DLB 130; DLBY 83

Farah, Nuruddin 1945- .... **CLC 53; BLC**
See also CA 106; DLB 125

Fargue, Leon-Paul 1876(?)-1947 ... **TCLC 11**
See also CA 109

Farigoule, Louis
See Romains, Jules

Farina, Richard 1936(?)-1966 .... **CLC 9**
See also CA 81-84; 25-28R

Farley, Walter (Lorimer)
1915-1989 .... **CLC 17**
See also CA 17-20R; CANR 8, 29; DLB 22;
JRDA; MAICYA; SATA 2, 43

Farmer, Philip Jose 1918- .... **CLC 1, 19**
See also CA 1-4R; CANR 4, 35; DLB 8;
MTCW

Farquhar, George 1677-1707 .... **LC 21**
See also DLB 84

Farrell, J(ames) G(ordon)
1935-1979 .... **CLC 6**
See also CA 73-76; 89-92; CANR 36;
DLB 14; MTCW

Farrell, James T(homas)
1904-1979 .... **CLC 1, 4, 8, 11, 66**
See also CA 5-8R; 89-92; CANR 9; DLB 4,
9, 86; DLBD 2; MTCW

Farren, Richard J.
See Betjeman, John

Farren, Richard M.
See Betjeman, John

Fassbinder, Rainer Werner
1946-1982 .... **CLC 20**
See also CA 93-96; 106; CANR 31

Fast, Howard (Melvin) 1914- ...... **CLC 23**
See also CA 1-4R; CAAS 18; CANR 1, 33;
DLB 9; SATA 7

Faulcon, Robert
See Holdstock, Robert P.

Faulkner, William (Cuthbert)
1897-1962 ..... **CLC 1, 3, 6, 8, 9, 11, 14,
18, 28, 52, 68; DA; SSC 1; WLC**
See also AAYA 7; CA 81-84; CANR 33;
CDALB 1929-1941; DLB 9, 11, 44, 102;
DLBD 2; DLBY 86; MTCW

Fauset, Jessie Redmon
1884(?)-1961 .... **CLC 19, 54; BLC**
See also BW; CA 109; DLB 51

Faust, Frederick (Schiller)
1892-1944(?) .... **TCLC 49**
See also CA 108

Faust, Irvin 1924- .... **CLC 8**
See also CA 33-36R; CANR 28; DLB 2, 28;
DLBY 80

Fawkes, Guy
See Benchley, Robert (Charles)

Fearing, Kenneth (Flexner)
1902-1961 .... **CLC 51**
See also CA 93-96; DLB 9

Fecamps, Elise
See Creasey, John

Federman, Raymond 1928- ...... **CLC 6, 47**
See also CA 17-20R; CAAS 8; CANR 10,
43; DLBY 80

Federspiel, J(uerg) F. 1931- .... **CLC 42**

Feiffer, Jules (Ralph) 1929- .... **CLC 2, 8, 64**
See also AAYA 3; CA 17-20R; CANR 30;
DLB 7, 44; MTCW; SATA 8, 61

Feige, Hermann Albert Otto Maximilian
See Traven, B.

Fei-Kan, Li
See Li Fei-kan

Feinberg, David B. 1956- .... **CLC 59**
See also CA 135

Feinstein, Elaine 1930- .... **CLC 36**
See also CA 69-72; CAAS 1; CANR 31;
DLB 14, 40; MTCW

Feldman, Irving (Mordecai) 1928- .... **CLC 7**
See also CA 1-4R; CANR 1

Fellini, Federico 1920-1993 .... **CLC 16**
See also CA 65-68; 143; CANR 33

Felsen, Henry Gregor 1916- .... **CLC 17**
See also CA 1-4R; CANR 1; SAAS 2;
SATA 1

Fenton, James Martin 1949- .... **CLC 32**
See also CA 102; DLB 40

Ferber, Edna 1887-1968............ **CLC 18**
See also AITN 1; CA 5-8R; 25-28R; DLB 9,
28, 86; MTCW; SATA 7

Ferguson, Helen
See Kavan, Anna

Ferguson, Samuel 1810-1886..... **NCLC 33**
See also DLB 32

Ferling, Lawrence
See Ferlinghetti, Lawrence (Monsanto)

Ferlinghetti, Lawrence (Monsanto)
1919(?)- .... **CLC 2, 6, 10, 27; PC 1**
See also CA 5-8R; CANR 3, 41;
CDALB 1941-1968; DLB 5, 16; MTCW

Fernandez, Vicente Garcia Huidobro
See Huidobro Fernandez, Vicente Garcia

Ferrer, Gabriel (Francisco Victor) Miro
See Miro (Ferrer), Gabriel (Francisco
Victor)

Ferrier, Susan (Edmonstone)
1782-1854 .... **NCLC 8**
See also DLB 116

Ferrigno, Robert 1948(?)- .... **CLC 65**
See also CA 140

Feuchtwanger, Lion 1884-1958 ..... **TCLC 3**
See also CA 104; DLB 66

Feydeau, Georges (Leon Jules Marie)
1862-1921 .... **TCLC 22**
See also CA 113

Ficino, Marsilio 1433-1499 .... **LC 12**

Fiedeler, Hans
See Doeblin, Alfred

Fiedler, Leslie A(aron)
1917- .... **CLC 4, 13, 24**
See also CA 9-12R; CANR 7; DLB 28, 67;
MTCW

Field, Andrew 1938-.............. **CLC 44**
See also CA 97-100; CANR 25

Field, Eugene 1850-1895 .... **NCLC 3**
See also DLB 23, 42; MAICYA; SATA 16

Field, Gans T.
See Wellman, Manly Wade

Field, Michael .... **TCLC 43**

Field, Peter
See Hobson, Laura Z(ametkin)

Fielding, Henry
1707-1754 .... **LC 1; DA; WLC**
See also CDBLB 1660-1789; DLB 39, 84,
101

Fielding, Sarah 1710-1768 .... **LC 1**
See also DLB 39

Fierstein, Harvey (Forbes) 1954- ... **CLC 33**
See also CA 123; 129

Figes, Eva 1932-................. **CLC 31**
See also CA 53-56; CANR 4; DLB 14

Finch, Robert (Duer Claydon)
1900- .... **CLC 18**
See also CA 57-60; CANR 9, 24; DLB 88

Findley, Timothy 1930- .... **CLC 27**
See also CA 25-28R; CANR 12, 42;
DLB 53

Fink, William
See Mencken, H(enry) L(ouis)

Firbank, Louis 1942-
See Reed, Lou
See also CA 117

Firbank, (Arthur Annesley) Ronald
1886-1926 .... **TCLC 1**
See also CA 104; DLB 36

Fisher, M(ary) F(rances) K(ennedy)
1908-1992 .... **CLC 76**
See also CA 77-80; 138

Fisher, Roy 1930-.............. **CLC 25**
See also CA 81-84; CAAS 10; CANR 16;
DLB 40

Fisher, Rudolph
1897-1934 .... **TCLC 11; BLC**
See also BW; CA 107; 124; DLB 51, 102

Fisher, Vardis (Alvero) 1895-1968.... **CLC 7**
See also CA 5-8R; 25-28R; DLB 9

Fiske, Tarleton
See Bloch, Robert (Albert)

Fitch, Clarke
See Sinclair, Upton (Beall)

Fitch, John IV
See Cormier, Robert (Edmund)

Fitgerald, Penelope 1916- .... **CLC 61**

Fitzgerald, Captain Hugh
See Baum, L(yman) Frank

FitzGerald, Edward 1809-1883 .... **NCLC 9**
See also DLB 32

Fitzgerald, F(rancis) Scott (Key)
1896-1940 ..... **TCLC 1, 6, 14, 28; DA;
SSC 6; WLC**
See also AITN 1; CA 110; 123;
CDALB 1917-1929; DLB 4, 9, 86;
DLBD 1; DLBY 81; MTCW

Fitzgerald, Penelope 1916-...... **CLC 19, 51**
See also CA 85-88; CAAS 10; DLB 14

Fitzgerald, Robert (Stuart)
1910-1985 .... **CLC 39**
See also CA 1-4R; 114; CANR 1; DLBY 80

FitzGerald, Robert D(avid)
1902-1987 .... **CLC 19**
See also CA 17-20R

Fitzgerald, Zelda (Sayre)
1900-1948 .... **TCLC 52**
See also CA 117; 126; DLBY 84

Flanagan, Thomas (James Bonner)
1923- .... **CLC 25, 52**
See also CA 108; DLBY 80; MTCW

Flaubert, Gustave
1821-1880 .... **NCLC 2, 10, 19; DA;
SSC 11; WLC**
See also DLB 119

Flecker, (Herman) James Elroy
1884-1915 .... **TCLC 43**
See also CA 109; DLB 10, 19

Fleming, Ian (Lancaster)
1908-1964 .... **CLC 3, 30**
See also CA 5-8R; CDBLB 1945-1960;
DLB 87; MTCW; SATA 9

Fleming, Thomas (James) 1927- .... **CLC 37**
See also CA 5-8R; CANR 10; SATA 8

Fletcher, John Gould 1886-1950... **TCLC 35**
See also CA 107; DLB 4, 45

Fleur, Paul
See Pohl, Frederik

Flooglebuckle, Al
See Spiegelman, Art

Flying Officer X
See Bates, H(erbert) E(rnest)

Fo, Dario 1926-.................. **CLC 32**
See also CA 116; 128; MTCW

Fogarty, Jonathan Titulescu Esq.
See Farrell, James T(homas)

Folke, Will
See Bloch, Robert (Albert)

Follett, Ken(neth Martin) 1949- .... **CLC 18**
See also AAYA 6; BEST 89:4; CA 81-84;
CANR 13, 33; DLB 87; DLBY 81;
MTCW

Fontane, Theodor 1819-1898 ..... **NCLC 26**
See also DLB 129

Foote, Horton 1916-.............. **CLC 51**
See also CA 73-76; CANR 34; DLB 26

Foote, Shelby 1916- .... **CLC 75**
See also CA 5-8R; CANR 3; DLB 2, 17

Forbes, Esther 1891-1967......... **CLC 12**
See also CA 13-14; 25-28R; CAP 1;
CLR 27; DLB 22; JRDA; MAICYA;
SATA 2

Forche, Carolyn (Louise) 1950-..... **CLC 25**
See also CA 109; 117; DLB 5

Ford, Elbur
See Hibbert, Eleanor Alice Burford

Ford, Ford Madox
1873-1939 .... **TCLC 1, 15, 39**
See also CA 104; 132; CDBLB 1914-1945;
DLB 34, 98; MTCW

Ford, John 1895-1973............. **CLC 16**
See also CA 45-48

Ford, Richard 1944-.............. **CLC 46**
See also CA 69-72; CANR 11

Ford, Webster
See Masters, Edgar Lee

Foreman, Richard 1937-.......... **CLC 50**
See also CA 65-68; CANR 32

Forester, C(ecil) S(cott)
1899-1966 .... **CLC 35**
See also CA 73-76; 25-28R; SATA 13

Forez
See Mauriac, Francois (Charles)

Forman, James Douglas 1932-...... **CLC 21**
See also CA 9-12R; CANR 4, 19, 42;
JRDA; MAICYA; SATA 8, 70

Fornes, Maria Irene 1930-...... **CLC 39, 61**
See also CA 25-28R; CANR 28; DLB 7;
HW; MTCW

Forrest, Leon 1937- .... **CLC 4**
See also BW; CA 89-92; CAAS 7;
CANR 25; DLB 33

Forster, E(dward) M(organ)
1879-1970 ..... **CLC 1, 2, 3, 4, 9, 10, 13,
15, 22, 45, 77; DA; WLC**
See also AAYA 2; CA 13-14; 25-28R;
CAP 1; CDBLB 1914-1945; DLB 34, 98;
DLBD 10; MTCW; SATA 57

Forster, John 1812-1876 .... **NCLC 11**

Forsyth, Frederick 1938-...... **CLC 2, 5, 36**
See also BEST 89:4; CA 85-88; CANR 38;
DLB 87; MTCW

Forten, Charlotte L. .... **TCLC 16; BLC**
See also Grimke, Charlotte L(ottie) Forten
See also DLB 50

Foscolo, Ugo 1778-1827.......... **NCLC 8**

Fosse, Bob .... **CLC 20**
See also Fosse, Robert Louis

Fosse, Robert Louis 1927-1987
See Fosse, Bob
See also CA 110; 123

Foster, Stephen Collins
1826-1864 .... **NCLC 26**

Foucault, Michel
1926-1984 .... **CLC 31, 34, 69**
See also CA 105; 113; CANR 34; MTCW

Fouque, Friedrich (Heinrich Karl) de la Motte
1777-1843 .... **NCLC 2**
See also DLB 90

Fournier, Henri Alban 1886-1914
See Alain-Fournier
See also CA 104

Fournier, Pierre 1916- .... **CLC 11**
See also Gascar, Pierre
See also CA 89-92; CANR 16, 40

Fowles, John
1926- .... **CLC 1, 2, 3, 4, 6, 9, 10, 15, 33**
See also CA 5-8R; CANR 25; CDBLB 1960
to Present; DLB 14; MTCW; SATA 22

Fox, Paula 1923-................ CLC 2, 8
See also AAYA 3; CA 73-76; CANR 20,
36; CLR 1; DLB 52; JRDA; MAICYA;
MTCW; SATA 17, 60

Fox, William Price (Jr.) 1926- ..... CLC 22
See also CA 17-20R; CANR 11; DLB 2;
DLBY 81

Foxe, John 1516(?)-1587 .... LC 14

Frame, Janet .... CLC 2, 3, 6, 22, 66
See also Clutha, Janet Paterson Frame

France, Anatole.................... TCLC 9
See also Thibault, Jacques Anatole Francois
See also DLB 123

Francis, Claude 19(?)- .... CLC 50

Francis, Dick 1920- .... CLC 2, 22, 42
See also AAYA 5; BEST 89:3; CA 5-8R;
CANR 9, 42; CDBLB 1960 to Present;
DLB 87; MTCW

Francis, Robert (Churchill)
1901-1987 .... CLC 15
See also CA 1-4R; 123; CANR 1

Frank, Anne(lies Marie)
1929-1945 ..... TCLC 17; DA; WLC
See also CA 113; 133; MTCW; SATA 42

Frank, Elizabeth 1945-........... CLC 39
See also CA 121; 126

Franklin, Benjamin
See Hasek, Jaroslav (Matej Frantisek)

Franklin, Benjamin 1706-1790... LC 25; DA
See also CDALB 1640-1865; DLB 24, 43,
73

Franklin, (Stella Maraia Sarah) Miles
1879-1954 .... TCLC 7
See also CA 104

Fraser, Antonia (Pakenham)
1932- .... CLC 32
See also CA 85-88; MTCW; SATA 32

Fraser, George MacDonald 1925-.... CLC 7
See also CA 45-48; CANR 2

Fraser, Sylvia 1935-............. CLC 64
See also CA 45-48; CANR 1, 16

Frayn, Michael 1933-...... CLC 3, 7, 31, 47
See also CA 5-8R; CANR 30; DLB 13, 14;
MTCW

Fraze, Candida (Merrill) 1945- ..... CLC 50
See also CA 126

Frazer, J(ames) G(eorge)
1854-1941 .... TCLC 32
See also CA 118

Frazer, Robert Caine
See Creasey, John

Frazer, Sir James George
See Frazer, J(ames) G(eorge)

Frazier, Ian 1951-............... CLC 46
See also CA 130

Frederic, Harold 1856-1898...... NCLC 10
See also DLB 12, 23

Frederick, John
See Faust, Frederick (Schiller)

Frederick the Great 1712-1786 ...... LC 14

Fredro, Aleksander 1793-1876..... NCLC 8

Freeling, Nicolas 1927- .... CLC 38
See also CA 49-52; CAAS 12; CANR 1, 17;
DLB 87

Freeman, Douglas Southall
1886-1953 .... TCLC 11
See also CA 109; DLB 17

Freeman, Judith 1946-........... CLC 55

Freeman, Mary Eleanor Wilkins
1852-1930 .... TCLC 9; SSC 1
See also CA 106; DLB 12, 78

Freeman, R(ichard) Austin
1862-1943 .... TCLC 21
See also CA 113; DLB 70

French, Marilyn 1929-...... CLC 10, 18, 60
See also CA 69-72; CANR 3, 31; MTCW

French, Paul
See Asimov, Isaac

Freneau, Philip Morin 1752-1832.. NCLC 1
See also DLB 37, 43

Freud, Sigmund 1856-1939 .... TCLC 52
See also CA 115; 133; MTCW

Friedan, Betty (Naomi) 1921-...... CLC 74
See also CA 65-68; CANR 18; MTCW

Friedman, B(ernard) H(arper)
1926- .... CLC 7
See also CA 1-4R; CANR 3

Friedman, Bruce Jay 1930-.... CLC 3, 5, 56
See also CA 9-12R; CANR 25; DLB 2, 28

Friel, Brian 1929-.......... CLC 5, 42, 59
See also CA 21-24R; CANR 33; DLB 13;
MTCW

Friis-Baastad, Babbis Ellinor
1921-1970 .... CLC 12
See also CA 17-20R; 134; SATA 7

Frisch, Max (Rudolf)
1911-1991 ..... CLC 3, 9, 14, 18, 32, 44
See also CA 85-88; 134; CANR 32;
DLB 69, 124; MTCW

Fromentin, Eugene (Samuel Auguste)
1820-1876 .... NCLC 10
See also DLB 123

Frost, Frederick
See Faust, Frederick (Schiller)

Frost, Robert (Lee)
1874-1963 .... CLC 1, 3, 4, 9, 10, 13, 15,
26, 34, 44; DA; PC 1; WLC
See also CA 89-92; CANR 33;
CDALB 1917-1929; DLB 54; DLBD 7;
MTCW; SATA 14

Froude, James Anthony
1818-1894 .... NCLC 43
See also DLB 18, 57

Froy, Herald
See Waterhouse, Keith (Spencer)

Fry, Christopher 1907-....... CLC 2, 10, 14
See also CA 17-20R; CANR 9, 30; DLB 13;
MTCW; SATA 66

Frye, (Herman) Northrop
1912-1991 .... CLC 24, 70
See also CA 5-8R; 133; CANR 8, 37;
DLB 67, 68; MTCW

Fuchs, Daniel 1909-1993 .... CLC 8, 22
See also CA 81-84; 142; CAAS 5;
CANR 40; DLB 9, 26, 28

Fuchs, Daniel 1934-............. CLC 34
See also CA 37-40R; CANR 14

Fuentes, Carlos
1928- ...... CLC 3, 8, 10, 13, 22, 41, 60;
DA; HLC; WLC
See also AAYA 4; AITN 2; CA 69-72;
CANR 10, 32; DLB 113; HW; MTCW

Fuentes, Gregorio Lopez y
See Lopez y Fuentes, Gregorio

Fugard, (Harold) Athol
1932- .... CLC 5, 9, 14, 25, 40, 80; DC 3
See also CA 85-88; CANR 32; MTCW

Fugard, Sheila 1932- .... CLC 48
See also CA 125

Fuller, Charles (H., Jr.)
1939- .... CLC 25; BLC; DC 1
See also BW; CA 108; 112; DLB 38;
MTCW

Fuller, John (Leopold) 1937-....... CLC 62
See also CA 21-24R; CANR 9; DLB 40

Fuller, Margaret .... NCLC 5
See also Ossoli, Sarah Margaret (Fuller
marchesa d')

Fuller, Roy (Broadbent)
1912-1991 .... CLC 4, 28
See also CA 5-8R; 135; CAAS 10; DLB 15,
20

Fulton, Alice 1952-............... CLC 52
See also CA 116

Furphy, Joseph 1843-1912....... TCLC 25

Fussell, Paul 1924-............... CLC 74
See also BEST 90:1; CA 17-20R; CANR 8,
21, 35; MTCW

Futabatei, Shimei 1864-1909 ..... TCLC 44

Futrelle, Jacques 1875-1912 ...... TCLC 19
See also CA 113

G. B. S.
See Shaw, George Bernard

Gaboriau, Emile 1835-1873 ...... NCLC 14

Gadda, Carlo Emilio 1893-1973 .... CLC 11
See also CA 89-92

Gaddis, William
1922- .... CLC 1, 3, 6, 8, 10, 19, 43
See also CA 17-20R; CANR 21; DLB 2;
MTCW

Gaines, Ernest J(ames)
1933- .... CLC 3, 11, 18; BLC
See also AITN 1; BW; CA 9-12R; CANR 6,
24, 42; CDALB 1968-1988; DLB 2, 33;
DLBY 80; MTCW

Gaitskill, Mary 1954-............. CLC 69
See also CA 128

Galdos, Benito Perez
See Perez Galdos, Benito

Gale, Zona 1874-1938 .... TCLC 7
See also CA 105; DLB 9, 78

Galeano, Eduardo (Hughes) 1940-... CLC 72
See also CA 29-32R; CANR 13, 32; HW

Galiano, Juan Valera y Alcala
See Valera y Alcala-Galiano, Juan

Gallagher, Tess 1943-......... CLC 18, 63
See also CA 106; DLB 120

Gallant, Mavis
1922- .... CLC 7, 18, 38; SSC 5
See also CA 69-72; CANR 29; DLB 53;
MTCW

Gallant, Roy A(rthur) 1924- .... **CLC 17**
See also CA 5-8R; CANR 4, 29; CLR 30;
MAICYA; SATA 4, 68

Gallico, Paul (William) 1897-1976 ... **CLC 2**
See also AITN 1; CA 5-8R; 69-72;
CANR 23; DLB 9; MAICYA; SATA 13

Gallup, Ralph
See Whitemore, Hugh (John)

Galsworthy, John
1867-1933 .... **TCLC 1, 45; DA; WLC 2**
See also CA 104; 141; CDBLB 1890-1914;
DLB 10, 34, 98

Galt, John 1779-1839 .... **NCLC 1**
See also DLB 99, 116

Galvin, James 1951- .... **CLC 38**
See also CA 108; CANR 26

Gamboa, Federico 1864-1939 ..... **TCLC 36**

Gann, Ernest Kellogg 1910-1991 .... **CLC 23**
See also AITN 1; CA 1-4R; 136; CANR 1

Garcia, Cristina 1958- .... **CLC 76**
See also CA 141

Garcia Lorca, Federico
1898-1936 .... **TCLC 1, 7, 49; DA;**
DC 2; HLC; PC 3; WLC
See also CA 104; 131; DLB 108; HW;
MTCW

Garcia Marquez, Gabriel (Jose)
1928- .... **CLC 2, 3, 8, 10, 15, 27, 47, 55;**
DA; HLC; SSC 8; WLC
See also Marquez, Gabriel (Jose) Garcia
See also AAYA 3; BEST 89:1, 90:4;
CA 33-36R; CANR 10, 28; DLB 113;
HW; MTCW

Gard, Janice
See Latham, Jean Lee

Gard, Roger Martin du
See Martin du Gard, Roger

Gardam, Jane 1928- .... **CLC 43**
See also CA 49-52; CANR 2, 18, 33;
CLR 12; DLB 14; MAICYA; MTCW;
SAAS 9; SATA 28, 39, 76

Gardner, Herb .... **CLC 44**

Gardner, John (Champlin), Jr.
1933-1982 ..... **CLC 2, 3, 5, 7, 8, 10, 18,**
28, 34; SSC 7
See also AITN 1; CA 65-68; 107;
CANR 33; DLB 2; DLBY 82; MTCW;
SATA 31, 40

Gardner, John (Edmund) 1926- ..... **CLC 30**
See also CA 103; CANR 15; MTCW

Gardner, Noel
See Kuttner, Henry

Gardons, S. S.
See Snodgrass, W(illiam) D(e Witt)

Garfield, Leon 1921- .... **CLC 12**
See also AAYA 8; CA 17-20R; CANR 38,
41; CLR 21; JRDA; MAICYA; SATA 1,
32, 76

Garland, (Hannibal) Hamlin
1860-1940 .... **TCLC 3**
See also CA 104; DLB 12, 71, 78

Garneau, (Hector de) Saint-Denys
1912-1943 .... **TCLC 13**
See also CA 111; DLB 88

Garner, Alan 1934- .... **CLC 17**
See also CA 73-76; CANR 15; CLR 20;
MAICYA; MTCW; SATA 18, 69

Garner, Hugh 1913-1979 .... **CLC 13**
See also CA 69-72; CANR 31; DLB 68

Garnett, David 1892-1981 .... **CLC 3**
See also CA 5-8R; 103; CANR 17; DLB 34

Garos, Stephanie
See Katz, Steve

Garrett, George (Palmer)
1929- .... **CLC 3, 11, 51**
See also CA 1-4R; CAAS 5; CANR 1, 42;
DLB 2, 5, 130; DLBY 83

Garrick, David 1717-1779 .... **LC 15**
See also DLB 84

Garrigue, Jean 1914-1972 .... **CLC 2, 8**
See also CA 5-8R; 37-40R; CANR 20

Garrison, Frederick
See Sinclair, Upton (Beall)

Garth, Will
See Hamilton, Edmond; Kuttner, Henry

Garvey, Marcus (Moziah, Jr.)
1887-1940 .... **TCLC 41; BLC**
See also BW; CA 120; 124

Gary, Romain .... **CLC 25**
See also Kacew, Romain
See also DLB 83

Gascar, Pierre .... **CLC 11**
See also Fournier, Pierre

Gascoyne, David (Emery) 1916- .... **CLC 45**
See also CA 65-68; CANR 10, 28; DLB 20;
MTCW

Gaskell, Elizabeth Cleghorn
1810-1865 .... **NCLC 5**
See also CDBLB 1832-1890; DLB 21

Gass, William H(oward)
1924- ... **CLC 1, 2, 8, 11, 15, 39; SSC 12**
See also CA 17-20R; CANR 30; DLB 2;
MTCW

Gasset, Jose Ortega y
See Ortega y Gasset, Jose

Gautier, Theophile 1811-1872 ..... **NCLC 1**
See also DLB 119

Gawsworth, John
See Bates, H(erbert) E(rnest)

Gaye, Marvin (Penze) 1939-1984 ... **CLC 26**
See also CA 112

Gebler, Carlo (Ernest) 1954- .... **CLC 39**
See also CA 119; 133

Gee, Maggie (Mary) 1948- .... **CLC 57**
See also CA 130

Gee, Maurice (Gough) 1931- .... **CLC 29**
See also CA 97-100; SATA 46

Gelbart, Larry (Simon) 1923- ... **CLC 21, 61**
See also CA 73-76

Gelber, Jack 1932- .... **CLC 1, 6, 14, 79**
See also CA 1-4R; CANR 2; DLB 7

Gellhorn, Martha Ellis 1908- ... **CLC 14, 60**
See also CA 77-80; DLBY 82

Genet, Jean
1910-1986 ... **CLC 1, 2, 5, 10, 14, 44, 46**
See also CA 13-16R; CANR 18; DLB 72;
DLBY 86; MTCW

Gent, Peter 1942- .... **CLC 29**
See also AITN 1; CA 89-92; DLBY 82

Gentlewoman in New England, A
See Bradstreet, Anne

Gentlewoman in Those Parts, A
See Bradstreet, Anne

George, Jean Craighead 1919- ...... **CLC 35**
See also AAYA 8; CA 5-8R; CANR 25;
CLR 1; DLB 52; JRDA; MAICYA;
SATA 2, 68

George, Stefan (Anton)
1868-1933 .... **TCLC 2, 14**
See also CA 104

Georges, Georges Martin
See Simenon, Georges (Jacques Christian)

Gerhardi, William Alexander
See Gerhardie, William Alexander

Gerhardie, William Alexander
1895-1977 .... **CLC 5**
See also CA 25-28R; 73-76; CANR 18;
DLB 36

Gerstler, Amy 1956- .... **CLC 70**

Gertler, T. .... **CLC 34**
See also CA 116; 121

Ghalib 1797-1869 .... **NCLC 39**

Ghelderode, Michel de
1898-1962 .... **CLC 6, 11**
See also CA 85-88; CANR 40

Ghiselin, Brewster 1903- .... **CLC 23**
See also CA 13-16R; CAAS 10; CANR 13

Ghose, Zulfikar 1935- .... **CLC 42**
See also CA 65-68

Ghosh, Amitav 1956- .... **CLC 44**

Giacosa, Giuseppe 1847-1906 ...... **TCLC 7**
See also CA 104

Gibb, Lee
See Waterhouse, Keith (Spencer)

Gibbon, Lewis Grassic .... **TCLC 4**
See also Mitchell, James Leslie

Gibbons, Kaye 1960- .... **CLC 50**

Gibran, Kahlil 1883-1931 .... **TCLC 1, 9**
See also CA 104

Gibson, William 1914- .... **CLC 23; DA**
See also CA 9-12R; CANR 9, 42; DLB 7;
SATA 66

Gibson, William (Ford) 1948- ... **CLC 39, 63**
See also CA 126; 133

Gide, Andre (Paul Guillaume)
1869-1951 .... **TCLC 5, 12, 36; DA;**
SSC 13; WLC
See also CA 104; 124; DLB 65; MTCW

Gifford, Barry (Colby) 1946- .... **CLC 34**
See also CA 65-68; CANR 9, 30, 40

Gilbert, W(illiam) S(chwenck)
1836-1911 .... **TCLC 3**
See also CA 104; SATA 36

Gilbreth, Frank B., Jr. 1911- .... **CLC 17**
See also CA 9-12R; SATA 2

Gilchrist, Ellen 1935- .. **CLC 34, 48; SSC 14**
See also CA 113; 116; CANR 41; DLB 130;
MTCW

Giles, Molly 1942- .... **CLC 39**
See also CA 126

Gill, Patrick
See Creasey, John

Gilliam, Terry (Vance) 1940-...... **CLC 21**
See also Monty Python
See also CA 108; 113; CANR 35

Gillian, Jerry
See Gilliam, Terry (Vance)

Gilliatt, Penelope (Ann Douglass)
1932-1993 .... **CLC 2, 10, 13, 53**
See also AITN 2; CA 13-16R; 141; DLB 14

Gilman, Charlotte (Anna) Perkins (Stetson)
1860-1935 .... **TCLC 9, 37; SSC 13**
See also CA 106

Gilmour, David 1949-............ **CLC 35**
See also Pink Floyd
See also CA 138

Gilpin, William 1724-1804....... **NCLC 30**

Gilray, J. D.
See Mencken, H(enry) L(ouis)

Gilroy, Frank D(aniel) 1925-........ **CLC 2**
See also CA 81-84; CANR 32; DLB 7

Ginsberg, Allen
1926- ...... **CLC 1, 2, 3, 4, 6, 13, 36, 69;**
DA; PC 4; WLC 3
See also AITN 1; CA 1-4R; CANR 2, 41;
CDALB 1941-1968; DLB 5, 16; MTCW

Ginzburg, Natalia
1916-1991 .... **CLC 5, 11, 54, 70**
See also CA 85-88; 135; CANR 33; MTCW

Giono, Jean 1895-1970........ **CLC 4, 11**
See also CA 45-48; 29-32R; CANR 2, 35;
DLB 72; MTCW

Giovanni, Nikki
1943- ...... **CLC 2, 4, 19, 64; BLC; DA**
See also AITN 1; BW; CA 29-32R;
CAAS 6; CANR 18, 41; CLR 6; DLB 5,
41; MAICYA; MTCW; SATA 24

Giovene, Andrea 1904-............ **CLC 7**
See also CA 85-88

Gippius, Zinaida (Nikolayevna) 1869-1945
See Hippius, Zinaida
See also CA 106

Giraudoux, (Hippolyte) Jean
1882-1944 ....TCLC 2, 7
See also CA 104; DLB 65

Gironella, Jose Maria 1917-....... **CLC 11**
See also CA 101

Gissing, George (Robert)
1857-1903 .... **TCLC 3, 24, 47**
See also CA 105; DLB 18, 135

Giurlani, Aldo
See Palazzeschi, Aldo

Gladkov, Fyodor (Vasilyevich)
1883-1958 .... **TCLC 27**

Glanville, Brian (Lester) 1931-...... **CLC 6**
See also CA 5-8R; CAAS 9; CANR 3;
DLB 15; SATA 42

Glasgow, Ellen (Anderson Gholson)
1873(?)-1945 .... **TCLC 2, 7**
See also CA 104; DLB 9, 12

Glassco, John 1909-1981 .... **CLC 9**
See also CA 13-16R; 102; CANR 15;
DLB 68

Glasscock, Amnesia
See Steinbeck, John (Ernst)

Glasser, Ronald J. 1940(?)-........ **CLC 37**

Glassman, Joyce
See Johnson, Joyce

Glendinning, Victoria 1937-........ **CLC 50**
See also CA 120; 127

Glissant, Edouard 1928-........ **CLC 10, 68**

Gloag, Julian 1930- .... **CLC 40**
See also AITN 1; CA 65-68; CANR 10

Gluck, Louise (Elisabeth)
1943- .... **CLC 7, 22, 44, 81**
See also Glueck, Louise
See also CA 33-36R; CANR 40; DLB 5

Glueck, Louise.................. CLC 7, 22
See also Gluck, Louise (Elisabeth)
See also DLB 5

Gobineau, Joseph Arthur (Comte) de
1816-1882 .... **NCLC 17**
See also DLB 123

Godard, Jean-Luc 1930-.......... **CLC 20**
See also CA 93-96

Godden, (Margaret) Rumer 1907-... **CLC 53**
See also AAYA 6; CA 5-8R; CANR 4, 27,
36; CLR 20; MAICYA; SAAS 12;
SATA 3, 36

Godoy Alcayaga, Lucila 1889-1957
See Mistral, Gabriela
See also CA 104; 131; HW; MTCW

Godwin, Gail (Kathleen)
1937- .... **CLC 5, 8, 22, 31, 69**
See also CA 29-32R; CANR 15, 43; DLB 6;
MTCW

Godwin, William 1756-1836...... **NCLC 14**
See also CDBLB 1789-1832; DLB 39, 104

Goethe, Johann Wolfgang von
1749-1832 ....**NCLC 4, 22, 34; DA;**
PC 5; WLC 3
See also DLB 94

Gogarty, Oliver St. John
1878-1957 .... **TCLC 15**
See also CA 109; DLB 15, 19

Gogol, Nikolai (Vasilyevich)
1809-1852 .... **NCLC 5, 15, 31; DA;**
DC 1; SSC 4; WLC

Goines, Donald
1937(?)-1974 .... **CLC 80; BLC**
See also AITN 1; BW; CA 124; 114;
DLB 33

Gold, Herbert 1924-....... **CLC 4, 7, 14, 42**
See also CA 9-12R; CANR 17; DLB 2;
DLBY 81

Goldbarth, Albert 1948-........ **CLC 5, 38**
See also CA 53-56; CANR 6, 40; DLB 120

Goldberg, Anatol 1910-1982 .... **CLC 34**
See also CA 131; 117

Goldemberg, Isaac 1945-.......... **CLC 52**
See also CA 69-72; CAAS 12; CANR 11,
32; HW

Golden Silver
See Storm, Hyemeyohsts

Golding, William (Gerald)
1911-1993 .... **CLC 1, 2, 3, 8, 10, 17, 27,**
58, 81; DA; WLC
See also AAYA 5; CA 5-8R; 141;
CANR 13, 33; CDBLB 1945-1960;
DLB 15, 100; MTCW

Goldman, Emma 1869-1940...... **TCLC 13**
See also CA 110

Goldman, Francisco 1955-........ **CLC 76**

Goldman, William (W.) 1931-... **CLC 1, 48**
See also CA 9-12R; CANR 29; DLB 44

Goldmann, Lucien 1913-1970 ...... **CLC 24**
See also CA 25-28; CAP 2

Goldoni, Carlo 1707-1793 .... **LC 4**

Goldsberry, Steven 1949-......... **CLC 34**
See also CA 131

Goldsmith, Oliver
1728-1774 .... **LC 2; DA; WLC**
See also CDBLB 1660-1789; DLB 39, 89,
104, 109; SATA 26

Goldsmith, Peter
See Priestley, J(ohn) B(oynton)

Gombrowicz, Witold
1904-1969 .... **CLC 4, 7, 11, 49**
See also CA 19-20; 25-28R; CAP 2

Gomez de la Serna, Ramon
1888-1963 .... **CLC 9**
See also CA 116; HW

Goncharov, Ivan Alexandrovich
1812-1891 .... **NCLC 1**

Goncourt, Edmond (Louis Antoine Huot) de
1822-1896 .... **NCLC 7**
See also DLB 123

Goncourt, Jules (Alfred Huot) de
1830-1870 .... **NCLC 7**
See also DLB 123

Gontier, Fernande 19(?)-.......... **CLC 50**

Goodman, Paul 1911-1972.... **CLC 1, 2, 4, 7**
See also CA 19-20; 37-40R; CANR 34;
CAP 2; DLB 130; MTCW

Gordimer, Nadine
1923- .... **CLC 3, 5, 7, 10, 18, 33, 51, 70;**
DA
See also CA 5-8R; CANR 3, 28; MTCW

Gordon, Adam Lindsay
1833-1870 .... **NCLC 21**

Gordon, Caroline
1895-1981 ...... **CLC 6, 13, 29; SSC 15**
See also CA 11-12; 103; CANR 36; CAP 1;
DLB 4, 9, 102; DLBY 81; MTCW

Gordon, Charles William 1860-1937
See Connor, Ralph
See also CA 109

Gordon, Mary (Catherine)
1949- .... **CLC 13, 22**
See also CA 102; DLB 6; DLBY 81;
MTCW

Gordon, Sol 1923-................ **CLC 26**
See also CA 53-56; CANR 4; SATA 11

Gordone, Charles 1925-.......... **CLC 1, 4**
See also BW; CA 93-96; DLB 7; MTCW

Gorenko, Anna Andreevna
See Akhmatova, Anna

Gorky, Maxim............. TCLC 8; WLC
See also Peshkov, Alexei Maximovich

Goryan, Sirak
See Saroyan, William

Gosse, Edmund (William)
1849-1928 .... **TCLC 28**
See also CA 117; DLB 57

Gotlieb, Phyllis Fay (Bloom)
    1926- . . . . **CLC 18**
    See also CA 13-16R; CANR 7; DLB 88

Gottesman, S. D.
    See Kornbluth, C(yril) M.; Pohl, Frederik

Gottfried von Strassburg
    fl. c. 1210- . . . . **CMLC 10**

Gould, Lois . . . . **CLC 4, 10**
    See also CA 77-80; CANR 29; MTCW

Gourmont, Remy de 1858-1915 . . . . **TCLC 17**
    See also CA 109

Govier, Katherine 1948- . . . . **CLC 51**
    See also CA 101; CANR 18, 40

Goyen, (Charles) William
    1915-1983 . . . . **CLC 5, 8, 14, 40**
    See also AITN 2; CA 5-8R; 110; CANR 6;
    DLB 2; DLBY 83

Goytisolo, Juan
    1931- . . . . **CLC 5, 10, 23; HLC**
    See also CA 85-88; CANR 32; HW; MTCW

Gozzi, (Conte) Carlo 1720-1806 . . **NCLC 23**

Grabbe, Christian Dietrich
    1801-1836 . . . . **NCLC 2**
    See also DLB 133

Grace, Patricia 1937- . . . . **CLC 56**

Gracian y Morales, Baltasar
    1601-1658 . . . . **LC 15**

Gracq, Julien . . . . **CLC 11, 48**
    See also Poirier, Louis
    See also DLB 83

Grade, Chaim 1910-1982 . . . . **CLC 10**
    See also CA 93-96; 107

Graduate of Oxford, A
    See Ruskin, John

Graham, John
    See Phillips, David Graham

Graham, Jorie 1951- . . . . **CLC 48**
    See also CA 111; DLB 120

Graham, R(obert) B(ontine) Cunninghame
    See Cunninghame Graham, R(obert)
    B(ontine)
    See also DLB 98, 135

Graham, Robert
    See Haldeman, Joe (William)

Graham, Tom
    See Lewis, (Harry) Sinclair

Graham, W(illiam) S(ydney)
    1918-1986 . . . . **CLC 29**
    See also CA 73-76; 118; DLB 20

Graham, Winston (Mawdsley)
    1910- . . . . **CLC 23**
    See also CA 49-52; CANR 2, 22; DLB 77

Grant, Skeeter
    See Spiegelman, Art

Granville-Barker, Harley
    1877-1946 . . . . **TCLC 2**
    See also Barker, Harley Granville
    See also CA 104

Grass, Guenter (Wilhelm)
    1927- . . . . . **CLC 1, 2, 4, 6, 11, 15, 22, 32,
                    49; DA; WLC**
    See also CA 13-16R; CANR 20; DLB 75,
    124; MTCW

Gratton, Thomas
    See Hulme, T(homas) E(rnest)

Grau, Shirley Ann
    1929- . . . . **CLC 4, 9; SSC 15**
    See also CA 89-92; CANR 22; DLB 2;
    MTCW

Gravel, Fern
    See Hall, James Norman

Graver, Elizabeth 1964- . . . . **CLC 70**
    See also CA 135

Graves, Richard Perceval 1945- . . . . **CLC 44**
    See also CA 65-68; CANR 9, 26

Graves, Robert (von Ranke)
    1895-1985 . . . . . . **CLC 1, 2, 6, 11, 39, 44,
                            45; PC 6**
    See also CA 5-8R; 117; CANR 5, 36;
    CDBLB 1914-1945; DLB 20, 100;
    DLBY 85; MTCW; SATA 45

Gray, Alasdair 1934- . . . . **CLC 41**
    See also CA 126; MTCW

Gray, Amlin 1946- . . . . **CLC 29**
    See also CA 138

Gray, Francine du Plessix 1930- . . . . **CLC 22**
    See also BEST 90:3; CA 61-64; CAAS 2;
    CANR 11, 33; MTCW

Gray, John (Henry) 1866-1934 . . . . **TCLC 19**
    See also CA 119

Gray, Simon (James Holliday)
    1936- . . . . **CLC 9, 14, 36**
    See also AITN 1; CA 21-24R; CAAS 3;
    CANR 32; DLB 13; MTCW

Gray, Spalding 1941- . . . . **CLC 49**
    See also CA 128

Gray, Thomas
    1716-1771 . . . . . . **LC 4; DA; PC 2; WLC**
    See also CDBLB 1660-1789; DLB 109

Grayson, David
    See Baker, Ray Stannard

Grayson, Richard (A.) 1951- . . . . **CLC 38**
    See also CA 85-88; CANR 14, 31

Greeley, Andrew M(oran) 1928- . . . . **CLC 28**
    See also CA 5-8R; CAAS 7; CANR 7, 43;
    MTCW

Green, Brian
    See Card, Orson Scott

Green, Hannah
    See Greenberg, Joanne (Goldenberg)

Green, Hannah . . . . **CLC 3**
    See also CA 73-76

Green, Henry . . . . **CLC 2, 13**
    See also Yorke, Henry Vincent
    See also DLB 15

Green, Julian (Hartridge) 1900-
    See Green, Julien
    See also CA 21-24R; CANR 33; DLB 4, 72;
    MTCW

Green, Julien . . . . **CLC 3, 11, 77**
    See also Green, Julian (Hartridge)

Green, Paul (Eliot) 1894-1981 . . . . . . **CLC 25**
    See also AITN 1; CA 5-8R; 103; CANR 3;
    DLB 7, 9; DLBY 81

Greenberg, Ivan 1908-1973
    See Rahv, Philip
    See also CA 85-88

Greenberg, Joanne (Goldenberg)
    1932- . . . . **CLC 7, 30**
    See also CA 5-8R; CANR 14, 32; SATA 25

Greenberg, Richard 1959(?)- . . . . **CLC 57**
    See also CA 138

Greene, Bette 1934- . . . . **CLC 30**
    See also AAYA 7; CA 53-56; CANR 4;
    CLR 2; JRDA; MAICYA; SAAS 16;
    SATA 8

Greene, Gael . . . . **CLC 8**
    See also CA 13-16R; CANR 10

Greene, Graham
    1904-1991 . . . . **CLC 1, 3, 6, 9, 14, 18, 27,
                        37, 70, 72; DA; WLC**
    See also AITN 2; CA 13-16R; 133;
    CANR 35; CDBLB 1945-1960; DLB 13,
    15, 77, 100; DLBY 91; MTCW; SATA 20

Greer, Richard
    See Silverberg, Robert

Greer, Richard
    See Silverberg, Robert

Gregor, Arthur 1923- . . . . **CLC 9**
    See also CA 25-28R; CAAS 10; CANR 11;
    SATA 36

Gregor, Lee
    See Pohl, Frederik

Gregory, Isabella Augusta (Persse)
    1852-1932 . . . . **TCLC 1**
    See also CA 104; DLB 10

Gregory, J. Dennis
    See Williams, John A(lfred)

Grendon, Stephen
    See Derleth, August (William)

Grenville, Kate 1950- . . . . **CLC 61**
    See also CA 118

Grenville, Pelham
    See Wodehouse, P(elham) G(renville)

Greve, Felix Paul (Berthold Friedrich)
    1879-1948
    See Grove, Frederick Philip
    See also CA 104; 141

Grey, Zane 1872-1939 . . . . **TCLC 6**
    See also CA 104; 132; DLB 9; MTCW

Grieg, (Johan) Nordahl (Brun)
    1902-1943 . . . . **TCLC 10**
    See also CA 107

Grieve, C(hristopher) M(urray)
    1892-1978 . . . . **CLC 11, 19**
    See also MacDiarmid, Hugh
    See also CA 5-8R; 85-88; CANR 33;
    MTCW

Griffin, Gerald 1803-1840 . . . . **NCLC 7**

Griffin, John Howard 1920-1980 . . . . **CLC 68**
    See also AITN 1; CA 1-4R; 101; CANR 2

Griffin, Peter . . . . **CLC 39**

Griffiths, Trevor 1935- . . . . **CLC 13, 52**
    See also CA 97-100; DLB 13

Grigson, Geoffrey (Edward Harvey)
    1905-1985 . . . . **CLC 7, 39**
    See also CA 25-28R; 118; CANR 20, 33;
    DLB 27; MTCW

Grillparzer, Franz 1791-1872 . . . . . . **NCLC 1**
    See also DLB 133

Hammett, (Samuel) Dashiell
1894-1961 . . . . **CLC 3, 5, 10, 19, 47**
See also AITN 1; CA 81-84; CANR 42;
CDALB 1929-1941; DLBD 6; MTCW

Hammon, Jupiter
1711(?)-1800(?) . . . . **NCLC 5; BLC**
See also DLB 31, 50

Hammond, Keith
See Kuttner, Henry

Hamner, Earl (Henry), Jr. 1923- . . . **CLC 12**
See also AITN 2; CA 73-76; DLB 6

Hampton, Christopher (James)
1946- . . . . **CLC 4**
See also CA 25-28R; DLB 13; MTCW

Hamsun, Knut . . . . **TCLC 2, 14, 49**
See also Pedersen, Knut

Handke, Peter 1942- . . **CLC 5, 8, 10, 15, 38**
See also CA 77-80; CANR 33; DLB 85,
124; MTCW

Hanley, James 1901-1985 . . . **CLC 3, 5, 8, 13**
See also CA 73-76; 117; CANR 36; MTCW

Hannah, Barry 1942- . . . . **CLC 23, 38**
See also CA 108; 110; CANR 43; DLB 6;
MTCW

Hannon, Ezra
See Hunter, Evan

Hansberry, Lorraine (Vivian)
1930-1965 . . . . . . **CLC 17, 62; BLC; DA;
DC 2**
See also BW; CA 109; 25-28R; CABS 3;
CDALB 1941-1968; DLB 7, 38; MTCW

Hansen, Joseph 1923- . . . . **CLC 38**
See also CA 29-32R; CAAS 17; CANR 16

Hansen, Martin A. 1909-1955 . . . . . **TCLC 32**

Hanson, Kenneth O(stlin) 1922- . . . . **CLC 13**
See also CA 53-56; CANR 7

Hardwick, Elizabeth 1916- . . . . **CLC 13**
See also CA 5-8R; CANR 3, 32; DLB 6;
MTCW

Hardy, Thomas
1840-1928 . . . . . . **TCLC 4, 10, 18, 32, 48,
53; DA; PC 8; SSC 2; WLC**
See also CA 104; 123; CDBLB 1890-1914;
DLB 18, 19, 135; MTCW

Hare, David 1947- . . . . **CLC 29, 58**
See also CA 97-100; CANR 39; DLB 13;
MTCW

Harford, Henry
See Hudson, W(illiam) H(enry)

Hargrave, Leonie
See Disch, Thomas M(ichael)

Harlan, Louis R(udolph) 1922- . . . . . **CLC 34**
See also CA 21-24R; CANR 25

Harling, Robert 1951(?)- . . . . **CLC 53**

Harmon, William (Ruth) 1938- . . . . . **CLC 38**
See also CA 33-36R; CANR 14, 32, 35;
SATA 65

Harper, F. E. W.
See Harper, Frances Ellen Watkins

Harper, Frances E. W.
See Harper, Frances Ellen Watkins

Harper, Frances E. Watkins
See Harper, Frances Ellen Watkins

Harper, Frances Ellen
See Harper, Frances Ellen Watkins

Harper, Frances Ellen Watkins
1825-1911 . . . . **TCLC 14; BLC**
See also BW; CA 111; 125; DLB 50

Harper, Michael S(teven) 1938- . . **CLC 7, 22**
See also BW; CA 33-36R; CANR 24;
DLB 41

Harper, Mrs. F. E. W.
See Harper, Frances Ellen Watkins

Harris, Christie (Lucy) Irwin
1907- . . . . **CLC 12**
See also CA 5-8R; CANR 6; DLB 88;
JRDA; MAICYA; SAAS 10; SATA 6, 74

Harris, Frank 1856(?)-1931 . . . . . . **TCLC 24**
See also CA 109

Harris, George Washington
1814-1869 . . . . **NCLC 23**
See also DLB 3, 11

Harris, Joel Chandler 1848-1908 . . . **TCLC 2**
See also CA 104; 137; DLB 11, 23, 42, 78,
91; MAICYA; YABC 1

**Harris, John (Wyndham Parkes Lucas)
Beynon** 1903-1969 . . . . **CLC 19**
See also CA 102; 89-92

Harris, MacDonald
See Heiney, Donald (William)

Harris, Mark 1922- . . . . **CLC 19**
See also CA 5-8R; CAAS 3; CANR 2;
DLB 2; DLBY 80

Harris, (Theodore) Wilson 1921- . . . . **CLC 25**
See also BW; CA 65-68; CAAS 16;
CANR 11, 27; DLB 117; MTCW

Harrison, Elizabeth Cavanna 1909-
See Cavanna, Betty
See also CA 9-12R; CANR 6, 27

Harrison, Harry (Max) 1925- . . . . . . **CLC 42**
See also CA 1-4R; CANR 5, 21; DLB 8;
SATA 4

Harrison, James (Thomas)
1937- . . . . **CLC 6, 14, 33, 66**
See also CA 13-16R; CANR 8; DLBY 82

Harrison, Kathryn 1961- . . . . **CLC 70**

Harrison, Tony 1937- . . . . **CLC 43**
See also CA 65-68; DLB 40; MTCW

Harriss, Will(ard Irvin) 1922- . . . . . . **CLC 34**
See also CA 111

Harson, Sley
See Ellison, Harlan

Hart, Ellis
See Ellison, Harlan

Hart, Josephine 1942(?)- . . . . **CLC 70**
See also CA 138

Hart, Moss 1904-1961 . . . . **CLC 66**
See also CA 109; 89-92; DLB 7

Harte, (Francis) Bret(t)
1836(?)-1902 . . . . **TCLC 1, 25; DA;
SSC 8; WLC**
See also CA 104; 140; CDALB 1865-1917;
DLB 12, 64, 74, 79; SATA 26

Hartley, L(eslie) P(oles)
1895-1972 . . . . **CLC 2, 22**
See also CA 45-48; 37-40R; CANR 33;
DLB 15; MTCW

Hartman, Geoffrey H. 1929- . . . . **CLC 27**
See also CA 117; 125; DLB 67

Haruf, Kent 19(?)- . . . . **CLC 34**

Harwood, Ronald 1934- . . . . **CLC 32**
See also CA 1-4R; CANR 4; DLB 13

Hasek, Jaroslav (Matej Frantisek)
1883-1923 . . . . **TCLC 4**
See also CA 104; 129; MTCW

Hass, Robert 1941- . . . . **CLC 18, 39**
See also CA 111; CANR 30; DLB 105

Hastings, Hudson
See Kuttner, Henry

Hastings, Selina . . . . **CLC 44**

Hatteras, Amelia
See Mencken, H(enry) L(ouis)

Hatteras, Owen . . . . **TCLC 18**
See also Mencken, H(enry) L(ouis); Nathan,
George Jean

Hauptmann, Gerhart (Johann Robert)
1862-1946 . . . . **TCLC 4**
See also CA 104; DLB 66, 118

Havel, Vaclav 1936- . . . . **CLC 25, 58, 65**
See also CA 104; CANR 36; MTCW

Haviaras, Stratis . . . . **CLC 33**
See also Chaviaras, Strates

Hawes, Stephen 1475(?)-1523(?) . . . . . **LC 17**

Hawkes, John (Clendennin Burne, Jr.)
1925- . . . . . . **CLC 1, 2, 3, 4, 7, 9, 14, 15,
27, 49**
See also CA 1-4R; CANR 2; DLB 2, 7;
DLBY 80; MTCW

Hawking, S. W.
See Hawking, Stephen W(illiam)

Hawking, Stephen W(illiam)
1942- . . . . **CLC 63**
See also BEST 89:1; CA 126; 129

Hawthorne, Julian 1846-1934 . . . . . **TCLC 25**

Hawthorne, Nathaniel
1804-1864 . . . . . . **NCLC 39; DA; SSC 3;
WLC**
See also CDALB 1640-1865; DLB 1, 74;
YABC 2

Haxton, Josephine Ayres 1921- . . . . **CLC 73**
See also CA 115; CANR 41

Hayaseca y Eizaguirre, Jorge
See Echegaray (y Eizaguirre), Jose (Maria
Waldo)

Hayashi Fumiko 1904-1951 . . . . **TCLC 27**

Haycraft, Anna
See Ellis, Alice Thomas
See also CA 122

Hayden, Robert E(arl)
1913-1980 . . . . . . **CLC 5, 9, 14, 37; BLC;
DA; PC 6**
See also BW; CA 69-72; 97-100; CABS 2;
CANR 24; CDALB 1941-1968; DLB 5,
76; MTCW; SATA 19, 26

Hayford, J(oseph) E(phraim) Casely
See Casely-Hayford, J(oseph) E(phraim)

Hayman, Ronald 1932- . . . . **CLC 44**
See also CA 25-28R; CANR 18

Haywood, Eliza (Fowler)
1693(?)-1756 . . . . **LC 1**

Hazlitt, William 1778-1830 . . . . . . **NCLC 29**
See also DLB 110

Hazzard, Shirley 1931- . . . . **CLC 18**
See also CA 9-12R; CANR 4; DLBY 82;
MTCW

Head, Bessie 1937-1986 . . . **CLC 25, 67; BLC**
See also BW; CA 29-32R; 119; CANR 25;
DLB 117; MTCW

Headon, (Nicky) Topper 1956(?)- . . . **CLC 30**
See also Clash, The

Heaney, Seamus (Justin)
1939- . . . . **CLC 5, 7, 14, 25, 37, 74**
See also CA 85-88; CANR 25;
CDBLB 1960 to Present; DLB 40;
MTCW

Hearn, (Patricio) Lafcadio (Tessima Carlos)
1850-1904 . . . . **TCLC 9**
See also CA 105; DLB 12, 78

Hearne, Vicki 1946- . . . . **CLC 56**
See also CA 139

Hearon, Shelby 1931- . . . . **CLC 63**
See also AITN 2; CA 25-28R; CANR 18

Heat-Moon, William Least . . . . **CLC 29**
See also Trogdon, William (Lewis)
See also AAYA 9

Hebbel, Friedrich 1813-1863 . . . . . **NCLC 43**
See also DLB 129

Hebert, Anne 1916- . . . . **CLC 4, 13, 29**
See also CA 85-88; DLB 68; MTCW

Hecht, Anthony (Evan)
1923- . . . . **CLC 8, 13, 19**
See also CA 9-12R; CANR 6; DLB 5

Hecht, Ben 1894-1964 . . . . **CLC 8**
See also CA 85-88; DLB 7, 9, 25, 26, 28, 86

Hedayat, Sadeq 1903-1951 . . . . **TCLC 21**
See also CA 120

Heidegger, Martin 1889-1976 . . . . . . **CLC 24**
See also CA 81-84; 65-68; CANR 34;
MTCW

Heidenstam, (Carl Gustaf) Verner von
1859-1940 . . . . **TCLC 5**
See also CA 104

Heifner, Jack 1946- . . . . **CLC 11**
See also CA 105

Heijermans, Herman 1864-1924 . . . **TCLC 24**
See also CA 123

Heilbrun, Carolyn G(old) 1926- . . . . . **CLC 25**
See also CA 45-48; CANR 1, 28

Heine, Heinrich 1797-1856 . . . . **NCLC 4**
See also DLB 90

Heinemann, Larry (Curtiss) 1944- . . **CLC 50**
See also CA 110; CANR 31; DLBD 9

Heiney, Donald (William)
1921-1993 . . . . **CLC 9**
See also CA 1-4R; 142; CANR 3

Heinlein, Robert A(nson)
1907-1988 . . . . . . **CLC 1, 3, 8, 14, 26, 55**
See also CA 1-4R; 125; CANR 1, 20;
DLB 8; JRDA; MAICYA; MTCW;
SATA 9, 56, 69

Helforth, John
See Doolittle, Hilda

Hellenhofferu, Vojtech Kapristian z
See Hasek, Jaroslav (Matej Frantisek)

Heller, Joseph
1923- . . . . **CLC 1, 3, 5, 8, 11, 36, 63; DA;**
WLC
See also AITN 1; CA 5-8R; CABS 1;
CANR 8, 42; DLB 2, 28; DLBY 80;
MTCW

Hellman, Lillian (Florence)
1906-1984 . . . . . . **CLC 2, 4, 8, 14, 18, 34,**
44, 52; DC 1
See also AITN 1, 2; CA 13-16R; 112;
CANR 33; DLB 7; DLBY 84; MTCW

Helprin, Mark 1947- . . . . . **CLC 7, 10, 22, 32**
See also CA 81-84; DLBY 85; MTCW

Helyar, Jane Penelope Josephine 1933-
See Poole, Josephine
See also CA 21-24R; CANR 10, 26

Hemans, Felicia 1793-1835 . . . . . . **NCLC 29**
See also DLB 96

Hemingway, Ernest (Miller)
1899-1961 . . . . **CLC 1, 3, 6, 8, 10, 13, 19,**
30, 34, 39, 41, 44, 50, 61, 80; DA; SSC 1;
WLC
See also CA 77-80; CANR 34;
CDALB 1917-1929; DLB 4, 9, 102;
DLBD 1; DLBY 81, 87; MTCW

Hempel, Amy 1951- . . . . **CLC 39**
See also CA 118; 137

Henderson, F. C.
See Mencken, H(enry) L(ouis)

Henderson, Sylvia
See Ashton-Warner, Sylvia (Constance)

Henley, Beth . . . . **CLC 23**
See also Henley, Elizabeth Becker
See also CABS 3; DLBY 86

Henley, Elizabeth Becker 1952-
See Henley, Beth
See also CA 107; CANR 32; MTCW

Henley, William Ernest
1849-1903 . . . . **TCLC 8**
See also CA 105; DLB 19

Hennissart, Martha
See Lathen, Emma
See also CA 85-88

Henry, O. . . . . **TCLC 1, 19; SSC 5; WLC**
See also Porter, William Sydney

Henry, Patrick 1736-1799 . . . . **LC 25**

Henryson, Robert 1430(?)-1506(?) . . . . **LC 20**

Henry VIII 1491-1547 . . . . **LC 10**

Henschke, Alfred
See Klabund

Hentoff, Nat(han Irving) 1925- . . . . . **CLC 26**
See also AAYA 4; CA 1-4R; CAAS 6;
CANR 5, 25; CLR 1; JRDA; MAICYA;
SATA 27, 42, 69

Heppenstall, (John) Rayner
1911-1981 . . . . **CLC 10**
See also CA 1-4R; 103; CANR 29

Herbert, Frank (Patrick)
1920-1986 . . . . **CLC 12, 23, 35, 44**
See also CA 53-56; 118; CANR 5, 43;
DLB 8; MTCW; SATA 9, 37, 47

Herbert, George 1593-1633 . . . . **LC 24; PC 4**
See also CDBLB Before 1660; DLB 126

Herbert, Zbigniew 1924- . . . . **CLC 9, 43**
See also CA 89-92; CANR 36; MTCW

Herbst, Josephine (Frey)
1897-1969 . . . . **CLC 34**
See also CA 5-8R; 25-28R; DLB 9

Hergesheimer, Joseph
1880-1954 . . . . **TCLC 11**
See also CA 109; DLB 102, 9

Herlihy, James Leo 1927-1993 . . . . . . **CLC 6**
See also CA 1-4R; 143; CANR 2

Hermogenes fl. c. 175- . . . . **CMLC 6**

Hernandez, Jose 1834-1886 . . . . . . **NCLC 17**

Herrick, Robert 1591-1674 . . . . . **LC 13; DA**
See also DLB 126

Herring, Guilles
See Somerville, Edith

Herriot, James 1916- . . . . **CLC 12**
See also Wight, James Alfred
See also AAYA 1; CANR 40

Herrmann, Dorothy 1941- . . . . **CLC 44**
See also CA 107

Herrmann, Taffy
See Herrmann, Dorothy

Hersey, John (Richard)
1914-1993 . . . . **CLC 1, 2, 7, 9, 40, 81**
See also CA 17-20R; 140; CANR 33;
DLB 6; MTCW; SATA 25;
SATA-Obit 76

Herzen, Aleksandr Ivanovich
1812-1870 . . . . **NCLC 10**

Herzl, Theodor 1860-1904 . . . . **TCLC 36**

Herzog, Werner 1942- . . . . **CLC 16**
See also CA 89-92

Hesiod c. 8th cent. B.C.- . . . . **CMLC 5**

Hesse, Hermann
1877-1962 . . . . **CLC 1, 2, 3, 6, 11, 17, 25,**
69; DA; SSC 9; WLC
See also CA 17-18; CAP 2; DLB 66;
MTCW; SATA 50

Hewes, Cady
See De Voto, Bernard (Augustine)

Heyen, William 1940- . . . . **CLC 13, 18**
See also CA 33-36R; CAAS 9; DLB 5

Heyerdahl, Thor 1914- . . . . **CLC 26**
See also CA 5-8R; CANR 5, 22; MTCW;
SATA 2, 52

Heym, Georg (Theodor Franz Arthur)
1887-1912 . . . . **TCLC 9**
See also CA 106

Heym, Stefan 1913- . . . . **CLC 41**
See also CA 9-12R; CANR 4; DLB 69

Heyse, Paul (Johann Ludwig von)
1830-1914 . . . . **TCLC 8**
See also CA 104; DLB 129

Hibbert, Eleanor Alice Burford
1906-1993 . . . . **CLC 7**
See also BEST 90:4; CA 17-20R; 140;
CANR 9, 28; SATA 2; SATA-Obit 74

Higgins, George V(incent)
1939- . . . . **CLC 4, 7, 10, 18**
See also CA 77-80; CAAS 5; CANR 17;
DLB 2; DLBY 81; MTCW

Higginson, Thomas Wentworth
1823-1911 . . . . **TCLC 36**
See also DLB 1, 64

Highet, Helen
See MacInnes, Helen (Clark)

Highsmith, (Mary) Patricia
1921- . . . . CLC 2, 4, 14, 42
See also CA 1-4R; CANR 1, 20; MTCW

Highwater, Jamake (Mamake)
1942(?)- . . . . CLC 12
See also AAYA 7; CA 65-68; CAAS 7;
CANR 10, 34; CLR 17; DLB 52;
DLBY 85; JRDA; MAICYA; SATA 30,
32, 69

Hijuelos, Oscar 1951- . . . . . . CLC 65; HLC
See also BEST 90:1; CA 123; HW

Hikmet, Nazim 1902(?)-1963 . . . . . . CLC 40
See also CA 141; 93-96

Hildesheimer, Wolfgang
1916-1991 . . . . CLC 49
See also CA 101; 135; DLB 69, 124

Hill, Geoffrey (William)
1932- . . . . CLC 5, 8, 18, 45
See also CA 81-84; CANR 21;
CDBLB 1960 to Present; DLB 40;
MTCW

Hill, George Roy 1921- . . . . CLC 26
See also CA 110; 122

Hill, John
See Koontz, Dean R(ay)

Hill, Susan (Elizabeth) 1942- . . . . CLC 4
See also CA 33-36R; CANR 29; DLB 14;
MTCW

Hillerman, Tony 1925- . . . . CLC 62
See also AAYA 6; BEST 89:1; CA 29-32R;
CANR 21, 42; SATA 6

Hillesum, Etty 1914-1943 . . . . TCLC 49
See also CA 137

Hilliard, Noel (Harvey) 1929- . . . . . . CLC 15
See also CA 9-12R; CANR 7

Hillis, Rick 1956- . . . . CLC 66
See also CA 134

Hilton, James 1900-1954 . . . . TCLC 21
See also CA 108; DLB 34, 77; SATA 34

Himes, Chester (Bomar)
1909-1984 . . . . CLC 2, 4, 7, 18, 58; BLC
See also BW; CA 25-28R; 114; CANR 22;
DLB 2, 76; MTCW

Hinde, Thomas . . . . CLC 6, 11
See also Chitty, Thomas Willes

Hindin, Nathan
See Bloch, Robert (Albert)

Hine, (William) Daryl 1936- . . . . CLC 15
See also CA 1-4R; CAAS 15; CANR 1, 20;
DLB 60

Hinkson, Katharine Tynan
See Tynan, Katharine

Hinton, S(usan) E(loise)
1950- . . . . CLC 30; DA
See also AAYA 2; CA 81-84; CANR 32;
CLR 3, 23; JRDA; MAICYA; MTCW;
SATA 19, 58

Hippius, Zinaida . . . . TCLC 9
See also Gippius, Zinaida (Nikolayevna)

Hiraoka, Kimitake 1925-1970
See Mishima, Yukio
See also CA 97-100; 29-32R; MTCW

Hirsch, E(ric) D(onald), Jr. 1928-... CLC 79
See also CA 25-28R; CANR 27; DLB 67;
MTCW

Hirsch, Edward 1950- . . . . CLC 31, 50
See also CA 104; CANR 20, 42; DLB 120

Hitchcock, Alfred (Joseph)
1899-1980 . . . . CLC 16
See also CA 97-100; SATA 24, 27

Hitler, Adolf 1889-1945 . . . . TCLC 53
See also CA 117

Hoagland, Edward 1932- . . . . CLC 28
See also CA 1-4R; CANR 2, 31; DLB 6;
SATA 51

Hoban, Russell (Conwell) 1925- . . CLC 7, 25
See also CA 5-8R; CANR 23, 37; CLR 3;
DLB 52; MAICYA; MTCW; SATA 1, 40

Hobbs, Perry
See Blackmur, R(ichard) P(almer)

Hobson, Laura Z(ametkin)
1900-1986 . . . . CLC 7, 25
See also CA 17-20R; 118; DLB 28;
SATA 52

Hochhuth, Rolf 1931- . . . . CLC 4, 11, 18
See also CA 5-8R; CANR 33; DLB 124;
MTCW

Hochman, Sandra 1936- . . . . CLC 3, 8
See also CA 5-8R; DLB 5

Hochwaelder, Fritz 1911-1986 . . . . . . CLC 36
See also CA 29-32R; 120; CANR 42;
MTCW

Hochwalder, Fritz
See Hochwaelder, Fritz

Hocking, Mary (Eunice) 1921- . . . . . CLC 13
See also CA 101; CANR 18, 40

Hodgins, Jack 1938- . . . . CLC 23
See also CA 93-96; DLB 60

Hodgson, William Hope
1877(?)-1918 . . . . TCLC 13
See also CA 111; DLB 70

Hoffman, Alice 1952- . . . . CLC 51
See also CA 77-80; CANR 34; MTCW

Hoffman, Daniel (Gerard)
1923- . . . . CLC 6, 13, 23
See also CA 1-4R; CANR 4; DLB 5

Hoffman, Stanley 1944- . . . . CLC 5
See also CA 77-80

Hoffman, William M(oses) 1939- . . . CLC 40
See also CA 57-60; CANR 11

Hoffmann, E(rnst) T(heodor) A(madeus)
1776-1822 . . . . NCLC 2; SSC 13
See also DLB 90; SATA 27

Hofmann, Gert 1931- . . . . CLC 54
See also CA 128

Hofmannsthal, Hugo von
1874-1929 . . . . TCLC 11; DC 4
See also CA 106; DLB 81, 118

Hogan, Linda 1947- . . . . CLC 73
See also CA 120

Hogarth, Charles
See Creasey, John

Hogg, James 1770-1835 . . . . NCLC 4
See also DLB 93, 116

Holbach, Paul Henri Thiry Baron
1723-1789 . . . . LC 14

Holberg, Ludvig 1684-1754 . . . . LC 6

Holden, Ursula 1921- . . . . CLC 18
See also CA 101; CAAS 8; CANR 22

Holderlin, (Johann Christian) Friedrich
1770-1843 . . . . NCLC 16; PC 4

Holdstock, Robert
See Holdstock, Robert P.

Holdstock, Robert P. 1948- . . . . CLC 39
See also CA 131

Holland, Isabelle 1920- . . . . CLC 21
See also CA 21-24R; CANR 10, 25; JRDA;
MAICYA; SATA 8, 70

Holland, Marcus
See Caldwell, (Janet Miriam) Taylor
(Holland)

Hollander, John 1929- . . . . . . CLC 2, 5, 8, 14
See also CA 1-4R; CANR 1; DLB 5;
SATA 13

Hollander, Paul
See Silverberg, Robert

Holleran, Andrew 1943(?)- . . . . CLC 38

Hollinghurst, Alan 1954- . . . . CLC 55
See also CA 114

Hollis, Jim
See Summers, Hollis (Spurgeon, Jr.)

Holmes, John
See Souster, (Holmes) Raymond

Holmes, John Clellon 1926-1988 . . . . CLC 56
See also CA 9-12R; 125; CANR 4; DLB 16

Holmes, Oliver Wendell
1809-1894 . . . . NCLC 14
See also CDALB 1640-1865; DLB 1;
SATA 34

Holmes, Raymond
See Souster, (Holmes) Raymond

Holt, Victoria
See Hibbert, Eleanor Alice Burford

Holub, Miroslav 1923- . . . . CLC 4
See also CA 21-24R; CANR 10

Homer c. 8th cent. B.C.- . . . . . CMLC 1; DA

Honig, Edwin 1919- . . . . CLC 33
See also CA 5-8R; CAAS 8; CANR 4;
DLB 5

Hood, Hugh (John Blagdon)
1928- . . . . CLC 15, 28
See also CA 49-52; CAAS 17; CANR 1, 33;
DLB 53

Hood, Thomas 1799-1845 . . . . NCLC 16
See also DLB 96

Hooker, (Peter) Jeremy 1941- . . . . . . CLC 43
See also CA 77-80; CANR 22; DLB 40

Hope, A(lec) D(erwent) 1907- . . . . CLC 3, 51
See also CA 21-24R; CANR 33; MTCW

Hope, Brian
See Creasey, John

Hope, Christopher (David Tully)
1944- . . . . CLC 52
See also CA 106; SATA 62

Hopkins, Gerard Manley
1844-1889 . . . . NCLC 17; DA; WLC
See also CDBLB 1890-1914; DLB 35, 57

Hopkins, John (Richard) 1931- . . . . . . CLC 4
See also CA 85-88

Hopkins, Pauline Elizabeth
　　1859-1930 . . . . **TCLC 28; BLC**
　　See also CA 141; DLB 50

Hopkinson, Francis 1737-1791 . . . . . . **LC 25**
　　See also DLB 31

Hopley-Woolrich, Cornell George 1903-1968
　　See Woolrich, Cornell
　　See also CA 13-14; CAP 1

Horatio
　　See Proust, (Valentin-Louis-George-Eugene-)
　　Marcel

Horgan, Paul 1903- . . . . **CLC 9, 53**
　　See also CA 13-16R; CANR 9, 35;
　　　DLB 102; DLBY 85; MTCW; SATA 13

Horn, Peter
　　See Kuttner, Henry

Hornem, Horace Esq.
　　See Byron, George Gordon (Noel)

Horovitz, Israel 1939- . . . . **CLC 56**
　　See also CA 33-36R; DLB 7

Horvath, Odon von
　　See Horvath, Oedoen von
　　See also DLB 85, 124

Horvath, Oedoen von 1901-1938. . . **TCLC 45**
　　See also Horvath, Odon von
　　See also CA 118

Horwitz, Julius 1920-1986. . . . . **CLC 14**
　　See also CA 9-12R; 119; CANR 12

Hospital, Janette Turner 1942- . . . . . **CLC 42**
　　See also CA 108

Hostos, E. M. de
　　See Hostos (y Bonilla), Eugenio Maria de

Hostos, Eugenio M. de
　　See Hostos (y Bonilla), Eugenio Maria de

Hostos, Eugenio Maria
　　See Hostos (y Bonilla), Eugenio Maria de

Hostos (y Bonilla), Eugenio Maria de
　　1839-1903 . . . . **TCLC 24**
　　See also CA 123; 131; HW

Houdini
　　See Lovecraft, H(oward) P(hillips)

Hougan, Carolyn 1943- . . . . **CLC 34**
　　See also CA 139

Household, Geoffrey (Edward West)
　　1900-1988 . . . . **CLC 11**
　　See also CA 77-80; 126; DLB 87; SATA 14,
　　59

Housman, A(lfred) E(dward)
　　1859-1936 . . . . . . **TCLC 1, 10; DA; PC 2**
　　See also CA 104; 125; DLB 19; MTCW

Housman, Laurence 1865-1959 . . . . . **TCLC 7**
　　See also CA 106; DLB 10; SATA 25

Howard, Elizabeth Jane 1923- . . . **CLC 7, 29**
　　See also CA 5-8R; CANR 8

Howard, Maureen 1930- . . . . . **CLC 5, 14, 46**
　　See also CA 53-56; CANR 31; DLBY 83;
　　MTCW

Howard, Richard 1929- . . . . . . **CLC 7, 10, 47**
　　See also AITN 1; CA 85-88; CANR 25;
　　DLB 5

Howard, Robert Ervin 1906-1936. . . **TCLC 8**
　　See also CA 105

Howard, Warren F.
　　See Pohl, Frederik

Howe, Fanny 1940- . . . . **CLC 47**
　　See also CA 117; SATA 52

Howe, Julia Ward 1819-1910 . . . . . **TCLC 21**
　　See also CA 117; DLB 1

Howe, Susan 1937- . . . . **CLC 72**
　　See also DLB 120

Howe, Tina 1937- . . . . **CLC 48**
　　See also CA 109

Howell, James 1594(?)-1666 . . . . **LC 13**

Howells, W. D.
　　See Howells, William Dean

Howells, William D.
　　See Howells, William Dean

Howells, William Dean
　　1837-1920 . . . . **TCLC 7, 17, 41**
　　See also CA 104; 134; CDALB 1865-1917;
　　　DLB 12, 64, 74, 79

Howes, Barbara 1914- . . . . **CLC 15**
　　See also CA 9-12R; CAAS 3; SATA 5

Hrabal, Bohumil 1914- . . . . **CLC 13, 67**
　　See also CA 106; CAAS 12

Hsun, Lu . . . . **TCLC 3**
　　See also Shu-Jen, Chou

Hubbard, L(afayette) Ron(ald)
　　1911-1986 . . . . **CLC 43**
　　See also CA 77-80; 118; CANR 22

Huch, Ricarda (Octavia)
　　1864-1947 . . . . **TCLC 13**
　　See also CA 111; DLB 66

Huddle, David 1942- . . . . **CLC 49**
　　See also CA 57-60; DLB 130

Hudson, Jeffrey
　　See Crichton, (John) Michael

Hudson, W(illiam) H(enry)
　　1841-1922 . . . . **TCLC 29**
　　See also CA 115; DLB 98; SATA 35

Hueffer, Ford Madox
　　See Ford, Ford Madox

Hughart, Barry 1934- . . . . **CLC 39**
　　See also CA 137

Hughes, Colin
　　See Creasey, John

Hughes, David (John) 1930- . . . . **CLC 48**
　　See also CA 116; 129; DLB 14

Hughes, (James) Langston
　　1902-1967 . . . . . **CLC 1, 5, 10, 15, 35, 44;**
　　　　　　BLC; DA; DC 3; PC 1; SSC 6; WLC
　　See also BW; CA 1-4R; 25-28R; CANR 1,
　　34; CDALB 1929-1941; CLR 17; DLB 4,
　　7, 48, 51, 86; JRDA; MAICYA; MTCW;
　　SATA 4, 33

Hughes, Richard (Arthur Warren)
　　1900-1976 . . . . **CLC 1, 11**
　　See also CA 5-8R; 65-68; CANR 4;
　　DLB 15; MTCW; SATA 8, 25

Hughes, Ted
　　1930- . . . . **CLC 2, 4, 9, 14, 37; PC 7**
　　See also CA 1-4R; CANR 1, 33; CLR 3;
　　DLB 40; MAICYA; MTCW; SATA 27,
　　49

Hugo, Richard F(ranklin)
　　1923-1982 . . . . **CLC 6, 18, 32**
　　See also CA 49-52; 108; CANR 3; DLB 5

Hugo, Victor (Marie)
　　1802-1885 . . **NCLC 3, 10, 21; DA; WLC**
　　See also DLB 119; SATA 47

Huidobro, Vicente
　　See Huidobro Fernandez, Vicente Garcia

Huidobro Fernandez, Vicente Garcia
　　1893-1948 . . . . **TCLC 31**
　　See also CA 131; HW

Hulme, Keri 1947- . . . . **CLC 39**
　　See also CA 125

Hulme, T(homas) E(rnest)
　　1883-1917 . . . . **TCLC 21**
　　See also CA 117; DLB 19

Hume, David 1711-1776. . . . . **LC 7**
　　See also DLB 104

Humphrey, William 1924- . . . . **CLC 45**
　　See also CA 77-80; DLB 6

Humphreys, Emyr Owen 1919- . . . . . **CLC 47**
　　See also CA 5-8R; CANR 3, 24; DLB 15

Humphreys, Josephine 1945- . . . . **CLC 34, 57**
　　See also CA 121; 127

Hungerford, Pixie
　　See Brinsmead, H(esba) F(ay)

Hunt, E(verette) Howard, Jr.
　　1918- . . . . **CLC 3**
　　See also AITN 1; CA 45-48; CANR 2

Hunt, Kyle
　　See Creasey, John

Hunt, (James Henry) Leigh
　　1784-1859 . . . . **NCLC 1**

Hunt, Marsha 1946- . . . . **CLC 70**
　　See also CA 143

Hunt, Violet 1866-1942 . . . . **TCLC 53**

Hunter, E. Waldo
　　See Sturgeon, Theodore (Hamilton)

Hunter, Evan 1926- . . . . **CLC 11, 31**
　　See also CA 5-8R; CANR 5, 38; DLBY 82;
　　MTCW; SATA 25

Hunter, Kristin (Eggleston) 1931- . . . **CLC 35**
　　See also AITN 1; BW; CA 13-16R;
　　CANR 13; CLR 3; DLB 33; MAICYA;
　　SAAS 10; SATA 12

Hunter, Mollie 1922- . . . . **CLC 21**
　　See also McIlwraith, Maureen Mollie
　　Hunter
　　See also CANR 37; CLR 25; JRDA;
　　MAICYA; SAAS 7; SATA 54

Hunter, Robert (?)-1734. . . . . **LC 7**

Hurston, Zora Neale
　　1903-1960 . . . . **CLC 7, 30, 61; BLC; DA;**
　　　　　　　　　　　　　　　　　　　　　　　SSC 4
　　See also BW; CA 85-88; DLB 51, 86;
　　MTCW

Huston, John (Marcellus)
　　1906-1987 . . . . **CLC 20**
　　See also CA 73-76; 123; CANR 34; DLB 26

Hustvedt, Siri 1955- . . . . **CLC 76**
　　See also CA 137

Hutten, Ulrich von 1488-1523. . . . . . . **LC 16**

Huxley, Aldous (Leonard)
　　1894-1963 . . . . . **CLC 1, 3, 4, 5, 8, 11, 18,**
　　　　　　　　　　　　　　　　　35, 79; DA; WLC
　　See also CA 85-88; CDBLB 1914-1945;
　　DLB 36, 100; MTCW; SATA 63

Author Index

Jeffers, (John) Robinson
1887-1962 .... **CLC 2, 3, 11, 15, 54; DA;
WLC**
See also CA 85-88; CANR 35;
CDALB 1917-1929; DLB 45; MTCW

Jefferson, Janet
See Mencken, H(enry) L(ouis)

Jefferson, Thomas 1743-1826 .... **NCLC 11**
See also CDALB 1640-1865; DLB 31

Jeffrey, Francis 1773-1850 ...... **NCLC 33**
See also DLB 107

Jelakowitch, Ivan
See Heijermans, Herman

Jellicoe, (Patricia) Ann 1927- ...... **CLC 27**
See also CA 85-88; DLB 13

Jen, Gish .... **CLC 70**
See also Jen, Lillian

Jen, Lillian 1956(?)-
See Jen, Gish
See also CA 135

Jenkins, (John) Robin 1912- .... **CLC 52**
See also CA 1-4R; CANR 1; DLB 14

Jennings, Elizabeth (Joan)
1926- .... **CLC 5, 14**
See also CA 61-64; CAAS 5; CANR 8, 39;
DLB 27; MTCW; SATA 66

Jennings, Waylon 1937- .... **CLC 21**

Jensen, Johannes V. 1873-1950 .... **TCLC 41**

Jensen, Laura (Linnea) 1948- ...... **CLC 37**
See also CA 103

Jerome, Jerome K(lapka)
1859-1927 .... **TCLC 23**
See also CA 119; DLB 10, 34, 135

Jerrold, Douglas William
1803-1857 .... **NCLC 2**

Jewett, (Theodora) Sarah Orne
1849-1909 .... **TCLC 1, 22; SSC 6**
See also CA 108; 127; DLB 12, 74;
SATA 15

Jewsbury, Geraldine (Endsor)
1812-1880 .... **NCLC 22**
See also DLB 21

Jhabvala, Ruth Prawer
1927- .... **CLC 4, 8, 29**
See also CA 1-4R; CANR 2, 29; MTCW

Jiles, Paulette 1943- .... **CLC 13, 58**
See also CA 101

Jimenez (Mantecon), Juan Ramon
1881-1958 .... **TCLC 4; HLC; PC 7**
See also CA 104; 131; DLB 134; HW;
MTCW

Jimenez, Ramon
See Jimenez (Mantecon), Juan Ramon

Jimenez Mantecon, Juan
See Jimenez (Mantecon), Juan Ramon

Joel, Billy .... **CLC 26**
See also Joel, William Martin

Joel, William Martin 1949-
See Joel, Billy
See also CA 108

John of the Cross, St. 1542-1591 .... **LC 18**

Johnson, B(ryan) S(tanley William)
1933-1973 .... **CLC 6, 9**
See also CA 9-12R; 53-56; CANR 9;
DLB 14, 40

Johnson, Benj. F. of Boo
See Riley, James Whitcomb

Johnson, Benjamin F. of Boo
See Riley, James Whitcomb

Johnson, Charles (Richard)
1948- .... **CLC 7, 51, 65; BLC**
See also BW; CA 116; CAAS 18;
CANR 42; DLB 33

Johnson, Denis 1949- .... **CLC 52**
See also CA 117; 121; DLB 120

Johnson, Diane 1934- .... **CLC 5, 13, 48**
See also CA 41-44R; CANR 17, 40;
DLBY 80; MTCW

Johnson, Eyvind (Olof Verner)
1900-1976 .... **CLC 14**
See also CA 73-76; 69-72; CANR 34

Johnson, J. R.
See James, C(yril) L(ionel) R(obert)

Johnson, James Weldon
1871-1938 .... **TCLC 3, 19; BLC**
See also BW; CA 104; 125;
CDALB 1917-1929; CLR 32; DLB 51;
MTCW; SATA 31

Johnson, Joyce 1935- .... **CLC 58**
See also CA 125; 129

Johnson, Lionel (Pigot)
1867-1902 .... **TCLC 19**
See also CA 117; DLB 19

Johnson, Mel
See Malzberg, Barry N(athaniel)

Johnson, Pamela Hansford
1912-1981 .... **CLC 1, 7, 27**
See also CA 1-4R; 104; CANR 2, 28;
DLB 15; MTCW

Johnson, Samuel
1709-1784 .... **LC 15; DA; WLC**
See also CDBLB 1660-1789; DLB 39, 95,
104

Johnson, Uwe
1934-1984 .... **CLC 5, 10, 15, 40**
See also CA 1-4R; 112; CANR 1, 39;
DLB 75; MTCW

Johnston, George (Benson) 1913- ... **CLC 51**
See also CA 1-4R; CANR 5, 20; DLB 88

Johnston, Jennifer 1930- .... **CLC 7**
See also CA 85-88; DLB 14

Jolley, (Monica) Elizabeth 1923- ... **CLC 46**
See also CA 127; CAAS 13

Jones, Arthur Llewellyn 1863-1947
See Machen, Arthur
See also CA 104

Jones, D(ouglas) G(ordon) 1929- .... **CLC 10**
See also CA 29-32R; CANR 13; DLB 53

Jones, David (Michael)
1895-1974 .... **CLC 2, 4, 7, 13, 42**
See also CA 9-12R; 53-56; CANR 28;
CDBLB 1945-1960; DLB 20, 100; MTCW

Jones, David Robert 1947-
See Bowie, David
See also CA 103

Jones, Diana Wynne 1934- .... **CLC 26**
See also CA 49-52; CANR 4, 26; CLR 23;
JRDA; MAICYA; SAAS 7; SATA 9, 70

Jones, Edward P. 1950- .... **CLC 76**
See also CA 142

Jones, Gayl 1949- .... **CLC 6, 9; BLC**
See also BW; CA 77-80; CANR 27;
DLB 33; MTCW

Jones, James 1921-1977.... **CLC 1, 3, 10, 39**
See also AITN 1, 2; CA 1-4R; 69-72;
CANR 6; DLB 2; MTCW

Jones, John J.
See Lovecraft, H(oward) P(hillips)

Jones, LeRoi .... **CLC 1, 2, 3, 5, 10, 14**
See also Baraka, Amiri

Jones, Louis B. .... **CLC 65**
See also CA 141

Jones, Madison (Percy, Jr.) 1925- ... **CLC 4**
See also CA 13-16R; CAAS 11; CANR 7

Jones, Mervyn 1922- .... **CLC 10, 52**
See also CA 45-48; CAAS 5; CANR 1;
MTCW

Jones, Mick 1956(?)- .... **CLC 30**
See also Clash, The

Jones, Nettie (Pearl) 1941- .... **CLC 34**
See also CA 137

Jones, Preston 1936-1979 .... **CLC 10**
See also CA 73-76; 89-92; DLB 7

Jones, Robert F(rancis) 1934- .... **CLC 7**
See also CA 49-52; CANR 2

Jones, Rod 1953- .... **CLC 50**
See also CA 128

Jones, Terence Graham Parry
1942- .... **CLC 21**
See also Jones, Terry; Monty Python
See also CA 112; 116; CANR 35; SATA 51

Jones, Terry
See Jones, Terence Graham Parry
See also SATA 67

Jones, Thom 1945(?)- .... **CLC 81**

Jong, Erica 1942- .... **CLC 4, 6, 8, 18**
See also AITN 1; BEST 90:2; CA 73-76;
CANR 26; DLB 2, 5, 28; MTCW

Jonson, Ben(jamin)
1572(?)-1637 .... **LC 6; DA; DC 4; WLC**
See also CDBLB Before 1660; DLB 62, 121

Jordan, June 1936- .... **CLC 5, 11, 23**
See also AAYA 2; BW; CA 33-36R;
CANR 25; CLR 10; DLB 38; MAICYA;
MTCW; SATA 4

Jordan, Pat(rick M.) 1941- .... **CLC 37**
See also CA 33-36R

Jorgensen, Ivar
See Ellison, Harlan

Jorgenson, Ivar
See Silverberg, Robert

Josipovici, Gabriel 1940- .... **CLC 6, 43**
See also CA 37-40R; CAAS 8; DLB 14

Joubert, Joseph 1754-1824 .... **NCLC 9**

Jouve, Pierre Jean 1887-1976 ...... **CLC 47**
See also CA 65-68

Joyce, James (Augustine Aloysius)
1882-1941 ..... **TCLC 3, 8, 16, 35; DA;
SSC 3; WLC**
See also CA 104; 126; CDBLB 1914-1945;
DLB 10, 19, 36; MTCW

Jozsef, Attila 1905-1937......... **TCLC 22**
See also CA 116

Juana Ines de la Cruz 1651(?)-1695 ... **LC 5**

Judd, Cyril
See Kornbluth, C(yril) M.; Pohl, Frederik

Julian of Norwich 1342(?)-1416(?) .... **LC 6**

Just, Ward (Swift) 1935-........ **CLC 4, 27**
See also CA 25-28R; CANR 32

Justice, Donald (Rodney) 1925- .. **CLC 6, 19**
See also CA 5-8R; CANR 26; DLBY 83

Juvenal c. 55-c. 127 .... **CMLC 8**

Juvenis
See Bourne, Randolph S(illiman)

Kacew, Romain 1914-1980
See Gary, Romain
See also CA 108; 102

Kadare, Ismail 1936- .... **CLC 52**

Kadohata, Cynthia.................. **CLC 59**
See also CA 140

Kafka, Franz
1883-1924 .... **TCLC 2, 6, 13, 29, 47, 53;
DA; SSC 5; WLC**
See also CA 105; 126; DLB 81; MTCW

Kahn, Roger 1927-................ **CLC 30**
See also CA 25-28R; SATA 37

Kain, Saul
See Sassoon, Siegfried (Lorraine)

Kaiser, Georg 1878-1945 .... **TCLC 9**
See also CA 106; DLB 124

Kaletski, Alexander 1946-......... **CLC 39**
See also CA 118; 143

Kalidasa fl. c. 400- .... **CMLC 9**

Kallman, Chester (Simon)
1921-1975 .... **CLC 2**
See also CA 45-48; 53-56; CANR 3

Kaminsky, Melvin 1926-
See Brooks, Mel
See also CA 65-68; CANR 16

Kaminsky, Stuart M(elvin) 1934- ... **CLC 59**
See also CA 73-76; CANR 29

Kane, Paul
See Simon, Paul

Kane, Wilson
See Bloch, Robert (Albert)

Kanin, Garson 1912-.............. **CLC 22**
See also AITN 1; CA 5-8R; CANR 7;
DLB 7

Kaniuk, Yoram 1930-............. **CLC 19**
See also CA 134

Kant, Immanuel 1724-1804 ...... **NCLC 27**
See also DLB 94

Kantor, MacKinlay 1904-1977 ...... **CLC 7**
See also CA 61-64; 73-76; DLB 9, 102

Kaplan, David Michael 1946- ...... **CLC 50**

Kaplan, James 1951- .... **CLC 59**
See also CA 135

Karageorge, Michael
See Anderson, Poul (William)

Karamzin, Nikolai Mikhailovich
1766-1826 .... **NCLC 3**

Karapanou, Margarita 1946-....... **CLC 13**
See also CA 101

Karinthy, Frigyes 1887-1938..... **TCLC 47**

Karl, Frederick R(obert) 1927- ..... **CLC 34**
See also CA 5-8R; CANR 3

Kastel, Warren
See Silverberg, Robert

Kataev, Evgeny Petrovich 1903-1942
See Petrov, Evgeny
See also CA 120

Kataphusin
See Ruskin, John

Katz, Steve 1935-................. **CLC 47**
See also CA 25-28R; CAAS 14; CANR 12;
DLBY 83

Kauffman, Janet 1945-............ **CLC 42**
See also CA 117; CANR 43; DLBY 86

Kaufman, Bob (Garnell)
1925-1986 .... **CLC 49**
See also BW; CA 41-44R; 118; CANR 22;
DLB 16, 41

Kaufman, George S. 1889-1961..... **CLC 38**
See also CA 108; 93-96; DLB 7

Kaufman, Sue .... **CLC 3, 8**
See also Barondess, Sue K(aufman)

Kavafis, Konstantinos Petrou 1863-1933
See Cavafy, C(onstantine) P(eter)
See also CA 104

Kavan, Anna 1901-1968...... **CLC 5, 13, 82**
See also CA 5-8R; CANR 6; MTCW

Kavanagh, Dan
See Barnes, Julian

Kavanagh, Patrick (Joseph)
1904-1967 .... **CLC 22**
See also CA 123; 25-28R; DLB 15, 20;
MTCW

Kawabata, Yasunari
1899-1972 .... **CLC 2, 5, 9, 18**
See also CA 93-96; 33-36R

Kaye, M(ary) M(argaret) 1909-..... **CLC 28**
See also CA 89-92; CANR 24; MTCW;
SATA 62

Kaye, Mollie
See Kaye, M(ary) M(argaret)

Kaye-Smith, Sheila 1887-1956..... **TCLC 20**
See also CA 118; DLB 36

Kaymor, Patrice Maguilene
See Senghor, Leopold Sedar

Kazan, Elia 1909-........... **CLC 6, 16, 63**
See also CA 21-24R; CANR 32

Kazantzakis, Nikos
1883(?)-1957 .... **TCLC 2, 5, 33**
See also CA 105; 132; MTCW

Kazin, Alfred 1915- .... **CLC 34, 38**
See also CA 1-4R; CAAS 7; CANR 1;
DLB 67

Keane, Mary Nesta (Skrine) 1904-
See Keane, Molly
See also CA 108; 114

Keane, Molly.................... **CLC 31**
See also Keane, Mary Nesta (Skrine)

Keates, Jonathan 19(?)- .... **CLC 34**

Keaton, Buster 1895-1966 .... **CLC 20**

Keats, John
1795-1821 ... **NCLC 8; DA; PC 1; WLC**
See also CDBLB 1789-1832; DLB 96, 110

Keene, Donald 1922-............. **CLC 34**
See also CA 1-4R; CANR 5

Keillor, Garrison .... **CLC 40**
See also Keillor, Gary (Edward)
See also AAYA 2; BEST 89:3; DLBY 87;
SATA 58

Keillor, Gary (Edward) 1942-
See Keillor, Garrison
See also CA 111; 117; CANR 36; MTCW

Keith, Michael
See Hubbard, L(afayette) Ron(ald)

Keller, Gottfried 1819-1890....... **NCLC 2**
See also DLB 129

Kellerman, Jonathan 1949- .... **CLC 44**
See also BEST 90:1; CA 106; CANR 29

Kelley, William Melvin 1937-...... **CLC 22**
See also BW; CA 77-80; CANR 27; DLB 33

Kellogg, Marjorie 1922-............ **CLC 2**
See also CA 81-84

Kellow, Kathleen
See Hibbert, Eleanor Alice Burford

Kelly, M(ilton) T(erry) 1947-....... **CLC 55**
See also CA 97-100; CANR 19, 43

Kelman, James 1946-............. **CLC 58**

Kemal, Yashar 1923- .... **CLC 14, 29**
See also CA 89-92

Kemble, Fanny 1809-1893 .... **NCLC 18**
See also DLB 32

Kemelman, Harry 1908-............ **CLC 2**
See also AITN 1; CA 9-12R; CANR 6;
DLB 28

Kempe, Margery 1373(?)-1440(?) ..... **LC 6**

Kempis, Thomas a 1380-1471 .... **LC 11**

Kendall, Henry 1839-1882....... **NCLC 12**

Keneally, Thomas (Michael)
1935- ...... **CLC 5, 8, 10, 14, 19, 27, 43**
See also CA 85-88; CANR 10; MTCW

Kennedy, Adrienne (Lita)
1931- .... **CLC 66; BLC**
See also BW; CA 103; CABS 3; CANR 26;
DLB 38

Kennedy, John Pendleton
1795-1870 .... **NCLC 2**
See also DLB 3

Kennedy, Joseph Charles 1929-...... **CLC 8**
See also Kennedy, X. J.
See also CA 1-4R; CANR 4, 30, 40;
SATA 14

Kennedy, William 1928-... **CLC 6, 28, 34, 53**
See also AAYA 1; CA 85-88; CANR 14,
31; DLBY 85; MTCW; SATA 57

Kennedy, X. J...................... **CLC 42**
See also Kennedy, Joseph Charles
See also CAAS 9; CLR 27; DLB 5

Kent, Kelvin
See Kuttner, Henry

Kenton, Maxwell
See Southern, Terry

Kenyon, Robert O.
See Kuttner, Henry

Kerouac, Jack ..... **CLC 1, 2, 3, 5, 14, 29, 61**
See also Kerouac, Jean-Louis Lebris de
See also CDALB 1941-1968; DLB 2, 16;
DLBD 3

Kerouac, Jean-Louis Lebris de 1922-1969
See Kerouac, Jack
See also AITN 1; CA 5-8R; 25-28R;
CANR 26; DA; MTCW; WLC

Kerr, Jean 1923-................ **CLC 22**
See also CA 5-8R; CANR 7

Kerr, M. E. .... **CLC 12, 35**
See also Meaker, Marijane (Agnes)
See also AAYA 2; CLR 29; SAAS 1

Kerr, Robert .... **CLC 55**

Kerrigan, (Thomas) Anthony
1918-..................... **CLC 4, 6**
See also CA 49-52; CAAS 11; CANR 4

Kerry, Lois
See Duncan, Lois

Kesey, Ken (Elton)
1935- ...... **CLC 1, 3, 6, 11, 46, 64; DA;
WLC**
See also CA 1-4R; CANR 22, 38;
CDALB 1968-1988; DLB 2, 16; MTCW;
SATA 66

Kesselring, Joseph (Otto)
1902-1967 .... **CLC 45**

Kessler, Jascha (Frederick) 1929-.... **CLC 4**
See also CA 17-20R; CANR 8

Kettelkamp, Larry (Dale) 1933- .... **CLC 12**
See also CA 29-32R; CANR 16; SAAS 3;
SATA 2

Keyber, Conny
See Fielding, Henry

Keyes, Daniel 1927-......... **CLC 80; DA**
See also CA 17-20R; CANR 10, 26;
SATA 37

Khayyam, Omar
1048-1131 .... **CMLC 11; PC 8**

Kherdian, David 1931-......... **CLC 6, 9**
See also CA 21-24R; CAAS 2; CANR 39;
CLR 24; JRDA; MAICYA; SATA 16, 74

Khlebnikov, Velimir .... **TCLC 20**
See also Khlebnikov, Viktor Vladimirovich

Khlebnikov, Viktor Vladimirovich 1885-1922
See Khlebnikov, Velimir
See also CA 117

Khodasevich, Vladislav (Felitsianovich)
1886-1939 .... **TCLC 15**
See also CA 115

Kielland, Alexander Lange
1849-1906 .... **TCLC 5**
See also CA 104

Kiely, Benedict 1919-......... **CLC 23, 43**
See also CA 1-4R; CANR 2; DLB 15

Kienzle, William X(avier) 1928- .... **CLC 25**
See also CA 93-96; CAAS 1; CANR 9, 31;
MTCW

Kierkegaard, Soren 1813-1855.... **NCLC 34**

Killens, John Oliver 1916-1987..... **CLC 10**
See also BW; CA 77-80; 123; CAAS 2;
CANR 26; DLB 33

Killigrew, Anne 1660-1685.......... **LC 4**
See also DLB 131

Kim
See Simenon, Georges (Jacques Christian)

Kincaid, Jamaica 1949- ... **CLC 43, 68; BLC**
See also BW; CA 125

King, Francis (Henry) 1923-..... **CLC 8, 53**
See also CA 1-4R; CANR 1, 33; DLB 15;
MTCW

King, Stephen (Edwin)
1947-..............**CLC 12, 26, 37, 61**
See also AAYA 1; BEST 90:1; CA 61-64;
CANR 1, 30; DLBY 80; JRDA; MTCW;
SATA 9, 55

King, Steve
See King, Stephen (Edwin)

Kingman, Lee..................... **CLC 17**
See also Natti, (Mary) Lee
See also SAAS 3; SATA 1, 67

Kingsley, Charles 1819-1875..... **NCLC 35**
See also DLB 21, 32; YABC 2

Kingsley, Sidney 1906-........... **CLC 44**
See also CA 85-88; DLB 7

Kingsolver, Barbara 1955-...... **CLC 55, 81**
See also CA 129; 134

Kingston, Maxine (Ting Ting) Hong
1940-............. **CLC 12, 19, 58**
See also AAYA 8; CA 69-72; CANR 13,
38; DLBY 80; MTCW; SATA 53

Kinnell, Galway
1927- .... **CLC 1, 2, 3, 5, 13, 29**
See also CA 9-12R; CANR 10, 34; DLB 5;
DLBY 87; MTCW

Kinsella, Thomas 1928-......... **CLC 4, 19**
See also CA 17-20R; CANR 15; DLB 27;
MTCW

Kinsella, W(illiam) P(atrick)
1935- .... **CLC 27, 43**
See also AAYA 7; CA 97-100; CAAS 7;
CANR 21, 35; MTCW

Kipling, (Joseph) Rudyard
1865-1936 ...... **TCLC 8, 17; DA; PC 3;
SSC 5; WLC**
See also CA 105; 120; CANR 33;
CDBLB 1890-1914; DLB 19, 34;
MAICYA; MTCW; YABC 2

Kirkup, James 1918- .... **CLC 1**
See also CA 1-4R; CAAS 4; CANR 2;
DLB 27; SATA 12

Kirkwood, James 1930(?)-1989 ...... **CLC 9**
See also AITN 2; CA 1-4R; 128; CANR 6,
40

Kis, Danilo 1935-1989 .... **CLC 57**
See also CA 109; 118; 129; MTCW

Kivi, Aleksis 1834-1872 .... **NCLC 30**

Kizer, Carolyn (Ashley)
1925- .... **CLC 15, 39, 80**
See also CA 65-68; CAAS 5; CANR 24;
DLB 5

Klabund 1890-1928.............. **TCLC 44**
See also DLB 66

Klappert, Peter 1942-............. **CLC 57**
See also CA 33-36R; DLB 5

Klein, A(braham) M(oses)
1909-1972 .... **CLC 19**
See also CA 101; 37-40R; DLB 68

Klein, Norma 1938-1989 .... **CLC 30**
See also AAYA 2; CA 41-44R; 128;
CANR 15, 37; CLR 2, 19; JRDA;
MAICYA; SAAS 1; SATA 7, 57

Klein, T(heodore) E(ibon) D(onald)
1947-...................... **CLC 34**
See also CA 119

Kleist, Heinrich von
1777-1811 .... **NCLC 2, 37**
See also DLB 90

Klima, Ivan 1931-............... **CLC 56**
See also CA 25-28R; CANR 17

Klimentov, Andrei Platonovich 1899-1951
See Platonov, Andrei
See also CA 108

Klinger, Friedrich Maximilian von
1752-1831 .... **NCLC 1**
See also DLB 94

Klopstock, Friedrich Gottlieb
1724-1803 .... **NCLC 11**
See also DLB 97

Knebel, Fletcher 1911-1993........ **CLC 14**
See also AITN 1; CA 1-4R; 140; CAAS 3;
CANR 1, 36; SATA 36; SATA-Obit 75

Knickerbocker, Diedrich
See Irving, Washington

Knight, Etheridge
1931-1991 .... **CLC 40; BLC**
See also BW; CA 21-24R; 133; CANR 23;
DLB 41

Knight, Sarah Kemble 1666-1727 ..... **LC 7**
See also DLB 24

Knowles, John
1926- .... **CLC 1, 4, 10, 26; DA**
See also AAYA 10; CA 17-20R; CANR 40;
CDALB 1968-1988; DLB 6; MTCW;
SATA 8

Knox, Calvin M.
See Silverberg, Robert

Knye, Cassandra
See Disch, Thomas M(ichael)

Koch, C(hristopher) J(ohn) 1932- ... **CLC 42**
See also CA 127

Koch, Christopher
See Koch, C(hristopher) J(ohn)

Koch, Kenneth 1925-......... **CLC 5, 8, 44**
See also CA 1-4R; CANR 6, 36; DLB 5;
SATA 65

Kochanowski, Jan 1530-1584....... **LC 10**

Kock, Charles Paul de
1794-1871 .... **NCLC 16**

Koda Shigeyuki 1867-1947
See Rohan, Koda
See also CA 121

Koestler, Arthur
1905-1983 .... **CLC 1, 3, 6, 8, 15, 33**
See also CA 1-4R; 109; CANR 1, 33;
CDBLB 1945-1960; DLBY 83; MTCW

Kogawa, Joy Nozomi 1935-........ **CLC 78**
See also CA 101; CANR 19

Kohout, Pavel 1928-.............. **CLC 13**
See also CA 45-48; CANR 3

Koizumi, Yakumo
See Hearn, (Patricio) Lafcadio (Tessima Carlos)

Kolmar, Gertrud 1894-1943...... **TCLC 40**

Konrad, George
See Konrad, Gyoergy

Konrad, Gyoergy 1933- ...... **CLC 4, 10, 73**
See also CA 85-88

Konwicki, Tadeusz 1926-..... **CLC 8, 28, 54**
See also CA 101; CAAS 9; CANR 39; MTCW

Koontz, Dean R(ay) 1945-........ **CLC 78**
See also AAYA 9; BEST 89:3, 90:2; CA 108; CANR 19, 36; MTCW

Kopit, Arthur (Lee) 1937- .... **CLC 1, 18, 33**
See also AITN 1; CA 81-84; CABS 3; DLB 7; MTCW

Kops, Bernard 1926-.............. **CLC 4**
See also CA 5-8R; DLB 13

Kornbluth, C(yril) M. 1923-1958.... **TCLC 8**
See also CA 105; DLB 8

Korolenko, V. G.
See Korolenko, Vladimir Galaktionovich

Korolenko, Vladimir
See Korolenko, Vladimir Galaktionovich

Korolenko, Vladimir G.
See Korolenko, Vladimir Galaktionovich

Korolenko, Vladimir Galaktionovich
1853-1921 .... **TCLC 22**
See also CA 121

Kosinski, Jerzy (Nikodem)
1933-1991 .... **CLC 1, 2, 3, 6, 10, 15, 53, 70**
See also CA 17-20R; 134; CANR 9; DLB 2; DLBY 82; MTCW

Kostelanetz, Richard (Cory) 1940-.. **CLC 28**
See also CA 13-16R; CAAS 8; CANR 38

Kostrowitzki, Wilhelm Apollinaris de
1880-1918
See Apollinaire, Guillaume
See also CA 104

Kotlowitz, Robert 1924-............ **CLC 4**
See also CA 33-36R; CANR 36

Kotzebue, August (Friedrich Ferdinand) von
1761-1819 .... **NCLC 25**
See also DLB 94

Kotzwinkle, William 1938- ... **CLC 5, 14, 35**
See also CA 45-48; CANR 3; CLR 6; MAICYA; SATA 24, 70

Kozol, Jonathan 1936-............ **CLC 17**
See also CA 61-64; CANR 16

Kozoll, Michael 1940(?)-.......... **CLC 35**

Kramer, Kathryn 19(?)-.......... **CLC 34**

Kramer, Larry 1935- .... **CLC 42**
See also CA 124; 126

Krasicki, Ignacy 1735-1801....... **NCLC 8**

Krasinski, Zygmunt 1812-1859 .... **NCLC 4**

Kraus, Karl 1874-1936......... **TCLC 5**
See also CA 104; DLB 118

Kreve (Mickevicius), Vincas
1882-1954 .... **TCLC 27**

Kristeva, Julia 1941- .... **CLC 77**

Kristofferson, Kris 1936-.......... **CLC 26**
See also CA 104

Krizanc, John 1956-.............. **CLC 57**

Krleza, Miroslav 1893-1981........ **CLC 8**
See also CA 97-100; 105

Kroetsch, Robert 1927- ...... **CLC 5, 23, 57**
See also CA 17-20R; CANR 8, 38; DLB 53; MTCW

Kroetz, Franz
See Kroetz, Franz Xaver

Kroetz, Franz Xaver 1946- .... **CLC 41**
See also CA 130

Kroker, Arthur 1945-............. **CLC 77**

Kropotkin, Peter (Aleksieevich)
1842-1921 .... **TCLC 36**
See also CA 119

Krotkov, Yuri 1917-.............. **CLC 19**
See also CA 102

Krumb
See Crumb, R(obert)

Krumgold, Joseph (Quincy)
1908-1980 .... **CLC 12**
See also CA 9-12R; 101; CANR 7; MAICYA; SATA 1, 23, 48

Krumwitz
See Crumb, R(obert)

Krutch, Joseph Wood 1893-1970.... **CLC 24**
See also CA 1-4R; 25-28R; CANR 4; DLB 63

Krutzch, Gus
See Eliot, T(homas) S(tearns)

Krylov, Ivan Andreevich
1768(?)-1844 .... **NCLC 1**

Kubin, Alfred 1877-1959 .... **TCLC 23**
See also CA 112; DLB 81

Kubrick, Stanley 1928-............ **CLC 16**
See also CA 81-84; CANR 33; DLB 26

Kumin, Maxine (Winokur)
1925-................... **CLC 5, 13, 28**
See also AITN 2; CA 1-4R; CAAS 8; CANR 1, 21; DLB 5; MTCW; SATA 12

Kundera, Milan
1929-........... **CLC 4, 9, 19, 32, 68**
See also AAYA 2; CA 85-88; CANR 19; MTCW

Kunitz, Stanley (Jasspon)
1905-................... **CLC 6, 11, 14**
See also CA 41-44R; CANR 26; DLB 48; MTCW

Kunze, Reiner 1933-............. **CLC 10**
See also CA 93-96; DLB 75

Kuprin, Aleksandr Ivanovich
1870-1938 .... **TCLC 5**
See also CA 104

Kureishi, Hanif 1954(?)-.......... **CLC 64**
See also CA 139

Kurosawa, Akira 1910-............ **CLC 16**
See also CA 101

Kushner, Tony 1957(?)- .... **CLC 81**

Kuttner, Henry 1915-1958........ **TCLC 10**
See also CA 107; DLB 8

Kuzma, Greg 1944-................ **CLC 7**
See also CA 33-36R

Kuzmin, Mikhail 1872(?)-1936 .... **TCLC 40**

Kyd, Thomas 1558-1594...... **LC 22; DC 3**
See also DLB 62

Kyprianos, Iossif
See Samarakis, Antonis

La Bruyere, Jean de 1645-1696...... **LC 17**

Lacan, Jacques (Marie Emile)
1901-1981 .... **CLC 75**
See also CA 121; 104

Laclos, Pierre Ambroise Francois Choderlos
de 1741-1803 .... **NCLC 4**

Lacolere, Francois
See Aragon, Louis

La Colere, Francois
See Aragon, Louis

La Deshabilleuse
See Simenon, Georges (Jacques Christian)

Lady Gregory
See Gregory, Isabella Augusta (Persse)

Lady of Quality, A
See Bagnold, Enid

La Fayette, Marie (Madelaine Pioche de la
Vergne Comtes 1634-1693...... **LC 2**

Lafayette, Rene
See Hubbard, L(afayette) Ron(ald)

Laforgue, Jules 1860-1887........ **NCLC 5**

Lagerkvist, Paer (Fabian)
1891-1974 .... **CLC 7, 10, 13, 54**
See also Lagerkvist, Par
See also CA 85-88; 49-52; MTCW

Lagerkvist, Par
See Lagerkvist, Paer (Fabian)
See also SSC 12

Lagerloef, Selma (Ottiliana Lovisa)
1858-1940 .... **TCLC 4, 36**
See also Lagerlof, Selma (Ottiliana Lovisa)
See also CA 108; CLR 7; SATA 15

Lagerlof, Selma (Ottiliana Lovisa)
See Lagerloef, Selma (Ottiliana Lovisa)
See also CLR 7; SATA 15

La Guma, (Justin) Alex(ander)
1925-1985 .... **CLC 19**
See also BW; CA 49-52; 118; CANR 25; DLB 117; MTCW

Laidlaw, A. K.
See Grieve, C(hristopher) M(urray)

Lainez, Manuel Mujica
See Mujica Lainez, Manuel
See also HW

Lamartine, Alphonse (Marie Louis Prat) de
1790-1869 .... **NCLC 11**

Lamb, Charles
1775-1834 .... **NCLC 10; DA; WLC**
See also CDBLB 1789-1832; DLB 93, 107; SATA 17

Lamb, Lady Caroline 1785-1828.. **NCLC 38**
See also DLB 116

Lamming, George (William)
1927-.............. **CLC 2, 4, 66; BLC**
See also BW; CA 85-88; CANR 26; DLB 125; MTCW

L'Amour, Louis (Dearborn)
    1908-1988 . . . . **CLC 25, 55**
    See also AITN 2; BEST 89:2; CA 1-4R;
    125; CANR 3, 25, 40; DLBY 80; MTCW

Lampedusa, Giuseppe (Tomasi) di . . . **TCLC 13**
    See also Tomasi di Lampedusa, Giuseppe

Lampman, Archibald 1861-1899 . . **NCLC 25**
    See also DLB 92

Lancaster, Bruce 1896-1963 . . . . **CLC 36**
    See also CA 9-10; CAP 1; SATA 9

Landau, Mark Alexandrovich
    See Aldanov, Mark (Alexandrovich)

Landau-Aldanov, Mark Alexandrovich
    See Aldanov, Mark (Alexandrovich)

Landis, John 1950- . . . . **CLC 26**
    See also CA 112; 122

Landolfi, Tommaso 1908-1979 . . . **CLC 11, 49**
    See also CA 127; 117

Landon, Letitia Elizabeth
    1802-1838 . . . . **NCLC 15**
    See also DLB 96

Landor, Walter Savage
    1775-1864 . . . . **NCLC 14**
    See also DLB 93, 107

Landwirth, Heinz 1927-
    See Lind, Jakov
    See also CA 9-12R; CANR 7

Lane, Patrick 1939- . . . . **CLC 25**
    See also CA 97-100; DLB 53

Lang, Andrew 1844-1912 . . . . **TCLC 16**
    See also CA 114; 137; DLB 98; MAICYA;
    SATA 16

Lang, Fritz 1890-1976 . . . . **CLC 20**
    See also CA 77-80; 69-72; CANR 30

Lange, John
    See Crichton, (John) Michael

Langer, Elinor 1939- . . . . **CLC 34**
    See also CA 121

Langland, William
    1330(?)-1400(?) . . . . **LC 19; DA**

Langstaff, Launcelot
    See Irving, Washington

Lanier, Sidney 1842-1881 . . . . **NCLC 6**
    See also DLB 64; MAICYA; SATA 18

Lanyer, Aemilia 1569-1645 . . . . **LC 10**

Lao Tzu . . . . **CMLC 7**

Lapine, James (Elliot) 1949- . . . . **CLC 39**
    See also CA 123; 130

Larbaud, Valery (Nicolas)
    1881-1957 . . . . **TCLC 9**
    See also CA 106

Lardner, Ring
    See Lardner, Ring(gold) W(ilmer)

Lardner, Ring W., Jr.
    See Lardner, Ring(gold) W(ilmer)

Lardner, Ring(gold) W(ilmer)
    1885-1933 . . . . **TCLC 2, 14**
    See also CA 104; 131; CDALB 1917-1929;
    DLB 11, 25, 86; MTCW

Laredo, Betty
    See Codrescu, Andrei

Larkin, Maia
    See Wojciechowska, Maia (Teresa)

Larkin, Philip (Arthur)
    1922-1985 . . . . **CLC 3, 5, 8, 9, 13, 18, 33,**
                      39, 64
    See also CA 5-8R; 117; CANR 24;
    CDBLB 1960 to Present; DLB 27;
    MTCW

Larra (y Sanchez de Castro), Mariano Jose de
    1809-1837 . . . . **NCLC 17**

Larsen, Eric 1941- . . . . **CLC 55**
    See also CA 132

Larsen, Nella 1891-1964 . . . . . **CLC 37; BLC**
    See also BW; CA 125; DLB 51

Larson, Charles R(aymond) 1938- . . . **CLC 31**
    See also CA 53-56; CANR 4

Latham, Jean Lee 1902- . . . . **CLC 12**
    See also AITN 1; CA 5-8R; CANR 7;
    MAICYA; SATA 2, 68

Latham, Mavis
    See Clark, Mavis Thorpe

Lathen, Emma . . . . **CLC 2**
    See also Hennissart, Martha; Latsis, Mary
    J(ane)

Lathrop, Francis
    See Leiber, Fritz (Reuter, Jr.)

Latsis, Mary J(ane)
    See Lathen, Emma
    See also CA 85-88

Lattimore, Richmond (Alexander)
    1906-1984 . . . . **CLC 3**
    See also CA 1-4R; 112; CANR 1

Laughlin, James 1914- . . . . **CLC 49**
    See also CA 21-24R; CANR 9; DLB 48

Laurence, (Jean) Margaret (Wemyss)
    1926-1987 . . **CLC 3, 6, 13, 50, 62; SSC 7**
    See also CA 5-8R; 121; CANR 33; DLB 53;
    MTCW; SATA 50

Laurent, Antoine 1952- . . . . **CLC 50**

Lauscher, Hermann
    See Hesse, Hermann

Lautreamont, Comte de
    1846-1870 . . . . **NCLC 12; SSC 14**

Laverty, Donald
    See Blish, James (Benjamin)

Lavin, Mary 1912- . . . . . . **CLC 4, 18; SSC 4**
    See also CA 9-12R; CANR 33; DLB 15;
    MTCW

Lavond, Paul Dennis
    See Kornbluth, C(yril) M.; Pohl, Frederik

Lawler, Raymond Evenor 1922- . . . . **CLC 58**
    See also CA 103

Lawrence, D(avid) H(erbert Richards)
    1885-1930 . . . . . . **TCLC 2, 9, 16, 33, 48;**
                   DA; SSC 4; WLC
    See also CA 104; 121; CDBLB 1914-1945;
    DLB 10, 19, 36, 98; MTCW

Lawrence, T(homas) E(dward)
    1888-1935 . . . . **TCLC 18**
    See also Dale, Colin
    See also CA 115

Lawrence of Arabia
    See Lawrence, T(homas) E(dward)

Lawson, Henry (Archibald Hertzberg)
    1867-1922 . . . . **TCLC 27**
    See also CA 120

Lawton, Dennis
    See Faust, Frederick (Schiller)

Laxness, Halldor . . . . **CLC 25**
    See also Gudjonsson, Halldor Kiljan

Layamon fl. c. 1200- . . . . **CMLC 10**

Laye, Camara 1928-1980 . . . **CLC 4, 38; BLC**
    See also BW; CA 85-88; 97-100; CANR 25;
    MTCW

Layton, Irving (Peter) 1912- . . . . . **CLC 2, 15**
    See also CA 1-4R; CANR 2, 33, 43;
    DLB 88; MTCW

Lazarus, Emma 1849-1887 . . . . **NCLC 8**

Lazarus, Felix
    See Cable, George Washington

Lazarus, Henry
    See Slavitt, David R(ytman)

Lea, Joan
    See Neufeld, John (Arthur)

Leacock, Stephen (Butler)
    1869-1944 . . . . **TCLC 2**
    See also CA 104; 141; DLB 92

Lear, Edward 1812-1888 . . . . **NCLC 3**
    See also CLR 1; DLB 32; MAICYA;
    SATA 18

Lear, Norman (Milton) 1922- . . . . . . **CLC 12**
    See also CA 73-76

Leavis, F(rank) R(aymond)
    1895-1978 . . . . **CLC 24**
    See also CA 21-24R; 77-80; MTCW

Leavitt, David 1961- . . . . **CLC 34**
    See also CA 116; 122; DLB 130

Leblanc, Maurice (Marie Emile)
    1864-1941 . . . . **TCLC 49**
    See also CA 110

Lebowitz, Fran(ces Ann)
    1951(?)- . . . . **CLC 11, 36**
    See also CA 81-84; CANR 14; MTCW

le Carre, John . . . . **CLC 3, 5, 9, 15, 28**
    See also Cornwell, David (John Moore)
    See also BEST 89:4; CDBLB 1960 to
    Present; DLB 87

Le Clezio, J(ean) M(arie) G(ustave)
    1940- . . . . **CLC 31**
    See also CA 116; 128; DLB 83

Leconte de Lisle, Charles-Marie-Rene
    1818-1894 . . . . **NCLC 29**

Le Coq, Monsieur
    See Simenon, Georges (Jacques Christian)

Leduc, Violette 1907-1972 . . . . **CLC 22**
    See also CA 13-14; 33-36R; CAP 1

Ledwidge, Francis 1887(?)-1917 . . . **TCLC 23**
    See also CA 123; DLB 20

Lee, Andrea 1953- . . . . **CLC 36; BLC**
    See also BW; CA 125

Lee, Andrew
    See Auchincloss, Louis (Stanton)

Lee, Don L. . . . . **CLC 2**
    See also Madhubuti, Haki R.

Lee, George W(ashington)
    1894-1976 . . . . **CLC 52; BLC**
    See also BW; CA 125; DLB 51

Lee, (Nelle) Harper
1926- .... **CLC 12, 60; DA; WLC**
See also CA 13-16R; CDALB 1941-1968;
DLB 6; MTCW; SATA 11

Lee, Julian
See Latham, Jean Lee

Lee, Larry
See Lee, Lawrence

Lee, Lawrence 1941-1990 .... **CLC 34**
See also CA 131; CANR 43

Lee, Manfred B(ennington)
1905-1971 .... **CLC 11**
See also Queen, Ellery
See also CA 1-4R; 29-32R; CANR 2

Lee, Stan 1922- .... **CLC 17**
See also AAYA 5; CA 108; 111

Lee, Tanith 1947- .... **CLC 46**
See also CA 37-40R; SATA 8

Lee, Vernon .... **TCLC 5**
See also Paget, Violet
See also DLB 57

Lee, William
See Burroughs, William S(eward)

Lee, Willy
See Burroughs, William S(eward)

Lee-Hamilton, Eugene (Jacob)
1845-1907 .... **TCLC 22**
See also CA 117

Leet, Judith 1935- .... **CLC 11**

Le Fanu, Joseph Sheridan
1814-1873 .... **NCLC 9; SSC 14**
See also DLB 21, 70

Leffland, Ella 1931- .... **CLC 19**
See also CA 29-32R; CANR 35; DLBY 84;
SATA 65

Leger, Alexis
See Leger, (Marie-Rene Auguste) Alexis
Saint-Leger

Leger, (Marie-Rene Auguste) Alexis
Saint-Leger 1887-1975........ **CLC 11**
See also Perse, St.-John
See also CA 13-16R; 61-64; CANR 43;
MTCW

Leger, Saintleger
See Leger, (Marie-Rene Auguste) Alexis
Saint-Leger

Le Guin, Ursula K(roeber)
1929- .... **CLC 8, 13, 22, 45, 71; SSC 12**
See also AAYA 9; AITN 1; CA 21-24R;
CANR 9, 32; CDALB 1968-1988; CLR 3,
28; DLB 8, 52; JRDA; MAICYA;
MTCW; SATA 4, 52

Lehmann, Rosamond (Nina)
1901-1990 .... **CLC 5**
See also CA 77-80; 131; CANR 8; DLB 15

Leiber, Fritz (Reuter, Jr.)
1910-1992 .... **CLC 25**
See also CA 45-48; 139; CANR 2, 40;
DLB 8; MTCW; SATA 45;
SATA-Obit 73

Leimbach, Martha 1963-
See Leimbach, Marti
See also CA 130

Leimbach, Marti .... **CLC 65**
See also Leimbach, Martha

Leino, Eino .... **TCLC 24**
See also Loennbohm, Armas Eino Leopold

Leiris, Michel (Julien) 1901-1990 ... **CLC 61**
See also CA 119; 128; 132

Leithauser, Brad 1953- .... **CLC 27**
See also CA 107; CANR 27; DLB 120

Lelchuk, Alan 1938- .... **CLC 5**
See also CA 45-48; CANR 1

Lem, Stanislaw 1921- ...... **CLC 8, 15, 40**
See also CA 105; CAAS 1; CANR 32;
MTCW

Lemann, Nancy 1956- .... **CLC 39**
See also CA 118; 136

Lemonnier, (Antoine Louis) Camille
1844-1913 .... **TCLC 22**
See also CA 121

Lenau, Nikolaus 1802-1850 ..... **NCLC 16**

L'Engle, Madeleine (Camp Franklin)
1918- .... **CLC 12**
See also AAYA 1; AITN 2; CA 1-4R;
CANR 3, 21, 39; CLR 1, 14; DLB 52;
JRDA; MAICYA; MTCW; SAAS 15;
SATA 1, 27, 75

Lengyel, Jozsef 1896-1975......... **CLC 7**
See also CA 85-88; 57-60

Lennon, John (Ono)
1940-1980 .... **CLC 12, 35**
See also CA 102

Lennox, Charlotte Ramsay
1729(?)-1804 .... **NCLC 23**
See also DLB 39

Lentricchia, Frank (Jr.) 1940-...... **CLC 34**
See also CA 25-28R; CANR 19

Lenz, Siegfried 1926- .... **CLC 27**
See also CA 89-92; DLB 75

Leonard, Elmore (John, Jr.)
1925- .... **CLC 28, 34, 71**
See also AITN 1; BEST 89:1, 90:4;
CA 81-84; CANR 12, 28; MTCW

Leonard, Hugh
See Byrne, John Keyes
See also DLB 13

Leopardi, (Conte) Giacomo (Talegardo
Francesco di Sales Save
1798-1837 .... **NCLC 22**

Le Reveler
See Artaud, Antonin

Lerman, Eleanor 1952- .... **CLC 9**
See also CA 85-88

Lerman, Rhoda 1936- .... **CLC 56**
See also CA 49-52

Lermontov, Mikhail Yuryevich
1814-1841 .... **NCLC 5**

Leroux, Gaston 1868-1927........ **TCLC 25**
See also CA 108; 136; SATA 65

Lesage, Alain-Rene 1668-1747........ **LC 2**

Leskov, Nikolai (Semyonovich)
1831-1895 .... **NCLC 25**

Lessing, Doris (May)
1919- ..... **CLC 1, 2, 3, 6, 10, 15, 22, 40;**
DA; SSC 6
See also CA 9-12R; CAAS 14; CANR 33;
CDBLB 1960 to Present; DLB 15;
DLBY 85; MTCW

Lessing, Gotthold Ephraim
1729-1781 .... **LC 8**
See also DLB 97

Lester, Richard 1932-............. **CLC 20**

Lever, Charles (James)
1806-1872 .... **NCLC 23**
See also DLB 21

Leverson, Ada 1865(?)-1936(?) .... **TCLC 18**
See also Elaine
See also CA 117

Levertov, Denise
1923- .... **CLC 1, 2, 3, 5, 8, 15, 28, 66**
See also CA 1-4R; CANR 3, 29; DLB 5;
MTCW

Levi, Jonathan.................... **CLC 76**

Levi, Peter (Chad Tigar) 1931-..... **CLC 41**
See also CA 5-8R; CANR 34; DLB 40

Levi, Primo
1919-1987 .... **CLC 37, 50; SSC 12**
See also CA 13-16R; 122; CANR 12, 33;
MTCW

Levin, Ira 1929- .... **CLC 3, 6**
See also CA 21-24R; CANR 17; MTCW;
SATA 66

Levin, Meyer 1905-1981 .... **CLC 7**
See also AITN 1; CA 9-12R; 104;
CANR 15; DLB 9, 28; DLBY 81;
SATA 21, 27

Levine, Norman 1924- .... **CLC 54**
See also CA 73-76; CANR 14; DLB 88

Levine, Philip 1928-.. **CLC 2, 4, 5, 9, 14, 33**
See also CA 9-12R; CANR 9, 37; DLB 5

Levinson, Deirdre 1931-.......... **CLC 49**
See also CA 73-76

Levi-Strauss, Claude 1908- .... **CLC 38**
See also CA 1-4R; CANR 6, 32; MTCW

Levitin, Sonia (Wolff) 1934- .... **CLC 17**
See also CA 29-32R; CANR 14, 32; JRDA;
MAICYA; SAAS 2; SATA 4, 68

Levon, O. U.
See Kesey, Ken (Elton)

Lewes, George Henry
1817-1878 .... **NCLC 25**
See also DLB 55

Lewis, Alun 1915-1944............ **TCLC 3**
See also CA 104; DLB 20

Lewis, C. Day
See Day Lewis, C(ecil)

Lewis, C(live) S(taples)
1898-1963 ..... **CLC 1, 3, 6, 14, 27; DA;**
WLC
See also AAYA 3; CA 81-84; CANR 33;
CDBLB 1945-1960; CLR 3, 27; DLB 15,
100; JRDA; MAICYA; MTCW;
SATA 13

Lewis, Janet 1899-.............. **CLC 41**
See also Winters, Janet Lewis
See also CA 9-12R; CANR 29; CAP 1;
DLBY 87

Lewis, Matthew Gregory
1775-1818 .... **NCLC 11**
See also DLB 39

Author Index

Lord Jeffrey
See Jeffrey, Francis

Lorenzo, Heberto Padilla
See Padilla (Lorenzo), Heberto

Loris
See Hofmannsthal, Hugo von

Loti, Pierre . . . . **TCLC 11**
See also Viaud, (Louis Marie) Julien
See also DLB 123

Louie, David Wong 1954- . . . . **CLC 70**
See also CA 139

Louis, Father M.
See Merton, Thomas

Lovecraft, H(oward) P(hillips)
1890-1937 . . . . **TCLC 4, 22; SSC 3**
See also CA 104; 133; MTCW

Lovelace, Earl 1935- . . . . **CLC 51**
See also CA 77-80; CANR 41; DLB 125;
MTCW

Lovelace, Richard 1618-1657 . . . . **LC 24**
See also DLB 131

Lowell, Amy 1874-1925 . . . . **TCLC 1, 8**
See also CA 104; DLB 54

Lowell, James Russell 1819-1891 . . **NCLC 2**
See also CDALB 1640-1865; DLB 1, 11, 64,
79

Lowell, Robert (Traill Spence, Jr.)
1917-1977 . . . **CLC 1, 2, 3, 4, 5, 8, 9, 11,**
15, 37; DA; PC 3; WLC
See also CA 9-12R; 73-76; CABS 2;
CANR 26; DLB 5; MTCW

Lowndes, Marie Adelaide (Belloc)
1868-1947 . . . . **TCLC 12**
See also CA 107; DLB 70

Lowry, (Clarence) Malcolm
1909-1957 . . . . **TCLC 6, 40**
See also CA 105; 131; CDBLB 1945-1960;
DLB 15; MTCW

Lowry, Mina Gertrude 1882-1966
See Loy, Mina
See also CA 113

Loxsmith, John
See Brunner, John (Kilian Houston)

Loy, Mina . . . . **CLC 28**
See also Lowry, Mina Gertrude
See also DLB 4, 54

Loyson-Bridet
See Schwob, (Mayer Andre) Marcel

Lucas, Craig 1951- . . . . **CLC 64**
See also CA 137

Lucas, George 1944- . . . . **CLC 16**
See also AAYA 1; CA 77-80; CANR 30;
SATA 56

Lucas, Hans
See Godard, Jean-Luc

Lucas, Victoria
See Plath, Sylvia

Ludlam, Charles 1943-1987 . . . . . **CLC 46, 50**
See also CA 85-88; 122

Ludlum, Robert 1927- . . . . **CLC 22, 43**
See also AAYA 10; BEST 89:1, 90:3;
CA 33-36R; CANR 25, 41; DLBY 82;
MTCW

Ludwig, Ken . . . . **CLC 60**

Ludwig, Otto 1813-1865 . . . . **NCLC 4**
See also DLB 129

Lugones, Leopoldo 1874-1938 . . . . . **TCLC 15**
See also CA 116; 131; HW

Lu Hsun 1881-1936 . . . . **TCLC 3**

Lukacs, George . . . . **CLC 24**
See also Lukacs, Gyorgy (Szegeny von)

Lukacs, Gyorgy (Szegeny von) 1885-1971
See Lukacs, George
See also CA 101; 29-32R

Luke, Peter (Ambrose Cyprian)
1919- . . . . **CLC 38**
See also CA 81-84; DLB 13

Lunar, Dennis
See Mungo, Raymond

Lurie, Alison 1926- . . . . **CLC 4, 5, 18, 39**
See also CA 1-4R; CANR 2, 17; DLB 2;
MTCW; SATA 46

Lustig, Arnost 1926- . . . . **CLC 56**
See also AAYA 3; CA 69-72; SATA 56

Luther, Martin 1483-1546 . . . . **LC 9**

Luzi, Mario 1914- . . . . **CLC 13**
See also CA 61-64; CANR 9; DLB 128

Lynch, B. Suarez
See Bioy Casares, Adolfo; Borges, Jorge
Luis

Lynch, David (K.) 1946- . . . . **CLC 66**
See also CA 124; 129

Lynch, James
See Andreyev, Leonid (Nikolaevich)

Lynch Davis, B.
See Bioy Casares, Adolfo; Borges, Jorge
Luis

Lyndsay, Sir David 1490-1555 . . . . . . **LC 20**

Lynn, Kenneth S(chuyler) 1923- . . . . **CLC 50**
See also CA 1-4R; CANR 3, 27

Lynx
See West, Rebecca

Lyons, Marcus
See Blish, James (Benjamin)

Lyre, Pinchbeck
See Sassoon, Siegfried (Lorraine)

Lytle, Andrew (Nelson) 1902- . . . . . . **CLC 22**
See also CA 9-12R; DLB 6

Lyttelton, George 1709-1773 . . . . **LC 10**

Maas, Peter 1929- . . . . **CLC 29**
See also CA 93-96

Macaulay, Rose 1881-1958 . . . . . **TCLC 7, 44**
See also CA 104; DLB 36

Macaulay, Thomas Babington
1800-1859 . . . . **NCLC 42**
See also CDBLB 1832-1890; DLB 32, 55

MacBeth, George (Mann)
1932-1992 . . . . **CLC 2, 5, 9**
See also CA 25-28R; 136; DLB 40; MTCW;
SATA 4; SATA-Obit 70

MacCaig, Norman (Alexander)
1910- . . . . **CLC 36**
See also CA 9-12R; CANR 3, 34; DLB 27

MacCarthy, (Sir Charles Otto) Desmond
1877-1952 . . . . **TCLC 36**

MacDiarmid, Hugh . . . . . **CLC 2, 4, 11, 19, 63**
See also Grieve, C(hristopher) M(urray)
See also CDBLB 1945-1960; DLB 20

MacDonald, Anson
See Heinlein, Robert A(nson)

Macdonald, Cynthia 1928- . . . . . . **CLC 13, 19**
See also CA 49-52; CANR 4; DLB 105

MacDonald, George 1824-1905 . . . . . **TCLC 9**
See also CA 106; 137; DLB 18; MAICYA;
SATA 33

Macdonald, John
See Millar, Kenneth

MacDonald, John D(ann)
1916-1986 . . . . **CLC 3, 27, 44**
See also CA 1-4R; 121; CANR 1, 19;
DLB 8; DLBY 86; MTCW

Macdonald, John Ross
See Millar, Kenneth

Macdonald, Ross . . . . . **CLC 1, 2, 3, 14, 34, 41**
See also Millar, Kenneth
See also DLBD 6

MacDougal, John
See Blish, James (Benjamin)

MacEwen, Gwendolyn (Margaret)
1941-1987 . . . . **CLC 13, 55**
See also CA 9-12R; 124; CANR 7, 22;
DLB 53; SATA 50, 55

Machado (y Ruiz), Antonio
1875-1939 . . . . **TCLC 3**
See also CA 104; DLB 108

Machado de Assis, Joaquim Maria
1839-1908 . . . . **TCLC 10; BLC**
See also CA 107

Machen, Arthur . . . . **TCLC 4**
See also Jones, Arthur Llewellyn
See also DLB 36

Machiavelli, Niccolo 1469-1527 . . **LC 8; DA**

MacInnes, Colin 1914-1976 . . . . . . **CLC 4, 23**
See also CA 69-72; 65-68; CANR 21;
DLB 14; MTCW

MacInnes, Helen (Clark)
1907-1985 . . . . **CLC 27, 39**
See also CA 1-4R; 117; CANR 1, 28;
DLB 87; MTCW; SATA 22, 44

Mackay, Mary 1855-1924
See Corelli, Marie
See also CA 118

Mackenzie, Compton (Edward Montague)
1883-1972 . . . . **CLC 18**
See also CA 21-22; 37-40R; CAP 2;
DLB 34, 100

Mackenzie, Henry 1745-1831 . . . . **NCLC 41**
See also DLB 39

Mackintosh, Elizabeth 1896(?)-1952
See Tey, Josephine
See also CA 110

MacLaren, James
See Grieve, C(hristopher) M(urray)

Mac Laverty, Bernard 1942- . . . . **CLC 31**
See also CA 116; 118; CANR 43

MacLean, Alistair (Stuart)
1922-1987 . . . . **CLC 3, 13, 50, 63**
See also CA 57-60; 121; CANR 28; MTCW;
SATA 23, 50

Mariner, Scott
See Pohl, Frederik

Marinetti, Filippo Tommaso
1876-1944 . . . . **TCLC 10**
See also CA 107; DLB 114

Marivaux, Pierre Carlet de Chamblain de
1688-1763 . . . . **LC 4**

Markandaya, Kamala . . . . **CLC 8, 38**
See also Taylor, Kamala (Purnaiya)

Markfield, Wallace 1926- . . . . **CLC 8**
See also CA 69-72; CAAS 3; DLB 2, 28

Markham, Edwin 1852-1940 . . . . . **TCLC 47**
See also DLB 54

Markham, Robert
See Amis, Kingsley (William)

Marks, J
See Highwater, Jamake (Mamake)

Marks-Highwater, J
See Highwater, Jamake (Mamake)

Markson, David M(errill) 1927- . . . . **CLC 67**
See also CA 49-52; CANR 1

Marley, Bob . . . . **CLC 17**
See also Marley, Robert Nesta

Marley, Robert Nesta 1945-1981
See Marley, Bob
See also CA 107; 103

Marlowe, Christopher
1564-1593 . . . . . **LC 22; DA; DC 1; WLC**
See also CDBLB Before 1660; DLB 62

Marmontel, Jean-Francois
1723-1799 . . . . **LC 2**

Marquand, John P(hillips)
1893-1960 . . . . **CLC 2, 10**
See also CA 85-88; DLB 9, 102

Marquez, Gabriel (Jose) Garcia . . . . . . **CLC 68**
See also Garcia Marquez, Gabriel (Jose)

Marquis, Don(ald Robert Perry)
1878-1937 . . . . **TCLC 7**
See also CA 104; DLB 11, 25

Marric, J. J.
See Creasey, John

Marrow, Bernard
See Moore, Brian

Marryat, Frederick 1792-1848 . . . . **NCLC 3**
See also DLB 21

Marsden, James
See Creasey, John

Marsh, (Edith) Ngaio
1899-1982 . . . . **CLC 7, 53**
See also CA 9-12R; CANR 6; DLB 77;
MTCW

Marshall, Garry 1934- . . . . **CLC 17**
See also AAYA 3; CA 111; SATA 60

Marshall, Paule
1929- . . . . **CLC 27, 72; BLC; SSC 3**
See also BW; CA 77-80; CANR 25;
DLB 33; MTCW

Marsten, Richard
See Hunter, Evan

Martha, Henry
See Harris, Mark

Martin, Ken
See Hubbard, L(afayette) Ron(ald)

Martin, Richard
See Creasey, John

Martin, Steve 1945- . . . . **CLC 30**
See also CA 97-100; CANR 30; MTCW

Martin, Violet Florence
1862-1915 . . . . **TCLC 51**

Martin, Webber
See Silverberg, Robert

Martindale, Patrick Victor
See White, Patrick (Victor Martindale)

Martin du Gard, Roger
1881-1958 . . . . **TCLC 24**
See also CA 118; DLB 65

Martineau, Harriet 1802-1876. . . . **NCLC 26**
See also DLB 21, 55; YABC 2

Martines, Julia
See O'Faolain, Julia

Martinez, Jacinto Benavente y
See Benavente (y Martinez), Jacinto

Martinez Ruiz, Jose 1873-1967
See Azorin; Ruiz, Jose Martinez
See also CA 93-96; HW

Martinez Sierra, Gregorio
1881-1947 . . . . **TCLC 6**
See also CA 115

Martinez Sierra, Maria (de la O'LeJarraga)
1874-1974 . . . . **TCLC 6**
See also CA 115

Martinsen, Martin
See Follett, Ken(neth Martin)

Martinson, Harry (Edmund)
1904-1978 . . . . **CLC 14**
See also CA 77-80; CANR 34

Marut, Ret
See Traven, B.

Marut, Robert
See Traven, B.

Marvell, Andrew
1621-1678 . . . . **LC 4; DA; WLC**
See also CDBLB 1660-1789; DLB 131

Marx, Karl (Heinrich)
1818-1883 . . . . **NCLC 17**
See also DLB 129

Masaoka Shiki. . . . . **TCLC 18**
See also Masaoka Tsunenori

Masaoka Tsunenori 1867-1902
See Masaoka Shiki
See also CA 117

Masefield, John (Edward)
1878-1967 . . . . **CLC 11, 47**
See also CA 19-20; 25-28R; CANR 33;
CAP 2; CDBLB 1890-1914; DLB 10;
MTCW; SATA 19

Maso, Carole 19(?)- . . . . **CLC 44**

Mason, Bobbie Ann
1940- . . . . **CLC 28, 43, 82; SSC 4**
See also AAYA 5; CA 53-56; CANR 11,
31; DLBY 87; MTCW

Mason, Ernst
See Pohl, Frederik

Mason, Lee W.
See Malzberg, Barry N(athaniel)

Mason, Nick 1945- . . . . **CLC 35**
See also Pink Floyd

Mason, Tally
See Derleth, August (William)

Mass, William
See Gibson, William

Masters, Edgar Lee
1868-1950 . . . . . **TCLC 2, 25; DA; PC 1**
See also CA 104; 133; CDALB 1865-1917;
DLB 54; MTCW

Masters, Hilary 1928- . . . . **CLC 48**
See also CA 25-28R; CANR 13

Mastrosimone, William 19(?)- . . . . . **CLC 36**

Mathe, Albert
See Camus, Albert

Matheson, Richard Burton 1926- . . . **CLC 37**
See also CA 97-100; DLB 8, 44

Mathews, Harry 1930- . . . . **CLC 6, 52**
See also CA 21-24R; CAAS 6; CANR 18,
40

Mathias, Roland (Glyn) 1915- . . . . . **CLC 45**
See also CA 97-100; CANR 19, 41; DLB 27

Matsuo Basho 1644-1694. . . . . **PC 3**

Mattheson, Rodney
See Creasey, John

Matthews, Greg 1949- . . . . **CLC 45**
See also CA 135

Matthews, William 1942- . . . . **CLC 40**
See also CA 29-32R; CAAS 18; CANR 12;
DLB 5

Matthias, John (Edward) 1941- . . . . . . **CLC 9**
See also CA 33-36R

Matthiessen, Peter
1927- . . . . **CLC 5, 7, 11, 32, 64**
See also AAYA 6; BEST 90:4; CA 9-12R;
CANR 21; DLB 6; MTCW; SATA 27

Maturin, Charles Robert
1780(?)-1824 . . . . **NCLC 6**

Matute (Ausejo), Ana Maria
1925- . . . . **CLC 11**
See also CA 89-92; MTCW

Maugham, W. S.
See Maugham, W(illiam) Somerset

Maugham, W(illiam) Somerset
1874-1965 . . . . . . **CLC 1, 11, 15, 67; DA;
                              SSC 8; WLC**
See also CA 5-8R; 25-28R; CANR 40;
CDBLB 1914-1945; DLB 10, 36, 77, 100;
MTCW; SATA 54

Maugham, William Somerset
See Maugham, W(illiam) Somerset

Maupassant, (Henri Rene Albert) Guy de
1850-1893 . . . . **NCLC 1, 42; DA; SSC 1;
                              WLC**
See also DLB 123

Maurhut, Richard
See Traven, B.

Mauriac, Claude 1914- . . . . **CLC 9**
See also CA 89-92; DLB 83

Mauriac, Francois (Charles)
1885-1970 . . . . **CLC 4, 9, 56**
See also CA 25-28; CAP 2; DLB 65;
MTCW

Mavor, Osborne Henry 1888-1951
See Bridie, James
See also CA 104

Maxwell, William (Keepers, Jr.)
   1908- .... **CLC 19**
   See also CA 93-96; DLBY 80

May, Elaine 1932- .... **CLC 16**
   See also CA 124; 142; DLB 44

Mayakovski, Vladimir (Vladimirovich)
   1893-1930 .... **TCLC 4, 18**
   See also CA 104

Mayhew, Henry 1812-1887 ..... **NCLC 31**
   See also DLB 18, 55

Maynard, Joyce 1953- .... **CLC 23**
   See also CA 111; 129

Mayne, William (James Carter)
   1928- .... **CLC 12**
   See also CA 9-12R; CANR 37; CLR 25;
   JRDA; MAICYA; SAAS 11; SATA 6, 68

Mayo, Jim
   See L'Amour, Louis (Dearborn)

Maysles, Albert 1926- .... **CLC 16**
   See also CA 29-32R

Maysles, David 1932- .... **CLC 16**

Mazer, Norma Fox 1931- .... **CLC 26**
   See also AAYA 5; CA 69-72; CANR 12,
   32; CLR 23; JRDA; MAICYA; SAAS 1;
   SATA 24, 67

Mazzini, Guiseppe 1805-1872 .... **NCLC 34**

McAuley, James Phillip
   1917-1976 .... **CLC 45**
   See also CA 97-100

McBain, Ed
   See Hunter, Evan

McBrien, William Augustine
   1930- .... **CLC 44**
   See also CA 107

McCaffrey, Anne (Inez) 1926- ...... **CLC 17**
   See also AAYA 6; AITN 2; BEST 89:2;
   CA 25-28R; CANR 15, 35; DLB 8;
   JRDA; MAICYA; MTCW; SAAS 11;
   SATA 8, 70

McCann, Arthur
   See Campbell, John W(ood, Jr.)

McCann, Edson
   See Pohl, Frederik

McCarthy, Charles, Jr. 1933-
   See McCarthy, Cormac
   See also CANR 42

McCarthy, Cormac .... **CLC 4, 57**
   See also McCarthy, Charles, Jr.
   See also DLB 6

McCarthy, Mary (Therese)
   1912-1989 ... **CLC 1, 3, 5, 14, 24, 39, 59**
   See also CA 5-8R; 129; CANR 16; DLB 2;
   DLBY 81; MTCW

McCartney, (James) Paul
   1942- .... **CLC 12, 35**

McCauley, Stephen (D.) 1955- ..... **CLC 50**
   See also CA 141

McClure, Michael (Thomas)
   1932- .... **CLC 6, 10**
   See also CA 21-24R; CANR 17; DLB 16

McCorkle, Jill (Collins) 1958- ...... **CLC 51**
   See also CA 121; DLBY 87

McCourt, James 1941- .... **CLC 5**
   See also CA 57-60

McCoy, Horace (Stanley)
   1897-1955 .... **TCLC 28**
   See also CA 108; DLB 9

McCrae, John 1872-1918........ **TCLC 12**
   See also CA 109; DLB 92

McCreigh, James
   See Pohl, Frederik

McCullers, (Lula) Carson (Smith)
   1917-1967 .... **CLC 1, 4, 10, 12, 48; DA;**
                       SSC 9; WLC
   See also CA 5-8R; 25-28R; CABS 1, 3;
   CANR 18; CDALB 1941-1968; DLB 2, 7;
   MTCW; SATA 27

McCulloch, John Tyler
   See Burroughs, Edgar Rice

McCullough, Colleen 1938(?)- ...... **CLC 27**
   See also CA 81-84; CANR 17; MTCW

McElroy, Joseph 1930- .... **CLC 5, 47**
   See also CA 17-20R

McEwan, Ian (Russell) 1948- ... **CLC 13, 66**
   See also BEST 90:4; CA 61-64; CANR 14,
   41; DLB 14; MTCW

McFadden, David 1940-........... **CLC 48**
   See also CA 104; DLB 60

McFarland, Dennis 1950- .... **CLC 65**

McGahern, John 1934-........ **CLC 5, 9, 48**
   See also CA 17-20R; CANR 29; DLB 14;
   MTCW

McGinley, Patrick (Anthony)
   1937- .... **CLC 41**
   See also CA 120; 127

McGinley, Phyllis 1905-1978 ...... **CLC 14**
   See also CA 9-12R; 77-80; CANR 19;
   DLB 11, 48; SATA 2, 24, 44

McGinniss, Joe 1942-............. **CLC 32**
   See also AITN 2; BEST 89:2; CA 25-28R;
   CANR 26

McGivern, Maureen Daly
   See Daly, Maureen

McGrath, Patrick 1950-........... **CLC 55**
   See also CA 136

McGrath, Thomas (Matthew)
   1916-1990 .... **CLC 28, 59**
   See also CA 9-12R; 132; CANR 6, 33;
   MTCW; SATA 41; SATA-Obit 66

McGuane, Thomas (Francis III)
   1939-...............**CLC 3, 7, 18, 45**
   See also AITN 2; CA 49-52; CANR 5, 24;
   DLB 2; DLBY 80; MTCW

McGuckian, Medbh 1950-...... **CLC 48**
   See also CA 143; DLB 40

McHale, Tom 1942(?)-1982....... **CLC 3, 5**
   See also AITN 1; CA 77-80; 106

McIlvanney, William 1936-........ **CLC 42**
   See also CA 25-28R; DLB 14

McIlwraith, Maureen Mollie Hunter
   See Hunter, Mollie
   See also SATA 2

McInerney, Jay 1955- .... **CLC 34**
   See also CA 116; 123

McIntyre, Vonda N(eel) 1948- ..... **CLC 18**
   See also CA 81-84; CANR 17, 34; MTCW

McKay, Claude ..... **TCLC 7, 41; BLC; PC 2**
   See also McKay, Festus Claudius
   See also DLB 4, 45, 51, 117

McKay, Festus Claudius 1889-1948
   See McKay, Claude
   See also BW; CA 104; 124; DA; MTCW;
   WLC

McKuen, Rod 1933-............. **CLC 1, 3**
   See also AITN 1; CA 41-44R; CANR 40

McLoughlin, R. B.
   See Mencken, H(enry) L(ouis)

McLuhan, (Herbert) Marshall
   1911-1980 .... **CLC 37**
   See also CA 9-12R; 102; CANR 12, 34;
   DLB 88; MTCW

McMillan, Terry (L.) 1951-..... **CLC 50, 61**
   See also CA 140

McMurtry, Larry (Jeff)
   1936-........ **CLC 2, 3, 7, 11, 27, 44**
   See also AITN 2; BEST 89:2; CA 5-8R;
   CANR 19, 43; CDALB 1968-1988;
   DLB 2; DLBY 80, 87; MTCW

McNally, T. M. 1961- .... **CLC 82**

McNally, Terrence 1939-...... **CLC 4, 7, 41**
   See also CA 45-48; CANR 2; DLB 7

McNamer, Deirdre 1950-......... **CLC 70**

McNeile, Herman Cyril 1888-1937
   See Sapper
   See also DLB 77

McPhee, John (Angus) 1931- ...... **CLC 36**
   See also BEST 90:1; CA 65-68; CANR 20;
   MTCW

McPherson, James Alan
   1943- .... **CLC 19, 77**
   See also BW; CA 25-28R; CAAS 17;
   CANR 24; DLB 38; MTCW

McPherson, William (Alexander)
   1933- .... **CLC 34**
   See also CA 69-72; CANR 28

McSweeney, Kerry .... **CLC 34**

Mead, Margaret 1901-1978........ **CLC 37**
   See also AITN 1; CA 1-4R; 81-84;
   CANR 4; MTCW; SATA 20

Meaker, Marijane (Agnes) 1927-
   See Kerr, M. E.
   See also CA 107; CANR 37; JRDA;
   MAICYA; MTCW; SATA 20, 61

Medoff, Mark (Howard) 1940- ... **CLC 6, 23**
   See also AITN 1; CA 53-56; CANR 5;
   DLB 7

Meged, Aharon
   See Megged, Aharon

Meged, Aron
   See Megged, Aharon

Megged, Aharon 1920-............ **CLC 9**
   See also CA 49-52; CAAS 13; CANR 1

Mehta, Ved (Parkash) 1934-....... **CLC 37**
   See also CA 1-4R; CANR 2, 23; MTCW

Melanter
   See Blackmore, R(ichard) D(oddridge)

Melikow, Loris
   See Hofmannsthal, Hugo von

Melmoth, Sebastian
   See Wilde, Oscar (Fingal O'Flahertie Wills)

Meltzer, Milton 1915- . . . . **CLC 26**
See also AAYA 8; CA 13-16R; CANR 38;
CLR 13; DLB 61; JRDA; MAICYA;
SAAS 1; SATA 1, 50

Melville, Herman
1819-1891 . . . . **NCLC 3, 12, 29; DA;**
SSC 1; WLC
See also CDALB 1640-1865; DLB 3, 74;
SATA 59

Menander
c. 342B.C.-c. 292B.C. . . . . **CMLC 9; DC 3**

Mencken, H(enry) L(ouis)
1880-1956 . . . . **TCLC 13**
See also CA 105; 125; CDALB 1917-1929;
DLB 11, 29, 63; MTCW

Mercer, David 1928-1980 . . . . **CLC 5**
See also CA 9-12R; 102; CANR 23;
DLB 13; MTCW

Merchant, Paul
See Ellison, Harlan

Meredith, George 1828-1909 . . . **TCLC 17, 43**
See also CA 117; CDBLB 1832-1890;
DLB 18, 35, 57

Meredith, William (Morris)
1919- . . . . **CLC 4, 13, 22, 55**
See also CA 9-12R; CAAS 14; CANR 6, 40;
DLB 5

Merezhkovsky, Dmitry Sergeyevich
1865-1941 . . . . **TCLC 29**

Merimee, Prosper
1803-1870 . . . . **NCLC 6; SSC 7**
See also DLB 119

Merkin, Daphne 1954- . . . . **CLC 44**
See also CA 123

Merlin, Arthur
See Blish, James (Benjamin)

Merrill, James (Ingram)
1926- . . . . **CLC 2, 3, 6, 8, 13, 18, 34**
See also CA 13-16R; CANR 10; DLB 5;
DLBY 85; MTCW

Merriman, Alex
See Silverberg, Robert

Merritt, E. B.
See Waddington, Miriam

Merton, Thomas
1915-1968 . . . . **CLC 1, 3, 11, 34**
See also CA 5-8R; 25-28R; CANR 22;
DLB 48; DLBY 81; MTCW

Merwin, W(illiam) S(tanley)
1927- . . . . . . **CLC 1, 2, 3, 5, 8, 13, 18, 45**
See also CA 13-16R; CANR 15; DLB 5;
MTCW

Metcalf, John 1938- . . . . **CLC 37**
See also CA 113; DLB 60

Metcalf, Suzanne
See Baum, L(yman) Frank

Mew, Charlotte (Mary)
1870-1928 . . . . **TCLC 8**
See also CA 105; DLB 19, 135

Mewshaw, Michael 1943- . . . . **CLC 9**
See also CA 53-56; CANR 7; DLBY 80

Meyer, June
See Jordan, June

Meyer, Lynn
See Slavitt, David R(ytman)

Meyer-Meyrink, Gustav 1868-1932
See Meyrink, Gustav
See also CA 117

Meyers, Jeffrey 1939- . . . . **CLC 39**
See also CA 73-76; DLB 111

Meynell, Alice (Christina Gertrude Thompson)
1847-1922 . . . . **TCLC 6**
See also CA 104; DLB 19, 98

Meyrink, Gustav . . . . **TCLC 21**
See also Meyer-Meyrink, Gustav
See also DLB 81

Michaels, Leonard 1933- . . . . **CLC 6, 25**
See also CA 61-64; CANR 21; DLB 130;
MTCW

Michaux, Henri 1899-1984 . . . . . . **CLC 8, 19**
See also CA 85-88; 114

Michelangelo 1475-1564 . . . . **LC 12**

Michelet, Jules 1798-1874 . . . . **NCLC 31**

Michener, James A(lbert)
1907(?)- . . . . **CLC 1, 5, 11, 29, 60**
See also AITN 1; BEST 90:1; CA 5-8R;
CANR 21; DLB 6; MTCW

Mickiewicz, Adam 1798-1855 . . . . . **NCLC 3**

Middleton, Christopher 1926- . . . . . . **CLC 13**
See also CA 13-16R; CANR 29; DLB 40

Middleton, Stanley 1919- . . . . **CLC 7, 38**
See also CA 25-28R; CANR 21; DLB 14

Migueis, Jose Rodrigues 1901- . . . . . **CLC 10**

Mikszath, Kalman 1847-1910 . . . . . **TCLC 31**

Miles, Josephine
1911-1985 . . . . **CLC 1, 2, 14, 34, 39**
See also CA 1-4R; 116; CANR 2; DLB 48

Militant
See Sandburg, Carl (August)

Mill, John Stuart 1806-1873 . . . . . **NCLC 11**
See also CDBLB 1832-1890; DLB 55

Millar, Kenneth 1915-1983 . . . . **CLC 14**
See also Macdonald, Ross
See also CA 9-12R; 110; CANR 16; DLB 2;
DLBD 6; DLBY 83; MTCW

Millay, E. Vincent
See Millay, Edna St. Vincent

Millay, Edna St. Vincent
1892-1950 . . . . . . **TCLC 4, 49; DA; PC 6**
See also CA 104; 130; CDALB 1917-1929;
DLB 45; MTCW

Miller, Arthur
1915- . . . . **CLC 1, 2, 6, 10, 15, 26, 47, 78;**
DA; DC 1; WLC
See also AITN 1; CA 1-4R; CABS 3;
CANR 2, 30; CDALB 1941-1968; DLB 7;
MTCW

Miller, Henry (Valentine)
1891-1980 . . . . **CLC 1, 2, 4, 9, 14, 43;**
DA; WLC
See also CA 9-12R; 97-100; CANR 33;
CDALB 1929-1941; DLB 4, 9; DLBY 80;
MTCW

Miller, Jason 1939(?)- . . . . **CLC 2**
See also AITN 1; CA 73-76; DLB 7

Miller, Sue 1943- . . . . **CLC 44**
See also BEST 90:3; CA 139

Miller, Walter M(ichael, Jr.)
1923- . . . . **CLC 4, 30**
See also CA 85-88; DLB 8

Millett, Kate 1934- . . . . **CLC 67**
See also AITN 1; CA 73-76; CANR 32;
MTCW

Millhauser, Steven 1943- . . . . **CLC 21, 54**
See also CA 110; 111; DLB 2

Millin, Sarah Gertrude 1889-1968 . . **CLC 49**
See also CA 102; 93-96

Milne, A(lan) A(lexander)
1882-1956 . . . . **TCLC 6**
See also CA 104; 133; CLR 1, 26; DLB 10,
77, 100; MAICYA; MTCW; YABC 1

Milner, Ron(ald) 1938- . . . . **CLC 56; BLC**
See also AITN 1; BW; CA 73-76;
CANR 24; DLB 38; MTCW

Milosz, Czeslaw
1911- . . . **CLC 5, 11, 22, 31, 56, 82; PC 8**
See also CA 81-84; CANR 23; MTCW

Milton, John 1608-1674 . . . **LC 9; DA; WLC**
See also CDBLB 1660-1789; DLB 131

Minehaha, Cornelius
See Wedekind, (Benjamin) Frank(lin)

Miner, Valerie 1947- . . . . **CLC 40**
See also CA 97-100

Minimo, Duca
See D'Annunzio, Gabriele

Minot, Susan 1956- . . . . **CLC 44**
See also CA 134

Minus, Ed 1938- . . . . **CLC 39**

Miranda, Javier
See Bioy Casares, Adolfo

Miro (Ferrer), Gabriel (Francisco Victor)
1879-1930 . . . . **TCLC 5**
See also CA 104

Mishima, Yukio
. . . . **CLC 2, 4, 6, 9, 27; DC 1; SSC 4**
See also Hiraoka, Kimitake

Mistral, Frederic 1830-1914 . . . . . . **TCLC 51**
See also CA 122

Mistral, Gabriela . . . . **TCLC 2; HLC**
See also Godoy Alcayaga, Lucila

Mistry, Rohinton 1952- . . . . **CLC 71**
See also CA 141

Mitchell, Clyde
See Ellison, Harlan; Silverberg, Robert

Mitchell, James Leslie 1901-1935
See Gibbon, Lewis Grassic
See also CA 104; DLB 15

Mitchell, Joni 1943- . . . . **CLC 12**
See also CA 112

Mitchell, Margaret (Munnerlyn)
1900-1949 . . . . **TCLC 11**
See also CA 109; 125; DLB 9; MTCW

Mitchell, Peggy
See Mitchell, Margaret (Munnerlyn)

Mitchell, S(ilas) Weir 1829-1914 . . **TCLC 36**

Mitchell, W(illiam) O(rmond)
1914- . . . . **CLC 25**
See also CA 77-80; CANR 15, 43; DLB 88

Mitford, Mary Russell 1787-1855 . . **NCLC 4**
See also DLB 110, 116

Mitford, Nancy 1904-1973........ **CLC 44**
See also CA 9-12R

Miyamoto, Yuriko 1899-1951 ..... **TCLC 37**

Mo, Timothy (Peter) 1950(?)-...... **CLC 46**
See also CA 117; MTCW

Modarressi, Taghi (M.) 1931-...... **CLC 44**
See also CA 121; 134

Modiano, Patrick (Jean) 1945-..... **CLC 18**
See also CA 85-88; CANR 17, 40; DLB 83

Moerck, Paal
See Roelvaag, O(le) E(dvart)

Mofolo, Thomas (Mokopu)
1875(?)-1948 .... **TCLC 22; BLC**
See also CA 121

Mohr, Nicholasa 1935-...... **CLC 12; HLC**
See also AAYA 8; CA 49-52; CANR 1, 32;
CLR 22; HW; JRDA; SAAS 8; SATA 8

Mojtabai, A(nn) G(race)
1938-................. **CLC 5, 9, 15, 29**
See also CA 85-88

Moliere 1622-1673 .... **LC 10; DA; WLC**

Molin, Charles
See Mayne, William (James Carter)

Molnar, Ferenc 1878-1952........ **TCLC 20**
See also CA 109

Momaday, N(avarre) Scott
1934-................. **CLC 2, 19; DA**
See also CA 25-28R; CANR 14, 34;
MTCW; SATA 30, 48

Monette, Paul 1945-.............. **CLC 82**
See also CA 139

Monroe, Harriet 1860-1936...... **TCLC 12**
See also CA 109; DLB 54, 91

Monroe, Lyle
See Heinlein, Robert A(nson)

Montagu, Elizabeth 1917-........ **NCLC 7**
See also CA 9-12R

Montagu, Mary (Pierrepont) Wortley
1689-1762 .... **LC 9**
See also DLB 95, 101

Montagu, W. H.
See Coleridge, Samuel Taylor

Montague, John (Patrick)
1929-................... **CLC 13, 46**
See also CA 9-12R; CANR 9; DLB 40;
MTCW

Montaigne, Michel (Eyquem) de
1533-1592 .... **LC 8; DA; WLC**

Montale, Eugenio 1896-1981... **CLC 7, 9, 18**
See also CA 17-20R; 104; CANR 30;
DLB 114; MTCW

Montesquieu, Charles-Louis de Secondat
1689-1755 .... **LC 7**

Montgomery, (Robert) Bruce 1921-1978
See Crispin, Edmund
See also CA 104

Montgomery, L(ucy) M(aud)
1874-1942 .... **TCLC 51**
See also CA 108; 137; CLR 8; DLB 92;
JRDA; MAICYA; YABC 1

Montgomery, Marion H., Jr. 1925-.. **CLC 7**
See also AITN 1; CA 1-4R; CANR 3;
DLB 6

Montgomery, Max
See Davenport, Guy (Mattison, Jr.)

Montherlant, Henry (Milon) de
1896-1972 .... **CLC 8, 19**
See also CA 85-88; 37-40R; DLB 72;
MTCW

Monty Python .... **CLC 21**
See also Chapman, Graham; Cleese, John
(Marwood); Gilliam, Terry (Vance); Idle,
Eric; Jones, Terence Graham Parry; Palin,
Michael (Edward)
See also AAYA 7

Moodie, Susanna (Strickland)
1803-1885 .... **NCLC 14**
See also DLB 99

Mooney, Edward 1951-........... **CLC 25**
See also CA 130

Mooney, Ted
See Mooney, Edward

Moorcock, Michael (John)
1939-................. **CLC 5, 27, 58**
See also CA 45-48; CAAS 5; CANR 2, 17,
38; DLB 14; MTCW

Moore, Brian
1921-........ **CLC 1, 3, 5, 7, 8, 19, 32**
See also CA 1-4R; CANR 1, 25, 42; MTCW

Moore, Edward
See Muir, Edwin

Moore, George Augustus
1852-1933 .... **TCLC 7**
See also CA 104; DLB 10, 18, 57, 135

Moore, Lorrie .... **CLC 39, 45, 68**
See also Moore, Marie Lorena

Moore, Marianne (Craig)
1887-1972 .... **CLC 1, 2, 4, 8, 10, 13, 19,**
                                    47; DA; PC 4
See also CA 1-4R; 33-36R; CANR 3;
CDALB 1929-1941; DLB 45; DLBD 7;
MTCW; SATA 20

Moore, Marie Lorena 1957-
See Moore, Lorrie
See also CA 116; CANR 39

Moore, Thomas 1779-1852....... **NCLC 6**
See also DLB 96

Morand, Paul 1888-1976 .... **CLC 41**
See also CA 69-72; DLB 65

Morante, Elsa 1918-1985........ **CLC 8, 47**
See also CA 85-88; 117; CANR 35; MTCW

Moravia, Alberto....... **CLC 2, 7, 11, 27, 46**
See also Pincherle, Alberto

More, Hannah 1745-1833 .... **NCLC 27**
See also DLB 107, 109, 116

More, Henry 1614-1687............. **LC 9**
See also DLB 126

More, Sir Thomas 1478-1535 .... **LC 10**

Moreas, Jean.................... **TCLC 18**
See also Papadiamantopoulos, Johannes

Morgan, Berry 1919-.............. **CLC 6**
See also CA 49-52; DLB 6

Morgan, Claire
See Highsmith, (Mary) Patricia

Morgan, Edwin (George) 1920-..... **CLC 31**
See also CA 5-8R; CANR 3, 43; DLB 27

Morgan, (George) Frederick
1922-...................... **CLC 23**
See also CA 17-20R; CANR 21

Morgan, Harriet
See Mencken, H(enry) L(ouis)

Morgan, Jane
See Cooper, James Fenimore

Morgan, Janet 1945-.............. **CLC 39**
See also CA 65-68

Morgan, Lady 1776(?)-1859...... **NCLC 29**
See also DLB 116

Morgan, Robin 1941-.............. **CLC 2**
See also CA 69-72; CANR 29; MTCW

Morgan, Scott
See Kuttner, Henry

Morgan, Seth 1949(?)-1990 .... **CLC 65**
See also CA 132

Morgenstern, Christian
1871-1914 .... **TCLC 8**
See also CA 105

Morgenstern, S.
See Goldman, William (W.)

Moricz, Zsigmond 1879-1942 ..... **TCLC 33**

Morike, Eduard (Friedrich)
1804-1875 .... **NCLC 10**
See also DLB 133

Mori Ogai .... **TCLC 14**
See also Mori Rintaro

Mori Rintaro 1862-1922
See Mori Ogai
See also CA 110

Moritz, Karl Philipp 1756-1793 ...... **LC 2**
See also DLB 94

Morland, Peter Henry
See Faust, Frederick (Schiller)

Morren, Theophil
See Hofmannsthal, Hugo von

Morris, Bill 1952-................ **CLC 76**

Morris, Julian
See West, Morris L(anglo)

Morris, Steveland Judkins 1950(?)-
See Wonder, Stevie
See also CA 111

Morris, William 1834-1896 .... **NCLC 4**
See also CDBLB 1832-1890; DLB 18, 35, 57

Morris, Wright 1910-... **CLC 1, 3, 7, 18, 37**
See also CA 9-12R; CANR 21; DLB 2;
DLBY 81; MTCW

Morrison, Chloe Anthony Wofford
See Morrison, Toni

Morrison, James Douglas 1943-1971
See Morrison, Jim
See also CA 73-76; CANR 40

Morrison, Jim.................... **CLC 17**
See also Morrison, James Douglas

Morrison, Toni
1931-.. **CLC 4, 10, 22, 55, 81; BLC; DA**
See also AAYA 1; BW; CA 29-32R;
CANR 27, 42; CDALB 1968-1988;
DLB 6, 33; DLBY 81; MTCW; SATA 57

Morrison, Van 1945-.............. **CLC 21**
See also CA 116

Nessi, Pio Baroja y
See Baroja (y Nessi), Pio

Nestroy, Johann 1801-1862...... **NCLC 42**
See also DLB 133

Neufeld, John (Arthur) 1938- ...... **CLC 17**
See also CA 25-28R; CANR 11, 37;
MAICYA; SAAS 3; SATA 6

Neville, Emily Cheney 1919-....... **CLC 12**
See also CA 5-8R; CANR 3, 37; JRDA;
MAICYA; SAAS 2; SATA 1

Newbound, Bernard Slade 1930-
See Slade, Bernard
See also CA 81-84

Newby, P(ercy) H(oward)
1918-..................... **CLC 2, 13**
See also CA 5-8R; CANR 32; DLB 15;
MTCW

Newlove, Donald 1928- .... **CLC 6**
See also CA 29-32R; CANR 25

Newlove, John (Herbert) 1938-..... **CLC 14**
See also CA 21-24R; CANR 9, 25

Newman, Charles 1938-.......... **CLC 2, 8**
See also CA 21-24R

Newman, Edwin (Harold) 1919- .... **CLC 14**
See also AITN 1; CA 69-72; CANR 5

Newman, John Henry
1801-1890 .... **NCLC 38**
See also DLB 18, 32, 55

Newton, Suzanne 1936- .... **CLC 35**
See also CA 41-44R; CANR 14; JRDA;
SATA 5

Nexo, Martin Andersen
1869-1954 .... **TCLC 43**

Nezval, Vitezslav 1900-1958 ...... **TCLC 44**
See also CA 123

Ng, Fae Myenne 1957(?)-......... **CLC 81**

Ngema, Mbongeni 1955- .... **CLC 57**
See also CA 143

Ngugi, James T(hiong'o)........ **CLC 3, 7, 13**
See also Ngugi wa Thiong'o

Ngugi wa Thiong'o 1938-..... **CLC 36; BLC**
See also Ngugi, James T(hiong'o)
See also BW; CA 81-84; CANR 27;
DLB 125; MTCW

Nichol, B(arrie) P(hillip)
1944-1988 .... **CLC 18**
See also CA 53-56; DLB 53; SATA 66

Nichols, John (Treadwell) 1940-.... **CLC 38**
See also CA 9-12R; CAAS 2; CANR 6;
DLBY 82

Nichols, Leigh
See Koontz, Dean R(ay)

Nichols, Peter (Richard)
1927- .... **CLC 5, 36, 65**
See also CA 104; CANR 33; DLB 13;
MTCW

Nicolas, F. R. E.
See Freeling, Nicolas

Niedecker, Lorine 1903-1970.... **CLC 10, 42**
See also CA 25-28; CAP 2; DLB 48

Nietzsche, Friedrich (Wilhelm)
1844-1900 ....**TCLC 10, 18**
See also CA 107; 121; DLB 129

Nievo, Ippolito 1831-1861 .... **NCLC 22**

Nightingale, Anne Redmon 1943-
See Redmon, Anne
See also CA 103

Nik.T.O.
See Annensky, Innokenty Fyodorovich

Nin, Anais
1903-1977 ...... **CLC 1, 4, 8, 11, 14, 60;**
SSC 10
See also AITN 2; CA 13-16R; 69-72;
CANR 22; DLB 2, 4; MTCW

Nissenson, Hugh 1933-........... **CLC 4, 9**
See also CA 17-20R; CANR 27; DLB 28

Niven, Larry .... **CLC 8**
See also Niven, Laurence Van Cott
See also DLB 8

Niven, Laurence Van Cott 1938-
See Niven, Larry
See also CA 21-24R; CAAS 12; CANR 14;
MTCW

Nixon, Agnes Eckhardt 1927-...... **CLC 21**
See also CA 110

Nizan, Paul 1905-1940........... **TCLC 40**
See also DLB 72

Nkosi, Lewis 1936-.......... **CLC 45; BLC**
See also BW; CA 65-68; CANR 27

Nodier, (Jean) Charles (Emmanuel)
1780-1844 .... **NCLC 19**
See also DLB 119

Nolan, Christopher 1965-.......... **CLC 58**
See also CA 111

Norden, Charles
See Durrell, Lawrence (George)

Nordhoff, Charles (Bernard)
1887-1947 .... **TCLC 23**
See also CA 108; DLB 9; SATA 23

Norfolk, Lawrence 1963-.......... **CLC 76**

Norman, Marsha 1947- .... **CLC 28**
See also CA 105; CABS 3; CANR 41;
DLBY 84

Norris, Benjamin Franklin, Jr.
1870-1902 .... **TCLC 24**
See also Norris, Frank
See also CA 110

Norris, Frank
See Norris, Benjamin Franklin, Jr.
See also CDALB 1865-1917; DLB 12, 71

Norris, Leslie 1921-.............. **CLC 14**
See also CA 11-12; CANR 14; CAP 1;
DLB 27

North, Andrew
See Norton, Andre

North, Anthony
See Koontz, Dean R(ay)

North, Captain George
See Stevenson, Robert Louis (Balfour)

North, Milou
See Erdrich, Louise

Northrup, B. A.
See Hubbard, L(afayette) Ron(ald)

North Staffs
See Hulme, T(homas) E(rnest)

Norton, Alice Mary
See Norton, Andre
See also MAICYA; SATA 1, 43

Norton, Andre 1912- .... **CLC 12**
See also Norton, Alice Mary
See also CA 1-4R; CANR 2, 31; DLB 8, 52;
JRDA; MTCW

Norway, Nevil Shute 1899-1960
See Shute, Nevil
See also CA 102; 93-96

Norwid, Cyprian Kamil
1821-1883 .... **NCLC 17**

Nosille, Nabrah
See Ellison, Harlan

Nossack, Hans Erich 1901-1978..... **CLC 6**
See also CA 93-96; 85-88; DLB 69

Nosu, Chuji
See Ozu, Yasujiro

Nova, Craig 1945-.............. **CLC 7, 31**
See also CA 45-48; CANR 2

Novak, Joseph
See Kosinski, Jerzy (Nikodem)

Novalis 1772-1801 .... **NCLC 13**
See also DLB 90

Nowlan, Alden (Albert) 1933-1983 .. **CLC 15**
See also CA 9-12R; CANR 5; DLB 53

Noyes, Alfred 1880-1958 .... **TCLC 7**
See also CA 104; DLB 20

Nunn, Kem 19(?)-............... **CLC 34**

Nye, Robert 1939-............. **CLC 13, 42**
See also CA 33-36R; CANR 29; DLB 14;
MTCW; SATA 6

Nyro, Laura 1947-.............. **CLC 17**

Oates, Joyce Carol
1938-...... **CLC 1, 2, 3, 6, 9, 11, 15, 19,**
33, 52; DA; SSC 6; WLC
See also AITN 1; BEST 89:2; CA 5-8R;
CANR 25; CDALB 1968-1988; DLB 2, 5,
130; DLBY 81; MTCW

O'Brien, E. G.
See Clarke, Arthur C(harles)

O'Brien, Edna
1936-... **CLC 3, 5, 8, 13, 36, 65; SSC 10**
See also CA 1-4R; CANR 6, 41;
CDBLB 1960 to Present; DLB 14;
MTCW

O'Brien, Fitz-James 1828-1862... **NCLC 21**
See also DLB 74

O'Brien, Flann........ **CLC 1, 4, 5, 7, 10, 47**
See also O Nuallain, Brian

O'Brien, Richard 1942-........... **CLC 17**
See also CA 124

O'Brien, Tim 1946-.......... **CLC 7, 19, 40**
See also CA 85-88; CANR 40; DLBD 9;
DLBY 80

Obstfelder, Sigbjoern 1866-1900... **TCLC 23**
See also CA 123

O'Casey, Sean
1880-1964 .... **CLC 1, 5, 9, 11, 15**
See also CA 89-92; CDBLB 1914-1945;
DLB 10; MTCW

O'Cathasaigh, Sean
See O'Casey, Sean

Ochs, Phil 1940-1976............. **CLC 17**
See also CA 65-68

Page, Louise 1955- . . . . CLC 40
See also CA 140

Page, P(atricia) K(athleen)
1916- . . . . CLC 7, 18
See also CA 53-56; CANR 4, 22; DLB 68;
MTCW

Paget, Violet 1856-1935
See Lee, Vernon
See also CA 104

Paget-Lowe, Henry
See Lovecraft, H(oward) P(hillips)

Paglia, Camille (Anna) 1947- . . . . CLC 68
See also CA 140

Paige, Richard
See Koontz, Dean R(ay)

Pakenham, Antonia
See Fraser, Antonia (Pakenham)

Palamas, Kostes 1859-1943 . . . . TCLC 5
See also CA 105

Palazzeschi, Aldo 1885-1974 . . . . . . CLC 11
See also CA 89-92; 53-56; DLB 114

Paley, Grace 1922- . . . . CLC 4, 6, 37; SSC 8
See also CA 25-28R; CANR 13; DLB 28;
MTCW

Palin, Michael (Edward) 1943- . . . . . CLC 21
See also Monty Python
See also CA 107; CANR 35; SATA 67

Palliser, Charles 1947- . . . . CLC 65
See also CA 136

Palma, Ricardo 1833-1919 . . . . TCLC 29

Pancake, Breece Dexter 1952-1979
See Pancake, Breece D'J
See also CA 123; 109

Pancake, Breece D'J . . . . CLC 29
See also Pancake, Breece Dexter
See also DLB 130

Panko, Rudy
See Gogol, Nikolai (Vasilyevich)

Papadiamantis, Alexandros
1851-1911 . . . . TCLC 29

Papadiamantopoulos, Johannes 1856-1910
See Moreas, Jean
See also CA 117

Papini, Giovanni 1881-1956 . . . . TCLC 22
See also CA 121

Paracelsus 1493-1541 . . . . LC 14

Parasol, Peter
See Stevens, Wallace

Parfenie, Maria
See Codrescu, Andrei

Parini, Jay (Lee) 1948- . . . . CLC 54
See also CA 97-100; CAAS 16; CANR 32

Park, Jordan
See Kornbluth, C(yril) M.; Pohl, Frederik

Parker, Bert
See Ellison, Harlan

Parker, Dorothy (Rothschild)
1893-1967 . . . . CLC 15, 68; SSC 2
See also CA 19-20; 25-28R; CAP 2;
DLB 11, 45, 86; MTCW

Parker, Robert B(rown) 1932- . . . . . . CLC 27
See also BEST 89:4; CA 49-52; CANR 1,
26; MTCW

Parkes, Lucas
See Harris, John (Wyndham Parkes Lucas)
Beynon

Parkin, Frank 1940- . . . . CLC 43

Parkman, Francis, Jr.
1823-1893 . . . . NCLC 12
See also DLB 1, 30

Parks, Gordon (Alexander Buchanan)
1912- . . . . CLC 1, 16; BLC
See also AITN 2; BW; CA 41-44R;
CANR 26; DLB 33; SATA 8

Parnell, Thomas 1679-1718 . . . . LC 3
See also DLB 94

Parra, Nicanor 1914- . . . . CLC 2; HLC
See also CA 85-88; CANR 32; HW; MTCW

Parrish, Mary Frances
See Fisher, M(ary) F(rances) K(ennedy)

Parson
See Coleridge, Samuel Taylor

Parson Lot
See Kingsley, Charles

Partridge, Anthony
See Oppenheim, E(dward) Phillips

Pascoli, Giovanni 1855-1912 . . . . . . TCLC 45

Pasolini, Pier Paolo
1922-1975 . . . . CLC 20, 37
See also CA 93-96; 61-64; DLB 128;
MTCW

Pasquini
See Silone, Ignazio

Pastan, Linda (Olenik) 1932- . . . . . . CLC 27
See also CA 61-64; CANR 18, 40; DLB 5

Pasternak, Boris (Leonidovich)
1890-1960 . . . . . . CLC 7, 10, 18, 63; DA;
PC 6; WLC
See also CA 127; 116; MTCW

Patchen, Kenneth 1911-1972 . . . CLC 1, 2, 18
See also CA 1-4R; 33-36R; CANR 3, 35;
DLB 16, 48; MTCW

Pater, Walter (Horatio)
1839-1894 . . . . NCLC 7
See also CDBLB 1832-1890; DLB 57

Paterson, A(ndrew) B(arton)
1864-1941 . . . . TCLC 32

Paterson, Katherine (Womeldorf)
1932- . . . . CLC 12, 30
See also AAYA 1; CA 21-24R; CANR 28;
CLR 7; DLB 52; JRDA; MAICYA;
MTCW; SATA 13, 53

Patmore, Coventry Kersey Dighton
1823-1896 . . . . NCLC 9
See also DLB 35, 98

Paton, Alan (Stewart)
1903-1988 . . . . . . CLC 4, 10, 25, 55; DA;
WLC
See also CA 13-16; 125; CANR 22; CAP 1;
MTCW; SATA 11, 56

Paton Walsh, Gillian 1937-
See Walsh, Jill Paton
See also CANR 38; JRDA; MAICYA;
SAAS 3; SATA 4, 72

Paulding, James Kirke 1778-1860 . . NCLC 2
See also DLB 3, 59, 74

Paulin, Thomas Neilson 1949-
See Paulin, Tom
See also CA 123; 128

Paulin, Tom . . . . CLC 37
See also Paulin, Thomas Neilson
See also DLB 40

Paustovsky, Konstantin (Georgievich)
1892-1968 . . . . CLC 40
See also CA 93-96; 25-28R

Pavese, Cesare 1908-1950 . . . . TCLC 3
See also CA 104; DLB 128

Pavic, Milorad 1929- . . . . CLC 60
See also CA 136

Payne, Alan
See Jakes, John (William)

Paz, Gil
See Lugones, Leopoldo

Paz, Octavio
1914- . . . . CLC 3, 4, 6, 10, 19, 51, 65;
DA; HLC; PC 1; WLC
See also CA 73-76; CANR 32; DLBY 90;
HW; MTCW

Peacock, Molly 1947- . . . . CLC 60
See also CA 103; DLB 120

Peacock, Thomas Love
1785-1866 . . . . NCLC 22
See also DLB 96, 116

Peake, Mervyn 1911-1968 . . . . CLC 7, 54
See also CA 5-8R; 25-28R; CANR 3;
DLB 15; MTCW; SATA 23

Pearce, Philippa . . . . CLC 21
See also Christie, (Ann) Philippa
See also CLR 9; MAICYA; SATA 1, 67

Pearl, Eric
See Elman, Richard

Pearson, T(homas) R(eid) 1956- . . . . CLC 39
See also CA 120; 130

Peck, Dale 1968(?)- . . . . CLC 81

Peck, John 1941- . . . . CLC 3
See also CA 49-52; CANR 3

Peck, Richard (Wayne) 1934- . . . . . . CLC 21
See also AAYA 1; CA 85-88; CANR 19,
38; JRDA; MAICYA; SAAS 2; SATA 18,
55

Peck, Robert Newton 1928- . . . . CLC 17; DA
See also AAYA 3; CA 81-84; CANR 31;
JRDA; MAICYA; SAAS 1; SATA 21, 62

Peckinpah, (David) Sam(uel)
1925-1984 . . . . CLC 20
See also CA 109; 114

Pedersen, Knut 1859-1952
See Hamsun, Knut
See also CA 104; 119; MTCW

Peeslake, Gaffer
See Durrell, Lawrence (George)

Peguy, Charles Pierre
1873-1914 . . . . TCLC 10
See also CA 107

Pena, Ramon del Valle y
See Valle-Inclan, Ramon (Maria) del

Pendennis, Arthur Esquir
See Thackeray, William Makepeace

Penn, William 1644-1718 . . . . LC 25
See also DLB 24

Puzo, Mario 1920- .... **CLC 1, 2, 6, 36**
See also CA 65-68; CANR 4, 42; DLB 6;
MTCW

Pym, Barbara (Mary Crampton)
1913-1980 .... **CLC 13, 19, 37**
See also CA 13-14; 97-100; CANR 13, 34;
CAP 1; DLB 14; DLBY 87; MTCW

Pynchon, Thomas (Ruggles, Jr.)
1937- ..... **CLC 2, 3, 6, 9, 11, 18, 33, 62,
72; DA; SSC 14; WLC**
See also BEST 90:2; CA 17-20R; CANR 22;
DLB 2; MTCW

Q
See Quiller-Couch, Arthur Thomas

Qian Zhongshu
See Ch'ien Chung-shu

Qroll
See Dagerman, Stig (Halvard)

Quarrington, Paul (Lewis) 1953- .... **CLC 65**
See also CA 129

Quasimodo, Salvatore 1901-1968 ... **CLC 10**
See also CA 13-16; 25-28R; CAP 1;
DLB 114; MTCW

Queen, Ellery.................. **CLC 3, 11**
See also Dannay, Frederic; Davidson,
Avram; Lee, Manfred B(ennington);
Sturgeon, Theodore (Hamilton); Vance,
John Holbrook

Queen, Ellery, Jr.
See Dannay, Frederic; Lee, Manfred
B(ennington)

Queneau, Raymond
1903-1976 .... **CLC 2, 5, 10, 42**
See also CA 77-80; 69-72; CANR 32;
DLB 72; MTCW

Quevedo, Francisco de 1580-1645.... **LC 23**

Quiller-Couch, Arthur Thomas
1863-1944 .... **TCLC 53**
See also CA 118; DLB 135

Quin, Ann (Marie) 1936-1973 .... **CLC 6**
See also CA 9-12R; 45-48; DLB 14

Quinn, Martin
See Smith, Martin Cruz

Quinn, Simon
See Smith, Martin Cruz

Quiroga, Horacio (Sylvestre)
1878-1937 .... **TCLC 20; HLC**
See also CA 117; 131; HW; MTCW

Quoirez, Francoise 1935-........... **CLC 9**
See also Sagan, Francoise
See also CA 49-52; CANR 6, 39; MTCW

Raabe, Wilhelm 1831-1910 .... **TCLC 45**
See also DLB 129

Rabe, David (William) 1940-... **CLC 4, 8, 33**
See also CA 85-88; CABS 3; DLB 7

Rabelais, Francois
1483-1553 .... **LC 5; DA; WLC**

Rabinovitch, Sholem 1859-1916
See Aleichem, Sholom
See also CA 104

Radcliffe, Ann (Ward) 1764-1823 .. **NCLC 6**
See also DLB 39

Radiguet, Raymond 1903-1923 .... **TCLC 29**
See also DLB 65

Radnoti, Miklos 1909-1944 .... **TCLC 16**
See also CA 118

Rado, James 1939-.............. **CLC 17**
See also CA 105

Radvanyi, Netty 1900-1983
See Seghers, Anna
See also CA 85-88; 110

Raeburn, John (Hay) 1941-........ **CLC 34**
See also CA 57-60

Ragni, Gerome 1942-1991 .... **CLC 17**
See also CA 105; 134

Rahv, Philip...................... **CLC 24**
See also Greenberg, Ivan

Raine, Craig 1944-.............. **CLC 32**
See also CA 108; CANR 29; DLB 40

Raine, Kathleen (Jessie) 1908- ... **CLC 7, 45**
See also CA 85-88; DLB 20; MTCW

Rainis, Janis 1865-1929.......... **TCLC 29**

Rakosi, Carl...................... **CLC 47**
See also Rawley, Callman
See also CAAS 5

Raleigh, Richard
See Lovecraft, H(oward) P(hillips)

Rallentando, H. P.
See Sayers, Dorothy L(eigh)

Ramal, Walter
See de la Mare, Walter (John)

Ramon, Juan
See Jimenez (Mantecon), Juan Ramon

Ramos, Graciliano 1892-1953 ..... **TCLC 32**

Rampersad, Arnold 1941-......... **CLC 44**
See also CA 127; 133; DLB 111

Rampling, Anne
See Rice, Anne

Ramuz, Charles-Ferdinand
1878-1947 .... **TCLC 33**

Rand, Ayn
1905-1982 ...... **CLC 3, 30, 44, 79; DA;
WLC**
See also AAYA 10; CA 13-16R; 105;
CANR 27; MTCW

Randall, Dudley (Felker)
1914- .... **CLC 1; BLC**
See also BW; CA 25-28R; CANR 23;
DLB 41

Randall, Robert
See Silverberg, Robert

Ranger, Ken
See Creasey, John

Ransom, John Crowe
1888-1974 .... **CLC 2, 4, 5, 11, 24**
See also CA 5-8R; 49-52; CANR 6, 34;
DLB 45, 63; MTCW

Rao, Raja 1909- .... **CLC 25, 56**
See also CA 73-76; MTCW

Raphael, Frederic (Michael)
1931- .... **CLC 2, 14**
See also CA 1-4R; CANR 1; DLB 14

Ratcliffe, James P.
See Mencken, H(enry) L(ouis)

Rathbone, Julian 1935- .... **CLC 41**
See also CA 101; CANR 34

Rattigan, Terence (Mervyn)
1911-1977 .... **CLC 7**
See also CA 85-88; 73-76;
CDBLB 1945-1960; DLB 13; MTCW

Ratushinskaya, Irina 1954- .... **CLC 54**
See also CA 129

Raven, Simon (Arthur Noel)
1927- .... **CLC 14**
See also CA 81-84

Rawley, Callman 1903-
See Rakosi, Carl
See also CA 21-24R; CANR 12, 32

Rawlings, Marjorie Kinnan
1896-1953 .... **TCLC 4**
See also CA 104; 137; DLB 9, 22, 102;
JRDA; MAICYA; YABC 1

Ray, Satyajit 1921-1992........ **CLC 16, 76**
See also CA 114; 137

Read, Herbert Edward 1893-1968.... **CLC 4**
See also CA 85-88; 25-28R; DLB 20

Read, Piers Paul 1941- ...... **CLC 4, 10, 25**
See also CA 21-24R; CANR 38; DLB 14;
SATA 21

Reade, Charles 1814-1884 .... **NCLC 2**
See also DLB 21

Reade, Hamish
See Gray, Simon (James Holliday)

Reading, Peter 1946-............. **CLC 47**
See also CA 103; DLB 40

Reaney, James 1926-............. **CLC 13**
See also CA 41-44R; CAAS 15; CANR 42;
DLB 68; SATA 43

Rebreanu, Liviu 1885-1944 .... **TCLC 28**

Rechy, John (Francisco)
1934- .... **CLC 1, 7, 14, 18; HLC**
See also CA 5-8R; CAAS 4; CANR 6, 32;
DLB 122; DLBY 82; HW

Redcam, Tom 1870-1933 .... **TCLC 25**

Reddin, Keith..................... **CLC 67**

Redgrove, Peter (William)
1932- .... **CLC 6, 41**
See also CA 1-4R; CANR 3, 39; DLB 40

Redmon, Anne.................... **CLC 22**
See also Nightingale, Anne Redmon
See also DLBY 86

Reed, Eliot
See Ambler, Eric

Reed, Ishmael
1938-... **CLC 2, 3, 5, 6, 13, 32, 60; BLC**
See also BW; CA 21-24R; CANR 25;
DLB 2, 5, 33; DLBD 8; MTCW

Reed, John (Silas) 1887-1920 ...... **TCLC 9**
See also CA 106

Reed, Lou....................... **CLC 21**
See also Firbank, Louis

Reeve, Clara 1729-1807 .... **NCLC 19**
See also DLB 39

Reid, Christopher (John) 1949-..... **CLC 33**
See also CA 140; DLB 40

Reid, Desmond
See Moorcock, Michael (John)

Reid Banks, Lynne 1929-
See Banks, Lynne Reid
See also CA 1-4R; CANR 6, 22, 38;
CLR 24; JRDA; MAICYA; SATA 22, 75

Reilly, William K.
See Creasey, John

Reiner, Max
See Caldwell, (Janet Miriam) Taylor
(Holland)

Reis, Ricardo
See Pessoa, Fernando (Antonio Nogueira)

Remarque, Erich Maria
1898-1970 . . . . **CLC 21; DA**
See also CA 77-80; 29-32R; DLB 56;
MTCW

Remizov, A.
See Remizov, Aleksei (Mikhailovich)

Remizov, A. M.
See Remizov, Aleksei (Mikhailovich)

Remizov, Aleksei (Mikhailovich)
1877-1957 . . . . **TCLC 27**
See also CA 125; 133

Renan, Joseph Ernest
1823-1892 . . . . **NCLC 26**

Renard, Jules 1864-1910 . . . . **TCLC 17**
See also CA 117

Renault, Mary . . . . **CLC 3, 11, 17**
See also Challans, Mary
See also DLBY 83

Rendell, Ruth (Barbara) 1930- . . **CLC 28, 48**
See also Vine, Barbara
See also CA 109; CANR 32; DLB 87;
MTCW

Renoir, Jean 1894-1979 . . . . **CLC 20**
See also CA 129; 85-88

Resnais, Alain 1922- . . . . **CLC 16**

Reverdy, Pierre 1889-1960 . . . . **CLC 53**
See also CA 97-100; 89-92

Rexroth, Kenneth
1905-1982 . . . . . . **CLC 1, 2, 6, 11, 22, 49**
See also CA 5-8R; 107; CANR 14, 34;
CDALB 1941-1968; DLB 16, 48;
DLBY 82; MTCW

Reyes, Alfonso 1889-1959 . . . . **TCLC 33**
See also CA 131; HW

Reyes y Basoalto, Ricardo Eliecer Neftali
See Neruda, Pablo

Reymont, Wladyslaw (Stanislaw)
1868(?)-1925 . . . . **TCLC 5**
See also CA 104

Reynolds, Jonathan 1942- . . . . **CLC 6, 38**
See also CA 65-68; CANR 28

Reynolds, Joshua 1723-1792 . . . . **LC 15**
See also DLB 104

Reynolds, Michael Shane 1937- . . . . **CLC 44**
See also CA 65-68; CANR 9

Reznikoff, Charles 1894-1976 . . . . **CLC 9**
See also CA 33-36; 61-64; CAP 2; DLB 28,
45

Rezzori (d'Arezzo), Gregor von
1914- . . . . **CLC 25**
See also CA 122; 136

Rhine, Richard
See Silverstein, Alvin

Rhodes, Eugene Manlove
1869-1934 . . . . **TCLC 53**

R'hoone
See Balzac, Honore de

Rhys, Jean
1890(?)-1979 . . . . **CLC 2, 4, 6, 14, 19, 51**
See also CA 25-28R; 85-88; CANR 35;
CDBLB 1945-1960; DLB 36, 117; MTCW

Ribeiro, Darcy 1922- . . . . **CLC 34**
See also CA 33-36R

Ribeiro, Joao Ubaldo (Osorio Pimentel)
1941- . . . . **CLC 10, 67**
See also CA 81-84

Ribman, Ronald (Burt) 1932- . . . . **CLC 7**
See also CA 21-24R

Ricci, Nino 1959- . . . . **CLC 70**
See also CA 137

Rice, Anne 1941- . . . . **CLC 41**
See also AAYA 9; BEST 89:2; CA 65-68;
CANR 12, 36

Rice, Elmer (Leopold)
1892-1967 . . . . **CLC 7, 49**
See also CA 21-22; 25-28R; CAP 2; DLB 4,
7; MTCW

Rice, Tim 1944- . . . . **CLC 21**
See also CA 103

Rich, Adrienne (Cecile)
1929- . . . . **CLC 3, 6, 7, 11, 18, 36, 73, 76;
PC 5**
See also CA 9-12R; CANR 20; DLB 5, 67;
MTCW

Rich, Barbara
See Graves, Robert (von Ranke)

Rich, Robert
See Trumbo, Dalton

Richards, David Adams 1950- . . . . . . **CLC 59**
See also CA 93-96; DLB 53

Richards, I(vor) A(rmstrong)
1893-1979 . . . . **CLC 14, 24**
See also CA 41-44R; 89-92; CANR 34;
DLB 27

Richardson, Anne
See Roiphe, Anne Richardson

Richardson, Dorothy Miller
1873-1957 . . . . **TCLC 3**
See also CA 104; DLB 36

Richardson, Ethel Florence (Lindesay)
1870-1946
See Richardson, Henry Handel
See also CA 105

Richardson, Henry Handel . . . . **TCLC 4**
See also Richardson, Ethel Florence
(Lindesay)

Richardson, Samuel
1689-1761 . . . . **LC 1; DA; WLC**
See also CDBLB 1660-1789; DLB 39

Richler, Mordecai
1931- . . . . **CLC 3, 5, 9, 13, 18, 46, 70**
See also AITN 1; CA 65-68; CANR 31;
CLR 17; DLB 53; MAICYA; MTCW;
SATA 27, 44

Richter, Conrad (Michael)
1890-1968 . . . . **CLC 30**
See also CA 5-8R; 25-28R; CANR 23;
DLB 9; MTCW; SATA 3

Riddell, J. H. 1832-1906 . . . . **TCLC 40**

Riding, Laura . . . . **CLC 3, 7**
See also Jackson, Laura (Riding)

Riefenstahl, Berta Helene Amalia 1902-
See Riefenstahl, Leni
See also CA 108

Riefenstahl, Leni . . . . **CLC 16**
See also Riefenstahl, Berta Helene Amalia

Riffe, Ernest
See Bergman, (Ernst) Ingmar

Riley, James Whitcomb
1849-1916 . . . . **TCLC 51**
See also CA 118; 137; MAICYA; SATA 17

Riley, Tex
See Creasey, John

Rilke, Rainer Maria
1875-1926 . . . . **TCLC 1, 6, 19; PC 2**
See also CA 104; 132; DLB 81; MTCW

Rimbaud, (Jean Nicolas) Arthur
1854-1891 . . . . . **NCLC 4, 35; DA; PC 3;
WLC**

Rinehart, Mary Roberts
1876-1958 . . . . **TCLC 52**
See also CA 108

Ringmaster, The
See Mencken, H(enry) L(ouis)

Ringwood, Gwen(dolyn Margaret) Pharis
1910-1984 . . . . **CLC 48**
See also CA 112; DLB 88

Rio, Michel 19(?)- . . . . **CLC 43**

Ritsos, Giannes
See Ritsos, Yannis

Ritsos, Yannis 1909-1990 . . . . . **CLC 6, 13, 31**
See also CA 77-80; 133; CANR 39; MTCW

Ritter, Erika 1948(?)- . . . . **CLC 52**

Rivera, Jose Eustasio 1889-1928 . . . **TCLC 35**
See also HW

Rivers, Conrad Kent 1933-1968 . . . . . . **CLC 1**
See also BW; CA 85-88; DLB 41

Rivers, Elfrida
See Bradley, Marion Zimmer

Riverside, John
See Heinlein, Robert A(nson)

Rizal, Jose 1861-1896 . . . . **NCLC 27**

Roa Bastos, Augusto (Antonio)
1917- . . . . **CLC 45; HLC**
See also CA 131; DLB 113; HW

Robbe-Grillet, Alain
1922- . . . . . . **CLC 1, 2, 4, 6, 8, 10, 14, 43**
See also CA 9-12R; CANR 33; DLB 83;
MTCW

Robbins, Harold 1916- . . . . **CLC 5**
See also CA 73-76; CANR 26; MTCW

Robbins, Thomas Eugene 1936-
See Robbins, Tom
See also CA 81-84; CANR 29; MTCW

Robbins, Tom . . . . **CLC 9, 32, 64**
See also Robbins, Thomas Eugene
See also BEST 90:3; DLBY 80

Robbins, Trina 1938- . . . . **CLC 21**
See also CA 128

Roberts, Charles G(eorge) D(ouglas)
1860-1943 . . . . **TCLC 8**
See also CA 105; CLR 33; DLB 92;
SATA 29

Roberts, Kate   1891-1985 . . . . **CLC 15**
See also CA 107; 116

Roberts, Keith (John Kingston)
1935- . . . . **CLC 14**
See also CA 25-28R

Roberts, Kenneth (Lewis)
1885-1957 . . . . **TCLC 23**
See also CA 109; DLB 9

Roberts, Michele (B.)   1949- . . . . **CLC 48**
See also CA 115

Robertson, Ellis
See Ellison, Harlan; Silverberg, Robert

Robertson, Thomas William
1829-1871 . . . . **NCLC 35**

Robinson, Edwin Arlington
1869-1935 . . . . **TCLC 5; DA; PC 1**
See also CA 104; 133; CDALB 1865-1917;
DLB 54; MTCW

Robinson, Henry Crabb
1775-1867 . . . . **NCLC 15**
See also DLB 107

Robinson, Jill   1936- . . . . **CLC 10**
See also CA 102

Robinson, Kim Stanley   1952- . . . . . . **CLC 34**
See also CA 126

Robinson, Lloyd
See Silverberg, Robert

Robinson, Marilynne   1944- . . . . **CLC 25**
See also CA 116

Robinson, Smokey . . . . **CLC 21**
See also Robinson, William, Jr.

Robinson, William, Jr.   1940-
See Robinson, Smokey
See also CA 116

Robison, Mary   1949- . . . . **CLC 42**
See also CA 113; 116; DLB 130

Rod, Edouard   1857-1910 . . . . **TCLC 52**

Roddenberry, Eugene Wesley   1921-1991
See Roddenberry, Gene
See also CA 110; 135; CANR 37; SATA 45

Roddenberry, Gene . . . . **CLC 17**
See also Roddenberry, Eugene Wesley
See also AAYA 5; SATA-Obit 69

Rodgers, Mary   1931- . . . . **CLC 12**
See also CA 49-52; CANR 8; CLR 20;
JRDA; MAICYA; SATA 8

Rodgers, W(illiam) R(obert)
1909-1969 . . . . **CLC 7**
See also CA 85-88; DLB 20

Rodman, Eric
See Silverberg, Robert

Rodman, Howard   1920(?)-1985 . . . . . **CLC 65**
See also CA 118

Rodman, Maia
See Wojciechowska, Maia (Teresa)

Rodriguez, Claudio   1934- . . . . **CLC 10**
See also DLB 134

Roelvaag, O(le) E(dvart)
1876-1931 . . . . **TCLC 17**
See also CA 117; DLB 9

Roethke, Theodore (Huebner)
1908-1963 . . . . . . **CLC 1, 3, 8, 11, 19, 46**
See also CA 81-84; CABS 2;
CDALB 1941-1968; DLB 5; MTCW

Rogers, Thomas Hunton   1927- . . . . . **CLC 57**
See also CA 89-92

Rogers, Will(iam Penn Adair)
1879-1935 . . . . **TCLC 8**
See also CA 105; DLB 11

Rogin, Gilbert   1929- . . . . **CLC 18**
See also CA 65-68; CANR 15

Rohan, Koda . . . . **TCLC 22**
See also Koda Shigeyuki

Rohmer, Eric . . . . **CLC 16**
See also Scherer, Jean-Marie Maurice

Rohmer, Sax . . . . **TCLC 28**
See also Ward, Arthur Henry Sarsfield
See also DLB 70

Roiphe, Anne Richardson   1935- . . . **CLC 3, 9**
See also CA 89-92; DLBY 80

Rojas, Fernando de   1465-1541 . . . . . . **LC 23**

Rolfe, Frederick (William Serafino Austin
Lewis Mary)   1860-1913 . . . . . **TCLC 12**
See also CA 107; DLB 34

Rolland, Romain   1866-1944 . . . . . . **TCLC 23**
See also CA 118; DLB 65

Rolvaag, O(le) E(dvart)
See Roelvaag, O(le) E(dvart)

Romain Arnaud, Saint
See Aragon, Louis

Romains, Jules   1885-1972 . . . . **CLC 7**
See also CA 85-88; CANR 34; DLB 65;
MTCW

Romero, Jose Ruben   1890-1952 . . . **TCLC 14**
See also CA 114; 131; HW

Ronsard, Pierre de   1524-1585 . . . . **LC 6**

Rooke, Leon   1934- . . . . **CLC 25, 34**
See also CA 25-28R; CANR 23

Roper, William   1498-1578 . . . . **LC 10**

Roquelaure, A. N.
See Rice, Anne

Rosa, Joao Guimaraes   1908-1967 . . . **CLC 23**
See also CA 89-92; DLB 113

Rosen, Richard (Dean)   1949- . . . . **CLC 39**
See also CA 77-80

Rosenberg, Isaac   1890-1918 . . . . . . **TCLC 12**
See also CA 107; DLB 20

Rosenblatt, Joe . . . . **CLC 15**
See also Rosenblatt, Joseph

Rosenblatt, Joseph   1933-
See Rosenblatt, Joe
See also CA 89-92

Rosenfeld, Samuel   1896-1963
See Tzara, Tristan
See also CA 89-92

Rosenthal, M(acha) L(ouis)   1917- . . . **CLC 28**
See also CA 1-4R; CAAS 6; CANR 4;
DLB 5; SATA 59

Ross, Barnaby
See Dannay, Frederic

Ross, Bernard L.
See Follett, Ken(neth Martin)

Ross, J. H.
See Lawrence, T(homas) E(dward)

Ross, Martin
See Martin, Violet Florence
See also DLB 135

Ross, (James) Sinclair   1908- . . . . **CLC 13**
See also CA 73-76; DLB 88

Rossetti, Christina (Georgina)
1830-1894 . . . **NCLC 2; DA; PC 7; WLC**
See also DLB 35; MAICYA; SATA 20

Rossetti, Dante Gabriel
1828-1882 . . . . **NCLC 4; DA; WLC**
See also CDBLB 1832-1890; DLB 35

Rossner, Judith (Perelman)
1935- . . . . **CLC 6, 9, 29**
See also AITN 2; BEST 90:3; CA 17-20R;
CANR 18; DLB 6; MTCW

Rostand, Edmond (Eugene Alexis)
1868-1918 . . . . **TCLC 6, 37; DA**
See also CA 104; 126; MTCW

Roth, Henry   1906- . . . . **CLC 2, 6, 11**
See also CA 11-12; CANR 38; CAP 1;
DLB 28; MTCW

Roth, Joseph   1894-1939 . . . . **TCLC 33**
See also DLB 85

Roth, Philip (Milton)
1933- . . . . . . **CLC 1, 2, 3, 4, 6, 9, 15, 22,**
31, 47, 66; DA; WLC
See also BEST 90:3; CA 1-4R; CANR 1, 22,
36; CDALB 1968-1988; DLB 2, 28;
DLBY 82; MTCW

Rothenberg, Jerome   1931- . . . . **CLC 6, 57**
See also CA 45-48; CANR 1; DLB 5

Roumain, Jacques (Jean Baptiste)
1907-1944 . . . . **TCLC 19; BLC**
See also BW; CA 117; 125

Rourke, Constance (Mayfield)
1885-1941 . . . . **TCLC 12**
See also CA 107; YABC 1

Rousseau, Jean-Baptiste   1671-1741 . . . **LC 9**

Rousseau, Jean-Jacques
1712-1778 . . . . **LC 14; DA; WLC**

Roussel, Raymond   1877-1933 . . . . . **TCLC 20**
See also CA 117

Rovit, Earl (Herbert)   1927- . . . . **CLC 7**
See also CA 5-8R; CANR 12

Rowe, Nicholas   1674-1718 . . . . **LC 8**
See also DLB 84

Rowley, Ames Dorrance
See Lovecraft, H(oward) P(hillips)

Rowson, Susanna Haswell
1762(?)-1824 . . . . **NCLC 5**
See also DLB 37

Roy, Gabrielle   1909-1983 . . . . **CLC 10, 14**
See also CA 53-56; 110; CANR 5; DLB 68;
MTCW

Rozewicz, Tadeusz   1921- . . . . **CLC 9, 23**
See also CA 108; CANR 36; MTCW

Ruark, Gibbons   1941- . . . . **CLC 3**
See also CA 33-36R; CANR 14, 31;
DLB 120

Rubens, Bernice (Ruth)   1923- . . . **CLC 19, 31**
See also CA 25-28R; CANR 33; DLB 14;
MTCW

Rudkin, (James) David 1936- ...... **CLC 14**
See also CA 89-92; DLB 13

Rudnik, Raphael 1933- .... **CLC 7**
See also CA 29-32R

Ruffian, M.
See Hasek, Jaroslav (Matej Frantisek)

Ruiz, Jose Martinez .... **CLC 11**
See also Martinez Ruiz, Jose

Rukeyser, Muriel
1913-1980 .... **CLC 6, 10, 15, 27**
See also CA 5-8R; 93-96; CANR 26;
DLB 48; MTCW; SATA 22

Rule, Jane (Vance) 1931- .... **CLC 27**
See also CA 25-28R; CAAS 18; CANR 12;
DLB 60

Rulfo, Juan 1918-1986 .... **CLC 8, 80; HLC**
See also CA 85-88; 118; CANR 26;
DLB 113; HW; MTCW

Runeberg, Johan 1804-1877 ...... **NCLC 41**

Runyon, (Alfred) Damon
1884(?)-1946 .... **TCLC 10**
See also CA 107; DLB 11, 86

Rush, Norman 1933- .... **CLC 44**
See also CA 121; 126

Rushdie, (Ahmed) Salman
1947- .... **CLC 23, 31, 55**
See also BEST 89:3; CA 108; 111;
CANR 33; MTCW

Rushforth, Peter (Scott) 1945- ..... **CLC 19**
See also CA 101

Ruskin, John 1819-1900 .... **TCLC 20**
See also CA 114; 129; CDBLB 1832-1890;
DLB 55; SATA 24

Russ, Joanna 1937- .... **CLC 15**
See also CA 25-28R; CANR 11, 31; DLB 8;
MTCW

Russell, George William 1867-1935
See A. E.
See also CA 104; CDBLB 1890-1914

Russell, (Henry) Ken(neth Alfred)
1927- .... **CLC 16**
See also CA 105

Russell, Willy 1947- .... **CLC 60**

Rutherford, Mark .... **TCLC 25**
See also White, William Hale
See also DLB 18

Ruyslinck, Ward
See Belser, Reimond Karel Maria de

Ryan, Cornelius (John) 1920-1974 ... **CLC 7**
See also CA 69-72; 53-56; CANR 38

Ryan, Michael 1946- .... **CLC 65**
See also CA 49-52; DLBY 82

Rybakov, Anatoli (Naumovich)
1911- .... **CLC 23, 53**
See also CA 126; 135

Ryder, Jonathan
See Ludlum, Robert

Ryga, George 1932-1987 .... **CLC 14**
See also CA 101; 124; CANR 43; DLB 60

S. S.
See Sassoon, Siegfried (Lorraine)

Saba, Umberto 1883-1957 .... **TCLC 33**
See also DLB 114

Sabatini, Rafael 1875-1950 .... **TCLC 47**

Sabato, Ernesto (R.)
1911- .... **CLC 10, 23; HLC**
See also CA 97-100; CANR 32; HW;
MTCW

Sacastru, Martin
See Bioy Casares, Adolfo

Sacher-Masoch, Leopold von
1836(?)-1895 .... **NCLC 31**

Sachs, Marilyn (Stickle) 1927- ..... **CLC 35**
See also AAYA 2; CA 17-20R; CANR 13;
CLR 2; JRDA; MAICYA; SAAS 2;
SATA 3, 68

Sachs, Nelly 1891-1970 .... **CLC 14**
See also CA 17-18; 25-28R; CAP 2

Sackler, Howard (Oliver)
1929-1982 .... **CLC 14**
See also CA 61-64; 108; CANR 30; DLB 7

Sacks, Oliver (Wolf) 1933- .... **CLC 67**
See also CA 53-56; CANR 28; MTCW

Sade, Donatien Alphonse Francois Comte
1740-1814 .... **NCLC 3**

Sadoff, Ira 1945- .... **CLC 9**
See also CA 53-56; CANR 5, 21; DLB 120

Saetone
See Camus, Albert

Safire, William 1929- .... **CLC 10**
See also CA 17-20R; CANR 31

Sagan, Carl (Edward) 1934- .... **CLC 30**
See also AAYA 2; CA 25-28R; CANR 11,
36; MTCW; SATA 58

Sagan, Francoise .... **CLC 3, 6, 9, 17, 36**
See also Quoirez, Francoise
See also DLB 83

Sahgal, Nayantara (Pandit) 1927- ... **CLC 41**
See also CA 9-12R; CANR 11

Saint, H(arry) F. 1941- .... **CLC 50**
See also CA 127

St. Aubin de Teran, Lisa 1953-
See Teran, Lisa St. Aubin de
See also CA 118; 126

Sainte-Beuve, Charles Augustin
1804-1869 .... **NCLC 5**

**Saint-Exupery, Antoine (Jean Baptiste Marie
Roger) de** 1900-1944 ... **TCLC 2; WLC**
See also CA 108; 132; CLR 10; DLB 72;
MAICYA; MTCW; SATA 20

St. John, David
See Hunt, E(verette) Howard, Jr.

Saint-John Perse
See Leger, (Marie-Rene Auguste) Alexis
Saint-Leger

Saintsbury, George (Edward Bateman)
1845-1933 .... **TCLC 31**
See also DLB 57

Sait Faik .... **TCLC 23**
See also Abasiyanik, Sait Faik

Saki .... **TCLC 3; SSC 12**
See also Munro, H(ector) H(ugh)

Salama, Hannu 1936- .... **CLC 18**

Salamanca, J(ack) R(ichard)
1922- .... **CLC 4, 15**
See also CA 25-28R

Sale, J. Kirkpatrick
See Sale, Kirkpatrick

Sale, Kirkpatrick 1937- .... **CLC 68**
See also CA 13-16R; CANR 10

Salinas (y Serrano), Pedro
1891(?)-1951 .... **TCLC 17**
See also CA 117; DLB 134

Salinger, J(erome) D(avid)
1919- ...... **CLC 1, 3, 8, 12, 55, 56; DA;
SSC 2; WLC**
See also AAYA 2; CA 5-8R; CANR 39;
CDALB 1941-1968; CLR 18; DLB 2, 102;
MAICYA; MTCW; SATA 67

Salisbury, John
See Caute, David

Salter, James 1925- .... **CLC 7, 52, 59**
See also CA 73-76; DLB 130

Saltus, Edgar (Everton)
1855-1921 .... **TCLC 8**
See also CA 105

Saltykov, Mikhail Evgrafovich
1826-1889 .... **NCLC 16**

Samarakis, Antonis 1919- .... **CLC 5**
See also CA 25-28R; CAAS 16; CANR 36

Sanchez, Florencio 1875-1910 ..... **TCLC 37**
See also HW

Sanchez, Luis Rafael 1936- .... **CLC 23**
See also CA 128; HW

Sanchez, Sonia 1934- .... **CLC 5; BLC**
See also BW; CA 33-36R; CANR 24;
CLR 18; DLB 41; DLBD 8; MAICYA;
MTCW; SATA 22

Sand, George
1804-1876 ...... **NCLC 2, 42; DA; WLC**
See also DLB 119

Sandburg, Carl (August)
1878-1967 .... **CLC 1, 4, 10, 15, 35; DA;
PC 2; WLC**
See also CA 5-8R; 25-28R; CANR 35;
CDALB 1865-1917; DLB 17, 54;
MAICYA; MTCW; SATA 8

Sandburg, Charles
See Sandburg, Carl (August)

Sandburg, Charles A.
See Sandburg, Carl (August)

Sanders, (James) Ed(ward) 1939- ... **CLC 53**
See also CA 13-16R; CANR 13; DLB 16

Sanders, Lawrence 1920- .... **CLC 41**
See also BEST 89:4; CA 81-84; CANR 33;
MTCW

Sanders, Noah
See Blount, Roy (Alton), Jr.

Sanders, Winston P.
See Anderson, Poul (William)

Sandoz, Mari(e Susette)
1896-1966 .... **CLC 28**
See also CA 1-4R; 25-28R; CANR 17;
DLB 9; MTCW; SATA 5

Saner, Reg(inald Anthony) 1931- .... **CLC 9**
See also CA 65-68

Sannazaro, Jacopo 1456(?)-1530 ...... **LC 8**

Sansom, William 1912-1976 .... **CLC 2, 6**
See also CA 5-8R; 65-68; CANR 42;
MTCW

Santayana, George 1863-1952 ..... **TCLC 40**
See also CA 115; DLB 54, 71

Scrum, R.
See Crumb, R(obert)

Scudery, Madeleine de 1607-1701..... **LC 2**

Scum
See Crumb, R(obert)

Scumbag, Little Bobby
See Crumb, R(obert)

Seabrook, John
See Hubbard, L(afayette) Ron(ald)

Sealy, I. Allan 1951- .... **CLC 55**

Search, Alexander
See Pessoa, Fernando (Antonio Nogueira)

Sebastian, Lee
See Silverberg, Robert

Sebastian Owl
See Thompson, Hunter S(tockton)

Sebestyen, Ouida 1924- .... **CLC 30**
See also AAYA 8; CA 107; CANR 40;
CLR 17; JRDA; MAICYA; SAAS 10;
SATA 39

Secundus, H. Scriblerus
See Fielding, Henry

Sedges, John
See Buck, Pearl S(ydenstricker)

Sedgwick, Catharine Maria
1789-1867 .... **NCLC 19**
See also DLB 1, 74

Seelye, John 1931- .... **CLC 7**

Seferiades, Giorgos Stylianou 1900-1971
See Seferis, George
See also CA 5-8R; 33-36R; CANR 5, 36;
MTCW

Seferis, George .... **CLC 5, 11**
See also Seferiades, Giorgos Stylianou

Segal, Erich (Wolf) 1937- .... **CLC 3, 10**
See also BEST 89:1; CA 25-28R; CANR 20,
36; DLBY 86; MTCW

Seger, Bob 1945-................ **CLC 35**

Seghers, Anna .... **CLC 7**
See also Radvanyi, Netty
See also DLB 69

Seidel, Frederick (Lewis) 1936-..... **CLC 18**
See also CA 13-16R; CANR 8; DLBY 84

Seifert, Jaroslav 1901-1986..... **CLC 34, 44**
See also CA 127; MTCW

Sei Shonagon c. 966-1017(?) ...... **CMLC 6**

Selby, Hubert, Jr. 1928- ..... **CLC 1, 2, 4, 8**
See also CA 13-16R; CANR 33; DLB 2

Selzer, Richard 1928-............. **CLC 74**
See also CA 65-68; CANR 14

Sembene, Ousmane
See Ousmane, Sembene

Senancour, Etienne Pivert de
1770-1846 .... **NCLC 16**
See also DLB 119

Sender, Ramon (Jose)
1902-1982 .... **CLC 8; HLC**
See also CA 5-8R; 105; CANR 8; HW;
MTCW

Seneca, Lucius Annaeus
4B.C.-65.................. **CMLC 6**

Senghor, Leopold Sedar
1906- .... **CLC 54; BLC**
See also BW; CA 116; 125; MTCW

Serling, (Edward) Rod(man)
1924-1975 .... **CLC 30**
See also AITN 1; CA 65-68; 57-60; DLB 26

Serna, Ramon Gomez de la
See Gomez de la Serna, Ramon

Serpieres
See Guillevic, (Eugene)

Service, Robert
See Service, Robert W(illiam)
See also DLB 92

Service, Robert W(illiam)
1874(?)-1958 ...... **TCLC 15; DA; WLC**
See also Service, Robert
See also CA 115; 140; SATA 20

Seth, Vikram 1952-.............. **CLC 43**
See also CA 121; 127; DLB 120

Seton, Cynthia Propper
1926-1982 .... **CLC 27**
See also CA 5-8R; 108; CANR 7

Seton, Ernest (Evan) Thompson
1860-1946 .... **TCLC 31**
See also CA 109; DLB 92; JRDA; SATA 18

Seton-Thompson, Ernest
See Seton, Ernest (Evan) Thompson

Settle, Mary Lee 1918- .... **CLC 19, 61**
See also CA 89-92; CAAS 1; DLB 6

Seuphor, Michel
See Arp, Jean

**Sevigne, Marie (de Rabutin-Chantal) Marquise
de** 1626-1696 .... **LC 11**

Sexton, Anne (Harvey)
1928-1974 .... **CLC 2, 4, 6, 8, 10, 15, 53;
DA; PC 2; WLC**
See also CA 1-4R; 53-56; CABS 2;
CANR 3, 36; CDALB 1941-1968; DLB 5;
MTCW; SATA 10

Shaara, Michael (Joseph Jr.)
1929-1988 .... **CLC 15**
See also AITN 1; CA 102; DLBY 83

Shackleton, C. C.
See Aldiss, Brian W(ilson)

Shacochis, Bob .... **CLC 39**
See also Shacochis, Robert G.

Shacochis, Robert G. 1951-
See Shacochis, Bob
See also CA 119; 124

Shaffer, Anthony (Joshua) 1926-.... **CLC 19**
See also CA 110; 116; DLB 13

Shaffer, Peter (Levin)
1926- .... **CLC 5, 14, 18, 37, 60**
See also CA 25-28R; CANR 25;
CDBLB 1960 to Present; DLB 13;
MTCW

Shakey, Bernard
See Young, Neil

Shalamov, Varlam (Tikhonovich)
1907(?)-1982 .... **CLC 18**
See also CA 129; 105

Shamlu, Ahmad 1925- .... **CLC 10**

Shammas, Anton 1951-............ **CLC 55**

Shange, Ntozake
1948- .... **CLC 8, 25, 38, 74; BLC; DC 3**
See also AAYA 9; BW; CA 85-88; CABS 3;
CANR 27; DLB 38; MTCW

Shanley, John Patrick 1950-....... **CLC 75**
See also CA 128; 133

Shapcott, Thomas William 1935- ... **CLC 38**
See also CA 69-72

Shapiro, Jane.................... **CLC 76**

Shapiro, Karl (Jay) 1913- .. **CLC 4, 8, 15, 53**
See also CA 1-4R; CAAS 6; CANR 1, 36;
DLB 48; MTCW

Sharp, William 1855-1905 .... **TCLC 39**

Sharpe, Thomas Ridley 1928-
See Sharpe, Tom
See also CA 114; 122

Sharpe, Tom.................... **CLC 36**
See also Sharpe, Thomas Ridley
See also DLB 14

Shaw, Bernard................... **TCLC 45**
See also Shaw, George Bernard

Shaw, G. Bernard
See Shaw, George Bernard

Shaw, George Bernard
1856-1950 .... **TCLC 3, 9, 21; DA; WLC**
See also Shaw, Bernard
See also CA 104; 128; CDBLB 1914-1945;
DLB 10, 57; MTCW

Shaw, Henry Wheeler
1818-1885 .... **NCLC 15**
See also DLB 11

Shaw, Irwin 1913-1984....... **CLC 7, 23, 34**
See also AITN 1; CA 13-16R; 112;
CANR 21; CDALB 1941-1968; DLB 6,
102; DLBY 84; MTCW

Shaw, Robert 1927-1978 .... **CLC 5**
See also AITN 1; CA 1-4R; 81-84;
CANR 4; DLB 13, 14

Shaw, T. E.
See Lawrence, T(homas) E(dward)

Shawn, Wallace 1943- .... **CLC 41**
See also CA 112

Sheed, Wilfrid (John Joseph)
1930- .... **CLC 2, 4, 10, 53**
See also CA 65-68; CANR 30; DLB 6;
MTCW

Sheldon, Alice Hastings Bradley
1915(?)-1987
See Tiptree, James, Jr.
See also CA 108; 122; CANR 34; MTCW

Sheldon, John
See Bloch, Robert (Albert)

Shelley, Mary Wollstonecraft (Godwin)
1797-1851 .... **NCLC 14; DA; WLC**
See also CDBLB 1789-1832; DLB 110, 116;
SATA 29

Shelley, Percy Bysshe
1792-1822 .... **NCLC 18; DA; WLC**
See also CDBLB 1789-1832; DLB 96, 110

Shepard, Jim 1956-.............. **CLC 36**
See also CA 137

Shepard, Lucius 1947- .... **CLC 34**
See also CA 128; 141

Sinyavsky, Andrei (Donatevich)
1925- .... **CLC 8**
See also CA 85-88

Sirin, V.
See Nabokov, Vladimir (Vladimirovich)

Sissman, L(ouis) E(dward)
1928-1976 .... **CLC 9, 18**
See also CA 21-24R; 65-68; CANR 13;
DLB 5

Sisson, C(harles) H(ubert) 1914- ..... **CLC 8**
See also CA 1-4R; CAAS 3; CANR 3;
DLB 27

Sitwell, Dame Edith
1887-1964 .... **CLC 2, 9, 67; PC 3**
See also CA 9-12R; CANR 35;
CDBLB 1945-1960; DLB 20; MTCW

Sjoewall, Maj 1935- .... **CLC 7**
See also CA 65-68

Sjowall, Maj
See Sjoewall, Maj

Skelton, Robin 1925- .... **CLC 13**
See also AITN 2; CA 5-8R; CAAS 5;
CANR 28; DLB 27, 53

Skolimowski, Jerzy 1938- .... **CLC 20**
See also CA 128

Skram, Amalie (Bertha)
1847-1905 .... **TCLC 25**

Skvorecky, Josef (Vaclav)
1924- .... **CLC 15, 39, 69**
See also CA 61-64; CAAS 1; CANR 10, 34;
MTCW

Slade, Bernard .... **CLC 11, 46**
See also Newbound, Bernard Slade
See also CAAS 9; DLB 53

Slaughter, Carolyn 1946- .... **CLC 56**
See also CA 85-88

Slaughter, Frank G(ill) 1908- ...... **CLC 29**
See also AITN 2; CA 5-8R; CANR 5

Slavitt, David R(ytman) 1935- .... **CLC 5, 14**
See also CA 21-24R; CAAS 3; CANR 41;
DLB 5, 6

Slesinger, Tess 1905-1945 .... **TCLC 10**
See also CA 107; DLB 102

Slessor, Kenneth 1901-1971 .... **CLC 14**
See also CA 102; 89-92

Slowacki, Juliusz 1809-1849 ..... **NCLC 15**

Smart, Christopher 1722-1771 .... **LC 3**
See also DLB 109

Smart, Elizabeth 1913-1986 .... **CLC 54**
See also CA 81-84; 118; DLB 88

Smiley, Jane (Graves) 1949- .... **CLC 53, 76**
See also CA 104; CANR 30

Smith, A(rthur) J(ames) M(arshall)
1902-1980 .... **CLC 15**
See also CA 1-4R; 102; CANR 4; DLB 88

Smith, Betty (Wehner) 1896-1972 ... **CLC 19**
See also CA 5-8R; 33-36R; DLBY 82;
SATA 6

Smith, Charlotte (Turner)
1749-1806 .... **NCLC 23**
See also DLB 39, 109

Smith, Clark Ashton 1893-1961 .... **CLC 43**
See also CA 143

Smith, Dave .... **CLC 22, 42**
See also Smith, David (Jeddie)
See also CAAS 7; DLB 5

Smith, David (Jeddie) 1942-
See Smith, Dave
See also CA 49-52; CANR 1

Smith, Florence Margaret
1902-1971 .... **CLC 8**
See also Smith, Stevie
See also CA 17-18; 29-32R; CANR 35;
CAP 2; MTCW

Smith, Iain Crichton 1928- .... **CLC 64**
See also CA 21-24R; DLB 40

Smith, John 1580(?)-1631 .... **LC 9**

Smith, Johnston
See Crane, Stephen (Townley)

Smith, Lee 1944- .... **CLC 25, 73**
See also CA 114; 119; DLBY 83

Smith, Martin
See Smith, Martin Cruz

Smith, Martin Cruz 1942- .... **CLC 25**
See also BEST 89:4; CA 85-88; CANR 6,
23, 43

Smith, Mary-Ann Tirone 1944- ..... **CLC 39**
See also CA 118; 136

Smith, Patti 1946- .... **CLC 12**
See also CA 93-96

Smith, Pauline (Urmson)
1882-1959 .... **TCLC 25**

Smith, Rosamond
See Oates, Joyce Carol

Smith, Sheila Kaye
See Kaye-Smith, Sheila

Smith, Stevie .... **CLC 3, 8, 25, 44**
See also Smith, Florence Margaret
See also DLB 20

Smith, Wilbur A(ddison) 1933- ..... **CLC 33**
See also CA 13-16R; CANR 7; MTCW

Smith, William Jay 1918- .... **CLC 6**
See also CA 5-8R; DLB 5; MAICYA;
SATA 2, 68

Smith, Woodrow Wilson
See Kuttner, Henry

Smolenskin, Peretz 1842-1885 .... **NCLC 30**

Smollett, Tobias (George) 1721-1771 .. **LC 2**
See also CDBLB 1660-1789; DLB 39, 104

Snodgrass, W(illiam) D(e Witt)
1926- .... **CLC 2, 6, 10, 18, 68**
See also CA 1-4R; CANR 6, 36; DLB 5;
MTCW

Snow, C(harles) P(ercy)
1905-1980 ...... **CLC 1, 4, 6, 9, 13, 19**
See also CA 5-8R; 101; CANR 28;
CDBLB 1945-1960; DLB 15, 77; MTCW

Snow, Frances Compton
See Adams, Henry (Brooks)

Snyder, Gary (Sherman)
1930- .... **CLC 1, 2, 5, 9, 32**
See also CA 17-20R; CANR 30; DLB 5, 16

Snyder, Zilpha Keatley 1927- ...... **CLC 17**
See also CA 9-12R; CANR 38; CLR 31;
JRDA; MAICYA; SAAS 2; SATA 1, 28,
75

Soares, Bernardo
See Pessoa, Fernando (Antonio Nogueira)

Sobh, A.
See Shamlu, Ahmad

Sobol, Joshua .... **CLC 60**

Soderberg, Hjalmar 1869-1941 .... **TCLC 39**

Sodergran, Edith (Irene)
See Soedergran, Edith (Irene)

Soedergran, Edith (Irene)
1892-1923 .... **TCLC 31**

Softly, Edgar
See Lovecraft, H(oward) P(hillips)

Softly, Edward
See Lovecraft, H(oward) P(hillips)

Sokolov, Raymond 1941- .... **CLC 7**
See also CA 85-88

Solo, Jay
See Ellison, Harlan

Sologub, Fyodor .... **TCLC 9**
See also Teternikov, Fyodor Kuzmich

Solomons, Ikey Esquir
See Thackeray, William Makepeace

Solomos, Dionysios 1798-1857 ... **NCLC 15**

Solwoska, Mara
See French, Marilyn

Solzhenitsyn, Aleksandr I(sayevich)
1918- ...... **CLC 1, 2, 4, 7, 9, 10, 18, 26,
34, 78; DA; WLC**
See also AITN 1; CA 69-72; CANR 40;
MTCW

Somers, Jane
See Lessing, Doris (May)

Somerville, Edith 1858-1949 ...... **TCLC 51**
See also DLB 135

Somerville & Ross
See Martin, Violet Florence; Somerville,
Edith

Sommer, Scott 1951- .... **CLC 25**
See also CA 106

Sondheim, Stephen (Joshua)
1930- .... **CLC 30, 39**
See also CA 103

Sontag, Susan 1933- ... **CLC 1, 2, 10, 13, 31**
See also CA 17-20R; CANR 25; DLB 2, 67;
MTCW

Sophocles
496(?)B.C.-406(?)B.C. ..... **CMLC 2; DA;
DC 1**

Sorel, Julia
See Drexler, Rosalyn

Sorrentino, Gilbert
1929- .... **CLC 3, 7, 14, 22, 40**
See also CA 77-80; CANR 14, 33; DLB 5;
DLBY 80

Soto, Gary 1952- .... **CLC 32, 80; HLC**
See also AAYA 10; CA 119; 125; DLB 82;
HW; JRDA

Soupault, Philippe 1897-1990 ...... **CLC 68**
See also CA 116; 131

Souster, (Holmes) Raymond
1921- .... **CLC 5, 14**
See also CA 13-16R; CAAS 14; CANR 13,
29; DLB 88; SATA 63

Southern, Terry 1926- . . . . **CLC 7**
See also CA 1-4R; CANR 1; DLB 2

Southey, Robert 1774-1843 . . . . . . **NCLC 8**
See also DLB 93, 107; SATA 54

Southworth, Emma Dorothy Eliza Nevitte
1819-1899 . . . . **NCLC 26**

Souza, Ernest
See Scott, Evelyn

Soyinka, Wole
1934- . . . . **CLC 3, 5, 14, 36, 44; BLC;**
DA; DC 2; WLC
See also BW; CA 13-16R; CANR 27, 39;
DLB 125; MTCW

Spackman, W(illiam) M(ode)
1905-1990 . . . . **CLC 46**
See also CA 81-84; 132

Spacks, Barry 1931- . . . . **CLC 14**
See also CA 29-32R; CANR 33; DLB 105

Spanidou, Irini 1946- . . . . **CLC 44**

Spark, Muriel (Sarah)
1918- . . . . **CLC 2, 3, 5, 8, 13, 18, 40;**
SSC 10
See also CA 5-8R; CANR 12, 36;
CDBLB 1945-1960; DLB 15; MTCW

Spaulding, Douglas
See Bradbury, Ray (Douglas)

Spaulding, Leonard
See Bradbury, Ray (Douglas)

Spence, J. A. D.
See Eliot, T(homas) S(tearns)

Spencer, Elizabeth 1921- . . . . **CLC 22**
See also CA 13-16R; CANR 32; DLB 6;
MTCW; SATA 14

Spencer, Leonard G.
See Silverberg, Robert

Spencer, Scott 1945- . . . . **CLC 30**
See also CA 113; DLBY 86

Spender, Stephen (Harold)
1909- . . . . **CLC 1, 2, 5, 10, 41**
See also CA 9-12R; CANR 31;
CDBLB 1945-1960; DLB 20; MTCW

Spengler, Oswald (Arnold Gottfried)
1880-1936 . . . . **TCLC 25**
See also CA 118

Spenser, Edmund
1552(?)-1599 . . . . **LC 5; DA; PC 8; WLC**
See also CDBLB Before 1660

Spicer, Jack 1925-1965 . . . . . . **CLC 8, 18, 72**
See also CA 85-88; DLB 5, 16

Spiegelman, Art 1948- . . . . **CLC 76**
See also AAYA 10; CA 125; CANR 41

Spielberg, Peter 1929- . . . . **CLC 6**
See also CA 5-8R; CANR 4; DLBY 81

Spielberg, Steven 1947- . . . . **CLC 20**
See also AAYA 8; CA 77-80; CANR 32;
SATA 32

Spillane, Frank Morrison 1918-
See Spillane, Mickey
See also CA 25-28R; CANR 28; MTCW;
SATA 66

Spillane, Mickey . . . . **CLC 3, 13**
See also Spillane, Frank Morrison

Spinoza, Benedictus de 1632-1677 . . . . **LC 9**

Spinrad, Norman (Richard) 1940- . . . **CLC 46**
See also CA 37-40R; CANR 20; DLB 8

Spitteler, Carl (Friedrich Georg)
1845-1924 . . . . **TCLC 12**
See also CA 109; DLB 129

Spivack, Kathleen (Romola Drucker)
1938- . . . . **CLC 6**
See also CA 49-52

Spoto, Donald 1941- . . . . **CLC 39**
See also CA 65-68; CANR 11

Springsteen, Bruce (F.) 1949- . . . . . . **CLC 17**
See also CA 111

Spurling, Hilary 1940- . . . . **CLC 34**
See also CA 104; CANR 25

Squires, (James) Radcliffe
1917-1993 . . . . **CLC 51**
See also CA 1-4R; 140; CANR 6, 21

Srivastava, Dhanpat Rai 1880(?)-1936
See Premchand
See also CA 118

Stacy, Donald
See Pohl, Frederik

Stael, Germaine de
See Stael-Holstein, Anne Louise Germaine
Necker Baronn
See also DLB 119

Stael-Holstein, Anne Louise Germaine Necker
Baronn 1766-1817 . . . . **NCLC 3**
See also Stael, Germaine de

Stafford, Jean 1915-1979 . . . **CLC 4, 7, 19, 68**
See also CA 1-4R; 85-88; CANR 3; DLB 2;
MTCW; SATA 22

Stafford, William (Edgar)
1914-1993 . . . . **CLC 4, 7, 29**
See also CA 5-8R; 142; CAAS 3; CANR 5,
22; DLB 5

Staines, Trevor
See Brunner, John (Kilian Houston)

Stairs, Gordon
See Austin, Mary (Hunter)

Stannard, Martin 1947- . . . . **CLC 44**
See also CA 142

Stanton, Maura 1946- . . . . **CLC 9**
See also CA 89-92; CANR 15; DLB 120

Stanton, Schuyler
See Baum, L(yman) Frank

Stapledon, (William) Olaf
1886-1950 . . . . **TCLC 22**
See also CA 111; DLB 15

Starbuck, George (Edwin) 1931- . . . . **CLC 53**
See also CA 21-24R; CANR 23

Stark, Richard
See Westlake, Donald E(dwin)

Staunton, Schuyler
See Baum, L(yman) Frank

Stead, Christina (Ellen)
1902-1983 . . . . **CLC 2, 5, 8, 32, 80**
See also CA 13-16R; 109; CANR 33, 40;
MTCW

Stead, William Thomas
1849-1912 . . . . **TCLC 48**

Steele, Richard 1672-1729 . . . . **LC 18**
See also CDBLB 1660-1789; DLB 84, 101

Steele, Timothy (Reid) 1948- . . . . **CLC 45**
See also CA 93-96; CANR 16; DLB 120

Steffens, (Joseph) Lincoln
1866-1936 . . . . **TCLC 20**
See also CA 117

Stegner, Wallace (Earle)
1909-1993 . . . . **CLC 9, 49, 81**
See also AITN 1; BEST 90:3; CA 1-4R;
141; CAAS 9; CANR 1, 21; DLB 9;
MTCW

Stein, Gertrude
1874-1946 . . . . . . **TCLC 1, 6, 28, 48; DA;**
WLC
See also CA 104; 132; CDALB 1917-1929;
DLB 4, 54, 86; MTCW

Steinbeck, John (Ernst)
1902-1968 . . . . . . **CLC 1, 5, 9, 13, 21, 34,**
45, 75; DA; SSC 11; WLC
See also CA 1-4R; 25-28R; CANR 1, 35;
CDALB 1929-1941; DLB 7, 9; DLBD 2;
MTCW; SATA 9

Steinem, Gloria 1934- . . . . **CLC 63**
See also CA 53-56; CANR 28; MTCW

Steiner, George 1929- . . . . **CLC 24**
See also CA 73-76; CANR 31; DLB 67;
MTCW; SATA 62

Steiner, K. Leslie
See Delany, Samuel R(ay, Jr.)

Steiner, Rudolf 1861-1925 . . . . **TCLC 13**
See also CA 107

Stendhal 1783-1842 . . . . **NCLC 23; DA; WLC**
See also DLB 119

Stephen, Leslie 1832-1904 . . . . **TCLC 23**
See also CA 123; DLB 57

Stephen, Sir Leslie
See Stephen, Leslie

Stephen, Virginia
See Woolf, (Adeline) Virginia

Stephens, James 1882(?)-1950 . . . . . . **TCLC 4**
See also CA 104; DLB 19

Stephens, Reed
See Donaldson, Stephen R.

Steptoe, Lydia
See Barnes, Djuna

Sterchi, Beat 1949- . . . . **CLC 65**

Sterling, Brett
See Bradbury, Ray (Douglas); Hamilton,
Edmond

Sterling, Bruce 1954- . . . . **CLC 72**
See also CA 119

Sterling, George 1869-1926 . . . . **TCLC 20**
See also CA 117; DLB 54

Stern, Gerald 1925- . . . . **CLC 40**
See also CA 81-84; CANR 28; DLB 105

Stern, Richard (Gustave) 1928- . . . **CLC 4, 39**
See also CA 1-4R; CANR 1, 25; DLBY 87

Sternberg, Josef von 1894-1969 . . . . . **CLC 20**
See also CA 81-84

Sterne, Laurence
1713-1768 . . . . **LC 2; DA; WLC**
See also CDBLB 1660-1789; DLB 39

Sternheim, (William Adolf) Carl
1878-1942 . . . . **TCLC 8**
See also CA 105; DLB 56, 118

Stevens, Mark   1951- . . . . CLC 34
See also CA 122

Stevens, Wallace
1879-1955 . . . . TCLC 3, 12, 45; DA;
PC 6; WLC
See also CA 104; 124; CDALB 1929-1941;
DLB 54; MTCW

Stevenson, Anne (Katharine)
1933- . . . . CLC 7, 33
See also CA 17-20R; CAAS 9; CANR 9, 33;
DLB 40; MTCW

Stevenson, Robert Louis (Balfour)
1850-1894 . . . . NCLC 5, 14; DA;
SSC 11; WLC
See also CDBLB 1890-1914; CLR 10, 11;
DLB 18, 57; JRDA; MAICYA; YABC 2

Stewart, J(ohn) I(nnes) M(ackintosh)
1906- . . . . CLC 7, 14, 32
See also CA 85-88; CAAS 3; MTCW

Stewart, Mary (Florence Elinor)
1916- . . . . CLC 7, 35
See also CA 1-4R; CANR 1; SATA 12

Stewart, Mary Rainbow
See Stewart, Mary (Florence Elinor)

Stifter, Adalbert   1805-1868 . . . . . . NCLC 41
See also DLB 133

Still, James   1906- . . . . CLC 49
See also CA 65-68; CAAS 17; CANR 10,
26; DLB 9; SATA 29

Sting
See Sumner, Gordon Matthew

Stirling, Arthur
See Sinclair, Upton (Beall)

Stitt, Milan   1941- . . . . CLC 29
See also CA 69-72

Stockton, Francis Richard   1834-1902
See Stockton, Frank R.
See also CA 108; 137; MAICYA; SATA 44

Stockton, Frank R. . . . . TCLC 47
See also Stockton, Francis Richard
See also DLB 42, 74; SATA 32

Stoddard, Charles
See Kuttner, Henry

Stoker, Abraham   1847-1912
See Stoker, Bram
See also CA 105; DA; SATA 29

Stoker, Bram . . . . TCLC 8; WLC
See also Stoker, Abraham
See also CDBLB 1890-1914; DLB 36, 70

Stolz, Mary (Slattery)   1920- . . . . CLC 12
See also AAYA 8; AITN 1; CA 5-8R;
CANR 13, 41; JRDA; MAICYA;
SAAS 3; SATA 10, 71

Stone, Irving   1903-1989 . . . . CLC 7
See also AITN 1; CA 1-4R; 129; CAAS 3;
CANR 1, 23; MTCW; SATA 3;
SATA-Obit 64

Stone, Oliver   1946- . . . . CLC 73
See also CA 110

Stone, Robert (Anthony)
1937- . . . . CLC 5, 23, 42
See also CA 85-88; CANR 23; MTCW

Stone, Zachary
See Follett, Ken(neth Martin)

Stoppard, Tom
1937- . . . . . . CLC 1, 3, 4, 5, 8, 15, 29, 34,
63; DA; WLC
See also CA 81-84; CANR 39;
CDBLB 1960 to Present; DLB 13;
DLBY 85; MTCW

Storey, David (Malcolm)
1933- . . . . CLC 2, 4, 5, 8
See also CA 81-84; CANR 36; DLB 13, 14;
MTCW

Storm, Hyemeyohsts   1935- . . . . CLC 3
See also CA 81-84

Storm, (Hans) Theodor (Woldsen)
1817-1888 . . . . NCLC 1

Storni, Alfonsina
1892-1938 . . . . TCLC 5; HLC
See also CA 104; 131; HW

Stout, Rex (Todhunter)   1886-1975 . . . CLC 3
See also AITN 2; CA 61-64

Stow, (Julian) Randolph   1935- . . CLC 23, 48
See also CA 13-16R; CANR 33; MTCW

Stowe, Harriet (Elizabeth) Beecher
1811-1896 . . . . NCLC 3; DA; WLC
See also CDALB 1865-1917; DLB 1, 12, 42,
74; JRDA; MAICYA; YABC 1

Strachey, (Giles) Lytton
1880-1932 . . . . TCLC 12
See also CA 110; DLBD 10

Strand, Mark   1934- . . . . . . CLC 6, 18, 41, 71
See also CA 21-24R; CANR 40; DLB 5;
SATA 41

Straub, Peter (Francis)   1943- . . . . . . CLC 28
See also BEST 89:1; CA 85-88; CANR 28;
DLBY 84; MTCW

Strauss, Botho   1944- . . . . CLC 22
See also DLB 124

Streatfeild, (Mary) Noel
1895(?)-1986 . . . . CLC 21
See also CA 81-84; 120; CANR 31;
CLR 17; MAICYA; SATA 20, 48

Stribling, T(homas) S(igismund)
1881-1965 . . . . CLC 23
See also CA 107; DLB 9

Strindberg, (Johan) August
1849-1912 . . . . . . TCLC 1, 8, 21, 47; DA;
WLC
See also CA 104; 135

Stringer, Arthur   1874-1950 . . . . . . TCLC 37
See also DLB 92

Stringer, David
See Roberts, Keith (John Kingston)

Strugatskii, Arkadii (Natanovich)
1925-1991 . . . . CLC 27
See also CA 106; 135

Strugatskii, Boris (Natanovich)
1933- . . . . CLC 27
See also CA 106

Strummer, Joe   1953(?)- . . . . CLC 30
See also Clash, The

Stuart, Don A.
See Campbell, John W(ood, Jr.)

Stuart, Ian
See MacLean, Alistair (Stuart)

Stuart, Jesse (Hilton)
1906-1984 . . . . CLC 1, 8, 11, 14, 34
See also CA 5-8R; 112; CANR 31; DLB 9,
48, 102; DLBY 84; SATA 2, 36

Sturgeon, Theodore (Hamilton)
1918-1985 . . . . CLC 22, 39
See also Queen, Ellery
See also CA 81-84; 116; CANR 32; DLB 8;
DLBY 85; MTCW

Sturges, Preston   1898-1959 . . . . . . TCLC 48
See also CA 114; DLB 26

Styron, William
1925- . . . . CLC 1, 3, 5, 11, 15, 60
See also BEST 90:4; CA 5-8R; CANR 6, 33;
CDALB 1968-1988; DLB 2; DLBY 80;
MTCW

Suarez Lynch, B.
See Bioy Casares, Adolfo; Borges, Jorge
Luis

Suarez Lynch, B.
See Borges, Jorge Luis

Su Chien   1884-1918
See Su Man-shu
See also CA 123

Sudermann, Hermann   1857-1928 . . TCLC 15
See also CA 107; DLB 118

Sue, Eugene   1804-1857 . . . . NCLC 1
See also DLB 119

Sueskind, Patrick   1949- . . . . CLC 44

Sukenick, Ronald   1932- . . . . . CLC 3, 4, 6, 48
See also CA 25-28R; CAAS 8; CANR 32;
DLBY 81

Suknaski, Andrew   1942- . . . . CLC 19
See also CA 101; DLB 53

Sullivan, Vernon
See Vian, Boris

Sully Prudhomme   1839-1907 . . . . . . TCLC 31

Su Man-shu . . . . TCLC 24
See also Su Chien

Summerforest, Ivy B.
See Kirkup, James

Summers, Andrew James   1942- . . . . . CLC 26
See also Police, The

Summers, Andy
See Summers, Andrew James

Summers, Hollis (Spurgeon, Jr.)
1916- . . . . CLC 10
See also CA 5-8R; CANR 3; DLB 6

Summers, (Alphonsus Joseph-Mary Augustus)
Montague   1880-1948 . . . . TCLC 16
See also CA 118

Sumner, Gordon Matthew   1951- . . . . CLC 26
See also Police, The

Surtees, Robert Smith
1803-1864 . . . . NCLC 14
See also DLB 21

Susann, Jacqueline   1921-1974 . . . . CLC 3
See also AITN 1; CA 65-68; 53-56; MTCW

Suskind, Patrick
See Sueskind, Patrick

Sutcliff, Rosemary   1920-1992 . . . . . . CLC 26
See also AAYA 10; CA 5-8R; 139;
CANR 37; CLR 1; JRDA; MAICYA;
SATA 6, 44; SATA-Obit 73

Sutro, Alfred 1863-1933........... **TCLC 6**
See also CA 105; DLB 10

Sutton, Henry
See Slavitt, David R(ytman)

Svevo, Italo.................. **TCLC 2, 35**
See also Schmitz, Aron Hector

Swados, Elizabeth 1951-......... **CLC 12**
See also CA 97-100

Swados, Harvey 1920-1972........ **CLC 5**
See also CA 5-8R; 37-40R; CANR 6;
DLB 2

Swan, Gladys 1934-............. **CLC 69**
See also CA 101; CANR 17, 39

Swarthout, Glendon (Fred)
1918-1992.................. **CLC 35**
See also CA 1-4R; 139; CANR 1; SATA 26

Sweet, Sarah C.
See Jewett, (Theodora) Sarah Orne

Swenson, May
1919-1989........ **CLC 4, 14, 61; DA**
See also CA 5-8R; 130; CANR 36; DLB 5;
MTCW; SATA 15

Swift, Augustus
See Lovecraft, H(oward) P(hillips)

Swift, Graham 1949-............. **CLC 41**
See also CA 117; 122

Swift, Jonathan
1667-1745.......... **LC 1; DA; WLC**
See also CDBLB 1660-1789; DLB 39, 95,
101; SATA 19

Swinburne, Algernon Charles
1837-1909...... **TCLC 8, 36; DA; WLC**
See also CA 105; 140; CDBLB 1832-1890;
DLB 35, 57

Swinfen, Ann.................... **CLC 34**

Swinnerton, Frank Arthur
1884-1982.................. **CLC 31**
See also CA 108; DLB 34

Swithen, John
See King, Stephen (Edwin)

Sylvia
See Ashton-Warner, Sylvia (Constance)

Symmes, Robert Edward
See Duncan, Robert (Edward)

Symonds, John Addington
1840-1893................. **NCLC 34**
See also DLB 57

Symons, Arthur 1865-1945....... **TCLC 11**
See also CA 107; DLB 19, 57

Symons, Julian (Gustave)
1912-.................. **CLC 2, 14, 32**
See also CA 49-52; CAAS 3; CANR 3, 33;
DLB 87; DLBY 92; MTCW

Synge, (Edmund) J(ohn) M(illington)
1871-1909.......... **TCLC 6, 37; DC 2**
See also CA 104; 141; CDBLB 1890-1914;
DLB 10, 19

Syruc, J.
See Milosz, Czeslaw

Szirtes, George 1948-............. **CLC 46**
See also CA 109; CANR 27

Tabori, George 1914-............. **CLC 19**
See also CA 49-52; CANR 4

Tagore, Rabindranath
1861-1941......... **TCLC 3, 53; PC 8**
See also CA 104; 120; MTCW

Taine, Hippolyte Adolphe
1828-1893................. **NCLC 15**

Talese, Gay 1932-................ **CLC 37**
See also AITN 1; CA 1-4R; CANR 9;
MTCW

Tallent, Elizabeth (Ann) 1954-..... **CLC 45**
See also CA 117; DLB 130

Tally, Ted 1952-................ **CLC 42**
See also CA 120; 124

Tamayo y Baus, Manuel
1829-1898................. **NCLC 1**

Tammsaare, A(nton) H(ansen)
1878-1940................. **TCLC 27**

Tan, Amy 1952-................ **CLC 59**
See also AAYA 9; BEST 89:3; CA 136;
SATA 75

Tandem, Felix
See Spitteler, Carl (Friedrich Georg)

Tanizaki, Jun'ichiro
1886-1965............ **CLC 8, 14, 28**
See also CA 93-96; 25-28R

Tanner, William
See Amis, Kingsley (William)

Tao Lao
See Storni, Alfonsina

Tarassoff, Lev
See Troyat, Henri

Tarbell, Ida M(inerva)
1857-1944................. **TCLC 40**
See also CA 122; DLB 47

Tarkington, (Newton) Booth
1869-1946................. **TCLC 9**
See also CA 110; 143; DLB 9, 102;
SATA 17

Tarkovsky, Andrei (Arsenyevich)
1932-1986.................. **CLC 75**
See also CA 127

Tartt, Donna 1964(?)-............. **CLC 76**
See also CA 142

Tasso, Torquato 1544-1595......... **LC 5**

Tate, (John Orley) Allen
1899-1979.... **CLC 2, 4, 6, 9, 11, 14, 24**
See also CA 5-8R; 85-88; CANR 32;
DLB 4, 45, 63; MTCW

Tate, Ellalice
See Hibbert, Eleanor Alice Burford

Tate, James (Vincent) 1943-... **CLC 2, 6, 25**
See also CA 21-24R; CANR 29; DLB 5

Tavel, Ronald 1940-............... **CLC 6**
See also CA 21-24R; CANR 33

Taylor, Cecil Philip 1929-1981..... **CLC 27**
See also CA 25-28R; 105

Taylor, Edward 1642(?)-1729.... **LC 11; DA**
See also DLB 24

Taylor, Eleanor Ross 1920-......... **CLC 5**
See also CA 81-84

Taylor, Elizabeth 1912-1975... **CLC 2, 4, 29**
See also CA 13-16R; CANR 9; MTCW;
SATA 13

Taylor, Henry (Splawn) 1942-...... **CLC 44**
See also CA 33-36R; CAAS 7; CANR 31;
DLB 5

Taylor, Kamala (Purnaiya) 1924-
See Markandaya, Kamala
See also CA 77-80

Taylor, Mildred D................. **CLC 21**
See also AAYA 10; BW; CA 85-88;
CANR 25; CLR 9; DLB 52; JRDA;
MAICYA; SAAS 5; SATA 15, 70

Taylor, Peter (Hillsman)
1917-...... **CLC 1, 4, 18, 37, 44, 50, 71;**
SSC 10
See also CA 13-16R; CANR 9; DLBY 81;
MTCW

Taylor, Robert Lewis 1912-........ **CLC 14**
See also CA 1-4R; CANR 3; SATA 10

Tchekhov, Anton
See Chekhov, Anton (Pavlovich)

Teasdale, Sara 1884-1933......... **TCLC 4**
See also CA 104; DLB 45; SATA 32

Tegner, Esaias 1782-1846........ **NCLC 2**

Teilhard de Chardin, (Marie Joseph) Pierre
1881-1955................. **TCLC 9**
See also CA 105

Temple, Ann
See Mortimer, Penelope (Ruth)

Tennant, Emma (Christina)
1937-................... **CLC 13, 52**
See also CA 65-68; CAAS 9; CANR 10, 38;
DLB 14

Tenneshaw, S. M.
See Silverberg, Robert

Tennyson, Alfred
1809-1892.. **NCLC 30; DA; PC 6; WLC**
See also CDBLB 1832-1890; DLB 32

Teran, Lisa St. Aubin de.......... **CLC 36**
See also St. Aubin de Teran, Lisa

Teresa de Jesus, St. 1515-1582...... **LC 18**

Terkel, Louis 1912-
See Terkel, Studs
See also CA 57-60; CANR 18; MTCW

Terkel, Studs.................... **CLC 38**
See also Terkel, Louis
See also AITN 1

Terry, C. V.
See Slaughter, Frank G(ill)

Terry, Megan 1932-.............. **CLC 19**
See also CA 77-80; CABS 3; CANR 43;
DLB 7

Tertz, Abram
See Sinyavsky, Andrei (Donatevich)

Tesich, Steve 1943(?)-.......... **CLC 40, 69**
See also CA 105; DLBY 83

Teternikov, Fyodor Kuzmich 1863-1927
See Sologub, Fyodor
See also CA 104

Tevis, Walter 1928-1984.......... **CLC 42**
See also CA 113

Tey, Josephine.................... **TCLC 14**
See also Mackintosh, Elizabeth
See also DLB 77

Thackeray, William Makepeace
1811-1863 .... **NCLC 5, 14, 22, 43; DA; WLC**
See also CDBLB 1832-1890; DLB 21, 55; SATA 23

Thakura, Ravindranatha
See Tagore, Rabindranath

Tharoor, Shashi 1956- .... **CLC 70**
See also CA 141

Thelwell, Michael Miles 1939- ..... **CLC 22**
See also CA 101

Theobald, Lewis, Jr.
See Lovecraft, H(oward) P(hillips)

Theodorescu, Ion N. 1880-1967
See Arghezi, Tudor
See also CA 116

Theriault, Yves 1915-1983 .... **CLC 79**
See also CA 102; DLB 88

Theroux, Alexander (Louis)
1939- .... **CLC 2, 25**
See also CA 85-88; CANR 20

Theroux, Paul (Edward)
1941- .... **CLC 5, 8, 11, 15, 28, 46**
See also BEST 89:4; CA 33-36R; CANR 20; DLB 2; MTCW; SATA 44

Thesen, Sharon 1946- .... **CLC 56**

Thevenin, Denis
See Duhamel, Georges

Thibault, Jacques Anatole Francois
1844-1924
See France, Anatole
See also CA 106; 127; MTCW

Thiele, Colin (Milton) 1920- .... **CLC 17**
See also CA 29-32R; CANR 12, 28; CLR 27; MAICYA; SAAS 2; SATA 14, 72

Thomas, Audrey (Callahan)
1935- .... **CLC 7, 13, 37**
See also AITN 2; CA 21-24R; CANR 36; DLB 60; MTCW

Thomas, D(onald) M(ichael)
1935- .... **CLC 13, 22, 31**
See also CA 61-64; CAAS 11; CANR 17; CDBLB 1960 to Present; DLB 40; MTCW

Thomas, Dylan (Marlais)
1914-1953 ... **TCLC 1, 8, 45; DA; PC 2; SSC 3; WLC**
See also CA 104; 120; CDBLB 1945-1960; DLB 13, 20; MTCW; SATA 60

Thomas, (Philip) Edward
1878-1917 .... **TCLC 10**
See also CA 106; DLB 19

Thomas, Joyce Carol 1938- .... **CLC 35**
See also BW; CA 113; 116; CLR 19; DLB 33; JRDA; MAICYA; MTCW; SAAS 7; SATA 40

Thomas, Lewis 1913-1993 .... **CLC 35**
See also CA 85-88; 143; CANR 38; MTCW

Thomas, Paul
See Mann, (Paul) Thomas

Thomas, Piri 1928- .... **CLC 17**
See also CA 73-76; HW

Thomas, R(onald) S(tuart)
1913- .... **CLC 6, 13, 48**
See also CA 89-92; CAAS 4; CANR 30; CDBLB 1960 to Present; DLB 27; MTCW

Thomas, Ross (Elmore) 1926- ...... **CLC 39**
See also CA 33-36R; CANR 22

Thompson, Francis Clegg
See Mencken, H(enry) L(ouis)

Thompson, Francis Joseph
1859-1907 .... **TCLC 4**
See also CA 104; CDBLB 1890-1914; DLB 19

Thompson, Hunter S(tockton)
1939- .... **CLC 9, 17, 40**
See also BEST 89:1; CA 17-20R; CANR 23; MTCW

Thompson, James Myers
See Thompson, Jim (Myers)

Thompson, Jim (Myers)
1906-1977(?) .... **CLC 69**
See also CA 140

Thompson, Judith .... **CLC 39**

Thomson, James 1700-1748 .... **LC 16**

Thomson, James 1834-1882 ...... **NCLC 18**

Thoreau, Henry David
1817-1862 ...... **NCLC 7, 21; DA; WLC**
See also CDALB 1640-1865; DLB 1

Thornton, Hall
See Silverberg, Robert

Thurber, James (Grover)
1894-1961 ... **CLC 5, 11, 25; DA; SSC 1**
See also CA 73-76; CANR 17, 39; CDALB 1929-1941; DLB 4, 11, 22, 102; MAICYA; MTCW; SATA 13

Thurman, Wallace (Henry)
1902-1934 .... **TCLC 6; BLC**
See also BW; CA 104; 124; DLB 51

Ticheburn, Cheviot
See Ainsworth, William Harrison

Tieck, (Johann) Ludwig
1773-1853 .... **NCLC 5**
See also DLB 90

Tiger, Derry
See Ellison, Harlan

Tilghman, Christopher 1948(?)- ..... **CLC 65**

Tillinghast, Richard (Williford)
1940- .... **CLC 29**
See also CA 29-32R; CANR 26

Timrod, Henry 1828-1867 .... **NCLC 25**
See also DLB 3

Tindall, Gillian 1938- .... **CLC 7**
See also CA 21-24R; CANR 11

Tiptree, James, Jr. .... **CLC 48, 50**
See also Sheldon, Alice Hastings Bradley
See also DLB 8

Titmarsh, Michael Angelo
See Thackeray, William Makepeace

Tocqueville, Alexis (Charles Henri Maurice Clerel Comte) 1805-1859..... **NCLC 7**

Tolkien, J(ohn) R(onald) R(euel)
1892-1973 ...... **CLC 1, 2, 3, 8, 12, 38; DA; WLC**
See also AAYA 10; AITN 1; CA 17-18; 45-48; CANR 36; CAP 2; CDBLB 1914-1945; DLB 15; JRDA; MAICYA; MTCW; SATA 2, 24, 32

Toller, Ernst 1893-1939 .... **TCLC 10**
See also CA 107; DLB 124

Tolson, M. B.
See Tolson, Melvin B(eaunorus)

Tolson, Melvin B(eaunorus)
1898(?)-1966 .... **CLC 36; BLC**
See also BW; CA 124; 89-92; DLB 48, 76

Tolstoi, Aleksei Nikolaevich
See Tolstoy, Alexey Nikolaevich

Tolstoy, Alexey Nikolaevich
1882-1945 .... **TCLC 18**
See also CA 107

Tolstoy, Count Leo
See Tolstoy, Leo (Nikolaevich)

Tolstoy, Leo (Nikolaevich)
1828-1910 ...... **TCLC 4, 11, 17, 28, 44; DA; SSC 9; WLC**
See also CA 104; 123; SATA 26

Tomasi di Lampedusa, Giuseppe 1896-1957
See Lampedusa, Giuseppe (Tomasi) di
See also CA 111

Tomlin, Lily..................... **CLC 17**
See also Tomlin, Mary Jean

Tomlin, Mary Jean 1939(?)-
See Tomlin, Lily
See also CA 117

Tomlinson, (Alfred) Charles
1927- .... **CLC 2, 4, 6, 13, 45**
See also CA 5-8R; CANR 33; DLB 40

Tonson, Jacob
See Bennett, (Enoch) Arnold

Toole, John Kennedy
1937-1969 .... **CLC 19, 64**
See also CA 104; DLBY 81

Toomer, Jean
1894-1967 ...... **CLC 1, 4, 13, 22; BLC; PC 7; SSC 1**
See also BW; CA 85-88; CDALB 1917-1929; DLB 45, 51; MTCW

Torley, Luke
See Blish, James (Benjamin)

Tornimparte, Alessandra
See Ginzburg, Natalia

Torre, Raoul della
See Mencken, H(enry) L(ouis)

Torrey, E(dwin) Fuller 1937-....... **CLC 34**
See also CA 119

Torsvan, Ben Traven
See Traven, B.

Torsvan, Benno Traven
See Traven, B.

Torsvan, Berick Traven
See Traven, B.

Torsvan, Berwick Traven
See Traven, B.

Torsvan, Bruno Traven
See Traven, B.

Urmuz
See Codrescu, Andrei

Ustinov, Peter (Alexander) 1921- .... **CLC 1**
See also AITN 1; CA 13-16R; CANR 25;
DLB 13

V
See Chekhov, Anton (Pavlovich)

Vaculik, Ludvik 1926- .... **CLC 7**
See also CA 53-56

Valenzuela, Luisa 1938-... **CLC 31; SSC 14**
See also CA 101; CANR 32; DLB 113; HW

Valera y Alcala-Galiano, Juan
1824-1905 .... **TCLC 10**
See also CA 106

Valery, (Ambroise) Paul (Toussaint Jules)
1871-1945 .... **TCLC 4, 15**
See also CA 104; 122; MTCW

Valle-Inclan, Ramon (Maria) del
1866-1936 .... **TCLC 5; HLC**
See also CA 106; DLB 134

Vallejo, Antonio Buero
See Buero Vallejo, Antonio

Vallejo, Cesar (Abraham)
1892-1938 .... **TCLC 3; HLC**
See also CA 105; HW

Valle Y Pena, Ramon del
See Valle-Inclan, Ramon (Maria) del

Van Ash, Cay 1918- .... **CLC 34**

Vanbrugh, Sir John 1664-1726 ...... **LC 21**
See also DLB 80

Van Campen, Karl
See Campbell, John W(ood, Jr.)

Vance, Gerald
See Silverberg, Robert

Vance, Jack .... **CLC 35**
See also Vance, John Holbrook
See also DLB 8

Vance, John Holbrook 1916-
See Queen, Ellery; Vance, Jack
See also CA 29-32R; CANR 17; MTCW

Van Den Bogarde, Derek Jules Gaspard Ulric
Niven 1921-
See Bogarde, Dirk
See also CA 77-80

Vandenburgh, Jane .... **CLC 59**

Vanderhaeghe, Guy 1951- .... **CLC 41**
See also CA 113

van der Post, Laurens (Jan) 1906-... **CLC 5**
See also CA 5-8R; CANR 35

van de Wetering, Janwillem 1931-.. **CLC 47**
See also CA 49-52; CANR 4

Van Dine, S. S. .... **TCLC 23**
See also Wright, Willard Huntington

Van Doren, Carl (Clinton)
1885-1950 .... **TCLC 18**
See also CA 111

Van Doren, Mark 1894-1972..... **CLC 6, 10**
See also CA 1-4R; 37-40R; CANR 3;
DLB 45; MTCW

Van Druten, John (William)
1901-1957 .... **TCLC 2**
See also CA 104; DLB 10

Van Duyn, Mona (Jane)
1921- .... **CLC 3, 7, 63**
See also CA 9-12R; CANR 7, 38; DLB 5

Van Dyne, Edith
See Baum, L(yman) Frank

van Itallie, Jean-Claude 1936-....... **CLC 3**
See also CA 45-48; CAAS 2; CANR 1;
DLB 7

van Ostaijen, Paul 1896-1928 ..... **TCLC 33**

Van Peebles, Melvin 1932- ...... **CLC 2, 20**
See also BW; CA 85-88; CANR 27

Vansittart, Peter 1920-............ **CLC 42**
See also CA 1-4R; CANR 3

Van Vechten, Carl 1880-1964 ...... **CLC 33**
See also CA 89-92; DLB 4, 9, 51

Van Vogt, A(lfred) E(lton) 1912-..... **CLC 1**
See also CA 21-24R; CANR 28; DLB 8;
SATA 14

Varda, Agnes 1928- .... **CLC 16**
See also CA 116; 122

Vargas Llosa, (Jorge) Mario (Pedro)
1936-....... **CLC 3, 6, 9, 10, 15, 31, 42;**
DA; HLC
See also CA 73-76; CANR 18, 32, 42; HW;
MTCW

Vasiliu, Gheorghe 1881-1957
See Bacovia, George
See also CA 123

Vassa, Gustavus
See Equiano, Olaudah

Vassilikos, Vassilis 1933-......... **CLC 4, 8**
See also CA 81-84

Vaughn, Stephanie................. **CLC 62**

Vazov, Ivan (Minchov)
1850-1921 .... **TCLC 25**
See also CA 121

Veblen, Thorstein (Bunde)
1857-1929 .... **TCLC 31**
See also CA 115

Vega, Lope de 1562-1635........... **LC 23**

Venison, Alfred
See Pound, Ezra (Weston Loomis)

Verdi, Marie de
See Mencken, H(enry) L(ouis)

Verdu, Matilde
See Cela, Camilo Jose

Verga, Giovanni (Carmelo)
1840-1922 .... **TCLC 3**
See also CA 104; 123

Vergil 70B.C.-19B.C. .... **CMLC 9; DA**

Verhaeren, Emile (Adolphe Gustave)
1855-1916 .... **TCLC 12**
See also CA 109

Verlaine, Paul (Marie)
1844-1896 .... **NCLC 2; PC 2**

Verne, Jules (Gabriel)
1828-1905 .... **TCLC 6, 52**
See also CA 110; 131; DLB 123; JRDA;
MAICYA; SATA 21

Very, Jones 1813-1880.......... **NCLC 9**
See also DLB 1

Vesaas, Tarjei 1897-1970......... **CLC 48**
See also CA 29-32R

Vialis, Gaston
See Simenon, Georges (Jacques Christian)

Vian, Boris 1920-1959 .... **TCLC 9**
See also CA 106; DLB 72

Viaud, (Louis Marie) Julien 1850-1923
See Loti, Pierre
See also CA 107

Vicar, Henry
See Felsen, Henry Gregor

Vicker, Angus
See Felsen, Henry Gregor

Vidal, Gore
1925- ..... **CLC 2, 4, 6, 8, 10, 22, 33, 72**
See also AITN 1; BEST 90:2; CA 5-8R;
CANR 13; DLB 6; MTCW

Viereck, Peter (Robert Edwin)
1916- .... **CLC 4**
See also CA 1-4R; CANR 1; DLB 5

Vigny, Alfred (Victor) de
1797-1863 .... **NCLC 7**
See also DLB 119

Vilakazi, Benedict Wallet
1906-1947 .... **TCLC 37**

Villiers de l'Isle Adam, Jean Marie Mathias
Philippe Auguste Comte
1838-1889 .... **NCLC 3; SSC 14**
See also DLB 123

Vincent, Gabrielle a pseudonym...... **CLC 13**
See also CA 126; CLR 13; MAICYA;
SATA 61

Vinci, Leonardo da 1452-1519....... **LC 12**

Vine, Barbara .... **CLC 50**
See also Rendell, Ruth (Barbara)
See also BEST 90:4

Vinge, Joan D(ennison) 1948-...... **CLC 30**
See also CA 93-96; SATA 36

Violis, G.
See Simenon, Georges (Jacques Christian)

Visconti, Luchino 1906-1976....... **CLC 16**
See also CA 81-84; 65-68; CANR 39

Vittorini, Elio 1908-1966...... **CLC 6, 9, 14**
See also CA 133; 25-28R

Vizinczey, Stephen 1933-.......... **CLC 40**
See also CA 128

Vliet, R(ussell) G(ordon)
1929-1984 .... **CLC 22**
See also CA 37-40R; 112; CANR 18

Vogau, Boris Andreyevich 1894-1937(?)
See Pilnyak, Boris
See also CA 123

Vogel, Paula A(nne) 1951-......... **CLC 76**
See also CA 108

Voight, Ellen Bryant 1943- .... **CLC 54**
See also CA 69-72; CANR 11, 29; DLB 120

Voigt, Cynthia 1942- .... **CLC 30**
See also AAYA 3; CA 106; CANR 18, 37,
40; CLR 13; JRDA; MAICYA;
SATA 33, 48

Voinovich, Vladimir (Nikolaevich)
1932-.................... **CLC 10, 49**
See also CA 81-84; CAAS 12; CANR 33;
MTCW

Voltaire
1694-1778 ... **LC 14; DA; SSC 12; WLC**

Wasserstein, Wendy
1950- .... **CLC 32, 59; DC 4**
See also CA 121; 129; CABS 3

Waterhouse, Keith (Spencer)
1929- .... **CLC 47**
See also CA 5-8R; CANR 38; DLB 13, 15;
MTCW

Waters, Roger 1944- .... **CLC 35**
See also Pink Floyd

Watkins, Frances Ellen
See Harper, Frances Ellen Watkins

Watkins, Gerrold
See Malzberg, Barry N(athaniel)

Watkins, Paul 1964- .... **CLC 55**
See also CA 132

Watkins, Vernon Phillips
1906-1967 .... **CLC 43**
See also CA 9-10; 25-28R; CAP 1; DLB 20

Watson, Irving S.
See Mencken, H(enry) L(ouis)

Watson, John H.
See Farmer, Philip Jose

Watson, Richard F.
See Silverberg, Robert

Waugh, Auberon (Alexander) 1939- .. **CLC 7**
See also CA 45-48; CANR 6, 22; DLB 14

Waugh, Evelyn (Arthur St. John)
1903-1966 ...... **CLC 1, 3, 8, 13, 19, 27,**
44; DA; WLC
See also CA 85-88; 25-28R; CANR 22;
CDBLB 1914-1945; DLB 15; MTCW

Waugh, Harriet 1944- .... **CLC 6**
See also CA 85-88; CANR 22

Ways, C. R.
See Blount, Roy (Alton), Jr.

Waystaff, Simon
See Swift, Jonathan

Webb, (Martha) Beatrice (Potter)
1858-1943 .... **TCLC 22**
See also Potter, Beatrice
See also CA 117

Webb, Charles (Richard) 1939- ...... **CLC 7**
See also CA 25-28R

Webb, James H(enry), Jr. 1946- .... **CLC 22**
See also CA 81-84

Webb, Mary (Gladys Meredith)
1881-1927 .... **TCLC 24**
See also CA 123; DLB 34

Webb, Mrs. Sidney
See Webb, (Martha) Beatrice (Potter)

Webb, Phyllis 1927- .... **CLC 18**
See also CA 104; CANR 23; DLB 53

Webb, Sidney (James)
1859-1947 .... **TCLC 22**
See also CA 117

Webber, Andrew Lloyd.............. **CLC 21**
See also Lloyd Webber, Andrew

Weber, Lenora Mattingly
1895-1971 .... **CLC 12**
See also CA 19-20; 29-32R; CAP 1;
SATA 2, 26

Webster, John 1579(?)-1634(?) .... **DC 2**
See also CDBLB Before 1660; DA; DLB 58;
WLC

Webster, Noah 1758-1843 .... **NCLC 30**

Wedekind, (Benjamin) Frank(lin)
1864-1918 .... **TCLC 7**
See also CA 104; DLB 118

Weidman, Jerome 1913- .... **CLC 7**
See also AITN 2; CA 1-4R; CANR 1;
DLB 28

Weil, Simone (Adolphine)
1909-1943 .... **TCLC 23**
See also CA 117

Weinstein, Nathan
See West, Nathanael

Weinstein, Nathan von Wallenstein
See West, Nathanael

Weir, Peter (Lindsay) 1944- .... **CLC 20**
See also CA 113; 123

Weiss, Peter (Ulrich)
1916-1982 .... **CLC 3, 15, 51**
See also CA 45-48; 106; CANR 3; DLB 69,
124

Weiss, Theodore (Russell)
1916- .... **CLC 3, 8, 14**
See also CA 9-12R; CAAS 2; DLB 5

Welch, (Maurice) Denton
1915-1948 .... **TCLC 22**
See also CA 121

Welch, James 1940- .... **CLC 6, 14, 52**
See also CA 85-88; CANR 42

Weldon, Fay
1933(?)- .... **CLC 6, 9, 11, 19, 36, 59**
See also CA 21-24R; CANR 16;
CDBLB 1960 to Present; DLB 14;
MTCW

Wellek, Rene 1903- .... **CLC 28**
See also CA 5-8R; CAAS 7; CANR 8;
DLB 63

Weller, Michael 1942- .... **CLC 10, 53**
See also CA 85-88

Weller, Paul 1958- .... **CLC 26**

Wellershoff, Dieter 1925- .... **CLC 46**
See also CA 89-92; CANR 16, 37

Welles, (George) Orson
1915-1985 .... **CLC 20, 80**
See also CA 93-96; 117

Wellman, Mac 1945- .... **CLC 65**

Wellman, Manly Wade 1903-1986 .. **CLC 49**
See also CA 1-4R; 118; CANR 6, 16;
SATA 6, 47

Wells, Carolyn 1869(?)-1942 ...... **TCLC 35**
See also CA 113; DLB 11

Wells, H(erbert) G(eorge)
1866-1946 .... **TCLC 6, 12, 19; DA;**
SSC 6; WLC
See also CA 110; 121; CDBLB 1914-1945;
DLB 34, 70; MTCW; SATA 20

Wells, Rosemary 1943- .... **CLC 12**
See also CA 85-88; CLR 16; MAICYA;
SAAS 1; SATA 18, 69

Welty, Eudora
1909- ...... **CLC 1, 2, 5, 14, 22, 33; DA;**
SSC 1; WLC
See also CA 9-12R; CABS 1; CANR 32;
CDALB 1941-1968; DLB 2, 102;
DLBY 87; MTCW

Wen I-to 1899-1946 .... **TCLC 28**

Wentworth, Robert
See Hamilton, Edmond

Werfel, Franz (V.) 1890-1945 ..... **TCLC 8**
See also CA 104; DLB 81, 124

Wergeland, Henrik Arnold
1808-1845 .... **NCLC 5**

Wersba, Barbara 1932- .... **CLC 30**
See also AAYA 2; CA 29-32R; CANR 16,
38; CLR 3; DLB 52; JRDA; MAICYA;
SAAS 2; SATA 1, 58

Wertmueller, Lina 1928- .... **CLC 16**
See also CA 97-100; CANR 39

Wescott, Glenway 1901-1987....... **CLC 13**
See also CA 13-16R; 121; CANR 23;
DLB 4, 9, 102

Wesker, Arnold 1932- .... **CLC 3, 5, 42**
See also CA 1-4R; CAAS 7; CANR 1, 33;
CDBLB 1960 to Present; DLB 13;
MTCW

Wesley, Richard (Errol) 1945-....... **CLC 7**
See also BW; CA 57-60; CANR 27; DLB 38

Wessel, Johan Herman 1742-1785 .... **LC 7**

West, Anthony (Panther)
1914-1987 .... **CLC 50**
See also CA 45-48; 124; CANR 3, 19;
DLB 15

West, C. P.
See Wodehouse, P(elham) G(renville)

West, (Mary) Jessamyn
1902-1984 .... **CLC 7, 17**
See also CA 9-12R; 112; CANR 27; DLB 6;
DLBY 84; MTCW; SATA 37

West, Morris L(anglo) 1916- ..... **CLC 6, 33**
See also CA 5-8R; CANR 24; MTCW

West, Nathanael
1903-1940 .... **TCLC 1, 14, 44**
See also CA 104; 125; CDALB 1929-1941;
DLB 4, 9, 28; MTCW

West, Owen
See Koontz, Dean R(ay)

West, Paul 1930- .... **CLC 7, 14**
See also CA 13-16R; CAAS 7; CANR 22;
DLB 14

West, Rebecca 1892-1983 .. **CLC 7, 9, 31, 50**
See also CA 5-8R; 109; CANR 19; DLB 36;
DLBY 83; MTCW

Westall, Robert (Atkinson)
1929-1993 .... **CLC 17**
See also CA 69-72; 141; CANR 18;
CLR 13; JRDA; MAICYA; SAAS 2;
SATA 23, 69; SATA-Obit 75

Westlake, Donald E(dwin)
1933- .... **CLC 7, 33**
See also CA 17-20R; CAAS 13; CANR 16

Westmacott, Mary
See Christie, Agatha (Mary Clarissa)

Weston, Allen
See Norton, Andre

Wetcheek, J. L.
See Feuchtwanger, Lion

Wetering, Janwillem van de
See van de Wetering, Janwillem

Wetherell, Elizabeth
See Warner, Susan (Bogert)

Whalen, Philip 1923- .... **CLC 6, 29**
See also CA 9-12R; CANR 5, 39; DLB 16

Wharton, Edith (Newbold Jones)
1862-1937 ...... **TCLC 3, 9, 27, 53; DA;
SSC 6; WLC**
See also CA 104; 132; CDALB 1865-1917;
DLB 4, 9, 12, 78; MTCW

Wharton, James
See Mencken, H(enry) L(ouis)

Wharton, William (a pseudonym)
.... **CLC 18, 37**
See also CA 93-96; DLBY 80

Wheatley (Peters), Phillis
1754(?)-1784 .... **LC 3; BLC; DA; PC 3;
WLC**
See also CDALB 1640-1865; DLB 31, 50

Wheelock, John Hall 1886-1978 .... **CLC 14**
See also CA 13-16R; 77-80; CANR 14;
DLB 45

White, E(lwyn) B(rooks)
1899-1985 .... **CLC 10, 34, 39**
See also AITN 2; CA 13-16R; 116;
CANR 16, 37; CLR 1, 21; DLB 11, 22;
MAICYA; MTCW; SATA 2, 29, 44

White, Edmund (Valentine III)
1940- .... **CLC 27**
See also AAYA 7; CA 45-48; CANR 3, 19,
36; MTCW

White, Patrick (Victor Martindale)
1912-1990 .. **CLC 3, 4, 5, 7, 9, 18, 65, 69**
See also CA 81-84; 132; CANR 43; MTCW

White, Phyllis Dorothy James 1920-
See James, P. D.
See also CA 21-24R; CANR 17, 43; MTCW

White, T(erence) H(anbury)
1906-1964 .... **CLC 30**
See also CA 73-76; CANR 37; JRDA;
MAICYA; SATA 12

White, Terence de Vere 1912- ...... **CLC 49**
See also CA 49-52; CANR 3

White, Walter F(rancis)
1893-1955 .... **TCLC 15**
See also White, Walter
See also CA 115; 124; DLB 51

White, William Hale 1831-1913
See Rutherford, Mark
See also CA 121

Whitehead, E(dward) A(nthony)
1933- .... **CLC 5**
See also CA 65-68

Whitemore, Hugh (John) 1936- ..... **CLC 37**
See also CA 132

Whitman, Sarah Helen (Power)
1803-1878 .... **NCLC 19**
See also DLB 1

Whitman, Walt(er)
1819-1892 ..... **NCLC 4, 31; DA; PC 3;
WLC**
See also CDALB 1640-1865; DLB 3, 64;
SATA 20

Whitney, Phyllis A(yame) 1903- .... **CLC 42**
See also AITN 2; BEST 90:3; CA 1-4R;
CANR 3, 25, 38; JRDA; MAICYA;
SATA 1, 30

Whittemore, (Edward) Reed (Jr.)
1919- .... **CLC 4**
See also CA 9-12R; CAAS 8; CANR 4;
DLB 5

Whittier, John Greenleaf
1807-1892 .... **NCLC 8**
See also CDALB 1640-1865; DLB 1

Whittlebot, Hernia
See Coward, Noel (Peirce)

Wicker, Thomas Grey 1926-
See Wicker, Tom
See also CA 65-68; CANR 21

Wicker, Tom .... **CLC 7**
See also Wicker, Thomas Grey

Wideman, John Edgar
1941- .... **CLC 5, 34, 36, 67; BLC**
See also BW; CA 85-88; CANR 14, 42;
DLB 33

Wiebe, Rudy (Henry) 1934- ... **CLC 6, 11, 14**
See also CA 37-40R; CANR 42; DLB 60

Wieland, Christoph Martin
1733-1813 .... **NCLC 17**
See also DLB 97

Wieners, John 1934- .... **CLC 7**
See also CA 13-16R; DLB 16

Wiesel, Elie(zer)
1928- .... **CLC 3, 5, 11, 37; DA**
See also AAYA 7; AITN 1; CA 5-8R;
CAAS 4; CANR 8, 40; DLB 83;
DLBY 87; MTCW; SATA 56

Wiggins, Marianne 1947- .... **CLC 57**
See also BEST 89:3; CA 130

Wight, James Alfred 1916-
See Herriot, James
See also CA 77-80; SATA 44, 55

Wilbur, Richard (Purdy)
1921- .... **CLC 3, 6, 9, 14, 53; DA**
See also CA 1-4R; CABS 2; CANR 2, 29;
DLB 5; MTCW; SATA 9

Wild, Peter 1940- .... **CLC 14**
See also CA 37-40R; DLB 5

Wilde, Oscar (Fingal O'Flahertie Wills)
1854(?)-1900 .... **TCLC 1, 8, 23, 41; DA;
SSC 11; WLC**
See also CA 104; 119; CDBLB 1890-1914;
DLB 10, 19, 34, 57; SATA 24

Wilder, Billy .... **CLC 20**
See also Wilder, Samuel
See also DLB 26

Wilder, Samuel 1906-
See Wilder, Billy
See also CA 89-92

Wilder, Thornton (Niven)
1897-1975 ...... **CLC 1, 5, 6, 10, 15, 35,
82; DA; DC 1; WLC**
See also AITN 2; CA 13-16R; 61-64;
CANR 40; DLB 4, 7, 9; MTCW

Wilding, Michael 1942- .... **CLC 73**
See also CA 104; CANR 24

Wiley, Richard 1944- .... **CLC 44**
See also CA 121; 129

Wilhelm, Kate .... **CLC 7**
See also Wilhelm, Katie Gertrude
See also CAAS 5; DLB 8

Wilhelm, Katie Gertrude 1928-
See Wilhelm, Kate
See also CA 37-40R; CANR 17, 36; MTCW

Wilkins, Mary
See Freeman, Mary Eleanor Wilkins

Willard, Nancy 1936- .... **CLC 7, 37**
See also CA 89-92; CANR 10, 39; CLR 5;
DLB 5, 52; MAICYA; MTCW;
SATA 30, 37, 71

Williams, C(harles) K(enneth)
1936- .... **CLC 33, 56**
See also CA 37-40R; DLB 5

Williams, Charles
See Collier, James L(incoln)

Williams, Charles (Walter Stansby)
1886-1945 .... **TCLC 1, 11**
See also CA 104; DLB 100

Williams, (George) Emlyn
1905-1987 .... **CLC 15**
See also CA 104; 123; CANR 36; DLB 10,
77; MTCW

Williams, Hugo 1942- .... **CLC 42**
See also CA 17-20R; DLB 40

Williams, J. Walker
See Wodehouse, P(elham) G(renville)

Williams, John A(lfred)
1925- .... **CLC 5, 13; BLC**
See also BW; CA 53-56; CAAS 3; CANR 6,
26; DLB 2, 33

Williams, Jonathan (Chamberlain)
1929- .... **CLC 13**
See also CA 9-12R; CAAS 12; CANR 8;
DLB 5

Williams, Joy 1944- .... **CLC 31**
See also CA 41-44R; CANR 22

Williams, Norman 1952- .... **CLC 39**
See also CA 118

Williams, Tennessee
1911-1983 ..... **CLC 1, 2, 5, 7, 8, 11, 15,
19, 30, 39, 45, 71; DA; DC 4; WLC**
See also AITN 1, 2; CA 5-8R; 108;
CABS 3; CANR 31; CDALB 1941-1968;
DLB 7; DLBD 4; DLBY 83; MTCW

Williams, Thomas (Alonzo)
1926-1990 .... **CLC 14**
See also CA 1-4R; 132; CANR 2

Williams, William C.
See Williams, William Carlos

Williams, William Carlos
1883-1963 .... **CLC 1, 2, 5, 9, 13, 22, 42,
67; DA; PC 7**
See also CA 89-92; CANR 34;
CDALB 1917-1929; DLB 4, 16, 54, 86;
MTCW

Williamson, David (Keith) 1942- .... **CLC 56**
See also CA 103; CANR 41

Williamson, Jack .... **CLC 29**
See also Williamson, John Stewart
See also CAAS 8; DLB 8

Williamson, John Stewart 1908-
See Williamson, Jack
See also CA 17-20R; CANR 23

Willie, Frederick
See Lovecraft, H(oward) P(hillips)

Willingham, Calder (Baynard, Jr.)
    1922- .... **CLC 5, 51**
    See also CA 5-8R; CANR 3; DLB 2, 44;
    MTCW

Willis, Charles
    See Clarke, Arthur C(harles)

Willy
    See Colette, (Sidonie-Gabrielle)

Willy, Colette
    See Colette, (Sidonie-Gabrielle)

Wilson, A(ndrew) N(orman) 1950- .. **CLC 33**
    See also CA 112; 122; DLB 14

Wilson, Angus (Frank Johnstone)
    1913-1991 .... **CLC 2, 3, 5, 25, 34**
    See also CA 5-8R; 134; CANR 21; DLB 15;
    MTCW

Wilson, August
    1945- .. **CLC 39, 50, 63; BLC; DA; DC 2**
    See also BW; CA 115; 122; CANR 42;
    MTCW

Wilson, Brian 1942- .... **CLC 12**

Wilson, Colin 1931- .... **CLC 3, 14**
    See also CA 1-4R; CAAS 5; CANR 1, 22,
    33; DLB 14; MTCW

Wilson, Dirk
    See Pohl, Frederik

Wilson, Edmund
    1895-1972 .... **CLC 1, 2, 3, 8, 24**
    See also CA 1-4R; 37-40R; CANR 1;
    DLB 63; MTCW

Wilson, Ethel Davis (Bryant)
    1888(?)-1980 .... **CLC 13**
    See also CA 102; DLB 68; MTCW

Wilson, John 1785-1854......... **NCLC 5**

Wilson, John (Anthony) Burgess 1917-1993
    See Burgess, Anthony
    See also CA 1-4R; 143; CANR 2; MTCW

Wilson, Lanford 1937- .... **CLC 7, 14, 36**
    See also CA 17-20R; CABS 3; DLB 7

Wilson, Robert M. 1944-......... **CLC 7, 9**
    See also CA 49-52; CANR 2, 41; MTCW

Wilson, Robert McLiam 1964- ..... **CLC 59**
    See also CA 132

Wilson, Sloan 1920- .... **CLC 32**
    See also CA 1-4R; CANR 1

Wilson, Snoo 1948-.............. **CLC 33**
    See also CA 69-72

Wilson, William S(mith) 1932- ..... **CLC 49**
    See also CA 81-84

Winchilsea, Anne (Kingsmill) Finch Counte
    1661-1720 .... **LC 3**

Windham, Basil
    See Wodehouse, P(elham) G(renville)

Wingrove, David (John) 1954-...... **CLC 68**
    See also CA 133

Winters, Janet Lewis .... **CLC 41**
    See also Lewis, Janet
    See also DLBY 87

Winters, (Arthur) Yvor
    1900-1968 .... **CLC 4, 8, 32**
    See also CA 11-12; 25-28R; CAP 1;
    DLB 48; MTCW

Winterson, Jeanette 1959-......... **CLC 64**
    See also CA 136

Wiseman, Frederick 1930-........ **CLC 20**

Wister, Owen 1860-1938 .... **TCLC 21**
    See also CA 108; DLB 9, 78; SATA 62

Witkacy
    See Witkiewicz, Stanislaw Ignacy

Witkiewicz, Stanislaw Ignacy
    1885-1939 .... **TCLC 8**
    See also CA 105

Wittig, Monique 1935(?)-......... **CLC 22**
    See also CA 116; 135; DLB 83

Wittlin, Jozef 1896-1976 .... **CLC 25**
    See also CA 49-52; 65-68; CANR 3

Wodehouse, P(elham) G(renville)
    1881-1975 ... **CLC 1, 2, 5, 10, 22; SSC 2**
    See also AITN 2; CA 45-48; 57-60;
    CANR 3, 33; CDBLB 1914-1945;
    DLB 34; MTCW; SATA 22

Woiwode, L.
    See Woiwode, Larry (Alfred)

Woiwode, Larry (Alfred) 1941-... **CLC 6, 10**
    See also CA 73-76; CANR 16; DLB 6

Wojciechowska, Maia (Teresa)
    1927- .... **CLC 26**
    See also AAYA 8; CA 9-12R; CANR 4, 41;
    CLR 1; JRDA; MAICYA; SAAS 1;
    SATA 1, 28

Wolf, Christa 1929- .... **CLC 14, 29, 58**
    See also CA 85-88; DLB 75; MTCW

Wolfe, Gene (Rodman) 1931-....... **CLC 25**
    See also CA 57-60; CAAS 9; CANR 6, 32;
    DLB 8

Wolfe, George C. 1954- .... **CLC 49**

Wolfe, Thomas (Clayton)
    1900-1938 ... **TCLC 4, 13, 29; DA; WLC**
    See also CA 104; 132; CDALB 1929-1941;
    DLB 9, 102; DLBD 2; DLBY 85; MTCW

Wolfe, Thomas Kennerly, Jr. 1931-
    See Wolfe, Tom
    See also CA 13-16R; CANR 9, 33; MTCW

Wolfe, Tom .... **CLC 1, 2, 9, 15, 35, 51**
    See also Wolfe, Thomas Kennerly, Jr.
    See also AAYA 8; AITN 2; BEST 89:1

Wolff, Geoffrey (Ansell) 1937- ..... **CLC 41**
    See also CA 29-32R; CANR 29, 43

Wolff, Sonia
    See Levitin, Sonia (Wolff)

Wolff, Tobias (Jonathan Ansell)
    1945- .... **CLC 39, 64**
    See also BEST 90:2; CA 114; 117; DLB 130

Wolfram von Eschenbach
    c. 1170-c. 1220 .... **CMLC 5**

Wolitzer, Hilma 1930- .... **CLC 17**
    See also CA 65-68; CANR 18, 40; SATA 31

Wollstonecraft, Mary 1759-1797...... **LC 5**
    See also CDBLB 1789-1832; DLB 39, 104

Wonder, Stevie .... **CLC 12**
    See also Morris, Steveland Judkins

Wong, Jade Snow 1922-........... **CLC 17**
    See also CA 109

Woodcott, Keith
    See Brunner, John (Kilian Houston)

Woodruff, Robert W.
    See Mencken, H(enry) L(ouis)

Woolf, (Adeline) Virginia
    1882-1941 ...... **TCLC 1, 5, 20, 43; DA;
        SSC 7; WLC**
    See also CA 104; 130; CDBLB 1914-1945;
    DLB 36, 100; DLBD 10; MTCW

Woollcott, Alexander (Humphreys)
    1887-1943 .... **TCLC 5**
    See also CA 105; DLB 29

Woolrich, Cornell 1903-1968....... **CLC 77**
    See also Hopley-Woolrich, Cornell George

Wordsworth, Dorothy
    1771-1855 .... **NCLC 25**
    See also DLB 107

Wordsworth, William
    1770-1850 .... **NCLC 12, 38; DA; PC 4;
        WLC**
    See also CDBLB 1789-1832; DLB 93, 107

Wouk, Herman 1915-......... **CLC 1, 9, 38**
    See also CA 5-8R; CANR 6, 33; DLBY 82;
    MTCW

Wright, Charles (Penzel, Jr.)
    1935- .... **CLC 6, 13, 28**
    See also CA 29-32R; CAAS 7; CANR 23,
    36; DLBY 82; MTCW

Wright, Charles Stevenson
    1932- .... **CLC 49; BLC 3**
    See also BW; CA 9-12R; CANR 26;
    DLB 33

Wright, Jack R.
    See Harris, Mark

Wright, James (Arlington)
    1927-1980 .... **CLC 3, 5, 10, 28**
    See also AITN 2; CA 49-52; 97-100;
    CANR 4, 34; DLB 5; MTCW

Wright, Judith (Arandell)
    1915- .... **CLC 11, 53**
    See also CA 13-16R; CANR 31; MTCW;
    SATA 14

Wright, L(aurali) R. 1939-......... **CLC 44**
    See also CA 138

Wright, Richard (Nathaniel)
    1908-1960 .... **CLC 1, 3, 4, 9, 14, 21, 48,
        74; BLC; DA; SSC 2; WLC**
    See also AAYA 5; BW; CA 108;
    CDALB 1929-1941; DLB 76, 102;
    DLBD 2; MTCW

Wright, Richard B(ruce) 1937- ...... **CLC 6**
    See also CA 85-88; DLB 53

Wright, Rick 1945-............... **CLC 35**
    See also Pink Floyd

Wright, Rowland
    See Wells, Carolyn

Wright, Stephen 1946- .... **CLC 33**

Wright, Willard Huntington 1888-1939
    See Van Dine, S. S.
    See also CA 115

Wright, William 1930- .... **CLC 44**
    See also CA 53-56; CANR 7, 23

Wu Ch'eng-en 1500(?)-1582(?)....... **LC 7**

Wu Ching-tzu 1701-1754 .... **LC 2**

Wurlitzer, Rudolph 1938(?)- ... **CLC 2, 4, 15**
    See also CA 85-88

Wycherley, William 1641-1715 .... **LC 8, 21**
    See also CDBLB 1660-1789; DLB 80

SSC Cumulative Nationality Index

SSC Cumulative Title Index

Title Index

Title Index

ISBN 0-8103-8930-4

90000

9 780810 389304